AF527628

A History of Sanskrit Literature
Classical Period

A HISTORY OF SANSKRIT LITERATURE

Classical Period

SURENDRA NATH DASGUPTA

SUSHIL KUMAR DE

MOTILAL BANARSIDASS PUBLISHERS
PRIVATE LIMITED • DELHI

1st MLBD Edition : ***Delhi, 2017***
First Published : Univesity of Calcutta, 1947 (1975)

ISBN : 978-81-208-4110-9 (Cloth)
ISBN : 978-81-208-4112-3 (Paper)

Motilal Banarsidass
41 U.A., Bungalow Road, Jawahar Nagar, Delhi 110 007
8 Mahalaxmi Chamber, 22 Bhulabhai Desai Road, Mumbai 400 026
203 Royapettah High Road, Mylapore, Chennai 600 004
236, 9th Main III Block, Jayanagar, Bangalore 560 011
8 Camac Street, Kolkata 700 017
Ashok Rajpath, Patna 800 004
Chowk, Varanasi 221 001

MLBD Cataloging-in-Publication Data
A History of Sanskrit Literature
Classical Period, Vol. I
by S.N. Dasgupta and S.K. De
ISBN : 978-81-208-4110-9 (Cloth)
ISBN : 978-81-208-4112-3 (Paper)
Includes Editor's Notes and Index
I. History II. Sanskrit Literature
III. Classical Period IV. Dasgupta, S.N.
V. De, S.K.

Published by
Motilal Banarsidass Publishers Private Limited
www.mlbd.com • mlbd@mlbd.com
Printed by Nice Printing Press

CONTENTS

BOOK I

CONTENTS, PREFACE AND INTRODUCTION

PAGE

CONTENTS iii

PREFACE v

INTRODUCTION

1. GENERAL REMARKS ... ... xiii-li

Functions of the *sūtas—sūtas* not repositories of heroic poetry xiii

Artificiality—not an indispensable character of Sanskrit Poetry xiv

Identification of Kāvya as "ornate poetry" untenable xv

Alaṃkāra in earlier literature xvi

Direct evolution of classical style from the Vedic literature... xvii

Continuity of the Kāvya literature xviii

Literature in the first six hundred years of the Christian era xix

Greater complexity of style in later times ... xix

Some characteristics of Sanskrit poetry—religio-social restrictions on society xxi

The development of the *Dharmaśāstra* and the Smṛti xxv

Effect of patternisation of life on literature ... xxviii

Varṇāśrama ideals in Kālidāsa xxx

Restriction of the scope of free love xxxii

Nature of the theme of subjects chosen... ... xxxiv

Kālidāsa's treatment of love of romances ... xxxv

The plot of the *Śakuntalā* and the view of Rabindranath xxxvi

O.P.—220 A

	Page
Patternisation and insulation of Indian Society ...	xxxviii
Function of poetry	xl
Relieving features of Sanskrit poetry	xli
Transcendent object of literary art	xli
Aesthetic emotion	xliii
Concept of Indian Drama	xlvi
The *Mahābhārata* and the *Rāmāyaṇa*	xlix
The essence of Kāvya as the heightened expression of experience	li
2. Social Background of Literature	lii-cxxvi
Choice of subjects—Literature and Life... ...	lii
Fashionable life in early India...	lv
Early academies	lvii
Life at the time of Bāṇa	lviii
Gradual separation of city life from the life in the villages	lx
Purāṇic legends—the source of the plots of Kāvya ...	lxii
Love in Sanskrit poetry	lxiii
Rasa and Rasābhāsa	lxiv
Growth of Indian civilisation from Vedic literature	lxv
The characteristics of Indian temperament ...	lxvi
Race peculiarities in the literature	lxviii
The idea of *dharma*	lxxii
Secular outlook and the doctrine of *Trivarga* ...	lxxiv
Dramatic art	lxxvii
Religious temperament and its effect on the choice of plots	lxxix
Drama—types and characteristics	lxxxii
The place of love in literature	lxxxix
Patternising tendency of Indian culture... ...	xc
Continuity of Indian culture	xciii
Ideal of *dharma* in law and politics	xcvi
Types of literature...	xcix
Political conditions and the early poetry ...	c

PAGE

Little Greek influence on Indian culture and literature ciii
Extension of Indian Empire up to Khotan and Afghanistan civ
Literature at the time of Kaṇiṣka cv
Rise of the Guptas... cvii
Fa Hien's evidence regarding India's social conditions and literature of the time cix
Gupta civilisation and colonisation by Indians ... cxi
Development of literature from the 7th to the 10th century cxiii
Political and literary contact with the neighbouring countries cxv
Political condition in India after Harṣa... ... cxvi
General review of the growth of Sanskrit literature cxvii
Literary Prākṛt—a standardised language ... cxx
Was Sanskrit a spoken language ? cxxi
Difficulties of appreciating Sanskrit poetry ... cxxv
Nature in Sanskrit poetry cxxvi

BOOK II

KĀVYA

CHAPTER I—ORIGINS AND CHARACTERISTICS

1. The Origin and Sources of the Kāvya 1
2. The Environment and Characteristics of the Kāvya 18
3. The Origin and Characteristics of the Drama ... 42

CHAPTER II—FROM AŚVAGHOṢA TO KĀLIDĀSA

1. Aśvaghoṣa and his School 69
2. The Avadāna Literature 81
3. The Literature of Tale and Fable 83
   (a) The Pañcatantra 86
   (b) The Bṛhatkathā of Guṇāḍhya 92
4. The Dramas Ascribed to Bhāsa 101

PAGE

CHAPTEP III—KALIDĀSA... 118

CHAPTER IV—SUCCESSORS OF KALIDĀSA IN POETRY

1. The Erotic Śatakas of Amaru and Bhartṛhari ... 156
2. The Stotra-Śatakas of Bāṇa, Mayūra and others ... 166
3. The Mahākāvya from Bhāravi to Māgha ... 173
   (*a*) Bhāravi 177
   (*b*) Bhaṭṭi 183
   (*c*) Kumāradāsa 185
   (*d*) Māgha 188
4. The Gnomic, Didactic and Satiric Poems ... 194

CHAPTER V—SUCCESSORS OF KALIDĀSA IN PROSE AND DRAMA

1. The Prose Kāvyas of Daṇḍin, Subandhu and Bāṇa ... 200
   (*a*) Daṇḍin 207
   (*b*) Subandhu 217
   (*c*) Bāṇabhaṭṭa 225
2. The Dramas from Śūdraka to Bhavabhūti ... 239
   (*a*) Śudraka 239
   (*b*) The Authors of the Caturbhāṇī and the Mattavilāsa 248
   (*c*) Harṣa 255
   (*d*) Viśākhadatta 262
   (*e*) Bhaṭṭanārāyaṇa 271
   (*f*) Bhavabhūti 277
   (g) Yaśovarman, Māyurāja and others 298

CHAPTER VI—THE LATER DECADENT POETRY AND PROSE

1. General Characteristics 304
2. The Mahākāvya... 316
3. Poems with Historical Themes 345
4. Shorter Pomes
   (*a*) The Erotic Poetry 364
   (*b*) The Devotional Poetry 375

PAGE

(c) The Didactic and Satiric Poetry 398
(d) The Anthologies and Women Poets ... 411
5. Prose Literature 418
(a) The Popular Tale 420
(b) The Prose Kāvya 429
(c) The Campū 433

CHAPTER VII—THE LATER DECADENT DRAMA
1. General Characteristics 441
2. Murāri and Rājaśekhara 449
3. Dramas with Legendary Themes and Comedies of Court-life. 462
4. Dramas of Middle-class Life and Plays of Semi-Historical Interest 474
5. The Allegorical Drama 479
6. Erotic and Farcical Plays 487
7. Dramas of an Irregular Type 501

BOOK III

HISTORY OF ALAMKĀRA

CHAPTER I—LITERARY AND CHRONOLOGICAL RELATIONS

Vyākaraṇa school and Alaṃkāra school 513
Alaṃkāra-śāstra—its name 517
Early Origin of the Alaṃkāra 520
Earlier Writers on Alaṃkāra-śāstra 525
Udbhaṭa 533
Alaṃkāra in the Agnipurāṇa 538
Ānandavardhana, Dhvanikāra and Abhinavaguptā ... 540
Rājaśekhara 546
Bhaṭṭatauta 548
Kuntaka 548
Dhanañjaya 550

Page

Mahimabhaṭṭa 551
Bhojadeva 552
Kṣemendra 554
Mammaṭa 556
Ruyyaka 556
Vāgbhaṭa I 559
Hemacandra 559
Jayadeva 560
Bhānudatta 561
Vidyādhara 561
Vidyānātha 562
Vāgbhaṭa II 563
Viśvanātha 563
Keśavamiśra 564
Appaya Dīkṣita 564
Jagannātha 565
Later minor writers 566

Chapter II—Principles of Literary Taste and Criticism

Introductory 567
Vakrokti 586
Theory of Rasa 592
Dhvani 604

BOOK IV

EDITOR'S NOTES

Some Earlier Writers... 610
Bhaṭṭikāvya and other cognate Caritakāvyas ... 614
Sanskrit Drama 630
Theory of the Greek Origin of the Indian Drama ... 650
Śakas and the Sanskrit Drama 654
Buddhistic Dramas 654
Lyric Poetry 656

	Page
Amaruśataka	668
Bhartṛhari	669
Gnomic Poetry	673
Historical Kāvyas	676
Prākṛt	683
Celebrated Writers of the Past—Little Known now ...	685
Guṇāḍhya	687
Pañcatantra	696
Bhāsa and the Dramas assigned to him	708
Kālidāsa	728
Subandhu	754
Bāṇa	755
Śūdraka	756
Harṣa—the Dramatist	758
Viśākhadatta	760
Murāri	760
Caturbhāṇī	761
Bhaṭṭanārāyaṇa	762
Bhavabhūti	763
Kumāradāsa	763
Nīlakaṇṭha Dīkṣita	764
Mahendravikrama-varman	765
Veṅkaṭanātha	765
Udayasundarī-kathā	766
Udayavarma-carita	766
Kumārapāla-pratibodha	767
Rūpaka-ṣaṭka	768
Pārtha-parākrama	769
Nara-nārāyaṇānanda	770
Śrīnivāsa-vilāsa-campū	770
Nalābhyudaya	771
Kathā-kautuka	771
Rāṣṭraudha-vaṃśa	772
Kamalinī-kalahaṃsa	772

PAGE

Acyutarāyābhyudaya 772
Ānandakanda-campū... 773
Nārāyaṇīya 774
Bharata-carita, Candraprabhā-carita, Kāvya-ratna and Bāla-mārtaṇḍa-vijaya 775

BOOK V

INDEX 777

PREFACE

The first information regarding the existence of Sanskrit and the literature of the Upaniṣads was carried to the West by the Latin translation, by Anquetil Duperron, of the 50 Upaniṣads from the Persian translation of Dara Shiko which at once elicited the highest approbation of Schopenhauer. There was a time when it was openly doubted in Europe whether there was any genuine Sanskrit language and the distinguished English philosopher Dugald Stewart (1753-1828) in one of his papers described Sanskrit as a forgery of the Brahmins. But the indefatigable work of Sir William Jones, Colebrooke and others made Sanskrit known to the Western world. It was then recognised that the Sanskrit language with its old and modern descendants represents the easternmost branch of the Indo-Germanic Aryan stock of speech. Numerous special coincidences of language and mythology between the Vedic Aryans and the people of Iran also prove incontestably that these two members of the Indo-Germanic family must have lived in close connection for some considerable period after the others had separated from them.

The origin of comparative philology dates from the time when European scholars became accurately acquainted with the ancient languages of India. Before this the classical scholars had been unable to determine the true relations between the then known languages of the Aryan stock. It is now almost universally recognised that Sanskrit is the eldest daughter of the old mother-tongue of the Aryan people and probably the only surviving daughter. But none of the other six principal members of the family has left any literary monuments and their original features have to be reproduced as best as possible from the materials supplied by their own daughter-languages.

Such is the case with regard to the Iranic, Hellenic, Italic, Celtic, Teutonic and Letto-Slavic languages. The oldest of the Indian speeches is to be found in the *Ṛgveda*. In the language of the *Ṛgveda*, one can trace a gradual and steady development of the language of the classical Sanskrit through the later Saṃhitās, the Brāhmaṇas and the Upaniṣads, The development, however, is not as spontaneous as the modifications that are effected by popular speech. It has been controlled by tradition and grammatical studies. Changes in the speech of the upper classes are largely prevented by the sacred devotion to it and this was further supplemented by the work of the early grammarians, whose analytical skill far surpassed anything achieved in the West up till recent times. The Sanskrit grammarians tried as far as possible to remove irregularities and they hardly allowed any scope to new formations and this preserved to a very great extent the purity of the language and its well-ordered nature which would otherwise have been impossible. The conservative tendency of Indian literary culture, which we have tried to demonstrate in the field of the development of Sanskrit literature in the Introduction, is remarkably manifested also in the permanent form that has been given to the Sanskrit language. The word *saṃskṛta* means *purified* and *well-ordered.* By 150 B.C., by the joint works of the 3 grammarians, Pāṇini, Kātyāyana and Patañjali, the language attained a stereotyped form which remained the same throughout the centuries, though it remained the literary language of the people. It can hardly be doubted that though Pāṇini recognised fully the Vedic accents and forms, yet in his time it was Sanskrit and not the older Vedic languages that were spoken. Yet Sanskrit cannot be regarded as an artificial cereation of the grammarians, for its development from the Vedas through the Brāhmaṇas and the Upaniṣads can be clearly traced. The Sanskrit language, which Pāṇini calls *bhāṣā,* or speech, is closely akin to the language of the Upaniṣads and the Brāhmaṇas. Though this *bhāṣā* Sanskrit is not so luxurious in form as the Vedic Sanskrit, yet there is no artificial symmetry and there is a profusion of *nipātas* or irregular forms which makes the study of Sanskrit so bewilderingly difficult to students.

Sanskrit was indeed the language not only of *kāvya* or literature but of all the Indian sciences, and excepting the Pāli of the Hīnayana Buddhists and the Prākṛt of the Jains, it was the only language in which the whole of India expressed all her best thoughts for the last 2 or 3 thousand years, and it has united the culture of India and given it a synchronous form in spite of general differences of popular speech, racial and geographical, economical and other differences. It is the one ground that has made it possible to develop the idea of Hindu nationhood in which kinship of culture plays the most important part. Under the shadow of one Vedic religion there had indeed developed many subsidiary religions, Śaiva, Vaiṣṇava, Śākta, etc., and within each of these, there had been many sects and sub-sects which have often emphasised the domestic quarrel, but in spite of it all there is a unity of religions among the Hindus, for the mother of all religious and secular culture had been Sanskrit.

Variations from Sanskrit as determined by Pāṇini, Kātyāyana and Patañjali may occasionally be noticed in the *Rāmāyaṇa*, the *Mahābhārata* and some of the other Purāṇas and Patañjali also noticed it when he said *chandovat kavayaḥ kurvanti* and an early poet such as Kālidāsa also sometimes indulges in such poetical licenses. Lesser poets who wrote inscriptions also often showed their inability to conform to the grammatical rules of Pāṇini. But apart from this the Sanskrit language has not suffered any change in the course of ages. It must, however, be noted that the technical and non-Brahminical works sometimes reveal a laxity of Sanskrit speech and in the case of the early Buddhist writers there was an intentional disregard to the rules of Pāṇini, probably in their effort towards the simplification of the Sanskrit language. The most notable example of this is the *gāthā* language of the *Lalitavistara* and similar other works. Sometimes even later Brahminical works which tried to bring a halo of antiquity, often made lapses in order to force upon the people the impression of their archaic nature as may be found in many of the Tantra works, or in the works of divination and incantation as found in the Bower manuscripts where there is ample evidence of Prākṛtism and careless Sanskrit. Instances, however, are not rare where actual Prākṛt forms were Sanskritised. The incorporation of Dravidian and other words into Sanskrit has also been widely recognised. The words formed by the *uṇādi* suffix will supply innumerable instances of how current words gained a footing into the Sanskrit language and fanciful derivations were attempted to justify such uses.

Not only in fairly early times was Prākṛt used for the edicts and the *praśastis* but it was also used in writing poetical and prose *kāvyas* in later times. The word *Prākṛta* is seldom used in early Sanskrit in the sense of a language. Its real meaning is 'original', 'natural', 'normal', and it has been used in this sense in the Vedic literature in the *Prātiśākhyas* and the *Śrautasūtras* and also in Patañjali's *Mahābhāṣya*. The word *prākṛtamānuṣa* is used in the sense of 'an ordinary man' or 'a man in the street.' Hemacandra says that *Prākṛta* is so called because it has been derived from Sanskrit which is the *prakṛti* or source (*prakṛtiḥ saṃskṛtaṃ tatra bhavaṃ tata āgatañca prākṛtam*). But there is another view as held by Pischel where the Prākṛt is derived as 'coming from nature' without any special instruction, *i.e.*, the folk language. But it is impossible for us to decide in what way the Prākṛt language grew. In the writings of the Prākṛt grammarians and writers on Poetics, the term denotes a number of distinctly artificial dialects, which, as they stand now, could hardly have been spoken vernaculars. Sir George Grierson divides Prākṛt into 3 stages, first, the primary Prākṛt, from which the Vedic language and Sanskrit were derived ; second, secondary Prākṛt, consisting of Pāli, the Prākṛts of the grammarians and literature and the Apabhraṃśas ; the third, Prākṛt consists of the modern vernaculars. But the inscriptions of Aśoka show at least the existence of three dialects, the Eastern dialect of the capital which was the official *lingua franca* of the Empire, the North-western and the Western dialects. We next find the post-Aśokan Prākṛts in the inscriptions and the Prākṛt of Aśvaghoṣa of the 1st century A.D. Here we find the old Ardha-māgadhī, the old Śaurasenī and old Māgadhī. According to the current tradition the Jaina doctrines preached by Mahāvīra were delivered in Ardha-māgadhī but the scriptures of Śvetāmbara Jainas that are now available have been very much influenced by the Mahārāṣṭrī and the later texts were written in Jaina Mahārāṣṭrī, while the Digambara scriptures are in Śaurasenī. The Paiśācī is also a from of Prākṛt though only few books written in this dialect are now available. Paiśācī was probably the language current in the Vindhya region. The charactaristics of the old Prākṛts consist largely in the transformation of the vowels ṛ and ḷ, ai and au, and in the reduction of the sibilants and nasals with also other changes in consonants. Literature of a secular character might have been composed in old Prākṛts until the 2nd century A.D. But about that date new changes were effected leading to the transformation of the old Prākṛt to a new stage of development. This resulted in the formation of the Mahārāṣṭrī in the dominions of the Sātavāhanas in the South-west and the rise of the Māgadhī and the Śaurasenī, as may be noticed in the dramas of Bhāsa and Aśvaghoṣa on the one hand and Kālidāsa on the other. By the 2nd century A.D. we find the Mahārāṣṭrī lyric in the pomes of Hāla. The Mahārāṣṭrī Prākṛt became important as the Prākṛt of the dramas and of the epic poetry. The Śaurasenī was but occasionally used in verse and sometimes in the drama. The Śaurasenī is more closely allied to Sanskrit than the Mahārāṣṭrī and it was generally used in dramas by men of good and noble position. The Māgadhī on the other hand was reserved for people of low rank. The *Nātya-śāstra* speaks, however, of different types of Prākṛt such as *Dākṣiṇātyā*, *Prācyā*, *Āvantī* and *Ḍhakkī*, which are the different types of the Śaurasenī, though *Cāṇḍālī* and *Śākārī* are types of the Māgadhī. The Prākṛt of the verses of the *Nātya-śāstra* need not be assumed to be the Prākṛt of a different type but it may well be regarded as a variant of the Śaurasenī. The poetry of Śaurasenī Prākṛt is closely akin to the Mahārāṣṭī. A separate note has been added regarding the Apabhraṃśa, the impotance of which for literary purposes may now be ignored.

A few Histories of Sanskrit Literature, such as *History of Sanskrit Literature* (1860) by Maxmüller, *History of Indian Literature* (1878) by Weber, *Indiens Litterature und Kultur* (1887) by L. V. Schroeder, *Literary History of India* by Frazer, *History of Sanskrit Literature* (1900) by Macdonell, *Die Literatur des alten Indiens* (1903) by Oldenberg, *Les Literatures de l' Inde* (1904) by V. Henry, *Geschichte der Indischen Litteratur* by Winternitz, *Sanskrit Drama* (1924), *History of Sanskrit Literature* (1928), as well as *Classical Sanskrit Literature* by Keith, and *Geschichte der Sanskrit-philologie und Indischen Altertumskunde* (1917, Vol. I and 1920, Vol. II) by Windisch, have been written. Of these, Winternitz's work in three volumes seems to be the most comprehensive treatment. The Calcutta University had completed the English translation of the first two volumes under the supervision of Professor Winternitz himself. The English translation of Volume III had advanced a little when Professor Winternitz died. The Calcutta University had then entered into correspondence with some European scholars about the supervision of the translation of Volume III. This correspodence having failed, I was approached by the University to undertake the work and it was proposed by me that as the translation of Volum III had only advanced but little, it would be better to plan another work deling with the subjects that form the content of Volume III of Professor Winternitz's work. It was also felt necessary that the title of the book, as it appeared in Professor Winternitz's work, *History of Indian Literature,* should be changed to *History of Sanskrit Literature,* as "Indian Literature" is too vast a subject to be taken up as a sort of appendage to the history of

Sanskrit literature, as Prof. Winternitz had done. As my hands at the time were too full with other works, it was arranged that under my chief editorship within an Editorial Board the work should be done by subscription by the scholars of Bengal. Volume I deals with Kāvya and Alaṃkāra and Volume II is expected to deal with other Technical Sciences. In Volume I, I had the good fortune to get the co-operation of Prof. Dr. S. K. De in writing out the portion on Kāvya. But for his valuable scholarly assistance and promptness of execution the publication of Volume I might have been long delayed. I have tried to supplement Prof. De's treatment with an Introduction and additional Editorial Notes and it is expected that these may also prove helpful to students. Our indebtedness to Prof. Winternitz's General Edition, Vol. III, and Prof. Keith's works, as well as to other Western and Indian scholars, cannot be exaggerated. For want of space it was not possible to go into greater details regarding the Alaṃkāra-Śāstra, but I hope that what appears there may be deemed sufficient for a general history of Sanskrit literature. The Introduction is intended to give a proper perspective for reviewing the history of Sanskrit literature in its background of racial, social and historical environment, an appreciation of which I consider essential for graspiag the significance of the Sanskrit literary culture.

It is to be regretted that some of the contributions, such as those on the Historical Kāvyas, or the elements of literature in the Inscriptions, or the Prākṛt literature, could not be incorporated in the present volume, though these should have been included here. This was due to the fact that those contributions were not received in time. It is expected, however, that these will appear in Volume II. In the meanwhile, both in the body of the book and in the Editorial Notes some general estimates have been taken of these, though very little has been said about the elements of literature in Inscriptions.

By way of confession of a hasty observation in the Alaṃkāra section that the Latin word *aurum* may be connected with the word *alam* in Sanskrit I beg to point out that since that section has ben printed, an eminent philologist has assured me that neither *aurum* is Latin nor can it be philologically connected with *alam* in Sanskrit.

In conclusion, I like to express my thanks to Mr. Krishnagopal Goswami, Sastri, M.A., P.R.S., Smriti-Mimansatirtha, Lecturer in the Post-Graduate Department of Sanskrit of the University of Calcutta, who has kindly prepared a list of contents and a detailed.Index for this volume.

S. N. DASGUPTA

NOTE

Since on account of circumstances over which there was no control the publication has been unusually delayed for nearly six years, I owe an apology for my inability in bringing the work up to date.

University of Dacca,
1946

S. K. D.

INTRODUCTION

Function of the *sūtas* according to Winternitz.

Winternitz, in Vol. III of his *History of Indian Literature*, German Edition, speaks of "the *Sūtas* as the representatives of the old heroic poetry who lived in the court of the princes and sang to extol them. They also went forth to battle so as to be able to sing of the heroic deeds of the warriors from their own observation. These court bards stood closer to the warriors than to the learned Brahmins. They also acted as charioteers of the warriors in their campaigns and took part in their martial life."

Sūtas were not repositories of heroic poetry.

But Winternitz does not give any reference from which he draws his views about the *sūta* as the traditional keeper of heroic poetry. The *sūta* occurs along with the *rathakāra* and *karmāra* in the *Atharva Veda* III, 5, 6, 7. We find reference to this *sūta* in *Gautama* (IV. 15), *Baudhāyana* (10. I. 9. 9.), *Vaśiṣṭha* (XVIII. 6), *Manu* (X. II), *Viṣṇu Dh. S.* (XVI. 6), *Yāj.* (I. 3), and the *Sūta-sāṃhitā*, where he appears as a *pratiloma* caste born of a Kṣattriya male and a Brahmin female. Kauṭilya says in his *Arthaśāstra* (III. 7) that Romaharṣaṇa, called also *sūta* in the Purāṇas, was not born out of a *pratiloma* marriage. The *sūta* has been referred to as sacred in the *Viṣṇupurāṇa* and the *Agnipurāṇa*. The duty of the *sūtas* according to *Manu* (X. 47) was to drive chariots and according to the *Vaikhānasa-smārta-sūtra* (X. 13) it was a part of his livelihood to remind the king of his duties and cook food for him. According to *Karṇaparva* (XXXII. 46. 47), *sūtas* were the servants (paricārakas) of the Kṣattriyas. According to *Vāyupurāṇa* (Ch. I.), the *sūtas* used to preserve the pedigrees of kings and great men and also the traditions of learning and books. But nowhere do we find that *sūtas* had any other work than those said above or that they ever played the part of a bard reciting the glories of the kings or were in any sense the depository of heroic poetry. His chief duty was the taming of elephants, driving chariots and riding horses. The difference between *sūta* and *rathakāra* is that the former was born from Kṣattriya male and Brahmin female in wedlock; the other out of wedlock through clandestine union.

Artificiality not an indispensable character of Sanskrit poetry.

The theory that these bards were gradually superseded by erudite poets also demands confirmation. It is also doubtful to affirm that the poets always described fights and battles from hearsay. Judging from the *Mahābhārata* and the state of events given in it in terms of *tithis* and *nakṣatras* which synchronise throughout the whole book, one should think that there were either dated notes of events or that the poets themselves according to some definite traditions synchronised the dates. Again, we know so little of the earlier poetry that we have no right to say that in earlier poetry greater stress was laid to form and erudition. The artificial poetry began at a much later date, from the 6th or the 7th century. Neither in the *Rāmāyaṇa* nor in the *Mahābhārata* do we find any influence of artificiality. Whatever may have been said in the *Tantrākhyāyikā* (I. 321), the *Mahābhārata* is regarded as an *itihāsa*, and seldom regarded as a *kāvya* which place is assigned to the *Rāmāyaṇa*. It is also doubtful (at least there is hardly any evidence) that the panegyrics were the first thing of *kāvya*. It is also wrong to hold that the *Kāvya* style means an ornate style.

At least none of the rhetoricians hold this view and there is hardly any evidence in its favour. Winternitz, therefore, is entirely wrong when he says, "The more strenuous the effort of the poet, the more 'ornate' his expressions, and the more difficult his work of art, the more did the prince feel flattered by it." The earliest Sanskrit rhetorician Bhāmaha holds a different view regarding *kāvya*. He says that even if *kāvya* requires explanatory interpretation like a *śāstra* ; then it would indeed be a matter of great regret for the common man. This signifies that at least Bhāmaha thought that *kāvya* should be written in such a manner that it should be intelligible to all. He says further that there are indeed different types of style but it is only that type of style which is intelligible to the ignorant, to women and children, that is sweet. Thus, in II. 1-3, he says : *mādhuryam abhivāñchantaḥ prasādaṃ ca sumedhasaḥ / samāsavanti bhūyāṃsi na padāni prayuñjate* ॥ *kecidojo' bhidhitsantaḥ samasyanti bahūnyapi* ॥ *śravyaṃ nātisamastārthaṃ kāvyaṃ madhuramiṣyate* । *āvidvadanganābālapratītārthaṁ prasādavat* ॥

Bhāmaha's idea of good poetry.

It should be noted that this opinion of Bhāmaha is based upon the study of previous good poetry and the opinions of other poets. Thus, he says in the colophon of his work :

avalokya matāni satkavīnām avagamya svadhiyā ca kāvyalakṣma ।

sujanāvagamāya bhāmahena grathitaṃ rakrilagomisūnunedam ।

Identification of kāvya as "ornate poetry" untenable.

This opinion may be confirmed by reference to the writings of other rhetoricians who followed Bhāmaha. It is a pity that Winternitz should have such an unfounded and uncharitable opinion of Indian poetry. It is also difficult to imagine why Winternitz should render *kāvya* as ornate poetry, which he defines as that in which "the poet makes it his highest ambition to astonish his readers or hearers by as numerous, as original and as elaborate similes as possible." His remarks about ornate poetry apply only to the poets of a degenerate time, when the true ideals of real poetry was lost sight of and when the poets had to pose themselves as great pundits. It is no doubt true that

Bhaṭṭi's view of poetry.

many of the famous poets like Bhaṭṭi, Māgha or Śrīharṣa follow the worst standard of artificial poetry and indeed Bhaṭṭi boasts that his *kāvya* is such that it is not intelligible without explanation ; yet it must be pointed ont that this was not the opinion of the critics of literature and that for that reason *kāvya* style should not be confounded with artificiality. During the period that many of these poets flourished there was such an ascendancy of the scholarly philosophers, that the poets often thought that learning was greater than poetry and they tried to pose their learning through their poetry. But I do not see how a poet like Aśvaghoṣa can be regarded as a representative of ornate poetry in the same sense in which Mahākṣattrapa Rudradāman's inscription-texts can be regarded as ornate.

Alaṁkāra in earlier literature.

Prof, Winternitz conteded that to know of the origin of ornate poetry we must know the origin of the Alaṃkāra literature and he seems to imply that that type of literature may be called ornate in which an acquaintance with the Alaṃkāra literature or its principles may be presupposed. He held further that surely Vālmīki did not as yet know any manual of poetics. But what is the reason for such an assurance ? We know that *upamās* were well-known even in Vedic times and Yāska deals with *upamā* in a fairly systematic manner. Pāṇini also seems to be fairly acquainted with some of the fundamental types of *upamā*. We have also reasons to believe that the *alcṃkāra* type cf thought had its origin in the Vyākaraṇa school. We do not also know that there were no treatises of *alaṃkāra* written before Vālmīki.

The comments that have been made above will show that the theory of ornate pcetry (Kunstdichtung) is beset with many difficulties. Though it is needless to trace the origin of Sanskrit Kāvyas to the Vedas or the Brāhmaṇas, it cannot be decided that some of the early Upaniṣads like the *Kaṭha, Muṇḍaka* and the *Śvetāśvatara* contain verses in the classical style. Indeed the style of the *Mahābhārata* and the *Gītā* may be regarded as the prolongation of the clssical style which had begun already at the time of the Upaniṣads. Among the early literature the *Rāmāyaṇa* and the *Mahābhārata* (though the latter is called *itihāsa*) must be regarded as the earliest literature of the Kāvya form that is available to us. Rhetoricians in a much later time have quoted verses from the *Mahābhārata* to demonstrate the theory of *vyañjanā* and *guṇībhūta-vyañjanā.*[1] Though there is a difference of atmosphere in the *Mahābhārata* which lays greater stress on the practical problems of life and conflict of ideals, yet the atmosphere of *Rāmāyaṇa* is not far removed from that of Kālidāsa. As Dr. De has shown, we can hardly trace the origin of Sanskrit Kāvyas to Prākṛt sources. It has also been pointed out by Dr. De that the theory of Renaissance of Sanskrit Kāvya in the 5th or 6th century A.D., as proposed by Maxmüller, cannot properly be supported. It is true that no extant

Direct evolution of the classical style from the Vedic literature.

The theor of the Renaissance of Sanskrit literature untenable.

[1] See *Mahābhārata, Strīparva,* Chap. XXIV, verse 17.—"ayaṁ sa rasanotkarṣī, etc.' Also, *Śāntiparva.* Āpaddharma, Chap. 103, verses 11 and 12. These have been referred to in the *Kāvyaprakāśa,* Chap. V, verses 45 and 46, as examples of *guṇībhūta vyaṅgya,* and Chap. IV, as example of *prabandha vyañjanā.*

kāvyas of any importance are available before Aśvaghoṣa. But there are plenty of references scattered over which suggest the existence of a fairly good field of Kāvya literature during the 5th to the 1st century B.C. Even Pāṇini is said to have written a work called *Jāmbavatīvijaya* and Patañjali refers to a *kāvya* by Vararuci.

Continuity of the Kāvya literature. Patañjali also refers to three ākhyāyikās, *Vāsavadattā*, *Sumanottarā*, and *Bhaimarathī*, and two dramas called *Kaṃsabadha* and *Balibandha*. He also quotes a number of verses from which the continuity is apparent. *Lalitavistara* also mentions *kāvya-kāraṇa* as a subject which was studied by Buddha. These and various other reasons adduced in the text show fairly conclusively the existence of Kāvya literature from the 2nd century B.C. to the 2nd century A.D. It has already been noticed that many of the verses of the Upaniṣads may well have been included in a classical work of *kāvya* in latter times. But most of the literature has now been lost.

Continuity of the Kāvya style. Aśvaghoṣa's Kāvya as well as Rudradāmana's inscriptions show an acquaintance with the principles of alaṃkāra. The Prākṛt inscriptions of the first two centuries of the Christian era as well as many texts of the Buddhists or the verses later found in the Pāli Jātakas all reveal the fact that they were written on the model of Sanskrit writings of their time. The writings of Matṛceṭa, Kumāralāta, Ārya-śūra, so far as they have been recovered, and the verses that are found in the *Caraka-saṃhitā* also confirm the view that the Kāvya style was flourishing at the time and this could not have been the case if there were no poetical texts at the time. There is also reason to believe that erotics, dramaturgy, the art of dancing and singing were all keeping pace with the literary development of the time.

Literature in the first six hundred years of the Christian era.

But definite dates of the poets in the history of Indian literature are difficult to be got. The Aihole inscription of 634 A.D. mentions the names of Kālidāsa and Bhāravi and we know that Bāṇa flourished in the 7th century A.D. They are the two fixed landmarks in the early chronology of Sanskrit poets. The testimony of Bāṇa as well as the other references that we find of the existence of many poets at the time prove fairly conclusively that the 4th and 5th centuries may be regarded as a very prominent period of literary production. This gets further confirmation from the evidence of inscriptions which are written in a fine literary style. Already from the evidence of Bhāmaha we know that many writers on *alaṃkāra* had flourished before him and that he had drawn on them in the composition of his work. The panegyric of Samudragupta by Hariṣeṇa (about 350 A.D.) may be taken as a typical case.

Greater complexity of style in later times from simplicity to pedantry.

But from the 6th century onwards we find that the poets often manifest a tendency for display of learning and scholarship and skill in the manipulation of words and verbosity and a studied use of *alaṃkāras*. We know that in the 4th century Vasubandhu had written his *Abhidharmakoṣa*. In this great work he mercilessly criticised not only other schools of Buddhism but also the Hindu schools of philosophy, such as *Sāṃkhya*, *Vaiśeṣika* and the like. Diṅnāga and Vātsyāyana flourished about the 5th century A.D. and from this time onward the quarrel of the philosophers and learned scholars of divergent schools began to grow into such importance that it practically influenced every other department of thought. The old simplicity of style which we find in Patañjali and Śavara had now disappeared. Śaṅkara and Jayanta who flourished probably in the 7th and 9th century are indeed noble exceptions, but even then the difference between their style and that of Patañjali and Śavara, is indeed very great. Learning appealed to people more than poetic freshness. We can well imagine that when most of the great poets flourished in the court atmosphere where great scholars came and showed their skill in debate and wrangle, learning and scholarship was more appreciated than pure fancy of poetry. Rabindranath draws a fine picture of such a situation in which he depicts the misfortune of the poet Śekhara.

Learning regarded as an important desideratum.

Dr. De has in a very impressive manner described the court atmosphere and how it left its mark on Sanskrit poetry. As a result of the particular demand in the court atmosphere the natural spontaneity of the poet was at a discount. The learning and adaptation to circumstances was given more importance than the pure flow of genius. Thus, Mammaṭa, the celebrated rhetorician in discussing the nature of poetic powers says that poetic power is the skill that is derived by a study of human behaviour, learning, familiarity with literature. history and the like, training taken from one who understands literature and exercise.[1] There was the other important thing for a court poet that he should be a *vidagdha* or possess the court culture, and Daṇḍin also says that even if the natural powers be slender, one may make himself suitable for the company of the *vidagdha* through constant practice. This shows that learning and exercise were given a greater place of importance than the natural spontaneity of poetic genius. As a result of this Sanskrit poetry not only became artificial but followed a traditional scheme of description and an adaptation of things. The magic of the Sanskrit language, the sonorousness of its word-

1 **śaktirnipuṇatā lokaśāstrakāvyādyavekṣaṇāt |**
kāvyajñaśikṣayābhyāsa iti hetustadudbhave |

jingle also led the poets astray and led them to find their amusement in verbal sonorousness. But whatever may be said against long compounds and puns it cannot also be denied that the Sanskrit language has the special genius of showing its grandeur and majesty through a noble gait. An Arab horse may be more swift and effective for all practical purposes but a well-adorned elephant of a high size has a grace in its movement which cannot be rivalled by a horse. These long compounds even in prose give such a natural swing when supplemented with the puns and produce an exhilaration which, though may not be exactly of the poetic type, has yet its place in the aesthetic atmosphere which is well illustrated in the writings of Bāṇa and in many inscriptions.

Some characteristics of Sanskrit poetry.

The *śloka* form in which the Sanskrit Kāvyas are generally written renders the whole representation into little fragmentary pictures—which stand independently by themselves and this often prevents the development of a joint effect as a unitary whole. The story or the plot becomes of a secondary interest and the main attention of the reader is drawn to the poetical effusions of the writer as expressed in little pictures. It is curious also to notice that excepting a few poets of the type of Bhavabhūti, the rugged, the noble and the forceful elements of our sentiments or of the natural objects could hardly be dealt with success. Even Kālidāsa failed in his description of sublime and sombre scenes. His description of the lamentation of Rati at the death of Madana in the *Kumārasambhava* has no tragic effect on us and it seems to be merely the amorous sentiment twisted upside down.

Religio-Social restrictions on society.

In studying the literature of a country, we cannot very well take out of our consideration a general cultural history of its people. The Aryans after their migration to India had come to live in a country peopled by aliens having a culture far below their own (excepting probably the Dravidians) whose cultural and other tastes were entirely different. The great problem before them was the problem of the fusion of races. It was the main concern of the leaders of society to protect the purity of the race, its culture and religion as far as possible. They initiated the system of *varṇāśrama* and enunciated rigorous regulations for the respective duties of the four *varṇas*. There is ample evidence in the Smṛtis that in spite of the rigorous regulations, these were often violated and as time passed on, rigours increased. Thus marriage with girls of lower *varṇas* which was allowed at one stage was entirely stopped in later times. There is, however, evidence to show that marriages took place not only with the girls of lower *varṇas* but many kings had devoted Greek wives. But still the problem of fusion of races gradually increased when the Huns, the Scythians and the Greeks not only entered the country and lived there, but became Hinduised. So long as many rulers of the country were given to military adventures and the people as a whole entered into commercial negotiations and intercourses with different countries and established settlements in different lands —the balance or the equilibrium of society had a dynamic vigour in it. Intercourse with other people on equal terms expanded the mental vista, but when, for reasons unknown, their came a period of stagnation and peple became more or less narrow and provincial, they lacked vigour and energy of free thought. In society the rigour of social rules increased, and people followed these rules in spite of the fact that obedience to such rules was in direct contradiction to the professed systems of philosophy. Philosophy became divested of

Stagnating effect of the rigorous injunctions of Smṛti.

social life and whatever divergence there might have been in the philosophical speculations of different sects and communities—they became equally loyal to the same *smṛti* laws. When the *smārta* followed the injunctions of *smṛti* on the belief that they all emanated from the Vedas, the Vaiṣṇava followed the same *smṛti* rules on the ground that they were the commandments of God. The maxim of the *Mīmāṃsā* was that no *smṛti* laws would have any validity if they are not supported by the Vedas. But there were really many *smṛti* laws about which no evidence could be found in the Vedas. The legal fiction was invented that where corroborative Vedic texts were not available, one should suppose that they existed but were lost. The whole effort was suicidal. It denied in principle the normal human fact that society is a human institution. With the change of condition and circumstances, material wants and means of production and external influences of diverse kinds, man must change and with the change of man, the social institutions, duties and obligations must also change. The attempt to bind with iron chains all movements of society, so that these must adapt themselves to the conditions that prevailed in Vedic times, was like the attempt of the Chinese to make the feet of the ladies manacled in iron shoes, so that when the lady grew to the adult age, her feet should remain like those of a baby. This extereme conservatism of social laws had an extremely depressive effect as regards the freedom of mind and it enslaved the temper of the mind and habituated it to respect the older traditions at the expense of common sense and wisdom. The elasticity of mind that we find in the *Mahābhārata* soon disappeared and people got themselves accustomed to think in terms invented for them by their predecessors. Yet it is not true that they were always faithful and loyal to the customs of Vedic times. Any Brahmin or community of Brahmins of influence could make a *smṛti* law which proved binding to successive generations of people. This may be illustrated by the case of beef-eating. Beef-eating is a recognised Vedic caustom and even to-day when marriage ceremonies are performed, there is a particular *mantra* which signifies that a cow has been brought for the feast of the bridegroom and the bridegroom replies out of pity that the cow need not be butchered for his gratification. But yet according to the later *smṛti*, cow-killing or beef-eating is regarded as one of the major crimes. Again, while sea-voyage was allowed in ancient times and therefore had the sanction of the Vedic literature, it has been prohibited by the later *smṛti*. The list of *kali-varjyas* may all be taken as instances of drawing up a tighter noose at the neck of the society. Thus, there was not merely the convenient fiction on behalf of the *smṛti* but even injunctions that were distinctly opposed to the older Vedic practices, which were forced upon the people by the later codifiers of *smṛti* for the guidance of society. It is difficult to understand how the injunctions of the *smṛti* writers derived any authoritative value. Probably in some cases many older instances had gone out of practice or become repugnant to the people, or that the codification of some *smṛti* writers might have had the backing of a ruling prince and was for the matter of that held sacred in his kingdom. But it may also have been that some *smṛti* writers had risen to great eminence and authority and by virtue of the peoples' confidence in him, his decisions became authoritative. In the case of Raghunandana, who lived in Navadwipa about 500 years ago, we find that either by personal influence or by propaganda he succeeded in making his views and interpretation stand supreme in Bengal in preference to the views of older *smṛti* authorities like Yājñavalkya or Vijñāneśvara.

The development of the *Dharmaśāstra* and the Smṛti

Dharmaśāstras were probably in existence before Yāska, but the important *Dharmaśāstras* of Gautama, Baudhāyana and Āpastamba probably flourished between 600 and 300 B. C. Before the *Dharmaśāstras* or the *Dharmasūtras* we have the *Gṛhyasūtras*. The *Hiraṇyakeśi Dharmasūtras* were probably written sometime about the 4th century A. D. The *Vāśiṣṭha Dharmasūtra* was probably in existence in the 1st or the 2nd century of the Christian era. The *Viṣṇu Dharmasūtra* had probably an earlier beginning, but was thoroughly recast in the 8th or the 9th century A. D. The *Hārīta* was probably written somewhere about the 5th century A. D. The versified *Śaṅkha* is probably a work of later date though it may have had an earlier version. We have then the *smṛtis* of Atri, Uśanas, Kanva, Kāśyapa, Gārgya, Cyavana, Jātukarṇa, Paithīnasi, Bṛhaspati, Bharadvāja, Śātātapa, Sumanta, of which the dates are uncertain. But most of the *smṛtis* other than the older ones were written during the period 400 to 1000 A. D. In ancient times the number of *smṛtis* must have been very small and the extent of limitations imposed by them was also not so great. Thus, Baudhāyana speaks only of Aupajaṅgham, Kātya, Kāśyapa, Gautama, Prajāpati, Maudgalya, Hārīta. Vaśiṣṭha mentions only Gautama, Prajāpati, Manu, Yama and Hārīta. Āpastamba mentions ten. Manu speaks of only six besides himself, such as Atri, Bhṛgu, Vaśiṣṭha, Vaikhānasa and Śaunaka. But in all their works the writers are mentioned only casually and there is no regular enumeration of writers on *Dharma* in one place. Yājñavalkya is probably the earliest writer who enumerated twenty expounders of *Dharma*. Kumārila who flourished in the 7th and the 8th century speaks of 18 *Dharma Saṃhitās.* We have then the 24 *Dharma Saṃhitās* which in addition to Yājñavalkya's list contains 6 more. There is another *smṛti* called *Ṣaṭtriṃśanmata* quoted by *Mitākṣarā* which contains 36 *smṛtis.* The *Vṛddhagautama Smṛti* gives a list of 57 *dharma-śāstras* and the *Prayoga-pārijāta* gives a list of 18 principal *smṛtis,* 18 *upasmṛtis* and 21 *smṛtikāras.* The

Later Smṛtis

Nirṇayasindhu and the *Mayūkha* of Nīlakaṇṭha gives a list of 100 *smṛtis.* Thus as time advanced the number of *smṛti* authorities increased and there was gradually more and more tightening. The *Manusmṛti* had probably attained its present form by the 2nd century A.D. and the *Yājñavalkyasmṛti* was probably composed in the 3rd or 4th century A.D. We find that though the *smṛtis* had begun at an early date and were supposed to have been based upon Vedic injunctions and customs, yet new *smṛti* authorities sprang up giving new injunctions which can hardly be traced to Vedic authorities. Many of the older authorities were again and again revised to harmonise the changes made and these revised editions passed off as the old ones as there was no critical apparatus of research for distinguishing the new from the old.

The Purāṇas also indulged in the accretions of the many materials of the *Dharma-śāstra.* From the 10th century onwards we have a host of commentators of *smṛtis* and writers of digests or *nibandhas* of *smṛtis.* A peep into the *smṛtiśāstras* and *nibandhas* of later times shows that there was a regular attempt to bind together all possible actions of men of different castes of society by rigorous rules of *smṛtis.* Such an attempt naturally has its repercussions on the mental freedom and spontaneity of the mind of the people.

This tendency may also be illustrated by a reference to the development of the philosophical literature.

Loyalty to the past, the chief characteristic of Indian culture.

It is curious, however, to note that though the Indian systems of philosophy diverged so diametrically from one another, they all professed to be loyal interpreters of the Upaniṣads. Śaṅkara's own interpretation of the Upaniṣads consists chiefly in showing the purport of the Upaniṣads as condensed in the *sūtras*. The *Brahmasūtra* itself says that there is no end to logical discussions and arguments and no finality can be reached by logical and philosophical debates. It is always possible to employ keener and keener weapons of subtle logic to destroy the older views. The scope and area of the application of logic must always be limited by the textual testimony of the Upaniṣads, which alone is the repository of wisdom. It is curious to note that the same Upaniṣadic text has been interpreted by some writers as rank nihilism, by others as absolutism and by others again as implying dualism, pluralism or theism. But the spirit was still there that the highest wisdom and truth are only available in the Upaniṣadic thought. So great has been the hold of the Upaniṣads on the Indian mind that even after centuries of contact with the Western world, its science and philosophy, Indian mind has not been able to shake off the tight hold of the Upaniṣads on its thought. The late poet Tagore, who happened to be probably the greatest poet and thinker of our age, drew most of his inspiration and ideas from Upanisads. In all his writings he largely expandend the Upaniṣadic thought assimilating with it some of the important tendencies of Western biology and philosophy, but always referring to Upaniṣads or interpreting them in that light for final corroboration.

The collapse of the Indian genius in formalistic lines and in artificiality in social customs, behaviours and actions, in philosophy and in art, is naturally reflected in the development of the Sanskrit literature of a later age. In the earlier age also the reverence for the past had always its influence on the genius of the poets of succeeding ages. It may be presumed that the court atmosphere of the Hindu kings was always dominated by a regard for the Hindu *Dharmaśāstras* as it was also the general attitude of the people. This tightening of the grip on the mind to follow the past was so much impressed upon the people that when after an age the poetical practice was established, the rhetoricians recorded this practice and made it a pattern for all kinds of literature. Just as the various writers on *Smṛti* had tried to record the customary practice and behaviour of all the daily actions of all class of people, so the rhetoricians also recorded the practice of the past poets and this served as a pattern or guide for the poets of succeeding generations.

The tightening grip of the Smṛtis affected freedom of thought and patternised life.

Its effect on literature.

When we read the works on rhetoric by Bhāmaha, Daṇḍin, Vāmana, Udbhaṭa and Rudrata, and other writers of earlier times, we find discussions on Kāvya of a structural nature. They discuss what constitutes the essence of Kāvya, the nature of adornments, the relative importance of the style, the adornment and the like, or whether or not suggestivity or rousing of sentiments should be regarded as being of primary importance in good literature, But seldom do we find an enumeration regarding requirements of the various kinds of poetry, *mahākāvya, khaṇḍa-kāvya,* etc., or a detailed description of the patterns of the different kinds of characters of heroes and heroines, or an enumeration of the subjects that have or have not to be described in works of poetry. These patterns when enumerated by the rhetoricians, becomes patterns of poetic behaviour which must be followed by the poets and loyalty to these patterns became often the criteria of good or bad poetry, just as the patterns of conduct recorded in the

Smṛti-śāstras became the criteria of good or bad conduct of the people.

Patternisation of life explains monotony regarding choice of subjects

It must also be noted that as the number of injunctions increased and as the *Smṛti-śāstra* demanded a complete patternisation of the conduct of all sections of people, freedom of life and behaviour gradually began to disappear. In whatever community or clan of people one may have had a chance of enquiring into, one would find the same pattern of behaviour as was running through the ages. It was an attempt towards a mummification of social life from which all novelty was gone. Even if there was anywhere any violation of the pattern, the poet could hardly utilise it without shocking the sense of decorum and religious tatse of the people. Thus, the poet had hardly any field of new experience. The freer life of older times became gradually encased within the iron casings of the laws of *Smṛti*. Thus Kālidāsa in describing his ideal king Dilīpa, says that his subjects did not deviate even by a line from the course that was followed from the time of Manu. It is thus easy to say that when life is unchangeably patternised and there is no freedom and spontaneity or change or variety in life, poetry cannot reflect any new problems of life and necessarily it must follow artificial patterns which had been current through centuries. This was further enhanced by the fact that the same tendency of working after a pattern out of a reverence for the past also intellectually compelled the poet to look for the pattern of his work to earlier poets or to generalisations made from them as recorded in the Alaṃkāra literature. I wish to affirm here that the reason why the earlier Sanskrit literature like the *Rāmāyaṇa* and the *Mahābhārata* and the works of Śūdraka, Bhāsa, etc., are more human, and the reason why poets of a later period became gradually more and more artificial, is largly due to the stagnation of society and social life. Kālidāsa, however, may be taken as an exception, but it seems that in his time the ideal of old *varṇāśrama-dharma* seemed still to inspire the ideal of the people. For this reason in two of his works, *Raghuvaṃśa* and *Abhijñana-śakuntala* he had taken a theme of antiquity and of history. Thus in *Raghuvaṃśa,* which is a history of the kings of Raghu race, he seems to have invented many episodes of the kings of the past about whom practically no record is available in Vālmīki. It is curious to note, however, that though he practically passed off the scenes of Rāma's life depicted by Vālmīki, yet he expressed his gratitude to him to the extent of comparing his work as being merely of the type of passing a thread through pearls through which holes have already been made by Vālmīki. Now, what may be the secret of Kālidāsa's feeling of greatfulness ?

Kālidāsa a portrayer of Varṇāśrama ideals.

Now it seems to me that Dilīp, Raghu, Aja, Daśaratha and Rāmacandra are really the pivotal characters of *Raghuvaṃśa.* If we take the lives of them all and roll them up into one, we can very well have a faithful picture of an ideal king, who is devoted to the rules of *varṇāśrama-dharma.* Throughout the *Rāmāyaṇa,* in the character of Rāma, beginning from the episode of his marriage to the killing of Śambūka, we have the picture of such a king, who is loyal to his father, loyal to his people, who marries for progeny, shows heroism by conquest and carries the fruits of civilisation to other countries. What Kālidāsa meant by threading the pearls is that he has really rolled up into one the great ideas of Vālmīki and manifested them in the character of different kings beginning from Dilīpa. His success with these two Kāvyas was largely due to his natural genius and also because the thing he took up

Kālidāsa's episodes of love.

was hallowed with the glory of the past. In *Śakuntalā* he staged his theme in a fairly supernormal manner. It was a prolongation of earth to heaven and as such it was not normal or natural. We find here also the same loyalty on the part of the king to *varṇāśrama-dharma* and the romance with Śakuntalā was also not clearly of the ordinary social order. Śakuntalā was the daughter on the one hand of Viśvāmitra and on the other, of Menakā, of an ascetic Kṣattriya and a heavenly nymph. As such the love was not unsocial In the other drama *Vikramorvaśī* also, he availed himself of a Vedic story and described the love of the king with a heavenly nymph. Had Kālidāsa been a modern man, he should have probably staged his drama in a different manner. Believer as he was in some amount of free love, the social conditions did not allow him to depict it otherwise than with an Apsarā. According to the older smṛtis and traditions available to us, we find that a love affair with a courtesan's daughter was thoroughly allowable in social practice. In the third love affair described by Kālidāsa, he takes a Yakṣa and his wife. In the fourth love affair in *Mālavikāgnimitra,* which was his maiden work, he was not so daring and took opportunity of the fact that it was the constant practice of the kings to have more than one wife. In that case also, Mālavikā was also a princess. She was brought in the family by circumstances of an unnatural character and though the queen had protected her from the sight of the king, he accidentlly saw her portrait and gradually fell into love with her. The *parivrājikā* performed her part in the manner somewhat foreshadowed in the *Kāmaśāstra*. The other love affair that Kālidāsa describes was that of Śiva and Pārvatī and here also only in the 5th canto, that we find a great ideal depicted in the effort of Pārvatī to attain, through penances, such proper worth as may make her deserving of her great husband, and this is the most important message of the book. Otherwise, the Kāvya, as a whole, falls flat on our ears. The 1st and the 2nd cantos are bores. The 3rd canto attains some vigour and the 4th canto is a mere parody of the tragic consequences following the effort of Kāma to fascinate Śiva. The 6th and 7th cantos can well be read or omitted. We thus see that the divine episode, even when delineated by a master genius like Kālidāsa, really failled because it had not the realities of life. Its value with us is the great idea that physical beauty by itself cannot really win the heart of great souls and also the idea that it is only then when a great souls is wedded with a woman who by her moral austerities can make herself pure and attract her husband through her purity and spiritual greatness and the crucifixion of the baser tendencies of life, that great leaders of nations such as Kārttikeya can be produced.

Patternisation of life by the Smṛtis restricted to the scope of free love—a natural desideratum for the development of poetry.

A member of the higher caste is to get married the very day he ceases to be a Brahmacārī according to the maxim that one cannot stay even a day without belonging to an *āśram*. Such marriages would naturally be arranged for him by his parents and relations and if after that he remains absolutely loyal to his wife, there is hardly any room for any intrigue or romance. Sanskrit poetry generally holds within it a charm or attraction which is almost inimitable by any other language, but owing to the patternised form of life enjoyed by the *smṛtis,* the scope of life depicted in the Kāvyas became so narrow and limited. The honest life formulated in the codes of duties, fixed once and for all, cannot be the fit atmosphere for the free development of poetic art. Freedom of love to some extent has to be tolerated in society and boys and girls have to remain unmarried up to an adult age in order that love episodes may be possible. Where the girls are married before they attain their puberty and when such marriges are arranged by their relations and when other forms of non-marital love are not recognised, the sphere of love poetry naturally becomes very limited. One has to find some instances of illicit love in royal spheres or one has to deal with heavenly nymphs or carry on with the tales of the *Rāmāyaṇa* or the *Mahābhārata*.

Yet in ancient times much wider freedom was recognised for sex relation.

Taking sex-love by way of illustration, we find that the *Kāmasūtra,* written probably towards the beginning of the Christian era, says (1.5.3) that sex behaviour to girls of lower caste, who are not untouchables, to prostitutes and to widows prepared to marry again, is neither recommended nor prohibited. It is only for pleasure.[1] The institution of prostitution of higher or lower orders was allowed in society without much objection. Thus when Cārudatta in *Mṛcchakaṭika* was challenged that how being an honourable man he had kept a prostitute though he had his wife, he says, "*yauvanamevātrāparāddhaṃ na cāritram*". "It is only the fault of my youth and not of my character". In the *Yājñavalkya* also we find in the *Vyavahāra-adhyāya,* Chap. 24, that primary and secondary sex behaviour was only prohibited in relation to married women, girls of higher castes and also other girls against their wish. There was thus a fair amount of latitude for free love and a study of the *Kuṭṭanīmatam* shows that even prostitutes were sometimes smitten with love though it is their profession to attract young people and deplete them of their riches. The fact that the transgression of young

1 *avaravarṇāsu aniravasitāsu veśyāsu punarbhūṣu ca na śiṣṭo na prati ṣiddhaḥ sukhārthatvāt.*

girls with regard to the secondary sex acts such as kissing, embracing and the like by other young men was treated very lightly, is realised by reference to *Yājñavalkya* and *Mitākṣarā*.[1] Again, it seems from *Yājñavalkya* (*Ācārādhyāya—Vivāhaprakaraṇa*) that transgression of married women unless it bore fruit, was treated very lightly. Thus Yājñavalkya (I.3.72) says, *vyabhicārād ṛtau śuddhiḥ, i.e.*, in the case of transgression the woman is purified by the next menstruation. The fact also that there were so many kinds of marriages and particularly the existence of a *gāndharva* marriage shows that life was much freer in ancient times than in later days. As the rigours of the Smṛti advanced with time and tried to stifle free social behaviour and as social customs became more and more puritanic and these again reacted upon the writers of the Smṛti and influence them gradually to tighten their noose more and more, the current of social life became gradually more and more stagnant and unfit for free literary productions.

Latitude of marriages latter on ruled out in practice through the influence of the *Smṛti* laws.

This also explains why the poets so often took the theme of their subject from older Kāvyas and Purāṇic legends. In itself there may be nothing wrong in taking themes from older legends, provided the poet could rejuvenate the legend with the spirit of his own times. Shakespeare also drew from the legends of Plutarch and other older writers. But though the general scheme of the story is the same, yet the

1 *somaḥ śaucaṁ dadāvāsaṁ gandharvaśca śubhāṁ giram |*
pāvakaḥ sarva-medhyatvaṁ medhyā vai yoṣito hyataḥ ||

Yājñavalkya, I. 3. 71.

somagandharvavahnayaḥ strīrbhuktvā yathākramaṁ tāsāṁ śauca-madhura-vacana-sarvamedhyatvāni dattavantaḥ tasmāt striyaḥ sarvatra sparśāliṅganādīṣu medhyāḥ śuddhāḥ smṛtāḥ ||

—Mitākṣarā, I. 3. 71.

characters have become living because Shakespeare lived through these characters in his own imagination and his sparkling genius took the materials of his own life from the social surroundings about him which became rekindled by his emotion and imagination and it was this burning colour of the characters, lived through in the mind of the poet, that was displayed in his dramatic creations. In the case of the Indian poets, the legend was drawn from older Kāvya or Purāṇic myths but the poet himself had but little life to infuse in the story (because in the social surroundings in which he lived, mind was not free to move) lest he might produce any shock on the minds of his readers who used to live a patternised life. The force of this remark will be easily appreciated if we remember that Sanskrit poets who deal with illicit love seldom make it the central theme of any big Kāvya and they utilised the little affairs of illicit love only in drawing little pictures. The writers of Alaṃkāra tell us that wherever such illicit love is described and howsoever beautifully may it be done, it must be taken as *rasābhāsa*, *i.e.*, semblance of literary aesthetic emotion and not real *rasa* or real asthetic amorous sentiments.

No theme of illicit love or love unsanctioned by the social rules could be described by poets without shocking the cultivated taste.

A poet like Kālidāsa made a successful venture in *Abhijñāna-śakuntala,* where though the love was not illicit yet it was going to shock the mind of his audience. In order to prevent such a catastrophe, he had to take his heroine as the daughter of a Kṣatriya and a heavenly nymph and as Duṣyanta was going to repress his emotion because it had no sanction of society—he was at once reminded of the fact that his mind was so much saturated with the proper discipline of the Vedic life that he could trust his passion as directing him to proper action. This very passage has been quoted by Kumārila in defence of actions that may be done

Kālidāsa's treatment of love of romances.

even without the sanction of the *śastra* in accordance with the customary behaviour of those whose minds are saturated with Vedic ideas through generations of loyal obedience to older customs. This also explains Manu's injunction of *sadācāra* as being one of the determinants of conduct.

Gāndharva marriages were probably out of date in Kālidāsa's time.

Kālidāsa also arranged the *gāndharva* marriage which was already becoming out of date at the time. He had however in his mind the instinct of compunction of a man whose mind is surcharged with sentiments of loyalty to the *Smṛti-śāstras* for staging such a romance which was not customary at the time. He therefore introduces a curse of ancient times through the fiery wrath of Durvāsā, creating a tragic episode which he really could not bridge except by the very unreal staging of a drama by making the king travel to heaven and kill demons there and meet Śakuntalā in the heavenly hermitage of Mārīca. For such a king who can travel to heaven and kill demons there, one is prepared to give any license. But Kālidāsa did not realise how unreal was this part of the drama which taken along the natural and normal environment of the first part. Of course Kālidāsa never hesitated to be unreal in his dramatic treatment. Śakuntalā's familiarity with nature in the poetic fancy that nature also loved her is expressed in a technique which is wholly unreal, *viz.*, that of making the trees offer ornaments for Śakuntalā.

This explains the plot of the *Śakuntala.*

Rabindranath in his criticism of the drama has interpreted it as embodying the conception of Kālidāsa that mere carnal love has a natural curse with it, unless it is chastened by self-mortification and *tapasyā*. I would supplement it with a further additional idea that this was probably Kālidāas's view in the case of such weddings as are to produce great sons like Bharata and Kārttikeya. He is not loyal to this view either in *Vikramorvaśī* or in *Mālavikāgnimitra.* In *Śakuntalā,* however, it may rightly be argued that the conception had taken place through passionate love and Śakuntalā was in fairly advanced state of pregnancy when she was repulsed from Duṣyanta's court. It may further be added that there was no wilful self-mortification and attempt to rouse purity through a sense of value for a great love, as was the case of Pārvatī's *tapasyā* in *Kumārasambhava,* for Śakuntalā lived with her mother in heaven and was nrturally pining through sorrow of separatian from Duṣyanta and wearing garment for lonely ladies as prescribed by the Śāstras. Strictly speaking there was no *tapasyā* for love ; it was merely a suffering for separation and as such we cannot apply the norm of *Kumārasambhava* to the drama *Śakuntalā.* From this standpoint Rabindranath's view cannot be strictly justified. For suffering through mere separation may chasten the mind and improve the sterner qualities of love, but it cannot fully affect the nature of the original worth and such occasions of suffering may arise even in normal curcumstances. We cannot also hold that Kālidāsa believed that suffering through separation chastens love, for we do not find it in the case of *Vikramorvaśī* and the *Meghadūta.* It seems therefore more pertinent to hold that the veil of unreality of a heavenly journey and meeting the son there were conceived as improvements on the *Mahābhārata* story because the *gāndharva* form of marriage had become obsolete and to make the issue of such a wedlock a great emperor like Bharata might not have pleased Kālidāsa's audience.

Rabindranath's review of *Śakuntalā* how far correct.

The unreality of *Vikramorvaṣī* is so patent that it needs no stressing. In the *Raghuvaṃśa* also there

Unreality of Kālidāsa's plots as compared with the plot of Śūdraka.

are many episodes which are wholly of a mythical nature. Why did this happen even with a genius like Kālidāsa? Our simple answer is that life had begun to be patternised even at the time of Kālidāsa. People would swallow anything that was mythical and that was the only place in which there was some latitude for depicting emotions. The normal life had begun to be undramatic and uneventful. Anything beyond the normal would have been resented as not contributing to good taste. But Śūdraka who flourished centuries before Kālidāsa, did not feel any compunction in making the love of a courtesan the chief theme of his drama. There, for the first and the last time, we find a drama which is surcharged with the normal realities of life.

Overflow of passion in the lyrics.

But the Sanskrit poets being thwarted in dealing with free passionate love as the chief theme of a glorious Kāvya gave indulgence to the repressed sex-motives in gross descriptions of physical beauty and purely carnal side of love both in long-drawn Kāvyas and also in lyrics. It is for this reason that the genius of Sanskrit writers in their realism of life has found a much better expression in small pictures of lyric poems than in long-drawn epics. The repressed motive probably also explains why we so often find carnal and gross aspects of human love so passionately portrayed.

I do not for a moment entertain the idea that Sanskrit poets as a rule had a puritanic temperament or suffered from any sense of prudery. They regarded amorous sentiment to be the first and most important of all *rasas.* Indeed, there have been writers on Alaṃkāra who had held the amorous sentiment to be the only sentiment to be portrayed.

Patternisation and insulation of Indian Society

But the patternised form of society and the unreal ways of living where every action of life was controlled by the artificial injunction of the *smṛti* which always attempted to shape the mould of a progressive society according to the pattern and model of a society which had long ceased to exist in its natural environments and which was merely a dream or imagination, hampered the poet's fancy to such an extent that it could seldom give a realistic setting to the creation of his muse. We may add to it the fact that Sanskrit poetry grew almost in complete isolation from any other literature of other countries. The great poetry of Rabindranath could not have been created if he were imprisoned only in the Sanskritic tradition. The society of the world and the poetry of the world in all ages are now in our midst. We can therefore be almost as elastic as we like, though it must be admitted that we cannot stage all our ideas in the present social environment of this country. Here again, we live in a time when there are different strata of society standing side by side. The present society has unfurled its wings towards future progress and in such a transitional stage, the actual process of becoming and the various stages of growth are lying one within the other. This may be well illustrated if we take the case of men and women living in the so-called polished and polite society of Chowringhee and the people living in the distant villeges of Bengal. We have now in our midst an immense number of societies having entirely different ideals and perspectives. There must have been some difference between people living in court atmosphere and people living in hermitages far away from the town such that the latter could hardly tolerate the former as is well-expressed in the words of Śārṅgarava and Śāradvata. But on the whole there was a much greater uniformity of society where all people followed the law of *Smṛti*.

Gradual stratification of society.

Artificiality and unreality of the life depicted in the Kāvyas.

In conclusion I wish to suggest that the cause of the artificiality and unreality of the life depicted in the Kāvyas is due to two facts : one, the gradual depletion of life form society due to the rigour of the *Smṛti* and absence of any intercourse with any foreign literature, and the other, the conservatism for which whatever foreign life was known to India could not in any way influence the character and perspective of the Indians.

Function of poetry.

In this connection it is not out of place to mention that the world of poetry was regarded as a new creation different from the world of Nature. The purpose of poetry is to give aesthetic enjoyment and not to give a replica of the hard struggles of life, miseries and sufferings. But I have reasons to think that this does not imply that poetry should be divested from life but it merely shows the spiritual nature of art which even through the depicting of sorrows and sufferings produces aesthetic pleasure. The object of poetry is mainly to rouse our sentiments of joy and everything else is to become its vehicle. This alone distinguishes the material world from the world of art. Thus Mammaṭa says that the world of Nature is uniform as it is produced by the power of destiny and is dependent upon the material atoms, energy and the accessory causes and is of the nature of pleasure, pain and delusion, whereas the world of words is a direct production of the poetic Muse and is through and through interpenetrated with aesthetic joy. It is also thought that poetry must carry with it the delineation of an ideal or ideals not communicated by way of authorisation, injunction or friendly advice, but by rousing our sympathy and interest, our joy and love for them. It was therefore committed to the production of something that would not in any way by shocking to the sense of the good as conceived by the people.

Relieving features of Sanskrit poetry:

But the relieving feature of the Sanskrit Kāvyas, in spite of the conventional themes, subjects and ways of description, is to be found in the fact that most of the legends drawn from the Purāṇas or the older Kāvyas, were often such that the people were familiar with them and were used normally and habitually to take interest in the heroes and heroines which were pretty well-known. People did not also miss naturalness and reality because they thought that in literature they were entering into a new world, which was bound to be different from the world of Nature they knew. The majesty and the grandeur of the Sanskrit language, the sonorousness of word-music, the rise and fall of the rhythm rolling in waves, the elasticity of meaning and the conventional atmosphere that appear in it have always made it charming to those for whom it was written. The unreality and conventionality appear only to a modern mind looking at it with modern perspectives. The wealth of imagery, the vividness of description of natural scenes, the underlying suggestiveness of higher ideals and the introduction of imposing personalities often lend great charm to Sanskrit poetry.

The transcendent object of literary art.

The atmosphere of artistic creation as displayed in a Sanskrit play, as distinguished from the atmosphere of ordinary reality has well been described by Abhinavagupta in his commentary on Bharata's *Nātya-Sūtra*. Thus, Abhinavagupta says that the constitutive words of a Kāvya produce in the mind of the proper reader something novel, something that is over and above the meaning of the poem. After the actual meaning of words is comprehended there is an intuition by virtue of which the spatio-temporal relation of particularity that is associated with all material events disappears and a state of universalisation is attained. When in the play of

Śakuntalā king Duṣyanta appeared on a chariot following a deer for piercing it with his arrows, the deer was running in advance, turning backward its neck from time to time to look at the chariot following it and expecting a stroke of the arrow at every moment, and drawing its hind legs towards the front, twisting the back muscles and rushing forth with open mouth dropping on the way the half-chewed grass, we have a scene of fear ; but our mind does not refer it to the deer of any particular time or place or to the particular king who was hunting the deer, and we have no idea of any fear as being of any particular kind or belonging to a particularly localised animal. The absence of this particularity is manifested in the fact that we have no feeling of sorrow or anxiety associated with it. It is because this fear arises in a special manner in which it is divested of all association of particularity that it does not get mixed up with any of our personal psychological feelings. For this reason the aesthetic experience produced by literature, the sentiment that is realised through delineation in art, is devoid of any association with any particular time, place or person. For this reason the aesthetic representation of fear or any other emotion is entirely different from any real psychological sentiment. And therefore, it is devoid of the ordinary associates that accompany any real psychological sentiment that is felt personally as belonging to a real person in a particular spatio-temporal setting. Abhinava says that in such a fear the self is neither absolutely hidden nor illuminated in its individual personal character *(tathāvidhe hi bhaye nātyantamātmā tiraskṛto na viśeṣataḥ ullikhitaḥ)*. The artistic creation and representation then appear in an atmosphere of light and darkness, shadow and illumination in which the reference to the real person and the real time and place is dropped. As when we infer the

Display of aesthetic conditions.

existence of fire from smoke we do not make any reference to any special fire or any special smoke, so here also the aesthetic sentiment has no localised aspect. When through the gestures of the players different sentiments are aroused in the minds of the observers, then the representation so intuited is divested of the spatio-temporal relations.

The sort of personality roused in art.

In the external world things exist in an inter-related manner and the negation of some of these relations imply also a negation of the other relations. For this reason when the mind becomes unrelated to the spatio-temporal relations and the actual personalities then the sentiment that is roused is divested of personalities and the actual conditions and the importance is felt of the roused sentiment alone.

Aesthetic emotion.

There is in our unconscious mind an instinctive attraction for different kinds of enjoyment as well as subconscious or unconscious impressions of various kinds of satisfactions. When aesthetic sentiments as dissociated from their actual environments of the original are roused in the mind, these become affiliated to or reconciled to the relevant root-impressions or instincts and that transforms the presentation into a real emotion though they are divested from the actual surroundings of the original. It is because the aesthetic emotion is roused by mutual affiliation of the representation and the in-lying dormant root-passions which are common to all that there can be a communion of aesthetic sentiments among observers, which is the ultimate message of art-communication (*ata eva sarva-sāmājikānāmekaghanatayaiva pratipatteḥ sutarāṃ rasa-paripoṣāya sarveṣām anādi-vāsanā-citrīkṛta-cetasāṃ vāsanāsaṃvādāt*).

Universalisation in poetry.

We thus see that universalisation is of two kinds. On the one hand, there is the universalisation of the representation consisting of the depletion from it of the actual conditions of the environment and the actual personalities. On the other hand, there is another kind of universalisation with reference to its enjoyment. The enjoyment is more or less of the same type for all qualified observers and readers. All persons have the same type of dormant passions in them and it is by being affiliated with those dormant passions that the aesthetic emotions bloom forth. For this reason in the case of all qualified observers and readers the aesthetic emotion enjoyed is more or less of the same type though there may be individual differences of taste on account of the existence of specific differences in the dormant passions and the nature of representations. In any case, where such aesthetic emotion is not bound with any ties and conditions of the actual world it is free and spontaneous and it is not trammelled or polluted by any alien feelings. The aesthetic quality called *camatkāra* manifests itself firstly, as an aesthetic consciousness of beauty, and secondly, as the aesthetic delight, and thirdly, as nervous exhilaration.

Status of aesthetic experience.

Abhinava is unable to define the actual mental status of aesthetic experience. It may be called an intuition, a positive aesthetic state, imagination, memory or a mere illumination (*sa ca sākṣatkāra-svabhāvo mānasā-dhyavasāyo vā saṃkalpo vā smṛtirvā tathātvena sphurann-astu*...*api tu pratibhānā-para-paryyāyā sākṣātkāra-svabhāveyam*). Our ordinary experiences are bound with spatio-temporal environments and conditions. In literature there cannot be such obstacles. When without any obstruction the rooted passions bubble forth as aesthetic emotion we have the emotion of literature. At the time of knowing ordinary objects we have the objects as actually transcending our knowledge which have an objective reality and which cannot be caught within the meshes of knowledge. When I see a tree standing before me I can only see certain colours spatially distributed before me but the actual tree itself is beyond that knowledge of colour. Being connected with an object which exist transcending my colour-perception and which cannot be exhausted within that colour-perception, our knowledge cannot stand by itself without that object. For this reason perceptual experience cannot wholly discover for us the object. So in our inner perception of pleasure or pain there is the ego within us which is unknown in itself and is known only so far as it is related to the emotions through which we live. For this reason here also there is the unknown element, the ego, which is not directly known. Our experience of pleasure and pain being integrally related to it, we have always an undiscovered element in the experience of ordinary pleasure and pain. Pleasure and pain, therefore, cannot reveal themselves to us in their entire reality or totality. Thus, both our inner experiences of pleasure and pain and our objective experience of things being always related to something beyond them cannot reveal themselves in their fulness. Our knowledge thus being incomplete in itself runs forth and tries to express itself through hundreds of relations. For this reason our ordinary experience is always relative and incomplete. Here our knowledge cannot show itself in its wholeness and self-complete absolute totality. Our knowledge is always related to an external object the nature of which is unknown to us. Yet it is on the basis of that unknown entity that knowledge manifests itself. It is therefore naturally incomplete. It can only express itself in and through a manifold of relations. But the aesthetic revelation is manifested without involving the actual object within its constituent content. It is, therefore, wholly unrelated to any localised object or subject. The aesthetic revelation is thus quite untrammelled by any objective tie.

Idealistic outlook of Indian Aesthetics.

I do not wish to enter any further into the recondite analysis of the aesthetic emotion as given by the great critic of literature, Abhinavagupta. But what I wish to urge is that the writers of Indian drama had not on the one hand the environment consisting of a social life that was progressive and free where concussions of diverse characters could impress their nature on them and on the other hand they regarded that the main importance of literature was not the actuality and concreteness of real life but they thought that the purpose of literature was the creation of an idealised atmosphere of idealised emotions divested from all associations of concrete actual and objective reality. Thus, Dr. De says: "Sanskrit drama came to possess an atmosphere of sentiment and poetry which was conducive to idealistic creation at the expense of action and characterisation, but which in lesser dramatists overshadowed all that was dramatic in it."

Concept of Indian drama.

According to the Sanskrit rhetoricians, Kāvya is divided into two classes—*dṛśya* and *śravya, i.e.,* what can be seen and what can be heard. Neither the Sanskrit rhetoricians nor the poets made any essential distinction between Kāvya and drama, because the object of them both is to create aesthetic emotion by rousing the dormant passions through the aesthetic representation or the art-communication. Our modren conception that drama should show the repercussions of human mind through a conflict of action and re-action in actual life cannot be applied in judging the Indian dramas. The supreme creator of the world, Brahman, produces the world out of Him as the representation of magical hallucination which has order and uniformity as well as unchangeable systems of relations, but which is all the same a mirage or *māyā* and is relatively temporary. The poet also moves his magic wand and drawing upon the materials of the world, weaves a new creation which possesses its own law but which is free from any spatio-temporal bondage of particularity in the objective world. It becomes spread out in our aesthetic consciousness where the aesthetic delight may show itself without being under the limitation of the objective world and the ordinary concerns and interests of the subjective mind. Yet there are some dramas at least like the *Mṛcchakaṭika* and the *Mudrārākṣasa* which satisfy our modern standards of judgment about drama.

The idea behind the happy ending of Indian dramas.

Consistent with the view that drama was not regarded by the Sanskrit poets as a composition in which the conflict of action and re-action and the struggle of passions are to be delineated, the Sanskrit poets as a rule abstained from showing any violent action or shocking scenes or shameful episodes or gross demonstration of passion or anything revolting in general on the stage. They had a sense of perfect decorum and decency so that the total effect intended by the drama might not in any way be vitiated. Consonant with this attitude and with the general optimism of Indian thought and philosophy that the world-process ultimately tends to beatitude and happiness whatsoever pains and sufferings there may be in the way—that Indian drama as a rule does not end tragically ; and to complete the effect we have often a benedictory verse to start with or a verse of adoration, and a general benediction for all in the end so that the present effect of the drama may leave a lasting impression on the mind. Indian culture as a rule does not believe that the world is disorderly and that accidents and chance-occurrences may frustrate good life and good intentions, or that the storms and stress of material events are purposeless and not inter-related with the moral life of man. On the other hand, the dominant philosophical belief is that the whole material world is integrally connected with the destiny of man and that its final purpose is the fulfilment of the moral development of man. Even the rigorous *Smṛtiśāstra* which is always anxious to note our transgressions has always its provisions for the expiation of our sins. No sins or transgressions can be strong enough to stick to a man ; it may be removed either by expiation or by sufferings. Freedom and happiness are the birth-right of a men. The rigorous life imposed upon an ascetic is intended to bring such beatitude and happiness as may be eternal. Consonant with such a view the ideal of art should be not one of laying emphasis on the changeful and accidental occurrences but on the law and harmony of justice and goodness and ultimate happiness. When we read the dramas of Shakespeare and witness the sufferings of King Lear and of Desdemona or of Hamlet, we feel a different philosophy. We are led to think that the world is an effect of chaotic distribution and redistribution of energy, that accidents and chance occurrences are the final determinanfs of events and the principle of the moral government of the world is only a pious fiction. But Indian culture as a rule being committed to the principle of the moral fulfilment of man's values as being ultimate does seldom allow the poets and artists to leave the destiny of the world to any chance occurrence. Chance occurrences and accidents do indeed occur and when the whole is not within our perspective they may seem to rule the world. But this is entirely contrary to Indian outlook. Granting that in our partial perspective this may appear to be true, yet not being reflective of the whole it is ugly, unreal and untrue and as such it is not worthy of being manifested through art, for the final appeal of art lies in a region where beauty, goodness and truth unite. The genuine art is supposed to rouse our *sattva* quality. It is these *sattva* qualities which in their tripartite aspects are the final source from which truth, goodness and beauty spring. According to the Hindu theory of Art, there cannot be any impure aesthetic delight and all aesthetic delight beautifies and purifies our soul. It is for this reason that even when the drama has a tragic end the effect of the tragic end is softened and mellowed by other episodes. Thus in the *Uttaracarita* the pivot of the drama is the desertion of Sītā. But the effect of this desertion is more than mollified by the episode of the third act in which Rama's passionate love for Sītā is so excellently portrayed and by the happy manner in which the drama ends.

The *Mahābhārata*, its dynamic character.

We may regard the *Mahābhārata* and the *Rāmāyaṇa* as the earliest specimens of great works written in the *kāvya* style. Though the *Mahābhārata* underwent probably more than one recension and though there have been many interpolations of stories and episodes yet it was probably substantially in a well-formed condition even before the Christian era. I have elsewhere tried to prove that the *Bhagavadgītā* was much earlier as a specimen of the *Vākovākya* literature which was integrated in the *Mahābhārata* as a whole. It is of interest to note that the whole tone of the *Mahābhārata* is in harmony with that of the *Gītā*. The *Mahābhārata* is not called a *kāvya*, it is called an *itihāsa* and judged by the standard of a *kāvya* it is unwieldy, massive and diffuse. It does not also follow any of the canons prescribed for a *mahākāvya* by later rhetoricians. But it is thoroughly dramatic in its nature, its personages often appear with real character and the conflict of actions and re-actions, of passions against passions, of ideals and thoughts of diverse nature come into constant conflict and dissolve themselves into a flow of beneficent harmony. It is a criticism of life, manners and customs and of changing ideals. It is free, definite and decisive and the entire life of ancient India is reflected in it as in a mirror. It contains no doubt descriptions of Nature, it abounds also in passages of love, but its real emphasis is one of life and character and the conflict of different cultures and ideals and it shows a state of society which is trying to feel its course through a chaotic conflict of different types of ideas and customs that mark the character of a society in a state of transition. Various stereotyped ideals of old are discussed here and dug to the roots as it were for discovering in and through them a certain fundamental principle which could be the basis of all morality and society. The scheme of the *Varṇāśrama-dharma* was still there and people were required to do their duties in accordance with their own *varṇas*. To do good to others is regarded in the *Mahābhārata* as the solid foundation of duty. Even truth had its basis in it. But still in the cause of one's duty and for the cause of right and justice the Kṣattriya was always bound to fight without attaching any personal interest in the fruits of his actions.

These and similar other principles as well as moral stories and episodes are appended with the main story of the *Mahābhārata* and thus it is a great store-house which holds within it at least implicitly a large part of ancient Indian culture and history of thoughts. The style of the whole is easy and flowing and there is seldom any attempt at pedantry or undue ornamentation, The style of the *Rāmāyana,* however, is much more delightful and it reveals genuine poetry of the first order. It is for this reason that the *Rāmāyaṇa* has always been looked upon as unappoachable model not only by lesser poets but also by poets like Kālidāsa and Bhavabhūti.

The essence of Kāvya as the heightened expression of experience.

Bhāmaha and other writers think, however, that the essential condition that contributes to the charm of *alaṃkāra* and *kāvya* as well is *atiśayokti* or the over-statement of the actual facts. This over-statement does not only mean exaggeration but a new way of approach to things, a heightening of value which also constitutes the essence of *vakrokti.* In whatever way one may heighten the value of that which was a mere fact of Nature it would contribute to poetry. In every type of poetry, even in *svabhāvokti,* the poet has to re-live within him the facts of Nature or the ordinary experiences of life and it is by such an inner enjoyment of the situation that the poet can contribute a part of his own inner enjoyment and spiritual perspective to the experiences themselves.[1] Mere statement of facts in which there is no sign that the poet lived through it cannot make literature. "The sun has set, the birds are going to their nests" —are mere informations. They do not constitute *kāvya.*[2] Thus the so-called *alaṃkāras* are often but

1. *saiṣā sarvaiva vakroktiranayārtho vibhāvyate* ।
yatno'syāṁ kavinā kāryaḥ ko'laṁkāro'nayā vinā ॥
—Bhāmaha, II. 85.

2. *gato'stamarko bhātīnduryānti vāsāya pakṣiṇaḥ* ।
ityevamādi kiṁ kāvyaṁ vārttāmenāṁ pracakṣate ॥
—Bhāmaha, II. 87,

the signs which show that the poet has re-lived through his ordinary experiences with his aesthetic functions and has thus created art. An over-emphasis of them, however, or a wilful effort at pedantry which does not contribute to beauty is indeed a fault. But in a poet like Bāṇa we find the oriental grandeur of decoration which, though majestic and pompous, is nevertheless charming.

Social Background of Literature

The choice of subjects. If we take a review of the subject matter of the various kāvyas and dramas, we find that the plots are mostly derived from the *Mahābhārata*, the *Rāmāyaṇa* and sometimes from some of the Purāṇas, sometimes from the stories of great kings, or religious and martial heroes, or sometimes from floating stories or from the great story-book of Guṇāḍhya and its adaptations, and sometimes from the traditional episodes about kings and sometimes also from stories invented by the poet himself. But as we move forward through the centuries, when the freedom of thought and views and ideas became gradually more and more curbed, the choice of subjects on the part of the poets became almost wholly limited to the stories of the *Rāmāyaṇa* and the *Mahābhārata*. This would be evident to anyone who will read the history of Sanskrit literature as presented here together with editorial comments at the end of the book.

Literature and life. Works of literature are not mere plays of imagination or of solitary caprices of the brain, but they may be said to be transcripts of contemporary manners or as representing types of certain kinds of mind. It is sometimes held that from the works of literature one might form a picture of the modes of human feelings and thoughts through the progressive march of history.

Mammaṭa in his *Kāvyaprakāśa* says that kāvya produces fame, one can know from it the manners and customs of the age and that it produces immediate artistic satisfaction of a transcendent order both for the reader and for the writer and it is also instructive by the presentation of great ideals in a sweet and captivating manner like that of one's lady love.

We can understand the history of literature of any country only by regarding it as being merely a product, a flower as it were, of the entire history rising upwards towards the sun like a gigantic tree with outspreading branches. It may be difficult to follow the tree from branch to branch and from leaf to leaf, but the tree has left its mark, the type to which it belongs, in its flowers. One can classify the histories of the various people by comparing the essential characteristics of the literature as much as one can classify the trees through the flowers. It is indeed true that an individual poet, though he may belong to his age, may have his own peculiarity of temperament and interest by which he may somewhat transcend the age. But such transcendence cannot altogether change the character of his mind which is a product of his society.

History and life.

Genuine history does not consist of the wars and battles that are fought, the accession and deposition of kings ; so if we judge of literature, it is not mere mythology or language or dogmas or creeds which may be discovered from certain documents that constitute literature, but it is the men that have created it. The general characteristics of an age can also become vivid if we can portray before our mind the individual men. Everything exists only through the individuals and we must become acquainted with the typical individual. We may discover the sources of dogmas, classify the poems, realise the political constitution of the country or analyse the language in accordance with the linguistic principles and so far clear the ground. But genuine history is brought to light only when the historian discovers and portrays across the lapse of centuries the living men as to how they worked, how they felt, how they are hemmed in by their customs, so that we may feel that we hear their voice, see their gestures, postures and features, their dress and garment, just we can do of friends whom we have visited in the morning or seen in the street.

If we want to study a modern French poet like Alfred de Musset, or Victor Hugo, we may imagine him, as Taine says, "in his black coat and gloves, welcomed by the ladies and making every evening his fifty bows and his score of *bon-mots* in society, reading the papers in the morning, lodging as a rule on the second floor ; not over-gay because he has nerves and specially because in this dense democracy where we choke one another, the discredit of the dignities of office has exaggerated his pretensions while increasing his importance and because the refinement of his feelings in general disposes him somewhat to believe himself a deity." Then again, if we take a poet like Racine of the 17th century, we can imagine him to be elegant, courtier-like, a fine speaker, with a majestic wig and ribbon-shoes, both Royalist and a Christian, clever at entertaining a prince, very respectful to the great, always knowing his place, assiduous and reserved, at Marly as at Versailles, among the regular pleasures of a polished society, brimming with salutations, graces, airs and fopperies of the Lords, who rose early in the morning to obtain the promise of being appointed to some office, in case of the death of the present holder, and among charming ladies who can count their genealogies on the fingers in order to obtain the right of sitting at a particular place in the court. So also when we read a Greek tragedy we must be able to imagine of well-formed beautiful figures living half-naked in the gymnasia or in the public squares under the most enchanting panorama of views ; nimble and strong, conversing, discussing, voting, yet lazy and temperate, waited on by slaves so as to give them leisure to cultivate their understanding and exercise their limbs and with no desire beyond attending to what is beautiful. We can get a picture of such a Greek life from thirty chosen passages of Plato and Aristophanes much better than we can get from a dozen of well-written histories.

Fashionable life in early India.

If we wish to picture before our mind the life of a city beau in ancient India we can imagine him as having a house beside a lake with a garden beside it, having many rooms for his works, for meeting people, for sleep and for bath—a house divided into an external and internal part, the internal part for the ladies. His bed is covered with a white sheet made fragrant with incense, pillowed on both sides, the head and the feet, and very soft in the middle, with a seat for an idol or image of a deity at the head-side of the bed, a small table with four legs of the same height as the bed on which there are flower-garlands, sandal-paste, a little wax in a vessel, a little fragrant fan, spices ; there is a spitoon on the ground, the 'Vīṇā' is hanging on a peg in the wall ; there is a number of pictures hanging in proper positions in the wall, articles for painting on a table, some books of poems and some garlands. The seats in the room are covered with beautiful covers ; outside in the verandah there are probably birds in a cage and arrangements of diverse sports in the yard, a swing hanging in a shady place ; and an elevated quadrangle for sitting at pleasure.

The beau rises in the morning, performs his morning ablutions, offers his morning prayers and other religious duties, besmears himself faintly with sandal-paste and wears clothes fragrant with the smoke of *aguru,* wears a garland on his hair, slightly paints his lips with red, chews betel leaves, and looking at his face at a mirror, will go out to perform his daily duties. He takes his bath everyday, cleanses his body with perfumes, gets himself massaged, sometimes takes vapour-baths, shaves generally every three days, takes his meals in the middle of the day, in the afternoon and also in the night ; after meals he would either play or go to sleep and in the evenings go out to the clubs for sport. The early part of the night may be spent in music and the night in love-making of diverse kinds, receiving ladies and attending to them. He arranges festivities on the occasions of worship of particular gods ; in the clubs he talks about literature in small groups, he sits together and drinks, goes out to gardens and indulges in sports. On festive occasions in the temple of Sarasvatī dramatic performances are held and actors and dancers from different temples come and meet together for the performance. Guests are received and well attended to. The clubs were generally located in the houses of courtesans or in special houses or in the houses of some members of the club. These clubs were often encouraged by the kings and in such places men more or less of the same age, intelligence, character and riches, met and spent their time in mutual conversation or conversation with courtesans. There they discussed literature, or practised dramatic art, dancing, singing, etc. They would often drink wines at each other's houses.

Life of a poet after Rājaśekhara

Rājaśekhara describes the daily life of a poet. He rises in the morning, performs his morning duties including religious practices. Then sitting at leisure in his study-room, he studies books relevant to poetry for about three hours and for about another three hours he engages himself in writing poetry. Towards midday, he takes his bath and meals, after which he again engages himself in literary conversations and literary work. In the afternoon, in association with chosen friends he criticises the work done in the morning, When a person writes something under the inspiration of emotion he cannot always be critical. It is therefore desirable that he should criticise his own work and try to better the composition in association with chosen friends. He then re-writes the work. He sleeps for six hours and in the early hours of the morning he reviews the work of the previous day. There are, however, poets who have no restrictions of time and are always engaged in writing poetry. Such poets have limitations of time as those engaged in services of some kind or other. Well-placed women such as princesses, daughters of high officials and courtesans as well as the wives of gay people became often highly learned and also poets.

Early academies

It is the business of the king to establish an assembly of poets. When the king himself is a poet, he would often make assembly halls for the poets where all learned people assemble as well as musicians, actors, dancers and singers. The kings Vāsudeva, Sātavāhana, Śūdraka, probably all had established such academies. Is for this reason that in the capitals of great kings learning had so often flourished. Thus, Kālidāsa, Meṇṭha, Amara, Rūpa, Sūra, Bhāravi, Bhaṭṭāra Harichandra and Candragupta flourished in Ujjayinī. So also Upavarṣa, Varṣa, Paṇini, Piṅgala,

Vyāḍi, Vararuci, Patañjali and others flourished in Pātaliputra.[1]

We know from *Arthaśāstra* that all kinds of teaching of fine arts and literature were ecouraged by the Mauryyas and that teachers of music, dancing, acting, etc., were maintained out of the provincial revenue. The kings held in their courts from time to time great exhibitions of poets and scholars, where they wrangled with one another and vied for victory in literary contests. There were often Poet Laureates attached to the king's court. Śrīharṣa says that in the court of Jayacandra a seat was reserved for him and he was offered two betel-leaves as a mark of honour.

Life at the time of Bāṇa.

Let us look at the autobiography of Bāṇa, who lived in the court of Śrīharṣa in the 7th century. He tells us that his mother died when he was quite young and his father also died when he was almost of the age of fourteen. He was studying at the time and he had sufficient wealth to maintain himself at home. But with the beginning of youth he was impatient and got into naughty habits. At this time he got a number of associates and friends. A little scrutiny into the host of associates that Bāṇa had may give us an idea of the sort of people that lived in the city and how in the city life all classes of people mixed together. Thus he says that he had for his asiociates Caṇḍasena and Matṛsena, who were born out of a Brahmin father and a Śūdra mother, the poet Iśāna, Rudra and Nārāyaṇa, who were learned scholars, Bharata, the composer of Sanskrit songs, Vāyu-vikāra, who was born in the

1 *iha kālidāsa-meṇṭhāv-atrā-mararūpa-sūra-bhāravayaḥ/*
haricandra-candraguptau-parīkṣitāv-iha viśālāyāṁ//
śrūyate ca pāṭaliputre śāstrakāra-parīkṣā—
atro-pavarṣa-varṣāv-iha pāṇini-piṅgalāv-iha-vyāḍiḥ/
vararuci-patañjalī iha parīkṣitāḥ khyātim upajagmuḥ//

—**Kāvyamīmāṁsā, Ch. X**

family of those who made songs in Prākrt, Anaṅgavāṇa and Sūcivāṇa, two ladies, Kātyāyanikā and Cakravākikā, Mayūraka the forester, Caṇḍaka the seller of betel-leaves Mandāraka the reader, Caṇḍaka the physician, Sudṛṣṭi the artist, Siddhasena the goldsmith and jeweller, Govinda the writer, Vīravarman the painter, Kumāradatta the varnisher, Jīmūta the drummer, Somila and Grahāditya the singers, Kuraṅgika the independent artisan girl, the pipers, Madhukara and Pārāvata, Darduraka the teacher of dancing, Keralikā the massage-girl, the dice-player Ākhaṇḍalaka, the dancing-master Tāṇḍavika, the actor Śikhaṇḍaka, the nun Sumati, the monk Vīradeva, the dancing-girl Haramikā, the reciter Jayasena, the śaiva Vakraghoṇa, the enchanter Karālakeśa, and the magician Cakorākṣa. Being overcome by such an association he went out of his home for seeing different countries in an irresponsible manner and after a time returned to his country. He then describes the atmosphere of Vedic studies and sacrifices that prevailed among his relations. Their houses rang always with the sound of Vedic recitations. People had their forehead besmeared with ashes, their long hairs were brown like fire. The children, who came to see the sacrificial ceremonies, sat on different sides. There were little hollows which were softened with the flowing soma-juice. The yards were green with grass. The skins of dark deer were lying about on which lay the sacrificial cakes and sacrificial rice. The *nīvāra* paddy were scattered about on the sands. Hundreds of holy disciples were bringing the green *kuśa,* the sacrificial wood, cowdung ; the yard was marked everywhere with the hoofs of cows that supplied milk for the sacrificial *āmīkṣā*. Many of the sacrificers were busy besmearing their *kamaṇḍalus* with mud. Heaps of branches of fig tree were lying about for sacrificial pegs. The whole ground was rendered brown by the sacrificial offerings. The smoke of the clarified butter had darkened the foliage of trees.

Gradual separation of city life from the life in the villeges.

We have again in *Harṣacarita* the description of splendour and magnificence of the capital and the court of a Hindu king and the description as to how he encouraged scholars and poets, artists, and scientists as also the pleasures of a city-life. As we read Kālidāsa describing court scenes many centuries before, we find that the court-life was not so far removed by its splendour and majesty from the life of ordinary people, the citizens, the members of the hermitage, and the like. Dilīpa in his journey to the hermitage of Vaśiṣṭha goes alone with his wife looking at the village scenes and talking with the rustic people on the way. His personal greatness, strength and vigour of character made such an appearance of his great personality that though alone he appeared as if he was in accompaniment of a host of retinue and army. There is a naïve simplicity in the portrayal of Dilīpa and Duṣyanta, of Vikrama and Puṣyamitra which we cannot find in Bāṇa's portrayal. As we move up to Bhāsa, we find that life in general, whether in court or outside, was more akin to the description that we find in the Arthaśāstra, with the difference that performances of Vedic sacrifices have a greater prominence in the lives of kings than what we find in the portrayal of royal lives in Kālidāsa or Bāṇa. Already in Kālidāsa the hermits from the forest cannot regard the city-life and the court-life with complacence. Śarṅgarava and Śāradvata think of the court of Duṣyanta as a hall surrounded with fire. Neither Vikrama nor Duṣyanta performs any sacrifice and when Puṣyamitra does it, he does so with a sense of majesty and greatness. Entirely different is the portrayal of the kings of the past age with whom performances of sacrifices and gifts are almost a normal routine. Even the great hero, Raghu, leaves up his all after his conquering career in his sacrifice.

We thus see that as we move along the centuries. the court-life becomes gradually separated from the life of the people as a whole. With this separation new types of characters and professionals of diverse description began to grow up and the court atmosphere and the city atmosphere gradually became alienated from the life of the people as a whole. Yet the older Vedic life and its ideals, as they became more and more hazy and dreamy, began to assume almost a supernatural hold consisting of fear and hope for the people at large. The influence of the legal literature with their injunctions and restrictions, became more and more stringent and more and more stiffened and inelastic as time went on. It seems that the people as a whole tolerated the court-life, but hardly assimilated it in their blood. An artificial division was thus created and more and more emphasised as we take a long perspective through the centuries from a position of an early eminence. With the inrush and settlement of Islamic supremacy and the practical destruction of Hindu court-life the breakage became almost complete. In a climate like that of India, people indeed appreciated the passionate side of life and even from the time of the Mauryyas or even earlier than that, the courtesans had almost an unrestricted importance and the urban taste often descended into vulgarity. We have the figure in terra cotta of a dancing girl discovered in the Mauryya level in Patna, where the girl is wearing shining apparels all over her body but her prominent breasts are shown uncovered. Most of the woman-figures in ancient art show the bosoms of young women in an uncovered manner. This tallies with the description of women's breasts in so many of our Sanskrit erotic verses which are shocking to our modern taste. More than this, we find Sanskrit poets vying with one another in the description of the most delicate acts of sex-life illustrating, as it were, the descriptions in the *Kāma-sūtra*. But be it as it may, the normal judgment of the audience had most often a sound inclination and in order to cater to this taste, we often find that a drama or a kāvya most often had a moral lesson to impart, though it ran always as an undercurrent. It is for this reason that stories from the *Rāmāyaṇa*, the *Mahābhārata* and the Purānas played such an important part for the formation of plots of Kāvyas and dramas. In decadent times, most of the dramas and kāvyas drew their inspiration from religious mythology, In and through such religious mythology the poets could gratify the expression of their erotic sentiments and could also cater to kindred sentiments among the audience without the fear of shocking their taste or appearing irreligious. In Sanskrit and particularly in Bengali poetry that flourished in the 16th and 17th centuries we find that erotic sentiments displayed through the divine personages of Kṛṣṇa and Rādhā became the religious creed of a particular sect of Vaiṣṇavism. Such expressions of eroticism were unrelated to marital restrictions and it was supposed that such dalliance between Kṛṣṇa and Rādhā took place in transcendental bodies to which criticisms from the standpoint of ordinary mundane life were not applicable. They were the demonstrations of love in life divine and a devotee may enjoy them from an upper sphere of spirituality with which the carnal being is out of contact. This idea of transforming eroticism into a religion had not its beginning only in the 15th or 16th century

Why Puranic legends were so extensively used.

literature of Bengal but it can be traced in the *Bhāgavata* and other literature as early as the 5th or 6th century A.D.

Love in Sanskrit poetry.

It may be pointed in this connection that sex liberty in fields other than marital were allowed in society and accepted by the legal literature, though not approved by the higher conscience of the people. The existence and persistence of *niyoga* for a long time in Hindu society shows that even in marital sphers sex liberty was allowed in a restricted form. The existence of various kinds of marriages and the legal rights allowed to children produced in a non-marital manner also illustrate the contention. In pre-Christain times, the Gāndharva form of marriage was regarded as quite respectable and a girl of a certain age was given the right to choose her own husband, if the parents had not married her within a prescribed age. We find in Kālidāsa that Duṣyanta says that tradition goes that daughters of kings had married according to the Gāndharva custom and that such marriages were approved by parents. This shows that in Kālidāsa's time at least the Gāndharva marriage was going out of fashion. But in the story of *Vāsavadattā* in Bhāsa and also in *Avimāraka,* it appears that no exception was taken to the Gāndharva marriage. But for the restriction by the Privy Council the law of Gāndharva marriage still holds according to Hindu Law. But as early as the story of Vilhaṇa we find that in spite of the provision of Hindu Law the Gāndharva form of marriage was not recognised by the society.

But side by side with this liberty of marriage of earlier times, the rules of Smṛti gradually made marriage of women more and more binding before the attainment of puberty. Thus, excepting in the case of nymphs or daughters of nymphs, or girls of kings from older stories, like that of Guṇāḍhya, themes of free love between adult men and women are indeed very rare in Sanskrit dramas. The *Mālatīmādhava* is a *prakaraṇa* or that type of drama where the plot is invented by the poet. But though the story as a whole is new, element of it are mostly found in the *Kathā-sarit-sāgara*. In Śūdraka's *Mṛcchakaṭika* we have a portrayal of love between the courtesan Vasantasenā and Cārudatta.

But yet we have a host of Sanskrit verses which deal with the love of *abhisārikās* or those women who themselves come to the houses of their beloved at night. In the *Kāma-sūtra* also we find that the houses of the *nāgaras* were visited by the *abhisārikās*. But there is hardly any instance, apart from the *kathā* literature, wherein any respectable girl has been depicted as playing the part of an *abhisārikā*. In the anthologies and *śatakas* we have almost a superabundance of love poems which are appearently of a non-marital character. But these are mostly single ślokas depicting a love scene, portraying a passion, or a love situation, without any reference to the sort of persons between whom this love was carried on.

Rasa and Rasābhāsa

Mammaṭa makes a distinction between *rasa* and *rasābhāsa* (semblance of *rasa*).[1] When a woman has many lovers or when illicit love is expressed, or when love is not responded to, or if the expression of love be with regard to intimate relations of a higher status, such expression of love is shocking to the audience and is called semblance of amorous sentiment *(rasābhāsa)*. Thus, some of the best erotic poems have been counted

1 *tadābhāsā anaucitya-pravartitāḥ*..............*Kāvya-prakāśa IV.* 49. *anaucityaṁ ca sahṛdaya-vyavahārato jñeyaṁ. yatra teṣām anucitamiti dhīḥ. tacca śṛṅgāre bahuviṣayatvena upanāyakādi-gatatvena nāyaka-nāyikānyatara-mātraviṣayatvena guru-jana gatatvena tiryagādi-gatatvādinā ca nānaiva. Uddyota* **commentary on the above as quoted in Jhalkikar's edition of** ***Kāvyaprakāśa.***

by many critics as examples of *rasābhāsa*. Sāradātanaya in his *Bhāva-prakāśana* of the 12th century modified this definition to a considerable extent and regarded that only when a description of love is such that it creates laughter that it is called *rasābhāsa*.

Gowth of Indian civilisation from Vedic literature.

If we take the general sweep of the growth of Indian civilisation and culture we find that Hindu life in India opens with the pretty vast collection of poems called the Vedas, which are surcharged with the impressions of Nature in its beautiful, tender, terrific and tempestuous aspects produced upon the extremely sensitive minds of the Indian people. The Aryans when colonising in India came amongst people who were either extremely barbaric and uncivilized, or who, as in the Indus Valley and in the South, were people who had a civilisation entirely different from theirs. The Aryans clung to their social order of the four *varṇas*, to their Vedas and to their original customs and rights in order to keep their integrity amongst an alien and barbaric people. Their original religion consisted of hymns to the Nature gods as preserved in the Vedas along with certain simple rites. It is difficult to reconstruct the nature of these rites as they have become merged in the complexity of rituals associated with the necessity of the preservation of fire The Vedic prose writings evolved by way of elaborating and systematising these sacrificial details. But as the Vedic families grew in number and expanded in different directions in the East and the South a separate secular life evolved and differentiated from the original Vedic structure and it gave rise to various professions as cities began to grow. The original motive of the early Vedic hymns was religious worship and as such Sanskrit literature has seldom been able to free itself from the religio-moral element. But with the expansion of life two other motives differentiated themselves in an absolutely clear and distinct form. The Vedic religion had its magical element with reference to supra-mundane happiness and all through the development of Indian religion and philosophy it had never been able to get rid of this magical element. The philosophies of the Vedānta, the Buddhism, the Yoga and the Sāṃkhya have always to depend upon the concept of magic and illusion as the fundamental pivot of the superstructure of these philosophies.

Natural scenery of India.

But with regard to the mundane affairs, the Indians have always been absolutely definite, concrete and realistic in their conceptions. There is no mysticism whatsoever in Sanskrit poetry. They are all based upon concrete and tangible emotions. The inexhaustible wealth cf natural phenomena in a country of tropical climate girdled by great mountain ranges, deep and extensive oceans interspersed with long and wide rivers ; where the seasons appear in so marked a manner with glorious colours of the sky, the glowing sunshine, silvery moonbeams, the pouring sonorous rains, the sweet and green verdure, the blossoming fragrant flowers of all hues and beauty ; where birds with brilliant feathers and sweet chirpings and cooings and animals of all description, the beautiful antelopes, the fleet steed, the majestic elephants and the royal lions are abundant in the forests ; all these captivated the sensitive minds of the Indians as much as the gazelleeyed damsels, with their ruddy cheeks and lips, the flowing raven hair, and healthy physique of emphatic outlines of figure.

The characteristics of Indian temperament.

On the other hand, the Indian mind is subtle, deep, logical to the extreme, imaginative and analytic. The Indian mind has as much appeal to passion and emotion, desire for enjoying the world at its best as for making provision for future post-mortem welfare which is as real to it as the world here on earth. At the same time, the Indian mind takes infinite delight in carrying on logical thoughts to their consistent conclusions in analysing, classifying, naming and arranging the data in any sphere of experience. Again, the climatic conditions in which the Aryans in India came to live were such that their very existence in life often depended upon favourable showers which alone could render their corn-fields fertile. They had thus to depend upon fate and Providence as the fundamental datum for their well-being. Yet they were fully conscious and alive to the efficiency of human will and action. Human beings are not mere playthings in the hands of Nature. The Indians in the history of their civilisation understood the value of human life and human existence as the end and purpose of the whole of natural existence. They therefore somehow belived that fate or destiny, howsoever unknown and unknowable may be its nature, can in reality be influenced and modified by our actions. Herein they fell back on faith which was an indispensable postulate for proper action. This world is for our enjoyment and so we have the world beyond the present, after death, which must be for our happy existence and it is somehow given to us that whatever may be the obstacles in the way of destiny or fate or in the way of the vagaries of natural phenomena, it lies in our power, which is itself a faith, that we can modify its nature and method of working in our favour. Early in the history of human civilisation they discovered the existence of a supreme power which not only controlled the phenomena of the external world but also all the biological phenomena of life, the functions of our cognitive and conative senses. They began to search for the secret of this power in the external world and being disappointed therein, turned inwardly to their own minds and discovered that the secret of this great power that ruled the life, the universe and the man, was nothing but the self. Thus, side by side with the development of the magical literature which elaborated the sacrificial doctrine that sought the source of all power outside man in his ritual dealings with the external world, we have the secret instructions of the Upaniṣads which reveal to us the ultimate philosophy and secret of human life and its place in Nature.

The genius and temperament of the race shows itself in the literature.

Literature is but a mode of the self-expression of the inner man. The external man is visible, the internal man is invisible. We can look at the articles of civilisation, the house, the furniture, the dress, the ordinary marks of refinement or rusticity, energy or constraint, customs and manners, intelligence, inventiveness and coolness, but all these are but different roads, the visible avenues that lead us to the invisible internal man as these are but his ways of expression. The internal man is but an organic unity of emotive and conative impulses which unroll themselves in accordance with the influences, physical and social. in which the person has to evolve. The gifts of a particular race are its own. The peculiarities of the Greek imagination that gave us the twin sister of the Antigone of Sophocles and the goddesses of Phidias are the peculiar expressions of the Greek mind. As there are differences in anatomical structure between the various species of animal and plant lives, so there are essential anatomical peculiarities in the struture of the different racial minds. If we take the life of a man like Cromwell as depicted by Carlyle we may discover a secret organic unity within him and an inner soul which would explain all his springs and action. We find how a soul is working with the troubling reverses of a melancholic imagination but with a tendency and temperment and instinct which is English to its very core, unintelligible to those who have not studied the peculiar English climate and still more the peculiarities of the genius of the English race. In and through his letters and mutilated speeches one may have the panorama of pictures that led him from his farm and team to the general's tent and the Protector's throne; all through the changes and vicissitudes of life, in his freaks of conscience and political conclusions, the entire machinary of his mind becomes directly visible; and all through his individuality we mark the peculiarities of the insulated Englishman. In understanding the peculiar transformation of the English life in the middle ages we can perceive how from under the meaningless theological discussions and monotonous sermons, how from underneath the beating of living hearts, the convulsions and apathies of monastic life, the unpredicted genius of English life re-asserts itself in wavy turmoils and how the inroads of surrounding worldliness and its struggles with the monastic ideal, the true appreciation of civic life in its exactness, balance and strength, reveals itself, and how the iron determination of the race shows itself through its constant struggle with the neighbouring states. How this English genius is well-contrasted with that of France, cultured and refined with her drawing-room manners and untiring analysis of character and actions, her keen irony and ready wit, her finesse so practised in the discrimination of shades of thought, her turbulent and uncontrollable emotions can be judged by any one who would care to study the representative literature of the two countries.

The idea of a supernatural world, of God and His relation to man is indeed common to most civilised human races, but it is the peculiar mode and apprehension distinctly unique in itself that has in one case resulted in the architecture of the churches being thrown down the old status, destruction of pictures and ornaments, curtailment of ceremonies, shutting up of worshippers in high pews and the like and in the other case in the erection of temple-structures, installation of images, abolition of windows, darkening of the inner chamber, and at the same time in the provision for individual worship for every person according to his needs and also in the provision for conceiving God as formless, graspable only in thought and devotion and purity of character. While truth is regarded as one in the European countries, the Indians have always regarded the reality of grades and aspects of truth. It is for this reason that evolution in Europe has always taken place by destroying or modifying the old, ushering in the new with a total disregard of the old except in so far as its elements lay hidden in the structure of the new. Indian genious, however, felt no contradiction between the old and the new. The development of Indian thought therefore is the ushering in of the new without the annulment of the old. While the development of the Upaniṣadic monism may on one hand be regarded as the annulment of the pluralism of Vedic sacrifices and rituals yet the latter persisted side by side with the former through centuries. The Indian always found such relations between the old and the new that it regarded every aspect of the evolution as true with reference to human history and the history of truth in evolution. The European who does not understand this peculiarity of the Indian genius, must necessarily fail to have a proper prespective of the evolution and development of Indian thought. The Indians do not feel any contradiction in taking to Vedic forms of rituals at the time of marriage and have the images of Śiva, Viṣṇu and Śakti installed in his family temples and at the same time regard the Brahman as the ultimate truth as formless, causeless and yet the cause of all.

Religious and secular ideas wedded together.

Many European scholars have discussed the question of the secular or religious origin of dancing and dramatic plays. They have failed to notice that the origin is both religious and secular and in the same performance even now both religious and secular value is attached. The Vaiṣṇava lyrics are tested from a literary point of view as excellent poems of love and at the same time they are enjoyed with deep religious fervour developing into religious frenzy and unconscious states of emotional depth.

Contact with alien races.

When the Aryan settlers entered India in successive hordes and found themselves amongst the aborigines of India, the most important concern with them was the maintenance of the integrity of their race and culture. They were, however, somewhat humane in their temperament and could not think of destroying absolutely those of the aborigines who submitted to them against the hostile ones, the Rākṣasas and the Asuras. They carried on an interminable war against the hostile ones until at least most of them were destroyed. It is not impossible that the civilization of the people of the Indus Valley which is almost universally admitted as being pre-Vedic was so destroyed. At the same time it would be unwise to think that even these hostile people had not infiltrated some of their customs and religious beliefs and other elements of their civilisation. The Śiva cult and the Yoga cult may be pointed out as specific instances of such infiltration. A close analysis and comparison of the elements of earliest Vedic civilisation may in course of time reveal many more instances of mutual contact and indebtedness.

The idea of *dharma* as social integrity.

But along with the successful war and occupation of the country and gradual extension of the civilisation towards the East along the course of the Ganges and towards the South beyond the Vindhyas, unobstructed at the time by any foreign invasions, the principal problem before these Aryans was to solve the question of social synthesis consistent with absolute social integrity. They felt that without such a social integrity their unity and fraternity would be lost and their influence and existence would be destroyed under the strange influence of an alien land. They therefore fell back for the preservation of their old customs and manners to the religious practices as preserved in the oral traditions of the Vedas and the subsequent Vedic literature as it developed gradually in course of time. Their chief motive urge was social preservation and social continuity and maintenance of its integrity and solidarity which the term '*dharma*' etymologically means. Such a problem need not arise in any appreciable manner in the case of those Aryans who had migrated to the Western countries for where the Aryans were in large multitude they destroyed the original aborigines and the inter-marriage between the various hordes of Aryans did not or could not lead to any disruption of their social integrity as Aryans. In Iran the Aryans preserved their integrity and thus their civilization till the advent of the Moslems and when they could not withstand the impact of Islamic invasion they largely lost their integrity and their civilisation merged with the civilisation of the Semitic people. But even there the best literature and philosophy of the Islamic world had been produced by the Persian converts. No other nation has been known to produce literature and philosophy of a standard higher than that of the Aryans.

As the preservation of the Vedic culture was thus regarded upon as the only means of social preservation and the maintenance of social integrity, and was thus looked upon as *dharma,* the idea of *dharma* as conformity to old customs and manners of Vedic times became the main spring not only of the evolution of the legal literature, the *Purāṇas* and the *Dharma-śāstras,* but it became ingrained in the society as the fundamental and indispensable structure and scheme of all its cultural products. Nothing could be allowed to prevail that would come into conflict with the *dharma.*

The concept of *dharma* depends on the Vedas.

This *dharma* again was based upon a literature and pre-eminently upon a poetic literature, *viz.*, the Vedas. Literature thus in one sense as a traditional storehouse of past customs and manners, was the source of *dharma* and it was *dharma* also that was in some sense at least the dominant influence or guide in the production and development of later literature. Practices of a secular nature that prevailed in old Vedic times became associated on the one hand with *dharma* and on the other they continued to have a development on secular lines such as would not be inconsistent with the practice of *dharma.*

Continuity of even the semi-secular practices through the ages.

I shal give one instance. In the *Ṛgveda* I. 92.4 there is a passage with describes the dancing of a courtesan (*nṛtu*)—*adhi peśāṃsi vapate nṛtur-iva-porṇute vakṣv ucchreva varjaham.* Sāyaṇa in commenting on the verse explains it as follows :—*nṛtur-iva nartayantī yoṣid-iva peśāṃsi, rūpa-nāmaitat sarvair-darśanīyāni rūpāṇi uṣā adhivapate svātmani adhikaṃ dhārayati vakṣaḥ svakīyam uraḥpradeśam porṇute anācchāditam karoti* *i.e.*, the Uṣas is like a dancing girl who carefully clothes herself in her best raiments but keeps her bosom uncovered in order to attract the eyes of all. Now, a terracotta figure of a dancing girl with beautiful and sparkling raiments over all her body but with bare bosoms has been discovered in the Maurya level of excavation near the site of the present Patna College. (See A. Banerjee-Śāstri's article, I. H. Q., 1933, p. 155.) Now, we find that exactly the same kind of dancing girl that used to dance before the audience in Vedic times appears in the same kind of dress keeping her bosoms bare and her body clothed in raiments before the audience in Maurya times. The continuty of the practice of the same kind of dancing with same kind of clothes for more than thousand years, cannot but appear to us surprising. Exactly the same sort of dancing of the Devadasis may even now be noticed in many of the temples of the South.

***Dharma*, the guiding principle of Hindu culture.**

We thus notice a strange continuity of secular practices and a strange association of these with religious practices which has led many scholars to conceive the development of Indian drama from religious sources. The point, however, that we wish to lay stress upon here, is that the motive of *dharma* being essentially of the nature of social preservation and maintenance of social solidarity, had never been lost sight of in the development of Indian literature. The importance of this would be realised when we consider that even to-day the indispensable definition of being a Hindu consists in his participation in and loyalty to the Vedic practices.

Secular outlook and the doctrine of *trivarga*.

If we closely review the tendencies of the Vedic culture, we find that in addition to the adherence to certain Vedic customs and manners and the doctrines of sacrifices, the Vedic people were anxious like other Aryan people to provide for wealth and enjoyment in this life and for making provision for happiness hereafter. As a matter of fact, most of their prayers are for mundane advantages, prosperity and happiness,

Even a cursory reading of the *Atharva Veda* will show that these Vedic people would offer prayers even for the meanest advantage and pleasure of vulgar types. The idea of *dharma* was later on supplemented with high moral ideals, self-control, control of passions and the like, culminating in the desire for liberation, but the idea of sense-enjoyment and the accumulation of articles of prosperity, *i.e.*, *kāma* and *artha*, remained all through the centuries more or less unaffected. The Hindu culture thus has been motivated principally by four impulses, the impulse of *dharma, artha, kama* and *mokṣa*. Of these the *mokṣa* literature consists primarily of the Upaniṣads, the work of the different philosophical systems, the religio-philosophical literature of the *Tantras* and the like. The impulse of *dharma* is to be found in the sacrificial literature and its accessories, the *Vedāṅgas*. The motive of *artha* forms the content of the *Vārttā* literature which is now mostly extinct. The motive of *kāma* in its special application to sexology has led to the development of a fairly large literature on the *Kāma-śāstra*. The *dharma, artha* and *kāma* together are called the *trivarga*. The literature of Political Science, the Kāvya and the like are supposed to have been motivated by the three fundamental emotive tendencies, *dharma, artha* and *kāma*. Of these the huge *stotra* literature is motivated by the impulse of *dharma* while the other forms of literature, *viz.*, Epic Kāvyas, Lyric Kāvyas, the Dramas, have been motivated by three principles, *dharma, artha* and *kāma* and so also is the *kathā* literature and the *nīti* literature.

We have said above that the genius of the Indian mind is at once extremely analytic and imaginative. For this reason we have a fairly large literature of *Nātya-śāstra* and *Alamkāra-śāstra*, which not only analyses in detail the various elements that constitute the complex act of dancing, acting and music, but which has also tried to review in detail the structure and technique of the Drama as well as the principles underlying the display of sentiments through the histrionic art as well as poetry in general.

Bharata in describing *nātya* has characterised it as productive of *dharma* and fame, as conductive to long life and increasing the understanding and as instructive to people in general. It is supposed to be the conjoint result of all knowledge, wisdom, art and craft. Its purpose is to produce a sort of imitation of human events and character. It produces satisfaction and rest for the suffering, the fatigued, the wretched and it consoles those that are troubled by grief.[1] Dramatic art is thus regarded by Bharata, the author of the earliest work on the science of dramaturgy now available, as the art of reproduction by imitation. Consistently with it, Dhanañjaya has defined *nātya* as the reproduction of a situation and as the different characters are given visible form (*rūpa*) in the person of the actors, a drama is called a *rūpaka*. Among the commentators of Bharata there are learned discussions regarding the sense in which a dramatic performance may be regarded as a reproduction in the sense of imitation and Abhinavagupta, the most penetrating and distinguished critic of art, strongly objects to the idea of imitation. He holds that through music, dancing, acting and the dress, dyeing, and the stage environment, the dramatic performance is entirely

[1] *nānā-bhāvopasampannaṁ nānā-vasthāntarātmakam |*
loka-vṛttānukaraṇaṁ nātyametanmayā kṛtam ||
duḥkhārtānāṁ śramārtānāṁ śokārtānāṁ tapasvinām |
viśrānti-jananaṁ kāle nāṭyametad bhaviṣyati ||
dharmyaṁ yaśasyamāyuṣyaṁ hitaṁ buddhi-vivardhanam |
loko-padeśa-jananaṁ nāṭyametad bhaviṣyati ||
na taj-jñānaṁ na tac-chilpaṁ na sā vidyā na sā kalā |
nāsau yogo na tat karma nāṭye'smin yanna dṛśyate ||

—Bharata's *Nāṭyaśāstra*.

a new art for the production of aesthetic joy and it is not imitation in any ordinary sense of the term. Abhinavagupta says that imitation of other's movements would produce the ludicrous and imitation of other's feelings and emotions is impossible. The influence of music, the sight of the other actors and the stage environment produce in the actor an influence by which he forgets his spatio-temporal, actual or local personality and thus transfigures himself into his dramatic personality and a new world consistent with the spirit of the dramatic situation appears in him and his performance produces in a similar manner a new influence, and a new type of communication emerges out of him and enlivens the mind of the audience. But we shall not enter here into any details of the nature of art-communication. We are only interested to point out that dramatic performance becomes an art when recitation in the form of dialogues associated with suitable gestures, postures, movement, dancing, dress and music, succeeds in giving expressions to sentiments and passions so as to rouse similar sentiments in the minds of the audience. Thus it becomes a dramatic art. Thus *Nāṭyadarpaṇa* says: *nāṭakamiti nāṭayati vicitraṃ rañjanāt praveśena sabhyānāṃ hṛdayaṃ nartayati iti nāṭakam.*[1] In this sense a dramatic performance should be distinguished from mere recitation which is not so effective. We have elsewhere in the editorial notes tried to show the manner in which the dramatic performance evoled through a combination of recitation, dancing and acting and the fact that there were at least in the 2nd century B.C. and in the time of the Mauryyas, schools and teachers for the training of the dramatic art.

Communication in dramatic art.

1 *yadyapi kathādayo'pi śrotṛhṛdayaṁ nāṭayanti tathāpi aṅk opāyādīnāṁ vaicitryahetūnāmabhāvāt na tathā rañjakatvam iti na te nāṭakam |*

Religious value of dramatic performances.

We have said above that the *kāvyas* and the *nāṭya* contributed to *dharma, artha* and *kāma* and Bharata's specification of the object of dramatic performance also confirms the view. Not only is *nāṭya* called a Veda for universal instruction and the author of the *Nāṭyaśāstra* called a *muni* (saint) but dramatic performances were generally held in times of religious festivities and when they consisted in the reproduction of the great characters of the *Rāmāyaṇa* and the *Mahābhārata*, they had not only an educative value in rousing noble passions but they were regarded also as productive of merit, both for those who performed them and for those who listened to and witnessed them. Even to-day the Rāmacarita is played in a peculiar manner in the United Provinces in India, where the players as well as the audience are surcharged with a religious emotion. Again, when a *kathaka* or a reciter would recite, say, the episode of the marriage of Sītā, religiously-minded persons would have the impression in their minds that the marriage of Sītā was actually taking place before them and those who can afford to do it, would willingly offer golden ornaments and jewels as articles of dowry for Sītā, which of course, are received by the Brahmin reciting as his fees. Even those who cannot afford to pay much would offer whatever they can, fruits and flowers, coins, grains, etc., on such an occasion. Here, again, we must note the imaginative character of the Indians, who can very easily lose their personality when they listen to the imaginary description of deeds that are dear to their hearts. I do not know if any other people in the world have such imaginary susceptibilities.

The episode of King Kulaśekhara.

In the *Prapannāmṛta* (Chap. 86) by Anantācārya there is a curious episode of King Kulaśekhara who was a Tamil king living in the 12th century, who was very fond of listening to the recitation of the *Rāmāyaṇa*.

When he listened to a verse to the effect that Rāma was alone to meet the fourteen thousand demons, he became so much excited with the affair that he immediately armed himself from head to foot and was on the point of marching with all his army to meet Rāvaṇa as an ally of Rāma.[1] Such imaginative predilection of the Indian people could easily be utilised by the poets by dealing with characters of the *Rāmāyṇa* and the *Mahābhārata* and the Purāṇas as a means of rousing the religious and moral interest of the audience and thereby contributing to *dharma*. We know that the *Rāmāyaṇa*, which is definitely called a *kāvya* and the *Mahābhārata*, which is called an *itihāsa* are regarded as invested with the holiness of the Vedas. Thus, there was an easy bridge between what may be called *dharma* and what may be called plain literature. We can also assume that the Indian people in general were as a rule religiously-minded and cared for that type of literature which initiated them to religious principles and strengthened their faith in a pleasurable manner through amusements. This may be a very important reason why most of the plots of Indian dramas and *kāvyaṣ* were taken from the *Rāmāyaṇa*, the *Mahābhārata* and the Purāṇas. There are indeed some plots derived either directly or indirectly from Guṇāḍhya or the floating materials used by him or from similar other sources. In other cases, the lives, of great kings or saints also form the subject-matter of the *kāvyas* and the dramas and in a few cases historical events have

Religious temperament of the people often explains the choice of plots.

1 *śuśrāva tam imaṁ ślokaṁ bhaktimān kulaśekharaḥ* ।
caturdaśa-sahasrāṇi rakṣasāṁ bhīma-karmaṇām ।
ekaśca rāmo dharmātmā kathaṁ yuddhaṁ bhaviṣyati ।
asahiṣṇustato' dharmayuddhaṁ śīghraṁ skhalad-gatiḥ ।
dhanurvāṇaṁ samādāya khaḍgaṁ carma ca vīryyavān ।
caturaṅgabalopeto janasthānaṁ kṛtatvaraḥ ।
pratasthe tatkṣaṇe tasya sahāyārthaṁ haripriyaḥ ॥

also been made the subject-matter of literature. Side by side with these historical *kāvyas* we have many *praśasti-kāvyas* in inscriptions which are of excellent poetic merit, such as, the *praśastis* by Kavīśvara Rāma (700-800 A.D.) and the Lalitaśūradeva of the 9th century A.D., &c,

Idealistic or religious motives sometimes inspired the poets in framing the plots.

Not only in the choice of subjects but also in the framing of the plots, poets were sometimes guided by idealistic motives. Thus Kālidāsa described the physical beauty of Pārvatī to its perfection in *Kumārasambhava,* but in the matter of the fruition of her love for a great *yogin* like Śiva, the fragile physical beauty was not deemed enough. She must go through the hardest penance in order that she may make her love fruitful. It is only the spiritual glory and spiritual attainment of spiritual beauty, beauty attained by self-control and the attainment of moral height that can become permanent and eternal.[1] In the case of the love of Śakuntalā, who in the intensity of her love had forgotten her duties in the hermitage, she had to suffer cruel rebuff and practical banishment in sorrow. The lusty love of Urvaśī was punished by her being turned into a creeper. Thus, the poet Kālidāsa, when describing the passion of love, is always careful to demonstrate that *kāma* should not in its intensity transgress the *dharma.* But the same poet was not in the least perturbed in giving us glowing experiences of conjugal satisfaction that took place between Śiva and Pārvtī, or conjugal yearning in the case of the Yakṣa for his

1 *iyeṣa sā kartumabandhya-rūpatāṁ samādhimāsthāya tapobhir-ātmanaḥ* ।
avāpyate vā kathamanyathādvayaṁ tathāvidhaṁ prema patiśca tādṛśaḥ ॥
—*Kumārasambhava,* Canto V, 2.

beloved spouse. *Kāma* in itself is not undesirable or bad, but when it transgresses *dharma* it becomes wicked. The *kāma* of King Agnivarṇa in *Raghuvaṃśa* led to his destruction. It is for this reason that the Sanskrit poets of India instead of portraying mere characters or giving expression to ardent love or other sentiments as such, or devising their plots at random from their everyday sphere of experiences, had to adopt a particular scheme, a framework of types, within which limitations they had to give vent to their poetic effusions. The scheme or the frame should be such that the fundamental principle that *dharma, artha* and *kāma* should not transgress one another leading to disastrous results, may be observed. But here again, with the exception of Bhāsa, most of the writers had conformed to the poetic convention that no drama should end with disastrous consequences. Here again, a drama as an work of art was regarded as a whole, as a cycle complete in itself. A drama ending with disastrous consequences would be a mutilated piece from the world of our experience—it would merely mean that the cycle has not been completed, or that it is only a partial view and not the whole. In spite of the charge of pessimism often laid at the door of Indian thought by the Westerners, it should be noted that the Indians who admit sorrow as a partial aspect of things would regard it as negative in the conception of the whole or totality. A drama in its totality must aim at some realisation. It is for this reason that the fully developed drama, *viz.*, a *nāṭaka*, should have in it five critical situations called the *mukha, pratimukha, garbha, vimarśa* and *nirvahaṇa*. Thus in the drama *Ratnāvalī*, the love of Sāgarikā at seeing the king Udayana at first sight, introduces the main theme

The ideal of *trivarga*.

Drama—an epitome of life.

The five critical situations.

of the drama which would culminate in the end in the happy union of Udayana with Sāgarikā. This is the seed, as it were, which would fructify in the whole drama. This seed of first love was somewhat obscured by the artifice of the king and other events that followed, but its shoot is again manifested when in Act II through the arrangement of Susaṅgatā king Udayana and Sāgarikā met each other. This is called the *pratimukha-sandhi.* The *garbha-sandhi* is that in which there are obstructive events which lead the reader to doubt whether the hopes raised would be fulfiled or not. Thus, when in *Sakuntalā* we have the curse of Durvāsā and later on, the repulsion of Śakuntalā by the king in the Court, and her disappearance, we have the *garbha-sandhi.* Later on, when at the sight of the ring the king is reminded of Śakuntalā, we have the *vimarśa-sandhi,* or in spite of the obstruction and doubt, the reader is again encouraged to hope and is partially satisfied with regard to the expected union. The last *nirvahaṇa-sandhi* is that in which the king Duṣyanta becomes again united with Śakuntalā in Act VII. Thus the five critical situations constitute a unity, an epitome of our life as a whole. Life has its crises, its difficulties and disappointments, but we have always to be hopeful regarding the final fulfilment. The drama is thus the reflection of life as a whole from the Indian point of view and contains its own philosophy. The critics, however, recommend further divisions of each of the critical stages into which we need not enter. What is important to note here is the general review of life.

Types of drama. Drama has several forms, *viz., nāṭaka, prakaraṇa, nāṭikā, prakaraṇī, vyāyoga, samavakāra, bhāṇa, ḍima, utsṛṣṭikāṅka, īhāmṛga, vīthi* and *prahasana.* The *prakaraṇa* deals with the plot consisting of the characters of ordinary people, such as the minister, Brahmin, merchant and the like and the plot generally is the poet's own invention, or taken from historical episodes. Thus *Mālatīmādhava* is a *prakaraṇa*. The heroine may either be a wife or a courtesan. In *Mṛcchakaṭika* we have a courtesan as a heroine and in *Mālatīmādhava* a wife. The other characters belong also to the sphere of common people. Among the women characters we have the procuresses and other common women. In a *prakaraṇa* there are generally troublous events and the principal hero is of a patient and peaceful temperament (*dhīraśānta*). The *nāṭikā* is a mixture of *nāṭaka* and *prakaraṇa*. The principal sentiment is generally love and the hero is generally of a soft and amorous temperament. It generally deals with the characters of kings. The hero king is always afraid of the queen in carrying on his amorous adventures. There are more heroines than heroes. It may be of one, two, three or four Acts. A *bhāṇa* portrays the character of a knave or rogue (*dhūrta*), wherein only one person acts in imaginary dialogues, *i.e.*, behaving as if the actor was responding to the question or speech of another and it consists only of one Act and it may include dancing as well. Though there is but only one actor, he carries on dialogues with imaginary persons not present on the stage. It may also include singing. Sometimes one may sit and recite with gestures. It generally portrays the amorous sentiment and sometimes heroism. The *prahasana* consists in portraying the sentiment of the ludicrous generally at the expense of the religious sects ; the actors and actresses are generally courtesans and their associates and the members of the sects at whose expense the fun is being enjoyed. It generally consists of one Act. A *ḍima* portrays the behaviours and characters of ghosts and ghostly beings, Gandharvas, Yakṣas and Rakṣasas. It generally portrays the sentiment of anger and that of the loathsome and disgusting and treats of dreadful things like the eclipse, the thunder and the comet. It generally consists of four Acts and has four critical situations. As examples of this, one may refer to the *Tripuradāha, Vṛtroddharaṇa* and *Tārakoddharaṇa.* A *vyāoga* has for its hero either gods or kings and has but few actors,—three, four or five, but not exceeding ten. The two critical situations, *garbha* and *vimarśa* are absent. It describes generally deeds of violence and fighting, but the fighting is not for the sake of any woman. It generally deals with the happenings of one particular day. A *samavakāra* deals with legendary episodes of the conflict between the gods and demons. It generally deals with the sentiment of heroism and generally consists of three Acts of three different times. It portrays siege of cities or battles or stormy destructions or destructions through fire. The *Samudramanthana* by Vatsarāja is a good illustration of *samavakāra.* A *vīthi* consists of one Act, like the *Vakulavīthi.* It generally portrays the sentiment of love and is sometimes accompanied with dancing and amorous gestures and generally there is one or two actors. The *utsṛṣṭikāṅka* deals with a known legend or a fairy tale and portrays cruel deeds and battles. Many young women are introduced as weeping and sorrowing. Though full of dreadful events, it would end in peace. Generally it contains three Acts. Actual killing should not be shown on the stage though sometimes violation of this rule is seen, as in the *utsṛṣṭikāṅka* called the *Nāgānanda,* where Jīmūtavāhana dies on the stage. An *īhāmṛga* portrays fighting for the sake of women and the hero may be godly or human and there may be great fights for the possession of heavenly nymphs. There are generally four Acts and the plot is derived from well-known stories modified by the dramatist.

Characteristics of a *nāṭaka*.

A review of these various forms of dramatic performance sheds some new light upon the problem of the evolution of the drama. Of these various forms of the drama it is only the *nāṭaka* and the *prakaraṇa* that may be regarded as full-fledged dramas. Of these two, again, the *nāṭaka* should be based upon a well-known story and the hero, who is generally a king, should be possessed of all kingly qualities. Though the story should be derived only from legends, yet whatever may be improper or undesirable should be left out. There should be many characters in it and there should be the five *sandhis* and a proper balance between the various Acts. The sentiment to be portrayed should be either heroic or amorous and nothing that may be shocking, dreadful or shameful should be shown on the stage. It should consist of at least five Acts and it should not have more than ten Acts and each should contain the event of one day or half a day. The *Vikramorvaṣī* is a five-Act drama, the *Rāmābhyudaya* a six-Act drama, the *Śakuntalā* a seven-Act drama, the *Nalavikrama* an eight-Act drama, the *Devīpariṇaya* a nine-Act drama and the *Bālarāmāyaṇa* a ten-Act drama. The *nāṭaka* form of drama is regarded as the best and it is supposed to contribute to *dharma, artha* and *kāma* in consistency with each other.[1] The *prakaraṇa* resembles the *nāṭaka,* only

1 *ato hi nāṭakasyā'sya prāthamyaṁ parikalpitam* ।
nāṭya-vedaṁ vidhāyādāvṛṣīnāha pitāmahaḥ ।
dharmādi-sādhanaṁ nāṭyaṁ sarva-duḥkhā-panodanam ।
āsevadhvaṁ tadṛṣayas tasyotthānaṁ tu nāṭakam ।
divya-mānuṣa-saṁyogo yatrāṅkairavidūṣakaiḥ ॥
—*Bhāvaprakāśana* of Śāradātanaya VIII, pp. 237-238.

the plot here may be either legendary or concocted by the poet. It also contributes to *dharma*, *artha* and *kāma*, but the characters are not taken from the higher sphere. There may be courtesans here or legally married wives or damsels in the state of courtship but they are all taken from the bourgeois, such as in the *Mṛcchakaṭika* or the *Mālatīmādhava*. The *nāṭikā* like the *Ratnāvalī* or the *Priyadarśikā* also deals with characters of the higher sphere and they are generally of the amorous type. There is not in it any attempt to contribute to *dharma*, *artha* and *kāma* in mutual consistency. We thus find that it has not the same high purpose as the *nāṭaka* or the *prakaraṇa* This accounts for the fact that *nāṭakas* have been more popular and we have an immensely larger number of *nāṭakas* than any other form of the drama. This is consistent with the ideal of the realisation of *trivarga*, *i.e.*, *dharma*, *artha* and *kāma*, in dramatic performance. It also accounts for the fact that we have so few of the *prahasana* and the *bhāṇa*, which are farces and parodies from common life. There may have been the earlier froms of popular play which gradually dwindled away into forgetfulness with the pronounced and pointed development of the ideal of *trivarga* among people in general, and we perceive that as time advanced the idea of *dharma* as a purpose of drama was more and more definitely demanded. When with the Mohamedan occupation the religious practices ceased to be encouraged by kings, people wanted to be reminded of the old ideals of holy characters in dramatic plays and this explains the fact why after the 12th or the 13th century we have such a superabundance of Epic *kāvyas* and dramas with religious themes.

Characteristics of some other fromsof the drama.

Taken at random, of about 68 dramatic pieces after the 12th century A.D., we find that the plot of about

41 of them were taken from the religious legends and only 27 from the secular legends, mostly built upon the story available from Guṇāḍhya's source. Of these 41 dramatic pieces drawn from the religious legends, 27 are *nāṭakas,* one is a *prakaraṇa,* 3 are *vyāyogas,* 2 *ḍimas,* one *īhāmṛga,* 4 *utsṛṣṭikāṅkas,* 2 *samavakāras.* Of the 27 dramatic pieces from secular sources, 6 are *nāṭakas,* 11 *prakaraṇas,* 3 *prahasanas,* 2 *vīthis,* 4 *nāṭikās* and one *īhāmṛga.* We thus see that the *nāṭakas* by far exceeded all other forms of dramatic compositions and most of them were taken from religious legends. All *vyāyogas* (three), *ḍimas* (two), *utsṛṣṭikāṅkas* (four) and *samavakāras* (two) are religious. There is one secular *īhāmṛga* and one religious. The *bhāṇa* and the *prahasana* cannot by nature be religious and we have only 4 *prahasanas* including the *Hāsyacūḍāmaṇi,* and there is one *bhāṇa* called the *Karpūracarita.* Among those derived from secular legends, there are some *nāṭakas, prakaraṇas,* two *vīthis* and 4 *nāṭikās.* The *ḍima,* we have already seen, deals with episodes of supernatural beings like the ghosts and goblins. The *vyāyoga* and the *samavakāra* deal generally with dreadful events, battles between the demons and the gods and it is probable that they existed as the earlier forms of dramatic representations portraying the defeats of the *asuras* and the aboriginal races in their conflict with the Aryans. The *bhāṇa* and the *prahasana* were generally comic representations from popular life of a lower status and they displayed no moralising tendency. These were the first to disappear. Those dramatic forms of representation like the *vyāyoga, ḍima* and *samavakāra* which represented military valour, anger or irascibility. of temper, could not also stand, as with the distance of time actual episodes of battles, etc. which had at one time agitated the public mind and

Dominance of religious motive in the dramatic literature.

Characteristics of different types of the drama.

represented the mock triumph of the Aryan people over their neighbours, ceased to interest the public mind. The fact that Bhāsa, whose works are the earliest representatives of our dramatic literature now available, gives equal importance to these as to the *nāṭakas* indicates the possibility of their existence in larger numbers in earlier times which are now lost. It is remarkable to note that Bhāsa also draws upon religious legends in a large measure. Of the two fragmentary dramas of Aśvaghoṣa, one is the *Śāriputra-prakaraṇa* and the other is a religious allegory like the *Prabodha-candrodaya* of later times, and the religious motive is apparent in both of them.

The subjects of dramas and Epics are mostly taken from religious sources.

In the drama of later times, *i.e.*, from the 12th to the 18th century, taking a review of about 33 dramas, we find that almost all of them are based on either the Rāma or the Kṛṣṇa legend. Hardly any drama had been written during this period which may be said to have been based upon the story-material of Guṇāḍhya which in the later centuries before Christ and throughout many centuries after the Christian era supplied materials to so many dramas. The same thing may be said with more emphasis regarding the Epic *kāvyas*. With the exception of the *Carita-kāvyas* or biographical epics there have hardly been any Epic *kāvyas* throughout the centuries which have not been based on the religious legends. Vālmīki's *Rāmāyaṇa*, the *Mahābhārata* and the Kṛṣṇa legends from the Purāṇas had stood as inexhaustible stores from which poets could either borrow or adapt legends with modifications for their *kāvya*. The *Praśasti kāvyas* were all inspired with feelings of loyalty to great kings or patrons and such loyalty could be compared only to devotion to God. Thus, both in the dramas and in the *kāvyas* the scope of the poet's treatment was limited by the considerations of *trivarga-siddhi*. The Sanskrit poets were as a rule very fond of delineating the amorous sentiment or the sentiment of love. But they could give play to the portrayal of their erotic predilections only in a limited manner in the *kāvyas* and the dramas so far as is consistent with normal, social and conjugal rules of life ; but in this sphere the elaborate description of feminine beauty and post-nuptial amorous enchantments gave the poets sufficient scope to indulge in their tendency to give expression to passions and longings. Long separations were also good situations for portraying amorous longings.

The place of love as a member of the *trivarga* in literature.

But whether in literature or not, the bodily side of the passion or the structural conditions of feminine beauty have found a place of importance and except in the works of a few artists or poets, the representations of the physical side seem to our taste to be rather crude. It does not, of course, prove that the passion was burning more in the blood of the Hindus than in the blood of other races. It probably simply means that *kāma* being one of the constituents of *trivarga,* voluptuousness and sensuality and appreciation of feminine beauty as sanctioned by *dharma* was quite innocent and had nothing to be abashed of. The passion of *kāma,* as has been mentioned above, had two spheres, one that was enjoined by *dharma* where non-indulgence of the passions would be a punishable sin, and the other when it was not enjoined by *dharma* but when such indulgence did not transgress the limits of *dharma*. So the poets also portrayed passionate love in the latter sphere and these portrayals in the *śatakas* and elsewhere form some of the best specimens of Sanskrit amorous poetry.

It has been said above that the drama or Epic *kāvya* was looked upon in this country not as a portrayal of any scene of life or any characters that came within the experience of the poet but that they were generally regarded as giving an epitome of complete life either of the great religious heroes or of kings famous in traditional or legendary accounts. Even the story of Guṇāḍhya had a sanctified atmosphere about it on account of the fact that it was often believed that it was originally narrated by Lord Śiva to Pārvatī (*hara-mukhodgīrṇā*). It is on this account that in the great *kāvyas* where royal life was depicted, wars and battles, *svayaṃvaras*, kingly magnanimity and royal episodes of love were narrated and in dramas also which were not professedly of a didactic character, the principal subject-matter was an episode of love and on some occassions heroism also.

Patternising tendency of Indian culture.

It is on account of a loyalty ingrained deeply in the mental structure of Hindu life that Hindu creations either in art, literature or philosophy have always followed the course of creating types, where individuality has always remained shy to express itself in its full height. Thus, in philosophy also we do not get a free response of thought moving forward largely untramelled by conditions, but always leaning towards certain fixed points which are like the Cartesian co-ordinates determining its exact situation. Thus, almost every Indian philosophy should admit the validity of the Vedas, the doctrine of re-birth or transmigration, the possibility of salvation and the root-cause of the world as being some form of ignorance. Within these limits each system of Indian philosophy develops its own views and predilections. Each system can criticise the above concepts, may explain its theory of knowledge and the nature of the world, a concept of bondage and salvation and the ways that may be adopted for that. So in art also, most forms of pictorial or statuary art and even the architectural art of India would have some message to communicate and a physical portrayal would rather sacrifice its faithfulness to nature in the interest of the message to be comunicated rather than be realistic and devote itself only to the delineation of beauty.

Under these circumstances, an Epic is supposed to have for its hero some king or kings of the same race. The story must be taken from a legend. It should include within it deprecatory remarks about evil deeds and the edification of the noble, description of natural scenes, mountains, forests and oceans, morning, evening, and the seasons.

The internal conditions of the genesis of art and literature.

Every kind of human production,—literature, music, fine arts, philosophy. science, statecraft,—has for its direct cause a moral disposition or a combination of moral dipositions which seems somehow internally to determine these products. The conditions of race, epoch and environmental conditions and circumstances bring out to prominence certain moral conditions which are suited to the production of particular types of architecture, painting, sculpture, music or poetry. Each has its special law and it is by virtue of this law, accidentally as it may appear, that development takes place amidst the diversion of its neighbours, like painting in Flanders and Holland in the 17th century, poetry in England in the 16th century, music in Germany in the 18th. At such times in such countries the conditions are fulfilled for one art rather than for another. There is a special kind of psychology, a mental perspective required for the development of each of these arts. There is a peculiar inner system of impressions and operations which makes an artist, a believer, a musician, a painter, a wanderer, or a man of society. Literature is like living monuments of the outstanding personalities of different times. Literature is instructive because it is beautiful. Its utility depends upon its perfection

It deals with visible and almost tangible sentiments and the more a book represents the important sentiment of the people the higher is its place in literature. It is by representing the mode of being of the whole Nature of a whole age that a writer can collect round him the sympathies of an entire age and an entire nation. It is not mere catechisms or chronicles that can impress upon us the inner nature of a person or a nation. It is the inner movement of sentiments and interests, ideals and emotions made living through artistic expression, that can hold before us the life of a people.

It is curious to notice that Indian life and manners continued to present a pattern for decades of centuries. There was growth and development but more or less on the same line. It was only after the Mahammadan invasion and finally with the occupation of the country by the British that the system of its life and manners and even the psychology of the people has undergone a rude change a change which at the first shock had stunned the mind of the people with the advent of the new sciences, new ways of thought, new perspectives which brought with it the whole history of Western culture with its massive strength hurled against the Indian people. During the first 130 years or so the nerve of the Indian mind was almost paralysed by this rude shock and during the past 50 years the Indian mind is again trying to understand the value of the contribution of this culture and has been trying to become self-conscious and rise above its influence--a fact which may be well appreciated not only by the growing political consciousness and demand for freedom but also from the history of the Bengali literature, culminating in the literature of Poet Rabindranath in whose writings we find a clear and concrete method as to how the Western culture can be synthesised with the

Indian genius without submitting and drooping down before the former but rising above it and yet assimilating its best fruits and introducing such changes in our outlook and perspective as are consonant with our past and yet capable of assimilating the new for a creative transfiguration.

Continuity of Indian culture.

The reason of the continuity of Indian culture is largely to be found in the insular character of our civilisation and the extreme doggedness and obstinacy amounting to haughtiness and national pride rising to the level of religion against the conscious acceptance of any contribution from any foreigner. This could be possible largely because of the fact that this national pride had become identified with our religion. Our legal literature is called *Dharmaśāstra* or religious literature. Manners, customs, professions and the like, the creation of our social classes with their restricted duties, divisions of life into different stages with their ordained duties, are not for us mere social adjustments due to diverse social and environmental causes but it has been the essence of Hindu religion. The Smṛtis or the Indian legal literature has codified for every member of every social class the nature of his duties. The law is not merely for regulating our conduct to our fellow-beings but for regulating the entire course of our daily life, eating, drinking and the like from birth to death. Though at different times people have more or less deviated from the strict programme laid down by the Smṛtis, yet, on the whole, the social life has strictly and uniformly followed not only the general scheme laid by the Smṛtis but also most of the particular details. I have said above that the stringent grip of the Smṛtis became more and more tightened with the advance of centuries. Thus, for example, the prescriptions of the medical science as regards food and drink as found in the *Caraka* in the 1st century A.D., is found wholly unacceptable in the legal literature of later times. Restrictions of food and drink and various other kinds of conduct and practice became more and more stringent, signifying thereby a slackening tendency in society.

Marx has said that division of the social classes has always been the result of conflict between the capitalists and the working classes and that the development of social culture, the production of literature, philosophy, music and the like, is the result of the change in economic conditions and means of production. But both these theses seem to lose their force in the case of India. Here we have the development of philosophy, art and literature though there has practically been no change in the means of economic production for more than 2,000 years. The Brahmins had a position which was even greater than that of a king, not to speak of a Vaiśya capitalist, and yet there was no theocracy in India like the Papal domination of the West or like the system of the Caliphs in Islam. The Brahmins were poor and self-abnegating persons who generally dedicated their lives to learning and teaching and to the practice of religious works. They did not interfere with the rules of kings except when some of them were appointed ministers but they laid down a scheme of life and a scheme of conduct which had to be followed by all persons from the king to the tanner. It was this enforcement of a universal scheme of life that often protected the people from misrule and tyranny on the part of kings. It is no doubt true that in a few exceptions there had been tyranny and misrule, but on the whole the kings had to follow a beneficent scheme for it was the law. It is pripcinally at the time of the Mauryas that we find many laws introduced which were advantageous to the king but the Mauryas were Śūdras. At the time of the Kṣatriya kings we again find the laws of Smṛti revived. The caste system had already come into force in its stringency in the 4th century B.C. Thus, Megasthenes says: "No one is allowed to marry out of his own caste or to exchange one profession or trade for another or to follow more than one business." The existence of the caste system means the allocation of particular duties in society to particular castes. The union of the Kṣatriya and the Brāhmaṇa, of the king and the law-giver in the council, was at the basis of the Hindu Government. There was a joint-family system very similar to what they had in Rome, but every individual member had a *locus standi* in the eye of the law and the father of the family was like the trustee of the family property. The king and the Brahamin were the trustees of society, the king by protecting and enforcing the laws of *dharma* and the Brahmin by promulgating them. The Brahmins, as it were, were the legislators, and the kings, the executives and the former were, so far as the legislation went, independent of the latter. This legislation, however, referred not only to ordinary juridical conduct but to all kinds of daily duties and conduct as well. But when the laws were codified, though the Brahmin as a *purohita* or priest retained his position of high honour and respect from the king, he was no longer a constituent of the Government. Thus, the seven *aṅgas* constituting the state (*svāmyā-mātya-suhṛt-koṣa-rāṣṭra-durga-balāni ca, i.e.,* king, councillor, allies, treasury, people and territory, fortresses and army), did not include Brahmins as a constituent. Gradually the importance of the king's office gained in strength as subserving the primary needs and interests of the people and the

Constitu-tion and structure of Hindu Society.

preservation of the society according to the principles of *dharma*. But even the king was bound to dispense justice in accordance with the principles of *dharma*. The dispensation of justice was not only necessary for social well-being but punishment was also regarded as having a purificatory value for a man's post-mortem well-being. The unrighteousness of a king destroys *dharma* in the society and creates social disturbances as well as physical misfortunes, such as, untimely death, famine and epidemic. Thus the dispensation of justice and its failure was regarded not only as having immediate but also transcendental effects. The king thus had a great responsibility. The king exists for the discharge of *dharma* and not for self-gratification (*dharmāya rājā bhavati na kāmakaraṇāya tu*). Almost all the sciences of polity are in thorough agreement with the view that a king must first of all be absolutely self-controlled. But in spite of all these, there were teachers like Bharadvāja who would advise any kind of unprincipled action for the maintenance of the king's power. But this was not accepted by most of the political authorities, but Kauṭilya's code leaned more or less to this type of action. In the *Mahābhārata* we find many passages in which the rôle of punishment is extolled and Bṛhaspati also held that view. Side by side with the view of divine authority of kings we have also in the *Mahābhārata* and the Buddhist canons the view that the king was elected by the people on the terms of contract which involved the exchange of the just exercise of sovereign power and obedience regarding payment of taxes on the part of the people. In Kauṭilya we find that he had due regard for the social order of *varṇāśrama* and he regarded the importance of the three Vedas, the *Vārtā-śāstra* and Polity. Kauṭilya lays great importance on the position

Ideal of *dharma* in law and politics.

of the king's office. The king constitutes within himself his kingdom and his subjects. Yet there are many passages in the *Arthaśāstra* to indicate that king's authority depends upon the will of the people whom he has always to keep satisfied, and we find there that it is the duty of the king to promote the security and prosperity of the people in lieu of which the subjects should pay taxes to him. Kauṭilya is also mainly loyal to the *Dharmaśāstra* principle that the king is an official who is entitled to receive taxes for the service of protection and that he is spiritually responsible for the discharge of his duties. Kauṭilya also lays down a very high standard of moral life for the king. Good education and self-control are the first requisites of good government. Though there are elaborate rules of foreign policy, Kauṭilya definitely lays down the view that no king should covet his neighbour's territories, and in case of battles with other kings it is his duty to restore to throne the most deserving from the near relations of the vanquished king—a policy entirely different from that of the imperialistic governments of to-day. A king should only attempt to secure safety for his kingdom and extend his influence on others. In later times, between 900 and 1200 A.D., when the commentaries of Medhātithi, Vijñāneśvara and Aparārka and the Jaina *Nītivākyāmṛta* were written, we have the view, particularly in *Medhātithi*, that the principles of *rājadharma* and *daṇḍanīti*, though principally derived from Vedic institutīons, are to be supplemented from other sources and elaborated by reason. Thus, Medhātithi would not restrict the office of kingship to a Kṣatriya alone but would extend it to any one who is ruling with proper kingly qualities. Kālidāsa also, we have seen, was consistent with the teaching of the old *Dharmaśāstra* that the term *kṣatra* was in meaning identical to the

position of the king.

term *nṛpa*. *Kṣatra* means *kṣatāt trāyate* and *nṛpa* means *nṛn pāti*. The older aspect of the king is that he should be popular, and this aspect is signified by the term *rājā* (*rājā prakṛtirañjanāt*). But Medhātithi uses the term *rājā, nṛpa* or *pārthiva* to mean any ruling prince. Medhātithi would apply the term *nṛpa* even to provincial governors. The subjects have the inalienable right of protection by the king by virtue of the taxes they pay to him, and for any mischief that comes to them, the king is responsible. If their property is stolen, the king will restore the value of the articles stolen. It seems also that Medhātithi not only concedes to the view that the subjects may even in normal times bear arms for self-protection, but when the king is incompetent, they have also the right to rebel and suspend the payment of taxes. But during the 12th to the 17th century in the works of Śukra, Mādhava and Parāśara, we find again the theory of divine right of kings coming to the forefront and the doctrine of the perpetual dependence of subjects on the king and of the king's immunity from harm advocated, which tended to contradict the earlier concept of king as the servant of the people.

From the above brief review we can well understand the light in which the kings were held during the really creative period of literature beginning from the 2nd or the 3rd century B.C. to the 12th century A.D. The ideal of a king depicted in the *Rāmāyaṇa* and also in the *Mahābhārata* as also in the works of Kālidāsa and other writers, reveals to us the integral relation of solidarity between the king and the subjects. Almost every drama ends with the prayer which is a sort of national anthem seeking the good of the king and the people. The concept of the king involved the principle that he would protect the people and be of such ideal character and conduct that he might be liked by all. The term *prakṛti*, etymologically meaning the source or origin, was a term to denote the subjects. This implied that the king drew his authority from the subjects. This is the reason why the kings often excited as much admiration as the gods and though many panegyric verses in literature may have as their aim the flattery of kings for personal gain, yet judging from the general relation between the king and his subjects it can hardly be doubted that in most cases there was a real and genuine feeling of sincere admiration and love for the king. This also gives us the reason why royal characters were treated in *kāvya* side by side with the characters of gods, for the king was god on earth not by his force or his power of tyranny but through love and admiration that was spontaneous about him on the part of the subjects. The cordial relation between subjects and royal patrons explains the origin of so many *praśasti* and *carita kāvyas*.

The place of King and god in literature.

Types of literature.

If we take a bird's-eye view of the Sanskrit literature we may classify them as Epic and Lyric *kāvyas*, the *carita kāvyas* (dealing with the lives of kings and patrons of learning), the *praśastis* or panegyrical verses, the different types of dramas, lyric *kāvyas*, the century collections or *śatakas*, the *stotra* literature or adoration hymns, the *Campūs* or works written in prose and verse, the *kathā* literature, the *nīti* literature, the didactic verses and stray verses such as are found in the anthologies. The sources of the materials of *kāvya* as held by Rājaśekhara, are *Śruti, Smṛti, Purāṇa, Itihāsa, Pramāṇavidyā, Samaya-vidyā* or the sectarian doctrines of the Śaivas, Pañcarātrins, etc., the *Arthaśāstra*, the *Nāṭyaśāstra* and the *Kāmaśāstra*, the local customs and manners, the different sciences and the literature of other poets.

Political conditions ane the early poetry.

Apart from the reference to poems written by Pāṇini and to the dramas referred to in the *Mahābhāṣya*, probably the earliest remains of good drama are the dramas of Bhāsa, which in some modified manner have recently been discovered. In the 1st century B.C. we have the works of Kālidāsa and in the 1st century A.D. we have the *Buddha-carita*, the *Sundarānanda*, the *Śāriputraprakaraṇa* and an allegorical drama written by Aśvaghoṣa, the Buddhist philosopher. This was the time of the Śuṅgas, the Kāṇvas and the Andhra dynasties. Puṣyamitra had slain his master Bṛhadratha Mauryya and had assumed sovereignty of the Mauryya dominions of Upper India and of South India up to the Nerbuda and had repulsed Minander, king of Kabul and the invader was obliged to retire to his own country. His son Agnimitra had conquered Berar and Puṣyamitra performed the *Aśvamedha* sacrifice and revived Hinduism. The *Mālavikāgnimitra* of Kālidāsa gives a glowing account of the *Rājasūya* sacrifice performed by Puṣyamitra. The Buddhist writers describe him as having persecuted the Buddhists. The last Śuṅga king Devabhūti lost his life and throne through the contrivances of his Brahmin minister, Vasudeva. He founded the Kāṇva dynasty, which was suppressed in 28 B.C. and the last Kāṇva king, Suśarman, was slain by the Andhras, who had already established themselves by the middle of the 3rd century B.C. on the banks of the Kṛṣṇā. The Andhra kings all claimed to belong to the Śātavāhana family. The name of Hāla the 17th king has come down to us because of his *Saptaṣatī* of Prākṛt erotic verses of great excellence. It seems that at this time Prākṛt rather than Sanskrit was the language of poetry in the South. It is difficult to ascertain the dates of Hāla's *Saptaśatī* (which have, however, in reality 430 stanzas common to all recensions, the rest may be an interpolation). Judging from the nature of the Prākṛt, one may think that the work was probably written about 200 A.D. though it is difficult to be certain of its date. In the meanwhile, we have some of the specimens of the earliest prose in the inscriptions of Rudradāmana in Girnār (A.D. 150). In the region of Bombay we get foreign rulers like the Kṣaharātas who were probably subordinate to the Indo-Parthian kings in the 1st century A.D. The next chief was Nahapāna. The Kṣaharātas, however, were extirpated by Gautamīputra-Śātakarṇi, the Andhra king. His son, Vāśiṣṭhiputra Srīpulumāyi, had married the daughter of Rudradāmana I, the Śaka Satrap of Ujjayinī, but much of the territory of the son-in-law was conquered by the father-in-law. As we have just seen, Sanskrit was the court language of Rudradāmana and Yajñaśrī, the son of Vāśiṣṭhiputra Srīpulumyāi, who was a great king of military exploits (173-202 A.D). The fall of the Andhra kings coincides approximately with the death of Vāsudeva, the last great Kuṣāṇ king of North India and with the rise of the Sassanian dynasty of Persia (A.D. 226). But the history of the 3rd century after Christ is rather very obscure. The only important tradition of literary growth during the Andhras is the legend about king Śātavāhana or Śālivāhana, in whose court Guṇāḍhya and Sarvavarmācārya are supposed to have lived. Guṇāḍhya was born at Pratiṣṭhāna in the Deccan on the banks of the Godāvarī. This city of Ptatiṣṭhāna is the capital of the Andhrabhṛtyas, though there is much doubt about the location of the city. But there is a Pratiṣṭhāna on the banks of the Ganges as mentioned in the *Harivaṃśa.* Bāṇa refers to Śātavāhana as having made the immortal repertory of beautiful passages and this seems to indicate that there was great

Political conditions in the 1st and 2nd centuries B.C. and the literature of the time.

cultivation of Sanskrit poetry even before Śātavāhana.[1]

Guṇāḍhya, Hāla and Sarvavarmā.

According to the legend, Śātavāhana's adopted father was Dīpakarṇī and this indicates that he may have belonged to the race of the Śātakarṇis. The *Hāla Saptaṣatī* also conclusively proves that there was an abundant literary production in the Prākṛt language and we have also strong reasons to believe that there must have been many dramas in Prākṛt. But we do no know anything more about the exact time when Hāla may have flourished. But if the legned is to be believed, the two great works, the *Kātantra* of Sarvavarmā and the *Bṛhatkathā* of Guṇāḍhya were written at this time. That stories used by Guṇāḍhya were floating about among the populace, is well evident from Kālidāsa's statement *udayana kathā-kavida-grāma vṛddhān* in the *Meghadūta* and the utilisation of those stories by Bhāsa. We know that in all probability, Kālidāsa had flourished at the time of the later Śuṅgas and Patañjali the grammarian was probably engaged as a priest in the Horse Sacrifice of Puṣyamitra. We also know that the Śaka kings like Rudradāmana had taken to the Sanskrit language and Vaiṣṇava religion. We also know from the inscriptions in the Besnagar Column that the Greek ambassador Heliodorus had accepted the Bhāgavata religion. It is also probable that Minander the Greek king had become a Buddhist.

Mithradates I, the Persian king (170-136 B.C.), had extended his dominions up to the Indus and this explains why the chiefs of Taxila and Mathurā had assumed Persian titles in early times and we have the remains of Persian culture in the excavations of Taxila.

1 *avināśinam-agrāmyam-akarot śātavāhanaḥ* ।
viśuddhajātibhiḥ koṣaṁ ratnairiva subhāṣitaiḥ ॥
—*Harṣa-carita.*

It is possible that a Christian Mission under St. Thomas had come to the court of the Indo-Parthian king Gondophares at the beginning of the Christian era, but the Mission seems to have left no impression. It may not be out of place here to mention that neither Alexander's conquest nor the association with Bactrian kings, seems to have left any permanent impression on the Indian mind. The Punjab or a considerable part of it with some of the adjoining regions remained more or less under Greek rule for more than two centuries (190 B.C. to 20 A.D.), but except the coins bearing Greek legends on the obverse, hardly any effect of Hellenisation can be discovered. It is surprising that not a single Greek inscription is available. There is no evidence of Greek architecture. The well-known sculptures of Gandhāra, the region around Peshawar, are much later indeed and are the offsprings of cosmopolitan Graeco-Roman art. The invasions of Alexander, Antiochus the Great, Demetrios, Eukratides and Minander were but military incursions which left no appreciable mark upon the institutions of India. The people of India rejected Greek political institutions and architecture as well as language.

Military occupations of the Greeks left but little influence on Indian culture and literature.

During the 2nd and the 3rd century, Śaivism had established itself very firmly in South. The Śiva cult had long been in existence among the Dravidians and by the 3rd century A.D. it attained almost its finished character in the noble and devout writings of Māṇikkavāchakara in Mālābar. The Vāsudeva cult had already penetrated into the south and by the 3rd and the 4th century A.D. the earliest Alwar thinkers had started the Bhakti literature.

Śaiva and Vaiṣṇava cults in the early centuries oi the Christian era.

In the meanwhile, the Yueh-chis being attacked by their foes, the Śakas, rushed forward and after subjugating Kabul, entered into India and conquered the Punjab

A career of the Śakas.

under Kadphises I. His son Kadphises II not only established his power in the Punjab but in a considerable part of the Gangetic plain in Benares (A.D. 45). But these parts were probably governed at this time by military Viceroys. In the meanwhile, the Yueh-chis were being attacked by the Chinese. Kaṇiṣka tried to repel the Chinese but his army was totally routed and he had to send several embassies to China to pay tributes. The conquest of Kabul by the Yueh-chis opened the land route towards the West and Roman gold of the early Roman Emperors, such as Tiberius (A.D. 14-38), began to pour into India in payment for silk, spices, gems and dye-stuff. Southern India at the same time was holding an active maritime trade with the Roman Empire and large quantities of Roman gold poured into India. Now, Kadphises II was succeeded by Kaṇiṣka (58 B.C.). His dominions extended all over North-Western India as far as the Vindhyas. A temporary annexation of Mesopotamia by Trajan, the Roman Emperor, in 116 A.D. brought the Roman frontier within 600 miles of the western limits of the Yueh-chi Empire. Kaṇiṣka had also conquered Kashmir and attacked the city of Pātaliputra from where he took away the Buddhist saint Aśvaghoṣa. His own capital was Puruṣapur or Peshawar. Kaṇiṣka had also conquered Kashgar, Yarkand and Khotan. Thus the limits of the Indian Empire extended up to Khotan, a fact which explains the migration of Buddhist culture and Indian works which are being occasionally discovered there. The most important thing about him for our purpose is that he was converted to Buddhism, as may be known from his coins. Buddhism had in his time developed into the Mahāyāna form of which Aśvaghoṣa was such an important representative and

Extension of Indian Empire up to Khotan and in the west to Afghanistan.

Kaṇiṣka converted to Buddhism.

the image of Buddha began to be installed in different parts of his Empire, taking a place with the older gods, such as Śiva or Viṣṇu and an elaborate mythology of Buddhism developed. It is at this time in the 2nd century A.D. that we have the style of sculpture described as the Gāndhāra school which was a branch of the cosmopolitan Graeco-Roman art. This style of art, which is much inferior to the indigenous Indian art, soon lost its currency. Kaṇiṣka called a council for the interpretation of Buddhist scriptures and about 500 members of the Sarvāstivāda school met in Kashmir and the Buddhist theological literature underwent a thorough examination and elaborations were made in huge commentaries on the *Tripiṭaka*. This included the *Mahāvibhāṣā* which still exists in its Chinese translation and it is said that these commentaries were copied on sheets of copper and these were deposited in a *stūpa* near Srīnagar. From the time of Kaṇiṣka we have the golden age of the development of Buddhist Mahāyāna and Sarvāstivāda literature as also the codification of most of the Indian philosophical *sūtras*. The first five or six centuries of the Christian era were also the age of great philosophical controversy between the Buddhists, the Hindus and the Jainas. Aśvaghoṣa himself had written the *Śraddhotpāda-sūtra* and the *Mahāyāna-sūtrālaṅkāra*. It has been urged by Cowell that Kālidāsa had borrowed from the *Buddhacarita*. But this point is very doubtful and the position may be reversed. The similarity of a few passages in the *Kumārasambhava* and the *Raghuvaṃśa* does not prove any conscious indebtedness on any side, so far as Aśvaghoṣa's *Buddhacarita* is concerned. Aśvaghoṣa also wrote a book of Buddhist legends called the *Sūtrālaṅkāra* and also the *Vajrasūcī*. More or less about this time we had also the poet Mātṛceṭa and also the

Rise of the Mahāyāna literature and the Gāndhāra art.

Rise of the philosophical literature.

Literature of the time.

Buddhist poet Ârya-śūra who wrote the *Jātakamālā* in imitation of Aśvaghoṣa's *Sūtrālaṅkāra*. His diction in prose and verse was of the *kāvya* style. Some of the important *Avadānas* were also written during the 1st or the 2nd century A.D. The *Aśokāvadāna* was actually translated into Chinese in the 3rd century A.D. It is curious to notice that these *Avadānas* which were written in Sanskrit, more or less at the time when the *Bṛhatkathā* of Guṇāḍhya was written in Paiśācī, were seldom utilised by the Sanskrit writers. Many of the *Avadāna* legends are found in Kṣemendra's work so far as the essential part of the tales is concerned. But the didactic element is preponderatingly much greater in the Buddhist treatments. The great Mahāyāna writers Nāgārjuna, Asaṅga, Vasubandhu, Candragomin, Śāntideva and others began to follow in close succession. The Mahāyāna literature gradually began to model itself on the Puraṇas and the introduction of the *Dhāraṇis* and other cults and rituals as well as the personification of powers into deities led to the rise of the Buddhist Tantras. The *Laṅkāvatāra*, a semi-philosophical and semi-Tantrik work, was written probably sometime in the 4th century and later on the Yoga doctrine modified according to the psychology of the different people—among the Tibetan, the Chinese and the Japanese—assumed diverse forms. The *stotra* literature also formed the model of the Buddhist *stotra* and through this the theatre of the mental operation extended not only from the Hindukush to Cape Comorin but it extended also to Further India, Tibet, China, Japan, Korea, the Malaya Archipelago and many islands in the Indian and the Pacific Ocean and also to Central Asia, Turkistan, Turfan and other places.

The reign of Kaṇiṣka terminated in or about 123 A.D. After him Vāsiṣka and Huviṣka succeeded and Huviṣka was succeeded by Vāsudeva I. The name signifies that he was converted into Hinduism and his coins exhibit the figure of Śiva attended by the bull, Nandī and the trident. Coins are found during the period 238-269 A.D. where a royal figure clad in the garb of Persia (an imitation of the effigy of Shahpur I, the Sassanian) is found, which indicates Sassanian influence in India. But we have no more details of it from any inscriptions of literary eminence. Probably numerous Rājās in India asserted their independence as may be inferred from muddled statements in the Purāṇas, such as the Ābhīras, Gardabhilas, Śakas, Yavanas, Vāhlikas and the successors of the Andhras. The imperial city of Pātaliputra maintained its influence as late as the 5th century A.D. but we practically know nothing about the condition of the interior of India at this time.

Uncertain political conditions after Kaṇiṣka·

The local Rājā near Pātaliputra called Candragupta married a Licchavi princess named Kumāradevī about the year 308 A.D. We do not hear much of the Licchavis in the intervening period of history since the reign of Ajātaśatru. Candragupta was strengthened by this alliance and he extended his dominion along the Gangetic Valley as far as the junction of the Ganges and the Jamuna, about 320 A.D. Between 330 and 335 A.D. he was succeeded by his son Samudragupta who immediately after his succession plunged himself into war. The multitude of *praśastis* in the inscriptions have immortalised his reign in Indian history. The elaborate composition of Hariṣeṇa with its contents is a historical document which iṣ remarkable also as a linguistic and literary landmark. Samudragupta's Empire extended on the North and the East from Kāmarūpa to Tāmralipti including the modern site of Calcutta and extended westwards in a straight line across the Vindhyas to Guzerat and Saurāṣṭra later on acquired

Rise of the Guptas.

by his son Candragupta II and on the north to the borders of Nepal up to the banks of the Chenab river in the Punjab. He performed an *Aśvamedha* ceremony and is reputed to have been an adept not only in music and song but it is said that he had also composed many metrieal works of great value and was called a King of Poets. He allowed the Buddhist king Meghavarṇa of Ceylon to erect a monastery and temple in Buddhagayā. In the 7th century when Hiuen-Tsang visited it, it was a magnificent establishment which accommodated 1000 monks of the Sthavira school and afforded hospitality to monks from Ceylon. Samudragupta had also received Vasuvandhu. Throughout his conquests he secured submission of the various chiefs but he seldom annexed their territory. He had removed his capital to Ayodhyā from Pātaliputra. Thus when Hiuen-Tsang came in the 7th century, he found Pātaliputra in ruins but when Rājeśekhara mentions the glory of Pātaliputra, he refers to Upavarṣa, Varṣa, Pāṇini, Piṅgala, Vyādi, Vararuci and Patañjali as having been tested according to the tradition in Pātaliputra.[1] His successor Candragupta, who had assumed the title of Vikramāditya, led his conquests to the Arabian Sea through Malwa, Guzerat and Kāthiāwad, which had been ruled for centuries by the Śaka dynasty. We know that the capital of Caṣṭana and his successors was Ujjayinī. Vidiśā was also the important centre of Agnimitra. But Samudragupta and his successors had made their capital in Ayodhyā. It will therefore be wrong to suppose that one should make Kālidāsa a resident of Ujjayinī and yet make him attached to the court of

[1] *Kāvyamīmāṁsā*, p. 55.

Candragupta II. Kauśāmbī, which stood on the high road to Ujjayinī and North India, had the Aśoka pillar on which there is inscribed an inscription of Samudragupta and it has been argued that Kauśāmbī also formed his temporary place of residence. Candragupta II destroyed the Śaka Satrapy by first dethroning and then executing Rudrasena. Though he was tolerant of Buddhism and Jainism he was an othodox Hindu and probably a Vaiṣṇava. From Fa Hien's accounts (405-411 A.D.) we find that people were enjoying good government and abundant prosperity at the time of Vikramāditya.

Vikramāditya Candragupta II.

Still then there were monasteries in Pāṭaliputra where about six to seven hundred monks resided, and Fa Hien spent three years there studying Sanskrit. At his time "charitable institutions were numerous. Rest houses for travellers were provided on the highways and the capital possessed an excellent free hospital endowed by benevolent and educated citizens—hither come all poor helpless patients suffering from all kinds of infirmities. They are well taken care of and a doctor attends them. Food and medicine are supplied according to their wants and thus they are made quite comfortable and when they are well they may go away."[1] In describing the state of the country Fa Hien speaks of the lenience of the criminal law. He further says: "throughout the country no one kills any living thing, or drinks wine or eats onions or garlic. They do not keep pigs or fowls, there are no dealings in cattle, no butchers' shops or distilleries in the market places. Only the *caṇḍālas,* hunters and fishermen lived a different way of life. The only source of revenue was rent on crown lands." Fa Hien never

Fa Hien's evidence regarding the condition of the country.

1 Smith's Early History of India, pp. 295-296.

speaks of brigands or thieves. At the death of Candragupta, Kumāragupta I ascended the throne in 413 A.D.

Literature of the time.

It will be wrong to suppose that Śaivism spread from the South to the North for even Kadphises II, the Kuṣāṇa conqueror, was an worshipper of Śiva and put the image of Śiva on his coins and during the whole period when Buddhism acquired ascendency in India, worship of Hindu gods had continued unabated. The only distinctly Buddhist coins were those that were struck by Kaṇiṣka but the next king Vāsudeva had been a Hindu, as has already been mentioned, and the Śaka Satraps were also Hindus. The Pāli language of the Buddhists were reserved only for Buddhist religious works. No *kāvya* or drama was written in Pāli and after Aśoka it was seldom used as the language of inscriptions and even the language of Aśoka's inscriptions was not Pāli. Though we are unable to place Kālidāsa in the Gupta period there was undoubtedly a great enlightenment of culture during the Gupta period which went on till the 11th or the 12th century. We have not only at this time Vatsabhaṭṭi and Hariṣeṇa but a galaxy of other writers. The panegyrics of both Hariṣeṇa and Vatsabhaṭṭi illustrate the highest style that Sanskrit had attained at this period. Bhāravi also probably lived in the 5th century and Bhaṭṭi also in all probability lived somewhere during the 5th or the 6th century. It has been suggested that Śūdraka may also have lived at this time, but we really know very little about Śūdraka. Āryabhaṭa, the celebrated astronomer, also probably lived towards the end of the 5th or the middle of the 6th century. The laws of Manu as we find it and also of Yājñavalka probably belong to this age. But as regards the poets, it will be rash to say that they were invariably attached to courts of kings. They probably lived well to be able to turn to their vocation of writing poetry, but it may be supposed that they had always some patrons among the rich people.

Art and architecture, both Buddhist and Brahminical, flourished during the 5th and the 6th century and though by the ravages of Moslem army almost every Hindu building was pulled to pieces and all large edifices of the Gupta age had been destroyed, yet recent researches have discovered for us a few specimens of architectural compositions of a considerable skill in out of the way places. The allied art of sculpture attained a degree of perfection, the value of which is being recently recognised. Painting as exemplified by the frescoes of Ajantā and the cognate works of Sigiria in Ceylon (479-97) are so many best examples of Indian art. Colonisation of the Malayan Archipelago, Java and Sumatra had begun probably at least in the early centuries of the Christian era and Indian civilisation, particularly Brahminic, had already been established in the Archipelago by 401 A.D. By the middle of the 7th century, according to the report of I-Tsing, Buddhism was in a flourishing condition in the island of Sumatra and it grew side by side with the Hindu culture. The study of Sanskrit was so much current there that I-Tsing spent about 6 months in order to acquaint himself with Sanskrit grammar. The earliest Sanskrit inscriptions, however, are found in Borneo and during the 4th century A.D. Borneo was being ruled by Hindu kings, such as Aśvavarman, Mūlavarman, etc. Already in the 5th century we hear of Pūrṇavarman in Western Java and the worship of Viṣṇu and Śiva was prevalent in those parts. Mahāyāna forms of Buddhism also flourished in the country in the 8th and 9th centuries. In India we find the Vaiṣṇava and the Śaiva worship flourish side by side

Gupta civilisation and colonisation by Indians during the early centuries of the Christian era.

with Buddhism. But the golden age of the Guptas lasted for a century and a quarter (330-455). Skandagupta came to the throne in 455 A.D. He successfully resisted the Puṣyamitras from the South and drove away the Huns. But in the second invasion of the Huns he was defeated, as we know from an inscription dated 458 A.D. He appointed Parṇadatta Viceroy of the West who gave Junāgaḍ or Girnār to his son. At about 465 and also in 470 the Huns began to pour in. Skandagupta probably died in 480 A.D. With his death the Empire vanished but the dynasty remained.

Contact with China during the later Guptas.

After his death Puragupta succeeded who reigned from 485 to 535 A.D. The importance of Maghdha, however, and the University of Nālandā survived the downfall of the Guptas. We have the account of a Chinese Mission sent to Magadha in 539 A.D. for the collection of original Mahāyāna texts and for obtaining services of scholars capable of translating them into Chinese. During the reign of Jīvitagupta I, Paramārtha was sent to China with a large collection of manuscripts. He worked for 23 years in China and died at the age of 70 in 569. During his reign Bodhidharma also went to China (502-549).

In the Western province of Malwa we find record of other kings such as Buddhagupta and Bhānugupta.

Valabhī and Anhilwāra the centres of learning from the 5th to the 15th century.

Towards the close of the 5th century Bhaṭārka established himself at Valabhī in Kāthiāwāḍ in 770. The great Buddhist scholars, Guṇamati and Sthiramati resided in Valabhī and Valabhī became a great centre of learning. After the overthrow of Valabhī its place was taken by Anhilwāra, which retained its importance till the 15th century.

The Huns, however, overthrew the Gupta Empire and became rulers of Malwa and Central India. But Mihirakula was defeated by a confederacy of kings headed by Bālāditya and Yaśodharman, a Rājā of Central India. Mihirakula fled to Kashmir. The Kashmirian king allowed him the charge of a small territory. Mihirakula then rebelled against his benefactor and killed his whole family. But this Hun leader had become a devotee of Śiva. With the death of Mihirakula India enjoyed immunity from foreign attacks for a long time.

The Huns supplanting the Guptas. Mihirakula becomes a Saiva.

We must now come to Harṣa (606-647). Harṣa was a great patron of learning and Bāṇa has given some account of him in his *Haṣacarita.* Harṣa's Empire was almost equivalent to that of Samudragupta. Harṣa was himself a great poet. He wrote three dramas, the *Ratnāvalī*, the *Priyadarśikā* and the *Nāgānanda.* Candra, probably Candragomin, the great grammarian, wrote a Buddhist drama called *Lokānanda* describing the story as to how a certain Maṇicūḍa gave away his wife and children to a Brahmin out of geneosity. He lived before 650 A.D. as he cited in the *Kāśikā Vṛtti.* A contemporary of his, Candradāsa, had dramatised the *Vessantara* legend. Whether Candra and Candragomin are identical, may be a matter of indecisive controversy. But Candra or Candraka's poems are quoted in the *Subhāṣitāvalī* and he was admired by the rhetoricians. Almost a contemporary of Harṣa was Mahendravikramavarman, son of the Pallava king Siṃhavikramavarman, and he also was himself a king who ruled in Kāñcī. He wrote s *prahasana* (*Mattavilāsa*) showing the same technique as that of Bhāsa. Bāṇa, we know, not only wrote the *Harṣacarita* and the *Kādambarī* but also the *Caṇḍī-śataka,* the *Mukuṭa-tāḍitaka* (a drama) and *Pārvatīpariṇaya* (a *rūpaka*). It is doubtful whether he or Vāmana Bhaṭṭa Bāṇa was the author of the *Sarvacarita-nāṭaka.* The great dramatist

Development of literature from the 7th to the 10th century.

Bhavabhūti also flourished about 700 A.D. His three plays, the *Mālatīmādhava,* the *Uttaracarita* and the *Vīracarita* are masterpieces of Sanskrit drama. Though the exact date of Subandhu, author of the *Vāsavadattā,* cannot be determined yet as both Bāṇa and Vāmana of the 8th century refer to him, he must have flourished in the 6th or the 7th century. Bhaṭṭi also probably flourished in the 6th or the 7th century. Bhāmaha was slightly junior to him. The *Nāṭyaśāstra* had been written probably in the 2nd century A.D. The poet Medhāvin and the Buddhist logician Dharmakīrti, who was also a poet, flourished probably in the 6th century and Daṇḍin, author of the *Kāvyādarśa* and the *Daśakumāracarita* probably also flourished in the 6th century. Diñnaga, the Buddhist logician, had flourished in the 5th century during which time Vātsāyana also wrote his *Bhāsya* on the *Nyāyasūtra.* The *Sāṃkhya-kārika* of Īsvarakṛṣṇa was probably written by the 3rd century A.D. and the *Nyāyasūtras* were probably composed near about that time and the *Vedānta-sūtras* of Bādarāyaṇa were probably composed by the 2nd century A.D. and we have already mentioned Vasuvandhu, author of the *Abhidharmakoṣa* and many important Buddhist works, who lived in the 4th century and was a senior contemporary of Samudragupta. Udbhaṭa probably flourished in the 8th century and the *Dhvanyāloka* was probably written in the latter half of the 9th century. Udbhaṭa was not only a rhetorician but he had also written a *Kumārasambhava.* We have already said that Vāmana lived probably in the 8th century, but as Vāmana quotes from Māgha, Māgha must have lived probably in the middle of the 7th century. The *Kāśikā* commentary was written about 600 A.D. and the *Nyāsa* was probably written between 700 and 750 A.D.

Rudrata also flourished before 900 and Abhinavagupta who wrote his *Locana* on the *Dhvanyāloka* probably about 150 years after, flourished in the 11th century and Rājaṣekhara probably lived in the first quarter of the 10th century. Viśākhadatta, the author of the *Mudrārākṣasa,* probably lived in the 9th century. Bhaṭṭanārāyaṇa, the author of the *Beṇīsaṃhāra,* is quoted by Vāmana, and must, therefore, have lived before 800 A.D. If he were one of the Brahmins who were brought to Bengal from Kanauj by king Ādiśūra, he may have lived in the 7th century A.D. Kumāradāsa, the author of the *Jānakīharaṇa,* was probably a king of Ceylon and probably lived in the beginning of the 6th century. Menṭha lived probably in the latter part of the 6th century and king Pravarasena, the author of *Setubandha,* must have lived during the same time. The Kashmirian author Bhūmaka who wrote his *Rāvanārjunīya* in 27 cantos, probably also lived at this time. Towards the close of the 9th century we have the *Kapphanābhyudaya* based on the tale of the *Avadānaśataka* by Śivasvāmī, one of the few exceptions where the *Avadāna* literature has been utilised. But there are some other poets like Bhaṭṭāra Haricandra or Guṇāḍhya or Āḍhyarāja whose works are not now available.

Political and literary contact with the neighbouring countries.

After Harṣa, the Empire was practically broken and we have a number of kingdoms in various parts of the country. China was trying to assert suzerainty in the northern frontier and when its power vanished in the first half of the 6th century, the domains of the White Huns were extending up to Gāndhāra and between 563 and 567 this country was held by the Turks. In 630 the Northern Turks were completely vanquished by the Chinese who extended their domains to Turfan and Kucha, thus securing the northern road communication from East to West. Gampo, the Tibetan king (A.D. 630) who had become a Buddhist, was friendly to India. In 659 China rose to the height of its power and was in possession of this country up to Kapiśā. The Turks were finally routed by the Chinese in A.D. 744 and between 665 and 715, the northern route from China to India between the Xaxartes and the Indus was closed and the southern route through Kashgar was closed by the Tibetans and the road over the Hindukush was closed by the Arabs with the rise of Islam. But again by 719 the Chinese regained influence on the border of India. Buddhism developed in Tibet as against the indigenous Bon religion. The Indian sages, Śāntarakṣita and Padmasambhava, were invited to Tibet. Contact between politics of India and that of China had ceased in the 8th century owing to the growth of the Tibetan power. In the 7th century, the Tāntrik form of the Mahāyāna, so closely allied to the Tāntrik worship in India, had established itself in Nepal. Nepal was conquered by the Gurkhas of the Hindu faith and there has been a gradual disintegration of Buddhism from that time. Kashmir was being ruled by Hindu kings and in the 8th century we had Candrāpīḍa, Muktāpīḍa and Jayāpīḍa, and in the 9th century there were the kings Avantīvarman and Śaṅkaravarman and in the 10th century we have the kings Pārtha, Unmattāvanti and later on Queen Diddā, all of whom were tyrannical. In the 11th century we have king Kalasa and Harṣa, after which it was conquered by the Moslems.

Political condition in India after Harṣa

After Harṣa's death, in the 8th century we have king Yaśovarman in Kanauj, a patron of Bhavabhūti and Vākpatirāja. At the end of the 8th century, the reigning monarch Indrāyudha was dethroned by Dharmapāla, king of Bengal, who enthroned a relative of his, Cakrāyudha, who was again dethroned by Nāgabhaṭa, the Gurjara-Pratihāra king, He transferred his capital to Kanauj. In the 9th century we have king Bhoja. Bhoja's son Mahendrapāla had for his teacher the poet Rājaśekhara. These kings were all Vaiṣṇavas. After this the power of Kanauj began to wane. In the 10th century Jayapāla, king of the Upper Valley of the Indus Region and most of the Punjab, attacked King Sabuktagīn and in the subsequent battles that followed was worsted and committed suicide. In Kanauj, king Rājyapāla was defeated by the Moslems. With the disappearance of the Gurjara-Pratihāra dynasty of Kanauj, a Rājā of the Gahaḍwār clan named Candradeva established his authority over Benares and Ayodhyā and also over Delhi. This is known as the Rathore dynasty. In the 12th century we have Rājā Jayacānd under whose patronage Srīharṣa, the poet, wrote his great work *Naiṣadhacarita*.

A general review of the growth of Sanskrit literature.

It is unnecessary to dilate more upon the political history of India. But from the body of the book and from what has been said in the Editorial Notes, it would appear that the current opinion that the glorious age of the Sanskrit literature synchronised with the glorious epoch of the Guptas, is not quite correct. On the other hand, great writers like Kālidāsa and Bhāsa flourished before the dawn of the Christian era—at the time probably of the Mauryas, and also shortly after the reign of Puṣyamitra at the time of the great Hindu ascendency ; the rise of Buddhism gave a great impetus to the development of sciences and particularly to philosophy ; but in spite of Buddhism, Hinduism became the prevailing religion of the kings of India and in many cases the kings themselves turned to be poets. In spite of the colossal political changes and turmoils in various parts of the country and various foreign inroads and invasions, we had a new era of literary culture and development till the 12th century, when the country was subjugated by the Mahommedans. Many writers have suggested that it is the foreign impact of the Śakas, the Hunas, the Turks, the Chinese, the Tibetans, that gave an incentive, by the introduction of new ideas, to literary development. But such a view will appear hardly to be correct, for to no period of the literary development of India can we ascribe any formative influence due to foreign culture. The Hindu literary development followed an insulated line of *Trivargasiddhi* all through its course from the 12th century onwards. With the occupation of Upper India by the Moslems and their inroads into Southern India and with the growth of stringency of the Smṛti rules and the insulating tendency, the former free spirit gradually dwindled away and we have mostly a mass of sterotyped literature to which South India, which was comparatively immune from the Moslem invasion, contributed largely. Southern India also distinguished itself by its contributions to Vaiṣṇava thought and the emotionalistic philosophy which had its repercussions in Norh India also. Some of the greatest thinkers of India, like Nāgārjuna and Śaṅkara and Rāmānuja, Jayatīrtha and Vyāsatīrtha, hailed from the South and devotionalism, which began with the Ārvārs in the 3rd or the 4th century A.D., attained its eminence in the 16th or the 17th century along with unparalleled dialectic skill of Veṅkaṭa, Jayatīrtha and Vyāsatīrtha. Philosophy in the North dwindled into formalism of the new school of Nyāya, the rise of emotionalism in Caitanya and his followers, and the stringency of the Smṛti in the *nivandhas* of Raghunandana.

Inexplicability of the appearance of geniuses in literature

In attempting to give a perspective of the growth and development of Sanskrit literary culture from the racial, religious, social, political and environmental backgrounds, we have omitted one fact of supreme importance, *viz.*, the rise of geniuses, which is almost wholly unaccountable by any observable data, and though poets of mediocre talents may maintain the literary flow yet in the field of literature as also in politics it is the great geniuses that stand as great monuments of the advancement of thought and action. No amount of discussion or analysis of environmental conditions can explain this freak of Nature just as in the field of Biology the problem of accidental variation cannot be explained. Why a Sūdraka, a Bhāsa, a Kālidāsa, a Bhavabhūti or a Bāṇa lifted up his head at particular epochs of Indian history, will for ever remain unexplained. Rājaśekhara regards poetic genius as being of a two-fold character, creative and appreciative. He alone is a poet to whom any and every natural or social surrounding provokes his creative activity to spontaneous flow of literary creation. This creative function may manifest itself through properly arranged words in rhyme or rhythm in the appreciation of literary art and also in the reproduction of emotion through histrionic functions. This individuality of genius in a way prevents the determination of great works of literary art as being the causal functions of historical cnnditions.

Rājaśekhara on the nature of poets.

But though the consensus of opinion among the rhetoricians point to the view that the mark of true poetry is the creation of sentiments, yet Rājaśekhara and others regard wide experience as an essential characteristic of a good poet. A poet's words should have a universality of application and the manner of his delivery should be such that his failures should be unnoticeable. Rajaśekhara further maintains that though genius is of supreme importance, yet learning is also essential. He distinguishes two types of poets, the Sāstra-kavi, who depicts sentiments and the *kāvya-kavi* who by his mode of delivery softens difficult ideas and thoughts. Both have their place in literature. Both reveal two tendencies which are complementary to each other. The acceptance of learning within the category of the essential qualities that go to make poetry, has well-established itself not only in the time of Rājaśekhara but long before him in the time of Bhaṭṭi and probably much earlier than him. Bhaṭṭi takes pride in thinking that his poems would not be intelligible to people who are not scholars. This wrong perspective arose probably from the fact that the grammatical and lexicographical sciences as well as the philosophical discipline had attained a high water-mark of respect with the learned people who alone could be the judges of poetry. This view, however, was not universal ; for as has elsewhere been noted, Bhāmaha urges that *kāvya* should be written in such a manner as to be intelligible even to those who have no learning or general education.

Literary Prākṛt—a standardised language.

We have seen that Sanskrit had become almost absolutely stereotyped by the middle of the 2nd century B.C. ; we have also seen that the Prākṛt, as we find in literature in spite of their names as Māgadhī, Śaurasenī and Mahārāṣṭrī, was not really the spoken language of those parts of the country. What we have are the standardised artificial forms of Prakṛt which were used for the purpose of literature. It is doubtful to what extent one can regard the Prakṛt of the Aśokan inscriptions to be the spoken dialect of any part of the country, though it has been held by many scholars that the

Eastern dialect was the *lingua franca* of the whole Empire and we assented to this view in the Preface. The variations found in the Girnār, the Kaliṅga, and the Siddāpur edicts would raise many problems of considerable difficulty,

Was Sanskrit a spoken language.?

Another important question that may arise particularly in connection with the drama and the prose literature, is the question as to whether Sanskrit was the spoken language at any time. In our Preface we pointed out that neither *Saṃskṛta* nor Prākṛta was regarded as the name of speech so far as it can be traced from the evidences of earlier Sanskrit literature. Pāṇini distinguishes between the Vedic and the Pāṇinian language, as *Vaidika* and *Bhāṣā* (spoken language). Patañjali in his *Bhāṣya* says that the object of grammar is to supply rules of control for current speech (*laukika* in the sense of being known to the common people, or as having sprung from the common people.)[1] But why should then there be at all rules for the control of speech ? The answer is : one, for the preservation of the integrity of the Vedas ;[2] and two, for making proper transformations of suffixes from the forms given in the *Saṃhitās* for practical sacrificial use ; and three, in pursuance of the general duty for all Brahmins to study the Vedas of which the chief accessory is grammar ; four, grammar is the shortest route for the study of correct words ; five, for arriving at certainty of meaning and for laying proper accents on words. In addition to this, Patañjali adds some supple-

1 *loke vidita iti lokasarvalokāṭṭhañ iti ṭhañ |*
athavā bhavārthe adhyātmāditvāt ṭhañ |
evaṁ vede bhavaiti vaidikaḥ | Mahābhāṣya—Paspaśāhnika.

2 There may be forms in the Vedas which are not found in the current speech and one who is not versed in grammar might easily be led to think that the Vedic form is erroneous.

mentary reason. These are as follows :—the Asuras who imitated the Brahmins in performing the sacrifices often misused the words or misplaced the accents. Thus, instead of putting the *pluta* accent on *he* and pronouncing the word *arayaḥ* after it, they used the words *helaya, helaya,* and were defeated for the reason that they could not get the benefit of the sacrifice for victory ; for this reason, a Brahmin should not mispronounce the words like the *mlecchas.* A wrong word or a wrong accent fails to denote the proper meaning. So to safeguard oneself from wrong usage one should study grammar. The study of grammar is also necessary for the comprehension of proper meaning. There are more wrong words and accents in currency than proper words and accents, for in place of one proper word or accent there may be many wrong words and accents and only the man who knows grammar can distinguish between the right and the wrong word. Here we find the purificatory influence of grammar. Moreover, rules of decorum require that the *pluta* accent should be given in offering salutations to respected persons, whereas in greeting a woman or a person coming from a distant place, one should omit the *pluta* accent. None but one versed in grammar can distinguish these. People often think that the Vedic words may be known from the Vedas and the current words from current speech, but the above discourse will show that there is a necessity for studying grammar for the acquirement in both.

A review of the above discourse reveals to us the following uncontestable facts—*viz.*, that even in the time of Patañjali the Pāṇinian language was used in current speech though many mispronounced and misaccented or corrupt or foreign words had crept into the current speech. The current speech was thus not exactly what we call Pāṇinian Sanskrit but Sanskrit in which there is a very large admixture of corrupt words, for Patañjali expressly says *bhūyāṃsaḥ apaśavdāḥ*' and a codified grammar was needed for sieving out the corrupt words though it cannot be denied that in spite of the sieving some popular words of foreign or aboriginal character were accepted as genuine Sanskrit words. The word *titau* occurring in a verse quoted by Patañjali is an instance of it. We also find that by Patañjali's time the tradition was that the Asuras had accepted Brahminic forms of sacrifice but they could not attain the fruits of them as they could not properly pronounce the Sanskrit words. The rules of accent prescribed for greeting persons also show that Sanskrit as mixed up with corrupt words was in use among the people. Those, however, who achieved the discipline of a grammatical study used the words recognised as chaste by the grammatical tradition. The mixed language as used by common folk was not unintelligible to the learned nor the speech of the learned unintelligible to the common people. A parallel may be drawn from the existing literary Bengali language and the spoken language varying from district to district with regard to words and accents. The learned Bengalees may not even understand properly in some cases the dialectical folk languages of another locality. Thus the Chittagong dialect of Bengali would hardly be intelligible to a learned Bengalee of Calcutta. A learned Chittagong-man may talk in standard Bengali with other learned men but may at the same time use his own dialect in talking with the common people of his native place or he may even intersperse Chittagong words with the words of standard Bengali. The standardisation of accent is still more difficult to be attained.

Dr. Hannes Sköld in his work on the *Nirukta* says that the derivations suggested by Yāska are only intelligible if we assume that he was conversant with some kind of Middle Indian Prākṛt speech. Prof. Lüders says that the language of Aśoka's Chancery was a high language but the actual spoken speech had almost advanced to a stage of the literary Prākṛts. Keith holds that Yāska spoke Sanskrit as he wrote it and the officials of Aśoka spoke in the language similar to what they wrote, while the lower classes of the people spoke in dialets which had undergone much phonetical transformation. From Patañjali's statement referred to above we can gather that the upper classes who were conversant with grammar spoke the chaster speech but as we go down the stratum the language was of a corrupt nature. The alien people on whom the Aryans had imposed their language could not also speak it correctly. The directions of royal edicts as found in the *Arthaśāstra*, Chapter 31, would lead to the presumption that the edicts were drafted in Sanskrit. Aśoka was probably the first to issue edicts in some form of Prākṛt as found in the inscriptions. It is also difficult to assert that Aśoka's inscriptions were written in accordance with the speech of the countries in which the edicts appeared ; for, though the language and the grammar of the edicts have many differences in different localities yet these would be too small in comparison with the actual dialectical varieties that might have existed between Mysore and Guzerat. We think therefore that though the Prākṛt speech was current in Aśoka's time and even in earlier times among the common people, among the higher classes Sanskrit was used in common speech. But the *tatsama* words flowed continuously into the current speech.

Difficulties of appreciating Sanskrit Poetry.

The study of Sanskrit *kāvyas* and their appreciation have their own difficulties. Excepting in the case of a few writers of elegance like Kālidāsa, Bhāsa or Śūdraka, most of the Sanskrit works in poetry are not easily accessible to those who have no proficiency in the language and even for the proficient it is not always an easy reading and at times one cannot make much of them without commentaries. The study of Sanskrit *kāvyas*, therefore, cannot be an easy pastime and cannot always be enjoyed as recreation in leisure hours. "The great poets of India," as Keith says, "wrote for audiences of experts ; they were masters of the learning of their day, long trained in the use of language and they aimed to please by subtlety, not simplicity of effect. They had at their disposal a singularly beautiful speech and they commanded elaborate and most effective metres." Under the circumstances, though the *kāvya* literature contains within it some of the great master-pieces of poetical works, it cannot hope to become popular with those who had a mere lisping knowledge of Sanskrit or who are unwilling to take the trouble of undertaking a difficult journey through the intricacies of the language To the trained ear the music of the poetry is so enthrallingly bewitching that the mere recitation of the verses in the proper manner produces a sense of exhilaration. I have seen that even in Europe, when I recited the verses, persons who had but little acquaintance with Sanskrit, had been tremendously affected by the sonorous rhythm of the Sanskrit verses and large audiences almost felt themselves spell-bound by the mystery of the music. Another difficulty regarding Sanskrit poetry is that, more than the poetry in other languages, the charm of Sanskrit poetry is untranslatable, as a large part of it is derived from the rhythm and the cadence. Thus,

Keith says : "German poets like Rückert can indeed base excellent work on Sanskrit originals, but the effects produced are achieved by wholly different means, while English eflorts at verse translations fall invariably below a tolerable mediocrity, their diffuse tepidity contrasting painfully with the brilliant condensation of style, the elegance of metre and the close adaptation of sound to sense of the original."

Nature in Sanskrit poetry.

Not a less attractive part of Sanskrit poetry is its charming descriptions of natural scences and the beauties of the seasons. As we go from poet to poet we often notice a change of outlook and prespective which cannot but leave a bright and exhilarating effect on our imagination. Thus, throughout the descriptions of natural scenes and objects as depicted by Kālidāsa, we find that the whole Nature is a replica of the human world--the same feelings and emotions, the same passions and sorrows, the same feelings of tenderness, love, affection and friendship that are found to reign in the human mind, are also revealed in the same manner for Kālidāsa in and through all the objects of Nature. The Yakṣa in the *Meghadūta* employs the cloud as the messenger to his love-lorn lady in the Alakāpurī, and the cloud itse f is made to behave as the friend, benefactor and lover of the flowers and rivers, mountains and forests, over which it may pass dropping showers of rain. Nature may be dumb but yet she understands the sorows of men and is friendly to them. In addressing the clouds he says : "Though you do not give any verbal response to my words yet I cannot think that you will not render me a friendly turn, for even in your silence you supply water to the *cātaka*." In the last verse of the *Meghadūta*, Kālidāsa says addressing the cloud : "Oh Cloud ! may you not be separated from the lightning who is your wife.

Either for the sake of friendship or for the sake of kindness or by finding me aggrieved, you may serve me as a messenger and after that you may go wherever you please" The seasons appeared to Kālidāsa almost as living beings. They are not merely the friends of man but throughout Nature the life and pesonality of the seasons are realised in joy and love, and in Kālidāsa's descriptions this aspect of Nature becomes extremely vivid.

But when Vālmīki looks at Nature, his general emphasis is on the realistic aspect of Nature. The aspect of its utility to man is thin and shadowy. But as we proceed onwards we find that gradually Nature begins to rise to the human level and often its practical utility to man is emphasised, *e.g.*, in the *Ṛtusaṃhāra* of Kālidāsa. The emphasis on the pragmatic aspect has indeed a deleterious effect on the nature of poetry, but oftentimes in the descriptions of the poets the pragmatic aspect is thinned away and human characters are ascribed to Nature, or Nature has been enlivened with the fulness of human consciousness. Starting from realism we often pass into idealism as self-reflection. In the *Rāmāyaṇa,* for example, Vālmīki is describing the situation of Rāma in his separation from Sītā and in contrasting it with the state of Sugrīva, describes the sorrow of Rāma. Thus he says : "I am without my wife and my throne and am being broken into pieces like the bank of a river As the rains make all places extremely impassable, so my sorrow is broad and wide and it seems to me as if I can never ford over to my great enemy Rāvaṇa" But Vālmīki here does not describe what Rāma would have done if his wife was nearby. He had seen the lightning by the side of the dark cloud and he was at once reminded as to how Sītā -might have been lying in the lap of Rāvaṇa. Looking at the new showers of rain he is reminded of the falling tears of Sītā. Nature thus reminds the human situation and events but there is no tinge of any pragmatic perspective regarding the rains. But human comparisons are quite common. Thus in describing the hills he speaks of them as if they were wearing garments of black deer-skin and he compares the rains with the the holy thread and music of the rains with the chanting of Vedic hymns. But apart from such human analogies the general tendency of Vālmīki's description is realism—descriptions of fruits and flowers, of birds and beasts, of muddy roads and moist winds, and so on. Bhavabhuti seems to have followed this realistic tendency of Vālmīki in his descriptions of Nature, which is sometimes sublime and sombre. Such a realistic tendency can be found in other poets also. Thus, the poet Abhinanda speaks of dreadful darkness torn sometimes into pieces by the gleaming lightning ; even the tree before us cannot be seen ; their existence can only be inferred from the collection of fire-flies ; the whole night is ringing with the humming of crickets.

Thus, the different poets of India had approached Nature from diverse points of view, some realistic, some pragmatic, some idealistic.

Thus, in spite of criticisms that may be levelled against Sanskrit poetry, to a learned Sanskritist who is acquainted with the trailing history of the allusive words and its penumbra, the double meanings and the associated myths, Sanskrit poetry with its luxurious images, cadence of rhyme, jingling alliteration of word-sounds, creates a wonderland of magic and joy that transports the reader to a new world of beauty. The delicate and passionate flickerings of love with which Sanskrit love poetry is surcharged are as much exciting to our primal tendencies as appealing to our cultured tastes. Though much of Sanskrit poetry has been lost through the ravages of time, yet what remains is worthy of the pride and satisfaction of any great nation. There is no compeer in the world of the *Mahābhārata* and the *Rāmāyaṇa* taken together, and Kālidāsa stands supreme before our eyes as a magic-creator of beauty and enchantment, and Bhavabhūti as the creator of the sombre and the sublime.

CHAPTER I

ORIGINS AND CHARACTERISTICS

1. The Origin and Sources of the Kāvya

Even if there is no direct evidence,[1] it would not be entirely unjustifiable to assume that the Sanskrit Kāvya literature, highly stylised though it is, had its origin in the two great Epics of India. The Indian tradition, no doubt, distinguishes the Itihāsa from the Kāvya, but it has always, not unjustly, regarded the *Rāmāyaṇa,* if not the *Mahābhārata,* as the first of Kāvyas.

[1] This rapid survey is only an attempt to give, from the literary point of view only, and from direct reading of the literature itself, a connected historical outline of a vast and difficult subject. It does not pretend to be exhaustive, nor to supersede the excellent and methodical presentations of Moritz Winternitz and Sten Konow, with their valuable bibliographical material, as well as the brilliant accounts of Sylvain Lévi and A. B. Keith, to all of which, as also to various monographs and articles of individual scholars, every writer traversing the same ground must acknowledge his deep indebtedness. But the aim of the present account is not to offer a mere antiquarian or statistical essay, not to record and discuss what has been said on Sanskrit literature (the value of which, however, is not and cannot be ignored), but to give, as concisely as possible, a systematic and literary account of the literarure itself. Even if strict chronology is not yet attainable, it should be recognised that our general knowledge of the subject is not today so nebulous as to make the applications of historical or literary methods altogether impossible. It is felt that Sanskrit literature, as literature, need no longer be looked upon as a literary curiosity, deserving merely a descriptive, erudite, apologetic or condescending treatment, but that it ranks legitimately as one of the great literatures of the world, to the appreciation of which broader historical and literary standards should be applied. The bibliographical references and purely learned discussions, which are available in their fulness elsewhere, are, therefore, reduced as much as possible to a minimum, and emphasis has been laid upon the literary aspects of the problems, which have, so far, not received adequate attention. It is not claimed that the work is final in this respect but it is hoped that a beginning has been made. The only apology that is necessary, apart from the obvious one of the writer's imperfect knowledge and capacity, is that it is written within certain limits of time, which allowed less provision of metarial than what could have been accomplished by longer preparation, and within certain limits of space, which did not permit him to enter fully into some of the difficult, but interesting, problems.

The *Mahābhārata* certainly afforded, by its diversified content, inexhaustible legendary and didactic material to later Kāvya poets ; but from the point of view of form, it is simpler and less polished, and conforms more to the epic standard. It could not, in spite of later addition and elaboration, afford such an excellent model for the factitious Kāvya as the more balanced and poetical *Rāmāyaṇa* did. The unity of treatment, elegancies of style and delicate verse-technique, which distinguish the *Rāmāyaṇa*, may not be studied, but they are none the less skilful and effective. It is probable that some part of its stylistic elaboration came into existence in later times, but there is nothing to show that most of these refinements did not belong to the poem itself, or to a date earlier than that of the Kāvya literature, which imitates and improves upon them. The literary standard and atmosphere of the epic are indeed different from those of Amaru and Kālidāsa, but the poem, as a whole, grounded like the *Mahābhārata* as it is in the heroic epos, is undoubtedly the product of a much more developed artistic sense.[1] The pedestrian naïvete of the mere epic narrative is often lifted to the attractive refinement of greater art, ; and the general tone of seriousness and gravity is often relieved by picturesque descriptions of the rainy season and autumn, of mountains, rivers and forests, as well as by sentimental and erotic passages and by the employment of metaphors and similes of beauty. If in the Kāvya greater importance is attached to the form, the *Rāmāyaṇa* can in a very real sense be called the first Kāvya ; and the literary embellishment that we find in it in the skilled use of language, metre and poetic figures is not wholly adventitious but forms an integral part of its poetic expression, which anticipates the more conscious ornaments and finish of the later Kāvya.

1 H. Jacobi, *Das Rāmāyaṇa*, Bonn, 1831, pp. 119-26 and A. B. Keith, *History of Sanskrit Literature*, Oxford, 1928 (cited throughout below as *HSL*), pp. 42-45, give some instances, which can be easily multiplied, of the formal excellences of the *Rāmāyaṇa*, which foreshadow the Kāvya. The Epics also show the transformation of the Vedic Anuṣṭubh into the Classical Śloka, and of the Vedic Triṣṭubh-Jagatī into a variety of lyrical measures which are further developed in the Kāvya.

There is no need, therefore, to trace back the origin of the Kāvya literature in the far-off Vedic hymns, and find its prototype in the Narāśaṃsa and Dānastuti panegyrics, in the semi-dramatic and impassioned Saṃvāda-Ākhyānas, in the heightening of style found in the glowing descriptions of deities like Uṣas, or in the legends and gnomic stanzas preserved in the Brāhmaṇas. The tradition of a non-religious literature was already there from remote antiquity surviving through long centuries as a strong undercurrent and occasionally coming to the surface in the more conventional literature ; but the immediate precursor of the Kāvya is undoubtedly the Epics, which themselves further develop these secular, and in a sense popular, tendencies of the earlier Vedic literature.

It is also not necessary to seek the origin of the Sanskrit Kāvya literature in the hypothetical existence of a prior Prakrit literature, on which it is alleged to have modelled itself. There is indeed no convincing evidence, tradition or cogent reason to support the theory that the Epics themselves or the Kāvya were originally composed in Prakrit and rendered later into Sanskrit. The existence of a Prakrit period of literature preceding the Sanskrit, which such theories presuppose, is inferred mainly from the epigraphical use of Prakrit in the period preceding the Christian era ; but it cannot be substantiated by the adducing of an evidence of value regarding the existence of actual Prakrit works in this period. Even assuming that a Prakrit literature existed, the co-existence of a Sanskrit literature in some form is not thereby excluded ; nor does it necessarily follow that the one was derived from the other. It is possible to assume the existence, from the Vedic times, of a popular secular literature, current in a speech other than the hieratic, from which the secular Vedic hymns derived their material ; and the tradition is possibly continued in heroic songs, lyrical stanzas, gnomic verses and folk-tales, which might have been composed in Prakrit ; but the very language and treatment of the Epics themselves show a stage of linguistic and literary development, in which a freer and less polished, but more practical, form of Sanskrit than the perfected speech of Pāṇini was employed for conveying a literature, not hieratic, but no less aristocratic. The influence of a concurrent popular Prakrit literature may be presumed, but the Epics, in form, substance and spirit, cannot be called popular in the same sense; they were loved by the populace, but in no sense composed or inspired by them. They possess linguistic and literary peculiarities of their own, which preclude the theory of Prakrit originals, and which must be traced ultimately, in unbroken tradition, to certain aspects of Vedic language and literature. There is, again, no evidence to justify the high antiquity claimed for the collection of Prakrit folk-tales of Guṇāḍhya, which is now lost, or for the Prakrit lyrics of Hāla, which have been misleadingly taken as the prototype of the Sanskrit lyrics. Not only does the Prakrit of Hāla's anthology show a fairly developed form of the language, far apart from the Prakrits of the early inscriptions and of the dramatic fragments of Aśvaghoṣa, but the Prakrit poetry which it typifies is as conventional as the Sanskrit, and is not folk-literature in its true sense. Both the *Mahābhārata* and the Jātakas, again, show the currency of the beast-fable, but in this sphere also we know nothing of any early Prakrit achievement. Nor can it be shown that an original Prakrit drama was turned into Sanskrit; and our earliest specimens of the Sanskrit drama in the Aśvaghoṣa fragments, which do not show it in a primitive or rudimentary form, are already written in Sanskrit, as well as in Prakrit.

The hypothesis of an earlier Prakrit literature started also from the supposition that Sanskrit was little used until it was recovered and restored sometime after the Christian era. The theory is thus a revival in another form of Max Müller's once famous but now discredited suggestion[1] of the cessation of literary

[1] *India: What can it teach us?* (London, 1882), p. 281 f. It is mainly on the basis of Fergusson's theory of the Vikrama era that Max Müller connected his suggestion with the legend of a king Vikramāditya of Ujjayinī, who was supposed to have driven out the Śakas from India and founded the Vikrama era in 544 A.D., but dated the era back to 57 B. C. Max

activity in India until the sixth century A.D., when a Sanskrit Renaissance was supposed to have begun. At a time when scanty facts gave room for abundant fancies, the theory appeared plausible ; it was apparently justified by the absence or paucity of literary works before and after the Christian era, as well as by the fact that the incursions of Greeks, Parthians, Kuṣāṇas and Śakas at this time must have affected the north-west of India. But the epigraphical and literary researches of Bühler, Kielhorn and Fleet have now confirmed beyond doubt the indication, first given by Lassen,[1] regarding the development of the Sanskrit Kāvya-form in the first few centuries of the Christian era, and have entirely destroyed Max Müller's theory of a literary interregnum. Bühler's detailed examination[2] of the evidence borne by the early inscriptions, ranging from the second to the fifth

Müller, however, had the sagacity to perceive that Fergusson's theory would at once collapse if any document were found dated in the Vikrama era before 544 A D The missing evidence is now found, and both the assumptions mentioned above are now shown to be untenable (see Fleet, *Gupta Inscriptions*. Introd. ; also *IA*, XXX, pp. 3-4). The Vikramāditya legend itself is fairly old. It owed its currency, no doubt, from an ill-authenticated verse of a late work, which associates Dhanvantari, Kṣapaṇaka, Amarasiṁha, Śaṅku, Vetālabhaṭṭa, Ghaṭakarpara, Kālidāsa, Varāhamihira and Vararuci as the nine gems of the court of this mythical king. While we know for certain that Varāhamihira flourished in the middle of the sixth century, Vararuci is undoubtedly a very old author to whom a Kāvya is ascribed in Patañjali's *Mahābhāsya* ; while of the other poets, some are mere names, and some, who are by no means contemporaries, are lumped together, after the manner of works like *Bhoja-prabandha*, which makes Kālidāsa, Bāṇa and Bhavabhūti contemporaries ! On this verse and on *Jyotirvidābharaṇa* (16th century in which it occurs, see Weber in *ZDMG*, XXII, 1868, pp. 708 f : also introd. to Nandargikar's ed. of *Raghu-vaṁśa* for references to work where this verse is discussed. It is remarkable, however, that the tradition of a great Vikramāditya as a patron of the Kāvya persists in literature. Subandhu laments that after the departure of Vikramāditya there is no true appreciator of poetry ; and an early reference in the same strain is found in a verse of Hāla (ed. *NSP*, v. 64). The Sanskrit anthologies assign some 20 verses to Vikramāditya, and he is associated with Bhartṛmeṇṭha, Mātṛgupta and Kālidāsa (see W. Thomas, introd. to *Kavīndra-vacana-samuccaya*, pp. 105-06 and references cited therein). There is no satisfactory evidence to connect him with the later Vikramādityas of the Gupta dynasty ; and if the original founder of the Vikrama era was a Vikramāditya, all search for him has, so far, not proved successful. For a recent discussion of the question, see Edgerton, introd. to *Vikramacarita*. pp. lviii-lxvi.

1 Lassen, *Indische Alterthumskunde*, II, p. 1159 f.

2 Die indischen Inschriften und das Alter der indischen Kuntspoesie in *SWA*, 1890 trs. *IA*, *xiii*, p. 291.

century A.D., not only proves the existence in these centuries of ā highly elaborate body of Sanskrit prose and verse in the Kāvya-style, but it also raises the presumption that most of the Praśasti-writers were acquainted with 'some theory of poetic art.' If Max Müller conjectured a decline of literary activity in the first two centuries of the Christian era on account of the incursions of the Śakas, we know now that there is nothing to justify the idea that the Western Kṣatrapas or Satraps of Śaka origin were great destroyers. Their inscriptions show that they became themselves rapidly Indianised, adopted Indian names and customs, patronised Indian art and religion, and adopted, as early as 150 A.D., Sanskrit as their epigraphical language. There is, therefore, no evidence for presuming a breach of literary continuity from the first to the fifth century A.D. If the theory is sometimes revived by the modified suggestion that the origin of the Sanskrit Kāvya is to be ascribed to the ascendancy of the Śakas themselves, the discovery and publication of Aśvaghoṣa's works directly negative the idea by affording further proof of an earlier bloom of the Sanskrit Kāvya literature in some of its important aspects, and perhaps push the period of its origin much further back. The fact that a Buddhist poet should, at the commencement of the Christian era, adopt the Sanskrit Kāvya-style for the avowed object[1] of conveying the tenets of his faith, hitherto generally recorded in the vernacular, is itself an indication of its popularity and diffusion ; and the relatively perfect form in which the Kāvya emerges in his writings pre-supposes a history behind it.

The history, unfortunately, is hidden from us. We can, however, surmise its existence in some from in Pāṇini's time in the 4th century B.C.,[2] if we consider that one of the direct results

1 As he declares at the close of his *Saundarānanda* that his object in adoptirg the Kāvya-form is to set forth the truth which leads to salvation in an attractive garb, so that it should appeal to all men.

2 Pāṇini's time is uncertain, but we take here the generally accepted date, as also Pantañjali's accepted date in relation to that of Pāṇini.

of his elaborate grammar, as also its object, had been the standardisation of Sanskrit, as distinguished from the Vedic (Chandas) and the spoken dialect (Bhāṣā). Although Pāṇini shows himself fully conversant with the earlier Vedic literature, there is no reason to suppose that the Śiṣṭa speech of his day was that of the priesthood alone; his object was not to regulate the hieratic speech but the language of polished expression in general. Pāṇini's own system, as well as his citation of the views of different schools of grammar, shows that grammatical studies must have been fairly well advanced in his time, and presupposes the existence of a respectable body of literature on which his linguistic speculations must have based themselves. Nothing, unfortunately, has survived ; and this literature, which must have been supplanted by the more mature writings of later times, is now only a matter of surmise.

The evidence would have been more definite if any reliance could be placed on the statement contained in a verse, ascribed to Rājaśekhara[1] in Jahlaṇa's *Sūkti-muktāvalī* (1257 A.D.) that Pāṇini wrote "first the grammar and then the Kāvya, the Jāmbavatī-jaya." A fragment[2] from Pāṇini's *Gāmbavatī-vijaya* is preserved by Rāyamukuṭa in his commentary on *Amara-kośa* (1.2.3.6), which was composed in 1431 A.D. Much earlier than this date, Nami-sādhu who wrote his commentary on Rudraṭa's *Kāvyālaṃkāra* in 1069 A.D.,[3] cites "from Pāṇini's Mahākāvya, the Pātāla-vijaya," a fragment (*saṃdhyā-vadhūṃ gṛhya kareṇa*) in illustration of the remark that great poets permit

1 *svasti Pāṇinaye tasmai yasya Rudra-prasādataḥ* | *ādau vyākaraṇaṁ kāvyam anu Jāmbavatī-jayam* || This Rājaśekhara could have been the Jaina Rajaśekhara, who wrote his *Prabandha-kośa* in 1348 A.D. ; but it is not clear if he was the dramatist Rājaśekhara, who flourished during the end of the 9th and the beginning of the 10th century ; for in the latter's *Kāvya-mīmāṁsā* there are references to Pāṇini's learned achievements but no mention of him as a poet.

2 *payaḥ-pṛṣantibhiḥ spṛṣṭā vānti vātāḥ śanaiḥ śanaiḥ*. Altogether Rāyamukuṭa quotes three fragments from Pāṇini (Bhandarkar, *Report*, 1883-84, pp. 62, 479). Another quotation from *Jāmbavatījaya* is given by Aufrecht in *ZDMG*, XLV, 1891, p. 308.

3 S. K. De, *Sanskrit Poetics*, I, p. 98.

themselves the licence of ungrammatical forms[1] and further gives as another example, a stanza "of the same poet" in which the un-Pāninian form *apaśyati* occurs.[2] Both these Kāvyas, ascribed to Pāṇini, are now lost, but their titles imply that they apparently dealt with Kṛṣṇa's descent into the lower world and winning of Jāmbavatī as his bride. It is not clear, however, from these separate and brief references, if they are two different works or one work with two different names. The tradition of Pāṇini's poetical achievement is also recorded in an anonymous stanza given in the *Sadukti-karṇāmṛta* (1206 A.D.),[3] while seventeen verses, other than those mentioned above, are also found cited in the Anthologies under the name of a poet Pāṇini,[4] of which the earliest citation appears to a verse given in the *Kavīndra-vacana-samuccaya*[5] (about 1000 A.D.). Most of these verses are in the fanciful vein and ornate diction, and some are distinctly

1 Ed. NSP, *ad* 2.8 : *mahākavīnām apy apaśabda-pāta-darśanāt*. Nami-sādhu also quotes in the same context similar solecisms from the poems of Bhartṛhari, Kālidāsa and Bhāravi

2 *gate'rdha-rātre parimanda-mandaṁ garjanti yat prāvṛṣi kāla-meghāḥ* ।
apaśyatī vatsam invedu-bimbaṁ tac charvarī gour iva huṁkaroti ॥

3 5.26.5, which extols Bhavabhūti along with Subandhu, Raghukāra (Kālidāsa,) Dākṣīputra (Pāṇini), Haricandra, Śūra and Bhāravi.

4 The Anthology verses are collected together and translated by Aufrecht in *ZDMG*, XIV, p. 581f ; XXVII. p. 46f ; XXXVI, p. 356f ; XLV, p. 308f. They are also given by Peterson, introd. to *Subhāṣitāvali*, pp. 54-58 and *JRAS*, 1891, pp. 311-19, and more fully by F. W. Thomas, *Kavīndravacana*°, introd., pp. 51-53. Also see Aufrecht in *ZDMG* XXVIII, p. 113, for quotations by Rāyamukuṭa.—The following abbreviations will be used for the Anthologies cited below : *Kvs*=Kavīndra-vacana-samuccaya, ed. F. W. Thomas, Bibl. Ind. Calcutta, 1912; *ŚP*=Śārṅgadhara-paddhati, ed. P. Peterson, Bombay, 1888 ; *Sbhv*=Subhāṣitāvali of Vallabhadeva, ed. P. Peterson. Bombay, 1886 ; *Sml*=Sūkti-muktāvalī of Jahlaṇa, ed. Gaekwad's Orient. Series, Baroda, 1939 ; *Skm*=Saduktikarṇāmṛta, ed. R. Sarma and H. Sarma, Lahore, 1933 ; *Pdv*=Padyāvalī, ed. S. K De, Dacca, 1934.

5 No. 186, *tanvaṅgīnāṁ stanau dṛṣṭvā*. As it will be clear from the concordance given by Thomas, the ascription in the Anthologies is not uniform, The *Sbhv* gives nine verses of which two only (*upoḍha-rāgeṇa* and *kṣapāḥ kṣāmīkṛtya*) are ascribed by *ŚP*. The *Skm* gives 8 verses including *upoḍha-rāgeṇa* ; while *Sml* assigns this verse, as well as *kṣapāḥ kṣāmīkṛtya*, which last verse is given also by *Sbhv* and *ŚP* but which is anonymous in *Kvs* and ascribed to Oṁkaṇṭha in *Skm*. The verses *pāṇau padma-dhiyā* and *pāṇau śoṇa-tale* are assigned to Pāṇini in *Skm*, but they are anonymous in *Kvs*, while the first verse is sometimes ascribed to Acala. Some of these verses are quoted in the Alaṁkāra works, but always anonymously, the oldest citations being those by Vāmana *ad* IV. 3 (*aindraṁ dhanuḥ*) and Ānandavardhana, p. 35 (*upoḍha-rāgeṇa*).

erotic in theme. Among the metres employed we have one verse in Śikhariṇī, two in Śloka, two in Śārdūlavikrīḍita, three in Sragdharā, three in Vaṃśasthavila and six in Upajāti. It is noteworthy that Kṣemendra, in his *Suvṛtta-tilaka* (iii. 30), tells us in the 11th century that Pāṇini excelled in composing verses in the Upajāti metre[1] ; and we find that, besides the six Anthology verses, both the verses quoted by Nami-sādhu, as well as two out of the three fragments given by Rāyamukṭa, are in the Upajāti.

Aufrecht, who first drew attention to the existence of a poet named Pānini, remarked that we did not as yet know of more than one author of that name ; and the question whether, despite the rarity of the name, we can assume the existence of more than one Pāṇini has not , in the interval, advanced much beyond that stage. As the Indian tradition, however, knows only of one Pāṇini who wrote the famous grammar and whom it does not distinguish from the poet Pāṇini, it has been maintained that the grammarian and the poet are identical.[2] While admitting that the evidence adduced is late, and that the ascription in the Anthologies, being notoriously careless, should not be taken as conclusive, one cannot yet lose sight of the fact that the tradition recorded from the 11th century, independently by various writers, makes no distinction between Pāṇini the grammarian and Pāṇini the poet. The genuineness of the Anthology verses may well be doubted, but the naming of the two poems, from which verses are actually quoted, cannot be so easily brushed aside. The silence of grammarians from

1 As, we are told further, Kālidāsa in Mandākrāntā, Bhavabhūti in Śikhariṇī, Bhāravi in Vaṁśasthavila, Ratnākara in Vasantatilaka, and Rājaśekhara in Śārdūlavikrīḍita, etc. The preponderance of Upajāti in Aśvaghoṣa's *Buddha-carita* (ed. E. H. Johnston, Pt. II. p. lxvi) undoubtedly indicates its early popularity, attested, also by its adoption of Kālidāsa in his two poems.

2 In the works and articles of Peterson cited above. Pischel, in *ZDMG*, XXXIX, 1885, p. 95f believes in the identity, but he makes it the ground of placing Pāṇini at about the fifth century A.D. ; Bühler however, rightly points out (*IA*, XV, 1886, p. 241) that "if the grammarian Pāṇini did write a Kāvya, it does not follow that he should be supposed to live in the 4th or 5th century A.D.; the Kāvya literature is much older."

Patañjali downwards is a negative argument[1] which proves nothing, while the least valid of all objections is that the Sanskrit of the poems could not have been the Sanskrit of Pāṇini, of that Pāṇini could not have used such ungrammatical forms as *gṛhya* and *apaśyati* in defiance of his own rules (vii. i. 37, 81). The occurrence of such archaisms, which are not rare in old poets,[2] is itself a strong indication of the antiquity of the poem or poems ; and when we consider that only two centuries later Patañjali refers to a Kāvay by Vararuci, who was also perhaps a grammarian-poet,[3] and quotes framents of verses composed in the same ornate manner and diction, the argument that the language of the poems is comparatively modern and could not have been that of Pāṇini loses much of its force. In the absence of further decisive evidence, however, the question must be regarded as open ; but nothing convincing has so far been adduced which would prove that the grammarian could not have composed a regular Kāvya.

The literary evidence furnished by the quotations and references in Patañjali's *Mahābhāṣya*, which show that the Sanskrit Kāvya in some of its recognised forms flourished in the 2nd century B.C.,[4] gives us the first definite indication regarding its early origin and development. Patañjali directly mentions a Vāraruca Kāvya (*ad* iv. 3.101),[5] although, un-

1 R. G. Bhandarkar in *JBRAS*, XVI, p. 344.

2 These archaisms are authenticated by the Epics, by Aśvaghoṣa and by what Patañjali says about poetic licence. Nami-sādhu, as noted above, rightly points out that such irregular forms are not rare evēn in later poets. The fragments quoted by Rāyamukuṭa and Nami-sādhu have undoubtedly the appearance of being old. Some of the Anthology verses contain instances of *lectio difficilior*, which have been discussed by Böhtlingk in *ZDMG*, XXXVI, p. 659.

3 Besides Vararuci, whose verses have been cited in the Anthologies (Peterson, introd. to *Sbhv* p. 103 ; *Skm*, introd., pp. 105-07), we have similar verses ascribed to Bhartṛhari (see Peterson in *Sbhv*, introd., p. 74 ; *Skm*, introd.. p. 82) and Vyāḍi (*Skm*, V. 32.2).

4 On the question of Patañjali's date, which is still uncertain, see Keith, *India Office Cat. of. MSS*, II, p. 243f.

5 One of Rājaśekhara's verses in the *Sūkti-muktāvalī* tells us that the name of Vararuci's poem was Kaṇṭhābharaṇa. Vararuci is one of the mysterious figures of early Sanskrit literature. He is sometimes identified with the Vārttikakāra Kātyāyana and extolled as one of the nine gems of the court of an equally mysterious Vikramāditya. To him a monologue-

fortunately, he supplies no further information about it. He refers to poetic licence, which was apparently not rare in his day, with the remark : *chandovat kavayaḥ kurvanti* (*ad* i.4.3). He appears to know various forms of the Kāvya literature other than poetry, although from his tantalisingly brief references or fragmentary quotations it is not always possible to determine in what exact form they were known to him. Like Pāṇini, Patañjali knows the Bhārata epic and refers to Granthikas, who were probably professional reciters. Tales about Yavakrīta, Priyaṅgu and Yayāti were current ; and commenting on Kātyāyana's oldest mention of the Ākhyāyika,[1] which alluded not to narrative episodes found in the Epics but to independent works, Patañjali gives the names of three Ākhyāyikās, namely, Vāsavadattā, Sumanottarā and Bhaimarathī. But, unfortunately, we have no details regarding their form and content. In an obscure passage (*ad* iii. 1.26), over the interpretation of which there has been much difference of opinion,[2] a reference is made to some kind of entertainment—possibly dramatic—in which a class of entertainers called Śaubhikas carry out, apparently by means of vivid action, the killing of Kaṃsa and the binding of Bali. Greater interest attaches to some *forty quotations*, mostly metrical, but often given in fragments, in which one can find eulogistic, erotic or gnomic themes in the approved style and language of the Kāvya. The metres in which they are conveyed are no longer

play entitled *Ubhayābhisārikā*, is attributed, as well as a lost work called *Cārumatī*, which was apparently a romance. He is vaguely referred to as an authority on the Alaṁkāra-śastra (S. K De, *Sanskrit Poetics*, I, p. 70) and regarded as the author of a Prakrit Grammar (*Prākṛta-prākaśa*), of a work on grammatical gender (*Liṅgānuśāsana)*, of a collection of gnomic stanzas *(Nīti-ratna)* and even of an eastern version of the colleetion of folk-tales known as *Siṁhāsana-dvātriṁśikā*. Apparently, he was one of the far-off apocryphal authors of traditional repute on whom all anonyma could be conveniently lumped.

[1] Vārttika on Pā., iv.3.87 and iv.2.60. Also see Patañjali, ed. Kielhorn, II, p. 284. Kātyāyana knows a work named Daivāsuram, dealing apparently with the story of the war of gods and demons.

[2] Ed. Kielhorn, II, p. 36. See Weber in *Ind. St.* XIII, p. 488f ; Lüders in *SBAW*, 1916, p. 698f ; Lévi in *Théâtre ind.*, I, p. 315 ; Hillebrandt in *ZDMG*, LXXII, p. 227f ; Keith in *BSOS*, I, Pt. 4, p. 27f and *Sanskrit Drama*, Oxford, 1924, p. 31f.

Vedic, but we have, besides the classical Śloka, fragments of stanzas in Mālatī, Praharṣiṇī, Vaṃśasthavila, Vasantatilaka, Pramitākṣarā, Indravajrā or Upendravajrā. In addition to this, there are about 260 scattered verses[1] treating of grammatical matters (sometimes called Śloka-vārttikas), which employ, besides the normal Śloka, Āryā, Vaktra and some irregular Triṣṭubh-Jagatī metres, such ornate lyrical measures as Vidyunmālā (3 stanzas), Samānī, Indravajrā and Upendravajrā (7 stanzas), Sālinī (4 stanzas), Vamśasthavila, Dodhnka (12 stanzas) and Toṭaka (2 stanzas).

This early evolution of lyrical measures, multitude of which is systematically defined and classified in the earliest known work on Prosody, attributed to Pingala,[2] takes us beyond the sphere of the Vedic and Epic metrical systems. The Epic poets, generally less sensitive to delicate rhythmic effects, preferred metres in which long series of stanzas could be composed with ease ; but the metrical variation in lyric and sentimental poetry, which had love for its principal theme, accounts for the large number of lyric metres which came into existence in the classical period. Some of the new metres derive their names from their characteristic form or movement : such as Druta-vilambita 'fast and slow', Vegavatī 'of impetuous motion,' Mandākrāntā 'stepping slowly,' Tvaritagati 'quickly moving' ; some are named after plants and flowers : Mālā 'garland' Mañjarī 'blossom' ; some are called after the sound and habit of animals, Śārdūla-vikrīḍita 'play of the tiger,' Aśva-lalita 'gait of the horse,' Hariṇī-pluta 'leap of the deer,' Haṃsa-ruta 'cackling of the geese,' Bhramara-vilasita 'sportiveness of the bees,' Gaja-gati 'motion of elephant' ; but it is also remarkable that the names given to a very large number

1. Kielhorn in *IA*, XV, p. 228 ; also *IA*, XIV, 1886, pp. 326-27.

2. M. Ghosh in *IHQ*, VII, 1931, p. 724f. maintains that the parts dealing with the Vedic and classical metres respectively cannot be attributed to the same author, and that the Vedic part should be assigned to *circa* 600 B.C. D. C. Sarcar, in *Ind. Culture*, VI, pp. 110f. 274, believes that the classical part cannot be placed earlier than the 5th century A.D.

of metres are epithets of fair maidens : Tanvī 'slender-limbed,' Rucirā 'dainty,' Pramadā 'handsome,' Pramitākṣarā 'a maiden of measured words,' Manjubhāṣiṇī 'a maiden of charming speech,' Śaśivadanā 'moonfaced,' Citralekhā 'a maiden of beautiful outlines,' Vidyunmālā 'chain of lightning,' Kanakaprabhā 'radiance of gold,' Cāruhāsinī 'sweetly smiling,' Kundadantī 'a maiden of budlike teeth,' Vasantatilaka 'decoration of spring,' Cañcalākṣī 'a maiden of tremulous glances,' Sragdharā 'a maiden with a garland,' and Kāntotpīḍā 'plague of her lovers' ! The names mentioned above undoubtedly indicate a more developed and delicate sense of rhythmic forms. The names of fair maidens, however, need not be taken as having actually occurred in poems originally composed in their honour by diverse poets, but they certainly point to an original connexion of thes lyric metres with erotic themes ; and Jacobi is right in suggesting[1] that they had their origin in the Sanskrit Kāvya poetry of a pre-Christian era, from which the Māhārāṣṭrī lyric also had its impetus and inspiration.

The difficulty of arriving at an exact conclusion regarding the origin and development of the Kāvya arises from the fact that all the Kāvya literature between Patañjali and Aśvaghoṣa has now disappeared ; and we cannot confidently assign any of the Kāvyas, which have come down to us, to the period between the 2nd century B.C. and the 1st or 2nd century A.D, We have thus absolutely no knowledge of the formative period of Sanskrit literature. The Kāvya does not indeed emerge in a definite and self-conscious form until we come to Aśvaghoṣa, the first known Kāvya-poet of eminence, who is made a contemporary of Kaniṣka by both Chinese and Tibetan traditions, and who can be placed even on independent grounds "between 50 B.C. and 100 A.D. with a preference to the first half of the first century A.D."[2] An examination of Aśvaghoṣa's works,

1 in *ZDMG*, XXXVIII, pp. 616-17.

2 See. *Buddha-carita*, ed. E. H. Johnston (Calcutta, 1936), Pt. II, introd., pp. xiii-xvii

however, shows[1] that although they are free from the later device of overgrown compounds, they betray an unmistakable knowledge, even in a somewhat rough and primitive form, of the laws of Kāvya poetry, by their skill in the use of classical metres,[2] by their handling of similes and other rhetorical figures, and by their growing employment of the stanza as a separate unit of expression.

A little later, we have a fairly extensive Sanskrit inscription, carved on a rock at Girnar of Mahākṣatrapa Rudradāman,[3] celebrating an event of about 150 A,D. and composed in the ornate Sanskrit prose familiar to us from the Kāvya. The literary merit of this Praśasti cannot be reckoned very high, but it is important as one of the earliest definite instances of high-flown Sanskrit prose composition. The inscription contains a reference to the king's skill in the composition of "prose and verse embellished and elevated by verbal conventions, which are clear, light, pleasant, varied and charming."[4] Making allowance for heightened statement not unusual in inscriptional panegyric, the reference can be taken as an interesting evidence of the early interest in Sanskrit culture evinced even by a king of foreign extraction. One can also see in the reference at least the author's, if not his patron's, acquaintance with some form of poetic art which prescribed poetic embellishment (Alaṃkāra) and conventional adjustment of words (Śabda-samaya), involving the employment of such excellences as clearness, light-

On the date of Kaniṣka a summary of the divergent views, with full references, is given by Winternitz, *History of Indian Literature* (referred to below as *HIL*), II, Calcutta, 1933, pp. 611-14. The limits of divergence are now no longer very large, and the date 100 A.D. would be a rough but not unjust estimate.

1. E. H. Johnston, *op. cit.*, pp. lxiii f.

2. Among the metres used (besides classical Anuṣṭubh) are Upajāti, Vaṃśasthavila, Rucirā, Praharṣiṇī, Vasantatilaka, Mālinī, Śikhariṇī, Śārdūlavikrīḍita, Suvadanā, Viyoginī, or Sundarī, Aupacchandasika, Vaitālīya, Puṣpitāgrā, and even unknown metres like Śarabhā, and rare and difficult ones like Kusumalatāvellita (called Citralekhā by Bharata), Udgātā and Upasthitapracupita.

3. *EI*, VIII, p. 36f.

4. *sphuṭa-laghu-madhura-citra-kānta-śabdasamayodārālaṃkṛta-gadya-padya°*.

ness, sweetness, variety, charm and elevation. It is notable that the composition itself is not free from archaism like *patinā* (for *patyā*), Prakritisms like *vīśaduttarāṇi* (for *viṃśad-*) or irregular construction like *anyatra saṃgrāmeṣu* ; but in respect of the employment of long sentences and sonorous compounds, of poetic figures like simile and alliteration, and of other literary devices, it exemplifies some of the distinctive characteristics of the Sanskrit Kāvya. The Nasik inscription of Siri Puḷumāyi[1] also belongs to the 2nd century A.D. and exhibits similar features, but it is composed in Prakrit, apparently by one who was familiar with Sanskrit models.

Not very far perhaps in time from Aśvaghoṣa flourished the Buddhist writers, Mātṛceṭa, Kumāralāta and Ārya Śūra, whose works, so far as they have been recovered, afford conclusive evidence of the establishment of the Kāvya style. To the third or fourth century A.D. is also assigned the *Tantrākhyāyika*, which is the earliest known form of the *Pañcatantra* ; and the oldest ingredients of the *Sattasaī* of Hāla and the *Bṛhatkathā* of Guṇāḍhya also belong probably to this period. It would also be not wrong to assume that the science of Erotics and Dramaturgy, typified by the works of Vātsyāyana and Bharata, took shape during this time ; and, though we do not possess any very early treatise on Poetics, the unknown beginnings of the discipline are to be sought also in this period, which saw the growth of the factitious Kāvya. The *Artha-śāstra* of Kauṭilya is placed somewhat earlier, but the development of political and administrative ideas must have proceeded apace with the growth of material prosperity and with the predominance of an entirely secular literature.

We have, however, no historical authority for the date of any of these works, nor of the great Kāvya-poets, until we come to the Aihole inscription of 634 A.D.,[2] which mentions Bhāravi,

1 *EI*, VIII, p. 60f.
2 *EI*, VI, p. 1f.

along with Kālidāsa, as poets of established reputation. Kālidāsa, however, speaking modestly of himself at the commencement of his *Mālavikāgnimita,* mentions Bhāsa, Somila (or Saumilla) and Kaviputra as predecessors whose works might delay the appreciation of his own drama. Although agreement has not yet been reached about the authenticity of the Trivandrum dramas ascribed to Bhāsa, there cannot be any doubt that as a dramatist Bhāsa attained, even in this early period, a reputation high enough to be eulogised by Kālidāsa, and later on by Bāṇabhaṭṭa. Of Somila we know from Rājaśekhara[1] that he was the joint author, with Rāmila,[2] of a *Śūdraka-kathā,* whith is now lost ; and only one verse of theirs is preserved by Jahlaṇa (59. 35) and Śārṇgadhara (No. 3822) in their anthologies.[3] Of Kaviputra also, who is cited in the dual, we have nothing but one verse only, given in the *Subhāṣitāvali* (No. 2227), but the verse now stands in Bhartṛhari's *Śatakas* (Śṛṅgāra , st. 3).

A definite landmark, however, in supplied by the *Harṣa-carita* of Bāṇabhaṭṭa who, as a contemporary of King Harṣavardhana of Thaneswar and Kanauj, belonged to the first half of the 7th century A.D., and who, in the preface to this work, pays homage to some of his distinguished predecessors. Besides. an unnamed author of a *Vāsavadattā,* who may or may not be Subandhu, he mentions Bhaṭṭāra Haricandra who wrote an unnamed prose work, Sātavāhana who compiled an anthology, Pravarasena whose fame travelled beyond the seas by his *Setu (bandha),* Bhāsa who composed some distinctive dramas, Kālidāsa whose flower-like honied words ever bring delight, the author of the *Bṛhat-kathā,* and Āḍhyarāja. Of Bhaṭṭāra

1 *tau Śūdrakakathā-kārau vandyau Rāmila-Somilau* | *yayor dvayoḥ kāvyam āsīd ardhanārīśvaropamau* ||, cited in Jahlaṇa, *op. cit.*

2 One verse under Rāmilaka is given by *Sbhv,* No. 1698. The *Śūdraka-kathā* is mentioned and quoted by Bhoja in his *Śṛṅgāra-prakāśa* ; the name of the heroine is given as Vinayavatī.

3 The stanza, however, is given anonymously in *Kvs* (No. 473) and attributed to Rājaśekhara in *Skm* (ii.86.5).

Haricandra[1] and Āḍhyarāja[2] we know nothing ; but it is clear that the fame of the remaining well known authors must have been widespread by the 7th century A.D. Although the respective dates of these works and authors cannot be fixed with certainty, it can be assumed from Bāṇabhaṭṭa's enumeration that the period preceding him formed one of the most distinguished epochs of Kāvya literature, the development of which probably proceeded apace with the flourishing of Sanskrit culture under the Gupta emperors in the 4th and 5th centuries of the Christian era.

This conclusion receives confirmation from the wide cultivation of the Kāvya form of prose and verse in the inscriptional records of this period, of which not less than fifteen specimens of importance will be found in the third volume of Fleet's *Corpus Inscriptionum Indicarum.*[3] Their Kāvya-features and importance in literary history have long since been ably discussed by Bühler.[4] His detailed examination not only proves the existence of a body of elaborate prose and metrical writings in Kāvya-style during these centuries, but also shows that the manner in which these Praśasti-writers conform to the rules of Alaṃkāra, crystallised later in the oldest available treatises like those of Bhāmaha and Daṇḍin, would establish the presumption of their acquaintance with some rules of Sanskrit

1 He is certainly not the Jaina Haricandra, author of the much later *Dharmaśarmābhyudaya* which gives a dull account of the saint Dharmanātha (ed. NSP, Bombay, 1899). Our Haricandra is apparently mentioned in a list of great poets in *Skm* (5.26.5), and quoted in the anthologies.

2 Most scholars have accepted Pischel's contention (*Nachrichten d. kgl. Gesellschaft d. Wissenschaften Göttingen*, 1901, p. 486 f.) that the word *āḍhyarāja* in st. 18 is not a proper name of any poet but refers to the poet's patron King Harṣa himself. But the verse has difficulties of interpretation, for which see F. W. Thomas and others in *JRAS*, 1903, p. 803 ; 1904, p. 155 f. ; 366, 544 ; 1905, p. 569 f. We also know from a stanza quoted in the *Sarasvatī-Kaṇṭhābharaṇa* that there was a Prakrit poet named Āḍhyarāja, who is mentioned along with Sāhasāṅka ; the commentary, however, explaining in a facile way that Āḍhyarāja stands for Śālivāhana and Sāhasāṅka for Vikrama !

3 Calcutta, 1888. Some of these inscriptional records will be found in a convenient form in Devanāgarī in D. B. Diskalkar's *Selections from Inscriptions*, Vol. I (Rajkot, 1925).

4 In *Die indischen Inschriften*, cited above.

poetics. The most interesting of these inscriptions is the panegyric of Samudragupta by Hariṣeṇa, engraved on a pillar at Allahabad (about 350 A.D.), which commences with eight stanzas (some fragmentary) describing vividly the death of Candragupta I and accession of his son Samudragupta, then passess over to one long sonorous prose sentence and winds up with an eulogistic stanza,—all composed in the best manner of the Kāvya. Likewise remarkable is the inscription of Vīrasena, the minister of Candragupta II, Samudragupta's successor. Some importance attaches also to the inscription of Vatsabhaṭṭi, which consists of a series of 44 stanzas celebrating (in 473 A.D.) the consecration of a Sun-temple at Daśapura (Mandasor), from the fact that the poetaster is alleged to have taken Kālidāsa as his model ; but the literary merit of this laboured composition need not be exaggerated.

2. The Environment and Characteristics of the Kāvya

It is noteworthy that in Hariṣeṇa's Praśasti, Samudragupta is mentioned not only as a friend and patron of poets but as a poet himself, who like Rudradāman before him, composed poems of distinction enough to win for himself the title of Kavirāja or king of poets.[1] Amiable flattery it may be, but the point is important ; for the tradition of royal authors, as well as of royal patrons of authors, continues througout the history of Sanskrit literature. The very existence of royal inscriptions written in Kāvya-style, as well as the form, content and general outlook of the Kāvya literature itself, indicates its close connexion with the courts of princes, and explains the association of Aśvaghoṣa with Kaṇiṣka, of Kālidāsa with a Vikramāditya, or of Bāṇabhaṭṭa with Harṣavardhana. The royal recognition not only brought wealth and fame to the poets, but also some leisure for

[1] For other examples of poet-kings see introduction to the edition of *Priyadarśikā* by Nariman, Jackon and Ogden, pp. xxxv-xxxix.

serious composition. In his *Kāvya-mīmāmsā* Rājaśekhara speaks of literary assemblies held by kings for examination of works and reward of merit ; and even if we do not put faith in this or in the unhistorical pictures of poetical contests at royal courts given in the *Bhoja-prabandha* and *Prabandha-cintāmaṇi*, a vivid account is furnished by Maṅkha in his *Srīkaṇṭha-carita* (Canto XV) of one such assembly actually held by a minister of Jayasiṃha of Kashmir towards the middle of the 12th century. As a matter of fact, the Kāvya literature appears to have been aristocratic from the beginning, fostered under the patronage of the wealthy or in the courts of the princes. Even if it does not lack serious interest, this literature naturally reflects the graces, as well as the artificialities, of courtly life ; and its exuberant fancy is quite in keeping with the taste which prevailed in this atmosphere. The court-influence undoubtedly went a long way, not only in fostering a certain langour and luxuriance of style, but also in encouraging a marked preference of what catches the eye to what touches the heart.

In order to appreciate the Kāvya, therefore, it is necessary to realise the condition under which it was produced and the environment in which it flourished. The pessimism of the Buddhistic ideal gradually disappeared, having been replaced by more accommodating views about the value of pleasure. Even the Buddhist author of the *Nāgānanda* does not disdain to weave a love-theme into his lofty story of Jīmūtavāhana's self-sacrifice and in his opening benedictory stanza he does not hesitate to represent the Buddha as being rallied upon his hard-heartedness by the ladies of Māra's train.[1] From Patañjali's references we find that from it very dawn love is establiahed as one of the dominant themes of the Kāvya poetry. Thy Buddhist conception

1 A similar verse with openly erotic imagery is ascribed to Aśvaghoṣa in *Kvs* No. 2.

2 One fragment, at least, of a stanza is clearly erotic in subject in its description of the morning : *varatanu sampravadanti kukkuṭāḥ* "O fair-limbed one, the cocks unite to proclaim". The full verse is fortunately supplied twelve centuries later by Kṣemendra, who quotes it in his *Aucitya-vicāra* but attributes it wrongly to Kumāradāsa.

of the love-god as Māra or Death gives way to that of the flower-arrowed deity, who is anticipated in the *Atharva-veda* and is established in the Epics, but whose appearance, names and personality are revived and developed in the fullest measure in the Kāvya. The widely diffused Kāvya manner and its prevailing love-interest invade even the domain of technical sciences ; and it is remarkable that the mathematician Bhāskaragupta not only uses elegant metre in his *Līlāvatī* but presents his algebraical theorems in the form of problems explained to a fair maiden, of which the phraseology and imagery are drawn from the bees, flowers and other familiar objects of Kāvya poetry. The celebration of festivals with pomp and grandeur, the amusements of the court and the people, the sports in water, the game of swing, the plucking of flowers, song, dance, music, dramatic performances and other diversions, elaborate description of which forms the stock-in-trade of most Kāvya-poets, bear witness not only to this sense of life but also to the general demand for refinement, beauty and luxury. The people are capable of enjoying good things of this world, while heartily believing in the next. If pleasure with refinement is sought for in life, pleasure with elegance is demanded in art. It is natural, therefore, that the poetry of this period pleases us more than it moves ; for life is seldom envisaged in its infinite depth and poignancy, or in its sublime heights of imaginative fervour, but is generally conceived in its playful moods of vivid enjoyment breaking forth into delicate little cameos of thought or fancy.

The dominant love-motif of the Kāvya is thus explained by the social environment in which it grows and from which alone it can obtain recognition. It is, however, not court-life alone which inspires this literature. At the centre of it stands the Nāgaraka, the polished man about town, whose culture, tastes and habits so largely mould this literature that he may be taken to be as typical of it as the priest or the philosopher is of the literature of the Brāhmaṇas or the Upaniṣads.[1] Apart from the

[1] H. Oldenberg, *Die Literatur des alten Indien*, Stuttgart und Berlin, 1903, pp. 198 f.

picture we got of him in the literature itself, we have a vivid sketch of an early protoype of the Nāgaraka in the *Kāma-sūtra* or Aphorism of Erotics, attributed to Vātsyāyana. We are told that the well-planned house of the Nāgaraka is situated near a river or tank and surrounded by a lovely garden ; in the garden there are, for amusement or repose, a summer house, a bower of creepers with raised parterre, and a carpeted swing in a shady spot. His living room, balmy with perfume, contains a bed, soft, white, fragrant and luxuriously furnished with pillows or cushions. There is also a couch, with a kind of stool at the head, on which are placed pigments, perfumes, garlands, bark of citron, canvas and a box of paint. A lute hanging from an ivory peg and a few books are also not forgotten. On the ground there is a spittoon, and not far from the couch a round seat with raised back and a board for dice. The Nāgaraka spends his morning in bathing and elaborate toilet, applying ointments and perfumes to his body, collyrium to his eyes and red paint to his lips, chewing betel leves and citron-bark to add fragrance to his mouth, and looking at himself in the glass. After breakfast he listens to his parrots, kept in a cage outside his room, witnesses ram and cock fights and takes part in other diversions which he enjoys with his friends and companions. After a brief midday sleep, he dresses again, and joins his friends ; and in the evening there is music, followed by joys of love. These are the habitual pleasures of the Nāgaraka, but there are also occasional rounds of enjoyment, consisting of festivals, drinking parties, plays, concerts, picnics in groves, excursions to parks or water-sports in lakes and rivers. There are also social gatherings, often held in the house of the ladies of th *demi-monde,* where assemble men of wit and talent, and where artistic and poetic topics are freely discussed. The part played by the accomplished courtesan in the polished society of the time is indeed remarkable ; and judging from Vasantasenā,[1] it must be said that in ancient India of this

[1] Also the picture of Kāmamañjarī in Ucchvāsa II of Daṇḍin's romance ; she is a typical courtesan, but highly accomplished and educated.

peiod, as in the Athens of Perikles, her wealth, beauty and power, as well as her literary and artistictastes, assured for her an important social position. She already appears as a character in the fragment of an early Sanskrit play discovered in Central Asia, and it is not strange that Sūdraka should take her as the heroine of his well-known drama ; for her presence and position must have offered an opportunity, which is otherwise denied to the Sanskrit dramatist (except through a legendary medium) of depicting romantic love between persons free and independent. The picture of the Nāgaraka and his lady-friend as we have it in literature, is undoubtedly heightened, and there is a great deal of the dandy and the dilettante in the society which they frequent ; but we need not doubt there is also much genuine culture, character and refinement. In later times, the Nāgaraka degenerates into a professional amourist, but originally he is depicted as a perfect man of the world, rich and cultivated, as well as witty, polished and skilled in the arts, who can appreciate poetry, painting and music, discuss delicate problems in the doctrine of love and has an extensive experience of human, especially feminine, character.

The science of Erotics, thus, exercised a profound influence on the theory and practice of the poetry of this period. The standard work of Vātsyāyana contains, besides several chapters on the art and practice of love, sections on the ways and means of winnning and keeping a lover, on courtship and signs of love, on marriage and conduct of married life, and not a little on the practical psychology of the emotion of love. On the last mentioned topic the science of Poetics, as embodied particularly in the specialised works on the erotic Rasa, went hand in hand ; and it is almost impossible to appreciate fully the merits, as well as the defects, of Sanskrit love-poetry without some knowlede of the habits, modes of thought, literary traditions and fundamental poetical postulates recorded in these Sāstras, the mere allusion to one of which is enough to call up some familiar idea or touch some inner chord of sentiment. There is much in these treatises which gives us an idealised or fanciful picture ; and the existence of the people of whom they speak was just as little a prolonged debauch as a prolonged idyll. There is also a great deal of scholastic formalism which loves subtleties and minutiae of classification. At the same time, the works bear witness to a considerable power of observation, and succeed in presenting a skilful and elaborate analysis of the erotic emotion, the theory of which came to have an intimate bearing on the psactice of the poets.

In this connexion a reference should be made to an aspect of Sanskrit love-poetry which has been often condemned as too sensual or gross, namely, its highly intimate description of the beauty of the feminine form and the delights of dalliance, as well as its daring indelicacies of expression. It should be recognised that much of this frankness is conventional ; the Sanskrit poet is expected to show his skill and knowledge of the Kāma-śāstra by his minute and highly flavoured descriptions. But the excuse of convention cannot altogether condone the finical yet flaunting sensuality of the elaborate picture of love-sports, such as we find in Bhāravi, Māgha and their many followers (including the composers of later Bhāṇas) and such as are admitted by a developed but deplorable taste. Even the Indian critics, who are not ordinarily squeamish, are not sparing in their condemnation of some of these passages, and take even Kālidāsa to task for depicting the love-adventures of the divine pair in his *Kumāra-sambhava*. A distinction, however, must be drawn between this conventional, but polished, and perhaps all the more regrettable, indecency of decadent poets, on the one hand, and the exasperatingly authentic and even blunt audacities of expression, on the other, with which old-time authors season their erotic compositions. What the latter-day poets lack is the naive exuberance or *bonhomie* of their predecessors, their easy and frank expression of physical affection in its exceedingly human aspect, and their sincere realisation of primal sensations, which are naturally gross or grotesque being nearer to life. It would be unjust and canting prudery to condemn these simpler moods of passion and their direct expression, unless they are meaninglessly vulgar. The point is too often forgotten that what we have here is not the love which dies in dreams, or revels in the mystic adoration of a phantom-woman. It does not talk about ideals and gates of heaven but walks on the earth and speaks of the passionate hunger of the body and the exquisite intoxication of the senses. The poets undoubtedly put a large emphasis on the body, and love appears more as self-fulfilment than as self-abnegation ; but in this preference of the body there is nothing debasing or prurient. The essential realism of passion, which cannot live on abstraction but must have actualities to feed upon, does not absolve a truly passionate poet from the contact of the senses and touch of the earth ; but from this, his poetry springs Antaeus-like into fuller being. Modern taste may, with reason, deprecate the intimate description of personal beauty and delights of love in later Sanskrit poetry, but even here it must be clearly understood that there is very seldom any ignoble motive behind its conventional sensuousness, that there is no evidence of delight in uncleanness, and that it always conforms to the standard of artistic beauty. Comparing Sanskrit poetry with European classical literature in this respect, a Western critic very rightly remarks that "there is all the world of difference between what we find in the great poets of India and the frank delight of Martial and Petronius in their dascriptions of immoral scenes." The code of propriety as well as of prudery differs with different people, but the Sanskrit poet seldom takes leave of his delicacy of feeling and his sense of art ; and even if he is ardent and luxuriant, he is more openly exhilarating than offensively cynical,

The Sanskrit poet cannot also forget that, beside his elegant royal patron and the cultivated Nāgaraka, he had a more exacting audience in the Rasika or Sahṛdaya, the man of taste, the connoisseur, whose expert literary judgment is the final test of his work. Such a critic, we are told, must not only possess technical knowledge of the requirements of poetry, but also a fine capacity of aesthetic enjoyment, born of wide culture and sympathetic identification with the feelings and ideas of the poet. The Indian ideal of the excellence of poetry is closely associated with a peculiar condition of artistic enjoyment, known as Rasa, the suggestion of which is taken to be its function, and in relation to which the appreciator is called Rasika. It is a reflex of the sentiment, which has been suggested in the poem, in the mind of the appreciator, as a relishable condition of impersonal enjoyment resulting from the idealised creation of poetry. The evoking of sentiment, therefore, is considered to be the most vital function of poetry ; and stress is put more and more on sentimental composition to the exclusion of the descriptive or ornamental. But here also the theorists are emphatic that in the art of suggesting this sentimental enjoyment in the reader's mind, the poetic imagination must show itself. As Oldenberg[1] remarks with insight, the Indian theorists permit intellectual vigour and subtlety, the masculine beauty, to stand behind that of the purely feminine enjoyment born of the finest sensibility. Both these traits are found in the literature from the beginning—the idea of delectable rapture side by side with a strong inclination towards sagacity and subtlety. It is true that the dogmatic formalism of a scholastic theory of poetry sinks to the level of a cold and monotonously inflated rhetoric ; but the theorists are at the same time not blind to finer issues, nor are they indifferent to the supreme excellence of real poetry[2] and the aesthetic pleasure resulting from it. They take care to add that, despite dogmas and formulas, the poetic imagination must manifest itself as the ultimate source of poetic charm. The demands that are made of the poet are, thus, very exacting ; he must not only be initiated into the intricacies of theoretic requirements but must also possess poetic imagination (Śakti), aided by culture

1 *Die Literatur des alten Indien*, p. 207 f.

2 *Cf.* Ānandavardhana, p. 29 : *asminn ati-vicitra-kaviparaṁparā-vāhini saṁsāre Kālidāsa-prabhṛtayo dvitrā pañcaṣā vā mahākavaya iti gaṇyate.*

(Vyutpatti) and practice (Abhyāsa). Even if we do not rely upon Rājaśekhara's elaborate account of the studies which go to make up the finished poet, there can be no doubt that considerable importance is attached to the "education" of the poet,[1] whose inborn gifts alone would not suffice, and for whose practical guidance in the devices of the crafts, convenient manuals[2] are elaborately composed.

It is not necessary to believe that the poet is actually an adept in the long list of arts and sciences[3] in which he is required to be proficient ; but it is clear that he is expected to possess (and he is anxious to show that he does possess) a vast fund of useful information in the various branches of learning. Literature is regarded more and more as a learned pursuit and as the product of much cultivation. No doubt, a distinction is made between the Vidvat and the Vidagdha, between a man versed in *belles lettres* and a dry and tasteless scholar ; but it soon becomes a distinction without much difference. The importance of inspiration is indeed recognised, but the necessity of appealing of a learned audience is always there. It is obvious that in such an atmosphere the literatue becomes rich and refined, but natural

1 See F. W. Thomas, *Bhandarkar Comm. Volume*, p. 397 f ; S. K. De, *Sanskrit Poetics*, II, pp. 357 f, 42 f.n., 52 ; Keith, *HSL*, pp. 338-41. Rājaśekhara gives an interesting, but somewhat heightened, picture of the daily life and duties of the poet, who is presented as a man of fashion and wealth, of purity in body, mind and speech, but assiduous and hard-working at his occupation.

2 These works furnish elaborate hints on the construction of different metres, on the display of word-skill of various kinds, on *jeux de mots* and tricks of producing double meaning, conundrums, riddles, alliterative and chiming verses, and various other device of verbal ingenuity. They give instructions on the employment of similes and enumerate a large number of ordinary parallelisms for that purpose. They give lists of Kavi-samayas or conventions observed by p ets, and state in detail what to describe and how to describe.

3 The earlist of such lists is given by Bhāmaha I. 9, which substantially agrees with that of Rudraṭa (I.18) ; but Vāmana (I.3.20-21) deals with the topic in some detail. The longest list includes Grammar, Lexicon, Metrics, Rhetoric, Arts, Dramaturgy, Morals, Erotics, Politics, Law, Logic, Legends, Religion and Philosophy, as well as such miscellaneous subjects as Medicine, Botany, Mineralogy, knowledge of precious stones, Elephant-lore, Veterinary science, Art of War and Weapons, Art of Gambling, Magic, Astrology and Astronomy, nomy, knowledge of Vedic rites and ceremonies, and of the ways of the world.

ease and spontaneity are sacrificed for studied effects, and refinement leads perforce to elaboration.

The Kāvya, therefore, appears almost from its very beginning as the careful work of a trained and experienced specialist. The technical analysis of a somewhat mechanical Rhetoric leads to the working of the rules and means of the poetic art into a system ; and this is combined with a characteristic love of adornment, which demands an ornamental fitting out of word and thought. The difficulty of the language, as well as its complexity, naturally involves prolonged endeavour and practice for effective mastery, but it also affords endless opportunity and temptation for astonishing feats of verbal jugglery, which perhaps would not be possible in any other language less accommodating than Sanskrit. Leaving aside the grotesque experiments of producing verses in the shape of a sword, wheel or lotus, or of stanzas which have the same sounds when read forwards or backwards, and other such verbal absurdities, the tricks in poetic form, and decorative devices are undoubtedly clever, but they are often overdone. They display learned ingenuity more than real poetry, and the forced use of the language is often a barrier to quick comprehension. Some poets actually go to the length of boasting[1] that this poem is meant for the learned and not for the dull-witted, and is understandable only by means of a commentary.[2] The involved construction, recondite vocabulary, laboured embellishment, strained expression, and constant search after conceits, double meanings and metaphors undoubtedly justify their boasting ; but they evince an exuberance of fancy and erudition rather than taste, judgement and real feeling. This tendency is more and more encouraged by the elaborate rules and definitions of Rhetoric, until inborn poetic fervour is

1 *Eg. Bhaṭṭi*, XXII. 34 ; *vyākyā-gamyam idaṁ kāvyam utsavaḥ sudhiyām alam | hatā durmedhasaś cāsmin vidvat-priyatayā mayā* ||. Here the Vidagdha is ignored deliberately for the Vidvat.

2 Some authors had, in fact, to write their own commentaries to make themselves intelligible. Even Ānandavardhana who deprecates such tricks in his theoretical work does not steer clear of them in his *Devi-śataka*.

entirely obscured by technicalities of expression. In actual practice, no doubt, gifted poets aspire to untrammelled utterance ; but the general tendency degenerates towards a slavish adherence to rules, which results in the overloading of a composition by complicated and laboured expressions.

Comments have often been made on the limited range and outlook of Sanskrit literature and on the conventionality of its themes. It is partly the excessive love of form and expression which leads to a corresponding neglect of content and theme. It is of little account if the subject-matter is too thin and threadbare to support a long poem, or if the irrelevant and often commonplace descriptions and reflections hamper the course of the narrative ; what does matter is that the diction is elaborately perfect, polished and witty, and that the poem conforms to the recognised standard,[1] and contains the customary descriptions, however digressive, of spring, dawn, sunset, moonrise, water-sports, drinking bouts, amorous practices, diplomatic consultations and military expeditions, which form the regular stock-in-trade of this ornate poetry. A large number of so-called poetic conventions (Kavi-samayas)[2] are established by theorists and mechanically repeated by poets, which descriptions of things, qualities and actions are stereotyped by fixed epithets, cliché phrases and restricted formulas. Even the various motifs which occur in legends, fables and plays[3] are worn out by repeti-

[1] See Daṇḍin, *Kāvyādarśa*, I. 14-19 ; Viśvanātha, *Sāhitya-darpaṇa*, VI. 315-25, etc.

[2] For a list of poetic conventions see Rājaśekhara, *Kāvya-mīmaṁsā*, XIV ; Amarasiṁha, *Kāvya-kalpalatā*, I. 5 ; *Sāhitya-darpaṇa*, VII. 23-24, etc. Some of the commonest artificial conventions are : the parting of the Cakravāka bird at night from its mate ; the Cakora feeding on the moonbeams ; the blooming of the Aśoka at the touch of a lady's feet ; fame and laughter described as white ; the flower-bow and bee-string of the god of love, etc. Originally the writers on poetics appear to have regarded these as established by the bold usage of the poet (*kavi-prauḍhokti-siddha*), but they are gradually stereotyped as poetical commonplaces.

[3] Such as the vision of the beloved in a dream, the talking parrot, the magic steed, the fatal effect of an ascetic's curse, transformation of shapes, change of sex, the art of entering into another's body, the voice in the air, the token of recognition, royal love for a lowly maiden and the ultimate discovery of her real status as a princess, minute portraiture of the heroine's personal beauty and the generous qualities of the hero, description of pangs of thwarted love and sentimental longing. M. Bloomfield (*Festscrift Ernst Windisch*, Leipzig,

tion and lose thereby their element of surprise and charm. The question of imitation, borrowing or plagiarism[1] of words or ideas assumes importance in this connexion; for it involves a test of the power of clever reproduction, or sometimes a criticism of some weakness in the passages consciously appropriated but improved in the caurse of appropriation.

The rigidity, which these commonplaces of conventional rhetoric acquire, is the result, as well as the cause, of the time-honoured tendency of exalting authority and discouraging originality, which is a remarkable characteristic of Indian culture in general and of its literature in particular, and which carries the suppression of individuality too far. It is in agreement with this attitude that Sanskrit Poetics neglects a most vital aspect of its task, namely the study of poetry as the individualised expression of the poet's mind, and confines itself more or less to a normative doctrine of technique, to the formulation of laws, modes and models, to the collection and definition of facts and categories and to the teaching of the means of poetic expression. This limitation not only hinders the growth of Sanskrit Poetics into a proper study of Aesthetic[2], but it also stands in the way of a proper appreciation and development of Sanskrit literature. The theory almost entirely ignores the poetic personality in a work of art, which gives it its particular shape and individual character. Sanskrit Poetics cannot explain satisfactorily, for

1914, pp. 349-61, *JAOS*, XXXVI, 1917, p. 54-89; XL, 1920, pp. 1-24; XLIV, 1924, pp. 202-42) W. Norman Brown (*JAOS*, XLVII, 1927, pp. 3-24), Penzer (in his ed. of Tawney's trs. of *Kathā-sarit-sāgara*, 'Ocean of Story') and others have studied in detail some of these motifs recurring in Sanskrit literature. Also see Bloomfield in *Amer. Journ. of Philology*, XI, pp. 1-36; XLI, pp. 309-35; XLIV, pp. 97-133, 193-229; XLVII, pp. 205-233; W. N. Brown in *ibid.*, XI, pp. 423-30; XLII, pp. 122-51; XLIII, pp. 289-317; *Studies in Honour of M. Bloomfield*, pp. 89-104, 211-24 (Ruth Norton); E. H. Burlingame is *JRAS*, 1917, pp. 429-67, etc.

1 The question is discussed by Ānandavardhana, *Dhvanyāloka*, III, 12 f.; Rājaśekhara *Kāvya-mīmāṁsā*, XI f.; Kṣemendra, *Kavikaṇṭhābharaṇa*, II, 1; Hemacandra, *Kāvyānuśāsana*, pp. 8 f. See S. K. De, *Sanskrit Poetics*, II, pp. 362-373.

2 See S. K. De, Sanskrit Poetics as a study of Aesthetic in *Dacca University Studies*, Vol. 1, No. 2, pp. 80-124.

instance, the simple question as to why the work of one poet is not the same in character as that of another, or why two works of the same poet are not the same. To the Sanskrit theorist a composition is a work art if it fulfils the prescribed requirements of 'qualities,' of 'ornaments,' of particular arrangements of words to suggest a sense or a sentiment ; it is immaterial whether the work in question is *Raghu-vaṃśa* or *Naiṣadha*. The main difference which he will probably see between these two works will probably consist of the formal employment of this or that mode of diction, or in their respective skill of suggesting this or that meaning of the words. The theorists never bother themselves about the poetic imagination, which gives each a distinct and unique shape by a fusion of impressions into an organic, and not a mechanic, whole. No doubt, they solemmly affirm the necessity of Pratibhā or poetic imagination, but in their theories the Pratibhā does not assume any important or essensial role ; and in practical application they go further and speak of making a poet into a poet. Bus it is forgotten that a work of art is the expression of individuality, and that individuality never repeats itself nor conforms to a prescribed mould. It is hardly recognised that what appeals to us in a poem is the poetic personality which reveals itself in warmth, movement and integrity of imagination and expression. No doubt, the poet can astonish us with his wealth of facts and nobility of thought, or with his cleverness in the manipulation of the language, but this is not what we ask of a poet. What we want is the expression of a poetic mind, in contact with which our minds may be moved If this is wanting, we call his work dull, cold or flat, and all the learning, thought or moralising in the world cannot save a work from being a failure. The Sanskrit theorists justly remark that culture and skill should assist poetic power or personality to reveal itself in its proper form, but what they fail to emphasise is that any amount of culture and skill cannot 'make' a poet, and that a powerful poetic personality must justify a work of art by itself.

The result is that Sanskrit poetry is made to confrom to certain fixed external standard attainable by culture and practice ; and the poetic personality or imagination, cramped wihin prescribed limits, is hardly allowed the fullest scope or freedom to create new forms of beauty. Although the rhetoricians put forward a theory of idealised enjoyment as the highest object of poetry, yet the padagogic and moralistic objects are enumerated in unbroken tradition. In conformity with the learned and scholastic atmosphere in which it flourishes, poetry is value for the knowledge it brings or the lessons it inclucates, and is regarded as a kind of semi-śāstra ; while the technical analysis and authority of the rhetorician tend to eliminate the personality of the poet by mechanising poetry. The exaltation of formal skill and adherence to the banalities of a formal rhetoric do not sufficiently recognise that words and ornaments, as symbols, are inseparable from the poetic imagination, and that, as such, they are not fixed but mobile, not an embalmed collection of dead abstractions, but an ever elusive series of living particulars. Sanskrit literature is little alive to these considerations, and accepts a normative formulation of poetic expression. But for the real poet, as for the real speaker, there is hardly an armoury of ready-made weapons ; he forges his own weapons to fight his own particular battles.

It must indeed be admitted that the influence of the theorists on the latter-day poets was not an unmixed good. While the poetry gained in niceties and subtleties of expression, it lost a great deal of its unconscious freshness and spontaneity. It is too often flawed by the very absence of flaws, and its want of imperfection makes it coldly perfect. One can never deny that the poet is still a sure and impeccable master of his craft, but he seldom moves or transports. The pictorial effect, the musical cadence and the wonderful spell of language are undoubted, but the poetry is more exquisite than passionate, more studied and elegant than limpid and forceful. We have heard so much about the artificiality and tediousness of Sanskrit classical poetry that is not necessary to emphasise the point ; but the point which has not been sufficiently emphasised is that the Sanskrit poets often succeed in getting out of their very narrow and conventional material such beautiful effects that criticism is almost afraid to lay its cold dry finger on these fine blossoms of fancy. It should no be fogotten that this literature is not the spontaneous product of an uncritical and ingenuous age, but that it is composed for a highly cultured audience. It presupposes a psychology and a rhetoric which have been reduced to a system, and which possesses a peculiar phraseology and a set of conceits of their own. We, therefore, meet over and over again with the same tricks of expression, the same strings of nouns and adjectives, the same the set of situations, the same groups of conceits and the same system of emotional analysis. In the lesser poets the sentiment and expression are no longer fresh and varied but degenerate into rigid artistic conventions. But the greater poets very often work up even these romantic commonplaces and agreeable formulas into new shapes of beauty. Even in the artificial bloom and perfection there is almost always a strain of the real and ineffable tone of poetry. It would seem, therefore, that if we leave aside the mere accidents of poetry, there is no inherent lack of grasp upon its realities. It is admitted that the themes are narrow, the diction and imagery are conventional, and the ideas move in a fixed groove ; but the true poetic spirit is not always wanting, and it is able to transmute the rhetorical and psychological banalities into things of art.

The Sanskrit poet, for instance, seldom loses an opportunity of making a wonderful use of the sheer beauty of words and their inherent melody, of which Sanskrit is so capable. The production of fine sound-effects by a delicate adjustment of word and sense is an art which is practised almost to prefection. It cannot be denied that some poets are industrious pedants in their strict conformity to rules and perpetrate real atrocities by their lack of subtlety and taste in matching the sense to the sound; but, generally speaking, one must agree with the appreciative remarks of a Western critic that "the classical poets of India have a sensitiveness to variations of sound, to which literatures of other contries afford few parallels, and their delicate combinations are a source of never-failing joy." The extraordinary flexibility of the language and complete mastery over it make this possible; and the theory which classifies Sanskrit diction on the basis of sound-effects and prescribes careful rules about them is not altogether futile or pedantic. One of the means elaborately employed for achieving this end is the use of alliteration and assonance of various kinds. Such verbal devices, no doubt, become flat or fatiguing in meaningless repetition, but in skilled hands they produce remarkable effects which are perhaps not attainable to the same extent in any other language. Similar remarks apply to the fondness for paronomasia or double meaning, which the uncommon resources of Sanskrit permit. In languages like English, punning lends itself chiefly to comic effects and witticisms or, as in Shakespeare[1], to an occasional flash of dramatic feeling; but in classical languages it is capable of serious employment as a fine artistic device.[2] It is true that it demands an intellectual strain disproportionate to the aesthetic pleasure, and becomes tiresome and ineffective in the incredible and incessant torturing of the language found in such lengthy triumphs of misplaced ingenuity as those of Subandhu and Kavirāja; but sparingly and judiciously used, the puns are often delightful in their terse brevity and twofold appropriateness. The adequacy of the language and its wonderful capacity for verbal melody are also utilised by the Sanskrit poet in a large number of lyrical measures of great complexity, which are employed with remarkable skill and sense of rhythm in creating an unparalleled series of musical word-pictures.

1 *Merchant of Venice*, IV 1, 123; *Julius Caeser*, I. 2, 156 (Globe Ed.)

2 *Cf.* Daṇḍin's dictum: *śleṣaḥ puṣṇāti sarvāsu prāyo vakroktiṣu śriyam.*

Th elegance and picturesqueness of diction are, again, often enhanced by the rolling majesty of long compounds, the capacity for which is inherent in the genius of Sanskrit and developed to the fullest extent. The predilection for long compounds, especially in ornate prose, is indeed often carried to absured excesses, and is justly criticised for the construction of vast sentences extending over several pages and for the trick of heaping epithet upon epithet in sesquipedalian grandeur ; but the misuse of this effective instrument of synthetic expression should not make us forget the extraordinary power of compression and production of unified picture which it can efficiently realise. It permits a subtle combination of the different elements of a thought or a picture into a perfect whole, in which the parts coalesce by inner necessity ; and it has been rightly remarked that "the impression thus created on the mind cannot be reproduced in an analytical speech like English, in which it is necessary to convey the same content, not in a single sentence syntactically merged into a whole, like the idea which it expresses, but in a series of loosely connected predications" Such well-knit compactness prevents the sentences from being jerky, flaccid or febrile, and produces undoubted sonority, dignity and magnificence of diction, for which Sanskrit is always remarkable, and which cannot be fully appreciated by one who is accustomed to modern analytical languages.

The inordinate length of ornate prose sentences is set off by the brilliant condensation of style which is best seen in the gnomic and epigrammatic stanzas, expressive of maxims of sententious wisdom with elaborate terseness and flash of wit. The compact neatness of paronomasia, antithesis and other verbal figures often enhances the impressiveness of these pithy sayings ; and their vivid precision is not seldom rounded off by appropriate similes and metaphors. The search for metaphorical expression is almost a weakness with the Sanskrit poets ; but, unless it is a deliberately pedantic artifice, the force and beauty with which it is employed cannot be easily denied. The various forms of metaphors and similes are often a source of fine surprise by their power of happy phraseology and richness of poetical fancy. The similarites, drawn from a fairly wide range, often display a real freshness of observation, though some of them become familiar conventions in later poetry; and comparison in some form or other becomes one of most effective means of stimulating the reader's imagination by suggesting more than what is said. When the similarity is purely verbal, it is witty and neat, but the poet seldom forgets to fit his comparison to the emotional content or situation.

Closely connected with this is the power of miniature painting, compressed in a solitary stanza, which is a characteristic of the Kavya and in which the Sanskrit poets excel to a marvellous degree. In the epic, the necessity of a continuous recitation, which should flow evenly and should not demand too great a strain on the audience, makes the poet alive to the unity of effect to be produced by subordinating the consecutive stanzas to the narrative as a whole. The method which is evolved in the Kāvya is different. No doubt, early poets like Aśvaghoṣa and Kālidāsa do not entirely neglect effective narration, but the later Kāvya attaches hardly any importance to the theme or story and depends almost exclusively on the appeal of art finically displayed in individual stanzas. The Kāvya becomes a series of miniature poems or methodical verse-paragraphs, loosely strung on the thread of the narrative. Each clear-cut stanza is a separate unit in itself, both grammatically and in sense, and presents a perfect little picture. Even though spread out over several cantos, the Kāvya really takes the form, not of a systematic and well knit poem, but of single stanzas, standing by themselves, in which the poet delights to depict a single idea, a single phase of emotion, or a single situation in a complete and daintily finished form. If this tradition of the stanza-form is not fully satisfactory in a long composition, where unity of effect is necessary, it is best exemplified in the verse-portion of the dramas, as well as in the Śatakas, such as those of Bhartṛhari and

Amaru, in which the Sanskrit poetry of love, resignation or reflection finds the most effective expression in its varying moods and phases. Such miniature painting, in which colours are words, is a task of no small difficulty ; for it involves the perfect expression, within very restricted limits, of a pregnant idea or an intense emotion with a few precise and elegant touches.

All this will indicate that the Sanskrit poet is more directly concerned with the consummate elegance of his art than with any message or teaching which he is called upon to deliver. It is indeed not correct to say that the poet does not take any interest in the great problems of life and destiny, but this is seldom writ large upon his work of art. Except in the drama which comprehends a wider and fuller life, he is content with the elegant symbols of reality rather than strive for the reality itself ; and his work is very often nothing more than a delicate blossom of fancy, fostered in a world of tranquil calm. Nothing ruffles the pervading sense of harmony and concord ; and neither deep tragedy nor great laughter is to be found in its fulness in Sanskrit literature. There is very seldom any trace of strife or discontent, clash of contrary passions and great conflicts ; nor is there any outburst of rugged feelings, any great impetus for energy and action, any rich sense for the concrete facts and forces of life. There is also no perverse attitude which clothes impurity in the garb of virtue, or poses a soul-weariness in the service of callous wantonness. Bitter earnestness, grim violence of darker passions, or savage cynicism never mar the even tenor and serenity of these artistic compositions which, with rare exceptions, smooth away every scar and wrinkle which might have existed. It is not that sorrow or suffering or sin is denied, but the belief in the essential rationality of the world makes the poet idealistic in his outlook and placidly content to accept the life around him, while the purely atistic attitude makes him transcend the merely personal. The Sanskrit poet is undoubtedly pessimistic in his belief in the inexorable law of Karman and rebirth, but his unlimited pessimism with regard to this world is toned down by his unlimited optimism with regard to the next. It fosters in him a stoical resignation, an epicurean indifference and a mystic hope and faith, which paralyse personal energy, suppress the growth of external life and replace originality by submission. On the other hand, this is exactly the atmosphere which is conducive to idealised creation and serenity of purely artistic accomplishment, in which Sanskrit poetry excels.

This complacent attitude towards life falls in with the view of Sanskrit Poetics which distinguishes the actual world from the world of poetry, where the hard and harsh facts of life dissolve themselves into an imaginative system of pleasing fictions. It results in an impersonalised and ineffable aesthetic enjoyment, from which every trace of its component or material is obliterated. In other words, love or grief is no longer experienced as love or grief in its disturbing poignancy, but as pure artistic sentiment of blissful relish evoked by the idealised poetic creation. To suggest this delectable condition of the mind, to which the name of Rasa is given is regarded both by theory and practice to be the aim of a work of art ; and it is seldom thought necessary to mirror life by a direct portrayal of fact, incident or character. It is for this reason that the delineation of sentiment becomes important—and even disproportionately important—in poetry, drama and romance ; and all the resources of poetic art and imagination are brought to bear upon it. Only a secondary or even nominal interest is attached to the story, theme, plot or character, the unfolding of which is often made to wait till the poet finishes his lavish sentimental descriptions or his refined outpourings of sentimental verse and prose.

This over-emphasis on impersonalised poetic sentiment and its idealised enjoyment tends to encourage grace, polish and fastidious technical finish, in which fancy has the upper hand of passion and ingenuity takes the place of feeling. Except perhaps in a poet like Bhavabhūti, we come across very little of rugged and forceful description, very little of naturalness and simplicity, hardly any genuine emotional directness, nor any love for all that is deep and poignant, as well as grand and awe-inspiring, in life and nature. Even Kālidāsa's description of the Himalayas is more pleasing and picturesque than stately and sublime. The tendency is more towards the ornate and the refined than the grotesque and the robust, more towards harmonious roundness than jagged angularity, more towards achieving perfection of form than realising the integrity and sincerity of primal sensations. It is, therefore, not surprising that there is no real lyric on a large scale in Sanskrit ; that is so-called dramas are mostly dramatic poems ; that its historical writings achieve poetical distinction but are indifferent to mere fact ; that its prose romances sacrifice the interest of theme to an exaggerated love of diction ; and that its prose in general feels the effect of poetry.

Nevertheless, the Sanskrit poet is quite at home in the depiction of manly and heroic virtues and the ordinary emotions of life, even if they are presented in a refined domesticated form. However self-satisfied he may appear, the poet has an undoubted grip over the essential facts of life ; and this is best seen, not in the studied and elaborate masterpieces of great poets, but in the detached lyrical stanzas, in the terse gnomic verses of worldly wisdom, in the simple prose tales and fables, and, above all, in the ubiquitous delineation of the erotic feeling in its infinite variety of moods and fancies. There is indeed a great deal of what is conventional, and even artificial, in Sanskrit love-poetry ; it speaks of love not in its simplicities but in its subtle moments. What is more important to note is that it consists often of the exaltation of love for love's sake, the amorous cult, not usually of a particular woman, a Beatrice or a Laura, but of woman as such, provided she is young and beautiful. But in spite of all this, the poets display a perfect knowledge of this great human emotion in its richness and variety and in its stimulating situations of joy and sorrow, hope and fear, triumph and defeat. If they speak of the ideal woman, the real woman is always before their eyes. The rhetorical commonplaces and psychological refinements seldom obscure the reality of the sentiment ; and the graceful little pictures of the turns and vagaries of love are often remarkable for their fineness of conception, precision of touch and delicacy of expression. The undoubted power of pathos which the Sanskrit poet possesses very often invests these erotic passages with a deeper and more poignant note ; and the poetical expression of recollective tenderness in the presence of suffering, such as we find in Kālidāsa and Bhavabhūti, is unsurpassable for its vividness of imagery and unmistakable tone of emotional earnestness. But here again the general tendency is to elaborate pathetic scenes in the theatrical sense, and to leave nothing to the imagination of the reader. The theorists are indeed emphatic that the sentiment should be suggested rather than expressed, and never lend their authority to the fatal practice of wordy exaggeration ; but this want of balance is perhaps due not entirely to an ineffective love of parade and futile adorning of trivialities, but also to an extreme seriousness of mind and consequent want of humour, which never allow the poet to attain the necessary sense of proportion and aloofness. There is enough of wit in Sanskrit literature, and it is often strikingly effective ; but there is little of the saving grace of humour and sense of the ridiculous. Its attempts at both comic and pathetic effects are, therefore, often unsuccessful ; and as we have said, it very seldom achieves comedy in its higher forms or tragedy in its deeper sense.

But the seriousness, as well as the artificiality, of Sanskrit literature is very often relieved by a wonderful feeling for natural scenery which is both intimate and real. In spite of a great deal of magnificently decorative convention in painting, there is very often poet's freshness of observation, as well as the direct recreative reproductive touch. In the delineation of human emotion, aspects of nature are very often skilfully interwoven, and most of the effective similes and metaphors of Sanskrit love-poetry are drawn from the surrounding familiar scenes. The *Ṛtu-saṃhāra,* attributed to Kālidāsa, reviews the six Indian seasons in detail, and explains elegantly, if not with deep feeling, the meaning of the seasons for the lover. The same power of utilizing nature as the background of human emotion is seen in the *Megha-dūta,* where the grief of the separated lovers is set in the midst of splendid natural scenery. The tropical summer and the rains play an important part in the emotional life of the people. It is during the commencement of the monsoon that the traveller returns home after long absence, and the expectant wives look at the clouds in eagerness, lifting up the ends of their curls in their hands ; while the maiden, who in hot summer distributes water to the thirsty traveller at the wayside resting places, the Prapā-pālikā as she is called, naturally evokes a large number of erotic verses, which are now scattered over the Anthologies. Autumn also inspires beautiful sketches with its clear blue sky, flocks of white flying geese and meadows ripe with corn ; and spring finds a place with its smelling mango-blossoms, southern breeze and swarm of humming bees. The groves and gardens of nature form the background not only to these little poems, and to the pretty little love-intrigues of Sanskrit plays, but also to the larger human drama played in the hermitage of Kaṇva, to the passionate madness of Purūravas, to the deep pathos of Rāma's hopeless grief for Sītā in the forest of Daṇḍaka, and to the fascinating love of Kṛṣṇa and Rādhā on the banks of the Yamunā.

It would appear that even if the Kāvya literature was magnificent in partial accomplishment, its development was considerably hampered by the conditions under which it grew, and the environment in which it flourished. If it has great merits, its defects are equally great. It is easier, however, to magnify the defects and forget the merits ; and it is often difficult to realise the entire mentality of these poets in order to appreciate their efforts in their proper light. The marvellous results attained even within very great limitations show that there was surely nothing wrong with the genius of the poets, but something was wrong in the literary atmosphere, which cramped its progress and prevented the fullest enfranchisement of the passion and the imagination. The absence of another literature for comparison—for the later Prakrit and allied specimens are mainly derivative—was also a serious drawback, which would partially explain why its outlook is so limited and the principles of poetic art and practice so stereotyped. India, through ages, never stood in absolute isolation, and it could assimilate and transmute what it received ; but Sanskrit literature had very few opprtunities of a real contact with any other great literature. As in the drama, so in the romance and other spheres, we cannot say that there is any reliable ground to suppose that it received any real impetus from Greek or other sources ; and it is a pity that such an impetus never came to give it new impulses and save it from stagnation.

It should also be remembered that the term Kāvya is not co-extensive with what is understood by the word poem or poetry in modern times. It is clearly distinguished from the 'epic,' to which Indian tradition applies the designation of Itihāsa ; but the nomenclature 'court-epic' as a term of compromise is misleading. The underlying conception, general outlook, as well as the principles which moulded the Kāvya are, as we have seen, somewhat different and peculiar. Generally speaking, the Kāvya, with its implications and reticences, is never simple and untutored in the sense in which these terms can be applied to modern poetry ; while sentimental and romantic content, accompanied by perfection of form, subtlety of expression and ingenious embellishment, is regarded, more or less, as essential. The Sanskrit Kāvya is wholly dominated by a self-conscious idea of art and method ; it is not meant for undisciplined enjoyment, nor for the satisfaction of casual interest The rationale is furnished by its super-normal or super-individual character, recognised by poetic theory, which rules out personal passion and emphasises purely artistic emotion. This is also obvious from the fact that the bulk of this literature is in the metrical form. But both theory and practice make the Kāvya extensive enough to comprehend in its scope any literary work of the imagination, and refuse to recognise metre as essential. It, therefore, includes poetry, drama, prose romance, folk-tale, didactic fable, historical writing and philosophical verse, religious and gnomic stanza,—in fact, every branch of literature which may be contained within the denomination of belles-letters in the widest sense, to the exclusion of whatever is purely technical or occasional. One result of this attitude is that while the drama tends towards the dramatic poem, the romance, tales and even historical or biographical sketches are highly coloured by poetical and stylistic effects. In construction, vocabulary and ornament, the prose also becomes poetical. It is true that in refusing to admit that the distinction between prose and poetry lies in an external fact, namely the metre, there is a recognition of the true character of poetic expression ; but in practice it considerably hampers the development of prose as prose. It is seldom recognised that verse and prose rhythms have entirely different values, and that the melody and diction of the one are not always desirable in the other. As the instruments of the two harmonies are not cearly differentiated as means of literary expression, simple and vigorous prose hardly ever develops in Sanskrit ; and its achievement is poor in comparison with that of poetry, which almost exclusively predominates and even approximates prose towards itself.

3. The Origin and General Characteristics of the Drama

The question of the origin and individual characteristics of the various types of literary composition comprised under the Kāvya will be discussed in their proper places ; but since drama like poetry, forms one of its important branches, we may briefly consider here its beginnings, as well as its object, scope and method. The drama, no doubt, as a subdivision of the Kāvya, partakes of most of its general characteristics, but since its form and method are different, it is necessary to consider it separately.

The first definite, but scanty, record of the Sanskrit drama is found in the dramatic fragment, discovered in Central Asia and belonging to the early Kuṣāṇa period, one of these fragments being actually the work of Aśvaghoṣa. The discovery, of which we shall speak more later, is highly important from the historical point of view; for the features which these fragments reveal undoubtedly indicate that the drama had already attained the literary form a technique which persist throughout its later course; and its fairly developed character suggests that it must have had a history behind it. This history, unfortunately, cannot be traced today, for the earlier speciments which might have enabled us to do so, appear to have perished in course of time. The orthodox account of the origin of the Sanskrit drama, by describing it as a gift from heaven in the form of a developed art invented by the divine sage Bharata, envelops it in impenetrable mist of myth; while modern scholarship, professing to find the earliest manifestation of a ritual drama in the dialogue-hymns of the *Ṛgveda* and presuming a development of the dramatic from the religious after the manner of the Greek drama, shrouds the question of its origin in a still greater mist of speculation.

The orininal purpose[1] of some fifteen hymns of the *Ṛgveda*, which are obviously dialogues and are recognised as such by the Indian tradition,[2] is frankly obscure. Most of them, like those of Purūravas and Urvaśī (x. 95), Yama and Yamī (x. 10), Indra, Indrāṇī and Vṛṣākapi (x. 86), Saramā and the Paṇis (x, 108), are not in any way connected with the religious sacrifice,

1 For a summary and discussion of the various theories and for references, see Keith in *ZDMG*, *lxiv*, 1910, p. 534 f, in *JRAS*, 1911, p. 979 f and in his *Sanskrit Drama* (hereafter cited as *SD*), p. 13 f.

2 Both Śaunaka and Yāska apply the term Saṁvāda-sūkta to most of these hymns, but sometimes the terms Itihāsa and Ākhyāna are also employed. Even assuming popular origin and dramatic elements, the hymns are in no sense ballads or ballad-plays.

nor do they represent the usual type of religious hymns of prayer and thanksgiving ; but they appear to possess a mythical or legendary content. It has been claimed that here we have the first signs of the Indian drama. The suggestion is that these dialogues call for miming ; and connected with the ritual dance, song and music, they represent a kind of refined and sacerdotalised dramatic spectacle,[1] or in fact, a ritual drama, or a Vedic Mystery Play in a nutshell,[2] in which the priests assuming the rôles of divine, mythical or human interlocutors danced and sang[3] the hymns in dialogues. To this is added the further presumption[4] that the hymns represent an old type of composition, narrative in character and Indo-European in antiquity, in which there existed originally both prose and verse ; but the verse, representing the points of interest or feeling, was carefully constructed and preserved, while the prose, acting merely as a connecting link, was left to be improvised, and therefore never remained fixed nor was handed down. It is assumed that the dialogues in the Ṛgvedic hymns represent the verse, the prose having disappeared before or after their incorporation into the Saṃhitā ; and the combination of prose and verse in the Sanskrit drama is alleged to be a legacy of this hypothetical Vedic Ākhyāna.

It must be admitted at once that the dramatic quality of the hymns is considerable, and that the connexion between the drama and the religious song and dance in general has been made clear by modern research. At first sight, therefore, the theory appears plausible ; but it is based on several unproved and unnessary assumptions. It is not necessary, for instance, nor is there any authority, for finding a ritual explanation of these hymns ; for

1 S. Lévi, *Téâtre indien*, Paris, 1890, p. 333f.

2 L. von Schroeder, *Mysterium und Mimus im Ṛgveda*, Leipzig, 1908 ; A. Hillebrandt, *Uber die Anfänge des indischen Dramas*, Munich, 1914, p. 22f.

3 J. Hertel in *WZKM*, XVIII, 1904, p. 59f, 137 f ; XXIII, p. 273 f ; XXIV, p. 117 f. Hertel maintains that unless singing is presumed, it is not possible for a single speaker to make the necessary distinction between the different speakers presupposed in the dialogues of the hymns.

4 H. Oldenberg in *ZDMG*, XXXII, p. 54 f ; XXXIX, p. 52 ; and also in *Zur Geschichte d. altindischen Prosa*, Berlin, 1917, p. 53f.

neither the Indian tradition nor even modern scholarship admits the presumption that everything contained in the *Ṛgveda* is connected with the ritual. As a matter of fact, no ritual employment for these hymns is prescribed in the Vedic texts and commentaries. We have also no record of such happenings as are complacently imagined, nor of any ritual dance actually practised by the Vedic priests ; the Ṛgvedic, as opposed to the Sāmavedic hymns were recited and not sung ; and later Vedic literature knows nothing of a dramatic employment of these hymns. It is true that some of the Vedic ritual, especially the fertility rites, like the Mahāvrata, contains elements that are dramatic, but the existence of a dramatic ritual is no evidence of the existence of a ritual drama. It is also not necessary to conceive of these Ṛgvedic dialogue-hymns as having been in their origin a mixture of poor prose and rich verse for the purpose of explaining the occurrence of prose and verse in the Sanskrit drama from its very beginning ; for the use of prose in drama is natural and requires no explanation, and, considering the epic tradition and the general predominance of the metrical form in Sanskrit literature, the verse is not unexpected. Both prose and verse in the Sanskrit drama are too intimately related to have been separate in their origin.

The modified form of the avove theory,[1] namely, that the Vedic ritual drama itself is borrowed from an equally hypothetical popular mime of antiquity, which is supposed to have included dialogue and abusive language, as well as song and dance, is an assumption which does not entirely dismiss the influence of religious ceremonies, but believes that the dramatic element in the ritual, as well as the drama itself, had a popular origin. But to accept it, in the absence of all knowledge about popular or religious mimetic entertainment in Vedic times,[2] is extremely

1 Sten Konow, *Das ind. Drama*, Berlin and Leipzig, 1920, p. 42f.

2 The analogy of the Yātrā, which is as much secular as bound up with religion in its origin, is interesting, but there is nothing to show that such forms of popular entertainment actually existed in Vedic times.

difficult The influence of the element of abusive language and amusing antics in the Horse-sacrifice, as well as in the Mahāvrata,[1] appears to have been much exaggerated ; for admittedly it is an ingredient of magic rites, and there is no evidence either of its popular character or of its alleged impetus towards the growth of the religious drama. The history of the Vidūṣaka of the Sanskrit drama,[2] which is sometimes cited in support, is at most obscure. He is an anomalous enough character, whose name implies that he is given to abuse and who is yet rarely such in the actual drama, who is a Brahmin and a 'high' character and who yet speaks Prakrit and indulges in absurdities ; but his derivation from an imaginary degraded Brahmin of the hypothetical secular drama, on the one hand, is as unconvincing as his affiliation to a ritual drama, on the other, which is presumed from the abusiva dialogue of the Brahmin student and the hataera in the Mahāvrata ceremony. An interesting parallel is indeed drawn from the history of the Elizabethan Fool, who was originally the ludicrous Devil of mediaeval Mystery Plays ;[3] but an argument from analogy is not a proof of fact. The Vidūṣaka's attempts at amusing by his cheap witticisms about his gastronomical sensibilities are inevitable concessions to the groundlings and do not require the far-fetched invocation of a secular drama for explanation. The use of Prakrit and Prakritic technical terminology in the Sanskrit drama, again, has been adduced in support of its popular origin, but we have no knowledge of any primitive Prakrit drama or of any early Prakrit drama turned into Sanskrit, and the occurrence of Prakritic technical terms may be reasonably referred to the practice of the actors.

It seems, therefore, that even if the elements of the drama were present in Vedic times, there is no proof that the drama,

1 A. Hillebrandt, *Rituallitteratur*, Strassburg, 1897, p. 157.

2 Sten Konow, *op. cit.*, pp. 14-15. See also J. Huizinga, *De Vidūṣaka in het indisch tooneel*, Groningen, 1897, p. 64 f, and M. Schuyler, The Origin of the Vidūṣaka in *JAOS*, XX, 1899, p. 338f.

3 A. Hillebrandt, *Die Anfänge*, p. 24 f.

in however rudimentary form, was actually known. The actor is not mentioned, nor does any dramatic terminology occur. There may have been some connexion between the dramatic religious ceremonies and the drama in embryo, but the theory which seeks the origin of the Sanskrit drama in the sacred dance, eked out by song, gesture and dialogue, on the analogy of what happened in Greece or elsewhere, is still under the necessity of proving its thesis by actual evidence ; and little faith can be placed on arguments from analogy. The application of Ridgeway's theory[1] of the origin of drama in general in the animistic worship of the dead is still less authenticated in the case of the Sanskrit drama ; for the performance is never meant here for the gratification of departed spirits, nor are the characters regarded as their representatives.

As a reaction against the theory of sacred origin, we have the hypothesis of the purely secular origin of the Sanskrit drama in the Puppet-play[2] and the Shadow-play[3] ; but here again the suggestions do not bear critical examination, and the lack of exact data precludes us from a dogmatic conclusion. While the reference to the puppet-play in the *Mahābhārata*[4] cannot be exactly dated, its supposed antiquity and prevalence in India, if correct, do not necessarily make it the source of the Sanskrit drama ; and its very name (from putrikā, puttalikā) implies that it is only a make-believe or imitation and presupposes the existence of the regular play. The designations Sūtradhāra and Sthāpaka need not refer to any original manipulation of puppets by 'pulling strings' or 'arranging' but they clearly refer to the original

[1] As set forth in *Dramas and Dramatic Dances of Non-European Races*, Cambridge, 1918, also in *FRAS*, 1916, p. 821 f. 1917, p. 143 f. effectively criticised by Keith in *JRAS*, 1916, p. 335 f, 1917, p. 140 f.

[2] R. Pischel in *Die Heimat des Puppenspiels*, Halle, 1900 (trs. into English by Mildred C. Twaney, London, 1902).

[3] Pischel in *Das altindische Schattenspiel* in *SBAW*, 1916, pp. 482-502, further elaborated by H. Lüders in Die Śaubhikas : ein Beitrag zur Geschichte d. indischen Dramas in *SBAW*, 1916, p. 698 f.

[4] XII, 294. 5, as explained by Nīlakaṇṭha.

function of the director or stage-manager of laying out and constructing the temporary playhouse. With regard to the shadow-play, in which shadow-pictures are produced by projection from puppets on the reverse side of a thin white curtain, the evidence of its connexion with the drama is late and indefinite,[1] and therefore inconclusive. Whatever explanation[2] may be given of the extremely obscure passage in Patañjali's *Mahābhāṣya* (*ad.* iii. 1. 26) on the display of the Śaubhikas, there is hardly any foundation for the view[3] that the the Śaubhikas discharged the function of showing shadow-pictures and explaining them to the audience. The exact meaning, again, of the term Chāyā-nāṭaka, found in certain plays, is uncertain ; it is not admitted as a known genre in Sanskrit dramatic theory, and none of the so-called Chāyā-nāṭakas is different in any way from the normal drama. The reference to the Javanese shadow-play does not strengthen the position, for it is not yet proved that the Javanese type was borrowed from India or that its analogue prevailed in India in early times ; and its connexion with the Sanskrit drama cannot be established until it is shown that the shadow-play itself sprang up without a previous knowledge of the drama.

Apart from the fact, however, that the primitive drama in general shows a close connexion with religion, and apart also from the unconvincing theory of the ritualistic origin of the Sanskrit drama, there are still certain facts connected with the Sanskrit drama itself which indicate that, if it was in its origin not exactly of the nature of a religious drama, it must have been considerably influenced in its growth by religion or religious cults. In the absence of sufficient material, the question does

1 On the whole question and for references see Keith in *SD*, pp. 53-57 and S. K. De in *IHQ*, VII, 1931, p. 542 f.

2 Various explanations have been suggested by Kayyaṭa in his commentary ; by A. Weber in *Ind. Studien.*, XIII, p. 488 f. ; by Lévi, *op. cit.*, p. 315 ; by Lüders in the work cited above ; by Winternitz in *ZDMG.*, LXXIV, 1920, p. 118 ff. ; by Hillebrandt in *ZDMG*, LXXII, 1918, p. 227 f. ; by Keith in *BSOS*, I. pt. 4. p. 27 f., and by K. G. Subrahmanya in *JRAS*, 1925, p. 502.

3 Lüders, *op. cit.*, supported by Winternitz, but effectively criticised by Hillebrandt and Keith.

not admit of clear demonstration, but it can be generally accepted from some undoubted indications. One of the early descriptions of scenic representation that we have is that given by Patañjali, mentioned above; it is interesting that the entertainment is associated with the Viṣṇu-Kṛṣṇa legend of the slaying of Kaṃsa and the binding of Bali. It may not have been drama proper, but it was not a mere shadow-play nor recitation of the type made by the Granthikas; it may have been some kind of pantomimic, or even dramatic, performance distinctly carried out by action. It should be noted in this connexion that, on the analogy of the theory of the origin of the Greek drama from a mimic conflict of summer and winter, Keith sees[1] in the legend of the slaying of Kaṃsa a refined version of an older vegetation ritual in which there was a demolition of the outworn spirit of vegetation, and evolves an elaborate theory of the origin of Indian tragedy from this idea of a contest. But the tendency to read nature-myth or nature-worship into every bit of legend, history or folklore, which was at one time much in vogue, is no longer convincing; and in the present case it is gratuitous, and even misleading, to invoke Greek parallels to explain things Indian. It is sufficient to recognise that here we have an early indication of the close connexion of some dramatic spectacle with the Viṣṇu-Kṛṣṇa legend, the fascination of which persists throughout the history of Sanskrit literature. Again, it may be debatable whether Śaurasenī as the normal prose Prakrit of the Sanskrit drama came from the Kṛṣṇa cult, which is supposed to have its ancient home in Śūrasena or Mathurā; but there can be no doubt that in the fully developed Sanskrit drama the Kṛṣṇa cult[2] came to play an important part. The Holi-festival of the Kṛṣṇa cult, which is essentially a spring festival, is sometimes equated with the curious ceremony of the decoration and worship of Indra's flagstaff (Jarjara- or Indradhvaja-pūjā)

1 In *ZDMG*, LXIV, 1910, p. 534 f.; in *JRAS*, 1911, p. 979, 1912, p. 411; in *SD*, p. 37f.
2 On the Kṛṣṇa cult, see Winternitz in *ZDMG*, LXXIV, 1920, p. 118f.

prescribed by Bharata as one of the preliminaries (Pūrva-raṅga) of enacting a play, on the supposition that it is analogical to the Maypole ceremony of England and the pagan phallic rites of Rome. The connexion suggested is as hypothetical as Bharata's legendary explanation that with the flagstaff Indra drove away the Asuras, who wanted to disturb the enacting of a play by the gods, is fanciful ; but it has been made the somewhat slender foundation of a theory[1] that the Indian drama originated from a banner festival (Dhvaja-maha) in honour of Indra. The existence of the Nāndī and other religious preliminaries of the Sanskrit drama is quite sufficient to show that the ceremony of Jarjara-pūjā, whatever be its origin, is only a form of the customary propitiation of the gods, and may have nothing to do with the origin of the drama itself. It is however, important to note that religious service forms a part of the ceremonies preceding a play ; and it thus strengthens the connexion of the drama with religion. Like Indra and Kṛṣṇa, Śiva[2] is also associated with the drama, for Bharata ascribes to him and his spouse the invention of the Tāṇḍava and the Lāsya, the violent and the tender dance, respectively ; and the legend of Rāma has no less an importance than of Kṛṣṇa in supplying the theme of the Sanskrit drama.

All this, as well as the attitude of the Buddhist and Jaina texts towards the drama,[3] would suggest that, even if the theory of its religious origin fails, the Sanskrit drama probably received a great impetus from religion in its growth. In the absence of decisive evidence, it is better to admit our inability to explain the nature and extent of the impetus from this and other sources, than indulge in conjectures which are of facts, fancies and theories all compact. It seems probable, however, that the literary antecedents of the drama, as of poetry, are to be sought mainly in the great Epics of India. The references to

1 Haraprasad Sastri in *JPASB*, V. 1909, p. 351f.
2 Bloch in *ZDMG*, LXII, 1908, p. 655.
3 Keith, *SD*, pp. 43-44.

the actor and dramatic performance in the composite and undatable texts of the Epics and the *Hari-vaṃśa* need not be of conclusive value, nor should stress be laid on the attempted derivation of the word Kuśīlava,[1] denoting an actor, from Kuśa and Lava of the *Rāmāyaṇa* ; but it seems most probable that the early popularity of epic recitation, in which the reciter accompanied it with gestures and songs, can be connected with the dramatisation of epic stories. How the drama began we do not know, nor do we know exactly when it began ; but the natural tendency to dramatisation, by means of action, of a vivid narrative (such, for instance, as is suggested by the *Mahābhāṣya* passage) may have been stimulated to a great degree by the dramatic recitation of epic tales. No doubt, the developed drama is not a mere dramatisation of epic material, and is also not clear how the idea of dramatic conflict and analysis of action in relation to character were evolved ; but the Sanskrit drama certainly inherits from the Epics, in which its interest is never lost throughout its history, its characteristic love of description, which it shares with Sanskrit poetry ; and both drama and poetry draw richly also upon the narrative and didactic content of the Epics. The close approximation also of drama to poetry made by Sanskrit theory perhaps points to the strikingly parallel, but inherently diverse, development from a common epic source ; and it is not surprising that early poets like Aśvaghoṣa and Kālidāsa were also dramatists. The other

1 Lévi, *op. cit.*, p. 312 ; Sten Konow, *op. cit.*, p. 9. It is not clear if the term is really a compound of irregular formation ; and the etymology *ku+śīla*, 'of bad morals,' is clever in view of the proverbial morals of the actor, but far-fetched. The word Bharata, also denoting the actor, is of course derived from the mythical Bharata of the *Nāṭya-śāstra*, and has nothing to do with Bhārata, still less with Bhāṭa which is clearly from Bhaṭṭa. The name Naṭa, which is apparently a Prakritisation of the earlier root nṛt 'to dance' (*contra* D. R. Mankad, *Types of Sanskrit Drama*, Karaci, 1926, p. 6 f.) probably indicates that he was originally, and perhaps mainly, a dancer, who acquired the mimetic art. The distinction between Nṛtta (Dancing) Nṛtya (Dancing with gestures and feelings) and Nāṭya (Drama with histrionics), made by the *Daśarūpaka* (1.7-9) and other works, is certainly late, but it is not unhistorical ; for it explains the evolution of the Rūpaka and Uparūpaka techniques.

literary tendency of the drama, namely, its lyric inspiration and metrical variety of sentimental verses, however, may have been supplied by the works of early lyrists, some of whose fragments are preserved by Patañjali. The extant dramatic literature, like the poetic, does not give an adequate idea of its probable antiquity[1], but that the dramatic art probably developed somewhat earlier even than the poetic can be legitimately inferred from the admission of the rhetoricians that they borrow the theory of sentiment from dramaturgy and apply it to poetics, as well as from the presumably earlier existence of the *Nāṭya-ṣāstra* of Bharata than that of any known works on poetics.

The extreme paucity of our knowledge regarding the impetus which created the drama has led to the much discussed suggestion[2] that some influence, if not the entire impetus, might have come from the Greek drama. Historical researches have now established the presence of Greek principalities in India ; and it is no longer possible to deny that the Sanskrit drama must have greatly developed during the period when the Greek influence was present in India. As we know nothing about the causes of this development, and as objections regarding chronology and contact

1 Pāṇini's reference to Naṭa-sūtras composed by Śilālin and Kṛśāśva (IV. 3. 110-111) has been dismissed as doubtful, for there is no means of determining the meening of the word Naṭa (see above), which may refer to a mere dancer or mimer. But the drama, as well as the dramatic performance, is known to Buddhist literature, not only clearly to works of uncertain date like the *Avadāna-śataka* (II. 24, the *Divyāvadāna* (pp. 357, 360-61), and the *Lalita-vistara* (XII, p. 178), but also probably to the Buddhist Suttas, which forbid the monks watching popular shows. The exact nature of these shows is not clear, but there is no reason to presume that they were not dramatic entertainments. See Winternitz in *WZKM*, XXVII, 1913, p. 39f. ; Lévi, *op. cit.*, p. 319f.—The mention of the word Naṭa or Nāṭaka in the undatable and uncertain texts of the Epics (including the *Hari-vaṁśa*) is of little value for chronological purposes.

2 A. Weber in *Ind. Studien*, II, p. 148 and Die Griechen in Indien in *SBAW*, 1890,p.920; repudiated by Pischel in *Die Rezension der Śakuntalā*, Breslau, 1875, p. 19 and in *SBAW*, 1906, p. 502 ; but elaborately supported, in a modified form, by Windisch in *Der griechische Einfluss im indischen Drama* (in *Verhl. d. V. Intern. Orient. Congress*) Berlin 1882, p. 3 f. See Sten Konow, *op. cit.*, pp. 40-42 and Keith, *SD*, pp. 57-68, for a discussion of thetheoryand further references. W. W. Tarn reviews the whole question in his *Greeks in Bactria and India*, Cambridge, 1938, but he is extremely cautious on the subject of Greek influence on the Sanskrit drama ; See Keith's criticism in *D. R. Bhandarkar Volume*, Calcutta, 1940, p. 224 f.

are not valid, is nothing *a priori* impossible in the presumption of the influence of the Greek drama on the Indian. The difficulty of Indian exclusiveness and conservatism is neutralised by instances of the extraordinary genius of India in assimilating what it receives from foreign sources in other spheres of art and science, notwithstanding the barrier of language, custom and civilisation.

But there are difficulties in adducing positive proof in support of the presumption. The evidence regarding actual performance of Greek plays in the courts of Greek princes in India is extremely scanty ;[1] but more important is the fact that there are no decisive points of contact, but only casual coincidences,[2] between the Sanskrit drama and the New Attic Comedy, which is regarded as the source of the influence. No reliance can be placed on the use of the device of token of recognition[3] common to the two dramas. Although the forms in which it has come down to us do not antedate the period of supposed Greek influence, the Indian literature of tales reveals a considerable use of this motif ; and there are also epic instances[4] which seem to preclude the possibility of its being borrowed from the Greek drama. It is motif common enough in the folk-tale in general, and inevitable in primitive society as a means of identification ; and its employment in the Sanskrit drama can be reasonably explained as having been of independent origin. No satisfactory inference, again, can be

1 Lévi, *op. cit.*, p. 60, but *contra* Keith, *SD*, p. 59.

2 Such as division into acts, number of acts, departure of all actors from the stage at the end of the acts, the scenic convention of asides, the announcing of the entry and identity of a new character by a remark from a character already on the stage, etc. The Indian Prologue is entirely different from the Classical, being a part of the preliminaries and having a definite character and object.—Max Lindenau's exposition (*Beiträge zur altindischen Rasalehre*, Leipzig 1913, p. v) of the relation between Bharata's *Nātya-śāstra* and Aristotle's *Poetik* is interesting, but proves nothing.

3 *E.g.*, the ring in *Mālavikāgnimitra and Śakuntalā*, stone of union and arrow (of Āyus) in *Vikramorvaśīya*, necklace in *Ratnāvalī*, the jewel falling from the sky in *Nāgānanda*, the garland in *Mālati-mādhava* and *Kunda-mālā*, the Jṛmbhaka weapons in *Uttara-carita*, the clay cart in *Mṛcchakaṭika*, the seal in *Mudrā-rākṣasa*, etc.

4 Keith, *SD*, p. 63.

drawn from the resemblance of certain characters, especially the Viṭa, the Vidūṣaka, and the Śakāra. The parasite occurs in the Greek and Roman comedy, but he lacks the refinement and culture of the Indian Viṭa ; the origin of the Vidūṣaka, as we have seen, is highly debatable, but his Brahmin caste and high social position distinguish him from the vulgar slave (*servus currens*) of the classical comedy, and we know from Patañjali that the Śakāra was originally a person of Śaka descent and was apparently introduced into the Sanskrit drama as a boastful, ignorant and ridiculous villain at a time when the marital alliance of Indian kings with Śaka princesses had fallen into disfavour.[1] These characters are not rare in any soicety, and can be easily explained as having been conceived from actual life in India. The argument, again, from the Yavanikā[2] or curtain, which covered the entrance from the retiring room (Nepathya) or stood at the back of the stage between the Raṅga-pīṭha and the Raṅgaśīrṣa, and which is alleged to have received its name from its derivation from the Ionians (Yavanas) or Greeks, is now admitted to be of little value, for the simple reason that the Greek theatre, so far as we know, had no use for the curtain. The theory is modified with the suggestion that the Indian curtain

1 He is represented as the brother of the king's concubine ; cf. *Sāhitya-darpaṇa*, III, 44. Cf. E. J. Rapson's article on the Drama (Indian) in *ERE*, Vol. IX, p. 885.

2 Windisch, *op. cit.*, p. 24 f. The etymology given by Indian lexicograp'ers from *java*, 'speed' (in the Prakrit Javanikā form of the word), or the derivation from the root *yu* 'to cover,' is ingenious, but not covincing. There is nothing to confirm the opinion that the form Jamanikā is a scribal mistake (Böthlingk and Roth) or merely secondary (Sten Konow), for it is recognised in the Indian lexicons and occurs in some MSS. of plays. If this was the original form, then it would signify a curtain only (form the root *yam*, 'to restrain, cover'), or double curtain covering the two entrances from the Nepathya (from yama, 'twin') ; but there is no authority for holding that the curtain was parted in the middle. See *IHQ*, VII, p. 480 f. The word Yavanikā is apparently known to Bharata, as it occurs at 5. 11-12 in the description of the elements of the Pūrvaraṅga. Abhinavagupta explains that its position was between the Raṅgaśīrṣa and Raṅgapīṭha (ed. GOS, p. 212). The other names are Paṭī, Pratiśirā and Tiraskaraṇī. There was apparently no drop curtain on the Indian stage.—The construction of the Indian theatre, as described by Bharata, has little resemblance to that of the Greek ; and Th. Bloch's discovery of the remains of a Greek theatre in the Sitavenga Cave (*ZDMG*, LVIII, p. 455 f.) is of doubtful value as a decisive piece of evidence.

is so called because the material of the cloth was derived from the Greek merchants ; but even this does not carry us very far to prove Greek influence on the Indian stage arrangement.

It will be seen that even if certain striking parallels and coincidences are urged and admitted between the Greek and the Sanskrit drama, the search for positive signs of influence produces only a negative result. There are so many fundamental differences that brorwing or influence is out of the question, and the affinities should be regarded as independent developments. The Sanskrit drama is essentially of the romantic rather than of the classical type, and affords points of resemblance to the Elizabethan, rather than to the Greek, drama. The unities of time and place are entirely disregarded between the acts as well as within the act. Even twelve years elapse between one act and another, and the time-limit of an act[1] often exceeds twenty-four hours ; while the scene easily shifts from earth to heaven. Romantic and fabulous elements are freely introduced ; tragi-comedy or melodrama is not infrequent ; verse is regularly mixed with prose ; puns and verbal cleverness are often favoured. There is not chorus, but there is metrical benediction and a prologue which are, however, integral parts of the play and set the plot in motion. While the parallel of the Vidūṣaka is found in the Elizabethan Fool, certain dramatic devices, such as the introduction of a play within a play[2] and the use of a token of recognition, are common. There is no limit in the Sanskrit drama to the number of characters, who may be either divine, semi-divine or human. The plot may be taken from legend or from history, but it may also be drawn from contemporary life and manners. With very rare exceptions, the main interest almost invariably centres in a love-story, love being, at least in practice, the only passion which forms

1 On time-analysis of Sanskrit plays (Kālidāsa and Harṣa), see Jackson in *JAOS* XX, 1899, pp. 341-59 ; XXI, 1900, pp. 88-108.

2 As in *Priyadarśikā, Uttara-rāma-carita* and *Bāla-rāmāyaṇa*. See Jackson's appendix to the ed. of the first play, pp. cv-cxi.

the dominant theme of this romantic drama. Special structures of a square, rectangular or triangular shape for the presentation of plays are described in the *Nāty-śāstra,*[1] but they have little resemblance to the Greek or modren theatre and must have been evolved independently. Very often plays appear to have been enacted in the music hall of the royal palace, and there were probably no special contrivances, nor elaborate stage-properties, nor even scenery in the ordinary sense of the word. The lack of these theatrical makeshifts was supplied by the lively imagination of the audience, which was aided by a profusion of verses describing the imaginary surroundings, by mimetic action and by an elaborate system of gestures possessing a conventional significance.

Besides these more or less formal requirements, there are some important features which fundamentally distiguish the Sanskrit drama from all other dramas, including the Greek. The aim of the Sanskrit dramatists, who were mostly idealists in outlook and indifferent to mere fact or incident, is not to mirror life by a direct portrayal of action or character, but (as in poetry) to evoke a particular sentiment (Rasa) in the mind of the audience, be it amatory, heroic or quietistic. As this is regarded, both in theory and practice, to be the sole object as much of the dramatic art as of the poetic, everything else is subordinated to this end. Although the drama is described in theory as an imitation or representation of situations (Avasthānukṛti), the plot as well as characterisation, is a secondary element ; its complications are to be avoided so that it may not divert the mind from the appreciation of the sentiment to other interests. A well known theme, towards which the reader's mind would of itself be inclined, is normally preferred ; the poet's skill is concerned entirely with the developing of its emotional possibilities, The criticism, therefore, that the Sanskrit dramatist shows little fertility in the invention of

1 On the theatre see D. R. Mankad in *IHQ*, VIII, 1932, pp. 480-99.

plots may be just, but it fails to take into account this peculiar object of the Sanskrit drama.

Thus, the Sanskrit drama came to possess an atmosphere of sentiment and poetry, which was conducive to idealistic creation at the expense of action and characterisation, but which in the lesser dramatists overshadowed all that was dramatic in it. The analogy is to be found in Indian painting and sculpture, which avoid the crude realism of bones and muscles and concentrate exclusively on spiritual expression, but which often degenerate into formless fantastic creation. This, of course, does not mean that reality is entirely banished; but the sentimental and poetic envelopment certainly retards the growth of the purely dramatic elements. It is for this reason that sentimental verses, couched in a great variety of lyrical measures and often strangely undramatic, preponderate and form the more essential part of the drama, the prose acting mainly as a connecting link, as a mode of communicating facts, or as a means of carrying forward the story. The dialogue is, therefore, more or less neglected in favour of the lyrical stanza, to which its very flatness affords an effective contrast. It also follows from this sentimental and romantic bias that typical characters are generally preferred to individual figures. This leads to the creation of conventional characters, like the king queen, minister, lover and jester, who become in course of time crystallised into permanent types; but this does not mean that the ideal heroic, or the very real popular, characters are all represented as devoid of common humanity. Cārudatta, for instance, is not a mere marvel of eminent virtues, but a perfect man of the world, whose great qualities are softened by an equally great touch of humanity; nor is Duṣyanta a merely typical king-lover prescribed by convention; while the Śakāra or the Viṭa in Śūdraka's play are finely characterised. These and others are taken from nature's never-ending variety of everlasting types, but they are no less living individuals. At the same time, it cannot be denied there is a tendency to large generalisation and a reluctance to deviate from the type. It means an indifference to individuality, and consequently to the realities of characterisation, plot and action, as well as a corresponding inclination towards the purely ideal and emotional aspects of theme. For this reason also, the Sanskrit drama, as a rule, makes the fullest use of the accessories of the lyric, dance, music, song and mimetic art.

As there is, therefore, a fundamental difference in the respective conception of the drama, most of the Sanskrit plays, judged by modern standards, would not at all be regarded as dramas in the strict sense but rather as dramatic poems. In some authors the sense of the dramatic becomes hopelessly lost in their ever increasing striving after the sentimental and the poetic, and they often make the mistake of choosing lyric or epic subjects which were scarcely capable of dramatic treatment. As, on the one hand, the drama suffers from its close dependence on the epic, so on the other, it concentrates itself rather disproportionately on the production of the polished lyrical and descriptive stanzas. The absence of scenic aids, no doubt, makes the stanzas necessary for vividly suggesting the scene or the situation to the imagination of the audience and evoking the proper sentiment, but the method progressively increases the lyric and emotional tendencies of the drama, and elegance and refinement are as much encouraged in the drama as in poetry. It is not surprising, therefore, that a modern critic should accept only *Mudrā-rākṣasa,* in the whole range of Sanskrit dramatic literature, as a drama proper. This is indeed an extreme attitude ; for the authors of the *Abhijñāna-śakuntala* or of the *Mṛcchakaṭika* knew very well that they were composing dramas and not merely a set of elegant poetical passages ; but this view brings out very clearly the characteristic aims and limitations of the Sanskrit drama. There is, however, one advantage which is not often seen in the modern practical productions of the stage-craft. The breath of poetry and romance vivifies the Sanskrit drama ; it is seldom of a prosaic cast ; it does not represent human beings insipidly under ordinary and commonplace circumstances ; it has often the higher and more poetic naturalness, which is no less attractive in revealing the beauty, as well as the depth, of human character ; and even when its dramatic qualities are poor it appeals by the richness of its poetry.

As the achievement of concord is a necessary corollary to the ideal character of the drama, nothing is allowed to be represented on the stage which might offend the sensibility of the audience and obstruct the suggestion of the desired sentiment by inauspicious, frivolous or undesirable details. This rule regarding the observance of stage-decencies includes, among other things, the prohibition that death should not be exhibited on the stage. This restriction, as well as the serene and complacent attitude of the Indian mind towards life, makes it difficult for the drama, as for poetry, to depict tragedy in its deeper sense. Pathetic episodes, dangers and difficulties may contribute to the unfolding of the plot with a view to the evoking of the underlying sentiment, but the final result should not be discord. The poetic justice of the European drama is unknown in the Sanskrit. The dramatist, like the poet, shows no sense of uneasiness, strife or discontent in the structure of life, nor in its complexity or difficulty, and takes without question the rational order of the world. This attitude also accepts, without incredulity or discomfort, the intervention of forces beyond control or calculation in the affairs of men. Apart from the general idea of a brooding fate or destiny, it thinks nothing of a curse or a divine act as an artificial device for controlling the action of a play or bringing about a solution of its complication. It refuses to rob the world or the human life of its mysteries, and freely introduces the marvellous and the supernatural, without, however, entirely destroying the motives of human action or its responsibility. The dramatic conflict, under these conditions, hardly receives a full or logical scope ; and however much obstacles may hinder the course of love or life, the hero and the heroine must be rewarded in the long run, and all is predestined to end well by the achievement of perfect happiness and union. There are indeed exceptions to the general rule, for the *Ūru-bhaṅga*[1] has a tragic ending ; while the death of Daśaratha occurs on the stage in the *Pratimā*, like that of Kaṃsa in the *Bāla-carita*. There are also instances where the rule is obeyed in the letter but not in spirit ; for Vasantasenā's apparent murder in the *Mṛcchakaṭika* occurs on the stage, and the dead person is restored to life on the stage in the *Nāgānanda*. Nevertheless, the injunction makes Kālidāsa and Bhavabhūti alter the tragic ending of the Urvaśī legend and the *Rāmāyaṇa* story respectively into one of happy union, while the sublimity of the self-sacrifice of Jīmūtavāhana, which suggests real tragedy, ends in a somewhat lame denouement of divine intervention and complete and immediate reward of virtue at the end. In the Western drama, death overshadows everything and forms the chief source of poignant tragedy by its uncertainty and hopelessness ; the Indian dramatist, no less pessimistic in his belief in the inexorable law of Karman, does not deny death, but, finding in it a condition of renewal, can hardly regard it in the same tragic light.

It is, however, not correct to say that the Sanskrit drama entirely excludes tragedy. What it really does is that it excludes the direct representing of death as an incident, and insists on a happy ending. It recognises some from of tragedy in its pathetic sentiment and in the portrayal of separation in love ; and tragic interest strongly dominates some of the great plays. In the *Mṛcchakaṭika* and the *Abhijñāna-śakuntala*, for instance, the tragedy does not indeed occur at the end, but it occurs in the middle ; and in the *Uttara-rāma-carita* where the tragic interest prevails throughout, it occurs in an intensive form at the beginning of the play. The theorists appear to maintain

[1] It has, however, been pointed out (Sukthankar in *FBRAS*, 1925, p. 141) that the *Ūru-bhaṅga* is not intended to be a tragedy in one act ; it is only the surviving intermediate act of a lengthy dramatised version of the *Mahābhārata* story ; the Trivandrum dramas, therefore, from no exception to the general rule prohibiting a *final* catastrophe.

that there is no tragedy in the mere fact of death, which in itself may be a disgusting, terrible or undignified spectacle and thus produce a hiatus in the aesthetic pleasure. Cruelty, murder, dark and violent passions, terror and ferocity need not have a premium. Undigested horrors are gloomy, depressing and unhealthy ; they are without dignity or decorum and indicate a morbid taste ; they do not awaken genuine pity or pathos. The Sanskrit drama generally keeps to the high road of life and never seeks the by-lanes of blood-and-thunder tragedy, or representation of loathsome and unnatural passions. Grim realism, in its view, does not exalt but debase the mind, and thereby cause a disturbance of the romantic setting. The theory holds that tragedy either precedes or follows the fact of death, which need not be visually represented, but the effect of which may be utilised for evoking the pathetic. It appears, therefore, that tragedy is not totally neglected, but that it is often unduly subordinated to the finer sentiments and is thus left comparatively undeveloped. The theory, however, misses the inconsolable hopelessness which a tragic ending inevitably brings ; and the very condition of happy ending makes much of the tragedy of the Sanskrit drama look unconvincing. In spite of the unmistakable tone of earnestness, the certainty of reunion necessarily presents the pathos of severance as a temporary and therefore needlessly exaggerated sentimentality.

There are also certain other conditions and circumstances which seriously affect the growth of the Sanskrit drama, in the same way as they affect the growth of Sanskrit poetry. From the very beginning the drama, like poetry, appears to have moved in an aristocratic environment. It is fostered in the same elevated and rarefied atmosphere and is expected to show the same characteristics, being regarded both by theory and practice, as a subdivision of the Kāvya, to the general aim and method of which it was more and more approximated. In the existing specimens there is nothing primitive ; we have neither the infancy of the drama nor the drama of infancy. The Sanskrit drama was never popular in the sense in which the Greek drama was. It is essentially a developed literary drama, inspired by the elegant poetic conventions of the highly cultured Sahṛdaya, whose recognition was eagerly coveted ; and its dominant love-motif reflects the tastes and habits of the polished court-circle, as well as of the cultivated Nāgaraka. The court-life in particular, which forms the theme of a number of plays on the amourettes of philandering princes, gives an opportunity of introducing song, dance and music ; and the graceful manner and erotic sentiment become appiopriate. In course of time, Poetics, Erotics and Dramaturgy conventionalised these tastes and habits ; and refined fancy and search after stylistic effect came in with the gradual preference of the subtle and the finical to the fervid and the spontaneous. The graces and artificialities of poetry become reflected in the drama, which soon loses its true accent of passion and fidelity to life.

Although the theorists lay down an elaborate classification of the various categories of sentiments, it is yet curious to note that in practice the sentiments that are usually favoured are the heroic and the erotic, with just an occasional suggestion of the marvellous. This accords well with the ideal and romantic character of the drama, as well as with the fabulous and supernatural elements which are freely introduced. The comic, under the circumstances, hardly receives a proper treatment. The Prahasana and the Bhāṇa profess to appeal to the comic sentiment, but not in a superior form ; and the survival of an insignificant and limited number of these types of composition shows that they did not succeed very well. The other sentiments are also suggested but they hardly become prominent. Even in the heroic or lofty subjects, an erotic underplot is often introduced ; and in course of time the erotic overshadows every other sentiment, and becomes the exclusive and universally appealing theme. It is true that the love-plots, which predominate in the drama, are not allowed to degenerate into mere portrayals of the petty domestic difficulties of a polygamic system, but the dramatists often content themselves with the developing of the pretty erotic possibilities by a stereotyped sentimental scheme of love, jealousy, parting and reunion. The sciences of Poetics and Erotics take a keen delight *ex accidenti* in minutely analysing the infinite diversities of the amatory condition and in arranging into divisions and subdivisions according to rank, character, circumstances and the like, all conceivable types of the hero, the heroine, their assistants and adjuncts, as well as the different shades of their feelings and gestures, which afford ample opportunities to the dramatic poect for utilising them for their exuberant lyrical stanzas. This technical analysis and the authority of the theorists lead to the establishment of fixed rules and rigid conventions, resulting in a unique growth of refined artificiality.

There is indeed a great deal of scholastic formalism in the dramatic theory of sentiment, which had a prejudicial effect on the practice of the dramatist. The fixed category of eight or nine sentiments, the subordination to them of a large number of transitory emotions, the classification of determinants and consequents, the various devices to help the movement of the intrigue, the normative fixing of dramatic junctures or stages in accordance with the various emotional states, the arrangement of the dramatic modes (Vṛttis)[1] into the elegant (Kauśikī), the energetic (Sāttvatī), the violent (Ārabhaṭī), and the verbal (Bhāratī) according as the sentiment is the erotic, the heroic, the marvellous, or only general, respectively—all these, no doubt, indicate considerable power of empirical analysis and subtlety, and properly emphasise the emotional effect of the drama ; but, generally speaking, the scholastic pedantry concerns itself more with accidents than with essentials, and the refinements of classification are often as needless[2] as they are

1 Bharata's description shows that the Vṛttis do not refer to mere dramatic styles, but also to dramatic machinery and representation of incidents on the stage.

2 *E.g.*, classification of Nāṭyālaṁkāras and Lakṣaṇas, the subdivisions of the Saṁdhyaṅgas, etc.

confusing. Although the prescriptions are not always logical but mostly represent generalisations from a limited number of plays, the influence of the theory on later practice is undoubted. As in the case of poetry, the result is not an unmixed good ; and, after the creative epoch is over, we have greater artificiality and unreality in conception and expression. Apart from various limitations regarding form, theme, plot and character, one remarkable drawback of the dramatic theory, which had a practical effect on the development of the drama as drama, lies in the fact that it enforces concentration of the sentiment round the hero or the heroine, and does not permit its division with reference to the rival of the hero, who therefore becomes a far inferior character at every point. The theorists are indeed aware of the value of contrast. To preserve the usual romantic atmosphere the ideal heroes are often contrasted with vicious antagonists. But the possibility is not allowed of making an effective dramatic creation of an antagonist (like Rāvaṇa, for instance), who often becomes a mere stupid and boastful villain. The Sanskrit drama is thereby deprived of one of the most important motifs of a real dramatic conflict.

Ten chief (Rūpaka) and ten to twenty minor (Uparūpaka) types of the Sanskrit drama are recognised by the Sanskrit dramatic theory.[1] The classification rests chiefly on the elements of subject-matter (Vastu), hero (Nāyak) and sentiment (Rasa), but also secondarily on the number of acts, the dramatic modes and structure. The distinctions are interesting and are apparently based upon empirical analysis ; they show the variety of dramatic experiments in Sanskrit ; but since few old examples of most of the types exist, the discussion becomes purely academic. The generic term of the drama is Rūpaka, which is explained as denoting any visible representation ; but of its ten forms, the highest is the Nāṭaka which is taken as the norm. The heroic or erotic

1 For an analysis of the various types and specimens, see D. R. Mankad, *Types of Sanskrit Drama,* cited above.

Nāṭaka, usually consisting of five to ten acts, is given a legendary subject-matter and a hero of elevated rank ; but the practice shows that it is comparatively free from minor restrictions. The Prakaraṇa is of the same length and similar structure, but it is a comedy of manners of a rank below royalty, with an invented subject and characters drawn from the middle class or even lower social grades, including the courtesan as the heroine and rogues of all kind. These two types, the Nāṭaka and the Prakaraṇa, are variations of the full-fledged drama ; but the details of the other types are not clear, and some of them are hardly represented in actual specimens. The Samavakāra, in three acts, is the supernatural and heroic drama of gods and demons, involving fight, fraud and disturbance, but of this we have no early specimen. For a similar want of authentic specimens, it is difficult to distinguish it from the Ḍima, usually in four acts, which is inadequately described, but which is given a similar legendary theme with a haughty hero, fight and sorcery, and the furious sentiment, its name being derived accordingly from a hypothetical root *ḍim*, 'to wound.' The Vyāyoga, as its name suggests, is also a military spectacle, with a legendary subject and a divine or human hero engaged in strife and battle ; but it is in one act, and the cause of disturbance is not a woman, the erotic and the comic sentiments being debarred. The type is old, and we have some specimens left, but they are of no great merit. We have, however, no living tradition of the Ihāmṛga, the Vīthī and the Utsṛṣṭāṇka. The first of these, usually extending to four acts but allowed to have only one, has a fanciful designation, supposed to be derived from its partly legendary and partly invented theme of the pursuit (Ihā) of a maiden, as attainable as the gazelle (Mṛga), by a divine or human hero of a haughty character ; but it in there is only a show of conflict, actual fight being avoided by artifice. The other two agree in having only one act and in having ordinary heroes, but the erotic and the pathetic sentiments (with plenty of wailings of women !) respectively predominate. The obscure name Vīthī, 'Garland,' is explained by its having a string of other subsidiary sentiments as well.[1] The name Utsṛṣṭāṅka is variously explained,[2] but since one of the explanations[3] speaks of its having a kind of inverted action, it is suggested that it may have had a tragic ending, contrary to ordinary practice. The Bhāṇa, on the other hand, is fortunate in having some old and late specimens. It is also a one-act play, erotic in character, but with only one hero-actor, namely the Viṭa ; it is carried on in monologue, the theme progressing by a chain of answers given by him to imaginary words 'spoken in the air,' and usually describing the love-adventures of the hero.[4] The comic is sometimes introduced in it ; and in this feature, as well as in the ribald character of the "hero," it has affinity with the next type, namely, the Prahasana, the one-act farce, the theme of which consists of the tricks and quarrels of low characters ; but the Sanskrit farce has little appeal because of its lack of invention and somewhat broad and coarse laughter.

As the very name Uparūpaka implies, the eighteen minor forms of the drama were evolved much later, but it is difficult to say at what period they came into existence. Bharata does not deal with any Uparupaka, except the Nāṭī (xviii. 106); and the first enumeration of seventeen varieties, without the designation of Uparūpaka and without any discussion, occurs in the Alaṃkāra section of the *Agni-purāṇa* (*c.* 9th century). Abhinavagupta only incidentally mentions nine, and the commentary on the *Daśarūpaka*

1 But the *Nātya-darpaṇa* suggests : *vakrokti-mārgeṇa gamanād vīthīva vīthī.*

2 *E.g.*, *utkramaṇonmukhā sṛṣṭir jīvitaṁ yāsāṁ tā utsṛṣṭikā śocantyaḥ striyas tābhir aṅkitatvād utsṛṣṭikāṅkaḥ* from the *Nāṭya-darpaṇa* (ed. GOS, Baroda, 1929, p. 130). Or, Viśvanātha's alternative suggestion : *nāṭakādyantaḥpātyaṅka-paricchedārthaṁ utsṛṣṭāṅkāḥ.*

3 *utsṛṣṭā viloma-rūpā sṛṣṭir yatra,* Viśvanātha in *Sahitya-darpaṇa.*

4 It is curious that in the Bhāṇa, Bharata forbids the Kauśikī mode, which gives scope to love and gallantry and which is eminently suitable to an erotic play ; but the element of Lāsya is allowed, of which, however, little trace remains in the existing specimens, but which is probably a survival in theory of what probably was a feature in practice. D. R. Mankad (*op. cit.*) puts forward the attractive, but doubtful, theory that the one-act monologue play the Bhāṇa, was the first dramatic type to evolve ; but in spite of its seemingly loose dramatic technique, it is too artificial in device to be primitive, or even purely popular in origin, while the existing specimens are late and have a distinctly literary form.

only seven in the same way. Some of the minor forms are doubtless variations or refinements on the original Rūpaka varieties, but there is some substance in the contention[1] that, as the Nāṭya came to be distinguished from the Nṛtya, the Rūpaka was mainly based on the Nāṭya and the Uparūpaka on the Nṛtya. It is highly possible that while the rhythmic dance was incorporating histrionics into itself, it was at the same time developing the minor operatic forms, in which dance and music originally predominated, but which gradually modelled itself on the regular drama. The Nāṭikā, for instance, is the lesser heroic and erotic Nāṭaka, just as the Prakaraṇikā, admitted by some, is a lesser Prakaraṇa ; but in both these there are opportunities of introducing song, dance and music. The Saṭṭaka is only a variation of the Nāṭikā in having Prakrit as the medium of expression ; while the Troṭaka, but for the musical element, is hardly distinguishable in itself from the Nāṭaka. The remaining forms have no representative in early literature and need not be enumerated here ; they show rather the character of pantomime, with song, dance and music, than of serious drama. Whatever scholastic value these classifications may possess, it is not of much significance in the historical development of the drama, for most of the varieties remain unrepresented in actual practice. The earlier drama does not appear to subscribe fully to the rigidity of the prescribed forms, and it is only in a general way that we can really fit the definitions to the extant specimens.

In the theoretical works, everything is scholastically classified and neatly catalogued ; forms of the drama, types of heroes and heroines, their feelings, qualities, gestures, costumes, make-up, situations, dialects, modes of address and manner of acting. All this perhaps gives the impression of a theatre of living marionetts. But in practice, the histrionic talent succeds in infusing

1 Mankad in the work cited. The term Uparūpaka is very late, the earlier designations being Nṛtyaprakāra and Geyarūpaka. On the technical difference between Rūpaka and Uparūpaka, see Hemacandra, *Kāvyānuśāsana*, ed. NSP, Comm. p. 329 f.

blood into the puppets and translating dry formulas into lively forms of beauty, while poetic genius overcomes learned scholasticism and creates a drama from the conflict of types and circumstances.

CHAPTER II

FROM ASVAGHOṢA TO KĀLIDĀSA

1. AŚVAGHOṢA AND HIS SCHOOL

Fifty years ago Aśvaghoṣa was nothing more than a name, but to-day all his important works have been published, and he is recognised as the first great Kāvya-poet and precursor of Kālidāsa. Very little however, is known of his personal history except what is vouchsafed by legends[1] and what can be gathered from his works themselves. The colophons to his Kāvyas agree in describing him as a Bhikṣu or Buddhist monk of Sāketa (Ayodhyā) and as the son of Suvarṇākṣī, 'of golden eyes,' which was the name of his mother. They also add the style of Ācarya and Bhadanta, as well as of Mahākavi and Mahāvādin. As an easterner, Aśvaghoṣa's admiration of the *Rāmāyaṇa*[2] is explicable, while it is probable that he belonged to some such Buddhist school of eastern origin as the Mahāsāṅghika or the Bahuśrutika.[3] He makes little display of purely scholastic knowledge; but the evidence of his works makes it clear that he had a considerable mastery over the technical literature which a Sanskrit poet was expected to possess, and a much wider acquaintance than most other Buddhist writers of the various branches of Brahmanical learning. His Sanskrit is not strictly faultless, but his easy command over it is undoubtedly not inferior to that of most

[1] A legendary biography of Aśvaghoṣa was translated into Chinese by Kumārajīva between 401 and 409 A.D.; extracts from it in W. Wassiljew, *Der Buddhismus*, St. Petersburg, 1860, p. 231 f. Cf. *JA*, 1908, II, p. 65 for Chinese authorities on the Aśvaghoṣa legend.

[2] On the poet's indebtedness to the *Rāmāyana*, which Cowell and Johnston deal with in the introductions to their respective editions of the *Buddha-carita*, see also A. Gawronski, *Studies about the Sanskrit-Buddhist Lit.*, Krakow 1919, pp. 27-40; C. W. Gurner in *JASB*, XXII, 1927, p. 347 f.; Winternitz, *HIL*, I, p. 512 f.

[3] See Johnston, *op. cit.*, pt. II, indrod, xxxi f.

Sanskrit writers. Everywhere great respect is shown to Brahmanical ideas and institutions, and it is not improbable that he was born a Brahman and given a Brahman's education before he went over to Buddhism. The obvious interest he shows in the theme of conversion in at least two of his works and the zeal which he evinces for his faith perhaps fortify this presumption. The Chinese tradition makes[1] Aśvaghoṣa a contemporary and spiritual counsellor of king Kaniṣka. The poet did not probably live later than the king, and it would not be wrong to put the lower limit of his date at 100 A.D. But in associating with Aśvaghoṣa the Sarvāstivādin Vibhāṣā commentary on the Abhidharma, or in naming the Vibhāṣā scholar Pārśva or his pupil Puṇyayaśas as having converted Aśvaghoṣa, the tradition, which cannot be traced further than the end of the 4th century and which shows more amiable than historical imagination, is perhaps actuated by the motive of exalting the authority of this school; for neither the date of the commentary is certain, nor can the special doctrines of the Sarvāstivādins be definitely traced in the unquestioned works of Aśvaghoṣa. That he was a follower of Hīnayāna and took his stand on earlier dogmatism admits of little doubt, but he was less of a scholastic philosopher than an earnest believer, and his emphasis on personal love and devotion to the Buddha perhaps prepared the way for Mahāyāna Bhakti, of which he is enumerated as one of the patriarchs. It is not necessary for us to linger over the question of his scholarship or religion;[2] but it should be noted that, while his wide scholarship informs his poems with a richer content, it seldom degenerates into mere pedantry, and the sincerity of his religious convictions

[1] On Chinese and other Buddhist sources concerning Aśvaghoṣa, see S. Lévi in *JA*, 1892, p. 201f.; 1896, II, p. 444 f.; 1908, II, p. 57 f.; 1928, II, p. 193; M. Anesaki in *ERE*, II, 1909, p. 159 f. and reff.; T. Suzuki in the work cited below. On Kaṇiṣka's date, see Winternitz, *HIL*, II, App. V, pp. 611-14 for a summary of different views.

[2] The question is discussed by Johnston in his introduction. Some doctrines peculiar to Mahāyāna have been traced in Aśvaghoṣa's genuine works, but his date is too early for anything other than primitive Mahāyāna. The recommendation of Yogācāra in *Saundarānanda* XIV. 18 and XX. 68 need not refer to the Yogācāra school, but perhaps alludes only to the practice of Yoga in general.

imparts life and enthusiasm to his impassioned utterances, and redeems them from being mere dogmatic treatises or literary exercises.

To later Buddhism Aśvaghoṣa is a figure of romance, and the Chinese and Tibetan translations of Sanskrit works, made in later times, ascribe to him a number of religious or philosophical writings, some of which belong to developed Mahāyāna.[1] In the absence of Sanskrit originals, it is impossible to decide Aśvaghoṣa's authorship ; but since they have not much literary pretensions it is not necessary for us to discuss the question. Among these doubtful works, the *Mahāyāna-śraddhotpāda-śāstra*, which attempts a synthesis of Vijñāna-vāda and Mādhyamika doctrines, has assumed importance from its being translated into English,[2] under the title 'Aśvaghoṣa's Discourse on the Awakening of Faith,' from the second Chinese version made about 700 A.D. ; but the internal evidence of full-grown Mahāyāna doctrine in the work itself puts Aśvaghoṣa's authorship out of the question. Another work, entitled *Vajrasūcī* 'the Diamond-needle,'[3] a clever polemic on Brahmanical caste, has also been published, but it is not mentioned among Aśvaghoṣa's works by the Chinese pilgrim Yi-tsing (7th century) nor by the *Bstan-ḥgyur*, and it shows little of Aśvaghoṣa's style or mentality ; the Chinese translation, which was made between 973 and 981 A.D., perhaps rightly ascribes it to Dharmakīrti. Of greater interest is the *Gaṇḍī-stotra-gāthā*, a small poem of twenty-nine stanzas, composed mostly in the Sragdharā metre, the Sanskrit text of which has been restored[4] and edited. It is in praise of the Gaṇḍī, the

1 A full list is given by F. W. Thomas in *Kvs*, introd., p. 26 f.

2 By T. Suzuki, Chicago 1900. Takakusu states that the earlier catalogue of Chinese texts omits the name of Aśvaghoṣa as the author of this work. The question of several Aśvaghoṣas is discussed by Suzuki and Anesaki, cited above. On this work see Winternitz *HIL*, II, pp. 361-62 and reff.

3 Ed. and trs. by Weber, *Über die Vajrasūcī*, in Abhandl. d. Berliner Akad., 1859, pp. 205-64, where the problem of authorship is discussed.

4 By A. Von Staël-Holstein, in Bibl. Buddh., no. XV, St. Petersburg 1913, and re-edited by E. H. Johnston in *IA*, 1933, pp. 61-70, where the authorship of Aśvaghoṣa has been questioned. Cf. F. W. Thomas in *JRAS*, 1914, p. 752 f.

Buddhist monastery gong, consisting of a long symmetrical piece of wood, and of the religious message which its sound is supposed to carry when beaten with a short wooden club. The poem is marked by some metrical skill, but one of its stanzas (st. 20) shows that it was composed in Kashmir at a much later time.[1]

The next apocryphal work is the *Sūtrālaṃkāra*,[2] over the authorship of which there has been a great deal of controversy.[3] The Chinese translation of the work, made by Kumārajīva about 405 A.D. assigns it to Aśvaghoṣa ; but fragments of the same work in Sanskrit were discovered in Central Asia and identified by H. Lüders,[4] who maintains that the author was Kumāralāta, probably a junior contemporary of Aśvaghoṣa, and that the work bore in Sanskrit the title of *Kalpanā-maṇḍitikā* or *Kalpanālamkṛtikā*. As the name indicates, it is a collection of moral tales and legends, told after the manner of the Jātakas and Avadānas in prose and verse, but in the style of the ornate Kāvya. Some of the stories, such as those of Dīrghāyus and Śibi, are old, but others clearly inculcate Buddha-bhakti in the spirit of the Mahāyāna. The work illustrates the ability to turn the tale into an instrument of Buddhist propaganda, but it also displays wide culture, mentions the two Indian Epics, the Sāṃkhya and Vaiśeṣika systems, the Jaina doctrines and the law-book of Manu, and achieves considerable literary distinction. It is unfortunate that the Sanskrit text exists only in fragments. Yuan Chwang informs us that Kumāralāta was the founder of the Sautrāntika school and came from Taxila ; it is not surprising, therefore, that

1 A work, entitled *Tridaṇḍa-mālā*, is ascribed to Aśvaghoṣa in *JBORS*, XXIV, 1938, pp. 157-60, but Johnston, *ibid*, XXV, 1939, p. 11 f. disputes it.

2 Translated into French on the Chinese version of Kumārajīva, by Ed. Huber, Paris 1908.

3 For references see Tomomatsu in *JA*, 1931, II, p. 135 f. Also L. de la Vallée Poussin, *Vijñaptimātrāsiddhi*, pp. 221-24.

4 *Bruchstücke der Kalpanāmaṇḍitikā des Kumāralāta* in Kongl Preuss Turfan-Expeditionen, Kleinere Sanskrit-Texte II, Leipzig 1926. The fragments are valuable, but unfortunately they are too few in number, and the work is still to be judged on the basis of the Chinese version. Some scholars hold that Aśvaghoṣa was the real author, and Kumāralāta only refashioned the work ; but it is now generally agreed that Aśvaghoṣa had nothing to do with its composition.

the work pays respect to the Sarvāstivādins, from whom the Sautrāntikas originated, or that some of its stories can be traced in the works of the school. In two stories (nos. 14 and 31), Kaniṣka appears as a king who has already passed away; the work, apparently written some time after Kaniṣka's death, cannot, therefore, be dated earlier than the 2nd century A.D.[1]

The three works, which are known for certain to be Aśvaghoṣa's, are; the *Buddha-carita*, the *Saundarananda* and the *Sāriputra-prakaraṇa*; and his fame as a great Sanskrit poet rests entirely on these. The first, in its original form of twenty-eight cantos, known to Yi-tsing and to the Chinese and Tibetan versions, is complete Mahākāvya on the life of the Buddha, which begins with his birth and closes with an account of the war over the relics, the first Council, and the reign of Aśoka. In Sanskrit[2] only cantos two to thirteen exist in their entirety, together with about three quarters of the first and the first quarter of the fourteenth (up to st. 31), carrying the narrative down to the Buddha's temptation, defeat of Māra and his enlightenment. It is the work of a real poet who, actuated by intense devotion to the Buddha and the truth of his doctrine, has studied the scripture and is careful to use the authoritative sources open to him, but who has no special inclination to the marvellous and the miraculous, and reduces the earlier extravagant and chotic legends to the measure and form of the Kāvya. Aśvaghoṣa does not depart in

1 If, however, Harivarman, a pupil of Kumāralāta, was a contemporary of Vasubandhu, then Kumāralāta could not have been a younger contemporary of Aśvaghoṣa, but should be dated not earlier than the 3rd century A.D.

2 Ed. E. B. Cowell, Oxford 1893, containing four additional cantos by Amṛtānanda, a Nepalese Pandit of the 19th century, who records at the end that he wrote the supplement in 1830 A.D., because he could not find a complete manuscript of the text. Also trs. into English by Cowell in *SBE*, vol. 49; into German by C. Cappeller, Jena 1922; into Italian by C Formichi, Bari 1912. Re-edited more critically, and translated into English, by E. H. Johnston in 2 vols., Calcutta 1936 (Panjab Univ. Orient. Publ. Nos. 31-32), which may be consulted for bibliography of other Indian editions and for critical and exegetical contributions to the subject by various scholars. Johnston remarks: "The textual tradition of the extant portion is bad, and a sound edition is only made possible by comparison with the Tibetan and Chinese translations." The Tibetan text, with German translation, under the title *Das Leben des Buddha von Aśvaghoṣa*, is given by F. Weller, in two parts, Leipzig 1926, 1928.

essentials from the received tradition, but he succeeds in infusing into his well conceived and vivid narrative the depth of his religious feeling and the spontaneity of his poetic emotion. Not unworthily praised is the skilful picture he draws of the young prince Sarvārthasiddhi's journey through the city, of the throng of fair women who hasten to watch him pass by, of the hateful spectacle of disease, old age and death which he encounters on the way, of the womanly blandishments and the political arguments of wisdom set forth by the family priest, which seek to divert the prince's mind from brooding thoughts of resignation, as well as of the famous night-scene of sleeping women, who in their moment of unconsciousness present all the loathsome signs of human misery and thereby hasten the flight of the prince from the palace. The requirement of a battle-scene in the Kāvya is fulfilled by the pleasingv ariation of the spirited description of the Buddha's fight with Māra and his hosts.[1] The work is, therefore, not a bare recital of incident, nor is it a dry and dogmatic exposition of Buddhist doctrine, but the Buddha-legend is conceived in the spirit of the Kāvya in respect of narrative, diction and imagery, and the poet's flame of faith makes the best lines of the poem quiver with the needed glow.

The *Saundarananda*,[2] all the eighteen cantos of which are preserved in Sanskrit, is connected also with the story of the Buddha ; but its actual theme is the conversion of his reluctant half-brother, Nanda, nicknamed Sundara for his handsome appearance. Nothing more than a mention of the fact of

[1] Perallelisms between Aśvaghoṣa and Kālidāsa in some of these passages, not only in ideals but also in diction and imagery, have been set forth in detail in Nandargikar's introduction to his edition of *Raghu-vaṁśa* (3rd ed., Bombay 1897, pp. 163-96) ; but the argument based thereon that Kālidāsa was earlier and Aśvaghoṣa imitated him has not found general support and is very unlikely.

[2] Discovered and edited by Haraprasad Shastri, Bibl. Ind., Calcutta 1910 ; critically re-edited and translated into English by E. H. Johnston, Oxford Univ. Press, 1928, 1932, which gives full bibliography. In spite of the richer content and wider interest of the *Buddha-carita*, Johnston is of opinion that "the handling of the *Saundarānanda* is altogether more mature and assured than that of the *Buddha-carita*" ; *contra* Winternitz, *HIL*, II, p. 262 note.

conversion is found in the *Mahāvagga* and the *Nidāna-kathā* ; and the subject is perhaps too slender to support an extensive poem. But the opportunity is taken, in the earlier part of the poem, to expand the legend with the proper Kāvya-embellishments, and in the latter part, to give expression at length to the poet's religious ideas and convictions. The first six cantos, therefore, describe the mythical foundation of Kapilavastu, its king, the birth of the Buddha and Nanda, the latter's love for his wife Sundarī, the forcible conversion of Nanda to the life of a monk, which he intensely dislikes, his conflict of feelings, and Sundarī's lament for her lost husband. All this is pictured skilfully in the manner and diction of the Kāvya, and possesses considerable narrative interest ; but in the rest of the poem there is not much of description or narration except the account of Nanda's ascent to heaven and yearning for Apsarases. Entire space is, therefore, devoted to an impassioned exposition of the evils of pride and lust, the vanities of the world and the joys of enlightenment. Here, more than in the imaginative presentation of the Buddha-legend, Aśvaghoṣa the preacher, no doubt, gets the upper hand of Aśvaghoṣa the poet ; but in this very conflict between his poetic temperament and religious passion, which finds delight in all that is delightful and yet discards it as empty and unsatisfying, lies the secret of the spontaneity and forcefulness which forms the real appeal of his poetry. It is not merely the zeal of the convert but the conviction of the importance of what he has to say that often makes him scorn mere verbal polish and learned ostentation and speak with an overmastering directness, the very truth and enthusiasm of which sharpen his gift of pointed phrasing, balance his sentences and add a new zest to his emotional earnestness.

In this respect Aśvaghoṣa's poetry lacks the technical finish and subtlety of the later Kāvya ; but it possesses freshness of feeling in the simplicity and nobility born of passionate faith. Aśvaghoṣa is fully conversant with the Brahmanical and Buddhistic learning of his day, while his metrical skill and use of rhetorical ornaments betoken his familiarity with the poetic art ;[1] but the inherent contrast between the poet and the artist, on the one hand, and the scholar and the preacher, on the other, often results in strange inequalities of matter and manner. At the conclusion of his poems, Aśvaghoṣa declares that he is writing for a larger public, and not merely for a learned audience, for the attainment of peace and not for the display of skill in the Kāvya. The question, therefore, whether he belongs to this or that school of thought, or whether he employs this or that metre or ornament in his poems is immaterial ; what is material to recognise is that religion is not his theme, but religious emotion, which supplies the necessary impetus and evolves its own form of expression without making a fetish of mere rhetoric or mere dogma. Aśvaghoṣa is a poet by nature, a highly cultivated man by training, and a deeply religious devotee by conviction. This unique combination is often real and vital enough to lift his poetry from the dead level of the commonplace and the conventional, and impart to it a genuine emotional tone which is rare in later poetry. What is most pleasing in his work to modern taste is his power of combining a sense of reality and poetry with the skill of art and scholarship. His narrative, therefore, is never dull, his choice of incident and arrangement never incoherent, his diction seldom laboured and his expression rarely devoid of elegant simplicity. If he is not a finished artist in the sense in which his successors are, nor even a great poet capable of great things, his poetic inspiration is genuine, and he never speaks in a tiresome falsetto. If his poetry has not the stress and discipline of chiselled beauty, it has the pliability and promise of unrefined form ; it has the sincerity and the throb, if not the perfectly ordered harmony, of full-grown music.

Aśvaghoṣa's versatility is indicated by his third work,[2] a Prakaraṇa or nine-act drama, entitled *Śāriputra-prakaraṇa* (or

1 On Aśvaghoṣa as scholar and artist, see Johnston, *op. cit.*, p. II, pp. xliv-lxxix.

2 H. Lüders, Das Śāriputraprakaraṇa, ein Drama des Aśvaghoṣa, in *Sitzungsberichte d Berliner Akad.*, 1911, p. 388 f.

Śāradvatīputra°), of which only fragments on palm leaf were discovered in Central Asia and a few passages restored by Lüders. Fortunately the colophon exists, and the question of authorship and name of the work is beyond doubt. Its theme is, again, an act of conversion connected with the Buddha, namely, that of Śāriputra and Maudgalyāyana, but the fragments give us little idea of the way in which the story, well-known from such older sources as the *Mahāvagga*, was handled. In having a Prakrit-speaking Vidūṣaka as one of the characters and in conforming to the requirements regarding division into acts, use of literary Prakrits,[1] ornamental metrical excursions[2] and other details, the fragments, however, afford clear testimony that the method and technique of a fairly developed Sanskrit drama[3] were already established in the 1st or 2nd century A.D. This presumption is confirmed also by the fragments of two other plays,[4] which were discovered with the remains of *Śāriputra-prakaraṇa*, but which bear no testimony of authorship and may or may not have been written by Aśvaghoṣa. The first has for its theme a Buddhist allegory, of which the details are not clear, although a whole leaf of the manuscript has ben recovered. It has Kīrti 'Fame,' Dhṛti 'Firmness' and Buddhi 'Wisdom' as characters, and apparently foreshadows such allegorical plays as Kṛṣṇamiśra's *Probodha-candrodaya* of a much later time. The Buddha himself appears, as in the drama described above, and all the characters, so far as the fragments go, speak Sanskrit. In having real, as well as allegorical, figures, it

1 On the Prakrits employed in this and the following plays, see Lüders in the works cited, and Keith, *HSL*, pp. 85-89. The Prakrit is literary and shows the influence of Sanskrit.

2 The metres employed (besides Śloka) are the usual classical ones ; Āryā, Upajāti, Śālinī, Vaṁśasthavila, Vasantatilaka, Mālinī, Śikhariṇī, Hariṇī, Suvadanā, Śārdūlavikrīḍita and Sragdharā.

3 *Contra* Sten Konow, *Indische Drama*, Berlin and Leipzig 1920, p. 50, but the grounds are weak.

4 H. Lüders, *Bruchstücke buddhistischer Dramen*, Kongl. Preuss. Turfan-Expeditionen, Kleinere Sankrit-Texte I, Berlin 1911, The question of authorship is undecided ; see Johnston, *op. cit.*, pp. xx-xxii.

resembles more the *Caitanya-candrodaya* of Kavikarṇapūra in its manner of treatment, but no definite conclusion is possible. The other play appears to have been also intended for religious edification, but from what remains of it we may infer that it was a social drama of middle class life of the type of the *Mṛcchakaṭika*. It concerns a young voluptuary, called simply the Nāyaka and probably named Somadatta, and his mistress Magadhavatī, apparently a courtesan converted to Buddhism. There are also a Prince (Bhaṭṭidālaka), an ever-hungry Vidūṣaka, named Kaumudagandha, a maid-servant, and a Duṣṭa or Rogue. The fragments are few in number and not consecutive, and it is difficult to make out the story. But in view of the uncertainty of the origin and antiquity of the Sanskrit Drama, these specimens, which belong probably to the same age, are highly interesting ; for they reveal the drama in its first appearance in a relatively perfected form, and clearly indicate that its origin should antedate the Christian era.

From the literary point of view, Aśvaghoṣa's achievement, we have seen, is marked not so much by crudity and primitiveness as by simplicity and moderation in language and style ; it is artistic but not in the extravagant manner of the later Kāvya. Its matter and poetic quality, therefore, more appealing than its manner and artistic effect. This is certainly different from the later taste and standard of verse-making ; and it is not surprising that with the exception of Kālidāsa, who is nearer his time, Aśvaghoṣa exercised little influence on later Sanskrit poets,[1] although the exception itself is a sure indication of the essential quality of his literary effort. Despite their religious zeal, the literary works of Aśvaghoṣa could not have been approved whole-heartedly also by the learned monks for his freedom of views and leaning towards Brahmanical learning.

1 The only quotation from Aśvaghoṣa in Alaṁkāra literature occurs in Rājaśekhara's *Kāvya-mimāṁsā*, ed. Gaekward's O. S., p. 18 (=*Buddha-c.* viii. 25). For other quotations see Johnston, *op. cit.*, pp, lxxix-lxxx, and F. W. Thomas, *Kvs*, introd., p. 29.

With the Buddhist writers of the Kāvya, on the other hand, Aśvaghosa was deservedly popular ; and some of their works were modelled so closely on those of Aśvaghoṣa that they were indiscriminately assigned to him in later times, with the result that the authors themselves came to be identified with him.[1]

Of the successors of Aśvaghoṣa, who are to be taken into account, not because they were Buddhists but because their works possess a wider literary appeal, we have already spoken of Kumāralāta, one of whose works is ascribed by the Chinese tradition to Aśvaghoṣa himself. Some of the poems[2] of Mātṛceṭa have likewise been attributed to Aśvaghoṣa by the Tibetan tradition, one of whose famous chroniclers, Tāranātha being of opinion that Mātṛceṭa is another name for Aśvaghoṣa ! Of the twelve works ascribed to Mātṛceṭa in Tibetan and one in Chinese, most of which are in the nature of Stotras and some belonging distinctly to Mahāyāna, only fragments *Śatapañcāśataka-stotra*[3] and *Catuḥśataka-stotra,*[4] or panegyric of one hundred and fifty and four hundred stanzas respectively, are recovered in Sanskrit. Both these works are simple devotional poems in Ślokas. They are praised by Yi-tsing, to whom Mātṛceṭa is already a famous poet, and who himself is said to have translated the first work into Chinese ; but they do not appear to possess much literary merit. That Mātṛceṭa, in spite of his name occurring distinctly in Yi-tsing and in the inscriptions was confused with Aśvaghoṣa, may have been due to the fact that he belonged to the same school and was probably a contemporary. A Tibetan version of another

1 Concerning the identifications, see F. W. Thomas in *Album Kern*, Leiden 1903, pp. 405-08 and *IA*, 1903, pp 345-60 ; also see *ERE*, VIII (1915), p 495f.

2 For a list of the works see F. W. Thomas, *Kvs*, introd., pp. 26-28.

3 Fragments published by S. Lévi in *JA*, XVI, 1910, pp. 433-56 and L de la Vallée Poussin in *JRAS*, 1911, pp. 759-77. Siegling is reported to have reconstructed about two-thirds of the Sanskrit text ; see Winternitz, *HIL*, II, p. 271 note. Both these works exist in Tibetan and Chinese.

4 The work is called Varṇanārha-varṇana in the Tibetan version and Central Asian fragments. For a translation of this text from Tibetan, see F. W. Thomas is *IA*, XXVIV, 1905, pp. 145-163.

work, called *Mahārāja-kanika-lekha*, in eighty-five stanzas, ascribed to Mātṛcitra, has been translated into English by F. W. Thomas,[1] who is probably right in thinking that Mātṛcitra is identical with Mātṛceṭa, and that king Kanika of the Kuśa dynasty addressed in this epistle of religious admonition is no other than the Kuṣāṇa king Kaniṣka.[2]

Of greater interest than the rather meagre works of Mātṛceṭa is the *Jātaka-mālā*[3] of Ārya Śūra, which consists of a free but elegant Sanskrit rendering, in prose and verse, of thirty-four[4] selected legends from the Pali *Jātakas* and the *Cariyā-piṭaka*, illustrating the Pāramitās or perfections of a Bodhisattva. Although sometimes marked by exaggeration, the tales are edifying. They were apparently composed for supplying ready illustrations to religious discourses, but the interest is more than religious. The work reveals a close study of Aśvaghoṣa's manner, and is inspired by the same idea of conveying in polished, but not too highly artificial, diction and noble doctrine of universal compassion ; and it is not surprising, therefore, that the author should be identified sometimes with Aśvaghoṣa. The attractive form in which the old stories are retold in the Kāvya-style shows that it was meant for a wider but cultivated audience, and we have Yi-tsing's testimony, confirmed by the existence of Chinese and Tibetan translations, that the work was at one time popular in India and outside. Ārya Śūra's date is unknown, but as another work of his[5] was translated into

1 *IA*, XXII, 1903, p. 345 f. The epistle is supposed to be Mātṛcitra's reply declining king Kanika's invitation to his court. The vogue of such epistolary exhortation is borne out by Nāgārjuna's *Suhṛllekha* and Candragomin's *Śiṣya-lekha*.

2 But *contra* S. C. Vidyabhusan in *JASB*, 1910, p. 477 f.

3 Ed. H. Kern in Harvard O. S. 1891 ; trs. J. S. Speyer in Sacred Books of the Buddhists, Oxford University Press, 1895. The title is a generic term for various poets have written 'garlands' of Jātakas.

4 The Chinese version contains only 14 stories.

5 For a list of other works ascribed to Ārya Śūra by Chinese and Tibetan traditions, see F. W. Thomas, *Kvs*, introd., p. 26 f.

Chinese in 434 A.D., he cannot be dated latter than the 4th century A.D.[1]

2. The Avadāna Literature

Closely connected with the *Jātaka-mālā*, which is also entitled *Bodhisattvāvadāna-mālā*, are the works belonging to what is called the Avadāna literature ; for the Jātaka is nothing more than an Avadāna (Pali Apadāna) or tale of great deed, the hero of which is the Boddhisattva himself. Their matter sometime coincides, and actual Jātaka stories are contained in the Avadāna works.[2] The absorbing theme of the Avadānas being the illustration of the fruit of man's action, they have a moral end in view, but the rigour of the Karman doctrine is palliated by a frank belief in the efficacy of personal devotion to the Buddha or his followers. The tales are sometimes put, as in the Jātaka, in the form of narration by the Buddha himself, of a past, present or future incident ; and moral exhortations, miracles and exaggerations come in as a matter of course. As literary productions they are hardly commendable, but their historical interest is considerable as affording illustration of a peculiar type of story-telling in Sanskrit.

The oldest of these collections is perhaps the *Avadāna-śataka*,[3] which is well known from some of its interesting narratives, but its literary merit is not high. The tales are arranged schematically, but not on a well conceived plan, into

1 We do not take here into account the works of other and later Buddhist writers, such as the *Catuḥ-śataka* of Āryadeva, the *Suhṛllekha* of Nāgārjuna, the *Śiṣya-lekha* and *Lokānanda-nāṭaka* of Candragomin, or the *Bodhicaryāvatāra* of Śāntideva, for they contribute more to doctrine or philosophy than to literature.

2 See Serge d'Oldenberg in *JRAS*, 1893, p. 304 ; and for Avadāna literature in general, see L. Feer's series of articles in *JA* between 1878 and 1884, and introd, to his translation of the *Avadāna-śataka*.

3 Ed. J. S Speyer, Bibl. Buddh., St. Petersburg 1902-09 ; trs. into French by L. Feer in *Annales du Musée Guimet*, Paris 1891. An earlier but lost Aśokāvadāna was composed, according to Przyluski, by a Mathurā monk about two centuries before Kaniṣka.

ten decades, each dealing with a certain subject, and are told with set formulas, phrases and situations. The first four decades deal with stories of pious deeds by which one can become a Buddha, and include prophecies of the advent of the Buddhas ; while the fifth speaking of the world of souls in torments, narrates the causes of their suffering with a tale and a lesson in morality. The next decade relates stories of men and animals reborn as gods, while the last four decades are concerned with deeds which qualify persons to become Arhats. The legends are often prolix, and there is more of dedactic than literary motive in the narration. The date of the work is uncertain, but while the mention of the Dīnāra as a current coin (Roman Denarius) is supposed to indicate 100 A.D. as the upper limit, the lower limit is supplied more convincingly by its translation, into Chinese in the first half of the 3rd century.

Hardly more interesting from the literary point of view is the *Divyāvadāna,*[1] the date of which is also uncertain, but which, making extensive use of Kumāralāta's work, cannot be earlier than the 1st century A.D. It is substantially a Hīnayāna text, but Mahāyāna material has been traced in it. Being probably a compilation of polygenous origin, extending over different periods of time, its matter and manner are unequal. The prose is frequently interrupted by Gāthās and pieces of ornate stanzas, but this is a feature which is shown by other works of this type. The language is reasonably correct and simple ; but debased Sanskrit, marked by Prakritisms, is not absent, and the diction is sometimes laboured and ornamental. We have here some really interesting and valuable narratives, specially the cycle of Aśoka legends, but they are scarcely well told ; the arrangement is haphazard and chaotic ; and the work as a whole possesses little literary distinction.[2]

1 Ed. E. B. Cowell and R. A. Neil, Cambridge 1886. Almost all the stories have been traced to other works.

2 For other collections of unpublished Avadānas, see Speyer and Feer, in the works cited, and Writernitz, *HIL*, II, pp. 290-92.

To the first century of the Christian era probably also belongs some parts of the *Mahāvastu,*[1] the 'Book of Great Events,' even if its substantial nucleus probably took shape in an earlier period. Although its subject is Vinaya, it contains, besides the life-story of the Buddha, some narratives of the Jātaka and Avadāna type ; but in its jumbling of confused and disconnected matter and for its hardly attractive style, it has small literary, compared with its historical, interest. The same remark applies more or less to the *Lalita-vistara,*[2] the detailed account of the 'sport' of the Buddha, the date of which is unknown and origin diverse. Whatever may be its value as a biography of the Buddha, its style is not unlike that of the Purāṇas. The narrative in simple but undistinguished Sanskrit prose is often interrupted by long metrical passages in mixed Sanskrit, and its literary pretensions are not of a high order.

3. The Literature of Tale and Fable

The Buddhist anecdotal literature perhaps reflects an aspect of the literary, as well as popular, taste of the time, which liked the telling of tales in a simple and unadorned, but distinctly elegant, manner ; for the origin of the Sanskrit *Pañcatantra* and the Prakrit *Bṛhatkathā,* which represent story-telling from another point of view, is perhaps synchronous, although the various extant versions of the two works belong to a much later period. The Avadāna, the didactic beast-fable and the popular tale are indeed not synonymous. While the Avadāna, closely related to the Jātaka, is clearly distinguishable as a Buddhist *gest,* which has a definite religious significance, the other two species are purely secular in object and character. The method of story-telling is also different ; for in the Jātaka or Avadāna, we have generally the application of a past legend

1 Ed. E. Senart, 3 vols, Paris 1882-97, with detailed sommary of contents and notes.

2 Ed, Rajendralal Mitra, Bibl. Ind., Calcutta 1877 ; English trs. by same (up to ch. xv), Bibl. Ind. 1881-86 ; re-editited by S. Lefmann, Halle 1902, 1908 ; complete French trs. by P. E. Foucaux in *Annales du Musée Guimet*, Paris 1884, 1892.

to a tale of to-day. In the Jātaka the Bodhisattva tells a tale of his past experience, but it is not narrated in the first person ; the device of first-hand narrative as well as of enclosing a tale, is a feature which characterises the classical method. The Sanskrit poetic theory ignores the Jātaka and Avadāna, presumably because they have a religious objective and seldom rises to the level of art, but it does not also clearly define and discriminate between the fable and the tale. The elaborate attempt to distinguish between the Kathā and the Ākhyāyikā,[1] as the invented story and the traditional legend respectively, is more or less academic, and has hardly any application to the present case. Some of the stories of the *Pañcatantra* are indeed called Kathās, but one of the versions of the entire work is styled *Tantrākhyāyikā*, while Guṇāḍhya's work is designated as the Great Kathā. Possibly no fine distinction is meant, and the terms Kathā and Ākhyāyikā are employed here in the general sense of story. A rigid differentiation, however, cannot perhaps be made in practice between the fable and the tale ; for the different elements in each are not entirely excluded in the other, nor isolated. The beast-fable, as typified by the *Pañcatantra*, is not seldom enriched by folk-tale and spicy stories of human adventure, while the tale, as represented by *Bṛhatkathā*, sometimes becomes complex by absorbing some of the elements of the fable and its didactic motive. Both these types, again, should be distinguished from the prose romance, the so-called Kathā and Ākhyāyikā, such as the *Harṣa-carita* and the *Kādambarī*, in which all the graces and refinements of the Kāvya are transferred from verse to prose, either to create an exuberantly fanciful story or to vivify and transform a legend or folk-tale.

The currency of tales and fables of all kinds may be presumed from remote antiquity, but they were perhaps not used for a definite purpose, nor reduced to a literary form, until

1 See S. K. De, The Kathā and the Ākhyāyikā in Classical Sanskrit in *BSOS*, III, p. 307f.—Daṇḍin (i-28) speaks of Ākhyāna as a general species, in which collections of tales like the *Pañcatantra* were probably included.

at a comparatively late period. The ancestor of the popular tale may have been such Vedic Ākhyānas as are preserved, for instance, in the Ṛgvedic dialogue-hymn of Purūravas and Urvaśī, or in such Brāhmaṇic legends as that of Śunaḥśepa; but it is futile to seek the origin of the beast-fable in the Ṛgvedic hymn of frogs (vii. 103), which panegyrises the frogs more from a magical than didactic motive, or in the Upaniṣadic parable of dogs (*Ch. Up*. i. 12), which represents the dogs as searching out a leader to howl food for them, but which may have been either a satire or an allegory. Nor is there any clear recognition of the fable in the Epics as a distinct literary *genre*, although the motifs of the clever jackāl, the naughty cat and the greedy vulture are employed for the purpose of moral instruction. But all these, as well as the Jātaka device of illustrating the virtues of Buddhism by means of beast-stories,[1] may have suggested the material out of which the full-fledged beast-fable developed in the *Pañcatantra*. In its perfected form, it differed from the simple parable or the mere tale about beasts, in having the latent didactic motive clearly and deliberately brought out and artistically conveyed in a definite framework and a connected grouping of clever stories, in which the thoughts and deeds of men are ascribed to animals. There is nothing simple or popular in such a form; and the beast-fable as an independent literary creation diverged considerably in this respect from the popular tale, which is free from didactic presentation and in which the more or less simple ideas of the people and their belief in myth and magic, as well as racy stories of human life, find a direct expression. In the case of beast-fable, again, the connexion with the courts of princes is cleared. The popular tale, no doubt, speaks of romantic prince and princess of a fairly-land; but the framework of collection of beast-fables like the *Pañcatantra*, which is delivered in the form of

[1] The Barhut Stūpa reliefs, depicting some of the stories, establish the carrency of the beast-fable at least in the 2nd Century B.C.

instruction to tender-minded young princes in statecraft and practical morality, leaves no doubt about one form of its emyloyment. It is thus closely related to the Nīti-śāstra and Arthaśāstra,[1] but it is not directly opposed to the Dharma-śāstra. The fact is important ; for even if the beast-fable inculcates political wisdom or expediency in the practical affairs of life, rather than a strict code of uprightness, it seldom teaches cleverness at the expense of morality.[2]

a. *The Pañcatantra*

The only collection of beast-fable and the solitary surviving work of this kind in Sanskrit is the *Pañcatantra,* which has come down to us in various forms ; but it is ā work which has perhaps a more interesting history than any in world-literature.[3] There can be little doubt that from the very beginning it had a deliberate literary form. Each of its five parts, dealing respectively with the themes of separation of friends (Mitra-bheda), winning of friends (Mitra-prāpti), war and peace (Saṃdhi-vigraha), loss of one's gains (Labdha-nāśa) and hasty action (Aparīkṣita-kāritva), is a narrative unit in itself ; but all together they form a perfect whole fitted into the frame of the introduction.

1 No direct influence of Kauṭily's *Artha-śāstra* can be traced in the *Pañcatantra.*

2 F. Edgerton in *JAOS,* XL, p, 271 f.

3 J. Hertel (*Das Pañcatantra, seine Geschichte und seine Verbreitung,* Leipzig and Berlin, 1914' Index, p. 451 f.) records over 200 different versions of the work known to exist in more than 50 languages (three-fourths of the languages being extra-Indian) and spreading over a region extending from Java to Iceland. For a brief résumé of this history, as well as for brief summary of the work, see Winternitz, *GIL,* III, pp. 294-311 ; Keith, *HSL,* pp. 248 f, 357 f.—The question whether the individual tales or the Indian fable itself as a species, were borrowed in their origin, from Greece is much complicated. Chronology is in favour of the priority of Greece, but the suggestion that India consciously borrowed from Greece is not proved. Some points of similarity may be admitted, but they may occur without borrowing on either side, At any rate, if reciprocal influences and exchanges occurred, India seems to have given more than it took. Benfey's position that the tale is entirely Indian, while the fable came from Greece, need not be discussed, for folklorists to-day no longer seek to find the birthplace of all tales and fables in any one country.

The stories are told, as in the case of the popular tale, in simple but elegant prose, and there is no attempt at descriptive or sentimental excursions or elaborate stylistic effects. The combining of a number of fables is also a characteristic which it shares with the popular tale, but they are not merely emboxed; there is, in the weaving of disjointed stories, considerable skill in achieving unity and completeness of effect. The insertion of a number of general gnomic stanzas in the prose narrative is a feature which is dictated by its didactic motive; but the tradition is current from the time of the Brāhmaṇas and the Jātakas. More interesting and novel, if not altogether original, is the device of conveniently summing up the moral of the various stories in pointed memorial stanzas, which are not general maxims but special labels to distinguish the points of individual fables. The suggestion[1] of a hypothetical prose-poetic Vedic Ākhyāna, in which the verse remained fixed but the prose mysterionsly dropped out, is not applicable to the case of the blend of prose and verse in the fable literature; for the prose here can never drop out, and the essential nature of the stanzas is gnomic or recapitulatory, and not dramatic or interlocutory. There must have existed a great deal of floating gnomic literature in Sanskrit since the time of the Brāhmaṇas, which might have been utilised for these passages of didactic wisdom.

The *Pañcatantra*, however, is not a single text, but a sequence of texts; it exists in more versions than one, worked out at different times and places, but all diverging from a single original text. The original,[2] which must have existed long before 570 A.D. when the Pahlavi version was made, is now lost; but neither its date nor its title nor provenance, is known with

[1] H Oldenberg in *ZDMG*, XXXVII, p. 54 f. XXXIX, p. 52 f; also in his *Zur Geschichte d. altindischen Prosa*, Berlin 1917, p. 53 f and *Lit. d. alten Indien*, cited above, pp. 44 f, 125 f. 153 f.

[2] The idea of a Prakrit original is discredited both by Hertel and Edgerton. The literature on the Pañcatantra is vast and scattered, but the results of the various studies will be found summarised in the works, cited below, of these two scholars.

certainty. The character and extent of the transformation, to which the work was subjected in course of time, make the problem of reconstruction one of great intricacy, but the labours of Hertel[1] and Edgerton[2] have succeeded in a great measure in going back to the primary *Pañcatantra* by a close and detailed examination of the various existing versions. That it originally contained five books with a brief introduction and was called *Pañcatantra*, is now made fairly certain, but there is a considerable discussion of the meaning of the word Tantra. It may denote nothing more than a book or its subject-matter, but since it occurs in the title *Tantrākhyāyikā* of one of the versions,[3] it may indicate a text of polity as an art. There is no evidence at all of authorship ; for the name Viṣṇuśarman, applied in the introduction to the wise Brahman who instructs, with these stories, the ignorant sons of king Amaraśakti of Mahilāropya in Deccan, is obviously as fictitious as the names of the king and the place. Hertel thinks that the work was composed in Kashmir, but his arguments are inadequate ; while nothing can be confidently inferred from the mention of Gauḍa or Ṛṣyamūka or of well known places of pilgrimage like Puṣkara, Vārāṇasī, Prayāga and Gaṅgādvāra.

The various important recensions of the *Pañcatantra* have been classified into four main groups,[4] which represent diversity of tradition but all of which emanate from the lost original. The first is the lost Pahlavi version,[5] from which were derived

1 *Das Pañcatantra*, cited above, as well as works and editions cited below.

2 *The Pañcatantra Reconstructed*, Text, Critical Apparatus, Indroduction and Translation 2 vols., American Orient. Soc., New Haven, Conn., 1924.

3 Jacobi, however, would translate it apparently as a collection of ākhyāyikā in tantras, 'die in bücher eingeteilte Erzählungssammlung.' See F. W. Thomas in *JRAS*, 1910, p. 1347.

4 Heetel, however, believes in two versions of one Kashmirian recension only as the archetype of the other three recensions, namely, the *Tantrākhyāyikā* and what he calls 'K'.—For a short genealogical table, setting forth the relationship of the four main recensions or groups, see Edgerton, *op. cit.*, II, p. 48, and for a full and detailed table of all known versions see Penzer's *Ocean of Story*, Vol. V. p. 242 (also by Edgerton).

5 Made by the physician Burzoë under the patronage of Chosroes Anūshīrwān (531-79 A.D.) under the title Karaṭaka and Damanaka.

the old Syriac[1] and Arabic[2] versions ; and it was through this source that the *Pañcatantra,* in a somewhat modified form, was introduced into the fable literature of Europe. The second is a lost North-western recension, from which the text was incorporated into the two North-western (Kashmirian) Sanskrit versions of Guṇāḍhya's *Bṛhatkathā,* made respectively by Kṣemendra and Somadeva (11th century A.D.).[3] The third is the common lost source of the Kashmirian version, entitled *Tantrākhyāyikā,*[4] and of the two Jaina versions, namely, the Simplicior Text, well known from Bühler and Kielhorn's not very critical edition,[5] and the much amplified Ornatior Text, called *Pañcākhyāna,* of Pūrṇabhadra (1199 A.D.).[6] The fourth is similarly the common lost source of the Southern Pañcatantra,[7]

1 Made by Būd, a Persian Christian, about 570 A.D. under the title Kalilag wa Damnag. Ed Schulthess, Berlin 1911.

2 Made by 'Abdallāh Ibnu'l-Muquffa about 750 A.D. under the style Kalīla wa Dimna. Ed. L Cheikho, 2nd Ed., Beyrouth 1923.

3 *Bṛhatkathā-mañjarī* xvi. 255 f ; *Kathā-sarit-sāgara* lx-lxiv. Leo von Mankowski has edited, with trans. etc., (from only one imperfect MS), Kṣemendra's version separately in *Der Auszug aus dem Pañcatantra in Kṣemendras Bṛhatkathāmañjarī,* Leipzig 1892. Lacôte, Hertel and Edgerton make it probable that the original *Bṛhatkathā* of Guṇāḍhya did not contain the *Pañcatantra.*—Somadeva's version of the *Pañcatantra* (according to Emenau's computation in *JAOS,* LIII, 1933, p. 125) contains 539 Ślokas, while Kṣemendra's in Mankowski's edition, has 306 ; but deducting tne stories not found in Somadeva, Kṣemendra's total would be about 270 only.

4 Ed, J. Hertel, Berlin 1910, containing two sub-versions ; also ed. J. Hertel in Harvard O. S., Cambridge Mass. 1915 ; trs J. Hertel, 2 vols., Leipzig and Berlin 1909.

5 Bomby Skt. Ser. 1868-69 ; also ed. L. Kosengarten Bonn 1848 ; ed. K. P. Parab, NSP, Bombay 1896 (revised Parab and V. L. Panshikar 1912). J. Hertel, Über die Jaina Recensionen des Pañcatantra in *BSGW,* LIV, 1902, pp. 23-134, gives selections of text and translation.

6 Ed. J. Hertel, Harvard Orient Ser., Cambridge Mass., 1908-12 ; trs into German by Schmidt, Leipzig 1901 ; into English by A. W. Ryder, Chicago 1925.—Pūrṇabhadra uses both the *Tantrākhyāyikā* and the Simplicior text.

7 Ed. J. Hertel (Text of recension *β*, with variants from recension *a*), Leipzing 1906 Text of recension *a*, ed. Heinrich Blatt, Leipzig 1930. See also J. Hertel, Über einen südlichen textus amplior des Pañcatantra in *ZDMG,* 1906-07 (containing translation of text). Of the Nepalese version' Bk. i-iii are included in Hertel's ed. mentioned above, while Bk. iv-v in his ed. of *Tantrākhyāyikā,* introd., p. xxvii. Selections from the Nepalese version published with trs. by Bendall in *JRAS,* 1888, pp. 465-501. See Hertel in *ZDMG,* LXIV, 1910, p. 58 f and *Das Pañcatantra,* pp. 37 f, 313 f.

the Nepalese version and the Bengali *Hitopadeśa.*[1] A detailed study of the character and interrelation of the various recensions and versions is not possible here, but some of their general characteristics may be briefly noted. The *Tantrakhyāyika* is perhaps the oldest Sanskrit version, and preserves the original text better and more extensively than any other version. But none of the recensions—not even the *Tantrākhyāyikā,* the claims of which have been much exaggerated by Hertel—represents in its entirety the primitive text. The North-western original of Ksemendra and Somadeva must have been a version made much later in Kashmir. Kṣemendra's fairly faithful, but dry, abstract suffers from its brevity, but Somadeva's narrative, in spite of a few omissions and some interruption of sequence by the introduction of extraneous tales, is normally clear and attractive. There is a great deāl of reshuffling of stories, as well as intrusion of additional matter, in both the Simplicior and Ornatior Texts, the former adding seven and the latter twenty-one new stories. The Southern recension exists in several sub-versions ; it is much abbreviated, but nothing essential appears to have been omitted, and only one complete story (The Shepherdess and her Lovers) is added. The *Hitopadeśa,*[2] which has currency mostly in Bengal, is practically an independent work, containing only four and not five books, by one Nārāyaṇa, whose patron was Dhavalacandra and who must have lived before 1373 A.D., which is the date of one of the manuscripts of the work. The compiler amplifies the stories derived in the main from the *Pañcatantra,* by drawing upon an unknown source, considerably omits, alters, remodels

1 Repeatedly printed in India, but not yet critically edited. The better known ed. is by P. Peterson, Bomb. Skt. Ser., 1887 ; also *Hitopadeśa nach Nepalischen Handschrift.* ed. H. Blatt, Berlin 1930 (Roman characters). The earliest ed. is that of A. Hamilton, London 1810, and the earliest trs. by C. Wilkins, London, 1787.

2 See J. Hertel, *Über Text und Verfasser des Hitopadeśa nach* (Diss.) Leipzig 1897, p. 37, and *Das Pañcatantra,* p. 38 f. In spite of omissions and alterations, the *Hitopadeśa* preserves over half the entire sub-stories of the Pañcatantra, and follows closely the archetype which it shares with the Southern recension.

the sequence of books and stories, and inserts large selections of didactic matter from *Kāmandakīya Nīti-sāra.*

Although Hertel is right in believing that the *Pañcatantra* was originally conceived as a work for teaching political wisdom, yet the fact should not make us forget that it is also essentially a story-book, in which the story-teller and the political teacher are unified, most often successfully, in one personality. There are instances where the professed practical object intrudes itself, and tedious exposition of polity prevails over simple and vivid narration ; but these instances are happily not too numerous, and the character of the work as a political text-book is never glaring. Inequalities doubtless appear in the stories existing in the different versions, but most of them being secondary ; it can be said without exaggeration that the stories, free from descriptive and ornamental digressions, are generally very well and amusingly told. They show the author as a master of narrative, as well as a perfect man of the world, never departing from an attitude of detached observation and often possessed of a considerable fund of wit and humour veiled under his pedagogic seriousness. If he makes his animals talk. he makes them talk well and the frankly fictitious disguise of the *fabliau* eminently suits his wise and amusing manner. With a few exceptions, the individual stories are cleverly fitted together into a complex but well planned form. The language is elegantly simple, and the author shows taste and judgment in never saying a word too much, except for a touch of the mock-heroic, and in realising that over-elaboration is out of place. The gnomic stanzas, if not the title-verses, are not always demanded by the narrative, but they are meant to give sententious summary of worldly wisdom and impressive utterance to very ordinary, but essential, facts of life and conduct. We do not know how far these stanzas are original, for some of them occur in the Epics and elsewhere ; but they are generally phrased with epigrammatic terseness, and form an interesting feature, in spite of the tendency to over-accumulate them. It is not

O.P. 220—12

without reason, therefore, that the work enjoyed, and still enjoys such unrivalled popularity as a great story-book in so many different times and lands.

b. *The Bṛhatkathā of Guṇāḍhya*

The popular tale is represented by a number of works in Sanskrit, but the earliest appears to have been the *Bṛhatkathā*, or 'the Great Story', of Guṇāḍhya, the Prakrit original of which is lost, but which is now known from three comparatively late Sanskrit adaptations. Its exact date[1] cannot be determind, but that it already received recognition before 600 A.D. is clear from the references to its importance by Bāṇa[2] and Subandhu[3] ; and there is nothing to show that it cannot be placed much earlier. If it belongs to a period after Christian era, it is not improbable that the work took shape at about the same time as the lost original of the *Pañcatantra* ; and to assign it to the fourth century A.D. would not be an unjust conjecture.[4] The recorded tradition informs us that the original *Bṛhatkathā* was composed in Paiśācī Prakrit ; and it is noteworthy that the literary form which the popular tale first assumed was one in Prakrit. Like the *Pañcatantra*, the work of Guṇāḍhya was undoubtedly a new literary creation, but the medium of expression perhaps indicates a difference in method and outlook.

1 On the question of date and author, see J. S. Speyer, *Studies about Kathāsaritsāgara*, Amsterdam 1908, p. 44 f. Bühler in his *Kashmir Report* summarily places the work in the first century A.D., with which F. Lacôte (*Mélanges Lévi*, p. 270) appears to agree ; but S. Lévi (*Théâtre indien*, 1891, p. 317) cautiously adjusts it to the 3rd century. See Keith in *JRAS*, 1909, p. 145f. Both Daṇḍin's *Daśa-kumāra-carita* and Subandhu's *Vāsavadattā* refer to the story of Naravāhanadatta.

2 *Harṣa-carita*, Introductory st. 17.

3 Ed. F. E. Hall, p. 110.

4 The alleged Sanskrit version of Durivinīta of the 6th century (R. Narasimhachar in *IA*, LXII, 1913, p. 204 and *JRAS*, 1913, p. 489 f ; Fleet in *JRAS*, 1911, pp. 186 f) and the supposed Tamil version of the 2nd century A.D. (S. K. Aiyangar in *JRAS*, 1906, p. 689 f ; and *Ancient India*, London 1911, pp. 328, 337) are too doubtful to be of any use for chronological purposes. See Lacôte, *Essai sur Guṇāḍhya et la Bṛhatkathā*, Paris 1908, p. 198 f.

An obviously legendary account of the origin of the work and the personality of the author is given, with some variations, in the introductory account of the two Kashmirian Sanskrit versions and in the apocryphal *Nepāla-māhātmya*[1] of a pseudo-Purāṇic character. It makes Guṇāḍhya an incarnation of a Gaṇa of Śiva, who under a curse is born at Pratiṣṭhāna on the Godāvarī and becomes a favourite of king Śātavāhana ; but the king has another learned favourite in Śarvavarman, the reputed author of the *Kātantra* grammar. Having lost a rash wager with Śarvavarman, with regard to the teaching of Sanskrit to the king, who had been put to shame by the queen for his ignorance of the language, Guṇāḍhya abjures the use of Sanskrit and society, and retires to the wild regions of the Vindhya hills. There, having learnt from another incarnated Gaṇa of Śiva the story of the *Bṛhatkathā*, originally narrated by Śiva to Pārvatī, he records it in the newly picked up local Paiśācī dialect, in 700,000 Ślokas, of which only one-seventh was saved from destruction and preserved in the work as we have it ! The Nepalese version of the legend, howeved, places Guṇāḍhya's birth at Mathurā and makes king Madana of Ujjayinī his patron ; it knows nothing of the wager but makes Guṇāḍhya, on being vanquished by Śarvavarman, write the story in Paiśācī for no other explicit reason than the advice of a sage named Pulastya. The legend is obviously a pious Śaiva invention modified in different ways in Kashmir and Nepal[2] ; from the reference in the *Harṣa-carita*, one may infer that it was known in some form to Bāṇabhaṭṭa ; but the value of biographical and other details is not beyond question. If Śarvavarman is introduced, Pāṇini, Vyāḍi and Vararuci-Kātyāyana also figure in the legend as contemporaries, although the Nepalese compiler does not appreciate the grammatical interest, nor the use of

1 Given in Lacôte, *op. cit.*, Appendix p. 291 f.

2 It is as a saint of Śaivism that Guṇāḍhya figures in the Nepalese work, as well as in a Cambodian inscription of about 875 A.D., which is of Śaivite inspiration (S. Lévi in *JA*, 1885, p. 412).

Prakrit. The association with Sātavāhana recalls one of the brilliant periods of Prakrit literature, and probably suggests that the employment of Sanskrit by the Kṣatrapa rulers probably found a counter-movement in favour of the patronage of Prakrit literature ; but Sātavāhana being a dynastic name, which may denote any of several kings, it does not help to solve the chronological problem.[1]

But much controversy has naturally centred round the value of the Guṇāḍhya legend regarding its testimony on the form of the lost work and its language. The legend speaks of Guṇāḍhya's work being written in Śloka and in the dialect of the wild people of the Vindhya regions, which is called the dialect of the Piśācas or Paiśācī. Daṇḍin, in his *Kāvyādarśa* (i. 38), appears to know the legend in some form, and states that the work was written in the Bhūta-bhāṣā ; but he thinks that it was a type of the prose romance known as Kathā, in which, of course, verse was allowed to be inserted. The three existing Sanskrit versions are all metrical, but this need not invalidate Daṇḍin's statement, if Daṇḍin can be presumed to have possessed a direct knowledge of the work already famous in his time. More inconclusive is the evidence regarding the nature and location of the dialect in which the work was composed. In accordance with the legend, the Paiśācī Prakrit is localised[2] as the dialect of the Vindhya regions lying near about Ujjayinī, but it is also maintained[3] that it was a North-western Prakrit of Kekaya and eastern Gāndhāra, which is regarded as the ancestor of the group of Dardic dialects now spoken in Kafirstan, Swat valley,

1 On the alleged Greek influence on Guṇḍhya's work, see Lacôte, *op. cit.*, pp. 284-86 who argues the opposite way to show that the Greek romance was influenced by the Indian. See Keith, *HSL*, p. 366 f.

2 Sten Konow in *ZDMG*, LXIV, 1910 p. 95 f and *JRAS*, 1921, p. 244 f ; Keith, *HSL* P. 269. Rājaśekhara (*Kāvya-mīmāṁsā*, p. 51) apparently holds the same view. Sten Konow's view, in brief, is that the Paiśācī was an Indo-Aryan language spoken by Dravidians in Central India.

3 G. Grierson in *JRAS*, 1905, p. 285 f, *ZDMG*, LXVI, 1912, pp. 49 f, at pp. 73-86, *JRAS*, 1921, p. 424 f, as well as in his *Linguistic Survey*, 1919, Vol. III, pt. 2 and in Hastings *ERE*, under Paiśāca, Vol. X (1918), p. 43 f.

Citral and adjacent places. The difficulty of arriving at a final conclusion[1] lies in the fact that the statements of fairly late Prakrit grammarians about Paiśācī Prakrit, as well as the doubtful fragments cited by them as specimens,[2] are meagre and uncertain. It is also not safe to argue back from the character and location of present-day dialects to those of a hypothetical Prakrit. The designation Paiśācī was perhaps meant to indicate that it was an inferior and barbarous dialect, and the sanction of a vow was required for its employment; but what we know about it from Prakrit grammarians and other sources makes it probable that it was an artificial from of speech nearer in some respects to Sanskrit than the average Prakrit. If it hardened *t* and *d* alone, it is a characteristic which may be equally applicable to a Vindhya dialect influenced by Dravidian and to a dialect of the North-west. The question, therefore, does not admit of an easy solution, although greater plausibility may be attached to the linguistic facts adduced from the Dardic dialects.

The exact content and bulk of the original *Bṛhatkathā* cannot also be determined, even to the extent to which we can approximate to those of the original *Pañcatantra*. We have two main sources of knowledge, derived from Kashmir and Nepal respectively, but both of them employ a different medium of expression, and are neither early nor absolutely authentic. The first is given by two metrical Sanskrit adaptations of Kashmir, namely, the *Bṛhatkathā-mañjarī*,[3] 'the Bouquet of Great

1 Lacôte, *op. cit.*, p. 51 f. Lacôte believes the Paiśācī to be based upon the Indo-Aryan language of the North-west, but spoken by non-Aryan people. He suggests a *via media* by stating that Guṇāḍhya picked up the idea of the dialect from travellers from the North-west, but his sphere of work lay around Ujjayinī! *Cf.* F. W. Thomas, Foreword to Penzer's ed. of *Ocean of Story*, Vol. IV pp. ix-x.

2 Hemacandra's Prakrit Grammar, ed. Pischel, iv. 303-24; for Mārkeṇḍeya, see Grierson in *JRAS*, 1913, p. 391. For a discussion of the Passages, see Lacôte, *op. cit.*, p. 201 f. Vararuci speaks of one Paiśācī dialect; Hemacandra appears to distinguish three varieties; Mārkaṇḍeya increases the number to thirteen! Different localities are mentioned, but one locality is agreed upon, *viz.*, Kekaya or N. W. Punjab.

3 Ed. Sivadatta and Parab, NSP, Bombay, 1901. Parts of it (introduction and first two stories), translated with the Roman text, by S. Lévi in *JA*, 1885-86.

Tale,' of the polymath Kṣemendra, and the *Kathā-sarit-sāgara,*[1] 'the Ocean of Rivers of Tales,' of Somadeva, the latter written between 1063 and 1082 A.D. and the former about a quarter of a century earlier.[2] Like Somadeva's work, that of Kṣemendra is divided into eighteen Lambhakas,[3] but it is of the nature of a condensed abstract, industriously and perhaps (as his other Mañjarīs shows) faithfully compiled. It consists of about 7,500 ślokas, as against more than 21,000 of Somadeva's work ; but Kṣemendra makes up for the brevity and dreariness of his narrative by a number of elegant, but mannered, descriptive and erotic passages.[4] Somadeva, on the other hand, is not anxious to abridge ; but he shows considerable restraint in avoiding useless elaboration, and tells his stories with evident zest and in a clear and attractive manner. At one time it was thought that these two Kashmirian versions drew directly from the Prakrit original, but the idea has now been discarded, not only from the comparative evidence of their contents but also in view of the discovery in Nepal in 1893 of the second important source, namely, the *Bṛhatkathā-śloka-saṃgraha* of Budhasvāmin,[5] which is also in Śloka, but unfortunately incomplete. Its date is unknown, but it is assigned, mainly on the probable date and

1 Ed. Durgaprasad and Parab, NSP, Bombay 1889 (reprinted 1903, 1915 etc.). H. Brokhaus edited i-v (with trs), 2 vols. Leipzig 1843, and vi-viii, iv-xviii (text only) in Abh für die Kunde d. Morgenlandes, II and IV, Leipzig 1862 and 1866. The work is well known from its Eng. trs. by C. H. Tawney under the title *Ocean of Story* in Bibl. Ind., Calcutta 1880-87, reprinted with notes and essays, etc., by N. M. Penzer in 10 vols., London 1924-28.

2 See Bühler, *Über das Zeitalter des kaśmirischen Dichters Somadeva,* Wien 1885. Somadeva wrote the work to please Sūryamatī, princess of Jalaṁdhara, wife of Ananta and mother of Kalaśa. Kṣemendra also wrote most of his works under king Kalaśa of Kashmir.

3 The division does not seem to be original, being missing in Budhasvāmin's version, which has Sarga division. The sections are called Gucchakas 'clusters' in Kṣemendra, and Taraṅgas 'billows' in Somadeva, according to the respective titles of their works.

4 On these descriptive passages, see Speyer, *op .cit.,* p. 17 f. Speyer estimates that Kṣemendra's work contains 7, 561 ślokas, Somadeva's 21, 388.

5 Ed. F. Lacôte, with trs., Paris 1908-29 (i-xxviii). The work was first discovered by Haraprasad Sastri in Nepal, but its importance was not realised till Lacôte edited the work and published the results of his investigations. The MS is from Nepal, but otherwise there is no sign of the Nepalese origin of the work.

tradition of the manuscript, to the 8th or 9th century A.D. Although this work is a fragment of 28 Sargas and 4,539 stanzas and also, as its name implies, an abbreviated abstract, its evidence is highly important regarding the existence of two distinct traditions of the text, which show considerable and remarkable divergences.[1]

The main theme of both the recensions appears to be the adventures of Naravāhanadatta, son of the gay and amorous Udayana, famed in Sanskrit literature, and his final attainment of Madanamañjukā as his bride and the land of the Vidyādharas as his empire ; but in the course of the achievement, he visits many lands and contracts a large number of marriages with beautiful maidens of all kinds and ranks. A vital difference, however, occurs in the treatment of the theme. While the Nepalese recension concentrates upon the main theme and gives a simple and connected narrative, comparatively free from extraneous matters, the Kashmirian recension is encumbered by a stupendous mass of episodic stories, indiscriminately accumulated and remotely connected, regardless of the constant break and obscuration of the original theme. The Nepalese recension, for instance, omits the introductory Guṇāḍhya legend, which occurs in the Kashmirian, and plunges at once into the story of Gopāla and Pālaka and of the love of Gopāla's son for Suratamañjarī, connecting it with the story of Naravāhanadatta, who is made the narrator of the tale of his twenty-six marriages. The Kashmirian authors are apparently aware of this beginning, but the necessity of commencing with the Guṇāḍhya legend and making Guṇāḍhya the narrator of the tale makes them shift the story of Gopāla, Pālaka and Suratamañjarī, and place it, unconnectedly, as a kind of appendix at the end. The Nepalese recension omits also the unnecessary tale of Udayana's winning of

[1] See Lacôte, *Essai* cited above, for a discussion of the Kashmirian versions, pp. 61-145, the Nepalese version, pp. 146-195, comparison of the two versions, pp. 207-18, and of the original *Bṛhatkathā*, pp. 1-59.

Padmāvatī, and does not think it desirable to provide royal ancestry for the courtesan Kaliṅgasenā, mother of Madanamañjukā, in order to conceal the questionable origin of the heroine. In the Kashmirian recension, the hero Naravāhanadatta does not even make his appearance till his birth in Bk. IV (in both versions), but the narrative of the hero is interrupted for two more books by the stories of Śaktivega and Sūryaprabha, who, recognising in the infant the destined emperor of the Vidyādharas, relate their own adventures as aspirants to the same rank. In this way, the main theme is constently interrupted by a vast cycle of legends, although Kṣemendra and Somadeva are not in perfect agreement, after Bk. IV, regarding the sequence and arrangement of the extra mass of material. It is clear that both the Kashmirian versions do not, in their zeal for collection, succeed in producing a unified or well-constructed work, although the narrative of Somadeva, who is a consummate story-teller, is marked, in spite of its bulk, by greater coherence and desire to preserve, however strenuously, the effect of the main story. The accretions, for example, not only bring in entirely irrelevent stories of Mṛgāṇkadatta and Muktāphalaketu, of expedition to the Camphor Land and the White Island for the winning of Ratnaprabhā and Alaṃkāravatī respectively, but also incorporate the Vikramāditya cycle of legends and interpolate versions of the entire *Pañcatantra* and the *Vetāla-pañcaviṃśati*. All this, with the addition of countless number of small tales, legends and witty stories, would justify the quaint, but appropriate, name of Somadeva's largest collection as the ocean of the streams of stories, and which in their rich mass would make the overwhelmed reader exclaim that here is indeed God's plenty !

How far these episodes and legend-cycles belonged to the original *Bṛhatkathā* cannot be precisely determined, but it is clear that much of them is remotely and sometimes confusedly connected with the main theme, and is entirely missing in the Nepalese recension. It is true that Budhasvāmin's work is specially styled a compendium (Saṃgraha) and that his omissions may have been dictated by a desire for abbreviation ; it is also possible[1] that Budhasvāmin is an independent writer rather than a mere epitomator, although he may have adhered to Guṇāḍya's narrative in the main. But it is clear, from the way in which the thread of the main story of Naravāhanadatta is kept from being lost in an interminable maze of loosly gathered episodes, that these interruptions or deviations from the predominant interest could not have occurred on a large scale in the original, if we are to presume from its reputation that it was a work of no small literary merit. It seems, therefore, that Budhasvāmin follows the original with greater fidelity[2] than Kṣemendra and Somadeva, who, apart from minor stories which they individually insert, are following a recension refashioned and much enlarged in Kashmir. In this recension the central theme appears to occupy, after the fashion of Kāvya-poets, a subordinate interest ; their essentials are often abridged and throughout sacrificed to the elaboration of subsidiary adventures, as well as to a somewhat confused insertion of tales derived from other sources. Whether this Kashmirian recension was in Paiśācī or in Sanskrit is not known ; but Somadeva distinctly speaks of having altered the language, and there are not enough verbal similarities[3] between Somadeva and Kṣemendra to warrant the supposition of a common Sanskrit original.

In the absence of the original work of Guṇāḍhya, an estimate of its literary merit would be futile. Each of the three adaptations have their own characteristics, which may or may not have been inherited from the original. Kṣemendra's abridged compilation is rapid, dreary and uninspiring, except in ornamental passages, which doubtless show the influence of the Kāvya. Somadeva's larger and more popular masterpiece has

1 Winternitz, *GIL*, III, pp. 315-17.

2 Lacôte, *Essai*, p. 207 f. Lacôte believes that the Kashmir recension is far removed form the original *Bṛhatkathā*, and was compiled about the 7th century A.D.

3 Speyer, *op. cit.*, p. 27 f.

been rightly praised for its immensely superior quality of vivid story-telling and its elegantly clear, moderate and appropriate style. Budhasvāmin's abstract, considered nearer to the original, is marked by a sense of proportion both in matter and manner, rapid narration, power of characterisation and simple description, as well as by a more bourgeois spirit and outlook suiting the popular tale ; but, in spite of these qualities, it is of a somewhat prosaic cast. It is difficult to say how far all the praiseworthy qualities, if not the blemishes, of these late versions, produced under different conditions, were present in the primary *Bṛhatkathā*, a verbal or even a confident substantial reconstruction of which is wellnigh impossible. To judge, however, from the principal theme, stories and characters, as well as from the general method and outlook, it is possible to assert that Guṇāḍhya must have been a master at weaving into his simple story of romantic adventure all the marvels of myth, magic and fairy tale, as well as a kaleidoscopic view of varied and well-conceived characters and situations. Although Naravāhanadatta is a prince, the story is not one of court life or courtly adventure, nor even of heroic ideals ; it is essentially a picture consonant with the middle class view of life and sublimated with the romance of strange adventure in fairy lands of fancy. It is certainly a work of larger and more varied appeal, containing a gallery of sketches from life, romantic as well as real ; and Keith is perhaps just in characterising it as a kind of bourgeois epic. The loves of the much-married Naravāhanadatta are perhaps too numerous and too light-hearted, like those of his famed father Udayana, but his chief and best love, Madanamañjukā, has only one parallel in Vasantasenā of the *Mṛcchakaṭika*; while in Gomukha we have a fine example of an energetic, resourceful and wise courtier and friend. It cannot be determined with certainty if the numerous tales of fools, rogues and naughty women existed in the original ; but they form an unparalleled store-house of racy and amusing stories, which evince a wide and intimate experience of human life and are in keeping with the humour and robust good sense of people at large.

4. The Dramas ascribed to Bhāsa

From the dramatic fragments of Aśvaghoṣa it is not unreasonable to assume that between him and Kālidāsa, there intervened a period of cultivation of the dramamatic art, which we find fully developed in the dramas of Kālidāsa, and which is warranted by Kālidāsa's own references to the works of Bhāsa, Somila and Kaviputra. Of the dramatic works of the last two authors we know nothing, but a great deal of facts and fancies are now available about Bhāsa's dramas.

Before 1912 Bhāsa was known only by reputation, having been honoured by Kālidāsa and Bāṇa as a great predecessor and author of a number of plays, and praised and cited by a succession of writers in later times[1] but since then, much discussion has centred round his name with the alleged discovery of his original dramas. Between 1912 and 1915, T. Ganapati Sastri published from Trivandrum thirteen plays of varying size and merit, which bore no evidence of authorship, but which, on account of certain remarkable characteristics, he ascribed to the far-famed Bhāsa. All the plays appear to have been based upon legendary material, but some draw their theme from the Epic and Purāṇic sources. From the Rāmāyaṇa, we have the *Pratimā* and the *Abhiṣeka*; from the Mahābhārata, the *Madhyama, Dūta-vākya, Dūta-ghaṭotkaca, Karṇa-bhāra, Uru-bhaṅga* and *Pañcarātra*; but the *Svapna-vāsavadatta, Pratijñā-yaugandharāyaṇa, Avi-māraka* and *Cārudatta* have legendary or invented plots, while the *Bāla-carita* deals with the Purāṇic Kṛṣṇa legend.[2] The

1 S. Lévi, *Théâtre indien*, Paris 1890, i. p. 157 f. and ii, pp. 31-32 gives a résu... literary references to Bhāsa known up to that time; other np-to-date references are collected together in Appendix C to C. R. Devadhar's ed. of the plays, cited below.

2 The legend is, of course, also found in the *Harivaṁśa*.—All the plays are available in a handy form in *Bhāsa-nāṭaka-cakra or Plays ascribed to Bhāsa*, published by C. R. Devadhar, Poona 1937, but it is better to consult the original Trivandrum editions, to which references are given below. Trs into English in two volumes by W. C, Woolner and L. Sarup, Oxford University Press, 1930-31. There are also numerous editions of some of the individual plays, but it is not necessary to enumerate them here.

plays were hailed with enthusiasm as the long-lost works of Bhāsa, but the rather hasty approbation of a novelty soon died down in a whirlwind of prolonged controversy. A large number of scholars of emience and authority whole-heartedly supported the attribution to Bhāsa,[1] but the reasons adduced did not win entire and universal satisfaction.[2] This led to a further and more detailed examination of the question, yielding some fruitful results, and new facts regarding the plays were also brought to light. Important arguments were advanced on both sides; but it is remarkable that there is not a single argument on either side which can be regarded as conclusive, or which may not be met with an equally plausible argument on the opposite side.[3] The problem to-day is delicately balanced; but since emphasis may be laid on this or that point, according to personal predilection, scholars, with a few exception, appear to have taken up unflinching attitudes and arrayed themselves in opposite camps. Between the two extremes lies the more sober view[4] which recognises that

1 For a bibliographical note of publications on Bhāsa till 1921, see V. S. Sukthankar in *JBRAS*, 1921-22, pp. 230-49. The following publications after 1921 are of interest: S. Lévi in *JA*, 1923, p. 19 f.; A. K. and K. R. Pisharoti in *BSOS* III, p. 107 f.; T. Ganapati Sastri in *JRAS*, 1924, p. 668 and *BSOS*, III, p. 627; A. K. Pisharoti, *Bhāsa's Works* (reprinted from Malayālam journal, Rasikaratna), Trivandrum 1925; K. R. Pisharoti in *BSOS*, III, p. 639, in *IHQ*, I. 1925, p. 103 f. in *JBRAS*, 1925 p. 246 f.; C. R. Devadhar in *ABORI*, 1924-25, p. 55 f.; C. Kunhan Raja in *Zeitschr, f. Ind. und Iran*, II' p. 247 f. and *Journal of Orient. Research*, Madras 1927, p. 232 f.; W. E. Clarke in *JAOS*, XLIV, p 101 f.; F. W. Thomas in *JRAS* 1922, p. 79 f. 1925, p. 130 f. and 1927, p, 877 f.; Keith in *BSOS*, III, p. 295 f.; H. Weller in *Festgabe Harmann Jacobi*, Bonn 1926, pp. 114-125; Winternitz in *Woolner Comm. Volume* 1940, p. 297 f.; A.D. Pusalker, *Bhāsa, a Study*, Lahore 1940, etc.

2 The first doubt appears to have been voiced independently by Ramavatar Sarma in *Śāradā*, I, Allahabad 1914-15, and by L. D. Barnett in *JRAS*, 1919, p. 233 f and in *BSOS*, 1920. I, pt. 3, pp. 35-38 (also *JRAS*, 1921, pp. 587-89, *BSOS*, III, pp. 35, 519, *JRAS*, 1925, p. 99). Among dissenters are also Bhattanatha Svamin in *IA*, XLV, 1916, pp. 189-95; K. R. Pisharoti in works cited above; and Hiranandra Sastri in *Bhāsa and Authorship of the Trivandrum Plays* in Memoirs of Arch. Surv. of India, No. 28, Calcutta 1926; S. Kuppusvami Sastri in Introd. to Śaktibhadra's *Āścarya-cūḍāmaṇi*, ed. Balamanorama Press, Madras 1929.

3 An admirably judicious summary of the important arguments on both sides is given by V. S. Sukthankar in the bibliographical note cited above, and in *JBRAS*, 1915, p. 126 f.

4 Notably Sukthankar, cited above, and Winternitz in *GIL*, III, pp.. 186, 645; but later on Winternitz is reported to have expressed the opinion that he is no longer a believer in Bhāsa's authorship of the plays (C. R. Devadhar's Preface to the ed. cited above).

a *prima facie* case for Bhāsa's authorship can be made out, but the evidence available does not amount to conclusive proof.

It will not be profitable to enter into the details of the controversy, but certain facts and arguments are to be taken into account before we can enter into a consideration of the plays. Since learned opinion is, not without reason, strangely divided, nothing is gained by dogmatic and sweeping assertions ; and it should be frankly recognised that the problem is neither simple nor free from difficulties. The first difficulty is the absence of the name of the author, in the prologues and colophons, of all the thirteen plays. It has been argued that this would testify to the great antiquity of the plays ; and it has ben assumed, plausibly but without proof, that the colophons were not preserved or that such details were left out in pre-classical times. But while nothing can be argued from our absolute lack of knowledge of pre-classical practice, the accidental and wholesale loss of the colophons of all manuscripts of all the thirteen plays by the same author is an assumption which demands too much from probability. On the other hand, the fact should be admitted at the outset that these plays are not forgeries, but form a part of the repertoire of a class of hereditary actors of Kerala (Cakkyars), that manuscripts of the plays are by no means rare, and that in omitting the name of the author, they resemble some of the plays of other classical authors similarly preserved by actors in Kerala. That they are not the absolutely original dramas of Bhāsa follows from this ; and the assumption that they are adaptations, in which the adapters had obvious reasons to remain nameless, is at least not less plausible. The next argument regarding the technique of the plays is perhaps more legitimate ; for there is undoubtedly a lack of conformity to the dramaturgic regulations of Bharata and his followers, which are more or less obeyed by the normal classical drama. But the argument is not as sound as it appears. The technical peculiarities[1] relate to the commencement of the Prologue by the Sūtradhāra, which is

1 M. Lindenau, *Bhāsa-studien*, Leipzig 1918, pp. 10-37.

supposed to have been noticed by Bāṇabhaṭṭa, the use of the word Sthāpanā for Prastāvanā, the introduction of stage-fights and death-scenes, the tragic ending in some plays, and the difference in the Bharata-vākya. It has been shewn in reply that, while Bāṇa's reference is either obscure, misunderstood or entirely irrelevant[1] the formal features recur also in Malayālam manuscripts of quite a number of Sanskrit plays of other authors and are capable of other explanations equally plausible. In the absence of adequate knowledge of pre-classical technique, such peculiarities, as are not confined to the dramas in question alone, are hardly of decisive value ; at most, we can infer the interesting existence of a different dramaturgic tradition, bur this does not prove the antiquity of the Trivandrum plays.

It has been also argued by the supporters of the attribution that expressions and ideas from these plays have been borrowed or exploited by authors like Kālidāsa and Bhavabhūti. While no strict proof or criterion of indebtedness is possible, it can be equally well argued, on the contrary, that the author or adapter of these anonymous plays plagiarised the alleged passages from standard sanskrit authors. The citations, again, from Bhāsa, or criticisms in the rhetorical or anthological literature,[2]

1 It is pointed out that Bāṇa's reference merely speaks of the Bhāsa dramas being commenced by the Sūtradhāra, a characteristic which, being true of all Sanskrit plays, has no special application here. The formula *nāndyante*, found in the Southern manuscripts *before* and *not after* the Nāndī-śloka is now known to be a characteristic of most South Indian manuscripts of Sanskrjt plays in general, and was, thus appearently a local practice, which is neither material nor relevant to the discussion. It is not clear if Bāṇa is really alluding to such technical innovations as the shortening of the preliminaries or the combining of the functions of the Sūtradhāra and the Sthāpaka. The rhetorical works are neither unanimous nor perfectly clear regarding the position of the *nāndyante* formula or the use of the word Sthāpanā. With regard to the employment of the Bharata-vākya, again, the Trivandrum plays do not follow a uniform practice which would support any definite conclusion regarding them. There are no such extraordinary Patākās in the Trivandrum plays as suggested by Bāṇa's description.

2 The thirteen anthology verses ascribed to Bhāsa (one of which occurs in the *Matta-vilāsa* and four are attributed to other authors) are missing in the Trivandrum plays. Even if this is suspicious, it proves nothing because of the notoriously uncertain and fluctuating character of anthological attributions. See F. W. Thomas in *JRAS*, 1927, p. 883 f.

relied upon by the supporters of the theory, have some plausibility, but they do not prove much ; for these authors do not unfortunately name the plays from which the passages are taken. It is true that one of the famous dramas of Bhāsa is cited and styled Svapna-vāsavadatta by some old authors ;[1] but here again the difficulty is that our present text of the Trivandrum Svapnanāṭaka does not contain some verses quoted by certain rhetoricians.[2] The difficulty is indeed not insuperable, inasmuch as one can imagine that they are misquotations, or that they are lost in the present recension ; but the wholly conjectural character of such an explanation is obvious. The discussion regarding references in the plays to Medhātithi's Bhāṣya on Manu[3] or to the *Artha-śāstra*[4] has not also proved very fruitful. And the least valid of all appears to be the Prakrit argument,[5] which presumes that archaisms in the Prakrit of the plays prove their earliness ; for it is now clear that some of them are obvious blunders, and that, of those which are genuine, archaisms of a similar type recur in the Malayālam manuscripts[6] of the plays of other authors, including those of Kālidāsa and Harṣa ; they are apparently local developments and cannot be made the safe basis of any chronological or literary conclusion.[7]

1 The argument regarding the impossibility of the plagiarism of the title does not, as Barnett points out, carry much weight, since we know of three *Kumāra-saṁbhavas*.

2 Sukthankar in *JARAS*, 1925, p. 135 f., shews that the reference of Rāmacandra and Guṇacandra in their *Nāṭya-darpaṇa* contains a situation and a stanza, quoted from a *Svapna-vāsavadatta* of Bhāsa, which really belongs, with some textual difference, to the Trivandrum play. F. W. Thomas in *JRAS*, 1928, p. 885 f., similarly deals with Abhinavagupta's citation missing in the Trivandrum play. *Cf* also F. W. Thomas in *JRAS*, 1922, p. 100 f.

3 Barnett in *BSOS*, III, pp. 35, 520-21 ; Keith in *BSOS*, III, p. 623 f. ; Sukthankar in *JBRAS*, 1925, pp. 131-32.

4 See Hirananda Sastri, *op. cit.*, p. 13 f.

5 W. Printz, *Bhāsa's Prakrit*, Frankfürt 1921 ; Keith in *BSOS*, III, p. 296 ; V. Lesny in *ZDMG*. LXXII, 1918, p. 203 f. ; Sukthankar in *JAOS*, XL, 1920, pp. 248-59, and *JBRAS*, 1925, pp. 103-117.

6 Pisharoti in *BSOS*, III, p. 109.

7 Sukthankar in *JBRAS*, 1925, p. 103 f. Even where the archaisms are genuine, it is, as R. L. Turner points out (*JRAS*, 1925, p. 175), dangerous to argue about date without full appreciation of possible dialectical differences, because a form may not necessarily indicate difference of age but only a difference of dialect or locality.

The historical discussion, again, regarding the identity of Bhāsa's patron, alleged to be mentioned in the word *rājasiṃha* of the Bharata-vākya, is similarly shown to be of very doubtful value.[1]

Leaving aside minor questions, these are, in brief, some of the important problems that arise out of the Trivandrum plays. It will be seen that the same material has led to absolutely contradictory results ; but none of the arguments advanced in support of Bhāsa's authorship is incontrovertible or resonably conclusive. Opinion, again, is sharply divided about the age of the plays,[2] between those who place them in the 5th century B.C. and those who bring them down by different stages to the 11th century A.D., the estimate varying by about sixteen centuries ! It is no wonder, therefore, that the whole question has run the normal course of enthusiastic acceptance, sceptical opposition and subdued suggestion of a *via media.* But beneath all this diversity of opinion lurks the fundamental divergence about the literary merits of the plays, the supporters claiming high distinction, worthy of a master-mind, and the dissenters holding that the works are of a mediocre or even poor quality. As the question of literary excellence is not capable of exact determination, the difference of opinion is likely to continue, according to the personal bias of the particular critic, until some objective factor or material would supply a conclusive solution to the problem. But it should be made clear that the whole discussion has now come to a point where the plays need no longer be made the fertile ground of romantic speculations. Already different aspects of the plays have been searchingly investi-

1 Sten Konow, *Ind. Drama,* p. 51, would assign the author of the plays to the reign of Kṣatrapa Rudrasiṁha I, *i.e.,* 2nd century A.D., but the arguments are not conclusive. Barnett conjectures that *rājasiṁha* is a proper name and refers to Paṇḍya Tēr-Māran Rājasiṁha I (c. 675 A.D.).

2 See Sukthankar, *JBRAS,* 1922, p. 233, for different estimates of the date by different scholars.

gated ;[1] and even if no definite solution is yet logically justified by the results of these intensive studies, they have helped to clear up misconceptions, negative baseless presumptions, and bring together a mass of material for further research.

These studies have now made it reasonable to asume that the Trivandrum plays, whether they are by Bhasa or by some other playwright, are of the nature of adaptations or abridgements made for the stage, and they have in fact been regularly used as stage-plays in the Kerala country. This very important fact should not be lost sight of in any discussion of the plays. It explains the traditional handing down of the plays without mention of the author's name, in closely resembling prologues, which are probably stage-additions, as well as the coincidence of formal technique and a large number of repetitions and parallels, which recur in these, as also in some other Sanskrit plays of Kerala.[2] Some unquestionably old Prakritic forms and genuine grammatical solecisms may have in this way been fossilised and preserved, although they do not necessarily prove the antiquity or authorship of the plays. The thirteen Trivandrum plays reveal undoubted similarities, not only verbal and structural, but also stylistic and ideological, which might suggest unity of authorship, —a theory indicated by the reference of Baṇa and others to a Bhasa Nāṭaka-cakra ; but since these are adaptations, and the originals are not known, it would be unsafe to postulate common authorship on similarities which occur also in plays of other known authors preserved in Kerala.

1 *E.g.*, on the Prakrits of the plays, by Printz, Sukthankar and others, as noted above ; on lexicographical and grammatical peculiarities, by C. J. Ogden in *JAOS*, XXXV, 1915, pp. 269 f. (a list of solecisms are given in App. B in Devadhara's ed.) ; on metrical questions, by V. S. Sukthankar in *JAOS*, XLI, 1921, pp. 107-30 ; on the sources of the Udayana legend, by F. Lacôte in *JA*, XIII, 1919, pp. 493-525 and P. D. Gune in *ABORI*, I, 1920-21, pp. 1-21 ; on a concordance of parallel and recurrent passages, by Sukthankar in *ABORI*, IV, 1923, p. 170 f. ; on the relationship between the *Cārudatta* and the *Mṛcchakaṭika* by Morgenstierne, *Ürber das Verhaltnis zwischen Cārudatta und Mṛcchakaṭika*, Leipzig 1921, S. K. Belvalkar in *Proc. of the First Orient Conf.*, 1922, p. 189 f., Sukthankar in *JAOS*, XLII, 1922, pp. 59-74, and J. Charpentier in *JRAS*, 1923, p. 599 f. ; etc.

2 Some of these are collected together in Hirananda Sastri, *op. cit.*, pp. 14-16.

A modified form of the theory makes an exception in favour of a limited number of the dramas, the merits of which have received wide recognition. It suggests that possibly Bhāsa wrote a *Svapna-vāsavadatta*[1] and a *Pratijñā-yaugandharāyaṇa*, closely related to it, of which the present texts give Malayālam recensions, and that the present *Cārudatta* is the fragmentary original of the first four acts of the *Mṛcchakaṭika* of Śūdraka, or at any rate it has preserved a great deal of the original upon which Śūdraka's drama is based.[2] But the authorship of the remaining plays is as yet quite uncertain. It must be said that the reasons adduced for these views undoubtedly make out a strong case ; but they are still in a great measure conjectural, and do not lead to any finality. It is possible also that the five one-act Mahābhārata pieces form a closely allied group, as the surviving intermediate acts of a lengthy dramatised version of the Mahābhārata story ; but here also we have no definite means of ascertaining it for a fact.

In view of these difficulties and uncertainties, it is clear that it behoves the sober student to adopt an attitude free from susceptibility to any hasty or dogmatic conclusion. The objective criterion proving insufficient, the ultimate question really comes to an estimate of the literary merits of the plays ; but on a point like this, opinion is bound to be honestly divergent and naturally illusive. The circumstance that all these plays, even including the limited number which may be, with some reason, ascribed to Bhāsa, are Malayālam adaptations or recensions of the original, causes a further difficulty ; for the plays are in a sense by Bhāsa, but in a sense they are not. The fact of their being recasts does not, of course, make them

1 Sukthankar, in *JBRAS*, 1925, 134 f., and Thomas in *JRAS*, 1928, p, 876 f., believe that the Trivandrum *Svapna* has probable minon changes, but has not undergone any great transformation.

2 Morgenstierne, Sukthankar and Belvalkar, as cited above. The *Cārudatta* is undoubtedly a fragment, but from internal evidence it is probable that the author or the compiler never contemplated writing only four acts. It is, however, not explained why this work alone is recovered as a fragment. See below under Śūdraka.

forfeit their connexion with the original, but the extent to which older material has been worked over or worked up by a later hand is unknown and uncertain. The suggestions that have been made about distinguishing the apparently older from the more modern matter and manner are more or less arbitrary ; for, in spite of unquestionably primitive traits, the process involves the difficulty of distinguishing the true Bhāsa from the pseudo Bhasa, not merely play by play, but scene by scene, and even verse by verse. It must also be admitted that all the plays are not, by whatever standard they are judged, of equal merit, and cannot be taken as revealing the alleged master-mind. One must feel that some of the scenes are very inferior and some of the verses are of feeble workmanship. At the same time, it can hardly be denied that here we have a series of plays, which are of varying merit but not devoid of interest ; that in part or in entirety they may not belong to Bhāsa, but they certainly represent a somewhat different tradition of dramatic practice ; and that, if they are not as old as some critics think, they are of undoubted importance in the literary history of the Sanskrit drama.

Leaving aside the fragmentary *Cārudatta* in four acts.[1] the two dramas which have won almost universal approbation are the *Svapna-vāsavadatta* and the *Pratijñā-yaugandharāyaṇa* ; and, in spite of obvious deficiencies, the approbation is not unjust. Both these works are linked together by external similarities and internal correspondences ; and their theme is drawn from the

1 Ed. T. Ganapati Sastri, Trivandrum Sansk. Ser., 1914, 1922 ; the text along with correspondences to Śūdraka's *Mṛcchakaṭika*, is reprinted by Morgenstiene, *op. cit.* The fragment has no Nāndī verse, and abruptly ends with the heroine's resolve to start out for Cārudatta's house. The dramatic incidents do not show any material divergence of a literary significance from Śūdraka's drama.—The Bhāsa plays are published in the following order by T. Ganapati Sastri from Trivandrum : *Svapna* (also 1915, 1916, 1923 1924), *Pratijñā* (also 1920), *Avi-māraka*, *Pañcarātra* (also 1917), *Bāla-carita*, *Madhyama* (also 1917), *Dūta-vākya* (also 1918, 1925), *Dūta-ghaṭotkaca*, *Karṇa-bhāra* and *Ūru-bhaṅga*—all in 1912, the last five in one volume, the others separately ; *Abhiṣeka* 1913 ; *Cārudatta* 1914 (also 1922) ; and *Pratimā* 1915 (also 1924).

same legend-cycle of Udayana,[1] the semi-historical beau ideal of Sanskrit literature, whose story must have been so popularised by the *Bṛhatkathā* that Kālidāsa assures us of its great popularity in his time at Avantī. The story of Udayana's two pretty amourettes supply the romantic plot to Harṣa's two elegant plays; but what we have here is not the mere banality of an amusing court-intrigue. In the *Pratijñā*, Udayana and Vāsavadattā do not make their appearance at all, but we are told a great deal about them, especially about Udayana's accomplishments, his courage, his love and impetuous acts. It is really a drama of political intrigue, in which the minister Yaugandharāyaṇa, as the title indicates, is the central figure; but it achieves a more diversified interest than the *Mudrā-rākṣasa* by interweaving the well-known romance of Udayana's love and adventure into the plot. Although the whole drama is characterised by simplicity and rapidity of action, it cannot be said that the plot is clearly and carefully developed. The ruse of the artificial elephant appears to have been criticised by Bhāmaha (iv. 40) as incredible, especially, as Udayana is described as one well-versed in the elephant-lore, but it is a device which is not unusual in the popular tale and need not be urged as a serious defect. It is, however, not made clear at what stage the incident of the music lesson, alluded to in IV. 18, actually took place,[2] nor why the captive king, at first treated with honour and sympathy, was thrown into prison

[1] On the legend of Udayana, see Lacôte cited above, and A. V. W. Jackson's introduction to *Priyadarśikā*, p. lxiii f. and references cited therein.

[2] It could not have come between Acts II and III for the jester and the minister know nothing of it; and Udayana's famous lute is sent by Pradyota to Vāsavadattā in Act II, while Udayana lies wonded in the middle palace. In Act III we are told Udayana, now in prison. somehow recovers the lute and catches sight of Vāsavadattā, as she goes in an open palanquin to worship at a shrine opposite the prison-gate. Nor is the music lesson made the occasion of the first meeting between Acts III and IV; and yet no other version is given in the play. Lacôte is perhaps right in pointing out that the allusive way in which the theme is doveloped in these plays proves that it was already familiar to their audience, and the details which the dramatist casually introduces or omits, are to be supplied from popular tradition. The hiatus, therefore, did not perhaps prove very serious or material to the audience of the plays.

so that "his fetters clank as he bows before the gods." Nevertheless, the drama finely depicts the sentiment of fidelity of a minister who is prepared even by sacrifice of himself to bring about a successful royal alliance. Some of the episodes, especially the domestic scene at the palace of Mahāsena Pradyota and the amusing interlude of the intoxicated page, are skilfully drawn; the characterisation, especially of Yaugandharāyaṇa, is vivid and effective; and the sustained erotic sub-plot, despite the non-appearance of the principal characters, enhances its main interest of political strategy.

The much praised *Svapna-vāsavadatta*, on the other hand, is less open to criticism. It is more effectively devised in plot,[1] and there is a unity of purpose and inevitableness of effect. The general story belongs to the old legend; but the motif of the dream is finely conceived, the characters of the two heroines are skilfully discriminated, and the gey old amourist of the legend and of Harṣa's dramas is figured as a more serious, faithful, if somewhat love-sick and imaginative, hero. The main feature of the play, however, is the dramatic skill and delicacy with which are depicted the feelings of Vāsavadattā, to whose noble and steadfast love no sacrifice is too great; while her willing martyrdom is set off by the equally true, but helpless, love of Udayana as a victim of divided affections and motives of statecraft.. It is a drama of fine sentiments; the movement is smooth, measured and dignified, and the treatment is free from the intrusion of melodrama, or of rant and rhetoric, to which such sentimental plays are often liable. If it is rough-hewn and unpolished, it also reveals the sureness of touch of a great dramatist; and to stint the word masterpiece to it is absurd and ungenerous,

1 But there are some trifling inconsistencies and lack of inventive skill, *e.g.*, the false report of Vāsavadattā's death is made the pivot of the plot, but the audience knows from the beginning that the queen is not really dead. One may, however, justify it by Coleridge's dictum of dramatic expectation, instead of dramatic surprise.

It must be frankly admitted, however, that these happy features are not possessed by the ten remaining Trivandrum plays, although each of them possesses some striking scenes or remarkable characteristics. Excepting the *Pañcarātra*, which extends to three acts, the Mahābhārata plays, whose literary merit has been much exaggerated, consist of one act each, and form rather a collection of slight dramatic scenes than complete and finished dramas. But they are meant to be of a sterner stuff, and make up by vigour what they lack in finish, although a lurking fondness is discernible for mock-heroic or violent situations. The *Madhyama* has a theme of the nature of a fairy tale, of which there is no hint in the Epic ; but the motif of a father meeting and fighting his own son unawares is not original, nor is the idea of the 'middle one', though cleverly applied, unknown, in view of the Brāhmaṇa story of Śunaḥśepa (*Ait. Br.*, vii. 15). What is original is the imagining of the situation out of the epic tale ; but the possibilities of the theme are hardly well-developed within the narrow limits of one act. There is also in the Epic no such embassy of Bhīma's son as is dramatised in the *Dūta-ghaṭotkaca*, which describes the tragic death of Abhimanyu and the impending doom of the Kurus ; there is some taunting and piquancy, but no action, and the whole scene is nothing more than a sketch. The *Dūta-vākya* is more directly based on the account of the embassy of Kṛṣṇa,, described in the Udyoga-parvan ; but it suffers also from the same lack of action, and the theme is exceedingly compressed and hardly completed. While the introduction of the painted scroll of Draupadī is an ingenious invention to insult the envoy effectively, the appearance of Viṣṇu's weapons, though original, is silly in serving no useful dramatic purpose. In spite of its tragic note and simplification of the original story, the *Karṇa-bhāra*, which describes the sad end of Karṇa, is scarcely dramatic and the only feature which appeals is the elevation of Karṇa's character ; it is not only a one-act play but really a one-character play. The same sympathy for the fallen hero is seen in the *Ūru-bhaṅga*, which represent the theme of Duryodhana's tragic death somewhat differently from that of the Epic. The noble resignation of Duryodhana and the invention of the poignant passage, which brings the blind king and his consort on the scene and makes Duryodhana's little son attempt to climb on his father's broken thighs, reveal some dramatic power ; but the introductory long description of the unseen fight is not happily conceived, and the play is also remarkable in having as many as sixty-six stanzas in one act alone ! The *Pañcarātra*, in three acts, is longer in extent, and perhaps shows more invention and possesses greater interest. It selects, from the Virāṭa-parvan, the dramatic situation of the Pāṇḍavas in hiding being forced into battle with the Kurus ; but it simplifies the epic story, the details of which are freely handled. While Trigarta's attack is omitted, Duryodhana's sacrifice, the motif of his rash promise, Abhimanyu's presence on the Kaurava side and capture by Bhīma are invented ; and Duryodhana and Karṇa are represented in more favourable light, Śakuni being the only villain in the piece. The number of characters is large in proportion to its length. The play is ingeniously titled, and there are some striking dramatic scenes ; but regarded as a story, it is far inferior to that of the Epic, and there is no substance in the suggestion that it is closer to the epic feeling and characterisation. The epic plays are, no doubt, of a heroic character, but they are far removed from the heroic age ; their novelty wins a more indulgent verdict than is perhaps justified by their real merit.

The Rāmāyaṇa plays are more ambitious and much larger in extent. The *Pratimā* seeks, in seven acts, to dramatise, with considerable omission and alteration, the almost entire Rāmāyaṇa story, but its interest centres chiefly round the characters of Bharata and Kaikeyī. Kaikeyī is conceived as *une femme incomprise*, a voluntary victim of public calumny, to which she patiently submits for the sake of her husband's honour and the life of her dear step-son ; and here again we find the same sympathy for the martyr and the persecuted. The development of the plot is skilfully. made to depend on the secrecy of Kaikeyī's noble motive for the seemingly greedy conduct of demanding the throne for her own son ; but for this, the plea of a Śulka (dowry) promised to her by Daśaratha has to be substituted for the two boons of the original, and the explanation of the secrecy of her motive itself at the end is rather far-fatched. The scene of the Statue Hall is connected with the same motif and create a situation ; but it is hardly worked out as the key-note of the play, as the title would suggest. The liberty taken in modifying the scene of Sītā's abduction, no doubt, substitutes a noble motive for the vulgar one of the greed for a golden deer ; but it fails to be impressive by making Rāma a childishly gullible person and Rāvaṇa a rather common, boastful villain. One of the striking scenes of the drama is that of Daśaratha's sorrow and death, which reveals a delicate handling of the pathos of the situation ; but, on the whole, the merits and defects of this drama appear to be evenly balanced. The *Abhiṣeka,* on the other hand, takes up the Rāmāyaṇa story at the point of the slaying of Vālin and consecration of Sugrīva, and supplies, in six acts, the episodes omitted in the other play, ending with the ordeal of Sītā and the consecration of Rāma. The play is perhaps so named because it begins and ends with a consecration. But there is not much dramatic unity of purpose behind the devious range of epic incidents. Its main feature is the sympathetic characterisation of Vālin and Rāvaṇa, but the other figures are of much less interest. Rāma is directly identified with Viṣṇu ; but he is here, more or less, a ruthless warrior, of whose treacherous slaying of Vālin no convincing explanation is oftered. In crossing the ocean, the mircale of divided waters is repeated from the episode of Vāsudeva's crossing the Yamunā in the *Bāla-carita*. Even if the *Abhiṣeka* is not a dreary summary of the corresponding parts of the Epic, it contains a series of situations rather than a sequence of naturally developed incidents, and is distictly feebler in dramatic character and quality than the *Pratimā*.

The *Bāla-carita,* in five acts, is similarly based upon a number of loosely joined incidents from the early life of Kṛṣṇa, but there are some features which are not found in the epic and Purāṇic legends.[1] If they are inventions, some of them (such as the great weight of the baby Kṛṣṇa, the gushing of water from the sands, or the incursion of Garuḍa and Viṣṇu's weapons) are clumsy and serve no dramatic purpose, while the introduction of Caṇḍāla maidens and of Kārtyāyanī, though bizzarre, is scarcely impressive. The erotic episodes of Kṛṣṇa's career are missing and the softer feeling is not much in evidence. There is a great deal of killing in most of the epic dramas mentioned above, but the *Bāla-carita* perhaps surpasses them all in melodramatic violence and ferocity. There is the slaying of the bull-demon, of the baby-girl hurled on the stone, as well as of the two prize-fighters and Kaṃsa himself, rapidly slaughtered in two stanzas! Kaṃsa, however, is not an entirely wicked person, but, as a fallen hero, is represented with much sympathy. There is, however, little unity or completeness of effect; the play is rather a dramatisation of a series of exciting incidents. As such, it is a drama of questionable merit; at least, it hardly deserves the high praise that has been showered on it with more zeal than reason.

The *Avi-māraka* depicts the love-adventure of a prince in disguise, whom a curse has turned, for the time being, into an outcast sheep-killer. It is interesting for its somewhat refreshing, if not original, plot, based probably on folk-tale,[2] of the love of an apparent plebeian for a princess. But from the outset it is clearly indicated that the handsome and accomplished youth must be other than what he seems; and the suspense is not skilfully maintained up to the unravelling of the plot at the end. As in the *Pratijñā,* the Vidūṣaka here is lively and interesting, but a Brahmin companion to an apparent outcast is oddly fitted. The denouement of a happy marriage, with the introduction of the

1 On the Kṛṣṇa legend see Winternitz in *ZDMG,* LXXIV, 1920, pp. 125-37.

2 The motifs of recognition and of the magic ring conferring invisibility are clearly important elements of the plot, derived apparently from folk-tale.

celestial busy-body, Nārada, is rather lame ; and the drama is not free from a sentimental and melodramatic atmosphere, in which the hero seeks suicide twice and the heroine once. For diversion from excess of sentiment, there are amusing scenes, such as the dialogue of the hero with the nurse and the small episode of the jester and the maid ; but there is enough of over-strained brooding and one long monologue in the course of the hero's sentimental burglary, in which the question is not merely of the number of lines, but one of vital connexion. There is, however, no justification for the claim that the *Avi-māraka* is a drama of love primitive in its expression and intensity.

It will be seen that all these plays are more or less faulty and are not as great as they are often represented to be. Judgment must ultimately pass in respect of the *Svapna* and the *Pratijñā*, which have the greater probability, at least from the literary point of view, of being attributed to Bhāsa. They also are not faultless ; but what appeals most to a student of the Sanskrit drama in these, as well as in the other plays, is their rapidity of action, directness of characterisation and simplicity of diction, which are points often neglected in the normal Sanskrit drama in favour of poetical excursions, sentimental excesses and rhetorical embellishments. The number of characters appearing never worries our author, but the stage is never overcrowded by the rich variety ; and, while most of the major characters are painted with skill and delicacy, the minor ones are not, normally, neglected. There is considerable inventive power ; and even if the constructive ability is not always praiseworthy, the swift and smooth progress of the plot is seldom hindered by the profusion of descriptive and emotional stanzas, and monostichs are freely employed. There is no lack of craftsmanship in transforming a legend or an epic tale into a drama, and daring modifications are introduced, although it may be admitted that the craftsmanship is not always admirable, nor the modifications always well judged. The style and diction are clear and forcible, but not uncouth or inelegant ; they have little of the succulence and 'slickness' of the ornate Kāvya. Even a casual reader will not fail to notice that the dramas do not possess elaborate art and polish of the standard type, but that there is, without apparent effort, vigour and liveliness of a rare kind. The plays defy conventional rules, and even conventional expression, but are seldom lacking in dramatic moments and situations. Perhaps a less enthusiastic judgment would find that most of the plays are of a somewhat prosaic cast, and miss in them the fusing and lifting power of a poetic imagination ; but it would be unjust to deny that they possess movement, energy and vividness of action as well as conisderable skill of consistent characterisation. There is nothing primitive in their art, on the one hand, and nothing of dazzling excellence, on the other, but there is an unadorned distinction and dignity, as well as an assurance of vitality. Even after deductions are made from exaggerated estimates, much remains to the credit of the author or authors of the plays. Whether all the aberrations, weaknesses and peculiarities indicate an embryonic stage of art, or an altogether different dramatic tradition, or perhaps an individual trait, is not definitely known ; nor is it certain that all or any one of these plays really belong to Bhāsa and to a period of comparative antiquity ; nor, again, can we determine the extent and nature of the recast to which they were submitted ; but what is still important to consider is that here we have, at least in some of the fascinatitg plays like *Svapna* and *Pratijñā*, a dramatist or dramatists of real power, whose unlaboured, but not forceless, art makes a direct and vitally human appeal. The deficiencies are patent, and a critic with a tender conscience may feel inclined to justify them ; but they need not diminish or obscure the equally patent merits. The dramas have wrestled with and conquered time ; and even if we cannot historically fit them in, they have an unmistakable dramatic, if not poetic, quality, and this would make them deserve a place of their own in the history of the Sanskrit drama.

CHAPTER III

KĀLIDĀSA

Of Kālidāsa's immediate predecessors we know little, and with the doubtful exception of the plays ascribed to Bhāsa, we know still less of their works. Yet, it is marvellous that the Kāvya attains its climax in him and a state of perfection which is never paralleld in its later history. If Aśvaghoṣa prepared the way and created the new poetry and drama, he did not finish the creation ; and the succession failed. In the interval of three or four centuries we know of other kinds of literary effort, but we have little evidence of the type which would explain the finished excellence of Kālidāsa's poetry. It must have been a time of movement and productivenes, and the employment of ornate prose and verse in the Gupta inscriptions undoubtedly indicates the flourishing of the Kāvya ; but nothing striking or decisive in poetry or drama emerges, or at least survives. What impresses us in Kālidāsa's works is their freedom from immaturity, but this freedom must have been the result of prolonged and diverse efforts extending over a stretch of time. In Kālidāsa we are introduced at once to something new which no one hit upon before, something perfect which no one achieved, something incomparably great and enduring for all time. His outstanding individual genius certainly accounts for a great deal of this, but it appears in a sudden and towering glory, without being buttressed in its origin by the intelligible gradation of lower eminences. It is, however, the effect also of the tyrannical dominance of a great genius that it not only obscures but often wipes out by its vast and strong effulgençe the lesser lights which surround it or herald its approach.

Of the predecessors of whom Kālidāsa himself speaks, or of the contemporaries mentioned by legends, we have very little information. There are also a few poets who have been confused, identified or associated with Kālidāsa ; they may have been contemporaries or immediate successors. Most of these, however, are mere names, and very scanty and insignificant works have been ascribed to them by older tradition or by more modern guess-work. Of these, the only sustained work is that of Pravarasena whose date is unknown, but who may have reigned in Kashmir in the 5th century A.D.[1] He wrote the *Setu-bandha* or *Rāvaṇa-vadha*[2] in fifteen cantos, but if it is in Prakrit, it is obviously modelled on the highly artificial Sanskrit Kāvya. The anthologies,[3] however, assign to him three Sanskrit stanzas, but they are hardly remarkable. Kahlaṇa (ii-16) mentions Candraka or Candaka as a composer of dramas under Tuñjina of Kashmir ; but of him and his work nothing is known, excepting small fragments preserved by Srīvara in his *Subhāṣitāvali*; and the identity of this dramatist with the Buddhist grammarian Candragomin, who also composed a drama (now preserved in Tibetan and entitled Lokānanda) is extremely hypothetical. Of Mātṛgupta, who is said to have been Pravarasena's predecessor on the throne of Kashmir, and who may or may not be identical with dramaturgist Mātṛguptācarya,[4] nothing remains except two stanzas contextually attributed by the Kashmirian Kahlaṇa in his *Rāja-taraṅgiṇī*

1 See Peterson in *Sbhv*, pp. 60-61. But Stein in his translation of the *Rāja-taraṇgiṇī*, i, pp. 66, 84 f., would place Pravarasena II as late as the second half of the 6th century. The ascription of the *Kauntaleśvara-dautya* to Kālsdāsa by Kṣemendra and Bhoja is used to show that Pravarasena, as the Vākāṭaka ruler of Kuntala, was a contemporary of Kālidāsa, but it is only an unfounded conjecture.

2 Ed. S. Goldschmidt, with German trs. (and word index by P. Goldschmidt), Strassburg and London 1880, 1884 ; ed. Sivadatta and K. P. Parab, with Skt. comm. of Rāmadāsa, NSP, Bombay 1895.

3 *Kvs.* introd., pp. 54-55.

4 S. K. De, *Sanskrit Poetics*, i, p. 32 ; fragments of this writer have been collected from citations in later works published by T. R. Chintamani in the *Journal of Oriental Research*, Madras, II (1928), pp. 118-28.

(iii. 181, 252), and one by another Kashmirian, Kṣemendra, in his *Aucitya-vicāra-carcā* (*ad* 22). Mātṛgupta, himself a poet, is said to have patronised Meṇṭha or Bhartṛmeṇṭha,[2] whose *Hayagrīva-vadha* elicited royal praise and reward. The first stanza of this work, in Śloka, is quoted by Kṣemendra,[3] as well as by some commentators and anthologists,[4] but it is obviously too inadequate to give an idea of the much lauded lost poem. Tradition associates Kālidāsa also with Ghaṭakarpara and Vetālabhaṭṭa. It has been suggested[5] that Ghaṭakarpara may be placed even earlier than Kālidāsa; but the laboured composition of twenty-four stanzas,[6] which passes under his name, hardly deserves much notice. It reverses the motif of the *Megha-dūta* by making a love-lorn woman, in the rainy season, send a message to her lover, and aims chiefly at displaying skill in the verbal trick of repeated syllables, known as Yamaka, exclusively using, however, only one variety of it, namely, the terminal. It employs a variety of metres,[7] but shows little poetic talent. Nor

1 These are also given as Mātṛgupta's in *Sbhv*, nos. 3181 and 2550. It is curious that the first stanza is assigned to Karpaṭika by Kṣemndra (*Aucitya-vicāra ad* 15).

2 Kahlaṇa, iii 125 f. 260-62. The word *meṇṭha* means an elephant-driver, and this meaning is referred to in a complimentary verse in *Sml* (4.61). The poet is sometimes called Hastipaka. Maṅkhaka (ii. 53) places Meṇṭha as a poet in the same rank with Bhāravi, Subandhu, and Bāṇa ; Śivasvāmin (xx. 47) equals him with Kālidāsa and Daṇḍin ; while Rājaśekhara thinks that Vālmīki re-incarnated as Meṇṭha !

3 *Suvṛtta-tilaka ad* iii. 16. The poem is also mentioned in Kuntaka's *Vakrokti-jīvita* (ed. S. K. De, Calcutta 1928, p. 243), and in the *Nāṭya-darpaṇa* of Rāmacandra and Guṇacandra (ed. GOS, Baroda 1929, p. 174).

4 Peterson. *op. cit.*, pp. 92-94. Small fragments are preserved in Śrīvara's *Subhāṣitavali*, nos. 203-204.

5 H. Jacobi, *Das Rāmāyaṇa*, p. 125 note. Jacobi relies mainly on the wager offered by the poet at the close that he would carry water in a broken pitcher for any one who would surpass him in the weaving of Yamakas ; but the poem may have been anonymous, and the author's name itself may have had a fictitious origin from the wager itself. The figure Yamaka, though deprected by Ānandavardhana, is old, being comprehended by Bharata, and need not of itself prove a late date for the poem.

6 Ed. Haeberlin in Kāvya-saṁgraha, p. 120 f., which is reprinted by Jivananda Vidyasagar in his Kāvya saṁgraha, I, Calcutta 1886, p. 357-66 ; ed. with a Skt. comm. by G. M. Dursch, Berlin 1828, with German verse trs.

7 Sundarī. Vasantatilaka, Aupacchandasika, Rathoddhatā, Puṣpitagrā, Upajāti and Drutavilambita, among which Rathoddhatā predominates.

is there much gain if we accept the attribution to this poet of the *Nīti-sāra*[1] which is simpler in diction but which is merely a random collection of twenty-one moralising stanzas, also composed in a variety of metres.[2] Of the latter type is also the *Nīti-pradīpa*[3] of sixteen stanzas, which is ascribed to Vetālabhaṭṭa ; but some of the verses of this shorter collection are indeed fine specimens of gnomic poetry, which has been much assiduously cultivated in Sanskrit.[4]

The doubtful poems of Kālidāsa, which comprise some twenty works form an interesting subject, but no serious or complete study has yet been made of them. Some of them, such as the elaborate Yamaka-kāvya, called the *Nalodaya*[5] in four cantos, and the slight *Rākṣasa-kāvya*[6] in some twenty stanzas, are now

1 Ed. Haeberlin, *op. cit.*, p. 504 f. ; Jivananda, *op. cit.*, pp. 374-80.

2 Upajāti, Śārdūlavikrīḍita, Bhujaṅgaprayāta, Śloka, Vaṁśasthavila, Vasantatilaka, Mandākrāntā, the Śloka predominating. Some of the stanzas are fine, but they recur in other works and collections.

3 Ed. Haeberlin, *op. cit.*, p. 526 f. ; Jivananda, *op. cit.*, pp. 366-72. The metres used are, Upajāti, Vasantatilaka, Śardūlavikrīḍita, Drutavilambita, Vaṁśasthavila, Mandākrāntā and Śloka.

4 Śaṅku is also regarded as a contemporary of Kālidāsa. He cannot be be indentical with Śaṅkuka, whom Kahlaṇa mentions as the author of the *Bhuvanābhyudaya*, a poem now lost ; for he belongs to the time Ajitāpīḍa of Kashmir (about 813-16 A.D.) ; see S. K. De, *Sanskrit Poetics*, i, p. 38. Śaṅkuka is also cited in the Anthologies, in one of which he is called son of Mayūra ; see Peterson in *Sbhv*, p. 127 and G· P. Quackenbos, *Poems of Mayūra*, pp. 50-52. Perhaps to this Śaṅkuka, cited as Amātya Śaṅkuka, is also attributed a drama, entitled *Citrotpalālambitaka* Prakaraṇa, from which a passage is quoted in the *Nāṭadapaṇa* of Rāmacandra and Guṇacandra (p. 86).

5 Ed. with the Subodhinī comm. of the Maithila Prajñākara-miśra, and with introd., notes and trs. in Latin by F. Benary, Berlin 1830 ; ed. Jagannath Sukla, with the same comm., Calcutta 1870 ; also ed. W. Yates, with metrical Engl. trs., Calcutta 1844. Pischel (*ZDMG*, LVI, p. 626) adduces reasons for ascribing its authorship to Ravideva, son of Nārāyaṇa and author probably also of the *Rākṣasa-kāvya*. With this view R. G. Bhandarkar (*Report, 1883-84*, p. 16) agrees. Ravideva's date is unknown, but Peterson (*JBRAS*, XVII, 1887, p. 69, note, corrected in *Three Reports*, 1887, p. 20 f.) states that a commentary on the *Nalodaya* is dated in Saṁvat 1664=1608 A.D. But A. R. Ramanatha Ayyar (*JRAS*, 1925, p. 263) holds that the the author of the *Nalodaya* was a Kerala poet, named Vāsudeva, son of Ravi, who lived in the court of Kulaśekhara and his successor Rāma in the first half of the 9th century (?), and wrote also another Yamaka-kāvya, *Yudhiṣṭhira-vijay* (ed. NSP, Bombay 1897) and an unpublished alliterative poem called *Tripura-dahana* : see below under ch. vi.

6 Ed. A. Hoefer in *Sanskrit Lesebuch*, Berlin 1849 ; ed. K.P. Parab, NSP, Bombay 1890, 1900 ; also in Jivananda, *op. cit.*, III, pp. 343-53 ; trs. by F. Belloni-Filippi in *GSAI*, XIX,

definitely known to be wrongly ascribed ; but it is possible that some of the Kālidāsa Apocrypha belongs to his contemporaries and followers. A more serious claim for Kālidāsa's authorship is made for the *Ṛtu-saṃhāra*[1] as a youthful production of the poet. It has been contested, however, that the poem may be young, but not with the youth of Kālidāsa. The Indian tradition on the question is uncertain ; for while it is popularly ascribed, Mallinātha, who comments on the other three poems of Kālidāsa, ignores it ;[2] and the artistic conscience of Sanskrit rhetoricians did not accept it, as did the other three poems, for purposes of illustration of their rules ; nor is any citation from it found in the early anthologies.[3] The argument that the poem is an instance of Kālidāsa's juvenilia[4] and is, therefore, not taken into account by commentators, anthologists and rhetoricians, ignores niceties of style, and forgets that the poem does not bear the obvious stigmata of the novice.[5] The Indian literary sense never thought it fit to preserve immaturities. The work is hardly immature in the sense that it lacks craftsmanship for its,

1906, p. 83 f. It is sometimes called Buddhivinoda or Vidvadvinoda Kāvya, a text of which is published by D. R. Mankad in *IHQ*, XIII, 1936, p. 692 f. ; see S. K. De in *IHQ*, XIV, pp. 172-76. There is a poet named Rākṣasa or Rākṣasa Paṇḍita, cited respectively in *Skm* (i. 90. 5) and *ŚP* (nos. 3810-11), although the stanzas in the anthologies are not taken from the poem. P. K. Gode (*Journal of Indian Hist.*, XIX, 1940, pp. 312-19) puts the lower limit of the date of the *Rākṣasa-kāvya* at 1000 A.D. on the strength of the date 1159 A.D. of a Jaina commentary on it.

1 Ed. W. Jones, Calcutta, 1792 (reproduced in fasc. by H. Kreyenborg Hannover 1924) ; ed. with a Latin and German metrical trs. by P. von Bohlen, Leipzig 1840 ; ed. W. L. Pansikar, with the comm. of Maṇirāma NSP, Bombay, 6th ed. 1922 (1st ed. 1906).

2 Mallinātha at the outset of his commentary on *Raghu*°, speaks of only three Kāvyas of Kālidāsa on which he himself comments.

3 Excepting four stanzas in *Sbhv*, of which nos, 1674, 1908 (=*Ṛts* vi. 16, 19) are assigned expressly to Kālidāsa, and nos- 1703, 1704 (=*Ṛts* i. 13, 20) are cited with *kayor api.* But on the composite text of this anthology, which renders its testimony doubtful, see S. K. De in *JRAS*, 1927, pp. 109-10.

4 Hillbrandt, *Kālidāsa*, Breslau 1921, p. 66 f. ; Keith in *JRAS*, 1912, pp. 1066-70, *JRAS*, 1913, pp 410-12, *HSL*, pp. 82-84 ; J. Nobel in *ZDMG*. LXVI, 1912, pp. 275-82, LXXIII, 1919, p. 194 f. and *JRAS*, 1913, pp, 401-10 ; Harichand Sastri, *L'Art poétique de 'Inde* (Paris 1917), pp. 240-42.

5 E. H. Johnston, introd. to *Buddha-carita*, p. lxxxi.

descriptions are properly mannered and conventional, even if they show some freshness of observation and feeling for nature ; its peculiarities and weaknesses are such as show inferior literary talent, and not a mere primitive or undeveloped sense of style.[1] It has been urged that Vatsabhaṭṭi in his Mandasor inscription borrows expressions and exploits two stanzas of the *Ṛtu-saṃhāra*. The indebtedness is much exaggerated,[2] but even if it is accepted, it only shows the antiquity of the poem, and not Kālidāsa's authorship. If echoes of Kālidāsa's phrases and ideas are traceable (e.g. ii. 10), they are sporadic and indicative of imitation, for there is nowhere any suggestion of Kālidāsa as a whole.[3] The poem is, of course, not altogether devoid of merit ; otherwise there would not have been so much controversy. It is not a bare description, in six cantos, of the details of the six Indian seasons, nor even a *Shepherd's Calender*, but a highly cultured picture of the seasons viewed through the eyes of a lover. In a sense it has the same motif as is seen in the first part of the *Megha-dūta* ; but the treatment is different, and there is no community of character between the two poems. It strings together rather conventional pictures of kissing clouds, embracing creepers, the wildly rushing streams and other tokens of metaphorical amorousness in nature, as well as the effect and significance of the different seasons for the lover. It shows flashes of effective phrasing, an easy flow of verse and sense of rhythm, and a diction free from elaborate complications, but the rather stereotyped descriptions lack richness of content and they are not blended sufficiently with human feeling.

1 This would rather rule out the suggestion that inasmuch as it shares some of Aśvaghoṣa's weaknesses, it is a half-way house between Aśvaghoṣa and Kālidāsa.

2 Cf. G. R. Nandargikar, *Kumāradāsa*, Poona 1908, p. xxvi, note.

3 Very pertinently Keith calls attention to Kālidāsa's picture of spring in *Kumāra*° iii and *Raghu*° ix, and of summer in *Raghu*° xvi (to which scattered passages from the dramas can also be added) ; but the conclusion he draws that they respectively show the developed and undeveloped style of the *same* poet is a matter of personal preference rather than of literary judgment.

Unlike lāter Sanskrit poets, who are often confident self-puffers, Kālidāsa expresses modesty and speaks little of himself. The current Indian anecdotes about him are extremely stupid, and show that no clear memory remained of him. He is one of the great poets who live and reveal themselves only in their works. His date, and even approximate time, is at worst uncertain, at best conjectural. His works have been ransacked for clues, but not very successfully ; but since they bear general testimony to a period of culture, ease and prosperity, they have been associated with the various great moments of the Gupta power and glory. The hypotheses and controversies on the subject need not occupy us here,[1] for none of the theories are final, and without further and more definite material, no convincing conclusion is attainable. Let it suffice to say that since Kālidāsa is mentioned as a poet of great reputation in the Aihole inscription of 634 A.D., and since he probably knows Aśvaghoṣa's works and shows a much more developed form and sense of style (a position which, however, has not gone unchallenged),[2] the limits of his time are broadly fixed between the 2nd and the 6th century A.D. Since his works reveal the author as a man of culture and urbanity, a leisured artist probably enjoying, as the legends say, royal patronage under a

[1] The literature on the subject, which is discussed threadbare without yielding any definite result, is bulky and still growing. The various views, however, will be found in the following : G. Huth, *Die Zeit des Kālidāsa* (diss.), Berlin 1890 ; B. Liebich, *Das Datum des Candragomin's und Kālidāsa's*, Breslau 1903, p. 28, and in *Indogerm. Forschungen*, XXXI, 1912-13, p. 198 f. ; A. Gawronski, *The Digvijaya of Raghu*, Krakau 1914-15 ; Hillebrandt, *Kālidāsa*, Breslau 1921 ; Pathak in *JBRAS*, XIX, 1895, pp. 35-43 and introd. to *Megha-dūta* ; Keith in *JRAS*, 1901, p. 578, 1905, p. 575, 1909, p. 433, *Ind. Office Cat.*, Vol. 2, pt. ii, p. 1201, *SD*, p. 143 f. ; also references cited in Winternitz, *HIL*, III, p. 40 f. W. F. Thomas, in *JRAS*, 1918, pp. 118-22, makes an attempt to revive the Diṇnāga legend.

[2] See Nandargikar, introd. to *Raghu*° ; Kshetresh Chattopadhyay in *Allahabad Univ. Studies*, II, p. 80, f. ; K. G. Sankar in *IHQ*, I, p. 312 f. To argue that Aśvaghoṣa is later than Kālidāsa is to presume, without sufficient reason, a retrogressive phase in literary evolution.

Vikramāditya,[1] it is not unnatural to associate him with Candragupta II (cir. 380-413 A.D.), who had the style of Vikramāditya, and whose times were those of properity and power. The various arguments, literary and historical, by which the position is reached, are not invulnerable when they are taken in detail, but their cumulative effect cannot be ignored. We neither know, nor shall perhaps ever know, if any of the brilliant conjectures is correct, but in the present state of our knowledge, it would not be altogether unjustifiable to place him roughly at 400 A.D. It is not unimportant to know that Kālidāsa shared the glorious and varied living and learning of a great time ; but he might not have done this, and yet be the foremost poet of Sanskrit literature. That he had a wide acquaintance with the life and scenes of many parts of India, but had a partiality for Ujjayinī, may be granted ; but it would perhaps be hazardous, and even unnecessary, to connect him with any particular geographical setting or historical environment.

Kālidāsa's works are not only singularly devoid of all direct personal reference, but they hardly show his poetic genious growing and settling itself in a gradual grasp of power. Very few poets have shown a greater lack of ordered development. Each of his works, including his dramas, has its distinctive characteristics in matter and manner , it is hardly a question of younger or older, better or worse, but of difference of character and quality, of conception and execution. All efforts,[2] therefore, to arrive at a relative

1 S. P. Pandit (Preface to *Raghu*°) admits this, but believes that there is nothing in Kālidāsa's works that renders untenable the tradition which assigns him to the age of the Vikramādity of the Saṁvat era, *i.e.*, to the first century B.C. The view has been developed in some recent writings, but arguments are hardly conclusive.

2 Huth attempts to ascertain a relative chronology on the basis of metres, but Kā idāsa is too finished a metrist to render any conclusion probable on metrical evidence alone ; see Keith's effective criticism in *SD*, p. 167. That *Kumāra*° and *Megha*° are both redolent of love and youth and *Raghu*° is mature and meditative, is not a

chronology of his writings have not proved very successful, and it is not necessary to indulge in pure guess-work and express a dogmatic opinion.

The *Kumāra-saṃbhava*[1] is regarded as one of Kālidāsa's early works, but it is in its own way as admirably conceived and expressed as his other poems. To the extent to which it has survived, it does not, however, complete its theme,—a defect which it shares with the *Raghu-vaṃśa,* also apparently left incomplete. The genuineness of the first seven cantos of the *Kumāra-saṃbhava* is beyond doubt ; but it brings the narrative down to the marriage of Śiva and Pārvatī, and the promise of the title, regarding the birth of the Kumāra, is not fulfilled. Probably canto viii is also genuine ; along with the first seven cantos, it is commented upon by Mallinātha and Aruṇagiri, and is known to writers on Poetics, who somewhat squeamishly censure its taste in depicting the love-sports of adored deities;[2] it also possesses Kālidāsa's characteristic style and diction. The same remarks, however, do not apply to the rest of the poem (ix-xvii) as we have it now. These

criterion of sufficienly decisive character. The dramas also differ in quality and character of workmanship, but is pure conjecture to infer from this fact their earliness or lateness. Similar remarks apply to the elaborate attempt of R. D. Karmarkar in *Proc. Second Orient. Conference*, Calcutta 1923, pp. 239-47. It must be said that the theories are plausible ; but their very divergence from one another shows that the question is incapable of exact determination.

1 Ed. A F. Stenzler, with Latin trs. (i-vii, London 1838) ; ed. T. Ganapati Sastri, with comm. of Aruṇagiri and Nārāyaṇa (i-viii), Trivandrum Skt. Ser. 1913-14. cantos viii-xvii first published in *Pandit'* Old Series, I-II, by Vitthala Sastri, 1866. Also ed. N. B. Parvanikar, K. P. Parab and W. L. Pansikar, with comm. of Mallinātha (i-viii) and Sitārāma (ix-xvii), NSP, 5th ed., Bombay 1908 (10th ed. 1927)) ; ed. with comm. of Mallinātha, Cāritravardhana and Sītārāma, Gujrati Printing Press, Bombay 1898. Eng. trs. by R. T. H. Griffith, 2nd ed., London 1879. It has been translated into many other languages, and edited many times in India—The NSP ed. contains in an Appendix Mallinātha's comm. on canto-viii, which is accepted as genuine in some South Indian manuscripts and editions (see *India Office Cat*, vii, p. 1419, no. 3764).

2 For a summary of the opinions, see Harichand Sastri, *Kālidāsa et l'Art poétique de l'Inde,* Paris 1917, p. 235 f.

cantos probably form a supplement[1] composed by some later zealous admirer, who not only insists upon the birth of Kumāra but also brings out the motive of his birth by describing his victory over the demon Tāraka. It is unbelievable that Kālidāsa abruptly left off his work ; possibly he brought it to a proper conclusion ; but it is idle to speculate as to why the first seven or eight cantos only survived. The fact remains that the authentic-city of the present sequel has not been proved.

Nevertheless, apart from the promise of the title, these genuine cantos present a finished and unified picture in itself. The theme is truly a daring one in aspiring to encompass the love of the highest deities ; but, unlike the later Greek poets to whom the Homeric inspiration was lost, the Sanskrit poets never regard their deities as playthings of fancy. Apart from any devotional significance which may be found, but which Kālidāsa, as poet never emphasised, the theme was a living reality to him as well as to his audience ; and its poetic possibilities must have appealed to his

1 Jacobi in *Verhandl. d. V Orient. Kongress*, Berlin 1881, II. 2, pp. 133-56 ; Weber in *ZDMG*, XXVII, p. 174 f. and in *Ind. Streifen*, III, pp. 217 f. 211 f. The arguments turn chiefly on the silence of the commentators and rhetoricians, and on grammatical and stylistic evidence, which need not be summarised here. Although the intrinsic evidence of taste, style and treatment is at best an unsafe guide, no student of Sanskrit literature, alive to literary niceties, will deny the obvious inferiority of the supplement. The extreme rarity of MSS for these additional cantos is also significant ; and we know nothing about their s urce, nor about the source of the commentary of Sītārāma on them (the only notice of a MS occurring in R. L. Mitra, *Notices*, x, no. 3289, p. 38). It must, however, be admitted that, though an inferior production, the sequel is not devoid of merit ; and there are echoes in it not only from Kālidāsa's works but also lines and phrases which remind one of later great Kāvya-poets. The only citation from it in later writings is the one found in Ujjvaladatta's commentary on the *Uṇādi-sūtra* (ed. T. Aufrecht, Bonn 1859, *ad* iv. 66, p. 106), where the passage *ravaḥ pragalbhāhata-bheri-saṁbhavaḥ* is given as a quotation with *iti Kumāraḥ* (and not *Kumāre*). It occurs as a variant of *Kumāra*° xiv. 32*a* in the NSP edition ; but it is said to occur also in Kumāradāsa's *Jānakī haraṇa*, which work, however, is cited by Ujjvaladatta (iii. 73) by its own name and not by the name of its author. If this is a genuine quotation from the sequel, then the sequal must have been added at a fairly early time, at least before the 14th century A.D., unless it is shown that the passage in question is a quotation from Kumāradāsa and an appropriation by the author of the sequel. The questionis re-opened by S. P. Bhattacharya in *Proceedings of the Fifth Orient. Conf.*, Vol. I, pp. 43-44.

imagination. We do not know exactly from what source[1] Kālidāsa derived his material, but we can infer from his treatment of the Śakuntalā legend, that he must have entirely rehandled and reshaped what he derived. The new mythology had life, warmth and colour, and brought the gods nearer to human life and emotion. The magnificent figure of the divine ascetic, scorning love but ultimately yielding to its humanising influence, the myth of his temptation leading to the destruction of Kāma as the emblem of human desire, the story of Umā's resolve to win by renunciation what her beauty and love could not achieve by their seduction, and the pretty fancy of the coming back of her lover, not in his ascetic pride but in playful benignity,—this poetic, but neither moralistic nor euhemeristic, working up of a scanty Purāṇic myth in a finished form is perhaps all his own. If there is a serious purpose behind the poem, it is merged in its total effect. It is, on the other hand, not bare story-telling or recounting of a myth ; it is the careful work of a poet, whose feeling, art and imagination invest his pictures with a charming vividness, which is at once finely spiritual and intensely human. His poetic powers are best revealed in his delineation of Śiva's temptation in canto iii, where the mighty effect of the few swift words, describing the tragic annihilation of the pretty love-god by the terrible god of destruction, is not marred by a single word of elaboration, but produces infinite suggestiveness by its extreme brevity and almost perfect fusion of sound and sense. A fine example also of Kālidāsa's charming fancy and gentle humour is to be found in the picture of the young hermit appearing in Umā's hermitage and his depreciation of Śiva, which evokes an angry but firm rebuke from Umā, leading on to the hermit's revealing himself as the god of her desire.

1 The story is told in *Mahābhārata,* iii. 225 (Bombaby ed.) and *Rāmāyaṇa,* i. 37 It is known to Aśvaghoṣa in some form, *Buddha-carita,* i. 88, xiii. 16.

The theme of the *Raghu-vaṃśa*[1] is much more diversified and extensive, and gives fuller scope to Kālidāsa's artistic imagination. The work has a greater height of aim and range of delivery, but has no known predecessor. It is rather a gallery of pictures than a unified poem; and yet out of these pictures, which put the uncertain mass of old narratives and traditions into a vivid poetical form, Kālidāsa succeeds in evolving one of the finest specimens of the Indian Mahākāvya, which exhibits both the diversity and plenitude of his powers.[2] Out of its nineteen cantos there is none that does not present some pleasing picture, none that does not possess an interest of its own; and there is throughout this long poem a fairly uniform excellence of style and expression. There is hardly anything rugged or unpolished anywhere in Kālidāsa, and his works must have been responsible for setting the high standard of formal finish which grew out of all proportion in later poetry. But he never sacrifices, as later poets often do, the intrinsic interest of the narrative to a mere elaboration of the outward form. There is invariably a fine sense of equipoise and an astonishing certainty of touch and taste. In the *Raghu-vaṃśa,*, Kālidāsa goes back to early legends for a theme, but it is doubtful if he seriously wishes to reproduce its spirit or write a Heldengedicht. The quality of the poem, however, is more important than its fidelity to the roughness of heroic times in which the scene is laid. Assuming that what he gives us is only a glorified picture of his own times, the vital question is whether he has painted excellent individuals or mere abstractions. Perhaps Kālidāsa is prone to depicting blameless regal characters, in whom a little blameworthiness had better

1 Ed. A. F. Stenzler, with a Latin trs., London 1832; ed. with the comm. Mallinātha by S. P. Pandit, Bombay Skt. Ser., 3 vols., 1869-74, and by G. R. Nandargikar, with English trs., 3rd revised ed., Bombay 1897; ed. with comm. of Aruṇagiri and Nārāyaṇa (i-vi), Mangalodaya Press, Trichur, no date. Often edited and translated in parts or as a whole.

2 The Indian opinion considers the *Raghu-vaṁśa* to be Kālidāsa's greatest poem, so that he is often cited as the Raghukāra *par excellence*. Its popularity is attested by the fact that about forty commentaries on this poem are known.

been blended ; but if they are meant to be ideal they are yet clearly distinguished as individuals ; and, granting the environment, they are far from ethereal or unnatural. Kālidāsa introduces us to an old-world legend and to an atmosphere strange to us with its romantic charm ; but beneath all that is brilliant and marvellous, he is always real without being a realist.

The earlier part of the *Raghu-vaṃśa* accords well with its title, and the figure of Raghu dominates, being supported by the episodes of his father Dilīpa and his son Aja ; but in the latter part Rāma is the central figure, similarly heralded by the story of Daśaratha and followed by that of Kuśa. There is thus a unity of design, but the entire poem is marked by a singularly varied handling of a series of themes. We are introduced in first canto to the vows and austerities of the childless Dilīpa and his queen Sudakṣiṇā in tending Vasiṣṭha's sacred cow and submitting to her test, followed by the birth of Raghu as a heavenly boon. Then we have the spirited narrative of young Raghu's fight with Indra in defence of his father's sacrificial horse, his accession, his triumphant progress as a conqueror, and his generosity which threatened to impoverish him,—all of which, especially his Digvijaya, is described with picturesque brevity, force and skill. The next three cantos (vi-viii) are devoted to the more tender story of Aja and his winning of the princess Indumatī at the stately ceremonial of Svayaṃvara, followed, after a brief interval of triumph and happiness, by her accidental death, which leaves Aja disconsolate and broken-hearted. The story of his son Daśaratha's unfortunate hunt, which follows, becomes the prelude to the much greater narrative of the joys and sorrows of Rāma.

In the gallery of brilliant kings which Kālidāsa has painted, his picture of Rāma is undoubtedly the best ; for here we have realities of character which evoke his powers to the utmost. He did not obviously wish to rival Vālmīki on his own ground, but wisely chooses to treat the story in his own way. While Kālidāsa devotes one canto of nearly a hundred stanzas to the romantic possibilities of Rāma's youthful career, he next accomplishes the very difficult task of giving, in a single canto of not much greater length, a marvellously rapid but picturesque condensation, in Vālmīki's Śloka metre, of the almost entire *Rāmāyaṇa* up to the end of Rāma's victory over Rāvaṇa and winning back of Sītā. But the real pathos of the story of Rāma's exile, strife and suffering is reserved for treatment in the next canto, in which, returning from Laṅkā, Rāma is made to describe to Sītā, with the recollective tenderness of a loving heart, the various scenes of their past joys and sorrows over which they pass in their aerial journey. The episode is a poetical study of reminiscent love, in which sorrow remembered becomes bliss, but it serves to bring out Rāma's great love for Sītā better than mere narration or description,—a theme which is varied by the pictures of the memory of love, in the presence of suffering, depicted in the *Megha-dūta*, and in the two lamentations, in different situations, of Aja and Rati. Rāma's passionate clinging to the melancholy, but sweet, memories of the past prepares us for the next canto on Sītā's exile, and heightens by contrast the grief of the separation, which comes with a still more cruel blow at the climax of their happiness. Kālidāsa's picture of this later history of Rāma, more heroic in its silent suffering than the earlier, has been rightly praised for revealing the poet's power of pathos at its best, a power which never exaggerates but compresses the infinite pity of the situation in just a few words. The story of Rāma's son, Kuśa, which follows, sinks in interest ; but it has a remarkably poetic description of Kuśa's dream, in which his forsaken capital city, Ayodhyā, appears in the guise of a forlorn woman and reproaches him for her fallen state. After this, two more cantos (xviii-xix) are added, but the motive of the addition is not clear. They contain some interesting pictures, especially that of Agnivarṇa at the end, and their authenticity is not questioned ; but they present a somewhat colourless account of a series of unknown and shadowy kings. We shall never know whether Kālidāsa intended to bring the narrative down to his own times and connect his own royal patron with the dynasty of Raghu ; but the poem comes to an end rather abruptly in the form in which we have it.[1] It will be seen from this brief sketch that the theme is not one, but many ; but even if the work has no real unity its large variety of subjects is knit together by the powers of colour, form and music of a marvellous poetic imagination. Objects. scenes, characters, emotions, incidents, thoughts—all are transmuted and placed in an eternising frame and setting of poetry.

The *Megha-dūta*,[2] loosely called a lyric or an elegy, is a much smaller monody of a little over a hundred stanzas[3] in the stately and melodious Mandākrāntā metre ; but it is no less characteristic

1 The last voluptuous king Agnivarṇa meets with a premature death ; but he is not childless ; one of the queens with a posthumous child is said to have succeeded. The Purāṇas speak at least of twenty-seven kings who came after Agnivarṇa, and ther is no reason why the poem should end here suddenly, but not naturally (see S. P. Pandit, Preface, P. 15 f. Hillebrandt, *Kālidāsa*, p. 42 f.). It has been uged that the poet's object is to suggest a moral on the inglorious end of a glorious line by depicting the depth to which the descendants of the mighty Raghu sink in a debauched king like Agnivarṇa, who cannot tear himself from the caresses of his women and who, when his loyal subjects and ministers want to have a sight of him, puts out his bare feet through the window for them to worship ! Even admitting this as a not unnatural conclusion of the poem, the abrupt ending iş still inexplicable.—C. Kunhan Raja (*Annals of Orient. Research*, Univ. of Madras, Vol. V, pt. 2, pp. 17-40) even ventures to question the authenticity of the entire second half of the *Raghu°*, starting with the story of Daśaratha ; but his reasons are not convincing.

2 The editions, as well as translations in various languages, are numerous. The earliest editions are those of H. H. Wilson (116 stanzas) with metrical Eng. trs.. Calcutta 1813 (2nd ed. 1843) ; of J. Gildemeister, Bonn 1841 ; of A. F. Stenzler, Breslau 1874. The chief Indian and European editions with different commentaries are : With Vallabhadeva's comm., ed. E. Hultzsch, London 1911 ; with Mallinātha's comm., ed. K. P. Parab, NSP, 4th ed., Bombay 1881, G. R. Nandargikar, Bombay 1894, and K. B. Pathak, Poona 1894 (2nd ed. 1916) (both with Eng. trs.) ; with Dakṣiṇāvartanātha's comm., ed. T. Ganapati Sastri, Trivandrum 1919 ; with Pūrṇa-sarasvatī's comm., ed. K. V. Krishnamachariar, Śrīvāṇī-Vilāsa Press Srirangam 1909 ; with comm. of Mallinātha and Cāritravardhana, ed. Narayana Sastri Khiste, Chowkhamba Skt. Ser., Benares 1931. English trs. by Col. Jacob, Poona 1870. For an appreciation, see H. Oldenberg, *op. cit.*, p. 217 f. The popularity and currency of the work are shown by the existence of some fifty commentaries.

3 The great popularity of the poem paid the penalty of interpolations, and the total number of stanzas vary in dsfferent versions, thus ; as preserved in Jinasena's Pārśvābhyudaya (latter part of the 8th century) 120, Vallabhadeva (10th century) 111, Dakṣiṇāvartanātha (*c.* 1200) 110, Mallinātha (14th century) 121, Purṇasarasvatī 110, Tibetan version 117, P'anabokke (Ceylonese version) 118. A concordance is given in Hultzsch, as well as a list of spurious stanzas.—On text-criticism, see introd. to eds. of Stenzler, Pathak

of the vitality and versatility of Kālidāsa's poetic powers. The theme is simple enough in describing the severance and yearnings of an imaginary Yakṣa from his beloved through a curse ; but the selection of the friendly cloud as the bearer of the Yakṣa's message from Rāmagiri to Alakā is a novel, and somewhat unreal, device,[1] for which the almost demented condition of the sorrowful Yakṣa is offered as an apology by the poet himself. It is perhaps a highly poetical, but not an unnatural, personification, when one bears in mind the noble mass of Indian monsoon clouds, which seem almost instinct with life when they travel from southern tropical sky to the snows of the Himalayas ; but the unreality of the poem does not end there. It has been urged that the temporary character of a very brief separation and the absolute certainty of reunion make the display of grief unmanly and its pathos unreal. Perhaps the sense of irrevocable loss would have made the motif more effective ; the trivial setting gives an appearance of sentimentality to the real sentiment of the poem. The device of a curse, again, in bringing about the separation—a motif which is repeated in another form in the *Abhijñāna-śakuntala*—is also criticised ; for the breach here is caused not by psychological complications, so dear to modern times. But the predominantly fanciful character of Sanskrit poetry recognises not only this as a legitimate means, but even departure on a journey,—on business as we should say to-day ; and even homesickness brings a flood of tears to the eyes of grown-up men and women !

and Hultzsh ; J. Hertel's review of Hultzsch's ed. in *Götting. Gelehrte Anzeigen*, 1912 : Macdonell in *JRAS*, 1913, p. 176 f. ; Harichand, *op. cit.*, p. 238 f. ; Herman Beckh, *Ein Beitrag zur Textkritik von Kālidāsa's Meghadūta* (Diss), Berlin 1907 (chiefly on the Tibetan version). A Sinhalese paraphrase with Eng. trs. published by the T. B. Panabokke, Colombo 1883.

1 Bhāmaha (i. 42) actually considers this to be a defect. The idea of sending message may have been suggested by the embassy of Hanūmat in the *Rāmāyaṇa* (cf. st. 104, Pathak's ed.), or of the Swan in the story of Nala in the *Mahābhārata*. Cf. also Kāmavilāpa Jātaka (no. 297), where a crow is sent as a messenger by a man in danger to his wife. But the treatment is Kālidāsa's own.

It is, however, not necessary to exaggerate the artistic insufficiency of the device ; for, the attitude is different, but not the sense of sorrow. If we leave aside the setting, the poem gives a true and poignant picture of the sorrow of parted lovers, and in this lies its real pathos. It is true that the poem is invested with a highly imaginative atmosphere ; it speaks of a dremland of fancy, its characters are semi-divine beings, and its imagery is accordingly adapted ; but all this does not negate its very human and genuine expression of the erotic sentiment. Its vividness of touch has led poeple even to imagine that it gives a poetic form to the poet's own personal experience ; but of this, one can never be sure. There is little of subjectivity in its finished artistic execution, and the lyric mood does not predominate ; but the unmistakable warmth of its rich and earnest feeling, expressed through the melody and dignity of its happily fitting metre, redeems the banality of the theme and makes the poem almost lyrical in its effect. The feeling, however, is not isolated, but blended picturesquely with a great deal of descriptive matter. Its intensity of recollective tenderness is set in the midst of the Indian rainy season, than which, as Rabindranath rightly remarks, nothing is more appropriate for an atmosphere of loneliness and longing ; it is placed also in the midst of splendid natural scenery which enhances its poignant appeal. The description of external nature in the first half of the poem is heightened throughout by an intimate association with human feeling, while the picture of the lover's sorrowing heart in the second half is skilfully framed in the surrounding beauty of nature. A large number of attempts[1] were made in later times to imitate the poem, but the *Megha-dūta* still remains unsurpassed as a masterpiece of its kind, not for its matter, nor for its description, but purely for its poetry.

Kālidāsa's deep-rooted fame as a poet somewhat obscures his merit as a dramatist ; but prodigal of gifts nature had been to him, and his achievement in the drama is no less striking. In the judgment of many, his *Abhijñāna-śakuntala* remains his

1 On the Dūta-kāvyas, see Chintaharan Chakravarti in *IHQ*, III, pp. 273-97.

greatest work ; at the very least, it is considered to be the full-blown flower of his genius. Whatever value the judgment may possess, it implies that in this work we have a unique alliance of his poetic and dramatic gifts, which are indeed not contradictory but complementary ; and this fact should be recognised in passing from his poems to his plays. His poems give some evidence of skilful handling of dramatic moments and situations ; but his poetic gifts invest his dramas with an imaginative quality which prevents them from being mere practical productions of stage-craft. It is not implied that his dramas do not possess the requisite qualities of a stage-play, for his *Śakuntalā* has been often successfully staged ; but this is not the only, much less the chief, point of view from which his dramatic works are to be judged. Plays often fail, not for want of dramatic power or stage-qualities, but for want of poetry ; they are often too prosaic. It is very seldom that both the dramatic and poetic qualities are united in the same author. As a dramatist Kālidāsa succeeds, mainly by his poetic power, in two respects : he is a master of poetic emotion which he can skilfully harmonise with character and action, and he has the poetic sense of balance and restraint which a dramatist must show if he would win success.

It is significant that in the choice of theme, character and situation, Kālidāsa follows the essentially poetic bent of his genius. Love in its different aspects and situations is the dominant theme of all his three plays, care-free love in the setting of a courtly intrigue, impetous love as a romantic and undisciplined passion leading to madness, and youthful love, at first heedless but gradually purified by suffering. In the lyrical and narrative poem the passionate feeling is often an end in itself, elegant but isolated ; in the drama, there is a progressive deepening of the emotional exprience as a factor of larger life. It therefore, affords the poet, as a dramatist, an opportunity of depicting its subtle moods and fancies in varied circumstances, its infinite range and intensity in closeness to common realities. His mastery of humour and pathos, his wisdom and humanity, come into play ;

and his great love of life and sense of tears in mortal things inform his pictures with all the warmth and colour of a vivid poetic imagination.

The *Mālavikāgnimitra*[1] is often taken to be one of Kālidāsa's youthful productions, but there is no adequate reason for thinking that it is his first dramatic work. The modesty shown in the Prologue[2] repeats itself in those of his other two dramas, and the immaturity which critics have seen in it is more a question of personal opinion than a real fact; for it resolves itself into a difference of form and theme, rather than any real deficiency of power.[3] The *Mālavikā* is not a love-drama of the type of the *Svapna-vāsavadatta*, to which it has a superficial resemblance, but which possesses a far more serious interest. It is a light-hearted comedy of court-life in five acts, in which love is a pretty game, and in which the hero need not be of heroic proportion, nor the heroine anything but a charming and attractive maiden. The pity of the situation, no doubt, arises from the fact that the game of sentimental philandering is often played at the expense of others who are not in it, but that is only an inevitable incident of the game. The motif of the progress of a courtly love-intrigue through hindrances to royal desire for a lowly maiden and its denouement in the ultimate discovery of her status as a princess was perhaps not as banal in Kālidāsa's

1 Ed. F. Bollenson, Leipzig 1879; ed. S. P. Pandit, with comm. of Kāṭayavema (*c.* 1400 A.D.), Bombay Sansk. Ser., 2nd ed., 1889, and by K. P. Parab, NSP, Bombay 1915. Trs. into English by C. H. Twney, Calcutta 1875 and London 1891; into German by Weber, Berlin 1856; into French by V. Henry Paris 1889. On Text criticism see C. Cappeller, *Observationes ad Kālidāsae Mālavikāgnimitram* (Diss.), Regimonti 1868; F. Haag, *Zur Textkritik und Erklärung von Kālidāsas Mālavikāgnimitra*, Frauenfeld 1872; Bollensen in *ZDMG*, XIII, 1859, p. 480 f.; Weber in *ibid.*, XIV, 1860, p. 261 f., Jackson in *JAOS*, XX, p. 343 f. (Time analysis). For fuller bibliography see Sten Konow, *op. cit.*, p. 63.

2 If the work is called *nava*, with a reference to far-famed predecessors, the same word is used to designate his *Abhijñāna-śakuntala*, which also modestly seeks the satisfaction of the learned as a final test; and his *Vikramorvaśīya* is spoken of in the same way in the Prologue as *apūrva*, with reference to former poets (*pūrva kavi*). In a sense, all plays are *nava* and *apūrva*, and no valid inference is possible from such descriptions.

3 Wilson's unfounded doubt about the authorship of the play led to its comparative neglect, but Weber and S. P. Pandit effectively set the doubts at rest. For a warm eulogy, see V. Henry, *Les Littératures de l'Inde*, p. 305 f.

time[1] as we are wont to think ; but the real question is how the theme is handled. Neither Agnimitra nor Mālavikā may appear impressive, but they are appropriate to the atmosphere. The former is a care-free and courteous gentleman, on whom the burden of kingly responsibility sits but lightly, who is no longer young but no less ardent, who is an ideal Dakṣiṇa Nāyaka possessing a great capacity for falling in and out of love ; while the latter is a faintly drawn ingénue with nothing but good looks and willingness to be loved by the incorrigible king-lover. The Vidūṣaka is a more lively character, who takes a greater part in the development of the plot in this play than in the other dramas of Kālidāsa. The interest of the theme is enhanced by the complications of the passionate impetuousity and jelousy of the young discarded queen Irāvatī, which is finely shown off against the pathetic dignity and magnanimity of the elderly chief queen Dhāriṇī. Perhaps the tone and tenor of the play did not permit a more serious development of this aspect of the plot, but it should not be regarded as deficiency. The characterisation is sharp and clear, and the expression polished, elegant and even dainty. The wit and elaborate compliments, the toying and trifling with the tender passion, the sentimentalities and absence of deep feeling are in perfect keeping with the outlook of the gay circle, which is not used to any profounder view of life.[2] One need not wonder, therefore, that while war is in progress in the kingdom, the royal household is astir with the amorous escapades of the somewhat elderly, but youthfully inclined, king. Gallantry is undoubtedly the keynote of the play, and its joys and sorrows should not be reckoned at a higher level. Judged by its own standard, there is nothing immature, clumsy or turgid in the drama. If Kālidāsa did not actually

1 The source of the story is not known, but it is clear thnt Kālidāsa owes nothing to the Purāṇic stories. As st. 2 shows, accounts of Agnimitra were probably current and available to the poet.

2 K. R. Pisharoti in *Journal of the Annamalai Univ.*, II, no. 2, p, 193 f., is inclined to take the play as a veiled satire on some royal family of the time, if not on Agnimitra himself, and would think that the weakness of the opening scene is deliberate.

originate the type, he must have so stamped it with the impress of his genius that it was, as the dramas of Harṣa and Rājaśekhara show, adopted as one of the appealing modes of dramatic expression and became banalised in course of time.

In the *Vikramovaśīya,*[1] on the other hand, there is a decided weakness in general treatment. The romantic story of the love of the mortal king Purūravas and the divine nymph Urvaśī is old, the earliest version occuring in the *Ṛgveda* x. 95 ; but the passion and pathos, as well as the logically tragic ending, of the ancient legend[2] is changed, in five acts, into an unconvincing story of semi-courtly life with a weak denouement of domestic union and felicity, brought about by the intervention of a magic stone and the grace of Indra. The fierce-souled spouse, *la belle dame sans merci* of the *Ṛgveda,* is transformed into a passionate but selfish woman, an elevated type of the heavenly courtesan, and later on, into a happy and obedient wife. The modifying hand of folk-tale and comedy of courtly life is obvious ; and some strange incidents and situations, like the first scene located in the air, is introduced ; but accepting Kālidāsa's story as it is, there is no deficiency in characterisation and expression. If the figures are strange and romantic, they are still transcripts from universal nature. Even when the type does not appeal, the character lives. The

1 Ed. R. Lenz, with Lain notes etc., Berlin 1833 ; ed. F. Bollensen, St. Petersberg, 1846 ; ed. Monier Williams, Hertford 1849 ; ed. S. P. Pandit and B. R. Arte, with extracts from comm. of Kāṭayavema and Raṅganātha, Bom. Skt. Ser., 3rd ed. 1901 (1st ed. 1879) ; ed. K. P. Parab and M. R. Talang, NSP, with comm. of Raṅganātha Bombay 1914 (4th ed.) ; ed. Charudev Sastri, with comm. of Kāṭyavema, Lahore 1929. Trs. into English by E. B. Cowell, Hertford 1851 ; into German by L. Frize. Leipzig 1880 ; into French by P. E. Foucaux, Paris 1861 and 1879. The recension according to Dravidian manuscripts is edited by Pischel in *Monatsber. d. kgl. preuss. Akad. zu Berlin,* 1875, p. 609 f. For fuller bibliography see Sten Konow, *op. cit.*, p. 65-66.

2 Kālidāsa's source, again, is uncertain. The story is retold with the missing details in the *Śatapatha Brāhmaṇa,* but Purāṇic accounts entirely modify it not to its advantage. The *Viṣṇu-purāṇa* preserves some of its old rough features, but in the *Kathā-saritsāgara* and in the *Matsya-purāṇa* we find it in the much altered form of a folk-tale. The latter version closely resembles the one which Kālidāsa follows, but it is not clear if the *Matsya-purāṇa* version itself, like the *Padma-purāṇa* version of the Śakuntalā-legend, is mopelled on Kālidāsa's treatment of the story.

brave and chivalrous Purūravas is sentimental, but as his madness shows, he is not the mere trifler of a princely amorist like Agnimitra ; while the jealous queen Auśinarī is not a repetition of Irāvatī or Dhāriṇī. Although in the fifth act, the opportunity is missed of a tragic conflict of emotion between the joy of Purūravas in finding his son and his sorrow at the loss of Urvaśī resulting from the very sight of the child, there is yet a skilful delineation of Kālidāsa's favourite motif of the recognition of the unknown son and the psychological climax of presenting the offspring as the crown of wedded love. There are also features in the drama which are exceptional in the whole range of Sanskrit literature, and make it rise above the decorum of courtly environment. The fourth act on the madness of Purūravas is unique in this sense. The scene is hardly dramatic and has no action, but it reaches an almost lyric height in depicting the tumultuous ardour of undisciplined passion. It is a fantasy in soliloquy, in which the demented royal lover, as he wanders through the woods in search of his beloved, demands tidings of his fugitive love from the peacock, the cuckoo, the flamingo, the bee, the elephant, the boar and the antelope ; he deems the cloud, with its rainbow, to be a demon who has borne his beauteous bride away ; he searches the yielding soil softened by showers, which may perchance, if she had passed that way, have retained the delicate impression of her gait, and may show some vestige of the red tincture of her dyed feet. The whole scene is melodramatically conceived ; and if the Prakrit verses are genuine,[1] they are apparently meant to be sung behind the scenes. The stanzas are changed with exuberance of emotion

1 The authenticity of the Prakrit verses has been doubted, chiefly on the ground that the Apabhraṁśa of the type found in them is suspicious in a drama of such early date, and that they are not found in the South Indian recension of the text. The Northern recension calls the drama a Troṭaka, apparently for the song-element in the verses, but according to the South Indian recension, it conforms generally to the essentials of a Nāṭaka. See U. N. Upadhye, introd. to *Paramātma-prakāśa* (Bombay 1937), p. 56, note, who argues in favour of the genuineness of the Apabhraṁśa verses.

and play of fancy, but we have nothing else which appeals in the drama but the isolation of individual passion. The inevitable tragedy of such a love is obvious ; and it is a pity that the play is continued after the natural tragic climax is reached, even at the cost of lowering the heroine from her divine estate and making Indra break his word !

That the *Abhijñāna-śakuntala*[1] is, in every respect, the most finished of Kālidāsa's dramatic compositions, is indicated by the almost universal feeling of genuine admiration which it has always evoked. The old legend of Śakuntalā, incorporated in the Ādiparvan of the *Mahābhārata*, or perhaps some version of it,[2] must have suggested the plot of this drama ; but the difference between the rough and simple epic narrative and Kālidāsa's refined and delicate treatment of it at once reveals his distinctive dramatic genius. The shrewd, straightforward and taunting girl of the Epic is transformed into the shy, dignified and pathetic heroine, while the selfish conduct of her practical lover in the Epic, who refuses to recognise her out of policy, is replaced by an irreprehensible forgetfulness which obscures his

1 The earliest edition (Bengal Recension) is that by A. L. Chézy Paris 1830. The drama exists in four recensions : (*i*) Devanāgarī, ed. O. Böhtlingk, Bonn 1842, but with better materials, ed. Monier Williams 2nd ed., Oxford 1876 (1st ed. 1853) ; with comm. of Rāghavabhaṭṭa, ed. N. B. Godbole and K. P. Parab, NSP, Bombay 1883, 1922. (*ii*) Bengali, ed. R. Pischel, Kiel 1877 ; 2nd ed. in Harvard Orient. Ser., revised by C. Cappeller, Cambridge Mass. 1922 (*iii*) Kāśmīrī, ed. K. Burkhard, Wien 1884. (*iv*) South Indian, no critical edition ; but printed with comm. of Abhirāma, Śrī Vāṇī Vilāsa Press, Sriangam 1917, etc. Attempts to reconstruct the text, by C. Cappeller (Kürzere Textform), Leipzig 1909, and by P. N. Patankar (called Purer Devanāgarī Text). Poona 1902. But no critical edition, utilising all the recensions, has yet been undertaken. The earliest English trs. by William Jones, London 1790 ; but trs. have been numerous in various languages. On Text-criticism, see Pischel, *De Kālidāsae Cakuntali recensionibus* (Diss.), Breslau 1872 and *Die Rezensionen der Cakuntalā*. Breslau 1875 ; A. Weber, *Die Recensionen de Śakuntalā* in *Ind. Studien*, XIV, pp. 35-69, 161-311 ; Harichand Sastri, *op. cit.*, p. 243 f. For fuller bibliography, see Sten Konow, *op. cit.*, pp. 68-70, and M. Schuyler in *JAOS*, XXII, p. 237 f.

2 The *Padma-Purāṇa* version is perhaps a recast of Kālidāsa's story, and there is no reason to think (Winternitz, *GIL*, III, p. 215) that Kālidāsa derived his material from the Purāṇa, or from some earlier version of it. Haradatta Sarma, *Kālidāsa and the Padmapurāṇa*, Calcutta 1925, follows Winternitz.

love. A dramatic motive is thereby supplied, and the prosaic incidents and characters of the original legend are plastically remodelled into frames and shapes of beauty. Here we see to its best effect Kālidāsa's method of unfolding a charactcr, as a flower unfolds its petals in rain and sunshine ; there is no melodrama, no lame denouement, to mar the smooth, measured and dignified progress of the play ; there is temperance in the depth of passion, and perspicuity and inevitableness in action and expression ; but, above all this, the drama surpasses by its essential poetic quality of style and treatment.

Some criticism, however, has been levelled against the artificial device of the curse and the ring[1] which brings in an element of chance and incalculable happening in the development of the plot. It should be recognised, however, that the psychological evolution of action is more or less, a creation of the modern drama. The idea of destiny or divinity shaping our ends, unknown to ourselves, is not a peculiarly Indian trait, but is found in ancient drama in general ; and the trend has been from ancient objectivity to modern subjectivity[2] Apart from judging a method by a standard to which it does not profess to conform, it cannot also be argued that there is an inherent inferiority in an external device as compared with the

1 Criticised severely, for instance, by H. Oldenberg in *Die Lit. d. alten Indien*, p. 261. The curse of Caṇḍabhārgava and the magic ring in the *Avi-māraka*, which have a different purpose, have only a superficial similarity, and could not have been Kālidāsa's source of the idea. On the curse of a sage as a motif in story and drama, see L. H. Gray in *WZKM*, XVIII. 1904, pp. 53-54. The ring-motif is absent in the *Mahābhārata*, but P. E. Pavolini (*GSAI*, XIX, 1906, p. 376 ; XX, p. 297 f.) finds a parallel in Jātaka no. 7. It is perhaps an old Indian story-motif.

2 C. E. Vaughan, *Types of Tragic Drama*, London 1908, p. 8 f. On the idea of Destiny in ancient and modern drama, see W. Macneille Dixon, *Tragedy*, London 1924, pp. 35-46 The device of the Ghost as the spirit of revenge in Euripides' *Hecuba* and Seneca's *Thyestes* is also external, although it was refined in the Elizabethan drama, especially in Shakespeare. The supernatural machinery in both *Macbeth* and *Hamlet* may be conceived as hallucination projected by the active minds in question, but it still has an undoubted influence on the development of the plot of the respective plays, which can be regarded as dramas of a man at odds with fate.

complication created by the inner impetus, to which we are in the present day more accustomed, perhaps too superstitiously. It is not really a question of comparative excellence, but of the artistic use which is made of a particular device. It is true that in Kālidāsa's *Abhijñāna-śakuntala*, the dramatic motive comes from without, but it is effectively utilised, and the drama which is enacted within and leads to a crisis is not thereby overlooked. The lovers are betrayed also by what is within, by the very rashness of youthful love which reaps as it sows ; and the entire responsibility in this drama is not laid on the external agency. Granting the belief of the time, there is nothing unreal or unnatural ; it is fortuitous but not unmotived. We have here not merely a tragedy of blameless hero and heroine ; for a folly, or a mere girlish fault, or even one's very virtues may bring misfortune, The unriddled ways of life need not always be as logical or comprehensible as one may desire ; but there is nothing illogical or incomprehensible if only Svādhikāra-pramāda, here as elsewhere, leads to distress, and the nexus between act and fate is not wholly disregarded. If the conflict, again, between the heart's desire and the world's impediment can be a sufficient dramatic motive, it is not of very great poetic consequence if the impediment assumes the form of a tragic curse, unknown to the persons affected, and plays the rôle of invisible but benevolent destiny in shaping the course of action. It is true that we cannot excuse ourselves by arraigning Fate, Chance or Destiny ; the tragic interest must assuredly be built on the foundation of human responsibility ; but at the same time a human plot need always be robbed of its mystery, and simplified to a mere circumstantial unfolding of cause and effect, all *in nostra potestate*. Fate or Ourselves, in the abstract, is a difficult question ; but, as in life so in the drama, we need not reject the one for the other as the moulder of human action.

Much less convincing, and perhaps more misconceived, is the criticism that Kālidāsa evinces no interest in the great problems of human life. As, on the one hand, it would be a misdirected effort to find nothing but art for art's sake in Kālidāsa's work, so, on the other, it would be a singularly unimaginative attempt to seek a problem in a work of art and turn the poet into a philosopher. It is, however, difficult to reconcile the view mentioned above with the well-known eulogy of no less an artist than Goethe, who speaks of finding in Kālidāsa's masterpiece "the young year's blossom and the fruit of its decline," and "the earth and heaven combined in one name." In spite of its obvious poetical exaggeration, this metaphorical but eloquent praise is not empty ; it sums up with unerring insight the deeper issues of the drama, which is bound to be lost sight of by one who looks to it merely for a message or philosophy of life.

The *Abhijñāna-śakuntala,* unlike most Sanskrit plays, is not based on the mere banality of a court-intrigue, but has a much more serious interest in depicting the baptism of youthful love by silent suffering. Contrasted with Kālidāsa's own *Mālavikāgnimitra* and *Vikramorvaśīya,* the sorrow of the hero and heroine in this drama is far more human, far more genuine ; and love is no longer a light-hearted passion in an elegant surrounding, nor an explosive emotion ending in madness, but a deep and steadfast enthusiasm, or rather a progressive emotional experience, which results in an abiding spiritual feeling. The drama opens with a description of the vernal season, made for enjoyment (*upabhoga-kṣama*) ; and even in the hermitage where thoughts of love are out of place, the season extends its witchery and makes the minds of the young hero and heroine turn lightly to such forbidden thoughts. At the outset we find Śakuntalā, an adopted child of nature, in the daily occupation of tending the friendly trees and creepers and watching them grow and bloom, herself a youthful blossom, her mind delicately attuned to the sights and sounds in the midst of which she had grown up since she had been deserted by her *amānuṣī* mother. On this scene appears the more sophisticated royal hero, full of the pride of youth and power, but with a noble presence which inspires love and confidence, possessed of scrupulous regard for rectitude but withal susceptible to rash youthful impulses, considerate of others and alive to the dignity and responsibility of his high station, but accustomed to every fulfilment of his wishes and extremely self-confident in the promptings of his own heart. He is egoistic enough to believe that everything he wishes must be right because he wishes it, and everything does happen as he wishes it. In his impetuous desire to gain what he wants, he does not even think it necessary to wait for the return of Kaṇva. It was easy for him to carry the young girl off her feet ; for, though brought up in the peaceful seclusion and stern discipline of a hermitage, she was yet possessed of a natural inward longing for the love and happiness which were due to her youth and beauty. Though fostered by a sage and herself the daughter of an ascetic, she was yet the daughter of a nymph whose intoxicating beauty had once achieved a conquest over the austere and terrible Viśvāmitra. This beauty and this power she had inherited from her mother, as well as an inborn keenness and desire for love ; is she not going to make her own conquest over this great king ? For such youthful lovers, love can never think of the morrow ; it can only think of the moment. All was easy at first ; the secret union to which they commited themselves obtains the ratification of the foster-father. But soon she realises the pity of taking love as an end in itself, of making the moment stand for eternity. The suffering comes as swiftly and unexpectedly as the happiness was headlong and heedless.

To these thoughtless lovers the curse of Durvāsa comes to play the part of a stern but beneficient providence. With high hopes and unaware of the impending catastrophe, she leaves for the house of her king-lover, tenderly taking farewell from her sylvan friends, who seem to be filled with an unconscious anxiety for her ; but very soon she finds herself standing utterly humiliated in the eyes of the world. Her grief, remorse and self-pity are aggravated by the accusation of unseemly haste and secrecy from Gautamī, as well as by the sterner rebuke of Śārṅgarava: "Thus does one's heedlessness lead to disaster!" But the unkindest cut comes from her lover himself, who insultingly refers to instincts of feminine shrewdness, and compares her, without knowing, to the trubid swelling flood which drags others also in its fall. Irony in drama or in life can go no further. But the daughter of a nymph as she was, she had also the spirit of her fierce and austere father, and ultimately emerges triumphant from the ordeal of sorrow. She soon realises that she has lost all in her gambling for happiness, and a wordy warfare is useless. She could not keep her lover by her youth and beauty alone. She bows to the inevitable; and chastened and transformed by patient suffering, she wins back in the end her husband and her happiness. But the king is as yet oblivious of what is in store for him. Still arrogant, ironical and self-confident, he wonders who the veiled lady might be; her beauty draws him as irresistibly as it once did, and yet his sense of rectitude forbids any improper thought. But his punishment comes in due course; for he was the greater culprit, who had dragged the unsophisticated girl from her sylvan surroundings and left her unwittingly in the mire. When the ring of recognition is recovered, he realises the gravity of his act. Her resigned and reproachful form now haunts him and gives him no peace in the midst of his royal duties; and his utter helplessness in rendering any reparation makes his grief more intense and poignant. The scene now changes from earth to heaven, from the hermitage of Kaṇva and the court of the king to the penance-grove of Mārīca; and the love that was of the earth changes to love that is spritual and divine. The strangely estranged pair is again brought together equally strangely, but not until they have passed through the trial of sorrow and become ready for a perfect reunion of hearts. There is no explanation, no apology, no recrimination, nor any demand for reparation. Śakuntalā has now learnt in silence the lessons of suffering ; and with his former self-complacency and impetuous desires left behind, the king comes, chastened and subdued, a sadder and wiser man. The young year's blossom now ripens into the mellow fruit of autumnal maturity.

Judged absolutely, without reference to an historical standard, Kālidāsa's plays impress us by their admirable combination of dramatic and poetic qualities ; but it is in pure poetry that he surpasses even in his dramatic works. It should be admitted that he has the powers of a great dramatist ; he can merge his individuality in the character he represents ; he can paint distinct individuals, and not personified abstractions, with consistent reality and profound insight into human nature ; all his romantic situations may not be justified, but he is always at the height of a situation ; within certain limits, he has constructive ability of a high order, and the action is perspicuous, naturally developed and adequately motived ; he makes a skilful use of natural phenomenon in sympathy with the prevailing tone of a scene ; he gives by his easy and unaffected manner the impression of grace which comes from strength revealed without unnecessary display or expenditure of energy ; he never tears a passion to tatters nor does he overstep the modesty of nature in producing a pathetic effect ; he does not neglect the incident in favour of dialogue or dainty stanzas ; all this and more may be freely acknowledged. But the real appeal of his dramas lies in the appeal of their poetry more than in their purely dramatic quality. His gentle pathos and humour, his romantic imagination and his fine poetic feeling are more marked characteristics of his dramas than mere ingenuity of plot, liveliness of incident and minute portraiture of men and manners. They save him from the prosaic crudeness of the realist as well as from an oppressive and unnatural display of technical skill. The elegant compliment of the author of the *Prasanna-rāghava* that Kālidāsa is the 'grace of poetry' emphasises the point ; but poetry at the same time is not too seductive for him. He is a master of sentiment, but not a sentimentalist who sacrifies the realities of life and character ; he is romantic, but his romance is not divorced from common nature and common sense. He writes real dramas and not a series of elegant poetical passages ; the poetic fancy and love of style do not strangle the truth and vividness of his presentation. He is also not in any sense the exponent of the opera of the lyrical drama, or the dramatic poem. He is rather the creator of the poetical drama in Sanskrit. But the difficult standard which he set could not be developed except in an extreme form by his less gifted successors.

In making a general estimate of Kālidāsa's achievement as a poet, one feels the difficulty of avoiding superlatives ; but the superlatives in this case are amply justified. Kālidāsa's reputation has always been great ; and this is perhaps the only case where both Eastern and Western critics, applying not exactly analogous standards, are in general agreement. That he is the greatest of Sanskrit poets is a commonplace of literary criticism, but if Sanskrit literature can claim to rank as one of the great literatures of the world, Kālidāsa's high place in the galaxy of world-poets must be acknowledged. It is not necessary to prove it by quoting the eulogium of Goethe and Ānanda-vardhana ; but the agreement shows that Kālidāsa has the gift of a great poet, and like all great poetic gifts, it is of universal appeal.

This high praise does not mean that Kālidāsa's poetic art and style have never been questioned or are beyond criticism. Leaving aside Western critics whose appreciation of an alien art and expression must necessarily be limited, we find the Sanskrit rhetoricians, in spite of their great admiration, are not sparing in their criticism ; and, like Ben Jonson who wanted to blot out a thousand lines in Shakespeare, they would give us a fairly long list of "faults" which mar the excellence of Kālidāsa's otherwise perfect work. We are not concerned here with the details of the alleged defects, but they happily demonstrate that Kālidāsa, like Shakespeare, is not faultily faultless. That his rhetoric is of the best kind is shown by the hundreds of passages approved by the rhetoricians themselves ; but that they sometimes disapprove his not conforming rigidly to their laws is also significant. If his obedience is successful, his disobedience is often no less successful in giving him freedom of idea and expression and saving him from much that is wooden and merely conventional.

Even in the imposing gallery of Sanskrit poets who are always remarkable for technical skill, Kālidāsa has an astonishing display of the poetic art ; but he never lends himself to an over-development of the technical to the detriment of the artistic. The legend which makes Kālidāsa an inspired idiot and implies a minimum of artistic consciousness and design is perhaps as misleading as the counter-error of too great insistence upon the consciousness and elaboration of his art. There is little doubt that he shared the learning of his time, but he wears his learning lightly like a flower ; while the depeptive clarity and simplicity of his work conceal the amount of cultivation and polish which goes into its making. It is not spontaneous creation ; but while lesser poets lack the art to conceal art, he has the gift of passion, imagination, music and colouring to give an effective appearance of spontaneity and inevitability. He belongs to a tradition which insists upon literature being a learned pursuit but he is one of the great and limpid writers who can be approached with the minimum of critical apparatus and commentatorial lucubrations.

This marvellous result is made possible because Kālidāsa's works reveal a rare balance of mind, which harmonises the artistic sense with the poetic, and results in the practice of singular moderation. No other Sanskrit poet can approach him in the command of that mysterious instrument, the measured word. Kālidāsa has a rich and sustained elevation of diction, but it is never overwrought and very rarely rhetorical in the bad sense. Conceits and play upon words are to be found in him, as in Shakespeare, but there are no irritating and interminable puns ; no search after strained expressions, harsh inversions or involved constructions; no love for jewels five words long; no torturing of words or making them too laboured for the ideas. Even Kālidāsa's love of similitude,[1] for which he has been so highly praised, never makes him employ it as a mere verbal trick, but it is made a natural concomitant of the emotional content for suggesting more than what is expressed. On the other hand, his ideas, emotions and fancies never run riot or ride rough-shod over the limits of words, within which they are compressed with tasteful economy and pointedness of phrasing. The result is a fine adjustment of sound and sense, a judicious harmony of word and idea, to a point not often reached by other Sanskrit poets. This is seen not only in the extraordinary vividness and precision of his presentment of images and ideas, but also in the modulation of letter, syllable, word, line and stanza to produce a running accompaniment at once to the images and ideas. The felicity of expression, its clarity and ease, which have been recognised in Kālidāsa as the best instance of the Prasāda Guṇa, come from this careful choice of a rich store of words, both simple and compound, which are not only delicately attuned but also made alive with the haunting suggestion of poetry. If it is simplicity, it is simplicity made more elegant than ornateness itself by sheer genius for proportion and vividity. There are hundreds of words, phrases and lines in Kālidāsa, echoing passages and vertitable gems of expression, giving us an infinity of fresh and felt observations, which fasten themselves on the memory; such is the distinctness of his vision and the eleborate, but not laboured, accuracy of his touch. If the gift of phrasing is one of the tests of a great writer, Kālidāsa possesses this happy gift; but it is also combined with the still more rare gifts, seen in prefection in great poets, of putting *multum in parvo* and of opening up unending vistas of thought by the magic power of a single line or phrase.

1 A study of Kālidāsa's Upamā has been made by P. K. Gode in *Proc. of the First Orient. Conf.*, Poona 1922, pp. 205-26. On Kālidāsa's retation to Alaṁkāra literature in general, see Hillebrandt, *Kālidāsa*, p. 107 f.

Kālidāsa is indeed careful of form, but he is not careless of matter. Like later Sanskrit poets he does not make his narrative a mere peg on which he can luxuriously hang his learning and skill. Whatever may be said about his choice of themes, he is seldom unequal to them. The wide exploration of subjects, legendary, mythical, emotional and even fantastic, and his grasp over their realities, are seen in the way in which he handles his huge and diverse material in the *Raghu-vaṃśa,* creates a human story out of a divine myth in his *Kumāra-saṃbhava* and depicts the passionate love of hapless lovers in an environment of poetical fancy in his *Megha-dūta* and his dramas. He may not always be at the height of his power through the entire length of a work, but he is always at the height of a particular situation. His sources are not exactly known, but it is clear that his subjects serve him for the stuff out of which he *creates* ; and Kālidāsa perhaps borrows nothing from his supposed originals that makes him Kālidāsa. He is not so much the teller of a story as the maker of it, and his unerring taste and restraint accomplish this making by not allowing either the form or the content to overwhelm or exceed each other.

The same sense of balance is also shown by the skilful adjustment of a mobile and sensitive prosody to the diction and theme of the poems. The total number of different metres which Kālidāsa employs is only about twenty. With the exception of Mandākrāntā of his short poem, they are either Śloka,[1] or a few moric metres like Vaitālīya, Aupacchandasika or Puṣpitāgra, but the general bulk consists normally of the relatively short lyrical measures of the Triṣṭubh-Jagatī family or metres akin to it. In the drama, of course, there is greater metrical variety suited to the different situations and emotions. In the bigger poems the

1 It is remakable that the Śloka is used not only for the condensation of the Rāmāyaṇa story in *Raghu*° xii, but also for the Stotra of deities both in *Raghu*° x and *Kumāra*° ii, as well as for the narration of Raghu's Digvijaya. For repetition of the same metre for similar theme, *cf.* Viyoginī in Aja-vilāpa and Rati-vilāpa ; Upajāti in describing marriage in *Raghu*° vii and *Kumāra*° vii ; Rathoddhatā in depicting amorous pastimes in *Raghu*° xix and *Kumāra*° viii, etc.

short lyrical measures are perhaps meant for facility of cotinued narration ; the simplicity and swing of the stanzas make his narrative flow in a clear and attractive stream ; but even in the leisurely descriptive and reflectively serious passages, they never cramp the thought, feeling or imagination of the poet. The stately and long-drawn-out music of the Mandākrāntā, on the other hand, very well suits the picturesque and melancholy recollections of love in his *Megha-dūta*. It is, however, clear that Kālidāsa is equally at home in both short and long measures ; and though a part of canto ix of the *Raghu-vaṃśa* is meant deliberately to display the poet's skill in varied metres, the variation is not unpleasing. But, normally, it is not a question of mere metrical skill, but of the developed and delicate sense of rhythmic forms and the fine subtlety of musical accompaniment to the power of vivid and elegant presentation.

With the same sense of equipoise Kālidāsa's imagination holds in perfect fusion the two elements of natural beauty and human feeling. His nature-pictures grow out of the situations, and his situations merge into the nature-pictures. This iș palpable not only in his *Megha-dūta*, but practically throughout, his other two poems and his dramas. The pathos of the destruction of Kāma is staged in the life and loveliness of spring ; Rāma's tender recollection of past joys and sorrows is intimately associated with the hills, rivers and trees of Daṇḍaka ; the pretty amourette of Agnimitra, the madness of Purūravas, or the woodland wooing of Duṣyanta is set in the midst of the sights and sounds of nature. A countless number of Kālidāsa's beautiful similes and metaphors is drawn from his loving observation of natural phenomena. The depth and range of his experience and insight into human life is indeed great, but the human emotion is seldom isolated from the beauty of nature surrounding it. Kālidāsa's warm humanism and fine poetic sensibility romanticise the natural as well as the mythological world, and they supply to his poetry the grace and picturesqueness of background and scenic variety.

It will be seen that the sense of universality in Kālidāsa's work springs not merely from its humanity and range of interests, but also from the fact that it reveals him as a great master of poetic thought who is at the same time a master of poetic style. Diction, imagery, verbal music, suggestion,—all the elements of poetry are present in intense degree and in many forms and combinations novel and charming ; but they all exhibit a marvellous fusion of the artistic consciousness with poetic imagination and feeling. Kālidāsa's poetic power, which scorns anything below the highest, is indeed not narrow in its possibilities of application, but its amplitude and exuberance are always held in restraint by his sense of art, which, however, does not act as an incubus, but as a chastener. His work, therefore, is never hampered or hurried ; there is no perpetual series of ups and downs in it, no great interval between his best and his worst ; it maintains a level of excellence and stamp of distinction throughout. All ruggedness and angularity are delicately smoothed away ; and the even roundness of his full-orbed poetry appeals by a haunting suggestion of serene beauty, resulting from a subtle merging of thought and feeling in sound and visual effect.

But from this spring both the strength and weakness of Kālidāsa's poetic achievement. If tranquil contemplation of recollected emotions. in both eastern and western theory, denotes the aesthetic attitude and forms the essence of true poetry, Kālidāsa's work is certainly marked by it in an eminent degree. His tranquility, considered as an attitude towards life, is not easy-going indifference or placid acquiescence in the order of things ; there is enough of earnestness and sense of sorrow to indicate that it must have been hard-won, although we are denied the sight of the strife and struggle which led to its attainment, or of the scars or wrinkles which might have been left behind. In his poetry, it bore fruit in the unruffled dignity and serenity of artistic accomplishment. At the same time, it encouraged a tendency towards reserve more than towards abandon. Kālidāsa's poetry seldom surprises us by its fine excess ; it is always smooth, measured and even. The polished and the ornate is as much natural to Kalidasa as, for instance, the rugged and the grotesque to Bhavabhūti. While Kalidasa broiders the exquisite tissue of poetry, Bhavabhūti would have it rough and homespun. This is perhaps not so much a studied effect as a temperamental attitude in both cases. The integrity and sincerity of primal sensations and their fervid expression, which Bhavabhūti often attains, are rare in Kalidasa's highly refined and cultured utterances. It is not that Kalidasa is averse to what is intense and poignant, as well as grand and awe-inspiring, in life and nature, but the emotions are chastened and subdued in the severity, strength and dignity of finished poetic presentation. There is nothing crude, rugose or tempestuous in Kalidasa, not a jarring note of violence or discord, but everything is dissolved in the harmony and beauty of reposeful realisation. The limitation of this attitude is as obvious as its poetic possibility. While it gives the perfect artistic aloofness conducive to real poetry, it deprives the poet of robust and keen perceptions, of the concrete and even gross realism of undomesticated passion, of the freshness of the drossy, but unalloyed, one direct from the mine. Kalidasa would never regard his emotions as their own excuse for being, but would present them in the embalmed glamour of poetic realisation, or in the brocaded garb of quintessenced rhetoric. Kalidasa has perhaps as much optimism for civilasation as Bhavabhūti has for savagery ; but he does not often attain the depths and heights which Bhavabhūti does by his untamed roughness. It is for this reason that some of Kalidasa's pictures, both of life and nature, finely poetic as they are, are still too refined and remote. The Himalayas do not appear to Kalidasa in their natural grandeur and sublimity, nor the Daṇḍaka forest in its wild beauty and ruggedness ; all these pictures are to be properly finished and framed, but thereby they lose much of their trenchant setting and appeal.

But all this is not mere suavity or finicality. Kalidasa's poetry does not swim in longour, cloyed with its own sweetness ;

the chastity and restraint of his imagination, the precision and energy of his phrasing, and the austerity of his artistic vigilance save him from mere sensuous ideality. Nor is it classical correctness in the narrow sense that might be learned in the schools of literature. The ornate in Kālidāsa, therefore, means very rarely mere prettiness or aesthetic make-believe; it is the achievement of the refined effect of a thought or feeling chiselled in its proper form of beauty and becoming thereby a poetic thought or feeling. It thus involves the process through which the poet lifts his tyrannical passion or idea to the blissful contemplation of an aesthetic sentiment. Kālidāsa can keep himself above his subject in the sense of command, as Bhavabhūti too often merges himself in it in the sense of surrender; and the difference is best seen in their respective treatment of pathos, in which Kālidāsa's poetic sense of restraint and balance certainly achieve a more profound effect. This is nowhere more clear than in the picture of Rāma's suffering on the occasion of Sītā's exile, drawn respectively by the two poets. Bhavabhūti's tendency is to elaborate pathetic scenes almost to the verge of crudity, omiting no circumstances, no object animate or inanimate which he thinks can add to their effectiveness; and, like most Sanskrit poets, he is unable to stop even when enough has been said. But Kālidāsa, like Shakespeare, suggests more than he expresses. Not one of those who gather round the body of Cordelia makes a phrase; the emotion is tense, but there is no declamation to work it up. The terrible blow given by the reported calumny regarding his beloved makes Rāma's heart, tossed in a terrible conflict between love and duty, break in pieces, like the heated iron beaten with a hammer; but he does not declaim, nor faint, nor shed a flood of tears. It is this silent suffering which makes Kālidāsa's Rāma a truly tragic figure. Not until Lakṣmaṇa returns and delivers the spirited but sad massage of his banished wife that the king in him breaks down and yields to the man; but even here Kālidāsa has only one short stanza (xiv. 84) which sums up with infinite suggestion the entire pity of the situation.

CHAPTER IV

THE SUCCESSORS OF KĀLIDĀSA IN POETRY

The difficulty of fixing an exact chronology, as well as the paucity and uncertainty of material, does not permit an orderly historical treatment of the poets and dramatists who, in all probability, flourished between Kālidāsa, on the one hand, and Māgha and Bhavabhūti, on the other. It must have been a period of great vitality and versatility ; for there is not a single department of literature which is left untouched or left in a rudimentary condition. But a great deal of its literary productions is probably lost, and the few that remain do not adequately represent its many-sided activity. We know nothing, for instance, of the extensive Prakrit literature, which presupposes Hāla's poetical compilation, and which sums up its folk-tale in the lost collection of Guṇāḍhya's *Bṛhatkathā*. No early collection also of the popular tale in Sanskrit has survived ; and of the possible descendants of the beast-fable, typified by the *Pañcatantra*, we know nothing. Concurrently with the tradition of Prakrit love-poetry in the stanza-form, illustrated by the *Sattasaī* of Hāla, must have started the same tradition in Sanskrit, which gives us the early Śataka of Amaru and which is followed up by those of Bhartṛhari and others ; but the exact relationship between the two traditions is unknown. The origin of the religious and gnomic stanzas, such as we find crystallised in the Stotra-Śatakas of Mayūra and Bāṇa and the reflective Śatakas of Bhartṛhari, is equally obscure. Nor do we know much about the beginnings of the peculiar type of the Sanskrit prose romance ; and we possess no earlier specimens of them than the fairly mature works of Daṇḍin, Bāṇa and Subandhu, who belong to this period. The dramatic works of Bhāsa and Kālidāsa must have inspired many a dramatist, but with the exception of Śūdraka, Viśākhadatta, Harṣa and the writers of four early Monologue Plays (Bhāṇas), ascribed respectively to Vararuci, Śūdraka, Īśvaradatta and Śyāmilaka, all other names have perished; while Bhaṭṭa Nārāyaṇa probably, and Bhavabhūti certainly, come at the end of this period. The number of early poetical works in Sanskrit, the so-called Mahākāvyas, is still fewer. If the poetical predecessors of Kālidāsa have all disappeared, leaving his finished achievement in poetry to stand by itself, this is still more the case with his succesors. Bhāravi, Bhaṭṭi, Kumāradāsa and Māgha, with just a few minor poets, practically complete the list of the composers of the Mahākāvya of this period. With the example of a consummate master of poetry to guide them, the general level of merit should have been fairly high and wide-spread; but, since much is apparently lost, the solitary altitudes become prominent and numerous in our survey.

1. The Erotic Śatakas of Amaru and Bhartṛhari

Although love-poetry blooms in its fullness in the Sanskrit literature, more than in the Vedic and Epic, its earliest specimens are lost. It should not be supposed that the passionate element in human nature never found expression. The episode of the love of Nanda and Sundarī painted by Aśvaghoṣa, the erotic theme of the poem of Ghaṭakarpara, as well as the very existence of the *Megha-dūta*, show that erotic poetry could not have been neglected. Love may not yet have come to its own in the Kunstpoesie, the polished and cultured Kāvya; but the example of Hāla's *Sattasaī*, whose stanzas are predominantly erotic, makes it possible that in folk-literature, the tradition of which is at least partially preserved in Prakrit, it finds an absorbing theme. The Prakrit poetry here is doubtless as conventional as Sanskrit, and is not folk-literature in its true sense; but it is clear that, while these early Prakrit stanzas, popular among the masses, have love for their principal subject, the early Sanskrit poems, so far as they have survived, do not often accept it as their exclusive theme. There is indeed no evidence to show that the Prakrit love-lyric is the prototype of the Sanskrit, but the presumption is strong that the erotic sentiment, which had diffused itself in the popular literature, survived in Prakrit poetry, and gradually invaded the courtly Sanskrit Kāvya, which provided a naturally fertile soil for it, and of which it ultimately became the almost universal theme.

It is remarkable, however, that, with the exception of a few works like the *Megha-dūta*, the Ghaṭakapara monody and the *Gīta-govinda*, which, again, are not unalloyed love-poems, the Sanskrit erotic poetry usually takes the form, not of a systematic well-knit poem, but of a single poetical stanza standing by itself, in which the poet delights to depict a single phase of the emotion or a single situation within the limits of a finely finished form. Such is the case mostly with the seven hundred Prakrit stanzas, which pass under the name of Hāla Sātavāhana. If in Prikrit the highest distinction belongs to Hāla's *Sattasaī* for being a collection which gives varied and charming expression to the emotion of love, the distinction belongs in Sanskrit without question[1] to the *Śataka* of Amaru, about whose date and personality, however, as little is known as about those of Hāla. It is a much smaller work, but it is no less distinctive and delightful.

A Śataka, meaning a century of detached stanzas, is usually regarded as the work of a single poet, although it is probable that Hāla's seven centuries, in the main form an anthology. The form, however, allows easy interpolation; and most of the early Śatakas contain much more than a hundred

1 Although the commentator Ravicandra finds a philosophical meaning in Amaru's stanzas! And Vemabhūpāla, another commentator, would take the work to be merely a rhetorical text-book of the same type as Rudra Bhaṭṭa's *Śṛṅgāra-tilaka*, meant to illustrate the various classes of the Nāyikā and the diversity of their amorous conditions!

stanzas. It is not always possible, however, for several reasons,[1] to separate the additions with certainty, and arrive at a definitive text. The *Amaru-śataka*,[2] for instance, is known to exist in at least four recensions,[3] in which the text fluctuates between totals of 96 and 115 stanzas,[4] the number of stanzas common to all the recensions, but given in varying sequence, being only 51. The uncertainty of the text not only makes an estimate of the work difficult, but also diminishes the value of any chronological conclusion which may be drawn from the citation of a particular stanza in later works. Vāmana's quotation,[5] for instance, in the beginning of the 9th century, of three stanzas without naming the work or the author, establishes nothing, although these stanzas occur in the present text of Amaru's *Śataka*. The earliest mention of Amaru as a poet of eminence is found in the middle of the 9th century in Ānandavardhana's work,[6] but it is of little assistance, as Amaru is perhaps a much earlier writer.

1 The attribution in the anthologies, which often quote from Amaru, is notoriously unreliable; and there is a great deal of divergence regarding the number and sequence of stanzas in the texts of the commentators and in the manuscripts of the work.

2 Ed. R. Simon, in four recensions (Roman characters), Kiel 1893 (Cf. *ZDMG*, XLIX, 1895, p. 577f); ed. Calcutta 1808 (see J. Gildemeister, *Bibliothecae Sanskritae*, Bonn 1847, p. 73, no. 162), with the comm. of Ravicandra (*alias* Jñānānanda Kalādhara); ed. Durgaprasad, with comm. of Arjunavarmadeva, with addl. stanzas from commentators and anthologies, NSP, 3rd ed., Bombay 1916 (1st ed., 1889).

3 Viz., South Indian (comm. Vemabhūpāla and Rāmānandanātha), Bengal (comm. Ravicandra), West Indian (comm. Arjunavarmadeva and Kokasaṁbhava), and Miscellaneous (comm. Rāmarudra, Rudramadeva, etc.). Simon bases his text chiefly on the South Indian recension, but it hardly supersedes the text of Arjunavarmadeva of Dhārā (circa 1215 A.D.), who is the oldest known commentator. No certainty, of course, is possible without further critical examination of materials.

4 Arjunavarman's printed text contains 102 stanzas; in the NSP. (Bombay) ed., the appendices add 61 verses from other commentators and anthologies. Aufrecht's suggestion (*ZDMG*, XXVII, p. 7f), on the analogy of one-metre Śatakas of Bāṇa and Mayūra, that only stanzas in the Śārdūlavikrīḍita metre are original, would give us about 54 to 61 in recensions i-iii, and only 33 in recension iv. For the anthology stanzas, some of which are fine pieces, but ascribed sometimes to other authors, see Thomas, *Kvs*, p. 22f; some of these are not traceable in the printed text; they are in varied metres.

5 Ed. Simon, nos. 16, 30, 89—Vāmana, *Kāvyālaṁkāra*, iii. 2. 4; iv. 3. 12; v. 2. 8.

6 *Dhvanyāloka* ed iii. 7.

The suggestion that he is later than Bhartṛhari proceeds chiefly on the debatable ground of style and technique ; but after the poetic art of Kālidāsa, elaboration and finish of expression may be expected in any writer, and need not prove anything. Even if Amaru is later than Bhartṛhari, the works of both exhibit certain charactersistics which would preclude a date later than this period, and probably they could not have been very far apart from each other in time.

Amaru is less wide in range than Hāla, but he strikes perhaps a deeper and subtler note. Amaru's poems lack a great deal of the homeliness and rough good sense of Hāla's erotic stanzas ; but they do not present, as more or less Hāla's verses do, the picture of simple love set among simple scenes. Amaru describes, with great delicacy of feeling and gracefulness of imagery, the infinite moods and fancies of love, its changes and chances, its strange vagaries and wanton wiles, its unexpected thoughts and unknown impulses, creating varied and subtle situatione. His language, with all the resources of Sanskrit, is carefully studied, but not extravagantly ornate ; and his gift of lyric phrasing gives it the happy touch of ease and naturalness. Amaru does not confine himself to the narrow limits of Hāla's slow-moving moric stanza, but appears to allow himself greater metrical variety and more freedom of space. His employment of long sonorous metres, as well as short lyric measures,[1] not only relieves the monotony of metrical effect, but adds richness, weight and music to his little camoes of thought and feeling.

In spirit of inequalities, almost every stanza in this collection possesses a charm of its own ;[2] and the necessity of compressing

[1] The metres employed in their order of frequency are : Śārdūlavikrīḍita, Hariṇī, Śikhariṇī, Mandākrāntā, Sragdharā, Vasantilaka and Mālinī ; while Drutavilambita, Vaktra and Vaṁśasthavila occur sporadically in some recensions only. See Simon's metrical analysis p. 46.

[2] For some specimens, with translation, S. K. De, *Treatment of Love in Sanskrit Literature*, Calcutta 1929, p. 28f ; C. R. Narsimha Sarma, *Studies in Sanskrit Lit.*, Mysore 1936, pp. 1-30.

synthetically one whole idea or image within the limits of a single stanza not only gives a precision and restrained elegance to the diction, but also presents, in each stanza, a complete picture in a finely finished form. In this art of miniature word-painting, of which we have already spoken, Amaru unquestionably excels. The love depicted in his stanzas is often youthful and impassioned, in which the sense and the spirit meet, with all the emotions of longing, hope, ecstasy, jealousy, anger, disappointment, despair, reconciliation and fruition. Amaru's world is indeed different from ours, but his pictures are marked by a spirit of closeness to life and common realities, not often seen in the laboured and sustained masterpieces of this period, as well as by an emotional yet picturesque directness, by a subtle harmony of sound and sense, and by a freedom from mere rhetoric,—qualities which are not entirely devoid of appeal to modern taste. But, on the surface, the light of jewelled fancy plays, and makes beautiful even the pains and pangs which are inseparable from the joys and hopes of love. It is not love tossed on the stormy sea of manhood and womanhood, nor is it that infinite passion and pain of finite hearts which lead to a richer and wider life. But, as we have already said, the Sanskrit poet delights in depicting the playful moods of love, its aspects of Līlā, in which even sorrow becomes a luxury. When he touches a deeper chord, the tone of earnestness is unmistakable, but its poignancy is rendered pleasing by a truely poetic enjoyment of its tender and pathetic implications. Rightly does Ānandavardhana praise the stanzas of Amaru as containing the veriable ambrosia of poetry; and in illustrating the theme of love as a sentiment in Sanskrit poetry, all writers on Poetics have freely used Amaru as one of the original and best sources. In Sanskrit sentimental poetry, Amaru should be regarded as the herald of a new development, of which the result is best seen in the remarkable fineness, richness of expression and delicacy of thought and feeling of the love-poems of later Śatakas, of the numerous anthologies, and even of the poetical drama.

The same traits as we notice in the *Śataka* of Amaru are found more or less in later centuries of love-poems, among which the *Śṛṅgāra-śataka* of Bhartṛhari must be singled out, not only for its early date and literary excellence, but also for the interest which attaches to the legends surrounding the mysterious personality of the author. Tradition ascribes to him also two other Śatakas, on wise conduct (*Nīti*) and resignation (*Vairāgya*), respectively, as well as an exposition of the philosophy of speech, entitled *Vākyapadīya*.[2] Although the last named work shows little of the softer gift of poetry, it is not inherently impossible for the poet to turn into a philosophical grammarian. From the Buddhist pilgrim Yi-tsing we know that a grammarian Bhartṛhari, apparently the author of the *Vākyapadīya*, died about 651 A.D.; and even if his reference does not make it clear whether Bhartṛhari was also the poet of the three Śatakas, his ignoring or ignorance of them need not be exaggerated. Bhartṛhari, the grammarian, was probably a Buddhist,[3] but the fact that the Śatakas reveal a Śaiva of the Vedānta persuasion[4] does not necessarily justify the supposition of two Bhartṛharis; for, apart from the question of interpolation,

1 Ed. P. Bohlen, with Latin trs., Berlin 1833; also ed., in Haeberlin's Kāvya-saṁgraha p. 143 f., reprinted in Jivananda's Kāvya-saṁgraha, II, p. 53 f., which also contains the Nīti and Vairāgya at pp. 125 f., 172 f. The Nīti and Vairāgya have been edited. from a number of Mss, and with extracts from commentaries, by K. T. Telang, Bomb. Skt. Ser., 1874, 1885. Thr three Śatakas are also printed, under the title Subhāṣitatriśatī, with comm. of Rāmacandra Budhendra, NSP, [6th revised ed., Bombay 1922 (1st ed. 1902)] A critical edition of the Śatakas is still a necessity. Eng. trs., in verse, of Nīti and Vairāgya by C. H. Tawney in *IA*, V, 1876 (reprinted, separately, Calcutta 1877); all the Śatakas trs. B. H. Wortham, Trübner: London 1886; J. M. Kennedy, London 1913; C. W. Gurner, Calcutta 1927.

2 Sometimes the grammatical poem *Bhaṭṭi-kāvya* is ascribed to him, but there is nothing more than the name Bhaṭṭi as a Prakritised form of Bhartṛ to support the attribuiion. The legends which make Bhartṛhari a brother of the still more mysterious Vikramāditya is useless for any historical purpose. The story has been dramatised in later times in the *Bhartṛhari-nirveda* of Harihara, ed. NSP, Bombay 1912. Cf. Gray in *JAOS*, XXV, 1904, p. 197 f.; A.V. W. Jackson in *JAOS*, XXIII, 1902, p. 313 f.

3 See Pathak in *JBRAS*, XVIII, 1893, p. 341 f.; but this view has not found general acceptance.

4 Telang. *op. cit.*, p. ix f.

Harṣa likewise invokes the Buddha in his *Nāgānanda*, but pays homage to Śiva in his *Ratnāvalī*.

The texts of the Śatakas of Bhartṛhari, as they stand, are much more uncertain and devoid of definite structure than that of Amaru's Śataka ; and stanzas from them occur in the works of other well-known writers,[1] or ascribed to other authors in the anthologies. The fact, however, should not be made the ground of the presumption that Bhartṛhari, like Vyāsa and Cāṇakya, is only a name under which miscellaneous compilations were passed,[2] or that Bhartṛhari himself incorporated stanzas from other writers to make up his own poem.[3] The argument lacks neither ingenuity nor plausibility, but very few Śatakas, early or later, have escaped the misfortune of tampering and interpolation ; and a critical examination of the textual question is necessary before the problem can be satisfactorily solved. There is still nothing to prevent us from accepting the tradition of Bhartṛhari's original authorship, which is almost uniform and unbroken, and which does not relegate him to the position of a mere compiler.

Nor is there any cogency in the suggestion that the *Śṛṅgāra-śataka* alone is genuine, made on the allged ground that it shows individuality and unity of structure as the product of a single creative mind. As the text itself is admittedly uncertain, regarding both originality and order of stanzas, such surmises, based on content and style, are always risky ; but there is hardly anything to justify the position that the *Śṛṅgāra-śataka* can be sharply distinguished in this or other respects from the *Nīti-* and *Vairāgya-śatakas*. If there is any substance in the legend recorded by Yi-tsing that Bhartṛhari vacillated no less than seven times between the comparative charms of the monastery and the world, it signifies that the poet who wrote a century of passionate

1 E.g. in *Abeijñāna-śakuntala, Mudrā-rākṣasa* and *Tantrākhyāyika* ; see Peterson *Sbhv*, pp. 74-75.

2 Aufrecht *Leipzig Catalogue*, no. 417.

3 Bohlen, *op. cit.*, Prefatio, p. viii.

stanzas could very well write the other two centuries on worldly wisdom and renunciation.

The susceptibility to contrary attractions is evident in all the three Śatakas. The *Nīti-śataka* should not be taken as a mere collection of moral maxims or an epitome of good sense and prudence ; it shows at once a lurking attachment to the world and an open revulsion from its sordidness. The poet says, with considerable bitterness, at the outset : "Those who are capable of understanding me are full of envy ; men in power are by arrogance disqualified ; all others labour under stupidity ; all my good sayings have, therefore, grown old within myself." In the same strain, the poet refers to the haughtiness of kings, to the power of wealth, to the humiliation of servitude, to the clash of passion and prejudice with culture and education, to the wicked and the ignorant reviling the good and the wise, and to the distressing things of life, which he calls darts rankling in his heart. Nor is the *Vairāgya-śataka* the work of an ascetic or inelastic mind. It gives expression to the passionate pain of an idealist, whose inborn belief in the goodness of the world is shattered by the sense of its hollowness and wickedness. It refers to the never-ending worries of earning and spending, of service and perpetual insults to one's self-respect, and of the wreck of human hopes in the striving for an ideal ; it condemns the smug complacency of humanity in the midst of disease, decay and death, and falls back upon the cultivation of a spirit of detachment.

The vehemence with which Bhartṛhari denounces the joys of life and attractions of love in these two poems is on a level with his attitude disclosed in his stanzas on love ; for the *Śṛṅgāra-śataka* is not so much a poem on love as on the essential emptiness of love, an outburst not so much on its ecstasies and sunny memories by a self-forgetful lover, as on its darkening sorrows and wrongs by a man in bitter earnest. It indicates a frame of mind wavering between abandon and restraint ; "either the fair lady or the cave of the mountains," "either youth or the forest," "either an abode on the sacred banks of the Ganges or in the delightful embrace of a young woman"—sentiments like these are scattered throughout. The delights of life and love are as much captiviting as they are reprehensible ; the bitterness of the denunciation only indicates the measure of the terrible fascination which love and life exert on the poet ; it arises not so much from any innate repugnance as from the distressing necessity of convincing himself and tearing away from them. Bhartṛhari's philosophy of love is simple : woman is both joy and sorrow, trouble and appeasement ; there is continual attraction and continual repulsion ; from loving too much the poet ceases to love at all and takes to asceticism. A man of artistic temperament and strong passions, the poet frankly delights in all that is delightful, but it gives him no peace nor any sure foothold anywhere. The tone is not sombre, but pungent, and even vitriolic. Bhartṛhari inevitably reminds one of Aśvaghoṣa, by the side of whose indignant outburst against woman, can be placed his biting interrogation : "Who has created woman as a contrivance for the bondage of all living creatures : woman, who is the whirlpool of all doubt, the universe of indiscipline, the abode of all daring, the receptacle of all evil, the deceitful soil of manifold distrust, the box of trickery and illusion, a poison coated with ambrosia, the hindrance to heaven and a way to the depth of hell ?" If the poet sometimes attains a calmer frame of mind in his two other Śatakas on Nīti and Vairāgya, his intense conviction is hard-won, and can be best understood in the light of the powerful longings and their attendant sufferings which he describes in his Śataka on love. It is no wonder that his assumption of the yellow garb so often conflicted with his craving for worldly delights.

Bhartṛhari, therefore, differs from Amaru both in attitude and expression. He is too earnest to believe in the exaltation of woman as such, even though he cannot withstand the fascination ; he is too serious to depict in swift succession the hundreds of tender memories and pleasing pains of love, its flying thoughts and dancing feelings, its delicate lights and shades, in the same way as they reflect themselves in Amaru's little poems in their playful warmth and colour. Bhartṛhari's miniature love-stanzas have not the same picturesqueness of touch, the same delicacy and elegance of expression, but they gain in intensity, depth and range,[1] because they speak of things which lie at the core of his being ; they have enough piquancy and sharpness to require any graceful trimming. If Amaru describes the emotion of love and the relation of lovers for their own sake and without any implication for connecting them with larger aspects of life, Bhartṛhari is too much occupied with life itself to forget its worries, and consider love and women[2] apart from it in any fanciful or ideal aspect. Amaru has perhaps more real poetry, but Bhartṛhari has more genuine feeling.[3]

There is a large number of erotic and reflective stanzas scattered throughout the Sanskrit anthologies, but the absence or uncertainty of chronological data makes it difficult to separate the early from the late compositions. If, however, the anthology poet Dharmakīrti, who is sometimes cited also with the epithet Bhadanta, be the Buddhist logician and philosopher, he should

1 The metres employed by Bhartṛhari in the present texts of his three pomes are diversified, but his inclination to long sonorours measures is shown by his use of Sragdharā twenty-two times. See L. H. Gray, The Metres of Bhartṛhari in *JAOS*, XX, 1899, pp, 157-59.

2 It is notworthy that Amaru always speaks of man's fickleness, and never echoes the almost universal bitterness regarding woman's inconstancy, which characterises much of the poetical, as well as religious and didactic, literature. Bhartṛhari, in one passage, recommends boldness and even aggressiveness in dealing with women, which the commentator facetiously explains by saying that otherwise woman will dominate man !—For a general appreciation of Bhartṛhari; see C. R. Narsimha Sarma, *op. cit.*, pp. 23-56 ; H. Oldenberg, *Lit. d. alten indien*, p. 221 f. ; S. K. De, *op. cit.*, p. 34 f.

3 The attitude of mind, which leaves no alternative between the world and the monastery, between love and renunciation, is not only an individuai trait, but seems to have marked the outlook of a class of Sanskrit poets, who wrote stanzas, applicable by *doubte entente* at once to the themes of enjoyment and resignation. In general also, the Sanskrit poets have enough simplicity and integrity of feeling to make them grateful for the joys of life, but penitent when they have exceeded in enjoying them. In such an atmosphere, it is clear, the idea of the chivalrous Platonic love or the so-called intellectual love could not develop at all.

belong to a period between the 6th and 7th century A.D. The total number of stanzas independently assigned to him in the different anthologies[1] is about sixteen.[2] There is nothing of the scholar or the pedant in these elegant little poems, which are generally of an erotic character, and some of them are worthy of being placed by the side of those of Amaru and Bhartṛhari. If Dharmakīrti, in the intervals of heavier work, wrote such a collection, its loss is much to be regretted.

2. The Stotra-Śatakas of Bāṇa, Mayūra and others

The vogue into which the Śataka style of poetry came in this period is also illustrated by the Stotras of Mayūra and Bāṇa, but their spirit, theme and method are different. The production of hymns in praise of deities obtained from the Vedic times, but the ancients possessed the secret of making their religion poetry and their poetry religion. Their descendants lost the art, but evolved a new type of Stotras or poem of praise and prayer. The Epics, as well as the Purāṇas and Tantras of uncertain date, abound in liturgical poems in which the gods of the new Hindu mythology receive adoration ; while the Jainas and Buddhists do not stay behind in addressing a large number of similar religious poems to the deities and teachers of their own pantheon and hagiology. Some of these compositions are meant solely for the purpose of sects and cults ; some are mere theological collections of sacred epithets or

1 For a complete list, see Thomas, *Kvs*, pp. 47-50, which gives also a list of Dharmakīrti's poetical works translated into Tibetan, including two Stotras. Also see Peterson, *Sbhv*, pp. 46-48, and in *JBRAS*, XVI, pp. 172-73 ; Aufrecht in *Ind. Stud.*, XVI, pp. 204-7, *ZDMG*, XXVII, p. 41.

2 Of these, Ānandavardhana quotes one (iii, p. 216 ; *lāvaṇya-draviṇa°*) with the remark: *tathā cāyaṁ Dharmakīrteḥ śloka iti prasiddhiḥ, saṁbhāvyate ca tasyaiva* ; and he adds another stanza (p. 217) by Dharmakīrti, which is not found in the anothologies. The first of these stanzas is also quoted and ascribed to Dharmakīrti by Kṣemendra in his *Aucitya-vicāra*.

strings of a hundred or thousand sacred names ; most of them have a stereotyped form and little individuality ; but the higher poetry and philosophy also invaded the field. Aśvaghoṣa's early eulogy of the Buddha in *Buddha-carita* xxvii is unfortunately lost in Sanskrit, while the Stotras of his school, as well as the spurious *Gaṇḍī-stotra* of a somewhat later time, are hardly of much poetical worth. We have, however, two remarkable Stotras to Viṣṇu and Brahman, both in the Śloka metre, uttered by the gods in Kālidāsa's *Raghu°* (x. 16-32) and *Kumāra°* (iii. 4-15) respectively, although it is somewhat strange that there is no direct Stotra to his beloved deity Śiva. In this connexion, a reference may be made to a similar insertion of Stotras in the Mahākāvyas of the period, such as the Stava of Mahādeva by Arjuna in the closing canto of Bhāravi's poem, that of Kṛṣṇa by Bhīṣma in *Śiśupāla-vadha* xiv, and that of Caṇḍī by the gods in Ratnākara's *Hara-vijaya* xlvii (167 stanzas). But praise and panegyric very early became the individual theme of separate poems ; and an endless number of Stotras has survived.[1] They are mostly late, and of little literary worth ; for many have attempted but very few have succeeded in the exceedingly difficult task of sacred verse. Their theme and treatment do not always concern Vairāgya, but their devotional feeling is undoubted, and they are seldom merely doctrinal or abstract. Their objective, however, is not poetry, and they seldom attain its proper accent. It is no wonder, therefore, that the Sanskrit poeticians and anthologists do not give much prominence to the Stotra works, nor consider them worthy of a separate treatment.

The early efforts of Mayūra and Bāṇabhaṭṭa are not very impressive for their purely poetic merit, but they illustrate the early application of the elegant, but distinctly laboured, manner of the Kāvya and its rhetorical contrivances to this kind of litera-

1 For religious hymnology, in general, a subject which has not yet been adequately studied, see S. P. Bhattacharyya, The Stotra-Literature of Old India in *IHQ*, I, 1925, pp. 340-60, for an eloquent appreciation.

ture. Mayūra is associated,[1] chiefly by late Jaina legends, assertions of late commentators and recorded traditions of anthologists, with Bāṇabhaṭṭa as a literary rival in the court of Harṣa and as related by marriage either as brother-in-law or father-in-law.[2] The legends also speak of Mayūra's affliction with leprosy by the angry curse of Bāṇa's wife, Mayūra's alleged sister or daughter, whose intimate personal beauty he is said to have described in an indiscreet poem. This work is supposed to be identical with the highly erotic, but rather conventional, poem of eight fragmentary stanzas, which goes by the name *Mayūrāṣṭaka*,[3] and which describes a fair lady returning from a secret visit to her lover. Three of its stanzas are in Sragdharā (the metre of *Sūrya-śataka*) and the rest in Śārdūlavikrīḍita ; it refers, with more wit than taste, to the "tiger-sport" of the lady with the "demon of a lover," and to the beauty of her limbs which makes even an old man amorously inclined.[4] If the poem is genuine, it is possible that such descriptions in the poem itself started the legend ; but the legend also adds that a miraculous recovery from the unhappy disease was effected, through the grace of the sun-god, by Mayūra's composing his well-known poem, the *Sūrya-*

1 All that is known of Mayūra and his genuine and ascribed works will be found in G. P. Quackenbos, *The Sanskrit Poems of Mayūra*, New Vork 1917 (Columbia Univ. Indo-Iranian series) ; it gives the works in Roman transliteration, with Eng. trs. and notes, and also contains the *Caṇḍī-śataka* of Bāṇa with trs. and notes.

2 In the enumeration of the friends of his youth, who are said to have been of the same age (*vayasā samānāḥ*), Bāṇa refers in his *Harṣa-carita* (ed. A. A. Führer, Bombay 1909, p. 67 ; ed. Parab, NSP, Bombay 1892, p. 47, 4th ed., 1914, p. 42) to a certain Jaṅgulika or snake-doctor, appropriately named Mayūraka, who may or may not be our poet ; but the earliest mention of the poet Mayūra, along with Bāṇa, in the court of Harṣa occurs in the *Navasāhasāṅka-carita* (ii. 18) of Padmagupta (about 1005 A. D.). The later eulogistic stanza of Rājaśekhara in *Sml.* (iv. 68), however, punningly alludes to the art of the snake-doctor. The earliest anonymous quotation of two stanzas (Nos. 9, 23) from the *Sūrya-śataka* of Mayūra occurs in Ānandavardhana's *Dhvanyāloka* (2nd half of the 9th century), ii, p. 92 and 99-100. There is another much inferior tradition which connects him, along with many other Sanskrit poets, with king Bhojo of Dhārā.

3 Quackenbos, *op. cit.*, pp. 72-79, text and trs. ; also in *JAOS*, XXXI, 1911, pp, 343-54.

4 *Kenaiṣā rati-rākṣasena ramitā śārdūla-vikrīḍitā*, st. 3 ; and *dṛṣṭvā rūpam idaṁ priyāṅga-gahanaṁ vṛddho'pi kāmāyate*, st. 5.

śataka,[1] in praise of the deity. But it must be said that the Śataka gives the impression of being actuated not so much by piety as by the spirit of literary display. The theme of the work, which retains in its present form exactly one hundred stanzas,[2] consists of an extravagant description and praise of the sun-god and his appurtenances, namely, his rays, the horses that draw his chariot, his charioteer Aruṇa, the chariot itself and the solar disc. The sixth stanza of the poem refers to the sun's power of healing diseases, which apparently set the legend rolling; but the belief that the sun can inflict and cure leprosy is old, being preserved in the Iranian story of Sām, the prototype of the Purāṇic legend of Sāmba; it may not have anything to do with the presumption that the cult of the sun was popular in the days of Harṣa, even if Harṣa's father is described in the *Harṣa-carita* as a devotee of the sun. With all its devotional attitude, the poem is written in the elaborate Sragdharā metre; and its diction, with its obvious partiality for compound words, difficult construction, constant alliteration, jingling of syllables and other rhetorical devices,[3] is equally

1 Ed. G. P. Quackenbos, as above. Also ed. in Haeberlin, *op. cit.*, p. 197 f., reproduced in Jivananda, *op. cit.*, II, pp. 222 f.; ed. Durgaprasad and K. P. Parab with comm. of Tribhuvanapāla, NSP, Bombay 1889, 1927; ed. with comm. of Yajñeśvara, in Pothi form, Baroda Saṁvat 1928 (=1872 A.D.). The Ceylonese paraphrase (Sanna) by Vilgammūla Mahāṭhere, with text, ed. Don A. de Silva Devarakkhita Baṭuvantuḍave, Colombo 1883 (see *JRAS*. XXVI, 1894, p. 555 and XXVIII, 1896, pp. 215-16).

2 With an apparently spurious stanza at the end, not noticed by the commentator, in NSP ed., giving the name of the author and the Phala-śruti. The order of the stanzas, however, is not the same in all editions and manuscripts; but this is of little consequence in a loosely constructed poem of this kind.

3 It is remarkable that puns are *not* frequent; and the poem has some clever, but very elaborate, similes and metaphors, e.g., that of the thirsty traveller (st. 14), of antidote against poison (st. 31), of the day-tree (st. 34), of the dramatic technique (st. 50); there is a play on the numerals from one to ten (st. 13; cf. *Buddha-carita* ii. 41); harsh-sounding series of syllables often occur (st. 6, 98 etc.); while st. 71 is cited by Mammaṭa as an instance of a composition, where facts are distorted in order to effect an alliteration. The Akṣara-ḍambara, which Bāṇa finds in the diction of the Gauḍas, is abundant here, as well as in his own *Caṇḍī-śataka*; and it is no wonder that one of the commentators, Madhusūdana (about 1654 A.D.), gives to both Mayūra and Bāṇa the designation of eastern poets (Paurastya).

elaborate. The quality of graceful and dignified expression and the flowing gorgeousness of the metre may be admitted ; in fact, the majesty which this compactly loaded metre can put on has seldom been better shown ; but the highly stilted and recondite tendencies of the work have little touch of spontaneous inspiration about them. Whatever power there is of visual presentation, it is often neutralised by the delibrate selection and practice of laboured tricks of rhetoric. The work is naturally favoured by the rhetoricians, grammarians and lexicographers, and frequently commented upon,[1] but to class it with the poems of Kālidāsa and Bhavabhuti shows the lack of ability to distinguish between real poetry and its make-believe.[2]

The *Caṇḍī-śataka*[3] of Bāṇa is of no higher poetical merit ; it is cited even less by rhetoricians[4] and anthologists, and commentaries on it are much fewer.[5] Written and composed in the same sonorous Sragdharā metre[6] (102 stanzas) and in the same elaborate rhetorical diction, the poem shows noteworthy similarity to Mayūra's Śataka, and lends plusibility to the tradition that it was composed in admiring rivalry. The myth of Caṇḍī's slaying of the buffalo-demon is old, being mentioned in the *Mahābhārata* (ix. 44-46) and amplified in the Purāṇas ; but Bāṇa makes use of it, not for embellishing the story, but for a high-flown panegyric of Caṇḍī, including a glorification

1 The number of commentaries listed by Aufrecht is 25 ; see Quackenbos, *op. cit.*, p. 103.

2 About 20 stanzas in various metres, not traceable in this work, are assigned to Mayūra in the anthologies ; some of them are clever and less artificial, but are not of much poetical value. For these see Quackenbos, pp. 229-42. Some of these verses are ascribed to other poets as well ; see Thomas, *Kvs*, p. 67f.

3 Ed. in Kāvyamālā, Gucchaka iv, with a Sanskrit comm. : ed. G. P. Quackenbos, as above, pp. 243-357. There is nothing improbable in Bāṇa's authorship of the work. Arjunavarmadeva in the 12th century (on Amaru, st. 1) expressly ascribes this work to Bāṇa and quotes a stanza from it. There is a picturesque description of a temple of Caṇḍikā in Bāṇa's *Kādambarī*.

4 The earliest quotation is by Bhoja, who cites st. 40 and 66.

5 Only two or three commentaries are, so far, known.

6 With the exception of six stanzas in Śārdūlavikrīḍita (nos. 25, 32, 49, 55, 56, 72), which may or may not be original, for the variation has no special motive.

of the power of Caṇḍī's left foot which killed the demon by its marvellous kick ! Bāṇa does not adopt Mayūra's method of systematic description of the various objects connected with Caṇḍī, but seeks diversion by introducing, in as many as forty-eight stanzas, speeches in the first person (without dialogue) by Caṇḍī, Mahiṣa, Caṇḍī's handmaids Jayā and Vijayā, Śiva, Kārttikeya, the gods and demons—and even by the foot and toe-nails of Caṇḍī ! Bāṇa has none of Mayūra's elaborate similes, but puns are of frequent occurrence and are carried to the extent of involving interpretation of entire individual stanzas in two ways. There is an equally marked tendency towards involved and recondite constructions, but the stylistic devices and love of conceits are perhaps more numerous and prominent. The work has all the reprehensible features of the verbal bombast with which Bāṇa himself characterises the style of the Gauḍas. Even the long-drawn-out and never sluggish melody of its voluminous metre does not fully redeem its artificialities of idea and expression, while the magnificent picturesqueness, which characterises Bāṇa's prose works, is not much in evidence here. To a greater extent than Mayūra's Śataka, it is a poetical curiosity rather than a real poem ; but it is an interesting indication of the decline of poetic taste and growing artificiality of poetic form, which now begin to mark the growth of the Kāvya.

One of Rājaśekhara's eulogistic stanzas quoted in the *Sūktimuktāvalī* (iv. 70) connects Bāṇa and Mayūra with Mātaṅga (*v. l.* Caṇḍāla)[1] Divākara as their literary rival in the court of king Harṣa. Nothing remains of his work except four stanzas quoted in the *Subhāṣitāvali*, of which one (no. 2546), describing the sea-girdled earth successively as the grandmother, mother, spouse and daughter-in-law, apparently of king Harṣa, has been censured for inelegance by Abhinavagupta. It has been suggested[2] that the

1 The GOS edition (Baroda 1938, p. 45) reads Caṇḍāla, without any variant, but with the note that the reading Mātaṅga is found in *ŚP*. Apparently the latter reading is sporadic.

2 F. Hall, introd. to *Vāsavadattā*, Calcutta 1859, p. 21, and Maxmüller, *India*, p. 330. note 5.

poet should be identified with Mānatuṅga, the well known Jaina Ācārya and author of two Stotras (namely, the *Bhaktāmara*[1] in Sanskrit and *Bhayahara*[2] in Prakrit), on the ground that some Jaina tales of miracles[3] connect him with Bāṇa and Mayura. But the evidence is undoubtedly weak,[4] and the presumption that the three Stotras of Bāṇa, Mayūra and this poet were meant respectively to celebrate sun-worship, Śaktism and Jainism is more schematic than convincing. The date of Mānatuṅga is uncertain ; the Jaina monastic records place him as early as the 3rd century A.D., but other traditions bring him down to periods between the 5th and the 9th century A.D. There is little basis of comparison between Mānatuṅga's Stotra and the Śatakas of Bāṇa and Mayūra. It consists of 44 or 48 stanzas, in the lighter and shorter Vasantatilaka metre, in praise of the Jina Ṛṣabha as the incomparable and almost deified saint ; but it is not set forth in the Āśir form of Bāṇa and Mayūra's Śatakas, being directly addressed to the saint. It is in the ornate manner, but it is much less elaborate, and the rhetorical devices, especially punning, are not prominent. Its devotional feeling is unmistakable, but there is little that is distinctive in its form and content.[5]

To the king-poet Harṣavardhana himself are ascribed, besides the three well known plays, some Buddhist Stotras of doubtful poetical value, if not of doubtful authorship. Of these,

1 Ed. Kāvyamālā, Gucchaka vii, pp. 1-10 ; also ed. and trs. H. Jacobi in *Ind. Stud.*, XIV, p. 359f. The title is suggested by the opening words of the poem.

2 Addressed to Jina Pārśvanātha, but the work is not yet printed. In 1309 A. D. Jinaprabha Sūri wrote a commentary on it (Peterson, *Report 1882-83*, p. 52).

3 The legend of the Jina's delivering Mānatuṅga from his self-imposed fetters, on the parallel of Caṇḍīs healing the self-amputated limbs of Bāṇa, is probably suggested by the general reference in the poem itself to the Jina's power, apparently in a metaphorical sense of releasing the devotee from fetters.

4 See Quackenbos, *op. cit.*, p. 10f.

5 The later Jaina Stotras, in spite of their devotional importance, are not of much literary value ; see Winternitz, *HIL*, II, p. 551f. Even the *Kalyāṇa-mandira* Stotra (ed. Kāvyamālā and *Ind. Stud., loc. cit.*) of Siddhasena Divākara is a deliberate and much more laboured imitation of the *Bhaktāmara* in the same metre and same number (44) of stanzas.

the *Suprabha* or *Suprabhāta* Stotra,[1] recovered in Sanskrit, is a morning hymn of twenty-four stanzas addressed to the Buddha, in the Mālinī metre. About a dozen occasional stanzas, chiefly of an erotic character, but of a finer quality than the Stotra, are assigned to Harṣa in the anthologies, in addition to a large number which can be traced mainly in the *Ratnāvalī* and the *Nāgānanda.*[2]

3. The Mahākāvya from Bhāravi to Māgha

One of the most remarkable offshoots of the literature of this period is represented by a group of Kālidāsa's direct and impressive poetical descendants, who made it their business to keep up the tradition of the sustained and elevated poetical composition, known in Sanskrit as the Mahākāvya, but who developed and established it in such a way as to stereotype it for all time to come. The impetus, no doubt, came from Kālidāsa's two so-called Mahākāvyas, but the form and content of the species were worked out in a different spirit. It would be unhistorical in this connexion to consider the definitions of the Mahākāvya given by the rhetoricians,[3] for none of them is earlier than Kālidāsa, and the question whether Kālidāsa conformed to them

1 Ascribed wrongly to king Harṣadeva of Kashmir in *Bstan-hgyur* and in Minayeff's manuscripts. It is given in extenso by Thomas in *JRAS*, 1903, pp. 703-22 and reproduced in App. B. to P. V. Kane's ed. of *Harṣa-carita*, Bombay 1918 See *Sbhv*, Introd. under Suprabhāta.

2 The anthological and inscriptional verses ascribed to Harṣa are collected together in introd. to *Priyadarśikā*, ed. Nariman, Jackson and Ogden, New York 1923, p. xlivf, and Thomas, *Kvs*. See M. L. Ettinghausen, *Harṣavardhana*, Louvain 1906, pp. 161-79.

3 J. Nobel, *The Foundations of Indian Poetry*, Calcutta 1925, p. 140f. The Mahākāvya or 'Great Poem' is a poetical narrative of heroic characters and exploits, but it is not a work of the type of the Great Epics, the *Mahābhārata* or the *Rāmāyaṇa*, which correspond to our sense of a heroic poem, but which are classified and distinguished as Itihāsas. The eminence denoted by the prefix 'great' does not refer to the more primitive epic or heroic spirit nor to directness and simplicity, but rather to the bulk, sustained workmanship and general literary competence of these more sophisticated and deliberate productions. If an analogy is permissible, the Mahākāvyas stand in the same relation to the Great Epics as the work of Milton does to that of Homer.

does not arise. Nor should the group of early poets, with whom we are occupied here, be supposed to have followed them. On the contrary, the norm, which even the two earliest rhetoricians, Bhāmaha (i. 19-23) and Daṇḍin (i. 14-19), lay down appears to have been deduced from the works of these poets themselves, especially from those of Bhāravi, the main features of which are generalised into rules of universal application. As such, the definitions are, no doubt, empirical, but they deal with accidents rather than with essentials, and do not throw much light upon the historical or poetic character of these compositions.

Perhaps for this reason, Vāmana (i. 3. 22) brushes aside the definitions as of no special interest ; but it is important to note that the rather extensive analysis of Rudraṭa (xvi. 7-19), more than that of earlier rhetoricians, emphasises at least one interesting characteristic of the Mahākāvya, as we know them, when it prescribes the rules for the development of the theme. Like his predecessors, he speaks indeed of such formal requirements as the commencement of the poem with a prayer, blessing or indication of content, the pursuit of the fourfold ends of life (conduct, worldly success, love and emancipation) the noble descent of the hero, the occurrence of sentiments and ornaments, the division into cantos, the change of metre at the end of each canto, and so forth ; but he also gives a list of diverse topics which may be introduced into the main narrative. These include not only subjects like political consultation, sending of messengers and spies, encampment, campaign and triumph of the hero, but also descriptions of towns, citizens, oceans, mountains, rivers, seasons, sunset, moonrise, dawn, sport in park or in water, drinking bouts and amorous dalliance. All this is, of course, prescribed as it is found conspicuously in Bhāravi and Māgha ; but Rudraṭa adds that in due time the poet may resume the thread of the main narrative, implying thereby that these descriptions, no matter what their relevancy is, should be inserted as a matter of conventional amplification and embellishment, and may even hold up and interrupt the story itself for a considerable length. This seldom happens in Kālidāsa, in whom the narrative never loses its interest in subsidiary matters ; but in Bhāravi and Māgha these banal topics, loosely connected with the main theme, spread over at least five (iv, v, viii-x) and six (vi-xi) entire cantos respectively, until the particular poet has leisure to return to his narrative. While Bhaṭṭi is sparing in these digressions, which are found mostly scattered in cantos ii, x and xi, Kumāradāsa devotes considerable space to them (cantos i, iii, viii, ix and xii). Although there is, in these passages, evidence of fluent, and often fine, descriptive power, the inventiveness is neither free nor fertile, but moves in the conventional groove of prescribed subjects and ideas, and the over-loading of the parts necessarily leads to the weakening of the central argument.

The motive for such adventitious matter is fairly obvious. It is meant to afford the poet unchartered freedom to indulge in his luxuriant descriptive talent and show off his skill and learning. While it tends to make the content of the poem rich and diversified, one inevitable result of this practice is that the story is thereby pushed into the background, and the poetical embellishments, instead of being incidental and accessory, become the main point of the Mahākāvya. The narrative ceases to be interesting compared to the descriptive, argumentative or erotic divagations of unconscionable length ; there is abundance, but no sense of proportion. The theme, therefore, is often too slender and insignificant ; whatever may be there of it is swamped by a huge mass of digressive matter, on which the poet chiefly concentrates ; and the whole poem becomes, not an organic whole, but a mosaic of poetic fragments, tastelessly cemented together.

It must be admitted that there is no lack of interesting matter in these Mahākāvyas, but the matter is deliberately made less interesting than the manner. The elegant, pseudo-heroic or succulent passages are generally out of place, but they are an admirable outlet for the fantastic fancy and love of rhetoric and declamation which characterise these poets. At the time we have reached, the stream of original thought and feeling, after attaining its high-water mark in Kālidāsa, was decidedly slackening. The successors of Kālidāsa pretend to hand down the tradition of their predecessor's great achievement, but what they lack in poetic inspiration, they make up by rhetoric in its full and varied sense. The whole literature is indeed so saturated with rhetoric that everything, more or less, takes a rhetorical turn. It seeks to produce, most often successfully, fine effects, not by power of matter, but by power of form, not by the glow of inspiration, but by the exuberance of craftsmanship ; and one may truly say that it is the age of cultivated form. If Kālidāsa left Sanskrit poetry a finished body, the subsequent ages did no more than weave its successive robes of adornment.

There is, therefore, an abundance of technical skill—and technical skill of no despicable kind—in the Mahākāvyas of this period, but there is a corresponding deficiency of those subtle and indefinable poetic powers, which make a composition vital in its appeal. The rhetoric, no doubt, serves its own purpose in these poems, and no one can deny its vigour and variety ; but it never goes very far, and often overreaches itself by its cleverness and excess. It breeds in the poets an inordinate love for itself, which seduces them to a prolixity, disproportionate to their theme, and to an extravagance of diction and imagery, unsuitable to their thought and emotion. This want of balance between matter and manner, which is rare in Kālidāsa and which a true poetic instinct always avoids, is very often prominent in these lesser poets ; and their popularity makes the tradition long and deeply rooted in Sanskrit poetical literature. It degenerates into a deliberate selection of certain methods and means wholly to achieve style, and loses all touch of spontaneity and naturalness. To secure strength, needless weight is superadded, and elasticity is lost in harmony too mechanically studied. The poets are never slipshod, never frivolous ; they are indeed far too serious, far too sober either to soar high or dive deep. Theirs is an equable merit, producing a dainty and even effect, rather than a throbbing response to the contagious rapture of poetic thought and feeling. As they never sin against art, they seldom reach the heaven of poetry.

Nevertheless, the poets we are considering are not entirely devoid of purely poetic merit, even if they are conscious and consummate artists. The period, as we see it, is neither sterile nor inanimate, nor is it supported by the prestige of a single name. It is peopled with striking figures ; and, apart from smaller poems of which we have spoken, the body of larger works produced is fairly extensive in quantity and not negligible in quality. Even if they do not reach the highest level, it is not necessary to belittle them. The qualities of the literature may not awaken the fullest critical enthusiasm, but it is certainly marked by sustained richness and many-sided fullness. Of the four greater poets of this period, namely, Bhāravi, Bhaṭṭi, Kumāradāsa and Māgha, it is curious that we possess only a single work of each. It is not known whether they wrote more works than what have survived. The verse quoted from these poets in the anthologies and rhetorical works are generally traceable in their extant poems ; but in view of the uncertain and fluctuating character of these attributions, the surplus of untraceable verses need not prove loss of other works which they are conjectured to have written. While Bhāravi and Māgha select for their themes particular episodes of the *Mahābhārata*, Bhaṭṭi and Kumāradāsa conceive the more ambitious project of rehandling the entire story of the *Rāmāyaṇa*. All the four agree in choosing a heroic subject from the Epics but their inspiration is not heroic, and their treatment has little of the simplicity and directness, as well as the vivid mythological background, of the Epics.

a. *Bhāravi*

Of the composers of the Mahākāvaya who succeeded Kālidāsa, Bhāravi is perhaps the earliest and certainly the formost. All that is known of him is that he must be placed much earlier than 634 A.D., at which date he had achieved poetic fame enough to be mentioned with Kalidāsa in the Aihole inscription of Pulakeśin II.[1] As the inscription belongs to the same half-century as that in which Bāṇa flourished, Bāṇa's silence about Bhāravi's achievement is somewhat extraordinary ; but it need not be taken to imply Bhāravi's contemporaneity or nearness of time to Bāṇa.

The subject-matter of the *Kirātārajunīya*[2] of Bhāravi is derived from one of the episodes of Arjuna's career described in the Vana-parvan of the *Mahābhārata.*[3] Under the vow of twelve years' exile the Pāṇḍavas had retired to the Dvaita forest, where the taunt and instigation of Draupadī, supported by the vehement urging of Bhīma, failed to move the scrupulous Yudhiṣṭhira to break the pledge and wage war. The sage Vyāsa appears, and on his advice they move to the Kāmyaka forest, and Arjuna sets out to win divine weapons from Śiva to fight the Kauravas. Indra, in the guise of a Brahman ascetic, is unable to dissuade Arjuna, but pleased with the hero's firmness, reveals himself and wishes him success. Arjuna's austerities frighten the gods, on whose appeal Śiva descends as a Kirāta, disputes with him on the matter of killing a boar, and, after a fight, reveals his true form and grants the devotee the desired weapons. This small and simple epic episode is selected for expanded and embellished treatment in eighteen cantos, with all the resources of a refined and elaborate art. Bhāravi adhers to the outline of the story,

1 For the alleged relation of Bhāravi and Daṇḍin, see S. K. De in *IHQ*, I, 1925, p. 31 f. III, 1927, p. 295 ; also G. Harihara Sastri in *IHQ*, III, 1927, p. 169 f., who would place Bhāravi and Daṇḍin at the close of 7th century. The quotion of a pāda of *Kirāta* XIII. 14 in the *Kāśikā* on Pāṇ. i. 3, 23, pointed out by Kielhorn (*IA*, XIV, p. 327), does not advance the solution of the question further.

2 Ed. N. B. Godabole and K. P. Parab, with the comm. of Mallinātha, NSP, Bombay 1885 (6th ed. 1907) ; only i-iii, with comm. of Citrabhānu. ed. T. Ganapati Sastri, Trivandrum Skt. Ser., 1918 ; trs. into German by C. Cappeller in Harvard Orient. Ser., xv, 1912.

3 Bomb. ed., iii. 27-41.

but he fills it up with a large mass of matter, some of which have hardly any direct bearing on the theme. The opening of the poem with the return of Yudhiṣṭhira's spy, who comes with the report of Suyodhana's beneficient rule, at once plunges into the narrative, but it also supplies the motive of the following council of war and gives the poet an opportunity of airing his knowledge of statecraft. The elaborate description of autumn and the Himalayas, and of the amorous sports of the Gandharvas and Apsarases in land and water, repeated partially in the following motif of the practice of nymphal seduction upon the young ascetic, is a disproportionate digression, meant obviously for a refined display of descriptive powers. Apart from the question of relevancy, Bhāravi's flavoured picture of amorous sports, like those af Māgha and others who imitated him with greater gusto and created a tradition, is gracelss in one sense but certainly graceful in another; and there is, in his painting of natural scenery, a real feeling for nature, even if for nature somewhat tricked and trounced. The martial episode, extending over two cantos, of the rally of Śiva's host under Skanda's leadership and the fight with magic weapons, is not derived form the original; but, in spite of elaborate literary effort, the description is rather one of a combat as it should be conducted in artificial poetry, and the mythical or magical elements take away much of its reality.

Bhāravi's positive achievement has more often been belittled than exaggerated in modern times. Bhāravi shares some of the peculiarities of his time and falls into obvious errors of taste, but in dealing with his poetry the literary historian need not be wholly apologetic. His attempt to accomplish astonishing feats of verbal jugglery in canto xv (a canto which describes a battle !)[1]

[1] The puerile tricks of Citra-bandha, displayed in this canto, are said to have originated from the art of arraying armies in different forms in the battle-field ! But it is more plausible that they arose from the practice of writing inscriptions on swords and leaves. They are recognised for the first time by Daṇḍin ; but Māgha appears to regard them (xix. 41) as indispensable in a Mahākāvya. Rudraṭa deals with them in some detail, but they are discredited by Ānandavardhana, suffered by Mammaṭa in deference to poetic practice, and summarily rejected by Viśvanātha.

by a singular torturing of the language is an instance of the worst type of tasteless artificiality, which the Sanskrit poet is apt to commit ; but it must have been partly the fault of his time that it liked to read verses in which all or some of the feet are verbally identical, in which certain vocables or letters are exclusively employed, in which the lines or feet read the same backwards or forwards, or in a zigzag fashion. One never meets with such excesses in Kālidāsa ; it is seen for the first time in Bhāravi. We cannot be sure, however, if Bhāravi originated the practice ; the deplorable taste might have developed in the interval ; but there can be no doubt that Bhāravi succumbed to what was probably a powerful temptation in his day of rhetorical display in general and of committing these atrocities in particular. His pedantic observation of grammar. his search for recondite vocabulary, his conscious employment of varied metres are aspects of the same tendency towards laboured artificiality. His subject, though congenial, is not original ; it is capable of interesting treatment, but is necessarily conditioned by its mythical character, and more so by Bhāravi's own idea of art. But these patent, though inexcusable, blemishes, which Bhāravi shares with all the Mahākāvya writers of this period, do not altogether render nugatory his great, though perhaps less patent, merits as a poet and artist.

Bhāravi as a poet and artist is perhaps not often first-rate, but he is never mediocre. It is seldom that he attains the full, haunting grace and melody of Kālidāsa's poetry, but he possesses not a little of Kālidāsa's charm of habitual ornateness, expressed with frequent simplicity, force and beauty of phrase and image. There are occasional bursts of rare and elsewhere unheard music, but what distinguishes Bhāravi is that, within certain narrow but impregnable limits, he is a master of cultivated expression. He has the disadvantage of coming after and not in the first flush of the poetic energy of the age ; his poetry is more sedate, more weighted with learning and technique ; but, barring deliberate artificialities, he is seldom fantastic to frigidity or meditative to dulness.

Bhāravi's subject does not call for light treatment. With his command of polished and stately phrase, he is quite at home in serious and elevated themes ; but the softer graces of his style and diction are also seen in the elegant effect which he imparts to the somewhat inelegant episode, not on love, but on the art of love, which is irrelevantly introduced, perhaps chiefly for this purpose. The beauty of nature and of maidens is an ever attractive theme with the Sanskrit poets, but even in this sphere which is so universally ultivated, Bhāravi's achievement is of no mean order. Bhāravi's metrical form is also skilled and developed, but his practice is characterised by considerable moderation. He employs about twenty-four different kinds of metre in all, most of which, however, are sporadic, only about twelve being principally employed.[1] Like Kalidāsa in his two Mahākāvyas, he employs mostly short lyrical measures, which suit the comparative ease of his manner, and avoids larger stanzas which encourage complexities of expression. There is, therefore, no unnecessary display of metrical skill or profusion, nor any desire for unlimited freedom of verse. He gives us, in general, a flawless and equable music, eminently suited to his staid and stately theme ; but there is not much of finer cadences or of more gorgeous melody.

Bhāravi's strength, however, lies more in the descriptive and the argumentative than in the lyric touch ; and this he attains by his undoubted power of phraseology, which is indeed not entirely free from indulgence in far-fetched conceits, but which is never over-gorgeous nor over-stiff. His play of fancy is constant and brilliant, but there is always a calm and refined dignity of diction. Bhāravi has no love for complicated

1 In each of cantos v and xviii, we find sixteen different kinds of metre, but Bhāravi does not favour much the use of rare or difficult metres. The only metres of this kind, which occur but only once each, are Jaloddhatagati. Jaladharamālā, Candrikā, Mattamayūtā, Kuṭilā and Vaṁśapatrapatitā. He uses, however, Vaitālīya in ii, Pramitākṣarā in iv, Praharṣiṇī in vii, Svāgatā in ix, Puṣpitāgrā in x, Udgatā in xii and Aupacchandasika in xiii.

compounds ; his sentences are of moderate length and reasonably clear and forceful ; there is no perverse passion for volleys of puns and inversions, for abundence of laboured adjectives, or for complexities of tropes and comparisons. He has the faculty of building up a poetical argument or a picture by a succession of complementary strokes, not added at haphazard, but growing out of and on to one another ; the amplification has vigour and variety and seldom leads to tedious verbiage. His phrases often give a pleasing surprise ; they are expressed with marvellous brevity and properiety ; it is impossible to improve upon them ; to get something better one has to change the kind.

Bhāravi's poetry, therefore, is seldom overdressed, but bears the charm of a well-ordered and distinctive appearance. Of the remoter and rarer graces of style, it cannot be said there is none, but Bhāravi does not suggest much of them. The Artha-gaurava or profundity of thought, which the Sanskrit critics extol in Bhāravi, is the result of his profundity of expression ; but it is at once the source of his strength and his weakness. His maturity of expression is pleasing by its grace and polish ; it is healthful by its solidity of sound and sense ; but it has little of the contagious enthusiasm or uplifting magnificence of great poetry. One comes across fine things in Bhāravi, striking, though quaintly put, conceits, vivid and graceful images, and even some distinctly fascinating expressions ; but behind every clear image, every ostensible thought or feeling, there are no vistas, no backgrounds ; for the form is too methodical and the colouring too artificial. Nevertheless, Bhāravi can refine his expression without making it jejune ; he can embellish his idea without making it fantastic. His word-music, though subdued, is soothing ; his visual pictures, though elaborate, are convincing. If he walks with a solemn tread, he knows his foothold and seldom makes a false step. In estimating Bhāravi's place in Sanskrit poetry, we must recognise that he cannot give us very great things, but what he can give, he gives unerringly ; he is a sure master of his own craft.

b. *Bhaṭṭi*

Bhaṭṭi, author of the *Rāvaṇa-vadha*,[1] which is more usually styled *Bhaṭṭi-kāvya* presumably after his name, need not detain us long. The poet's name itself cannot authorise his identification with Vatsabhaṭṭi of the Mandasor inscription,[2] nor with Bhartṛhari, the poet-grammarian. We are told in the concluding stanza[3] of the work that it was composed at Valabhī ruled over by Śrīdharasena, but since no less than four kings of this name are known to have ruled at Valabhī roughly between 495 and 641 A. D., Bhaṭṭi lived, at the earliest, in the beginning of the 6th century, and, at the latest, in the middle of the 7th.[4]

The so-called Mahākāvya of Bhaṭṭi seeks to comprehend, in twenty cantos, the entire story of the *Rāmāyaṇa* up to Rāma's return from Laṅkā and coronation; but it is perpetrated deliberately to illustrate the rules of grammar and rhetoric. It is, in the words of the poet himself, like a lamp to those whose eye is grammar; but without grammar, it is like a mirror in the hands of the blind. One can, of course, amiably resolve to read the work as a poem, ignoring its professed purpose, but one will soon recognise the propriety of the poet's warning that the composition is a thing of joy to the learned, and that it is not easy for one, who is less gifted, to understand it without a commentary. Sound literary taste will hardly justify the position, but there is not much in the work itself which evinces sound literary taste.

1 Ed. Govinda Sankar Bapat, with comm. of Jayamaṅgala, NSP, Bombay 1887; ed. K. P. Trivedi, with comm. of Mallinātha, in Bomb. Skt. Ser., 2 volṣ., 1898; ed. J. N. Tarkaratna, with comm. of Jayamaṅgala and Bharatamallika, 2 vols., Calcutta 1871-73; (reprint of Calcutta ed. in 2 vols., 1808).

2 As suggested by B. C. Majumdar in *JRAS*, 1904, p. 306f.; see Keith in *JRAS* 1909, p. 435.

3 The stanza is not commented upon by Mallinātha.

4 See Hultzsch in *ZDMG*, LXXII, 1909, p. 145f. The work is of course known to Bhāmaha, but since Bhāmaha's date itself is uncertain, the fact is not of much chronological value. On the relation of Bhaṭṭi's treatment of poetic figures to that of Bhāmaha, see S. K. De, *Sanskrit Poetics*, I, pp. 51-57.

Apart from its grammatical ostentation, the poem suffers from a banal theme. Bhaṭṭi attempts some diversity by introducing speeches and conceity, as well as occasional description of seasons and objects, but the inventions are negligible, and the difficult medium of a consciously laboured language is indeed a serious obstacle to their appreciation. What is a more serious brawback is that the poet has hardly any freedom of phraseology, which is conditioned strictly by the necessity of employing only those words whose grammatical forms have to be illustrated methodically in each stanza ; and all thought, feeling, idea or expression becomes only a slave to this exacting purpose. It must be said, however, to Bhaṭṭi's credit that his narrative flows undisturbed by lengthy digression ; that his diction, though starched and weighted by grammatical learning, is without complexities of involved construction and laboured compounds ; that, in spite of the inevitable play of word and thought, there is nothing recondite or obscure in his ideas ; and that his versification,[1] though undistinguished, is smooth, varied and lively.

Even very generous taste will admit that here practically ends all that can be said in favour of the work, but it does not very much improve its position as a poem. If one can labour through its hard and damaging crust of erudition, one will doubtless find a glimmering of fine and interesting things. But Bhaṭṭi is a writer of much less original inspiration than his contemporaries, and his inspiration comes from a direction other than the purely poetic. The work is a great triumph of artifice, and perhaps more reasonably accomplished than such later triumphs of artifice as proceed even to greater excesses ; but that is a different thing from poetry. Bhaṭṭi's scholarliness has justly propitiated scholars, but the self-imposed curse of artificiality

[1] Like the early Mahākāvya poets, Bhaṭṭi limits himself generally to shorter lyrical metres ; longer metres like Mandākrāntā, Śārdūlavikrīḍita and Sragdharā being used but rarely. The Śloka (iv-ix, xiv-xxii) and Upajāti i, ii, xi, and xii) are his chief metres. Of uncommon metres, Aśvalalita, Nandana, Narkūṭaka, and Praharaṇakalikā occur only once each.

neutralises whatever poetic gifts he really possesses. Few read his worst, but even his best is seriously flawed by his unfortunate outlook ; and, unless the delectable pursuit of poetry is regarded as a strenuous intellectual exercise, few can speak of Bhaṭṭi's work with positive enthusiasm.

c. *Kumāradāsa*

Kumāradāsa, also known as Kumārabhaṭṭa or Bhaṭṭa Kumāra. deserves special interest as a poet from the fact that he consciously modelled his *Jānakī-haraṇa*,[1] in form and spirit, on the two Mahākāvyas of Kālidāsa, even to the extent of frequently plagiarising his predecessor's ideas and sometimes his phrases. This must have started the legend[2] which makes this great admirer and follower of Kālidāsa into his friend and contemporary, and inspired the graceful but extravagant, eulogy of Rājaśekhara,[3] quoted in the *Sūkti-mukāvalī* (4. 76) of Jahlaṇa. A late Ceylonese tradittion of doubtful value identifies our author with a king of Ceylon, named Kumāradhātusena or Kumāradāsa (*circa* 517-26 A.D.), son of Maudgalāyana. Even if the identity is questioned,[4] the poet's fame was certainly widely spread in the 10th century ; for the author of the *Kāvya-mimāṃsā* (p. 12) refers to the tradition of the poet's being born

1 Reconstructed and edited (with the Sinhalese Sanna) cantos i-xv and one verse of xxv, by Dharmarama Sthavira, in Sinhalese characters, Colombo 1891 ; the same prepared in Devanāgarī, by Haridas Sastri, Calcutta 1893 ; i-x, ed. G. R. Nandargikar, Bombay 1907 (the ed. utilises some Devanāgarī Mss, but most of these appear to owe their origin to the Sinnhalese source) ; xvi, ed. L. D. Barnett from a Malayālam Ms in *BSOS*, IV, p. 285f. (Roman text), to which addl. readings furnished from a Madras Ms by S. K. De in *BSOS*, IV, p. 611f.

2 Rhys Davids in *JRAS*, 1888, pp. 148-49.

3 The stanza punningly states that no one, save Kumāradāsa, would dare celebrate the abduction of Sītā (*Jānakī-haraṇa*) when *Raghuvaṁśa* was current, as no one but Rāvaṇa would dare accomplish the deed when Raghu's dynasty existed.

4 Keith in *JRAS*, 1901, p. 578f. Nandargikar, *Kumāradāsa and his Place in Skt. Lit*, Poona 1908, argues for a date between the last quarter of the 8th and the first quarter of the 9th century A. D., which seems quite reasonable. Rājaśekhara (*Kāvya-mīmāṁsā* ed. GOS, 1916, p. 26) quotes anonymously *Jānakī-haraṇa*, xii. 37 (*madaṁ navaiśvarya*).

blind, and Kumāradāsa's stanzas are quoted in the Sanskrit anthologies dating from about the same time.[1]

The entire Sanskrit text of the *Jānakī-haraṇa* has not yet been recovered, but the Sinhalese literature has preserved a Sanna or word-for-word gloss of the first fourteen cantos and of the fifteenth in part,[2] which brings the story down to Aṅgada's embassy to the court of Rāvaṇa. From this gloss it has been possible to piece together a text, which is perhaps not a perfect restoration, but which cannot diverge very far from the original.[3] The extent of the original work is not known, but since the gloss also preserves the colophon and the last stanza of canto xxv, giving the name of the work and the author, it is probable that the poem concluded with the theme of Rāma's coronation apparently handled in this canto. If this is correct, then it is remarkable that Kumāradāsa's poem exactly coincides, in the extent of its subject-matter, with the work of Bhaṭṭi.[4] Like the *Rāvaṇa-vadha,* again, the *Jānaki-haraṇa* suffers from a banal theme derived from the Epic, although Kumāradāsa's object and treatment are entirely different. In the handling of the story, Kumāradāsa follows his original fairly faithfully ; but, for diversity, poetical descriptions and episodes are freely introduced. In the first canto, for instance, a picture of Ayodhyā, which is rivalled by the account of Mithilā in canto vi, is given, while the sports of Daśaratha

1 For the citations see Thomas, *Kvs.* pp. 34-36. Kṣemendra in his *Aucitya-vicāra* (*ad* 24) wrongly ascribes a stanza to Kumāradāsa, of which one foot is already quoted by Patañjali. Whether the poet knew the *Kāśikā* (*circa* 650 A. D.) is debatable (see Thomas in *JRAS,* 1901, p. 266) ; and Vāmana's prohibition (v. 1.5) of the use of *khalu* has no particular reference to Kumāradāsa. These and such other references are too indefinite to admit of any decisive inference.

2 The Madras Ms existing in the Govt. Orient. Mss Library, contains twenty cantos, but it is a very corrupt transcript of an unknown original, and it is not known how far it is derived ultimately from the Sinhalese Sanna. The last verse of the Ms describes Kumāradāsa as king of Ceylon and son of Kumāramaṇi.

3 Leumann in *WZKM,* VII, 1893, pp. 226-32 ; F. W. Thomas in *JRAS,* 1901, pp. 254-58.

4 For an analysis of the poem, see the article of Thomas, cited above.

and his wives in the garden are described in canto iii. We have a fine description of the rainy season in canto xi, while the next canto matches it with a picture of autumn. In most of these passages the influence of Kālidāsa is transparent. Daśaratha's lecture to Rāma on the duties of kingship has no counterpart in Kālidāsa's poems ; but the appeal to Viṣṇu in canto ii, the description of spring in canto iii, the entire canto viii on the dalliance of Rāma and Sītā after marriage, and Sītā's lovelorn condition (Pūrva-rāga) before marriage in the preceding canto, inevitably remind one of similar passages and episodes in Kālidāsa's two poems. But these digressions are neither too prolix nor too numerous, and the interest of the narrative is never lost. In this respect Kumāradāsa follows the manner of Kālidāsa rather than that of Bhāravi, and has none of the leisurely and extendend scale of descriptive and erotic writing which prevails in the later Mahākāvyas.

The incomplete and not wholly satisfactory recovery of Kumāradāsa's work makes it difficult to make a proper estimate ; but the remark is not unjust that the *Jānakī-haraṇa,* as a poem, is more artificial than the *Raghu-vaṃśa* and the *Kumārasaṃbhava,* perhaps more than the *Kirātārjunīya,* but it does not approach, in content, from and diction, the extravagance of the later Kāvya. Some of Kumāradāsa's learned refinements take the form of notable grammatical and lexicographical peculiarities, and of a decided love for circumlocution, alliteration and dainty conceits, but none of these propensities take an undue or elaborate prominence. His metrical skill is undoubted, but like Kālidāsa in his two longer poems, he prefers short musical metres and does not seek the profusion or elaboration of shifting or recondite rhythmic forms.[1] Although Kumāradāsa has a weakness for the pretty and the grandiose, which sometimes strays into the ridiculous, he is moderate in the use of poetic figures ; there is some play upon words, but no complex puns.

[1] The only uncommon, but minor, metre is Avitathā.

Although Kumāradāsa's poem furnishes easy and pleasent reading, his poetic power is liable to be much overrated. The compliment which ranks him with Kālidāsa, no doubt, perceives some superficial similarity, but Kumāradāsa's originality in treatment, idea and expression is considerably impaired by his desire to produce a counterfeit. Possessed of considerable ability, he both gains and loses by coming after Kālidāsa. He has a literary tradition, method and diction prepared for him for adroit employment, but he has not the genius to rise above them and strike out his own path. With inherited facility of execution, he loses individuality and distinction. Kumāradāsa is a well-bred poet who follows the way of glittering, but not golden, poetic mediocrity : he is admirable but not excellent, learned but not pedantic, neat but not overdressed, easy but not simple. He has a gift of serviceable rhetoric and smooth prosody, but he is seldom brilliant and outstanding. He has a more than competent skill of pleasing expression, but he lacks the indefinable charm of great poetry. It is not easy to feel as much enthusiasm for Kumāradāsa as for Bhāravi ; but it is not just on that account to deny to him a fair measure, though by comparison, of the extraordinarily diffused poetic sprit of the time.

d. *Māgha*

The usually accepted date for Māgha is the latter part of the 7th century A.D. The approximation is reached by evidence which is not altogether uncontestable ; but what is fairly certain is that the lower terminus of his date is furnished by the quotation from his poem by Vāmana and Ānandavardhana[1] at the end of the 8th and in the middle of the 9th century A.D. respectively,

1 *Dhvanvāloka*, ed. NSP, 1911, Second Uddyota, pp. 114, 115=*Śiṣu* v. 26 and iii. 53. A little earlier (end of the 8th century) Vāmana quotes from Māgha (*Śiśu*° i. 12, 15=*Kāvyāl.* v. 1.10, v. 2.10 ; x. 21=v. 1. 13 ; xiv. 14=iv. 3.8). Mukulabhaṭṭa in his *Abhidhā-vṛtti-mātṛkā* (ed. NSP, Bombay 1916, p. 11) similarly quotes *Śiśu*° iii. 33 anonymously.

and the upper terminus by the very likely presumption that he is later than Bhāravi whom he appears to emulate. There are five stanzas appended to Māgha's poem which give, in the third person, an account of his family, and which are commented upon by Vallabhadeva, but not by Mallinātha. From these verses we learn that Māgha's father was Dattaka Sarvāśraya, and his grandfather Suprabhadeva was a minister of a king named Varmala. An attempt has been made to identify this Varmala (*v.l.* Varmalāta, Dharmanābha or-nātha and Nirmalāta) with king Varmalāta, of whom an inscription of about 625 A.D. exists.[1] But neither is this date beyond question, nor the identification beyond all doubt.

Like Bhāravi, with whom Māgha inevitably invites comparison, Māgha derives the theme of his *Śiśupāla-vadha*[2] from a well known episode of the *Mahābhārata*,[3] but the difference of the story, as well as perhaps personal predilection, makes Māgha glorify Kṛṣṇa, in the same way as Bhāravi honours Śiva. At Yudhiṣṭhira's royal consecration, Bhīṣma advises the award of the highest honour to Kṛṣṇa, but Śiśupāla, king of the Cedis, raises bitter protest and leaves the hall. In the quarrel which ensues, Śiśupāla insults Bhīṣma and accuses Kṛṣṇa of mean

1 See Kielhorn in *Göttinger Nachrichten*, 1906, pp. 143-46, and in *JRAS*, 1908, 409f.; R. G. Bhandarkar, *Report 1897*, pp. xviii, xxxix; D. R. Bhandarkar in *EI*, IX, p. 187f.; Pathak in *JBRAS*, XXIII, pp. 18-31; Kane in *JBRAS*, XXIV, pp. 91-95; D. C. Bhattacharyya in *IA*, XLVI, 1917, p. 191f.; H. Jacobi in *WZKM*, III, 1889, pp. 121f., and IV, 1890, p. 236f.; Klatt in *WZKM*, IV, p. 61f. The minor arguments that Māgha knew the *Kāśikā* or the *Nyāsa* of Jitendrabuddhi (*Śiśu*° ii. 112), or the *Nāgānanda* of Harṣa (xx. 44) are, for the indefiniteness of the allusions, hardly worth much. The Jaina legends have been invoked to prove that Māgha was a contemporary of the poet Siddha (about 906 A.D.), but the legends only show that the Jainas made use of famous men in their anecdotes, and nothing more. More worthless is the *Bhoja-prabandha* account which makes Māgha, as also many other poets, a contemporary of King Bhoja. The legend related in Merutuṅga's *Prabandha-cintāmani* is equally useless.

2 Ed. Atmaram Sastri Vetal and J. S. Hosing, with comm. of Vallabhadeva and Mallinātha, Kāshi Skt. Ser. no 69, 1919; ed. Durgaprasad and Sivadatta, NSP, Bombay 1888, 9th ed. 1927, with comm. of Mallinātha only. Trs. into German by E. Hultzsch, Leipzig 1929, and in extracts, by C. Cappeller (Bālamāgha), Stuttgart 1915, with text in roman characters.

3 Bomb. ed. ii, 33-45.

tricks, including theft of his affianced bride. Having endured Śiśupāla's insolence so far, on account of a promise to his mother to bear a hundred evil deeds of her son, Kṛṣṇa now feels that he is relieved of the pledge, and severs the head of Śiśupāla with his discus. The epic story here is even simpler and more devoid of incidents than the episode of Arjuna's fight with the Kirāta but it contains a number of rival speeches, which give Māgha an opportunity of poetical excursions into the realm of politics and moralising, vituperation and panegyric. The outline of the epic story is accepted, but its slenderness and simplicity are expanded and embellished, in twenty cantos, by a long series of descriptive and erotic passages deliberately modelled, it seems, upon those of Bhāravi. A variation is introduced in the first canto by the visit of Nārada to Kṛṣṇa at the house of Vasudeva, with a message from Indra regarding the slaying of Śiśupāla; but it has its counterpart in Bhāravi's poem in the visit of Vyāsa to Yudhiṣṭhira. A similar council of war follows, in which Baladeva advises expedition and Uddhava caution; and the knowledge of statecraft displayed by Uddhava corresponds to that evinced by Bhīma in Bhāravi's poem. After this, Māgha, like Bhāravi, leaves the narrative and digresses into an even more luxuriant, but disproportionate, mass of descriptive matter extending practically over nine cantos (iv-xii), as against Bhāravi's seven. Kṛṣṇa's journey to Indraprastha to attend Yudhiṣṭhira's consecration and the description of the mount Raivataka, which comes on the way, correspond to Arjuna's journey and description of the Himalayas; and Māgha wants to surpass Bhāravi's in the display of his metrical accomplishment by employing twenty-four different metres in canto iv, as opposed to Bhāravi's sixteen in canto v. The amours and blandishments of the Apsarases and Gandharvas in Bhāravi are rivelled with greater elaboration and succulence by the amorous frolics of the Yādavas with women of fulsome beauty; and it is remarkable that in some of these cantos Māgha selects the same metres (Praharṣiṇī and Svāgatā) as Bhāravi does. Māgha makes a similar, but more extensive, exhibition of his skill in the over-ingenious construction of verses known as Citra-bandha (canto xix), and follows his predecessor in introducing these literary acrobatics in the description of the battle, although the battle-scenes are depicted, in both cases, by poets who had perhaps never been to a battle-field !

It is clear that the tradition, for once, is probably right in implying that Māgha composed his *Śiśupāla-vodha* with a view to surpass Bhāravi's *Kirātārjunīya* by entering into a competition with him on his own ground.[1] The orthodox Indian opinion thinks (with a pun upon their respective names) that Māgha has been able to eclipse Bhāravi completely, and even goes further in holding that Māgha unites in himself Kālidāsa's power of metaphorical expression, Bhāravi's pregnancy of thought and Daṇḍin's gracefulness of diction. While making allowance for exaggeration not unusual in such indiscriminate praise, and also admitting freely that Māgha can never be mentioned lightly by any one who loves Sanskrit poetry, it is difficult for a reader of the present day to share this high eulogy. Māgha's deliberate modelling of his poem on that of Bhāravi, with the purpose of outdoing his predecessor, considerably takes away his originality, and gives it the appearance of a tremendous effort. He can claim the literary merits of Bhāravi, but he also exaggerates some of Bhārabi's demerits. In respect of rhetorical skill and exuberance of fancy, Māgha is not unsuccessful, and may have even surpassed Bhāravi ; but the remark does not apply in respect of real poetic quality, although it would not be just to deny to him a gift, even by comparison, of real poetry.

But Māgha's work, though not great, has been distinctly undervalued in modern times, as it was once overvalued. It is

1 The question of Māgha's relationship to Bhāravi has been discussed by Jacobi (in *WZKM*, III, 1889, pp. 121-40) by a detailed examination of the structure of the two poems, their form, content and parallel passages, with the conclusion that Bhāravi's poem served as a model for that of Māgha. Jacobi (p. 141 f.) further wants to show that Bāṇa and Subandhu borrowed from Māgha, but the parallelisms adduced are not definite enough to be of much use for chronological or literary purpose.

impossible to like or admire Māgha heartily, and yet there are qualities which draw our reluctant liking and admiration. His careful and conscientious command of rhetorical technique is assured. He has an undoubted power of copious and elegant diction, and his phraseology and imagery often attain a fine, though limited, perfection. His sentences have movement, ease and balance ; and the variety of short lyrical metres,[1] which he prefers, gives his stanzas swing and cadence. Māgha himself tells us that a good poet should have regard for sound and sense, and so he cultivates both. Like Bhāravi, he is a lover of harmonic phrases and master of cultivated expression, but he is perhaps more luxuriant, more prone to over-colouring, and more consciously ingenious. He can attain profundity by a free indulgence in conceit, but he is never abstruse. Fine felicities or brilliant flashes are not sporadic ; and Māgha's faculty of neat and pointed phrasing often rounds off his reflective passages with an epigrammatic charm. He does not neglect sense for mere sound, but the narrative is of little account to him, as to most Kāvya poets ; and the value of his work lies in the series of brilliant and highly finished word-pictures he paints. From the hint of a single line in the Epic, he gives an elaborate picture of Yudhiṣṭhira's consecration ; and he must bring in erotic themes which are even less relevant to his subject than that of Bhāravi. In his poetry the Śāstric learning and the rhetorical art of the time come into full flower, but it lacks the flush and freshness of natural bloom. At every step we go, we are stopped to admire some elegant object, like walking in a carefully trimmed garden with a guide. Māgha can make a clever use of his knowledge of grammar, lexicon, statecraft, erotics and poetics ; he can pour his fancy into a faultless mould ; but it is often an uninspired and uninspring accomplishmet. He would like to raise admiration to its

1 On metres which Māgha employs, see Belloni-Phillipi, *La Metrica degli Indi*, Firenze 1912, ii, p. 55 ; Keith, *HSL*, pp. 130-31. On metrical licences of Māgha, see Jacobi in *Ind Stud*, xvii, p. 444 f. and in *Verhandl. des V Orientalisten-Congress*. p. 136 f.

height in every line, so that in the end the whole is not admirable. Of real passion and fervour he has not much, and he does not suggest much of the supreme charm of the highest poetry ; but he has a soft richness of fancy, which often inclines him towards sweetness and prettiness. Like Bhāravi, he is a poet, not of love, but of the art of love ; but he can refine the rather indelicate theme of amorous sports with considerable delicacy. It is perhaps not fortuitous that Māgha selects Kṛṣṇa, and not Śiva, as his favourite god. The Indian opinion speaks highly of his devotional attitude, and Bhīṣma's panegyric of Kṛṣṇa, to which Bhāravi has nothing corresponding, is often praised ; but one at once observes here the difference in the temperament of the two poets.

There can be no doubt that Māgha is a poet, but his poetic gift is considerably handicapped by the fact that he is in verse a slave, and a willing slave, to a cut-and-dried literary convention. He appears to possess a great reserve of power, but he never seems to let himself go. He does not choose to seek out an original path for himself, but is content to imitate, and outstrip, if possible, his predecessor by a meretricious display of elaborateness and ingenuity. The sobriquet Ghaṇṭā-Māgha, which he is said to have won by his clever fancy in comparing a hill, set in the midst of sunset and moonrise, to an elephant on whose two sides two bells are hung, is perhaps appropriate in bringing out this characteristic ; but it only emphasises his rhetorical quality, which is a different thing from the poetical, although the quaint simile is not a just specimen of what he can do even in the rhetorical manner. Māgha's extraordinary variety, however, is conditioned by corresponding inequality. His poem is a careful mosaic of the good and the bad of his predecessors, some of whose inspiration he may have caught, but some of whose mannerisms he develops to no advantage. Apart from deliberate absurdities, the appearance of his poeery is generally irreproachable, with its correct make-up, costume and jewellery, but one feels very often that its features are insignificant and its expression devoid of fire and air. The fancy and vividness of some of his pictures, the brilliancy and finish of his diction make one feel more distinctly what is *not* there, but of which Māgha is perhaps not incapable. The extent of his influence on his successors, in whose estimation he stands even higher than Kālidāsa and Bhāravi, indicates the fact that it is Māgha, more than Kālidāsa and Bhāravi, who sets the standard of later verse-making; but the immense popularity of his poem also shows that there is always a demand for poetry of a little lower and more artificial kind.

4. The Gnomic, Didactic and Satiric Poems

Although it is difficult to distinguish between gnomic and didactic verse, the two Śatakas of Bhartṛhari on Nīti and Vairāgya may be taken as partially typical of the didactic spirit and possessing a higher value than, say, the collection of gnomic stanzas, which pass current under the name of Cāṇakya and contain traditional maxims of sententious wisdom. Of the pronounced didactic type this period does not possess many other specimens than the Śatakas of Bhartṛhari, unless we regard the *Moha-mudgara*[1] (or *Dvādaśa-pañjarikā* Stotra) as one of the genuine works of the great Śaṃkara. This latter work, however, is a small lyric, rather than didactic, outburst of seventeen stanzas, finely inspired by the feeling of transitoriness of all mortal things; while its moric Pajjhaṭikā metre and elaborate rhyming give a swing and music to its verses almost unknown in Sanskrit, and probably betoken the influence of Apabraṃśa or vernacular poetry. As such, it is doubtful if it can be dated very early, but it is undoubtedly a poem of no small merit.

The gnomic spirit, however, finds expression from remote antiquity in many aspects of Indian literature. Such tersely

1 Ed. J. Haeberlin in Kāvyasaṁgraha, Calcutta 1847, p. 263f., reprinted in J. Vidyasagar in Kāvyasaṁgraha, Calcutta 1888, p. 352; text and trs. by F. Nève in *JA*, xii, p 607f. For Stotras ascribed to Śaṁkara, see below under ch. VI (Devotional Poetry).

epigrammatic sayings, mostly composed in the Śloka metre, appear in the Nīti sections of the two great Epics, in the Purāṇas, in the law-books and in the tales and fables, while some of the earlier moral stanzas occurring in the Brāhmaṇas perhaps helped to establish the tradition in the later non-Sanskritic Buddhist and Jaina literature. But the stanzas are mostly scattered and incidental, and no very early collection has come down to us, although the *Mahābhārata* contains quite rich masses of them in the Śānti, Anuśāsana, Prajāgara section of the Udyoga and other Parvans. That a large number of such stanzas formed a part of floating literature and had wide anonymous currency is indicated by their indiscriminate appropriation and repetition in various kinds of serious and amusing works mentioned above ; but it would be hardly correct to say that they represent popular poetry in the strict sense of the term. They rather embody the quintessence of traditional wisdom, the raw materials being turned into finished literary products, often adopted in higher literature, or made the nucleus of ever-growing collections. They are of unknown date and authorship, being the wit of one and wisdom of many ; but they were sometimes collected together and conveniently lumped upon some apocryphal writer of traditional repute, whether he be Vararuci, Vetālabhaṭṭa or Cāṇakya. But the collections are often dynamic, the process of addition going on uninterruptedly for centuries and bringing into existence various versions, made up by stanzas derived from diverse sources. The content of such compilations is thus necessarily varied, the stanzas being mostly isolated but sometimes grouped under particular heads, and embraces not only astute observations on men and things but also a great deal of polity, practical morality and popular philosophy. There is nothing deeply original, but the essential facts of life and conduct are often expressed with considerable shrewdness, epigrammatic wit and wide experience of life. The finish of the verses naturally varies, but the elaborately terse and compact style of expression, sometimes with appropriate antithesis, metaphors and similes, often produces the pleasing effect of neat and clever rhetoric ; and their deliberate literary form renders all theories of popular origin extremely doubtful.

It is unfortunate that most of the early collections are lost while those which exist are undatable ; but the one ascribed to Cāṇakya and passed off as the accumulated sagacity of the great minister of Candragupta appears to possess a fairly old traditional nucleus, some of the verses being found also in the Epics and elsewhere. It exists in a large number of recensions, of which at least seventeen have been distinguished,[1] and it is variously known as *Cāṇakya-nīti,*[2] *Cāṇakya-śataka,*[3] *Cāṇakya-nīti-darpaṇa,*[4] *Vṛddha-cāṇakya*[5] or *Laghu-cāṇaka.*[6] The number of verses in each recension varies considerably, but the largest recension of Bhojarāja, in eight chapters, preserved in a Śāradā manuscript, contains 576 verses in a variety of metres, among which the Śloka predominates.[7] Whether the lost original, as its association with Cāṇakya would imply, was a deliberate work on polity is not clear, as the number of verses devoted to this topic in all recensions is extremely limited ; but there can be no doubt that, both in its thought and expression, it is one of the richest and finest collections of gnomic stanzas in Sanskrit, many of which must have been derived from fairly old sources.

1 Oscar Kressler, *Stimmen indisoher Lebensklugheit* (Indica, Heft 4), Leipzig 1907, pp. 38-45. Five recensions (*viz.*, Cāṇakya-nīti-śāstra, Cāṇakya-nīti-śataka, Laghu-cāṇakya, Vṛddha-cāṇakya and Cāṇakya-śloka) are printed in Roman transliteration, with translation of previously unpublished stanzas, by Eugène Mọnseur, Paris : Ernest Leroux 1887. See also Weber *Ind. Streifen*, I, pp 253-78

2 Ed. Mirzapore 1877 ; also a somewhat different version, ed. Agra 1920, mentioned by Kressler.

3 Ed. J. Haeberlin, *op. cit.*, reprinted by J. Vidyasagar, *op. cit.*, II, p. 385 f.

4 Ed. Mathuraprasa Misra, Benares 1870 ; reprinted many times at Benares.

5 Ed. Bombay 1858 ; trs. by Kressler, *op. cit.*. p. 151 f. It has 340 verses in 17 chapters of equal length.

6 Ed. Agra 1920, as above ; also ed. E. Teza (from Galanos Ms), Pisa 1878.

7 The other metres in their order of frequency are : Indravajrā,, Śārdūlavikrīḍita, Vasantatilaka, Vamśathavila, Śikhariṇī, Āryā and Sragdharā, besides sporadic Drutavilambita, Puṣpitāgrā, Pṛthvī, Mandākrāntā, Mālinī, Rathoddhatā, Vaitālīya, Vaiśvadevī Śālini and Hariṇī. See Kressler, *op. cit.*, p. 43.

Of satire, or satiric verses in the proper sense, Sanskrit has very little to show. Its theory of poetry and complacent attitude towards life precluded any serious cultivation of this type of literature. Invective, lampoon, parody, mock-heroic or pasquinade—all that the word satire connotes—were outside the sphere of the smooth tenor and serenity of Sanskrit artistic compositions; and even in the farce and comic writing the laughter, mostly connected with erotic themes, is hardly keen or bitter. They may touch our sense of comedy, but rarely our sense of satire, for the arrant fools and downright knaves are objects not of indignant detestation but of mild ridicule. Some amount of vivid realism and satirical portraiture will be found in the early Bhāṇas, as well as in the stories of Daṇḍin, but they seldom reach the proportion and propriety of a real satire.

The earlist datable work of an erotic-comic, if not fully satiric, tendency is the *Kuṭṭanī-mata*[1] or 'Advice of Procuress' of Dāmodaragupta, which in spite of its ugly title and unsavoury subject, is a highly interesting tract, almost creating this particular *genre* in Sanskrit. The author was a highly respectable person, who is mentioned by Kahlaṇa as a poet and minister of Jayāpiḍa of Kashmir (779-813 A.D.), and the fact that his work is quoted extensively in the Anthologies, as well as by Mammaṭa, Hemacandra and others, bears testimony to its high literary reputation. The theme is slight. A courtesan of Benares, named Mālatī, unable to attract lovers, seeks advice of an old and experienced bawd, Vikarālā, who instructs her to ensnare Cintāmaṇi, son a of high official, and describes to her in detail the cunning art of winning love and gold. To strengthen her discourse, Vikarālā narrates the story of the courtesan Hāralatā and her lover Sudarśana, in which the erotic and the pathetic sentiments intermingle, as well as the

1 Ed. Durgaprasad in Kāvyamālā, Gucchaka iii, NSP, Bombay 1887 ; but with ampler materials, ed. Tansukhram Manassukhram Tripathi, with a Sanskrit commentary, Bombay 1924. Trs. into German by J. J. Meyer, Leipzig 1903.

tale of the dancing girl Mañjarī and king Samarabhaṭa of Benares, in which Mañjarī gives an enactment of Harṣa's *Ratnāvalī* and succeeds by her beauty and blandishments to win much wealth from the prince and leave him impoverished. With graceful touches of wit and humour, delicate problems in the doctrine of love are set forth ; and in spite of the obvious grossness of its dangerous content, the work does not lack elegance of treatment, while the characters, though not wholly agreeable, are dawn with considerable skill and vividness from a direct observation of certain social types. The pictures are doubtless heightened, but they are in all essentials true, and do not present mere caricatures. The chief interest of the work lies in these word-pictures, and not in the stories, which, though well told, are without distinction, nor in the subject-matter, which, though delicately handled, is not above reproach.

Although the *Kuṭṭanī-mata* displays a wide experience of men and things, it is based undoubtedly upon a close study of the art of Erotics, the Vaiśika Upacāra or Vaiśikī Kalā, elaborated by Vātsyāyana and Bharata for the benefit of the man-about-town and the courtesan ; but, on this ground, to reject it lightly as mere pornography is to mistake the real trend of the lively little sketch. There is indeed a great deal of frankness and even gusto, in describing, in no squeamish language, the art and mystery of satisfying the physical woman ; and the heroines of the stories are made the centres of coarse intrigues. Modern taste would perhaps regard all this as foul and fulsome ; but there is no proof of moral depravity. On the contrary, the moral depravity, perhaps of his own times (as we learn from Kahlaṇa), is openly and amusingly depicted by the author, not with approval, but with object of making it look ludicrous. As in most comic writings in Sanskrit, the erotic tendency prevails, and there is not much direct satire. But, even if his scope is narrow, Dāmodaragupta is a real humourist, who does not seek to paint black as white but leaves the buęstion of qlack and white for the most part one. At theal conclusion of his poem, he tells us that any one who reads it will not fall victim to the deceit of rogues, panderers, and procuresses ; but his work is not a mere guide-book for the blind, the weak and the misguided. It is a work of art in which there is no didactic moralising, but which is characterised by direct and animated, but not merciless, painting of droll life, essentially of the higher grades of society. The poet sees two kinds of men in all walks of life—rogues and fools ; but he neither hates the one nor despises the other. The result is comedy rather than satire, not virtuous indignation but entertaining exposure of human frailty. Dāmodaragupta is a perfect artist in words and also a poet ; and the fecetious style, couched in slow-moving and serious Āryā stanzas, is elegantly polished, yet simple and direct in polite banter and power of gentle ridicule. There is hardly anywhere any roughness or bitterness ; and the witty, smooth and humorous treatment makes the work unique in Sanskrit. If the atmosphere is squalid, it is not depressing, but amusing. Dāmodaragupta is daring enough to skate on thin ice, but he has balance and lightness to carry him through ; and if his onset is not biting, it is not entirely toothless. That the extraordinary coarseness of his subject never hindered the popularity of his work with men of taste and culture is a tribute to its innate literary merit. But we shall see that later authors like Kṣemendra, also a Kashmirian, in trying to imitate him without his gifts, lapsed into bald realism, acrid satire or unredeemed vulgarity. The difficult type of literature, thus inaugurated, had great possibilities, but it never developed properly in Sanskrit.

CHAPTER V

SUCCESSORS OF KĀLIDĀSA IN PROSE AND DRAMA

1. The Prose Kāvyas of Daṇḍin, Subandhu and Bāṇa

a. *General Remarks*

The peculiar type of prose narrative, which the Sanskrit theory includes under the category of Kathā and Ākhyāyikā, but which, on a broader interpretation, has been styled Prose Romance or Kunstroman, first makes its appearance, in this period, in a fully developed form in the works of Daṇḍin, Subandhu and Bāṇa. But the origin of this species of literature is shrouded in greater obscurity than that of the Kāvya itself, of which it is presumed to be a sub-division. We know at least of Aśvaghoṣa as a predecessor who heralded the poetic maturity of Kālidāsa, but of the forerunners of Daṇḍin, Subandhu and Bāṇa we have little information. The antiquity of this literature is undoubted, but no previous works, which might have explained the finished results diversely attained by these authors, have come down to us. We have seen that the Ākhyāyikā is specifically mentioned by Kātyāyana in his Vārttika ; and Patañjali, commenting on it, gives the names of three Ākhyāyikās known to him, namely, Vāsavadattā, Sumanottarā and Bhaimarathī ; but we know nothing about the form and content of these early works. The very title of the *Bṛhatkathā* and the designation Kathā applied to the individual tales of the *Pañcatantra*, one of whose versions is also called *Tantrākhyāyikā*, indicate an early familiarity with the words Kathā and Ākhyāyikā, but the terms are apparently used to signify a tale in general, without any specific technical connotation.[1] We know nothing, again, of the *Cārumatī* of Vararuci,

[1] The Kathā and the Ākhyāyikā are mentioned in *Mahābhārata* ii. 11.38 (Bomb.Ed.), but Winternitz has shown (*JRAS*, 1903, pp. 571-72) that the stanza is interpolated.—The Sanskrit Ākhyāyikā, as we know it, has no similarity to Oldenberg's hypothetical Vedic Ākhyāna ;

from which a stanza is quoted in Bhoja's *Śṛṅgāra-prakāśa*, nor of the *Śūdraka-kathā* (if it is a Kathā) of Kālidāsa's predecessor Somila (and Rāmila), nor of the *Taraṅgavatī* of Śrīpālitta,[1] who is mentioned and praised in Dhanapāla's *Tilakamañjarī* and Abhinanda's *Rāma-carita* as a contemporary of Hāla-Sātavāhana. Bāṇa himself alludes to the two classes of prose composition, called respectively the Kathā and the Ākhyāyika, clearly intimating that his *Harṣa-carita* is intended to be an Ākhyāyikā and his *Kādambarī* a Kathā. He also offers a tribute of praise to writers of the Ākhyāyika who preceded him, and refers, as Subandhu also does,[2] to its division into chapters called Ucchvāsas and to the occurrence of Vaktra metres as two of its distinguishing characteristics. Bāṇa even mentions Bhaṭṭāra Haricandra, to us only a name, as the author of a prose composition of high merit ; to this testimony the Prakrit poet Vākpati, in the 9th century, subscribes by mentioning Haricandra along with Kālidāsa, Subandhu and Bāṇa.

It seems clear, therefore, that Bāṇa is no innovator, nor is Haricandra the creator of the Prose Kāvya, which must have gradually evolved, with the narrative material of the folk-tale, under the obvious influence of the poetic Kāvya during a considerable period of time. But an effort[3] has been made to prove,

for in the Ākhyāyikā the prose is essential and the verse negligible. See Keith in *JRAS* 1911, p. 979 for full discussion and references.

1 This is obviously the Dharama-kathā or Jaina religious story, called *Taraṅgavatī*, of Śri-pādalipta or Siri-pālitta, who is already mentioned as Taraṅgavatīkāra in the *Aṇuogadāra*, and therefore must have flourished before the 5th century A.D. The scene of the story is laid at Śrāvastī in the time of Udayana ; but the work is lost. Its romantic love-story, however, is preserved in the *Taraṅgalolā*, composed in Prakrit verse in 1643 A.D. According to E. Leumann, who has translated the *Taraṅgalolā* (München 1921), Śrī-pādalipta lived as early as the 2nd or 3rd century A.D. There is a tradition that he lived in the time of Śālivāhana. A MS of the Prakrit work is noticed in the *Descriptive Cat. of MSS in the Jaina Bhandar at Pattan* by L. B. Gandhi (GOS, Baroda 1937), introd., p. 58.

2 Ed. F. Hall, p. 184.

3 Weber in *SBAW*, XXXVII, p. 917 and *Ind. Stud.* XVIII, p. 456 f. ; Peterson introd, to *Kādambarī*, 2nd ed., Bombay 1889. pp. 101-04. But Lacôte comes to the opposite conclusion of the borrowing by the Greek romance from the Sanskrit ! See discussion of the question by L. H. Gray, introd. to *Vāsavadattā* (cited below), p. 35 f. ; Keith in *JRAS*, 1914, p. 1103 ; 1915, p. 784 f. ; *HSL*, p. 365 f. ; and Winternitz, *GIL*, III, p. 371 f.

by adducing parallels of incident, motif and literary device, that the Sanskrit romance was directly derived from the Greek. Even admitting some of the parallels, the presumption is not excluded that they might have developed independently, while the acutal divergence between the two types, in form and spirit, is so great as to render any theory of borrowing no more than a groundless conjecture. The Sanskrit romance, deriving its inspiration directly from the Kāvya, to which it is approximated both by theory and practice, is hardly an exotic ; it is differentiated from the Greek romance by its comparative lack of interest in the narrative, which is a marked quality of the Greek romance, as well as by its ornate elaboration of form and exprssion,[1] which is absent in the naivete and simplicity of the Greek stories. It is true that the fact of difference need not exclude the possibility of borrowing ; but, as in the case of the drama, no substantial fact has yet been adduced, which would demonstrate the positive fact of borrowing by Sanskrit.

So far as the works of the rhetoricians are concerned, the earliest forms of the Kathā and the Ākhyāyikā are those noticed by Bhāmaha and Daṇḍin.[2] In the Ākhyāyikā, according to Bhāmaha, the subject-matter gives facts of actual experince, the narrator being the hero himself; the story is told in pleasing prose, divided into chapters called Ucchvāsas and containing metrical pieces in Vaktra and Aparavaktra metre, indicative of future happening of incidents ; scope may be allowed to poetic invention, and the theme may embrace subjects like the abduction of a maiden (Kanyā-haraṇa), fighting, separation and final triumph of the hero ; and it should be composed in Sanskrit. In the

[1] The Greek romance has, not doubt, a few specific instance of rhetorical ornaments, such as homoiteleuta, parisosis, alliteration and strained compounds, but they are not comparable to those in the Sanskrit romance, which essentially depends on them. There is hardly anything in Greek corresponding to the picaresque type of story which we find in Daṇḍin.

[2] See, on this question, S. K. De, The Ākhyāyikā and Kathā in Classical Sanskrit in *BSOS*, III, 1925, p. 507-17 ; also J. Nobel, *op. cit.*, p. 156 f.

Kathā, on the other hand, the subject-matter is generally an invented story, the narrator being some one other than the hero; there is no division into Ucchvāsas, no Vaktra or Aparavaktra verses; and it may be composed either in Sanskrit or in Apabhraṃśa. It will be seen at once that the prototypes of this analysis are, strictly, not the two prose narratives of Bāṇa, nor those of Daṇḍin and Subandhu, but some other works which have not come down to us. It is worth noting, however, that the older and more rigid distinctions, embodied by Bhāmaha, were perhaps being obliterated by the innovations of bolder poets; and we find a spirit of destructive criticism in the *Kāvyādarśa* of Daṇḍin, who considers these refinements not as essential, but as more or less formal requirements. Accordingly, Daṇḍin does not insist upon the person of the narrator, nor the kind of metre, nor the heading of the chapter, nor the limitations of the linguistic form as fundamental marks of difference. This is apparently in view of current poetical usage, in which both the types were perhaps converging under the same class of prose narrative, with only a superficial difference in nomenclature. It must have been a period of uncertain transition, and Daṇḍin's negative criticism (as also Vāmana's brushing aside of the whole controversy) implies that no fixed rules had yet been evolved to regulate the fluctuating theory or practice relating to them.

It is clear that the uncertain ideas of early theorists, as well as the extremely small number of specimens that have survived, does not give us much guidance in definitely fixing the nomenclature and original character of the Sanskrit Prose Kāvya. Nevertheless, the whole controversy shows that the two kinds of prose narrative were differentiated at least in one important characteristic. Apart from merely formal requirements, the Ākhyāyikā was conceived, more or less, as a serious composition dealing generally with facts of experience and having an autobiographical, traditional or semi-historical interest; while the Kathā was essentially a fictitious narrative, which may sometimes (as Daṇḍin contends) be recounted in the first person, but whose chief interest resides in its invention.[1] These older types appear to have been modified in course of time ; and the modification was chiefly on the lines of the model popularised by Bāṇa in his two prose Kāvyas. Accordingly we find Rudraṭa doing nothing more than generalising the chief features of Bāṇa's works into rules of universal application. In the Ākhyāyikā, therefore, Rudraṭa authorises the formula that the narrator need not be the hero himself, that the Ucchvāsas (except the first) should open with two stanzas, preferably in the Āryā metre, indicating the tenor of the chapter in question, and that there should be a metrical introduction of a literary character. All these injunctions are in conformity with what we actually find in Bāṇa's *Harṣa-carita*. The Kathā was less touched by change in form and substance, but the erotic character of the story, consisting of the winning of a maiden (Kanyā-lābha), and not abduction (Kanyā-haraṇa) of the earlier theorists, was expressly recognised ; while, in accordance with the prevalent model of the *Kādambarī*, a metrical introduction, containing a statement of the author's family and motives of authorship, is also required. This practically stereotypes the two kinds in Sanskrit literature. It is noteworthy, however, that later rhetoricians do not expressly speak of the essential distinction based upon tradition and fancy, although they emphasise the softer character of the Kathā by insisting that its main issue is Kanyā-lābha, which would give free scope to the delineation of the erotic sentiment.

It is obvious that the prescriptions of the theorists are interesting historical indications of later developments, but they do not throw much light upon the origin and early history of the Sanskrit Prose Kāvya. In the absence of older material, the problem is difficult and does not admit of a precise determination. There can hardly be any affinity with the beast-fable of the *Pañcatantra* type, which is clearly distinguishable in form,

1 The old lexicon of Amara also accepts (i. 5. 5-6) this distinction when it says : *ākhyāyikopalabdhārthā*, and *prabandhakalpanā kathā*.

content and spirit ; but it is perhaps not unreasonable to assume that there was an early connexion with the popular tale of heroes and heroines, including the fairy tale of magic and marvel. This appears to be indicated by the very designation of the *Bṛhatkathā* as a Kathā and the express mention of this work as a Kathā by Daṇḍin ; and the indication is supported by the suggestion that this early collection was drawn upon by Daṇḍin, Subandhu and Bāṇa. If this is granted, a distinction should, at the same time, be made ; for the *Bṛhatkathā*, in conception and expression, was apparently a composition of a different type. The available evidence makes it more than probable that the popular tale never attained any of the refinement and elaboration which we find in the prose romance from its beginning,—in a less degree in Daṇḍin and in more extravagant manner in Subandhu and Bāṇa. From this point of view, the prose romance cannot be directly traced back to the popular tale represented by Guṇāḍhya's work ; its immediate ancestor is the ornate Kāvya itself, whose graces were transferred from verse to prose for the purpose of rehandling and elaborating the popular tale. It is not known whether the new form was applied first to the historical story and then employed to embellish the folk-tale, as the basis of the distinction between the Ākhyāyikā and the Kathā seems to imply ; but it is evident that the prose romance was evolved out of the artistic Kāvya and influenced by it throughout its history. The theorists, unequivocally and from the beginning, include the prose romance in the category of the Kāvya and regard it as a kind of transformed Kāvya in almost every respect, while the popular tale and the beast-fable are not even tardily recognised and given that status.

It seems probable, therefore, that the prose romance had a twofold origin. It draws freely upon the narrative material of the folk-tale, rehandles some of its natural and supernatural incidents and motifs, adopts its peculiar emboxing arrangement of tales and its contrivance of *deux ex machina*, and, in fact, utilises all that is the common stock-in-trade of the Indian story-teller. But its form and method of story-telling are different, and are derived essentially from the Kāvya. Obviously written for a cultured audience, the prose romance has not only the same elevated and heavily ornamented diction, but it has also the same enormous development of the art of description. In fact, the existing specimens combine a legendary content with the form and spirit of a literary *tour de force*. The use of unwieldy compounds, incessant and elaborate puns, alliterations and assonances, recondite allusions and other literary devices, favourite to the Kāvya, receive greater freedom in prose ; but stress is also laid on a minute description of nature and on an appreciation of mental,. moral and physical qualities of men and women. From the Kāvya also comes its love-motif, as well as its inclination towards erotic digressions. Not only is the swift and simple narrative of the tale clothed lavishly with all the resources of learning and fancy, but we find (except in Daṇḍin's *Daśakumāra-carita*) that the least part of the romance is the narrative, and nothing is treated as really important but the description and embellishment. From this point of view, it would be better to call these works Prose Kāvyas or poetical compositions in prose, than use the alien nomenclature Prose Romances, which has a connotation not wholly applicable.

The evolution of the peculiar type of the Prose Kāvya from the Metrical Kāvya, with the intermediary of the folk-tale, need not have been a difficult process in view of the fact that the term Kāvya includes any imaginative work of a literary character and refuses to make verse an essential. The medium is immaterial ; the poetical manner of expression becomes important both in prose and verse. If this is a far-off anticipation of Wordsworth's famous dictum that there is no essential distinction between verse and prose, the direction is not towards simplicity but towards elaborateness. In the absence of early specimens of imaginative Sanskrit prose, it is not possible to decide whether the very example of the Prose Kāvya is responsible for this attitude, or is itself the result of the attitude ; but the approximation of the Prose Kāvya to the Metrical Kāvya appears to have been facilitated by the obliteration of any vital distinction between literary compositions in verse and in prose. But for the peculiar type of expository or argumentative prose found in technical works and commentaries, verse remains thoughout the history of Sanskrit literature the normal medium of expression, while prose retains its conscious character as something which has to compete with verse and share its rhythm and refinement. At no period prose takes a prominence and claims a larger place ; it is entirely subordinated to poetry and its art. The simple, clear and yet elegant prose of the *Pañcatantra* is considered too jejune, and never receives its proper development ; for poetry appears to have invaded very early, as the inscriptional records show, the domain of descriptive, romantic and narrative prose. An average prose-of-all-work never emerges, and even in technical treatises pedestrian verse takes the place of prose.

b. *Daṇḍin*

The *Daśakumāra-carita*[1] of Daṇḍin illustrates some of the peculiarities of the Sanskrit Prose Kāvya mentioned above, but it does not conform strictly to all the requirements of the theorists. This disregard of convention in practice may, with plausibility, be urged as an argument in support of the identity of our Daṇḍin with Daṇḍin, author of *Kāvyādarśa*, who, as we have seen above, also advocates in theory a levelling of distinctions. But from the rhetorician's negative account no conclusive inference

[1] Ed. H. H. Wilson, London 1846 ; ed. G. Bühler and P. Peterson, in two pts., Bombay 1887, 1891, revised in one vol. by G. J. Agashe, Bombay 1919 ; with four comms. (Padacandrikā, Padadīpikā, Bhūṣaṇā and Laghudīpikā), ed. N. B. Godabole and Vasudeva L Pansikar, NSP, 10th ed., Bombay 1925. (1st ed. with two comm., 1883 ; 2nd ed. with three comm., 1889). Trs. into English (freely) by P. W. Jacob (Hindu Tales), London 1873, revised by C. A. Rylands, London 1928 ; by A. W. Ryder, Chicago 1927. Trs. into German by J. J. Meyer, Leipzig 1902, and by J. Hertel, in *Ind. Erzähler* 1-3, Leipzig 1902 ; trs. into French by H. Fauche in Une Tétrade, ou drame, hymne, roman et poème, ii, Paris 1862. Editions with Engl. trs. also published in India by M. R. Kale, Bombay 1926, and by C. Sankararama Sastri, Madras 1931.

is possible, and the romancer may be creating a new genre without consciously concerning himself with the views of the theorists. The problem of identity cannot be solved on this slender basis alone ; and there is, so far, no unanimity nor impregnable evidence on the question. Some critics are satisfied with the traditional ascription of both the works to one Daṇḍin,[1] and industriously search for points to support it. However good the position is, errors in traditional ascription are not rare and need not be final. On the other hand, the name Daṇḍin itself, employed to designate a religious mendicant of a certain order, may be taken as a title capable of being applied to more than one person, and therefore does not exclude the possibility of more than one Daṇḍin. A very strong ground for denying identity of authorship is also made out[2] by not a negligible amount of instances in which Daṇḍin the prose-poet offends against the prescriptions of Daṇḍin the rhetorician. It is a poor defence to say that a man need not practise what he teaches ; for the question is more vital than mere mechanical adherence to rules, but touches upon niceties of diction and taste and general outlook. The presumption that the *Daśakumāra* belongs to the juvenilia of Daṇḍin and the *Kāvyādarśa* is the product of more mature judgment is ingenious, but there is nothing immature in either work. The general exaltation of the Vaidarbha Mārga in the *Kāvyādarśa* and its supposed illustration in the *Daśakumāra* supply at best a vague argument, which need not be considered seriously. That both the authors were Southerners is suggested, but not proved ; for while the indications in the *Kāvyādarśa* are inconclusive, there is nothing to show that, apart from conventional geography,[3] the author of the romance knows familiarly the eighteen different countries

1 The attribution of three works to Daṇḍin by Rājaśekhara and the needless conjectures about them are no longer of much value ; see S. K. De, *Sanskrit Poetics*, I, p. 62 note and p. 72.

2 Agashe, *op. cit.*, pp. xxv-xxxv.

3 See Mark Collins, *The Geographical Data of the Raghuvaṁśa and the Daśakumāracarita* (Diss.), Leipzig 1907, p. 46.

mentioned in the course of the narrative. The geographical items of the *Daśakumāra* only reveal a state of things which existed probably in a period anterior to the date of Harṣavardhana's empire,[1] and suggest for the work a date much earlier than what is possible to assign to the *Kāvyādarśa*. It is true that the time of both the works is unknown ; but while the date of the *Kāvyādarśa* is approximated to the begining of the 8th century,[2] there is nothing to show that the *Daśakumāra* cannot be placed much earlier.[3] The use of rare words, grammatical solecisms and stylistic peculiarities of the *Daśakumāra* again, on which stress is sometimes laid for a comparatively late date, admit of an entirely opposite, but more reasonable, explanation of an early date, which is also suggested by the fact that the romance has certainly none of the affected prose and developed form of those of Subandhu and Bāṇa. The picture of the so-called degenerate society painted by Daṇḍin is also no argument for a late date ; for it would apply equally well to the *Mṛcchakaṭika* and the *Caturbhāṇī*, the earliness of which cannot be doubted and to which the *Daśakumāra* bears a more than superficial resemblance in spirit, style and diction.[4]

1 Mark Collins, *op. cit.* p. 9 f.

2 S. K. De, *Sanskrit Poetics*, I. p. 58 f., in spite of Keith's advocacy (*Indian Studies in honour of Lanman*, Cambridge Mass., 1929, p. 167 f.) of an earlier date for the *Kāvyādarśa* on the ground of Daṇḍin's priority to Bhāmaha. This is not the place to enter into the reopened question, but there is still reason to believe that the presumption of Bhāmaha's priority will survive Keith's strenuous onslaught.

3 The alleged relation of Bhāravi to Daṇḍin of the *Daśakumāra*° (see S. K. De in *IHQ*, I, p. 31 f. ; III, p. 395-96 ; G. Harihara Sastri in *ibid*, III, pp. 169-71), would place him towards the close of the 7th and beginning of the 8th century A. D.,—a date which is near enough to that of Daṇḍin of the *Kāvyādarśa* ; but the reliability of the account is not beyond question (see Keith, *HSL*, preface, p. xvi).

4 Weber (*Indische Streifen*, Berlin 1868, pp. 311-15, 353), Meyer (*op. cit.*, pp. 120-27) and Collins (*op. cit.*, p. 48) would place *Daśakumāra*° some time before 585 A. D. In discussing the question, however, it is better not to confuse the issue by presuming beforehand the identity of the romancer and the rhetorician. Agashe's impossible dating at the 11th or 12th century is based on deductions from very slender and uncertain data. The fact that the *Daśakumāra* is not quoted in the antnological literature before the 11th century or that adaptations in the vernacular were not produced before the 13th, are arguments from silence which do not prove much. Agashe, however, does not rightly accept the worthless

The *Dasrkumāra-carita* in its present form, shows, with Bāṇa's two romances, the peculiarity of having been left unfinished, but it also lacks an authentic beginning. The end is usually supplied by a supplement in four Ucchvāsas, called Uttara-pīthikā or Śeṣa, which is now known to be the work of a comparatively modern Deccan writer named Cakrapāṇi Dīkṣita,[1] son of Candramauli Dīkṣita ; but a ninth or concluding Ucchvāsa by Padmanābha[2] and a continuation by Mahārājādhirāja Gopīnātha[3] are also known to exist. The beinning is found similarly in a Prelude, called Pūrva-pīṭhikā,[4] in five Ucccvāsas, which is believed on good grounds to be the work of some other hand than that of Daṇḍin. The title *Daśakumāra-carita* suggests that we are to expect accounts of the adventures of ten princes, but the present extent of Daṇḍin's work proper contains, with an abrupt commencement, eight of these in eight Ucchvāsas. The Pūrva-pīṭhikā was, therefore, obviously intended to supply not only the framework of the stories but also the missing stories of two more princes ; while the Uttara-pīṭhikā undertakes to conclude the story of Viśruta left incomplete in the last chapter of Daṇḍin's work. Like the Uttara-pīṭhikā, the Pūrva-pīṭhikā which was apparently not accorded general acceptance, exists in various forms,[5] and the details of the tales

legend, relied upon by Wilson, which makes Daṇḍin an ornament of the court of Bhoja. The reference to Bhoja-vaṁśa in Ullāsa viii (ed. Agashe, p. 129) does not support this hypothesis, for Kālidāsa also uses the name Bhoja, referring probably to the rulers of Vidarbha.

1 Eggeling, *Ind. Office Cat.*, vii, no. 4069/2934, p. 1553.

2 Agashe, *op. cit.*, p. xxiv.

3 Wilson, introd., p. 30 ; Eggeling, *op. cit.*, vii, no. 4070/1850, p. 1554.

4 Some MSS (*e.g.*, India Office MS. no. 4059/2694 ; Eggeling, *op. cit.*, vii, p. 1551) and some early editions (*e.g.*, the Calcutta ed. of Madan Mohan Tarakalamkar, 1849) do not contain the Pūrva-pīṭhikā. The ed. of Wilson and others include it. Wilson ventured the conjecture that the Prelude is the work of one of Daṇḍin's disciples ; but in view of the various forms in which it is now known to exist and also because it is missing in some MSS, this conjecture must be discarded. Some of the versions are also obviously late productions.

5 The version, which begins with the solitary benedictory stanza *brahmāṇḍa-echatra-daṇḍa°* and narrates, in five Ucchvāsas, the missing stories of the two princes Puṣpodbhava and Somadatta, along with that of the missing part of the story of Rājavāhana and his lady-love

do not agree in all versions nor with the body of Dandin's genuiue text.

So far as Daṇḍin's own narrative goes, each of the seven princes, who are the friends and associates of the chief hero, Rājavāhana, recounts his adventure, in the course of which each carves out his own career and secures a princely spouse But the work opens abruptly with an account of Rājavāhana, made captive and led in an expedition against Campā, where in the course of a turmoil he finds all the rest of his companions. By his desire they severally relate their adventures, which are comprised in each of the remaining seven chapters. The rather complex story of Apahāravarman, which comes in the second Ucchvāsa, is one of the longest and best in the collection, being rich in varied incidents and interesting characters. The seduction practised on the ascetic Marīci by the accomplished courtesan, Kāmamañjarī, who also deceives the merchant Vastupāla, strips him to the loin-cloth and turns him into a Jaina monk ; the adventure in the gambling house ; the ancient art of thieving[1] in which the hero is proficient ; the punishing of the old misers of Campā who are taught that the goods of the world are perishable ; the motif of the inexhaustible purse ; all these, described with considerable humour and vividness, are woven cleverly into this tale of the Indian Robin Hood,

Avantisundarī is the usually accepted Prelude, found in most MSS. and printed editions. Its spurious character has been shown by Agashe. It is remarkable that the usual metrical beginning required by theory at the outset of a Kathā or Ākhyāyikā is missing here. The benedictory stanza however, is quoted anonymously in Bhoja's *Sarasvatī-kaṇṭhābharaṇa* (ed. Borooah, 1884, p. 114) ; the fact would indicate that this Prelude must have been prefixed at least before 11th century. Another Prelude by Bhaṭṭa Nārāyaṇa is given in App. to Agashe's ed., while still another in verse by Vināyaka in three chapters is noticed by Eggeling. *op. cit.*, vii, no. 40671/586a, p. 1553. M. R. Kavi published (Madras 1924) a fragmentary *Avantisundarī-kathā* in prose (with a metrical summary called °*Kathā-sāra*), which is ascribed to Daṇḍin as the lost Pūrva-pīṭhikā of his romance, but this is quite implausible ; see S. K. De in *IHQ* I, p. 31 f. and III, p. 394 f.

1 On the art of thieving., see Bloomfield in *Amer. Journ. of Philology*, XLIV, 1923, pp. 97-123, 193-229 and *Proc. of the Amer. Philosophical Soc.*, LII, pp. 616-50. On burglary as a literery theme, see L. H. Gray in *WZKM*, XVIII, 1904, pp. 50-51. Śarvilaka in the *Mṛcchakaṭika* is also a scientific thief, with his paraphernalia, like Apahāravarman.

who plunders the rich to pay the poor, unites lovers and reinstates unfortunate victims of meanness and treachery. The next tale of Upahāravarman is not equally interesting, but it is not devoid of incident and character ; it is the story of the recovery of the lost kingdom of the hero's father by means of a trick, including the winning of the queen's favour, murder and pretended transformation[1] by power of magic into the dissolute king who had usurped. The succeeding story of Arthapāla is very similar in its theme of resuscitation of his father's lost rank as the disgraced minister of the king of Kāśī, and incidental winning of Princess Maṇikarṇikā, but it has nothing very striking except the pretended use of the device of snake-charm. The fifth story of Pramati introduces the common motif of a dream-vision of the Princess Navamālikā of Śrāvastī, and describes how the hero, in the dress of a woman, contrives (by the trick of being left as a deposit) to enter the royal apartments and have access to the princess ; but it also gives an incidental account of the somewhat unconventional watching of a cock-fight by a Brahman ! The sixth story of Mitragupta, who wins Princess Kandukavatī of Dāmalipta in the Suhma country, is varied by introducing adventures on the high seas and on a distant island, and by enclosing, after the manner of the *Vetāla-pañcaviṃśati,* four ingenious tales, recounted in reply to the question of a demon, namely, those of Bhūminī, Gominī, Nimbavatī and Nitambavatī, all of which illustrate the maxim that cunning alone is the way to success. The seventh tale of Mantragupta is a literary *tour de force,* in which no labial letters are used by the narrator, because his lips have been made sore by the passionate kisses of his beloved. It begins with the episode of a weird ascetic and his two ministering goblins, repeats the device of pretended transformation through magic into a murdered man, and places the incidents on the seacoast of Kaliṅga and Andhra. The last incomplete narrative of

1 On the art of entering another's body as a fiction-motif, see M. Bloomfield in *Proc. American Philosophical Soc.*, LVI, 1917, pp. 1-43.

Viśruta relates the restoration of the hero's protégé, a young prince of Vidarbha, to power by a similar clever, but not over-scrupulous, contrivance, including the ingenious spreading of a false rumour, the use of a poisoned chaplet and the employment of a successful fraud in the name and presence of the image of Durgā ; but the arguments defending idle pleasures, which speak the language of the profligate of all ages, as well as the introduction of dancers and jugglers and their amusing sleight of hand, are interesting touches.

It will be seen at once that Daṇḍin's work differs remarkably from such normal specimens of the Prose Kāvya as those of Subandhu and Bāṇa ; and it is no wonder that its unconventionality is not favoured by theorist, in whose rhetorical treatises Daṇḍin is not cited till the 11th century A.D. The *Daśakumāra-carita* is rightly described as a romance of roguery. In this respect, it is comparable, to a certain extent, to the *Mṛcchakaṭika,* which is also a drama full of rascals, and to the four old Bhāṇas, ascribed to Śyāmilaka, Īśvaradatta and others ; but rescality is not the main topic of interest in Śūdraka's drama, nor is the Bhāṇa, as a class of composition, debarred by theory from dealing with low characters and themes of love, revelry and gambling. Daṇḍin's work, on the other hand, derives its supreme flavour from the vivid and picturesque exposition of such characters and themes. Although the romantic interest is not altogether wanting, and marvel and magic and winning of maidens find a place, it is concerned primarily with the adventures of clever tricksters. Daṇḍin deliberately violates the prescription that the Prose Kāvya, being a sub-division of the Kāvya in general, should have a good subject (Sadāśraya) and that the hero should be noble and high-souled. Gambling, burglary, cunning, fraud, violence murder, impersonation, abduction and illicit love form, jointly and severally, the predominating incidents in every story ; and Mantragupta's definition of love as the determination to possess —*de l'audace* in Danton's famous phrase—is indeed typical of its erotic situations. Wilson, with his mid-Victorian sense of propriety speaks of the loose principles and lax morals of the work, and the opinion has been repeated in a modified form by some modern critics; but the point is over-looked that immorality, rather than morality, is its deliberate theme. The *Daśakumāra* is imaginative fiction, but it approaches in spirit to the picaresque romance of modern Europe, which gives a lively picture of rakes and ruffians of great cities. It is not an open satire, but the whole trend is remarkably satirical in utilising, with no small power of observation and caricature, the amusing possibilities of incorrigible rakes, unscrupulous rogues, hypocritical ascetics, frudulent priests, light-hearted idlers, fervent lovers, cunning bawds, unfaithful wives and heartless courtesans, who jostle with each other within the small compass of the swift and racy narratives. The scenes are accordingly laid in cosmo-politan cities where the scum and refuse of all countries and societies meet. Even the higher world of gods, princes and Brahmans is regarded with little respect. The gods are brought in to justify disgraceful deeds in which the princes engage them-selves; the Buddhist nuns act as procuresses; the teaching of the Jina is declared by a Jaina monk to be nothing but a swindle; and the Brahman's greed of gold and love of cock-fights are held up to ridicule. Two chief motives which actuate the princes of wild deeds are the desire for delights of love and for the possession of a realm, but they are not at all fastidious about the means they employ to gain their ends. Their frankness often borders on cynicism and, if not on a lack of morality, on fundamental non-morality.

It is a strange world in which we move, life-like, no doubt, in its skilful portraiture, but in a sense unreal, being sublimated with marvel and magic, which are seldom dissociated from folk-tale. We hear of a collyrium which produces invisibility, of a captive's chains transformed deliciously into a beautiful nymph, of burglar's art which turns beggars into millionaires, and of magician's charms which spirit away maidens. This trait appears to have been inherited from the popular tale, and Daṇḍin's indebtedness to the *Bṛhatkathā* has been industriously traced.[1] But the treatment undoubtedly is Daṇḍin's own. He is successful in further developing the lively elements of the popular tale, to which he judiciously applies the literary polish and sensibility of the Kāvya ; but the one is never allowed to overpower the other. The brier of realism and the rose of romance are cleverly combined in a unique literary form. In the laboured compositions of Subandhu and Bāṇa the exclusive tendency towards the sentimental and the erotic leads to a diminishing of interest in the narrative or in its comic possiblities. The impression that one receives from Daṇḍin's work, on the other hand, is that it delights to caricature and satirise certain aspects of contemporary society in an interesting period. Its power of vivid characterisation realises this object by presenting, not a limited number of types, but a large variety of individuals, including minor characters not altogether devoid of reality and interest. There can be little doubt that most of these are studies from life, heightened indeed, but faithful ; not wholly agreeable, but free from the touch alike of mawkishness and affectation. It is remarkable that in these pictures the realistic does not quench the artistic, but the merely finical gives way to the vividly authentic. We pass from pageantry to conduct, from convention to impression, from abstraction to fact. There are abundant instances of the author's sense of humour, his wit and polite banter, his power of gentle satire and caricature, which effectively contribute to the realism of his outlook. For the first time, these qualities rare enough in the normal Sanskrit writing, reveal themeselves in a literary from, and make Daṇḍin's delightfully unethical romancero picaresco, not a conventional Prose Kāvya, but a distinct literary creation of a new type in Sanskrit.

There is more matter, but the manner has no difficulty in joining hands with it. Daṇḍin's work avoids the extended scale and leisurely manner of proceeding, the elaborate descriptive and

1 Agashe, *op. cit.*, p. xli f.

sentimental divagations, the eccentricities of taste and extravagance of diction, which are derived from the tradition of the regular Kāvya and developed to its utmost possibilities or impossibilities in the imaginative romances of Subandhu and Bāṇa. The arrangement of the tales is judicious, and the comparatively swift and easy narrative is never overloaded by constant and enormous digressions. The episodic method is old and forms a striking feature of Indian story-telling, but in the *Daśakumāra* the subsidiary stories never beat out, hamper nor hold up the course of the main narrative. Even the four clever stories in the sixth Ucchvāsa are properly emboxed, and we are spared the endless confusion of curses and changing personalities and stories within stories.

Not only Daṇḍin's treatment, but also his style and diction are saved from the fatal fault of over-elaboration by his sense of proportion and restraint. He is by no means an easy writer, but there are no fatiguing complexities in his diction ; it is energetic and yet elegantly articulated. It is not marked by any inordinate love for disproportionate compounds and sesquipedalian sentences, nor by a weakness for far-fetched allusions, complex puns and jingling of meaningless sounds. The advantage of such a style, free from ponderous construction and wearisome embellishment, is obvious for the graphic dressing up of its unconventional subjects of a cheat, a hypocrite, an amorist or a braggadacio ; and the Kāvya-refinements would have been wholly out of place. Occasionally indeed Daṇḍin indulges in florid descriptions, such as we find in the pictures of the sleeping Ambālikā or the dancing Kandukavatī, but even in these cases he keeps within the limits of a few long sentences or only one printed page. There is an attempt at a literary feat in the avoidance of labial sounds in the seventh Ucchvāsa, but it is adequately motived ; and Dṇḍin wisely confines himself to a sparing use of such verbal ingenuity. It is not suggested that Daṇḍin makes no pretension to ornament, but, in the main, his use of it is effective, limited and pretty, and not recondite, incessant and tiresome.

The highest praise goes to Daṇḍin as the master of vigorous and elegant Sanskrit prose ; and his work, in its artistic and social challanges, is undoubtedly a unique masterpiece, the merits of which need not be reluctantly recognised by modern taste for not conforming to the normal model.

c. SUBANDHU

In theory and accepted practice, the normal type of the Prose Kāvya is illustrated, not by the work of Daṇḍin, but by those of Subandhu and Bāṇa. In these typical prose Kāvyas, however, there is less exuberance of life, the descriptions are more abundant and elaborate, the narrative is reduced to a mere skeleton, learning loads the wings of fancy, and the style and treatment lack ease and naturalness. They have no ruffian heroes, nor dubious adventures, but deal with chaste and noble, if somewhat sentimental and bookish, characters. They employ all the romantic devices, derived from folk-tale, of reborn heroes and transformed personages in a dreamland of marvellous but softer adventure, and present them in a gorgeous vehicle of elaborately poetical, but artificial, style.

The date of Subandhu, author of the *Vāsavadattā*,[1] is not exactly known. Attempts have been made to establish its upper and the lower terminus, respectively, but Subandhu's punning allusion, on the one hand, to the Uddyotakara[2] and a supposed work of Dharmakīrti,[3] belonging at least to the middle of the

1 Ed. F. Hall, Bibl. Ind., with comm. of Śivarāma Tripāṭhin, Calcutta 1859, reprinted almost *verbatim* by J. Vidyasagar, Calcutta 1874, 3rd ed. 1907 ; ed. R. V. Krishnamachariar with his own comm. Śrī Vāṇī-vilāsa Press, Srirangam 1906 ; ed. Louis H. Gray, in roman characters, Columbia University Press, New York 1913. Śivarāma belongs to the 18th century ; see S. K De, *Sanskrit Poetics*, I, p. 318. There is also an earlier comm. of Jagaddhara which deserves publication.

2 *nyāya-sthitim* (v. l. *-vidyām*) *ivoddyotakara-svarūpām* (ed. Hall, p. 235 ; ed. Srirangam, p. 303 ; ed. Gray, p. 180).

3 *bauddha-saṁgatim* (v. l. *sat-kavi-kāvya-racanām*) *ivālaṁkāra-bhūṣitām*, *loc. cit.* It is remarkable that the reading is not found in all Mss (Hall, p. 236), and no work of Dharmakīrti's called Buddhasaṁgatyalaṁkāra has yet been found. Lévi (*Bulletin de l'E'cole Français d'Extrême-Orient*, 1903, p. 18) denies that Subandhu alludes to Dharmakīrti's literary activity.

sixth century A.D., and, on the other, by Bāṇa's allusion to a *Vāsavadattā*. which is supposed to be the same as Subandhu's work of that name, in the preface to his *Harṣa-carita*,[1] composed early in the seventh century.[2] But it must be recognised that the question is not free from difficulty. Neither the date of Dharmakīrti nor that of the Uddyotakara can be taken as conclusively settled ; nor is it beyond question, in the absence of the author's name, that Bāṇa really alludes to Subandhu's work. Even if the early part of the 7th century is taken to be the date of Dharmakīrti and the Uddyotakara, it would make Subandhu a contemporary of Bāṇa. The traditional view that Bāṇa wrote his romance to surparss that of Subandhu probably arose from Bāṇa's qualification of his own *Kādambarī* (st. 20) by the epithet *ati-dvayī* 'surpassing the two,' these two being, according to the very late commentator,[3] Subandhu's *Vāsavadattā* and Guṇāḍhya's *Bṛhatkathā*. But the doubt expressed,[4] though later abandoned,[5] by Peterson has been lately revived. Since the arguments on both sides of the question[6] proceed chiefly on the

1 Stanza II. The argument that Bāṇa, by the use of Śleṣa in this stanza, means to imply Subandhu's fondness for it, is weak ; for Bāṇa uses Śleṣa also in the stanzas on Bhāsa and the *Bṛhatkathā*.

2 Among other literary or historical allusions made by Subandhu, the reference to Vikramāditya and Kaṅka in the tenth introductory stanza has been made the basis of entirely problematic conjectures by Hall (p. 6), Hoernle (*JRAS*, 1903, p. 545 f) and B. C. Mazumdar (*JRAS*, 1907, p. 406 f.) ; see L. H. Gray, introd., p. 8f. The description of Kusumapura and Subandhu's practice of the Gauḍī Rīti may suggest that he was an eastern writer, but the geography of the work is too conventional and the argument on Rīti too indefinite to be decisive. There are two other punning allusions by Subandhu, apparently to a Gaṇa-kārikā with a Vṛti by Surapāla (ed. Srirangam, p. 314) and an obscurely mentioned work by Kamalākara-bhikṣu (p. 319) ; but these have not yet been sufficiently recognised and traced.

3 Bhānudatta, the commentator, belong to the 16th century. But the phrase *atidvayī* is not grammatically correct, and the reading appears to be doubtful. Possibly it is a graphical scribal error for *aniddhayā* (qualifying *dhiyā*) read by other commentators (*cf. OLD*, IV, no. 2, 1941, p. 7).

4 Introd. to *Kādambarī*, pp. 71-73. 5 Introd. to *Sbhv*, p. 133.

6 See Kane, introd. to *Harṣa-carita*, p. xif ; Weber, *Indische Streifen*, Berlin 1868, I, pp. 369-86 ; Telang in *JBRAS* XVIII, 1891, p. 147 f. ; W. Cartellieri in *WZKM*, I, 1887, pp. 115-32 ; F. W. Thomas in *WZKM*, XII, 1898, pp. 21-23, also in *JRAS*, 1920, pp. 386-87 ; Mankowski in *WZKM*, XV, 1901, p. 246f. Keith in *JRAS*, 1914 (arguing that Subandhu cannot be safely ascribed to a period substantially

debatable grounds of the standard of taste and morals, and of style and diction, it is scarcely possible to express a final opinion without being dogmatic. The only one characteristic difference of Subandhu's prose from that of Bāṇa, apart from its being uninspiring, is the excessive, but self-imposed, use of paronomasia (Śleṣa); but this argues neither for priority nor posteriority, but only suggest the greater currency of this figure of speech in this period. The only certain point about Subandhu's date is the fact that in the first half of the 8th century, Vākpati in his Prakrit poem *Gauḍavaho* (st. 800) connects Subandhu's name with those of Bhāsa, Kālidāsa and Haricandra, and a little later in the same century, Vāmana quotes anonymously[1] a passage which occurs, with a slight variation, in Subandhu's *Vāsavadattā.*[2]

With the Vāsavadattā of the Udayana legend, made famous by various poets in Sanskrit literature, Subandhu's romance has nothing common except the name; and since the story, as told by Subandhu, does not occur elsewhere in any form, it appears to be entirely invented and embellished by our poet. But the plot is neither rich nor striking. The handsome prince Kandarpaketu,

before 650 A.D.); Sivaprasad Bhattacharya in *IHQ*, IV, 1929, p. 699f.—There is one passage to which attention does appear to have been drawn, but it is no less important. It describes the passionate condition of Vāsavadattā at the sight of Kandarpaketu and runs thus: *hṛdayaṁ vilikhitam iva utkīrṇam iva, pratyuptam iva, kīlitam iva..... vajralepa-ghaṭitam iva......marmāntara-sthitam iva,* which appears to be reproduced in a metrical form in the following three lines from Bhavabhūti's *Mālatī-mādhava* (v. 10):

> *līneva pratibimbiteva likhitevotkīrṇa-rūpeva ca*
> *pratyupteva ca vajralepa-ghaṭitevāntarnikhāteva ca* |
> *sā naś cetasi kīliteva viśikhaiś cetobhuvaḥ pañcabhiḥ...*

The verbal resemblance cannot be dismissed as accidental; but considering that Bhavabhūti here improves upon what he weaves into the texture of his poem and also the fact that Bhavabhūti is known to have borrowed phrases from Kālidāsa, the presumption of borrowing on the part of Bhavabhūti is likely.

1 *Kāvyālaṁkāra* i. 3. 25 (*kuliśa-śikhara-khara-nakhara*°)—*Vāsavadattā*, ed. Srirangam, p. 331 and ed. Hall, p. 226.

2 For other references to Subandhu and his work see Gray, pp. 3-4. Gray is right in thinking that the reference in the *Daśakumāra*° to Vāsavadattā clearly alludes to the story of Udayana and Vāsavadattā, and not to Vāsavadattā of Subandhu's romance.

son of Cintāmaṇi, beholds in a dream a lovely maiden ; and, setting out with his friend Makaranda in search of the unknown beloved and resting at night in the Vindhya hills under a tree, he overhears the conversation of a couple of parrots that princess Vāsavadattā of Pāṭaliputra, having similarly dreamt of Kandarpaketu, has sent her pet parrot, Tamālikā, to find him. With the help of the kindly bird, the lovers unite ; but as Śṛṅgāraśekhara, father of the princess, plans her marriage with a Vidyādhara chief, the lovers elope on a magic steed to the Vindhya hills. Early in the morning, while Kandarpaketu is still asleep, Vāsavadattā, straying into the forest, is chased by two gangs of Kirātas ; but as they fall out and fight for her, she eludes them but trespasses into a hermitage, where she is turned into stone by the curse of the unchivalrous ascetic. Kandarpaketu, deterred from self-destruction by a voice from the sky, finds her after a long search, and at his touch the curse terminates.

It will be seen that the central argument of such tales is weak and almost insignificant. The general scheme appears to consist of the falling in love of a passionate hero with a heroine of the fair and frail type, and their final union after a series of romantic adventures, in which all the naraative motifs[1] of dream-vision, talking parrots, magic steed, curse transformation and voice in the air are utilised. But the interest of the story-telling lies not in incident, but in minute portraiture of personal beauty of the lovers and their generous qualities, their ardent, if sentimental, longing for each other, the misfortune obstructing the fulfilment of their desires, their pangs of thwarted love, and the preservation of their love through all trials and difficulties until their final union. All this is eked out lavishly by the romantic commonplaces of the Kāvya, by highly flavoured descriptions of cities, battles, oceans, mountains, seasons, sunset, descriptions of cities, battles, occens, mountains, seasons, sunset, moonrise and the like, and by the display of enormous Śāstric

1 A list of these are made out by Cartellieri, *op. cit.* For a study of these motifs as literary devices see Gray in *WZKM*, XVIII, 1904, p. 39 f.

learning and technical skill. Subandhu's poverty of invention and characterisation, therefore, is not surprising ; and criticism has been, not unjustly, levelled against the absurdities and inconsistencies of his story. But the slenderness of the theme is not so much a matter of importance to subandhu as the manner of developing or over-developing it. Stress has been rightly laid on his undoubted, if somewhat conventional, descriptive power ; but the more than occasional descriptive digressions, forming the inseparable accessory of the Kāvya, constitute the bulk of his work, and are made merely the means of displaying his luxuriant rhetorical skill and multifarious learning. The attractiveness of the lady of Kandarpaketu's vision, for instance, is outlined in a brief sentence of some one hundred and twenty lines only ! The wise censure of Ānandavardhana[1] that the poets are often regardless of theme and sentiment and exceedingly engrossed in verbal tricks is more than just in its application to the Prose Kāvya of this type.

It must, however, be said to Subandhu's credit that he is not overfond of long rolling compounds, and even when they occur, they are not altogether devoid of majesty and melody. When he has no need for a long sentence, he can write short ones, and this occurs notably in the beief dialogues. The sound-effects are not always tedious, nor his use of words always atrocious. What becomes wearisome in its abundance is Subandhu's constant search for conceits, epithets and similes expressed in endless strings of paronomasia (Śleṣa) and apparent incongruity (Virodhābhāsa). For this reason, even his really coruscating ideas and images become more brilliant than luminous. When we are told that a lady is *rakta-pāda* like a grammatical treatise, her feet being painted with red lacquer as sections of grammar with red lines, or that the rising sun is blood-coloured, because the lion of dawn clawed the elephant of the night, we are taken to the verge of ludicrous fancy ; but

1 *Dhvanyāloka*, ed. NSP, Bombay 1911, p. 151.

such instances abound from page to page.[1] In a stanza, the genuineness of which, however, is doubted, Subandhu describes his own work as a treasure-house of literary dexterity, and declares that he had woven a pun in every syllable of his composition. We have indeed the dictum of the *Kāvyādarśa* (ii. 362) that paronomasia generally enhances the charm of all poetic figures, and the extraordinary resources of Sanskrit permit its effective use, but the rhetorician probably never means that the paronomasia should overshadow everything. The richness of Subandhu's fancy and his ingenuity in this direction is indeed astonishing and justifies his boasting ; but it cannot be said that he has used this figure with judgment or with the sense of visualisation which makes this, as well as other, figures a means of beautiful expression. Subandhu's paronomasias are often far-fetched and phantas-magoric, adduced only for the sake of cleverness, and involve much straining and even torturing of the language. It is true that in the stringing together of puns Subandhu does not stand alone. Bāṇa also makes much use of it, and refers to this habit of the Kathā when he describes it as *nirantara-śleṣa-ghana*. But Bāṇa never indulges in unceasing fireworks of puns and other devices, and his poetic imagination and power of picturesque description make ample amends for all his weakness for literary adornment. Subandhu, on the other hand, lacks these saving graces ; nor does he command the humour, vigour and variety of Daṇḍin. He becomes, therefore, a willing victim of the cult of style, which believes that nothing great can be produced in the ordinary way.

In order to appreciate Subandhu's literary accomplishment this fact should be borne in mind ; and it is as unnecessary as it is hypercritical either to depreciate or exaggerate his merits unduly. It should be conceded that, in spite of its fancy, pathos and sentiment, Subandhu's work is characterised by an element

[1] Krishnamachariar has given (*op. cit.*, p. xixf) an almost exhaustive list of instances ofSubandhu's verbal accomplishment.

of mere trick which certainly impairs its literary value ; but it should not be assumed that it is a stupendous trifle, which enojoyed a fame and influence disproportionate to its worth. Bāṇa is doubtless a greater poet and can wield a wonderful spell of language, but Subandhu's method and manner of story-telling do not differ much from those of Bāṇa, and conform to the general scheme of the Prose Kāvya. But for his excessive fondness for paronomasia, Subandhu's style and diction are no more tyrannically mannered than those of Bāṇa ; and parallelisms in words and ideas have been found in the respective works of the two poets. It is true that Subandhu's glittering, but somewhat cold, fancy occupies itself more with the rhetorical, rather than with the poetical, possibilies of his subject ; but making allowance for individual traits, one must recognise the same technique and paraphernalia in both Subandhu and Bāṇa. They deal with the self-same commodities ; and if richness of vocabulary, wealth of description, profusion of epithets, similes and conceits, and frequency of learned allusions are distinctive of Subandhu, they are also found in Bāṇa. Whatever difference there is between the two romancers, it is one not in kind but in degree.

It would appear, therefore, that both Subandhu and Bāṇa exhibit in their works certain features of the Sanskrit prose narrative which, being of the same character, must have belonged to the general literary tendency of the time. The tendency is not so apparent in Daṇḍin, but in Subandhu and Bāṇa it is carried to its extreme ; and we find, more or less, a similar phenomenon in poetry, as we pass from Bhāravi to Māgha. It is, however, a facile explanation which puts it down to incompetence, bad taste or queer mentality ; the question has a deeper historical significance, perhaps more in prose than in poetry. Louis H. Gray calls attention to certain stylistic similarities between Subandhu's *Vāsavadattā* and Lyly's *Eupheus* ; but if there is any point in drawing a parallel, it lies precisely in the fact that the work of the Sanskrit stylist, like that of the Elizabethan mannerist, is a deliberate attempt to achieve a rich.

variegated and imaginative prose style, although like all deliberate attempts it is carried to fantastic excess. The ornate and fanciful style tends to the florid and extravagant, and needs to be restrained and tamed ; but the plain style inclines equally towards the slipshod and jejune, and needs to be raised and inspired. The plain style, evidenced in the *Pañcatantra,* is indeed well proportioned, clear and sane, and is suitable for a variety of literary purpose, but it is ill fitted for fanciful, gorgeous or passionate expression ; it is constantly liable, when not used with something more than ordinary scholarship and taste, to degenerate into commonness or insipidity. Neither Subandhu nor Bāṇa may have evolved a properly ornate style, suitable for counteracting these perils and for elevated imaginative writing, but their inclination certainly points to this derection. It is not the rhetorical habit in these writers which annoys, but their use of rhetoric not in proportion, but out of proportion to their narrative, description, idea or feeling. Perhaps in their horror of the commonplace and in their eagerness to avoid the danger of being dull, they proceed to the opposite extreme of too heavy ornamentation, and thereby lose raciness, vigour and even sanity ; but for this reason the worthiness of their motive and the measure of success which they achieved should not be missed. We have an interesting illustration here of what occurs everywhere, namely the constantly recurring struggle between the plain and the ornate style ; but in trying to avoid plainness, these well-meaning but unbalanced writers practically swamp it with meaningless ornateness, by applying to prose the ill-fitting graces and refinements of poetry. The gorgeous standard, which they set up, is neither faultless nor easy to follow, but it is curious that it is never questioned for centuries. It is a pity that their successors never realise their literary motive, but only exaggerate their literary mannerisms. It was for the later writers to normalise the style by cutting down its early exuberant excesses, but it is strange that they never attempted to do so. Perhaps they fell under the fascination of its poetical magnificence, and were actuated by the theory which approximated prose to poetry and affiliated the prose Kāvya to the metrical. There has never been, therefore, in the later history of Sanskrit prose style, a real ebb and flow, a real flux between maxima and minima. It is for this reason perhaps that the perfect prose style, which keeps the golden mean between the plain and the ornate, never developed in Sanskrit.

There is, thus, no essential difference of literary inspiration between Subandhu and Bāṇa ; only, Subandhu's gifts are often rendered ineffectual by the mediocrity of his poetic powers. There is the sameness of characteristics and of ideas of workmanship ; but while Subandhu often plods, Bāṇa can often soar. The extreme excellence, as well as the extreme defect, of the literary tendency, which both of them represent in their individual way, are, however, better mirrored in Bāṇa's works, which reach the utmost limit of the peculiar type of the Sanskrit prose narrative.

d. *Bāṇabhaṭṭa*

In the first two and a half chapters of his *Harṣa-carita* and in the introductory stanzas of his *Kādambarī*,[1] Bāṇabhaṭṭa gives an account of himself and his family as prelude to that of his royal patron. He was a Brahman of the Vātsyāyana-gotra, his ancestry being traced to Vtsa, of whom a mythological account is given as the cousion of Śāradvata, son of Sarasvatī and Dadhīca. In the family was born Kubera, who was honoured by many Gupta kings, and whose youngest son was Pāśupata. Pāśupata's son was Arthapati ; and among the many sons of Arthapati, Citrabhānu was Bāṇa's father. They lived in a place called Prītikuṭa on the banks of the Hiraṇyabāhu, otherwise known

1 The accouts agree, eccept in one omission, namely, the name of Bāṇa's great-grandfather, Pāśupata, is not found in the *Kādambarī*. For a recent summary of all relevant questions regarding Bāṇa and his works, as well as for a full bibliography, see A. A. Maria Sharpe, *Bāṇa's Kādambarī* (Diss., N. V. de Vlaamsche, Leuven 1937), pp. 1-108, which also contains Dutch trs. of work, with indices and concordances.

as the river Śoṇa. Bāṇa's mother Rājyadevī died while he was yet young, but his father took tender care of him. When he was about fourteen, his father died ; and in the unsettled life which followed, Bāṇa wandered about from place to place, mixed in dubious company, acquired evil repute as well as rich experience, returned home and lived a life of quiet study. He was summoned to the presence of king Harṣavardhana, ostensibly for being taken to task for his misspent youth, at his camp near the town of Maṇitārā on the Ajiravatī. He was at first received with coldness, but afterwards with much favour.[1] After some time, on a visit home, Bāṇa was requested by his relatives to speak of the great king. He began his narrative, after having warned his audience of his inability to do full justice to his theme. The story is told in the remaining five Ucchvāsas, but it is left unfinished. It was possibly never his intention to offer a complete account ; for he tells us that even in a hundred lives he cannot hope to recount the whole story of Harṣa's mighty deeds, and asks his audience if they would be content to hear a part.[2]

We have already spoken of the value of the important metrical preface to the *Harṣa-carita*,[3] which speaks of the famous literary predecessors of Bāṇa. The story begins with a description of Sthāṇvīśvara and of the glorious kings, sprung from

1 It is not known at what stage of Harṣa's career Bāṇa met him. It is assumed that Bāṇa was fairly young when Harṣa in his greatness patronised him, and that there is no reason to presume that Bāṇa wrote in the early part of Harṣa's reign, which ended in 647 A.D. Bāṇa never alludes to troubles of poverty among other troubles he mentions in Ucchvāsa i, and we are also told that he inherited wealth from his ancestors. He acknowledges gifts from his patron, but there is nothing to support the legend that he sold some of his literary works to Harṣa.

2 The earliest quotation from Bāṇa, though anonymous, occurs in Vāmana's *Kāvyālaṁkāra* (2nd half of the 8th century) v. 2. 44, *anukaroti bhagavato nārāyaṇasya* (= *Kādambarī*, ed. Peterson, p. 6). In the middle of the 9th century, Bāṇa and his two works are mentioned by Ānandavardhana in his *Dhvanyāloka* (ed. NSP, pp. 87, 100, 101, 127).

3 Ed. A. A. Führer, with comm. of Śaṁkara, Bomb. Skt. Ser., 1909 ; ed. K. P. Parab, with same comm. NSP, Bombay 1892 (5th ed. 1925) ; ed. P. V. Kane (without comm. but with notes etc.), Bombay 1918. Trs. into English by E. B. Cowell and F. W. Thomas, London 1907.

Puṣpabhūti, from whom is descended Harṣavardhana's father, Prabhākaravardhana. Harṣa's elder brother is Rājyavardhana; and his sister Rājyaśri is married to Grahavarman of the Maukhari family of Kānyakubja. Then we have a more brilliant than pathetic picture of the illness and death of Prabhākaravardhana, whose queen Yaśomati also ascends the funeral pyre, of the return of Rājyavardhana from his successful campaign against the Hūṇas, and of his reluctance to ascend the throne. But before Harṣa could be installed, news reaches that the king of Mālava his slain Grahavarman and imprisoned Rājyaśrī. Rājyavardhana succeeds in defeating the Mālava king, but he is treacherously killed by the king of Gauḍa. Harṣa's expedition to save his sister follows, but in the meantime she escapes from prison and is rescued by a Buddhist sāge. The story abruptly ends with the meeting of Harṣa and Rājyaśrī while the tale of her recovery is being told. The work gives us nothing about the later career of Harṣa, nor any information regarding the later stages of Bāṇa's own life.

The *Harṣa-carita* has the distinction of being the first attempt at writing a Prose Kāvya on an historical theme.[1] Subandhu's *Vāsavadattā*, as well as Bāṇa's other prose narrative, the *Kādambarī*, deals with legendary fiction and everything is viewed in these works through a highly imaginative atmosphere. The *Harṣa-carita* is no less imaginative, but the author takes his own sovereign as his hero and weaves the story out of some actual events of his career. In this respect it supplies a contemporary picture, which, in the paucity of other records, is indeed valuable; but its importance as an historical document should not be overrated. The sum-total of the story, lavishly embellished as it is, is no more than an incident in Harṣa's career; and it cannot be said that the picture is either full or satisfactory from the historical point of view. Many points in the narrative, especially the position, action and identity of the Malava

1 See below, ch. VI, under Poems with Historical Themes.

and the Gauḍa kings, are left obscure ; and the gorgeously descriptive and ornamental style leaves little room for the poor thread of actual history. Even if the work supplies picturesque accounts, into which the historian may profitably delve, of the actualities of life in camp and court, in monastery and village retreat, of military expeditions, and of social religious observances and practices, we learn very little indeed of the political facts of the great emperor's reign as a whole.

It is clear that Bāṇa writes his *Harṣa-carita* more as a romantic story than as a sober history of the king's life, and stops when he is satisfied that his Muse has taken a sufficiently long flight. The term 'Historical Kāvya,' which is often applied to this and other works of the same kind, is hardly expressive ; for, in all essential, the work is a Prose Kāvya, and the fact of its having an historical theme does not make it historical in style, spirit and treatment. The reproach that India had little history and historical sense is perhaps not entirely just, but India was little interested in historical incident as such, and never took seriously to chronicling, much less to what is known as history in modern times. The uncertainties of pre-history, therefore, continue in India to a comparatively late period ; and it is also important to note that the idea of evolution is, in the same way, scarcely recognised in the sphere of thought and speculation. Perhaps the explanation is to be sought in the psychology of the Indian mind, which takes the world of imagination to be more real than the world of fact ; perhaps we in modern times attach too much importance to fact or incident and make a fetish of history or evolution. In any case, history had little place in the Kāvya, which apparently considered the mythological heroes to be more interesting than the actual rulers of the day. Even when a real personage is taken for treatment, as in the case of Harṣa, he is elevated and invested with all the glory and some of the fiction of the mythological hero. The Sanskrit theory of art also, in its emphasis on imaginative and impersonalised creation, encouraged abstraction, admitted belief in fate and miracle, and had little feeling for the concrete facts and forces of human nature and human life. The same spirit, which tended against the creation of a vigorous and sensitive drama, stood also in the way of clear and critical historiography. The poets who, like Bāṇa, write on historical themes, never claim merit as historians, but conceive their duty to be that of a poet. It would not be proper, therefore, to attach the qualification 'historical' to what is essentially a Kāvya.

The imposition of keeping even within the semblance of fact is absent in the *Kādambarī*, which is an entirely imaginative creation, but which like the *Harṣa-carita*, is also left unfinished. It was, however, death, which cut off the work; and we are told by Bāṇa's son, Bhūṣaṇa,[1] that he wrote the latter part, not out of literary ostentation, but as a task of filial duty. We do not know in what way Bāṇa himsels would have rounded off the inherent difficulties of the remainder of the plot, but the inferiority of the supplement is generally admitted. It gives the impression of introducing complexities, but there is also an anxiety of bringing the story to a somewhat hurried close. The command over the ornate style and diction is undoubted, and the son possesses some of the excellences of the father; but to the mannerisms of the father, which are often exaggerated, are added a few peculiar to the son.

The story of the *Kādambarī*,[2] which deals with the lives and loves of two heroes, each of whom is reborn twice, is too well known to require a detailed summary here. But it is noteworthy that Bāṇa's portion of the composition stops even

[1] In some MSS (*e.g.*, Stein, *Jammu Cat.*, Bombay 1894, p. 299), he is called Pulina or Pulinda. Dhanapāla in his *Tilaka-mañjarī* (Pref. verse 26) seems to suggest that Pulinda was the name.

[2] Ed. P. Peterson, Bomb. Skt. Ser., 1883; ed. P. V. Kane, Bombay 1911, 1920; (3rd ed. 1921, Pūrvabhāga only); ed. K. P. Parab, with comm. of Bhānucandra and Siddhacandra, NSP, Bombay 1890 (7th ed., revised by V. L. Panshikar 1928). Engl. trs. (with occasional omissions) C. M. Ridding, London 1896. Summaries of the story will be found in these editions.

before the theme is properly developed. It introduces the Caṇḍala maiden and her speaking parrot itto the court of Śūdraka and puts the entire narrative in the mouth of the parrot.[1] Apart from absurdity of the device, it is noteworthy that the old method of emboxing tale within tale is also retained; for the parrot's tale includes that of the sage Jābāli concerning Candrāpīḍa and Vaiśaṃpāyana, along with the story told by Mahāśvetā of her love for Puṇḍarīka. After the meeting of Candrāpīḍa with Kādambarī, whose entrance into the story is too long delayed, and his hurried return to Ujjayinī, Bāṇa's work ends abruptly with the welcome news which Patralekhā brings to him of Kādambarī's assurance of love. It is clear that, like Spenser, Bāṇa conceived of too large a plan and never lived to finish it. The plot is only begun but hardly unfolded. It is completed ingeniously enough by his son, but we have no means, except from scattered and uncertain hints in the narrative itself, of knowing whether Bāṇa wanted to develop it with all its later bewildering turn and confusion of curses and changing personalities of reborn heroes. Half-told as the tale is by him, we cannot be sure if he meant Śūdraka, the hearer of the story, but a redundant figure at the outset, is to become the real hero in the end as the reborn Candrāpīḍa, who in his turn is to be the moon-god in his former birth, or whether Vaiśaṃpāyana is to turn out as the transformed parrot itself recounting the tale; for these elaborate intricacies occur in the second part of the work. This important fact is ignored when one criticises Bāṇa for his highly complex plot, and charges him wich deficiency of constructive power. The striking parallelism of the story of the *Kādambarī* to the much humbler one of King Sumanas (or Sumānasa), narrated in the two Kashmirian versions of the *Bṛhatkathā*,[2] may suggest that Bāṇa may have

1 On the rôle of the Parrot in story literature, see L. H. Gray in ***WZKM***, XVIII, 1904, p. 42.

2 Somadeva's *Kathā-sarit-sāgara*, x. 3 (Tawney's trs., Calcutta 1884, ii, p. 17 f.; the whole passage is reproduced in Peterson's introd. to the *Kādambarī*, pp. 84-95); Kṣemendra's *Bṛhatkathā-mañjarī*, xvi. 185 f.

wanted to utilise the motif of curse and rebirth, but it is useless to speculate whether he would have done it in the same way as we have it now. The complications of the plot, as developed in Bhūṣaṇa's supplement, can hardly be inferred from the dry bones of the much simpler and less refined original, occurring in the versions of the *Bṛhatkatha*, which has a somewhat different denouement and which attaches degrading forms of birth to the heroine Mandārikā and her father, on the rather frivolous ground of a curse proceeding from wild grief in the one case and repentance for pronouncing the curse in the other.

That the method of emboxing tales can be carried to a confusing extent is seen in the arrangement of Somadeva's *Kathā-sarit-sāgara*, where, often with an insignificant framework, we have A's account of B's report of C's recounting of D's relating of what E said, and so forth, until we have the disentangling of the entire intricate progression, or reversion to the main story, which the reader in the meantime probably forgets. The form is not ill suited to a succession of disconnected tales, as in the *Pañcatantra*, where they are narrated generally by the characters of the frame-story or of the inset stories. There is further improvement in the *Daśakumāra-carita*, where their several experiences are narrated, with a semblance of realism, by the princes themselves in the first person, and in the *Vetāla-pañca-viṃśati*, where all the separate tales are connected to serve one main purpose. In the *Kādambarī*, the old machinery is adapted, with a clever plan, to the conditions of the complex narrative. The device of first-hand narration is made an essence of the form ; for the inset stories explain matters which the main narrator could not himself know and which each subsidiary narrator is allowed to describe as coming within the scope of personal experience. The main narrative here is not recounted by the hero, but in effect by the sage Jābāli, who is supposed by his insight to know vividly what he relates, and who can describe freely and objectively ; but each of the minor narratives, like that of Mahāśvetā gives effective expression to intimate knowledge and feeling, and is made essential to the development of the plot.

The denouement, as developed by Bhūṣaṇa, is sometimes criticised as flat. To a certain extent, this is true ; but, making allowance for the device of curse and rebirth common enough in folk-tale,[1] one should admit that there is an element of surpise in the discovery at the end that Śūdraka, who is only the listener to the story, is himself the real hero, who had loved in vain in two lives, and whose listening to the story is a necessary condition of the reawakening of his love for Kādambarī and of brininging his second life to an end by his revived longing for reunion. As a rule, the romance-writers, like the poets, are rather poor inventors of plot, and make use of all the paraphernalia of conventional story-telling, as well as of the fantastic ornateness of an overworked diction ; but there is more arrangement, progress and interest in Bāṇa's narrative than in Subandhu's ; and, in spite of the complexes of past and present lives, there cannot be much doubt that the threads of the stories of the loves of the two maidens, which form his main theme, are skilfully interlaced.

The chief obstacle to our appreciation of Bāṇa's constructive gift, however, is his weakness for elaborating the tales, by dwelling too much on details, in a style which draws prose and poetry together in an unnatural alliance. The lack of proportion is due partly to largeness of handling, and partly to a prodigal imagination which prefers lawless splendour to decent insipidity. But the sense of proportion is the very foundation of style and treatment. There is no need, for instance, to lose sight of the narrative in a lavish description of Ujjayinī, of Śukanāsa's palace, of the Vindhya forest and hermitage, of the temple of

1 For a study of these motifs as literary devices, see L. H. Gray in *WZKM*, XVIII, 1904, pp. 53-54. Gray cites an instance from the story of Arthapāla in *Daśakumāra°*, where there is a hint not fully developed, of a very complex scheme of three incarnations involving six persons. It is noteworthy, however, that it is Bāṇa's heroes, and not his heroines, who undergo three rebirths each.

Caṇḍikā, of night and moonrise, all of which give us wonderful word-pictures, no doubt, but most of which are certainly overdone. Bāṇa's power of observation and picturesque description, his love of nature, his eye for colour and ear for music, the richness of his fancy and his wealth of words, are excellences which are unquestioned ; but they are seldom kept within moderate bounds. His choice of subject may be good, but his choice of scale is fatal. The readiness of his resources is truly astonishing, but the exaggeration often swamps the reality of his pictures. The description of Ujjayinī, for instance, is too extravagant in its terms to give us a vivid notion of what it actually was in his time. The delineation of Mahāśvetā's beauty is too undiscriminating in its heaping of metaphors and epithets to present a convincing visual picture. Nor are absurdities excluded in matters of detail. The physician, a youth of eighteen, who attends upon the dying Prabhākaravardhana, is so fanatically attached to his king that he must also burn himself on the funeral pyre on his patron's death. It is not that Bāṇa's imageries lack visualisation and proper phrasing ; Bāṇa can be forcible and direct when he chooses ; the sense of humour is not altogether wanting in his picture, for example, of the Drāviḍa ascetic, or in his description of Skandagupta as having a nose as long as his sovereign's pedigree ; the advantage of contrast is utilised in the characterisation of the pairs of lovers ; all this and more is admitted. But the censure is just that Bāṇa allows no topic to pass until he can squeeze no more out of it. Whether in description or in speeches of lamentation and exhortation, no possible detail is missed, no existing variety of synonymous epithets omitted, no romantic symbolism and conceit overlooked, nor any brilliant rhetorical device ignored.

It is clear that Bāṇa's evident relish in this extended and over-ostentatious method is a hindrance not only to vigorous narrative, but also to the realities of sentiment and character. Comments have been made, not unjustly, on the shadowy nature of his personages, some in their second and even third birth, and their exaggerated sentiments. But, making allowance for aberrations inevitable in a rich and exuberant talent, it must be said that Bāṇa's power of characterisation or delineation of sentiment is not entirely divorced from reality. The world he depicts is removed in time and character, but not in appreciation and sympathy, from our own. The tale is strange, as also its manner of telling, but the element of marvel and magic is a recognised concomitant of the popular tale and need not of itself diminish its value as a romance, any more than the imaginative character of Spenser's *Faery Queene* impairs its interest as a poem. The scene is laid as much in Kādambarī's home, situated beyond the Himalayas and peopled by Gandharvas and Kinnaras, as in Ujjayinī where Candrāpīḍa's very human father Tārāpīḍa and his practical minister Śukanāsa hold court in royal splendour. The world of fancy is conceived as vividly as the world of humanity ; but the whole unreal machinery fades away when we are brought face to face with a tale of human love and sorrow, set forth in its idyllic charm as well as in its depth of pathos. It cannot be denied indeed that these old-time romancers are not always good at assessing the fine shades of human conduct ; they see life as an affair in which black is black and white is white, black and white seldom merge in dubious grey. Bāṇa attempts to infuse some diversity of colouring into his Patralekhā and his Śukanāsa, but they are too fine to be life-like. His two heroes are endowed with nobility, courtesy, devotion and charm, but they give the impression, more or less. of broad types of character ; they are hardly human beings. All this must be frankly admitted. But it must also be admitted that Bāṇa possesses a wonderful insight into the currents of youthful passion and virgin modesty, in their varying impulses of joy and grief, hope and despair ; and this forms the pith of his work in its surrounding embroidery, It is perhaps for this reason that he is more successful in delineating his two heroines. The maidenly love of Kādambarī. with its timid balancing of the new-born longing and cherished filial duty, is finely set off by the pathetic fidelity of the lovelorn Mahāśvetā, awaiting her lover for long years on the shores of the Acchoda lake. If they are overdressed children of Bāṇa's poetic imagination, his romantic ideas of love find in them a vivid and effective embodiment ; they are no less brilliant types, but they are at the same time individualised by the sharpness of the impression.

Indeed, the chief value of Bāṇa's unique romance lies, not in its narrative, not in its characterisation, nor in its presentation, but in its sentiment and poetry. In this extraordinary tale Bāṇa gives us a poetic treatment, in two different ways, of youthful love, having its root not only in the spontaneous emotion of this life, but in the recollective affection of cycles of existence, in what Kālidāsa and Bhavabhūti describe as friendships of former births firmly rooted in the heart. It is a study of the poetic possibilities of the belief in transmigration ; it conceives of a longer existence which links the forgotten past and the living present in bonds of tender and unswerving memories. If love in this romance moves in a strange and fantastic atmosphere of myth and folk-tale, the unreality of the dream-pageant acquires a vitality and interest from the graceful and poetic treatment of the depth and tenderness of human love, chastened by sorrow and death, enlivened by abiding hope and faith, and heightened by the touch of an intrepid idealism. And the extravagance of its luxuriant diction is perhaps a fit vehicle for this extravagantly romantic tale of love.

There are some critics, however, who on formal grounds would deny to Bāṇa a high rank as a prose writer ; and the classic onslaught of Weber[1] has been repeatedly quoted. The charge, in brief, is that Bāṇa's style and diction suffer from the vices of an unduly laboured vocabulary, syntax and ornamentation. His prose has been compared to an Indian jungle, where progress is rendered impossible by luxuriant undergrowths,

1 In *ZDMG*, 1853, quoted by Peterson, *op. cit.*, introd., p. 38. On this romance, see Weber, *Indische Streifen*, i. pp. 308-86.

until the traveller cuts out a path for himself, and where wild beasts lie in wait for him in the shape of recondite words, far-fetched allusions, vast sentences, undiscriminated epithets upon epithets in a multitude of aggressive compounds and of a whole battalion of puns, similes, hyperboles, alliterations and assonances. His erudition, it is complained, is heavy in its outrageous tendency to overloading and subtlety ; his sense of proportion is faulty in its excessive use of literary embellishments and in the construction of really enormous sentences, in which the verb or the subject is held over to the second, third, nay, even to the sixth page of print, all the interval being filled with more dazzling than illuminating series of phrases and phrases upon phrases ; his weakness for play upon thought or word is incessant and irritating ; he is dominated by the perverse desire of producing the graces of poetry in prose ; the grandeur of his style is ponderous and affected and often falls into the grandiose,—in fact, he has all the worst faults of verbal and mental bombast which can characterise a prose writer. While some measure of imperfect sympathy may be suspected in this unqualified denunciation, there is a great deal in this view which is justifiable. But it should not be forgotten that richness of vocabulary, wealth of description, frequency of rhetorical ornaments, length of compounds and elaborateness of sentences, a grandiose pitch of sound and sense are common features of the Prose Kāvya ; and in this respect Bāṇa is perhaps less reprehensible than Subandhu, whose unimaginative stolidity aggravate, rather than lessen, the enormity of the blemishes. The author of the *Kāvyādarśa* asserts that a profusion of compact compounds is the very life of Sanskrit prose, and that paronomasia is the very soul of poetic figures ; this dictum is exemplified only too well by these writings. Whether Bāṇa felt himself fettered by the literary canons of the rhetoricians, or whether these fetters themselves were forged on the model of the works composed by himself and his compeers, is a question which need not be discussed here ; but it must be admitted at once that in Bāṇa's romance, floridity, subtlety and horror of the obvious gets altogether the upper hand, as compared with succinctness, simplicity and directness. That Bāṇa can write with force and beauty and achieve considerable diversity of style has been pointed out by his apologists, but this cannot be taken as his general practice. He can seldom write without elegancies, and his manner has a tendency to generate into mannerism. He is often unable to concentrate in a terse phrase the force of pathos and passion, but reduces its strength by diffusing it into gracefully elaborated sentences. All this and even more cannot be denied. Bāṇa is not faultless ; he is indeed very faulty. But all this should not lead us to compare his works with those of Daṇḍin, which are differently conceived and executed, nor emphasise points in which he is obviously deficient. We should judge him on his own merits, and not by any standard which he does not profess to follow. It is useless to expect things which he does not aim at, but it is necessary to find out in what he is truly efficient.

It seems strange that one should be capable of denying the splendour of Bāṇa's prose at its best. It is eccentric, excessive and even wasteful, but its organ-voice is majestic in movement and magnificent in volume and melody. It would often seem that the nobly wrought diction moves along in its royal dignity and its panorama of beautiful pictures, while the poor story lags behind in the entourage and the humble sentiment hobbles along as best as it can. But it should not be forgotten that it is mainly by its wonderful spell of language and picturesqueness of imagery that Bāṇa's luxuriant romances retain their hold on the imagination, and it is precisely in this that their charm lies. It is an atmosphere of gracious lunar rainbows rather than that of strong sunlight. No one denies that Bāṇa's prose is useless for average purposes, but the question is whether it suites the purpose for which it is intended, whether the high-flown style is able to shape the rough stones of popular literature into gems of romantic beauty. It may be said that a more terse and simple style would have been appropriate for his account of king Harsa, but the work, as we have already said, should be taken more as a Prose Kāvya than as an historcal production, more as a stupendous panegyric than as a real biography. Still more should the *Kādambarī* be taken as a gorgeous and meandering tapestry work, in which an over-fancy fertile weaves endless patterns of great but fantastic beauty. It is conceded that prose in its normal proportion is hardly Bāṇa's natural organ of speech, nor is poetry, if one is to judge from his *Caṇḍī-śataka* ; but he affects a kind of prose-poetry in which he is unique. If he is swayed by the rhetorical passion of the Sanskrit poets, he is not merely rhetorical ; if he writes long sentences, his sentences are seldom obscure ; if he has a fondness for epithets and compounds, they are not always devoid of vividness, harmony and stateliness. Bāṇa is neither an imaginative recluse, nor a lover of the abstruse and the difficult, but he has an undoubted gift for the picturesque, the tender and the pathetic. He has a rare mastery over a certain gamut of feeling and fancy, but his prettiness or succulence never lack dignity nor become namby-pamby. In spite of their long-drawn-out brilliance and overwhelming profusion, his elaborate sentence-pictures are seldom wanting in the variety, swing and cadence of balanced phrase. Bāṇa has an amazing command over words and an irrepressible talent for melodious and majestic phrase ; but he is not so much a creator of words and phrases as an architect of sentences and paragraphs. In the combination of pictorial effect with the elegance and splendour of word-music, they form an unparalleled series of vignettes of astonishing lavishness. He would be monotonous and tiresome to one who determines to plod doggedly through the whole work, but he is attractive if attention is confined at a time to the marvellous richness of his fancy revealed in one or two of his delightful episodes and descriptions. Bāṇa pours out the whole farrago of his ideas, and has a provoking, and sometimes meaningless, habit of heaping them up in the enormous mass of a single sentence. He is verbose, not in the sense that he takes many words to express an idea, but in the sense that he gives expression to a multitude of ideas where a few would suffice. He is always in the danger of being smotherd by his own luxuriance. Indeed, Bāṇa's work impresses us by its unfailing and unrestrained wealth of power ; we have here not an abundance, but a riot. It is useless to seek a motive behind his work or sobriety of judgment and workmanship ; what we have here is the sheer delight of voluminous expression, the largeness of tumultuous fancy, and the love of all that is grand and glorious in fact or fiction.

2. The Drama from Śūdraka to Bhavabhūti

As in poetry, so in the drama, the period which followed Kālidāsa is still an expansive age in which stagnation has not yet set in. Unfortunately, only a limited number of dramatic works has survived ; but, fortunately, they show greater elasticity, variety and vitality than the poetical works of this period. With the exception of Amaru and Bhartṛhari, we have, on the one hand, Bhāravi, Bhaṭṭi, Mayūra, Kumāradāsa and Māgha, who do nothing more than work variations in the same tradition of poetry ; but we have, on the other hand, Śūdraka, the writers of four early Bhāṇa's, Harsa, Viśākhadatta, Mahendravikrama, Bhaṭṭa Nārāyaṇa and Bhavabhūti, each of whom represents a different and interesting type of the drama.

a. *Śūdraka*

In the long and varied history of the Sanskrit drama the *Mṛcchākaṭika*[1] of Śūdraka occupies a unique place. It is some-

1 Ed. A. F. Stenzler, Bonn 1847 ; ed. N. B. Godabole, with comm. of Lalla Dikṣita and Pṛthvīdhara, Bomb. Skt. Ser., 1896 ; ed. K. P. Parab, with comm. of Pṛthvīdhara, NSP, Bombay 1900, 3rd revised ed. 1909, 5th ed. 1922, Trs. into English by A. W. Ryder, Harvard Orient. Ser., Cambridge Mass., 1905 ; also by R. P. Oliver, Univ. of Illinois, U.S.A., 1938. The work has been translated several times into German and French, and also in other languages. For fuller bibliography see Sten Konow, *op. cit.*, p. 59.—For fuller bibliographies of dramatic writings dealt with in the following pages, one should consult, besides Sten Konow, M. Schuyler's ***Bibliography of the Sanskrit Drama*****, New**

times taken as one of the oldest extant Sanskrit dramas, and sometimes as a mere recast and continuation, by a clever but anonymous playwright, of the fragmentary *Cārudatta* ascribed to Bhāsa. But we have no exact knowledge of its date, origin and authoriship, nor of its relation to the *Cārudatta*. The work has been variously assigned to periods ranging from the 2nd century B.C. to the 6th century A.D.,[1] but even if none of the opinions advanced carries complete conviction, there can hardly be any doubt that it is a fairly old work. In spite of the number of legends which have gathered round the name of Śūdraka, its reputed author, nothing is known of him beyond the somewhat fanciful account[2] given in the Prologue of the play. We are told in this eulogistic reference that the author was a great Brahman king[3] of the name of Śūdraka ; and among the curious details of his excellences, we find that he was proficient in the Ṛgveda and the Sāmaveda, in mathematics, in the art concerning the courtesan and and in the lore of elephants,—statements which it is not impossible to support, to a limited extent, from the knowledge betrayed in the drama itself. The royal author is also said to have obtained the grace

York 1906, and Winternitz, *GIL*, iii, under respective authors and works. Only important editions and works on the plays are mentioned here. Analyses of the plots of the plays dealt with below are given by Sylvaien Lévi, Sten Konow and Keith ; as they are thus available in French, German and English respectively, we have avoided repetition as much as possible.

1 The various opinions are summarised by Sten Konow, *Ind. Drama*, p. 57, which see for references ; also K. C. Mehendale in *Bhandarkar Comm. Vol.*, Poona 1917, p. 367 f. Sten Konow himself would identify Śūdraka with the Ābhīra king Śivadatta (about 250 A.D.), while Jolly shows (*Hindu Law of Partition, Inheritance and Adoption*, Tagore Law Lectures, Calcutta 1883, p. 68 f.) that the knowledge of legal procedure evidenced in act ix follows what we find in the law books belonging to the 6th and 7th centuries. Jacobi (*Bhavisatta-kaha*, Munich 1918, p. 83 note), on the astrological data in act iv, believes that the drama could not have been written before the 4th century A.D. Sten Konow's view is effectively criticised by J. Charpentier in *JRAS*, 1923, p. 595 f., who discusses the question in some detail.

2 The use of the perfect tense, indicative of an event long past, in stanzas 3, 4, and 7 of the prologue is significant ; but it need not imply that the information is not based upon tradition or is not trustworthy.

3 See Charpentier, *loc. cit.*

of Śiva ; and after performing the horse-sacrifice and placing his son on the throne, he died by entering the fire at the astonishing age of a hundred years and ten days.

Whether all this describes an historical or a mythical king is not certain ; and Śūdraka's identity and authorship must yet be regarded as unsolved problems. The fact that Kālidāsa's predecessor, Somila (with Rāmila) wrote a *Śūdraka-kathā* perhaps indicates Śūdraka's legendary character accepted even before Kālidāsa's time ; and to later authors like Daṇḍin, Bāṇa, Kalhaṇa (iii. 343) and Somadeva he is already a figure of romance,[1] associated with Vidiśā, Pratiṣṭhāna, Vardhamāna and other places. Late legends connect him with the Andhrabhṛtyas and Sātavāhana (or Śālivāhana), but to melt down the legends and recoin historic truth from them, when they bear upon their very face the stamp of myth, is possible but not convincing. Some facts may have been drawn into the legends, and probably real incidents and names of real persons occur, but the attempt to separate the real from the unreal is, more or less, a pastime of ingenuity. The external evidence failing, the internal is equally elusive. Even assuming that the *Mṛcchakaṭika* is a *réchauffé* or recension of the *Cārudatta*, there is yet no decisive evidence regarding Bhāsa's authorship of the drama ; and even if the ascription is correct, it is insufficient to suggest a definite date for either of the two works. As royal authors in historic times were not averse to having works written for themselves, it have been maintained by those who believe in an historical Śūdraka that the real author, like a wise and greatful courtier, ascribed his work to his royal patron and allowed his own name to perish. This suggestion, wholly lacking proof, stands on a par with the equally fanciful

1 A later romance called *Śūdraka-vadha* (!), is quoted by Rāyamukuta (*ZDMG*, xxviii, p. 117) and a drama entitled *Vikrānta-śūdraka* is quoted in Bhoja's *Sarasvati-kaṇṭhā-bharaṇa* (p. 378) and *Śṛṅgāra-prakāsa* ; both the authors apparently make Śūdraka the hero. Hemacandra in his *Kāvyānuśāsana* (ed. NSP, Bombay 1901, p. 335) mentions a *Śūdraka-kathā* by Pañcaśikha, which is also cited by Bhoja in his *Śṛṅgāra-prakāśa* (see S. K. De in *BSOS*, IV, 1926, p. 281).

presumption that some late but skilful author composed this drama on the basis of the *Cārudatta*,[1] or revised a recension of the original on which the *Cārudatta* itself was based, and concealed his identity by passing off his work under the far-off famous name of Śūdraka. Much less convincing, for want of proof, again, is the hypothesis[2] of an early date based upon some accidental similarites with the New Greek Comedy. We are, therefore, left to no more than impressions. But even on this ground, however inadequate, it is not possible to assign a very late date to the *Mṛcchakaṭika*. Vāmana already in the 8th century refers (iii. 2. 4.) to a composition by Śūdraka, and also quotes two passages anonymously,[3] one of which occurs also in the *Cārudatta*, but the other does not.[4]

1 In *Cārudatta* the total number of verses in the four acts is 55, of which 13 are not found in the *Mṛcch*°, the remaining 42 being identical; but the total number of verses in the first four acts of Śūdraka's play is 129 —See above, under Bhāsa. Belvalkar shows by an examination, chiefly of incident and expression, that the *Cārudatta* could not have been an abridgment or adaptation of Śūdraka's drama. Sukthankar adds a critical review of the technique, Prakrit, versification, dramatic incident (especially with regard to time-scheme) of the two plays and furnishes *prima facie* reasons for holding that "the Cārudatta version is, on the whole, older than the Mṛcchakaṭika version, and hence (as a corollary), if our Cārudatta is not itself the original of the Mṛcchakaṭika, then, we must assume, it has preserved a great deal of the original upon which the Mṛcchakaṭika is based." But C. R. Devadhar, in introd. to his recent ed. *Cārudatta* (Poona 1939), expresses the view that the *Cārudatta* is abridged from the first four acts of the *Mṛcchakaṭika*. He maintains, by adducing the main differences of the two versions, that "the author of the *Cārudatta*, whoever he was, wanted to make a pleasing comedy out of the first four acts of the *Mṛcchakaṭika*, and hence has avoided reference to the political revolution, to Rohasena and to the law-suit, which is contempleted by the vengeful Śakāra."

2 Windisch, *Einfluss*, cited above, p. 12 f., see Keith's criticism in *SD*, pp. 63-64, and Sten Konow in *IA*, XLIII, 1914, pp. 65-66.

3 *Kāvyālaṁkāra, ad.* iv. 3. 23, *dyūtaṁ hi nāma puruṣasyāsiṁhāsanaṁ rājyam* (=*Mṛcch*°, act, ii, but missing in *Cāru*°); and *ad* v. 1. 3, the entire stanza, *yāsāṁ balir bhavati* (=*Mṛcch*°, i. 9; *Cāru*°, i. 2).

4 Only one verse from Śūdraka, not traceable in the drama, is quoted in the anthologies, namely, *Sbhv*, no, 1271. A Bhāṇa is also ascribed to him, for which see below, under *Caturbhāṇī*.—Gray (*JAOS*, XXVII, 1907, p. 419 f.) shows that Śūdraka's grammar does not conform closely to the norm, a fact which indicates not only his departure from convention but probably also his early date.

Whatever may have been the date and whoever may have been the author, there can be no doubt that the *Mṛcchakaṭika* is one of the few Sanskrit dramas in which the dramatist departs from the beaten track and attempts to envisage directly a wider, fuller and deeper life. He has paid for his boldness and originality by the general disregard of his great work by the Sanskrit theorists ;[1] but he knows that he is writing a drama, and not an elegant series of sentimental verses in accordance with the prescribed mode. It is, thus, not the usual type of a dramatic poem, but possesses distinctly dramatic qualities, which make a greater appeal to modern taste and idea. Apart from the graphic picture it presents of some phases of contemporary life,[2] the work is truly worthy of a great dramatist in its skilful handling of a swift-moving plot of sustained interest,[3] in its variety of incidents and characters, in its freedom from the usual fault of over-elaboration,[4] in its sharpness of characterisation, in its use of direct and homely imageries conveyed in a clear, forcible and unaffected diction, in its skilful employment of a variety of Sanskrit and Prakrit metres,[5] in its witty dialogue, in its general

1 The earliest quotation in dramaturgic works occur in the *Avaloka* on *Daśarūpaka*, i. 46 (=ii. 4), etc. See Mehendale, *op. cit*, p. 370.

2 See R. G. Basak in *IHQ*, 1929, p. 229-325.

3 The unity of action is questioned by Gray in introd. to his trs. But the criticism is really based on a misconception of acts ii-v, which he thinks to be episodic, forming a subplot of little connexion with the main plot. But all these so-called episodes are necessary for characterising Vasantasenā and her love, and therefore essential to the main theme.—It is remarkable that there are six shifting scenes in act i, which take place in Cārudatta's house and in the street outside,—a difficult feat indeed for the stage-manager ! This feature is also noticeable in the *Mudā-rākṣasa* and probably points to the existence of a enlarged stage.

4 Except perhaps the elaborate description of Vasantasenā's house and the Abhisārikā scene.

5 It is significant that the Śloka is greatly favoured being apparently suitable for rapidity and directness of style. The four most commonly employed metres, next to the Śloka, are, in their order of frequency, Vasantatilaka, Śārdūlavikrīḍita, Āryā, and Indravajrā (including Upajāti) ; of more unusual metres there are Vidyunmālā and Vaiśvadevī. No other Sanskrit play exhibits such a variety of Prakrits as found in the *Mṛcch*°. On the use of the Prakrits see Pischel, *Grammatik der Prakrit-sprachen* (Strassburg 1900), p. 25 f. ; *JRAS*, 1913, p. 882, 1918, p. 513 ; Keith, *SD*, pp. 140-42. Śaurasenī predominates and Māhārāstri. siare

liveliness and dramatic effect, in its mastery of deep pathos and in its rare quality of quiet humour. In spite of its somewhat conventional happy ending, which, however, is adequately developed, it verges almost upon tragedy ; and neither the plot nor the characters can be regarded as conventional. All these excellences invest the simple love-story of this ten-act comedy of middle-class life with a charm peculiarly its own ; and the remark that it is the most Shakespearian of all Sanskrit plays is, in some respect, not undeserved.

The drama has not only a curious title[1] but an equally curious theme and treatment. The title "The Little Clay-cart" is derived from an episode, which leads to the leaving of the heroine's jewels in the toy clay-cart of the hero's little son and gives rise to complications of the plot, which are finally resolved in the denouement ; and the episode of the clay-cart also has a psychological significance in the turn of the heroine's life. What is more remarkable is that in this drama, for the first time, we turn from the stories of kings and queens to a more plebeian atmosphere[2] from the dramatisation of time-worn legends[3] to a more refreshing plot of everyday life, the scene of

1 It is noteworthy that Śūdraka defies the convention of naming his play after the names of the hero and the heroine, as we have it in Bhavabhūti's Prakaraṇa, the *Mālatī-mādhava*. In contravention of dramaturgic prescription, Cārudatta does not appear at all in acts ii, iv, vi and viii ; while his simple-minded and whole-hearted friend, Maitreya, with his doglike faithfulness, does not conform to the technical definition and has none of the grosser traits of the typical Vidūṣaka. The presence of shady characters is, obviously, not entirely legitimate, for this makes the author of the *Daśarūpaka* call it a Saṁkīrṇa Prakaraṇa (cf. *Nāṭya-darpaṇa*, p. 119) inasmuch as such characters are apparently appropriate to the Bhāṇa or Prahasana.

2 The *Avi-māraka* is not as plebeian as it appears.

3 Apart from the question of the relation of the *Mṛcch°*. to the *Cārudatta*, which work, however, covers the same ground only up to the first four acts, the source of the story is unknown. We cannot be sure that the idea of a courtesan falling in love with a Brahman is derived from the story of Kumudikā and Rūpiṇikā, as we find it in Somadeva's version of the *Bṛhatkathā*, for the story may not have occurred in the original ; but the example of Madanamañjukā was probably there. The courtesan is also a heroine already of the Central Asian dramatic fragment, of which we have spoken. The sub plot of Gopāla and Pālaka is also known to be an old legend. But all this, as well as, the relation of the play to the *Cārudatta*, does not detract from its originality, which by

which is laid in a cosmopolitan city like Ujjayinī. When we turn from the two masterpieces of Kālidāsa and Bhavabhūti to this third great Sanskrit drama, we find ourselves descending, as it were' from a refined atmosphere of potery and sentiment to the firm rock of grim reality. And yet the drama is not at all shorn of real poetry and sentiment, which flourish no less in the strange world unfolded by the drama,—a world in which thieves, gamblers, rogues, political schemers, mendicants, courtiers, idlers, police constables, housemaids, bawds and courtesans jostle along freely. The love that it depicts is not the sad and romantic love of Dusyanta and his woodland beloved, nor yet the fond and deep conjugal affection idealised in Bhavabhūti's story of Rāma and Sītā, but simply and curiously, the love of a man about town for a courtesan, which is nevertheless as pure, strong and tender. The strange world supplies a fitting background to the strange love ; and an inventive originality[1] is displayed by linking the private affairs of the lovers with a political intrigue which involves the city and the kingdom. Into the ingenious plot are also freely thrown a comedy of errors leading to disaster and act of burglary leading to happiness, a murder and a court-scene ; and considerable fertility of dramatic imagination is displayed in working out the details of the plot, its only serious defect being its great length. The drama is also singular in conceiving a large number of interesting characters, drawn from all grades of society, from the high-souled Brahman to the sneaking thief ;

itself would, at least from the literary point of view, exclude the work from being stigmatised as "an inexcusable plagiarism." Even though it may have borrowed, it certainly transmutes what it borrows by a fine dramatic sense and workmanship.

1 The political background which practically permeates the entire drama, even from its prologue, in which there is a reference to king Pālaka, is entirely absent in the *Cārudatta.* Charpentier, however, thinks (*JRAS,* 1925, p. 604 f.) that the episode of Pālaka is loosely connected and adventitious. But the point is missed that it is neither a detached nor a fully developed subplot ; and even if it is considered unessential to the main story, it never becomes conspicuous but runs through the thread of the central theme, supplying motives to some of the incidents. What is more important is that the episode is necessary to create the general atmosphere of the bizarre society, in which the whole host of rascals are capable at any moment of all kinds of acts, ranging from stealing a gem-casket to starting a revolution.

they are presented not as types, but as individuals of diversified interest ;[1] and it includes, in its broad scope, farce and tragedy, satire and pathos, poetry and wisdom, kindliness and humanity.[2]

In the midst of all the motley assemblage of characters, who are mostly rogues and rascals and are yet true, and not altogether unlovable, gentlemen, stand out prominently the hero and the heroine. The Śakāra Saṃsthānaka, with his ignorant conceit and brutal lust, presents an excellent contrast, but the author's power of effective characterisation is best seen in his conception of the two main characters. The noble Cārudatta, a large-hearted Brahman by birth and wealthy merchant by profession, does not represent the typical Nāgaraka, whose whole round of life consists of love and pleasure ; for there is nothing of the gilded dandy and dilettante in his refined character and his chief interest is not gallantry. There is a note of quiet self-control in most of his acts ; and even in love most of the courtship is done by Vasantasenā. He is a young man of breeding, culture and uprightness, whose princely liberality wins the admiration of the whole city, but reduces him to lonely poverty. If the change of fortune makes him bitter, it does not make him a misanthrope nor does it debase his mind ; it only teaches him to take life at its proper value. Cārudatta is endowed with great qualities, but like the conventional hero he is not made a paragon of virtue. He is by no means austere or self-denying. He is a perfect man of the world, who loves literature, music and art, does not disdain gambling, nor share his friend Maitreya's bias against the hetarae. He never assumes a self-righteous attitude ; his great virtues are softened by the milk of human kindness. His youth does not exhibit indifference, and the most outstanding feature of his character is his quiet and deep love for Vasantasenā.

1 Śūdraka's men are perhaps better individualised than his women.

2 For a brief appreciation of the play, see S. K. De, *Treatment of Love in Sanskrit Literature*, Calcutta 1929, pp. 80-87 ; and for a summary of the story see S. K. De in *Tales from Sanskrit Dramatists*, Madras 1930, pp. 62-96.

The wrong of this unconventional love disapears in the ideal beauty which gathers round it ; and its purity, strength and truth make it escape degradation, Vasantasenā has neither the girlish charm of Śakuntalā nor the mature womanly dignity of Sītā. Witty and wise, disillusioned and sophisticated, she has seen much of a sordid world ; she has yet a heart of romance, and her love is true and deep even in a social status which makes such a feeling difficult. Much wealth and position she has achieved by an obligatory and heredit ry calling, but her heart is against it, and it brings her no happiness. Her meeting with Cārudatta affords a way of escape, but she is sad and afraid lest her misfortune of birth and occupation should stand in the way. It is a case of love at first sight, and for the first time she is really in love. The touch of this new emotion quickens rapidly into a pervading flame and burns to ashes her baser self. It is all so strange even to herself. She can yet hardly believe that she, an outcast of society, has been able to win the love of the great Cārudatta, the ornament of Ujjayinī, and asks, half incredulously, the morning after her first union with her beloved, if all that is true. She is fascinated by the lovely face of Cārudatta's little son and stretches out her arms in the great hunger for motherhood which has been denied to her. But the child in his innocence refuses to come to her and take her as his mother, because she wears such fine things and ornaments of gold : a harsh speech from a soft tongue, which makes her take off her ornaments, fill the toy clay-cart of the child and ask him to get a gold cart to play with. Her love makes her realise the emptiness of riches and the fulness of a pure and true affection. When the Śakāra threatens to kill her for not submitting to himself, and taunts her as "an inamorata of a beggarly Brahman," she is not ashamed but replies : "Delightful words ! Pray, proceed, for you speak my praise." Growing furious, the brutal and cowardly Śakāra takes her by the throat. She does not cry out for succour, but she remembers her beloved Cārudatta and blesses his name. "What, still dost thou repeat that name," spits out the Śakāra, blinded by rage, as he strangles her ; but on the verge of imminent death the name of Cārudatta is still on her lips, and she murmurs in a struggling voice : *nama Cārudattassa*, "My homage be to Cārudatta !"

The dramatic action reaches a natural climax, and the work might have ended here with a tragic note ; but the tragedy is converted into a comedy of reunion, which may appear as a weak denouement, but which is logically developed by a skilful handling of the incidents. The happy ending is a convention enforced by theory, but in this drama convention is nowhere respected as mere convention. It is a drama of social and artistic challenges, and the dramatist is perfectly aware of his strength in putting them forth. The *Mṛcchakaṭika* may not have been, as one of its critics contends, "a transcript from real life," but its author never sacrifices real life for a stereotyped manipulation of the threadbare sentiment and action. If he really works up the fragmentary *Cārudatta*, or some previous original, as Shakespeare is said to have reworked old pieces, he succeeds in producing a masterpiece, which stands by itself in its entire conception and execution.

b. *The Authors of the Caturbhāṇī*

Somewhat closely connected with the *Mṛcchakaṭika* in atmosphere and spirit, but limited in scope and inferior in literary quality, are the four one-act monologue plays, discovered and published ih 1922 under the title *Caturbhāṇī*,[1] one of which is actually ascribed to Śūdraka. The four Bhāṇas are : the *Ubhayābhisārikā*, the *Padma-prābhṛtaka*, the *Dhūrta-viṭa-saṃvāda* and the *Pāda-tāḍitaka*, ascribed respectively to Vararuci,

1 Ed. M. Ramkrishna Kavi and S. K. Ramanatha Sastri, Sivapuri, (Trichur) 1922. The works deserve to be better printed and known. For studies of these works, see F. W. Thomas in *Centenary Supplement* to *JRAS*, 1924, pp. 129-36, and *JRAS*, 1924, p. 262 f. ; S. K. De in *JRAS*, 1926, pp. 63-90. Sukumar Sen has translated the *Ubhayābhisārikā* into English in *Calcutta Review*, 1926, pp. 127-47.

Śūdraka,[1] Īśvaradatta and Śyāmilaka, on the authority chiefly of a traditional verse. Except in Śyāmilaka's *Pāda-tāḍitaka*, neither the author's name nor the occasion of the performance is mentioned in the rudimentary prologue to these plays. The lower limit of the *Pāda-tāḍitaka*, however, is obtained by the references of Abhinavagupta,[2] Kuntaka[3] and Kṣemendra[4] all of whom belong to the end of the 10th century ; while the lower limits of the date of *Padma-prābhṛtaka* and *Dhūrta-viṭa-saṃvāda* are given by Hemacandra's quotation and reference in his *Kāvyānuśāsana*[5] at the end of the 11th and beginning of the 12th century ; but the lower limit of the *Ubhayābhisārikā* is not known. Since, however, they exhibit similar characteristics and form a group by themselves, between which and the later specimens of the Bhāṇa (the earliest of which is certainly not earlier than the 13th century) a considerable time must have elapsed, there can be little doubt that the four Bhāṇas belong to the age of the earlier classical dramatists ; and, on the strength of facts revealed in the plays themselves, their general atmosphere, the types of men and nations that they deal with, their tone and temper, their lexicographical and stylistic peculiarities, Thomas is perhaps not wrong in placing them, or at least one of the Bhāṇas, "in the time of Harṣa of Kanauj or even that of the later Guptas." A comparative study of these Bhāṇas with the later specimens, in the light of the prescriptions of the dramaturgists, would also show a method and manner, which would justify the general inference that

1 There is nothing to show that the play is by Śūdraka, nor anything to dispute the authorship.

2 See the editor's Preface to the Bhāṇas. The referencc occurs in the comm. on Bharata, ch. xiv.

3 Ed. S. K. De, Calcutta 1928, i. 111 (=*Pāda-tāḍitaka* 55) anonymously.

4 *Pāda*-t. 33, 125=*Aucitya-vicāra, ad* 16 and *Suvṛtta-tilaka, ad* ii. 31. The colophon says that Śyāmilaka is an Udīcya ; the statement is apparently confirmed by these citations by Kashmirian authors.

5 Ed. NSP, p. 339. The identity of Īśvaradatta with Īsvarasena (*c.* 236-239 A.D.), son of the Abhīra king Śivadatta, is suggested but not proved.

these Bhāṇas, as a group, should be assigned to a period later than that of Bharata's *Naṭya-śāstra*, but much earlier than that of the standard work of Dhanañjaya (end of the 10th century).

Compared with later plays of the same type, the *Caturbhāṇī* presents more variety, greater simplicity, a larger amount of social satire and comic relief, a more convincing power of drawing individuals rather than abstractions, easier and more colloquial style, and some measure of real poetry in spite of certain rough coarseness. Except in the *Dhūrta-viṭa-saṃvāda*, the Viṭa is not exactly the "hero" ; but, as the friend and emissary of the hero, who never appears, he fills the stage as the sole actor. The plot, of course, in such one-act monologue plays, is slight, but it does not here consist merely of the conventional amorous adventures of the Viṭa and usual reunion at the end ; on the contrary, as much variety is introduced as is possible within its narrow scope. In the *Padma-prābhṛtaka*, Karṇīputra Mūladeva,[1] in love with Devasenā, sister to his beloved hetaera Devadattā, commissions his friend Śaśa the Viṭa, to ascertain the state of Devasenā's mind. The Viṭa walks through the streets of Ujjayinī, exchanging imaginary conversation with various kinds of amusing people and taking an interest in their affairs, discharges his commission successfully, and returns with a gift of lotus-flower as a souvenir from Devasenā, from which the play takes its name. In the *Dhūrta-viṭa-saṃvāda*, the clever and experienced Viṭa, finding the rainy season too depressing, comes out to spend the day in some amusement. He cannot afford dice and drinking—even his clothes are reduced to one garment—so he wends his way towards

1 The legend of Mūladeva Karṇīsuta, which is alluded to by Bāṇa, probably goes back to the *Bṛhatkathā*, Karṇīsuta being regarded traditionally as the author of a manual on theft. In Bāṇa's reference : *karṇīsuta-katheva saṁnihita vipulācalā śaśopagatā ca* (*Kadambari* ed. Peterson, 1900, p. 19, ll. 16-17), punning allusion is made to Śasī and Vipula of the story, both of whom occur in this play. On the character and adventures of Mūladeva see M. Bloomfield in *Proc. American Philosophical Soc.*, LII, 1913, pp. 616-50.

the street where courtesans live, meeting various kinds of people and ultimately reaching the house of the roguish couple Viśvalaka and Sunandā, where he passes the day in discussing certain knotty problems of Erotics put to him by Viśvalaka. The title "Dialogue between a Rogue and a Rake," therefore, appropriately describes its content; and it gives an amusing epitome of the aesthetic and erotic laws which govern the life of a rake, and forms a companion volume to such works as Dāmodaragupta's *Kuṭṭanī-mata.* In the *Ubhayābhisārikā,* the Viṭa is requested by his friend Kuberadatta to propitiate his offended lady Nārāyaṇadattā; but when, after the usual series of wayside adventures, he reaches the house of the latter, he finds that the lovers, urged by the witchery of the season, had already set out in search of each other and forestalled him in effecting a reunion. In the *Pāda-tāḍitaka,* the theme is more interesting and novel, if less edifying. The Viṭa sets out to attend an assembly of rogues and rakes, who have met to consider the question of expiation referred to them by Tauṇḍikoki Viṣṇunāga, the nominal hero, the son of a Mahāmātra, and himself an officer of the king, for the indignity he has suffered by allowing an intoxicated courtesan, a Saurāṣṭra girl, named Madanasenikā, to kick him, in playfulness, on such a sacred spot of his body as his head! Some think that it is not Viṣṇunāga, but the girl herself, who should expiate for setting her foot upon such a beast; others suggest that Viṣṇunāga should rub and shampoo her dishonoured foot; another proposes that he should bathe his head with the water with which she washes her feet, and drink the same; the poet Rudravarman prescribes that his dishonoured head should be shorn; but in the end, it is agreed, on the proposal of the presiding rake, that Madanasenikā should put more sense into her lover by setting her foot on the president's own head in the sight of Viṣṇunāga!

The scene of action of all these plays is laid in imperial cities like Ujjayinī or Kusumapura; and in one case (*Pāda-tāḍitaka*) the author probably wants to disguise the name of the actual city, whose scandals are recorded, by calling it Sārva-bhauma-nagara, an imaginary cosmopolitan city somewhere in Western India. Of course, the Viṭa takes his usual promenade in the hetaera's street and carries on imaginary conversations, but the characters are not the conventional types of the man about town and the courtesan ; they are sufficiently diversified to keep up the interest of the narrative ; and a zest is added, in spite of the erotic theme, by a decided leaning towards satirical and comic portraiture, which is rare in later Bhāṇas entirely engrossed in eroticism. One would seek in vain in later decadent writings for the power of observation and reproduction of the classes of peoples and personages who are described or ridiculed in the *Caturbhāṇī*. Characters like Sārasvatabhadra, the sky-gazing poet with a verse on the spring recorded on the wall, Dattakalasi the pedantic Pāṇinian with his sesquipedalian affectation and war on the Kātantrikas, Saṃdhilaka, the Śākya-bhikṣu, who consoles the hetaera Saṃghadāsikā with words of the Buddha, Mṛdaṅgavāsulaka the decrepit Nāṭaka-viṭa, nicknamed "Bhāva Jaradgava," the thoughtless young rake Śreṣṭhiputra Krsnilaka averse to marriage, the penniless impotent Nagna-śramaṇa Viśva-laka and his dried-up mistress Sunandā, Vilāsakauṇḍinī the hypocritical Buddhist Parivrājikā of easy virtue who always quotes the scriptures—to mention only a few—are specimens which are unknown to later Bhāṇas.[1] The Viṭa, who is the central figure, is also not altogether a despicable character here, not such a worthless amorist as the later Bhāṇas depict him to be. As a character, he is neglected in the serious drama, but he appears in the *Cārudatta* and attains considerable development in the *Mṛcchakaṭika*. In the Bhāṇa he is in all his glory ; he appears, no doubt, as an erotic character in these early works, but he is still figured as a poet skilled in the arts, and has not yet become

1 The Buddhist monks and nuns, who figure also in the *Bhagavadajjuka* and *Mattavilāsa*, disappear from later Bhāṇa and Prahasana, and their place is taken by absurd Śrotriyas, wicked Paurāṇikas, Śaivas, Vaiṣṇavas and Bhāgavatas. The large number of foreigners mentioned and caricatured in the *Caturbhāṇī* is also a notworthy feature.

a gallant in the worst sense in which he appears in the later Bhāṇas.[1]

Apart from their naive exuberance of robust grossness, the *Caturbhāṇī* stand unique for their amusing pictures of the lives and adventures, scandals and gossips, of a class of people who infest all imperial cities, and would not be unworthy of the pen of the author of the *Mṛcchakaṭika*, to whom one of the Bhāṇas is actually ascribed. The language employed is Sanskrit throughout, with the exception of two short Prakrit passages in the *Pāda-tāḍitaka* (pp. 21, 23); and its racy, well turned and conversational tone, very unlike that of the affected prose of the romances of Subandhu and Bāṇa, is rightly characterised by an appreciative critic as "the veritable ambrosia of Sanskrit speech." The metrical variety is skilful and vigorous, and does not hamper the interest by unnecessary display and profusion. The literary importance of the *Caturbhāṇī*, therefore, cannot be gainsaid. The Bhāṇas in later times become mere literary exercises, devoid of variety and monotonous in their cloying insistence on the erotic sentiment; they subside into a conventional and lifeless form of the art. The *Caturbhāṇī*, on the other hand, have more life and greater freedom of handling and draws upon other legitimate sources of interest than the erotic. Their marked flair for comedy and satire, their natural humour and polite banter, their presentation of a motley group of interesting characters, not elaborately painted but suggested with a few vivid touches of the brush, are characteristics which are not frequently found in Sanskrit literature; and, apart from their being the earliest specimens of a peculiar type of dramatic composition, they possess a real literary quality in their style and treatment, which makes them deserve a place of their own in the history of the Sanskrit drama.

1 Bharata lays down that the Bhāṇa should be *dhūrta-viṭa-samprayojya*; the Viṭa need not be "the hero," as he is not in most of these early Bhāṇas, but he is the only character who fills the stage, and the heroship is naturally transferred to him in later Bhāṇas, in which however, he becomes a poor shadow of his former self.

Of the same lively and satirical character, but inferior in scope, treatment and literary quality, is the *Matta-vilāsa*[1] of Mahendravikrama-varman. The prologue of the play, fortunately, gives the name of the author and describes him as a king of the Pallava dynasty and son of Siṃhavarman ; the scene is laid in Kāñcī, the modern Conjevaram and the ancient capital of the Pallava kingdom. All this enables us to identify the author with the king of that name, known to us from inscriptions, which mention the *Matta-vilāsa* as a work of his, and also give him the titles of Guṇabhara, Avanībhājana, Mattavilāsa and Śatrumalla, all found in the play itself. The king ruled in Kāñcī about 620 A.D., and was thus a contemporary of Harṣavardhana and Bāṇa.

The play is a slight farcical sketch in one act, technically belonging to the category of the Prahnsana, which is closely allied to the Bhāṇa. It depicts with some liveliness the drunken revelry of a Śaiva mendicant, bearing a human skull in lieu of alms-bowl and accordingly calling himself a Kapālin, his wandering with his wench through the purlieus of Kāñcī on his way to a tavern, his scuffle with a hypocritical Buddhist monk[2] whom he accuses of the theft of the precious bowl which he has lost, his appeal to a degenerate Pāśupata to settle the dispute, and the final recovery of the bowl from a mad man who had retrieved it from a stray dog. The incident is amusing but trivial, and the

1 Ed. T. Ganapati Sastri, Trivandrum Skt. Ser., 1917. On this drama see L. D. Barnett in *JRAS*, 1919, pp. 233-34, *BSOS*, 1920, I, pt. 3, pp. 36-38. Eng trs. L. D. Barnett, *BSOS*, V, 1930, pp. 697-710.—Except that he author is named in the prologue, the play shows the same technique of stage-craft and other peculiarities as the plays attributed to Bhāsa. Barnett makes this fact the basis of the suggestion that the Bhās dramas are the products of an anonymous playwright of a Southern dramatic school who composed them at about the same period as that of Mahendravikrama. But since the features are shown also by several other plays of other dramatists of known or unknown dates, the conclusion, we have seen, cannot be justified in the form in which it is stated.

2 It is significant that the monk, a frail son of the Church, bears the name of Nāgasena, the famoes Buddhist divine and protagonist of the *Milindapañho* ; and his mumbling of the Śikṣāpada and his inward fretting about restrictions regarding wine and women are interesting touches. On false ascetics and nuns in Indian fiction in general, see M. Bloomfield in *JAOS*, XLIV, 1924, pp. 202-942.

satire caustic but broad. It evinces no distinctive literary characteristics of a high order, but within its limits it shows some power of vivid portraiture in a simple and elegant style, and certainly deserves an indulgent verdict as the earliest known specimen[1] of the Prahasana or farce, which in later times becomes marked by greater vulgarity and less literary skill.

c. *Harṣa*

Three dramas, entitled respectively *Priyadarśikā*, *Ratnāvalī* and *Nāgānanda*, have come down to us under the name of Śrī-Harṣa ; and in spite of some discussions[2] about the identity of the author and ascription of the works, there cannot be much doubt that the dramatist was identical with king Śrī-Harsa-vardhana Śīlāditya of Sthāṇvīśvara and Kānyakubja, who was the patron of Bāṇabhaṭṭa and of the Chinese pilgrim Yuan Chwang, and who reigned in the first half of the 7th century (circa 606-648 A.D.). The authorship of the plays is now assured by abundant evidence, partly external and partly internal. Doubts do not appear to have exsited on the subject from the 7th to the 9th century; for Dāmodaragupta, in the 9th century, describes

1 The *Bhagavadajjuka* ascribed to Bodhāyana (see below) is probably a much later work. —Although a small farce, as many as nine different metres are employed in the *Matta-vilāsa* ; apparently varieties of Prakrit are employed, but the uncertainty of scribal modifications in South Indian manuscripts precludes any positive inference from such archaic forms as are also found in the Bhāsa dramas.

2 For a summary of the discussion, see A. V. W. Jackson's introd. to ed. of *Priya-darśikā*. Doubts regarding authorship appears to have been raised by the remarks of some scholiasts on an opening passage of the *Kāvya-prakāśa* of Mammaṭa (i. 2), in which it is stated that Dhāvaka (v. l. Bāṇa) and others obtained wealth from Śrīharṣa and the like. In explaining the passage some commentaries ascribe the *Ratnāvalī* to Dhāvaka, although allowing that it bears Harṣa's name ; and since the reading Bāṇa, instead of Dhāvaka, is sometimes found in Kashmirian MSS, it is assumed that Bāna, who was a protégé and littérateur at Harṣa's court, received recompense for writing some of the dramas which now pass in the king's name. It must be admitted that the evidence is extremely late and weak, for Mammaṭa's statement merely refers to Harṣa's well-known generosity as a patron of letters. Of Dhāvaka we known nothing, and disparity of style would make Bāṇa's authorship highly implausible.

in his *Kuṭṭanī-mata*[1] a performance of the *Ratnāvalī*, and ascribes the work distinctly to Harṣa ; while Yi-tsing,[2] in the last quarter of the 7th century, clearly refers to a dramatisation of the subject of *Nāgānanda* by Harṣa.[3] That all the three plays are by the same hand is also rendered certain by the almost verbatim repetition of the same Prologue-stanza which praises Harṣa as the author, as well as by the close likeness which exists in all the three plays with regard to theme, treatment, structural peculiarity, parallel situations, kindred ideas, repeated phrases and recurring stanzas.[4]

Although the *Nāgānanda*[5] is somewhat different in character as a drama, the *Priyadarśikā*[6] and the *Ratnāvalī*[7] are practically variations of a single theme in almost identical form[8] ; and the striking similarity of structure, characters and situations is more than merely accidental. Each of the two plays is a four-act Nāṭika, and is based on one of the numerous amourettes of the gay and gallant Udayana, famed in legend, whose romantic

1 Ed. Kāvyamālā, Gucchaka iii, NSP, Bombay 1887, pp. 98-99, 104-06.

2 J. Takakusu, *A Record of the Buddhist Religion*, Oxford 1896, pp. 163-64.

3 Bāṇabhaṭṭa also refers more than once to Harṣa's gifts as a poet (*Harṣa-carita*, ed. Führer, pp. 112-21) ; and in the Anthologies, as we have already noted, stanzas chiefly from the dramas are attributed to Harṣa.

4 See Jackson, introd. to *Priyadarśikā*, pp. lxxviif, for a detailed study of the relation of the three plays and examples of parallelisms of style and treatment.

5 Ed. G. B. Brahme and S. M. Paranjpe, Poona 1893 ; ed. T. Ganapati Sastri with comm. of Śivarāma, Trivandrum Skt. Ser., 1917. Eng trs. by Palmar Boyd, London 1872, and by Hale Wartham, London and New York 1911.

6 Ed. V. D. Gadre, Bombay 1884 ; ed. R. V. Krishnamachariar, Sri-Vani-Vilasa Press, Srirangam, 1906 ; ed. G. K. Nariman, A. V. W. Jackson and C J. Ogden, Text in roman characters, Eng. trs. and notes, etc., Columbia Univ. Indo-Iran. Ser., New York 1923.

7 Ed. C. Cappeller in Böhtlingk's Sanskrit *Chrestomathie*, 3rd ed., Leipzig, 1903, p. 326 f ; ed. K. P. Parab, with comm. of Govinda, NSP, Bombay 1895 ; ed. Krishnath Nyayapanchanan, with comm. of Śivarāma, Calcutta 1864.

8 In the *Ratnāvalī*, which appears to have been the most current of the three plays, the question of interpolation of stanzas or passages may arise, but the textual corruption in all the three plays is not conspicuous, nor are the variations of such consequence as would justify the assumption of different recensions. Although MSS are abundant, the *Priyadarśikā* appears to have been comparatively neglected, and only one quotation from it (i. 1) occurs in *Skm* (i. 114) and only two in the *Daśarūpaka*.

ādventures, familiar to the audience of the day,[1] made him a suitable hero for the erotic and elegant court-plays of this type. In conformity with the old legend, both the plays exhibit Udayana as the hero, Vasantaka his jester, Vāsavadattā as his chief queen, and Kāñcanamālā as her principal attendant. The two heroines, Sāgarikā and Āraṇyakā, both for the time being so named from the peculiar circumstances of their rescue from the sea and the forest, are indeed not traceable in the legend, but in their conception and presentation, they afford unmistakable parallelism thoughout. It is true that the characters of the hero and the chief members of his entourage are, in a large measure, fixed by tradition, but the main action of the two plays centres respectively round the two heroines, who being independent of the legend, could have been developed, not only with originality but also as characters more definitely distinguished from each other ; and it is certainly not praiseworthy to create them as replicas with only slight variations. The incidents of the two plays, again, are almost the same in general outline, even to the repetition of similar situations,[2] and are such as one would normally expect in a comedy of court-life, of which the earliest example is found in Kālidāsa's *Mālavikāngimitra.* They consist of the light-hearted love-intrigue of the king with a lowly maiden of unknown status, their secret meetings chiefly through the help of the jester and the damsel's friend, the jealousy of the queen (*cosi fan tutte !*) and her final acceptance of the

1 *loke hāri ca vatsarāja-caritam*, Prologue-stanza.

2 *Eg.*, the garden-scene in act ii ; the avowal of heroine's hopeless passion ; her attempt at suicide ; the intrigue which leads, though differently worked out, to the meeting of the lovers ; the imprisonment of the jester and the heroine by the queen and their subsequent release ; the rescue of the heroine by the king, supposed in each case to be at the point of death ; recognition of the heroine as a princess and cousin and acceptance by the queen as a co-wife ; announcement of the victory of the royal army at the end, and general rejoicing, etc.—Some of the common tricks of plot are utilised, *e.g.*, the device of the picture, monkey escaping from its cage and causing disturbance (elephant in Kālidāsa and tiger in Bhavabhūti), rescue of the heroine by the hero from a danger, the Vasantotsava and Kaumudī-mahotsava, etc. On some of these motifs in Indian story-telling and drama, see L. H. Gray in *WZKM*, XVIII, 1904, pp. 43 f.

situation in the last act, when the maiden is discovered as her long-lost cousin. In the invention of the plot, therefore, there is perhaps not much opportunity, nor is there much inclination, of showing fertility of imagination, which is confined chiefly to the detailed management of the intrigue. Indeed, the extraordinary similarity of plot-development, however neatly conducted, as well as the close resemblance of the characters, make the one play almost a repetition or recast of the other. The only original feature of the *Priyadarśikā* is the effective introduction of a play within a play (Garbhāṅka) as an integral part of the action, and its interruption (as in *Hamlet*) brought on by its vivid reality. But, barring this interesting episode, the *Priyadarśikā*, by the side of the *Ratnāvalī*, which is undoubtedly the better play in every respect, is almost superfluous for having hardly any striking incident, character or idea which does not possess its counterpart in its twin-play.

The subject, form and inspiration of the *Nāgānanda* is different. It is a five-act Nāṭaka, a more serious drama, on the obviously Buddhist legend of the self-sacrifice of Jīmūtavāhana, which is told in the two Sanskrit versions of the *Bṛhatkathā*, in a longer and a shorter version in both.[1] The Prologue, however, speaks of a Vidyādhara Jātaka in which the story is found related, but of this work we know nothing. Although the Buddha is invoked in the benedictory stanza, Gaurī is introduced as a *deus ex machina*, and purely Buddhistic traits are not prominent, except in its central theme of universal benevolence.[2] The benedictory stanza, however, in introducing an erotic note, probably anticipates the general tenor of the play, which brings

[1] *Kathā-sarit-s.* xxii. 16-257, xc. 3-201 ; *Bṛhatkathā-m.* iv 50-108, ix. 2. 776-903. A comparative analysis is given in introd. to P. V. Ramanujasvami's ed. of the *Nāgānanda* (Madras 1932). On the legend see F. D. K. Bosch, *De Legende van Jīmūtavāhana in de Sanskrit Litteratur*, Leiden 1914 (on Harṣa's treatment of the legend, p. 90 f).

[2] From Bāṇa we learn of Harṣa's intention to become a Buddhist, while Yuan Chwang's testimony makes him a Buddhist in old age. Harṣa himself pays homage to Śiva (in *Priya°* and *Ratnā°*) and to the Buddha alike ; and it is probable that as a king he practised religious toleration.

in an erotic sub-plot on the hero's love for Malayavatī and connects it with the main quietistic theme of his heroic sacrifice. The episode is a simpler story of love and marriage without much intrigue, but it occupies the first three acts almost entirely, and its tone and treatment show considerable likeness to those of the author's other two erotic plays, not only in isolated passages, but also in particular situations.[1] The result is that the first three acts are almost completely separated from the last two, which depict the different theme of supreme charity, and on which the chief interest of the drama rests. The one part is not made essential to the development of the other; there is thus no unity of action or balance between the two isolated parts. It is difficult to reconcile also the picture of Jīmūtavāhana's unlimited benevolence and resolution in the face of death, which draws Garuḍa's praise of him as the Bodhisattva himself, but during which he does not even think of Malayavatī, with the unnecessary and unrelated preliminary account of him as the conventional love-sick hero, or of Malayavatī as the simple, sentimental heroine. It is not his love which inspires his great act of sacrifice, nor is it rendered difficult by the memory of that love; and an inexplicable hiatus is, therefore, felt when one passes from the one episode to the other. The plot of the drama does not also appear to be as carefully developed as in the other two plays.[2] The denouement is also weak; for the great sacrifice suggests a real tragedy, and the divine intervention of Gaurī to turn into a comedy and reward of virtue is an unconvincing artificial device. The free use of the supernatural is, of course, not out of place in the atmosphere of the drama, of which the hero is a Vidyādhara and the heroine is a Siddhā, but it offers too easy a solution of the

1 Such as the meeting of the lovers in the sandal-bower by the help of the jester, the love-sickness of the heroine, and her attempt to commit suicide, etc.

2 *E.g.* the somewhat unnatural want of curiosity on the part of the lovers to know each other's identity, even when they had friends at hand who might have enlightened them, or even their ignorance of each other, is inexplicable; the heroine's melodramatic attempt to commit suicide (repeated from the other two plays) is not sufficiently motived here, the exit of Śaṅkhacūḍa and his mother in act iv is poorly managed, etc.

final tragic complication and destroys the grandeur of its appeal. Nor can Harṣa be said to succeed in the comic interlude, apparently introduced for the sake of contrast in the third act; for the Vidūṣaka, who is lively enough in the other two plays, is here stupid and vulgar,[1] and the Viṭa a poor sot and sensualist, while the whole passage is a paltry farce or burlesque, rather than a necessary picture of character. Nevertheless, these defects need not altogether negate the real merits of the drama. However strange the setting, the embodiment in Jīmūtavāhana of the high and difficult ideal of self-sacrificing magnanimity, in a romantic atmosphere of pathos and poetry, is not altogether unsuccessful.

If the *Nāgānanda* had ended with the first three acts, it would have, in spite of a few scattered references to the hero's generosity, passed for a short comedy of love like the *Priyadarśikā* and the *Ratnāvalī*. While Harṣa's power of depicting sentiments other than love is acknowledged, it is clear that he excels in his three plays in his fine gift of delineating the pretty sentiment in pretty environment. Sometimes perhaps he deals with it in a maudlin and melodramatic fashion, but he shows himself capable of treating it with purity and tenderness. His works throughout show unmistakable traces of the influence of the greater dramatists,[2] but he is a clever borrower, who catches not a little of the inspiration and power of phrasing of his predecessors; and perhaps in light plays of the type he favoured, elegance was more expected than originality. In the *Ratnāvalī*, if not to the same

1 This late instance of a degraded buffoon does not support Schuyler's suggestion (*JAOS*, XX, 1899, p. 399 f.) that the character is a relic of earlier popular plays, allowing as it does full opportunity (which the author as a Buddhist is supposed to have availed himself) of ridiculing the Brahmans.

2 Apart from the general outline of the theme, which must have been popularised by Kālidāsa's *Mālavikā*, we find reminiscences of Kālidāsa in the incident of the bees tormenting the heroine, the heroine's ruse to delay her departure from the sight of her lover, the part played by the jester in bringing about the meeting of the lovers, his talk in sleep revealing the secret, the imprisonment of the heroine, the use of magic spells to counteract the effect of poison, etc The influence of *Svapna-vāsavadatta* is not clearly traceable, unless the fire-scene brought about by magic is taken as being suggested by the fire-incident at Lāvāṇaka.

degree in his other two plays, Harṣa is great in lightness, vivacity and sureness of tender touch, although in brilliancy depth of feeling and real pathos he falls below some of his fellow-dramatists. It is remarkable that even if his *Priyadarśikā* and *Ratnāvalī* inexplicably choose the same theme and pattern they are still separately enjoyable as pretty little plays of light-hearted love, effectively devised and executed. If Kālidāsa supplied the pattern, Harsa has undoubtedly improved upon it in his own way, and succeeded in establishing the comedy of court-intrigue as a distinct type in Sanskrit drama. The situations are prepared with practised skill ; they are admirably conducted, adorned, but not over-embellished, with poetical sentiment and expression, and furnished with living characters and affecting incidents ; it is no wonder that the Sanskrit dramaturgists quote the *Ratnāvalī*, which is undoubtedly Harṣa's masterpiece, as the standard of a wėll-knit play. Harṣa is graceful, fluent and perspicuous ; he possesses a quaint and dainty, if not original and soaring, fancy, and a gift of writing idyllic and romantic poetry, with frequent felicities of expression and musical cadence[1] Essentially a decorative artist, he embroiders a commonplace tale with fine arabesques, and furnishes feasts of colour and sound by pictures of a sping or moonlight festival and of refined luxuries and enjoyments of the court-life of his day. But considering his contemporary and protégé, Bāṇa, his style is markedly simple, and his prose is unadorned ; the emotional and descriptive comments in the poetical stanzas are neither profuse nor inappropriate. The types of conquering heroes and frail heroines he draws may not possess great appeal, but they have a tender and attractive quality of romance, and their creator does not lack insight into human nature, nor the power of developing

[1] It is notable that unlike earlier dramatists, Harṣa is decidedly fond of employing long and elaborate metres, his favourite metres being the Śārdūlavikrīḍita and the Sragdharā, which occur quite frequently in all his plays ; but his versification is smooth and tuneful. The Prakrits employed are mainly Śaurasenī and Māhārāṣṭrī ; they are easy and elegant but offer no special features.

character by action. There is, however, a certain trimness about Harṣa's plays, a mastery of technique which is too smooth and unmodulated. They give the impression of a remarkably fine, but even, writer, seldom rising far above or sinking much below a uniform level of excellence. Apart from the importance attached to him as a royal author and patron of authors, Harṣa claims place among the worthies of this period, not so much by any transcendent genius, but by a pleasing gift of delicate workmanship, conscious but not too studied, assured but not too ingenious.

d. *Viśākhadatta*

Of Viśākhadatta, author of the *Mudrā-rākṣasa*,[1] we know only what he himself tells us in the Prologue to his play, namely, that he was son of Mahārāja Bhāskaradatta (or according to most manuscripts, Pṛthu) and grandson of Sāmanta Vaṭeśvaradatta ; and in spite of all the conjectures and theories that have centred round his date and personality, we shall probably never know anything more. In the concluding stanza (vii. 21), which, however, is not an integral part of the play but is meant to be spoken by the actor and hence called Bharata-vākya, there is a mention of a king Candragupta, whose kingdom is said to be troubled (*udvejyamāna*) by the Mlecchas. As a reference to Candragupta Maurya, who is the subject of the play itself, would be unusual in the Bharata-vākya, it is taken as the eulogy of a reigning sovereign ; and some scholars are inclined to see[2] in

1 Ed. K. T. Telang, with comm. (written 1713 A.D.) of Dhuṇḍirāja, Bomb. Skt. Ser. 1884 (7th ed. 1928) ; ed. A. Hillebrandt, Breslau 1912 ; ed. K. H. Dhruva, 2nd ed., Poona 1923, with English trs. All the known commentaries are of comparatively modern date ; for an account see Dhruva, introd., p. xix. On the MSS material and an edition of the Prakrit verses, see Hillebrandt, Zur Kritik des Mudrā-rākṣasa in *NGGW*, 1905, pp. 429-53. No good Engl. trs., except Wilson's free rendering in *Select Specimens* vol. ii ; French trs. by V. Henry, Paris 1888 ; German trs. by L. Frize, Leipzig 1883.—The *Cāṇakya kathā* of Ravi-nartaka (ed. S. C. Law, Cal. Orient. Ser. 1921), like Dhuṇḍirāja's summary printed in Telang's ed., is a résumé of the traditional story, although the work pretends to derive its material from a prose original, and gives some new points of interest.

2 K. P. Jayaswal in *IA*, XLII, 1913, pp. 265-67 ; Sten Konow, in *IA*, XLIII, 1914 p. 66 f. and *Ind. Drama*, p. 70 f. ; Hillebrandt in *ZDMG*, XXXIX, 1885, p. 130 f., LXIX

Viśakhadatta a contemporary of Candragupta II of the Gupta dynasty (*cir.* 375-413), and apparently of Kalidasa. But since the readings Dantivarman, Rantivarman or Avantivarman, instead of Candragupta, are also found, no finality is reached on the question. The first two of these names cannot be traced anywhere; but since two Avantivarmans are known, the author's patron is identified sometimes with the Maukhari king Avantivarman, who flourished in the 7th century[1] and married his son Grahavarman to Harsavardhana's sister Rajyaśrī, and sometimes with Avantivarman, king of Kashmir, who reigned in the middle of the 9th century.[2] From Hillebrandt's critical edition of the text, however, it appears that the variant Avantivarman is most

1915, p. 363 (4th century A.D.); S. Srikantha Sastri in *IHQ*, VII, 1931, pp. 163-69. The difficulty, however, of taking the term *mleccha* in the sense of the Hūnas (even though they are mentioned as allies of Malayaketu in v. 11) and of explaining the word *udvejyamāna* satisfactorily in terms of the known facts of Candragupta's time should be recognised; while Jayaswal's identification of Pravartaka and Malayaketu are wholly fanciful. J. Charpentier, in *JRAS*, 1923, p, 586 f. (also *IHQ*, VII, 1931, p. 629), would, however, take Viśākhadatta to be a contemporary of one of the last Guptas, probably Samudragupta, but he confesses inability to adduce much historical or literary evidence in support of his theory. *Raghu*° vii. 56 and *Śiśu*° i. 47 are adduced as parallels to the stanza in question (vii. 21), as well as *Raghu*° vii. 43 to *Mudrā*° v. 23; but it is admitted that such literary coincidences by themselves are of not much use in fixing a date. The presumption of Konow and Charpentier that the drama must have been composed before the destruction of Pāṭaliputra, because the town plays an important part in it, should not be pressed too far in view of the conventional geography which we often find in Sanskrit imaginative writings. —The assumption (*JASB*, 1930, pp. 241-45) that the drama is a Bengal work is purely gratuitous and conjectural.

1 K. H. Dhruva in *WZKM*, V. p. 25 f. (2nd half of the 6th century); V. J. Antani in *IA*, LI, 1922, pp. 49-51. Dhruva rightly points out that the way in which the king of Kashmir is mentioned in the play itself would preclude any reference to Avantivarman of Kashmir.

2 Telang, introd. to his ed.; Jacobi in *WZKM*, II, pp. 212-16. Jacobi adduces also passages which Ratnākara, who flourished in Kashmir at about the same time, is said to have imitated from the *Mudrā*°; but Dhruva points out that the passages are not conclusive. By astronomical calculation, again, Jacobi would identify the eclipse mentioned in the play as having occurred on December 2, 860 A.D, when, he holds, Śūra, Avantivarman's minster, had the play performed. Some passages from *Mudrā*° occurs, with some variation, in other works, *e.g*, *Mudrā*° ii. 13=*Tantrākhyāyika* i. 46; ii. 18=Bhartṛhari's *Nīti*° 27 and *Pañcatantra* etc., but there is nothing to suggest that Viśākhadatta could not have utilised the floating stock of Nīti verses, and such passages are of doubtful use in question of chronology. See also Hertel in *ZDMG*, LXX, 1916, pp. 133-42; Keith in *JRAS*, 1909, p. 145 (9th century).

probably a later emendation ; and if this is so, the theories based upon the name lose much of their force. In view of these difficulties, the problem must still be regarded as unsolved ; but there is nothing to prevent Viśākhadatta from belonging to the older group of dramatists who succeeded Kālidāsa, either as a younger contemporary, or at some period anterior to the 9th century A.D.[1]

Whatever may be its exact date, the *Mudrā-rākṣasa* is undoubtedly one of the great Sanskrit dramas. In theme, style and treatment, however, it stands apart from the normal Sanskrit play, even to a greater degree than the *Mṛcchakaṭika*. It is partly for its originality that its merits have been even less appreciated than those of Śūdraka's play by orthodox Sanskrit theorists. It breaks away from the banal subject of love, having only one minor female character ; and poetic flights are naturally circumscribed by its more matter-of-fact interest. If the *Mṛcchakaṭika* gives a literary form to the bourgeois drama, its theme is still an affecting story of love and suffering, and politics merely forms its background ; the *Mudrā-rākṣasa,* on the other hand, is a drama of purely political intrigue, in which resolute action in various forms constitutes the exclusive theme. The action, however, does not involve actual fight, war or bloodshed.[2] There is enough martial spirit, but there is no fondness for violent situations, no craving for fantastic adventures and no taste for indecorous afrightments. The action takes the form essentially of a conflict of wills, or of a game of skill, in which the interest is made to depend on the plots and counterplots of two rival politicians. One may wonder if such a subject is enough to absorb the mind of the audience, but the action of the play never flags, the characters are drawn admirably to support it,

1 The earliest quotation from the work occurs in *Daśarūpaka* (10th century A.D.)

2 The antecedent incidents of the drama are not indeed bloodless, for we are told of the extirpation of the Nandas and of the murders of Sarvārthasiddhi and Pravartaka, but in the drama itself Cāṇakya's policy is directed rather towards preventing the shedding of blood.

and the diction is appropriate in its directness, force and clarity. The *Pratijñā-yaugandharāyaṇā* is also another drama of political intrigue, but the plotting in it centres round the romantic legend of Udayana's love for Vāsavadattā, both of whom do not make their appearance indeed, but of whom we hear a great deal throughout the play. The *Mudrā-rākṣasa* is unique in avoiding not only the erotic feeling but also the erotic atmosphere. It is a drama without a heroine. There is nothing suggestive of tenderness or domestic virtues, no claim to prettiness of romance, no great respect even for religion and morality. Politics is represented as a hard game for men ; the virtues are of a sterner kind ; and if conduct, glorified by the name of diplomacy, is explained by expediency, its crookedness is redeemed by a high sense of duty, resolute fidelity to a cause, and unselfish devotion. There is a small scene between Candanadāsa and his family indicative of affection, but it is of no great importance to the development of the plot, and there is nothing of sentimentality in it even in the face of death.

Perhaps the suggestion is correct[1] that the *Bṛhatkathā* of Guṇāḍhya could not have been the source[2] of the plot of the *Mudrā-rākṣasa* ; for the events narrated there might have supplied the frame (as Viśākhadatta did not certainly invent the tale),[3] but the main intrigue appears to be the work of the dramatist himself. It is also not necessary to assume that the drama is historical in all its details, or to see in the working out

1 Speyer, *Studies about the Kathāsaritsāgara*, p. 54 ; the drama is held here to belong to the 4th century A.D.

2 In the printed text of the *Daśarūpaka* (i. 61) we have the statement in Dhanika's Vṛtti : *bṛhatkathā-mūlaṁ mudrārākṣasam*, followed by the quotation of two verses ; but these verses are obviously interpolated from Kṣemendra's *Bṛhatkathā-mañjarī* (ii. 216, 217). See G. C. O. Haas, Introd. to *Daśarūpaka* (New York, 1912), p. xxiii.

3 The story of the downfall of the Nandas and the rise of the Mauryas occurs also in Hemacandra's *Pariśiṣṭa-parvan* and other works, and is probably traditional. The details of Cāṇakya's intrigue, and even the name of Rākṣasa, are not found in these sources. The very name of the drama, derived from the signet ring (Mudrā) which plays an important part in the winning over of Rākṣasa, as well as the employment of the old idea of a token in this particular form, appears to be entirely Viśākhadatta's own.

of a political plot a tendencious piece of literature, which may be conveniently referred to this or that period of Indian political history. It is unquestionable that Candragupta and Cāṇakya are historical personages, and so are possibly Rākṣasa and Sarvārthasiddhi, although these latter names do not occur in the traditional accounts we possess ; but how far they are historically or purposively presented is a different question ; at lest, the occurrence of historical facts or persons does not justify the designation of a historical drama to the work of art, which must necessarily owe a great deal to the author's imagination in the ingenious maturing of the story.

The main theme of the drama is the reconciliation of Rākṣasa, the faithful minister of the fallen dynasty of the Nandas, by that traditional master of statecraft, Cāṇakya, who wants to win him over, knowing his ability and honesty, into the service of Candragupta Maurya, who has been established on the throne by Cāṇakya's cleverness and his own bravery. To the crafty machinations of Cāṇakya are inseparably linked the almost co-extensive plots of Rākṣasa, acting in alliance with Malayaketu, son of Candragupta's former ally, now alienated by the treacherous murder of his father by Cāṇakya's agents. The detailed development of the plot of the drama is complicated, but perspicuous ; ingenious, but not unnecessarily encumbered. The first act plunges at once into the story and gives us a glimpse into Cāṇakya's resolution and his deeply laid schemes, cunningly devised and committed to properly selected agents, which set the entire plot in motion. The second act shows, by way of contrast, the counter-schemes of Rākṣasa and the character of his agents, as well as the traps of Cāṇakya into which he unsuspectingly walks. The next act is an ably constructed dramatic scene of a pretended but finely carried out open quarrel between Candragupta and Cāṇakya, meant as a ruse to entrap Rāksasa further into the belief that Cāṇakya has fallen from royal favour. In the next three acts the plot thickens and moves rapidly, drawing the net more and more firmly round Rākṣasa, and ending in

Malayaketu's suspicion of the treachery of his own friends, execution of the allied Mleccha kings, and dismissal of Rākṣasa, who is left to soliloquise deeply on the heart-breaking failure of his aims and efforts, and on the fate of his friend Candanadāsa who is led to death The misguided but valiant and pathetic struggle of Rākṣasa perhaps suggests tragedy as the natural end, by making him a victim of the misunderstandings created by Cāṇakya ; but the intrigue is developed into a happy end, not in a forced or illogical manner, but by a skilful handling of the incidents, which are made to bring about the denouement in the natural way. Cāṇakya's intention from the beginning is not tragedy but a happy consummation. He makes, therefore, an accurate estimate of both the strength and weakness of his opponent's character and prepares his scheme accordingly. Cāṇakya knows that the only way to subdue Rākṣasa and impel him to a supreme act of sacrifice is through an attack on his dearly loved friends, especially Candanadāsa, whose deep affection and spirit of sacifice for Rākṣasa is equally great. In the last act, cornered and alone, Rākṣasa is ultimately compelled to accept, with dignity, the yoke which he never inteded to bear, not to save his own life, but to protect those of Candanadāsa and his friends. The acts are complete in themselve, but they are not detached ; no situation is forced or developed unnaturally ; all incidents, characters, dialogues and designs are skilfully made to converge towards the denouement, not in casual strokes, but in sustained grasp ; and there is no other drama in Sanskrit which achieves organic unity of action and inevitableness with greater and more complete effect.

In characterisation, Viśākhadatta fully realises the value of contrast, which brings distinctive traits into vivid relief ; and one of the interesting features of his delineation is that most of his characters are dual portraits effectively contrasted, but not made schematically symmetrical. Both Cāṇakya and Rākṣasa are astute politicians, bold, resourceful and unscrupulous, but both are unselfish and unflinchingly devoted, from different motives, to their respective cause. Any possible triviality or sordidness of the plot is redeemed by the purity of their motives and by the great things which are at stake. Both are admirable as excellent foils to each other ; Cānakya is clear-headed, self-confident and vigilant, while Rāksasa is soft, impulsive and blundering ; the one is secretive, distrustful and unsparing, while the other is frank, amiable and generous ; the one is feared, while the other is loved by his friends and followers ; the hard glitter of the one shows off the pliable gentleness of the other. The motive of Cāṇakya's unbending energy is not any affectionate sentiment for Candragupta, for in his methodical mind there is no room of tender feelings ; Rākṣasa, on the other hand, is moved by a high sense of duty and steadfast loyalty, which draws the unwilling admiration even of his political adversary. It is precisely Rākṣasa's noble qualities which prompt Cāṇakya to go to the length of elaborate schemes to win him over ; and it is precisely these noble qualities which lead ultimately to his downfall. He is made a victim of his own virtues ; and the pathos of the situation lies not in an unequal fight so much as in the softer features of his character. Rākṣasa is, of course, also given to intrigue, but he does not live and breathe in intrigue as Cāṇakya does. There is, however, no feeling in Cāṇakya's strategy ; there is too much of it in Rākṣasa's. Although sharp and relentless, Cāṇakya is indeed not a monster, and whatever one may think of his deception, impersonation and forgery, one admires his cool and ingenious plotting ; but our sympathy is irresistibly drawn towards the pity of Rākṣasa's stumbling and foredoomed failure, his noble bitterness on the break up of his hopes and efforts, his lofty desire to sacrifice himself for his friend, and his dignified but pathetic submission. The same contrast is seen in the presentation of Candragupta and Malayaketu. Although they are pawns in the game, they yet are not mere puppets in the hands of the rival statesmen. Though low-born and ambitious, the Maurya is a sovereign of dignity and strength of character, well trained, capable and having entire faith in his preceptor and minister, Cāṇakya ; but the capricious young mountaineer, moved as he is by filial love, is conceited, weak and foolishly stubborn, and has his confidence and mistrust equally misplaced. It is clear that the characters of this drama are not fair spirits from the far-off and unstained wonderland of fancy, nor are they abstract embodiments of perfect goodness or incredible evil. Even the minor characters, none of whom is fortuitous or unmotived, are moulded skilfully with a natural blend of good and evil. The secret agents of Cāṇakya, Bhāgurāyaṇa and Siddhārthaka, faithfully carry out their commissions, not with spontaneous enthusiasm, but from a feeling of awe and meek submission ; they are, however, finely discriminated as individuals, for while the one hates his work and feels secret compunctions, the conscience of the other is more accommodating. Rākṣasa's agents, the disguised Virādhagupta and the honest Śakaṭadāsa, on the other hand, are moved by a sincere attachment to Rākṣasa and honest desire to serve. One of the most touching minor characters of the play is Candanadāsa, the head of the guild ot lapidaries, whose affection for Rākṣasa is as sincere as that of Induśarman for Cāṇakya, but it is strong and undefiled enough to rise to the height of facing death for the sake of friendship and to be used, for that very reason, as a lever by Cāṇakya to play upon the magnanimous weakness of Rākṣasa. It is true that the characters of the drama are not always of a pleasant type, but they have a consistent individuality, and are drawn as sharply and coloured as diversely as the shady characters in the *Mṛcchakaṭika*.

The mastery of technique which the work betrays is indeed considerable, but there is no aggressive display of technical skill or any wooden conformity, so far as we know, to fixed modes and models. Nor is there any weakness for the commonplace extravagances of poetic diction affected by some of his contemporaries. Viśākhadatta's style is limpid, forcible and fluent ; and he appears to be fully aware of the futility of a laboured and heavily embellished diction for the manly strain of sentiment and vigorous development of character which his drama wants to attain. His metrical skill[1] and literary use of Prakrits[2] are considerable, but in no way conspicuous. Perhaps as a stylist he does not claim a high rank with his great compeers, and yet some of his stanzas stand out among the loftiest passages in Sanskrit literature. We do not indeed find in him the poetic imagination and artistic vigilance of Kālidāsa, the dainty and delicate manner of Harṣa, the humour, pathos and kindliness of Śūdraka, the fire and energy of Bhaṭṭa Nārāyaṇa, or the earnest and tearful tenderness of Bhavabhūti; but there can be no doubt that his style and diction suit his subject, and, in all essentials, he is no meaner artist. He uses his images, similes and embellishments, with considerable skill and moderation; and, if he does not indulge profusely in elaborate poetical and descriptive passages, it is because his sense of dramatic propriety recoils from them. The soliloquy of Rākṣasa is indeed long, but it is not longer than some of the soliloquies in *Hamlet*. It shows, however, that the author was not incapable of truly emotional outbursts; and the paucity of citations from his work in later rhetorical and anthological works need not prove that his drama is devoid of poetical or emotional touches. The kind of poetry and sentiment, which are normally favoured, are perhaps not to be found here; but in easy and subdued elegance of its own poetry and sentiment, the work is certainly successful. Viśākhadatta never thinks less of his subject and more of himself, so as to make his work a convenient vehicle for the display of his literary ingenuities; nor does he pitch his voice too high and exhaust himself by the violence of his effort. He has the gift of projecting himself into the personality of his characters; his dialogues and stanzas have

1 The metres most employed (beisdes the Śloka) in order of frequency are Śārdūlavikrīḍita, Sragdharā, Vasantatliaka and Śikhariṇī. Other metres are sporadic, but no rare kind is attempted.

2 The usual Prakrits are Śaurasenī and Māhārāṣṭrī, but Māgadhī also occurs. Hillebrandt rightly points out that, as in *Śakuntalā*, *Mṛcchakaṭika* and other earlier plays there is no justification in this case for the assumption that Śaurasenī was exclusively employed for the prose.

the dramatic quality necessary for rapidity and directness of action and characteristion; and if his work is necessarily of a somewhat prosaic cast, it still conforms more to the definition of the drama as the literature of action than some of the greater Sanskrit plays. The only serious defect is that the drama lacks grandeur, with a grand subject; it also lacks pity, with enough scope for real pathos. The downfall of a dynasty and fight for an empire are concerns only of personal vanity, wounded by personal insult; they are matters of petty plotting. Our moral sense is not satisfied even by the good result of placing Candragupta more securely on the throne; and the atmosphere of cold, calculated strategy and spying is depressing enough for a really great and noble cause.[1]

e. *Bhaṭṭa Nārāyaṇa*

Both Vāmana[2] and Ānandavardhana[3] cite passages anonymously from the *Veṇī-saṃhāra*[4] of Bhaṭṭa Nārāyaṇa, who must,

1 Passages from a drama, entitled *Devī-candragupta*, are quoted seven times in the *Nāṭya-darpaṇa* of Rāmacandra and Guṇacandra (12th century); ed. GOS, Baroda 1929, pp. 71, 84, 86, 118, 141-42, 193, 194), and the work is attributed to Viśākhadeva, who is probably identical with our author Viśākhadatta (whose name, however, does not occur in the anonymous quotations from the *Mudrā-rākṣasa*). The work has not been recovered, but it probably dealt with the story (*cf.* Rājaśekhara, *Kāvya-mīmāṁsā*, p. 46) of Kumāra Candragupta's rescue (in the disguise of a woman) of Dhruvadevī who had been abducted by a Śaka prince. This is perhaps the same story as is alluded to by Bāṇa in *Harṣa-carita* (*aripure ca para-kalatra-kāmukaṁ kāminī-veśa-guptaś candraguptaḥ śaka-nṛpatim aśātayat*); see *IA*, LII, 1923, pp. 181-84, where this Candragupta is taken to be Candragupta II of the Gupta dynasty. From the citations it appears that the drama extended at last to five acts. Abhinavagupta also quotes the work, without the name of the author, in his commentary on Bharata; so does also Bhoja in his *Śṛṅgāra-prakāśa* (see S. K. De in *BSOS*, IV, 1926, p. 282). Another work of Viśākhadeva's, entitled *Abhisārikā-vañcitaka* (°*vandhitaka*) is also cited by Abhinavagupta and Bhoja. It appears to have been based on another love-legend of Udayana, in which Padmāvatī wins back the lost affection of Udayana, who suspects her of having killed his son, by disguising herself as a Śabarī and in the rôle of an Abhisārikā, making her tender-minded husband fall in love with her again!—It is curious that a drama called *Pratijñā-cāṇakya* on the same theme appears to have been composed by one Bhīma, as we knew from its citation also by Abhinavagupta and Bhoja; apparently it was modelled on Viśākhadatta's play (see R. Ramamurthi in *JOR*, Madras, III, 1929, p. 80).

2 *Kāvyāl.* iv. 3. 28=*Veṇī*° v. 26d.

3 *Dhvan.* (ed. Kāvyamālā, 1911) *ad* ii. 10, pp. 80, 81=*Veṇī*° i. 21, iii. 31; *Dhvan. ad* iii. 44, p. 225=*Veṇī*° v. 26.

4 Ed. J. Grill, Leipzig 1871; ed. K. P. Parab, with comm. of Jagaddhara, NSP, Bombay 1898, 3rd ed. 1913. English trs. by Saurindra M. Tagore, Calcutta 1880.

therefore, belong to a period anterior to 800 A.D. ; and this lower limit is confirmed by the fact that the work, along with Harṣa's *Ratnāvalī,* is frequently quoted by the *Daśarūpaka,* in the last quarter of the 10th century, as one of the approved types of the Sanskrit drama. Beyond this, nothing definite is known about the exact date of the play ; and of the author, the Prologue gives us the only information that his other name or title was Mṛgarājalakṣman, about the significance of which there has been much conjecture but no certainty. The Bengal legend[1] that Bhaṭṭa Nārāyaṇa was one of the five Kānyakubja Brahmans who were invited by an equally fabulous king Ādiśūra of Bengal, should be relegated to the realm of fantastic fables which often gather round celebrated names. Serious attempts have been made to extract history from these legends of genealogists,[2] but unless corroborated by independent evidence, these so-called traditions of Bengal match-makers and panegyrists of big families are hardly of much value for historical purposes, particularly for events of comparatively early times. Traces of Pañcarātra tenets[3] are discovered in *Veṇī* i. 23 and iv. 43, 45, but the interpretation is far-fetched, while there is no justification for the view that the character of Cārvāka is meant to ridicule directly the materialistic doctrine of the reputed philosopher Cārvāka. Even if these ingenious conjectures are admitted, they are of little use for determining the age of the work.

Barring the epic pieces ascribed to Bhāsa, the *Veṇī-saṃhāra* is the only surviving work of the earlier group of dramatists, which takes valour as its ruling sentiment, but the presentation is too formless and rhetorical to be convincing. It attempts in six acts to dramatise a well-known episode of the *Mahābhārata,*

1 Sten Konow, *Ind. Drama,* p. 77 ; discussed also by Grill, *op. cit.*

2 It should be noted that while the historicity of Ādiśūra himself is doubtful, the genealogical works, are not agreed among themselves with regard to the names of the five Brahmans who were invited, the time and motive of their invitation, as well as their detailed genealogical account.

3 See Grill, introd. p. xviif and introd. to the edition of L. R. Vaidya and N. B. Godabole, Poona 1895.

but practically goes over the entire epic war ; and in subject, style and inspiration it differs from contemporary plays. The first act depicts Bhīma's revengeful pride of power. Draupadī's brooding resentment at the ignominious insult heaped on her by the Kauravas, as well as failure of Krsna's embassy, which makes war inevitable. With this menace of war hovering on the horizon, the second act introduces a frivolous and ineffective love-episode, censured even by the Sanskrit theorists, between Duryodhana and his queen Bhānumatī, relates her ominous dream, describes a sudden storm symbolical of the coming turmoil, and leaves Duryodhana gloating over the insult done to Draupadī at his instigation. The next act commences with a rather conventional, but loathsome, picture of the horrors of the battle-field, described by a couple of demons who feed on human flesh and blood, and we learn that most of the Kaurava heroes, including Droṇa, have in the meantime fallen ; but it goes on to a finely conceived scene of altercation between the suspicious Aśvatthāman and the sneering Karṇa, interrupted by Bhīma's boastful voice behind the scene. The dramatic possibilities, however, of the rivalry between these two Kaurava warriors are not at all developed ; the scene, therfore. becomes a lively but an uncalled for and unmotived episode. In act iv, we find Duryodhana wounded in battle and his brother Duḥśāsana, who had insulted Draupadī in public assembly by dragging her by the braid of her hair, killed by Bhīma ; but the account, given by the Kaurava messenger, Sundaraka, of Karṇa's death is too long and tedious, and serves no dramatic purpose. In the next act, the violent and insulting address of Bhīma to poor old Dhṛtarāṣṭra may be in the best heroic style, but it is gratuitous and only shows Bhīma as a wild, blood-thirsty and boasful bully. The last act, in which Duryodhana's death is announced introduces a poor comedy of mischief in the midst of all this fury and tragedy, through the instrumentality of the disguised demon Cārvāka, but it is as absurd as it is unnecessary ; and Bhīma's dragging Draupadī by her hair in mistake is perhaps an unwittingly ludicrous repetition of her rude treament by a similar method on a former and more serious occasion!

The title suggests that the main theme, to which all incidents are made to converge, is the satisfaction of Bhīma's ferocious revenge, celebrated by the killing of the Kaurava chiefs and by binding up, with blood-stained hands, the braid of Draupadī, which she had sworn to let down until the wrong to her is avenged. The subject is one of primitive savagery, but the polish of the drama has nothing primitive in it. There is undoubtedly much scope for fury and violence, but since violent situations have no sanction, the fury exhausts itself in declamatory blustering. There is enough of pathos and horror, but the pathos is tiresome and the horror uncouth; there is enough of action, but the action is devoid of dramatic conflict or motivation to carry it on with sustained interest; there is enough instinct for claptrap stage-effect, but the effect limits itself to a series of detached and disjointed scenes of excitement. We do not know whether the work chooses to follow faithfully the dramaturgic rules which we find elaborated by the theoists, or whether the theorists themselves faithfully deduce the rules from the model of this work; but the correspondence is undoubtedly close and almost slavish. Judged by the conventional standard, its dramatic merit may be reckoned very high,[1] but considered absolutely, it must be admitted that the plot is clumsily contrived, the situations are often incongruous, the scenes are disconnectedly put together, and the incidents do not inevitably grow out of one another. There is also considerable narrative digression after the manner of the Kāvya. The work is hardly a unified play, but is rather a panoramic procession of a large number of actions and incidents, which have no intrinsic unity except that they concern the well-known epic personages who appear, no naturally developed sequence except the sequence

1 But even the *Daśarūpaka* and the *Sāhitya-darpaṇa* are unable to find as proper illustrations of the Garbha and Vimarśa Saṁdhis from the *Veṇī*, as from *Ratnāvalī*, for instance.

in which they are found in the Epic. The drama suffers from the common mistake of selecting an epic theme, without the power of transforming it into a real drama, and the modifications introduced for the purpose are hardly effective. The presentation is rather that of a vivid form of story-telling, and the author might as well have written a Kāvya.

It is true that Bhaṭṭa Nārāyaṇa's characterisation of the peculiar types of "heroes" is interesting ; they are living figures, and not mere violently moved marionettes ; but, with the exception of the cautiously peaceful Yudhiṣṭhira and the wisely moderate Kṛṣṇa, the characters are hardly lovable. Bhīma has fire and energy, and his grandiloquent defiances do credit to the rhetorical powers of his creator ; but he is a boisterous, undisciplined and ferocious savage, and his equally valiant brother Arjuna is a worthy second in rant and fury. Draupadī's bitterness is well represented, but this is not made the only thing for which the brothers fight, and she is herself rather crude in her implacable hate and deisre for revenge. The duplicity of the weak Dhṛtarāṣṭra is suggested after the Epic, but not properly developed. The sneaky jealousy of Karṇa and the distrustful anger of Aśvatthāman offer dramatic opportunities, but the figures are made too short-lived in the drama ; and the vain, selfish and heartless arrogance of Duryodhana is scarcely relieved by his irrelevant amorousness befitting a conventional love-sick hero.

There is much good writing and some diffused pathos in the work, but since the dramatic construction is poor and the epic and narrative details hamper the action and mar the result of otherwise able, but unattractive, characterisation, the general effect is wholly undramatic. It is more so, because the diction, though polished and powerful, is laboured and generally unsuited for dramatic purpose. The author appears to be obsessed with the idea that long, high-sounding words and compounds are alone capable of imparting force, the so-called Ojas, to a composition. The procedure is sanctioned by the rhetoricians, but its excessive employment in Sanskrit and Prakrit prose and verse is rightly censured by Anandavardhana, especially with reference to dramatic writing. It should be noted, however, that the extravagances of grandiose expression and lengthy description are not only tedious, but they also indicate that the author perhaps conceives his work more as a poetical than a dramatic piece. And perhaps it would not be right to judge it otherwise. The *Veṇī-saṃhāra* is one of the earliest and best examples in Sanskrit of that peculiar kind of half-poetical and half-dramatic composition which may be called the declamatory drama ; and it shares all the merits and defects of this class of work. The defects are perhaps more patent, but they should not obscure the merits, which made the work so entertaining to the Sanskrit theorists. Even if overdone very often, there is considerable power of poetry and passion, vividness of portraiture of detached scenes and characters, command of sonorous and elevated phrasing, and remarkable skill and sense of rhythm in the manipulation of a variety of metres.[1] The work does not indeed pretend to any milder or refiner graces of poetry ; and the defect of dramatic form and method is almost fatal ; but it has energy, picturesqueness, and narrative motion. These qualities, which are best seen in detached passages, if not in the drama as a whole, are indeed not negligible, and perhaps eminently suit the type of composition affected. If the work is neither a well judged nor a well executed dramatisation of the epic story, it still attains a certain vigorous accomplishment and holds its popularity by this power of appeal and excitement. Notwithstanding these allowances, carefully but not grudgingly made, even a generous critic will find it difficult to assign a high rank to Bhaṭṭa Nārāyaṇa, both as a poet and as a

1 Next to the largest employment of the Śloka, Bhaṭṭa Nārāyaṇa favours Śārdūlavikrīḍita and Sragdharā equally with Śikhariṇī and Vasantatilaka as the principal metres of his play. His Prakrit with long compounds and absence of verse, like that of Bhavabhūti, is apparently modelled on Sanskrit and calls for no special remarks. Normally it is Śaurasenī, although Māgadhī is also traceable.

dramatist. It may be urged that if there is bad drama, there is good poetry in his play ; but even in poetry, as in drama, the fault which mars Bhaṭṭa Nārāyaṇa's forceful work is that it is too often rhetorical in the bad sense, and rhetoric in the bad sense is hardly compatible with the best poetry or drama.

f. *Bhavabhūti*

In the earlier group of great dramatists, Bhavabhūti is perhaps one of the youngest, but he occupies a very high place, which in Indian estimation has been often reckoned as next to that of Kālidāsa, as the author of three important plays. One of these, the *Mālatī-mādhava*[1] gives a fictitious romantic love-story of middle class life, and the other two, the *Mahāvīra-carita*[2] and the *Uttara-rāma-carita,*[3] deal respectively with the earlier and the later history of Rāma and derive their theme from the *Rāmāyaṇa.* Unlike most of his contemporaries and predecessors, Bhavabhūti is not entirely reticent about himself. In the Prologues to his

1 Ed. R. G. Bhandarkar, comm. of Jagaddhara, Bombay Skt. Ser., 1905 ; ed. M. R. Telang, with comms. of Jagaddhara, Tripurāri (i-vii) and Nānyadeva (viii-x), NSP, Bombay 1926. No Engl trs., except Wilson's free rendering in *Select Specimen*, ii ; French trs. by G Strehly, Paris 1885 ; Germantrsby. Ludwing Fritze, Leipzig, 1884. One of the earliest editions is that of C. Lassen, Bonn 1832.

2 The earlier editions of Trithen (London 1848) and Anundaram Boroooah (Calcutta 1877) are superseded by the critical ed., based on important manuscripts, by Todar Mall, Oxford Univ. Press, 1928 (Punjab Univ. Publ.). Also ed. T. R Ratnam Aiyar and K. P. Parab, with comm. of Vīrarāghava, NSP, 3rd. ed. Bombay 1910 (1st ed. 1892). Eng. trs. by John Piekford, London 1871.

3 Ed. T. R. Ratnam Aiyar and K. P. Parab, with comm. of Vīrarāghava, NSP, Bombay 1906 (1st ed. 1889) ; ed. with comm. of Rāmacandra Budhendra, Madras 1882 ; ed. P. V. Kane, with comm. of Ghanaśyāma (1st half of the 18th century ; *Journal of Orient. Research*, Madras, ii, 1929, pp. 231-43), Bombay 1921 ; ed. C. Sankarama Sastri, with comm. of Nārāyaṇa, Balamonorama Press, Madras 1932 ; ed. S. K. Belvalkar (Text only), Poona 1921 ; ed. S. K. Balvalkar, vol. i, containing Trs. and Introd. only, Harvard Orient. Ser., Cambridge Mss. 1915. Also Eng. trs. by C. H. Tawney, Calcutta 1871 ; French trs. by Félix Nève, Bruxelles and Paris 1880, and by P. d'Alheim, Bois-le-roi 1906. Besides Sten Konow and M. Schuyler cited above, see Schuyler in *JAOS*, XXV, 1904, pp. 189f. for fuller bibliography.

three plays he gives us some autobiographical details.[1] We are told that he belonged to a pious and learned Brahman family of the Kāśyapa Gotra, who followed and taught the Taittirīya branch of the Black Yajurveda, duly maintained the Five Fires, performed Soma sacrifices, bore the surname of Udumbara and lived in Padmapura, probably in Vidarbha (the Berars). Bhavabhūti was fifth in descent from one who was called Mahākavi (Great Poet) and who performed the Vājapeya sacrifice; and his grandfather was Bhaṭṭa Gopāla, his father Nīlakaṇṭha and his mother Jātūkarṇī. The poet himself was given the title of Śrīkaṇṭha, but commentators imagine that Bhavabhūti was also a title he won as a poet blessed with luck or the holy ashes (Bhūti) of Śiva (Bhava). His preceptor was a pious and learned ascetic, named appropriately Jñānanidhi.[2] He studied the Vedas and Upaniṣaḍs, the Sāṃkhya and Yoga, and mastered various branches of learning, including grammar, rhetoric and logic; a statement which it is not impossible to corroborate from the knowledge displayed in his works.[3] Although a scholar and given occasionally to a love of display, Bhavabhūti seldom pushes his scholarship to the verge of pedantry. He was essentially a poet; and like his predecessor Bāṇa, he had apparently a rich and varied experience of life, and stood, as he himself tells us, in friendly relation with actors, into whose hand he gave his plays; but this fact need not justify the efforts that have been made to trace evidence of revision of his plays for stage-purposes. All his plays were enacted at the fair of Lord

1 The account, scantiest in *Uttara*° and fullest in *Mahāvīra*°, is summarised and discussed by Bhandarkar, Todar Mall and Belvalkar in the works cited above.

2 The colophon to act iii of a manuscript of *Mālatī-mādhava* (see S. P. Pandit's introd. to *Gauḍavaho*, pp. ccv, et seq.) assigns the play to a pupil of Kumārila, while the colophon to act iv gives the name of this pupil as Umbekācārya. But undue weight need not be attached to the testimony of a single manuscript to prove that these acts are substitutions, or that Bhavabhūti is identical with the well-known pupil and commentator of Kumārila, although chronology is not incompatible and knowledge of Mīmāṁsā not impossible to infer from the plays.

3 On Bhavabhūti's scholarship, see Keith in *JRAS*, 1914, p. 719 f and Todar Mall, pp. xxv-xxvi, xliii-xliv; Peterson in *JBRAS*, XVIII, 1791, p. 109 f

Kālapriyānātha, usually identified with Mahākāla, whose famous shrine at Ujjayinī is mentioned by Kālidāsa and Bāṇa.

Although, like Bāṇa, Bhavabhūti has given us an interesting account of himself and his family, yet, unlike Bāṇa, he says nothing about the time when he lived. He shows familiarity with court-life, but does not refer to any royal favour. On the contrary, he is evidently distressed by the lack of contemporary appreciation of his works, and declares, with defiant but charming egotism, that there will some day arise a kindred spirit to do justice to his genius, for, time is boundless and the world is wide.' The inference is possible that he had to struggle hard for fame and fortune, although we do not know how far the bliss of conjugal love, which he idealises in his writings, proved a solace to him in reality.[1] In view of all this, it is surprising to find that the Kashmirian chronicler Kahlaṇa[3] mentions Bhavabhūti, along with Vākpatirāja, as having been patronised by king Yaśovārman of Kānyakubja. Obviously, this Vākpatirāja is the author of the enormous, but unfinished, Prakrit poem *Gauḍavaha* which glorifies Yaśovarman and in which the poet acknowledges indebtedness to Bavabhūti in eulogistic terms. As this poem is presumed to have been composed about 736 A.D. before Yaśovarman's defeat and humiliation by king Lalitāditya of Kashmir,[4] it is inferred that Bhavabhūti flourished, if not actually in the court of Yaśovarman, at least during his reign, in the closing years of the 7th or the first quarter of the 8th century. This date agrees with what is known of our poet's chronological relations with other writers. He is certainly

1 The view that Bhavabhūti is rural, as Kālidāsa is urban, is not justified by his works.

2 *Rāja-taraṅgiṇī*, iv. 144.

3 ed. S. P. Pandit, Bombay Skt. Ser., 1887, stanza 799 (the same reference in this revised edition by N. B Utgikar, Poona 1927).

4 The exact date is a matter of dispute ; see Stein's note on the point in his translation of the *Rāja-taraṅgiṇī*, introd. sec. 85 ; also the works of Bhandarkar, Pandit and Belvalkar cited above.

later than Kālidāsa, with whose writings he is familiar,[1] and apparently also than Bāṇa, who does not mention him. The earliest writer to eulogise Bhavabhūti (besides Vākpatirāja) is Rājaśekhara,[2] and the earliest work in which anonymous quotations from his works occur is the *Kāvyālaṃkāra*[3] of Vāmana; both these references set the lower limit of his date at the last quarter of the 8th century.

The plot of the *Mālatī-mādhava* is based on the time-worn theme of love triumphant over many obstacles, but we turn pleasantly from royal courts to a more plebeian atmosphere and find greater individuality of presentation. Bhavabhūti prides himself (i. 4) upon the ingenuity of his plot; to a certain extent, this is justifiable. But the general outline of the central story and some of the striking incidents and episodes have been industriously traced to the two Kashmirian adaptations of the *Bṛhatkathā*, respectively made by Kṣemendra[4] and Somadeva,[5] with the suggestion that Bhavabhūti derived them, or at least hints of them, from Guṇāḍhya's lost work. But even granting that the coincidences[6] are not accidental, it should be recognised that the evolving of the plot as a whole in ten acts by a dexterous combination of varied motifs and situations is apparently the poet's own. The central interest is made to rest, not upon one love-story, but upon to parallel love-stories, skilfully blended together and crowded with such exciting and unexpeted

1 See Todar Mall, pp. xxxix-xliii, and Belvalkar, p. xl.

2 *Bāla-rāmāyaṇa*, i. 16.

3 *Kāvyā*° i. 2. 12=*Mahāvīra*° i. 54; iv. 3. 6.=*Uttara*° i. 38. For other citations in rhetorical and anthological literature, see Todar Mall, p. xxix; but, curiously enough, Todar Mall omits these two citations of Vāman.

4 xi. 9-88 (Madirāvatī); iii. 218-30; v. 100-163 (Aśokadatta)

5 xiii. 1. 17-215 (Madirāvatī); v. 2 (Aśokadatta); xviii. 2 (Madanamañjarī and Khaṇḍakapāla).

6 Such as, impersonation and marriage in disguise, meeting of lovers in a temple, rescue from a wild animal (the conventional elephant being replaced by the tiger), offering of human flesh and seeking the aid of ghosts, in the cemetery, attempted immolation by a magician, abduction and rescue of the heroine, etc. But some of the motifs belong to the floating stock-in-trade of story-telling.

turn of incidents as is not normally found in such stories. There is also some real comic relief—a rare thing in Bhavabhūti—and a free use of the terrible, horrible and supernatural sentiments. The main plot moves round the love of Mādhava, a young student and Mālatī, daughter of a cabinet minister ; it is thwarted by the interposition of a powerful suitor in Nandana, nominated by the king, but it ends with achievements of success, partly through accidents and partly through the diplomacy of a shrewd, resourceful and kind-hearted Buddhist nun,[1] Kāmandakī, a friend and class-mate of the fathers of Mādhava and Mālatī. The by-plot, which is obviously meant to be a parallel as well as a contrast, is concerned with the love of Makaranda and Madayantikā ; it is linked to the main plot by presenting Madayantikā as a sister of Mālatī's rival suitor Nandana, and by making Mādhava's friend Makaranda fall in love with her. The interweaving of the plot and the by-plot is complicated and diversified by the comic episode of the pretended marriage of Nandana to Makaranda disguised as Mālatī, as well as by two sensational escapes of Mālatī from violent death. Makaranda's impersonation, which also involves Madayantikā's mistaking him for Mālatī and confessing her own love to him unawares, ending in their elopement, is made parallel to the imposition on Mālatī, with a similar result, by Mādhava's taking the place of Mālatī's companion Lavaṅgikā ; while Mādhava's valiant rescue of Mālatī from the clutches of a Kāpālika becomes, in the same way, a natural counterpart of Makaranda's heroic, but somewhat conventional, rescue of Madayantikā from the claws of a tiger.

There can be no doubt that the dramatist knows the value of contrast, but he also knows the value of suspense ; and in

1 The Buddhist nun as a go-between, or more euphemistically a match-maker, is a familiar figure in Indian story-telling, and occurs in the *Daśakumāra-carita*, where she helps Apahāravarman to meet Kāmamañjarī, Ratnāvatī to regain her husband Balabhadra, and Kalahakaṇṭha to evolve the scheme of winning Nimbavatī ; but in this drama she is a much more dignified person. Even if she freely discusses matters of love *a la* Kāmā-śāstra, she is a sincere, wise and loving woman, who promotes the love of the young couples partly out of affection for them and partly out of the memory of her old friendship with their fathers.

spite of the length of the drama, the interest is sustained by skilful inventiveness and by a naturally developed interplay of two parallel, but contrasted, plots. The defect, however, is that the subsidiary plot and its chief characters tend to overshadow the main plot and its hero and heroine. This happens partly on account of the important part played by the daring and resourceful Makaranda, by whose side the love-sick and melodramatic Mādhava pales into the conventional hero, and partly by the extremely arresting character of the shrewd and lively Madayantikā, who similarly surpasses Mālatī the shy and hesitating official heroine. The action also, notwithstanding a series of exciting incidents, suffers as a whole from a vital weakness in the central conception. Kāmandakī, with her kindly scheming, is undoubtedly meant to hold the key-position in the drama (the Kārya-vidhāna, as Kalahaṃsa says), far greater than the role of Friar Laurence in the *Romeo and Juliet*, or of the Parivrājikā in *Mālavikāgnimitra* ; but the action of the drama is made to depend more on a series of accidents than on her clever diplomacy. It is true that she takes the fullest advantage of lucky occurrences, but too many important events happen by pure accident to further her design. The tiger-episode, which leads to the love of Makaranda and Madayantikā, is a veritable godsend to Kāmandakī, while Mālatī, twice on the verge of death, is saved by the merest chance, as the dramatist himself admits in v. 28. The incidents are, of course, dramatically justified, and the element of chance cannot be entirely ruled out of a drama, as out of life, but their convenient frequency demands too much from credulity. They are consistent perhaps with the supernatural atmosphere, in which uncanny things might happen ; but they leave the general impression that the play moves in an unreal world of folk-tale, in which tigers run wild in the streets, ghosts squeak in cemeteries, Kāpālikas perform gruesome rites unhindered, maidens are abducted with murderous intent, and people adept in occult sciences fly through the air with both good and bad purposes,—but all miraculously resolved into a final harmonious effect!

The lack of a sense of proportion is also seen in prolonging the play even after it naturally ends with act viii, in which the king moved by the valour of Mādhava and Makaranda, is disposed to pardon them and acknowledge the marriage. The episodes of the two abductions of Mālatī hardly arise out of the story, but they are added to satisfy the sensational craving for the terrible and the gruesome, and to fill the whole of act ix and a part of act x with the grief and lamentation of the hapless Mādhava, separated from his beloved, in the approved manner of a man in Viraha. It may be said that the first abduction is meant to establish a parallelism by showing that Mādhava is no less heroic than his friend in the rescue of his own beloved, and that the second abduction by Kapālakundalā is a natural act of revenge for the slaying of Aghoraghaṇṭa , but these purposes need not have been realised by clumsy appendages, involving fortuitous coincidences, by the introduction of terrible scenes, which are too unreal to inspire real terror, as well as by an unnecessary display of poetic sentimentality, modelled obviously on the madness of Purūravas in Kālidāsa's drama.

It is clear that, however lively, interesting and original the plot-construction of the play is, it lacks restraint, consistency and inevitableness. But a still greater defect lies in Bhavabhūti's tendency to over-emphasise and his inability to stop at the right moment, seen in a damaging degree in the highly poetical, but unhindered, sentimental passages. In his attempt to evoke tragic pathos, Bhavabhūti, with his unhumorous disposition, makes his hero faint too often, and this happens even at a time when he should rush to save his friend's life in danger. The love-agony frequently becomes prolonged, unmanly and unconvincing. The exuberant descriptive and emotional stanzas and elaborate prose speeches,[1] the high sounding phrases

[1] *E.g.*, the long Prakrit passages in acts iii and vii, the description of the cremation-ground at night in act v, and the forest scene in act ix.

and lengthy compounds (albeit not so formidable as they look) had perhaps a special relish, as much for the poet as for his audience. Some of the passages are highly poetical and picturesque ; but they indicate an expansiveness and lack of moderation, which are fatal to dramatic movement and propriety ; and the fact that some of these stanzas are repeated in the other two plays gives the impression that the poet had them ready-made to be utilised whenever an opportunity presents itself. Much of the talk of love and grief, therefore, becomes unreal and tends to overwhelm action and characterisation.

Nevertheless, the *Mālatī-mādhava* possesses, in many respects, a unique interest in the history of the Sanskrit drama, not only as an attractive picture of certain aspects of middle-class life, but also because of its genuine poetic quality. It is really an interesting story cast in a loose dramatic form, rather than an accomplished drama, but inventiveness and movement are not wanting. There is little individuality in its chief hero and heroine, who are typically sentimental lovers, making a lot of fuss about themselves, but Makaranda and Madayantikā, as well as Kāmandakī, show that the author's power of characterisation is not of a mean order. There is indeed a great deal of melodrama, of which it is difficult for a romantic play to steer clear entirely, but which often mars its pathetic and dramatic effect ; and the gratuitious introduction of supernatural and horrible scenes may be pertinently questioned. It must, however, be admitted that there is a great deal of real poetry and passion in Bhavabhūti's picture of youthful love, which reaches its most mature and mellow expression in his *Uttara-rāma-carita*. If the *Mālatī-mādhava* is one of his earliest works,[1] the faults are those of youth and inexperience ; but Bhavabhūti, even in this sentimental play, is far more serious than most light-hearted Sanskrit poets, and the intense poetic quality of his

1 The *Mahāvīra-carita* is often taken to be Bhavabhūti's earliest work, but it is difficult to dogmatise on the question of its priority to the *Mālati-mādhava*. The *Uttara-carita* is unquestionably the most mature work, as the poet himself indicates.

erotic stanzas, with their music,[1] colouring and fervour, relieves their banality. The picture of Mālatī, tossed between love and duty and reluctantly yielding to a stolen marriage, of the description of the first dawning of the passion in Mādhava and its effect on his youthful mind, is in the best manner of the poet and is much superior to what one finds normally in Sanskrit sentimental literature. The key-note of this weird but passionate love-story is perhaps given in the works of Makaranda (i. 17) when he says that the potent will of love wanders unobstructed in this world, youth is susceptible, and every sweet and charming thing shakes off the firmness of the mind. It is a study of the poetic possibilities of the undisciplined passion of youth ; but no other Sanskrit poet, well versed as he is in the delineation of such sentiment, has been able to present it with finer charm and more genuine emotional inflatus.

If the *Mālatī-mādhava* is defective in plot-construction, much improvement is seen in this respect in the *Mahāvīra-carita* which reveals a clearer conception of dramatic technique and

1 In this play Bhavabhūti employs a large number of metres, about twenty-five, with considerable skill, including rarer metres like Daṇḍaka (v. 23 ; fifty-four syllables in each foot), Nardaṭaka (v. 31, ix. 18) and Aparavaktra (ix. 23). The Śloka is not frequent (occurring about 14 times), but other chief metres, in their order of frequency, are Vasantatilaka, Śārdūlavikrīḍita, Śikhariṇī, Mālinī, Mandākrāntā and Hariṇī, the shorter metres being generally used for softer sentiments and the longer for the heroic and the awe-inspiring. There are eleven Āryās, to which Kālidāsa also shows partiality. In the *Mahāvīra-carita* Bhavabhūti uses twenty different metres, in which the Śloka appears in about one-third of the total number of stanzas, the Śārdūlavikrīḍita, Vasantatilaka, Śikhariṇī, Sragdharā, Mandākrāntā and Upajāti coming next in order of frequency ; the only unusual metre is Mālyabhārā found in a sigle stanza, while the Āryā occurs only thrice. The *Uttara-carita* has the same metres as above, but here the Śloka easily leads and the Śikhariṇī comes next to it, after which comes the Vasantatilaka and Śārdūlavikrīḍita, while the Sragdharā, Drutavilambita and Mañjubhāṣiṇī are sporadic here, as in *Mālatī*. It is noteworthy that there is not a single Prakrit verse in all the three plays. Bhavabhūti's Prakrit in prose passages, with their long compounds (which remind one of Vākpatirāja's laboured verse), is obviously influenced by Sanskrit usage, but it is sparingly employed in the *Mahāvīra*. His vocabulary, both in Sanskrit and Prakrit, has a tendency to prolixity, but it is extensive and generally adequate, while his poetic style is fully consistent with his poetical imagery and feeling.

workmanship, even if it is feebler in characterisation and in the literary quality of its poetical stanzas. It dramatises in seven acts[1] the early history of Rāma, beginning a little before his marriage and ending with his return from Laṇkā and coronation. The theme is found ready-made, but since the epic story is in the form of a narrative, containing a large number of episodes, incidents and characters, a mere panoramic reproduction of a series of pictures is hardly enough for a drama proper. The problem before the dramatist is not only to select such incidents and characters as are necessary and appropriate, but also where such selection is difficult, to modify and adjust them in such a way as to make the different units well arranged with adequate dramatic motive and unity of action. In making daring, but judicious, changes even in a well-known and accepted story, Bhavabhūti gives evidence not only of his boldness and power of ingenious invention, but also of his sense of dramatic construction. Accordingly the whole action is conceived as a feud of Rāvaṇa against Rāma. The seed of dramatic conflict and movement is found in Rāvaṇa's discomfiture as a suitor by the rejection of his messenger and by the betrothal of Sītā to Rāma at the Svayaṃvara. Rāvaṇa's desire for revenge at this insult to his pride and valour is further inflamed by death of Tāṭakā, Subāhu and other demons at the hands of Rāma ; and the action is set in motion by the diplomacy of Rāvaṇa's valiant minister Mālyavat, which includes the crafty instigation by him of

[1] Unfortunately, the genuineness of the last two acts, namely, the sixth and the seventh, and the concluding part of the fifth act is not beyond question. Bhavabhūti's authorship of the text up to v. 46 alone is proved by the agreement of all manuscripts and printed editions ; but for the rest we have (*i*) the Vulgate text, found in most North Indian manuscripts and generally printed in most editions (*ii*) the text of Subrahmaṇya, found in South Indian manuscripts, (printed in Ratnam Aiyar's edition as such) and (*iii*) the text of Vināyaka (printed in Todar Mall's ed.), which agrees with the Vulgate in having the same text for acts vi and vii, but differs from it, as well as from Subrahmaṇya's text, in the portion from v. 46 to the end of that act. None of these supplementary texts probably represents Bhavabhūti's own text, which is perhaps lost. For a discussion of the whole question see Todar Mall's introduction, reviewed in detail by S. K. De in *IA*, LIX, 1930, pp. 13-18.

Paraśurāma and the despatch of Śūrpaṇakhā in the clever disguise of the nurse Mantharā, the second episode ingeniously exonerating Kaikeyī and supplying a motive for Śūrpaṇakhā's later conduct. The first scheme fails, the second succeeds, after which the abduction of Sītā becomes easy. In order to frustrate Rāma's efforts, there is then the intrigue of Mālyavat with Vālin, which serves the twofold purpose of exculpating the dubious conduct of Rāma and avoiding the unseemly fraternal quarrel between Vālin and Sugrīva. But Vālin dies; and on the failure of diplomacy, nothing remains but the use of force, leading to the denouement of Rāvaṇa's defeat and death, rescue of Sītā and coronation of Rāma. The changes, therefore, in the original story are many, but they are justified by the necessity of evolving a well-knit and consistent plot; and the action is developed mainly on the basis of a conflict between strategy and straightforwardness. Whatever may be said about its adequacy, the attempt to motivate the episodes shows considerable dramatic sense and skill.

But the plot fails to impress us as a whole. The central conception of the dramatic conflict is weak. The strategy of Mālyavat fails, not because it is met with an equally ingenious counter-strategy, not even because Rāma has superior strength and resources, but because it is destined that Rāma, with virtue in his favour, must ultimately win. On the side of villainy, Bhavabhūti was doubtless permitted to take as much liberty with the original story as he wished, but perhaps he could not do so with equal impunity on the side of virtue; the entire dramatic conflict, therefore, becomes unconvincing. The plot also suffers from Bhavabhūti's usual lack of restraint and of the sense of proportion, which is so glaring in his *Mālatī-mādhava*, from a greater feebleness of characterisation and from a heavier and more uncouth style and diction. As in his *Uttara-carita*, Rāma here is human and normal, but he is conceived as the ideal hero of valour, nobility and chivalry, and the human traits of his character (as also those of Sītā, who is here presented as fidelity incarnate) are not made as appealing as they are in Bhavabhūti's more mature play. Mālyavat is shrewd and resourceful and has a sense of better things, but he falls far below Cāṇakya or Rākṣasa. Parśurāma's great prowess is balanced by his furious temper ; Vālin's magnanimity by his susceptibility to bad advice ; Rāvaṇa's qualities of body and mind by his inclination to thoughtless passion ; but none of these characters rises above modiocrity, and there is hardly any development of character by action, hardly any fine colouring or diversity of shading. Bhavabhūti also appears to be less successful in the heroic than in the softer sentiments ; it is a kind of flaunting, but really meek and bookish, heroism that he paints even in his Rāma. Moreover, action is often substituted by narration of events in long and tedious speeches. The Bharata-episode at the end of act iv and the scene between Vālin and Sugrīva are indeed ably executed, but Mālyavat's self-revelation is carried to an unnecessary and tiresome length. Like the lamentation of Mādhava, spread over an act and a half, the wordy warfare between Paraśurāma, on the one hand, and Janaka, Daśaratha, Rāma and their friends on the other, is dragged tediously through two acts. All such passages reveal the author's multifarious knowledge and rhetorical power, but they also show a distinct desire for parade and tend to hamper reality and rapidity of action, as well as effectiveness of characterisation. In all this, Bhavabhūti may have been carried away by convention, but temperamentally he appears to be too prone to over-elaboration by means of description and declamation ; and even if his language in this play is often vigorous and adequate, it lacks his usual ease and grace.

Even if still deficient in action, for which the theme hardly affords much scope, the *Uttara-rāma-carita* shows a much greater command of dramatic technique and characterisation.[1] It is undoubtedly Bhavabhūti s masterpiece, the product, as the poet

1 A detailed appreciative study of Bhavabhūti's dramatic art and technique will be found in Belvalkar's introduction to the play, pp. lxxvi-lxxxv,

himself declares, of his mature genius, and has deservedly enrned the high reputation of having equalled the dramatic masterpiece of Kālidāsa, It depicts in seven acts the later history of Rāma extending from the exile of Sītā to the final reunion ; and Bhavabhūti's literary characteristics may be studied to the best advantage in this work, which reaches a high level as a drama but which undoubtedly ranks higher for its intense poetic quality. Bhavabhūti derives his theme from the *Rāmāyaṇa*, but to suit his dramatic purpose he does not, as in his earlier Rāma-drama, hesitate to depart in many points from his authoritative epic original. The conception, for instance, of the picture-gallery scene, derived probably from a hint supplied by Kālidāsa (*Raghu*° xiv. 25), and of the invisible presence of Sītā in a spirit-form during Rāma's visit to Pañcavaṭī, of Rāma's meeting with Vāsantī and confession, the fight between Lava and Candraketu, the visit of Vasiṣṭha and others to Vālmīki's hermitage, and the enactment of a miniature play or masque on Rāma's later history composed by Vālmīki, are skilful details which are invented for the proper development of his dramatic theme, as well as for the suitable expression of his poetic powers. Here again, Bhavabhūti's principal problem is not the creation but the adequate motivation of an already accepted story. While not monotonously adhering to his original, he accepts for his particular dramatic purpose the epic outlines of a half-mythical and half-human legend of bygone days, which had already tāken its hold on the popular imagination by its pathos and poetry, but he reshapes it freely with appropriate romantic and poetical situations, which bring out all the ideal and dramatic implications of a well-known story. In taking up the theme of conjugal love as a form of pure, tender and spiritual affection, ripening into an abiding passion, Bhavabhūti must have realised that its beauty and charm could be best brought out by avoiding the uncongenial realism of contemporary life and going back to the poetry and idealism of olden days. It was not his purpose to draw the figures on his canvas on the generous and heroic scale of the Epic; but he wanted to add to the ancient tale an intensity of human feeling, which should transform an old-world legend into one of everyday experience, the story of high ideals into one of vivid reality.

In this drama Bhavabhūti idealises conjugal love through the chastening influence of sorrow, and he does this in a way which is unparalleled in Sanskrit, or perhaps in any literature. There are indeed some charming pictures of domestic happiness in Indian literature; but the causes, both social and religious, which lowered women in public estimation by depriving them of their early freedom and dignity, naturally hindered the evolution of a free conjugal relation. It is conceivable that the larger and more heterogeneous group comprising the family in ancient India may have also hampered its growth; for a girl left her father s home to enter the home, not of her husband, but of her father-in-law, and the husband is often merely one of the factors of the big family. Wedded love was indeed highly prized, but ordinary marriages were .perhaps often prompted by motives of convenience, among which must be reckoned the necessity of having a son for religious purposes; and self-choice of husband was almost entirely confined to the Epics, being forbidden by the customary Smṛtis, even if permitted by the Kāma-śāstra. The Aśokan edicts, though now and then didactic on family relations, are silent on conjugal life. Buddhism brought greater freedom to women; but the Epics, as well as the Dharmaśāstras, are full of utilitarian precepts—not merely priestly generalisation—sregarding marriage, and domestic happiness is still summed up in the loyalty of a fuitful, patient and thrifty wife. Moreover, the existence of polygamy, which was perhaps the Dharma more of the higher classes than of the people in general, rendered the position of the wife difficult and sometimes less than real. When, like queen Dhāriṇī, she finds herself treated by her husband with scant grace and deserted for a younger rival, it becomes useless for her to show her temper and jealousy like Irāvatī; she can, if she is shrewd and discreet, only say pathetically : *na me eso maccharassa kālo* ('this is not for me a time for jealousy'), and all that is possible for her to do is to make the best of a bad job by falling back upon her own sense of dignity and pride. The author of the *Mṛcchakaṭika* discreetly keeps Cārudatta's wife in the background ; on the very rare occasions in which she does appear, we have just a sad and dignified picture, in which her gentleness and generosity are not feigned indeed but are apparently virtues made of helpless necessity.

It is natural, therefore, that even from antiquity Indian opinion represents the god of love as different from the deities who preside over marriage and fertility. No doubt, restrictions placed on the physical gratification of love, except in marriage, are due not only to moral and social necessity, but they also indicate a tendency which harmonises with the biological law that mating is the final cause of love. But in a society where mating was also a religious duty and where conjugal relation was moulded by a peculiar social evolution, an errant tendency was inevitable ; and many writers have not hesitated to express a startlingly heterodox view. There are indeed genuine praises of the wife, but one poet, for instance, represents married life as a prison-house, and the usual note is that of the glorification of the love-union permitted by Kāma-śāstra. It is not difficult to understand a similar attitude, occasionally, on the part of the wife. Apart from the numberless tales of naughty and cunning wife's intrigues in Sanskrit folk-tale, a more refined sentiment is expressed by one woman-poet who is impatient with the perfect spouse, who has all the virtues of a stage-hero, but none of a lover, which alone can make her happiness perfect. Free and continuous courtship is thus recognised as a stimulus of permanent love. Married love can remain unspoiled by time and familiarity and retain its romance and beauty only where there is enough of that idealism which can make such continuous courtship possible and redeem it from the debasing contact of the littleness of life's daily experience. In such a discouraging atmosphere, where the tendency to take the marriage-vow lightly was not uncommon, Bhavabhūti had the courage to represent conjugal love as a serious and abiding human passion, as a blend of sex-feeling, parent-feeling and comradeship, or as expressed in the words of the wise Kāmandakī (vi.) : "Know, my dear children, that to a wife her husband and to a husband his lawful wife, are, each to each, the dearest of friends, the sum-total of relationships, the completeness of desire, the perfection of treasures, even life itself." The implications, both real and ideal, of such love, are best brought out, in the idea of our poet, not by an invented plot, nor by a story based on the narrow realism of actual life, but by the idealism, pathos and poetry of an intensely human legend of the past, round which a hundred romantic associations have already gathered.

Bhavabhūti's Rāma and Sītā are from the beginning man and woman of more strenuous and deeper experience than Duṣyanta and his woodland love. In the opening act, which has been praised so often and which strikes the keynote of the drama, the newly crowned king of Ayodhyā with his beloved spouse and his ever faithful brother is looking over pictures which recall the dear memory of their past sorrow. This scene, which is made the occasion for the tender and deep attachment of Rāma and Sītā to show itself, also heightens by contrast the grief of separation which immediately follows. There is a fine note of tragic irony not only in Rāma's assurance that such a separation as they had suffered would never happen again, in Lakṣmaṇa's inadvertent allusion to the fire-ordeal and Rāma's instant declaration of his disbelief in baseless rumours, but also in Sītā's passionate clinging to the memories of past joy and sorrow on the verge of a still more cruel fate. The blow comes just at a moment when the tired, timid and confiding Sītā falls asleep on the arms of her husband, who is lost in his own thoughts of love. When the cup of happiness, full to the brim, was raised to his lips it was dashed off from Rāma's hand ; and one can understand the sentimental breakdown which immediately follows in the conflict between his love and his stern sense of kingly duty. With the responsibilites of the state newly laid on his shoulders, Rāma is perhaps more self-exacting than is right or just to himself and his beloved ; but having abandoned the faithful and dear wife, who was his constant companion ever since childhood, his suffering knows no bounds. Both his royal and personal pride is deeply wounded by the thought that such an unthinkable stain should attach to the purity of his great love and to the purity of the royal name he bears.

The scene of the next two acts is laid in the old familiar surroundings of Daṇḍaka and Pañcavaṭī, which Rāma revisits. Twelve years have elapsed ; his grief has mellowed down ; but he is still loyal and devoted to the memory of his banished wife. The sorrow, which has become deep-seated, is made alive with the recollection of their early experience of married love in these forests, where even in exile they had been happy. The situation is dramatically heightened by making the pale, sorrowing but resigned Sītā appear in a spirit-form, unseen by mortals, and become an unwilling, but happy, listener to the confessions which her husband makes unknowingly to Vāsantī of his great love and fidelity. Sītā's resentment is real and reasonable, and she is still mystified as to why Rāma abandoned her. She comes on the scene with despair and resignation in her heart, but it is not for her to sit in judgment on his conduct. She appears as the true woman and loving wife which she has not ceased to be, and is willing to be convinced. Unknown to each other, the reconciliation of hearts is now complete ; and with an admirable delicay of touch the dramatist describes her gradual, but generous, surrender to the proof that, though harsh, he deeply loves her and has suffered no less. When Vāsantī, who cannot yet take kindly to Rāma, reproves him on his heartless act to his wife in a half-finished, but bitter, speech (iii. 26) and denounces him in her righteous wrath, her pitiless words aggravate his grief ; but the unseen Sītā, with a characteristic want of logic but with the true instinct of a loving heart, now defends her husband and resents all disparagement from outside. The denouement of reunion is only a logical development of this scene ; and the recognition scene in act iv in which Bhavabhūti, like Kālidāsa, represents the offspring as the crown of wedded love, forms a natural psychological climax. By removing the inevitable tragedy of the original story, Bhavabhūti runs the risk of weakening the artistic effect of his drama, but the denouement of happy ending is not here a mere observance of convention, brought about in a forced way. It is naturally developed by rehandling the entire theme and creating new situations, and no other conclusion is possible from the poet's skilful readjustment of motives and incidents. It is a drama in which the tragic climax occurs, with the sorrow and separation at the beginning ; and it requires a considerable mastery of the dramatic art to convert it from a real tragedy into a real comedy of happiness and reunion. It cannot be said that Bhavabhūti does not succeed.

Bhavabhūti praises himself for his "mastery of speech', and claims merit for felicity and richness of expression as well as for depth of meaning ; and the praise that he arrogates for himself is not undeserved. The qualities in which he excels are his power of vivid and often rugged, or even grotesque, description, the nobility and earnestness of his conception, a genuine emotional tone, and a love for all that is deep and poignant, as well as grand and awe-inspiring, in life and nature. Contrasted with Kālidāsa, however, he lacks polish and fastidious technical finish : but, as we have already said, his tendency was not towards the ornate and the finical but towards the grotesque and the rugged, not towards reserve but towards abandon. This would explain, to a certain extent, why his so-called dramas are in reality dramatic poems, and his plot is, at least in his earlier plays, a string of incidents or pictures without any real unity. Bhavabhūti cannot write in the lighter vein, but takes his subject too seriously ; he has no humour, but enough of dramatic irony ; he can hardly attain perfect artistic aloofness, but too often merges himself in his subject ; he has more feeling than real poetry.

His *Uttara-rāma-carita* shows indeed considerable dramatic skill, but it appeals more as an exceedingly human story of love and suffering, steeped in the charm of poetry and sentiment. It is chiefly in this that its merit lies. The story is drawn from the Epic, but the picture is far more homely, far more real ; the emotion is far more earnest than is usual in Sanskrit love-poetry. Bhavabhūti is not concerned with romantic and light-hearted intrigues, nor does his theme, in spite of the introduction of the supernatural, consist of the treatment of a legendary subject, removed from the reality of common experience. His delineation of love as an emotion is finely spiritual and yet intensely human. His descriptions are marked by an extraoridinary realism of sensation and vividness of touch. While preserving the essential ideality of a theme, which was cherished through ages as an elevated conception, he invests it with a higher poetical naturalness, based on the genuine emotions of common manhood and womanhood. In this he vies successfully with Kālidāsa.

It is natural, therefore, that in Indian estimation Bhavabhūti should rank next to Kālidāsa as a poet, if not as a dramatist. To be judged by this lofty standard is itself a virtual acknowledgment of high merit ; and it is not an altogether unjust praise. Bhavabhūti's shortcomings are those of an exuberant poetic mind, lacking the much-desired restraint of an artist, and they are manifest on the surface ; but he has excellences which place him very high. As a dramatist he does not certainly lack power, but perhaps he is not as successful as Kālidāsa, much less than Śūdraka or Viśākhadatta. His tendency to exaggerate, to strain deliberately after effect and accumulate series of them, to indulge in sentimental prolixity, to take things too earnestly and identify himself with them, are faults which are fatal to a good dramatist. His lack of humour, which is partially responsible for these aberrations, does not indicate a disorganised mind, but it is perhaps a temperamental insufficiency, which makes his mind too elevated and inelastic to appreciate fully the lighter side of life and embrace in broad and sparkling sympathy all kinds of men and things. He is too profoundly interested in his characters and their sentiments to care for action as such. In a narrative we are told what occurs, in a drama we see the actual occurrence ; in Bhavabhūti's plays, comparatively little happens, though much is said. And yet he does not excel in mere narrative. His genius is lyrical, implying a development of feeling and reflection at the expense of action ; it is too often so in principle, even when it is not so in form. He cannot project himself properly into his characters ; he is too personal to be entirely self-effacing, too impetuous to be smooth and even. Bhavabhūti is indeed not a shadowy figure, but lives vividly in his works ; he is one of the few charmingly egoistic poets in Sanskrit, who seldom loses sight of himself, but permeates his writings (even though they are dramas) with the flavour of a rugged but lovable personality. It is not surprising, therefore that his emotions carry him away, often further than the limits of art. His sentiment becomes sentimentality, and his pathos the spectacular sensibility of the man of feeling rather than the poignant rush of tragic sorrow. He is a master of aggravated pathos rather than of heroic agony. He does not condense a world of emotion in one terse pregnant phrase of concentrated passion, but dilutes the strength of the poetic nucleus by diffusing it into graceful and sonorous periods. Perhaps popular taste did not disapprove of such naked wallowing in the pathetic ; and very few Sanskrit poets, in accordance with the accepted theory of sentiment, would resist the opportunity of a free outpouring in sentimental verse and prose. But these are not mere concessions to the groundlings, nor is theory not emphatic in the sound view that sentiments should be suggested rather than expressed. The unauthorised practice of wordy emphasis springs rather from an excess of sensibility inherent in Bhavabhūti's poetic imagination, whiah is never tired by unchartered freedom. Leaving aside his Mādhava, even his Rāma's prolonged lamentations, tears and faintings, however poetic, are overdone and become undignified.

There can be no denying these facts, which are obvious even to a superficial reader of Bhavabhūti's plays. Bhavabhūti is fortunate in having good editors and apologists.—the kindred spirits for whom he cried in his life-time ; but his merits are also too obvious to require a justification of his demerits. It is not of much consequence if his dramas, judged by a strict standard, are really dramatic poems ; it is the type in which Bhavabhūti excels, and he should be judged by what he actually aims at and achieves. Other dramatists may exhibit a greater degree of some characteristic quality, but it is scarcely too much to say that none among the successors of Kālidāsa surpasses Bhavabhūti in pure poetry. It is not necessary to prove it by quoting instances of his mastery of poetical imagery, thought and expression in every variety of melting modulation or sounding pomp ; the spirit of poetry, quite indefinable but easily perceivable, pervades all his writings in their theme and treatment, and more especially, in the charming series of lyric stanzas which Bhavabhūti alone could write. If he is a poet of human passion, having a strong perception of the nobility of human character and its deeply felt impulses and emotions, he is no less a lover of the overwhelming grandeur of nature, enthroned in the solitude of dense forests, sounding cataracts and lofty mountains. It is not often that his passionate humanism and naturalism yield to mere academicism. If he expresses his sensations with a painful and disturbing intensity[1] and often

1 In his description of primal sensations Bhavabhūti is as often direct as he is uncouth, but terribly appropriate, in his selection of words. The word *grāvan*, for instance, in his famous line, describing Rāma's poignant sorrow (*Uttara*° i. 28), is not dainty like Kālidāsa's *upala*, but it cannot be substituted for a weaker word. His jagged description of the Daṇḍaka forest, though often bizarre and even grotesque, can be contrasted in this respect to the refined charm of Kālidāsa's pictures of nature. Bhavabhūti is one of the few Sanskrit poets who can describe a sensation in its intense vividness, without investing it with an ideal glamour or domesticating it. Witness, for instance, his description of the sensation of touch in *Uttara*° i. 35, *Mālatī*° vi. 12 and *Mahāvīra*° ii. 22. He is not gross nor sensual, but it is not correct to say that his ideas and objects are spiritually rarefied ; on the

strays into the rugged and the formless (or, shall we say, evolves his own form of art and expression ?), he thereby drinks deep at the very fountain of life ; he realises the man's joy, even he loses the artist's serenity. His unevenness and inequality, even his verbosity and slovenliness, are thus explicable. Bhavabhūti suffers from the excess of his qualities, but the qualities are those of a great, but powerfully sensitive, poetic mind. His contemporaries called him Śrīkaṇṭha "Divine Throat", perhaps in homage to his divine music ; but since it is also the name of the rugged and powerful deity, who swallowed poison in lieu of nectar, the epithet is justified by Bhavabhūti's mastery of overmastering passion, by his nervous energy and terrible sincerity, which scorn mere polish and finish, but speak, with palpitating warmth, of things lying at the very core of his being.

g. *Yaśovarman, Māyurāja and Others*

The *Mallikā-māruta,*[1] a Prakaraṇa in ten acts, was at one time ascribed to Daṇḍin, but it is now known to be the work of Uddaṇḍin or Uddaṇḍanātha, who was patronised by the Zamorin Mānavikrama of Calicut (Kukkuṭakroḍa) at about the middle of the 17th century. A poor imitation of *Mālatī-mādhava,* it describes the love of Mallikā, daughter of a Vidyādhara king, and Māruta, a Kuntala prince, with the subsidiary episode of the love of his friend Kalakaṇṭha and her maid Ramayantikā ; it has also a female magician Mandākinī, two escapes from mad elephants and two abductions. To Bāṇa is sometimes attributed a drama of little merit, entitled *Parvatī-pariṇaya*[2] in five acts,

contrary, the touch of sensuousness is too warmly conspicuous to be ignored. The comparison with sublimely academic Milton and the coldly polished Thomas Gray, suggested by Lanman, is barely justifiable.

1 Ed. Jivananda Vidyasagar, with comm. of Raṅganātha, Calcutta 1878. See Pischel, introd. to *Śṛṅgāra-tilaka,* p. 10 ; S. Kuppusvami, *Descript. Cat. Madras Govt. Orient. Library,* vol. xxi, Madras 1918, No. 12580.

2 Printed many times, *e.g.* by M. R. Telang, NSP, Bombay 1892, 1911 ; by T. R. Ratnam Aiyar, Madras 1898 ; by R. V. Krishnamachariar, Śrī-Vāṇī-Vilāsa Press, Srirangam 1906 : by R. Schmidt, Leipzig 1917. For bibliography, see Sten Konow, p. 105, note. On the

which has a theme similar to (or, one might say, which is an undramatic dramatisation of) that of the *Kumāra-saṃbhava* ; but it is really the work of a comparatively modern Abhinava Bāṇa, named Vāmana Bhaṭṭa Bāṇa, who was a court-poet of the Reḍḍi prince Vema of Koṇḍviḍu at the end of the 14th and the beginning of the 15th century, and who also wrote a small but highly erotic Bhāṇa entitled *Śṛṅgāra-bhūṣaṇa.*[1] Of the lost drama, *Mukuṭa-tāḍitaka,* cited and ascribed to Bāṇa by Bhoja in his *Śṛṅgāra-prakāśa*[2] and by Caṇḍapāla in his commentary on the *Nala-campū,*[3] nothing is known, except that the drama apparently dealt with the Mahābhārata episode of Bhīma's fight with Duryodhana. Another drama, called *Śārada-candrikā,* by Bāṇa is known only by Śāradātanaya's reference in his *Bhāvaprakśa.*[4]

Yaśovarman, king of Kānyakubja, who is mentioned by Kahlaṇa as a patron of Bhavabhūti and Vākpatirāja, was the author of a lost Nāṭaka, entitled *Rāmābhyudaya,* which is cited by Ānandavardhana,[5] and which, according to Śāradā-

work and the author, see K. T. Telang in *IA*, III, 1874, p. 219 f ; K. Glaser, *Über Bāṇas, Pārvatīpariṇaya-nāṭaka, SWA* 1883 (reprint, Wien 1883), gives the text in Roman, as in Bombay, ed., but badly edited ; R. Schmidt in *IA*, XXXV, 1906, p. 215 f.

1 Ed. Sivada and Parab, NSP, Bombay, 1896, 1910.

2 See S. K. De in *BSOS*, IV, 1926, p. 282.

3 Keith, *SD*, p. 182, note 3.

4 Ed. Gaekwad's Orient. Ser., p. 252 ; It is surmised that the plot of this play referred to Bāṇa's story of Candrāpīḍa's death and revival. In this connexion it is noteworthy that commenting on an erotic stanza, ascribed to Bāṇa, Kṣemendra in his *Aucitya-vicāra*° (*ad,* śl. 14), thinks that the stanza in question describes the Viraha of Kādambarī ; but it does not occur in Bāṇa's romance. Considering the fact that Bāna never lived to finish his romance, it is very unlikely that he wrote either a dramatic or metrical version of the story, especially because the revival of Candrāpīḍa is not an item in Bāṇa's portion of the romance. A large number of verses, untraceable in Bāṇa's known works, are cited in the anthologies (see Thomas, *Kvs,* pp. 55-59) : but no safe conclusion is possible from them regarding his authorship of other works ; and some of the stanzas might belong to Abhinava Bāṇas of later times.

5 *Dhvanyāloka,* ed. NSP, Bombay 1911, pp. 133, 148 (name of the author given by Abhinavagupta). The play is also cited in the *Daśarūpaka* (ed. NSP, Bombay, 1917), i. 46 ; in the *Nāṭyadarpaṇa* (ed. Gaekwad's Orient. Series, Baroda 1929), pp. 45, 56, 72-91, 95 109, 116, 144, 158 (the references are to different acts) ; in *Nāṭaka-lakṣaṇa-ratna-kośa* (ed. M. Dillon, Oxford Univ. Press, 1933), pp. 33, 130, as well as in Bhoja's *Śṛṅgāra*° (*BSOS,* IV. 1926, p. 282).

tanaya, consisted of six acts. Some of the large number of quotations found under Yaśovarman's name in the anthological and rhetorical literature[1] probably belonged to this drama, which presumably dealt with the entire Rāmāyaṇa story.[2]

Of Māyurāja, author of another lost Rāma-drama, named *Udātta-rāghava*, we have no information ; but his work is cited five times in the *Daśarūpaka*[3] and is known earlier to Abhinavagupta[4] and Kuntaka.[5] One of the eulogistic verses of Rājaśekhara, given in the *Sūkti-muktāvalī* of Jahlaṇa (iv. 82),[6] speaks of Māyurāja as a Kalacuri poet, but since our knowledge of the Kalacuri dynasty of this period is meagre, the poet, if he was a Kalacuri prince, cannot be identified.

Anaṇgaharṣa Mātrarāja,[7] son of king Narendravardhana, is more fortunate in the fact that his drama, *Tāpasa-vatsarāja-carita*,[8] has survived in a unique Śāradā manuscript. Nothing is known of him, but his work offers in six acts a variation of the theme of the *Svapna-vāsavadatta* by making Udayana, king of Vatsa, turn into an almost demented ascetic out of grief for his queen's alleged death, while Yaugandharāyaṇa succeeds by a ruse to marry the king of Padmāvatī who is enamoured of Udayana from a portrait. The reunion with Vāsavadattā, who also turns

1 See Thomas, *Kvs*, pp. 75-76, and references cited therein.

2 For a conjectural summary of the plot of this play from later citations, see R. Ramamurthi in *Jour. Orient. Research*, Madras, III, 1929, pp. 268-72.

3 ii. 58 ; iii. 3, 24 (with name of the author) ; iv. 13, 28.

4 In his commentary on Bharata, ch. xix.

5 Ed. S. K. De, Calcutta 1928, pp. 225, 254 (author's name not given).

6 Two of Māyurāja's verses are also quoted in this anthology (90. 10 ; 92.5). The *Nāṭya-darpaṇa* also quotes this work thrice (pp. 66, 116, 194) without the name of the author. The Kulapatyaṅka, cited several times in the *Nāṭaka-ratna-kośa*, probably refers to an act of this drama in which the abduction of Sītā occurs. It appears from these and other citations that Māyurāja made certain modifications in the original Rāmāyaṇa story by making Lakṣmaṇa pursue the golden deer and Rāma follow him later, and by eliminating, after Bhavabhūti, the element of treachery in the slaying of Vālin.

7 There is no authority for identitifying him with Māyurāja ; see S. K. De in *JRAS*, 1924, p. 664.

8 Ed. Yadugiri Yatiraja, Bangalore 1928, from the Berlin manuscript of the play Weber, No. 2166, which is described and quoted by Hultzsch in *Nachrichten d. Göttingischen Gesselschaft*, 1886, p. 224 f.

into a Parivrājikā, occurs at Prayāga at a melodramatic moment when the king and Vāsavadattā, both tired of life, are about to commit suicide. The play has some real poetry and pathos, with a great deal of lamentation in elegant and touching verses, clearly after *Vikramorvaśīya* ; but there is hardly any action or any convincing characterisation. The work is known to Ānanda vardhana and Abhinavagupta,[1] as well as to Kuntaka,[2] and there can be no doubt that it belongs to a period earlier than the middle of the 9th century[3]

Both Abhinavagupta[4] and Kuntaka mention and quote from a large number of lost dramas, which are of unknown date and mostly of unknown authorship, but which, being cited by them, presumably belongs to this period. They are : *Chalita-rāma, Kṛtyārāvaṇa, Māyā-puṣpaka* (all three Rāma-dramas), *Pratimā-niruddha* (ascribed by *Nāṭya-darpaṇa* to Vasunāga, son of Bhīmadeva), *Pāṇḍavānanda,*—all Nāṭakas, and a Prakarna called *Puṣpa-dūṣitaka* (or °*bhūṣitaka*).[5] To this list may be added the following plays mentioned by Abhinavagupta alone : *Pratijñā-*

1 In this *Locana* and his commentary on Bharata Ānandavardhana quotes anonymously (p. 131) *utkampinī bhayā*° from iii. 16. Also cited by Bhoja in *Śṛṅgāra*°. The qutations are fully traced in the edition mentioned above.

2 Kuntaka quotes, without naming the author, from acts ii (pp. 151-52), iii-iv (pp. 229-30). The play is also cited extensively in the *Nāṭya-darpaṇa*, pp. 30, 34, 43, 66, 67, 100, 106, 107.

3 A *Manoramā-vatsarāja* by Bhīmaṭa is also cited in the *Nāṭya-darpaṇa* (p. 144). We know that Manoramā is a handmaid of Priyadarśikā in Harṣa's drama ; does this play deal with another amour of Udayana with her ? Another work of Bhīmaṭa, named *Svapana-daśānana*, is mentioned by Bhoja and Rājaśekhara, the later describing Bhīmaṭa as Kaliñjara-pati and author of five plays ; see Sten Konow, p. 87, Keith, *SD*, p. 239. He may or may not be identical with Bhima, author of *Pratjñā-cāṇakya*. The *Vīṇā-vāsavadatta* (ed. Kuppusvami Sastri and C. Kunhan Raja, Madras 1931), which is an incomplete anonymous play breaking off at the beginning of the fourth act, resembles the Bhāsa plays, and appears to be another version of the *Pratijñā*° theme, in which the ruse of elephant, imprisonment of Udayana and music-lession on the Vīṇā to Vāsavadattā are utilised as important incidents. It is suggested that this play is identical with the lost *Unmāda-vāsavadatta* of Śaktibhadra, but this is of course an unsupported conjecture.

4 In his commentary on Bharata.

5 All these works are cited in the *Daśarūpaka* (excepting *Māyāpuṣpaka*) and in the *Nāṭya-darpaṇa*.

cāṇakya (ascribed to Bhīma),[1] two lyrical or musical plays, named respectively *Cūḍāmaṇi* and *Guṇamālā*, (both Dombikā), as well as *Devī-candragupta* and *Abhisārikā-vañcitaka* (both Nāṭakas) which we have already mentioned. The *Daśarūpaka* adds another play of unknown authorship, named *Taraṅgadatta*,[2] probably a Prakaraṇa, which has a courtesan as a heroine and which was apparently modelled on Śūdraka's play. The *Nāṭya-darpaṇa* which cites most of these works, further mentions another play, which probably belongs to the 9th century, namely, a Prakaraṇa, called *Citrotpalālambitaka*, assigned to Amātya Śaṅkuka, apparently the Śaṅkuka who belonged to the time of Ajitāpīḍa of Kashmir.[3] The meagre citations do not, unfortunately, give us an adequate idea of these unrecovered plays, but their popularity is indicated by the large number of references in dramaturgic treatises. Some information, however, is available about the plot of the oft-quoted *Puṣpa-dūṣitaka*, mentioned above, from the accounts given by Kuntaka and by the authors of the *Nāṭyadarpaṇa*.[4] A Prakaraṇa in six acts, it had for its theme the lovestory of a merchant Samudradatta and Nandayantī, which involved their secret marriage, opposition from Samudradatta's father Sāgaradatta, her pregnancy, suspicion of her chastity, and the final reunion of the lovers by means of a ring of recognition and by the identification of the constellation under which their child wss born.

The *Āścarya-cūḍāmaṇi* of Śaktibhadra[5] is claimed to be the oldest South Indian play (the author having declared in the

1 See R. Ramamurthi in *Jour. Orient. Research*, III, 1929, pp. 80-89. It appears to have een written to emulate Viśākhadatta's work.

Also quoted by Bhoja and Śāradātanaya.

The *Nāṭya-darpaṇa* also cites a *Abhinava-rāghava* of Kṣīrasvāmin, pupil of Bhaṭṭendurāja, who was Abhinavagupta's Guru ; but this work obviously belongs to the end of the 10th century.

4 See pp. 226, 236, 243. See R. Ramamurthy in *JOR*, Madras, IV, 1930, pp. 78-81.

5 Ed. C. Sankaraja Sastri, with introd. by Kuppusvami Sastri, Bālamanorama Press Madras 1926 ; Eng. trs. by the same editor, 1927 separately. It has been claimed that the *Abhiṣeka* and the *Pratimā* were also written by Śaktibhadra, and that the *Unmādavāsavadatta*, mentioned by Śaktibhadra himself as another work of his, is the same work as the *Pratijñā*. ! But these suggestions lack proof.

Prologue that he belonged to Dakṣiṇāpatha), and is assigned, not on very adequate grounds, to the 9th century. It dramatises, in seven acts, the story of the *Rāmāyaṇa*, and betrays knowledge of Bhavabhūti's plays. Although it contains some fine stanzas and good prose, it is poorly executed as a drama, and there is nothing remarkable in it except the prettydevice, from which the play takes its name, of the magic crest-jewel of Sītā as a token of recognition. The first two acts deal with the Śūrpaṇakhā episode in the forest as one of the motives of the feud ; the third and fourth, with Sītā's abduction by Rāvaṇa approaching in the magic disguise of Rāma ; the fifth, with Rāvaṇa's love-making to Sītā interrupted by Mandodarī ; the sixth, with the embassy of Hanūmat who presents to Sītā the miraculous ring of Rāma for recognition, and returns with the marvellous crest-jewel of Sītā as a token ; and the last act winds up with the fire-ordeal. The incident of the crest-jewel and magic-ring, which is mentioned for the first time in act iii and utilised in act vi, is of course suggested by Vālmīki's Cūḍāmaṇi and Aṅgulīyaka, but it is employed as a mere device and is neither the central motive nor a dramatically effective idea. The play contains some fine verses, but it is really a series of narrative episodes, with some inventiveness (as for instance, Rāvaṇa's disguise as Rāma, but it is perhaps suggested by Bhavabhūti's Śūrpaṇakhā disguised as Mantharā), and with a slight dramatic unity of action, derived from Bhavabhūti's idea of a central feud between Rāvaṇa and Rāma.

CHAPTER VI

THE LATER DECADENT POETRY AND PROSE

1. General Characteristics

As a term of popular criticism, the epithet 'decadent' would at first sight appear too vague and facile to be applied to a literature which extends over several centuries and comprises abundance and variety of talent and effort ; but when we consider the strange combination of elaborate pains and insufficient accomplishment of interminable prolixity and endless dreariness, characterising the poetical and dramatic literature which was produced from the 10th century onwards, the appropriateness of the description will be obvious. It is true that no strict theory of evolution is applicable to literature, and that occasional burst of individual excellence upsets all complacent labelling ; but there can be no doubt that in the period we are considering the truly creative epoch of Sanskrit literature had exhausted itself ; and there was no ability to rise to a new form of art, no turning point, nor any return to the earlier manner of the great poets. The entire literature was imitative and reproductive ; and even if some brilliant flashes are perceptible here and there, the general characteristics are so even and uniform that there is hardly any breach of continuity in its monotonously long course of history. The poets of the period suggest facility rather than inspiration, subtlety rather than judgment, immense and varied learning rather than vigour and versatility of spontaneous power. With all their inherited affluence and inborn talent for elaborate composition, the greatest of them is scarcely a poet at all, but a consummate versifier, who sums up all the traditions of poetic art that can be learned by clever artisan. If there is no innovation, there is also no adaptability of old-world art to new-world usage. What was once living and organic becomes mechanical and fossilised. All this means not progress, but decided decline, or at least stagnation, in which the shallow streams of poetic fancy move sluggishly within the confines of conventional matter and manner.

This is nowhere so evident in this period as in the cultivation of the Mahākāvya, the so-called great poem, which makes no attempt to escape from its stiff limitations, but contents itself with a cotinuation of the established tradition. The moulder of its form and spirit is not Kālidāsa but his stalwart successors, among whom Bhaṭṭi and Māgha appear to have wielded the greatest influence. The admiration for Kālidāsa is doubtless unfeigned, but the failure to take him as a model arose from an incapacity to comprehend his spirit. Bhāravi had certainly vigour and variety, but he was, in the opinion of later generations, entirely eclipsed by Māgha, while Kumāradāsa's mediocre attempt to reproduce Kālidāsa's simpler method produced little impression. Bhaṭṭi and Māgha, therefore, were preferred by authors of laborious talents as models of imitative literary exercises ; for here it was possible to make up by learning and rhetoric what was lacking in passion and poetry On the one hand, the work of Bhaṭṭi became the precursor of some marvellous triumphs of literary ingenuity, Māgha's poem, on the other, started a long series of artificially sustained compositions, which seldom went beyond the stereotyped form, theme, manner and method, and included all the customary appendages and embellishments. No one would deny that Māgha was a poet, but very few would assert that he was one of the greatest kind ; and yet he became practically the sole arbiter of poetic taste to later generations. This was possible because the standard of verse-making, which he brought into vogue, confirmed the tendency to limit poetry to prescribed and prescribable form, to abstention as much as possible from what is individual and conformation to what is conventional. On the positive side of his excellence, Māgha himself was indebted to this process of conscious or unconsious conventionalising, which he brought to its acme and which all his successors adored. But while Māgha was a poet, not many of his successors were ; they had his qualities without his genius, his defects without the power of redeeming them. The fine sense of restraint and balance which we find in Kālidāsa is something quite different from the new standard of erudite correctness and massive craftsmanship, in which hardly any one can be put above Māgha, but which, up to a point, can be acquired and applied by labour and dexterity.

The tendency to uniformity and consequent monotony is also perceptible, though in a less obvious degree, in the shorter poems of this period. Perhaps in no other sphere than that of erotic poetry there is greater opportunity for individual variation, but the convention established by Amaru and Bhartṛhari is seldom overstepped. One comes across almost invariable touches of consummate elegance and occasional freshness of conception and execution, to which the large number of erotic stanzas quoted in the Anthologies bear witness ; but the elegance is often the product of mechanical adroitness, and refined ingenuity replaces spontaneity of poetic inspiration. In the Stotra literature of this period there is perhaps greater personal element, which inspires more impressive devotional fervour, but in course of time this type of composition also becomes, like erotic poety, decrepit and confined to the narrow limits of standardised topic, mood and phraseology. The small body again of didactic and satiric writing, which presents wise and earnest reflections or mocking arabesques of men and manners, has a piquancy of its own ; but here also the earlier models are too slavishly followed, and the descriptions and reflections are of a too broad and obvious character. A new field of poetic adventure is afforded by the opportunities of historical themes, but the method is too favourable to rhetoric not to be perilous to history. There are also a few Prose Kāvyas, but Bāṇabhaṭṭa had set an example too dangerous for smaller men, while the Campū, as an off-shoot of the Prose Kāvya, is late, secondary and incompetent. The fact that outside exegetical and scholastic writings this period cannot show much prose and that the small amount of literary prose that it can show is not of much consequence, would of itself indicate the poverty of the literature in one of its important aspects. A greater interest, therefore, attaches to the prose story-books, which show some sense of the value of a straightforward style, rare in the studied masterpieces of the Prose Kāvya and the Campū; but the collections, though always amusing, are often pedestrian and sometimes unredeemingly gross, and they seldom pass beyond conventional assumptions to an original or superior vein of literature.

It is evident that one of the outstanding features of the poetical literature of this period in almost all its branches is its extraordinary lack of originality and independence. The writers are undoubtedly gifted with considerable literary skill, but they are capable masters, as well as unfortunate victims, of a rigid convention. The convention believed that the general alone was orthodox, and that there was no room for the individual; in practice, it led to a standardisation of idea and expression, of form and theme. On the positive side, it aimed at a well-informed utilisation of accumulated experience and experiment, at the achievement of order, regularity and correctness in accordance with fixed principles and patterns, at the establishment of a kind of literary etiquette regarding what to say and how to say it, and at the stabilising of a poetic diction as the proper uniform of poetry. Once we accept the scheme and the standard, there is much excellent writing in this period, if not much excellent literature. Within his limits, the author is a master of his craft; if he does not betray any knowledge of other modes and ideals, he never stumbles in regard to his own mode and ideal, for which no labour is too arduous for him, no ingenuity too refined; moments of greatness are rare, but there is nothing slipshod or slovenly; and above all, he has that indescribable but real quality called breeding.

The works of the period, therefore, are based upon solid and extensive acquirements; they are careful and sustained products of an urbane and highly cultured poetic art. The poets have no hesitation to treat the most worn-out and commonplace subjects on the tenaciously conservative plan and procedure; but in the extraordinary command of a rich and recondite vocabulary, in the grace and fluency of phrasing, in the painful accuracy of grammatical forms, in the elaborate adjustment of sonorous sound and sense, in the skilled use of difficult and diverse metres, in the ingenuity of wielding a weighty, ornamented and complex diction, their achievements possess a degree of massively and mechanically polished efficiency which is indeed astonishing. The process is lower but surer; it cannot attain pinnacles nor plumb profundities, but it can float on a conscientious level of equable and pleasant accomplishment. In no other period, and perhaps in no other literature, we have such a large number of productions, ranging over many centuries, which may not have given us poetry of the right kind, but which are perfect triumphs of poetic artifice in its best and worst senses. For bulk of work, unfailing workmanship and general competence, it is impossible to ignore them entirely, but it is also impossible to admire them heartily.

But whatever we may in our day think of it, the literature itself never shows any dissatisfaction with the fetters and limitations that it creates for itself, nor is its audience ever puzzled or repelled by them. There is always a complete agreement and understanding between the poets and their admirers, involving a perfect accommodation of the works to the standard of excellence demanded and the mental attitude or aptitude of their readers. Otherwise, the vast and contented multiplication, with only small variations, of the same types of composition for several centuries would not be intelligible. That the claims of most of these writers to the name of poet could be disputed probably never entered into their own conscience, nor into the head of their admiring contemporaries and imitators; but when one considers the question absolutely, and not with reference to particular conditions, one cannot fail to recognise that this literature seldom possesses the freedom which emphasises creative imagination and aims at achieving anything other than what accepted tradition approves. The literature will never lack its fit readers, though few, but it will never have any wide appeal.

For, all this means an attempt to mechanise an activity of the human mind which refuses to be mechanised, to reduce to norms and categories what can never be normal and categorical, to immobilise the mobile by throwing a bridle on the neck of Pegasus. That the art of poetry could be systematised, after the method of positive sciences, appears to have been one of the tacitly fundamental postulates of the system of Poetics, which had sprung up in the meantime, and which concerned itself chiefly with a pedagogic and practical exposition of the decorative devices of literary expression. The belief that the explanation of the verbal arrangement was enough for understanding the process of poetic creation led naturally to the formulation of definite canons and conventions for the benefit of the aspiring poets.[1] The rhetorical works, therefore, taught craftsmanship rather than creation, a doctrine of technique rather than free exercise of the poetic imagination, a respect for convention rather than individuality of treatment. Sanskrit Poetics reached the rank of an independent discipline at about the time when Sanskrit poetry itself, in the hands of less imaginative writers, was becoming a highly factitious product of verbal specialists. The Poetics naturally reflected the temper and encouraged the tendency of the poetry. With surprising assiduity and astuteness, it analysed precedents and formulated prescriptions; and in a period in which industry was reckoned higher than inspiration it came to have perforce an authority disproportionate to its importance. Both in theory and practice, therefore, we have a willing and unquestioned

[1] For a discussion of the whole question, see S. K. De, Sanskrit Poetics as a study of Aesthetic in *Dacca University Studies*, Vol. i, pt. 2, p. 83 f.

obedience to modes and models, laws and means, in accordance with a well defined and unalterable norm. The result was, on the one hand, a servere restriction of poetic imagination and expression, but, on the other, a correspondingly high proficiency in the attainment of mechanical excellence. The allied disciplines of Grammar, Lexicology, Erotics and Prosody also brought in their highly refined mass of rules, normatively defined and classified with equally fertile and elaborative acumen. If the poet was not an expert in the long list of sciences and arts prescribed for his mental equipment, he was at least well versed in the technical requirements and conventions of these studies, which were meant to instruct him in the artifices of his craft, in the adroit manufacturing of standardised poetry.

That the poetry of this period should be a product of high cultivation, meant chiefly for a highly cultivated audience, is also a natural corollary of the fact that it flourished in an age in which scholastic cultivation of learning was becoming universal. In almost every branch of knowledge, in the various arts and sciences, the really creative age was almost finished by the 10th century; it was succeeded necessarily by a scholastic stage of critical elaboration, the chief work of which consisted not only in systematising the accumulated stock of dogmas and doctrines but also in making fine and subtle distinctions in matters of detail. It was the age of commentaries and of commentaries on commentaries, of manuals and manuals of manuals. All this, of course, meant spread of learning and intellectual activity, but the learning was circumscribed and unfruitful, and the intellectual activity dissipated itself in elaborate but useless refinements. Under an astonishing mass of curious erudition and endlessly fertile dialectic acumen, there is, generally speaking, very little independent thinking or constructive ability; and the learned distinctions are in most cases trivial niceties which concern accidents rather than essentials. The different systems of speculative thought may now be supposed to have well nigh run their course and attained their natural termination in a stage of uncreative but prolix scholasticism.

In the literature of the period the scholastic tendency reflects itself in the portentuous employment of the intellect to a disproportionate finical end. With the general subsidence of the creative impulse, we have a stage of weighty and ingenious elaboration, made with talent, industry and learning, but with an exaggerated consciousness of art. The influence acted in twofold ways. The range and quality of poetic thought and expression become, on the one hand, extremely limited and studied in having its mechanism ponderously well established, and, on the other, extremely abundant and subtle in working out strange and unnatural variations. Marvellous erudition goes hand in hand with marvellous refining of trivialities. The lost art of an earlier generation is thereby not revived, nor is a new art created out of its ashes; but the accumulated resources become the means of parade and dexterity.

We have thus a class of admirable but secondary writers, in whom intellect and fancy become more powerful than sentiment and imagination, and technical skill and learning get the better of originality of conception and execution. They choose the broad and easy path of mechanical conventionality; and with ready-made words and ideas, forms and themes, it is not difficult to acquire impressive facility and attain respectable workmanship. But the productions become too much alike, being fashioned after the same pattern ; their subjects have too little variety, their treatment fundamentally similar, and their style and diction employ the same commonplaces of words, ideas, epithets and conceits. In order to counteract this monotony, inseparable from working with rigidly similar means and materials, it is inevitable that there should be an oppressive and unnatural display of erudition and technical cleverness. The key-word is grace, of which there is enough, but the word becomes almost synonymous with strained and strange refinements. Instead of reducing the encumbrance of ornament, the quest of the adorned becomes morbid and fanatical, but it is too often in the lower rhetoric that bedizenment is sought. It is not prodigality of beauty but of ingenuity. The poet is always on the watch for unexpected analogies and dexterous turns of expression; he cultivates astoundingly clever manipulation of words, their sound-effects in alliterative jingle and chiming assonance, the multifarious ways of splitting them up for diversity of meaning; an idea is turned to every conceivable distortion; the most far-fetched conceits, which bear the same relation to beautiful ideas as play upon words bear to charming wit, are laboriously discovered; the most obscure recesses of learned or mythological allusions are ransacked. It is needless to comment on this subtle pedantry and appalling taste, which do not wait upon nature but try to anticipate her and thereby defeat themselves. The whole procedure of the decadent poetry bears an analogy to the methods of the scholastic pedagogue, but the effect is one of a conjuror's tricks, astonishing but puerile.

All these excesses betoken the close of the literary age, but the history of Sanskrit poetry does not, curiously enough, close formally with the 10th century. It loses all genuine interest thereafter, but works continued to be produced plentifully and unbrokenly for several centuries. The amazing profusion of production need not surprise us, nor need it prove that the works are not decadent. The volubility of bad poets is a parallel to the prolixity of scholastic pedants. Working on well defined lines and with well established mechanism, it is possible for average ability and industry to multiply the accepted patterns in vast number and imposing magnitude. The quantity here is, therefore, not an index to quality; it is a kind of mass production on a regular scale; and it would be idle to value the products in the higher sphere of poetry. The average poetry may have attained a respectable level, but there is hardly any great poetry. The hundreds of names that range over several centuries include indeed those of some poets who are not yet utterly discrowned, but on their brows, the laurels are thin and brittle; and it is difficult to say if most of them will ever recover much or anything of the great reputation which they long held. New names are also being constantly unearthed by the pious care of assiduous scholars, but it cannot be said that in their totality they add much of real worth to the store of Sanskrit poetry. It is even doubtful if most of the versifying authors who have been 'discovered' really deserve a resurrection from the limbo of oblivion. Amiable antiquarians who have made the attempt have succeeded only in keeping a few names half alive and in securing a limited recognition of the merits of a few others. Even as 'minor' poets they are hardly of much importance. A true minor poet ought to be more than a mere name and to be fairly readable; but few, save scholars, know more than the names (if so much) of these obscure scribblers of the period.

Much of the artificial and recondite tendencies of this literature would have been counteracted had it been popular in the proper sense of the term, or had real contact with life and its realities. But from the very beginning it was sequestered for the study or for cultured society, which was hardly the nourishing soil of human interest and intercourse. It had little, therefore, of the *gaité de cœur*, the bold and joyous popular sentiment, its rough good sense,its simplicity, directness and freedom; the poetry was lofty, exclusive, refined and cultivated. It was composed for an urban and sophisticated audience, and had its own system of phraseology,its own set of ideas and conceits and its own refinement of emotional analysis. It course of time, its stylistic elegancies and sentimental subtleties must have spread down and reached the masses, and there is no reason to suppose that their appreciation was always restricted to a privileged circle. But in the less creative stage, the poetry had less universality of appeal and became more factitious and remote. In receded further from common life and common realities and became almost exclusively a product of artificial and erudite fancy. Its environment, innate characteristics and conditions of growth encouraged, to its extreme limit, a taste which preferred the fantastic and the elaborate to the fervid and the spontaneous. In the cultivation of all that is odd, weighty and elaborate, the poet became indifferent to the natural graces of thought and emotion in their most simple forms, and his subtle and ponderous style ceased to have a really wide appeal.

There may have been in this period a close touch between Sanskrit and Prakrit poetry, but there is no evidence to show that Prakrit poetry, at least in this period, was in any sense popular poetry. As a matter of fact, it was as stilted as Sanskrit, and was doubtless influenced by the same literary tradition. Even in the preceding period, the *Setu-bandha* and the *Gauḍa-vaha* are in no way less artificially constructed than the contemporary Sanskrit Kāvyas, while Rājaśekhara's Prakrit verse and prose in the present period show that they were composed by a poet and for an audience who were both familiar with Sanskrit models. The remark is also applicable, to a certain extent, to the Apabhraṃśa poetry, which was gradually coming into prominence, but which never received as much literary recognition as the Prakrit. Being essentially derivative, neither Prakrit nor Apabhraṃśa poetry proved a solvent for the stiffness and pedantry of Sanskrit poetry, which, on the contrary, reacted upon them and made them share its artificialities. If there existed a popular literature, it was never adequately represented by Prakrit or Apabhraṃśa poetry, nor was its influence palpably perceptible on Sanskrit. Occasionally, here and there, a new trait, like the use of rhyme, emerges; but even rhyme is sparingly used in Sanskrit, only in some Stotras and lyric stanzas. It is not until we come to Jayadeva's *Gīta-govinda* that we find the first positive instance of the reaction of popular literature on Sanskrit and the first successful attempt to rennovate the older form and substance by the absorption of the newer life and spirit. This was indeed not an isolated phenomenon, but the result apparently of a fairly widespread tendency, the importance of which cannot be exaggerated. It did not, however, prove powerful and extensive enough to renew and remodel entirely the declining Sanskrit poetry or save it from its approaching stagnation. It is curious, therefore, that the extreme and affected classicality of Sanskrit poetry and drama continued uninterrupted for a long stretch of centuries, and a true romantic reaction never set in. It is only with the advent of British rule in the 19th century and at the touch of contemporary European literature, that the romantic art came to prevail, not in Sanskrit poetry which was all but dead, but in modern Indian literature, which started vigorously in a new environment and under totally new influences.

There was, thus, in its long course of history from the 10th century onwards, no absorption of new influence nor any attempt to deviate from the beaten track. The average Sanskrit poet could never refuse or defy convention, and there were few rebels among the hundreds of self-satisfied imitators. But the process appears to have commenced even before the 10th century. The poetic convention was not conscious work of a single mind, but it was spread over a long period of time and established by degrees by the influence of several great writers, commencing from Bhaṭṭi and Māgha. Inherent drawbacks in the literature itself, the whole cast of its thought and expression, its general outlook, its monotony of subject, conservative taste and limitation of treatment, its adoption of an affected poetic diction—all these, combined with declining poetic power, which concerned itself more with elaboration than creation, became fatal to the growth of real poetry and indicated that the literature now badly needed a change. Such a change, however, did not come with the Muhammadan occupation of the country, either for better or for worse. Although there is evidence to show that imperial rulers from Akbar to Shah Jahan, as well as local Muslim potentates, were patrons of Sanskrit learning and literature, the equilibrium does not appear to have been much disturbed. It is, therefore, not correct to say that the process of decadence was brought about or hastened by foreign rule and its attendant disturbances, for the seeds of decadence were already there and were germinating for some time. We have seen that the epoch of really great and creative writers had already gone by, and the decline had commenced, not only in literature, but more widely in various branches of Sanskrit learning. The foreign dominion, therefore, was never responsible for the process ; but it must be said that it never brought in its wake any vigorous poetic or dramatic literature, contact with which could have retarded the decline or furnish fresh impetus for revival. If a literaturef, after creating great things in the past, does nothing more of the same kind for several centuries and practically limits itself to the abundant reproduction of laborious trifles, then the conclusion is obvious that it has come to its natural termination ; and it is futile to lay the blame upon external disturbances, which might have seriously affected men's mind, but which never actively discouraged nor caused any paucity of literary production, nor even broke in upon its atmosphere of aloofness from real life.[1]

2. The Mahākāvya

Māgha is the last sturdy figure among the earlier group of Mahākāvya writers ; and he naturally becomes, by his popularity and position, the puissant and glorious founder of the tribe in later times. In accepting his work, as well as that of Bhaṭṭi in some cases, the Mahākāvya does not, however, connect itself with the best and highest tradition ; for there is no return to the earlier and more limpid manner of Aśvaghoṣa and Kālidāsa, whose classic examples never made it feel entitled to emancipate itself from the bondage of an inferior convention. Even Māgha's influence is badly and inadequately represented ; for his obvious

1 The utilisation of Persian literature is late and scanty. The *Kathā-kauntuka* (ed. Sivadatta and K. P. Parab, NSP, Bombay 1901), for instance, of Śrīvara, who flourished in the 15th century and wrote to please his patron Zain-u'l-'Ābidīn of Kashmir, renders into facile Sanskrit the theme of Yūsuf and Zulaikha. The work, in 14 chapters, is composed entirely in Śloka, and is virtually a rendering of Mullā Jāmī Nūr-u'd-dīn's work, for a comparison with which see R. Schmidt, *Das Zathākautukam des Śrīvara vergleichen mit Dschāmī's Jusuf und Kuleikha*, Kiel 1898.

rhetorical mannerisms are reproduced rather than his rare poetic qualities. The Mahākāvya, as an extensive and elevated poetic endeavour, probably came to be regarded as the highest type of composition and as the indispensable test of a great poet. It had a prodigious vogue ; but, notwithstanding high pretensions and conscientious effort, it is perhaps the most laboured and least animated of all the types of poetic composition affected in this period. The works have received praise for their sustained and careful conformity to the recognised standard of erudite fancy and verbal proficiency, but they have deserved censure because they are so obviouly elaborate exercises in metre and language rather than fruits of poetic inspiration. In different circumstances and in other times, the worthy authors might have achieved individuality and distinction, but here they content themselves with a mastery of the conventional style and ignore qualities which we demand of those whom we designate masters.

We have already spoken of the general characteristics and particular tendencies of the Mahākāvya as practised by Kālidāsa's great successors. In this period they are so firmly established by the authority and popularity of these distinguished writers that we find little variation of the general scheme, method, topic and style. As a rigidly fixed type, the Mahākāvya ceases to develop, but there is progressive increase of artificiality and decrease of taste. The theme, placidly accepted from well known legendary sources, are, as before, too slender to support a lofty and extensive poem, and there is no sense of the central story and its regular unfolding. For the human drama it lacks sinew ; it contents itself with romance and fantasy. The prodigality of loosely connected divagations, descriptive. argumentative or erotic, is wearisomely similar in every poem. It hampers, interrupts and buries under its load the inadequate and unsubstantial narrative. but it is a convenient outlet for the exhibition of technical skill and learning. In poetry, there is perhaps nothing wrong if the subject is of little importance, but the treatment in this case is also narrowly conditioned, and the manner displays all the deadly weaknesses of pseudo-classicism, the climax being reached in the childish tricks of the Citra-bandhas, which are repeated in almost unbroken tradition.[1] The poets may be uninspired but they are exceedinly active. They do not know what tedium means ; they can go on weaving hundreds of elaborate stanzas and build up a verbal edifice of magnificence, in which scholarly ingenuity masquerades under the name of poetry and reduces it to a magnificence of futility.

The Mahākāvya writers of this period, therefore, both gain and lose by their chronological position. They find ready to their hands a system of poetic composition, working on well defined lines, and following recognised principles and an established tradition, as well as an audience trained to the manner by a succession of brilliant writers. But with consequent facility and finish of execution, the freedom of conception and treatment is forfeited. There must either be the reproduction, in varied combinations, of stock situations and familiar motives, or the forced invention of strange and unnatural themes ; the one tending to monotonous repetition, the other to unhealthy wildness. With diminishing poetic power and increasing verbal skill, the poets of this period choose the former alternative. If they had not the genius to rise superior to their circumstances and leave the beaten path, they had at least the genius, in a flawed and limited sense, to work out finical variations and produce *tour de force* of considerable rhetorical cunning, if not of poetical brilliance. It is true that all the works cannot be outright condemned, and some of them are curious mosaics of the good and bad of their exemplars ; but the task of sifting much dross to find pure gold may be a delight to the scholar, but hardly repays the trouble of the ordinary reader.

1 The tricks are progressively discredited even by the rhetoricians, although they become the subject, as we shall see, of specialised treatises. As an evidence of the author's extraordinary command over the language, they may be regarded as curiosities, but when an apologist of Sanskrit poetry speaks of them as "giving word-puzzles in a poetic garb," he indulges in an enthusiastic confusion between word-puzzles and poetry !

We have thus in the Mahākāvya of the period industrious monuments of poetic skill, but not much of real poetry. Most of them are hardly human documents; they embody cold and methodical practice in conventional art and artifice. They all think the same thought and speak the same speech. It is difficult to maintain that the passion in these poems is ever genuine, but the poets need not have taken so much pains to cover up whatever trace there is of it under a prodigious amount of pedantry and bad rhetoric. Some of the poems still possess a limited popularity, and can still be declaimed by school-boys; but most of them are hopelessly dead and require little criticism.

A typical instance of the decadent Mahākāvya is furnished by the *Hara vijaya*[1] of the Kashmirian Ratnākara, son of Amṛtabhānu, who flourished under Cippaṭa Jayāpīḍa (832-44 A.D.) and Avantivarman (855-84 A.D.) in a period of considerable literary activity. It is a stupendous work of 50 cantos and 4, 321 verses, but main narrative is extremely scanty, and the interest is made to dissipate itself into a number of subsidiary channels. It relates the story of the slaying by Śiva of the demon Andhaka who, born blind of Śiva himself, regained sight by his austerities and became a menace to the gods. But the author must show his knowledge of polity in eight cantos (ix-xvi) and of erotic practice in another ten or eleven (xvii-xx, xxii-xxviii); the latter digression concerning Śiva's host, who appear to be better lovers than warriors, works out the usual paraphernalia of purely descriptive matter, such as plucking of flowers, sporting in water, sunset, moonrise, stormy sea, pangs of lover's separation, feminine toilet and blandishments, drinking bouts and merriment, love-play, and sunrise! The opening description in six cantos (i-vi) of the city of Śiva, his Tāṇḍava dance, the Seasons, Śiva's capital on Mount Mandara, and praise (in terms of Kashmirian Śaiva philosophy!) and

[1] **Ed. Durgaprasad and K. P. Parab, with comm. of Alaka, NSP, Bombay 1890.—On Ratnākara's imitation of Māgha see Jacobi in *WZKM*, IV, 1890, p. 240 f. On the lexical meterials in the poem see R. Schmidt in *WZKM*, XXIX, p. 259 f.**

appeal to Śiva by the Seasons fleeing for protection to him, are balanced by the closing accounts of the sending of messenger, the demon's kingdom in heaven, exchange of defiances, preparation for the campaign and the imaginative battle lacking the virtue of imagination, all of which occupy twenty cantos (xxxi-l) and include the tricks of the Citra-bandha (canto xlviii) and a tremendous hymn to Caṇḍī (canto xlvii) in 167 Vasantatilaka stanzas! Ratnākara's work, with its utter lack of taste and sense of proportion, persistent straining of effort and interminable dreariness, beautifully exemplifies the desperate state to which the Mahākāvya had already descended. Ratnākara is styled Vāgīśvara and Vidyāpati; his mastery of speech and specialised learning perhaps justify the titles; but he is hardly a poet of distinction. He fancied his powers of writing a Mahākāvya, but his own assertion that one who is not a poet can become a poet, and even a great poet, is characteristic of the attitude which is apt to confuse pedantry with poetry. Although Kahlaṇa (v. 35) mentions him, Alaka writes a gloss on his work, the anthologists take notice of some of his verses[1] and Kṣemendra praises his command of the Vasantatilaka metre, yet the rarity of copies of his work in later times, even in Kashmir,[2] is perhaps singificant of the fact that the work could never live and was not unjustly consigned to oblivion.

The *Kapphiṇābhyudaya*[3] of Ratnākara's younger contemporary Śivasvāmin, who also adorned the court of Avantivarman, is a work of exactly the same type. Notwithstanding a limited recognition by anthologists, rhetoricians and lexicographers,

1 For the anthology verses see Peterson, *Subhāṣitāvali*, p. 96; Aufrecht in *ZDMG*, XXXVI, p. 372 f. Some of the verses are undoubtedly striking, but they shine in the reflected glory of conventional words and ideas.

2 The first detailed account of the work was given by Bühler in his *Kashmir Report* (extra no. of *JBRAS*), Bombay 1877, pp. 43-45. The published text contains many lacunae for want of good manuscripts.

3 Ed. Gaurishankar, Panjab Univ. Orient. Publication Series, Lahore 1937. The first notable account of the work was given by Seshagiri Sastri in his *Report of Sanskrit and Tamil MSS.*, No. 2, Madras 1899.

this work also suffered a similar, but not unexceptionable, neglect.[1] Like Katnākara, Śivasvāmin, son of Arkasvāmin, was probably a Rashmirian Śaiva, and his poem is dedicated to Śiva (xx. 45) ; but he does not disdain to invoke and glorify the Buddha. Contrary to general practice, but probably on the advice of a Buddhist monk and teacher named Candramitra, Śivasvāmin selects for his theme the Buddhist legend[2] of Kapphiṇa, which exists in two different versions in the Sanskrit *Avadāna-śataka* and in the Pali commentaries. Śivasvāmin shows a first-hand knowledge of Buddhist doctrine and its terminology, but he selects the simple Avadāna story of king Kapphiṇa of Dakṣiṇāpatha, who invades the territory of Prasenajit of Śrāvastī but is converted into Buddhism by a miracle, and works it out of all recognition and in the full and approved manner of the Mahākāvya, as prescribed by the rhetoricians. Although he speaks of having studied Kālidāsa, Bhartrmeṇṭha[3] and Daṇḍin, his work is obviously modelled on those of Bhāravi, Māgha and even Ratnākara.[4] Although it is less ambitious in having the respectable limit of twenty cantos, against fifty of Ratnākara, it is composed in no less difficult and ornate diction and with no less leisurely display of abundant skill and learning in the employment of language, metre[5] and rhetorical ornament. He cannot, of course, omit the customary appendages of disproportionately lengthy descriptions (cantos viii-xv) of the six seasons, enjoyment of water-sports, plucking of flowers, toilet, sunset, moonrise, drinking parties, union of lovers and sunrise, as well

1 It is noteworthy that manuscripts are rare even in its place of origin. No Kashmirian MSS were available for the above edition, which is based chiefly, but unsatisfactorily, on fragmentary Oḍiyā and Newāri copies.

2 This is in no way surprising when we remember that in the next century Kṣemendra, another Kashmirian, includes the Buddha among the Avatāras in his *Daśāvatāra-carita*.

3 The title of Śivasvāmin's work, however, reminds one of the *Bhuvanābhyudaya* of his predecessor Śaṅkuka, which is mentioned by Kahlaṇa (iv. 704).

4 For the close resemblances, see Gaurishankar, *op. cit.*, pp. li-lxix.

5 For metrical analysis, see Gaurishankar, pp. lxx-lxxiii. Śivasvāmin employs altogether 42 different metres, but in canto vi he makes a display of 37 kinds of metre, as against Bhāravi's 16 and Māgha's 22 in cantos v and iv respectively of their poems.

as of sending of messengers, councils of war, political discussion and artificial battle-scenes, including the tricks of the Citrabandha (vi-xviii) and a hymn to the Buddha in Prakrit and his replying sermon in Sanskrit (xix-xx) ! In spite of the novelty of his central theme, Śivasvāmin can claim no more merit than that of producing a literary curiosity of Śāstric knowledge, technical facility and misplaced ingenuity ; and as a successor of the great composers of artificial verse, he is entitled to all the censure and perhaps to some of the praise allotted to Bhaṭṭi and Māgha, as well as to his contemporary Ratnākara[1]

The *Śrīkaṇṭha-carita*[2][3] of Maṅkhaka, another Kashmirian work in twenty-five cantos, composed between 1135 and 1145 A.D., shows the same stereotyped form, method and diction, but reverts for its theme to the Purāṇa legend of Śiva's overthrow of Tripura. As usual, the story here is of the slightest importance, and the whole stock-in trade of accessories is liberally brought in. After preliminary prayers and benedictions in one canto, the work dilates upon the theme of good and bad people (canto ii) and gives an account (canto iii) of the author, his family and his country. Maṅkhaka's father was Viśvāvarta, son of Manmatha, and his three brothers Śṛṅgāra, Bhaṅga and Alaṃkāra (familiarly called Laṅkaka) were all, like himself, scholars and employed as state officials. Ruyyaka, mentioned in the last canto (xv. 30, 135 f), is probably the same as Ruyyaka, author of the *Alaṃkāra-sarvasva*,[3] who apparently instructed the poet in the art of rhetoric. The story is taken up, in cantos iv and v, with a description of Kailāsa and its deity, but

1 We are told in an apocryphal verse of the *Sūkti-muktāvalī* that Śivasvāmin wrote some seven Mahākāvyas, several dramatic works and eleven lacs of hymns and narratives composed day by day in praise of Śiva. We are mercifully spared of them.

2 Ed. Durgaprasad and K. P. Parab, with comm. of Jonarāja (*c.* 1417-67 A.D.). The first detailed account of the work appeared in Bühler's *Kashmir Report*, cited above, pp. 50-52.

3 Ruyyaka's work cites five verses from Maṅkhaka's poem without naming the author (see Jacob in *JRAS*, 1897, p. 293 for these verses). The Southern tradition of Maṅkhaka's collaboration with Ruyyaka in the *Alaṁkāra-sarvasva* does not seem to be authentic ; see S. K. De, *Sanskrit Poetics*, i, pp. 191-93.—Maṅkhaka appears to have written his work a few years earlier than the date of Kahlaṇa's historical poem.

it is interrupted for several cantos (vi-xvi) with the digressive descriptions of the spring and the usual erotic sports and amusements, and of sunset, moonrise and morning. We return to the martial exploits, involved in the story but handled in the conventional manner, in the following cantos (xvii-xxiv), ending with the burning of Tripura. In the last canto, however, which was probably added later, we have an account of some historical and literary interest, written in the simpler and easier Śloka metre, of an assembly of learned men, held under the patronage of the poet's brother Alaṃkāra, a minister of Jayasiṃha of Kashmir (1127-1150 A.D.), on the occasion of the completion and reading of the poem. It includes thirty names of scholars, poets and officials, stating their capacities and their tastes. But for these personal details, which have a value of their own, the *Śrīkaṇṭha-carita* shows only a faithful observance of the rules of Poetics regarding the composition of a Mahākāvya, and is consequently a work of little originality. As a pupil of Ruyyaka, Maṅkhaka shows much cleverness in the use of rhetorical ornaments, and succeeds in achieving some rich and charming effects in language and metre; but, generally speaking, his work lacks lucidity of expression,[1] as well as freshness and variety.

It is not necessary to take further detailed notice of the form and content of other Mahākāvyas of this period, which are even more stiff productions, composed in strict accordance with the established norm. Some of the more extensive poems, again, like the *Hara-carita-cintāmaṇi*[2] of Jayadratha, are not

1 If our Maṅkhaka is identical with the author of the *Maṅkha-kośa*, then he was also a lexicographer, whose partiality for recondite words would not be surprising.

2 Ed. Sivadatta and K. P. Parab, NSP, Bombay 1897, the text going up to 22 Prakāśas. The form Jayadratha, and not Jayaratha, of the author's name occurs in the printed text, as well as in Bühler's account, while the Kashmirian titles Rājānaka and Mahāmāheśvara indicate that he was a Kashmirian Śaiva. It is possible that he should be distinguished from and was in fact a brother of Jayadratha, the well known commentator on Abhinavagupta's *Tantrāloka* and Ruyyaka's *Alaṁkāra-sarvasva* (see S. K. De, *Sanskrit Poetics*, i, p. 197 f). He flourished in the first quarter of the 13th century under Rājadeva of Kashmir.

really Mahakavyas, but works of the Mahatmya type, which retell in the Śloka metre old and new Śaiva myths and legends, some of which are directly connected with places of pilgrimage in Kashmir. Similarly, the *Kādambarī-kathā-sāra*[1] of still another Kashmirian Abhinanda, son of Jayanta Bhaṭṭa, is not a regular Mahakavya, but is only an elegant metrical summary of Bāṇa's romance in eight cantos, composed mostly in Śloka ; it has the honour of being quoted by Abhinavagupta, Kṣemendra and Bhoja, and apparently belongs to the first half of the 9th century. Although the author mentions one of his ancestors in the seventh degree as a Gauḍa, it is not clear if he is identical with the Gauḍa Abhinanda,[2] who is cited extensively in the Anthologies, but whose verses are not traceable in the *Katha-sāra*, or with Abhinanda, son of the Śatānanda and author of the *Rāma-carita*, whose date and place of origin is uncertain.[3] This last-named work,[4] incomplete even in thirty-six cantos, weaves a Mahakavya of the elaborate kind out of the well-worn Rāmāyaṇa story, commencing from the abduction of Sītā and ending with the death of Kumbha-Nikumbha ; four supplementary cantos written by other hands complete the narrative. The *Daśāvatāra-carita*[5] of Kṣemendra, also composed in Kashmir in 1066 A.D. is again, not strictly a Mahakavya, nor a religious poem, but

1 Ed. Durgaprasad and K. P. Parab, NSP, Bombay 1888, 1899 ; ed. Acintyaram Sarman, Lahore 1900 ; also ed. in the *Pandit*, vols. i-ii. Kṣemendra in his *Kavikaṇṭhā-bharaṇa* also refers to a *Padya-kādambarī* composed by himself.

2 For references and discussion of the question, see S. K. De, *Padyāvalī*, pp. 182-84 and *New Ind. Antiquary*, II, p. 85.

3 Of the anthology verses quoted under the name Abhinand, only two in *Sadukti-karṇamṛta* (out of 22) and two in *Sūkti-muktāvalī* are traceable in the *Rāma-carita* (see introd., pp. vii-xiii). The earliest reference to this poet is that by Soḍḍhala in his *Udayasundarī-kathā* (pp. 2-3), which belongs to the first quarter of the 11th century, while Bhoja quotes extensively, but anonymously, from the poem at about the same time. The problem is complicated by the fact that the editor of the *Ramā-carita* makes a plausible case of its author having belonged to Gauḍa ; but the identity of his patron Hāravarṣa Yuvarāja, son of Vikramaśīla, with Devapāla, son of Dharmapāla of Gauḍa, is, without further evidence, highly problematic.

4 Ed. K. S. Ramaswami Sastri, Gaekwad's Orient. Series, Baroda 1930.

5 Ed. Durgaprasad and K. P. Parab, N.S.P, Bombay 1891.

gives an interesting account of the ten incarnations[1] in the regular Kāvya style, being an abstract, more or less, of Purāṇic stories; but, like Kṣemendra's other abstracts,[2] it is of little distinction in its eulogy or narrative.

The only Mahākāvya which need detain us is the *Naiṣadha-carita*[3] of Śrīharṣa, not so much for its intrinsic poetic merit as for the interesting evidence it affords of the type of enormously laboured metrical composition which was widely and enthusiastically favoured.[4] The work is regarded as one of the five great Mahākāvyas is Sanskrit; it is undoubtedly the last masterpiece of industry and ingenuity that the Mahākāvya can show, but to class it with the masterpieces of Kālidāsa, Bhāravi and even Māgha is to betray an ignorance of the difference between poetry and its counterfeit. The question of the date and place of activity of Śrīharṣa, who is described as the son of Śrīhīra and Māmalladevī, is not free from difficulty. In one of the four additional verses found at the end of the poem, the genuineness of which, however, is not beyond question, it is said that the poet received honour from the king of Kānya-kubja. As this assertion agrees with the story recorded in Jaina

1 *Viz.*, Matsya, Kūrma, Varāha, Nṛsiṁha, Vāmana, Paraśurāma, Rāma, Kṛṣṇa, the Buddha and Karkya—a list slightly different from that of Jayadeva.

2 The *Rāmāyaṇa-mañjarī* (ed. Bhavadatta and K. P. Parab) and the *Mahābhārata-mañjarī* (ed. Sivadatta and K. P. Parab), NSP, Bombay 1903 and 1898 : and the *Bṛhatkathā-mañjarī* mentioned above. The *Bhārata-mañjarī* is dated 1037 A.D.

3 Ed. Bibl. Ind., Calcutta, vol. i (Pūrva i-xi), with comm. of Premchandra Tarkavagisa, 1836, vol. ii (Uttara xii-xxii), ed. E. Röer, with the comm. of Nārāyaṇa, 1855; ed. Jivananda Vidyasagara with comm. of Mallinātha, 2 vols., Calcutta 1875-76, ed. K. L. V. Sastri and others, with the comm. of Mallinātha, (i-xii only), in two parts, Palghat 1924; ed. Sivadatta and V. L. Panashikar, with comm. of Nārāyaṇa, NSP, Bombay 1894, 6th ed. 1928; ed. Nityasvarup Brahmacari, with comm. of Nārāyaṇa, Bharatamallika and Vaṁśivadana (i-iii only), Calcutta 1929-30; Eng. trs., with extracts from eight comms. (Vidyādhara, Cāṇḍūpaṇḍita, Īśānadeva, Narahari, Viśveśvara, Jinarāja, Mallinātha and Nārāyaṇa), by K. K. Handiqui, Lahore 1934.

4 The work is extensively quoted in the anthologies and is the subject of more than twenty different commentaries, including those of Mallinātha and Cāritravardhana. But the legend, more witty than authentic, that Mammaṭa thought that this one work was sufficient to illustrate all the faults mentioned in his rhetorical work also indicates that its artificialities did not escape notice.

Rajaśekhara Sūri's *Prabandha-kośa* (composed in 1348 A.D.), it has been held[1] that Śrīharṣa probably flourished under Vijayacandra and Jayacandra of Kanauj in the second half of the 12th century.[2] He was probably also a logician and philosopher, and wrote the Vedāntic treatise *Khaṇḍana-khaṇḍa-khādya*; for, apart from the mention of the work (vi. 113) and of his labours in the science of logic (x. 137) in two epilogue-stanzas,[3] the *Naiṣadha-carita* itself passes in review a number of philosophical doctrines including those of the Buddhists, Jainas and Cārvākas.

The *Naiṣada-carita* selects for treatment the well known Mahābhārata story of Nala and Damayantī, but deals with a very small part of it, carrying the narrative only as far as their

1 G. Bühler in *JBRAS*, X, 1871, p. 31 f.; XI, 1874, p. 279. K. T. Telang (*IA*, II, p. 71f.; III, p. 81f.) and R. P. Chanda (*IA*, XIII, 1913, pp. 83 f, 286 f), however, question the trustworthiness of Rājaśekhara's account, and suggest the 9th or the 10th century as the date of Śrīharṣa.—The attempt to demonstrate (N. K. Bhattacharya in *Sarasvati Bhavana Studies*, Benares 1924, iii, pp. 159-94; see also *Ind. Culture*, II, p. 576 f.) that Śrīharṣa belonged to Bengal is wholly unconvincing; see S. K. De in *New Indian Antiquary*, II, p. 81, note.

2 The date is not unlikely in view of the fact that Cāṇḍūpaṇḍita's commentary on the Naiṣadha is dated 1297 A.D., and itself refers to a still earlier commentary by Vidyādhara.

3 At the end of each canto, an epilogue-stanza in Śārdūlavikrīḍita is repeated with some variations, giving us a few personal details about the author and his work, and including a reference to the *Khaṇḍana-khaṇḍa-khādya* as the author's own work. This treatise in its turn mentions the *Naiṣadha-carita*. While mutual reference is not unusual, it is somewhat curious that, while the reference in the philosophical work is to the twenty-first canto of the poem, the reference in the poem to the other work occurs at the end of the sixth! Again, the last concluding verse of canto xvi declares that the poem was honoured by the learned people of Kashmir, but it demands too much from credulity to believe that the work was appreciated even before the sixteenth canto was completed. These and other considerations render the genuineness of the epilogue-stanzas doubtful, although it is quite possible that they embody a genuine tradition. The other works of Śrīharṣa mentioned in these stanzas are: Sthairya-vicāra-prakaraṇa (iv. 123), Śrīvijaya-praśasti (v. 138), Gauḍorvīśa-praśasti (vii. 109), Arṇava-vivaraṇa (ix. 160), Chinda-praśasti (xxii. 222), Śivaśakti-siddhi (xviii. 154) and Navasāhasāṅka-carita Campū (xxiii. 151). We know nothing about the nature and content of these works, and all historical speculations based upon them are idle. But Śrīharṣa's writing of panegyrics in praise of Chinda or king of Gauḍa need not be incompatible with his being patronised by the king of Kanauj.

4 There is no evidence to show that the poem was left incomplete; but even if it were so the twenty-two cantos which exist are quite sufficiently characteristic.

romantic marriage and the advent of Kali in Nala's capital. The broad outlines of the epic legend are accepted, but there are some significant changes, one of which is meant to show Nala's character in a somewhat different light.[1] In delivering the message of the gods, Nala's anxiety in the *Mahābhārata* is to reconcile his own interest with what he conceives to be his duty to the gods, but in the poem a higher and subtler motive of the conflict of his honour with his sense of failure of his mission is conceived. But the episode of Nala's story (for it is no more than an episode), to which Śrīharṣa devotes about two thousand and eight hundred verses, is related in less than two hundred Ślokas in the *Mahābhārata*. The simple epic story is perhaps one of the most romantic and pathetic to be found in any literature, but Śrīharṣa confines himself, significantly enough, to the lighter side of Nala's career. The concern of the undoubtedly talented master of diction and metre is not with the possibilities of the story itself, but with the possibilities of embellishing it, disproportionately in twenty-two cantos, by his forensic and rhetorical fancy with a pedantic mass of descriptive matter, supposed to be indispensable in the Mahākāvya. The Svayaṃvara of Damayantī, for instance, takes only a few lines in the Epic, but Śrīharṣa devotes to it five long cantos (x-xiv) of more than five hundred stanzas. It is she most gorgeous and elaborate description of its kind in Sanskrit; but it is not the question of magnificence and proportion alone that is here significant. To present to Damayantī the five Nalas, or rather the real Nala and the four divine suitors who have assumed his form, is a task of no small difficulty; in Śrīharṣa's opinion, the task is worthy of Sarasvatī, the goddess of learning, who is made to undertake it; for each of the eighteen verses must have a twofold meaning, overtly applying to Nala, but characterising at the same time one of the four gods who also pose as Nala. For the sake of uniformity and impartiality, even the verses which describe the real Nala are also made to possess

1 Handiqui, *op. cit.*, p. xxvi.

double meaning ; and in the closing stanza, the address is capable of five interpretations, one for each of the dissembling gods and the fifth for Nala himself. The situation in ingeniously conceived, and the display of marvellous punning is not altogether out of place ; but it certainly sets a perplexing task to poor Damayantī, to whom the verses perhaps would not be intelligible forthwith without a commentary !

But not rhetoric alone,—Śrīharṣa's philosophical studies supply the theme of one whole canto (xvii), irrelevantly introduced, in which the trickish gods appear in the rôle of the protagonists of different systems of thought and belief, while there are throughout the poem abundant allusions to philosophical theories and doctrines. Śrīharṣa is careful, however, to show that his learned preoccupations in no way rendered him unfit for dealing with the refinements of the erotic art. One whole canto (vii), for instance, of more than a hundred stanzas impedes the progress of the narrative by a minute and frankly sensuous inventory of Damayantī's beauty of limbs commencing from the hair of the head and ending with the toe-nails of her feet ; but what is indicative of a singular lack of taste is that the description comes from Nala himself who views her from an invisible distance ! The poet never loses an opportunity of erotic digression. The unveiled succulence of some of the passages may be only a practical illustration of his knowledge of the Kāma-śāstra as a Śāstra ; but, notwithstanding the grace of a complex diction, the passages are extremly graceless in many places. Apart from the usual description of married bliss, to which the Epic makes only a passing reference, but which is an established convention in the Mahākāvya, one may cite such episodes as the feast of Dama (canto xvi) to show that the poet does not hesitate to introduce vulgar innuendos in what is supposed to be witty repartee of a more or less cultured society. It is no wonder, therefore, that, judging by modern standards, an impatient Western critic should stigmatise the work as a perfect amsterpiece of bad taste and bad style !

At the same time it must be said to Śrīharṣa's credit that even if his Damayantī is conventional, he shows considerable skill in the general picture of Nala's character depicted with its conflict of the emotions of love and honour. Despite laboured language, there are animated and quite witty speeches and dialogues, and not a little of remarkable epigrams and wise reflections. There can also be no doubt about Śrīharṣa's extraordinarily varied learning and command of the entire resources of traditional technique, even though the learning tends towards the obscure and the technique towars the artificial. His metrical skill is also considerable; he employs about twenty different metres in all[1] which are mostly short lyrical measures, the Mandākrānta, Śikhariṇī and Sragdharā occurring only rarely; but his predilection towards harsh and recondite forms of words and phrases does not always make his metres smooth and tuneful. Without any avowed grammatical, rhetorical or lexicographical object, his diction is deliberately difficult, his fancy is abundant but often fantastic, and his *feux d' artifice* of metaphor, simile, antithesis and other tricks of expression are more brilliant than illuminating. They are not so much means of beautiful and limpid expression as of ingenious straining of words and ideas. Śrīharṣa's descriptive power, which has been so much praised, is astonishing in its profusion and cleverness; but his extreme partiality for romantic commonplaces and the fatiguing ornateness of his overworked diction make it phantasmagoric and devoid of visualisation. This is nowhere so unfortunately displayed as in the description of natural scenery, which, as a rule, is a strong point with Sanskrit poets, but which in Śrīharṣa becomes lifeless and unconvincing.

Notwithstanding his limitations, it is clear that Śrīharṣa possesses a truly high gift, but it is a gift not of a high poetic character. It should be recognised at once that the *Naiṣadha-carita* is not only a learned poem, but is in many ways a repository of traditional learning, and should, therefore, be

1 In order of preference, the frequently used metres are: Upajāti, Vaṁśasthavila, Śloka, Vasantatilaka, Svāgatā, Drutavilambita, Rathoddhatā, Vaitālīya and Hariṇī.

approached with the full equipment of such learning. It is also a treasure-house of literary dexterity and involves for its appreciation an aptitude in this direction. The modern reader often perhaps lacks this equipment and aptitude, and therefore finds little interest in a work which, for its cult of style, has always been so popular with scholars of the traditional type. But, however much its learning and dexterity may win over a limited class of readers, its appeal can never be wide, not so much for its solid crust of scholarship and rhetoric, but for the extremely limited power and range of its purely poetic quality. It very often happens, as in this case, that wherever there is a lack of poetic inspiration, there is a tendency to astonish us by the hard glitter of technical skill and sheer erudition. Śrīharṣa not only shares but emphasises to an extreme degree the worst artificialities of his tribe ; and no sound-hearted, sound-minded reader will ever include him in the small class of great poets. Even as a rhetorical writer, Śrīharṣa does not rank high ; for his rhetoric is there, not because it is a natural accompaniment of the emotion or imagination, but because it is loved for its own sake. It indicates not only a tendency towards the artificial, but an inability to achieve the natural. Like Subandhu and like most writers of the kind, Śrīharṣa is obsessed with the idea that nothing great can be attained in the ordinary way. Even if a modern critic has the inclination to share the enthusiasm of Śrīharṣa's admirers, the poet's impossible and incessant affections rise up in witness against such an attitude.

If the reputed Mahākāvya writers of the period deserve such measured praise, what shall be said of the legion of lesser authors who weakly imitate them ? If in their own day they enjoyed some popularity, they did so because they supplied, not the right kind of poetry, but the kind which was readily favoured. It is upon the artistic skill of expression that they chiefly concentrate ; but their ideas are too often commonplace and their poetic speech stored with phrases and formulas of generations of older poets. In these writings the vision of romance never fades, but the vision of nature is never born. Their language is never pliant nor their verse supple ; while their fancy loves to play with the fantastic and the extravagant. It will be enough for our purpose, therefore, if we mention here only some of the more well known works which have been so far published. The Nala legend, for instance, is attempted in its entirety, in fifteen cantos, by the *Sahṛdayānanda*[1] of Kṛṣṇānanda, a Kāyastha of the Kapiñjala family and Mahāpātra to the king of Puri, as well as by the *Nalābhyudaya*,[2] in eight cantos, of Vāmanabhaṭṭa Bāṇa, whom we have already mentioned above for an insipid dramatisation of one of Kālidāsa's poems. On the Epics and the Purāṇas are also based several elaborate attempts, including grammatical and rhetorical poems to be mentioned below, as well as metrical adaptations by Jaina writers.[3] One such close adaptation, in nineteen Parvans (and not cantos !), of the Mahābhārata is the *Bāla-bhārata*[4] of Amaracandra Sūri, pupil of Jinadatta Sūri, who flourished under Viśaladeva of Gujarat in the first half of the 13th century. The *Jānakī-pariṇaya*[5] of Cakrakavi, son of Lokanātha and Ambā, deals in eight cantos with the well known Bāla-kāṇḍa episode of Sītā's marriage ; but the *Udāra-rāghava*[6] of Sākalyamalla, *alias* Mallācārya of Kavimalla son of Mādhava and a contemporary of Śiṅgabhūpāla (c. 1330 A.D.). is a highly artificial recast of the entire Rāmāyaṇa story,

1 Ed. Durgaprasad and K. P. Parab, NSP, Bombay 1892 ; the Śrī Vāṇī Vilāsa Press ed. prints only six cantos. As the work is cited in the *Sāhitya-darpaṇa*, its date cannot be later than the 14th century.

2 Ed. T. Ganapati Sastri, Trivandrum Sanskrit Series, 2nd ed. 1913

3 Only a selected number of such Jaina works are mentioned below ; for a more detailed account, see Winternitz, *HIL*, ii, p. 495f.

4 Ed. in the *Pandit*, Old Series, iv-vi, Benares 1869-71 ; also ed. Sivadatta and K. P. Parab, NSP, Bombay 1894. See Weber in *ZDMG*, XXVII, 1873, p. 170f. and *Ind. Streifen* iii, p. 211f. The industrious author wrote, some seven works of which the better known are the *Padmānanda* (see below), a comm. on his friend Arisiṁha's *Kāvya-kalpalatā* and a work on Prosody, called *Chandoratnāvalī*. For the author, see introd. to *Padmānanda* and S. K. De, *Sanskrit Poetics*, i, p. 210f.

5 Ed. T. Ganapati Sastri, Trivandrum Skt. Ser. The author also wrote Campūs on the marriages of Rukmiṇī Gaurī and Draupadī. He appears to have lived in the 17th century.

6 Printed Gopal Narayan Co., Bombay, no date.

but only nine out of its reputed eighteen cantos are available. The *Naranārāyaṇānanda*[1] of Vastupāla, minister of Vīradhavala of Dholka (Kathiawad) is a more pretentious work in sixteen cantos, describing the friendship of Arjuna and Kṛṣṇa and ending with the abduction and marrige of Subhadrā. The *Pāṇḍava-carita*[2] of Maladhārin Devaprabha Sūri, who lived about 1200 A.D., lapses into summarising in eighteen cantos the contents of the eighteen parvans of the Mahābhārata, remodelling many details but hardly rising above the Purāṇic style. The *Surathotsava*[3] of Someśvara, son of Kumāra and Lakṣmī and court-poet of Viradhavala and Viśaladeva of Gujarat (c. 1219-71 A.D.), brings in some diversity by relating in fifteen cantos the mythical story of Suratha, his penance in the Himalayas and slaying of demons, albeit in the approved manner and diction. There is no reason to regard it as a political allegory, but it has an interesting conclusion, which gives some personal history of the poet and his patrons.

The Kṛṣṇa legend claims the *Hari-vilāsa*[4] of Lolimbarāja, composed in five cantos, at about the middle of the 11th century, on the early exploits of Kṛṣṇa up to the slaying of Kaṃsa, the subject affording some opportunity of erotic flavour and lyric fluency. But the *Yādavābhudaya*[5] of the well known South Indian teacher and scholar Veṅkaṭanātha or Veṅkatadeśika, is a

1 Ed. C. D. Dalal and R. Anantakrishna Sastri, Gaekwad's Orient. Ser., Baroda 1916. The work appears to have been composed between 1220 and 1230 A.D.

2 Ed. Sivadatta and K. P. Parab, NSP, Bombay 1911.

3 Ed. Sivadatta and K. P. Parab, NSP, Bombay 1902.

4 Ed, Kāvyamālā, Gucchaka xi, Bombay 1895, pp. 94-113 ; also ed. in the *Pandit*, Old Series, ii, pp. 79f. 101f. The author, who lived under the South Indian king Harihara, a contemporary of Bhoja of Dhārā, is better known for his works on medicine.—Another poem on the Kṛṣṇa legend, called *Gopāla-līlā*, by Tailaṅga Rāmacandra (born in 1484 A.D.) is edited in the *Pandit*, vi.

5 Ed. with comm. of Appayya Dīkṣita, in three parts, Śrī Vāṇī Vilāsa Press, Srirangam 1907-24. The introduction contains an account of the author, who lived mostly in Kāñcī and Śrīraṅgam, and his numerous poetical and philosophical works, including the allegorical play, *Saṁkalpa-sūryodaya* (see below), the Stotra *Pādukā-sahasra* (ed. NSP, Bombay) and philosophical poem *Haṁsa-saṁdeśa* (see below). On the author, see *Journal of Orient. Research*, Madras, II, pts. iii-iv.

long and laborious production of great literary, but small poetic merit, composed between the second half of the 13th and the first half of the 14th century. The *Rukmiṇī-kalyāṇa,*[1] dealing with the abduction and marriage of Rukmiṇī, is a similarly dreary but much less extensive work of another South Indian scholar and polymath, Rājacūḍāmaṇi Dīkṣita, who flourished under Raghunātha Nāyaka of Tanjore in the earlier part of the 17th century. The Bengal Vaiṣṇava movement also produced some elaborate poems,[2] but they concentrate chiefly on the Rādhā legend and present it in a background of highly sensuous charm. Such, for instance, is the *Govinda-līlāmṛta*[3] of Kṛṣṇadāsa Kavirāja, which describes in twenty-three cantos (2511 verses) the erotic sports and pastimes of Kṛṣṇa and Rādhā, occuring at different parts of the day (Aṣṭakālika-Līlā) ; whatever may be the devotional value of the work, its poetic merit cannot be reckoned highly. The Śaiva legends are also handled with equal zeal and facility. They find a novel and interesting treatment in the *Bhikṣāṭana*[4] of Gokula, better known by his title .Utprekṣā-vallabha, who flourished sometime before the 14th century. Even the austere and terrible Śiva is depicted in this poem in an erotic surrounding ; for the theme of its forty Paddhatis is Śiva's wandering

1 Ed. Adyar Library, Madras 1929, with comm of Bāla Yajña-vedeśvara. The intoduction by T. R. Cintamani gives an interesting account of the voluminous author and his other works. See also S. K. De, *Sanskrit Poetics*, i, pp. 307-8.

2 Also some shorter poems, Stotras and Campūs (see below).

3 Ed. Sachinandan Gosvami, Brindavan 1903 (in Bengali characters). For the author, who is better known for his Bengali metrical biography of Caitanya, see S. K. De, *Kṛṣṇa-karṇāmṛta*, Dacca 1938, pp. lv.-lxiii. The work is divided into three parts : Prātar-līlā i-vii, Madhyāhna-līlā viii-xviii and Niśa-līlā xix-xxiii. In spite of its erotico-religious theme, it is a highly artifical and laboured work, and the author's pedantry and learning are conspicuous throughout, especially in several cantos which purport to illustrate various figures of speech and metres—Other Kāvyas, dealing with the same theme and composed by the followers of Caitanya of Bengal, are the *Kṛṣṇāhnika-kaumudī* in six Prakāśas, of Paramānanda Kavikarṇapūra and the *Kṛṣṇa-bhāvanāmṛta* of Viśvanātha Cakravartin (A.D. 1786), in twenty cantos, for which see below under Devotional Poetry.

4 Ed. Kāvyamālā, Gucchaka xii, Bombay 1897, pp. 54-163. As the work (sometimes with the name Utprekṣāvallabha of the author) is quoted extensively in the *Śārṅgadhara-paddhati* (no. 3333, 3353=i. 14, 15 ; 3523, 3524=iv. 6, 5) as well as in the *Sbhv* and *Smt*, it cannot be dated later than the 14th century.

about as a mendicant for alms and the feelings of the Apsarases of Indra's heaven at his approach. More conventional is the *Śiva-līlārṇava*[1] of Nīlakaṇṭha Dīkṣita who lived under Tirumala Nāyaka of Madura in the first half of the 17th century, and who inherited the varied learning and prolixity of his well known ancestor Appayya Dīkṣita.[2] It is a laboured composition in twenty cantos, but selects for its subject the local legend of the sixty-four feats of the god Sundaranātha Śiva of Madura, the supposed source being the Hālāsya-māhātmya of the Skanda Purāṇa. Nīlakaṇṭha's *Gaṅgāvataraṇa*,[3] however, is a small attempt in nine cantos, which deals with the well known myth of the descent of the Ganges through the austerities of Bhagīratha. The courts of Madura and Tanjore in the 17th century were scenes of varied literary activity, but it is hardly necessary to take into account these late and stilled productions, except where (as noticed below) they have special features to offer.

If Māgha's example produced a prolific series of progressively artificial Mahākāvyas, Bhaṭṭi appears to have been the spiritual godfather of a more factitious line of peculiar metrical composition, in which the frank object is no narrative, nor poetry, but direct illustration of grammatical niceties or rhetorical ingenuities. The ingenuities concern the exclusive employment of such external verbal devices as the Yamaka and the Śleṣa, the former consisting of chiming repetition, with or without meaning, of the same group of vocables in different positions in a stanza,[4] and the latter, ordinarily known as paronomasia or punning,

1 Ed. T. Ganapati Sastri, Trivandrum Sanskrit Series 1909 ; ed. Śrī Vāṇī Vilāsa Press Srirangam 1911.

2 For the author, see introd. to *Gaṅgāvataraṇa*, NSP. ed. ; also S. K. De, *Sanskrit Poetics*, i p. 266, 301. Nīlakaṇṭha was the son of Nārāyaṇa and Bhūmidevi and grandson of Appayya Dīkṣita's brother Accā Dīkṣita. His *Nīlakaṇṭha Campū* (see below) was completed in 1637 A.D.

3 Ed. Bhavadatta and K. P. Parab, NSP, Bombay 1902.

4 The Yamaka occurring at the end of the feet was fovoured as a not unlikely substitute for rhyme ; but properly speaking, rhyme is not Antya-yamaka (because here the vowel-groups remaining the same, the penultimate syllable is not preceded by a different consonant) but ntyānuprāsa, as defined by Viśvanātha, x. 6.

arising out of the coalescence of two or more words as one in appearance, but not in meaning, or resulting from the same word having different meanings either in its entirety or by its being split up in different ways.[1] The tradition of the Yamaka Kāvya goes back, as we have seen, to Ghaṭakarpara, while the artifice of the Śleṣa, favoured from the very beginning, was made use of by earlier poets chiefly as additional ornament which imparted piquancy and variety, with the result that we have no early Śleṣa Kāvya in which the figure is used for its sake. Its cultivation must have received an impetus from its systematic elaboration in the works of Subandhu and Bāṇa ; and we find in the present period its extreme employment as a device spread over the entire extent of a poem, which, by this contrivance, is made to have a twofold or even threefold application to totally different themes. Such playing with the languages producing incredible feats of verbal jugglery, is possible because of the special advantages afforded by Sanskrit, by its flexibility as well as complexity of grammatical forms, by the susceptibility of its words to a large number of recondite meanings and delicate subtleties, by the different modes of compounding words, and

1 There are other types of Durghaṭa and Citra Kāvya, but for obvious reasons they are not taken into account. Thus, we have poems of deliberately difficult construction like the *Durghaṭa-kāvya* (noticed by Eggeling in *Ind. Office Cat.* vii, p. 1488, no. 3926) ; poems which are meant to illustrate various figures of speech, such as Vakrokti in Ratnākara's *Vakrokti-pañcāśikā* (ed. Kāvyamālā, Gucchaka i, pp. 101-114 ; the figure consisting of the deliberate misunderstanding of one's words for the purpose of making a clever retort generally by means of punning) ; enigmatic poems, like the *Bhāva śataka* of Nāgarāja (ed. Kāvyamālā, Gucchaka, iv, p. 37 f), which propose ingenious riddles of a literary character in each verse, expecting a suitable reply ; poems which practice Citrabandhas or verses written in the form of a sword, cross, wheel and so forth, like the *Devī-śataka* of Ānandavardhana and *Īśvara śataka* of Avatāra (both ed. Kāvyamālā, Gucchaka, ix, pp. 1 f. 31 f), *Kavīndra-karṇābharaṇa* of Viśveśvara (ed. Kāvyamālā, Gucchaka, viii, p. 51 f ; see S. K. De *Sanskrit Poetics*, i, p. 312 f), *Catur-hārāvali-citra-stava* of Jayatilaka Sūri (ed in Stotra-ratnākara, pt. ii. Bombay, 1913) or *Citra-bandha-rāmāyaṇa* of Veṅkaṭeśvara, (noticed in P. P. S. Sastri's *Tanjore Catalogue*, vi, nos. 2728-35). The Citrabandha is also the subject of specialised treatises like the *Vidagdha-mukha-maṇḍana* of Dharmadāsa Sūri (ed. Haeberlin, 262 f ; also ed. NSP. Bombay 1914 ; see S. K. De, *op. cit.*, i. pp. 297-98). It is clear that all these works require commentaries, without which they are not easily intelligible.

by diverse ways in which the syllables comprising a word or a line can be disjoined. Such adaptability is perhaps found in no other language, but it is clear that these misplaced but astounding efforts have only a nominal claim to be called poetical compositions.

Of the purely grammatical poems of the type of the *Bhaṭṭi-kāvya,* there are no very early specimens except the *Rāvaṇ-ārjunīya*[1] of Bhaṭṭa Bhīma (Bhauma or Bhaumaka) probably a Kashmirian production, which is mentioned next to Bhaṭṭi's work as a "Śāstra-kāvya" by Kṣemendra,[2] and which must, from this reference, belong to a period earlier than the 11th century.[3] It relates, in twenty-seven cantos imperfectly recovered, the story of Rāvana's fight with Kārtavīryārjuna and illustrates at the same time the grammatical rules of Pāṇini in the regular order of the Aṣṭādhyāyī. In the same way, the *Kavi-rahasya*[4] of Halāyudha is composed as a metrical guide to poets in the employment of verbal forms, but it is also an eulogy of Kṛṣṇarāja III of the Rāṣṭrakūṭa family (940-56 A.D.). The *Vāsudeva-vijaya,*[5] a work of unknown date on the Kṛṣṇa legend, by Vāsudeva of Puruvana in Kerala, traverses in three cantos the entire Aṣṭādhyāyī; it was apparently left incomplete and was supplemented on the topic of the Dhātupāṭha by the *Dhātu-kāvya*[6] of Nārāyaṇa in another three cantos, bringing the narrative down to the death of Kaṃsa. Hemacandra's *Kumārapāla-carita,* of which we shall speak presently, also incidentally illustrates Sanskrit grammar in twenty and Prakrit grammar in eight cantos.

1 Ed. Sivadatta and K. P. Parab, NSP, Bombay 1900.

2 *Suvṛtta-tilaka,* iii. 4.

3 The editors of the work do not agree with the allegation that it is cited in the *Kāśikā.*

4 Ed. L. Heller, in both longer (299 verses, generally in Śloka) and shorter (273 verses) recensions, Greifswald 1900. On the author see R. G. Bhandarkar, *Report 1883-94,* p. 8f; Heller, *Halāyudha's Kavirahasya,* Diss., Göttingen 1894; Zachariae, *Ind. Wörterbücher* (Grundriss), p. 26.

5 Ed. Kāvyamālā, Gucchaka x Bombay 1915, pp. 52-121.

6 Ed. *ibid.* pp. 121-232. It follows generally Bhīmasena and Mādhava.

Although in *Bhaṭṭi-kāvya* x we have an elaborate illustration of different kinds of Yamaka in as many as twenty verses, the earliest Yamaka-kāvya of Ghaṭakapara is a short poem of twenty-two stanzas, which almost exclusively employs end-chiming. The next sustained Yamaka-kāvya, the *Kīcaka-vadha,*[1] of Nītivarman, who flourished earlier than the 11th century in some eastern province, keeps to the less complex scheme of Ghaṭakarpara and uses only final and some medial chimings. It is an embellished presentation, in five cantos (117 verses), of the simple and vigorous Mahābhārata episode of Bhīma's slaying of Kīcaka. There is nothing striking in the narrative itself, but the work has the unique distinction of employing not only Yamaka in four cantos but also Śleṣa in one (canto iii), in which Draupadī's speech to Virāṭa is made by clever punning indirectly significant for the Pāṇḍavas.[2] The Yamaka-kāvyas of the Kerala poet Vāsudeva, son of Ravi and contemporary of Kulaśekhara-varman, are, however, noteworthy for the manipulation, in the difficult moric Ārya metre, of more multifarious and difficult schemes of Yamaka. His *Nalodaya*[3] in four cantos (217 verses), which was at one time stupidly ascribed to Kālidāsa and sometimes taken as the work of Ravideva, deals with the story of Nala and succeeds in managing with merciless torturing of the language, the exacting demands of even quadruple Yamaka in a single verse. His *Yudhiṣṭhira-vijayodaya,*[4] which deals in eight Āśvāsas (719 verses) with the Mahābhārata story, beginning from the hunting sports of Pāṇḍu and ending with the coronation of Yudhiṣṭhira, is also a curious literary effort of the same

1 Ed. S. K. De, with comm. of Janārdana-sena and extracts from the comm. of Sarvānanda-nāga, and with an introd. on the work and the author, Dacca University Orient. Text Publ., Dacca 1929.

2 The work is also cited as one of the rare instances of a Kāvya opening with an Āśis (benediction), and not, as usual, with Namaskriyā or Vastu-nirdeśa. The work is naturally quoted by a large number of grammarians, historians and lexicographers, one of the earliest quotations occurring in Nami-sādhu's commentary on Rudraṭa's *Kāvyālaṁkāra* in 1069 A. D.

3 See above, p. 121 footnote 5 for references.

4 Ed. Sivadatta and K. P. Parab with comm. of Rājānaka Ratnakaṇṭha, NSP, Bombay 1897.

kind.[1] It is needless to enlarge the list by mentioning other work, like the *Vṛndāvana-yamaka*[2] of Manāṅka, or the *Rāma-yamakārṇava*[3] of Veṅkaṭeśa, son of Śrīnivāsa, the latter author being also credited with an extensive Mahākāvya in thirty cantos on the Rāma story, entitled *Rāmacandrodaya.*[4] The *Kṛṣṇa-līlā*[5] of Madana, son of Kṛṣṇa, composed in 1523 A.D. (84 verses) on the theme of Kṛṣṇa's separation from the Gopīs, is a short Yamaka-kāvya of the Samasyā-pūraṇa type, in which one foot in each stanza is taken from Ghaṭakarpara's poem, so that its four consecutive stanzas give, by appropriation, the text of one entire verses of Ghaṭakarpara. Some Jaina writers appear to be fond of the artificial tricks of Yamaka; as for instance, Devavijaya-gaṇi in his *Siddhi-priya* Stotra[6] employs the same order of syllables over nearly half the foot in two consecutive feet of each stanza, while Śobhana in his *Caturviṃśati-jina-stuti*[7] constructs his verses in such a way that the second and fourth feet of each verse have the same order of syllables.

1 On Vāsudeva's two other Yamaka-kāvyas, the ***Tripura-dahana*** and ***Śauri-kathodaya,*** not yet published (MSS in Govt. Oriental Manuscripts Library, Madras, nos. 1852a and 1852b), see A. S. Ramanatha Ayyar in *JRAS*, 1925, p. 265f. The date assigned by Ayyar is the first half of the 9th century, but its correctness depends on that of Kulaśekhara which is still uncertain. Venkatarama Sarma (Yamaka-kavi Vāsudeva in ***Proceedings of the Tenth All-India Orient. Conference***, Tirupati, 1940, pp. 187-202) gives a list of 21 works of Vāsudeva, of which 14 appear to be genuine. Of these the following eight (all available is MSS in Govt. Orient. MSS Library, Madras) are Yamaka Kāvyas: *Yudhiṣṭhīravijayodaya, Śauri-kathodaya, Tripura-dahana, Acyuta-līlodaya, Nalodaya, Śivodaya, Devīcaritodaya,* and *Satya-tapaḥ-kathodaya.* Vāsudeva is described as the son of Maharṣi and Gopālī: he lived in Vedāraṇya or Kunnamkulam in Malabar, and his poems glorify the three deities Śiva, Durgā (Devī) and Kṛṣṇa worshipped in that place. *Satya-tapaḥ-kathodaya,* however, relates the story of Satya-tapas, a devout ancestory of the author.

2 Ed. Haeberlin, Kāvya-saṁgraha, pp. 453-62; Jivananda's Kāvaya-saṁgraha iii, p. 416f. It is a short poem of 43 (mostly Āryā) verses (52 verses in Eggeling, no 3911, pt. vii, p. 1466). Date unknown. It is in the form of a dialogue between Rāma and Kṛṣṇa at Vṛndāvana. The poet justly describes himself as a Varṇa-kavi.

3 P. P. S. Sastri, *Tanjore Catalogue*, vi, p. 2681f. Composed in 1656 A.D.

4 *Ibid.*, p. 2658 f. Composed in 1635 A.D.

5 Eggeling, *Ind. Office Catalogue*, vii, p. 1361. As one of the verses of the original (no. 21 in Haeberlin) is omitted here the total number of verses in this work becomes 84 and not 88.

6 Ed. Kāvyamālā, Gucchaka vii, 2nd ed. 1907, p. 30f.

7 Ed. *Ibid*, p. 132 f.

Although the Śleṣa is a favourite figure of speech with Sanskrit poets, the practice of the Śleṣa-kāvya does not connect itself with any tradition earlier than the 11th century. Barring the Śleṣa-canto of *Kīcaka-vadha*, the first sustained specimen is the *Rāma-carita*[1] of Saṃdhyākara nandin. The author, who was the son of Prajāpati-nandin and grandson of Pināka-nandin of Puṇḍravardhana in North Bengal, completed the work in the reign of Madanapāla, son of Ramapāla of Bengal and third in succession from him, at the close of the 11th century ; but since the author's father held the office of a minister under Rāmapāla, the inner history of the stirring political events recorded in the poem, must have been a matter of direct knowledge. Saṃdhyākara proudly calls himself Kalikāla-Vālmīki, and undertakes in this work of four chapters to relate in 220 Aryā verses the story of Rāma of the Rāmāyaṇa and the history of Rāmapāla of Bengal, simultaneously in each verse, by the device of punning and of splitting up of word-units in different ways. He claims that his puns are not distressing (akleśana). To his contemporaries who were familiar with the incidents narrated, they might not have presented much difficulty, but today the loss of the commentary to a part of the work makes the application of the uncommented verses to the history of the time not easily intelligible. The main theme of the work is an account of a successful revolution in North Bengal, the murder of Mahīpāla II, occupation of Varendra by the rebels, and restoration of Rāmapāla, Mahīpāla's youngest brother, to his paternal kingdom ; but since the work could not be completed before three more kings came to rule, the story is continued even after the death of Rāmapāla and concludes with some allusions to Madanapāla's reign. The work undoubtedly possesses, in spite of its

[1] Ed. Haraprasad Sastri, in Memoirs of ASB, Calcutta 1910. There is an anonymous commentary to the poem up to ii. 35, which is not composed by the author but which is useful in its explanation of allusions to contemporary history. The work has been re-edited, with improved materials and a new commentary on the uncommented portion, by R. C. Majumdar, R. G. Basak, and N. G. Banerji, Varendra Research Society, 1939.

apparently partisan sririt, a great value as a contemporary record of historical incidents, but the poetical merit of this extremely artificial composition is obviously very small; and on account of its limited and local interest it failed in its appeal to posterity and became forgotten. This device of handling different tales or themes in the same poem has been quite fruitful in Sanskrit. We see it in the *Rāghava-pāṇḍavīya,*[1] descriptively called *Dvisaṃdhāna-kāvya,*[2] of Dhanañjaya, surnamed Śrutakīrti Traividya, son of Vāsudeva and Śrīdevī and a Digambara Jaina, who wrote between 1123 and 1140 A.D. Each verse of its eighteen cantos apply equally, as the name of the work implies, to the story of the two Epics at the same time. A little later, we have another and better known *Rāghava-pāṇḍavīya*[3] by Kavirāja, whose personal name probably was Mādhava Bhaṭṭa[4] and who flourished (i. 13)[5] under Kādamba Kāmadeva (1182-87 A.D.) of Jayantapurī.[6] It relates in the same way, in thirteen cantos, the double story of Rāghava and the Pāṇḍavas. The author compares himself to Subandhu and Bāṇabhaṭṭa in the matter of verbal dexterity, but his very restricted method and objective do not obviously allow much scope for any poetic gift that he might have possessed, and his work

1 Ed. Sivadatta and K. P. Parab, with comm. of Badarīnātha, NSP, Bombay 1895. See R. G. Bhandarkar, *Report 1884-87*, p. 19 f; Pathak in *JBRAS*, XXI, 1904, p. i f; Fleet in *IA*, XXIII, p. 279.

2 The word 'Dvi-saṁdhāna,' meaning a work of twofold application, is used by Daṇḍin; it becomes the generic name of such works. It is significant that our Dhanañjaya wrote a lexicon, called *Dhanañjaya-nāma-mālā*.

3 Ed. Bibl. Ind., with the modern comm. of Premachandra Tarkavagisa, Calcutta 1854 (reprinted by Bhavadeva Chatterji, Calcutta 1892); ed. Sivadatta and K. P. Parab, with the comm. of Śaśadhara, NSP, Bombay 1897; ed. Granthamālā, with comm. of Lakṣmaṇa Sūri, son of Śrīdatta, Bombay 1889.

4 See Pathak in *JBRAS*, XXII, 1905.

5 R. G. Bhandarkar, *Report 1884-87*, p. 20, thinks that Kavirāja belongs to the end of the 10th century; but the comparison of his own patron with Muñja need not prove the author's contemporaneity with Muñja of Dhārā. See Pischel *Die Hofdtchier des Lakṣmaṇasena* Göttingen 1893, p. 37 f.—Kavirāja also wrote another poem, *Pārijāta-haraṇa*, in ten cantos, but it does not employ Śleṣa.

6 Vanavāsi, the seat of the Kādambas, in North Canarese district is said to be still known as Jayantī-kṣetra.

remains a brilliant example of a bad kind. To the same class of composition belongs the *Rāghava-naiṣadhīya*,[1] probably a comparatively recent work, of Haradatta Sūri, son of Jayaśaṃkara of Gārgya Gotra, which relates by the same method the stories of Rāma and Nala. The number of such works is not small, but very few of them have been thought worthy of printing. Thus, Vidyāmādhava, who flourished in the court of Cālukya Somadeva plausibly Someśvara of Kalyāṇa (1126-38 A.D.), gives in nine cantos of his *Pārvatī-rukmiṇīya*[2] the double story of the marriages of Śiva and Pārvatī and of Kṛṣṇa and Rukmiṇī ; while Veṇkaṭādhvarin, better known as the author of the *Viśvaguṇādarśa Campū*[3] (1st half of the 17th century), deals with the stories of the Rāmāyaṇa and the Bhāgavata, with the Viloma device in his *Yādava-rāghavīya*,[4] a short poem of three hundred stanzas. A further development of this device is seen in the use of treble punning for relating three different stories at a time, of which an extreme example is the *Rāghava-pāṇḍava-yādavīya*[5] or *Kathā trayī* of Cidambara, son of Anantanārāyaṇa and protégé of Veṅkaṭa I of Vijayanagar (1586-1614 A.D.), the stanzas of its three cantos being worded in such a way as to describe at the same time the stories of the Rāmāyaṇa, the Mahābhārata and the Bhāgavata.

There is also a number of smaller erotic-ascetic poems which utilise the device of Śleṣa in having the simultaneous themes of

1 Ed. Sivadatta and K. P. Parab, with the author's own comm., NSP, 1896, 2nd ed., Bombay 1926. Since the commentary cites Bhaṭṭojī Dīkṣita as Dīkṣita, it could not have been earlier than the 17th century.

2 *Descriptive Cat. of Škt. Mss in Govt. Orient. Mss Library*, Madras, vol. xx (Kāvya), pp. 7777-79, No. 11606.

3 See below, under Campū. The author belonged to the first half of the 17th century. See E. V. Viraraghavacharia in *Ind. Culture*, VI, pp. 225-34.

4 *Descriptive Cat., Madras Govt. Orient. Mss Library*, xx, p. 7956 f. (No. 11821). Printed in Telugu characters, with the author's own commentary, Vidyātaraṅgiṇī Press, 1890. It is not a Śleṣa-kāvya, but employs the Viloma device, in which the verses read in the usual orders gives the story of Rāma, and read in the reverse order gives th e (1) Kṛṣṇa.

5 *Ibid*, p. 7829 f ; also P. P. S. Sastri, *Tanjore Catalogue*, vi, p. 2700.

Love (Śṛṅgāra) and Renunciation (Vairāgya). Such, for instance, are the *Rasika-rañjana*[1] of Rāmacandra, son of Lakṣmaṇabhaṭṭa, or the *Śṛṅgāra-vairāgya-taraṅgiṇī*[2] of the Jaina Somaprabhācārya. Without using Śleṣa, however, Daivajña Sūrya, son of Jñānadhirāja of Pārthapura and an astronomer of some repute,[3] shows another method of applying the verses to two themes simultaneously in his *Rāma-kṛṣṇa-viloma-kāvya.*[4] It is a small production of 36 or 38 stanzas, which praises in alternate half verses Rāma and Kṛṣṇa, the text given by the second half when read backward is the same as that of the first half read forward. It is clear that, however much we may admire the extraordinary cleverness displeyed in the works described above, they are not poems but poetical monstrosities, which hardly deserve even a mention in a literary history of Sanskrit poetry.

One of the interesting applications of the form and spirit of the Mahākāvya is seen in the works of a group of Jaina writers, who adopt them, not unsuccessfully, for presenting Jaina legends in a poetical garb, as well as for historical or biographical accounts. Some of these, however, are mere eulogies of saints, some frankly ethical or doctrinarian, while some are of the Māhātmya or Purāṇa type, composed in pedestrian Sanskrit. As most of them do not properly conform to the standard of a Mahākāvya, we need mention here a few which have greater pretensions. One of the earliest of these is the anonymous *Varāṅga-*

1 Ed. Kāvyamālā, Gucchaka iv, 2nd ed., NSP, Bombay 1899, pp, 80-121 (130 verses). Composed at Ayodhyā in 1524 A.D.

2 Ed. Kāvyamālā, Gucchaka v, 2nd ed., 1908, pp. 124-142 (46 verses), with a comm. Somaprabha's *Śabdārtha-vṛtti*, which is referred to in the colophon to this work, illustrates the achme of variable interpretation; for in it a single verse of his own composition is explained in one hundred different ways! Somaprabha's date is about 1276 A.D.

3 The authot wrote his astronomical work, *Sūrya-prakāśa*, in 1539 A.D., and his commentary on *Līlāvatī* in 1542 A.D. One of his ancestors lived in the court of Rāma of Devagiri.

4 Ed. Kāvyamālā, Gucchaka ix, NSP, Bombay 1899, pp. 80-121 (36 verses); ed. Haeberlin, reprinted in Jivananda's Kāvyasaṁgraha iii, pp. 463-85 (38 verses).

carita,[1] ascribed to Jaṭāsiṁhanandi, a Jaina monk of Karṇāta, whose date, as attested by later citations, would be earlier than the 10th century. It narrates in thirty-one cantos the Jaina legend of Varāṅga. In the colophon it is described as a Dharma-kathā ; and, being distinctly monkish in its outlook, it contains as many as nine cantos on Jaina dogmatics, which have no direct connexion with the narrative ; but at the same time the work is not a mere doctrinal treatise. It is a regular Mahākāvya in form, diction and metrical characteristics. The slender theme of the jealously of the step-mother, treachery of a minister, the wanderings of the hero in the forest, his adventures and martial exploits and final restoration to his kingdom is neither original nor enthralling ; but it is fully embellished in the customary manner and with the customary digressive matter, which forms the stock-in-trade of the Mahākāvya. Similarly, the legend of king Yaśodhara is dealt with in the *Yaśodhara-carita*[2] of Vādirāja Sūri in four cantos, in the beginning of the 11th century, as well as by Māṇikya Sūri in his *Yaśodhara-carita*[3] of unknown date. A great impetus to the poetical treatment of Jaina legend appears to have been given by the *Triṣaṣṭi-śalākā-puruṣa-caritra*[4] (with its supplementary *Pariśiṣṭa-parvan* or *Sthavirāvali*[5]) of the famous Jaina Ācārya Hemacandra, who composed it at the desire of his converted royal disciple Kumārapāla of Anhilvad,

1 Ed. A. N. Upadhye, Māṇikacandra Digambara Jaina Granthamālā, Bombay 1938. The date and authorship are frankly uncertain, but are determined chiefly from the external evidence of Jaina literary tradition. The editor is inclined to push the date to the 7th century A.D. and identify the author with Jaṭāsiṁhanandi mentioned in Koppala inscription, the date of which, however, is equally uncertain. The archaisms and solecisms, though interesting, need not be a conclusive evidence ; for we know that such characteristics are found in some South Indian manuscripts, especially in Kerala manuscripts of Sanskrit plays.

2 Ed. T. A. Gopinath Rao, Sarasvatī Vilāsa Series, Tanjore 1912. The author wrote his *Pārśvanātha-carita* in 1025 A.D.

3 Ed. Hiralal Hansaraj, Jamnagar 1910. It is difficult to identify our author with the known Māṇikya Sūri who flourished between the 13th and the 16th century. The same story is also treated in Somadeva Sūri's *Yaśastilaka Campū* (see below).

4 Ed. Jaina Dharma-prasāraka Sabhā, Bhavnagar 1906-13.

5 Ed. H. Jacobi. Bibl. Ind. Calcutta 1883-1891, 2nd ed. 1932.

between 1160 and 1172 A.D. The sixty-four Śalākā-puruṣas or Great Men, whose stories are presented in ten Parvans, are the twenty-four Jinas, the twelve Cakravartins, the nine each of Vasudevas, Baladevas and Viṣṇudviṣas of Jaina hagiology. The work calls itself a Mahākāvya, but its main purpose is religious edification, the intrusion of which affects its long and tedious narrative. The later instances of the working up of Jaina legends and tales are numerous, but their literary value, in most cases, is not of an outstanding character. In addition to the *Bālabhārata* already mentioned, Amaracandra also wrote, for the delectation of the minister Padma, the *Padmānanda*,[1] in which he undertook to present, in the regular Kāvya form and diction, but with much religious and ethical matter, an account of all the twenty-four Jinas[2] ; but the ambitious project does not appear to have been fulfilled, and we have in nineteen cantos only the life of the first Jina. The legend of Śālibhadra, already told briefly by Hemacandra, engages Dharmakumāra in his *Śālibhadra-carita*,[3] composed in seven cantos in 1277 A.D. The *Kṣatra-cūḍāmaṇi*[4] of Oḍeyadeva Vādībhasiṃha, who lived in the beginning of the 11th century, gives a treatment in eleven Lambhakas, mostly in Śloka of the Uttara-purāṇa legend of Jīvaṃdhara, which theme has also been treated in 509 Ślokas by Guṇabhadrācārya in his *Jīvaṃdhara-caritra*[5] and by Haribhadra in his *Jīvaṃdhara-campū*.[6] This Haribhadra may or may not be identical with Haricandra, who wrote in twenty-one cantos the *Dharmaśarmābhyudaya*,[7] dealing with the story of Dharmanātha, the fifteenth Tīrthaṃkara, on the direct model of Māgha's poem. As a typical Mahākāvya of this period, it possesses some interest ; as

1 Ed. H. R. Kapadia, Gaekwad's Orient. Series, Baroda 1932.

2 For works of this type by various authors, see H. R. Kapadia's ed. of *Caturviṁśati-jinānanda-stuti* of Meruvijaya-gaṇi, Āgamodaya-samiti Series, Bombay 1929.

3 Ed. in Yaśovijaya Jaina Granthamālā, Benares 1910. See Bloomfield in *JAOS*, XLIII, 1923, p. 257 f.

4 Ed. T. S. Kuppusvami Sastri, Sarasvatī Vilāsa Series, Tanjore 1905.

5 Ed. *ibid.*, Tanjore 1907.

6 Ed. *ibid.*, Tanjore 1905.

7 Ed. Durgaprasad and K. P. Parab, NSP, Bombay 1899.

also does the *Nemi-nirvāṇa*,[1] on the life of Neminātha is fifteen cantos, of Vāgbhaṭa, who lived under Jayasiṃha of Gujarat (1093-1154 A.D.), but who need not be identical with the author of the rhetorical work *Vāgbhaṭālaṃkāra*. A similarly constructed Mahākāvya is the *Jayanta-vijaya*[2] of Abhayadeva Sūri, composed in 1221 A.D., which describes in nineeten cantos the legend of king Jayanta. It is noteworthy that all these Jaina productions include the regular Kāvya topics and digressive descriptions of the seasons, battles and erotic sports, the last topic being treated with equal zest by the Jaina monks including the pious Hemacandra ! It is interesting also that one of the many versions of the Udayana legend is treated by Maladhārin Devaprabha in his *Mṛgavatī-caritra*,[3] while Cāritrasundara, who probably lived in the middle of the 15th century, deals in fourteen cantos with the fairy story of Mahīpāla in his *Mahīpāla-caritra*.[4]

There is not much of meritorious poetical writing of later Buddhist authors, whose energy was directed more towards religious than literary matters. The *Padya-cūḍāmaṇi*[5] of Buddhaghoṣa relates in ten cantos the legend of the Buddha up to the defeat of Māra, which differs in some details from the versions of the *Lalita-vistara* and the *Buddha-carita*. There is nothing either to prove or disprove the identity of the author with the famous Pali writer Buddhaghoṣa. In spite of its well worn theme and its obvious imitation of Aśvaghoṣa and Kālidāsa, the work is not without merit as a well-written Kāvya.

2. Poems with Historical Themes

The earlier classical documents, which are concerned with historical events or personages, are the elaborate Praśastis or

1 Ed. Sivadatta and K P. Parab, NSP, Bombay 1896.

2 Ed. Bhavadatta and K. P. Parab, NSP, Bombay 1902. See Peterson, *Fourth Report*, p. vii.

3 Ed. Hiralal Hansaraj, Jamnagar 1909.

4 Ed. Hiralal Hansaraj, Jamnagar 1909. For the story see Winternitz, *HIL*, ii, p, 536.

5 Ed. M. Rangacharya and S. Kuppusvami Sastri, Madras 1921.

panegyrics embodied in inscriptional records. Their obvious object is to celebrate in sonorous prose and verse some meritorious acts of a particular ruler, eulogise his valour and munificence, and give genealogical and other relevant descriptions of some value. But while the genealogy beyond one or two generations is often amiably invented and exaggerated, and glorification takes the place of sober statement of facts, the laudatory accounts are generally composed by poets of modest power. The result is neither good poetry nor good history. They are yet interesting as the first poetical treatment of historical themes ; and the agreeable practice which they establish of mixing fact with fiction was accepted by more earnest and ambitious writers, but perhaps it was accepted with a greater leaning towards pleasant fiction than towards hard facts.

There is indeed no tradition, from the beginning, of meticulous chronicling or critical appreciation of historical facts as such. Neither the Purāṇas nor the Buddhist or Jaina records, which were meant more for attractive edification than serious history, show any historical sense in their complacent confusing of fact and fiction, in their general indifference to chronology, in their intermingling of divine and human action, in their unhesitating belief in magic and miracle, and in their deep faith in incalculable human destiny. It is true that later records give us some interesting facts and dates, while glimpses of history have been laboriously retrieved from earlier records, but even the most enthusiastic believer in them would not for a moment claim that they give us instances of clear, consistent and adequate historiography. No nearer approach is made by the large number of poems, dramas and romances, which deal ostensibly with historical themes but really with the poetic, dramatic or romantic possibilities of them. While considering Bāṇa's *Harṣa-carita*, which is the earliest known specimen of a sustained character, we have briefly indicated the general characteristics of such writings, and little need be added to what has been said. These literary efforts contain historical material, but the extent and value of such material are immensely variable, and do not in any sense represent a proper step towards history. It is not surprising, however, that India failed to produce, in spirit of its abundance of intellect, history in the modern sense, just as it failed to produce some other categories of modern literature; but the result has to us a decided lack of understanding of the evolution of ancient life and thought. It is not only poverty in a particular branch of literature, but also absence of trustworthy information regarding the complex movements of human act and idea in their panoramic procession. The reason lies perhaps in the innate and deep-rooted limitations of the ancient ideal, outlook and environment, as well as in the peculiarity of the literary objective, method and tradition, which affected the sustained and assiduous practice of Sanskrit literature as a whole, no less than in its haphazard and uninterested attempt at definite historical writing. Apart from a deep philosophy or artistic setting, ordinary history is in fact a prosaic idea. As a matter of research, it aims at knowledge of facts; as an idea, it professes to bring out larger principles governing human affairs; as a method, its leaning is towards objective accuracy. It is thus, entirely out of harmony with the spirit of Sanskrit literature, and could not be disciplined by its formal conception of art. The idea of composing history for its own sake was, thus, naturally slow to emerge; and when it did emerge in a small way, it could not divest itself of its legendary and poetic associations.

The attitude remained imperfect, and the treatment was necessarily conditioned by it. The authors themselves never felt uneasy, because the tradition ordained no deep interest in mere fact or incident, but even authorised unrestrained fancy or over-dressed fiction. Both theory and practice established that wroks, which dealt with facts of experience or had a biographical and historical content, did not require any specialised form and method, but should be considered only as types of the Kavya and be embellished with all its characteristic graces, refinements and fanciful elaboration. The fact of having an historical theme seldom made a difference; and such works are, in all essentials, as good or as bad as are all fictitious narratives. The authors therefore, claim merit, not for historicity, but for poetry. As poets, they need not keep within the limits of ascertained or ascertainable verities; it is even not necessary to ascertain, much less to appreciate or interpret, them. It matters little if the credulity is immense and unrestrained, if the representation is not faithful or accurate, if there is no depth or sense of proportion in the drawing of characters, who may be either downright devils or incredible saints, or if the slender and uneven thread of actual history is buried under a mass of luxuriant poetry or poetical bombast. As in the normal Kāvya so also here, there is no sense of the tragic contradictions and humorous dissonances of life, no situations of moral complexity, no unfolding of an intensely human drama. Even if an historical personage is taken as the central figure, he may be magnified and surrounded with all the glory and glamour of a legendary hero like Rāma or Yudhiṣṭhira, who is, to these writers, as real and perhaps more interesting than the petty rulers of their own day, although the old heroic flame could not be fanned anew.

In making an estimate of these works, therefore, it should be borne in mind that they are, in conception and execution deliberately meant to be elegant poetical works rather than sober historical or human documents. They are sometimes politely called 'Historical Kāvyas', but the description not only involves contradiction in terms, but is also misleading. It is not on their historical matter so much that they should be reckoned as on the poetic quality and treatment, for which alone they strive. As in the case of the ordinary Kāvya, the historical narrative is only the occasion, the elaborate poetry woven round it is alone essential. The incidents and characters are all lifted from the sphere of matter-of-fact history to the region of fancy and fable; and we have, more or less, the normal tradition of the Kāvya,—the same general scheme, the same descriptive digressions and the same ornate manner and diction. The qualification 'historical,' therefore, serves no useful purpose except indicating imperfectly that these Kāvyas have an historical, instead of a legendary or invented, theme ; but the historical theme is treated as if it is no better nor worse than a legendary or invented one.

We have already briefly indicated some of these characteristics in connexion with the Prose Kāvya, the *Harṣa-carita*, of Bāṇabhaṭṭa. In the period under consideration, we have also in verse a large number of similar works, which do not pretend much towards history but offer themselves as regular Kāvyas even though they sometimes euphemistically call themselves 'Caritas'. Kahlaṇa mentions (iv. 704f) that Śaṅkuka, in the reign of Ajitāpīḍa of Kashmir (1st half of the 8th century), described the terrible battle between the regents Mamma and Utpala in his *Bhuvanābhyudaya*. Had the work survived, it would have given us an early specimen of the type of Kāvya we are now considering. The next work is the *Navasāhasāṅka-carita*[1] of Padmaguptā, also called Parimala, son of Mṛgāṅkadatta. The work was composed probably in 1005 A.D. as a compliment to the poet's patron, the Paramāra Sindhurāja of Dhārā, who was also called Navasāhasāṅka. It describes in eighteen cantos (1525 verses), in the conventional manner and diction of a Mahākāvya, the marriage of the king with Śaśiprabhā, daughter of the Nāga king Śaṅkhapāla. Śaśiprabhā finds her pet deer pierced by an arrow, on which she recognises the name of the king, while the king in his turn, in pursuit of the deer, comes to a lake and finds a swan with a pearl necklace on its beak, which bears the name of Śaśiprabhā. Śaśiprabhā sends her maiden in search of the necklace, and an interview with the king follows. He is asked to invade Nāgaloka, kill the demon Vajrāṅkuśa and bring the golden

1 Ed. Vaman Islampurkar, Bombay Sansk. Series, 1895, Pt. i. (all published). From the poem we learn that the poet was patronised by both Muñja Vākpatirāja and his brother Sindhurāja. On the work and the author, see G. Bühlerd and Th. Zachariae, Über das Navasāhasāṅkacarita in *Sitzungsberichte d. Wiener Akademie*, p. 583f, reprinted Wien 1888, pp. 1-50 ; trs. into English in *IA*, XXXVI, pp. 624f. An account of the Paramāra dynasty is given in the poem in xi. 64-102 ; see Bühler and Zachariae, p. 604f (reprint, p. 24f).

lotus from its pleasure-pond ; all of which being accomplished, the lovers are united. The characteristically complacent confusion of heroic myth and historical fact makes the story a kind of a heightened fairy tale, and probably, as such, a gratifying compliment. If as history it is not of much value, as Kāvya it is written in the fully embellished, but comparatively pleasant style ; and in spite of the usual descriptive degressions, the narrative is not entirely sacrificed.

The *Vikramāṅkadeva-carita*[1] of Bihlaṇa, son of Jyeṣṭhakalaśa and Nāgadevī, has perhaps a little more historical matter and interest, but it is also very distinctly a Kāvya and conforms to the normal method and manner in its poetical amplifications and other characteristics. The last canto of the work, as the first Ucchvāsa of the *Harṣa-carita*, gives an interesting account of the poet's family, his country and its rulers, his wandering and literary adventures.[2] Born at Koṇamukha, near Pravarapura in Kashmir, of a pious and learned family of Midland Brahmans, Bihlaṇa was educated there and obtained proficiency in grammar and poetics, his father having been himself a grammarian who wrote a commentary on the *Mahābhāṣya* He set out on his wanderings in quest of fame and fortune at about the time of the nominal succession of Kalaśa to the throne of Kashmir ; and his literary career, which now began, extended over the third and fourth quarters of the 11th century. After visiting Mathurā, Kānyakubja, Prayāga and Vārāṇasī, he received welcome at the court of Kṛṣṇa of Dāhala (Bundelkhand), where he appears to have composed a poem on Rāma. He might have visited king Bhoja at Dhārā but did not. After spending some time perhaps, as his *Karṇasundarī* shows, in the court of Karṇadeva Trailokya-

1 Ed. G. Bühler, Bombay Sanskrit Series. 1875.

2 Such accounts are doubtless inspired by the poet's natural desire to secure his own immortality with that of his patron, but they are not a special feature of poems on historical subjects. While Bāṇa's *Harṣa-carita* and Vākpatirāja's Prakrit *Gauḍavaha* contain them, we have them, on the other hand, in Maṅkhaka's *Śrīkaṇṭha-carita* and Someśvara's *Svrathotsava,*

malla (1064-94 A.D.) of Aṇhilvad, he appears to have embarked from there for Southern India and spent some time in pilgrimage. He came to Kalyāṇa, where the Cālukya king Vikramāditya VI Tribhuvanamalla (1076-1127 A.D.), honoured him and gave him the office of Vidyāpati, in return for which he composed, before 1088 A.D., the present work in eighteen cantos to celebrate certain incidents of his patron's career.

The main theme of this laudatory poem consists of royal wars and royal marriages. It commences with a short account of the Cālukyas and passes on to Tailapa (973-97 A.D.), from whom the dynasty had its proper inauguration; but the story of the earlier kings is brief and fragmentary. After a somewhat fuller, but not connected, narrative of the deeds of Vikramāditya's father Āhavamalla, we have the birth of his three sons, Vikramāditya's youthful career of conquest before accession, a truly touching picture of Āhavamalla's death, Vikrama's exploits during the reign of his elder brother Someśvara II, his marriage with the Cola princess and expeditions in Southern India, and his own accession after a fratricidal war, all these in the earlier cantos, as well as Vikrama's capture and defeat of his younger brother Jayasiṃha and his numerous wars with the Colas in the later cantos, are given generally with the zest and style, but not always with the precision and accuracy, of a poetic chronicler. But the history of Vikrama's winning of his queen Candralekhā (or Candaladevī), daughter of a Śilahāra, ruler of Karahāta, is disproportionately enlarged *con amore* over seven and a half cantos (vii-xiv) by the safer introduction of the customary amplifications of palpable Kāvya topics, including description, for instance, of the spring season, minute depiction of the birde's physical charms (beginning, as in Śrīharṣa's *Naiṣadha*, with toe-nail and finishing with her head!), account of the Svayaṃvara and marriage, followed by the particular sports of the pair bathing scenes, drinking revelry, hunting expedition and amusements, as well as the general pleasures of the autumn, the monsoon and the cool season!

Divested of such traditionally poetic and flatteringly rhapsodic envelopment, Bihlaṇa's poems contains ampler historical information than that found in most poems of this kind ; and his account is generally confirmed by the evidence of inscriptions. But from the point of view of history, his narrative is inadequate and unsatisfactory. Like Bāṇa's romance, many of whose characteristics it shares, Bihlaṇa's poem gives us neither a connected and consistent, nor a full and accurate, account of his hero's entire career. It leaves us with a few fragmentary facts about Vikrama's predecessors, his own early career and his accession, embellished with much that is fanciful, and lapses into an exuberant poetic treatment of the first two years of his reign, his later career being disposed of with some hurried and sketchy references. In characterisation, sharply contrasted lights and shades are replaced by a vague moral chiaroscuro. One can realise the difficulties of a court-poet, whose amiableness must gloss over unpleasant aspects, whitewash his hero and blacken his enemies, and leave many things beautifully vague, uneven and obscure. Bihlaṇa has excellent reasons, therefore, for glorifying for instance, the circumstances of Vikrama's birth as a matter of Śiva's divine favour, as well as magnifying his youthful valour, with which he is said to have perfected his art of annihilation on the Colas, although these hereditary and ubiquitous enemies appear inexterminable and cause repeated troubles at every step! The chronological order to the wars does not matter, nor accuracy regarding their nature and extent ; it is enough that the hero must conquer many countries, including even the far-off Gauḍa and Kāmarūpa! All this is evidently a part of the plan of representing Vikrama as the favourite of the gods, entitled to supplant his elder brother on the throne and crush the improper rebellion of his younger brother; and the poet does not hesitate invoking the intervention of Śiva thrice to justify the awkwardness of these unfraternal acts!

These limitations are natural and obvious, but they do not permit Bihlaṇa much freedom to exercise his undoubted gift for historical narrative and attain impartiality and precision either with regard to incident or characterisation. He has to be content with the application of the traditional form and method of the Kāvya to an historical subject, in order to evolve an embellished poetical picture, rather than compile a faithful record of the deeds of his royal patron. It is not necessary to speculate what the results might have been in other circumstances ; it is enough to recognise that Bihlaṇa intended to compose, no history, but Kāvya, not independently, but in grateful complaisance to his patron's glorification. His work has much less mythical element than Padmagupta's fanciful poem, much less confusing gorgeousness than Bāṇa's romance ; but, in all essentials, it is no more than a Kāvya, having the mere accident of an historical kernel. The lengthy diversion from serious matter, therefore, found in the romantic story of the winning of Chandralekhā, occupies him, quite appropriately after the established tradition of the Mahākāvya, with luxuriantly poetical description of Svayaṃvara, seasons and court-amusements. It is as a poet that Bihlaṇa excels ; and, in spite of his obvious conventionalism, he often succeeds in imparting a fine poetical charm to his graphic pictures. What Bihlaṇa lacks, like most poets of this period, is confident originality and independence, but within his limits he is undoubtedly an impressive artist and poet. His style is not easy, but elegant and normally attractive ; it is doubtless studied, but not overdone with subtleties of thought and expression ; it is fully embellished, but reasonably clear and effective in its verbal and metrical skill. This is no mean praise in an age of mechanical conventionality, which reproduced colourless imitations of little merit. Comparatively speaking, Bihlaṇa's work remains a graphic document for the subject and a pleasant poem in itself.

The only work in Sanskrit, which to a certain extent approaches the standard of a sustained chronicle, if not of critical history, is the well known *Rāja-taraṅgiṇī*[1] of Kahlaṇa, but it is

[1] Ed. M. A. Stein, vol. (Text), Bombay 1892 Eng. trs. separately published, with introduction etc. in two vols., Westminster 1900. Also ed. Durgaprasad, in 3 vols. 1

no less a poetical narrative than a matter-of-fact chronicle. Like Bihlaṇa, whose poem he appears to have studied, Kahlaṇa was also a Kashmirian, but he was neither a courtier nor a court-poet. His father Campaka was a minister of the wicked and hapless Harṣa of Kashmir (1089-1101 A.D), whom, unlike the average Kashmirian of his time, he followed faithfully through all the vicissitudes of fortune ; but after Harṣa's tragic death, he seems to have retired from active life, and young Kahlaṇa deprived of opportunities of ministerial office, was never drawn directly into the whirlpool of the stormy political life of his time. Since the accession to power of Uccala and Sussala, the contemporary history of Kashmir was one of intrigue, oppression and bloodshed. Kahlaṇa had the good fortune of standing apart and viewing the sad and dreary state of his country, without illusion and with a sense of dispassion and resignation which is reflected in his story. He was at the same time not a recluse, but a keen observer of current events, and possessed an inherited understanding of political affairs, which never lost sight of reality. He had also admirable literary gifts, being well versed not only in Sanskrit literature, but also in the legendary lore of his country, and had enough catholicity of mind to respect other religious creeds than Kashmirian Śaivism, which he professed but of whose degeneration in pratice he was well aware. The combination of these qualities justified his ambition of writing a systematic chronicle of the kings of Kashmir, to which he was probably urged by his patron Alakadatta. The work mentions Jayasiṃha (1127-1159 A.D.), son of Sussala, as the reigning sovereign ; [1] it was commenced in Śaka 1070 (= 1148-49 A.D.) and completed in the next year.

(i-vii), vol 2 (viii), vol. 3 (supplements of Jonarāja, Śrīvara and Prājyabhaṭṭa, Bombay 1892, 1894, 1896. The *editio princeps*, with the three supplements, was published by the Asiatic Society of Bengal, Calcutta 1835.

[1] From Ratnākara's citation in his *Sāra-samuccaya*, we learn that Kahlaṇa composed a Kāvya on this king, entitled *Jayasiṁhābhyudaya*.

For periods of remoter antiquity Kahlaṇa appears to have freely utilised the works of his predecessors. He consulted eleven such sources, including the still extant *Nīlamata-purāṇa* ; but he tells us that the extensive royal chronicles (Rāja-kathās) of earlier times were unfortunately lost through the misplaced learning of one Suvrata, who condensed them in a lengthy but difficult poem. Kṣemendra, we are informed, drew up a list of kings, called *Nṛpāvalī* ; but no part of it was free from mistake. Among other authorities, Kahlaṇa mentions Helārāja, who composed a similar work in twelve thousand *granthas*, and whose opinion was followed by Padmamihira in his own work ; while Chavillākara furnished Kahlaṇa with some information about Aśoka and his devotion to Buddhism. We know nothing about there authors and their works, nor are we told anything about their agreements and disagreements. The present heterogenous text of the *Nīlamata-purāṇa*,[1] a work of the Māhātmya type, with its rich information regarding the sacred places of Kashmir and their legends might show, to some extent, how Kahlaṇa used his sources for the traditional history of earlier periods ; but we do not know how he used his other materials, what he received, what he added and what he rejected. Although Kahlaṇa often betrays extreme credulity, he is conscientious enough to consult, wherever possible, inscriptions, records of land grants, coins and manuscripts, in order to overcome "the worry arising from many errors". The extent of his researches in this direction cannot be determined, but the result is often seen in his minute knowledge of local topography, his generally correct assertions about literary history and the detailed information he gives about the building of temples and edifices, all of which possess considerable historical value.

The first three comparatively short chapters of Kahlaṇa's work deal with a series of fifty-two fabulous kings, the first king Gonanda being made contemporaneous with the epic Yudhiṣṭhira. This is obviously an attempt to connect the history of Kashmir,

1 Ed. Ramalal Kanjilal and Jagaddhar Zadoo, Lahore 1924 ed. K. St. J. M. de Vreese, Leiden (E. J. Brill) 1936.

which does not play any part in the Mahābhārata war, with the imaginary date of a glorious legendary event ; but the account is naturally hazy and unhistorical. Kahlaṇa frankly admits that he took some of the kings from his predecessor's accounts, while others are patched up, apparently from heresay and tradition, for the sake of a continuous narrative. It was perhaps not possible for him to sift and weigh the meagre and uncertain evidence that was available to him, but he feels no uneasiness in accepting all kinds of romantic tales, legendary names and impossible dates. Of historical figures, Aśoka is barely mentioned ; and though Kahlaṇa speaks of Huṣka, Juṣka and Kaniṣka, he dismisses the Turuṣka kings of Kashmir in a few lines, misplacing them by four hundred years in relation to Aśoka. But chronology in this remote period does not worry him , history and legend are hopelessly mixed up ; and he has no difficulty in believing that Aśoka lived in 1260 B.C., or that Raṇāditya, one of the last kings of the restored Gonanda line, reigned for three hundred years, or that Mihirakula and Toramāṇa, apparently the well known Hūṇa kings, belonged to the Gonanda dynasty ! With the fourth chapter begins the story of the Karkoṭa dynasty, to whom a mythical origin is assigned. It covers, with some semblance of historical treatment, a period apparently from 600 to 855 A.D., and includes a number of kings from Durlabhavardhana to Anaṅgāpīḍa. The dynasty ends with its overthrow by Avantivarman, son of Sukhavarman and grandson of Utpala ; and real history begins from this stage in the fifth chapter, the sixth chapter bringing it down to the death of the lascivious and blood-thirsty queen Diddā in 1003 A.D. In the seventh chapter, the Lohara dynasty succeeds with Diddā's nephew, and takes us down, in 1731 verses, to the assassination of Harṣa in 1101 A.D., that is practically to the author's own time. The eighth and last valuable chapter deals at greater length (3449 verses) with contemporary events of the troublous times which began with the accession of Uccala.

It will be seen that the scope of Kahlaṇa's work is comprehensive, but its accomplishment is uneven. If the earlier part of his chronicle is defective and unreliable, and if his chronology is based upon groundless assumptions, he does not move in the high clouds of romance and legend when he comes nearer his own time, but attains a standard of vividness and accuracy, like which there is nothing anywhere in Sanskrit literature, nothing in his predecessors Bāṇa, Padmagupta or Bihlaṇa. The work is also a rich source of the culture-history of a great country. Kahlaṇa doubtless has his limitations as a critical investigator and betrays the peculiar attitude of Sanskrit writers towards historical matters. His unquestioning acceptance of myth and legend ; his faith in witchcraft and miracle ; his belief in omens and portents ; his inability to withstand the distant glamour of ancient glory or the improbabilities of the older chronology , his reckoning of fate or destiny, of sins of previous birth, or of intervention of gods and demons as a sufficient explanation of human action,—from all this it is difficult to expect a proper appreciation of historical events or motives. The attitude precludes depth of insight into the complexities of human mind and character, except of a certain type with which the author was too familiar ; it never leads to a breadth of vision to consider his country, secluded as it is, in relation to the outer world. In the narration of more recent events, however, his personal knowledge or direct information makes him achieve much better results. He shows a masterly grasp of the petty politics of a small principality, of its hostile factions, of its usual course of intrigue, strife, treason, assassination and massacre ; and he can ably depict the characters which throng and fight within its limited arena, its series of royal debauchees, treacherous sycophants, plotting ministers, turbulent landlords, immoral teachers, intriguing priests, untamed soldiers and lawless ladies. Here he is in contact with reality, and being unconcerned, can attain his own ideal of a judge, free alike from love and hatred (i. 7). But here also his outlook is narrow. He is an interesting chronicler rather than a philosophic historian. He can give minute exposition of facts and criticise acts and incidents according to a limited standard, but he never feels it to be his business to draw broader conclusions or apply large principles of history.

But in making an estimate of Kahlaṇa's work it should not be forgotten that, like most Sanskrit authors who attempt historical subjects, he conceives his duty to be that of a poet more than that of an historian. The dark days of his boyhood and the unpleasant and tragic history of Harṣa, Uccala and Sussala must have produced a deep impression on his mind, and bred in him a spirit of wisdom and resignation. His work, therefore, is grave and moral, being wrought under the shadow of a disturbed order of things; he is a poet whom the fleeting nature of human power and pomp moves earnestly. It is natural, therefore, that he should write a Kāvya, concerning the strife and struggle of kings, with Śānta or the quietistic mood as the prevailing sentiment (i.23) and with obvious lessons to princes and people. The didactic tendency may have been imbibed from the Epics; but Kahlaṇa's motive in selecting, as his text, the theme of earthly fame and glory, and his comparatively little interest in mundane events for their own sake, must have also been the result of his particular experience of men and things. To such a frame of mind the doctrine of fate may be a sensible solution of acts and incidents; and exaggerations and insufficiencies of facts may not prove formidable. It does not lead twoards history, but certainly towards poetry; and it is as a poet that Kahlaṇa would like to be judged. Doubtless some of his weaknesses spring from this attitude, but it is also the source of his strength. As a simple but diversified and deeply affecting poetical narrative, the merit of his work can never be questioned; and if the verdict be that he is not a great historian, no one would deny that he is a poet whose originality of achievement is certainly remarkable in a singularly unoriginal and unpoetical age. Kahlaṇa regrets (i. 6) that the character and amplitude of his subject do not permit much indulgence in the usual Kāvya topics and embellishments; but his enforced moderation is perhaps productive of better results than he imagines. It enables him to wield a graphic style, usually in the Śloka metre, elegant yet not devoid of directness, rapid yet not too condensed. The complexities of the highly ornamented and unwieldy Kāvya style and diction would have been out of place in a narrative like his. Kahlaṇa's occasional modest digression into the sphere of ornate poetry displays no lack of inclination or skill, but it is well that he is kept restrained by the interest of a clear, flowing and forcible narrative. Arid stretches of prosaic verse or the bald manner of the mere chronicler are inevitable in such a long poem, but they are sometimes even better than the artificialities of Bāṇa and Bihlaṇa. Some of Kahlaṇa's fine passages, however, show how he can make effective use of the resources of the poetic style, without burdening it with intricacies of elaborate expression and without at the same time descending to mere versified prose. By the nature and interest of his subject, he has been able to avoid beaten tracks and banal topics, and attain considerable independence of treatment and expression ; and this, as well as the large sweep of his work, distinguishes it in a high degree from every other poetical narrative of the same type in Sanskrit.

The difference becomes abundantly clear when we compare Kahlaṇa's work with its three continuations[1] composed in Kashmir by Jonarāja, Śrīvara and Prājyabhaṭṭa respectively, or with other Kāvyas of this class, which are either dry and bare annals or exuberant poems with little historical interest. We have already spoken of the *Rāma-carita* of Saṃdhyākara Nandin, which describes, by means of Śleṣa, the double story of Rāma, king of Ayodhyā, and Rāmapāla, king of Bengal ; but its literary

1 The three continuations of the *Rāja-taraṅgiṇī* will be found printed in the *editio princeps*, Calcutta 1835, p. 278 f as well as in Durraprasad's ed. mentioned above. The first by Jonarāja, intended to bring the chronicle down to the time of the author's patron Zain-u-'l-'Ābidīn (1417-67 A.D.), was left incomplete in 681 verses by the author's death in 1459. His pupil Śrīvara wrote the second continuation in four chapters for the period between 1459 and 1486. The *Rājāvalī-patākā* of Prājyabhaṭṭa and his pupil Suka deals in nearly a thousand verses with the story of a few more years till the annexation of Kashmir by Akbar (1586 A.D.). They are far less original and accurate works. See Stein, Trs. of *Raja-ta*, ii°, p. 373 f.

value is negligible, and its abstruse punning method renders its historical information vague and difficult of application to contemporary events. The Kashmirian Jahlana, who is mentioned by Maṅkhaka (xxv. 75) as a minister of Rājapurī, appears to have written an account of his patron Somapāla[1], son of Saṃgrāmapāla of Rājapurī, in his *Somapāla-vilāsa,* but nothing is known of the contents of the work which is now lost. The fragmentary and unfinished *Pṛthvīrāja-vijaya*[2] of unknown date and authorship, commented upon by Jonarāja (15th century) and quoted by Jayaratha, may have also been a Kashmirian work. It deals, in conventionally poetical manner (canto v, for instance, illustrates varieties of figures of speech) and apparently on the model of Bihlaṇa's poem, with the victories of the Cāhumāna prince Pṛthvīrāja of Ajmer and Delhi, who fought with Shāhabuddīn Ghori and fell in 1193 A.D., the prince being presented in the poem as an incarnation of Rāma. There are also a few ornate Kāvyas of this type which celebrate rulers of local and limited renown, but they are of little poetic or historic interest, and most of them are yet unpublished. Among those which have been printed, mention may be made of the *Rāṣṭrauḍha-vaṃśa*[3] of Rudra; son of Ananta and grandson of Keśava, of Southern India ; it gives in twenty cantos the story of Bāgulas of

1 Kahlaṇa, viii. 621 f, 146.

2 Ed. S. K. Belvalkar, Bibl. Ind., Calcutta 1914-22. The author's name is missing but Belvalkar conjectures its author to be a Kashmirian poet named Jayānaka, who is one of the figures in the poem. It may have been composed between 1178 and 1193 A.D. and left unfinished on account of the prince's change of fortune, Jayaratha, who flourished in the first quarter of the 13th century cites v. 50 in his commentary on Ruyyaka's *Alaṁkāra-sarvasva* (ed. NSP, p. 64). The recent edition of the *Pṛthvīrāja-vijaya,* however, by Gourishankar H. Ojha and C. S. Gulleri(Ajmer 1941), with the commentary of Jonaraja, also gives the poem in an incomplete form in 12 cantos, but makes out Jayānaka to be the author. It is edited from the birch-bark MS of the work discovered by Bühler in Kashmir in 1876 and now deposited in the Bhandarkar Oriental Institute at Poona. A summary of the contents of the work is given by Har Bilas Sarda in *JRAS,* 1913, pp. 259-81.

3 Ed. Ember Krishnamacharya, Gaekwad's Orient. Series, Baroda 1917, with an historical introd. by C. D. Dalal. Some cantos, e.g. xii, display diversity of metres, The author is said to have composed also a *Jāhāṅgīra-sāha-carita* at the command of Pratāpa Sāha, son ofh is patron.

Mayūragiri, commencing from the originator of the dynasty, Rāṣṭrauḍha, king of Kanauj, and ending with Nārāyaṇa Śāha, ruler of Mayūragiri, who was the patron of the author. The *Raghunāthābhyudaya*,[1] in twelve cantos, of Rāmabhadrāmba, a mistress of Raghunātha Nāyaka of Tanjore, is also interesting as the work of a cultured woman-writer of modest poetic merit and historic sense on some incidents connected with the author's hero, which took place about 1620 A.D ; while the *Madhurā-vijaya* or *Vīrakamparāya-carita* of another woman-poet, Gaṇgādevī, queen of Acyutarāya of Vijayanagara, gives an account of her husband's conquest of Madura.[2]

The Jaina writers also proved themselves adepts at this kind of composition, but the literary and historical interest of their works is variable. The most extensive but the least animated is the *Kumārapāla-carita* or *Dvyāśraya-kāvya*[3] of the Jaina Ācārya Hemacandra (1089-1173 A.D.)[4] whose versatility and encyclopaedic knowledge embraced many fields of Sanskrit and Prakrit learning, and through whose efforts Gujarat became the stronghold of Śvetāmbara Jainas for many centuries. The work gives in twenty-eight cantos an account of the rulers of Aṇhilvad, bringing it down to the time of Kumārapāla, who came to the throne in 1142 A,D., and whom Hemacandra himself converted into Jainism in 1152 A.D. Tht first twenty cantos, a part of which (xvi-xx) deals with Kumārapāla but the

1 Ed. T. R. Cintamani, University of Madras, 1934.

2 For *Varadāmbikā-pariṇaya* of Tirumalāmbā, as well as for these works, see below under Women-poets. Also see *Vemabhūpāla-carita* under Prose-kāvya.—On Acyutarāya of Vijaynagar, Rājanātha also wrote *Acyutarāyābhyudaya* (ed. Śrī Vāṇīvilāsa Press, 1907) in 12 cantos ; see P. P. Sastri, *Tanjore Catalogue*, vii, pp. 3238-43.

3 Ed. A. V. Kathvate, cantos i-xx (Sanskrit) in two parts, Bombay Sanskrit Series, 1885, 1915 ; and ed. S. P. Pandit, cantos xxi-xxviii (Prakrit), in the same series, 1900 ; 2nd revised edition by P. L. Vaidya, with an appendix containing Hemacandra's Prakrit Grammar, in the same series, 1936.

4 On the author, see G. Bühler, *Über das Leben des Jaina-Mönches Hemacandra*, Wien 1889, and H. Jacobi in *Encyclop. of Religion and Ethics*, vi, p. 591. On the author's rhetorical, grammatical and lexicographical works, see S. K. De, *Sanskrit Poetics*, i. p. 203 f ; S. K. Belvalkar, *Systems of Sanskrit Grammar*, Poona 1915, p. 73 f ; Th. Zachariae, *Ind. Woerterbücher*, Strassburg 1897, p, 30 f.

rest with Kumārapāla's predecessors, have a distinct importance for the history of the Calukyas of Gujarat. This portion is written in Sanskrit ; but the last eight cantos are written in Prakrit and are concerned entirely with Kumārapāla, although the two concluding cantos contain no historical matter but moral and religious reflections. The alternative title refers to this twofold medium, as well as to the intention of the work to illustrate the rules of the author's own Sanskrit and Prakrit grammars, which makes it Dvisaṃdhāna. The work possesses great interest for the picture it gives of Kumārapāla's efforts to make Gujarat into a model Jaina state ; but it is, by its very learned and propagandist object, a highly artificial and laborious production, which brings in the usual Kāvya topics, but which is scarcely interesting as a Kāvya.[1]

Of other Jaina Kāvyas, which have an historicel subject, a brief mention of the published texts will suffice ; they are worthy efforts, but present neither adequate history nor attractive poetry. There are, for instance, several poems and dramas[2] concerned with some of their ruling dynasties of Gujarat, especially with the history of the Vāghelā rulers Vīradhavala and Vīsaladeva and their astute ministers, Vastupāla and Tejaḥpāla. Someśvara, who wrote between 1179 and 1262 and whose *Surathotsava* we have already mentioned, composed his *Kīrtikaumudī*[3] as a panegyric of Vastupāla, in the form more of a Campu than that of a regular Kāvya. Another eulogistic work on the same personage, chiefly with reference to his pilgrimages

[1] There is another *Kumārapāla-carita* by Jayasiṁha Sūri, composed in 1265 A.D. (ed. Hiralal Hamsaraj, Jainh Bhāskarodaya Press, Jamnagar). Other works dealing with Kumārapāla are : the Prakrit poem, *Kumārapāla-pratibodha* of Somaprabhācārya (composed in 1185 A.D.), ed. Gaekwad's Orient. Ser., Baroda 1920 ; he allegorical drama *Moha-parājaya* of Yaśaḥpāla, to be noticed below ; *Kumārapāla-prabandha* of Jinamaṇḍanā (ed. Bhavnagar 1915). There is also a *Kumārapāla-caritra* of Cāritrasundara, published by the Jaina Ātmānanda Sabhā, Bhavnagar 1914.

[2] Vastupāla is one of the heroes of the drama *Hammīra-mada-mardana* of Jayasiṁha, to be noticed below.

[3] Ed. A. V. Kathvate, Bombay Sanskrit Series, 1883.

and religious activities, is the *Sukṛta-saṃkīrtana*[1] of Arisiṃha, son of Lavaṇasiṃha, in eleven cantos (553 verses) ; but the first two cantos give an account of the Cāpotkaṭa or Cauḍa family and the Caulukya rulers of Gujarat respectively, mixed up in the later cantos with Kāvya topics like the description of seasons and of the hero's entry into the city. A still third work on the same subject is the *Vasanta-vilasa*[2] of Bālacandra Sūri, pupil of Haribhadra Sūri and author of the drama *Karuṇā-vajrāyudha* ;[3] it was composed after Vastupāla's death (1242 A.D.) for the delectation of his son Jaitrasiṃha, and gives in fourteen cantos a similar account of the rulers of Gujarat and of the various episodes, religious and political, in Vastupāla's career.[4] Some two centuries later, Nayacandra Sūri wrote the *Hammīra-mahākāvya*[5] in fourteen cantos, with Hammīra, the Cauhān king of Mewar, as his hero. The narrative is uneven, and the author often lapses into poetic rhapsody to cover his ignorance of historical facts ; and more than three cantos (v-vii, and a part of viii) are devoted to the usual descriptions of seasons, sports, amusements and erotic activities of the hero.

There are also short poems of panegyric on particular rulers, such as the *Rajendra-karṇapūra*[6] of Śaṃbhu (75 verses in varied metres), eulogising Harṣa of Kashmir ; the *Sukṛta-kīrti-kallolinī*[7] of Udayaprabha Sūri (179 verses in varied metres)

1 Ed. Jaina Ātmānanda Sabbā Series, Bhavnagar 1917. For an account of the work and the author, see G. Bühler, *Das Sukṛtasaṁkīrtana des Arisiṁha* in *Sitz. d. Wiener Akad.*, Wien 1889 ; text on pp. 39-56, with an historical and literary introduction (Eng. trs. Burgess in *IA*, XXXI, pp. 477-95). See S. K. De, *Sanskrit Poetics*, i, p. 210f.

2 Ed. C. D. Dalal, Gaekwad's Orient. Ser., Baroda 1917. Vastupāla was poetically called Vasantapāla.

3 This work, for which see below, was composed at the temple of Ādinatha during Vastupāla's pilgrimage to Śatruñjaya.

4 Vastupāla himself wrote the *Nara-nārāyaṇānanda* noticed above ; he was not only a patron of poets, but also a poet himself ; and in these laudatory works he is figured as statesman, warrior, philanthropist and man of piety.

5 Ed. Nilkantha Janardan Kirtane, Bombay 1879, with an introd. See Kirtane in *IA*, VIII, 1879, p. 55f.

6 Ed. Kāvyamālā, Gucchaka i, NSP, Bombay 1886, pp. 22-34.

7 Printed as an appendix to Jayasiṁha Sūri's *Hammīra-mada-mardana* (Gaekwad's Orient. Series).

in honour of Vastupāla ; or the *Prāṇābharaṇa*[1] of Jagannātha (53 verses in varied metres) in praise of Prāṇanārāyaṇa of Kāmarūpa ; but there is not much of historical and literary worth in these extravagant laudations of grateful poets.

4. Shorter Poems

a. *The Erotic Poetry*

The tradition of erotic poetry, we have seen, is ubiquitous in Sanskrit literature ; and from the time of Aśvaghoṣa's *Saundarananda,* it is appropriated by the Mahākāvya (as also by drama) in its fulsome description of erotic acts and feelings, which occupy not a small place in these compositions, and of which even pious Hindu and Jaina writers are not abhorrent. But Sanskrit love-poetry, from the begining, is either mixed up with descriptive matter (as in the *Megha-dūta* and Ghaṭakarpara poem) and didactic drift (as in Aśvaghoṣa and Bhartṛhari), or it takes the form (as in Amaru) of single stanzas, standing by themselves, in which the poet delights to present a complete picture in an elegant and finished form. The Sanskrit Anthologies abound in such fine little stanzas ; in all likelihood they are taken from extensive works of particular poets, which are now lost ; but they are isolated in the stanza-form as complete units of expression. It is probable that they were sometimes composed as such, not in a particular context but independently, and were collected together in the frame of Śatakas. Even if it is possible to find out an entire significance from the detached stanzas in a Śataka, they seldom have any inner connexion or motive in relation to one another, or any totality of effect, each stanza by

1 Ed. Kāvyamālā, Gucchaka i, pp. 79-90. The author also wrote *Āsapha-vilāsa,* apparently a prose Ākhyāyikā, in praise of Nawāb Aṣaf Khān (d. 1641), a nobleman of the court of Shāh Jahān, *Jagadābharaṇa* in honour of Shāh Jahān's son Dārā Shikoh ; but these works do not appear to have been yet printed.

There is no need to deal here with geographical or topographical works (Deśa-vṛttas) which are hardly poems.

itself having a self-contained charm of its own. In this way, extraordinary variety, richness and subtlety are achieved by depicting single aspects of the infinite moods and fancies of love ; and the necessity of comperssing one whole idea or situation within the limits of a single stanza gives to the pictures the precision and elegance of exquisite cameos of poetic thought and feeling, This is one of the most remarkable characteristics of Sanskrit love-poetry, of which we have already spoken and which gives to it a value of its own. There is no systematic and well knit love-poem or love-lyric in the sense in which we understand it today. In the series of individual stanzas, the erotic poetry deals with niceties rather than simplicities of love, with fanciful vagaries rather than direct exaltations. It has very often a background of nature and natural feelings, but they are romanticised with elegancies of words and ideas, and there is nothing of the beauty that stings and thrills. The sentiment is more often artistic than personal, and expressed in perfect accordance with the poetic theory of impersonalised enjoyment, which would not permit the theme of a particular woman, but of woman as such, provided she is young and beautiful.[1] It is true that the particular woman is always there behind the universalised woman, and inspires the emotional earnestness and vivid imagery, but there is in its refined and idealised expression little of subjectivity or of the lyric mood ; and the poetry delights to move in an imaginative world of serene and pleasant fiction.

In later erotic poetry, with which we are concerned here, the rhetorical and psychological refinements come to dominate ; and even if the little pictures often possess delicacy of feeling and gracefulness of touch, the reality and richness of the emotion are obscured by deliberate straining after conventional literary effects. The love-poetry does not escape the taint of artificiality which marks the entire poetry of this period. We have the same want of independence, the same monotony inseparable from

1 See above, pp. 38-39.

similar series of ideas and similar treatment. The technical analysis and authority of Erotics and Poetics, which evolved a system of meticulous classification of the ways and means of love and their varied effects, eastablished a series of so-called poetic conventions, to be expressed with stock poetic phrases, analogies and conceits. All conceivable types of heroes and heroines ; their assistants and adjuncts ; the different shades of their feelings and gestures ; the generous sets of their excellences, physical and mental ; the varied moods and situations ; in fact, the entire sentiments of love, with its elaborate paraphernalia, is industriously defined, analysed and classified, with a great deal of observation, it is true, but with all the pedantry of scholastic formalism. The emotional and artistic formulas thus prescribed become the unalterable mechanism of erotic poetry. The result naturally is the growth of a refined artificiality in sentiment and expression ; and in uninspired poets, it becomes a clever but mechanical reproduction of romantic commonplaces and decorative shibboleths. The general tradition established by Amaru and Bhartṛhari is further refined, but seldom exceeded or advanced. Making allowance for these obvious limitations, it should nevertheless be conceded that the erotic poetry of this period is never so dull and dreary as the extensive Mahākāvya, but can often work up its aesthetic and emotional banalities into things of real beauty. The bloom is doubtless artificial, and the perfection is attained by careful culture ; there is no rush of passion or tumult of style ; but very often in the detached stanzas of the Anthologies, as well as in some sustained works of lesser poets, we have rare and pleasing moments of charm, which we miss in the more ambitious and elaborately composed Kāvyas. If they are dainty trifles, it is often in trifling things that poetry flourishes with daintiness of touch in metre, phrase, sound and sense, more than in massive productions of erudite industry. Perhaps the theme of love has a wider and more potent appeal ; perhaps the poets themselves are more readily moved and become better articulate by its intimate character.

Whatever may be the reasn, the fact remains that this poetry is often characterised by the tender and touching strain of a refined emotional inflatus, while the emotion of the greater Kāvya poets is almost always a matter of serious doubt.

It is also noteworthy that the erotic poetry of this period is very closely allied with its devotional and didactic poetry, not only in respect of quality but also on account of certain fundamental characteristics. Although commonsense and poetics would like to distinguish between love and religious devotion, or love and worldly wisdom, it is curious that in the actual poetic practice of Sanskrit, the three aspects of human thought and activity betray a tendency to intermingle. While mediaeval devotionalism is saturated with eroticism, of which it is sometimes a transfigured expression, the didactic reflectiveness cannot but concern itself earnestly with the mighty sex-impulse of human life. The old tradition of Śṛṅgāra, Nīti and Vairāgya, of Love, Wisdom and Resignation, going hand in hand, naturally persists, either in the Śataka form or in regular poems, the one adding a zest and piquancy to the other; and the lover, the moralist and the devotee dominate the lesser, but better, poetry of this period.

The Sanskrit erotic poetry is best exemplified, as we have said, in the hundreds of exquisite stanzas, scattered in the Anthologies and assigned to more than a thousand obscure and well nigh dateless poets; but the Anthologies, being repositories of diverse metter, do not bring erotic poetry alone into prominence. Nor is it possible for us to deal here in detail with the immense wealth and variety of material which they supply for a study of Sanskrit love-poetry. We shall confine ourselves here to separate poems, or collections of stanzas in the form of Śatakas. Of these, the earliest appears to be the *Caurī-* (or *Caura*) *surata-pañcāśikā*[1] shortly, *Caura-pañcāśikā*, of unknown date and author-

1 (*i*) Ed. P. von. Bohlen (along with Bhartṛhari's Śatakas), with comm. of Gaṇapati, Berlin 1833, and also ed. in Haeberlin's Kāvyasaṁgraha, Calcutta 1847, p. 227 (Devanāgarī and Bengali recension); (*ii*) ed. and trs. J. Ariel in *JA*, 1848, s. 4, t. xi, p. 469 f, and sd. in

ship, but generally ascribed to Bihlaṇa, around which romantic legends have gathered. It consists of fifty passionate stanzas in the Vasantatilaka metre, uttered in the first person, on the subject of secret love, which is apparently responsible for the title of the poem. Most of it is devoted to the description of feminine charm in particularly erotic situations; and the recollective word-pictures of stolen pleasure, with their lavish sensuous detail, appear vividly circumstantial. This fact probably became the starting point of a large number of anecdotes regarding the origin and authorship of the work; and the popularity of the luscious poem gave rise to at least three distinct recensions of the text. In one form of the South Indian recension, we find the text enclosed in a poem called *Bihlaṇa-kāvya*, in which the poet Bihlaṇa is made to utter these stanzas when caught in a secret intrigue with a princess and led to be executed, with the result that the king, impressed by the glowing verses, relents, orders his release and permits his marriage with the princess. The story occurs in various forms, and the names of the actors, as well as place of occurrence of the alleged incident, are also varied.[1] As in the case of most early collections of the Śataka type, the text is extremely fluctuating, only about thirty-three

Kāvyamālā, Gucchaka xiii, NSP, Bombay 1903, pp. 145-49, as imbedded in the *Bihlaṇa-kāvya* (South Indian recension); (*iii*) ed. and trs. W. Solf, Kiel 1886 (Kashmirian recension). The work, in its Vulgate text, is poetically, if freely, rendered into English verse by Sir Edwin Arnold (in litho, Trübner : London 1896). The work has been printed also in Jivananda Vidyasagar's Kāvya-saṁgraha, i, p. 596 f (3rd ed. 1888) and in Kāvyakalāpa, No. 1, pp. 100-05.

1 In Solf's edition there are no names, but there are two introductory verses which mention Bihlaṇa, an unnamed king of Kuntala and a princess. In Ariel's edition, the princess is Yāminī-pūrṇatilaka, daughter of the Pañcāla king Madanābhirāma; in the Kāvyamālā edition, she is Śaśikalā, Candrakalā or Candralekhā, dauthter of Virasiṁha of Mahilāpattana; in Gujarat manuscripts, she is a Cauḍa or Caura (*i.e.*, Cāpotkaṭa) princess; while in the Bengal tradition, she is Vidyā, daughter of king Vīrasiṁha, and the poet-hero is not Bihlaṇa, but Sundara (also called Cora-kavi), son of Guṇasāgara of Caurapallī in Rāḍha, while the stanzas of the *Pañcāśikā*, often absorbed in larger poems, are made by pun to have a twofold application simultaneously to Vidyā and the goddess Kālī whom Sundara propitiates in his distress. The last account occurs in various forms in Bengali poems, which appropriate the Sanskrit stanzas; but a Sanskrit version, ascribed to Vararuci, also exists in 53 verses (see Sailendranath Mitra in *Proc. of the Second Orient. Conference*, Calcutta 1923, p. 215f). The legend also forms the theme of a Sanskrit *Vidyā-sundara* (printed in Jivananda's Kāvya-saṁgraha

verses being common to the Kashmirian and the South Indian recensions. It is clear, therefore, that Bihlaṇa's authorship[1] can be asserted with as a little confidence as that of Cora (in spite of Jayadeva's mention of a poet of that name in his *Prasanna-rāghava*)[2] or of Sundara. It is, on the other hand, not improbable that the stanzas were old floating verses of forgotten authorship, which were ascribed to Bihlaṇa, Cora, Sundara, and Vararuci in turns, and different legendary frame-stories were supplied. But the work itself, as a whole, is indeed a fine specimen of Sanskrit erotic poetry. Notwithstanding repetition of conventional ideas, imageries and situations, the spring and resonance of its Vasanta-tilaka stanzas, the simplicity and swing of its comparatively smooth diction, and the vivid relish of its recollection of past scenes of pleasure relieve, by their descriptive richness and variety, the monotony inevitable in such series of verses, and render the poem unique in Sanskrit. No direct imitation of the work has survived, but occasionally we find its influence at work ; as for instance, in verses 92 and 99-114 of the apparently late poem, the *Tārā-śaśāṅka*[3] of Kṛṣṇa, son of Nārāyaṇa.

iii, pp. 441-63) ; but the stanzas *Pañcāśikā* do not occur, and the poem supplies a small part of the story without any preliminary account of Vidyā and Sundara. The idea of a tunnel made by Sundara under the palace for his clandestine meetings is old and occurs in the Mahāummaga Jātaka (Fausboll, vi, no. 546)

1 Apart from the fact that Bihlaṇa himself makes no claim to any royal intrigue in his autobiographical account, the fact that a stanza from the Kashmirian recension, which is supposed to be more genuine (*nidrā-nimīlita-dṛśaḥ* Solf, no. 36), is cited in Abhinavagupta's *Locana* (ed. NSP. p. 60) Kuntaka's *Vakrokti-jīvita* (ed. S. K. De, *ad* i, 51, 65) and Dhanika's commentary on *Daśa-rūpaka* (ed. NSP, iv 23) ; it indicates the existence of the text in some form already in the 10th century.

2 The suggestion that the name Cora or Caura, found in some versions of the legend, implies an original story of the love of a robber chief and a princess, is illusory ; for in one version Cora is the proper name of a Brahmin, and it is evident that the name was suggested by the very title of the poem relating to stolen love. The idea of a princess must have been a part of the original legend, for it is found in a stanza which occurs in the various versions (Solf nos. 37, 55 ; Bohlen nos. 11, 45 ; Jivananda nos. 10, 43), but the name Vidyā is obviously based upon a misunderstanding, deliberate or otherwise, of the simile *vidyāṁ pramāda-galitām iva*, occurring in one of the common opening stanzas of the poem.

3 Ed. Kāvyamālā, Gucchaka iv, NSP, Bombay 2nd ed., 1899, pp. 68-71. If the author is the son of the Kerala poet Nārāyaṇa Bhaṭṭa, then he would belong to the commencement of the 17th century.

The tradition of the Śataka form is followed by a large number of poets. Thus, Utprekṣāvallabha, whose *Bhikṣāṭana* is more an erotic than a religious poem, wrote before the 14th century the *Sundarī-śataka,*[1] a highly artifical eulogy of feminine beauty in the Āryā metre, at the request of king Madanadeva, whose identity, however, is not known ; while in the beginning of the 18th century, Viśveśvara, son of Lakṣmīdhara, of Almora, composed, among other works, the *Romāvalī-śataka*[2], in the same spirit of unblushingly describing intimate feminine charms with elaborate skill but with dubious taste. The Śṛṅgāra-śatakas are numerous ; but among those which have been printed, one need only mention those of Janārdana Gosvāmin[3] and Narahari,[4] and the three centuries, called *Śṛṅgāra-kalikā-triśatī,*[5] of Kāmarāja Dīkṣita, (beginning of the 18th century ?), son of Sāmarāja,[6] in which the first lines of the verses follow the alphabetical order ! Some poets attempt both the themes of Śṛṅgāra and Vairāgya, as for instance, Janārdana Gosvāmin, who also wrote a *Virāgya-śataka*[7] (his Nīti-śataka is perhaps missing !) ; some attempt (as we have already seen in the cases of the *Rasik-rañjan* of Rāmacandra and *Śṛṅgāra-vairāgya-taraṅgiṇī* of the Jaina Somaprabha) to utilise the device of punning to make their poems have a simultaneous double application to erotic and ascetic themes ; while others, like Dhanadadeva compose three separate centuries on Śṛṅgāra, Nīti and Vairāgya.[8] A work of greater pretension and reputation is the *Āryā-saptaśatī*[9] of Govardhana, a court-poet of

1 Ed. Kāvyamālā, Gucchaka ix, 1916, p. 100f.

2 Ed. Kāvyamālā, Gucchaka viii, 2nd ed., 1911, p. 135f.

3 Ed. Kāvyamālā, Gucchaka xi, 1925, p. 133f.

Ed. Kāvyamālā, Gucchaka xii, 1897, p. 37f.

5 Ed. Kāvyamālā, Gucchaka xiv, 2nd ed., 1938, p. 86f.

6 See S. K. De *Sanskrit Poetics*, i, p. 320.

7 Ed. Kāvyamālā. Gucchaka xiii, 2nd ed., 1916, p. 131f.

8 Ed. Kavyamālā, Gucchaka xiii, pp. 33-108 ; composed in 1434 A.D.

9 Ed. Durgaprasad and K. P. Parab, with the comm. of Ananta, NSP., 2nd e ., Bombay 1895 ; also ed. Somnath Sarman, Dacca 1864 (text only, in Bengali characters). The text in the two editions differ, the first containing 756 and the second 731 verses. See

Lakṣmaṇsena of Bengal and contemporary of Jayadeva who mentions him in the *Gīta-govinda*. There are more than 700 isolated verses in this poem, arranged alphabetically in Vrajyās and having a predominantly erotic theme. Govardhana obviously takes the Prakrit *Gāthā-saptaśati* of Hāla as his model. He attains a measure of success, but the verses, moving haltingly in the somewhat unsuitable medium of Sanskrit Āryā metre, are more ingenious than poetical, and lack the flavour, wit and heartiness of Hāla's miniature word-pictures. But the work achieved the distinction of having inspired the very interesting Hindi *Satsaī* of Vihārilāl,[1] which holds a high rank in Hindi poetry. The very late author Viśveśvara of Almora, mentioned above, also appears to have taken Govardhana's work as his model in his own Sanskrit *Āryā-saptaśatī*,[2] but it is a very poor production. A bare mention will suffice of other poems which do not adopt the Śataka form, but which are yet substantial assemblage, more or less, of independent stanzas, such as the *Svāhā-sudhākara*,[3] a comparatively short poem (26 verses) of the Campū type with a thin story, and the *Koṭi-viraha*,[4] a longer poem (107 verses) with a similarly scanty story of two imaginary lovers, their union and separation,—both composed by Nārāyaṇa, the Kerala author of the *Nārāyaṇīya* (Stotra), who lived towards the end of the 16th century. Much more interesting and well written is the *Bhāminī-vilāsa*[5] of the well-known Tailaṅga poet-rhetorician Jagannātha, son of Perubhaṭṭa and Lakṣmī, who

S.K. De in *Eastern and Indian Studies in honour of F.W. Thomas*, p. 64f (Extra no. of the *NIA*), p. 64f. All that is known of the author will be found discussed by Pischel in his *Holfdichter des Lakṣmaṇasena*, Göttingen 1893, pp. 30-33.

1 Grierson in *JRAS*, 1894, p. 110.

2 Ed. Visnuprasad Bhandari, Chowkhamba Sanskrit Series, with the author's own comm., Benares 1924.

3 Ed. Kāvyamālā, Gucchaka iv, p. 52f.

4 El. Kāvyamālā, Gucchaka v, 2nd ed., 1908, p. 142f. It is explained that Koṭi or Koḍiya in Malayālam means 'nūtana'.

5 Ed. K. P. Parab and M. R. Telang, with comm. of Acyutarāya, NSP, Bombay 1894; also ed. Granthamālā, iv, with the comm. of Mahādeva Dīkṣita, containing some extra verses. The work has been printed many times in India. Text, with Eng. trs., by Sesadri Iyer, Bombay 1894; French trs. by A. Bergaigne, Paris 1872. For the author, who

flourished during Shāh Jahān's reign. The work, however, is not entirely erotic, being divided into four parts, namely, Anyokti (101 verses) Śṛṅgāra (102), Karuṇa (19) and Śānta (31), but the preponderance is towards the erotic and the didactic. Although there is not much depth of feeling or height of imagination, a large number of the verses can be singled out for their neatness and elegance of expression and considerable pictorial fancy.

The general tendency in an unoriginal epoch to produce imitations or counterfeits is responsible for more than fifty Dūta-kāvyas,[1] which derive their impetus, but not inspiration, from Kālidāsa's *Megha-dūta.* Their interest lies not so much in their poetical worth as in their utilisation of the original form and motif in different ways and for different purposes, furnishing illuminating illustration of the variations that can be worked by ingenious and industrious talents, which could scarcely imbibe the poetic spirit of the original work. The Mandākrāntā metre is generally accepted, but we have also Śikhariṇī,[2] Vasantatilaka,[3]

lived in the 2nd and 3rd quarters of the 17th century, see S. K. De, *Sanskrit Poetics*, i, p. 275f. In the introduction to Lakshman Ramachandra Vaidya's ed. of the work (Bombay 1887) there is a list of Jagannatha's works.

1 A treatment of the Dūta-kāvya literature is given by Chintaharan Chakravarti in *IHQ, III*, pp. 273-97. Sequels to the *Megha-dūta* have also been thought of, and there are also a few Pratisaṁdeśas, containing the counter-message of the Yakṣa's wife !

2 As in *Haṁsa-dūta* of Rūpa Gosvāmin and *Manodūta* of *Vrajanātha.* The former work has been very often printed, *e.g.*, in Haeberlin's Kāvya-saṁgraha, p. 323f (Jivananda i, p. 441f), in Harichand Hirachand's Kāvyakalāpa, Bombay 1864, p. 35f, etc ; but there is no critical edition, the number of verses varying in the printed texts. The learned author, who flourished in the 15th century, was one of the disciples of Caitanya of Bengal (see S. K. De, introd, to *Padyāvalī*, for an account of the author and his works). In the present work, a swan is sent as messenger by the Gopīs of Vṛndāvana to Kṛṣṇa at Mathurā, the poem incidentdlly illustrating the Rasa-śāstra of Bengal Vaiṣṇavism. The *Manodūta* of Tailaṅga Vrajanātha, composed in 1758 A.D. (ed. Kāvyamālā, Gucchaka xiii, pp. 84-130), describes the sending of Mind as messenger to Kṛṣṇa by the helpless Draupadī when she was insulted at the court of Duryodhana.

3 As in *Manodūta* of Viṣṇudāsa and *Hṛdaya-duta* of Harihara. The first work (ed. Chintaharan Chakravari, Saṁskṛta Sāhitya Pariṣad, Calcutta 1937) is a pathetic appeal in 101 verses to Kṛṣṇa, with Mind as messenger and includes a description of Vṛndāvana. The Vaiṣṇava author is said to have been a maternal uncle of Caitanya of Bengal, and if so, lived in the 15th century. The second work is noticed by Weber, *Berlin Catalogue*, i, no. 571 (116 verses).

Mālinī[1] and even Śārdūlavikrīḍita.[2] Not only inanimate objects, like the Wind,[3] the Moon,[4] Footprints[5] and the sacred Tulasī plant,[6] but also various birds and animals, like the parrot, cuckoo, bee, swan,[7] peacock, cakora, cātaka and cakravāka,[8] as well as mythological beings like Uddhava[9] and Hanūmat,[10] are selected as messengers for imaginary journeys over various places

1 As in *Candra-dūta* of Jambū, noticed by Peterson, *Three Reports* 1887, p. 292. It contains 23 verses with various forms of Yamaka, and deals with an ordinary love-message of a woman to her lover. It belongs probably to the first half of the 10th century ed. (J. B. Chaudhuri, Calcutta 1941 ; also see *Modern Review*, Calcutta, lxx, no 2, August, 1941, pp. 158-61).

2 As in *Pika-dūta*, mentioned by Chakravarti (in *IHQ*, iii, p. 272), in 31 verses, describing the sending of a cuckoo as a messenger to Kṛṣṇa by the Gopīs. The same theme and the same metre occur also in the *Pāntha-dūta* of Bholānātha (Eggeling, *Ind. Office Cat*. vii, no. 3890), the messenger being a pilgrim on the way to Mathurā.

3 As in the *Pavana-dūta* of Dhoyī, ed. Manomohan Chakravarti, from a single MS in *JASB*, 1905, pp. 53-68 ; re-edited Chintaharan Chakravarti, Saṁskṛta Sāhitya Parisad, Calcutta 1926. The author, a court-poet of Lakṣmaṇasena of Bengal, is mentioned by Jayadeva as a contemporary. The work is noteworthy in taking up, without being a Carita, an historical personage, namely, the poet's patron Lakṣmaṇasena, as the hero. The poet makes Kūvalayavatī, a Gandharva maiden of the Malaya hills, fall in love with the king during the latter's career of conquest in the south, and send the south-easterly wind as a messenger. It is an elegent poem of 104 verses, but of no greater merit than most poems of its kind. There is another *Pavana-dūta* of Vādicandra Sūri, who flourished in the 17th century, in 101 verses, in which the wind carries a message from Vidyānareśa, king of Ujjayinī, to his wife Tārā, who has been abducted by a Vidyādhara (ed. Kāvyamālā, Gucchaka xiii, p. 9-24), a purely invented story.

4 As in the *Indu-dūta* of Vinayavijaya-gaṇi, and several *Candra-dūtas*. In the first-named work (ed. Kāvyamālā, Gucchaka xiv, pp. 40-60 ; 131 verses), the well known Jaina author (end of the 17th century), residing at Jodhpur, sends the moon as messenger, with a kind of Vijñapti-patra to his religious preceptor at Surat, incidentally describing Jaina temples and sacred places on the way. For other Candra-dūtas see Chakravarti, in *IHQ, III*, p. 276.

5 As in the *Padāṅka-dūta* of Kṛṣṇa Sārvabhauma. ed. Jivananda's Kāvyasaṁgraha, i, pp. 507-30 ; Kāvyakalāpa, i, p. 53f. The work, in which the footprints of Kṛṣṇa are asked by the Gopīs to carry their message to him at Mathurā, was composed at the court of Raghunātha Rāya of Nadia (Bengal) in 1723 A.D.

6 As in *Tulasī-dūta*, mentioned by Chakravarti, *op. cit*. It is in 34 verses, composed in Śaka 1706=1784 A.D., with the same theme of the Gopī's message to Kṛṣṇa.

7 *Haṁsa-duta* of Rūpa Gosvāmīn mentioned above, and *Haṁsa-dūta* of Veṅkaṭadeśika and anonymous *Haṁsa-saṁdeśa* mentioned below.

8 For numerous works with these devices, see Chakravarti, *op. cit*.

9 As in the *Uddhava-saṁdeśa* (138 verses) of Rūpa Gosvāmin (ed. in Haeberlin, p. 322f ; Jivananda, iii, p. 215f) and *Uddhava-dūta* (141 verses, ed. in Haeberlin, p. 348 f ; Jivananda i. p. 531f) of Mādhava Śarman. The theme is based on Bhāgavata Purāṇa x. 47.

10 As in *Kapi-dūta*, Dacca University Library, MS no. 975B (fragmentary).

in India, the topographical information being of variable value. The limit is reached when even abstract objects, like the Mind[1] and Devotion,[2] are made to discharge the function, the poems tending to become abstract and allegorical. Mythological subjects, such as the well known stories of Rāma and Sītā,[3] Kṛṣṇa and Rādhā,[4] Pārśvanātha and Neminātha[5] are utilised, besides those of historical personages in a few rare cases.[6] In the hands of Jaina and Vaiṣṇava authors the device easily becomes the means of religious instruction, reflection or propaganda. A curious literary application is also seen in the adoption of the trick of Samasyā-pūraṇa in the compostion of some Dūta-kāvyas. The Jaina imitations[7] sometimes adopt and

[1] Besides the *Manodūta* and *Hṛdaya-dūta* mentioned above, we have a *Cetodūta* (129 verses) of an unknown Jaina author, which describes the sending of the author's own mind as a messenger to his preceptor, but which also adopts the device of Samasyā-pūraṇa in having the fourth foot of every verse identical with the fourth corresponding foot of verses from the *Megha-dūta*.

[2] As in the *Bhakti-dūta* (23 verses) of Kālīprasāda (Mitra, *Notices*, iii, p. 27) in which Mukti is figured as the lady of the poet's desire and Bhakti acts as a messenger.

[3] Only in a limited number of poems, such as the *Kapi-dūta* mentioned above, the *Bhramara-dūta* of the Nyāya commentator Rudra Nyāyavācaspati, son of Vidyānivāsa (H, P. Sastri, *Notices*, ii, p. 153), the *Candra-dūta* of Kṛṣṇacandra Tarkālaṁkāra, (*ibid, loc. cit.*), and the *Haṁsa-dūta* (60+50 verses in two Aśvāsas) of the well known South Indian scholar teacher Veṅkatadeśika (ed Govt. Oriental Library, Mysore 1913).

[4] This is, of course, a favourite subject with Vaiśṇava writers, especially of Bengal; and the works, some of which are noted above, are numerous.

[5] See below.

[6] As in the *Pavana-dūta* of Dhoyī. The Jaina poems about the report of progress from a pupil to the preceptor are also not fictitious in respect of persons figuring in them.

[7] Besides the *Cetodūta* mentioned above, we have several Jaina works of this kind. The *Pārśvābhyudaya* of Jinasena, who wrote the *Adipurāṇa* in the 9th century, is not a Dūtakāvya, but gives the life-story of Pārśvanātha (ed. Yogiraj Panditacharya, NSP, Bombay 1909); the entire *Megha-dūta*, however, is incorporated by the device of inserting one or two lines of Kālidāsa in each verse. Similarly, the *Śīla-dūta*, which is not a Dūta-kāvya but a didactic poem on the story of Sthūlabhadra, is composed on the principle of Samasyāpūraṇa by Cāritrasundara-gaṇi (ed. Yaśovijaya Jaina Granthamālā, Benares 1915) in 1420 A.D. But there are also Jaina Dūta-kāvyas which employ the device. Thus the *Nemi-dūta* of Vikrama, son of Śṛṅgāra, describes in 123 verses (ed. Kāvyamālā, Gucchaka ii, 1886, p 85f), the sending of the cloud as a messenger by the Tīrthaṁkara Neminātha's wife Rājamatī to her husband, who had gone to Mount Abu to practise penance; but the last line of each verse is taken from Kālidāsa's poem in the manner of Samasyā-pūraṇa. Of the same type is the *Meghadūta-samasyā-lekha* (ed. Jaina Ātmānanda Granthamālā, Bhavnagar

incorporate one or two Pādas, ussually the fourth Pāda, of Kālidāsa's verses into the corresponding Pādas of their own verses, the rest being composed by the poets themselves as a kind of clever filling up of the entire stanza. It is ingenious, but the literary exercise naturally leads to artificiality and straining of the language. The original object of sending a love-message is also replaced in some works by the intention of making the poem a kind of descriptive Vijñapti-patra, sent by a disciple to his preceptor, to report progress in religious activities in a distant land. This finds a parallel to the Vaiṣṇava effort to make the poems vehicles for conveying devotional ideas, the sentiment of love being replaced by those of tranquillity and devotion.[1] The process reaches its climax as the Dūta-kāvya becomes a nominal form for conveying abstract philosophical ideas, as when a devotee sends the swan of his mind with a philosophical message to his beloved Bhakti for an imaginary flight to the world of Śiva ![2]

b. *The Devotional Poetry*

The devotional poetry of this period, connected closely with the erotic, presents two lines of literary growth, which sometimes blend, but which stand in no constant relation. We have, on the one hand, the tradition of elaborate Stotras of a descriptive or philosophical character, but, on the other, we have the steady development of highly impassioned devotional poems, which pass through the whole gamut of erotic motif, imagery and expression. The personal note is present in both the tendencies, but while in the one it is expressed in the guise of religious thought, religious motion in the other shapes and colours

1914) of Meghavijaya (end of the 17th century), in which the cloud is sent as a messenger to the author's preceptor Vijayaprabha Sūri.

1 In one case a note of parody appears, *e.g.*, in the *Kāka-dūta* (mentioned by M. Krishnamacharier, *Classical Sanskrit Literature*, Madras 1937, p. 365), in which a fallen Brahmin in prison seeks to send a message through a crow to his beloved Kādambarī (Drink)! —The *Vāṅmaṇḍana-guṇa-dūta* of Vīreśvara (ed. J. B. Chaudhuri, Calcutta 1941) is a religious philosophical poem which solicits the patronage of a king !

2 As in *Haṁsa-saṁdeśa*, ed. Sambasiva Sastri, Trivandrum Sanskrit Series 1930.

it. The intellectual satisfaction and moral earnestness, which characterise the earlier theistic devotionalism, inspire the high-toned trāditional Stotras ; but with the rise of mediaeval sects and propagation of emotional Bhakti movements, the basic inspiration of devotional writings is supplied, more or less, by a mood of erotic mysticism, which seeks to express religious longings in the intimate language and imagery of earthly passion. This brings about a new development in Sanskrit religious poetry, and relates it very closely with erotic literature, so much so that poems like the *Gīta-govinda* would appear, from different aspects, both as a religious and an erotic work. The mighty sex-impulse becomes transfigured into a deeply religious emotion; and, however mystic the devotional attitude may appear, the literary gain is beyond question. While the Stotras of more orthodox tradition beget a new series of grave, elevated and speculative hymns, the emotional and poetic possibilities of the newer quasi-amorous attitude become immense and diverse, and express themselves in mystically passionate poems, dramas and Campūs. These effusions of the devout heart are in a sense beyond criticism, but, strictly speaking, they do not always attain a high level of poetic excellence. Nevertheless, the more the religious sentiment becomes personal in ardour and concrete in expression, the more the pedantry of its theology and psychological rhetoric recedes to the background, and it is lifted to the idealism and romantic richness of intensely passionate expression. In the hands of these erotic-religious emotionalists, we have a fresh accession and interpretation of the romantic legends of the gods ; and the wistfulness, amazement and ecstasy of the new devotional sentiment lift its poetry from the dry dogmatism of scholastic thought into a picturesque and luscious spiritualisation of sensuous words and ideas.

The more orthodox mode of staid and sober Stotra-writing is, however, not less fruitful, prompted that it is by the extremely active impetus of speculative thought or scholastic learning of the time The large number of Vedāntic Stotras, for instance some of which are ascribed to the great Śaṃkara himself, the Kashmirian Śaivite poems, the Jaina and Buddhist Mahāyāna hymns, the South Indian Vaiṣṇava and Śaiva panegyric of deities, or the Bengal Tāntric and Vaiṣṇava eulogiums, are inspired by the different religious tendencies of the time. They spring no doubt, from depth of religious conviction ; but, composed generally that they are for the purposes of a particular cult, they are often weighted with its theological or philosophical ideas. When they are not of this learned type, or when they do not merely give a string of laudatory names and epithets of deities or a metrical litany of their glory and greatness, or when they are not merely liturgical verses, they possess the moving quality of attractive religious poems. These alone come within the sphere of literary criticism. The number of Stotras preserved is indeed vast,[1] and only a small percentage of them is yet in print ; but even those which have been published are mostly of unknown or late date, and their individual poetic traits are not always conspicuous. Only a few of them rise to the level even of a medicore poem, being burdened with didactic or doctrinal matter, or with dry recital of commonplace words and ideas. It is true that no other department of Sanskrit verse has been so prolific ; that it would not be just to ignore the Stotras as mere curiosities, even though Sanskrit rhetorical and anthological literature displays no special enthusiasm for them ; and that no adequate study of Jaina, Buddhist and Hindu hymnology has yet been made ; but at the same time, no case has been made that, apart from religious interest, the literature deserves a deeper investigation for its purely poetic worth, even though individual Stotras have been of modesty merit. Some of the hymns are undobtedly popular and have been uttered by thousands of devout minds from generation to generation, but mere

1 For printed collections of Jaina, Buddhist and Hindu Stotras, see below, but they hardly represent the vastness of this literature. The notice of Stotra manuscripts, for instance, in the Madras Government Oriental Manuscript Library covers three volumes (xviii-xx). The Purāṇas and Tantra works abound in Stotras.

popularity or liturgical employment is no index to literary quality. They are popular, not because they are always great religious poems of beauty, but because they give expression to cherished religious ideas. They are concerned more with religion than religious emotion, and have therefore different values for the devotee and the literary critic.

The later Buddhist Stotras[1] are true to the manner and diction of the Hindu Stotras, the only difference lying in the mode and object of adoration. Some of them choose the ornate style and elaborate metres of the Kāvya, while others are litanies of the type common in the Purāṇas. The *Lokeśvara-śataka*[2] of Vajradatta, who lived under Devapāla in the 9th century, is composed in the elaborate Sragharā verses,[3] describing in the form of a series of benedictions the physical features and mental excellences of the deity Avalokiteśvara, obviously on the model of the Śatakas of Mayūra and Bāṇa ; and tradition has also invented a similar legend of the poet's being cured of leprosy by this eulogy of the deity ! In the same Sragdharā metre and polished diction is composed a large number of Stotras to Tārā, the female counterpart of Avalokiteśvara, of which the *Āryā-tārā-sragdharā-stotra*[4] (37 verses) of the Kashmirian Sarvajñamitra, who lived in the first-half of the 8th century, is perhaps the most remarkable. The *Bhakti-śataka*[5] of Rāmacandra Kavibhāratī of Bengal, who came to Cylon under king Parākramabāhu at about 1245 A.D. and became a Buddhist, is of some interest as

1 For a bibliography and short treatment of Buddhist Stotras, see Winternitz, *HIL*, ii, p. 375 f.

2 Ed. Suzanne Karpelés, with Sanskrit and Tibetan texts and a Fr. trs , in *JA*, 1919, s. 11, t. xiv, pp. 357-465. *Cf.* F. W. Thomas in *JRAŚ.*, 1921, pp. 281-83.

3 It should be remembered that the *Gaṇḍī-stotra* ascribed to Aśvaghoṣa is composed in the Sragdharā metre, as also the Stotras of Mayūra and Bāṇa.

4 Ed. S. C. Vidyabhusan, with commentary and two Tibetan versions in Bauddha-Stotra-saṁgraha, vol. i. Bibl. Ind., Calcutta 1908. In the introduction, the editor mentions no fewer than 96 texts relating to Tārā. The author also wrote several other Stotras, which have been edited and translated by G. de Blonay in his *Materiaux pour servir á l'historie de la déesse Buddhique Tārā*, Paris 1895.

5 Ed. Haraprasad Sastri, with Eng. trs., in *JBTS*, i, 1893, pt. 2, pp. 21-43.

an example of the application of Hindu ideas of Bhakti to an extravagant eulogy of the Buddha, composed in the approved Kāvya style and diction. It is not necessary to deal with later Mahāyāna Tāntric Stotras, which are innumerable but which show little poetic merit.

The Jaina Stotras,[1] commencing with the *Bhaktāmara* of Mānatuṅga and the *Kalyāṇa-mandira* of his imitator Siddhasena Divākara,[2] are large in number, but they also exhibit the same form, style and characteristics, and therefore need not detain us long. Besides eulogies of particular saints or Jinas, there is quite a number of Stotras, generally known as *Caturviṃśati-jina-stuti* or *Caturviṃśikā*, in which all the twenty-four Jinas are extolled. Such Stotras are composed by well-known teachers and devotees, like Samantabhadra[3] (*c.* first half of the 8th century), Bappa-bhaṭṭi[4] (*c.* 743-838 A.D.), Śobhana[5] (second half of the 10th century), Jinaprabha Sūri[6] (beginnig of the 14th century) and others. As the glorification of Jinas and saints does not admit of much variation in subject-matter, some poems, as we have seen, are artificially constructed to show tricks of language in the use of Yamaka and other rhetorical figures in the regular Kāvya method; while others contain religious reflections and instructions, which conduce little towards literature.

Of the Hindu Stotras,[7] it is difficult to say if all the two hundred Vedāntic Stotras, which pass current under the name of

1 Collections of Jaina Stotras will be found in Kāvyamālā, Gucchaka vii, 3rd ed., Bombay 1907; in Jaina Stotra Saṁgraha, published in the Yaśovijaya Jaina Granthamālā, 1905; in Stuti-saṁgraha with Avacūri. NSP, Bombay 1912; and in Stotra-ratnākara, i, ii, ed. Yaśovijaya Jaina Saṁskṛta Pāṭhasālā, Mehasana, NSP, Bombay 1913-14. The more important of the Jaina Stotras have been noticed by Winternitz, *HIL*, ii, p. 548 f.

2 See above, pp. 171-72.

3 Ed. Pannalal Chaudhuri in Digambara Jaina Granthabhāṇḍāra, Benares 1924-25. Suali would place the author in the 6th century, S. C. Vidyabhusan in the 7th.

4 Ed. in Stuti-saṁgraha cited above.

5 Ed. Kāvyamālā, Gucchaka vii, 3rd ed. 1907, p. 30f; also ed. and trs. H. Jacobi in *ZDMG*, XXXII, 1878, p. 509f.

6 Ed. Kāvyamālā. Gucchaka vii, p. 115; also in Stuti-saṁgraha.

7 The collections of Hindu Stotras are numerous, of which the following larger ones are notable: Bṛhat-stotra-muktāhāra in two parts (416 stotras), Gujrati Printing Press, Pt. i,

the great Vedāntic philosopher Śaṃkara are rightly ascribed, but there is no reason to suppose that not one of them came from him; for devotion to a particular deity is not inconsistent with the profession of severe monistic idealism. Perhaps the majority of them were composed by later Śaṃkaras of the Saṃpradāya, or even passed off under the name; but since there is no criterion, except that of style and treatment, at best an unsafe guide, one can never be positive on the question.[1] Some of these Stotras, however, are undoubtedly inspired by religious enthusiasm and attain a charming quality of tender expression, in spite of occasional philosophical or didactic background. Such, in instance, are the *Śivāparādha-kṣamāpaṇa* in Sragdharā; the *Dvādaśa-pañjarikā*, commonly known as *Moha-mudgara*, and the *Carpaṭa-pañjarikā* in rhymed moric metre; the several short Stotras in Bhujaṅgaprayāta, namely, the *Daśa-ślokī*, *Ātma-ṣaṭka* (also called *Nirvāṇa-ṣaṭka*), *Hastāmalaka*, the *Vedasāra-śiva-stuti*;[2] and the shorter *Ānanda-laharī*[3] consisting of twenty stanzas in the Śikhariṇī metre. Not only ease and elegance of expression, but also the smooth flow of metre and use of rhyme make these

2nd ed. 1923, Pt. ii, Bombay 1916; Bṛhat-stotra-ratnākara (144 stotras), Kalpataru Press, Bombay 1888; also same title 240 stotras), Native Opinion Press, Bombay 1918; also same title, in two parts, Emperor of India Press, Madras 1897, 1905; Bṛhat-stotra-sarit sāgara (306 stotras), Gujarati News Press, Bombay 1927; Stava-samudra (41 stotras), ed. Purnachandra De. pt. i, Calcutta 1918. Among the Stotras published in the various Gucchakas of the Kāvyamālā, the more notable are: Śiva-stuti of Laṅkeśvara, Tripura-mahimnaḥ Stava and Lalita-stava-ratna of Durvāsas, Sudarśana-śataka of Kuraṇārāyaṇa, Ānandama dira-stava of Lalla Dīkṣita, and Dīnākrandana-stuti of Loṣṭaka, besides those which we notice below.

[1] The question has been briefly discussed by S. K. Belvalkar (*Sri Gopal Basu Malik Lectures on Vedanta Philosophy*, Poona 1929, p. 220ff). Chiefly on the ground of their being commented upon by more than one reliable and ancient commentary, he would consider the following stotras as probably genuine: (1) Ānandalaharī (of 20 stanzas) (2) Govindāṣṭaka (3) Dakṣiṇāmūrti Stotra (4) Daśaślokī (5) Dvādaśa-pañjarikā (Moha-mudgara) (6) Bhaja Govindam Stotra (7) Ṣaṭpadī or Viṣṇu-ṣaṭpadi and (8) Harimīḍe Stotra.

[2] These Stotras have been printed very often in India at Mysore, Srirangam, Poona and elsewhere. They will be found conventienly in the Bṛhat-stotra-ratnākara, NSP, Bombay, 3rd ed., 1899; also in *Select Works of Saṁkarācārya*, ed. H. R. Bhagavat, Poona 1925, pt. ii; also ed. Srī Vaṇī Vilāsa Press, Srirangam.

[3] There is another Ānanda-laharī or Saundarya-laharī in 100 verses ascribed to Śaṁkara, ed. in Haeberlin, p. 236, Jivananda, iii, p. 1f; trs. Avalon, Hymns to the Goddess, London 1913, p. 62f.

deservedly popular Stotras occupy a high rank in Sanskrit Stotra literature. The peculiarly titled *Śiva-mahimnaḥ Stotra*[1] of Puspadanta, which has been precursor of other Mahimnaḥ Stotras in praise of other deities, is perhaps earlier in date ;[2] but as numerous commentaries on it attest,[3] it is more recondite and philosophical both in thought and expression. Many of the apparently late Stotras are dateless and apocryphal, but are ascribed indiscriminately to Yājñavalkya, Vālmīki, Vyāsa, Rāvaṇa, Upamanyu, Durvāsas and Kālidāsa, even if their merit may not justify such attribution. Some Stotras are inserted into the Epics and the Purāṇas ; the undoubtedly spurious *Durgā-stava* in the Virāṭa-parvan (which exists in as many as six versions, besides the Vulgate !) being typical. The avowedly literary Śatakas, on the other hand, are within greater historical certainty. They are more elaborately constructed and sometimes attempt conventional tricks of style. The *Mukunda-mālā*[4] of the devout Vaiṣṇava king Kulaśekhara of Kerala is perhaps one of the earliest of such literary composition ; but if it has stylistic affectations, they are mostly redeemed by its unmistakable devotional earnestness, as well as by a proper sense of style.

Of the Kashmirian Śaivite poems, the twenty short hymns of Utpaladeva (c. 925 A.D.), son of Udayākara and pupil of Somānanda, in his *Stotrāvalī*[5] are uneven, some being conven-

1 Printed very often, the earliest ed. with trs. being by K. M. Banerji *JASB*, VIII, 1839, pp. 355-66. Ed. in Bṛhat-stotra-ratnākara, p. 98 (40 verses, in Śikhariṇī and other metres) ; ed. Chowkhamba Series, Benares 1924.

2 Being cited by Rājaśekhara in his *Kavya-mīmāṁsa* and the Kashmirian Jayantabhaṭṭa in his *Nyāya-mañjarī*, it cannot be later than the 10th century.

3 The hymn has been interpreted so as to apply to Viṣṇu as well !

4 Ed. in Haeberlin, p. 515f (22 verses) reprinted in Jivananda, i, p. 507f (22 verses) ; ed. Kāvyamālā, Gucchaka i, p. 11f (34 verses) ; and ed. K. Rama Pisharoti, with comm. of Rāghavendra (17th century), Annamalai Univ. Sanskrit Series, Annamalainagar 1933 (31 verses). Pisharoti dates Kulaśekhara very highly at the close of the 7th and beginning of the 8th century, but probably the poet flourished much later between the 10th and the 12th century. Hultzsch (*Epi. Ind.*, VII, p. 197) notes that a verse from this poem (Haeberlin 7, Kāvyamālā 6, Pisharoti 3) occurs in an inscription of so distant a place as Pagan in the 13th century.

5 Ed. Visnuprasad Bhandari, with the comm. of Kṣemarāja, Chowkhamaba Sanskrit Series, Benares 1902. See S. K. De, *Sanskrit Poetics*, i, p. 119, on the author.

tionally elaborate. The earlier *Devī-śataka*[1] of Ānandavardhna (c. 850 A.D.) and the *Iśvara-śataka*[2] of Avatāra of unknown date are stupid Durghaṭa poems, which have little devotional merit but concern themselves with verbal tricks and Citra-bandhas, wisely condemned by Ānandavardhana himself in his theoretical work. The *Vakrokti-pañcāśikā*[3] of Ratnākara, which makes the playful love of Śiva Pārvatī its theme, is a similar exercise in style, illustrating the clever use of punning ambiguities, and has scarcely any religious leaning. The *Ardhanārīśvara-stotra*[4] of Kahlaṇa, a short piece of eighteen Śardūlavikrīḍita stanzas, is much better in this respect, notwithstanding its partiality for alliteration. The *Sāmba-pañcāśikā,*[5] an eulogy of the sun-god in fifty (mostly) Mandākrāntā verses, is also probably a Kashmirian work, being commented upon by Kṣemarāja in the beginning of the 13th century ; but it is referred to the mythical Sāmba, son of Kṛṣṇa, even if it is an apparently late and laboured work, having a background of Kashmirian Śaiva philosophy.

From the later Stotras of a literary character or Stotra-kāvyas, all of which show, more or less, technical skill of the conventional kind and sometimes rise to fine words and ideas, it is difficult to single out works of really outstanding merit. The *Nārāyaṇīya*[6] of Nārāyaṇabhaṭṭa of Kerala, composed in 1585 A.D., is a devout but highly artificial poem of a thousand learned verses, divided symmetrically into ten decades and addressed to the deity Kṛṣṇa of Guruvayoor, who is said to have cured the author of rheumatism after listening to the verses ! The *Ānanda-mandākinī*[7] of the well known Bengali philosopher Madhusūdana

1 Ed. Kāvyamālā, Gucchaka xi, pp. 1-31, with comm. of Kayyaṭa.

2 Ed. *ibid*, pp. 31-63, with an anonymous commentary.

3 Ed. Kāvyamālā, Gucchaka i, pp. 101-14, with comm. of Vallabhadeva. These are no more religious poems than Ratnākara's own *Hara-vijaya* or Maṅkhaka's *Śrikaṇṭha-carita.*

4 Ed. Kāvyamālā, Gucchaka xiv, 2nd ed. 1938, pp. 1-4.

5 Ed. Durgaprasad and K. P. Parab with comm. of Kṣemarāja NSP, Bombay 1889 (also ed. 1910) :

6 Ed. T. Ganapati Sastri, Trivandrum Sanskrit Series, 1912.

7 Ed. Kāvyamālā, Gucchaka ii, p. 138f (102 verses) ; also in the *Pundit*, New Series, i, 1876-77, pp. 498-514.

Sarasvatī, who flourished at the middle of the 16th century, is a similar production, in praise of Kṛṣṇa, in the sonorous Śārdūla-vikrīḍita metre, in which both the learning and devoutness of the author express themselves equally well in a highly ornate style. The same remarks apply to a number of 17th century productions, such as the five *Laharīs* (*Amṛta°*,[1] *sudhā°*,[2] *Gaṅgā,°*[3] *Karuṇā°*[4] and *Lakṣmī°*[5]) of Jagannātha, the poet-rhetorician from Tailaṅga, the *Ānandasāgara-stava*[6] of Nīlakaṇṭha Dīkṣṭita in praise of the goddess Mīnākṣī, consort of Sundaranātha Śiva, of Madura, and the three stilted panegyrics of Rāma's weapons[7] by Nīlakaṇṭha's pupil, Rāmabhadra Dīkṣita, who also perpetrated an absurdity of alphabetically arranged eulogy of the same deity, called *Varṇamālā-stotra*.[8]

One of the noteworthy traits of some of the literary Stotra-kāvyas is that they are devoted either to a highly sensuous description of the love-adventures of the deities, or to a detailed enumeration of their physical charms, masculine or feminine. This may be one form of the mediaeval erotic mysticism, of which we shall speak more presently; but, apart from the sports of Rādhā and Kṛṣṇa, where such delineation is perhaps not out of place, there is a tendency, commencing from the tradition of *Kumāra-saṃbhava* viii, to ascribe sexual attributes to divine beings or paint their amours with lavish details. The gentle description of the love of deities, like those found in the benedictory stanzas of the *Ratnāvalī* and *Priyadarśikā*, does not

1 Ed. Kāvyamālā, Gucchaka i, p. 99 f. (10 verses in Śārdūlavikrīḍita), in praise of Yamunā.

2 Ed. Kāvyamālā, Gucchaka i, p. 16 f. (30 verses in Sragdharā), in praise of Sūrya.

3 Printed many times. Ed. NSP, Bombay 1924 (53 verses, mostly in Śikhariṇī, in praise of Gaṅgā. Also called Pīyūṣa-laharī.

4 Ed. Kāvyamālā, Gucchaka ii, p. 55 f (60 verses in Vaṁśastha, Viyoginī and other metres), in praise of Kṛṣṇa.

5 Ed. Kāvyamālā, Gucchaka ii, p. 104 f (41 verses in Śikhariṇī) in praise of Lakṣmī.

6 Ed. Kāvyamālā, Gucchaka xi, p. 76 f (108 verses in Vasantatilaka).

7 *Rāmāsṭaprāsa* in Kāvyamālā, Gucchaka x, p. 18 f (116 verses in Śardūlavikīḍita); and *Rāma-cāpa-stava* (111) verses in the same metre and *Rāma-bāṇa-stava* (108 verses n Sragdharā) in Kāvyamālā, Gucchaka xii, p. i f and 18 f.

8 Ed, Kāvyamālā, Gucchaka xiii, p. 1 f (51 verses).

exceed good taste, but some poets like to describe their deities in particularlary dubious amorous situations.[1] On the other hand, we have the description of Viṣṇu's divine limbs, from the hair to the toe-nail[2]; while Mūka Kavi, alleged to be Śaṃkara's contemporary,[3] attempts in his *Pañca-śatī*[4] a *tour de force* in five hundred erotic-religious verses, describing in each century of verse such physical charms and attributes of his deity (Kāmākṣī of Kāñcī) as her smile, her side-long glances, her lotus-feet and so forth. The climax is reached in Lakṣmaṇa Ācārya's *Caṇḍī-kuca-pañcāśikā*,[5] which describes in fifty verses the beauty of Caṇḍī's breasts! It is needless to comment on the amazing taste displayed in such works.

This makes the transition easier to the other series of erotic-devotional Stotras and short poems, which follow the conventional form and diction but entirely change the spirit and outlook. We have already noted that these works give expression to a phase of the mediaeval Bhakti movement, which was prominently emotional, and base the religious sentiment, mystically, upon the exceedingly familiar and authentic intensity of transfigured sex-passion. However figuratively the poems may be interpreted, they make erotic emotionalism their refined and sublimated essence. The Bhakti movement, in all its sectarian ramifications, centres chiefly round the early romantic life of Kṛṣṇa as it is described, not in the Epic, but in the Purāṇas. Although the sentiment of Bhakti came to be applied to other deities as well, including even the Buddha, the Kṛṣṇa, -Gopī legend

1 See, for instance, the benedictory verse quoted in *Kvs* no. 37, or the section on Lakṣmī-vihāra in *Skm.*

2 *E,g.*, in *Viṣṇu-pādādi-keśānta-varṇana-stotra* in Kavyamālā, Gucchaka ii, p. 1 f. The trait is found also in Bāṇa's *Caṇḍī-śataka* and Vajradatta's *Lokeśvara-stava*. Even the footwear of the deity is an object of eulogy in a thousand verses in the *Pādukā-sahasra* of Veṅkaṭadeśika (ed. Kedarnath and V. L. Panshikar, NSP, Bombay 1911).

3 Or, sometime identified with the 20th Ācārya, known as Mūkārbhaka Śaṁkara.

4 Ed. Kāvyamālā, Gucchaka v, p. 1 f.

5 Kāvyamālā, Gucchaka ix, p. 80 f. It is a comparatively modern work, containing 83 verses (18+50+15).

had perhaps the greatest erotic-religious possibilities, which were developed to the fullest extent. The *Śrīmad-bhāgavata*, as the great scripture of emotional devotion and store-house of such legends, becomes the starting point of the theology of the neo-Vaiṣṇava sects and supplies the basic inspiration to the new devotional poetry. The new standpoint vivifies religion, as well as its poetry, with a human element, and lifts one of the most powerful impulses of the human mind into the means of glorious exaltation. It thereby brings colour and beauty into religious life; and its essential truth lies in its assertion of the emotional and the aesthetic in human nature against the hard intellectuality of dogmas and doctrines.

But, in course of time, the new movement creates its own dogmas and doctrines. Along with its philosophy and theology, the sectarian devotionalism elaborates its appropriate system of emotional analysis, its refinements of psychology and poetics, its subtleties of phraseology, imagery and conceits. As the sentiment of Bhakti or religious devotion is approximated to the sentiment of literary relish, called Rasa, the whole apparatus of Alaṃkāra, as well as Kāma-śāstra, technicalities are ingeniously utilised and exalted, although the orthodox theory itself would not regard Bhakti as a Rasa. The new application becomes novel, intimate and inspiring; and the erotic sensibility in its devotional ecstasy often rises above the formalism of its rhetorical and psychological conventions, of its metaphysical and theological niceties. Even the subtled dogmas and formulas appear to have a charming effect on literary conception and phrasing, being often transmuted by its fervent attitude into things of art. The poems may not have always reached a high standard of absolute poetic excellence, but the standard it often reaches, in its rich and concrete expression of ecstatic elevation, is striking enough as a symptom of the presence of the poetic spirit which the emotional Bhakti movement brought in its wake.

But the attitude was not without its defect and danger. The Purāṇic life of Kṛṣṇa being brought to the foreground, the more ancient epic figure of Vāsudeva-Kṛṣṇa is transformed beyond recognition. The old epic spirit of godly wisdom and manly devotion is replaced by a new spirit of mystical-emotional theology, which goes into tender rapture over divine babyhood, into frankly sensuous ecstasy over the sportive loveliness of devine adolescence; and its god is moulded accordingly. The mediaeval expression of religious devotion dispenses with the necessity of intellectual conviction (Jñāna) or moral activity (Karman) in the orthodox sense, but takes its stand entirely upon a subtilised form of emotional realisation (Rasa). All worship and salvation are regarded as nothing more than a blissful enjoyment of the divine sports, involving personal consciousness and relation, direct or remote, between the enjoyer and the enjoyed. But as emphasis is laid upon the erotic sentiment involved in the sports of Kṛṣṇa, the attitude, however, metaphysically interpreted, becomes too ardent, borders dangerously upon sense-devotion and often lapses into a vivid and literal sensuousness. Whatever may be its devotional value, there can be no doubt that it became immensely fruitful in literature; but its abnormalities are often carried to flagrant and dubious extremel.

The earliest sustained composition, which illustrates these tendencies, appears to be the *Kṛṣṇa-karṇāmṛta*[1] of Līlāśuka, of which the text exists in two recensions. The Southern and Western manuscripts present the text in an expanded form in three Āśvāsas of more than a hundred verses in each; while,

1 The text has been printed many times in India The Southern recension, with Pāpayallaya Sūri's commentary (107+110+102 verses in three Āśvāsas) is published from Śrī-Vaṇī-Vilāsa Press, Srirangam (no date). The Bengal recension, consisting of the first Āśvāsa only in 112 verses, is critically edited by the present writer, in the Dacca Univeristy Orient. Publ. Series Dacca 1938, with three Bengal commentaries of the 15th century, *viz.*, those of Gopālabhaṭṭa, Caitanyadāsa and Kṛṣṇadāsa Kavirāja, with full critical apparatus and additional verses from Pāpayallaya Sūri's text and other sources. Several other collections of similar verses, called *Sumaṅgala-stotra, Bilvamaṅgala-stotra, Kṛṣṇa-stotra, Bāla-gopāla-stuti* and so forth, are attributed to our author. On the authenticity of such collectanea, as well as on textual questions, see Introd. to this edition, where they have been fully discussed. To Kṛṣṇa-līlā-śuka are asscribed the *Abhinava-kaustubha-mālā* and *Dakṣiṇāmūrti-stava,* ed. T. Ganapati Sastri, Trivandrum Sanskrit Series 1905.

curiously enough, the Bengal recension appears to have preserved this South Indian text more faithfully in one Āśvāsa only, namely the first, with 112 verses. One of the concluding self-descriptive verses in the the first Āśvāsa appears to make a punning, but reverential, mention of the poet's parents, Dāmodara and Nīvī, and his preceptor Īśānadeva ; while the opening stanza speaks of Somagiri, apparently a Śaṃkarite ascetic, as his spiritual Guru. The poet calls himself Līlāśuka, without the additional name Bilvamaṅgala, and does not give the fuller form Kṛṣṇalīlāśuka. The fact is important because of the possibility of existence of more than one Bilvamaṅgala and of a Kṛṣṇa-līlā-śuka who is known chiefly as a grammarian ; and we have nothing except the uncertain testimony of local anecdotes to equate the two names with that of Līlāśuka. Beyond this nothing authentic is known of the date and personal history of our author, although many regions and monastic orders of Southern India claim him and have their local legends to confirm the claim : and reliance on this and that legend would enable one to assign him to different periods of time ranging from the 9th to the 15th century.

The *Kṛṣṇa-karṇāmṛta* is a collection of devotional lyric stanzas in which Kṛṣṇa is the object of the poet s prayer and praise. It is not a descriptive poem on the life or sports of Kṛṣṇa, but a passionate eulogy of the beloved deity, expressed in erotic words and imageries, in a mood of semi-amorous self-surrender. If any analogy is permissible, it resembles, to some extent, the mediaeval Christian lyrics, which are laden with passionate yearning for the youthful Christ as the beloved, and of which the Song of Solomon—'I am my Beloved's, and my Beloved is mine'—is the sacred archetype ; but the difference lies in conceiving the youthful Kṛṣṇa in a background of extremely sensuous charm, in the vivid exuberance of erotic fancy, and in the attitude of pathetic supplication and surrender (Prapatti). Although made up of detached stanzas, the ardent longing of our poet-devotee for a vision of his beautiful deity, the wistfulness of his devotional hope and faith, and the evident burst of joy and amazemnt in the fulfilment of his desire supply an inner unity which weaves them into a passionate whole. In spite of emotional directness, the poem possesses all the distinctive features of a deliberate work of art. The sheer beauty and music of its words and the highly sensuous pictorial effect, authenticated by a deep sincerity of ecstatic passion, make it a finished product of lyric imagination. The uninterested critic will probably consider the excess of erotic sentiment to be pathological, but to appreciate the poem one must realise the entire mentality of our devotee-poet. It is easy to dismiss it as an exemplification of abnormal psychology, but it is difficult for the scoffer to realise the warmth and earnestness of the emotional belief, the transport and exaltation of the refined mysticism. These devout utterances do not represent a professional effort, but a born gift, or a gift acquired through the intensity of worship and adoration, a mood of that god-intoxicated madness which draws from visible and familiar things an intuition of elevating joy. It is not the systematic expression of religious ideas so much as their fusion into a whole in a remarkable poetical and devotional personality, which makes these spiritual effusions intensely attractive. The work, therefore, is not only a noteworthy poetical production of undoubted charm, but also an important document of Bhakti-devoutness, which illustrates finely the use of erotic motif in the service of religion, and deservedly holds a high place in mediaeval Śtotra literature.

Leaving aside stray poems of a similar type, we pass over to the *Gīta-govinda*[1] of Jayadeva, which is comparable to

1 Printed many times in India. The earliest edition is that of Lassen, Bonn 1846. Other notable editions with commentaries: With the Rasikapriyā of Kumbha and Rasamañjari of Śaṁkara Miśra, ed. M. R. Telang and W. L. Panshikar, NSP, Bombay 1899, 1923; with the Bālabodhinī of Caitanyadāsa, ed. Harekrishna Mukherji, in Bengali characters, Calcutta 1929 (this comm. was first printed in Calcutta 1872). The text will also be found in Haeberlin, pp. 69-114 (1847). For an account of the commentaries, see Lassen's Prolegomena to his edition, and Pischel, *Hofdichter des Lakṣmaṇasena*, Göttingen 1893. The poem has been translated into English by Sir William Jones (*Colleeted*

Līlāśuka's poem in many respects, and which representing, as it does, another aspect of the same devotional tendency becomes with it the rich source of literary and religious inspiration of mediaeval India. The fame of this extraordinary work has never been confined within the limits of Bengal; it has claimed more than forty commentators from different provinces of India, and more than a dozen imitations; it has been cited extensively in the Anthologies[1]; it has been regarded not only as a great poem, but also as a great religious work of mediaeval Vaiṣṇava Bhakti. It is no wonder, therefore, that the work should be claimed also by Mithilā and Orissa[2]. Of the author himself, however, our information is scanty, although we have a large number of legends[3] which are matters of pious belief rather than positive historical facts. In a verse occuring in the work itself (xii, 11)[4], we are informed that he was the son of Bhojadeva and Rāmādevī (variants Rādhā°, Vāma°), and the name of his wife was probably Padmāvatī alluded to in other verses.[5] His home was Kendubilva (iii. 10), which has been

Works, London 1807) and Edwin Arnold (*The Indian Song of Songs*, Trübner : London 1875; free verse rendering), and into French by G. Courtiller, Ernest Leroux : Paris 1904. But none of these versions reproduce the exquisite verbal melody and charm of the original.

1 Besides 31 verses quoted in *Skm*, of which only two (1.59. 4 ; ii. 37. 4) are traceable in the poem (xi. 11 and vi. 11), we have 24 quotations in *SP* and 4 in *Sbhv*. The *Sml* assigns two verses to Jayadeva, one of which occurs in the *Prasanna-rāghava* of his name-sake Jayadeva, who describes himself as the son of Mahādeva and Sumitrā, but with whom our Jayadeva is often confounded.

2 The question has been discussed by Manomohan Chakravarti in *JASB*, 1906, pp. 163-65.

3 The Hindi *Bhaktamāl* of Nābhādāsa re-written by Nārāyaṇadāsa in the middle of the 17th century, as well as the Sanskrit *Bhaktamālā* of Candradatta based on it, records some of these pious legends. See Pischel, *op. cit.*, pp. 19, 23, and Grierson, *Modern Vernacular Lit. of Hindustan*, Calcutta 1889, sec. 51 ; M. Chakravarti in *JASB*, 1906, p. 163 f. These legends, however, show in what light Jayadeva was glorified in the eyes of later devotees.

4 The verse is not commented upon by Knmbha in the middle of the 15th century, but it is accepted by other commentators and is found in Bühler's Kashmir MS (*Kashmir Report*, p. 64), as well as in the Nepal MS, dated 1494 A.D. (*JASB*, 1906, p. 166).

5 The implied personal reference to Padmavati in i. 2 is expressly disputed by Kumbha, who would interpret the word *padmāvatī* to mean the goddess Lakṣmī. In x. 8, again, we have *padmāvatī-ramaṇa-jayadeva-kavi°*, but there is a variant reading *jayatij ayadeva-kavi°*,

identified with Kendulī, a village on the bank of the river Ajaya in the district of Birbhum in Bengal, where an annual fair is still held in his honour on the last day of Māgha. The various songs in the poem, recorded along with appropriate Rāgas and Tālas, would indicate that the poet had also a knowledge of music. Jayadeva gives us no independent clue to his date, except referring to Govardhana, Dhoyī and Umāpatidhara, which point to the period of Sena rule; but traditional accounts agree in placing him in the court of Lakṣmaṇasena. This is confirmed by the fact that Śrīdharadāsa's *Sadukti-karṇāmṛta*, which was compiled in 1206 A.D., quotes from Jayadeva; and a verse from the *Gīta-govinda* occurs in an inscription, dated 1292 A.D.[1]

The work is not a Stotra of praise but a poem which deals with a highly erotic episode of Kṛṣṇa's vernalsports in Vṛndāvana. It is divided into twelve cantos, in the form, but not in the spirit, of the orthodox Kāvya. Each canto falls into sections, which contain Padāvalīs or songs, composed in rhymed moric metres and set to different tunes.[2] These songs, which are introduced briefly by a stanza or two, written in the orthodox classical metres, form the staple of the poem. They are placed in the mouth of three interlocutors, namely, Kṛṣṇa, Rādhā and her companion, not in the form of regular dialogues, but as lyric expressions of particular emotional predi-

which omits the word; while a third reference in xi. 8 is interpreted by Kumbha also in the same way. But Caitanyadāsa, Śaṁkara Miśra and other commentators take these passages as implying a reference to the proper name of Jayadeva's wife. The legend that Padmāvatī was a dancing girl, and Jayadeva supplied the musical accompaniment to her dancing, is said to be implied by means of punning in Jayadeva's self-description as *padmāvatī-caraṇa-cāraṇa-cakravartin* in i. 2.

1 See *JASB*, 1906, pp. 168-69. See M. R. Majumdar, A 15th Century Gitagovinda MS with Gujarati Paintings, in *Bombay University Journal*, May, 1938, p. 127, where an inscription, dated Saṁvat 1348(=1292 A.D.), of Śārṅgadeva's reign reproduces the Daśavatāra Stuti of Jayadeva's work (i. 16) as a benedictory stanza, Two poems ascribed to Jayadeva, in praise of Hari-govinda, are preserved in the Sikh *Adigranth* but in their present form they are in Western Apabraṁśa.

2 The name Aṣṭapadī found in some South Indian MSS is misleading, for the songs are not always found in groups of eight stanzas, nor is it the normal number.

cament, individually uttered or described by them in the musical mode. The theme, which is developed in this novel operatic form, is simple. It describes the estrangement of Rādha from Kṛṣṇa, who is sporting with other maidens, Rādha's sorrow, longing and jealousy, intercession of Rādha's companion, Kṛṣṇa's return, penitence and propitiation of Rādha, and the joy of their final reunion. Jayadeva's exact source is not known.[1] There are parallelisms between his extremely sensuous treatment of the Rādha-Kṛṣṇa legend and that of the *Brahmavaivarta Purāṇa*, but there is no conclusive proof of Jayadeva's indebtedness. Nor is it probable that the source of Jayadeva's inspiration was the Kṛṣṇa-Gopi legend of the *Śrīmad-bhāgavata*, which avoids all direct mention of Rādha (who is also not mentioned by Līlā-śuka),[2] and describes the autumnal, and not vernal, Rāsa-līlā. There existed, apparently, other obscure currents of erotic devotionalism, for which Jayadeva, like the *Brahmavaivarta Purāṇa* and like Vidyāpati of a later period, derived his inspiration. Even in Caitanya's time, when the Śrīmad-bhāgavata emotionalism was fully established in Bengal, we have evidences of other forms of Vaiṣṇava devotion, which did not accept nor did strictly conform to the Bhāgavata source.[3]

And yet the Caitanya movement in later time attempted to appropriate Jayadeva and transform him, as also Vidyāpati,[4] into a regular Caitanyaite Vaiṣṇava. It would regard the

1 For a discussion of the question see S. K. De, Pre-Caitanya Vaiṣṇavism in Bengal in *Festschrift M. Winternitz*, Leipzig 1933, p. 196 f and *Early History of Vaiṣṇava Faith and Movement in Bengal*, Calcutta 1942, pp. 7-10.

2 The Rādhā legend, however, is comparatively old, being referred to in Hāla's Prakrit *Sapta-śatī*, ed., NSP, Bombay 1911, i. 89, and in Ānandavardhan's *Dhvanyāloka*, ed. NSP, 1911, p. 87.

3 As evidenced by the Bengali *Śrīkṛṣṇa-kīrttana* of Baḍu Caṇḍīdāsa (*c*. end of the 14th century), and by the Pre-Caitanya Sahajiyā movements which continued their tradition even after Caitanya's time.

4 See Haraprasad Sastri, introd. to his ed. of Vidyāpati's *Kīrti-latā*. Calcutta 1904 (Hṛṣikeśa Series), which shows that Vidyāpati was normal Smārta Pañcopāsaka (worshipping, the five deities Gaṇeśa, Sūrya, Śiva, Viṣṇu and Durgā), who wrote Padāvalīs on Rādhā-Kṛṣṇa as well as on Śiva and Gaṅgā, besides composing in Sanskṛit series of Smṛti treatises and works on Śiva-Durgā worship.

Gīta-govinda not so much as a poetical or devotional composition of great beauty but as an authoritative religious text, illustrating the refined subtleties of its theology and Rasa-śāstra. The theme, as well as the spirit of Jayadeva's poem would doubtless lend themselves to such interpretation, but the attitude of sectarian exposition affects and obscures the proper appreciation of its purely literary quality. It should not be forgotten that Jayadeva flourished at least three centuries before the promulgation of the Rasa-śāstra of Rūpa Gosvāmin; and the Kṛṣṇaism, which emerges in a finished literary form in his poem, as in the Maithili songs of Vidyāpati, should not be equated with the sectarian dogmas and doctrines of later scholastic theologians. As a poet of undoubted gifts, he could not have made it his concern to compose a religious treatise according to any particular Vaiṣṇava dogmatics[1]; he claims merit as a poet, and his religious emotion or inspiration should not be allowed to obscure this proper claim. If his emotional temperament preferred an erotic theme and selected the love-story of Rādhā and Kṛṣṇa, fascinating to mediaeval India, the divine love that he depicts is considerably humanised in an atmosphere of passionate poetic appeal.

There cannot be any doubt that the *Gīta-govinda*, both in its emotional and literary aspects, occupies a distinctive place in the history of Sanskrit poetry. Jayadeva, it is true, emphasises the praise and worship of Kṛṣṇa, but his work is not, at least in its form and spirit, the expression of an intensly devotional personality in the sense in which Līlāśuka's poem is; and no influence of Līlāśuka is traceable in Jayadeva. If Jayadeva claims religious merit, he also prides himself upon the elegance,

1 That Jayadeva had no sectarian purpose is also shown by the fact that the Sahajiyā sect of Bengal also regards him as its Ādi-guru and one of its nine Rasikas. The Vallabhācāri sect also appears to have recognised the *Gīta-govinda*, in imitation of which Vallabhācārya's son Viṭṭhaleśvara introduced rhymed Padāvalīs into his *Sṛṅgāra-rasa-maṇḍana*. A curious instance of appropriation is furnished by the *Saśilekhā* commentary of Kṛṣṇadatta, son of Bhaveśa of Mithilā, which makes an attempt to interpret *Gīta-govinda* as applying simultaneously to the legends of Kṛṣṇa and Siva!

softness and music of his poetic diction, as well as upon the felicity and richness of his sentiments. The claims are in no way extravagant. Even if there is nothing new in it, the theme must have been a living reality to the poet as well as to his audience. But the literary form in which the theme is presented is extremely orginal. The work calls itself a Kāvya and conforms to the formal division into cantos, but in reality it goes much beyond the stereotyped Kāvya prescribed by the rhetoricians and practised by the poets. Modern critics have found in it a lyric drama (Lassen), a pastoral (Jones), an opera (Lévi), a melodrama (Pischel) and a refined Yātrā (von Schroeder). As a creative work of art, it has a form of its own, but defies conventional classification. Though cast in a semi-dramatic mould, the spirit is entirely lyrical ; though modelled perhaps on the prototype of the popular Kṛṣṇa-yātrā in its musical and melodramatic peculiarities, it is yet far removed from the old Yātrā by its want of improvisation and mimetic qualities ; though imbued with religious feeling, the attitude is not entrirely divorced from the secular ; though intended and still used for popular festival where simplicity and directness count, it yet possesses al the distinctive characteristics of a deliberate work of art. Except the introductory descriptive verses composed in the orthodox metres, the entire work consists of Padāvalīs, which are meant to be sung as musical speeches, but to which rhymed and alliterative moric metres are skilfully combined ; while the use of refrain with these songs not only intensifies their haunting melody, but also combines the detached couplets into a perfect whole. We have thus narration, description and speech finely interwoven with recitation and song, a combination which creates a type unknown in Sanskrit. Again, the erotic mysticism, in its expression of religious feelings in the intimate language and imagery of earthly passion, supplies the picturesque and emotional inflatus, in a novel yet familiar form, by transforming the urgent sex-impulse into an ecstatic devotional sentiment. All the conventions and commonplaces of Sanskrit love-poetry are skilfully utilised, and the whole effect is heightened by blending it harmoniously with the surrounding beauty of nature. All this, again, is enveloped in a fine excess of pictorial richness, verbal harmony and lyrical splendour, of which it is difficult to find a parallel. Jayadeva makes a wonderful use of the sheer beauty of words and their inherent melody, of which Sanskrit is so capable ; and like all artistic masterpieces, his poem becomes almost untranslatable. No doubt, there is in all this deliberate workmanship, but all effort is successfully concealed in an effective simplicity and clarity, in a series of passionate and extremely musical word-pictures.

In its novelty and completeness of effect, therefore, Jayadeva's poem is unique in Sanskrit, and it can be regarded as almost creating a new literary *genre*. It is clear that it does not strictly follow the tradition of the Sanskrit Kāvya, but bears closer resemblance to the spirit and style of Apabhraṃśa or Modern Indian poetry. The musical Padāvalīs, which form the vital element of the poem, are indeed composed in Sanskrit, but they really reflect the vernacular manner of expression ; and the rhymed and melodious metres, with their refrain, are hardly akin to older Sanskrit metres. The very term Padāvalī itself, which becomes so familiar in later Bengali song, is not found in this sense in Sanskrit, but is obviously taken from popular poetry. A consideration of these peculiarities makes Pischel suggest[1] that Jayadeva's work goes back to an Apabhraṃśa original ; but, apart from the fact that no such tradition exists, literary and historical considerations will entirely rule out the suggestion. It should not be forgotten that the *Gīta-govinda* was composed in an epoch when the classical Sanskrit literature was already on the decline, and when

1 *Op., cit.*, p. 27 ; repeated by S. K. Chatterji, *Origin and Development of Bengali Language*, Calcutta 1926, pp. 125-26, but the view is wrongly ascribed to Lassen. The fact that none of the Padāvalīs is quoted in the Anthologies proves nothing, it only shows that the Anthology-makers did not think that the songs strictly followed the Sanskrit tradition

it was possible for such irregular types to come into existence, presumably through the influence of musical and melodramatic tendencies of the vernacular literature, which was by this time emerging into definite existence. It is conceivable that popular festive performances, like the religious Yātrā, with their mythological theme, quasi-dramatic presentation and preference for song and melodrama, must have reacted upon the traditional Sanskrit literature and influenced its spirit and form to such an extent as to produce irregular and apparently nondescript types, which approximated more distinctly to the vernacular tradition, but which, being meant for more cultivated audience, possessed a highly stylised form. Jayadeva's *Gīta-govinda* appears to be a noteworthy example of such a type, indicating as it does, an attempt to renew and remodel older forms of composition by absorbing the newer characteristics of the coming literature in the vernacular. In these cases, the vernacular literature. developing side by side, appearently reacted upon Sanskrit, as it was often reached upon by Sanskrit ; and the question of re-translation does not arise. It should also be noted that, although the Padāvalīs follow the spirit and manner of vernacular songs, yet they accept the literary convention of Sanskrit in its highly ornamental stylistic mode of expression. The profusion of verbal figures, like chiming and alliteration, which are not adventitious but form an integral part of its literary expression, is hardly possible to the same extent in Prakrit or Apabhraṃśa, which involves dipthongisation, compensatory lengthening or epenthetic intrusion of vowels, as well as elision of intervocalic consonants. It would be strange indeed to suggest that these verbal figures did not exist in the original but were added or re-composed in the presumed Sanskrit version. Neither linguistic nor literary sense will admit that the *Gīta-govinda* was prepared in this artificial manner ; and the theory of translation becomes unbelievable when one considers that its achievement lies more in the direction of its verbally finished form, which is inseparable from its poetic expression.

It is not necessary to consider more than a dozen imitations which the *Gīta-govinda*, like the *Megha-dūta*, produced; for these literary counterfeits never became current coins of poetry. It is curious, however, that they sometimes substitute the theme of Rāma and Sītā,[1] and Hara and Pārvatī,[2] for Kṛṣṇa and Rādhā; while it is noteworthy that Viṭṭhaleśvara, son of Vallabhācārya, the founder of the Vallabhācāri sect, introduces, in his independent work *Śṛṅgāra-rasa-maṇḍana*, songs composed on the model of Jayadeva's Padāvalīs, just as Rāmānanda-rāya does in his drama *Jagannātha-vallabha*.[4] The *Kṛṣṇa-līlā-taraṅgiṇī*[5] of Nārāyaṇtīrtha, pupil of Śivarāmānanda-tīrtha, comprehends in twelve Taraṅgas the entire story of Kṛṣṇa from birth to establishment at Dvārakā and includes songs in musical modes; it is sometimes ranked with the poems of Līlāśuka and Jayadeva as the third great work on Kṛṣṇa-līlā; but it is a late and laboured imitation which never attained more than a limited currency. Indeed, with Jayadeva we are practically at the end of what is best not only in erotic-religious poetry, but also in Sanskrit poetry in general; and its later annals are dull and uninspiring. He blew the embers of poetry with a new breath, but the momentary glow did not arrest its

1 E.g., *Gīta-rāghava* of Prabhākara, mentioned in R. G. Bhandarkar's *Report*, 188-83, p. 130. The poet is mentioned as the son of Bhūdhara, and he wrote in 1618 A.D.

2 The *Gīta-gaurīpati* of Bhānudatta, ed. Grantharatna-mālā, vol. i, p. 32, vol. ii, pp. 33-92 Bombay 1888; separately printed, Gopal Narayan Co., Bombay 1891. On the author see S. K. De, *Sanskrit Poetics*, p. 245, where this work is also noticed. Other similar imitations are: *Gīta-gaṅgāhdara* of Kalyāṇa, *Gīta-giriśa* of Rāmabhaṭṭa, *Gīta-digambara* of Vaṁśamaṇi of Mithilā. *Gīta-rāghava* of Hariśaṁkara, *Gīta-gopāla* of Caturbhuja, etc.

3 Ed. Mulachandra Tulsidas Televala, Bombay 1919. For the songs, see pp. 5, 56-58, 60, 70 of this edition. The work is in nine Ullāsas.

4 See below, under Drama. This is done also by some followers of Caitanya in their poetical works; such songs, for instance, occur in Kavikarṇapūra's *Ānanda-vṛndāvana* Campū, in Jīva Gosvāmin's *Gopāla-campū*, in Prabodhānanda's *Saṁgīta-mādhava*, and in Rūpa Gosvāmin's *Gītāvalī*.

5 Eggeling, *India Office Catalogue*, vii, no. 3881, pp. 1462, MS incomplete in eight taraṅgas; Burnell, *Tanjore Catalogue*, pt. iii, p. 168. Cf. Sesagiri Sastri, *Report*, ii, Madras 1899, p. 57, where the importance of the work is much exaggerated. The author flourised in he Godavari district about 1700 A.D.

steady decline. Of emotional Bhakti-productions of later times, in which Bengal became prolific during the early years of the Caitanya movement, but which have more doctrinal value than poetic, mention need be made of only a few works. A typical example is furnished by the *Stava-mālā*[1] of Rūpa Gosvāmin. The author was one of the immediate disciples of Caitanya; as one of the authoritative teachers of the new faith, who wrote in Sanskrit, and as a poet, rhetorician and devotee, he became deservedly the centre of its arduous and prolonged literary activity at Vṛndāvana. In his *Padyāvalī*, of which we shall speak presently, he gives an anthological survey of devotional verses, new and old, which illustrate the many nuances of the emotional worship of Kṛṣṇa made current by the Caitanya sect. The *Stava-mālā* is a collection, made by his nephew Jīva, of some sixty Stotras and Gītas, composed by Rūpa himself, which bear witness alike to his devotion, learning and literary skill. The pieces are of unequal merit; but some, like the *Mukunda-muktāvalī*,[2] betray the influence of Līlāśuka; others, like the *Govinda-birudāvalī*, attempts but does not succeed in evolving new rhythmical forms; but for exquisite verbal melody and pictorial fancy, the poems on Rāsa-līlā in the moric metres, the piece entitled *Svayam-utprekṣita-līlā*, and the songs included in the part entitled *Gītāvalī*, stand out prominently and show fairly successful reproduction of Jayadeva's manner and diction. But rhetoric is still profuse and overwrought in these hymns and songs; it is fraught with devotional fancy but often prone to inane ingenuities. The *Stavavālī*[3] of Raghunātha-dāsa, his friend and fellow-disciple, is much inferior in art, but superior in sincere devotional passion, while the separate Stotras and devotional works like the *Caitanya-candrāmṛta* (143 verses of praise and panegyric) of Prabodhānanda, the *Kṛṣṇāhnika-kaumudī* (in

1 Ed. Bhavadatta Sastri and K. P. Parab, with comm. of Jīva Gosvāmin, NSP, Bombay 1903.

2 Also ed. (without the name of the author) in Kāvyamālā, Gucchaka ii, p. 157 f.

3 Ed. Radharaman Press, Berhampur (Murshidabad) 1923, in Bengali characters.

six Prakāśas) of Paramānanda-dāsa Kavikarṇapūrā (who also wrote a Sanskrit poetical biography of Caitanya, entitled *Caitanya-caritāmṛta*), the *Govinda-līlāmṛta* of Kṛṣṇadāsa Kavirāja and the *Camatkāra-candrikā*, *Gaurāṅga-līlāmṛta* and *Kṛṣna-bhāvanāmṛta* (dated 1786 A.D.) of Viśvanātha Cakravartin have a limited appeal and are hardly known outside Bengal.[1]

c. *The Didactic and Satiric Poetry*

It is difficult to define precisely the significance of the term 'didactic poetry', commonly applied to a group of heterogeneous compositions which are more or less of a moralising tendency; for the objection is not invalid that didacticism is incompatible with poetry. But the term is intended, in the popular sense, to include a series of poems, which are not tracts or text-books giving a metrical exposition of complex philosophical or moral themes, but which give impressive poetical expression to traditional wisdom or to wisdom which springs from intimate observation of men and manners. Such reflective poetry in Sanskrit sometimes expresses itself in cleverly turned gnomic stanzas, polarised into antithesis or crystallised into epigram; but it comprehends chiefly the theme of Nīti in the wide sense of practical sagacity, as well as of Vairāgya as the mood which realises the emptiness of human endeavour and leads to noble reflections on the sorrows and worries of life. There is also a thin surplus of light composition which ridicules men and their morals. From the very beginning, as an inheritance of the older Epic literature, the didactic vein runs through the entire body of Sanskrit poetry; but in these poems it comes directly to the surface, not always as moralising for its own sake, but as

[1] All these works, with the exception of *Kṛṣṇāhnika-kaumudī* and *Camatkāra-candrikā* (ed. Haridas Das, Navadvīpa, 1938, 1940, have been printed at the above press in Bengali characters). If they were printed in Devanāgarī, perhaps they would have been more widely known. For Bibliographical details and brief accounts of these works, see S. K. De, introductions and notes to the *Padyāvalī* and *Kṛṣṇa-karṇāmṛta* and *Early History of Vaiṣṇava Faith and Movement in Bengal*, ch. vii, cited above.

literary expression of the moral feeling. Humanity finds full expression, and poetry often displays richness, perspicacity and depth. It is clear that in its ethical attitude the Sanskrit didactic poetry leans very perceptibly towards Sanskrit devotional poetry, of which it is sometimes an accessory; but since eroticism is found to be a dangerous and eradicable element of human nature, erotic acts and ideas often form the subject of wise thought and sarcasm. From grave questions of morals, policy and peace to those of amusements, triflings and snares of love, the scope of didactic poetry is wide enough to make the designation, in the absence of better terminology, rather inadequate, if not misleading; but it is clear that it has a province of its own and deserves a separate treatment.

The didactic poetry, like the erotic and the devotional, generally takes the form of the traditional Śataka, or of a series of indefinite number of detached verses, with the exception of a few satirico-comic poems of a more well-knit form. Thus, we have polished reflective stanzas of elevated Śatakas, or highly finished Subhāṣitas which are pithy apophthegms of proverbial philosophy; but there is also another method known as Anyāpadeśa, in which the same purpose is achieved by an indirect appreciation or condemnation of analogical qualities of particular objects.[1] The general theme of all these forms of composition consists of the commonplaces of prevalent ethics, but there are acute observations, abundant and varied, expressed in skilled but often felicitous diction, and in a variety of melodious metres, on the sorrows and joys of life, fickleness and caprices of love, follies of men and wiles of women, right mode of life, futility of pomp and power, weariness of servitude, falsehood and instability of human effort and desire, delights of solitude and

1 As for instance, the poet describes the dust as insignificant, light by nature and trampled daily under our feet, but the fickle wind tosses it high, and it can sit on the summit of lofty mountains! The didactic implication is obvious. It is possible that the Anyāpadeśa is a development from the figure Anyokti or Aprastuta-praśaṁsā, but there is no reason to restrict it to this narrow connotation.

tranquillity, as well as witty and sometimes sardonically humorous reflections on humbug and hoax. As these and similar topics are repeated with slight variations, it will not be necessary in the following brief account to describe the contents of individual poems in detail, unless there is something out of the ordinary The example of Bhartṛhari appears to dominate ; but there is considerable originality of thought and expression, although there are tiresome writers who make misguided attemps to compose dull series of merely imitative Śatakas. Some works, again, like the *Bhāminī-vilāsa* of Jagannātha, make an effort to combine the three motifs of Love, Wisdom and Resignation in one poem; some authors vie with one another in producing double or triple Śataka on these themes, or one Śataka with double or triple punning application of meaning ; while others, like the Jaina Padmānanda[1] and the Vedāntist Appayya Dīkṣita,[2] content themselves with composing only Vairāgya-śatakas of moderate literary merit. Sometimes, in the case of most Jaina and some Hindu authors, the didatic poetical form is pressed into the service of religious instruction or propaganda, but these so-called poems may be neglected in a literary account.

A high antiquity is claimed for the *Nīti-dviṣaṣṭikā*[3] of Sundara-pāṇḍya, apparently of Madura, but, the fact that anonymous citation from it is found in the *Pañcatantra* proves nothing, nor is the author's identity with Sundara-pāṇḍya, who is said to have been mentioned as an ancestor of Arikeśarin in an inscription of about 750 A.D., proved beyond doubt. In any case, this collection of one hundred and fifteen highly artificial Āryā verses on diverse moral topics is scarcely of much outstanding literary

1 Ed. Kāvyamālā, Gucchaka vii, p. 71 f (in Sārdūlavikrīḍita).

2 Ed. Kāvyamālā, Gucchaka i, p. 91 f (in Āryā).

3 Ed. K. Markandeya Sarma, Kilpauk, Madras 1928. See *Descriptive Cat. Library, Orient Govt. MSS. Library*, xx, p. 8056, no. 12051 : *Des. Cat. Trivandrum Palace Library*, no. 1683. The *Sbhv* gives some of Sundara-pāṇḍya's verses under the names of Prakāśavarṣa, Argata and Ravigupta. But Sundara-pāṇḍya is also quoted in the *Sūkti-ratna-hāra* of Kaliṅgarāya (c. 13th century). The printed work contains 115 verses, with an appendix of 33 additional verses. The tradition of Āryā metre, which is favoured mostly in Southern India, is noteworthy.

importance. Of greater interest is the *Bhallaṭa-śataka*[1] of the Kashmirian Bhallaṭa, who flourished[2] under king Śaṃkaravarman (883-902 A.D.). The printed text of the poem contains 108 stanzas in a variety of lyrical metres; but, like most early Śatakas, the work must have suffered some tampering and interpolation, for two of its verses are ascribed to other poets in the Anthologies, and one of Ānandavardhana's verses is found in it.[3] In this Śataka there is not much obtrusive display of metrical or rhetorical skill, but most of the verses, in thought and expression, are elegantly moulded. Even if individuality is not conspicuous, the verses are varied and eminently readable, and the collection is by no means pedestrian. Judging from the name of the author, the *Śānti-śataka*[4] of Śihlaṇa probably belongs also to Kashmir, but nothing is known of its date and author, except that the poet, being quoted in the *Sadukti-karṇāmṛta* of Śrīdhara-dāsa, must belong to a period anterior to 1206 A.D.[5] The poem deals, by means of detached stanzas, in four chapters (Paritāpa-praśamana, Vivekodaya, Kartavyatā and Brahma-prāpti) with the merits of asceticism; but the various aspects of the attainment of tranquallity are described with considerable feeling and without much complexities of diction. The poetic reference to the inexorableness of the fruits of human action in the opening stanza[6] need not show that the poet was a Buddhist, and there is

1 Ed. Kāvyamālā, Gucchaka iv, p. 140f. The work is cited by Abhinavagupta (*Locana*), Kṣemendra (*Aucitya-vicāra*), Kuntaka, Mammaṭa and the anthologies. For a study of the text, see V. Raghavan, in *Annals of the Venkaṭeśvara Oriental Institute*, i, p. 37 f.

2 Kahlaṇa, v. 204.

3 No. 68=*Dhvanyāloka* (NSP *ed.*) p. 218 (*amī te dṛśyante nanu*).

4 Ed. K. Schönfied, with German trs., Leipzing 1910; also in Haeberlin, p. 410f, Jivananda ii. p. 278f. See Keith in *JRAS*, 1911, p. 257f. In view of the extremely uncertain text of most early Śatakas, there is no reason to hold, with Schönfield and Keith, that the *Śanti-śataka*, which must have (as the editor also admits) suffered similar textual tampering, is a mere compilation; and since the texts of Bhartṛhari's Śatakas themselves are not yet fixed, no conclusion is safe from the fact that 22 stanzas are common to the present texts of the works of Śihlaṇa and Bhartṛhari.

5 Perhsps the author knew Rājaśekhara's works; for i. 4d. appears to be a reminiscence of *Viddha-śāla*°, i. 23.

6 The stanza occurs in some versions of Bhartṛhari's *Nīti-śataka*.

much in the content of the poem which is of universal application. The inspirer of Śihlaṇa's thought and style is of course Bhartṛhari; even if Śihlaṇa does not possess the gifts of his predecessor, there can be no doubt that he is a poet of moderate competence. He is less pedantic than most of his fellow-writers, not wholly devoid of individuality, never low and seldom too affected. Of other Kashmirian works, the *Anyokti-muktālatā*[1] of Śambhu, who also wrote a high-flown panegyric already noticed above of Harṣa of Kashmir, is a collection of 108 datached stanzas which display stylistic tricks but no special poetic excellence.

Of unknown date and provenance, but probably later and certainly of less merit, are the *Dṛṣṭānta-kalikā-śataka*[2] of Kusumadeva, a collection of gnomic verses in the Śloka metre, and the *Upadeśa-śataka*[3] of Gumāni, which moralises, in Āryā verses, on some myths and legends from the Epics and the Purāṇas. On the other hand, the *Bhāva-śataka* of Nāgarāja,[4] son of Jalāpa and grandson of Vidyādhara of Karpaṭi Goṭra and Ṭāka family (probably a petty ruling family who flourished near Delhi), is a curious collection of enigmatic verses in various metres, in which the erotic motif is freely utilised and the peculiar condition or action of various persons is described with an implication of the reason for such condition or action.[5] The *Bhāva-vilāsa*[6] of the

1 Ed. Kāvyamālā, Gucchaka ii, p. 61f.

2 Ed. Kāvyamālā, Gucchaka xiv, p. 77f. The work is earlier than Vallabhadeva's *Subhāṣitāvali* which quotes 21 verses from it (nos. 287-307).

3 Ed. Kāvyamālā, Gucchaka ii, p. 20f.

4 Ed. Kāvyamāla, Gucchaka iv, p. 37 f. The author was probably some court-poet of Nāgarāja, to whom the work is ascribed *honoris causa*. See R. G. Bhandarkar, *Report* 1882-83, p. 97 and Peterson. *Three Reports*, p. 21f. On Jayaswal's theory of high antiquity (300 to 350 A-D.) of the poem, see Winternitz in *IHQ*, XII, 1936, pp. 134-37.

5 For instance, the fifth verse says that a damsel tormented by thirst went to the riverside, took water with both hands, looked at it, but did not drink it,—why? The answer supplied in the prose commentary is that it was on account of the flowing reflection of her own beautiful hands, she fancied the water to be blood! Sporting in a pavilion, a clever girl, decorated with jewels, kicked her lover with her feet without any fault of his,—why? Because, the commentary explains, she saw her own reflection in the jewels, but mistaking it for another woman, became jealous!

6 Ed. Kāvyamālā, Gucchaka ii, p. 111 f (verses in varied metres). The author flourished in the time of Akbar. He also wrote a *Bhramara-dūta*, already noticed above.

Nyāya commentator. Rudra Nyāyavācaspati, son of Vidyanivāsa, contains some well-written, but undistinguished, Anyāpadeśa stanzas, but about 20 verses are taken up with the panegyric of the author's patron Bhāvasimha, an ancestor of the present ruler of Jaipur (Rajputana). The *Lokokti-muktāvalī*[1] of Dakṣiṇamūrti is a composition of a similar, but more stilled construction. Other published Anyāpadeśa collections include the *Anyāpadeśa śataka* of Nīlakantha Dīksita (1st half of the 17th century) of Southern India,[2] of Madhusūdana of Mithilā[3] and of the Alamkārika Viśveśvara of Almora (beginning of the 18th century);[4] but Nīlakantha also wrote the *Sabhā-rañjana*,[5] a collection of 105 sententious verses in the Śloka metre, and the *Śānti-vilāsa*,[6] a Vairāgya work of 51 Śikharinī verses. These are compositions in which verse is not a synonym of poetry but an adjunct of laboured wit.

The collections of Subhāṣitas or Happy Sayings do not present any difference in form, theme and diction. Thus, we have the *Subhāṣita-nīvī*[7] of the prolific South Indian scholar and teacher Veṅkaṭadeśika, a highly artificial homily, containing 144 verses in a variety of metres, symmetrically divided into 12 Paddhatis of 12 verses in each, and dealing with such topics as pride, wickedness, servitude, nobility, tranquality and so forth. Much more extensive and diversified in content are the *Harihara-subhāṣita*[8]

1 Ed. Kāvyamālā, Gucchaka xi, p. 65 f (94 verses in varied metres).

2 Ed. Kāvyamālā, Gucchaka vi, p. 143 f (in Śārdūlavikrīḍita). Also the *Anyokti-muktāvalī* of Haṁsavijaya-gaṇi, ed. Kedarnath and V. L. Panshikar. NSP, Bombay 1907.

3 Ed. Kāvyamāla, Gucchaka ix, p. 64 f. In varied metres. The author is described as the son of Padmanābha and Subhadrā, but his date is not known.

4 Ed. Kāvyamālā, Gucchaka v, p, 89 f. In Śārdūlavikrīḍita, except the first verse which is in Sragdharā. For the author see S. K. De, *Sanskrit Poetics*, I, p. 312-13.

5 Ed. Kāvyamālā, Gucchaka ix, p. 156 f. Under the title 'Minor Poems of Nīlakṇtha Dikṣita,' the Śrī Vaṇī Vilāsa Press Srirangam 1911, publishes Kali-viḍambana, Sabhā-rañjana, Santi-vilāsa. Vairāgya-śataka, Ānandasagara-stava and Anyāpadeśa-śataka.

6 Ed. Kāvyamālā, Gucchaka vi, p. 12 f (51 verses).

7 Ed. M. T. Narasimha Aiyangar. Śrī Vāṇi Vilāsa Press, Srirangam 1908.

8 Ed. Kedarnath and W. L. Panshikar. NSP, 2nd ed., Bombay 1910 (1st ed. Bhavadatta and K. P. Parab 1905).

of Harihara and the *Subhāṣita-ratna-saṃdoha*[1] of Amitagati. The first work contains over six hundred verses in Śloka, Āryā and other metres, and includes sections on polity, erotics and spiritual knowledge. The second work, composed in 994 A.D., by a well known Digambara Jaina monk, is divided into thirty-two Prakaraṇas, usually having, on the Kāvya model, different metres for different sections. It is not only an earnest poetical epitome of the entire Jaina ethics and rules of conduct, but also contains severe reflections on woman, dice and drinking, the courtesan having a whole section to herself.

But these moralising poets are too serious to depict the sins and follies of men with the sparkle of wit and humour. The type of satrico-comic poetry, inaugurated by Dāmodaragupta, therefore, does not find any gifted exponent, but languishes in the hands of a limited number of industrious writers, who are indeed experts in erotics and shrewd observers of life, but who lack balance and lightness of touch in painting drolleries, as well as the power of polished wit and gentle ridicule to redeem the natural tendency to bitter sārcasm or coarse realism. The only writer who evinces an interesting bent in this direction is the Kashmirian Kṣemendra, whose works best exemplify the merits and defects of later attempts. This hard-working polymath,[2] surnamed Vyāsadāsa, was the son of Prakāśendra and grandson of Sindhu, and wrote in the reign of Ananta and his son and successor Kalaśa of Kashmir, Kṣemendra's literary activity thus falling in the middle and second half of the 11th century. He composed not only poems, plays, narratives, didactic and satiric sketches, a work on Nīti (*Nīti-kalpataru*), treatises on rhetoric, erotics and prosody, but also made abstracts of older poems, of the two Epics, of Guṇāḍhya's *Bṛhatkathā*, of the

1 Ed. Bhavadatta and W. L. Panshikar, NSP, 2nd ed., Bombay 1909. Ed. and trs. R. Schmidt and J. Hertel in *ZDMG*, LXIX. 1905, and LXI, 1907 separately published, Leipzig 1908. On the author, see Peterson, *Fourth Report*, Bombay 1894, p. ix.

2 On Kṣemendra and his works, see S. K. De, *Sanskrit Poetics*, i. pp. 139-43. On Kṣemendra's handling of his material in making abstracts, see M. B. Emeneau, Kṣemendra as a Kavi in *JAOS*, LIII, 1933, p. 124 f.

Buddhist Avadānas, of Bāṇa's Kādambarī and of Vātsyāyana's *Kāma-sūtra*. Hardly any other Sanskrit writer is so thorough a devotee of what may be called miscellaneous literature. He is versatile, accomplished and methodical; but he cannot be altogether dismissed as a mere adapter or miscellaneous compiler. Perhaps his enormous literary travail was not such drudgery as one would be inclined to think, for it certainly helped him to acquire an admirable literary skill and an amount of multiferious learning, which add a flavour to his best writings. But his originality is best seen, not in his laborious lucubrations, which are no more than literary exercises, but in the lighter things on which perhaps he did not spend so much labour and midnight oil.

In his *Samaya-mātṛkā*,[1] or Original Book of Convention for the courtesan, Kṣemendra is doubtless inspired by Dāmodargupta, and selects a similar theme of the snares and trickeries of the harlot. It gives in eight chapters, composed mostly in Śloka, but diversified by lyrical measures, the story of a young courtesan Kalāvatī, who is introduced by a roguish barber to an "owl-faced, crow-necked and cat-eyed" (iv. 7) old bawd, named Kaṇkālī, for detailed but witty instruction in her difficult profession, and who succeeds with the advice and assistance to ensnare a precocious young boy and rob his rich and foolish parents. The merit of the work lies not in its unsavoury story, but in its heightened, yet graphic, picture of droll life, painted with considerable sharpness of phrasing and characterisation, and with an undertone of mocking satire directed against many forms of prevalent deformity. The most curious part of the work is the amusing account, given with touches of local colour, of the adventures of Kaṅkālī and her wanderings in younger days through the length and breadth of Kashmir, as a whore, pretended wife and widow to many men, thief, nun, procuress, shop-girl, seller of cakes, barmaid, beggar-woman, flower-girl, woman-magician and holy saint; while her spicy

1 Ed. Durgaprasad and K. P. Parab, NSP, 2nd ed., Bombay 1925.

anecdotes, her erotic classification of different types of men after different birds and beasts, and her shady but ingenious ways of cheating fools and knaves are not without interest. Kṣemendra does not show any squeamishness regarding delicate, questionable and even repulsive topics, nor any tendency to romanticise them. He wields a rich, racy and pointed style, and has considerable skill in turning out keenly edged verses, suitable for depicting certain types of ludicrous men and scenes. But it cannot be said that his outspoken frankness does not often lapse into a gloating over bald and unnecessary vulgarities. It is difficult indeed for his subject to steer clear of the danger in all cases, but with his knowledge and zest for erotics, Kṣemendra appears to be a willing victim. He is more a satirist than a humorist, and is in a sense privileged to present things in a repulsively naked form ; but pungent and realistic that his descriptions often are, there is nothing to redeem the general atmosephere of prosy and depressing sordidness. Nevertheless, his work as *chronique scandaleuse* is not mere pornography, nor an immoral work with a moral tag ; it is, in spite of its obvious coarseness, an interesting specimen of an approach to satirical realistic writing which is so rarely cultivated in Sanskrit.

Kṣemendra's other works are not so richly descriptive ; they are compositions of a somewhat more didactic kind. They are not narratives, but are either astute homilies on human wickedness, with occassional flashes of trenchant wit and amusing word-pictures, or entertaining sketches of human follies and oddities, enlivened by cutting sarcasm and facetious anecdotes. Of the homilectic kind are his *Sevya-sevakopadeśa*,[1] *Cārucaryā*[2] and *Caturvarga-saṃgraha*.[3] The first is a short tract of sixty-one verses, containing shrewd reflections on the relation of master

1 Ed. Kāvyamālā, Gucchaka ii, p. 79f. The verses are in varied metres.

2 Ed. Kāvyamālā, Gucchaka ii, p. 128f.

3 Ed. Kāvyamālā, Gucchaka, v, p. 75f. In 107 verses in diverse metres. See Lévi in *JA*, 1885, t. vi, s, 8, p. 404 f.

and servant; the third is a poetical exposition, in four chapters of the four general objects of human activity, namely, virtue, wealth, love and salvation; while the second is a century of moral aphorisms in the Śloka metre on virtuous conduct, illustrated by pithy allusions to myths and legends ingeniously ransacked by the author's miscellaneous learning. In all these deliberately didactic works, it is the satirist who is turned a homilist; and his observations are not destitute of a witty and often epigrammatic flavour, to which his simple and elegantly direct style undoubtedly contributes.

More interesting are his satirical sketches of different types of human frailty. His *Darpa-dalana*[1] is a diatribe against human pride, which is described as springing from seven principal sources, namely, birth, wealth, learning, beauty, valour, charity and asceticism; they are treated separately in as many chapters, with illustration of each type of braggadocio by a tale invented for the purpose. Here the moralist is dominant, but the satirist is irrepressible and peeps out very often, as for instance, in the description of quacks in learning and pretenders to sanctity. In his *Kalā-vilāsa*[2] Kṣemendra reverts to his mode of satire, with less coarseness and greater sense of comedy, and adopts the moric Ārya metre of Dāmodaragupta's *Kuṭṭanī-mata*. It is a poem in ten cantos, in which Mūladeva, the legendary master of trickery, instructs his young disciple Candragupta, son of a merchant, in the arts of roguery practised by cheats, quack doctors, harlots, traders, goldsmiths, singers, actors, beggars, ascetics and so forth, and illustrates his exposition by amusing tales. The first canto gives a general account of the various forms of cheating and their exponents; the second describes greed; the third discusses the erotic impulse and wiles of women;

1. Ed. Kāvyamālā, Gucchaka vi, p. 66f. In varied metres. Trs. into German by R. Schmidt in *ZDMG, LXIX*, 1915, p. 1f. Extracts ed. and trs. B. A. Hirszbant (Über Kṣemendras Darpadalana), St. Petersburg 1892.

2. Ed. Kāvyamālā, Gucchaka, i, p. 34f. Trs. into German (v-x) by R. Schmidt in *WZKM*, XXVII, 1914, p. 406f.

the fourth is devoted entirely to the harlot; the fifth depicts the wicked Kāyasthas, skilled in crooked writing, who as high-placed executive officials, possessed with little conscince but with great power of mischief, form the target of Kṣemendra's special inventive; the sixth dilates upon the follies of pride; the seventh describes with much wit the wandering singer, bard, dancer, actor, who steal people's money by their device of making harmonious noise and meaningless antids; the eighth denounces the special tricks of the goldsmith, who steals your gold before your eyes; the ninth deals with various forms of roguery practised by the astrologer, the false doctor, the seller of patent medicine, merchants and *chevalier d'industrie* of the same feather; while the tenth and last canto winds up with a constructive lecture on what the arts should be. The work is thus a remarkably comprehensive discourse, with a legendary framework, on the various activities of notorious tricksters known to Kṣemendra; and his easy and elegant style makes the descriptions amusing and the satire effective.

The two works, *Deśopadeśa* and *Narma-mālā,*[1] which are in some repects complementary to each other, are conceived in the same spirit and style, and directed, more narrowly but with greater concentration, against oppression, hypocrisy and corruption which prevailed in Kashmir in Kṣemendra's days. The first work is put in the form of advice (Upadeśa), or rather ironical homage, the second in that of ridicule (Narma or Parihāsa); but the satirical attitude is not different. The *Deśopadeśa* deals, in eight sections, with the cheat (Khala), who builds castles in the air to delude innocent people ; the avaricious miser (Kadarya), miserable, dirty and desolate, who never enjoys what the hoards; the prostitute (Bandhakī), described as a restless but mechanical wooden puppet, with her cheap tricks and one hundred and one amulets worn on her body for luck; the snake-like old bawd (Kuṭṭanī), who can make the impossible possible and *vice-versa*;

1 Ed. Madhusudan Kaul, Kashmir Series of Texts and Studies, Poona 1923.

but who cannot help getting bruised in constant brawls ; the ostenatatious voluptuary (Viṭa), monkey-like with his foppish dress, curly hair, dental speech and love for loose women ; the students from foreign lands, especially from Gauḍa, who avoid touch of people lest their fragile body should break, but who, under the bracing climate of Kashmir, acquire overbearing manners refuse to pay shop-keepers and are ready to draw the knife on the slightest provocation ; the old man, marrying a young wife to the amusement and joy of other people, and begetting a child, like a withered and leafless tree bearing unexpected fruit ; the degraded Śaiva teacher, ignorant and lecherous, and the people who come to him, namely, the inevitable Kāyastha and his fickle wife favoured by the Guru, the poetaster struggling with his shabby verses, the crafty merchant, the bragging alchemist, the false ascetic, the boastful grammarian and the ignorant, ink-besmeared scribe. In the *Narma-mālā* we have a similar series of pen-pictures, but its three interesting chapters are meant to be a sharp satire on the misrule and oppression of the Kāyastha administration before the time of king Ananta. The Kāyastha, whose pen was his sword, monopolised all the key-positions in the state, as the Gṛhakṛtyādhipati or chief executive officer of internal administration, the Paripālaka or governor of a province, the Lekhopādhyāya or clerk-in-chief, the Gañjadivira or chief accountant, and the Niyogin or executive officer in the villages. In the first chapter are described the public activities of these and other officers, their parasites and myrmidons, and their enormities and atrocious misdeeds ; the rest of the work outlines, with vivid skill, the degarded private life of a typical Kāyastha and his frivolous wife, in the course of which we have again a quack doctor, a foolish astrologer, a Buddhist nun acting as a go-between, a surgeon-barber, and the inevitable Śaiva Guru who institutes a sacrifice to restore the mysteriously failing health of the Kāyastha's wife. Apart from the local interest and value of these works, they are indeed noteworthy satirical sketches, exaggerated *cum grano salis*, but substantially faithful, having less frequent lapses into squalor or coarseness, and composed in the best literary manner of Kṣemendra. There is nothing of melancholy wisdom in Kṣemendra. Knowing full well the castigating use of satire he deals out his blows too liberally, but with precision; with bitter and often foul-mouthed presumption, but with the unerring insight of a shrewd observer. His adroit epithets, *bons mots* and picturesquely abusive phrases show his piquant skill in metre, language and significance, eminently suitable to his subject and his method.

We have devoted some space to Kṣemendra's satirical writings, but it is not disproportionate when one considers their literary worth in the light of the vein of originality, which practically failed and ceased after him. We have some feeble attempts, like *Mugdhopadeśa*[1] of the Kashmirian Jahlaṇa (1st half of the 12th century), which in sixty-six verses, in the ill-chosen Śārdūlavikrīḍita metre, contains high-flown reflections on the lure and deception of the traditional, rather than the real, courtesan (*esto perpetua!*), in an erotically didactic rather than satiric style. These writers, anxious to maintain respectability are afraid of descending to repellent reality which their sucject demands, and only touch the fringe of it, from a safe distance, with the long end of the stick of romantic verse. Of different interest perhaps is the *Kali-viḍambana*[2] of the South Indian Nīlakaṇṭha Dīkṣita ; it is more polished, but witty, in describing in a century of well rounded Śloka verses the hopeless state of human affairs in the degraded Kali age. None of these and similar works of later times, however, give us such amusing sketches or piquant pictures of everyday society as are found in the works of Dāmodaragupta and Kṣemendra. All these later attempts may not indicate higher sanctitude but perhaps greater sanctimoniousness. The only later group of works which weakly attempts to carry on the tradition of satire is the

[1] Ed. Kāvyamālā, Gucchaka viii, p. 125 f. Jahlaṇa was also the author of *Somapāla-vilāsa* mentioned above. He should be distinguished from the anthologist Jahlaṇa.

[2] Ed. Kāvyamālā, Gucchaka v. p. 115 f.

Prahasana; but the Prahasana, we shall see, never flourished with convincing vigour, nor became an achievement of which Sanskrit literature can be legitimately proud.

d. *The Anthologies and Women Poets*

The greatest repositories of single stanzas of more than a thousand known and unknown poets are the Sanskrit Anthologies, which began to be compiled from the 10th century onwards. They preserve the verses of greater and more well known poets, but their importance consists in rescuing from oblivion a large number of fleeting verses of lesser and less known poets. It is true that the Anthologies belong to a comparatively late period; they furnish little account of the poets themselves or their works; the quotations are tantalisingly meagre; the notoriously careless and fluctuating ascriptions, as well as anonymous citations, do not yield much positive chronological result; but, in spite of these drawbacks, their literary importance is immense. Within the limits of space at our disposal, it would not be possible to give an adequate account of the Anthology-poets, but they certainly reflect an astonishing variety and a natural and charming quality, which one misses in the deliberate masterpieces of greater poets, and therefore deserve a detailed and separate study. Even admitting that stray stanzas cannot give us much, one can yet realise that the so-called minor poets often represent the spirit of an age or a country better than the more formidable members of the profession. As rich collections of erotic, gnomic, didactic, devotional and descriptive verses, the value of the Anthologies cannot be exaggerated; for, mosaics as they are, they are perhaps better represented here than in the extensive individual works of unequal and uneven workmanship. No doubt, the verses are produced from the same anvil and with the same tools, but the individual variations of the less pretentious poets are often worked with a cameo-like neatness out of the very limited and stereotyped means and materials. Most of them reach only a modest level, but they often show, in their small and unassuming way, dainty touches in metre and phraseology, a sense of harmony in sound and sense, and a pretty fancy, indicative, in their total effect, of the true poetic spirit. The lesser poet cannot indeed transgress the authority of the recognised tradition, but perhaps he can trust his own feelings to a greater degree. If he is not original, he can attain, within limits, a touch of nature and of lyric loveliness which are so rare in elaborate poems. We cannot illustrate here these observations by actual citation or consideration of individual poets, especially when the quantity and diversity of the verses are overwhelmingly extensive and the quality naturally variable; but even a careless glance through the Anthologies will bring charming surprises from page to page, which cannot but lead to an enhanced appreciation of Sanskrit poetry.

The earliest known Anthology is perhaps the incomplete and anonymous work, which has been published under the title of *Kavīndra-vacana-samuccaya*[1] from a unique manuscript in Nepalese characters of about the 12th century A.D. As none of the 113 poets, to whom its extant 525 verses are attributed, can be placed with certainty later than 1000 A.D., the anthology itself cannot belong to a later period. Its opening sections on the Buddha and Avalokiteśvara point to the probability of its unknown compiler having been a Buddhist; but with the exception of these eighteen or ninteen verses of a distinctly Buddhistic leaning, there is nothing Buddhistic about the work, which contains material, arrangement and division of subjects similar to those of most other Sanskrit anthologies. There is a fairly lengthy section on Hari as well, containing 53 verses, followed by sections of descriptive verses on spring, summer and the rainy season, but more than two-thirds of the work (350 verses) are devoted to the theme of love and the lover.

1 Ed. F. W. Thomas, Bill. Ind., Calcutta 1912. The title is lost in the MS, but supplied conjecturally from the introductory stanza.

The next anthology of importance is the *Subhāṣitāvali*[1] of the Kāśmīraka Vallabhadeva, which is quoted directly by Vandyaghaṭīya Sarvānanda in 1160 A.D. in his commentary on the *Amara-kośa,*[2] but the present text of which contains a large number of later additions and therefore cannot be placed earlier than the 15th century.[3] It is an extensive anthology, containing 3,527 verses in 101 sections or Paddhatis, and the number of authors and works cited, according to Peterson's list, is about 360. It contains stanzas on a large variety of subjects, including thoughts on and descriptions of love and other passions, the conduct of life, natural scenery and seasons, worldly wisdom and witty sayings. Of more definite date is the Bengal anthology, *Sadukti-karṇāmṛta,*[4] compiled by Śrīdhara-dāsa, son of Vaṭudāsa, in 1206 A.D. in the reign of Lakṣmaṇa-sena of Bengal, who appears to have been the patron of the compiler and his father. The five parts, called Pravāhas, are entitled respectively Deva, Śṛṅgāra, Cāṭu, Apadeśa and Uccāvaca, and contain 95, 179, 54, 72 and 76 sections or Vīcis. As each Vīci is arranged symmetrically to contain five verses, the total number of verses should have been 2,380, but as several verses appear to be lost in the printed text, the actual number of quoted verses is 2,370, the number of authors and works being 485. The compiler does not confine himself in his selection to Bengal, nor even to his own time; but his Vaiṣṇava inclination makes

1 Ed. P. Peterson and Durgaprasad, Bombay Sanskrit Series, 1886.

2 Ed. Trivandrum Sansk. Ser. 1914-17, pt. ii, Khaṇḍa ii, varga 4, p. 130 f.

3 See on this question, S. K. De, in *JRAS*, 1927, pp. 471-77 ; Keith's objections in *BSOS*, v, pt. i, p. 27 f, and S. K. De in *BSOS*, v, pt. iii, p. 499 f.

4 The work is also called Sūkti-karṇāmṛta in some MSS. Ed. Ramavatara Sarma, Bibl. Ind (till 1921), only two fascicules ; complete work edited by the same, and printed with an introduction and additional readings by Haradatta Sarma, Lahore 1933. The edition appears to be chiefly based on the Serampore College Library MS ; but no account is given of its MS material, and there is no critical apparatus. The method of editing is hardly critical; and as no account is taken of two important MSS of the work (viz. those in the Asiatic Society of Bengal and Calcutta Sanskrit College, its value is considerably impaired. For the work see Aufrecht in *ZDMG*, XXXVI 1882, p. 361 f, 509 f ; Pischel, *op. cit.*; Manomohan Chakravarti in *JAŚB*, 1906, pp. 157-76. The number of anonymous quotation in the Anthology appears to be more than 450.

him give a large number of Vaiṣṇava verses, which have been freely utilised in the later Bengal anthology of Rūpa Gosvāmin.

On the model of Vallabhadeva's *Subhāṣitāvali* was compiled in 1257 A.D. the *Subhāṣita-muktāvalī* or *Sūkti-muktāvalī*[1] of Jahlaṇa'[2] son of Lakṣmīdhara, the compiler as well as his father having flourished in the reign of the Yādava king Kṛṣṇa who came to the throne in 1247 A.D. It is a fairly extensive anthology, which appears to have existed in a shorter and a longer recension;[3] but the printed text makes no differentiation and gives the work eclectically in 2,790 verses, contained in 133 sections, and arranged on the plan and method of Vallabhadeva's anthology, the number of authors and works cited being more than 240. At the commencement of the anthology, there is an important section of traditional verses on Sanskrit poets and poetry, which is of great interest from the point of view of literary history. Of the same character is the *Śārṅgadhara-paddhati*,[4] compiled by Śārṅgadhara, son of Dāmodara, at about 1363 A.D. It contains 4,689 verses[5] in 163 sections, the number of works and authors cited being about 292. Its arrangement and subject-matter closely follow those of the two anthologies mentioned above, and a large number of its verses is also to be found in them. The *Sūkti-ratna-hāra*[6] of Sūrya Kaliṅgarāya, which could not have been compiled before the 1st half of the 14th century,[7] arranges its quotations, after six

[1] Ed. Ember Krishnamacharya, Gaekwad's Oriental Ser., Baroda 193.

[2] There are some verses at the end in the printed edition (cf. also *Descriptive Cat. Madras Govt. Orient. Library.* xx, p. 8109f), which tell us that the work was compiled by Vaidya Bhānu Paṇḍita for Jahlaṇa in Śaka 1179=1257 A.D.

[3] As R. G. Bhandarkar, who first gave an account of this anthology in his *Report 1887-91*, states.

[4] Ed. P. Peterson, Bombay Sanskrit Series, 1888. See Aufrecht in *ZDMG*, XXV, 1871, p. 455f; XXVII, 1873, p. 1f. Aufrecht notices and translates verses of 264 authors and works.

[5] But verse no. 56 gives the total number of verses in the anthology as 6,300!

[6] Ed. Sambasiva Sastri, Trivandrum Sanskrit Series, 1939. The edition is based upon a single Trivandrum manuscript. On the work and the author, see V. Raghavan in *Journal of Orient. Rasearch*, Madras. XIII, pp. 293-306.

[7] See V. Raghavan, *op. cit.*, p. 305f,

introductory Paddhatis (dealing chiefly with Namaskāra, Āśir, praise of the Vedas and so forth), into four Parvans concerned respectively with Dharma, Artha, Kāma and Mokṣa. As a South Indian compilation, the work is interesting for having preserved verses of South Indian authors, but the compiler appears to have known the *Subhāṣitāvali* of Vallabhadeva. The subject-matter, arrangement and method of compilation of the *Padyāvalī*[1] of Rūpa Gosvāmin, however, which is a Bengal Vaiṣṇava endeavour, is somewhat different. As all the verses are devoted to Kṛṣṇa and Kṛṣṇa-līlā, they are arranged in sections in accordance with the different doctrinarian aspects of Kṛṣṇa-Bhakti and different episodes of the erotic career of Kṛṣṇa; and the whole arrangement conforms generally to the rhetorical classification of the Vaiṣṇava Rasa-śāstra, to which the work may be regarded as an illustrative compendium. It is a compilation of 386 verses from over 125 authors. But Rūpa Gosvāmin does not confine himself to Bengal or to Vaiṣṇava authors alone. He selects older verses from Amaru, Bhavabhūti and others and arranges them in a Rādhā-Kṛṣṇa context, sometimes even modifying the text in order to make non-sectarian verses applicable to a sectarian purpose. To the second half of the fifteenth century belongs the *Subhāṣitāvali* of the Kashmirian Śrīvara, pupil of Jonarāja, which cites from 380 poets. To the 17th century probably belong the *Padya-veṇī* of Veṇīdatta, son of Jagajjīvana, the *Padya-racanā* of Lakṣmaṇabhaṭṭa Aṅkolakara (between 1625 and 1650 A.D.),[2] the *Padyāmṛta-taraṅgiṇī* (compiled 1673 A.D.) of Hari Bhāskara,[3] son of Āpājībhaṭṭa, and the *Subhāṣita-hārāvalī* of Hari-kavi[4]; but none of these,

[1] Ed. S. K. De, Dacca Univ. Oriental Publ. Series, Dacca 1934.

[2] Ed. NSP, Bombay 1908. On the date of this anthology, see P. K. Gode in *Journal of Oriental Research, Madras*, XIV, 1940, pp. 184-193 (a list of works and authors cited is also given).

[3] On this anthology, see P. K. Gode in *Calcutta Oriental Journal*, III, pp. 33-35.

[4] The author was the court-poet of the Maratha king Sambhāji, son of Śivāji (see P. K. Gode in *ABORI*, XVI, 1935, pp. 262-91). He also wrote *Śambhurāja-carita*, a pticaloe ife of his royal patron, in 1685 A.D.

except the *Padya-racanā*, has yet appeared in print. There are also many other anthologies, great and small, which are not yet published, but it is not necessary to mention them all here.

Although it has not been possible to deal here with the innumerable poets of the Anthologies, a few words should be spared for the women-poets, who are chiefly, but inadequately, represented in the Anthologies. We have[1] some 150 scattered verses of about 40 women-poets, of whom the names of Vijjā, Vikaṭanitambā, Śīlābhaṭṭārikā, Bhāvadevī, Gaurī, Padmāvatī and Vidyāvatī stand out prominently both in extent and variety of their verses. Unfortunately, the works from which their verses are quoted are not known, and we have no other means of determining the nature and value of their literary achievement. But, to judge from the extremly meagre specimens of stray verses, one cannot say that their contribution to Sanskrit poetry is either original or impressive both in quantity and quality. There is also not much variety. The verses are mostly dainty trifles, concerned with light erotic topics, in the conventional embroidery of romantic fancy. Almost all the women-poets are occupied with the theme of love; and even where the verse is descriptive there is most often an erotic implication. Sometimes there is a tender and touching note; here and there one may also find a glimpse into the heart of the woman; but, in general, there is not much that is truely feminine in these verses, which might have been as well written by men. It may be that love made up the entire life of the woman: but perhaps these verses, which give the impression that she is more fully ardent and less self-controlled than man, would lead to a dubious generalisation and give the entire question a wrong perspective. The w. man- cet looks suspiciously like a replica of the passionate he oine f the normal Sanskrit poetry and drama. One may even go urt :r and doubt if some of the verses are really written by

1 *Sanskrit Poetesses*, Part A (Select Verses), ed. J. B. Chaudhuri and trs. with an introduction by Roma Chaudhuri, Calcutta 1939; Pt. B. (containing the *Vaidyanātha-praśasti* Devakumārikā and *Sanātana-gopāla-kāvya* of Lakṣmī), Calcutta 1940.

women, or are passed off under fictitious feminine names with a mildly perverse motive ! Apart from the tone of the verses, the suspicion is not unnatural when one considers the rather strange and unusual names, like Vikatanitambā[1] and Jaghanacapalā, especially when the only one verse assigned to the latter is also composed in the Jaghanacapalā metre and cleverly constructed to contain the name itself, after the manner of signed verses not rare in Sanskrit. In any case, the specimens are insufficient and do not enable us to form a high opinion of woman's creative and artistic ability in a sphere in which, by her temperament, she is eminently fitted to attain a high rank.

Outside the Anthologies, there are just a few women writers who may be briefly mentioned here as composers of the Kāvya. Among these, we have already spoken of Rāmabhadrāmbā of Tanjore, who wrote the semi-historical poem *Raghunāthābhyudaya* to celebrate the greatness of her lover, Raghunātha-Nāyaka of Tanjore (c. 1614 A.D.). Another woman poet, who was honoured by Raghunātha-Nāyaka with the eulogistic title of Madhuravāṇī, translated Raghunātha's *Āndhra-Rāmāyaṇa* into elegant Sanskrit verse, in fourteen cantos, under the title *Rāmāyaṇa-sāra-kāvya.*[2] Another cultured woman-poet, Tirumalāmbā, in her *Varadāmbikā-pariṇaya,*[3] a highly artificial Campū, describes the romance of the love and wedding of Varadāmbikā with her

1. If the name occurs in Rājaśekhara's eulogistic verses on poets quoted in Jahlaṇa's *Śukti-muktāvalī,* there is no reason to think that it was not traditionally accepted ; and little is known about the poet herself. The information, however, vouched to us by Bhoja that she was married a second time (punarbhū) is more circumstantial, and, if it is reliable, may indicate a real person. Other names found in Jahlaṇa are : Vijjaka, Śīlābhaṭṭirikā, Vijayāṅkā and Prabhudevi ; while in a memorial verse ascribed to Dhanadadeva in *Śārṅgadhara-paddhati,* we have the praise of Śīlābhaṭṭārika, Mārulā and Morikā. All these names are found in the Anthologies, but there is no proof that all were names of real persons.

2 The only known MS of this work, which belonged to the Veda-vedānta-mandira, Mallesvaram, Bangalore, appears to have been lost, and the work is not printed.

3 Ed. Laksman Sarup, Lahore 1938 (?). See P. P. S. Sastri, *Tanjore Catalogue,* vii, pp. 3243-46, no. 4220. The editor notes that the Campū contains the largest compound to be found in Sanskrit, but this is hardly a compliment ! On some of these poets, see *Indian Review,* IX (1908), Madras, pp. 106-11 ; *JRAS,* 1908, p. 163 ; J. B. Chaudhuri, *Sanskrit Poetesses,* Pt. B. Introduction, cited above.

own husband or lover Acyutarāya, king of Vijayanagara, who came to the throne at about 1530 A.D. Another earlier and more gifted Vijayanagara poetess, Gaṅgādevī, queen (vii. 36-41) of Vīra Kampana or Kamparāya, son Bukka I (c. 1343-79 A.D.), composed the *Madhurā-vijaya*[1] or *Vīrakamparāya-carita,* now available only as a fragment, to celebrate her husband's conquest of Madura. It is written in a simple style, comparatively free from the pedantry of grammar and rhetoric. But all these works are of the usual conventional type, and do not show any distinctive features to call for special comment.

5. Prose Literature

The literary prose compositions of this period, compared with the poetical, form indeed a small and unpretentious branch ; for prose does not appear to have been as assiduously cultivated as verse. Even technical works were complacently composed in verse, presumably because verse is easier to memorise and utilise for condensed and effective expression. The verse invaded from the beginning, the domain of prose and ousted it from its legitimate employment. The result was that in technical treatises the verse became prosaic, while in literary works the prose assumed the colour and mode of verse and poetry. It was seldom realised that the two harmonies had different spheres and values, and that the characteristics of the one were not desirable in the other. The verse attained a far greater degree of maturity, circulation and importance, and the prose was consequently neglected. The preponderance of the one form of writing partially explains and is explained by the poverty of the other ; but it is more than a case of preponderance, it is one of almost exclusive monopoly, doubtless aided by the resulting inability to distinguish between the two modes of formal writing. In practice certainly, if not in theory, the separate existence of prose as a

1 Ed. Harihara Sastri and V. S. Sastri, Śrīdhara Press, Trivandrum 1916, with introd. by T. A. Gopinatha Rao.

vehicle of expression is sparingly recognised, the writers fancying that prose is but a species of verse itself and of poetry which is conveyed in verse, and making their prose, endowed with florid rhetorical devices, look as much as possible like their own verse and poetry.

The tradition of the highly ornamented and poetically gorgeous prose was, we have seen, established by Bāṇabhaṭṭa, but it is neither prose-poetry nor poetical prose as we understand it to-day ; it is an extremely artificial creation in which prose and poetry are drawn together in an astonishingly peculiar and unnatural alliance. The tradition is continued in this period, somewhat languidly, in the writing of that strange species of the Prose Kāvya, which, entirely lacking in narrative quality, yet went by the name of Kathā or narrative. The blend of realism and romance, of satire and sentiment which we found in Daṇḍin was no longer appreciated, but the example of Bāṇabhaṭṭa also does not seem to have inspired much literary enthusiasm. Partly because the standard set by Bāṇabhaṭṭa was perhaps too high and arduous, and partly because such extremely elaborate composition perhaps ceased to engage wide interest, the Prose Kāvya does not appear to have been much favoured by really talented writers. Perhaps also the craving for ornate exercise of prose, along with verse, was satisfied by the growth of a hybird species, called Campū, of mixed prose and verse, which, on the decline and break-up of the Prose Kāvya, combined some of its features with those of the metrical Kāvya, in a kind of curious, but not very brilliant, mosaic. But the most unassuming, and yet the most interesting, prose literature of this period is exemplified by a small number of popular tales, which continue the simpler prose tradition of the *Pañcatantra*, and contain racy stories of common life and folk-tale, denuded of high-flown romance but sublimated with myth and magic, and enforced with pithy gnomic verses of epigrammatic wit. Into the artificial and jaded atmosphere of the classical romantic tale they throw the freshness and naivete of folk-tradition and common experience ; and the story-form is seen in some of its proper vigour and pliability.

a. *The Popular Tale*

The popular prose tale of this period commands attention, not only by its interesting narrative content, but also because the works show a sense of the value of the simple and direct prose style, which we rarely find in the heavily constructed and devterously stylistic Prose Kāvya and Campū. The collections of prose tales, however, are mostly of unknown authorship, and the various redactions, made out of traditional material by different hands, naturally exhibit different kinds of style and diction. Thus, the Ornatior Text of the *Śuka-saptati* is written in a decidedly high-flown, if not too elaborate, style, compared with the almost bald and unattractive prose of the Simplicior Text. But even taking into account such inevitable differences, one can say that the prose tale in general, contrasted with the Prose Kāvya and the Campū, makes less claim to ornateness and certainly shows a reasonably clear and attractive manner, which effectively increases the intrinsic interest of its matter. Although still halting, what we have is not the mere lisping of prose, nor is it fully developed into the literary prose of the best kind. The most remarkable feature is that it is not always plain style, but when elegant, there are no intricacies of construction and elaborate ornamentation, no confused disregard of periods and interminable heaping of ingenious phrases, epithets and conceits, no love of punning and other affectations. It is for these reasons that the prose tale retained, as attested by the recensions of the works and their translations into modern Indian languages, greater popularity and wider currency, while the Prose Kāvya failed and the Campū flourished by artificial cultivation.

While the beast-fable died out with the *Pañcatantra* exhausting itself in a sequence of variations of the original text, the *Bṛhatkathā*, in spite of its great reputation, does not appear to have left behind a direct descendant. If there were imitative attempts, they are now lost. The next oldest collection of popular tales that we have is the *Vetāl-pañcaviṃśati*, but the extent of the gap between it and the *Bṛhatkathā* is not known. Although the earliest versions of this very interesting collection of twenty-five tales of the Vetāla is preserved in the two Kashmirian versions of the *Bṛhatkathā*[1] by Kṣemendra and Somadeva respectively (11th century), it is missing in the Nepalese version of Budhasvāmin. It is not clear, therefore, that it formed a part of the lost work of Guṇāḍhya ; on the contrary, it is highly probable that it belonged originally to an independent cycle, as several other more or less deverging versions have also survived. The most noteworthy of these versions is that of Śivadāsa[2] of unknown date and place of composition, which is in prose with interspersed verse ; but another anonymous prose recast of Kṣemendra's version[3] is also known. There is another abridged version attributed to Vallabhadeva,[4] but it exists only in not more than half a dozen known manuscripts, and is textually poorer and less important, being not substantially different from that of Śivadāsa. The version of Jambhaladatta[5]

1 *Bṛhatkathā-mañjari* ix. 2. 19-1221 ; *Kat ā-sarit-sāgara* 75-99. Kṣemendra's version is shorter and balder than Somadeva's and omits some minor incidents, but they have essentially the same content. See Lévi in *JA*, s. 8, t. vii, 1886, p. 190f ; M. B. Emeneau in *JAOS*, LIII, 1933, pp. 124-43. According to Emeneau's calculation, the number of Ślokas in Kṣemendra's version is 1206, in Somadeva's 2195. Hertel and Edgerton have made it probable that the original *Bṛhatkathā* did not contain the twenty-five tales of the Vetāla.

2 Ed. Heinrich Uhle, Leipzig 1884, on the basis of 11 comparatively modern MSS. The text is given in transliteration. In 1914 Uhle published, in *BSGW*, LXVI (Leipzig), pp. 2-87, the text of an earlier MS dated 1487 A.D. Hertel would not place Śivadāsa much before 1487 A.D. ; he believes that Śivadāsa used an earlier metrical version, and finds the influence of old Gujarati on the language of his text.

3 Also contained in Uhle's ed.

4 Eggeling, *India Office Catalogue*, vii, p. 1564. As its poor Sanskrit and vernacular forms and constructions indicate, the text is probably evolved from some vernacular version.

5 Ed. M. B. Emeneau, with Eng. trs. and text in transliteration, American Oriental Society, New Haven, Connecticut 1934.

is almost entirely in prose (with sporadic introductory verses), but its date and provenance are likewise unknown; it is nearer to the Kashmirian versions in respect of proper names, but the details of the stories differ. The *Vetāla-pañcaviṃśati* is also known in several forms in modern Indian languages.[1] A critical comparison of all the versions still awaits investigation, but it is doubtful if any of these extant versions fully represent the lost original. The metrical form in which we find the work in the Kashmirian versions does not prove that the original was in verse, nor do the versions justify any positive conclusion regarding the order and content of the stories.

There can be no doubt, however, that the *Vetāla-pañcaviṃśati* is one of the most interesting collection of shrewd and well-told tales in Sanskrit. The frame-story, in which the twenty-five inset tales are emboxed, is simply and cleverly conceived quite in the spirit of the folk-tale. In order to oblige an ascetic,[2] who brings to him everyday a fruit containing a concealed jem, king Trivikramasena or Vikramasena, who becomes Vikramaditya in later accounts, agree to bring, for the purpose of some magic rite, a corpse hanging from a tree. But a vampire or Vetala has already taken possession of the corpse. He agrees to leave the body if the king would answer his questions, but ingeniously frustrates the king's efforts twenty-five times by recounting to him an enigmatic story and asking him to solve it, thereby making the king break the condition of silence necessary for the successful accomplishment of his undertaking. The riddles are by no means easy of solution; and if the king's replies are casuistic, they are certainly ingeniously fitted. Who is the most

1 The work also exists in Kalmuck (ed. B. Jülg, Leipzig 1866) and Tibetan (ed. A. H. Francke in *ZDMG*, LXXV, 1925, pp. 72-96) adaptations.—On translations into various modern Indian languages, see Grierson. *The Modern Vernacular Literature of Hindustan*, Calcutta; Oesterly, Baitāl Pacīsī (in *Bibliothek Orientalischer Märchen und Erzählungen*, I, Leipzig 1873; Penzer's ed, of *Ocean of Story*, vol. vi, pp. 265-67.

2 In Somadeva's version he is a Bhikṣu, in Kṣemendra's a Śramaṇa, in Śivadāsa's a Digambara!

fastidious epicure—the man who would not touch the food because his fine sense of smell discovers that the paddy was grown in a field adjoining a cemetery, or the one who would not lie on a divinely soft and piled-up bed because somewhere below the heap of mattress there is a piece of hair, or the one who would not touch a woman because she smelt like a goat having been nourished with goat's milk in her infancy ? Who is the best lover —the one who perishes on the same funeral pyre with the body of the dead girl, or the one who builds a hut and lives in sorrow near the funeral ground, or the one who revives the dead girl by means of a charm he chances to discover ? Equally baffling is the question of tangled relationship of the children of a father, who espouses unwittingly the daughter of a woman wedded to his son, with the children of the son. We have also a difficult question of ceremonialism, when three hands appear to receive the oblation of a thief's son brought up by a Brahman and adopted by a king; or a difficult question of honour, in the case of a woman, allowed by her generous fiancée to keep an assignation, unharmed by an equally generous robber who allows her to pass, and returned untouched by the no less generous lover to whom she goes. Diversified indeed are the stories, and well conceived. From the literary point of view, however, the value of the different versions is, of course, different. The Kashmirian versions are in verse, mostly in Śloka, Kṣemendra's being terse and Somadeva's pleasantly amplified; Jambhaladatta's version is unadorned, and even bald and undistinguished; while Śiva-dāsa's is marked by considerable literary grace and narrative quality. How far these individual characteristics of style and treatment are inherited from the original cannot be exactly determined; but, judging from their general tendencies, one should think that the initial impetus must have been towards simple narrative vigour rather than towards sheer splender of style, and that the core of the work must have achieved popularity and distinction as much from its fine story-material as from the manner in which it was presented.

Much inferior in literary quality, as well as in the interest of the stories, is the *Siṃhāsana-dvātriṃśikā* or *Vikrama-carita.*[1] As the title implies, it purports to be a collection of thirty-two tales, told by the magic statues supporting Vikramāditya's unearthed throne, to king Bhoja who was about to ascend it,—all the stories celebrating the glorious qualities of king Vikrama,[2] and implying that no one who did not possess these qualities was entitled to sit on the throne. The work exists in two diverging recensions, Northern and Southern. The Northern has been distinguished into three versions, namely, the Jaina version of Kṣemendra Muni (alleged to be based on a Mahārāṣṭrī version), the Bengal version ascribed to Vararuci (which is merely based on the Jaina), and a short anonymous version; while the Southern, generally called *Vikrama-carita,* has a prose, as well as a secondary metrical version in the Śloka metre, both anonymous. The main thread of the narrative is more or less the same in all versions, but in verbal form and in the order of the tales they are independent of one another. A comparative examination[3] shows that none of the versions can be taken as preserving the work in its original form. Weber[4] and Hertel,[5] however, believe the tales to be of Jaina origin and naturally emphasise the superior antiquity of the Jaina version; but Edgerton makes it probable that, in the order of the tales, at least, the Southern recension is nearer to what he thinks to be the original form, while the Jaina version is marked by greater individuality

1 Ed. F. Edgerton, in two parts, containing the text in transliteration and Eng. trs., in four recensions, Harvard Oriental Series, Cambridge, Mass., 1926.

2 The Vikramāditya legend is also the subject of several poems, *e.g*, the *Vīra-caritra* of Ananta in thirty Adhyāyas, mostly in Śloka (Eggeling, *India Office Catalogue*, vii, pp. 1502-3; Jacobi in *Ind. Studien*, xiv, pp. 97-160); *Vikramodaya* in 28 cantos (*ibid.* vii, pp. 1501-2) *Śālivāhana-kathā* of Śivadāsa in 18 cantos (*ibid*, vii, pp. 1567-70); *Mādhavānala-kathā* (H. Schöl, *Die Strophen d. Mādhavānalakathā*, Diss., Halle 1914), etc.

3 Edgerton, *op. cit.*, p. xxix; also in *American Journal of Philology*. XXXIII, p. 271 f.

4 *Ind. Studien*, xv, Leipzig, 1878, pp. 185-453 (large section of the Jaina Text in Roman). The Jaina recension is edited by Hiralal Hamsaraj, Jaina Bhāskarodaya Press, Jamnagar 1914; the Southern recension, ed. Jivananda Vidyasagar, Calcutta 1881; the Vararuci's recension (Bengal), printed Serampore (1818): See Eggeling, *Ind. Office Catalogue*, vii, p. 1566f,

5 *BSGW*, LIV, p. 114 f.

and tendency to deliberate modifications. The date and authorship of the work are unknown, but since both the Southern and Jaina versions, apparently independently, refer to the Dānakhaṇḍa of Hemādri's *Caturvarga-cintāmaṇi*, it cannot date from a time earlier than the 13th century. Although a widely popular work, its special purpose of illustrating the generous deeds of a model king and reiterating moral lessons not only makes it an extreme example of the didactic method of story-telling, carried to its monotonous lengths, but also limits it to particular kinds of moral stories, which, barring a few good ones, lack variety and strikingness. The stories are told (leaving aside the metrical version) in easy and sometimes terse prose, but it is unimaginative (despite mannered descriptions of the Jaina version) and lacks elegance and distinction. The work appears to have enjoyed greater reputation than its literary or intrinsic worth justifies.

The *Śuka-saptati,* or Seventy Tales of a Parrot, is more lively and racy, even though the tales are of a merry cast and not always edifying. Of the two principal versions, the Simplicior[1] and the Ornatior,[2] the one is stylistically simple and the other embellished ; but the Simplicior, being greatly condensed and consequently obscure in places, may have been a secondary and abridged text. The Ornatior text appears to be the work of Cintāmaṇi Bhaṭṭa, who, having used Pūrṇabhadra's version of the *Pañcatantra,* cannot be earlier than the 12th century ; while the Simplicior text seems to have been redacted by a Śvetāmbara Jaina who may have used a Prakrit original. The work may be described generally as a collection of naughty wives' tales, which form one of the familiar topics of the popular tale in general. The wise parrot, finding the mistress of the house inclined to run after other men in the absence of

1 Textus Simplicior, ed. Richard Schmidt, Leipzig 1893 (Trs. into German, Kiel, 1894). A shorter version of this text is also edited by him in *ZDMG,* LIV and LV (1900-1901), pp. 515f, If.

2 Textus Ornatior, ed. R. Schmidt, München 1898-99 (Trs. into German, Stuttgart 1899) Analysis and comparison of the two texts, with trs. of some section, by R. Schmidt in *Der Textus Ornatior der Śukasaptati,* Stuttgart 1896.

her husband, and asking her if she has sufficient courage and coolness to get out of difficulties as so-and-so did, rouses her curiosity, narrates the tales and succeeds in keeping her interested every night till her husband returns. In spite of the apparently virtuous motive of the frame-story, the inset stories naturally describe how cunning women get out of embarrassing scrapes, deceive their foolish husbands and even exact apologies from them for their very suspicion. However disreputable some of the stories may be, they are certainly smart and generally amusing. They show a keen knowledge of humanity under their frivolous and easy gaiety. The diction of the Simplicior text, with its brief and bald sentences, is often abrupt and generally flat, but the Ornatior text, in spite of its conscious effort at stylistic skill, is more attractive in conveying its wealth of amusing incidents and observations.

Of other similar collections of tales, the *Bharaṭaka-dvātriṃśikā*[1] of unknown date and authorship is a collection of thirty-two stories of the ridiculous Bharaṭakas who were probably Śaiva mendicants ; but it is attractive neither in style nor in treatment. The work may or may not be of Jaina inspiration, but its contact with the literature of the people is betrayed by its interspersed vernacular verses, which are also in evidence occasionally in the Simplicior text of the *Śuka-saptati*. The *Purṣa-parikṣā*[2] of the Maithila Vidyāpati, on the other hand, is written in simple and graceful style and has deservedly enjoyed wider popularity for its forty-four tales on the question of what constitutes manly qualities, some of the stories having references to historical persons and incidents. The number of Jaina Kathānakas,[3]

[1] Ed. J. Hertel, Leipzig 1921.

[2] Ed. Gujarati Printing Press, Bombay 1882, with Gujarati trs. The author, who is best known for his exquisite Radha-Kṛṣṇa songs in Maithili, flourished under Śivasiṁha of Mithilā towards the latter part of the 14th century A.D.

[3] On the Jaina achievement in narrative literature, see Hertel, *Literature of the Śvetāmbaras of Gujarat*, Leipzing 1922. The word 'Kathānaka' does not appear to be a recognised term of orthodox poetics, although the *Agni-purāṇa* (337-20) speaks of Kathānikā as a variety of Gadya-kāvyā, along with Parikathā and khaṇḍakathā. Ānandavardhana (iii.7) recognises

consisting of narratives or books of narratives, is vast. But some of them are in Prakrit or Apabhraṃśa ; some, like the *Uttama-kumāra-carita*[1] or the *Pāpabuddhi-dharmabuddhi-kathānaka,*[2] are plainly allegorical and didactic ; some, like the *Campaka-śreṣṭhi-kathānaka*[3] and the *Pāla-gopāla-kathānaka,*[4] both of Jinakīrti, are of the nature of fantastic fairy tales ; while others, like the *Samyaktva-kaumudī,*[5] are of an openly propagandist character. Of collections of popular tales, the *Kathā-kośa*[6] of an unknown, but not old, compiler is a poor and insipid production in bad Sanskrit with inserted Prakrit verses ; but more interesting is the *Kathā-ratnākara*[7] of Hemavijaya-gaṇi (*c.* 17th century), not for its hardly elegant style and diction, but for its 258 miscellaneous short tales, fables and anecdotes, mostly of fools, rogues and artful women. There is no frame-story but the tales are loosely strung together, while the characterless Sanskrit prose is freely diversified by verses in Sanskrit, Prakrit and modern Indian languages. The Jaina authors are fond of stories and have produced them in amazing profusion, but the stories, in whatever form they are presented, are all essentially sermons, or have a moral tag attached to them ; they are seldom intended for mere entertainment. The well-known Sanskrit story-motifs are utilised, but good stories are sometimes spoiled by forcing them into a moral frame. With their unadorned, but pedestrian, prose and lack of artistic presentation, the Jaina writings in this sphere are scarcely remarkable as literary

Parikathā and Khaṇḍakathā, adding Sakalakathā (all these terms being explaind by Abhinavagupta in his commentary, but omits Kathānikā. The description of Kathānikā, however, given by the *Agni-purāṇa* does not apply to the so-called Jaina Kathānaka.

1 Ed. Weber in *SBAW,* 1884 i. p. 269f ; the metrical version in 686 Ślokas by Cārucandra is printed by the Jaina Bhāskarodaya Press, Jamnagar 1911.

2 Ed. E. Lovarini in *GSAI,* III, pp. 94-127 (with trs.).

3 Ed. J. Hertel in *ZDMG,* LXV, 1911, pp. 1-51, 425-47.

4 See J. Hertel, *Jinakīrtis Geschichte von Pāla und Gopāla,* Leipzig 1907 (*BSGW,* LXIX). Jinakīrti lived at about the middle of the 15th century.

5 A. Weber in *SBAW,* 1889, p. 731.

6 Trs. C. H. Tawney, London 1895.

7 Ed. Hiralal Hamsraj, Jaina Bhāskarodaya Press, Jamnagar 1911 ; trs. J. Hertel, München 1920.

productions, but they are interesting from their unmistakable contact with the general life of the people, especially those stories which are not of unrelieved moral and religious dreariness.

The Jaina Prabandhas, however, stand in a different category. They are semi-historical works, which pretend to deal with historical and literary personages, but really make a motley collection of curious legends and anecdotes. They are written in elegant prose, but freely introduce Prakrit and Apabhraṃśa, as well as Sanskrit, verses. The works are perhaps not satisfactory for their historical information of earlier times, but they have certainly an amusing content and a readable style. Two works of this type have earned a limited renown and deserve mention, namely, the *Prabandha-cintāmaṇi*[1] of Merutuṅga, completed in 1306 A.D., and the *Prahandha-kośa*[2] of Rājaśekhara Sūri, completed in 1348 A.D. Merutuṅga's work is divided into five Prakāśas, each of which contains several Prabandhas. The first Prakāśa relates the legend of Vikramāditya and Sātavāhana, the story of the Caulukya kings of Aṇhilvad and of the Paramāra kings Muñja and Bhoja of Dhārā. The second Prakāśa continues the story of Bhoja ; the third and fourth Prakāśas that of the Aṇhilvad rulers, bringing the narrative down to the reign of Kumārapāla. An account is also given of the Gujarat rulers Lavaṇaprasāda and Vīradhavala and the two well-known ministers of the latter, Tejḥpāla and Vastupāla, who furnish the subject-matter also of many plays, poems and panegyrics. The treatment is not systematically historical but attractively anecdotal ; but the part, which gives a picture of times nearer to the author's own, is not without some historical interest. The last Prakāśa is a collection of miscellaneous stories of Śīlāditya, Lakṣmaṇasena, Jayacandra, Bhartṛhari and others.

1 Ed. Jinavijaya, Pt. i, Text, Singhi Jaina Series, Santiniketan, Bengal 1933 ; also ed. Ramacandra Dinanath, Bombay, 1888 ; Eng. trs. by C. H. Tawney, Bibl. Ind., Calcutta 1901.

2 Ed. Jinavijaya, I, Text, same series, Santiniketan 1935.

The twenty-four Prabandhas of Rājaśekhara Sūri's work are concerned respectively with seven royal (including Lakṣmaṇasena and Madanavarman) and three lay personages, as well as with ten Jaina teachers (including Hemacandra) and four poets, namely, Śrīharṣa, Harihara, Amaracandra and Digambara Madanakīrti. Of these accounts, the last four appear to be most interesting and original. To the same class of composition, but not to Jaina inspiration, belongs the *Bhoja-prabandha*[1] of Ballāla (end of the 16th century), which, however, is entirely useless as an historical document and is not of much value as a literary production. Its chief object is to depict Bhoja, apparently Bhoja of Dhāra, in relation to many poets who are attracted to his court by his liberal and appreciative patronage ; but in doing this it sticks at no anachronism nor perversion of historical facts. It brings together in Bhoja's court a large number of literary celebrities, such as Kālidāsa, Bhavabhūti, Daṇḍin and Māgha, as well as less known poets like Sītā and Cittapa, who are made to display their readiness of wit and vie with each other in quick composition of smart verses in a series of amusing, but unconnected, anecdotes. The work makes some attempt at elegant writing, but its matter is not sufficiently diversified, and the prose diction, on the whole, nerveless and devoid of character, when compared with that of the Jaina Prabandhas.

b. *The Prose Kāvya*

The romantic Prose Kāvya with its traditional machinery and traditional pomp of style was no innovation ; but the achievements of Subandhu and Bāṇa inspired more unintelligent

1 Printed many times in India. There are several versions of the text (see L. Oster *Die Rezensionen des Bhojaprabandha*, Dios., Darmstadt, 1911). The Southern text is repeatedly printed, the earliest being ed. Madras 1851 ; whilst editions have appeared from Calcutta (*e.g.* Jivananda Vidyasagar's in 1872. 1883) and Bombay (*e.g.* ed. Vasudeva Panshikar, NSP, 1921). A shorter version is noticed by Eggeling in *India Office Catalogue*, vii, p. 1549. An eclectic edition from two Paris manuscripts is published, with trs. of some sections, by Théodore Pavie in *JA*, 1854-55, t. iii. p. 185 f ; t. iv, p. 385 f ; t. v, p. 76 f ; which is also published in litho by the same scholar, Callet : Paris 1855.

admiration than intelligent practice of the extremely difficult type of literary composition, in which the simple ends of story are sacrificed to enormous complexities of extravagant diction. It is perhaps not the effort involved which turned off later talents, for equally gorgeous and elaborate Mahākāvyas were zealously produced ; but perhaps the impossible prose form, with its superfluously ornamented and interminably prolonged sentences, never appealed widely to later taste, which preferred to display these strained ingenuities in the regular metrical form of the Kāvya. This might be one of the reasons which led to the development of the Campū ; for the Campū does not differ essentially from the Prose Kāvya but only allows greater scope to verse. The Prose Kāvya, therefore, is comparatively little cultivated in this period. It is limited its in range of topics, impossibly mannered in expression and deliberately devoid of all interest in pure narrative. It becomes an exclusixe and curious type. The poet overlays, diffuses, adorns, sentimentalises ; into the unsubstantial woof of story are woven iridescent pageants of preternatural exploits and fantastic adventures ; there is no simplicity nor directness, but whatever is pointed is wrapped in a loose but heavy garment of embroidered, indecisive heap of phrases. The alien attraction of poetry not only affects the disposition and behaviour of prose, which ceases to be real prose, but it also tends to detach story, which ceases to be story, from the root and mainstay of the whole *genre* in vigorous and terse narrative.

Bāṇa, however, found an imitator, who could copy most of his hyperbolic mannerisms, but could not reproduce much of his poetic excellences, in the Śvetāmbara Jaina Dhanapāla, son of Sarvadeva, who wrote his *Tilaka-mañjarī*[1] under Muñja Vākpati-

1 Ed. Bhavadatta and K. P. Parab, NSP, Bombay 1903. This Dhanapāla, who is different from the Digambara Jaina Dhanapāla, author of the Apabhraṁśa *Bhavisatta-kaha*, also wrote a Prakrit lexicon called *Paiya-lacchī-nāma-mālā*, and a Jaina Stotra, *Ṛṣabha-pañcāśikā*. Merutuṅga (ed. Santiniketan, p. 36 f ; Tawney, p. 60 f) places him in the court of Bhoja of Dhārā and narrates some legends about the origin of the present work.—The work gives continuous narrative, like Bāṇa's *Kādambarī*, without any division into chapters.

rāja of Dhārā at about 970 A.D. In the introductory verses Dhanapāla eulogises the Paramāra kings of Dhārā, and, among other poetical predecessors, mentions the author of *Taraṅgavatī* (the Jaina Śrīpālitta)[1] and Rudra, who composed a *Trailokya-sundarī-kathā*. He tells us in a punning verse that Bāṇa's Kādambarī was completed by Pulinda or Pulindhra, which apparently, in his opinion, was the name of Bāṇabhaṭṭa's son, The *Tilaka-mañjarī* is an elaborate tale of the love and union of Tilakamañjarī, and Samaraketu, the heroine being a regular image of Kādambarī, and most of the occasions of note in the story finding a parallel to those in Bāṇa's romance. In spite of considerable literary skill, the work is not impressive even as an imitation, and does not repay the exertion of wading through the tedious length of its brilliant, but hardly illuminating, magnificence.

The other Jaina efforts to imitate Bāṇa may be noted here, not so much for their poetic appeal as for the illustrative zest and talent of the authors. The *Udaya-sundarī-kathā*[2] of Soḍḍhala is sometimes classed as a Campū,[3] but like Dhanapāla, the author consciously takes Bāṇa as his model in producing an artificial Kathā. Barring the verse-prelude, the *Kādambarī* is essentially in prose, but both Dhanapāla and Soḍḍhala are liberal in their use of verse in the prose narrative, the number of verse increasing perceptibly in the latter. In the case of both, however, the prose is the normal vehicle, and the employment of verse is not so free and frequent as in a Campū ; nor is the form of these works different from what is expected in a Kathā[4] by later theorists. From Soḍḍhala's own account of himself and his family in the first Ucchvāsa, we learn that he was the son of Śūra and Padmāvatī of the Vālabha Kāyastha family

1 See above p. 201.

2 Ed. C. D. Dalal and E. Krishnamacharya, Gaekwad's Oriental Series, Baroda 1920.

3 A fact which would of itself show that the distinction between a Prose Kāvya and a Campū was becoming illusory.

4 With the exception that the work is not a continuous narrative but is divided, like an Ākhyāyikā, into Ucchvāsas.

of Gujarat and flourished under the patronage of Chittarāja, Nāgarjuna and Mummuṇirāja, rulers of Koṅkana, who had their capital at Sthānaka, modern Thānā, near Bombay. As the poet refers also to the patronage of Vatsarāja of Lāṭa, it is probable that his work was composed between 1026 and 1050 A.D. The romance describes, in eight Ucchvāsas, the fictitious story of the love and marriage of Udayasundarī, daughter of Sikhaṇḍatilaka, king of the Nāgas, and Malayavāhana, king of Pratiṣṭhāna, making full use of the ornate style and accessories of the Prose Kāvya. The author has considerable power of driving his slender narrative into the undulating eddies of spacious sentences, or making it subside now and then into elaborāte verses; but the story, as usual in such romances, halts and hobbles, and the literary dexterity and splendour of style do not compensate the loss of simple narrative force. The myth-world which these romances depict are remote indeed from nature and humanity, but the poets never show any intention of making it appear natural and human; on the other hand, they fasten, with the enthusiasm of pure artists, upon every fantastic or arabesque contortion of incident which offer a vantage-ground, not for such pictorial or poetic effects as riot in Bāṇa's romance, but for the hard and enamelled brilliance of traditional art and phrase. The story, it is clear, can never thrive well in such an atmosphere; it loses its native vigour in breathing the ethereal air and feeding on the romantic nourishment; but the story in the Prose Kāvya is of as little importance as it is in the metrical Kāvya, whose characteristics are reflected, not with limpid grace, but with gorgeous extravagance.

The few later specimens are even less meritorious. The *Gadya-cintāmaṇi*[1] of the Digambara Jaina Odeyadeva Vādīva-siṃha,[2] pupil of Puṣpasena, describes, in eleven Ḷambhakas,

1 Ed. T. S. Kuppusvami Sastri, Madras 1902 Since Puṣpasena was a pupil of Somadeva Sūri, author of *Yaśastilaka Campū*, the date of our author would be roughly the beginning of the 11th century.

2 See notice of the author's *Kṣatra-cūḍāmaṇi*, above p. 344.

the legend of Satyadhara and his son Jīvaṃdhara, culminating in the latter's seeking peace in asceticism, the story of course being derived, like other Jaina works on the Jīvaṃdhara legend, from Guṇabhadra's *Uttara-purāṇa*. Like the Jaina romances mentioned above, it is also a close adaptation of the luxuriance of Bāṇabhatta's romance ; four pages, for instance, are devoted to the description of Satyadhara in the approved style, and nearly three pages to his queen Vijayā ; but the ethical import in this work is perhaps more predominant, and the literary interest, in spite of tolerable rhetoric, much less absorbing. Of non-Jaina works, the *Vemabhūpāla-carita*[1] of Vāmana Bhaṭṭa Bāṇa, purporting to celebrate the Reddi ruler, Vemabhūpāla or Vīranārāyaṇa Koṇḍaviḍu (*c.* 1403-20 A.D.), deserves only a passing mention as a deliberate but dreary imitation of Bāṇa's *Harṣa-carita*. These hopeless compositions are enough to show the mortal collapse in which the Prose Kāvya lay stricken ; and it is not necessary to pursue its unprofitable history further.

c. *The Campū*

Though the term Campū is of obscure origin, it is already used by Daṇḍin in his *Kāvyādarśa* (i. 31) to denote a species of Kāvya in mixed verse and prose (*gadya-padyamayī*). Nothing, however, is said by Daṇḍin, or by any other rhetorician, about the relative proportion of verse and prose ; but since the Prose Kāvya (Kathā and Ākhyāyikā), which makes prose its exclusive medium, also makes limited use of verse, it has been presumed that the mingling of prose and verse in the Campū should not occur disproportionately. In actual practice, the question, in the absence of authoritative prescription, seems never to have worried the authors, who employ prose and verse indifferently for the same purpose. The verse is not always specially reserved, as one would expect, for an important idea, a poetic description, an

1 **Ed. R. Krishnamachariar. Srī-Vaṇī-Vilāsa Press, Srirangam 1910.**

impressive speech, a pointed moral, or a sentimental outburst, but we find that even for ordinary narrative and description verse is as much pressed into service as prose. In this respect, the Campū scarcely follows a fixed principle ; and its formlessness, or rather disregard of a strict form, shows that the Campū developed quite naturally, but haphazardly, out of the Prose Kāvya itself, the impetus being supplied by the obvious desire of diversifying the prose-form freely by verse as an additional ornament under the stress or the lure of the metrical Kāvya. In the Campū, therefore, the verse becomes as important a medium as the prose, with the result that we find a tendency, similar to that of the decadent drama, of verse gradually ousting prose from its legitimate employment. Although Daṇḍin is aware of this type of composition, we possess no specimen of the Campū earlier than the 10th century A.D. Its late appearance, as well as its obvious relation to the Prose Kāvya, precludes all necessity of connecting it, genetically, with the primitive mode of verse and prose narrative found in the Pali Jātaka or in the Fable literature, in which the verse is chiefly of a moralising or recapitulatory character, or in the inscriptional records, where the verse is evidently ornamental, or in the purely hypothetical Vedic Ākhyāna, which is alleged to have contained slender prose as the mere connecting link of more important verse.

The Campū, thus, shares the features of both Sanskrit prose and poetry, but the mosaic is hardly of an attractive pattern. Excepting rarely outstanding treatment here and there, the large number of Campūs that exist scarcely shows any special characteristic in matter and manner which is not already familiar to us from the regular metrical and prose Kāvya. The subject is generally drawn from legendary sources, although in some later Campūs miscellaneous subjects find a place. The Campū has neither the sinewy strength and efficiency of real prose, nor the weight and power of real poetry ; the prose seeking to copy *ex abundanti* the brocaded stateliness of the prose Kathā, and the verse reproducing the conventional ornateness of the metrical Kāvya. The form, no doubt, affords scope for versatility, but the Campū writer, as a rule, has no original voice of his own. The history of the Campū, therefore, is of no great literary interest, and it would be enough if we notice here some of the better known works which are in print,

The earliest known Campū appears to be the *Nala-campū* or *Damayanti-kathā*[1] of Trivikrama-bhaṭṭa, whose date is inferred from the fact that he also composed the Nausari inscription of the Rāṣṭrakūṭa king Indra III in 915 A.D.[2] The work pretends to narrate the old epic story of Nala and Damayantī, but the accessories and stylistic affectations of laboured composition entirely overgrow the little incident that there is in it, and only a small part of the story is told in its seven Ucchvāsas. The poet himself describes his work as abounding in puns and difficult constructions, for he believes in the display of verbal complexities after the manner of Bāṇa and Subandhu, and deliberately, but wearisomely, imitates their interminably descriptive, ingeniously recondite and massively ornamented style. He has a decided talent in this direction, as well as skill in metrical composition, and elegant verses from his Campū are culled by the Anthologists ;[3] but beyond this ungrudgingly made admission, it is scarcely possible to go in the way of praise.

To the same century and same category of artificial writing belongs the *Yaśastilaka-campū*[4] of the Digambara Jaina Somaprabha Sūri, an extensive work in eight Āśvāsas, composed in 959 A.D. in the reign of the Rāṣṭrakūṭa king Kṛṣṇa, under the patronage of his feudatory, a son of the Cālukya Arikesarin III.

1 Ed. Durgaprasad and Sivadatta, with the comm. of Caṇḍapāla (c. 1230 A.D.), NSP, 1885, 3rd ed., Bombay 1921 ; also ed. Chowkhamba Skt. Series, Benares 1932. The poet describes himself as the son of Nemāditya and grandson of Śrīdhara.

2 D. R. Bhandarkar in *Epi. Ind.*. IX, p. 28. Trivikrama also wrote *Madalasā-campū* (ed. J. B. Modaka and K. N. Sane. Poona 1882). He is quoted anonymously in Bhoja's *Sarasvati-kaṇṭhābharaṇa* (*parvata-bhedi pavitram, ad* iv. 36=*Nala-campū*, vi, 29).

3 All the verses quoted in *Sbhv*, *SP*, and *Pdv* are traceable in the *Nala-campū* ; see S. K. De, *Padyāvalī*, pp. 206-7.

4 Ed. Kedarnath and others, in two parts, with the comm. of Śrutasāgara Sūri, NSP, 2nd ed., Bombay 1916.

It relates the legend of Yaśodhara, lord of Avantī, the machinations of his wife, his death and repeated rebirths and final conversion into the Jaina faith. The story, based upon Guṇabhadra's *Uttara-purāṇa*, is not new, having been the subject of many a Jaina work, like the Apabhraṃśa *Jasahara-cariu*[1] of Puṣpadanta and the Sanskrit *Yaśodhara-carita* of Vādirāja Sūri; but it is narrated here, not normally, but in the embellished mode established by Bāṇabhaṭṭa's *Kādambarī*, one of its distinctive features being the treatment of the motif of rebirths. A large part of the narrative[2] indeed deals with experiences of different births, but a resolution is at last made to put an end to transmigration by following the teachings of a Jaina sage, named Sudatta. These teachings form the subject of the last three Āśvāsas of the work, added as a kind of popular manual of devotion (Upāsakādhyāyana or Readings for the Devotee) explanatory of the Jaina religious texts. This didactic motive and interweaving of doctrinal matter practically run through the entire work, which Somadeva, like most Jaina authors, makes a means to his religious end. A vast array of authorities, pedantic and poetical, for instance, is assembled in the king's polemic against the killing of animals in sacrifice, while a knowledge of polity is displayed in the elaborate discussion between the king and his ministers. It cannot be denied that Somadeva is highly learned, as well as skilled in constructing magniloquent prose sentences and turning out an elegant mass of descriptive and sentimental verses; but the purely literary value of his work has been much exaggerated. If his earnest religious motive is the source of an added interest, it is too obtrusive and dreary to be improved by his respectable rhetoric and pellucid prosody.

These two earlier Campū works are fair specimens of the type; and it is not necessary to make more than a bare mention of later and less meritorious attempts. The Jaina legend of

1 Ed. P. L. Vaidya, Karañja Series, Karañja, Berar 1931.

2 For an analysis of the work, see Peterson, *Second Report*, Bombay 1884, pp. 35-46.

Jīvaṃdhara, based on the *Uttara-purāṇa,* forms the subject-matter also of the *Jīvaṃdhara-campū*[1] of uncertain date, composed in eleven Lambhakas by Haricandra, who is probably identical with the Digambara Jaina Haricandra, whom we have already mentioned as the author of the *Dharma-śarmābhyudaya.* The later Campūs of Hindu authors are no better, their subjects being drawn from the Epics and the Purāṇas. The *Rāmāyaṇa-campū,*[2] ascribed to Bhoja, extends up to the Kiṣkindha-kāṇḍa of the epic story, the sixth of Yuddha-kāṇḍa being made up by Lakṣmaṇa-bhaṭṭa, son of Gaṇgādhara and Gaṇgāmbikā, while some manuscripts give a seventh or Uttara-kāṇḍa by Veṅkaṭarāja. Similarly, Anantabhaṭṭa wrote a *Bhārata-campū*[3] in twelve Stavakas. There are several *Bhāgavata-campūs,*[4] for instance, by Cidambara (in three Stavakas), by Rāmabhadra and by Rājanātha. On the separate episodes of the Epics and the Bhāgavata, there are also several Campūs, but they are not so well known. The Purāṇa myths also claimed a large number of Campūs ; for instance, the *Nṛsiṃha-campū* by Keśavabhaṭṭa,[5] son of Nārāyaṇa (in six Stavakas), by Daivajña Sūrya (in five Ucchvāsas),[6] and by Saṃkarṣaṇa (in four Ullāsas), all dealing with the story of Prahlād's deliverance by the Man-Lion incarnation of Viṣṇu. The *Pārijāta-haraṇa-campū*[7] of Śeṣa Kṛṣṇa, who flourished in the second half of the 16th century, is concerned with the well-known Purāṇa legend of Kṛṣṇa's exploit. The *Nīlakaṇṭha-vijaya-campū* of the South Indian

[1] Ed. T. S. Kuppusvami Sastri, Sarasvatī Vilāsa Series, Tanjore 1905.

[2] Printed many times in India. Ed. K. P. Parab, with the comm. of Rāmacandra Budhendra. NSP, Bombay 1898. This edition contains the 6th Kāṇḍa of Lakṣmaṇabhaṭṭa. Another supplement, entitled Yuddha-kāṇḍa-campū, by Rājacūḍāmaṇi Dīkṣita is known (ed. T. R. Cintamani in *IHQ.* VI, 1930, pp. 629-38).

[3] Ed. K. P. Parab, with comm. of Rāmacandra Budhendra, NSP, Bombay 1903 (also ed. 1916). Very often printed in India.

[4] See P. P. S. Sastri, *Tanjore Catalogue*, vii, p. 3082 f.

[5] Ed. Hariprasad Bhagavat, Krishnaji Ganapat Press, Bombay 1909.

[6] Ed. Durgaprasad and K. P. Parab, NSP, 2nd ed., Bombay 1889, 1900. The author also wrote the drama *Kaṁsa-vadha* (see below).

[7] Ed. C. Sankararama Sastri, Bālamanoramā Press, Madras 1924. Also ed. J. B. Moḍaka and K. N. Sane in Kāvyetihāsa-saṁgraha, Poona 1882.

Nīlakaṇṭha Dīkṣita was composed in 1637 A.D. on the myth of the churning of the ocean by gods. All these are rather literary exercises than creative works.

The Campū form composition appears to have been popular and largely cultivated in Southern India, but nothing will be gained by pursuing its history further than mentioning some curious developments in the hands of some later practitioners of the type. We find that not only myths and legends were drawn upon as themes, but that the form came to be widely and conveniently applied to purposes of description and exposition of various kinds. Thus, Samarapuṃgava Dīkṣita, son of Veṅkaṭeśa and Anantāmmā of Vādhūla-gotra, wrote towards the third quarter of the 16th century his *Yātrā-* (or *Tīrtha-yātrā-*) *prabandha,*[1] describing in nine Aśvāsas, with plenty of interspersed verses, a pilgrimage which he undertook with his elder brother to the holy shrines of Southern India, but incidentally enlarging upon the stock poetic subjects of the six seasons, sunrise, sunset, erotic sports and the like. This is a praiseworthy attempt to divert the Campū from its narrow groove, but the traditional rhetoric thwarts and prevents the assertion of a natural vein. We have already spoken above of *Varadāmbikā-pariṇaya* of the woman poet Tirumalāmba, who gives a highly romantic version, in the usual mannered style, of an historical incident in the career of the Vijayanagara king Acyutarāya. The versatile Veṅkaṭādhvarin,[2] son of Raghunātha and Sītāmbā of the Ātreya-gotra of Conjeevaram, whose literary activity was almost synchronous with that of Nīlakaṇṭha Dīkṣita, conceived the idea of quickening the Campū with a mild zest for disputation and satire. He composed a curious Campū, entitled *Viśva-*

1 Ed. Kedarnath and V. L. Panshikar, NSP, Bombay 1908. It is the same work as that noticed, but vaguely described, by Eggeling, *Ind. Office Cat.*, vii, p. 1533, no. 4036.

2 Veṅkaṭādhvarin was a voluminous writer, and composed, among other works, the *Yādava-rāghavīya* mentioned above, a supplement (the Uttara-kāṇḍa) to Bhoja's *Rāmāyaṇa-campū*, and several poems, plays and Stotras. See *Ind. Culture*, VI, p. 227, for other works of this author.

guṇādarśa,[1] in which two Gandharvas, Viśvāvasu and Kṛśānu, take a bird's-eye view of various countries from their aerial car, the former generous in appreciation of their qualities, the latter censorious of their defects. The device is adapted in the *Tattva-guṇādarśa*[2] of Annayārya, which describes the comparative merits of Śaivism and Vaiṣṇavism in the form of a conversation between Jaya and Vijaya, a Śaivite and a Vaiṣṇavite respectively. Local legends and festivals, or praise of local deities and personages also supply the inspiration of many a Campū.[3] The *Vedāntācārya-vijaya*[4] of Kavi-tārkika-siṃha Vedāntācārya describes the life of the South Indian teacher, Vedāntadeśika, the disputations held by him with Advaitins and his polemic successes. The *Vidvan-moda-taraṅgiṇī*[5] of Rāmacandra Ciranjīva Bhaṭṭācārya, a comparatively modern work, is a witty composition which brings together the followers of schools and sects, and, by means of their exposition, pools together the essence of various beliefs and doctrines. But the most strange application of the Campū form occurs in the *Mandāramaranda-campū*[6] of Krsna, which is nominally a Campū but is in fact a regular

1 Ed. B, G. Yogi and M. G. Bakre, NSP, 5th ed. Bombay 1923 ; also ed. with a comm., Karnatak Press, Bombay 1889.

2 See *Descriptive Cat., Madras Govt. Orient. Lib.*, xxi, p. 8223, no. 12295.

3 As for instance, the *Śrīnivāsa-vilāsa-campū* of Veṇkaṭeśa or Veṅkaṭādhvarin (ed. Durgaprasad and K. P. Parab, NSP, Bombay 1893), which describes the glory of the deity Śrī Veṅkateśvara of Tirupati in the highly artificial style of Subandhu ; the *Citra-campū* of Bāṇeśavara Vidyālaṁkāra, composed in 1744 A. D. (ed. Ramcharan Chakravarti, Benares 1940 ; Eggeling, *Ind. Office Cat.*, vii. pp. 1543-45, no. 4044), eulogising the author's patron, Citrasena of Vardhamāna (Burdwan), Bengal, and giving quasi-historical information about the Maratha raid of Bengal of 1742.

4 *Descriptive Cat. Madras Govt. Orient. Lib.*, xxi, p. 8290, no. 12365.

5 Ed. Veṅkaṭeśvara Press, Bombay 1912. The author's *Mādhava-campū* has been edited by Satyavrata Sāmaśramī, Calcutta 1881. For the author, see S. K. De, *Sanskrit Poetics*, i. p. 294. He lived in the 1st half of the 18th century, his *Vṛtta-ratnāvalī*, a work on Prosody in honour of Yaśovanta Siṁha, Nayeb-Dewan of Dacca under Suja-ud-daulah of Bengal, being dated 1731 A.D.

6 Ed. Kedarnath and V. L. Panshikar, NSP, Bombay, 2nd ed., 1924. As the work copies some definitions from Appayya Dīkṣita, it cannot be earlier than the 17th century. The *Rasa prakāśa* commentary on Mammata's *Kāvya-prakāśa* is probably his,

treatise on rhetoric and prosody, composed with elaborate definitions and illustrations.

As the Jaina writers made use of the Campū for religious propaganda, the Bengal Vaiṣṇava school also did the same in respect of their creed and belief in the Kṛṣṇa-legend, of which they presented erotico-religious pictures of great sensuous charm. The *Muktā-caritra*[1] of Raghunātha-dāsa, a disciple of Caitanya, relates a short tale, in which Kṛṣṇa demonstrates that pearls could be grown as a crop by sowing and watering them with milk, but of which the real object is to show the superiority of Kṛṣṇa's free love for Rādhā over his wedded love for Satyabhāmā. But the *Gopālā-campū*[2] of Jīva Gosvāmin, nephew of Rūpa Gosvāmin, and the *Ānanda-vṛndāvana-campū*[3] of Paramānanda-dāsa-sena Kavikarṇapūra are much more artificial, extensive and elaborate works, which describe, after the *Hari-vaṃśa* and *Śrīmad-bhāgavata*, the early childhood and youth of Kṛṣṇa in a lavishly luscious and rhetorical style. Kavikarṇapūra's work deals with the early life of Kṛṣṇa at Vṛndāvana ; but Jīva's huge Campū envisages the entire career of Kṛṣṇa, but making modification in the legends in accordance with the Vaiṣṇava theology of the Bengal school, of which it is more of the nature of a Siddhānta-grantha.

1 Ed. Nityasvarup Brahmacari, Devakinandan Press, Brindaban 1917, in Bengali characters.

2 Ed. Nityasvarup Brahmacari, in two parts (Purva and Uttara khaṇḍas), Devakinandan Press, Brindaban 1904 ; also ed. Rasavihari Samkhyatirtha, with comm. of Vīracandra, in two parts, Devakinandan Press, Calcutta 1908-1913, in Bengali characters.

3 Ed. in the *Pandit*, Old Series, vol. ix and x, New Series, vols. i-iii ; also published in parts, by Madhusudan Das, with comm. of Visvanatha Cakravartin, Hugli 1918 etc., in Bengali characters (incomplete).

CHAPTER VII

THE LATER DECADENT DRAMA

1. General Characteristics

With Bhavabhūti practically ends the great epoch of Sanskrit dramatic literature and begins the age of lesser achievement. There is profusion of talent and effort, but there is no drama of real dramatic quality. All kinds of so-called plays continued to be produced in amazing abundance for several centuries, and the number of works available today in print or in manuscript exceeds six hundred, but they are inferior and imitative productions, which seek to follow dramaturgic rules slavishly, but which reveal little sense of what a drama really is. They are rather narratives, cast in a loose dramatic form, or expanded with a series of lyric and descriptive stanzas loosely strung together. Of the large bulk of these, so little of any kind is retained by the general memory that, considering their poor quality, we can hardly say that they are consigned to any exceptional oblivion. Here and there individual manner and method are perceptible, and a few names are still cherished ; but the seeds of decadence, which we already find in Bhaṭṭa Nārāyaṇa and Bhavabhūti, come into full and lūxuriant bloom. The drama now shows no uneasiness in abjectly surrendering itself to the poetical Kāvya ; and, in course of time, it becomes a curious hybrid between a play and a poem.

On that side of the drama which is not literature but stagecraft, the Sanskrit dramatists, as a rule, never made a strong appeal. But if earlier dramatists did not reach the highest level as constructors of plot, inventors of incident, or creators of dramatic effect, their successors never attained, nor did they care to attain, any level at all. The disproportion between the acting and the literary value of a drama increases, until the literary motive overshadows everything. It is true that there never existed in Sanskrit any real distinction between the literary drama, which may be acted but not with real acting success, and the acting drama, which abandons all pretension to literature and succeeds only on the stage ; it is also true that the necessity never ceased of appealing to the highly cultivated audience of the royal court and polished society, and there existed the wide-spread influence and continual temptation of narrative and lyric matter, detrimental to action and characterisation ; but the inherent dramatic sense of earlier writers was never entirely eclipsed by the general demand for purely literary effect.

The root of the trouble lay in the fact that there was always a distinct cleavage between drama and life, and the gulf widened as dramatic enthusiasm subsided. Had the theatre been more popular, the tendency to reject reality and simplicity and to strain for artificial and recondite result would have been counteracted. But from the beginning the authors, as a rule, were dramatists of exclusive society, dealing preferably with kings and courts, *ego et rex meus* ; and it is very seldom that they came down from their pedestal. The common antithesis of facile criticism made between a poet of the people and one of the court is idle in this case, for the simple reason that there was hardly any real poet of the people. We can seldom take away from the dramatist the courtly atmosphere and the sham heroes and heroines with their conventional twaddle. But the earlier masters, in spite of this limitation, could still produce real dramatic interest ; they were not entirely indifferent to the realities of life or drama. If they were inclined to the poetic, they could invest their plays with a higher poetic naturalness ; and in this sense, there was no lack of vigour and variety, no complete divorce between the poetical drama and real life. Their successors continued to work with the same traditional material. There was as yet no strict limitation of form, and the immense fund of legends, as well as the unlimited diversity of life, was open to them ; but out of respect for texts and traditions, or out of contempt for the real life surrounding them, they preferred to draw upon the same epic and legendary cycles or fictitious amourettes of court-life, with a more conscious inclination towards poetic extravagance and greater lack of dramatic power and originality. The taste for elegancies in language and sentiment are indeed not absent in the earlier masterpieces. It appears to have spread down and diffused itself among the common people, and there is no hint that the demand for exuberant graces and refinements of poetry in dramatic composition was not almost universal. Even middle-class life is presented by Bhavabhūti in an apparently excessive poetic atmosphere; and the fact that in later times, the *Ratnāvalī* and the *Veṇī-saṃhāra* were preferred to the *Mṛcchakaṭika* and the *Mudrā-rākṣasa*, is typical of this traditional attitude. The heroic and erotic drama alone survived, with the thinnest surplus of plays of other kinds. Common life was left to inferior talents, and their productions were allowed to pass, in course of time, to neglect and oblivion.

The scanty remains of the earlier drama do not justify any sweeping conclusion, but it seems that there was, as we have already pointed out, hardly any living tradition for all the eighteen forms of the drama recognised in dramaturgic treatises. If some writers of later times, like Vatsarāja, attempted rarer types of plays, they were not following what was widely in vogue, but displaying, more or less, pedantry and book-learning, which prompted them to produce lifeless plays in accordance with fixed formulas. As such, they are literary curiosities, but useless as historical specimens. This slavish adherence to dramaturgic prescriptions, which gradually becomes a general feature of the decadent drama, is also found in the normally accepted heroic and erotic plays, as well as in these laboriously constructed specimens, and illustrates the more pronounced influence of theory on practice. Although based upon empirical analysis, the theory tended to enforce fixed rules and methods, and never proved advantageous to a free development of practice. In a period of decadence, in which inspiration was replaced by erudition, it naturally came to have a greater hold and authority, and the plays became too deliberately bound to precedent to be original to any extent. If some irregular types, like the *Mahānāṭaka* and *Gopāla-keli-candrikā*, were evolved, they came into existence through other causes; not in accordance with the theory but in spite of it. The general result was that the drama receded entirely from real life, and became nothing more than a rigid, but insipid, exercise in literary skill and ingenuity.

One of the disastrous results of this isolation of drama from life is seen in the wide separation of its language from the language of life. Since drama is not life, the language of drama, like that of poetry, has doubtless its own ways of expression, and neither Kālidāsa nor Shakespeare ever wrote in the common language of his time; but, however refined and elevated it may be, neither the drama nor its language can afford to lose its semblance of colour and vividness to those of life or its language. The stilted and laboured diction of the later Sanskrit drama, losing all touch with life, becomes wholly unconvincing. The distinction of class implied in the distinction of Prakrit dialects[1] becomes now a meaningless convention, and may be neglected, especially in view of the fact that its use (in spite of Rājaṣekhara's *tour de force*) becomes more artificial and sparing than what we find, for instance, in Bhavabhūti, who never employs Prakrit in verse, and in Bhaṭṭa Nārāyaṇa, who never uses more forms of Prakrits than he can help. The fact is, however, significant that in this decadent drama Prakrit is merely suffered to exist or relegated to an inferior position, and Sanskrit, with its learned possibilities, becomes the normal, but not natural, medium. In some works, like the *Mahānāṭaka*,

1 On dramatic Prakrits in general, see Pischel, *Grammatik der Prakrit-sprachen*, Strassburg 1900, sections 5f, 22-26, 28-30; Sten Konow in *JRAS*, 1901, p. 329 f, 1922, p. 434 f. and introd. to his ed. of *Karpūramañjarī*; Hultzsch in *ZDMG*, LXVI, 1912, p. 709 f; Hillebrandt in *Gottingische gelehrte Anzeigen*, 1908, p. 99 f; Manmohon Ghosh, introd. to his ed. of *Karpūramañjarī*.

Prakrit is entirely absent. If Sanskrit was more difficult, it was richer and more accommodating to stylistic extravagances ; if it was learned, it suited the learned atmosphere ; it also served the purpose of composing those lyric, narrative and reflective stanzas which came to predominate and oust the prose, in a greater degree, from its legitimate place, or to make it, with its sonorous length and excess of heavy compounds, approximate to the established method of verse.

It is clear that the whole cast of thought and style, the atmosphere, the stereotyped conventions and limited themes, and the highly poetical and affected diction become unfavourable, and almost fatal, to the writing of such plays as would be at once poetical and practical. The dramatists themeselves do not seem quite to know whether they are composing a play or a poem ; nor are they producing the right kind of either. For the prevailing heroic and erotic drama, poetry is, to some extent, necessary, but the poetry here is of the artificial kind ; the heroic degenerates into the pseudo-heroic and the erotic into the namby-pamby. The poetic frenzy, which describes the eyes of maidens as compendious oceans, or arms of men as capable of uprooting the Himalayas, is delightfully hyperbolic, but leaves us cold. The dramatist has verses enough for anything ; the verses have often the fascination of sonorous sound and sentimental sense, but their profusion and extravagance become undramatic and tiresome ; sometimes they have resonance, but no melody ; and being mechanically multiplied with set phrases and conceits, they have little originality in idea and expression. The prose and the dialogue are thereby reduced to a minimum ; and the little that remains of them loses all dramatic quality, for the simple reason that everything of importance is expressed in verse. In the leisurely progress of the exuberant stanzas, the action is left to take care of itself ; dramatic propriety, unity, or motive is of little concern ; a panorama of pictures or a loosely connected series of incidents is enough. The plot is even of less concern ; it is unredeemed by variety of presentation, and offers, in play after play, the same set of incidents and situations ; it is never hurried, nor does the dramatist expect us to follow it with breathless interest. All this inevitably affects characterisation and delineation of sentiment. The conventionally fixed types of character become only dim figures shadowed through a vague mist of luxuriant poetry. There are beautiful ladies, but their tender and fragile portraits combine in the memory into one delicate type which stands practically for all ; they are discriminated by names, but not by character. Virtues are idealised with an absurd neglect of proportion ; but the vicious persons are only harmless devils whose passion can run as high as the stiff manner of tirades alows. There is a vast amount of distress in what are meant to be pathetic scenes, but we read them comfortably without tears or undue emotion, unless the sham-tragic lingo becomes too much for our patience. The extreme rarity and, when they occur, the utter worthlessness of comic or pseudo-comic parts of the decadent drama are on a par with this diffused and rhetorical pathos, as well as with the huffiness and extravagant passion of its impossible stage-heroes.

The lack of humour explains and is explained by the lack of pathos, and both spring from a lack of grasp on the essentials of human nature. These sentimentally idealised writings hardly show any sense of the stress and contradiction from which both tragedy and comedy arise. The attitude is ethically clear and regular ; there is no situation of moral complexity, as well as no appreciation of the inherent inconsistencies of human character ; no shadow of tragic error qualifies heroic grandeur, as no shade of good is allowed to redeem foulness. We have consequently neither really tragic heroes, nor really lively rogues. As humour degenerates into coarse and boisterous laughter, by tragedy is understood, characteristically enough, a mere misfortune, a simple decline from good to evil hap, the nodus of which can be dissolved in sentiment or cut away by the force of merciful circumstances. Even when the hero undergoes real and grievous affliction, all obstacles and perils give away before him, and the poignancy of the tragedy is warded off. The calamity never rightly comes home, but becomes the means of sentimental effusion; and the hero is never brought to the point at which he utters the agonised cry of Oedipus or Lear in their last straits. The foreshadowing of all this we have seen in Bhavabhūti, but it becomes a definite posture with the decadent playwrights who succeed him; and they betray an equally unhumorous and inelastic disposition. The comedy is confined chiefly to insignificant characters and to equally insignificant farcical sketches. There is no breath of sympathy for the follies and oddities of life, no amused allowance for its ugliness and rascality, no inclination to look at life more widely and wisely, and no sense of tear in laughter, which consequently descends to puerile and tastless vulgarity.

If drama is the transference of human action on the stage, these works are not dramas, and very few of them are acceptable as stage-plays. Even considered as poems, their real value is obscured by convention and pedantry. It has been suggested that the natural progress of the dramatic art was obstructed and disordered, from this period onwards, by the depressing effect of Muhmmadan invasion and by the turmoil and uncertainty consequent upon it. As in poetry, so in drama, this is only partially true. The dislocation of social and political order undoubtedly reacted on literature, especially on the drama, which is necessarily meant to be closer to actual life; but this cannot be the entire explanation. The decadence, in the case of the drama, is neither an isolated phenomenon, nor is it brought about directly and immediately by the foreign invasion. The process was wide-spread; it is seen in poetry, as well as in the various arts and sciences, which produce nothing striking after the 9th or the 10th century, but concern themselves with the barren refinements of scholasticism. The decline had already commenced widely even before the foreign occupation became an actual fact. The drama lost all contact with real life and became an abstract thing of fancy, not as a consequence of external disturbances, but because the really creative .period of Sanskrit literature in almost all its aspects closed with the 10th century. The period ended with the standardisation of the forms and methods of the dramatic, as well as the poetic, art ; and though much was produced thereafter, there was nothing of real merit. The standard patterns were already there, and with a fund of ready-made words and ideas, it was not difficult for the proverbial prolixity of bad writers to turn out poems and dramas in vast number. But the vein of originality had exhausted itself, and the foeign incursion never brought in its train any vigorous dramatic literature which might have furnished the much needed impetus towards a revival. The foreign occupation, therefore, which was necessarily a slow and diffused process, could not save it from stagnation, and perhaps hastened the decline, but it was never responsible for a state of things which had commenced, independently and much beforehand, from causes inherent in the literature itself.

The history of the Sanskrit drama, therefore, does not close with the 10th century, but it loses genuine interest thereafter. There is no breach of community, and the general scheme of the various kinds of plays is so stereotyped that monotony inevitably results from the unvaried sameness, not only of form, manner and method, but also of incident, sentiment and characterisation. The drama becomes an uninspired and uninspiring record, which seldom rises above the dead leavel of convention and uniformity of characteristics. The literature which calls itself drama is neither good drama nor good poetry. Nothing will be gained, therefore, by pursuing its unprofitable history in detail, or by a bare recital of names, which might have an antiquarian but no literary importance. We have to reckon, in such cases, brilliant flashes, but even these become rare. Some of the writers, like Murāri, Rājaśekhara, Kṣemīśvara and Kṛṣṇamisra have enjoyed traditional reputation, but the validity of the praises showered upon them is not justified by actual reading.

They are poets who try the stage, but they are never to the manner born, nor is their gift of poetry high and arresting. Notwithstanding worthy and strenuous effort, they are not only chronologically behind (which was in itself a misfortune rather than a blessing), but recede as much from the first row of the dramatists as they fall back in point of time. These four writers, however, so completely represent the drama in its decline and fix the general characteristics so rigidly that, after considering their works, it would be hardly necessary to take up in detail those of their countless successors, who have little ability to swerve from the beaten track and produce anything of which Sanskrit drama or poetry may be legitimately proud.

2. Murāri and Rājaśekhara

The Prologue to Murāri's solitary play, named *Anargha-rāghava*,[1] tells us that he was son of Vardhamāṅka of Maudgalya Gotra and Tantumatī. Beyond this we know nothing of him, and his date is conjectural. Most probably he knew Bhavabhūti's *Mahāvīra-carita*,[2] from which he appears to have borrowed, but loosely utilised, the motif of Mālyavat's conspiracy. The earliest citation from the *Anargha-rāghava*, without the name of the author, occurs in the *Daśa-rūpaka*.[3] It would not be unjustifiable, therefore, to place Murāri at the end of the 9th or the beginning of the 10th century. This date accords well with a passage of the *Śrīkaṇṭha-carita* (xxv. 74), in which Maṅkhaka mentions and apparently makes him a predecessor

1 Ed. Premchandra Tarkavagis, Calcutta 1860; ed. Durgaprasad and K. P. Parab, with the commentary of Rucipati, NSP, Bombay 1894.

2 The alleged citation of the prose passage of *Uttara-carita* between vi. 30 and 31 in the prose passage of *Anargha*°, Prologue verses 6 and 7, made out by Sten Konow (p. 83), is illusory, for the verbal resemblance is uncertain.

3 *Daśa-rūpaka ad* ii. 1 (*rāma rāma*) = *Anargha*° iii, 21. The fact that the verse occurs in the *Mahānāṭaka*, which is notorious for is appropriation of verses from most Rāma-dramas. does not invalidate the position.

of Rājaśekhara.[1] The seventh act of Murāri's drama gives a rapid description of various well-known places, like Ujjayini, Vārāṇasī, Kailāsa, Prayāga, Tāmraparṇī on the sea, Campā in Gauḍa, Pancavaṭī. Kuṇḍina in Mahārāṣṭra, and Kāñcī in the Drāviḍa country ; but the singular mention of Māhiṣmatī as the seat of the Kalcuris in the Cedi-maṇḍala is curious, and perhaps suggests that the poet lived under the patronage of some king of that dynasty.[2]

The *Anargha-rāghava* dramatises the traditional narrative of the *Rāmāyaṇa,* with very slight modification, in seven acts. In a somewhat lengthy Prologue[3] the author justifies the choice of a banal theme, and explains how the splendid subject really deserves the epithet Anargha, hia own object being to relieve his audience, who had enough of horror, terror and disgust, with an elevated, heroic and charming composition. The smooth, even an excessively poetical, tenour of his writing perhaps bears out this claim and supports his own arrogation of the style of Bāla-Vālmīki ; but neither his choice of topic, which has been already so forcibly presented by Bhavabhūti, nor his undramatic and extravagant treatment, which is tediously prolonged, justifies the poet's confidence and the enthusiastic estimate of his admirers.[4]

1 The supposition that Ratnākara refers to Murāri in the middle of the 9th century in a punning passage of his *Hara-vijaya* (xxxviii. 68) cannot be supported, as the reference is not at all clear. See Bhattanatha Svamin in *IA*, XLI, 1912 p. 141 and Sten Konow, *loc. cit.* —Murāri is also mentioned by Rāmacandra, a pupil of Hemacandra (1st half of the 12th century) in his *Nāṭya-darpaṇa* (p. 193) and his *Kaumudi-mitrānanda* (Prologue) ; but the supposition of Hultzsch (*ZDMG,* LXXVI, 1921, p. 63) that Rāmacandra was Murāri's contemporary is not borne out by the terms of the reference,

2 The Sūtradhāra calls himself Madhyadeśīya. We are told that the work was presented at the procession (Yātrā) of Puruṣottama ; this cannot, in the absence of historical knowledge of the time of construction of the Jagannātha temple at Puri, refer to that deity in particular. There is no satisfactory evidence also for the late Bengal tradition which takes Murāri as the progenitor of a class of Bengali Brahmans.

3 The prolixity of some of the chief decadent dramatists is seen in the length of their boastful Prologues, in which they appear to vie with one another. Murāri is moderate in having only 13 stanzas, but Rājaśekhara (in his *Bāla-rāmāyaṇa*) has 20 and Jayadeva 23.

4 The popularity of Murāri's play is attested not only by the citation of anthologists but also by the existence of a large number of commentaries on his work.

After some poetic, but hyperbolic, compliments exchanged between Daśaratha and Viśvāmitra, the first act of the drama ends with the sighs and lamentations of the former at the departure of Rāma to the hermitage of Viśvāmitra. The second long act, containing more than eighty stanzas, opens with the recital of the history of Vālin, Rāvaṇa, Hanūmat and Tāṭakā by means of a lengthy prose conversation, interspersed with verse, between two pupils of Viśvāmitra. This is followed by the appearence of Rāma and Lakṣmaṇa and description by them, in a series of verses, of the hermitage, its occupants and their doings, as well as of the heat of midday, which, with a singular disregard of time, brings us to the evening, to a description of sunset, to the approach of Tāṭakā announced behind the scenes, Rāma's reluctant exit to kill her, a description of the fight by Lakṣmaṇa who stays behind on the stage, and Rāma's return to describe the moonrise in his turn. The end of the glorious day comes with Viśvāmitra's suggestion of a visit to Mithilā, which of course involves a description of the city and its ruler. In the third and fourth acts, the motif of Rāvaṇa's feud and Mālyavat's strategy is feebly borrowed from Bhavabhūti, but not developed as the basis of dramatic action or unity, to the necessity of which Murāri seems to be utterly indifferent. But he scatters liberally more than sixty sonorous stanzas in each of these acts, and spends all his strength on them. The arrival of Rāvaṇa's messenger and his discomfiture at Sītā's Svayamvara, and the subsequent device of Śūrpəṇakhās disguise as Mantharā, are elaborated, imitatively but without dramatic skill. Then we have grandiose exchange of defiances (again after Bhavabhūti) between Rāma and Paraśurāma. Though equally boastful and insulting, Paraśurāma, however, is not connected with the plot by Mālyavat's instigation, and Rāma is not as impolite as his friends, who carry on the campaign of vituperation from a safe distance behind the scenes. In the fifth act, most of Rāma's doing in the forest, as well as Sītā's abduction, is reported, till Rāma appears on the stage lamenting. Vālin is made to challenge him to a fight on a somewhat frivolous excuse; and Vālin's death and Sugrīva's coronation are again described second-hand. In the next long act, in which the number of stanzas is well over eighty, all the incidents from the building of the bridge over the ocean to the death of Rāvaṇa are similarly described by persons on the stage or by voices from behind the scenes. But the longest and most actionless act is the last, in which the aerial journey of Rāma and his party to Ayodhyā is modelled on *Raghu°* xiii and the last act of the Vulgate text of the *Mahāvīra-carita*; but the route is not only spread over a large number of terrestrial places, but also considerably diversified, deliberately for the purpose of poetical stanzas, by transporting it to the celestial regions, and by including a sight of the Mount Meru, Kailāsa and the world of the moon, the poet surpassing himself in this enormous act by composing more than one hundred and fifty stanzas.

It will be seen that there is incredibly little action in a work which calls itself a drama, almost everything being subordinated to metrical description and declamation, and the epic succession of incidents being panoramically reproduced by these means, without the slightest attempt to convert the whole into a drama. As mouthpieces chiefly of narration or verse, the characters in the play are well known and fixed types. There is little interest in the scanty prose dialogues, which are meant mostly to furnish information, while the poetical dialogues are merely long-drawn-out series of descriptive or sentimental monologues; both are hopelessly deficient in dramatic quality and effect. The pathos and passion are consequently diffused and rhetorical. The designedly profuse and extravagant volleys of description and declamation are, of course, excuses for elaborate excercise in ornate composition; but reckoning by the poetical stanzas alone, which make a total of nearly five hundred and forty, the work is more than double the size of the *Mālatī-mādhava*, as well as of the *Uttara-rāma-carita*, which, lengthy as they are, contain two hundred and thirty-four and two hundred fifty-five stanzas respectively. One wonders why the author did not attempt writing a regular poem instead. Perhaps the distinction was obliterated by the steady and disproportionate development of the reflective, narrative and sentimental aspect of the drama, of which we see the beginnings already in Bhaṭṭa Nārāyaṇa and Bhavabhūti.

We should like to remember Murāri more as an elegant poet, capable of turning out harmonious verses, than as a dramatist in the proper sense. But even in his poetry we see only the last glow of the ashes, and not the bright gleam of the older flame of poetry. While everything he writes is facile and never ungraceful, he does nothing first-rate. He has a fine gift of sonorous words, of pretty but strained conceits and of smooth and melodious versification ; but since poetry does not consist merely of all these, Murāri does not rank high even as a poet. In neither sound nor sense does he possess the finer touch of imagination and suggestiveness ; his sentiment has tenderness, but no strangeness, nor always strict tragic quality. The splendid rhetoric of some of his best passages almost excuses the enthusiasm of his admirers for a style and treatment full of glaring poetic and dramatic inadequacy ; but it only pleases, and does not thrill, being very seldom rhetoric of the best kind Murāri appears to have imitated Bhavabhūti, but he borrows Bhavabhūti's prolix sentimentality and looseness without profiting by his vigour and dramatic sense ; and he does not also possess the much higher poetic gift of his great predecessor.

If Murāri is typical of the decadent Sanskrit dramatists, Rājaśekhara is perhaps more so ; and some account of his works would be profitable for understanding the trend, method and treatment of the dramatic writings of this period of decline. Rājaśekhara, son of Darduka (or Duhika) and Śīlavatī, is never too modest to speak of himself ; and from his works we know a great deal about him, his family, his patrons and his career as a poet.[1] He belonged to the Yāyāvara family, in which were born poets and scholars like Sūrānanda, Tarala, Kavirāja and Akālajalada, the last-named person, famed in the Anthologies, being his great-grandfather. His ancestors lived in Mahārāṣṭra, but he himself must have spent much of his life in the midland as the preceptor (Upādhyāya) of king Mahendrapāla and his son Mahīpāla of Mahodaya (Kanauj), and later on as a protégé of Yuvarāja, who has been identified with Yuvarāja I Keyūravarṣa, the Kalacuri ruler of Tripurī. The poet's wife, Avantisundarī, was an accomplished Kṣatriya lady of Cahuan family, whom he quotes with respect in his *Kāvya-mīmāṃsā* and for whose pleasure his *Karpūramañjarī* was composed. But since marriage beneath one's own caste is not forbidden for a Brahman, the fact need not imply that Rājaśekhara himself was a Kṣatriya. On the other hand, his Kṣatriya descent is not negatived by his quite compatible position as an Upādhyāya, or by that of his father as the Mahāmantrin of some unnamed king. That Rājaśekhara was a man of multifarious learning admits of little doubt; and he appears to have composed a large number of works. In his *Bāla-rāmāyaṇa* (1.2) he describes himself as Bāla-kavi and author already of six works, while in his *Karpūra-mañjarī*, the style of Bāla-kavi is repeated with the addition of the proud title of Kavirāja, which he himself considers to be higher than that of a Mahākavi. If he began his career as a Bāla-kavi, apparently given to him from the word Bāla occurring in his two epic plays, then these are presumably his early productions; but the question whether his *Karpūra-mañjarī* or his *Viddha-śālabhañjikā* was the last is difficult to determine.[2] Of his six earlier works mentioned in the *Bāla-*

1 For a detailed account of Rājaśekhara's life and times, see V. S. Apte, *Rājaśekhara: His Life and Writings*, Poona 1886; F. Kielhorn in *EI*, I, pp. 162-179 and J. F. Fleet in *IA*, XVI, pp. 175-78; Sten Konow's ed. of *Karpūramañjarī*, pp. 177-76; Manomohan Ghosh's ed. of the same play, pp. lxv-lxxii; S. K. De, *Sanskrit Poetics*, i, pp. 122-28.

2 The chronological order of Rājaśekhara's plays is uncertain. See, besides Sten Konow and Ghosh cited above, V. V. Mirashi in *Pathak Commemoration Volume*, Poona 1934, p. 359 f.

rāmāyaṇa, the lost *Hara-vilāsa*, a Kāvya, mentioned and quoted by Hemacandra (p. 335 comm.) and Ujjvaladatta (*ad* ii. 28), may have been one. Besides his four plays, he also wrote a general work of miscellaneous information on poets and poetry, named *Kāvya-mīmāṃsā*,[1] in which there is a reference to another work of his, called *Bhuvana-kośa*, for information on general geography. From his explict references to Mahendrapāla, Mahīpāla and Yuvarāja, his date has been fixed with some certainty at the last quarter of the 9th and the first quarter of the 10th century. This date is supported by the fact that the latest writers quoted by Rājaśekhara are the Kashmirian Ratnākara and Ānandavardhana, both of whom belong to the middle of the 9th century, while the earliest writer to mention Rājaśekhara appears to be the Jaina Somadeva, whose *Yaśastilaka* is dated in 960 A.D.[2]

In his *Bāla-rāmāyaṇa*,[3] which loosely dramatises in ten acts the entire story of the *Rāmāyaṇa* up to Rāma's coronation, Rājaśekhara perpetrates, both by its bulk and execution, an appalling monstrosity of a so-called drama. Like Murāri, he makes the mistake not only of choosing, with little poetic and less dramatic power, a banal epic theme, but also of attempting to outdo his predecessors[4] in scattering, through its entire length, the debris of a too fertile talent, which, in the shape of unending quantities of descriptive and sentimental verses, come

1 On this work, see S. K. De, *Sanskrit Poetics*, i, p. 125 f. ii, p. 366 f.

2 Rājaśekhara's plays are also cited anonymously in the *Daśa-rūpaka*, and Rājaśekhara is mentioned in the *Udayasundarī-kathā* of Soḍḍhala, composed about the same time (990 A.D.). Most of the Anthology verses ascribed to Rājaśekhara (see Thomas, *Kvs*, pp. 81-92) are traceable in his four plays, but a large number remains untraced. The untraced memorial verses on Sanskrit poets (in *Sūkti-muktāvalī*) may or may not belong to him.

3 Ed. Govindadev Sastri, Benares 1869 (reprinted from the *Pandit*, Old Series, iii, 1862-69) ; ed. Jivananda Vidyasagar, Calcutta 1884. But a good edition is still desirable.

4 Indebtedness to Bhavabhūti is expressly acknowledged, and unmistakable evidence of imitation has been shown by Apte, *op. cit.*, p. 37 f ; but there can be little doubt that Murari's extravagant work also served as his model.

up to a total of nearly seven hundred and eighty. Even the Prologue itself which contains, with its twenty stanzas, a voluble account of himself and his indiscernible merits, reaches almost to the dimension of an act, while each of the ten acts, averaging more than seventy verses and once running up to one hundred, has almost the bulk of a small drama ! It has been calculated that more than two hundred stanzas are in the long Śārdūla-vikrīḍita metre and about ninety in the still longer Sragdharā. It is a wonder how such an enormous play could have been brought on the stage ; but the author takes an evident pride in its bulk (i. 12), and recommends it for *reading*, for whatever merit may be found in its diction. In the construction of plot, some variation is shown by making Rāvaṇa's misdirected passion for Sītā the prime cause of his feud, the feud itself being conceived, not originally but after Bhavabhūti, as the central motif. This substitution, however, of love and longing for mock-heroic ferocity is hardly an improvement. Rāvaṇa, with his amorousness and his disappointed hope, becomes more ludicrous than impressive, and it is not surprising that Paraśurāma, instead of lending him assistance, insults him openly. The diplomacy of Mālyavat is also repeated from Bhavabhūti with some slight variation, such as, the device of bringing about the banishment of Rāma by Mantharā and the demons in the disguise of Kaikeyī and Daśaratha.[1] The contrivance of a play within a play is also borrowed in act iii from Harṣa and Bhavabhūti. Rāvaṇa pines away with hopeless *crève-cœur* ; and for his amusement a troupe of actors which visits his palace enacts, by happy or unhappy chance, a miniature play on the betrothal of Sītā to Rāma ; the realism of the scence infuriates Rāvaṇa and the play is interrupted. The scene is not ineffectively conceived; but the motif is farcically repeated by a second cruder effort, in act v, to amuse Rāvaṇa by

[1] This device of tricking by disguise is carried to its ludicrous excess in the *Jānakī-pariṇaya* of Ramabhadra Dikṣita (17th century), in which Rāvaṇa, Śaraṇa, Vidyujjihva and Tāṭakā apear in disguise as Rāma, Lakṣmaṇa, Viśvamitra and Sītā, so that a confusion arises when they meet and results in a cheap comedy of errors !

means of marionettes dressed up as Sītā, with speaking parrots inside! The idea, however, seems to have pleased the author, for he again utilises the head of a similar speaking marionette, representing the severed head of Sītā, as a part of Mālyavat's stratagem to frighten the enemies. Rāvaṇa's Viraha, in which he demands tidings of his beloved in *furor poeticus* from nature, the seasons, streams and birds, is obviously a faint imitation of Purūravas's madness in the *Vikramorvaśīya* ; but it is as unnecessary as it is tedious. The narrative thereafter drags on with a profusion of description, and there is little action throughout. In the last act, Rājaśekhara describes, after Murāri, in nearly a hundred stanzas, the aerial tour of Rāma and his party, which includes a visit also to the world of the moon.

Rājaśekhara's second epic play, the *Bāla-bhārata*,[1] which is also called *Pracaṇḍa-pāṇḍava* (i.8), was probably projected, on the same scale and plan, to be a companion Nāṭaka on the Mahābhārata story ; but, mercifully, it is left incomplete. Of the two acts which remain, the first describes the Svayaṃvara of Draupadī ; the second deals with the gambling scene, ill-treatment of Draupadī and departure of the Pāṇḍavas to the forest ; but, with the exception of a few well turned verses, there is nothing remarkable in the fragment.

The two remaining plays are smaller works in four acts, and resemble each other in form and substance. The first, *Karpūramañjarī*,[2] is called a Saṭṭaka (i.6), and the second, *Viddha-śālabhañjikā*,[3] a Nāṭikā ; but the distinction does not appear to be substantial between the two types, except that the

1 Ed. C. Cappeller, Strassburg, 1885 : ed. Durgaprasad and K. P. Parab, NSP, Bombay 1887 (included in their ed. of *Karpūra*°, see below).

2 Ed. Durgaprasad and K. P. Parab, with comm. (incomplete) of Vasudeva, NSP, Bombay 1887 (also contains *Bāla-bhārata*) ; ed. Sten Konow, with Eng. trs. and notes by C. R. Lanman, Harvard Orient. Ser., Cambridge Mass., 1901 ; ed. Manomohan Ghosh, Calcutta Univ., 1939. Also ed. in the *Pandit*, Old Series, vii (1872-73).

3 Ed. Vamanacharya in the *Pandit*, Old Series, vi-vii (1871-73) ; ed. B. R. Arte, with comm. of Nārāyaṇa Dikṣita (18th century), Poona 1886 ; Eng. trs. by L. H. Gray in *JAOS*, XXVII, 1906, pp. 1-71. A critical edition of this work is desirable.

forms is written entirely in Prakrit.[1] The theme in both the plays is the traditional amorous intrigue of court-life ; but the flat rehandling would have made the plays insignificant had there not been song, dance, poetry and sentiment, even if the poetry is affected and the sentiment puny. There is an attempt at novelty in some scattered scenes and incidents, but the influence of Harṣa's *Ratnāvalī* is unmistakable. The influence, however, has not proved advantageous ; for, being weakly imitative, the treatment lacks vividness and coherence, the plot is poorly managed, and the characterisation is distinctly feeble. In the *Karpūramañjarī*, we have the conventional story of king Caṇḍapāla's light-hearted, but extremely sentimental, amour with a lovely maiden of unknown status, the machinations of the Vidūṣaka and the maiden's girl-friend to bring about the meeting of the lovers who pine helplessly for each other, the jealousy of the queen and the heroine's imprisonment. the final union and the queen's acceptance of the situation with the discovery that the heroine is a princess and her cousin and that marriage with her would lead to her husband's attainment of paramount sovereignty. The important variations are that there is no plotting minister behind the scheme, that the heroine is brought on the scene and into the palace by the Tāntric powers of the queen's spiritual guide, Bhairavānanda, that the king's access to the imprisoned girl is secured by making a subterranean passage, that another such passage is made enabling the prisoner to play an amusing, but silly, game of hide-and-seek with the queen, and that the queen is made to consent to the union by a hardly worthy trick played on her by her own preceptor Bhairavānanda.

1 The author himself states that the only difference is that the connecting scenes (Praveśakas and Viṣkambhakas) are wanting in the Saṭṭaka. It is suggested that a distinct kind of dancing was used in it. This play is practically the only example of the type we have. See Chintaharan Chakravarti in *IHQ*, VII, 1931, p. 169 f for a discussion of the nature of the Saṭṭaka. The definition of the *Sāhitya-darpana* is merely a generalisation of the characteristics of the present play.

We have the same general scheme of courtly comedy in the *Viddha-śālabhañjikā* ; but the intrigue is perhaps more varied between the two plays of Rājaśekhara than between the two similar plays of Harṣa. The unknown maiden, of course, turns out in the end to be a cousin becoming the co-wife ; but a better device is adopted in making her a hostage sent by her royal father to the palace of king Vidyādharamalla in the disguise of a boy, changing her name from Mṛgāṅkāvalī to Mṛgāṅka-varman. We have the old ruse of the minister Bhāgurāyaṇa (after Yaugandharāyaṇa) in arranging matters in such a way that the king falls headlong in love with the beautiful maiden. This is achieved through the motif of a dream-vision, which turns out to be an actual fact brought about by the minister's contrivance. The statue-device, from which the play takes its name, is in the same way not original, nor is it effectively employed as a central incident or motive. The entrance of the heroine is too long delayed, as she does not make her appearance till the middle of the third act and does not actually meet the king till a quarter of the fourth act is over. The usual complications and luxuriant descriptions of love, longing and secret meeting follow ; and there is nothing remarkable in them, except the trick which the king's friend, the Vidūṣaka, plays on the queen's foster-sister Mekhalā and the queen's induced design to avenge it by marrying the king to the boy of unsuspected sex, thereby outwitting herself by letting the king have what he desired. This last idea has points in its favour, but it is too much to make the *dénouement* follow from a puerile subsidiary incident concerning the Vidūṣaka alone, while the king is kept strangely in ignorance about the true import of the pretented marriage.

It must be admitted that Rājaśekhara has more inventiveness than Murāri, but, like Murāri, his style and treatment are chaotically poetic, rather than sensibly dramatic. In spite of a certain individuality and distinction, the note is essentially imitative ; the foot-marks of Harṣa, Bhavabhūti and even Murāri are too clear to be mistaken. Rājaśekhara claims the title of

Kavirāja and traces his poetic descent from the Ādi-kavi through Bhartṛmeṇṭha and Bhavabhūti, but this is only a mournful example of a bad poet and still worse dramatist not hesitating to put his own price on himself. Barring stray passages and incidents, Rājaśekhara's Rāma-drama, which mistakes quantity for quality, is an enormity in every sense. It would perhaps be unjust to criticise his two comedies of court-intrigue equally severely for lack of dramatic quality. Allowances should be made for the suggestion that they are conceived more as spectacular sentimental entertainments, having a slight plot, than as well-constructed plays, and that the main stress should be laid rather on beauty of diction and versification than on action and characterisation. But, apart from the fact that Rājaśekhara's poetry is facile and shallow, his diction conventional and his ideas full of far-fetched conceits, his two small plays of court-life lack the main interest of a comedy of intrigue, which should depend on a succession of lively incidents and lightly sketched pictures. The elaborate anatomy of theatrical passion, set forth in an equally elaborate mass of reflective and sentimental stanzas, is not only monotonous but hamper and disorganise the little action which the plays possess. The majority of these verse are, of course, out of place in a drama, but the illegitimate attraction of rhetorical poetry and tumid sentiment makes the author introduce them merely for the purpose of unnecessary display of his own skill and learning.

Rājaśekhara is conscious of this blemish of unnecessarily prolonged elaboration, which reaches its impossible limit in his *Bāla-rāmāyaṇa*, but he thinks (i. 12) that the main question is excellence of expression. In actual practice, however, this excellence degenerates into a varied and ingenious stylistic exercise and an entire disregard of all sense of proportion and propriety. His *forte* is not dramatic construction, nor is his hand competent to create living characters, but it is his inordinate love of style which kills all reality and vividness of his attempts in these directions. The pallid heroes and faint heroines are conventional and fail to be impressive with their sentimental effusiveness ; Rāvaṇa, with his amorous and pseudo-heroic rant, is no better ; Bhāgurāyaṇa is an insipid edition of Yaugandharāyaṇa ; while his typical Vidūṣakas are tedious with their pointless jokes and still more tasteless antics. The enlarged form of pathos and sentiment becomes a muddle of the lachrymose and the rhetorical. In fairness, it must be said, however, that Rājaśekhara can write elegant and swinging verses, and the introduction of song and dance diversifies the banality of his themes and sentimental outpourings. He has a considerable vocabulary of fine words and a fund of quaint conceits both in Sanskrit and in Prakrit, which bear out his boast that he is a master of languages. His decided ability to handle elaborate metres in Sanskrit and Prakrit, especially his favourite Śārdūlavikrīḍita (to which must be added Sragdharā and Vasantatilaka), justly deserves Kṣemendra's praise. Although his pictures of sunset, dawn and midday, or of the heroine's beauty and the hero's love-lorn condition, or of battles and mythical places, lose their interest on account of their artificial character, yet his weakness for elaborate description gives us some heightened, but vivid, accounts of the various aspects of court-life, its pleasures and its luxury. But Rājaśekhara does not seem to possess much critical sense, nor even the grace to be ashamed of faults which he has not the virtue to avoid. Even in poetry, for which he claims merit, his art is supremely conscious. His verses are often pleasant and always readable, but seldom touching ; and he flings out fine things and foolish things in *copia verborum* with equal enthusiasm or equal indifference. The rhetoricians and anthologists quote his verses with considerable admiration (though not always without censure); but even his best passages seek and receive applause more by meretricious rhetorical contrivances than by genuine poetic quality. He deliberately models his style and even copies from the splendid examples of poetry and drama of his predecessors, but he fails to transfer to his own works their ease and brilliancy.

3. Dramas with Legendary Themes and Comedies of Court-life

The popularity of Murāri and Rājaśekhara gave a charter to the production of a series of plays on the same worn out legendary and fictitious themes with greater artificiality and less dramatic power. Most of these plays are dramas of the Nāṭaka form, and also some Vyāyogas, which derive their themes from the two Epics and the Purāṇas ; while a few Nāṭikās still continue the tradition of the comedy of court-life. The number of Epic and Purāṇic plays is fairly large, but there is none of real merit which deserves detailed notice, although some of them are not altogether negligible and still retain their limited popularity. They do not fail entirely on the literary side, but as specimens of dramatic writing, they are mostly imitative and poor ; and over all of them presides the artificiality of decadence.

The *Prasanna-rāghava* of Jayadeva[1] is one such typical drama of this period, which is consciously based on earlier models, and stands for ever in a fatal bracket with the *Anargha-rāghava* of Murāri. The author is to be distinguished from several other Jayadevas, known to literary history, by his self-description that he was the son of Mahādeva of Kauṇḍinya Gotra and Sumitrā. His date is uncertain, but he can be assigned roughly to the 13th century.[2] Although in i. 18 he refers to his proficiency in logic, as well as in poetry, his identity with the logician Jayadeva Pakṣadhara of Mithilā lacks proof ; but he is certainly the author of a popular text-book on rhetoric, known as *Candrāloka*, from which he probably took the surname of Pīyūṣavarṣa. In rhetorical charm and smoothness of verse,[3] the

1 Ed. Govindadev Sastri, Benares 1868 (appeared in the *Pandit*, Old Series, ii-iii, 1867-69) ; ed. K. P. Parab, NSP, Bombay 1914 (1st ed. 1893) ; ed. S. M. Paranjpe and N. S. Panse, Poona 1894.

2 See S. K. De, *Sanskrit Poetics*, p. 215 f.

3 Jayadeva favours mostly the shorter Vasantatilaka metre, but the elaborate Śārdūla-vikrīḍita comes next. He knows much metrical variety and skill, and employs Svāgatā which si rare in the earlier drama.

play, like that of Murari, is naturally not wanting ; but it exhibits the same lack of dramatic sense, being deficient in unity of action and characterisation, and the same diffuse style and treatment. It adds more mannerisms and more insignificant (and even ludicrous) ideas and incidents. Jayadeva has no difficulty, for instance, in making a pupil of Yājñavalkya overhear the conversation of bees in Sanskrit, or in bringing the Asura Bāṇa, unnecessarily, as an insolent rival to Rāvaṇa for the hand of Sītā even before Rāma is thought of as such, or in arranging, after Duṣyanta and Śakuntalā, a preliminary meeting of Rāma and Sītā, in which they admire the union of the Vāsantī creeper and the mango-tree and whisper words of love, even before Śiva's bow is lifted ! After Sītā's abduction, Rāma is all but mad, and demands, after the approved style of Purūravas, his beloved from the moon and the birds, until a Vidyādhara, by his power of magic, shows the events of Laṇkā and gives ocular demonstration of Sītā's faithfulness and chastity. The coals at the fire-ordeal turn into perals ; and there is at the end the inevitable aerial journey of Rāma and his party. Some of the incidents in the play are of course, reported instead of being represented, but mercifully Jayadeva is not so prolix in description and declamation as Murāri and Rājaśekhara. His play attains a comparatively respectable dimension, the total number of verses being three hundred and ninety-two, although the last act alone includes ninety-four verses. The only novel feature, however, of the play is the interesting spectacular scene of the five river-goddesses gathered round the ocean, but it is loosely connected with the main action.

Of the existence of several Rāma-dramas even before the 12th century we have only meagre information from the *Nāṭya-darpaṇa*, in which Rāmacandra and Guṇacandra[1] mention and

1 Both were pupils of the Jaina Ācārya Hemacandra and lived in the times of Kumārapala and Ajayapāla (c. 1143-75 A.D.). Rāmacandra is the reputed author of a hundred works, including no less than eleven dramas. See introd. to *Nala-vilāsa* and *Nātya-darpaṇa*, ed. Gaekwad's Orient. Series, Baroda 1926, 1929.

quote from the *Jāmadagnya-jaya* (Vyāyoga), from the *Abhinava-rāghava* (Nāṭaka) of Kṣīrasvāmin, pupil of Bhaṭṭendurāja and from *Kundamālā* (Nāṭaka) of Vīranāga, besides from Rāma-candra's own *Raghu-vilāsa* and *Rāghavābhyudaya* (both Nāṭakas). None of these is available, except the *Kunda-mālā*.[1] This drama has the same theme, in six acts, as Bhavabhūti's *Uttara-rāma-carita*, on which it is obviously modelled ; but there is hardly anything remarkable in its style and treatment except the pretty but ineffective device of a garland of Kunda flowers as a token of recognition. The other Rāma-dramas are even much less interesting, and when they are not imitative they are insignificant. Most of them are still in manuscript. Of the published and better known of these, the *Unmatta-rāghava*,[2] called a Prekṣāṇaka, of Bhāskara is a curious little play in one act, which describes Rāma's search and maddened soliloquies (obviously after Purūravas of Kālidāsa) on Sītā's transformation into a gazelle by the curse of the ever irascible sage Durvāsas and her recovery with the help of Agastya. The *Adbhut-darpana*[3] in ten acts, of Mahādeva, son of Kṛṣṇa Sūri of the Kauṇḍinya Gotra, who belonged to Tanjore towards the middle of the 17th century, begins with Aṅgada's mission to Rāvaṇa and ends with Rāma's coronation, the work deriving its title from the interesting device of a magic mirror (conceived after *Prasanna-rāghava* iv) which shows to Rāma the happenings at Laṅkā.

[1] Ed. M. Ramkrishna Kavi and S. K. Ramanatha Sastri, Dakṣiṇabhāratī Series, Madras 1923. The attribution to Diṅnāga is unauthentic. See S. K. De in *JRAS*, 1924, pp. 663-64 ; Woolner in *ABORI*, XV, pp. 236-39 and S. K. De in *ibid*, XVI, 1935, p. 158. The work is quoted in the *Sāhitya-darpaṇa* vi. 36 (= Prologue, stanza 2, with prose). There are passages in the drama obviously imitative of Kālidāsa, Bhavabhūti and Bāṇabhaṭṭa ; and it shows little dramatic power.

[2] Ed. Durgaprasad and K. P. Parab, NSP, Bombay 1889, 1925. It was composed to entertain an assembly of learned men who had come to do honour to Vidyāraṇya. If this Vidyāraṇya is identical with the famous scholar of that name, then the work may be assigned to the 14th century. In his *Kāvyānuśāsana* (p. 97, comm.), Hemacandra quotes a passage from a drama entitled *Unmatta-rāghava*, but the passage is not traceable in Bhāskara's work.

[3] Ed. Sivadatta and K. P. Parab, NSP, Bombay 1906. The author's teacher Bālakṛṣṇa was a contemporary of Nīlakaṇṭha, whose *Nīlakaṇṭha-vijaya* Campū is dated 1636 A.D.

The *Jānakī-pariṇaya*[1] of Mahādeva's contemporary, Rāmabhadra Dīkṣita, son of Yajñarāma Dīkṣita and pupil of Nīlakaṇṭha Dīkṣita, is in seven acts, and has the only peculiarity of introducing a curious but silly jumble of confusing disguises, adopted by the Rākṣasas masquerading as Viśvāmitra, Rāma, Lakṣmaṇa and Sītā.[2]

The plays which deal similarly with the Mahābhārata legends are also numerous, but they do not call for any detailed account. The industrious Kashmirian polymath Kṣemendra, towards the second half of the 11th century, mentions a *Citra-bhārata* (Nāṭaka)[3] composed by himself, which has not survived. The other polymath Rāmacandra, pupil of the Jaina Ācārya Hemacandra, has left behind *Nala-vilāsa*,[4] a Nāṭaka in seven acts, on the well-worn story of Nala, and the *Nirbhaya-bhīma*,[5] a one-act Vyāyoga on the story of the slaying of the Baka-demon ; but both are laboured compositions by one who was well versed in dramaturgic rules. The Kerala prince Kulaśekhara, whose date is uncertain but who probably lived between the first half of the 10th and the first half of the 12th century,[6] produced two plays, named *Tapatī-saṃvaraṇa*[7] and *Subhadrā-dhanañjaya*,[8] the

[1] Printed many times. Ed. Laksmana Suri, Tanjore 1906. Rāmabhadra also wrote a Bhāṇa called *Śṛṅgāra-tilaka* (ed. Kedarnath and V. L. Panshikar, NSP, Bombay 1910, which see for an account of the author). See T. S. Kuppusvami Sastri in *IA*, XXXIII, 1904, p. 126 f, 176 f. Content of the drama summarised by Lévi, p. 286 f.

[2] The *Dūtāṅgada* and *Mahānāṭaka* will be dealt with below, under Dramas of an Irregular Type.

[3] *Aucityavicāra°* *ad* 31 ; *Kavikaṇṭhābharaṇa* v. 1. Also a *Kanaka-jānakī*, probably a drama, cited in the last work, apparently on the Rāmāyaṇa story.

[4] Ed. G. K. Srigondekar, Gaekwad's Orient. Ser., Baroda, 1926. It also uses the device of inset play. On the Nala-legend, Kṣemīśvara also appears to have written a *Naiṣa-dhānanda* in seven acts (MS, dated 1611 A.D., noticed by Peterson, *Three Reports*, pp. 340-42). Other plays on the same theme, like the *Bhaumī-pariṇaya* of Ratnakheṭa Dīkṣita are not yet in print, but the *Nala-caritra* of Nīlakaṇṭha Dīkśita (about 1636 A.D.), in seven acts, is edited by C. Sankararama Sastri, Bālamanoramā Press, Madras 1925.

[5] Ed. Haragovinda Das, Yaśovijaya Granthamālā no. 19, Benares, Vīra Era 2437 (=1911 A.D.).

[6] K. Rama Pisharoti (IHQ. VII, 1931, p. 319-30) would place the dramatist at the close of the 7th and beginning of the 8th century A.D., but his arguments are not convincing.

[7] Ed. T. Gaṇapati Sastri with the comm. of Śivarāma, Trivandrum Sansk. Ser., 1911.

[8] Ed. T. Ganapati Sastri, with comm. of Śivarāma, Trivandrum Sansk. Ser., 1912.

titles of which sufficiently explain their respective themes. The first, which deals with the legend of the Kuru king Saṃvaraṇa and Tapatī, daughter of the sun-god, is rather a narrative in a loose dramatic form of six acts, utilising the conventional devices of the vision of the beloved in dream, meeting of lovers in the course of a royal hunt, the inevitable longing and sentimentalities, union, abduction and final reunion, with plenty of supernatural and marvellous incidents ; while the second selects a theme, which has erotic and heroic possibilities, but less dramatic quality, and which does not improve by conventional treatment in five acts. Another Kerala prince Ravivarman, *alias* Saṃgrāmadhīra, of Kolambapura (Quillon), born in 1265 A.D., derives his story of Kṛṣṇa's son from the *Hari-vaṃśa* and the Purāṇas in his five-act drama *Pradyumnābhyudaya.*[1] Though the plot is scanty and conventionally constructed, it is interesting for its device of making Pradyumna join a troupe of actors in order to get an entry into the inaccessible city of Prabhāvatī's father, and in introducing a play within play for the first sight of the lovers at a theatre ; it also shows some dramatic sense and use of prose, as well as moderation in the size of the acts and in number of sentimental and descriptive stanzas ; but one whole act is devoted to the elaboration of the lovers' longings, and the general artificiality of style and treatment cannot be mistaken. The Yuvarāja Prahlādanadeva, son of Yaśodhara and brother Dhārāvarṣa ruler of Candrāvatī, wrote a Vyāyoga, entitled *Prātha-parākrama,*[2] in about 1208 A.D. It dramatises in one Act the martial story of Arjuna's recovery of the cows of Virāṭa raided by the Kurus ; but allowing the merit of smooth verses, which the author himself claims, it does not deserve any special recognition. The same theme in the same form of a Vyāyoga

1 Ed. T. Ganapati Sastri, Trivandrum Sansk. Ser., 1910. On the author see Kielhorn in *Epi. Ind.*, IV, p. 145 f.

2 Ed. C. D. Dalal, Gaekwad's Orient. Ser., Baroda 1917. It was enacted on the occasion of the festival of Acaleśvara, the tutelary deity of Maunt Abu. The prince is extolled by Someśvara in his *Surathotsava*.

is attempted also by Kāñcanācārya, son of Nārāyaṇa, in his *Dhanañjaya-vijaya*;[1] and the story of Subhadrā's elopement is adopted for dramatisation in one act by Mādhava Bhaṭṭa, son of Maṇḍaleśvara Bhaṭṭa and Indumatī, in his *Subhadrā-haraṇa* (called a Śrīgadita),[2] but with no better success. The Draupadī legend is similarly dramatised in two acts by Vijayapāla, son of Siddhapāla, who was a contemporary of the Caulukya Kumārapāla,[3] in his *Draupadī-svayaṃvara,*[4] but there is little originality in the handling of the old story. The *Saugandhikā-haraṇa*[5] of Viśvanātha, a protégé of the Kākatīya ruler Pratāparudra of Warangal (about 1291-1322 A.D.), is a lively one-act Vyāyoga, like the *Kalyāṇa-saugandhika*[6] of the Kerala author Nīlakaṇṭha, both of which deal with Bhīma's encounter and vehement altercation with Hanūmat, his unknown half-brother, in his adventure of fetching the Saugandhikā flowers for Draupadī from a mysterious lake belonging to Kubera.[7]

The allied Kṛṣṇa legend also claims a large number of plays. Perhaps on account of the more emotional nature of the theme, some variation is noticeable, but most of the plays are late and are not of much interest.[8] Besides the *Gopāla-keli-candrikā* of

1 Ed. Sivadatta and K. P. Parab, NSP, Bombay 1885, 1911. On the author, see Sten Konow, p. 118.

2 Ed. Durgaprasad and K. P. Parab, NSP, Bombay 1888 As a MS of the work belongs to Saṁvat 1667 (=1610 A.D.), the work is earlier than that date, and possibly later than that of the *Sāhitya-darpaṇa* vi, whose definition of Śrīgadita it follows.

3 See E. Hultzsch in *ZDMG*, LXXV, 1921, pp. 67-68.

4 Ed. Muni Jinavijaya, Jaina Ātmānanda Sabhā, Bhavnagar 1918. The work utilises the device of splitting up a verse and distributing its parts to different persons as a continuous metrical dialogue.—Hastimalla, pupil of Govindabhaṭṭa, wrote about 1290 A.D. in Southern India two epic dramas, *Vikrānta kaurava* in six acts and *Maithilī-ka yāṇa* in five acts. Both these works have been printed in Manikacandra Digambara Granthamālā, but they are of only modest merit.

5 Ed. Sivadatta and K. P. Parab, NSP, Bombay 1902.

6 Ed. L. D. Barnett in *BSOS*, III, 1923, pp. 33-50 (Roman characters); ed. L. Sarup, Hindi Press, Lahore, no date. It is also a Vyāyoga in one act. The common source of both these works is of course the Vanaparavan. The author was probably a contemporary of Kulaśekhara Varman of Kerala (see introd. to *Āścarya-cūḍāmaṇi*, p. 9).

7 For other Mahābhārata plays, see Sten Konow, pp. 102 f.

8 For a list of Kṛṣṇa-dramas, which are still in manuscript, see Sten Konow, pp. 99-102.

Rāmakṛṣṇa, to be mentioned presently, we have the *Yādavābhyudaya* of the indefatigable Rāmacandra, not yet published but mentioned in his *Nātya-darpaṇa*, the *Kṛṣṇa-bhakti-candrikā*[1] of Anantadeva, son of Āpadeva, the *Rukmiṇī-pariṇayā*[2] (in five acts) of Rāmavarman Vañci of Travancore (1755-87 A.D.), the *Vaidarbhī-vāsudeba*[3] of Sundararāja, son of Varadarāja (also of Kerala), the *Rukminī-haraṇa* of Śeṣa Cintāmaṇi, son of Śeṣa Nṛsiṃha (before 1675 A.D.), the *Vṛṣabhānujā*[4] (a four act Nāṭikā) of Kāyastha Mathurādāsa, and *Kaṃsa-vadha*[5] (in seven acts) of Śeṣa Kṛṣṇa, son of Nṛsiṃha. The Caitanya movement of Bengal and Orissa also produced, towards the middle of the 16th century, some devotional plays on Kṛṣṇa-Bhakti, among which mention may be made of the *Vidagdha-mādhava* (in seven acts), the *Lalita-Mādhava* (in ten acts) and *Dāna-keli-kaumudī*[6] (called a Bhāṇikā without acts divison) of Rūpa Gosvāmin, and the *Jagannātha-vallabha*[7] (in five acts) of Rāmānanda-rāya. The first three works are deliberate attempts to illustrate the doctrinal nuances of the emotional Bhakti in terms of the old romantic Kṛṣṇa-legend, while the last work describes itself as a Saṃgīta-nāṭaka and contains Padāvalis or songs in imitation of those of Jayadeva. There can be no doubt that these works constitute a departure, and are inspired by great devotional fervour of a refined erotico-religious character,

1 Ed. Kavyetihāsa-saṁgraha, Poona 1878-88 ; also ed. Granthamālā, Bombay 1887.

2 Ed. Sivadatta and K. P. Parab, NSP, Bombay 1894.

3 Ed. Tinnevelli, 1888.

4 Ed. Sivadatta and K. P. Parab, NSP, Bombay 1895 ; also ed. in the *Pandit*, Old Series, iii-iv (1868-69). The author probably flourished in the 15th century.

5 Ed. Durgaprasad and K. P. Parab, NSP, Bombay 1888. The author lived in the time of Akbar and wrote the work for Todar Mall's son.

6 All these works are published by the Radharaman Press, Berhampur, Murshidabad in Bengali characters, respectively in 1924, 1902 and 1926. The *Vidagdha-mādhava* is also ed. Bhavadatta and K. P. Parab, NSP, Bombay 1903 ; it was composed in 1533 A.D. The author was a disciple of Caitanya and one of the recognised Gosvāmins who systematised the dogmas and doctrines of the cult (see S. K. De, introd. to *Padyāvalī*, Dacca 1934).

7 Ed. Radharaman Press, Berhampur-Murshidabad 1882 (in Bengali characters).

as well as by acute scholastic learning (a strange combination !); but their interest is other than literary, and they have little pretension to the dramatic in the proper sense.[1]

On wider mythological subjects, it is more difficult to single out any striking work out of some forty, which are known to exist, but very few of which are in print. The *Hara-keli* of the Cāhamāna king, Vīsaladeva Vigraharāja of Śākambharī (Sambhar), has the same theme as Bhāravi's poem, but it is only partially preserved in a stone-inscription[2] at Ajmere ; while his protégé Somadeva, in the first half of the 12th century, wrote a similarly preserved Nāṭaka (engraved in 1153 A.D.) named *Lalita-vigraharāja*, in honour of the king, describing the king's love for princess Desaladevī of Indrapura. The *Pārvatī-pariṇaya*, which we have already mentioned, is an unorginal and undoubtedly late production, while there is little merit in the *Rati-manmatha* (a Nāṭaka in five acts)[3] of Jagannātha, son of Bālakṛṣṇa and Lakṣmī and pupil of Kāmeśvara. Out of the plays which deal with the Purāṇa story of Hariścandra, the *Satya-hariścandra*[4] (in six acts) of Rāmacandra, pupil of Ācārya Hemacandra, is of the same character as his *Nata-vilāsa* mentioned above. The *Caṇḍa-kauśika*[5] of Ācārya Kṣemīśvara deals

1 For a detailed account of these works and authors see S. K. De, *Early History of the Vaiṣṇava Faith in Bengal*, ch. vii,

2 F. Kielhorn, *Brūchstūcke indischer Schauspiele in Inschriften zu Ajmere*, Berlin 1901 ; Sanskrit Plays, partly preserved as inscriptions at Ajmere, in *IA*, XX, 1891, p. 201-12 (part of the text in Roman characters) ; also in *NGGW*, 1893, pp. 552-70 (Lalitavigraharāja, Text Roman).

3 Ed. Granthamala iii-iv, Bombay 1890-91. The *Manmatha-mohana* of Rāma of the Kauśikayāna Gotra (ed. with summary of contents by R. Schmidt in *ZDMG*, LXIII, 1909, p. 409 f, 629 f) deals with the same theme of Śiva's temptation, but it is probably a late work, one of its MSS being dated 1820 A.D.

4 Ed. B. R. Apte and S. V. Puranik, NSP, Bombay 1898, 1909. The work is cited in his *Natya-darpaṇa*.

5 Ed. Jaganmohan, Tarkalamkara, Calcutta 1867 (reprinted by Jivananda Vidyasagar, Calcutta 1884) ; ed. in Litho MS form, Krishna Sastri Gurjara Press, Bombay 1860 ; trs. into German verse under the title *Kauśika's Zorn* by Ludwig Fritze, Leipzig 1883. Kṣemīśvara describes himself as Ācārya ; but his father's name is not given.

with the same theme in five acts, but there is nothing distinctive in its style and treatment. Kṣemīśvara was probably a younger contempory of Rājaśekhara; for a verse in the Prologue states that the work was composed and produced at the court of Mahīpāla, who is sometimes taken to be Mahīpāla of Bengal,[1] but who is probably the same as Rājaśekhara's patron, Mahīpāla Bhuvanaikamalla of Kānyakubja.[2] The play works out the effect of a curse of the irascible sage Viśvāmitra upon the upright king Hariścandra, who unwittingly offends him; it involves the loss of kingdom, wife and child, but ends in restoration of everything to the satisfaction of all concerned. There is some interest in the idea of trial of character by suffering, but the piling up of disasters as an atonement of what appears to be an innocent offence unnecessarily prolongs the agony, and the divine intervention at the end is, as usual, dramatically too flat. The story itself, despite its pathos, lacks dramatic quality, and improves very little by the poor execution and mediocre poetry of Kṣemīśvara. The Jaina form of the Buddhist legend of the sacrifice of Śibi (the name changed to Vajrāyudha) is similarly dramatised in one act, with a Jaina background, by Ācarya Bālacandra,[3] a pupil of Haribhadra Sūri,

1 Suggested by H. P. Sastri (*Descriptive Cat. of Skt. Mss.* in *ASB*, vii, Calcutta 1934), on the ground that the Prologue speaks of king Mahīpāla as having driven away (in 1023 A.D.), the Karṇātakas, who, in Sastri's opinion, were the invading armies of Rājendra Cola I, or the Karṇāṭakas who came in the train of Cedi kings at a later time. It is noteworthy that the two oldest palm-leaf manuscripts of the drama, dated respectively in 1250 and 1387 A.D., were found in Nepal, and that the only Alaṁkāra work which cites the drama is the *Sāhitya-darpaṇa* of Viśvanātha, which belongs to Orissa in the first half of the 15th century.

2 Pischel in *Göttingische gelehrte Anzeigen*, 1883, p. 1220 f. Kṣemīśvara's assertion of his patron's victory over the Karṇāṭaka's is explained as the courtier's version of the conflict with Rāṣṭrakūta Indra III, who for his part claims victory over Kānyakubja (*IA*, XXXVI, pp. 175-79). See discussion of the question by S. K. Aiyangar in *Sir Asutosh Jubilee Comm. Vol*, Orientalia, pt. 2, p. 559 f; R. D. Banerji, *Pālas of Bengal*. p. 73, *JBORS*, XIV, p. 512 f; J. C. Ghosh in *Ind. Culture*, II, pp. 354-56; K. A. Nilkantha, Sastri in *JORM*, VI, pp. 191-98 and *Ind. Culture*, II, pp. 797-99.

3 See E. Hultzsch in *ZDMG*, LXXXV, 1921, p. 68.

in his *Karuṇā-vajrāyudha,*[1] but it is not necessary to linger over this and other specimens of mythological plays.[2]

The Nāṭikā, which generally deals with stories of court-life of a legendary or fictious character, appears to have induced even a smaller number of imitations, and the type is found even more rigidly fixed by the works of Harṣa and Rājaśekhara. There is still some literary skill in turning out fine verses, but the specimens that we possess are poorly conventional. They all speak the same language and have the same set of situations, feelings and ideas. In their tragic interest they court the hopelessly unreal, in their comedy the insipidly banal. A bare notice of a few typical plays will, therefore, suffice. Kṣemendra speaks of a *Lalita-ratna-mālā,* written by himself,[3] probably on the Udayana legend, but the work has not been recovered. The *Nāṭya-darpaṇa* also mentions a few Nāṭikās, now lost, namely, *Anaṅgavatī* (p. 153), *Indulekhā* (p. 114) and *Kauśalikā* by Bhavatanucūḍa Bhaṭṭa (p. 30), as well as *Vanamālā* by Rāmacandra himself (p. 171). Of extant plays, some comparatively early works may be briefly noticed here just to indicate their general tenor and treatment. The first is the *Karṇaśundarī*[4] of the Kashmirian Bihlaṇa, who belonged to the second half of the 11th century, and apparently wrote this work as a compliment to the Caulukya Karṇadeva Trailokyamalla of Aṇhilvad (1064-94 A.D.), whose actual marriage to a princess it celebrates under the guise of a romantic story. In four acts it rehandles, with little originality, the old theme of the king falling in love, first in a dream and then in a picture, with Karṇasundarī, who is introduced into the palace

1 Ed. Muni Caturvijaya, Jaina Ātmānanda Granthamālā, Bhavnagar 1916. It is called a Nāṭaka, but like the *Dūtāṅgada* mentioned below, it consists of only a Prastāvanā and one long act containing 135 stanzas. It is thus an irregular play having no act-division, and the long descriptive stage-direction (in 8 printed lines) on p. 22 is interesting in this connexion.

2 The Kuvalayāśva legend is also dealt with by some later plays of the 17th century, for which, as well as for other mythological dramas, see Sten Konow, pp. 103-107.

3 *Aucitya-vicara, ad* 21.

4 Ed. Durgaprasad and K. P. Parab, NSP, Bombay 1888.

through the usual minister's intrigue, of the queen's jealousy and attempt to marry the king, in revenge, to a boy in the heroine's disguise, frustrated by the minister's clever but expected substitution of the real person,—a poor recast obviously of the *Ratnāvalī* and the *Viddha-śālabhañjikā*. A similar theme, as well as treatment, is also seen in the *Pārijātamañjarī*[1] or *Vijayaśrī* of Madana, surnamed Bāla-sarasvatī of Gauḍa, who was a preceptor of the Paramāra king Arjunavarman of Dhārā and belonged to the first quarter of the 13th century. The play, composed at about 1213 A.D., is recovered incomplete, but it appears to be a distinct imitation of the *Ratnāvalī*. The only variation in the general scheme is that it takes (like *Karṇasundarī*) the contemporary king himself as the hero, and that the unknown beloved, apparently a girl not of royal blood but made into a princess by the fiction of reincarnation, is introduced into the palace in the form of a miracle and picturesque allegory of a garland of Pārijāta flowers,[2] dropping on the breast of the victorious king and changing into a beautiful maiden! A similar device of a magic lotus, presented to the queen, in which the heroine is discovered, is found in the *Kamalinī-kalahaṃsa*[3] of Rājacūḍāmaṇi Dīkṣita, a prolific South Indian writer, who was the son of Satyamaṅgala Ratnakheṭa Śrīnivāsādhvarin and flourished under Raghunātha Nāyaka of Tanjore in the earlier part of the 17th century: but the play is a close imitation, in four acts, of *Viddha-śalabhañjikā*, and introduces the well worn motifs of drama-vision, love in a picture, statue of the heroine, the jealous queen's attempt to marry the king in revenge to a disguised boy, who of course turns out to be the heroine, and the ultimate discovery of her

[1] Only the first two acts which remain are edited by E. Hultzsch. Leipzig and Bombay 1906. As these two acts are preserved in stone-inscription at Dhārā (1211-1215 A.D.), it probably contains a historical reference to Arjunavarman's marraige with the Caulukya princess, daughter of Bhīmadeva II of Aṇahillapāṭaka.

[2] The name of the Princess itself probably suggested to the poet the idea of her miraculous appearance, as a piece of graceful compliment.

[3] Ed. Śrī-vāṇīvilāsa Press, Srirangam 1917, with an introd. by T. H. Kuppusvamy Sastry on the author and his works. See also S. K. De, *Sanskrit Poetics*, i, pp. 307-8.

status as a princely cousin of the queen ; there is some stylistic display but little originality or variety. We shall close this account with a passing mention of the *Mṛgāṅkalekhā*[1] of Viśvanātha, son of Trimaladeva, as one of the latest specimens of such imitative comedies of court-life. It depicts in four acts the love of Karpūratilaka, king of Kaliṅga, for Mṛgāṅkalekhā, daughter of the king of Kāmarūpa ; she is met at a hunt and lodged in the palace as the friend of the queen, and then abducted to the temple of Kālī by a demon named Śaṅkhapāla, who is killed by the king with the help of a benevolent magician ; but a second rescue (after Bhavabhūti) is staged by the attack of Śaṅkhapāla's brother, who comes in the form of a wild elephant ![2]

The extreme form in which dramaturgic conventions reacted upon the mind of the aspiring dramatist is best seen in a series of four mythological and two erotic and comic plays,[3] composed deliberately to illustrate six, out of ten, recognised forms of Sanskrit drama, by Vatsarāja, who describes himself as the minister of Paramardideva of Kālañjara (1163-1203 A.D.). Although considerable literary craftsmanship of the conventional kind is displayed, the author is a sturdy devotee of the canons, and his artificially constructed plays are nothing but literary curiosities. The first, but probably composed last, is the one-act Vyāyoga, called *Kirātārjunīya* and based obviously on Bhāravi's poem of the same title ; the second is a Samavakāra in three acts, named *Samudra-mathana*, on the legend of the churning of the ocean by gods and demons, leading to the winning of Lakṣmī by Viṣṇu ; the third, *Rukminī-haraṇa*, is an Īhāmṛga

1 Ed. N. S. Khiste, Sarasvati Bhavana Texts, Benares 1929. Analysed by Wilson. The play was enacted during the festival of Viśveśvara at Benares. The author came originally from the banks of the Godāvarī.

2 Analysis, with extracts, of a Nātika, named *Vāsantika*, by Rāmacandra in four acts, given by Eggeling, *Catalogue of India Office Manuscripts*, vii, no. 4186 p. 1600 f ; of another Nātikā in four acts, named *Śṛṅgāra-vāṭikā* (or *vāpikā*) by Viśvanātha Bhaṭṭa, son of Mādhavabhaṭṭa of Cittapāvana family, no. 4196, p, 1615 f.

3 Ed. C. D. Dalal under the title *Rūpaka-ṣaṭka* in Gaekward's Orient Series, Baroda 1918. A verse of Vātsarāja is quoted by Jahlaṇa in his *Sūkti-muktāvali*, but it is not traceable in the plays.

in four acts, in which Kṛṣṇa successfully tricks and deprives Śiśupāla of his affianced bride ; the fourth is the *Tripura-dāha,*[1] a Ḍima in four acts, on the legend of Śiva's destruction of the city of the demon Tripura ; the fifth is the one-act Bhāṇa, entitled *Karpūra carita,* conventional but more lively than later Bhāṇas, giving the Viṭa Karpūraka's recital of his love, gambling and revelry ; and the last is a Prahasana or farce, named *Hāsya-cūḍāmaṇi,* in which are depicted the ways of Jñānaśrī, a Bhāgavata, who earns his livelihood by his amusing tricks based upon his pretension of supernatural powers for recovering lost articles. Barring the two lighter plays, which are not negligible, it would be idle to pretend that the productions have much dramatic force and vividness. The works are typical of one aspect of decadence, namely, its lifeless conformity to dramaturgic rules, regarding plot, diction, characterisation and sentiment, and, being comparatively late and obviously bookish, the works can scarcely be taken as representing a living tradition of such rare types of the drama as the Samavakāra, Īhāmṛga and Ḍima.

4. Dramas of Middle Class Life and Plays of Semi-historical Interest

An epoch of dramatic writing, which relegated real life to the background and took little interest in incident and action, cannot be expected to follow the difficult examples set by the authors of the *Mṛcchakaṭika* and the *Mudrā-rākṣasa.* As a specimen of the so-called Prakaraṇa type of plays, we have already dealt with the *Mallikā-māruta* of Uddaṇḍin, which is a curious but confused imitation of Bhavabhūti's *Mālatī-mādhava.* It would have been interesting if the *Kāmadatta,* cited and described as a Dhūrta-prakaraṇa by the author of the *Rasārṇava-sudhākara,* had survived ; but the general model of all later plays, mostly Prakaraṇas, of middle-class life, is not the *Mṛcchakaṭika* but the

[1] The themes of *Tripura-dāha* and *Samudra-mathana* are doubtless suggested by Bharata's reference to lost works of these names.

Mālatī-mādhava. They present (so far as we can judge from those which are extant) a curious medley of sentimental verses and well-worn Kathā incidents, with a free use of all the ordinary novelistic devices and of magic and marvel. The bourgeois spirit of the popular tale is naturally there ; but the works show little touch of life and freshness of observation, and the tales are hardly marked by the blithe realism of Daṇḍin tempered by strange romance. The lay man was probably still full of mercantile energy, but he was apparently not waking up to the new intelligence, or perhaps was losing the old zest in life. If he still retained a vivid interest in things around him, he had perhaps a greater inclination to beguile himself with weird tales of wonder and childish sentimentalities. The plays, therefore, faithfully reflect this attitude, and the little poetic realism, which developed in the earlier period, becomes lost in the extravagances of fancy and sentiment.

In his *Nāṭya-darpaṇa* Rāmacandra mentions and quotes from a Prakaraṇa, named *Anaṅgasenā-harinandi,* and also from three plays of the same class by himself, namely, *Mallikā-makaranda, Rohiṇī-mṛgāṅka* and *Kaumudī-mitrānanda.* Of these, the last-named Prakaraṇa in ten acts alone is published.[1] It is typical of the later play of this kind in having a complicated series of narrative, rather than dramatic, incidents.[2] The theme is the elopement of Mitrānanda, son of a merchant, with Kaumudī, the worldly-wise daughter of a sham-ascetic, from an imaginary island of Varuṇa, and their subsequent adventures in Siṃhala and other places, including the subsidiary story of the hero's friend Makaranda, who is married to Sumitrā, daughter of a merchant. With a frank zest for the strange and the marvellous, the plot utilises some of the common motifs of story telling, such as the device of a love-charm, of a magic spell (received from the goddess Jāṅgulī) for the cure of snake-bite, of magic herbs for removing disease, of human sacrifice, and of a

1 Ed. Muni Punyavijaya, Jaina Ātmānanda Granthamālā, Bhavnagar 1917.

2 The plot is summarised by Hultzsch in *ZDMG,* LXXV, pp. 63-65.

wicked Kāpālika breathing life into a corpse! The story resembles those of Daṇḍin's *Daśakumāra-carita*, and the author might have done well if he had attempted to write in the same strain and form; for there is not much merit in the play as a dramatic piece, nor is it remarkable on the poetic side. Even less meritorious is another Prakaraṇa, entitled *Prabuddha rauhiṇeya*,[1] by Rāmabhadra, pupil of Jinaprabha Sūri (about 13th century) of the school of the logician Devasūri, who died in 1169 A.D. In six acts it dramatises the Jaina story of the misdeeds, incarceration and penitence of a bandit, named Rauhiṇeya, but the plot is meagre and the play is wholly undramatic. The *Mudrita-kumudacandra*[2] of Yaśaścandra, son of Padmacandra and grandson of Dhanadeva, a minister of a prince of Śākambharī, hardly deserves mention in this connexion; for it is not so much a drama as a record in five acts of the controversy, which took place in 1124 A.D., in the presence of king Jayasiṃha of Gujarat (1094-1142), between two Jaina teachers, the Śvetāmbara Devasūri and the Digambara Kumudacandra, in which the latter, with a pun on his name, was completely sealed up (*mudrita*). The extremely limited number of Prakaraṇas, which followed these and which were composed more or less on the same pattern, need not detain us further, and very few of them are available in print.[3]

Of the plays of the type of the *Mudrā-rākṣasa* which possess a semi-historical interest, very great antiquity is claimed for the nameless drama, which has been published from the Madras transcript of a unique manuscript discovered in Malabar, and named *Kaumudī-mahotsava*[4] by its editor from the

1 Ed. Muni Punyavijaya, Jaina Ātmānanda Granthamālā, Bhavnagar 1918. Summarised by Hultzsch in above, pp. 66-67.

2 Ed. Jaina Yaśovijaya Granthamālā, Benares, Vīra Era 2432 (=A.D. 1906). Analysed by Hultzsch, as above, pp. 61-62.

3 For a list and running account, see Sten Konow, pp. 110-111.

4 Ed. M. Ramakrishna Kavi and S. K. Ramanatha Sastri, Dakṣiṇabhāratī Series, Madras 1929. The MS was transcribed for the Government Oriental MS Library, Madras. See *Quarterly Jour. af Andhra Research Soc.*, II-III, 1927-29.

expression being used in the Prologue. The name of the author is also not known, as nothing remains of the part which contained it in the Prologue, except the broken letters *kayā nibaddhaṃ nāṭakam*, from which it is conjectured that the author was a woman and her name was Vijjakā (reading *vijjakayā* in the lacuna), well known from the anthologies.[1] We are told in the Prologue that the play was enacted at the coronation of king Kalyāṇavarman of Pāṭaliputra, and its theme appears to be an episode of the king's life. It speaks of the defeat and death of Kalyāṇavarman's father Sundaravarman at the hands of Canḍasena, his general, who conspired with the Licchavis, and takes for its subject-matter the reinstatement of Kalyāṇavarman on the throne of Maghadha by the efforts of the minister Mantragupta. There is possibly some historic background to the plot, but we cannot with certainty identify the characters of the play with historic persons,[2] nor do we know anything about its authorship or period of composition.[3] The plot is a commonplace political intrigue, but it is eclipsed by the equally commonplace story of the love of Kalyāṇavarman for Kīrtimatī, daughter of Kīrtisena, a Yādava King of Śūrasena. There is a nun or Parivrājikā, named of Yogasiddhi, who has been once a nurse to Kalyāṇavarman, but who later on becomes attached to the royal family of Śūrasena and accompanies Kīrtimatī in a pilgrimage to Vindhya-

1 The date of Vijjā or Vijjakā is uncertain, but she is probably later than Daṇḍin of the *Kavyādarśa*. We cannot be sure whether she is identical with Vijaya-bhaṭṭārikā, queen of Candraditya.—In iv. 19, there is a mention of Vijaya and the god Anantanārāyaṇa, supposed to be the same as the deity of Trivandrum. But it is possible to make too much of the passage.—Jayaswal ingeniously infers the name of the author to be Kīśorikā from a supposed pun in verse 2.

2 K. P. Jayaswal (*ABORI*, XII, 1930-31, pp. 50-56; *JBORS*, XIX, p. 313f) would identify Candasena with Candragupta I and place the drama at about 340 A.D. But his views are entirely conjectural and lack corroboration.

3 The reference to the story of Udayana (i. 11), of Śaunaka and Bandhumatī, and of Avimaraka and Kuraṅgī (ii. 15, repeated v. 9), or to Dattaka (v. 7), Goṇikāputra and Mūladeva, do not warrant any definite chronological conclusion. There are obvious imitations of passages from Kālidāsa, Bhāravi and Bhavabhūti, and the drama must be placed later than the 8th century. The parallel passages are given by D. R. Mankad in *JBORS*, XVI 1934-35, pp. 155-57, and Dasaratha Sarma in *IHQ*, X, 1934, pp. 763-66.

vāsinī ; but the part she plays in bringing about the union of the lovers is almost negligible. Neither is the political intrigue nor the erotic theme developed in any striking manner ; and in spite of simplicity and directness, the diction and treatment, as the enthusiastic editors themselves admit, possess little dramatic realism or poetic distinction, and do not improve by the extreme mediocrity of the attempt.

Of some historical interest is the *Hammīra-mada-mardana*, composed at the instance of Vastupāla's son Jayantasiṃha between 1219 and 1299 A.D., by Jayasiṃha Sūri, pupil of Vīra Sūri and priest of the temple of Munisuvrata at Broach, in order to commemorate the exploits of Tejaḥpāla and his brother Vastupāla, ministers of Vīradhavala of Gujarat. It depicts in five acts Vīradhavala's conflicts with the Mleccha ruler Hammīra (or Amīr Shikār), Vastupāla's skill in diplomacy and the repulsion of the Muhammadan invasion of Gujarat. The main incident is historical, but whether in working out the plot the author meant his work to be more an eulogy than history does not concern us here. It is, however, a sustained attempt to write a drama of martial and political strategy. There is a succession of exciting incidents and enough of the sentiment of fear, but it cannot be said that the author succeeds in evolving a connected dramatic plot or creating distinctive characters. The ministers are endowed with exemplary intelligence, but the system of espionage and diplomacy is too obvious, the valour displayed too stagey, style and treatment too conventional, and the general atmosphere of the play too pedestrian. Other quasi-historical plays, like the *Pratāparudra-kalyāṇa*[2] of the rhetori-

1 Ed. C. D. Dalal, Gaekwad's Orient. Series, Baroda 1920, which gives, besides an analysis of the plot, all information about the work and historical matters connected with it. The author is to be distinguished from Jayasiṁha Sūri who wrote a *Kumārapālacarita* in 1265 A.D., and the present work from the *Hammīra-mahākāvya* written by Nayacandra Suri, already described, which deals with the Cauhan king Hammira.

2 Ed. Grantha-rantna-mālā, Bombay 1891. The work, written between the last quarter of the 13th and the first quarter of the 14th century, celebrates in five acts the poet's

cian Vidyānātha, or the *Gaṅgādāsa-pratāpa-vilāsa*[1] (in nine acts) of the Gujarat author Gaṅgadhara, or the *Bāla-martaṇḍa-vijaya*[2] of Devarāja, son of Śeṣādri of Sucīndram (Travancore), in five acts, are frankly panegyrics and not dramas.[3] The *Bhartṛhari-nirveda*[4] of Harihara is not even historical, but half legendary and half fanciful. It is still less dramatic, being in part a didactic glorification of the Haṭha-yoga system of Gorakṣanātha as a means of emancipation !

5. The Allegorical Drama

Although one of Aśvaghoṣa fragments contains some personifications of abstract virtues as *dramatis personae,* there is yet no evidence that the allegorical drama, like the Middle English Morality, played any important part in the early evolution of Sanskrit dramatic literature. It is also not clear if the type, of which we see the rudiments perhaps in the dramatic fragment mentioned above, was actually practised, even on a small scale, before or since Aśvaghoṣa's time, thus establishing a continuous tradition. All the plays of this kind belong

patron, the Kākatīya ruler Pratāparudra of Warangal, in whose honour is also written Vidyānātha's rhetorical work, *Pratāparudra-yaśobhūṣaṇa*. The short drama is included in the third chapter of this work. On the author, see Trivedi's introd. to the rhetorical work and S.K. De, *Sanskrit Poetics*, i, p. 229 f.

1 Eggeling, *India Office Catalogue*, vii, no. 4194, pp. 1608-15. It deals with the struggle of the poet's patron, Gangadasa Pratāpadeva, ruler of Champakapura (Champanir) with Muhammad Shah II of Gujarat (1443-51 A.D.).

2 Ed. K. Sambasiva Sastri, Trivandrum Sanskrit Series, 1931. The author was patronised by Mārtaṇḍavarman (1729-58 A.D.), whose exploits the work commemorates, including the renovation of the shrine of Padmanabha at Trivandrum.

3 The *Lalita-vigraharāja* of Somadeva is already mentioned above.

4 Ed. Durgaprasad and K. P. Parab, N.S.P., Bombay 1892, 1900 ; Eng. trs. by L. H. Gray in *JAOS*, XXV, 1904, pp. 197-225. The play is based upon the old legend of Bhatṛhari's Vairāgya, but the handling is free. In order to test the love of his wife Bhānumatī, king Bhartṛhari causes it to be reported that he has been killed by a tiger while hunting. His wife falls dead on hearing the news, and the king in grief wants to ascend the funeral pyre with his wife's body. He is, however, persuaded by the Yogic teachings of Gorakṣanātha ; and in consequence, he loses all attachment to the world and all interest in his wife, who, however, is revived by the ascetic ! As the famous saint Gorakṣanāthā is one of the characters, the drama is late, and its editors think that it belongs to mithilā.

to a very late period, the earliest known being the *Prabodha-candrodaya* of Kṛṣṇamiśra, which belongs to the second half of the 11th century. We do not know whether Kṛṣṇamiśra was merely reviving an old tradition or himself creating the peculiar type ; in any case, the credit belongs to him of attempting to produce a symbolical drama by means of purely personified abstractions, without making it differ at all in form and style from the normal drama. But it was like rowing off-stream, if not against it, up a backwater, which leads nowhere. In spite of numerous subsequent attempts, the type did not flourish well, nor did it develop into a new dramatic *genre*. Hardly any degree of literary talent or invention can long sustain the interest of an allegory; and it would be ideal to expect that our dramatists could greatly succeed in a sphere where success is indeed difficult to achieve.

The attempts, however, are interesting, not only for their novelty and cleverness, but also for the peculiar spirit of allegorising which they represent. The spirit is not a naive poetic trait but a deliberate decadent trend, which, in its remoteness from real life, revelled in abstract ideas and symbols. Even if the themes are sometimes childish, the plays do not belong to the childhood of the drama. They are inspired, not by a spirit of fancy and mythology, but by a tendency towards philosophical and scholastic thinking, being purposely composed to illustrate some doctrinal thesis. It is perhaps difficult to turn a dogma into a drama, but such philosophical allegories as the story of Puraṃjana[1] in the *Śrīmad-bhāgavata* (iii. 25-28) might have suggested the method. The weakness, however, of this class of composition is that in taking abstract ideas as *dramatis personae*, it either gives them so much individuality that their real intention is concealed, or so little that they are dull abstractions and nothing more. Most often they are cut-and-dried labels neatly defined by

[1] On this story there actually exist some later allegorical plays, *e.g.*, the *Puraṁjana-carita* of Kṛṣṇadatta (Rajendralala Mitra, *Notices*, no. 2000) and the *Puraṁjana-nāṭaka* of Haridāsa (Kielhorn, *Catalogue of MSS in Central Provinces*. no. 70).

reflective consciousness, logical concepts rather than natural facts, doctrinal formulas rather than live entities. The whole course of action is so clearly betrayed by the tell-tale characters that it loses all interest. Although conforming fully to the developed dramatic form and mode, the type touches the border of the real drama only when the tendency to symbolical, rather than literal, presentation prevails ; but in most cases we find that it is deliberately intended to convey religious and moral edification, or to glorify pedantic scholasticism, by means of allegorical action and characterisation. In this respect, the Sanskrit allegorical drama of a more self-conscious epoch differs from the Middle English Morality, to which it bears only a superficial resemblance in its origin, spirit and treatment. It does not also possess the religious ardour and exaltation found in such masterpieces of allegorical tales as Bunyan's *Grace Abounding* and *Pilgrim's Progress,* which, in their blend of the personal element with the mystic, admit us to the tremendous spectacle of the spiritual struggles of a human soul and its unspeakable agonies.

The date of Kṛṣṇamiśra is fixed with some certainty from his own references in the Prologue to one Gopāla, at whose command the play was written to commemorate the victory of his friend, king Kīrtivarman, over the Cedi king Karṇa.[1] As Karṇa is mentioned in an inscription dated 1042 A.D., and as an inscription of the Candella king Kīrtivarman is also dated 1098 A.D., it has been concluded that Kṛṣṇamiśra belonged to the second half of the 11th century.

The curious title of Kṛṣṇamiśra's solitary work, the *Prabodha-candrodaya,*[2] or 'the Moonrise of True Knowledge',

1 See Hultzsch and Kielhorn in *Ep. Ind.*, I, pp. 217 f, 325 ; V. A. Smith in *IA*, XXXVII, 1908, p. 143. The victory appears to have been won through the valour of Gopāla, who may have been an ally ; but the commentator Maheśvara thinks that he was a general (Senāpati) of Kīrtivarman.

2 Ed. Bhavanicharan Sarman, with the comm. of Maheśvara, Calcutta 1832 ; ed. H. Brockhaus, Leipzig 1835, 1845 ; ed. V. L. Pansikar, with Nāṇḍillagopa's Candrikā and Rāmadāsa Dīkṣita's Prakāśa comm., NSP, Bombay 1898 (2nd ed. 1904). Trs. into Eng. by J. Taylor, Bombay 1886, 1893, 1916 ; into German by T. Goldstücker, Konigsberg 1842 ; into French by G. Deveze in *Rev. de la Linguistique et de Philogie Comp.*, XXXII-XXXV, Paris 1899-1902. Bibliography by Schuyler in *JAOS*, XXV, 1904, pp. 194-96.

suggests its theme. It is a profound philosophical allegory, in six acts, of the whole life of man, and not of particular virtue or vice, cast in the form of a dramatic strife between the forces of the human mind which lead to true knowledge and those that are opposed to them. It is conceived as an internecine struggle between the two powerful sons of the regal Mind (Manas), born respectively of his two wives, Activity (Pravṛtti) and Repose (Nivṛtti) and named king Confusion (Moha) and king Discrimination (Viveka). Among the faithful adherents of king Confusion, stand Love (Kāma) and his wife Pleasure (Rati) ; Anger (Krodha) and Injury (Hiṃsā) ; Egoism (Ahaṃkāra) and his grandson Deceit (Dambha), born of Greed (Lobha) and Desire (Tṛṣṇā) ; Heresy (Mithyā-dṛṣṭi) described as a courtesan ; and Materialism represented by Cārvāka. On the other side are arrayed, but for the time being stand routed, the forces of king Discrimination, namely Reason (Mati), Duty (Dharma), Pity (Karuṇā), Goodwill (Maitrī), Peace (Śānti) and her mother Faith (Śraddhā), Forgiveness (Kṣamā), Contentment (Santoṣa), Judgement (Vastu-vicāra), Religious Devotion (Bhakti) and others. The plot is ingeniously developed by means of allegorical incidents, as well as by comic and erotic relishes, and centres round the accomplishment of the ultimate union of king Discrimination (Viveka) and Sacred Lore (Upaniṣad), from which is predicted the overthrow of king Confusion by the birth of True Knowledge (Prabodha) and Spiritual Wisdom (Vidyā). As the meeting ground of all faiths and heresies, Benares is aptly selected as the key-spot which both parties attempt to occupy, but which becomes at the outset the triumphant seat of Confusion. To this is linked the episode of Peace (Śānti), who has lost her mother Faith (Śraddhā), and of the trials of the assailed Faith who is saved by Devotion (Bhakti). The first episode, cleverly conceived, delineates the desperate plight of Peace, who searches in vain for Faith in Jainism, Buddhism and Brahmanism (Soma Cult) ; each appears with a wife claiming to be Faith, but Peace cannot recognise her mother in these distorted forms. After the vicissitudes of the great struggle and ultimate triumph of the good party, the old Mind is disconsolate over the loss of his progeny Confusion and his wife Activity ; but true Doctrine, the Vedānta, appears, disabuses him of false ideas and advises him to settle down with the other remaining wife, Repose, who is worthy of him. In the end, the Supreme Lord appears as Being or Puruṣa ; Discrimination is united with Sacred Lore ; and the prophecy is fulfilled by the birth of True Knowledge out of the union.

With such abstract and essentially scholastic subject-matter, it is difficult to produce a drama of real interest. But it is astonishing that, apart from the handicaps inherent in the method and purpose, Kṛṣṇamiśra succeeds, to a remarkable degree, in giving us an ingenious picture of the spiritual struggle of the human mind in the dramatic form of a vivid conflict, in which the erotic, comic and devotional interests are cleverly utilised. In form, the work is arranged as a regular comedy and does not differ from the ordinary play. With regard to dialogue and metrical arrangement, it is not inferior ; and the amusing scenes of the various forms of hypocrisy, arrogance and pedantry show considerable power of lively satire. On the doctrinal side, the composition attempts to synthesise Advaitic Vedānta with Viṣṇu-bhakti, but the philosophical and didactic content does not make it heavily pedantic nor insipidly doctrinarian. Even if represented by personified abstractions, the theme is made a matter of common internal experience, and not an abstruse theological exercise. The allegorising is consistent, and there is no frigidity in the plot ; we follow it with interest and curiosity as much as we follow the unfolding of a dramatic spectacle. On the literary side also Kṛṣṇamiśra can frame fine sentences and stanzas of both emotional and reflective kinds. Admitting all this, it would be idle, however, to pretend that the author, despite his dramatic grasp and inventiveness, is completely successful in shaping his abstract ideas into living persons. The method of presenting a single trait, instead of the whole man, in a magnified form, and of attaching a descriptive label to it, can hardly be expected to produce life-like results. The gift of satire and realism, as well as of poetry, which the author undeniably possesses, saves his pictures from being caricatures ; but his religious ardour is never so passionate and his poetic fancy never so enchanting as to enable him (as they enable Bunyan and Spenser partially) to clothe his abstract qualities with vivid personality, and compel our sympathy with his shadowy personages as with real beings. Nevertheless, of all such plays in Sanskrit, Kṛṣṇamiśra's work must be singled out as an attractive effort of much real merit.

The other allegorical plays are elaborate, but in no way commendable, productions. Their number is quite respectable,[1] but most of them are comparatively little known. Even their titles, without going further, often suggest and fully explain their theme and character. The work which stands next in date and sustained effort, but not in dramatic quality, is the *Moha-parājaya*[2] or 'Conquest of Confusion' of Yaśaḥpāla, son of Dhanadadeva and Rukmiṇī of the Moḍha family of Gujarat and himself a minister of Caulukya Kumārapāla's successor, Ajayapāla (1229-32 A.D.). It is a play in five acts, and the title itself indicates the influence of Kṛṣṇamiśra's work ; but it is composed chiefly in the interest of Jainism and is furnished with a few concrete historical characters, surrounded by personifications of abstract qualities. It describes the conversion of Kumārapāla into Jainism by the famous Ācārya Hemacandra, both of whom of course appear in the play, but it also utilises the erotic Nāṭikā motif of the king's marriage with Kṛpāsundarī, who is a real personage but who is figured from her name as the incarnation of Beautiful Compassion, the marriage taking place through the efforts of the minister Puṇyaketu, the Banner of Merit, and with the ministration of Hemacandra as the priest. As a pledge

1 For a list see Sten Konow, *op. cit.*, pp. 93-96.

2 Ed. Muni Caturvijaya, Gaekwad's Orient. Series, Baroda 1918.

Kumārapāla agrees to banish the seven sins (Gambling, Flesh-eating, Drinking, Slaughter, Theft and Adultery, Concubinage being overlooked) and abolishes the practice of confiscating the property of heirless persons ; while with the help of Hemacandra, armoured in his *Yoga-śāstra* and made invisible by his *Vītarāga-stuti*, the king succeeds in removing the siege laid on Man's Mind by king Confusion. There is some historical interest in the delineation of the activities of Jainism and Kumārapāla's beneficent regulations, but the literary merit of the work need not be exaggerated. The erotic episode is ineffective, and the presentation of the vices, on the model of Kṛṣṇamiśra's work, is a feeble and unconvincing attempt.

The *Caitanya-candrodaya*[1] of Paramānanda-dāsa-sena Kavi-karṇapūra, son of Śivānanda of Kāñcanapallī (Kāñcḍāpāḍā) Bengal, was composed in 1572 A.D. at the command of Gajapati Pratāparudra of Orissa. It is, in essence, a dramatised account of Caitanya's life at Navadvīpa and Puri. Even if it introduces allegorical (*e.g.*, Maitrī, Bhakti, Adharma, Virāga, etc.) and mythical (*e.g.*, Nārada, Rādhā, Kṛṣṇa, etc. in the inset play), figures as a subsidiary contrivance, as well as the device of a mythological play inserted into the real play, it is not really an allegorical play, for the action does not hinge upon the allegorical element. Kavikarṇapūra is a facile writer, but he conceives himself as a poet and devotee rather than as a sober historian. The work affords an interesting glimpse into the atmosphere of Caitanyaism and records some tradition which the poet's father (who figures in the play) as an elderly disciple of Caitanya might have handed down ; but with its muddled theological discourses, weak characterisation and rhetorical embellishments, it neither brings out adequately the spiritual significance of Caitanya's life nor attains much distinction as a dramatic or historical contribution.

1 Ed. Rajendralala Mitra, Bibl. Ind., Calcutta 1854 ; ed. Kedarnath and V. L. Panasikar, NSP, Bombay 1906. For a detailed account of the work and author, see S. K. De, *Vaiṣṇava Faith and Movement in Bengal*, chs. ii and vii.

It would be enough if such of the remaining plays of this type, as are better known, are briefly noticed here, for they are works of no outstanding literary merit. There is some vivid portraiture, as well as some sharp satire and ingenious fancy, but the reflective, theological and allegorical side gets altogether the better of the dramatic, pictorial and poetic. To the 16th century belongs the *Dharma-vijaya*[1] of Bhūdeva Śukla, which allegorises in five acts the advantages of a life of spiritual duty, and introduces, besides the usual personifications of virtues and vices, characters like Poetry (Kavitā), Prākṛta and Poetic Figure (Alaṃkāra). The *Vidyā-pariṇaya,*[2] composed by Vedakavi, but dutifully ascribed to the author's patron Ānandarāya Makhin, son of Nṛsiṃha of Bhāradvāja Gotra (who was Ānandarao Peshwā, minister of Śarabhojī of Tanjore, 1711-29 A.D.), describes in seven acts the marriage of king Jīva (Individual Soul) and Vidyā (Spiritual Wisdom), with the usual paraphernalia of theology and erotic imagery ; while the *Jīvānanda*[3] of the same poet, also in seven acts, apparently written earlier for Śāhjī of Tanjore (1687-1711 A.D.), is a work of similar import but of little dramatic merit. The *Amṛtodaya,*[4] in five acts, of the Maithila Gokulanātha, son of Pītāmbara and Umadevī, a court-poet of Fateh Shah of Srinagar (about 1615 A.D.), similarly depicts the allegorical progress of Jīva from creation to annhilation. The *Śrīdama-carita* of Sāmarāja Dīkṣita, composed in

1 Ed. Narayana Sastri Khiste in Sarasvati Bhavana Texts Series, Benares 1930 ; also ed. Grantha-ratna-mālā, iii, nos. 6-7, Bombay 1889-90. The *Rasa-vilāsa* of Bhūdeva Śukla was composed about 1550 A.D. (*ABORI*, XIII, p. 183).

2 Ed. Sivadatta and K. P. Parab, NSP, Bombay 1893. The work expressly mentions in the Prologue the *Prabodha-candrodaya*, *Saṁkalpa-sūryodaya* and *Bhavanā-puruṣottama*. The last-named work was composed in five acts by Śrīnivāsa Atitātrayājin, son of Bhāvasvāmin and Lakṣmī, of Surasamudra (between Tanjore and Madura). It is noticed by Burnell in his *Cat. of Skt. MSS in the Tanjore Palace Library*, p. 170.

3 Ed. Durgaprasad and K. P. Parab, NSP, Bombay 1891.

4 Ed. Sivadatta and K. P. Parab, NSP, Bombay 1897. The work was composed in 1693 A.D.

5 Analysed in Wilson, *Hindu Theatre*, vol. ii, p. 404 f. On Samaraja's date (latter part of the 17th century) and works, see S. K. De, *Sanskrit Poetics*, i, p. 320 ; P. K. Gode in *ABORI*, X, pp. 158-59, where mention is made of another work of Sāmarāja on

1681 A.D., deals, in a mixed allegorical form in five acts, with the legend of Śrīdāma, a companion of Kṛṣṇa, in which the hero, a favourite of Learning (Sarasvatī) but obnoxious to Prosperity (Lakṣmī), is assailed by Poverty and Folly, but is ultimately saved by the virtuous agents of Kṛṣṇa. Even less interesting are the elaborate South Indian plays, the *Saṃkalpasūryodaya*, in ten acts, of Veṅkatanātha Vedāntadeśika Kavitārkikasiṃha,[1] and the *Yatirāja-vijaya*[2] or *Vedānta-vilāsa*, in six acts of Varadācarya or Ammal Acārya, both of which give a dreary allegory of the triumph of Rāmānuja's doctrine, and illustrate in its extreme form the use of the allegorical drama for the purpose of sectarian propaganda.

6. Erotic and Farcical Plays

The peculiar type of one-act play, the Bhāṇa and the Prahasana, are closely allied to each other in having a farcical character ; but the Bhāṇa is predominantly erotic and consists entirely of a prolonged monologue carried on by means of suppositious dialogues. Both of them must have been popular, and, as attested by theory, undoubtedly old ; but with the exception of the *Caturbhāṇī* and the *Matta-vilāsa*, of which we have spoken above, the specimens of these forms of composition which exist belong to comparatively recent times. There is, however, no evidence to support the suggestion that more abundant specimens

Kāmaśāstra, entitled *Rati-kallolini*, and composed in 1719 A.D. His *Śṛṅgārāmṛta-laharī* is published in Kāvyamālā, Gucchaka xiv.

1 Ed. K. Srinivasacharya, Conjeevaram 1914 ; ed. K. Narayanacandra and D. R. Iyengar, Śrī-Vāṇī-vilāsa Press, Srirangam, 1917 (acts i-v), with Eng. trs. ; also ed. in the *Pandit*, xxviii-xxxii (1906-10), xxxiv (1912), xxxvii (1915) and xxxviii (1916). The author, better known as Vedantadeśika only, was a versatile teacher and polygraph, who flourished in the latter half of the 13th century. The work is written obviously on the model of Kṛṣṇamisra's *Prabodha-candrodaya*, but it is adapted to the tenets of the author's own school, and follows pedantically, in the arrangement of its acts, the order of topics of the *Vedānta-sūtra*.

2 Ed. K. Viraraghava Tatacarya, Kumbhakonam 1902.

3 The author, son of Ghaṭikāśata Sudarśanācārya, was a Vaiṣṇava teacher of Kāñchī the latter half of the 17th and the beginning of the 18th century. But see E. V. Vira Raghavacharya in *Journal of Veṅkaṭeśvara Oriental Institute*, II, pt. i ; (1941), who would place Varadācārya in the 14th century.

of Bhāṇa and Prahasana have not come down to us because they were intended for the people and were not considered worthy of preservation. To judge from the small number of such plays as have survived, it is clear that, in spite of a certain popular trait discernible in their theme and rough humour, they belong, not to the popular theatre, but to the literary drama. Apparently the polished society did not disdain the shallow gaiety of the farce and the erotic monologue play, which take for their characters debauches, rogues and vagrants and for their subjects shady and coarse acts, but which are composed in the elegant and polished manner of the normal literary drama. In this sense, they are artistic productions of the same kind, and exhibit the same stylistic merits and defects. The literary tradition is also indicated by the fact that these dramatic types chiefly develop the characters of the old Viṭa and Vidūṣaka of the regular drama, who become principal and not merely incidental. It is true that the Vidūṣaka does not directly occur[1] in the Prahasana and that the Viṭa in the later Bhāna is a much degarded character, but the connexion cannot be mistaken, and the Viṭa still retains an echo of his old polish. The degradation is due not to any supposed writing for the masses or to any supposed contact with the popular play, but to the general decadence of dramatic sense and power, which manifests itself in this period in almost all types of dramatic composition. The world which the Bhāṇa and Prahasana paint is more or less, a world of conventional caricature, but the exaggeration of oddity and vice is, on the whole, no more nor less removed from real life than the picture of ideal virtue in the serious drama. If the plays constantly verge upon real comedy without ever touching it, it is a characteristic which can be sufficiently explained by the universal lack of real dramatic gift, without the uncorroborated presumption of their being meant only for popular consumption.

1 Except in a small way in the *Bhagavad-ajjukīya* and *Dhūrta-samāgama*.

Indeed the group of Bhāṇas, with which we are concerned here, consists, in a narrow sense, of artistic productions imitative and reproductive of earlier works, and present a monotonous sameness of style and treatment, which suggests a sense of artificiality inseparable from all laboured composition. After the creative epoch of the *Caturbhāṇī*, the Bhāṇa as a specien of the drama does not appear to have developed much, and the definitions of the theorists are as little divergent on this point as the practice of the dramatists themselves. Of the limited number of such plays, only about a dozen have so far been published ; but since they do not present much variety in matter and manner it would not be necessary to take them in detail. The earliest of this is the *Karpūra-carita*[1] of Vatsarāja of Kalañjara (end of the 12th and beginning of the 13th century), of which we have spoken above. With its monologic Prologue, free use of Prakrit, enough comic relief and a somewhat diversified plot, it bears more affinities to the *Caturbhāṇī* than the later Bhāṇas, but it is in no way a very remarkable production.

With the exception of this noteworthy Bhāṇa, which is older in date and which does not belong to Southern India, all other later Bhāṇas bear a striking similarity to one another in their form and content, as well as in their place of origin. Of such Bhāṇas as have been so far published, we have the *Śṛṅgāra-bhūṣaṇa*[2] of Vāmana Bhaṭṭa Bāṇa, which belongs to the end of the 14th and beginning of the 15th century ; the *Vasanta-tilaka*[3] of Varadācarya or Ammalācarya, the Vaiṣṇava teacher of Kāñcī ; the *Śṛṅgāra-tilaka*[4] of his contemporary Rāmabhadra Dīkṣita (middle and second half of the 17th), written

1 Ed. C. D. Dalal, Gaekwad's Orient. Series, no. 8, Baroda 1918 (in Vatsarāja's *Rūpaka-ṣaṭka*). See above, p. 474.

2 Ed. Sivadatta and K. P. Parab, NSP, Bombay 1896, 1910.

3 Ed. Damaruvallabha Sarman, Calcutta 1868 ; ed. Vavilla Ramanujacharya, Madras 1872. Also ed. Jivananda Vidyasagar, Calcutta 1874, see above, p. 487, footnote 3.

4 Ed. Sivadatta and K. P. Parab, NSP, Bombay 1894, 1910. It is called Ayyābhāṇa to distinguish it from *Vasanta-tilaka* which is called Ammābhāṇa.

to rival Varadācarya's work ; the *Sṛṅgāra-sarvasva*[1] of Nallā Dīkṣita, son of Bālachandra Dīkṣita (about 1700 A.D.) ; the *Rasa-sadana*[2] of Yuvarāja of Koṭiliṅgapura in Kerala ; the *Pañcabāṇa-vijaya*[3] of Raṅgācarya ; the *Śāradā-tilaka*[4] of Śaṃkara ; and the *Rasika-rañjana*[5] of Śrīnivāsācarya.[6] The *Mukundānanda*[7] of Kāśīpati Kavirāja, who flourished at the court of Nañjarāja of Mysore, is a late Bhāṇa belonging to the early part of the 18th century. It calls itself a mixed or Miśra Bhāṇa, and alludes in the erotic adventures of its Viṭa, Bhujaṅgaśekhara, to the sports of Kṛṣṇa and the Gopīs. The double application differentiates it from the ordinary Bhāṇa, with which it cannot be strictly classified.

The Bhāṇa, as typified by these works, may not be unfittingly described as the picture of a Rake's progress, giving us the account of a glorious day of adventure of the Viṭa, who appears here, not as the cultured and polished wit of earlier Bhāṇas but a professional amourist, casting his favours right and left and boasting of a hundred conquests in the hetaera-world. His name is significant ; it is either Vilāsaśekhara, Anaṅgaśekhara, Bhujaṅgaśekhara, Śṛṅgāraśekhara, Rasikaśekhara or simply (but rarely) the Viṭa. The Prologue is not, as one would expect, in the form of a monologue, but consists of a dialogue (as in the normal drama) between the Sūtradhāra and his assistant. The Viṭa-hero, whose approach is indicated

[1] Ed. Sivadatta and K. P. Parab, NSP, Bombay 1902, 1911.

[2] Ed. Sivadatta and K. P. Parab, NSP, Bombay 1893, 1922.

[3] Ed. V. Ramasvami Sastrulu, in Telugu characters, Madras 1915.

[4] Analysed by Wilson, *op. cit.*, ii, p. 384. The author was a native of Benares.

[5] Ed. Mysore 1885.

[6] No trace has yet been found of *Śṛṅgāra-mañjarī* and *Līlā-madhukara*, mentioned respectively by Śiṅgabhūpāla and Viśvanātha. For a bibliography of unpublished Bhāṇas, see Sten Konow, *op. cit.*, pp. 121-23. For an account of the printed Bhāṇas, see S. K. De, A Note on the Sanskrit Monologue Play (Bhāṇa) in *JRAS*, 1926, pp. 63-90.

[7] Ed. Durgaprasad and K. P. Parab, NSP, Bombay 1889, 1894. On the author and his date, see M. P. L. Shastry in *New Indian Antiquary*, IV, 1941, pp. 150-54. Eulogising this ruler, Nañjarāja, the poet Nṛsiṁha, calling himself Abhinava Kālidāsa (!), composed his rhetorical work named *Nañjarāja-yaśobhūṣaṇa* (ed. Gaekwad's Orient. Series, Baroda 1930). Kāśīpati also appears to have written a commentary on Nañjarāja's *Saṁgīta-gaṅgādhara*.

at the end of the Prologue, enters the stage in a love-lorn condition, and begins a somewhat mawkish description of the early morning in terms of an erotic imagery. What brings him out so early is usually his vexation at being separated by force of circumstances from his beloved, who is generally a hetaera and sometimes an intriguing married woman ; but his object may also be a friendly visit, or his anxiety to keep his promise of looking after his friend's mistress. He makes a promenade through the street of the hetaera (Veśa-bāṭa), and carries on a series of imaginary conversations with friends, both male and female, who frequent such a place, speaking in the air to persons out of sight and repeating answers which he pretends to receive. He depicts in this way the rather shady lives and amorous adventures of a large number of his acquaintances, mostly rogues, hypocrites, courtesans and men-about-town, and describes ram-fights, cock-fights, snake-charming, wrestling, gambling with dice, magic shows, acrobatic feats, selling of bracelets, besides various kinds of fashionable, if feminine, sports.[1] He settles disputes between a hetaera (or her lover) and her grasping old mother, or between a hetaera and her unfaithful lover, incidentally describing the Kalatra-patrikā[2] or the document setting forth the terms of contract of a temporary union. He listens to music played on the Vīṇā and sometimes enters a dancing saloon, exchanging pleasantries with dancing girls. He succeeds in the end in achieving the object with which he set forth, executes the entrusted commission or meets his beloved, and concludes with a description of the evening and moonrise,—the end of a perfect day ! The scene of action is usually laid in some famous South Indian city, like Kāñcī, or, as in *Śāradā-tilaka,* in some imiginary

1 Such as Kanduka-krīḍā, Ḍolā-vihāra, Cakṣur-apidhāna, Ambara-karaṇḍaka, Maṇi-guptaka, Yugmāyugma-darśana, Caturaṅga-vihāra, Gajapati-kusuma-kanduka, .etc, none of which is mentioned by Vātsyāyana.

2 See, for instance, *Śṛṅgāra-bhūṣaṇa*, p. 15, *Śṛṅgāra-sarvasva*, p. 18. Besides money, the man stipulates to provide for his mistress a pair of cloth every month, as well as flower, wreaths, musk and camphored betel every day.

land of romantic fancy like Kolāhalapura, 'the city of noise'; and the normal occasion of the performance of the play is some festival in honour of a local deity.

One of the outstanding features of all these later Bhāṇas is their want of variety. There is a monotonous sameness of theme, sentiment, incidents, objects and characters, as well as of style and treatment, which suggests that the Bhāṇa in this epoch of artificiality became a mere literary exercise and subsided into a lifeless form of art. We come across some fine verses, both descriptive and erotic, but the descriptions are conventional in their conceits and tricks of expression. It is also noteworthy that the comic and satiric tendency, which should rightly find a place in the Bhāṇa from its close connexion with the Prahasana, and which is so prominent in the *Caturbhāṇī*, gradually disappears in the later Bhāṇas, which became in course of time entirely erotic. Some amount of satire is incidentally introduced in the description, for instance, of licentious Paurāṇikas, old Śrotriyas and fraudulent astrologers,[1] and some people like the Gurjaras are pungently ridiculed,[2] but this is not a common feature. The satire or real comedy is indeed very slight; and the erotic, and often hopelessly coarse, descriptions, incidents and imageries almost universally predominate. The characters are rarely diversified, but consist of specimens of courtesans bawds and libertines, all having the erotic stamp; they are types, rather than individuals, repeating themselves in all later Bhāṇas. The depressing atmosphere of such unedifying characters, none of whom rises above the middle class, is bound to be dull, as they are seldom seasoned with comic effects, individual traits, or variety of incidents and situations. The monotonous instance on the erotic sentiment tends to become cloying; and it is no wonder that the Bhāṇa, as a species of composition, though

1 Only in *Śāradā tilaka*, there is some satire directed against the Jaṅgamas, Śaivas and Vaiṣṇavas. The Bhāgavatas are ridiculed in Vatsarāja's farce *Hāsya-cūḍāmaṇi*, but not in his Bhāṇa, *Karpūra-carita*.

2 In the *Mukundānanda*.

popular in a limited sense, never made a permanent appeal, and was in course of time forgotten.

It is probable that the erotic tendency, in spite of the silence of Bharata and his commentator, was an inseparable feature of the Bhāṇa from its very beginning, and we find it present in the *Caturbhāṇī*. The erotic figure of the Viṭa as the only actor naturally kept up and fostered it. But what is significant is that the erotic element gets the upper hand in the later Bhāṇas, as they do not make the best of the comic possibilities of the society which they handle and which lend themselves finely to such treatment. The very names of the later Bhāṇas and of their principal Viṭas emphasise their exclusive tendency towards eroticism and their diminishing interest in comedy and satire. Bharata gives us no prescription regarding the sentiment to be delineated in the Bhāṇa, and the earlier authors of the *Caturbhāṇī*, therefore, were unfettered in this respect and could draw upon other legitimate sources of interest than the erotic. But from the time of the *Daśa-rūpaka* onwards, it is distinctly understood that the erotic and the heroic should be the sentiment proper to the Bhāṇa. The heroic was probably dropped as unsuitable to the essential character of the play, but the erotic came to prevail.[1] The erotic convention, in fact, overshadows everything, and one would seek in vain in these decadent writings for the power of observation and reproduction of real life which are so vividly exhibited by the *Caturbhāṇī*.

There is a greater scope for comedy and satire in the Prahasana, but by its exaggeration, hopeless vulgarity (allowed by theory) and selection of a few conventional types of characters, it becomes more a caricature, with plenty of horse-play, than a picture of real life, with true comedy. As a class of composition, the Prahasana is hardly entertaining, and has little literary

1 Viśvanātha's exception that the Kaiśiki Vṛtti may sometimes be allowed in the Bhāṇa is quite in keeping with the erotic spirit of the later writings, as this dramatic style gives greater scope to love and gallantry.

attraction. The erotic tendency is still there, but it is confined chiefly to the set stanzaṣ and descriptions, and entirely submerged in a series of grotesque and often coarse antics. The theme is invented, and consists generally of the tricks and quarrels of low characters of all kinds, which often include a courtesan. The action is slight, and the distinction made by theory between the mixed (Saṃkīrṇa) and unmixed (Śuddha) types is more or less formal and is of no practical significance. The earlier Prahasanas have only one act, like the Bhāṇa, but the later specimens extend to two acts, or divides the one act into two Saṃdhis.

The dramaturgic treatises mention sevaral Prahasanas which have not come down to us. Thus, the *Bhāva-prakāśa* of Śāradātanaya mentions *Sairaṃdhrikā*, *Sāgara-kaumudī* and *Kali-keli*; while the *Rasārṇava-sudhākara* cites *Ānanda-kośa*, *Bṛhat-subhadraka* and *Bhagavad-ajjuka*, of which the last-named work alone has been recovered. Of the three Prahasanas cited in the *Sāhitya-darpaṇa*, the *Laṭaka-melaka* alone has survived, but the *Dhūrta-carita* and *Kandarpa-keli* are lost. Of the existing Prahasanas, we have already spoken of the *Matta-vilāsa* of Mahendravikrama, which is undoubtedly the earliest known (620 A.D.), and of the *Hāsya-cuḍāmaṇi* of Vatsarāja, which belongs to the end of the 12th and beginning of the 13th century. Between these two works comes probably the *Bhagavad-ajjukīyas*,[1] which is an undoubtedly old Prahasana, but the date of which is unknown and authorship uncertain. Like most plays preserved in Kerala, the Prologue omits the name of the author, but a late commentary, which finds throughout a philosophical meaning in the farce, names (in agreement with two manuscripts of the play) Bodhāyana Kavi as the author, who is otherwise unknown, but whom the commentator might

1 Ed. A. Banerji Sastri in *JBORS*, 1924, from very imperfect materials, but ed. more critically with an anonymous commentary by P. Anujan Achan, and published from the Paliyam Manuscripts Library, Jayanta-mangalam, Cochin 1925. Also ed. Prabhakarạ Sạstri Vẹturi, Vavillạ Press, Madras 1925.

be confusing with the Vṛttikāra Bodhāyana quoted by Rāmānuja. The argument that the farce was composed at a time when Buddhism was still a living faith is clearly indefinite and inconclusive, but compared with later specimens of the Prahasana, it reveals features of style and treatment which render a date earlier than the 12th century very probable. One important feature of this well-written farce, which distinguishes it from all other farces in Sanskrit, is that the comic element is found not in the oddities of the characters but in the ludicrousness of the plot. In this farce of the Saint and the Courtesan, as it is curiously named, the saint is a true ascetic and learned teacher, well versed in Yoga, while his pupil Śaṇḍilya is the typical Vidūṣaka of the serious drama ; their conversation, with which the play begins, has comic features, but it is never grotesque and coarse, and the characters are not of that low and hypocritical type which is ordinarily ridiculed in the farce. The courtesan, who enters the neighbouring garden and awaits her lover, does not show the vulgar traits of the common harlot, which we find in the normal Prahasanas to be mentioned below. The funny situation arises when the girl falls dead bitten by a serpent, and the saint, finding an opportunity of impressing his scoffing pupil by a display of Yogic powers, enters the dead body of the courtesan. The messenger of Yama, coming to fetch the dead soul and finding that a mistake has been committed, allows the soul of the courtesan to enter the lifeless body of the saint. The curious exchange of souls make the saint speak and act like the courtesan, while the courtesan adopts the language and conduct of the saint, until the messenger of Yama restores the equilibrium and returns the souls to their respective bodies. Although a small piece, the play achieves real humour, not by cheap witticisms and clownish acts, but by a genuinely comic plot and commendable characterisation. It is easily the best of the Sanskrit farces.

We can dismiss the *Dāmaka-prahasana* of unknown date and authorship, the main incident of which covers about three printed pages,[1] as no one can seriously call the fragment a Prahasana or even a noteworthy work in any respect. The Dāmaka-incident is an obvious imitation of the usual Vidūṣaka-episode of the normal drama, while the two added pieces of a few lines are fragmentary and unconnected and have no comic element in it. The slight work looks like a selection of scenes or half-scenes, containing verses culled from well-known works and compiled for some kind of division. The *Nāṭa-vāṭa-prahasana*[2] of Yadunandana, son of Vāsudeva Cayani, is also of unknown date and does not strictly conform to the technical requirements, but there is no reason to suppose that it is an early work. It has the coarseness of later farces and does not exhibit any noteworthy literary characteristics. The Prologue, presented in the form of a Monologue, in which the Sūtradhāra carries on by means of Ākāśa-bhāṣita, may be an interesting relic of an old trait, but it may have been suggested by established technique of main body of the Bhāṇa itself. Although some characters are common, the two Saṃdhis of the play are entirely unconnected, and the suggestion that it was composed on the model of some popular dramatic spectacles of looser technique is not improbable.

The remaining farces, which have been so far published, are of a coarser type and have little to recommend them. There is some rough wit, as well as satire, but it is often defaced by open vulgarity, while the descriptive and erotic stanzas possess little distinction. The earliest of these is the *Laṭaka-melaka,*[3] or 'the Conference of Rogues', composed apparently in the first part of the 12th century, under Govindcandra of Kanauj, by Kavirāja Śaṅkhadhara. It describes in two acts the assembling of all kinds of roguish people at the house of the go-between

1 Ed. V. Venkatarama Sastri, Lahore 1926. On the false ascription of this work to Bhāsa, see J. Jolly in *Festgate Garbe*, Erlangen 1927, pp. 115-21.

2 Ed. Granthamālā, ii, Bombay 1887.

3 Ed. Durgaprasad and K. P. Parab, NSP, Bombay 1889, 3rd ed. 1923. There are several quotations from this work in the *Śārṅgadhara-paddhati* and the *Sāhitya-darpaṇa*, which undoubtedly place the work earlier than the 14th century.

Danturā for winning the favour of her daughter Madanamañjarī. They represent a number of types, each labelled with a particular foible, indicated by their very names. First comes, with his parasite Kulavyādhi, the profligate professor Sabhāsali who, having a ferociously quarrelsome wife Kalahapriyā, seeks diversion in the society of the courtesan. As Madanamañjarī has accidentally swallowed a fish bone, the quack doctor Jantuketu is called in ; his methods are absurd, but his words and acts make the girl laugh, with the happy result of dislodging the bone. Then appear the Digambara Jaṭāsura and the Kāpālika Ajñānarāśi quarrelling; the cowardly village headman Saṃgrāmavisara, accompanied by his sycophant Viśvāsaghātaka ; the hypocritical Brahman Mithyāśukla ; the fraudulent preceptor Phuṅkaṭamiśra ; the depraved Buddhist monk Vyasanākara, interested in a washerwoman, and other similar characters. There is a bargaining of the lovers, and in the end a marriage is satisfactorily arranged between the old bawd Danturā and the Digambara Jaṭāsura. The *Dhūrta-samāgama*[1] or 'the Meeting of Knaves' of the Maithila Jyotirīśvara Kaviśekhara, son of Dhaneśvara and grandson of Rāmeśvara of the family of Dhīreśvara, was composed under king Harasiṃha or Harisiṃha of Karṇāṭa family, who ruled in Mithilā during the first quarter of the 14th century.[2] It is a farce of the same type in one act, in which there is a contest between a wicked religious mendicant Viśvanagara and his pupil Durācāra over a charming courtesan Anaṅgasenā, whom the pupil saw first, but whom the preceptor meanly desires to appropriate to himself. On the suggestion of the girl, the matter is referred to arbitration by the Brahman Asajjāti who craftily decides, after the manner of the ape in the fable, to keep

1 Ed. C. Lassen in his *Anthologia Sanscritica* (not reprinted in the 2nd ed.), Bonn 1838 ; ed. C. Cappeller, in litho, Jena 1883. *Cf.* Lévi, *op. cit.*, p. 252 f.

2 In some MSS the name of the king is given as Narasiṁha, who has been identified by Sten Konow and Keith, following Lassen, with Narasimha of Vijayanagara (1487-1508 A.D.). But this is clearly incorrect. See discussion of the whole question by S. K. Chatterji in *Prceedings of the Oriental Conference*, Allahabad, vol. ii, pp. 559-69.

the girl for himself, although his Vidūṣaka also covets the prize. It should be remembered that the author wrote a work also on the art of love, entitled *Pañca-sāyaka*,[1] and the extreme erotic tendency of his farce, therefore, is not unexpected.

The other extant farces belong to a much later period. The *Hāsyārṇava*[2] of Jagadīśvara follows in two acts the general scheme, with a slight variation, of bringing rogues and rakes together in the house of the bawd Bandhurā, which the king Anaya-sindhu, Ocean of Misrule, visits to study the character of his people, as they are drawn there by the beauty of her daughter Mṛgāṅkalekhā. The series of characters who enter comprises the court chaplain Viśvabandhu and his pupil Kalahāṅkura, who quarrel over the possession of a courtesan ; the incompetent doctor Vyādhi-sindhu, son of Āturāntaka, who wants to cure colic by applying a heated needle to the palate ; the surgeon-barber Rakta-kallola who has cut his patient and left him in a pool of blood ; the police-chief Sādhu-hiṃsaka, Terror to the Good, who reports with great satisfaction that the city is in the hands of thieves ; the comic general Raṇa-jambūkā, who is valiant enough to cut a leach in two ; and the ignorant astrologer Mahāyāntrika. In the second act, the efforts of the chaplain and his pupil to obtain the damsel meet with opposition from those of another religious teacher, Madāndhamiśra and his pupil, who are birds of the same feather. The older men succeed, and the two pupils content themselves with the old hag, knowing that they would share the young girl on the sly. The work is disfigured by unredeemed vulgarity of words and acts, and cannot in any sense be regarded as an attractive production. The *Kautuka-sarvasva*[3] of Gopīnātha

1 Ed. Sadananda Sastri, Lahore 1921.

2 Ed. C. Cappeller, in litho print, Jena 1883 ; ed. Srinath Vedantavagis, 2nd ed., Calcutta 1896, with a Skt. commentary.

3 Ed. Ramacandra Tarkalamkara, Calcutta 1828. Analysed by Wilson, ii, p. 410 and by C. Cappeller in *Guru-pūjā-kaumudī* (Festschrift A. Weber), Leipzig 1896, pp. 59-62. Dacca University MS, no. 1580 D.

Cakravartin, composed for the Durgā-pūjā festival of Bengal, is also a late work, but it is less vulgar and more amusing. It describes in two acts the wicked pranks of king Kali-vatsala, Darling of Iniquity, of Dharma-nāśa city, addicted to the hemp-juice and fond of other men's wives, who oppresses the Brahman Satyācāra, proclaims free love, becomes involved in a dispute over a courtesan whom every one wants to oblige, and ends by banishing all good people from the realm. The king's advisers are his minister Śiṣṭāntaka, his chaplain Dharmānala, his followers Anṛta-sarvasva and Paṇḍita-pīḍā-viśārada, his courtier and nobleman Kukarma-pañcānana and Abhavya-śekhara, and his general Samara-jambūka, their names explaining the dominant traits of their character. Although less vulgar and more amusing, the work is of little merit and possesses no greater appeal in its plot and characterisation. The *Kautuka-ratnākara*,[1] another Bengal work, composed by the royal priest (unnamed but surnamed Kavitārkika, son of Vāṇīnātha) of Laksmaṇamāṇikya (end of the 16th century) of Bhuluyā (in Noakhali), ridicules an imbecile king Duritārṇava of Puṇya-varjita city, who relies on his knaves to recover his abducted queen. Although she was sleeping well protected in the arms of the police-chief Suśīlantaka, she was focibly taken away on the night preceding the spring-festival. The king acts on the advice of his minister Kumati-puñja, his priest Ācāra-kalakūṭa, his astrologer Aśubha-cintaka, the overseer of his harem obscenely named Pracaṇḍa-śepha, his general Samara-kātara and his guru Ajitendriya. He appoints a courtesan Anaṅga-taraṅgiṇi in her place to officiate at the festival, until a Brahman, named Kapaṭa-veṣa-dhārin, is accidentally revealed as the abductor. As in the other farces described above, the oddities and antics of these characters supply a great deal of vulgar merriment, but the work is not free from the faults of exaggeration and coareness, which take away the edge of its

1 Dacca University MS, no. 1821 (fragmentary). Analysed by C. Cappeller, *op. cit.* pp. 62-63.

satire and comic portraiture. To the latter part of the 17th century belongs the *Dhūrta-nartaka*[1] of Sāmarāja Dīkṣita,[2] son of Narahari Bindupuraṃdara, and author of a number of poems and of the play *Śrīdāma-caritā* mentioned above. It is a farce in one act but in two Saṃdhis, composed in honour of a festival of Viṣṇu, to ridicule chiefly the Śaiva ascetics. The ascetic Mureśvara is in love with a dancing girl, but his two pupils to whom he confides his passion, attempt to oust him and seek to expose him to the king Pāpacāra. The play is comparatively free from the usual grossness, but it has little fancy or humour to recommend it.

The Sanskrit Prahasana, as a whole, suffers from poverty of invention and lack of taste. The interest seldom centres in the cleverness of the plot or in well-developed intrigue, but in the follies and oddities of characters, which are often of a board and obvious type. Neither in the incidents nor in the characters there is any vivid and animated use of colour or any sense of proportion. The whole atmosphere is low and depressing. We have neither thoroughly alive rascals nor charmingly entertaining fools, for they are all thrown into fixed moulds without much regard for actualities. The characters are low, not in social position, but as unredeemingly base and carnal ; and there being no credit for any other quality, they are hardly human. The procession of unmitigated rogues or their rougher pastimes need not be without any interest ; but there is no merit in attempting to raise laughter by deliberately vulgar exhibitions and expressions, which mar the effect of the plays even as burlesques and caricatures. The parodies of high-placed people lose their point, not only from tasteless exaggeration, but also from their extremely sordid and prosaic treatment. Even if refinement is out of place in a farce, detailed and puerile coarseness is redundant and ineffective.

1 Analysed by Wilson, *op. cit.*, ii, p. 407.

2 On Sāmarāja and his date and works, see above. p, 486, footnote 5.

7. Dramas of an Irregular Type

The steady development of description and declamation by means of elaborate verses and the entire wiping out of action, which we have noticed in the normal drama of this period, reach their climax in some so-called later plays, like the *Dūtāṅgada* and the *Mahānāṭaka,* which exhibit also certain markedly irregular features. Although nominally keeping to the outward from of drama, the works are devoid of all dramatic action, being rather a collection of poetical stanzas, descriptive, emotional or narrative, with slight interspersed dialogues and quasi stage-directions. Having regard to the course of development of the Sanskrit drama in this decadent epoch, which more and more sacrificed action and characterisation to narrative and description, some of the general features are in themselves not inexplicable ; but since there are particular irregularities and since some of the specimens, like the *Dūtāṅgada,* describe themselves as Chāyā-nāṭakas, they have been cited as typical examples of a peculiar *genre* by expounders of the shadow-play hypothesis.[1] While the connotation of the term Chāyā-nāṭaka[2] itself is extremely dubious, the shadow-play theory, however, appears to be entirely uncalled for and without foundation, and there is hardly any characteristic feature which is not otherwise intelligible by purely historical and literary considerations.

1 R. Pischel, Das altindische Schattenspiel in *SBAW,* 1906, pp. 482-502 ; H. Lüders, Die Śaubhikas in *SBAW,* 1916, p. 698 f ; Sten Konow, *op. cit.,* pp. 89-90 ; Winternitz, *GIL,* iii, p. 243 (also in *ZDMG,* LXXIV, 1920, p. 118 f). For other plays of this type, which are also claimed as shadow-plays, and discussion of the entire question, see Keith, *SD,* pp. 33 f, 53 f, 269 f and S. K. De, The Problem of the Mahānāṭaka in *IHQ,* VII, 1931, p. 537 f.

2 The term is variously explained as 'outline of a drama of entr'cte' (Rajendralala Mitra and Wilson), 'shadow of a drama or half-drama' (Pischell), 'a drama in the state of shadow' (Lévi). Having regard to the derivative nature of the plays like the *Dūtāṅgada* and the *Mahānaṭaka,* which incorporate verses from known and unknown Rāma-dramas, it is not impossible to hold that the term Chāyā-nāṭaka means 'an epitomised adaptation of previous plays on the subject', the term Chāyā being a well known technical term used in the sense of borrowing or adaptation. It should be noted that the Chāyā-nāṭaka, in the sense of shadow play, is not a category of Sanskrit dramatic composition and is unknown to theories as a dramatic *genre,* early or late. Its prevalence in ancient times is extremely doubtful, and the part alleged to be played by it in the evolution of the Sanskrit drama is entirely problematic.

The *Dūtaṅgada*[1] of Subhaṭa describes in four scenes the embassy of Aṅgada,[2] who is sent to demand restoration of Sītā from Rāvaṇa. There is a regular prologue. After this, in the first scene, Aṅgada is sent as a messenger ; in the second, Bibhīṣaṇa and Mandodarī attempt to dissuade Rāvaṇa from his fatal folly ; in the third, Aṅgada executes his mission, but on Rāvaṇa's endeavour to persuade him, with the illusion of Māyā-Sītā, that Sītā is in love with the lord of Laṅkā, Aṅgada refuses to be deceived and leaves Rāvaṇa with threats ; and in the fourth, two Gandharvas inform us that Rāvaṇa is slain, and Rāma enters in triumph. The work exists in various forms ; but a longer and a shorter recension are distinguished. Characterising the longer recension,[3] Eggeling writes : "Not only is the dialogue itself considerably extended in this version by the insertion of many additional stanzas, but narrative verses are also thrown in, calculated to make the work a curious hybrid between a dramatic piece (with stage directions) and a narrative poem." Most of these supplementary verses are, however, traceable in other Rāma-dramas ; for instance, verses 4 and 5 (in Eggeling's citation) are taken from the *Prasanna-rāghava* and verse 5 from the *Mahāvīra-carita*.[4] The shorter recension also betrays the character of a similar compilation, and in the closing verse the author himself acknowledges his indebtedness to his predecessors. It is clear that the work does not pretend entire originality, but it was probably compiled for some particular purpose. The Prologue tells us that it was produced at the court of Tribhuvanapāla, who appears to be the Caulukya prince of that name

1 Ed. Durgaprasad and V. L. Pansikar, NSP, Bombay 1891, 4th revised ed. 1922 ; Eng. trs. by L. H. Gray in *JAOS*, XXXII, p. 59 f. The longer recension is given by the India Office MS, no 4189 (Eggeling, *Catalogue*, vii, p. 1604 f).

2 The theme is the same as that of act vii, Madhusūdana's version of the *Mahānāṭaka*, the word Dūtāṅgada being actually used in Dāmodara's recension, act xi, p. 149.

3 The longer recension, as given in the India Office MS (vii, no. 4189) contains 138 verses (as against 56 of the shorter printed recension), but the total number is still larger owing to irregular numbering of the verses in the MS.

4 Even gnomic stanzas, like *udyoginaṁ puruṣa-siṁham upaiti lakṣmīḥ*, which occurs in *Hitopadeśa*, are found in the work.

who reigned at Aṇhilvad at about 1242-43 A.D., and was presented at the spring festival held in commemoration of the restoration of the Śaive temple of Deva attana (Somnath) in Kathiawad by the deceased king Kumārapāla. Apart from prevalence of verse, more narrative than dramatic, over very scanty prose, which is a common enough feature of the decadent drama, there is nothing to distinguish it from the ordinary play and stamp it out as an irregular piece. Compared with the *Mahānāṭaka*, it is not anonymous, nor extensive; there is a regular prologue, as also some stage-direction and scene-division ; the theme is limited, and the number of persons appearing not large ; nor is Prakrit altogether omitted. To all appearance, it is a spectacular play of the popular type, composed frankly for a festive occasion, which fact will sufficiently explain (having regard to the expensive character of popular entertainments) its alleged laxity, as well as the existence of various recensions ;[1] but there is nothing to show that it was meant for shadow-pictures, except its doubtful self-description as a Chāya-nāṭaka, which need not necessarily mean a shadow-play.

This descriptive epithet is used in the prologue or colophon of some other plays also, which are otherwise different in no way from the ordinary dramatic compositions of this period, but which have been mentioned by some modern scholars as instances of Sanskrit shadow-play. Such is the *Dharmābhyudaya*[2] of Meghaprabhācārya, a short and almost insignificant play of one act but three or four scenes, having the usual prologue and stage-directions, enough prose and verse dialogues, and some Prakrit. There is, however, one stage-direction in it, which is said to support its claim to be recognised as a shadow-play. As the king takes a vow to become an ascetic,

1 Pischel points out that there are as many recensions of the work as there are manuscripts.

2 Ed. Muni Punyavijaya, Jaina Ātmānanda Granthamālā, Bhavanagar 1918. A brief résumé is given by Hultzsch in *ZDMG*, LXXV, p. 69.

the stage direction reads : *yamanikāntarād yati-veṣa-dhārī putrakas tatra sthāpanīyaḥ* (p. 15) "form the inner side of the curtain is to be placed a puppet wearing the dress of an ascetic." The direction, however, is meant to be nothing more than the symbolical representation of a fact ; it is difficult to see in it any reference to the shadow-play. No such directions, however, are found in the other so-called Chāyā-nāṭakas, not even in the *Dūtāṅgada* and the *Mahānāṭaka*, which are upheld as typical specimens of the hypothetical shadow-play. Of these plays, again, the three epic dramas of Rāmadeva Vyāsa, who was patronised by the Haihaya princes of the Kalacuri branch of Rāyapura and who thus belonged to the first half of the 15th century, are not admitted even by Lüders as shadow-plays at all. The first drama, *Subhadrā-pariṇaya*,[1] consisting of one act but three scenes, has a theme which is sufficiently explained by its title ; the second, *Rāmābhyudaya*,[2] also a short play in two acts, deals with the time-worn topic of the conquest of Laṅkā, the fire-ordeal of Sītā, and Rāma's return to Ayodhyā ; while the third play, *Pāṇḍavābhyudaya*,[3] also in two acts, deals with the birth and Svyaṃvara of Draupadī. If we leave aside the self-adopted title of Chāyā-nāṭaka, these plays do not differ in any respect from the ordinary play. The anonymous *Hari-dūta*,[4] which describes in three scenes Kṛṣṇa's mission to Duryodhana, has the same theme as the *Dūta-vākya* ascribed to Bhāsa, but there is nothing in it which would enable us to classify it as a shadow-play ; and it does not, moreover, describe itself as a Chāyā-nāṭaka. The *Ānanda-latikā*, again, which is regarded by Sten Konow as a shadow-play, is really a comparatively modern dramatic poem in five sections (called Kusumas) on the

1 See Bendall in *JRAS*, 1898, p. 231. MS noticed in Bendall's *Cat. of MSS in the British Museum*, no 271, p. 106 f. Analysis in Lévi, *op. cit.*

2 MS in Bendall, *op. cit.*, no. 272, pp. 107-3. Analysed by Lévi.

3 India Office MS no. 4187 (Eggeling, vii, p. 1602).

Bendall, *op. cit.*, no. 270, p. 106. Analysed by Lévi.

5 India Office MS no. 4203. (Eggeling, vii, p. 1624). Edited in the *Saṁskṛta-Sāhitya-Pariṣat-Patrikā*, vol. XXIII, *et sequel*, Calcutta 1940-42.

love of Sama and Revā, composed by Kṛṣṇanātha Sārvabhauma Bhaṭṭācārya, son of Durgādāsa Cakravartin. The same remarks apply to the modern *Citra-yajña* of Vaidyanātha Vācaspati (in five acts, on the Dakṣa-legend), described by Wilson, who is undoubtedly right in pointing out its similarities to the popular Yātrā of Bengal. It is possible that all these short pieces, not entirely original, were meant for popular festive entertainments, and therefore made some concession to popular taste by not conforming strictly to the orthodox requirements, and the shadow-play theory is not at all necessary to explain whatever peculiarities they possess on this account.

All the alleged irregular features of these small plays are found enormously emphasised in the huge, anonymous and semi-dramatic *Mahānāṭaka*. the peculiarities or real irregularities of which have started some amount of learned speculation centering round the obscure question of its character and origin. Though technically designated a Nāṭaka, it evinces characteristics which apparently justify Wilson's description of the work as a nondescript composition. It is a very extensive work, almost wholly in verse, on the entire Rāmāyaṇa story, but a large number of its verses is unblushingly plagiarised from most of the known, and probably some unknown, dramas on the same theme. There is little of prose and true dialogue ; the usual stage-directions are missing ; the number of characters appearing is fairly large ; there is a benediction, and in one recension we have a curious Prarocanā verse, which ascribes the play to the mythical Hanūmat, but there is no proper Prologue ; all the elements of the plot prescribed by theory are wanting, the work being a panoramic narration of the epic incidents without dramatic motive or action ; the number of acts, at least in one recension, is beyond the prescribed limit ; in short, the work, barely exhibiting a dramatic form, gives the impression of being a loose narrative composition, as opposed to dramatic, and might have been as well written in the regular form of a Kāvya.

The work exists in two principal recensions; the one, West Indian, redacted by Dāmodara Miśra in fourteen acts and 548 verses, is styled *Hanūman-nāṭaka*,[1] while the other, East Indian (Bengal), arranged by Madhusūdana in ten acts and 720 verses, is named the *Mahānāṭaka*.[2] The titles are clearly descriptive,[3] and the work is in reality anonymous; but both the recensions find it convenient to ascribe the apparently traditional work of unknown or forgotten authorship to the legendary Hanūmat, the faithful servant of Rāma. We have no historical information about the origin of the work, but fanciful accounts, recorded by the commentators and by the *Bhoja-prabandha*, associate the recovery of Hanūmat's work with Bhoja and suggest the redaction of an old anonymous composition. Although the two recensions are divergent, a considerable number of verses is common, and recent textual researches tend to show[4] that probably Dāmodara's version is the primary source and Madhusūdana's derivative. But there is nothing to negative the conjecture that originally there existed an essential nucleus, round which these elaborate recensions weave a large number of verses, culled chiefly from various Rāma-dramas. If Bhoja of the legendary account be Bhoja of Dhārā (second quarter of the 11th century), whose interest in encyclopaedic compilations is well known, then the earliest redaction may have taken place in his time; but the process of expansion must have continued, leading to divergence of recensions and incor-

1 Ed. Veṅkaṭeśvara Press, Bombay 1909, with the Dipakā comm. of Mohanadāsa.

2 Ed. Chandrakumar Bhattacharya, with the comm. of Candraśekhara, Calcutta 1874; ed. Jivananda Vidyasagar, 2nd. ed., Calcutta 1890.—The number of verses varies greatly in different MSS and editions; the number given here is that of Aufrecht's *Bodleian Catalogue*, p. 142b.

3 The term Mahānāṭaka is not really a designation, but a description. The term is not known to Bharata and the *Daśa-rūpaka*, but later writers like Viśvanātha explain it as a technical term which connotes a play containing all the episodes and possessing a large number (generally ten) of acts. The *Bāla-rāmāyaṇa* is apparrently a Mahānāṭaka in this sense. Śāradātanaya's description of a Māhānāṭaka throws little light on the subject (see S. K. De in *Pathak Commemoration Volume*, p. 139 f).

4 A. Esteller, *Die älteste Rezension des Mahānāṭaka*, Leipzig 1936.

poration of a large mass of stanzas from the leading dramatic works on the Rāmāyaṇa theme.[1]

What the original form of the text was we do not know,[2] but there can be little doubt that the present form of the text is comparatively late, and does not carry us back, as scholars have presumed, to the earliest stage of the development of the Sanskrit drama. That it is a drama of an irregular type, more than any of the works mentioned above, is admitted ; but the work also shows the general features of the decadent drama in a much more intensified manner, in its greater formlessness, in its preference of narration to action, and in the almost exclusive preponderance of poetical stanzas. This fact may not furnish a complete explanation, but since the quasi-dramatic presentation is not early and spontaneous but late and deliberate, it cannot be argued that the irregularities betoken a primitive stage in which the drama had not yet emerged from the epic condition. That some matter was worked up into an extensive compilation is fairly obvious, but it is difficult to separate the old matter for historical purposes ; and the work, as a whole, does not justify any conclusion regarding the early evolution of the Sanskrit drama. Nor can the origin of the *Mahānāṭaka* be sought in the far-fetched hypothesis of the shadow-play, the very existence of which in ancient India is not beyond doubt. We have here no description of the work as a Chāyā-nāṭaka, as we have in the case of *Dūtāṅgada* and some other plays ; and there is nothing in the work itself, in spite of its irregularities, to show that the composition was intended or ever used for shadow-pictures.

On the other hand, the late and derivative character of the *Mahānāṭaka* may very well suggest that it was a compilation or adaptation of existing works on the subject, for a particular

1 The citations from the work in rhetorical and anthological works do not prove its antiquity. See S. K. De in *IHQ*, VII, 1931, pp. 541-42.

2 Esteller's suggestion that the original *Mahānāṭaka* was an anthology of epic narration, and the title Nāṭaka was a subsequent addition is only an unproved conjecture.

purpose, around an original traditional nucleus. What this purpose was is not clear, but to suggest[1] that here we have only a literary drama or *tour de force*, never intended to be staged, is not to offer a solution but to avoid the question. In no sense can the *Mahānāṭaka* be regarded as a *tour de force*, its artistic merits, apart form its descriptive and emotional stanzas, which are mostly borrowed, being almost negligible. To say, again, that it is a Lesedrama *plus* Campū *plus* Ṭīkā[2] is to give a facile description, and not an explanation. There are indications, on the contrary, that the *Mahānāṭaka*, like other works of a similar type, was meant and probably utilised for some kind of performance,[3] in which there was more recitation and narration than action and dialogue ; and its form, as a recitable semi-dramatic poem, was moulded accordingly.

This presumption receives support from the fact that the work assumed its present shape at a time when it was possible for such nondescript types to come into existence. It is clear that we cannot assign any of the recensions of the *Mahānāṭaka* to a very early date, and that they should be explained in the light of the literary conditions which prevailed at a period when the classical drama was in its decline and the creative impulse had subsided. The break up of the old orthodox drama was almost synchronous with the rise of Apabhraṃśa and modern Indian literature ; and along with it came popular entertainments of the type of the semi-religious Yātrā, with its mythological subject, quasi-dramatic presentation and preference of recitation and singing. Having regard to these historical facts, as well as to the trend and treatment revealed by such works as

1 Keith, *SD*, p. 273.

2 Esteller in the work cited.

3 Keith admits this when he says that the work was composed in preparation for some kind of performance in which the dialogue was plentifully eked out by narration. S. P. Bhattacharya (*IHQ*, 1934, p. 492 f) suggests that the work was compiled as a manual for use of professional Purāṇa reciters of the Bengal class of Kathakas. But, on this theory, the occasional elaborate stage-directions, the chorus-like Vaitālīya-vākyas, the length and extended working out of the story are not satisfactorily explained. The Bengali manuals for Kathakas are certainly of a different character.

the *Mahānāṭaka*, the presumption is not unlikely that such vernacular semi-dramatic performances of popular origin reacted on the literary Sanskrit drama and influenced its form and manner to such an extent as to render the production of such apparently irregular types greatly probable. It is not suggested, in the absence of tradition, that such a pseudo-play was actually enacted as a Yātrā, which had little pretension to a literary character. It may or may not have been, but it is possible to maintain that such works were not merely literary exercises but were intended for popular spectacular shows of some kind. That they were stylised is intelligible from their having been composed for a more cultivated audience, who with the fading attraction of the mechanically reproductive Sanskrit drama, wanted something analogous, in spirit and mode of operation, to the living types of popular entertainments, but exhibiting outwardly some of the forms of the regular drama. The anonymity and secondary character of the *Mahānāṭaka*, as well as the existence of different but substantially agreeing recensions, are points in favour of this view. As the imperfect dialogues and narrative passages were frequently supplemented, it is not surprising that a work meant for such performance increased in bulk, incorporating into itself fine recitative passages from various sources ; and different versions accordingly came into circulation. The very existence of the versions shows that it was a living work, which was modified by the exigencies of time and place, and discredits the idea of a purely literary composition. All this presumption is perhaps more in keeping with the nature of the work and the period in which the recensions were redacted than the solution of an unwarranted shadow-play theory or the superficial Lesedrama explanation.

Although regrettably little information is available about the popular entertainments of the period, indications of their possible influence on Sanskrit literature are yet not altogether wanting. Keith rightly compares such nominal plays as the *Mahānāṭaka* with the *Gīta-govinda* of Jayadeva and the *Gopāla-keli-candrikā* of Rāmakṛṣṇa, both of which can be (and in the case of the *Gīta-govinda* it actually is) enjoyed as a lyrical narrative or song, but both of which are at the same time capable of similar quasi-dramatic presentation. In both the works, we find a sublimated outcome of the operatic and melodramatic Kṛṣṇa-Yātrā, and in the case of the *Gīta-govinda* we have to reckon with the deliberate art of a creative mind. But they resemble the *Mahānāṭaka* at least in one particular, namely, in the adaptation of traditional matter and form to newer and less rigid demands of a popular origin. The date of Rāmakṛṣṇa's *Gopāla-keli-candrikā*[1] is not known, but it is apparently a late work written in Gujarat. It is not an anonymous and extensive compilation like the *Mahānāṭaka*, but a semi-religious play in five acts on the youthful exploits of Kṛṣṇa with the Gopīs. It contains, however, a large number of stanzas in light lyrical metres, both descriptive and emotional, as well as rhymed Apabhraṃśa verses obviously meant to be sung. Caland, who has edited the work, touches upon its similarity to the Yātrā, and suggests its parallel to the Swang of North-western India, which unlike the regular play, is metrical throughout, and in which the actors recite the narrative portions as well as take part in the dialogues. Its connexion with the *Mahānāṭaka* is acknowledged in the Prologue (p. 44), where the Sūtradhāra alludes to the absence of Prakrit in that play, and there can be little doubt that the author was influenced by the same tendency towards narrative and recitative rather than dramatic presentation. Another work of similar semi-dramatic form but of greater operatic and melodramatic tenor is the *Pārijāta-haraṇa*[2] of Umāpati Upādhyāya of Mithilā, which

1 Ed. W. Caland (*Een onbekend Indisch tooneelstuk*), Amsterdam 1917. *Cf.* Winternitz in *ZDMG*, LXXIV, 1920, p. 137 f.

2 Ed. and trs. G. Grierson in *JBORS*, III, 1917, pp. 20-98. The author flourished under Hariharadeva of Mithilā reigning "after the Yavana rule", and appears to be familiar with Jayadeva's *Gita-govinda*. The *Hariścandra-nṛtya* (ed. A. Conrady, Leipzig 1891) of the Nepalese king Siddhi Narasiṁha (circa 1620-57 A.D.) is rightly called a Tanzspiel by its editor, but it is in the Nepalese dialect.

deals with Kṛṣṇa's well known exploit of carrying off Indra's Pārījāta tree, and actually contains songs composed in the Maithili dialect.[1] These works are not strictly plays of the orthodox type, and the introduction of song (especially vernacular song) and narration indicates that they were probably meant for some kind of quasi-dramatic performance of a popular character.[2] They are indeed distinguishable in many respects from the *Mahānāṭaka*, which is a unique production ; but what is important to note is that these irregular types, however isolated and scattered they might appear, are perhaps products of a distinct literary tendency to renew and remodel older forms of Sanskrit poetry and drama by absorbing the newer characteristics of the vernacular literature, which now reacted upon the Sanskrit, as it was often reacted upon by the Sanskrit ; and there is no reason why the *Mahānāṭaka* should not be regarded as illustrating an aspect of the same movement. It is curious, however, that the movement did not prove as fruitful as it should have been advantageous ; and it could not ultimately save Sanskrit literature from gradual stagnation or from being completely ousted by the stronger and fresher vitality of modern Indian literature.

1 Sanskrit songs, on the direct model of Jayadeva's work, occurs in the *Jangannātha-vallabha* of Rāmānanda-rāya, a Bhakti-drama inspired by the Caitanya movement, which is called a Saṁgīta-nāṭaka in its Prologue. See above, p. 468.

2 The *Nandighoṣa-vijaya* (or *Kamalā-vilāsa*), in five acts, described by Eggeling (vii, no. 4190, p. 1606), appears to be a similar semi-dramatic composition connected with the Ratha-yātrā festival of Jagannātha at Puri ; it was composed by Śivanārāyaṇa-dāsa in honour of his patron Gajapati Narasiṁhadeva of Orissa, in the middle of the 16th century.

CHAPTER I

LITERARY AND CHRONOLOGICAL RELATIONS

The Vyākarana School and the Alamkāra School

The word *alaṃkāra* is derived from the word *alam* (Gk. *aurum* —gold), which in Sanskrit primarily means adornment. *Alaṃkāra* thus means the making of adornments or ornaments or decorations. It is also used in relation to the *Alaṃkāraśāstra* or the Science of the Decoration of Speech, literary embellishments. The science of grammar deals with correctness of language or speech. Whatsoever development the Sanskrit language may have undergone since the time of the Vedas and whatsoever attempts may have been made in the various *śikṣā* literature and pre-Pāṇinian writers on Grammar, it attained a stability and is supposed to have fitted exactly to the scheme prepared for it by Pāṇini (5th or 6th century B. C.), Kātyāyana (probably 4th century B. C.), and Patañjali, the writer of the great commentary called the *Mahābhāṣya* (2nd century B. C.). The earliest systematic work on Alaṃkāra that has survived the ravages of time is that of Bhāmaha (who was in all probability a Buddhist of the 5th or 6th century A. D.), of which we shall have occasion to discuss later on. Bharata's *Nāṭyasūtra,* which is essentially a work on histrionic art, incidentally makes reference to many topics which might better come under a work on Alaṃkāra and which shows that in all probability works on Alaṃkāra must have existed in the time when the relevant passages referring to Alaṃkāra topics were written. The date of this *Nāṭya-śāstra* is also uncertain as would be evident from relevant discussions that would follow in due course.

The close association of the grammar and the Alaṃkāra literature may well be expected and it is also justified by tradition. The former deals with correctness of speech and the latter with literary embellishments.

In most works on Alaṃkāra we find a chapter dedicated to the three-fold powers of words. We know that Pāṇini's *prātipadikārtha*, etc., implies that there were five opinions regarding the signification of a word. The word *parimāṇa* in the above-mentioned rule has been interpreted by Bhaṭṭoji Dīkṣita as *droṇarūpaṃ yat parimāṇaṃ tatparicchinno brīhih pratyayārthe prakṛtyartho'bhedena saṃsargeṇa viśeṣaṇam.*" If this interpretation is accepted, it becomes clear that what has been regarded as *lakṣaṇā* by the writers on Alaṃkāra is regarded by Pānini as being nothing but primary sense. The author of the *Tattvabodhinī* commentary, Jñānendra Bhikṣu, in trying to effect a compromise between the two views as to whether the first case-ending here is in the primary sense or in the secondary sense, and in computing the value of the two suggestions, says that the difference lies in the two different aspects in which the word may be supposed to significate (*śabdabodha-kṛta-vailakṣaṇyam*). Pāṇini makes no provision for *lakṣaṇā* even in the case of *siṃho mānavakaḥ* or *agnir mānavakaḥ*. This appears to me to show conclusively that Pāṇini himself was not aware of the view propounded by the writers of Alaṃkāra, that *lakṣanā* is a power of signification of words different from the primary sense.

We know that when a word contradicts its context in the primary sense of the word, as recorded in the lexicons, it may yet in many cases significate another meaning—such significations many either be due to customary practice or for implying a special suggestion. Thus if I say, 'The imperialistic states are bound to be cannibals,'—the word 'cannibal' means one who eats human flesh—certainly the imperialistic states cannot be eating human flesh ; the word, therefore, simply means that they try to destroy one another. The use of the word 'cannibal' instead of simple expression that the imperialistic states destory one another, is intended to imply that their actions are as heinous and hateful as those of cannibals. Here the secondary sense of the word 'cannibal' has a relation with its primary sense, but this roundabout expression, on account of the force of its implication, contributes to the embellishment of the speech and hence comes within the province of Alaṃkāra. In witnessing a horse race, one may say that the black runs faster than the rest. Here the use of the word 'black' to denote the 'black horse' is a customary usage which may or may not add to the embellishment of speech.

The grammarians think that in the case of a primary sense the signification is due to the power of the word standing as the symbol (*saṃketa*) for the object. Here the fact that the symbol significates its object is due to the fact that there is really no distinction between the symbol and its connotation. This is the view of the grammarians as well as that of the Mīmāṃsaka and the Yoga authors. The writers of Alaṃkāra follow this view in preference to the Nyāya view which holds that it is by the will of God that from certain words we understand certain meanings. The understanding of a meaning is a subjective affair, while the significatory view as held by the grammarians and the Alaṃkāra authors is a purely objective view. The words significate certain objects and we learn it by practice. But however true it may be with regard to the primary-sense it would be obviously wrong to attribute the secondary or the indicatory signification as being due to the power of the word, for here the indicatory sense does not occur with the pronouncement of the word but after a long process of cogitation regarding its inappropriateness in the context and the possible manner in which this inappropriateness might be removed. For this reason *lakṣanā* can hardly be regarded as the significatory power of the word. The Alaṃkāra writers do not seem to be absolutely ignorant of this criticism, and we find them sometimes describing the operation of *lakṣaṇā* as an *āropita-kriyā* or an attributive function.

It is true no doubt that the older Alaṃkāra writer Bhamaha does not treat these, but the later Alaṃkāra writers like Mammaṭa and Viśvanātha take their fundamental start with the three-fold division of the power of words. We have said before that Pāṇini does not seem to admit the *lakṣaṇā* as a separate function of words. With the conception that words objectively by their own power denote things and are as a matter of fact one with the things, seems to be a Pāṇinian view, at least as interpreted by Patañjali and Bhartṛhari, the older commentator of Patañjali's *Mahābhāṣya* and the writer of the *Vākyapadīya.* We know that all the three schools, Mīmāṃsā, Vyākaraṇa and Yoga, admit the philosophical doctrine that the power and the possessor of power are identical. The Alaṃkāra school, in adopting the same significatory theory of words, naturally adopts the same philosophical doctrine at least by implication. That this idealism forms the basis of the Alaṃkāra school of thought can be well apprehended from the words of Dhvanikāra (*apāre kāvyasaṃsāre kavireva prajāpatiḥ* । *sa yat pramāṇaṃ kurute viśvaṃ tat parivartate* ॥ In the infinite world of literature the poet is the creator, and whatever appears to him to be valid, the world also changes accordingly). The last line should be read with caution. It does not mean merely that the imagination of the poet is valid, but it means that the world changes its form in accordance with the value-sense of the poet. Or, in other words, the world transforms itself into that form which is approved as valid in the poet's creation. It assumes, therefore, that the beauty created by the poet does not merely make the world appear beautiful to our eyes but the world transforms itself into beauteous forms in accordance with the creation of the poet. The *vāṅmaya-jagat* or the world of words is in reality identical with the world of nature.

Mammaṭa, again, classifies words as being of four kinds, as, meaning, *jāti* or class notion, quality or *guṇa, kriyā* or action, *dravya* or things, in accordance with the view of Patañjali. We thus find that there is a natural affinity of origin between the grammar school of thought and the Alaṃkāra school. It is also well-known that the Grammar school has always been referred to by the Alaṃkāra school as the wise men or *budha.*[1]

ALAṂKĀRA-ŚĀSTRA—ITS NAME

The ordinary treatises of Alaṃkāra like *Kāvya-prakāśa* or *Sāhitya-darpaṇa* generally consist of ten chapters and they deal generally with the following subjects:—(1) the definition of Kāvya, whether it is necessarly didactic or not; (2) the threefold signification of words, primary, indicatory, and implicatory; (3) the nature of poetic emotion; (4) the nature of the implicatory sense of a higher and lower order; (5) the special qualities of good literature, their defects, their style, their adornments or *alaṃkāra. Sāhitya-darpaṇa* treats along with it the various forms of Kāvya. In addition to this there are special treatises dealing only with a part of the subject.

Bhāmaha, the author of the oldest available treatise on Alaṃkāra, treats primarily of *guṅa, doṣa, rīti,* and *alaṃkāra,* and also makes incidental remarks on the usefulness of Kāvya. It may, therefore, naturally be asked why since a work on Alaṃkāra treats of so many subjects, it should be named as *alaṃkraśāstra.* The question acquires a point of force when we consider that in most of the recondite works on Alaṃkāra great emphasis is given on *dhvani* and *rasa* as the constitutive characteristics of a good Kāvya. The question is nowhere definitely faced in a work of Alaṃkāra, but it seems to me that the earlier works on Alaṃkāra that are now lost probably dealt with various types of literary ornaments or *alaṃkāras* which led, naturally, to the criticism and enquiry as to the further condition which would make the adornments really possess the adorning character. We find Bhāmaha actually raising such questions and introducing the topic of *rasa* or emotion as being the determinant factor of true

1 See *Dhvanyāloka.*

adornments. All adornments are also regarded by him as consisting of exaggeration (*atiśayokti*) and the covert way of suggestion which may be called *vakrokti*.

The 16th chapter of Bharata's *Nāṭya-śāstra* enumerates four adornments or *alaṃkāras*, ten excellences or *guṇas*, and thirty-six characteristics or *lakṣaṇās* of a good Kāvya. But I think that the first enquiry into the nature of poetic embellishments must have led the earliest thinkers to take note of the poetic imageries, spontaneous expressions of which are found also in the Vedas, and this must have given *alaṃkāra* its first title of importance.

In the time of Bharata there seemed to have been an excellent development of poetic literature and Bharata concerned himself particularly with one form of it, the Dramaturgy and the allied topics.

The word *upamā* or comparison is found in the *Ṛg-Veda* V. 34. 9; I. 31. 15, and Pāṇini II. 3. 72 mentions the word *upamāna*. The term *alaṃkāra* in the form *alaṃkariṣṇu* is explained by Pāṇini III. 2. 36, and the word occurs in *Śatapatha Brāhmaṇa* XIII. 8. 4. 7.; III. 5. 1. 36 and *Chāndogya Upaniṣad* VIII. 8. 5. But Yāska in his *Nighaṇṭu* III. 13 gives a list of particles for indicating *upamā*, which are illustrated in the *Nirukta* I. 4; III. 13-18, and IX. 6. These are such as, *iva, yathā, na, cit, nu, ā*, etc. These are called *nipāta* in the sense of *upamā*. He further mentions *bhūtopamā, rūpopamā*, and *siddhopamā* and *luptopamā* as varieties of *upamā*. The *luptopamā* is called *arthopamā* and is in essence the same as the *rūpaka* of the later Alaṃkāra writers. Yāska also quotes the definition of *upamā* as given by an earlier grammarian Gārgya (*athāto upamā yad atat tatsadṛśam iti gārgyaḥ*). From the rule, *upamānāni sāmānya-vacanaih* and the rule *upamitaṃ vyāghrādibiḥ sāmānyāprayoge* we can understand that the teachings of Gārgya were already assimilated by Pāṇini and we find there the various terms of imagery such as, *upamāna, upamita, sāmānya, aupamya, upamārtha,* and *sādṛśya* had all been used by Pāṇini in about fifty *sūtras* of his work. The place of *upamā* in modifying compounds and accents and in other grammatical constructions has been referred to by Pāṇini. Kātyāyana in his *Vārttika* and Śāntanava in his *Phiṭ-sūtras* follow Pāṇini. In the *Mahābhāṣya* II. 1. 55. Patañjali interprets Pāṇini's usage of the term *upamāna,* which is somewhat different from the later definition of the term.

My view that the Alaṃkāra school arose as an offshoot of the Grammar school, may be regarded to attain special point of force when the above facts are considered. The later definition of *śrautī* and *ārthī upamā* is based upon the fact as whether simile was based on a *kṛt* or a *taddhit* suffix and the distinction between the *śrautī* and the *ārthī upamā* was based on this criterion till the time of Udbhaṭa and this is controlled by Pāṇini's rule V. 1. 115-16. A *śrautī upamā* is supposed to be that where the comparison is indicated by *yathā, iva, vā,* or the suffix *vat* in the sense of *iva.* Again, Pāṇini II. 4. 71 inspires the *Vārttika,* which directs that *iva* may always be compounded as in *śabdārthāviva.* Pāṇini III. 1. 10 advises the *kyac* suffix in the sense of comparison.[1] It is needless to multiply examples but the above brief discussion seems to point to the view that poetic imageries had very largely evolved in the grammar school. Of the various *alaṃkāras* or the adornments of speech, imageries of divers types occupy practically more than three-fourths of the field. The high respect in which the grammarians were held by the Alaṃkāra writers is also evident from the remarks of Ānandavardhana.[2] Bhāmaha also devotes one whole chapter to the grammatical correctness of words and so does also Vāmana. It may also be pointed out that the discovery of the theory of *vyañjanā,* which is regarded as the high water mark of the genius of the great alaṃkāra writers, is

1 See S. K. De's *Sanskrit Poetics,* Vol. I, pp. 1-11.

2 *prathame hi vidvāṁso vaiyākaraṇāḥ, vyākaraṇamūlatvāt sarvvavidyānāṁ,* p, 47, *Dhvanyāloka.*

also, on the pattern of the *Sphoṭa* theory of the grammarians, as elaborated in *Vākyapadīya* and other works.

It is a known fact that the early *praśasti* writer, during the first few centuries of the Christian era, Aśvaghoṣa, in his *Buddha-carita* is well-acquainted with such figures of speech as *upamā, utprekṣā,* or *rūpaka, yathāsaṃkhya,* or *aprastuta praśaṃsa,* etc. The use of the various figures of speech by Kālidāsa is also too well-known. Subandhu takes pride in his skill of using *śleṣa* in every letter of his composition.[1] In Bhāmaha also we find a great aptitude and liking for diverse types of *alaṃkāra.* We hear also of Kāśyapa and Vararuci as early writers of *alaṃkāra,* as well as Medhāvin as referred to by Bhāmaha. All these seem to indicate that even before the other topics of the *alaṃkāra-sāstra* were developed there were probably treatises of Alaṃkāra dealing with manifest emphasis on the figures of speech, which had already developed in Pāṇini and the grammarians, who may be regarded as the inspirers of the *alaṃkāra-śāstra.*

The Early Origin of the Alaṃkāra

Many writers have in modern times discussed the subject of Alaṃkāra.[2] It is admitted on all hands that the *alaṃkāra-śāstra* attained in India the position of a science in very early times. But the question is how early did the *alaṃkāra-śāstra* become

[1] *pratyakṣara-śleṣamayaprapañca-vinyāsa-vaidagdhyanidhiṁ prabandham | sarasvatīdatta-vara-prasādāc cakre subandhuḥ sujanaika-bandhuḥ.* ||

[2] P. Regnaud, *La Rhetorique Sanskrite,* Paris 1884 ; R. Pischel, *Göttinger Gelehrte Anzeigen* 1885 ; G. A. Jacob, J.R.A.S., 1897 ; J. Nobel, *Beiträge zur älteren Geschichte des Alaṁkāra-śāstra, Din.,* Berlin 1911, and Z.D.M.G., 1912 1913, 1919 ; P. V. Kane, *Outlines of the History of Alaṁkāra Literature, Indian Antiquary* 41, 1912 ; his edition of *Sāhityadarpaṇa* ; H. Oldenberg, *Die Literatur des alten Indien,* Stuttgart and Berlin 1903 ; Harichānd, *Kālidāsa et l'art poetique de l'Inde,* Paris 1917 ; H. Jacobi, *Uber Begriff und Wesen Der poetischen Figuren in der indischen Poetik* ; *Nachrichten von der Kgl, Gesellschaft der Wissenschaften,* Göttingen, *Philolog—Histor. Klasse* 1908 ; and *Die Poetik und Äesthetik der Inder in der Internat Wochenschrift,* 29th Okt. 1910 ; Sovani's article in *Bhandarkar Commemoration Vol.*; S. K. De's *Sanskrit Poetics* ; S. N. Dasgupta's *Kavya-vicāra* (in Bengali).

really a *śāstra* or a science. From general considerations, since in our view the *alaṃkāra-śāstra* was inspired by the Grammar school of thought we expect it to have evolved slightly later than the middle of the 2nd century B.C., in the age of Patañjali. Let us see how far other considerations may justify this thesis.

Rājaśekhara, a man of the tenth century, in his *Kāvya-mīmāṃsā* speaking of the origin of the *alaṃkāra-śāstra* claimed that it was instructed by Śiva to Brahmā and from him it was handed down to others and then it became divided into 18 sections, each of which was taught by a particular teacher. Thus, Sahasrākṣa taught *Kavirahasya,* Muktigarbha, *Auktika,* Suvarṇanābha, *Rītinirṇaya,* Pracetāyana, *Anuprāsika,* Citrāṇgada, *Citra* and *Yamaka,* Śeṣa *Śabdaśleṣa,* Pulastya, *Vāstava,* Aupakāyana, *Aupamya,* Parāśara, *Atiśaya,* Utathya, *Arthaśleṣa,* Kuvera, *Arthālankārikā,* Kāmadeva, *Vainodika,* Bharata, *Rūpaka-nirūpaṇīya* Nandikeśvara, *Rasādhikārikā,* Dhīṣaṇa, *Doṣādhi kārikā,* Upamanyu, *Guṇaupādānikā,* Kucumāra *Aupaniṣadika.* It is interesting to note that the majority of the sections deal with figures of speech, and this lends support to our view that the earlier treatises on *Alaṃkāra* were mostly on the figures of speech. Of the writers mentioned above almost nothing is known to us except that Kucumāra and Suvarṇanābha are referred to in the *Kāma-sūtra* (I. 13-17) as the authors of the *Aupaniṣadika* and the *Sāmprayogika* sections of erotics. We do not know anything further of the time or the authenticity of the above-mentioned writers. According to the *Hṛdayaṅgama* commentary of the *Kāvyādarśa,* Kāśyapa and Vararuci had written works on poetics before Daṇḍin, whose works Daṇḍin had consulted. The Commentary *Śrutānupālinī* on the *Kāvyā-darśa* mentions Kāśyapa, Brahmadatta, and Nandisvāmī as predecessors of Daṇḍin.[1] These works are no longer available.

1 P V. Kane, *The Sāhityadarpaṇa,* 1923, Introduction (p. 1),

But nowhere in the earliest literature do we find any reference to *alaṃkāra-śāstra*. Thus the *Chāndogya Upaniṣad* gives a list of the old *śāstras* (VII, 1. 2. 4) ; but it does not refer to the *alaṃkāra-śāstra*. Āpastamba in II. 4. 11 refers to the six *aṅgas* and neither Yājñavalkya nor Viṣṇupurāṇa refers to the *alaṃkāra-śāstra*. In the *Lalitavistara* there is a reference to *Kāvya-karaṇa-grantha* and *Nāṭya*. *Kāvya-karaṇa-grantha* need not necessarily mean *Alaṃkāra*. The *Arthaśāstra* of Kauṭilya also does not make any reference to *Alaṃkāra*. Kauṭilya's *Arthaśāstra* in advising the language of the King's Edicts recommends sequence of meaning (*arthakrama*), completeness of sense (*paripūrṇatā*), sweetness (*mādhuryya*), clearness (*spaṣṭatva*) and width of meaning (*audāryya*), as excellences of style, to be observed. But this has nothing to do with *alamkāra-śāstra*, at best it may refer only to style. It thus appeares that there is no evidence that there was any *alaṃkāra śāstra* before Patañjali.

It is true that Bharata's *Nāṭya-śāstra* contains elements of *alaṃkāra-śāstra*, but its date is uncertain Macdonell assigns it to the 6th century A.D. and MM. Haraprasad Sastri to the 2nd century B.C., and Lé'vi to the Kṣatrapā period. The fact that Kālidāsa in his *Vikramorvaśī* refers to Bharata as a *muni*, only shows that he was much earlier than Kālidāsa. This would place the lower limit of Bharata to the 3rd or 4th century B.C. From the reference in Kālidāsa we are compelled to say that Dr. De's view that the lower limit of Bharata in the 8th century A.D., seems quite untenable. In any case there is but little evidence that the present *Nāṭya-śāstra* was written earlier than the commencement of the Christian era. Many writers have written on Bharata's *Nāṭya-sāstra*.[1]

1 W. Heymann, basing on a South Indian MSS. wrote upon it in the *Nachrichten von der Kgl. Gesellschaft der Wissenschaften*, Göttingen, *Philolog—Histo*. Klasse, 1874 ; P. Regnaud published also the *adhyāyas* six and seven in *La Rhétorique Sanskrite*, Paris 1884, and *adhyāyas* 15 to 17 in the *Annals of the Musée Guimet*, and also the *adhyāyas* 20 to 22, and 34 have been published by F. A. Hall. The 28th *adhyāya* was published by J. Grosset in contribution *a' l'étude de la Musique Hindue*, Paris 1888 ; a critical foreword to *adhyāyas* 1-14 was also published by him is Paris in 1898. The whole work was published

We thus see that there is no evidence that any *alaṃkāra-śāstra* existed beyond the commencement of the Christian era. Bharata, however, need not be regarded as the earliest writer on dramaturgy. We find references in Pāṇini of a *Bhikṣu-sūtra* and a *Naṭa-sūtra* and we do not know who is the original author of this *Naṭa-sūtra* and whether this *Naṭa-sūtra* is somewhat connected with our present *Nāṭya-śāstra.* We have also reference in Paṇini (IV. 3. 110) of Kṛśāśva and Śilālin, who were recondite writers on dramaturgy. But we know nothing further of these two writers. Bharata's *Nāṭya-śāstra* is said to have many commentaries. The names of the commentaries referred to by Abhinavagupta and Śārṅgadeva are the followings :—Udbhaṭa, Lollaṭa, Śaṅkuka, Bhaṭṭanāyaka, Rāhula, Bhaṭṭatauta, Kīrtidhara, Mātṛgupta. Only fragmentary portions of Abhinavagupta's commentary are available and have been printed in the Gaekwad Oriental Series by the name *Abhinava-bhāratī.*[1] *Śārṇgadhara-paddhati* refers to some of the verses of Śaṅkuka. It is doubtful, however, whether Śaṅkuka the poet and Śaṅkuka the commentator is one and the same person. Kalhaṇa mentions a poet Śaṅkuka and his poem *Bhubanābhyudaya.* Śaṅkuka probably lived in the early ninth century. If the two are identical, Saṅkuka's date becomes ascertainable, but we know nothing of the date of Lollaṭa, but he was probably later than Udbhaṭa as Lollaṭa controverts Udbhaṭa's view (9th century A.D.). There is a confusion as to whether Bhaṭṭanāyaka was the author of a work called *Hṛdaya-darpaṇa,* for while Hemacandra refers to it as belonging to Bhaṭṭanāyaka Abhinavagupta definitely seems to refer the work as belonging to a different person. So, though some scholars have maintained

in the Kāvyamālā series in 1894 and later on with parts of the commentary of Abhinavagupta, in the Gaekwad Oriental Series ; Pavolini in the *Giornale de la Societa Asiatic Italiana* discusses about the *Nāṭya-śāstra* in 1912 and refers to the work of F. Cimmino on the *Nāṭya-śāstra* published in Naples 1912 ; Prof. H. H. Dhruva also writes on the subject in *Asiatic Quarterly Review*, No. III, 2, 1896, and MM. Śāstri in J. A. S. B., 5, 1919. S. K. De's *Sanskrit Poetics* and Introductory Notes to P. V. Kane's edition of *Sāhityadarpaṇa.*

that Bhaṭṭanāyaka was the author of *Hṛdaya-darpaṇa,* I have definitely denied that in my *Kāvya-vicāra.* *Hṛdaya-darpaṇa,* however, though it may have supported Abhinavagupta in certain places, was in reality a work which had contradicted the *dhvani*-theory, and it was on this account that Mahima Bhaṭṭa to save his credit said that before writing his book he had not consulted *Hṛdaya-darpaṇa.*

But all this is a digression. *Hṛdaya-darpaṇa* does not appear to have been a commentary to Bharata's *Nāṭya-śāstra* as some maintain. Bhaṭṭanāyaka was in all probability conversant with the text of *Dhvanyāloka* and Ānandavardhana and was probably a contemporary of Abhinavagupta. But these discussions do not concern us here. We find that the *Nāṭya-śāstra* of Bharata was the earliest available work to us that contained *alaṃkāra* materials, and this work could not have been at least in its present form earlier than the 1st or 2nd century A.D.[1]

1 At the end of the work *Bharatīya Nāṭya-sāstra* the name of the author appears as Nandī Bharata. The same name occurs as the author of a work on music, and the name of Nandī or Nandikeśara occurs as the author of *Abhinaya-darpaṇa.* The word *Bharata* also stands for the director of the actor, and R. Pischel translates *Bharatiya Nāṭya-śāstra* as the book of instruction on the art of acting for the actors. In later literature the word 'Bharata' is also used in the sense of play-director, who appears on the stage at the conclusion of the play, and utters a benedictory verse called the *Bharatavākya.* In *Viṣṇupurāṇa* III. 6 Bharatamuni is said to be the author of the *Gandharva-veda* or the science of music. The *Nāṭya-śāstra,* as we have it, is the work of an encyclopaedic character. It is composed generally in verses of an epic nature and sometimes changes the metre, interspersed here and there with prose, and consists of 38 chapters or *adhyāyas.* It deals not only with the nature of the dramatic literature but also with the art of dancing and mimic and various other subject connected with the operation of acting. It deals also with the *rasa* and *bhāva* and alaṁkāra and the art of dramatic poetry and music. Regnaud and Oldenberg fix the date of *Nāṭya-śāstra* in the 1st century of the Christian era. Pischel, however, regarded this to be a work of the 6th or 7th century A.D. D. R. Bhandarkar thinks that the present *Nāṭya-śāstra* is based on an earlier work. Speaking of the chapter on music he says that it belongs to the 4th century A.D. or it may even be later. MM. Śāstrī regarded it to be a work of the 7th century A.D., and Jacobi places it in the 3rd century A.D. On this subject see the following literature :—(1) Oldenberg's *die Literatur des Alten Indien,* Stuttgart, und Berlin 1903, (2) R. Pischel in *Gottinger Gelehrte Anzeigen* 1886 (p. 763), (3) D. R. Bhandarkar in *Indian Antiquary* 41, 1912, (4) MM. Śāstrī's article in the J.A.S.B., 6, 1910, 307, (5) Jacobi in Bhavisatta Kahao. (6) P. V. Kane's Introduction to *Sāhitya-darpaṇa,* (7) Dr. S. K. De's *Sanskrit Poetics.*

The Earlier Writers on Alamkāra-Śāstra

Bhamaha, of whom we shall treat later on, refers to a writer, Medhavin, regarding the defects of *upamā* as pointed out by him. He also refers to him on the subject of the *alaṃkāras*, *yathāśaṅkhya* and *utprekṣā*.[1] But Medhavin's work on *alaṃkāras*, has not come down to us and we do not know of any MSS. also of Medhavin's work.

P. V. Kane, referring to the *anuvaṁśa* verses of the *Nāṭya-śāstra* mentions the name of Kohala, Vātsya, Śāṇḍilya and Dhūrtila, as persons stated there as destined to spread the *Nāṭya-śāstra*. The name Kohala as a writer of *Nāṭya-śāstra* occurs in *Kuṭṭanimatam* of Damodaragupta of the 8th century A.D. A work on *tāla*, attributed to Kohala, exists in the India Office Library, and Hemacandra in his *Kavyānusāśana* speaks of Kohalācārya as a writer on dramaturgy. The *Rasārṇava-sudhākara* of Siṁha-bhūpāla mentions Bharata, Śaṇḍilya, Kohala, Dattila, and Mataṅga as authors of works on *Nāṭya-śāstra*.

Rāghava Bhaṭṭa, in his commentary on *Śakuntalā*, quotes chapters and verses from Bharata's *Nāṭya-śāstra*, and refers to the commentary *Abhinava.bhāratī* by Abhinavagupta. This commentary occurs also under the name of *Nāṭyaveda-vivṛti*. Someśvara, a commentator of *Kāvya-prakāśa*, refers to a commentator of *Nāṭya-śāstra* by the name of Maṅgala. Māṇikya-candra also in his *Kāvya-prakāśasaṅketa* refers to Maṅgala. Maṅgala is referred to also by Hemacandra and Rājaśekhara. Sundara Miśra in his *Nāṭya-pradīpa*, composed in 1613 A.D. refers to a passage of *Nāṭya-śāstra* and speaks of Mātṛguptācāryya as having written a *Vyākhyāna* on it. Rāhula Bhaṭṭa also refers to the passage of *ārāmbha* and *vija* in the *Nāṭya-śāstra* and supports the view of Mātṛguptācāryya on it. Mr. Kane suggests that Mātṛgupta probably wrote a *vārttika* of the *Nāṭya-śāstra*. It is difficult to say whether this Mātṛgupta was the poet who was made King of Kashmir by Harṣavikramāditya of Ujjain as stated in *Rājataraṅgiṇī* III, 128-189.

1 *yathāsaṁkhyamathotprekṣām alaṁkāradvayaṁ viduḥ* ı *saṁkhyānamiti medhavinotprekṣābhihitā kvacit* ıı 2.88.

As it stands it means that Medhavin styles *utprekṣa* as *saṁkhyāna* but Daṇḍin has told us in the *Kāvyādarśa* II, 273 that *yathāsaṁkhya* has been styled as *saṁkhyāna* by other writers. Kane, therefore, suggests that in the second line the reading *medhavinotprekṣā* should read as *medhāvi notprekṣā*. The meaning under such a reading would be that Medhāvī calls *yathāsaṁkhya saṁkhyāna* and has not mentioned *utprekṣā*. Such a meaning tallies with that of Daṇḍin as above. Namisādhu in commenting on Rudraṭa's *Kāvyālaṁkāra*, 1. 2. refers to the name of one Medhāvi-rudra along with Daṇḍin and Bhāmaha as authors of *alaṁkāra-śāśtra*. But it is difficult to guess whether Medhāvi-rudra is one name or two names, Medhāvi and Rudra. We know of no Alamkāra author of the name of Rudra, and we know also that there were many names with Rudra as the second member, such as, Mālavarudra, Kapilarudra, etc. (See Kane's article in J.R.A.S., 1908). Namisādhu further quotes from Medhāvin on the subject of the defects of simile and on the four divisions of *śabda* that Medhāvin has not counted the *karmapravacanīyas*. The *Trikāṇḍaśeṣa* regards Medhāvirudra and Kālidāsa as synonymous and Rājaśekhara in his *Kāvyamīmāṁsā* calls Medhāvirudra a blind poet and Kālidāsa a writer on *alaṁkāra* (see Kane's *Sāhityadarpaṇa*).

Bhāmaha's *Kāvyālaṃkāra* is the earliest work on *alaṃkāra* that has come down to us. The existence of the work was at first guessed from a few quotations given by Colonel Jacob in J.R.A.S., 1897, and the work has been published by Mr. Trivedi as an appendix to his edition of his *Pratāparudra-yaśobhūṣaṇa* in the Bombay Sanskrit Series.[1] He is supposed to have been the son of Rakrilagomin and his work is written in verse. It is divided into six chapters and contains 398 verses. The first chapter, containing sixty verses, deals with the qualifications of a poet, the differentiation and division of Kāvya as prose and poetry, and as work in Sanskrit prose or *apabhraṃśa*, as epic poetry, drama, *ākhyāyikā* and *anubandha*, and also treats of the *Vaidarbhī* and the *Gauḍī* styles, and speaks of some literary defects. In the second chapter he deals with three *guṇas*, *mādhurya*, *prasāda*, and *ojas*, and takes up the subject of *alaṃkāra* which he continues through the third chapter. The *alaṃkāras* of which he speaks are two kinds of *anuprāsa*, five kinds of *yamaka*, *rūpaka*, *dīpikā*, *upamā* with its seven defects, *prativastūpamā* as a variety of *upamā*, *ākṣepa*, *arthāntaranyāsa*, *vyatireka*, *vibhāvanā*, *samāsokti*, *atiśayokti*, *yathāsaṃkhya*, *utprekṣā*, *svabāvokti*, *preyas*, *rasavat*, *ūrjasvī*, *paryāyokta*, *samāhita*, *udātta*, *śleṣa*, *apahnuti*, *viśeṣokti*, *virodha*, *tulyayogitā*, *aprastutapraśaṃsā*, *vyājastuti*, *nidarśanā*, *upamārūpaka*, *upameyopamā*, *sahokti*, *parivṛtti*, *sasandeha*, *ananvaya*, *utprekṣāvayava-saṃsṛṣṭi*, *bhāvika*, *āśīḥ*—thirty-nine in all. He denies the status of *alaṃkāra* to *hetu*, *sūkṣma*, *leśa*, and *vārttā* as they contain no *vakrokti*. These were counted as *alaṃkāra* by some of the predecessors of Bhāmaha. In the fourth chapter he deals with eleven kinds of defects of Kāvya and defines and illustrates them. In the 5th chapter he deals with logic and treats of the defects of Kāvya as arising from logical hiatus. In the 6th chapter he gives some practical hints to poets for observing grammatical purity, as Bhāmaha also did. Whether Bhāmaha was Buddhist in faith

[1] ...onel Jacob in Z.D.M.G., 64.

or not has been the subject of much discussion among many scholars, and while his being the son of Rakrilagomin and his adoring Śarva, a name of Buddha, has been the ground of suggestion that he was a Buddhist, Kane has given many arguments in favour of the view that he was not a Buddhist, but this does not concern us here. It appears from his writings that he had benefited himself by the works of his predecessors. The expressions given in his work may have been mostly composed by him but it would be too much to say that all the expressions were composed by him as could be said of Jagannātha, the author of *Rasagaṅgādhara.* Up till now no commentary on Bhāmaha's work has been found but Udbhaṭa has worked a commentary on it called *Bhāmaha-vivaraṇa,* but this work is not now available. He mentions many authors, such as Rāmaśarmā, Kaṇabhakṣa, Pāṇini, Sālāturīya, Medhāvin, Rājamitra, Śākhāvardhana, Aśmakavaṃśa and Ratnāharaṇa. But Ratnāharaṇa may well be the title of a book than of a man. Bharata's work has been referred to but he has not been mentioned by name. He also refers to the story of Vatseśa and Naravāhanadatta which were the principal chapters of *Bṛhatkathā.* He highly praises Pāṇini's grammatical system and is conversant with *daṇḍanīti* and *sphoṭavāda.* The *Kāmadhenu* quotes many verses from Bhāmaha which are not available in *Kāvyālaṃkāra* and Nārāyaṇa in his *Vṛttaratnākara* quotes long passages from Bhāmaha, which shows that Bhāmaha had also work on metrics. There is a Bhāmaha, who had written a commentary on Vararuci's grammar, but whether all these three Bhāmahas are one, is more than we can say.

Pratīhārendurāja, the commentator on Udbhaṭa, informs us that Udbhaṭa had written a commentary on Bhāmaha and this statement is confirmed by Abhinavagupta (see the *Locana,* pp. 10, 40, 50, and Hemacandra, Commentary, pp. 17 and 110). Ruyyaka also refers to this commentary (pp. 183). Vāmana also betrays his acquaintance with Bhāmaha as his definition of *upamā* is a mere paraphrase of that of Bhāmaha. Dr. De points out clearly (*Sanskrit Poetics*, Vol. I, pp. 16) Vāmana's acquaintance with Bhāmaha's work. Bhāmaha, therefore, preceded Vāmana and Udbhaṭa and belonged probably to the 8th century A.D. Bhāmaha also refers to *Nyāsa* of Jinendrabuddhi (Bhāmaha VI. 36). Jinendrabuddhi probably lived in 700 A.D. Bhāmaha therefore, must be anterior to Jinendra. But various doubts can be raised as to the exact date of Jinendrabuddhi, who has been placed by Kielhorn as being later than Haradatta, the author of *Padamañjarī*, who died in 878 A.D. So the date ascribed to Jinendra by Pāṭhaka cannot be regarded as certain. Trivedi in I.A., XLII has shown that the reference to Nyāsakāra need not necessarily be a reference to Jinendrabuddhi. Thus the hypothetic reference to the above regarding the date of Bhāmaha on the strength of his reference to Nyāsakāra is smashed to pieces. The supposition of Haricand in his *L'art Poetique de l' Ind*, that Bhāmaha in I. 42 refers to *Meghadūtam*, is as untenable as Pāṭhaka's view that Māgha II. 86 refers to Bhāmaha I. 16. We have already seen that no hint as regards Bhāmaha can be attained on the supposition that he was a Buddhist. Jacob, however, has shown that in Chapter 5, Bhāmaha makes a lot of reference to Dharmakīrtti. If this is correct then Bhāmaha was anterior to Dharmakīrtti who lived in the 7th century A.D. Bhāmaha then probably lived in the beginning of the 8th century A.D. and might have been a senior contemporary of Udbhaṭa.

Bhaṭṭi tells us in XXII. 35 that he composed his poem in Valabhī, ruled over by Śrīdharasena or Srī Dharasena,[1] where Śri

1 *Kāvyam idaṁ vihitaṁ mayā valabhyāṁ śrīdharasena-narendra-pālitāyām.*

The *Jayamaṅgalā* commentary reads '*Śrīdharasūnu*'! It appears that there were four Śrīdharasenas who ruled in Valabhī between 550 and 650 A. D. Whether the king be Śrīdharasena or Sridharasena's son we find that Bhaṭṭi lived in the first half of the 7th century A.D. He was probably slightly older than Bhāmaha, or if he was a young poet living in the court of Śrīdharasena and attained a long life, he might have lived also in the 8th century A.D., in which case he might have been a senior contemporary of Bhāmaha. In his tenth canto he gives illustrations of 38 *alaṁkāras* including *anuprāsa* and *yamaka* and in the eleventh he illustrates *mādhuryya guṇa*. in 47 verses and the twelfth canto is dedicated to the illustrations of *bhāvika*, which Bhāmaha describes in III. 52. In the thirteenth canto he illustrates *bhāṣāsama*, where the same verse may be regarded as composed is a decorative word, the last of whom was living in 651 A.D., that being the date of his latest grant. Bhaṭṭi therefore lived in the 7th century A.D. and might have continued to live in the 8th century A.D. and can thus be an earlier contemporary of Bhāmaha.[1] As it appears from Bhāmaha II. 20 that he covertly criticises Bhaṭṭi XXII. 34 (see foot-note) he probably have seen Bhaṭṭi's work, which is in confirmation with the date of Bhāmaha as adduced here.[2]

Daṇḍin's *Kāvyādarśa* is a well-known work on Sanskrit Poetics.[3] The 1st chapter differentiates Kāvya as *gadya, padya,*

both in Sanskrit and in Prākṛta. Now in the illustrations of the figures Bhaṭṭi mentions the same figures that are dealt with by Bhāmaha and Daṇḍin. His illustrations of the figures are also in the same order in which Bhāmaha defines the figures, with some deviations. These deviations show that probably both Bhaṭṭi and Bhāmaha drew upon the same sources and according to their individual liking.

1 Bhaṭṭi in XXII. 34, in describing his work, said :—

vyākhyāgamyam idaṁ kāvyam utsavaḥ sudhiyāmalam |
hatā durmedhasaś cāsmin vidvatpriyatayā mayā ||

Bhāmaha apparently referring to the above contention of Bhaṭṭi criticises him as follows :—

kāvyānyapi yadīmāni vyākhyāgamyāni śāstravat |
utsavaḥ sudhiyāmeva hanta durmedhaso hatāḥ || Bhāmaha II. 20

2 As for the modern attempts regarding study of Bhāmaha, see as follows :—Jacobi Z.D.M.G. 64, 1910 ; John Nobel, *Beiträge zur älteren Geschichte des Alaṅkāraśāstra* ; also Z.D.M.G. 73, 1919, K. P. Trivedi, *Pratāparudra-yaśobhūṣaṇa* (appendix, where the book is published), and also Introduction, page 28, etc.; *Indian Antiquary* 42, 1913 ; R. Narasiṁhacāra, *Indian Antiquary* 1912, 1913 ; T. Narasimghiyengar and P. V. Kane, J.R.A.S., 1905 and 1908, hold Bhāmaha as being younger than Daṇḍin. Gaṇapatiśāstrī in his Introduction, page 25, of Bhāsa's *Svapna-Vāsavadattā* holds that Bhāmaha lived in the 1st century B.C., but he was, probably as late as Kālidāsa. On this point see Nobel Z.D.M.G. 73 already referred to ; see also Haricand's *Kālidāsa*, p. 70 ; P. V. Kane's Introduction to *Sāhitya-darpaṇa* and S. K. De's *Sanskrit Poetics.*

It is curious to notice that several passages, which are quoted in the *Kāmadhenu* Commentary on Vāmana on *Kalās*, are not available in the present work. Probably these are chapters which are now lost.

3 It has been often printed in India since its Calcutta edition of 1863 with the commentary of Premcand Tarkavāgīśa of the Calcutta Sanskrit College. It has been printed with to commentaries, in Madras in 1910, and in Poona by Dr. Belvalkar and Śāstrī Raṅgācāryya Reddi. The work is divided into three chapters. In Professor Raṅgācāryya's edition there are four chapters, the third being split up into two. There are in all 660 verses in the Calcutta edition and 663 verses in the Madras edition.

and *miśra*. *Gadya* (prose) is again subdivided into *ākhyāikā* and *kathā*, though there is no real distinction between the two. A division of literature is also made of Sanskrit Prose into *apabhraṃśa* and *miśra*. He also speaks of the two styles, *vaidarbhī* and *gauḍī*, and the ten *guṇas*. He differentiates and illustrates *anuprāsa* and regards erudition (*śruta*), genious (*pratibhā*) and constant application (*abhiyoga*) as the constitutive qualities of a poet. The second chapter is dedicated to the treatment of *alaṃkāras* in the following order : – *svabhāvokti, upamā, rūpaka, dīpaka, āvṛtti, ākṣepa, arthāntaranyāsa, vyatireka, vibhāvanā samāsokti, atiśayokti, utprekṣā, hetu, sūkṣma, leśa, yathāsaṃkhya, preyas, rasavat, ūrjasvī, paryyāyokta, samāhita, udātta, apahnuti, śleṣa, viśeṣokti, tulyayogitā, virodha, aprastuta-praśaṃsā, vyājokti, nidarśanā, sahokti, parivṛtti, āśīḥ, saṃkīrṇa,* and *bhāvika*, thirty-five in all. In addition to this in the third chapter he deals with *yamaka* and defines and illustrates the *citrakāvyas, gomūtrikā, ardhabhrama, sarvatobhadra, svarasthāna, varṇaniyama* and the *prahelikā*.

Kane suggests that as in his illustrations the southern countries are often referred to, he most probably was a man from the Deccan.[1] He is said to have written thirteen works of which *Daśakumāra-carita* is belived to be one.[2] Regarding

[1] He mentions the following works by name :—*Chandoviciti* (I. 12), *Bṛhatkathā* (I. 38), *Setubandha* (I. 39). Though he does not mention by name he shows acquaintance with the *Mahābhāṣya* (*Kāvyādarśa* II. 227), Bharata's *Nāṭya-śāstra* (II. 367). He also, like Bhāmaha, speaks of *Pūrvācāryyas* or great writers of the past whom he had consulted in writing his work. He holds a discussion on the verse *limpatīva tamo'ṅgāni* which Pratīhārendurāja thinks as referring to Udbhaṭa. The verse in question is a quotation from *Mṛcchakaṭika* and is also in Bhāsa's *Cārudatta* and *Bālacarita*. In *Śārṅgadhara paddhati* a verse of Rājaśekhara is quoted to show that Daṇḍin wrote three works which were widely known.

[2] On this point, however, doubts have been raised by Mr. Trivedi (Introduction, *Pratāparudra-yaśobhūṣaṇa* p. 31), Mr. Agase, I.A. 1915 and in his Introduction to *Daśakumāra-carita*, p. 35, holds that the author of *Kāvyādarśa* cannot be the author of *Daśakumāra-carita* on the ground that the author of *Kāvyādarśa* was a fastidious critic and as such could not have been the author of *Daśakumāra-carita* which abounds in faults of grammar and good taste. But as Kane points out, this is no serious argument for practice is more difficult than preaching, as Mahimabhaṭṭa also says in his *Vyaktiviveka*,—

the ascertainment of Daṇḍin's date there has been much discussion and opposition among the scholars. There is a number of passages in *Kāvyādarśa* which agree with Bhāmaha word for word. P. V. Kane, for instance, wishes to place Daṇḍin before Bhāmaha, while most other scholars regard Bhāmaha to be earlier than Daṇḍin.[1]

svakṛtiṣa ayantritaḥ katham anuśiṣyād anyam ayam iti na *vācyam, vārayati bhiṣag apathyād itarān svayamācarannapi tat.* Kṣemendra in his *Aucitya-vicāra-carccā* finds fault with his own composition. The argument on the ground of the difference of style between *Daśakumāra-carita* and *Kāvyādarśa* also does not hold water for the one is written in poetry and the other in prose,

[1] Mr. Trivedi (Introduction to *Pratāparudra* and *Indian Antiquary* 1913, and Bhandarkar Commemoration Vol.; Dr. Jacobi. Z.D.M.G. 1910; Prof. Raṅgācāryya, Introduction to the edition of *Kāvyādarśa*; Mr. Ganapati Śāstri, Introduction to *Svapna-Vāsavadattā*; Prof. Pāṭhak, Introduction to *Kavirājamārga*; and Dr. S. K. De's *Sanskrit Poetics* place Bhāmaha before Daṇḍin; Prof. M. T. Narasimhiyengar (J.R.A.S., 1905) places Daṇḍin before Bhāmaha and Prof. Pāthak changes his former view in J.B.R.A.S. 23 and I.A. 1912 and places Daṇḍin before Bhāmaha.

The ascertainment of the reference of Bhāmaha in Daṇḍin or *vice versa* and the ground of agreement of views is difficult as both of them had utilized the works of their predecessors, and the views common between the two may be due to the existences of common sources. Both Daṇḍin and Bhāmaha are very early writers and are always referred to by later writers and therefore it is difficult to decide the priority between the two. Daṇḍin had preceded both Udbhaṭa and Vāmana by a considerable period and he cannot be placed later than the 8th century A.D.

Trivedi and Raṅgācāryya have pointed out that Bhāmaha has been referred to as *cirantana* in *Alaṁkāra-sarvasva* (p. 3) as *ākara* or source by Rāghava Bhaṭṭa (commentary to *Śakuntalā*, p. 14) and that it is only in Namisādhu's commentary on Rudraṭa that Daṇḍin has been placed earlier than Bhāmaha. The reference to Bhāmaha as very old does not determine the question of the priority of either Daṇḍin or Bhāmaha. Namisādhu wrote his commentary on Rudraṭa, as he himself declares in Sambat 1125 or 1061 A.D. The statement of Namisādhu that Daṇḍin preceded even Medhāvirudra referred to by Bhāmaha is regarded by Kane as being decisive of the priority of Daṇḍin over Bhāmaha. The reference to Bhāmaha in *Alaṁkārasarvasva* as being *cirantana* proves nothing, for the same epithet has been also applied to Udbhaṭa. It has been argued that Daṇḍin has an elaborate treatment of *yamaka* and *śabdālaṁkāra* and had made an elaborate subdivision of *upamā*, while Bhāmaha treats them only in the general manner, and for this reason Bhāmaha should be regarded as being earlier. But comparing Bharata and Bhāmaha we find that Bharata gives ten varieties of *yamaka* and Bhāmaha only five. *Yamaka* was highly praised even in much earlier times, as it occurs in Rudradamana's inscription in A.D. 150. In later times *yamaka* was not so much appreciated, and Udbhaṭa ignores it and Mammaṭa is exceedingly brief. Daṇḍin's treatment of *upamā* follows Bharata while Bhāmaha's scheme is that what has been followed by Udbhaṭa and Mammaṭa. But from this no conclusion is possible. The commentator Taruṇa Vācaspati, a late writer, says that in many

The upshort of the discussion, which has briefly been summed up (see P. N.), is that Bhāmaha lived after the 5th century

places Daṇḍin criticises Bhāmaha. Thus Namisādhu and Taruṇa Vācaspati hold different opinions regarding the priority or posteriority of Daṇḍin.

Again, the distinction between *kathā* and *ākhyāyikā* as given by Bhāmaha and Daṇḍin are different. This distinction between *kathā* and *ākhyāyikā* is also found in the *Mahābhāṣya* and Daṇḍin's treatement of the distinction between *kathā* and *ākhyāyikā* need not be regarded as a criticism of Bhāmaha. Daṇḍin speaks of four defects of *upamā* while Bhāmaha speaks of seven, following Medhāvin. Some illustrations that have been regarded as good poetry by Daṇḍin have been regarded as being no poetry at all but merely as *vārtā* or information by Bhāmaha. But this can hardly be regarded as determining the priority of Bhāmaha. The examples are old ones and on them two different opinions have been given by the two writers. Such and other arguments based on the different treatment of some of the *alaṁkāras* or *doṣas* by the two writers cannot be regarded as leading to any difinite conclusion.

But Bhāmaha has a part of a passage of which the whole is found in Daṇḍin, and if Śārṅgadhara is to be believed, Daṇḍin is prior to Bhāmaha. In many passages Bhāmaha refers to the view of other writers without mentioning names and criticises them, e. g., the distinction between *Vaidarbhī* and *Gauḍī*, and this distinction is found in Bhāmaha. Daṇḍin mentions ten *guṇas*, following Bharata, but Bhāmaha says nothing about the *guṇas*. He ridicules the view of the division of *guṇas* and reduces them to three like the author of the Dhvanikāra. But such a comprehensive view of Bhāmaha cannot be reduced to an argument for his anteriority, for Vāmana, who was posterior to both Daṇḍin and Bhāmaha also counts the ten guṇas. Again, Bhāmaha reduces upamā to three types, the same is done in *Kāvyādarśa* (II. 30-32). Of these three, *i.e.*, *nindopamā*, *Praśaṁsopamā*, and *ācikhysāu-upamā*, *Nāṭya-śāstra* gives the first two only. Daṇḍin not only gives the three *upamās* of Bhāmaha but many more types of *upamās*. There are also divergences of view on the subject of other *alaṁkāras*. But from this nothing can be argued.

But though the above arguments are inconclusive regarding the point at issue there are some other considerations which seem to throw further light. It is very probable that both Bhāmaha and Daṇḍin lived in more or less the same age, probably in the same century and probably they both derived their materials from older sources so that it is difficult to say anything as to which of them borrowed from whom. But in spite of the fact that Kane thinks that there is no evidence, that Bhāmaha was a Buddhist, it cannot be gainsaid that his definition of perception as *kalpanāpoḍha*, is borrowed directly from Dharmakīrtti. Bhāmaha in V. 6 says :—*pratyakṣaṁ kalpanāpoḍhaṁ tato'rthāditi kecana, kalpanāṁ nāma-jātyādi yojanām pratijānate*. Now, this is exactly the view of Dharmakirtti, who defines perception in his *Nyāyabindu* as *pratyakṣaṁ kalpanāpoḍham abhrāntam*. The definition of *anumāna* also agrees with that of *Nyāyabindu*. It may therefore be conveniently inferred that Bhāmaha was anterior to Dharmakīrtti. Dharmakīrtti in all probability lived in the 5th century A.D. and Bhāmaha, therefore, was anterior to that date.

About the date of Daṇḍin we are not so fortunate. Kane points out that the poetess Vijjakā may be identified with the Vijayā Bhaṭṭārikā, the queen of Candrāditya, the eldest son of Pulakeśin II, who lived about 660 A.D. ; and since Vijjakā quotes from Kāvyādarśa, Daṇḍin must be earlier than or at least contemporary of Vijjaka ; but the identification on which the ascertainment of the date rests is itself shaken.

A.D. and that he was in all probability a Buddhist. Daṇḍin lived in all probability more or less in the same century as Bhāmaha, but there is no direct means by which we can conclusively fix the date of Daṇḍin, but on the whole the weight of evidence, though not conclusive, seems to tend to the conclusion that is generally adopted that Bhāmaha was prior to Daṇḍin. Though Kane holds the opposite view, Daṇḍin's work *Kāvyādarśa* is very popular and has many commentators.[1]

UDBHAṬA

He wrote *Alaṃkāra-saṃgraha* and also a *vivṛti* on Bhāmaha's *Kāvyālaṃkāra*. Udbhaṭa's *Alaṃkāra-saṃgraha* was translated by Col. Jacob in J. R. A. S., 1897 and has been published by N.S.P., Bombay, in 1915 with the commentary of Pratīhārendurāja. The work contains six chapters and in 79 *kārikās* he defines 41 *alaṃkāras*. According to Pratīhārendurāja the illustrations are taken from Udbhaṭa's own work *Kumārasambhava*.[2]

1 These commentaries are :—(*a*) by Taruṇa Vācaspati (probably of the 11th century A.D.), (*b*) *Hṛdayaṅgama* by an anonymous author, (*c*) *Mārjjanā* by Harinātha, who wrote also a commentary on Bhoja's *Sarasvatīkaṇṭhamaṇi*, who was not only later than Bhoja but also later than Keśavamiśra ; (*d*) *Muktāvalī* by Narasiṁha Sūri ; (*e*) *Candrikā* by Triśaraṇataṭabhīma ; (*f*) *Rasikarañjanī* by Viśvanātha ; (*g*) *Vivṛti* by Kṛṣṇakānta Tarkavāgiśa.

There are also commentaries by Vādijaṅghāla, Bhagīratha, Vijayānanda, *Vaimalyavidhāyinī* by Tribhuvanacandra, Dharmavācaspati ; and two commentaries of unknown authors. Almost all these commentaries are in MSS. form except the commentary by Premcānd Tarkavāgiśa, published in Calcutta ; Taruṇa Vācaspati's commentary edited by Prof. Raṅgācāryya and *Hṛdayaṅgama* edited by the same professor.

Among the modern scholars who have contributed to the study of Daṇḍin the following names may be mentioned :—Jacobi in Z. D. M. G , 1910, argues that Daṇḍin lived probably in the 7th century A. D. ; G. A. Jacob, J. R. A. S., 1897 ; L. D. Barnett, J. R. A. S., 1905 ; Bern Heimer, Z. D. M. G. 63, 1909 ; P. V. Kane, *Indian Antiquary*, 1912 ; Gray's *Vasavadattā* (pp. 111) ; there exists also a Tibetan translation of Daṇḍin's *Kāvyādarśa* in the Tanjore collection as noticed by G. Huth in *Sitzungsberichte der Berliner Akademie der Wissenschaften* 1895 and Z. D, M. G. 49, 283 ; see also Dr. De's *Sanskrit Poetics* and Dr. Dasgupta's *Kāvya-vicāra* (in Bengali) ; *Kāvyādarśa* was translated in German by O. Böhtlingk, Leipzig 1890.

2 *anena granthakṛtā svoparacitakumārasambhavaikadeśo' trodāharaṇatvenopanyastaḥ.*

The alaṃkāras taken up by Ubdhaṭa may be enumerated as follows :—*punaruktavadābhāsa, chekānuprāsa, lāṭānuprāsa* and *anuprāsa* (of three kinds, *paruṣavṛtti, upanāgarika, and grāmya*), *rūpaka, upamā, dīpaka, pativastūpamā, ākṣepa, arthāntaranyāsa, vyatireka, vibhāvanā, samāsokti, atiśayokti, yathāsaṃkhya, utprekṣā, svabhāvokti, preyaḥ, rasavat, ūrjasvī, samāhita, paryyāyokta,* two kinds of *udātta, śliṣṭa, apahnuti, viśeṣokti, virodha, tulyayogitā, aprastutapraśaṃsā, vyājastuti, nidarśanā, upameyopamā, sahokti, saṃkara, parivṛtti, ananvaya, sasandeha, saṃsṛṣṭi, bhāvika, kāvyaliṅga, dṛṣṭānta.* It will be seen that these *alaṃkāras* are counted here almost in the same order as we find in Bhāmaha. He only omits Bhāmaha's *yamaka, upamārūpaka* and *utprekṣāvayava.* But he adds some *alaṃkāras* which are not counted by Bhāmaha, such as, *punaruktavadābhāsa, saṃkara, kāvyaliṅga,* and *dṛṣṭānta.*

Udbhaṭa was a great Alaṃkāra writer and was held in high esteem by later writers. He is even regarded as greater than Bhāmaha.[1]

1 He often also deviated from Bhāmaha. While Bhāmaha divided *anuprāsa* into two classes and *rūpaka* into four classes, Udbhaṭa drew two different types from the first kind *rūpaka.* While Bhāmaha showed three types of *śleṣa,* Udbhaṭa showed two types. While Bhāmaha regards *preyas* as an expression of inspired devotion to a preceptor, God, King or Sun, Udbhaṭa regards *bhāvālaṁkāra* as *preyas.* Bhāmaha does not speak of *paruṣā, grāmyā* and the *upanāgarikā vṛtti,* but, Udbhaṭa shows them. Udbhaṭa has often been referred to as *Cirantana* along with Bhāmaha (P. V. Kane's Introduction to S. D.).

Some special doctrines of Udbhaṭa are as follows :—(1) that words should be regarded as different when they have different meanings, (2) that *śleṣa* is an *arthālaṇkāra* even though it be *śabdaśleṣa*—this view has been criticised by Mammaṭa ; that even though *śleṣa* be mixed with other *alaṁkāras, śleṣa* should be regarded as dominant,—this view has also been criticised by Mammaṭa ; (4) that a *vākya* has a three-fold activity of *abhidhā* ; (5) both Rājaśekhara and Mahimabhaṭṭa ascribe to the disciples of Udbhaṭa the view that there are two kinds of meaning, (*a*) where the meaning comes out clearly by the analysis of the context as in the case of commentary literature or *śāstras.* (1) where the meaning cannot be got merely by the analysis of the word and its ordinary meaning separately, but when they jointly foreshadow a meaning, as in the case of kāvya, It has been further urged that though according to the older (*prācyānām,* should it mean eastern ?) works on *alaṁkāra, alaṁkāra* is regarded as the chief thing according to Udbhaṭa and others *guṇa* and *alaṁkāra* have been given the same position.

The date of Udbhata is not so difficult to ascertain. He was the *sabhāpati* of King Jayāpīḍa of Kashmir (779-813 A.D.).[1] Therefore he must have flourished in the 8th century A.D.

The commentator Pratīhārendurāja is probably the oldest commentator of Alaṃkāra works. He was a pupil of Mukula as appears from the colophon of the commentary. He flourished in the middle of the 10th century A.D. as he refers to *Dhvanyāloka*. Mukula is said to have lived in the first quarter of the 10th century A.D.[2] Vāmana's *Kāvyālaṅkāra Sūtra* is a well-known work on Alaṃkāra.[3] Vāmana's work consists of *sūtras* with short explanatory notes of the *Vṛtti* type. Vāmana has been referred to by Pratīhārendurāja and Abhinavagupta. Vāmana divides his work into five topics (*adhikāras*) and each topic is divided into two or three *adhyāyas*. There are in all twelve *adhyāyas*. The first *adhikaraṇa* deals with the need or *prayojana* of Kāvya, characterises the nature of those who are fit for studying *alaṃkāras*, and declares that style is the soul of poetry. The styles are three in number, *vaidarbhī*, *gauḍī*, and *pāñcālī*. In the second *adhikaraṇa* he deals with the defects of words, propositions and their meanings. In the third *adhikaraṇa* he deals with

1 See *Rājataraṅgiṇi*, IV. 495.

2 In Abhinava's commentary on *Bhagavadgītā* he mentions the name of Bhaṭṭendurāja, the son of Śrībhūtirāja, the grandson of Saucaka of the Kātyāyana *gotra* as being his teacher. Peterson appears to suggest in his Introduction to *Subhāṣitāvali* (pp. 11) that Bhaṭṭendurāja and Pratīhārendurāja are the same, but there is no evidence in favour of this identification, Bhaṭṭendurāja was a poet, not only on the strength of Abhinavagupta's declaration in his *Abhinavabhāratī*, but he is also quoted in Kṣemendra's *Suvṛtti-tilaka* and *Aucitya-vicāra-cintāmaṇi*. and his verses occur also in *Śārṅgadhara-paddhati*. But we have no evidence that Pratīhārendurāja had any poetical gift. He was not in sympathy with the *dhvani* theory of Abhinavagupta and further holds that in Udbhaṭa's handling of the poetic figures, the theory of *dhvani* was anticipated.

3 It was first edited by Cappeller, Jena 1875, in the *Kāvyamālā* series 1848, then by Anandarām Baruā, 1883, then in the Granthapradarśanī series, 1895, in the Benares Sanskrit series with *Kāmadhenu* commentary in 1908, and in the Śrīvāṇivilāsa series, Śrīraṅgam 1909. The last one is the best edition of the work. It was translated into English by Sir Gaṅgānātha Jhā, Allahabad. It has two commentaries, *Kāmadhenu* by Gopendra, probably of the 15th century. A.D. and *Sāhitya-sarvasva* by Maheśvara.

the *guṇas* and in the fourth he deals with *yamaka* and *anuprāsa*, the six *doṣas*, of *upamā* and other *alaṃkāras* based on *upamā*. The fifth *adhikaraṇa* is devoted to poetical conventions, observance of the rules of *sandhi*, necessity of grammatical purity and the like. The last chapter also deals with the purity of words. He defines and illustrates in addition to *anuprāsa*, *yamaka* and *upamā*, *prativastupamā*, *samāsokti*, *aprastutapraśaṃsā*, *apahnuti*, *rūpaka*, *śleṣa*, *vakrokti*, *utprekṣā*, *atiśayokti*, *sandeha*, *virodha*, *vibhāvanā*, *ananvaya*, *upameyopamā*, *parivṛtti*, *krama*, *dīpaka*, *nidarśanā*, *arthāntaranyāsa*, *vyatireka*, *viśeṣokti*, *vyājastuti*, *vyājokti*, *tulyayogitā*, *ākṣepa*, *sahokti*, *samāhita*, *saṃsṛṣṭi*, *upamārūpaka*, and *utprekṣāvayava*—in all thirty-three *alaṃkāras*.

Vāmana is the defender of the *rīti* school of poetics and has been severely criticised by the later writers on Alaṃkāra. Though Vāmana uses some of the older names of *alaṃkāras*, such as, *viśeṣokti*, *rūpaka*, or *ākṣepa*, he gives entirely different meanings to them. Vāmana's commentator, Sahadeva, says that Vāmana's work had gone quite out of use and that Mukula Bhaṭṭa restored it. As Vāmana is mentioned by Pratīhārendurāja of the 10th century A.D., it must have preceded him. Vāmana seems to have preceded even the Dhvanikāra (see *Dhvanyāloka*, pp. 37). Kalhaṇa says that Vāmana was a minister of Jayāpīḍa. Būḥler supposes that the two Vāmanas are identical. If this view be accepted, then Vāmana lived in 800 A.D. and would be a contemporary of Udbhaṭa. But none of them refers to either. There is a further point as to whether the Alaṃkara author Vāmana could be identified with Vāmana the writer of the *Kāśikā*, in which case Vāmana is to be placed in the 7th century A.D. It is curious, as Kane notes, that some of the grammatical views of Vāmana are in agreements with those of *Kāśikā*. If these two Vāmanas are identical then the Alaṃkāra author Vāmana should be regarded as having lived in the 7th century A.D.

The *Kāvyālaṃkāra* of Rudraṭa with the commentary of Namisādhu has been published in the *Kāvyamālā* series. According to Jacobi (Z.D.M.G. 56, 763) he lived under King Avantivarmā

(855-883). Rudraṭa was also called Śastānanda and was the son of Vāmana, and he should not be confused with Rudrabhaṭṭa, the author of *Śṛṅgāratilaka*. Pischel, however, in Z.D.M.G. 39, 314 and 42, 296 is in favour of identifying them.[1]

Rudraṭa's work is in 734 verses. In the first 16 chapters he deals with the objects of Kāvya, the definition of a poet and his requirements, the five *śabdālaṃkāras, vakrokti, anuprāsa, yamaka, śleṣa,* and *citra* ; the four styles, *vaidarbhī, pāñcālī, lāṭī* and *gauḍī* ; the six bhāṣās, *prākṛta, saṃskṛta, māgadhī, paiśācī śaurasenī, apabhraṃśa,* in which poetry is composed. He also defines *vakrokti* and *anuprāsa* and illustrates five *vṛttis, madhura lalita, prauḍha, paruṣa* and *rudra,* of *anuprāsa.* He also treats *yamaka* in details as well as *śleṣa* with its chief varieties and the tricky or *citrakāvyas.* He also treats of the defects of *pada* and *vākya.* He was, however, the earliest author on Alaṃkāra, who tried to classify the *alaṃkarās* according to certain rational principles. These principles are five,—*vāstava,* on which 23 *alaṃkāras* are based ; *aupamya,* on which 21 *alaṃkāras* are based ; *atiśaya,* on which 12 *alaṃkāras* are based ; and *śleṣa,* on which 10 *alaṃkāras* are based. Thus altogether it treats of 66 *alaṃkāras.* So far in Bhāmaha, Daṇḍin, Udbhaṭa and Vāmana, the number scarcely exceeds forty. He also deals with the defects of meaning and of four defects of *upamā.* He describes the ten *rasas* and the two varieties of *śṛṅgāra* and classifies different kinds of heroes and heroines.

On account of his rational method of classification, some of those *alaṃkāras,* such as, *upameyopamā* or *anvaya,* which, though in reality are varieties of *upamā,* have been counted as separate *alaṃkāras* and so defined, have not been taken as separate *alaṃkāras* by Rudraṭa but regarded as varieties of

1 See also Jacobi's article in *Wiener Zeitschrift Für die Kunde des Morgenlandes,* 2 151 and Z.D.M.G. 42, 425 ; also Jacob in J.R.A.S., 1897 (pp. 291) ; also Narasinghiengar in J.R.A.S, 1905. Rudraṭa should not be confused with Rudrabhaṭṭa author of *Śṛṅgāratilaka.*

Namisādhu is said to have been a Śvetāmbara Jaina, who wrote his commentary on Rudraṭa in 1068.

upamā. Then, again, his naming of certain *alaṃkāras* is different from his predecessors. Thus, what Bhāmaha calls *vyājastuti* and what Udbhaṭa calls *udātta* and what Daṇḍin calls *svabhāvokti*, have been called by Rudraṭa *vyājaśleṣa* and *jāti*. What other writers have called *atiśayokti* as the mutual change of place of antecedents between kāraṇa and *kāryya*, has been termed as *pūrva* by Rudraṭa. Again some of the *alaṃkāras*, such as *hetu*, *bhāva*, *mata*, *sāmya* and *pīḍita*, that have been counted by Rudraṭa, have been dismissed by later writers on the ground that they are instances of *guṇībhūtavyaṅga*, *i.e.*, where the implied sense instead of being superior has been subordinated to the primary sense.

As Kane has said, Rudraṭa represents the Alaṃkāra school. He repudiates the theory of Vāmana that *rīti* is the soul of kāvya. While the later writer Mammaṭa regards the existence of *guṇa* as an important constitutive desideratum of Kāvya, Rudraṭa does not define *guṇa* at all. It is probably from Rudraṭa that Mammaṭa had regarded the existence of *alaṃkāra* as a constitutive desideratum of kāvya.

As has been suggested above, he lived in the 9th century A.D. He was earlier than Pratīhārendurāja, who always quotes from him and is also earlier than Rājaśekhara.

Rudraṭa's work with the commentary of Namisādhu has already been published in the Kāvyamālā series, as already said above. But Vallabhadeva, a well-known commentator of Māgha, refers in his own commentary to Māgha (Māgha, IV. 21, VI. 28), to his commentary on Rudraṭa. But this earliest commentary on Rudraṭa is probably now lost. Vallabhadeva has not only commented on Māgha but Kālidāsa, Mayūra, and Ratnākara, and Dr. De says that he probably belonged to the 10th century, for his grandson, Kaiyaṭa, son of Candrāditya, wrote a commentary on Ānandavardhana's *Devīśataka* (977-78) during the reign of Bhīmagupta (971-82 A.D.). This Vallabhadeva is certainly different from the author of *Subhāṣitāvali*, who, according to Aufrecht, lived in the 16th century, and according to Bühler (*Kunst Poesie*) lived in the 15th century. Peterson refers to another Jaina commentator on Rudraṭa, called Āśadhara, who lived in the 13th century. After the invasion of Sahabuddin Ghori he migrated to Mālava and lived in the court of the king Dhārā. He wrote more than fiteen works. We hear also of another commentary *Rasataraṅgiṇī* by a son of Harivaṃśabhaṭṭa Drāviḍa. But the work is scarce.

ALAṂKĀRA IN THE AGNIPURĀṆA

The *Agnipurāṇa* is one of the encyclopaedic Purāṇas like the *Viṣṇudharmottara-purāṇa*, which deals with all sorts of subjects of Indian culture even including grammar and lexicon.[1] For considerations stated in the foot-note the *Agnipurāṇa* may be placed in the 9th or 10th century. It deals with four kinds of *rītis*, four kinds of *vṛttis—bhāratī, sātvatī, kaiśkī,* and *ārabhaṭī*. It deals also with different kinds of *abhinaya,* and differentiates various kinds of *kāvya* as *gadya, padya,* and *miśra* ; and its language is Sanskrit and Prakrit ; the modes of *kāvya,* as *kathā ākhyāyikā,* and *mahākāvya* ; the condition and modes of dramatic emotion and expression, such as, *sthāyibhāva, anubhāva, vyabhicāribhāva,* etc. ; it deals also with some *śabdālaṃkāras, arthālaṃkāras,* and *śabdārthālaṃkāras, guṇas* and *doṣas*.[2]

1 Regarding lexicon, *Agnipurāṇa* drew its materials from *Amarakoṣa,* which was translated into Chinese in the 6th century, as Maxmüller says in '*India—What It Can Teach Us.*' Mr. Oak Places *Amarakośa* in the 4th century and Telang in even an earlier date. But Hoernle in J. R. A. S. 1906 attempts to place it between the 7th and the 10th centu.ies.

The *Agnipurāṇa* knows Bharata's *Nāṭya-śāstra* and seems also to be acquainted with Bhāmaha's work and even the theory of *dhvani*. It can, therefore, be argued that at lea st the chapter on poetics of the *Agnipurāṇa* was composed after Abhinavagupta had written h is *Dhvanyāloka*. It is also significant that no early writer quotes from *Agnipurāṇa*. It is only in the 12th century that *Agnipurāṇa* is quoted as an authority. We may therefore roughly place *Agnipurāṇa* in the 9th or the 10th century A.D., preferably the latter

2 The *Agnipurāṇa* has been published at different times. Probably the earliest one is that of the Bibliotheca Indica, edited by Rajendralal Mitra, 1878, and Mr. M. N. Dutt published in English a translation of it in two volumes, Calcutta, 1903.

Ānandavardhana, the Dhvanikāra, and Abhinavagupta

The work that passes by the name of *Dhvanyāloka* consists of a number of *kārikās* with a *vṛtti* and an elaborate commentary called *Locana* by Abhinavagupta. The work is divided into four chapters or *uddyotas.* It appears that three different persons are responsible for the writing of the *kārikā,* the *vṛtti,* and the commentary on the *vṛtti.* The *kārikā* verses are called the *dhvanikārikās* and the author is called the Dhvanikāra. The Commentary on the *kārikā* is called the *Dhvanyāloka* and the elaborate commentary on it is called *Locana.* It appears further that there were other commentaries on the *Dhvanyāloka* than the *Locana.* One of these at least was called *Candrikā,* which was written by some ancestor of Abhinavagupta, in whose family the study of *Dhvanyāloka* was current for many generations.[1]

1. It is, therefore, wrong as sometimes it has been suggested that the author of the *kārikā* was the direct teacher of Abhinavagupta. It has been suggested by Mr. Kane that the *Locana* commentary of Abhinavagupta on *Dhvanyāloka* (the commentary on the *kārikā*) was written about 150 years after the *Dhvanyāloka* was composed. The *Dhvanyāloka* is the real work on which Abhinava was writing his *Locana.* For this reason he often refers to the author of the *Dkvanyāloka* as the *granthakāra.* The *kārikās* are sometimes called in *Locana* the *Mūlakārika* or simply the *Kārikās,* and its author was called the *kārikākāra.* The author of the *Dhvanyāloka* is also sometimes called the *vṛttikṛt.* The study of *Locana*—shows clearly that Abhinavagupta regarded the author of the *Kārikā* as being different from the author of the *vṛtti.* In p. 8 Abhinava refers to a poet Manoratha who was a contemporary of the author of the *Kārikā.* In pages 11 and 12 Abhinava tells us that the name of the author of the *Vṛtti* or the *Dhvanyālokā* is Ānandavardhanācarya. This work *Dhvanyāloka* is called by the name *Sahṛdayāloka* and *Kāvyālokā* in the colophons. In the penultimate verse at the end of the 4th *uddyota* there is a verse which runs as follows :—

kāvyākhye khilasaukhyadhāmani vivudhodyāne dhvanir darśitaḥ.

This suggests that the name of the original work on which Ānandavardhana commented was called *Kāvyadhvani* or some other name associated with Kāvya. It is for this reason that Ānandavardhana's *Vṛtti* was called *Kāvyāloka* or *Dhvanyāloka.* Prof. Sovani in J.R.A.S., 1910, suggested that it was called *Sahṛdayāloka* because probably the name of the author of the *Kārikā* was Sahṛdaya. P. V. Kane has further suggested that the passage in Mukula Bhaṭṭa's Abhidhāvṛttimātṛkā was considerably earlier than Abhinava's ;—the passage *dhvaneḥ sahṛdayair nūtanatayā upavarṇitasya* and also the passage in the same work, *sahṛdayaiḥ kāvyavartmani nirūpitā* and the

From the considerations stated in the foot-notes, we find that there is no certainty regarding the authorship of the *kārikās*, sometimes called the *Mulakārikā* or the *Dhvanikārikā*. The author is sometimes referred to as Dhvanikāra or Dhvanikṛt. There was probably for centuries before the advent of Abhinavagupta or even Ānandavardhana, the author of the *vṛtti* or the

reference by Pratīhārendurāja in his commentary on Udbhaṭa, *kaiścit sahṛdayair dhvanir-nāma vyañjakatvabhedātmā*, prove that Sahṛdaya was the name of the author of the *Kārikās*. But as to whether Sahṛdaya was or was not the author of the *Kārika*, the argument does not seem to be conclusive, for there is a plural number to the word and no honorific title attached to it, and as such Sahṛdaya may mean the intuitive school of poetry and not the name of any person.

The passage, *sahṛdaya-manaḥprītaye* occurring in the first *kārikā* would naturally suggest that the name of the author of the *Kārikā* could not have been Sahṛdaya, for in that case it would be very unusual for him to refer to himself in the third person and then say that the work was written for giving pleasure to him, unless of course the word *sahṛdaya* contained a pun. The other view that I venture to suggest is that the word *sahṛdaya* probably referred to a school of literaty critics who regarded the intuitive implication as appealing to the heart either by way of emotion or by way of suggesting truthṣ. So also the word, *sahṛdayodaya-lābha-hetu* means—for the benefit that there may arise the intuitive *connaissance* of poetic value. The word *sahṛdaya* and its synonym *sucetas* occur often in the *Kārikās*, the *Vṛtti* and the *Locana*. The *Dhvanyāloka*, in discussing the nature of *sahṛdayatva*, says (p. 11),—*yeṣāṁ kāvyānuśīlanābhyāsavāśād viśadībhūte manomukure varṇanīya-tanmayībhavanayogyatā te hṛdayasaṁvādabhājaḥ sahṛdayāḥ*—*i.e.*, those are to be called *sahṛdayas* whose mind after a long and continued practice of literature has become as transparent as a mirror such that whatever is described to them through literature enters into them in such a manner that they by their (natural or earned) capacity can exercise a sympathy by which they may identify themselves with the same and thereby the poet's heart, as revealed through literature, may communicate itself without restraint to them—not only the poets but other persons having similar capacities may find themselves in communication with one another through the poet's heart as revealed in literature. The *Locana* speaks of Ānandavardhana as *sahṛdaya-cakravartī* as the king of the sahṛdayas. In the last verse of the *Dhvanyāloka* Ānandavardhana says :—*satkāvyaṁ tattvaviṣayaṁ sphurita-prasupta-kalpaṁ manaḥsu paripakvadhiyāṁ yadāsīt tad vyākarot sahṛdayodayalābhahetau ānandavardhana iti prathitābhidhānaḥ*. The essence of the couplet is that what had appeared in the minds of literary connoisseurs of excellence but had remained there in a dreamy and inarticulate state, has been clearly explained and formulated in the *Dhvanyāloka* and with that very purpose the work has been written.

It is thus obvious that there were a large body of literary connoisseurs who had discovered the nature of *dhvani* and *rasa* as being the essence of poetry and it is this body of men who have often been referred to as *sahṛdayas*. I therefore cannot think that the name *sahṛdaya* was the name of the Kārikākāra and that it was the Kārikākāra who was referred to by the term *sahṛdaya* by Mukula and others.

kārikās which is referred to as the *grantha* or the text by Abhinavagupta in his *Locana* commentary, a school of poetical connoisseurs who regarded the essence of charm of poetry as being the truth of the emotion communicated to us by the poet through his art which so completely deluged the mind of the audience or the reader that it could not be distinguished from what was communicated in this manner.

The name of Ānandavardhana's *vṛtti* is *Dhvanyāloka* or *Kāvyāloka*, and the name of the *vṛtti* by Abhinavagupta is *Locana* as I have already mentioned.

By 900 A.D. Ānandavardhana had become a well-known writer and Rājaśekhara of the 10th century refers to Ānandavardhana and so does also Jalhaṇa in his *Sūkti-muktāvali.*[1]

It is curious to notice that already in early times there were some confusions among the old authors of Alaṃkāra regarding the identity of the author of the *Vṛtti*, as Mr. Kane points out. Thus Pratīhārendurāja refers to some of the doctrines in the *Vṛtti*, and also to a verse claimed by Ānandavardhana, as his own to Sahṛdaya. Kuntaka, the author of *Vakroktijīvita*, is said to refer to a verse of Ānandavardhana as belonging to Dhvani-kāra. Mahimabhaṭṭa, a contemporary of Abhinavagupta, makes no distinction between the authors of the *Kārikā* and the *Vṛtti*. Kṣemendra in his *Aucitya-vicāra-carccā* refers to the *kārikās* as belonging to Ānandavardhana and so does Hemacandra. Viśva-nātha in his *Sāhitya-darpaṇa* II. 12. quotes the first verse as belonging to Dhvanikāra and ascribes a *Vṛtti* to the Dhvanikāra. We thus see that there is a great conflict of poinion between

[1] *pratibhā-vyutpattyoḥ pratibhā śreyasī, sā hi kaver avyutpatti-kṛtaṁ doṣam aśeṣam ācchādayatī, tatrāha :—avyutpatti-kṛto doṣaḥ śaktyāsaṁvriyate kaveḥ, yastvaśakti-kṛtastasya sa jh ṭityavabhāsate* (*Dhvanyāloka*, p. 137).

—Rājaśekhara, *Kāvyamīmaṁsā* (p. 15).

Also

dhvaninātigabhīreṇa kāvyatattvaniveśinā, Ānandavardhanaḥ kasya nāsīdānanda-vardhanaḥ.

—Rājaśekhara as quoted by Jalhaṇa and as pointed out in J.B.R.A.S., Vol. 17, p. 57.

Abhinavagupta and these authors, and it is exceedingly difficult for us to come to a decisive conclusion.[1]

My own view is that the view of Abhinava that the Dhvanikāra and Ānandavardhana are two different persons is well-attested by an intimate study of Ānandavardhana's *vṛtti*, which in some places differs from that of the Dhvanikāra while in others it modifies and elaborates the meagre statements of the Dhvanikāra in such a manner that it is Ānandavardhana and not Dhvanikāra who can rightly take pride in having evolved an original system of *dhvani* in a systematic manner though elements of it are found in the Dhvanikāra's *Kārikās* and even before him. That this was the case was lost sight of on account of the fact that the views of Ānandavardhana have in general been in agreement with the teaching of the *Karikās*. This led to the confusion among many writers that the writer of the *Vṛtti*, Ānandavardhana, was identical with the writer of the *Kārikās*. Therefore, Ānandavardhana has often been referred to as the Dhvanikāra. It is almost impossible to say who really the Dhvanikāra was. Jacobi's attempt to fix the date of Dhvanikāra through the date of the poet Manoratha of the 8th century A.D.

1 Mr. Kane following Sovani has suggested that Sahṛdaya was the name of the author of the Kārikā to which I signified my dissent for it seems to me that there is ample evidence to show that though no elaborate treatise on the subject was written yet the dhvani view was current in tradition as Ānandavardhana himself says (p. 10),—*paramparayā samāmnātaḥ, i.e.,* carried through unbroken tradition, to which the *Locana* comments,—*vināpi viśiṣṭa-pustakeṣu vivecanāt ityabhiprayaḥ,* i.e., though the subject of *dhvani* was not treated in a special work yet the theory was known and propagated through unbroken tradition. It is this school of thinkers who are in my opinion referred to by the word *sahṛdaya.* He knew also that Pratihārendurāja after referring to the views of the *sahṛdayas* said that the views of the sahṛdayas regarding dhvani is already included in the theory of *alaṁkāras.* He then treats of the three kinds of *dhvani, vastu, alaṁkāra* and *rasa,* and there are examples given by Dhvanikāra as these three divisions of *dhvani* are but examples of *alaṁkāra.*

Winternitz also thinks that the ground of the Dhvanikārikās is to be found in Udbhaṭa's work,—*Die Lehre des Udbhaṭa, dass in der Stimmung das Wesen der Poesie zu suchen sei, bildete die Grundlage für die Dhvanikārikās, 120 Memorialstrophen über Poetik von einem ungenannten Verfasser, zu denen Anandavardhana von Kaschmir um* 850 *n. Chr. seinen überaus lehrreichen kommentar Dhvanyāloka geechreiben hat,* der *in der Tat ein selbständiges Werk über das Wesen der Dichtkunst ist,* pp. 17-18, *Geschichte der indischen Litterartur.*

(according to *Rājataṅgiṇī*, the minister of the king Jayāpīḍa) is also due to a confusion; for if Abhinava's opinion is to be accepted, Manoratha was not a contemporary of the Dhvanikāra but of Ānandavardhana. We thus see that both the name and the date of the Dhanikāra is uncertain. The fact that we find no references in the Dhvanikāra's *Kārikās* to either Daṇḍin or Bhāmaha or Vāmana, does not prove that he was not a contemporary of either of them. Ānandavardhana's date, however, may be regarded as the 8th century A.D. if the identity of the poet Manoratha and of the minister-poet Manoratha be accepted. Abhinava must have lived about 150 years since the date of Ānandavardhana. If Manoratha flourished in the reign of Jayāpīḍa, and he was a contemporary of Ānandavardhana, as stated by Abhinava, Ānandavardhana's date may be regarded as well-nigh fixed. Rājaśekhara says that Ānandavardhana flourished in the reign of Avantivarmā (855-83) of Kashmir.[1]

To the students of Indian Philosophy, Abhinavagupta is known for his prolific works on the *Pratyabhijñā* school of Kāśmir Śaivism. In addition to these he also wrote many verses, probably *kāvya* works, *stotra* works, as well as a commentary called *vivaraṇa* on the *Kāvyakautuka* of his teacher *Bhaṭṭatauta*. From the colophon to his *Pāratriṃśikā Vivaraṇa* we know that his grandfather was Varāhagupta, father Cukhala and his younger brother was called Manorathagupta. He had many *gurus*. Thus in the *Locana* commentary he not only refers to his teacher Bhaṭṭendurāja but also quotes verses from him. He is profuse in his praises of his *guru* Bhaṭṭendurāja. From the references in the *Locana* it appears that he had in all probability studied *Dhvanyāloka* with his teacher Bhaṭṭendurāja, who was not only a poet but a critic also. It has already been suggested that this Bhaṭṭendurāja should be regarded as

[1] ***muktākaṇaḥ śivasvāmī kavir ānandavardhanaḥ prathāṁ ratnākaraścāgāt sāmrājye' vantivarmaṇaḥ,—Rājataraṅgiṇī*, V. 3 .**

This is in harmony with the fact that he quotes Udbhaṭa who flourished in the 800 A D. and was quoted by *Rājataraṅgiṇī* of 900 A.D.

different from Pratīhārendurāja, the commentator of Udbhaṭa, as Pratīhārendurāja was not in favour of counting the independent importance of *dhvani*, and he was probably a southerner. It is however interesting to notice that in the *Samudrānanda* and the *Alaṃkārasarvasva* (p. 130, Trivandrum) Pratihārendurāja is regarded as identical with Bhaṭṭendurāja (see also p. 34 of *Alaṃkāra-sāra-saṃgraha-laghu-vṛttī*). Bhaṭṭa-tauta was another teacher of Abhinavagupta, whose work *Kāvyakautuka* was commented on by Abhinavagupta. Utpala is referred to in the Locana as his *parama-guru*. On the subject of *Pratyabhijñā* Philosophy his teacher was probably Lakṣmanaguru.

The *Dhvanyāloka* contains four *uddyotas* or chapters. In the first chapter he takes up the problem as to whether the claims of *dhvani* as being the essence of literature may be accepted as true or whether it can be included within *lakṣaṇā* or *abhidhā*. He holds that literature is appreciated not for its direct meaning or the information that it carries, but for the grace or beauty (like that of ladies) which is inexpressible but can be felt (*pratīyamāna*). This *pratīyamāna* or expression transcending the meaning is of three kinds, (1) it may manifest a truth (*vastu-dhvani*) ; (2) suggest a comparison (*alaṃkāra-dhvani*) ; or (3) communicate an emotion (*rasa-dhvani*). Mere grammarians and lexicographers do not understand the value of this suggestive expression. It is only when the suggestive expression supersedes the ordinary meaning that kāvya becomes a *dhvani-kāvya*. In *alaṃkāras* such as *samāsokti*, *ākṣepa*, *paryyāyokti*, etc., though there is a suggestive sense yet it is the primary sense that appears to be chiefly dominant there. *Dhvani* is of two kinds. (1) *avivakṣitavācya* and (2) the *vivakṣitānyaparavācya*. In the first case the primary meaning or the *vācya* has not the intended sense, it is only the suggested sense that is intended whereas in the latter case the suggestive sense is only more graceful and beautiful than the ordinary sense, though the ordinary sense is also conveyed. Abhinava and Ānandavardhana also try to distinguish here between *bhakti* or *lakṣaṇā* and *dhvaṇi*. In the second chapter the *avivakṣita-vācya-dhvani* is further subdivided into *arthāntara-saṃkramita* and *atyanta-tiraskṛta-vācya* and the *vivakṣitānyapara-vācya* is further subdivided into *asaṃlakṣya-krama* and *saṃlakṣya-krama*. The former is found in the case of the communication of *rasa* or *rasābhāsa*, etc. He also distinguishes there between the *alaṃkāras*, *rasavat*, *preya*, etc., and *rasadhvani* and also deals with the difference between the *guṇas* and *alaṃkāras*. He also further subdivides the *saṃlakṣyakrama-vyaṅga* and the *asaṃlakṣyakrama-vyaṅga*. In the 3rd chapter he further classifies *vyañjanā* as being from *pada*, *vākya*, *saṃghaṭanā* and *prabandha*, the manner in which the *rasa* is manifested, the figures which are particularly favourable to particular *rasas*, the plot in its relation to *rasas*, the subtle manner in which the particular suffixes, etc., may manifest the *asaṃlakṣyakrama-vyaṅga* dominance and subordination of *rasas* and their conflict. He also repudiates the view that *vyañjanā* is not *anumāna*. The *rītis* and *vṛttis* are also discussed. In the 4th chapter he discusses the nature of the *pratibhā* of poets, *guṇībhūta-vyaṅga*, or where the *dhvani* is either inferior or equal in status to the primary meaning. He also treats of the unlimited field of poetry which true geniuses may discover.

The *Locana* commentary has two other commentaries called *Locana-vyākhyā-kaumudī* by Parameśvarācāryya. None of these commentaries has yet been published.

Rajaśekhara

The *Kāvya-mīmāmsā* of Rājaśekhara, published in the Gaekwad Oriental Series, is a handbook for poets and is written in eighteen chapters, such as, *(i) śāstra-saṃgraha*, treating of the origin of *alaṃkāra-śāstra* ; *(ii) śastra-nirdeśa*, distinguishing between *śāstra* and *kāvya* ; *(iii) kāya-puruṣotpatti,* a mythical account of a *kāvya-puruṣa,* whose body is word and its sense and the various languages, its limbs, the *rasa* its self or *ātman,* and so on ; the *kāvya-puruṣa* is married to *sāhitya-vidyā-vadhū* ; *(iv) pada-vākya-viveka* dealing with *śakti, pratibhā vyutpatti* or erudition, *samādhi* (concentration) and *abhyāsa* (practice) as constitutive of the efficient art of writing poetry ; *(v) kāvyapākakalpa* dealing with *vyutpatti* or erudition, *śastrakavi, kāvya-kavi* and *ubhaya-kavi*; *(vi) padavākya-viveka* dealing with the nature of *śabda* and *vākya* ; *(vii) pāṭha-pratiṣṭhā* dealing with the proper language and style to be followed and the sort of intonation that is found in different parts of India ; *(viii) kāvyārthanaya* dealing with sources of the materials of literature ; *(ix) artha-vyāpti* dealing with the indispensable element kāvya as *rasa* ; (x) *kavi-caryyā* dealing with the discipline through which a poet must undergo and the external environment in which the poet should live ; (xi-xiii) the extent to which a poet can appropriate and utilise his predecessors' words and thoughts ; (xiv-xvi) dealing with conventions of poetry and fauna and flora of India ; (xvii) dealing with Geography of India together with economic and other products and the complexion of the different races of India ; (xviii) deals with the seasons, the winds, birds, etc. He quotes many old writers and has also been quoted in turn by Hemacandra, Vāgbhaṭa, Māṇikyacandra and Someśvara. He was probably a Mārhāṭṭā man who not only wrote the *Kāvya-mīmaṃsā* but also *Nala-rāmāyaṇa* and *Karpūra-mañjarī* in Prākṛt as well as *Viddhaśālabhañjikā* and *Bālabhārata,* otherwise called *Pracaṇḍapāṇḍava* and *Haravilāsa.* He is said to have lived in the first quarter of the 10th century.[1]

1 *Indian Antiquary,* Vol. 16, Vol. 34 and *Epigraphica Indica,* Vol. I, show that Mahendrapāla and Nirbhaya Narendra lived between 902 and 907, and the date of his son Mahīpāla is 917 A.D. Rājaśekhara was the teacher of Nirbhaya and he speaks of the king Mahīpāla, the son of Nirbhaya Narendra.

Bhaṭṭatauta

We have already referred the *Kāvyakautuka* of Bhaṭṭatauta, the teacher of Abhinavagupta, on which the latter had written a commentary called *Vivaraṇa.* So far we can collect his views as has already been done by Mr. Kane. We can say that he regarded *śāntarasa* as the most dominant one and superior to all other *rasas.* He further held that in understanding a poet the reader must undergo the same experiences as the poet has done.[1]

Kṣemendra in his *Aucitya-vicāra-carccā* and Hemacandra in his *Kāvyānuśāsana* and Someśvara in his commentary on *Kāvyaprakāśa* refers to *Kāvyakautuka.* The *Kāvyaprakāśāsaṃketa* of Māṇikyacandra also makes references to Bhaṭṭatauta. It has also been suggested by Hemacandra that Bhaṭṭatauta was against the view that the dramatic emotion was due to imitation and this has been elaborately shown in the *Abhinavabhāratī* commentary and Bharata's *Nāṭya-sūtra.*

Kuntaka

The *Vakrokti-jīvita* of Kuntaka has been edited and published by Dr. S. K. De. In this work *Vakrokti-jīvita* he profusely quotes Bhāmaha and Daṇḍin and sometimes Udbhaṭa also. The *Locana* of Abhinavagupta contains no reference to *Vakrokti-jīvita* and neither does he refer to the *Locana.* It is assumed therefore that he was a contemporary of Abhinavagupta and lived between 925 to 1025 A.D.[2]

His work is divided into 4 chapters and it consists of *kārikās* and their interpretations with examples. He held a theory that *vakrokti* was the soul of poetry but even in Bhāmaha we find that certain *alaṃkāras* were not regarded as

1 *"nāyakasya kaveḥ śrotuḥ samāno' nubhavastataḥ"* quoted in the *Locana,* p. 29.

2 The following literature may be consulted on Kuntaka :—Jacobi, Z.D.M.G. 56, 1902 ; also 69, 1908 ; T. Gaṇapati Śāstrī in the Trivendrum Sanskrit Series, Vol. V ; see also Haricānd's *Kālidāsa.*

alaṃkāras as there was no *vakrokti* in them. *Vakrokti* as the essence of Kāvya literature is therefore not a discovery or invention of Kuntaka, but it was he who gave it a finished form. It seems that in most cases various definitions given are Kuntaka's own and so also are most of the examples. Most of the later writers such as the author of *Ekāvali*, Someśvara, Māṇikyacandra, etc., all refer to the views of Kuntaka for refutation, preferring the *dhvani* theory to the *vakrokti*. But as I have showed elsewhere, that the idea of *vakrokti* includes *dhvani* in it.

The word *vakrokti* literaly means arch-speech. While anything is signified directly by the ordinary meaning of the words the speech may be regarded as straight and direct. But when the intended expression is carried by other means it may be called arch-speech. The word and its meaning constitute the kāvya. The word, however, that is constitutive of a kāvya should be such that though it has many meanings it only expresses or implies that particular meaning which the speaker intends to convey. The significance should be such that it can produce delight to men of literary taste, the meaning should be such that in its own spontaneous wave it should create beauty.[1] Real poetry must be the submission of an idea in a striking and charming manner.

The word and the sense both co-operate together in producing kāvya. But to what end do they co-operate? To this Kuntaka's reply is that they co-operate in producing an indescribable charm or beauty. Both the word and the sense play their own respective roles in producing the charm of poetry, and in the writings of a really great poet, they compete with one another in producing the effect. There are various ways in which this is effected. It may depend upon the alphabetic sounds, the words, the suffixes, the propositions, the contexts.

[1] *śabdo vivakṣitārthaika-vācakaḥ anyeṣu satsu api, arthaḥ sahṛdayāhlādakārī svaspandasundaraḥ ubhāvetāvalaṁkāryau tayoḥ punaralaṅkṛtiḥ, vakroktireva vaidagdhye-bhaṅgī-bhaṇitirucyate.*

He gives elaborate examples of the uniqueness and strikingness of different varieties of poetry. Mahimabhaṭṭa, however, criticised both Kuntaka and Abhinava.[1]

DHANAÑJAYA

The *Daśarūpa* of Dhanañjaya is a work on dramaturgy. It is a work of four chapters ; the first deals with the diflerent parts of a drama, the second with the several kinds of heroes and heroines ; the third deals with the practical problems concerned in connection with staging a drama and the varieties of dramatic demonstration, and the fourth deals with the *rasa* theory. It has a commentary by Dhvanika who had written also another work called *Kāvyanirṇaya.* His views were somewhat similar to that of Bhaṭṭanāyaka.

Dhanañjaya was the son of Viṣṇu and a member of the *rājasabhā* of Muñja (974, 979 and 991-94 A.D.) and Dhvanika, the commentator, was his brother.[2] Dhanañjaya practically remodelled and re-edited the dramaturgical portions of Bharata's *Nāṭya-śāstra* and has often been quoted in later times by writers on *alaṃkāra.*[3]

This dramaturgical work of Dhanañjaya became so famous in later times that both Viśvanātha and Vidyānātha have largely drawn upon this work for the materials of their treatment of dramaturgy. The commentator Dhvanika who wrote *Daśarūpāvaloka,* quotes from Padmagupta of 995 A.D. and is also quoted

1 On Kuntaka see Jacobi, Z.D.M.G., 1902 and 1906 and T. Ganapati Śāstri, Trivendrum Sanskrit Series, No. 5 ; Haricānd's *Kālidāsa* ; S. K. De's *Sanskrit Poetics* ; and Mr. Kane's Introduction to *Sāhitya-darpaṇa.*

2 See *Epigraphica Indica,* Vol. I, p. 235, Vol. 2, p. 180 ; *Indian Antiquary,* Vol. 6, p. 51.

The work has been published by F. Hall, Bibl.-Ind., Calcutta 1865, and by K. P. Parab, Bombay 1897. It has been translated into English by G. C. O. Haas, Columbia University, Indo-Iranian Series, New York 1912; see also Jacobi, Göttinger, Gelehrte Anzeigen 1913 and Barnett. J.R.A.S., 1913. See also S. Lévi, J. A. 1886. Jacobi holds with Lévi that Dhvanika was only the other name of Dhanañjaya.

3 *Das Daśarūpa ist viel übersichtiicher und systemarischer als das Bhāratīya-Nāṭya-Śāstra und wird daher in den späteren Werken über Poetic am häufigsten zitiert.* Winternitz, *History of Indian Literature,* Vol. III p. 20.

by Bhoja in his *Sarasvatī-kaṇṭhābharaṇa* in the first part of the 11th century. This suggestion by Jacobi and Lévi based on the inadvertent reference of a verse of Dhanañjaya to Dhvanika cannot be supported. For Vidyānātha refers to Dhanañjaya's *Daśarūpa* but not to the commentary, and Śārṅgarava quotes verses from Dhvanika's commentary referring them to Dhvanika. A few other commentaries were also written on *Daśarūpa* such as the commentary by Nṛsiṃhabhaṭṭa, the *Daśarūpa-ṭīkā* by Devapāṇi and *Daśarūpa-paddhati* by Kuravirāma.[1]

MAHIMABHAṬṬA

Rājānaka Mahimabhaṭṭa's *Vyakti-viveka,* with a commentary that breaks off in the middle of the 2nd *vimarśa,* has been published in the Trivendrum Series (1909). His chief purpose was to controvert the *dhvani* theory of Abhinavagupta. He does not deny that the soul of poetry is emotion, but he objects to the manner of communication as being of a special type called *dhvani.* He holds that the communication is by the process of inference.[2]

The work is divided into three chapters or *vimarśas.* In the very first verse he gives us the object of his work as leading to the demonstration of the fact that all that passes by the name of *dhvani* are really cases of inference.[3]

It is not the place here to enter into an elaborate statement of the arguments of Mahimabhaṭṭa for the destruction of the *dhvani* theory. But it may be pointed out that his attempt utterly failed as it left the later writers unconvinced of the rightness of his contention. He has often been referred to, by later writers, but always for refutation. As his views have

1 See De's *Sanskrit Poetics,* Vol. I, p. 135.

2 *asty abhisandhānāvasare vyanjakatvaṁ śabdānāṁ gamakatvaṁ tacca liṅgatvam ataś ca vyaṅgya-pratītir liṅga-pratītireveti liṅga-liṅgi-bhāva eva teṣaṁ vyaṅgya-vyañjaka-bhāvo nāparaḥ kaścit.* See Mahimabhaṭṭa's *Vyakti-viveka.*

3 *anumānāntarbhavaṁ sarvvasyaiva dhvaneḥ prakāśayitum, vyakti-vivekaṁ kurute praṇamya mahimā paraṁ vācam. Ibid.,* Verse I.

been summarised in the *Alaṅkārasarvasva* he must be earlier than 1100 A.D., and as he quotes the *Bālarāmāyaṇa* of Rājaśekhara and criticises the *Vakroktijīvita* he must be placed later than 1000 A.D. But Mahimabhaṭṭa has also been criticised by Mammaṭa in his *Kāvyaprakāśa.* It is therefore likely that he lived between 1020 and 1060 A.D. Again, Ruyyaka who flourished in the first half of the 12th century wrote a commentary on Mahimabhaṭṭa. Mahimabhaṭṭa therefore lived between Abhinava and Ruyyaka, which leads us to the conclusion, just arrived. Mahimabhaṭṭa's preceptor is Śyāmala, who was quoted by Kṣemendra, and this is quite in harmony with our view of Mahimabhaṭṭa's date. It is difficult to say whether Mahimabhaṭṭa was wholly original regarding his *anumāna* theory of *rasa,* for we know that Śaṅkuka had a similar theory and that Ānandavardhana refuted a similar theory which was current in his time. But at any rate, Mahimabhaṭṭa's work is the only elaborate treatise that we have on the *anumāna* theory. Mahimabhaṭṭa had also written another work called *Tattvoktikoṣa,* in which he discussed the nature of *pratibhā.* Mahimabhaṭṭa's work, with the commentary of Rājānaka Rujjaka, was published by Gaṇapati Śastrī in Trivendrum Sanskrit Series (1909).[1]

Bhoja

Bhoja's *Sarasvatī-kaṇṭhābharaṇa* is a merely compilatory work of great dimension. It was published in Calcutta by Ānandarām Baruā in 1884. It was written by King Bhoja who lived in the 11th century A.D. It is divided into five chapters of which the first deals with *padadoṣa, vākyadoṣa* and *vākyārthadoṣa* of 16 types and 24 *guṇas* of *śabda* and *vākyārtha.* In the 2nd chapter he deals with 24 *śabdālaṃkāras* and in the 3rd with 24 *arthālaṃkāras.* In the 4th chapter he deals with

[1] See Narasimhyienger's article in J.R.A.S., 1908 ; also Kane's Introduction to *Sāhityadarpaṇa*, and De's *Sanskrit Poetics*.

24 varieties of *śabdopamā* and 24 varieties of *arthopamā* and a number of other *alaṃkāras*, and in the 5th he deals with *rasas*, *bhāvas*, the nature of heroes and heroines, the five *sandhis* of drama and the four *vṛttis*.

He quotes profusely from Daṇḍin's *Kāvyādarśa*, Kālidāsa and Bhababhūti, Bāṇa and Śrīharṣa, Rājaśekhara, Rudraṭa and Māgha. In dealing with the figures, *upamā*, *ākṣepa*, *samāsokti* and *apahnuti*, he follows *Agnipurāṇa*. He counts 6 *rītis*, *vaidarbhī*, *pāñcālī*, *gauḍī*, *avantikā*, *lāṭīyā* and *māgadhī*, as instances of *śabdālaṃkāra*. He reduces the six *pramāṇas* of Jaimini to figures of speech, and though he speaks of eight *rasas*, he gives extreme emphasis to *śṛṅgāra*, and in his *Śṛṅgāraprakāśa* he admits only one *rasa*, viz., *śṛṅgāra*. It is curious enough to see that he regarded *guṇas* and *rasas* as *alaṃkāras*.

Numerous works are ascribed to Bhoja. He is said to have written one *Dharmaśāstra* and passages from this are found quoted in the *Mitākṣarā* and the *Dāyabhāga*. He wrote a commentary on the *Yogaśāstra* called the *Rājamārtaṇḍa* and an astronomical work called *Rājamṛgāṅka* (1042-43). The *Sarasvatīkaṇṭhābharaṇa* was probably composed between 1030 and 1050. It has a commentary called *Ratnadarpaṇa* by Ratneśvara.[1]

[1] Apart from *Ratnadarpaṇa* there are at least three other commentaries on *Sarasvatikaṇṭhābharaṇa*, viz., *Sarasvatikaṇhābharaṇa-mārjjanā* by Harinatha, *Duṣkaracitra-prakāśikā* by Lakṣmīnātha Bhaṭṭa, and *Sarasvatikaṇṭhābharaṇa-ṭīkā* by Jagaddhara, who wrote commentaries on the *Meghadūta*, *Vāsavadattā*, *Veṇisaṁhāra*, *Mālatīmādhava*, etc. Harikṛṣṇa Vyāsa ia also supposed to have written a commentary on *Sarasvatī-kaṇṭhābharaṇa* (see S. K. De's *Sanskrit Poetics*). Dr. Bhandarkar in his *Early History of the Deccan* came to the conclusion that Bhoja belonged to the first half of the 11th century. Dr. Būhler in his Introduction to the *Vikramāṅkadevacarita* holds that Bhoja flourished at a somewhat later date. *Rājataraṅgiṇī* refers to Bhoja as a man of great charity and Bühler thinks that the passage in question in *Rājataraṅgiṇī* refers to the period when Kalasa was crowned king of Kashmir in 1062. This has, however, been doubted by others and instead of Kalasa the reference is to king Ananta. Būhler further says that there is a quotation from *Caurapañcāśikā* in *Sarasvatīkaṇṭhābharaṇa*. *Caurapañcāśikā* was written by Bilhaṇa but this also is not absolutely certain. According to the *Bhojaprabandha* Bhoja reigned for 55 years. Muñja, the uncle of Bhoja, was killed by Tailaka between 994 and 997 A.D. and he was succeeded by his brother Sindhula, also called Navasāhasāṅka. An inscription of ayasiṁha is found dated 1112 Saṁvat, *i.e.*, 1055 A.D. This shows that Bhoja could not have been living beyond 1054 A,D. A land grant by Bhoja dated 1021 A.D. has also been found. Bhoja probably ascended the throne in 1005 A.D. and died before 1054.

Kṣemendra

He wrote two works on *Alaṃkāra*, the *Aucitya-vicāra-carccā* and the *Kavi-kanṭhābharaṇa*. In addition to this he wrote *Bhārata-mañjarī*, the *Bṛhatkathā-mañjarī*, the *Rājāvali* and forty other works. He also wrote on metre a work called *Suvṛtti-tilaka*.

In this *Aucitya-vicāra-carccā* he holds that propriety (*aucitya*) is the soul of poetry, and when any description, *alaṃkāra, rasa*, etc., oversteps its proper bounds it hurts the *rasa* and mars the poetry.[1]

In his *Kavi-kaṅṭhābharaṇa* he deals with the following subjects :—*kavitvaprāpti, śikṣā, camatkṛti, guṇadoṣabodha, paricayaprāpti*. He also gives certain directions regarding *guṇas* and *doṣas*. He also regarded the study of grammar, logic and drama as indispensable for a poet. He probably flourished in 1050 A.D. at the time of King Ananta who ruled in Kashmir (1020-1063).

Mammaṭa

Mammaṭa's *Kāvya-prakāśa* is a first class work of compilation. It became later on the model for any other similar works of compilation. In the first chapter he deals with the object of writing kāvya, the definition of kāvya and its subdivision as good and bad. The second chapter is devoted to the study of words, *abhidhā, lakṣaṇā* and *vyañjanā*, the third with the functions of different kinds of *vyañjanā* ; the fourth with the varieties of *dhvani* and the nature of *rasa* ; the fifth with *guṇībhūta-vyañga* and its eight subdivisions ; the sixth with *citra-kāvya*, the seventh with *doṣas*, the eighth with *guṇas* and their distinctions from *alaṃkāra*, the ninth with *śabdālaṃkāra* and *rīti* and the tenth with *alaṃkāras*.

1 *anaucityamṛte nānyat rasa-bhaṅgasya kāraṇam, praśiddhaucityabanahastu rasasyopaniṣat parā.*

2 For information about his work, see Bühler's *Kasmir Reports*, pp. 45-48, J.B.R.S., Vol. 16, pp. 167-79 and also the extra number, pp. 5-9.

Though a compiler, Mammaṭa is also an independent critic. Thus he criticises Bhaṭṭodbhaṭa, Rudraṭa, Mahimabhaṭṭa, Vāmana and others. He also finds fault with Bhāmaha and upholds the *dhvani* theory.

The work is divided into *kārikā* and *vṛtti*. Vidyābhūṣaṇa in his *Sāhityakaumudī*, Maheśvara and Jayarāma in his *Tilaka*, hold that the *kārikās* were written by Bharata and the *vṛti* by Mammaṭa.[1]

From considerations mentioned in the footnote, Kane defends the view that both the *vṛtti* and the *kārikā* were written by the same person. But whatever that may be, the whole of the work was not written by Mammaṭa. The commentator of *Kāvyaprakāśa*, Ruyyaka, in his *Saṃketa* commentary says that Mammaṭa could not finish the work but that it was finished by some other person. The apparent unity is due to his imitating the style of Mammata.[2]

Jayantabhaṭṭa, Someśvara, Narahari, Sarasvatītīrtha, Kamalākara, Ānanda Yajñeśvara, the commentators of *Kāvyaprakāśa*, also uphold this view. Rājānaka Ānanda in his commentary says that Mammaṭa wrote upto the *parikara alaṃkāra* and the rest was written by Allaṭa or Alāṭa.[3]

1 The ground for such an assertion is that some of the *kārikās* are identical with the verses of *Nāṭya-śāstra, e.g., śṛṅgāra-hāsya-karuṇa-rati rhāsaśca.* etc.

Again, in the *vṛtti* to the first *kārikā* the writer of the *kārikā* is referred to in the third person as *granthakṛt parāmṛśati* which seems to indicate that the writer of the *kārikā* is a different person than that of the *vṛtti.* There in the 10th *ullāsa* there is a difference of opinion between the *kārikā* and the *vṛtti,* in the *kārikā 'samasta-vastu-viṣayam.'* Against this it can be urged that out of the 142 *kārikās* only a few agree with Bharata's. So other *kārikās* may also be pointed out which are adaptations from Vāmana and the *Dhvanikārikā.* The use of the third person also is often a fashion with the commentators. The supposed point of difference is in reality an elucidation or modification rather than difference.

2 *esa grantho grantha-kṛtānena kathamapyasamāptatvāt apareṇa pūritāvaśeṣatvāt dvikhaṇḍo, pi akhaṇḍatayā yad avabhāsate tatra saṁghaṭanaiva hetuḥ.*

kṛtaḥ śrī-mammaṭācāryya-varryyaiḥ/parikarāvadhiḥ
prabandhaḥ pūritaḥ śeṣo vidhā-yāllaṭa.sūriṇā.

Aruna Varmā a commentator of *Amaruśataka,* of the 13th century, in quoting a verse from *Kāvyaprakāśa* says, *yathodāhṛtaṁ doṣanirṇaye mammaṭāllaṭabhyām.* Arjuna Varmā was almost a contemporary of Mammaṭa and his words are to be trusted. Allata's work commences from some part of the 7th chapter.

I agree, however, with Kane that there is no reason to suppose that the *kārikās* were written by Bharata, for in that case the *vṛtti* of the *rasakārikās* should not have supported the contention of the *kārikā* by quoting Bharata.

Mammaṭa refers to Abhinavagupta, and to Bhoja, and as such must have lived in or about 1055 A.D. *Kāvyaprakāśa* had many commentaries, such as, *Bālacittānurañjinī* by Narahari Sarasvatītīrtha, *Dīpikā* by Jayantabhaṭṭa, both belonging to the 13th century A.D. ; *Kavyādarśa* by *Someśvara, Kāvyaprakāśa-viveka* by Śrīdhara *Kāvyaprakāśa-dīpikā,* by Chaṇḍīdāsa, *Kāvyaprakāśa-darpaṇa* by Viśvanātha of the 14th century, *Sāhitya-dīpika* by Bhāskara, *Kāvyaprakāśa-vistārikā* by Paramānanda Cakravarttī, *Kāvyaprakaśa-dīpika* by Gobinda Ṭhakkura. On this last-mentioned work Vaidyanātha wrote a commentary called *Prabhā.* Nāgojībhaṭṭa wrote the *Uddyota,* Jayarāma Nyāyapañcānana wrote a commentary on the *Kāvyaprakāśa* called the *Kāvyaprakāśa-tilaka* and Śrivatsalāñchana wrote *Sārabodhinī.* Rabi wrote a commentary called *Madhumatī,* and Ratnapāṇi *Kāvyadarpaṇa.* Maheśvara Nyāyālaṃkāra wrote *Bhāvārtha-cintāmaṇi* and Rājānaka Ānanda wrote *Kāvyaprakāśa-nidarśanā.* Again, Rājānakaratnakaṇṭha wrote a commentary called *Sāra-samuccaya.* Narasiṃha Ṭhakkura wrote *Narasiṃha-manīṣā,* Vaidyanātha *Udāharaṇa-candrikā,* Bhīmasena Dīkṣita wrote *Sudhāsāgara,* Baladeva Vidyābhūṣaṇa wrote a commentary called *Sahitya-kaumudī* and a *Ṭippanī* called *Kṛṣṇānandinī.* Nāgojībhaṭṭa wrote two commentaries, *Laghūddyota* and *Bṛhaduddyota.* In addition to this we have a commentary by Vācaspati and also a commentary by Kamalākara Bhaṭṭa.

Ruyyaka

His work *Alaṃkāra-sarvasva* is a standard work on figures of speech. He summarises and compiles the views of Bhāmaha, Udbhaṭa, Rudraṭa Vāmana, the *Vakrokti-jīvita,* the *Vyakti-viveka* and the Dhvanikāra, and deals with about 75 *arthālaṃkaras* in addition to the *śabdālaṃkāras, punaruktivadābhāsa, chekānuprāsa*, *vṛttānuprāsa*, *yamaka*, *lāṭānuprāsa* and *citra*. He adds a few more *alaṃkāras* to Mammaṭa's list, such as, *pariṇāma*, *rasavat*, *preyas*, *ūrjjasvī*, *samāhita*, *bhāvodaya*, *bhāvasandhi*, *bhāvaśavalatā* and adds two new *alaṃkāras*, *vikalpa* and *vicitra*. Viśvanātha was inspired by Ruyyaka and drew some of his materials from him. So also did *Ekāvalī* and *Kuvalayānanda*. He also sometimes criticises some of the older writers, such as Abhinava, on the subject of *alaṃkāra*. He also often refers to *Kāvyaprakāśa*. He differs from Mammaṭa on the principle on which *śabdālaṃkāra* and *arthālaṃkāra* are to be distinguished. When Mammaṭa said that the principle should be *anvaya-vyatireka*, Ruyyaka said that it should be *āśrayāśrayibhāva*. The definitions of many of the *alaṃkāras*, however, are the same as in *Kāvyaprakāśa*.

There is some dispute regarding the authorship of the *Vṛtti*. In the Kāvyamālā edition the first verse says that the *Vṛtti* belongs to the author of the *Kārikā*.[1] This view is also supported by Jayaratha who commented upon the work 75 years later, and so did many of the later writers. But the Tangore MSS. says that the *Alaṃkārasūtras* were written by his teacher to which Ruyyaka supplied the *Vṛtti*.[2] In the Trivandrum edition, however, the commentator Samudrabandha says that the *Vṛtti* was written by one Maṅkhuka or Maṅkha. We know from Maṅkha's *Śrīkaṇṭha-carita* (25. 26-30) that Maṅkha was the pupil of Ruyyaka. It appears therefore that there was a tradition that Ruyyaka wrote the *Kārikā* and Maṅkha wrote the *Vṛtti*. But the conscientious opinion of such persons as Kumārasvāmī (Ratnāpaṇa), Jagannātha, Jayaratha and other writers being on the side that both the *Kārikā* and the *Vṛtti* were written by Ruyyaka, we may safely ignore the statement of Samudrabandha (1300 A.D.) who is a much later writer.[3] According to a colophon

1 *nijālaṁkāra-sūtrāṇāṁ vṛttyā tātparyam ucyate*
Alaṁkārasarvasva, Verse 1.

2 *gurvalaṁkārasūtrāṇaṁ vṛttyā tātparyam ucyate.*

3 P. V. Kane's Introduction to *Sāhityadarpaṇa*.

of the M.S. of the *Sahṛdaya-līlā,* Rucaka was another name of Ruyyaka and he was the son of Rājānakatilaka[1] According to Jayaratha Ruyyaka wrote a commentary on the *Kāvyaprakaśa* called *Kāvyaprakāśa-saṃketa.* The work *Alaṃkāra-sarvasva* is often referred to by later writers merely as *Sarvasva.* In addition to *Kāvyālaṃkāra-sarvasva,* Ruyyaka wrote many other works, such as, *Alaṃkārānusāriṇī, Kāvyaprakāśa-saṃketa, Nāṭaka-mīmāṃsā, Vyaktiviveka-vicāra, Śrīkaṇṭha-stava, Śahṛdaya-līlā, Sāhitya-mīmāṃsa, Harṣacarita-vārttika.*

As Ruyyaka quotes from *Vikramāṅka-deva-carita,* composed about 1085 A.D. according to Būḥler, and criticses the *Vyakti-viveka* and the *Kāvyaprakaśa,* he must have therefore lived after 1100 A.D. Maṅkha's *Śrīkaṇṭha-carita* is said to have been composed between 1135 and 1145 A.D., as *Alaṃkāra-sarvasva* contains quotation from this work it must have been composed not earlier than 1150 A.D. The *Kāvyaprakāśa-saṃketa* of Māṇikyacandra composed between 1159-60 often refers to the *Alaṃkāra-sarvasva.* Therefore the *Alaṃkāra-sarvasva* was probably composed between 1135 and 1153.[2]

Of the commentaries Jayaratha's *Vimarśinī* was particularly famous. It was probably written sometime in the 13th century. Jayaratha wrote also another work called *Tantrāloka-viveka.* The other commentator, Samudravandha, was in the court of

1 See Pischel's Introduction to *Śṛṅgāra-tilaka* (pp. 28-29).

2 The work was translated into German by Jacobi in Z.D.M.G. 62, 1908. Jacobi in J.R.A.S. 1897 held that it was possible that Ruyyaka wrote the sūtras and Maṅkha the *Vṛtti.* See also Haricānd's *Kālidāsa.*

Ruyyaka was also the author of *Sahṛdaya-līlā,* published by R. Pischel. See also De's *Sanskrit Poetics* in which the view held above regarding the identity of authorship of the *Vṛtti* and the *Kārikā* has been subscribed to.

The fact that five verses of *Śrīkaṇṭha-carita* occur in *A'aṁkārasarvasva* may be due to the reason that *Śrīkaṇṭha-carita* of Maṅkha was submitted to Ruyyaka among others for criticism.

The work has been published in the Kāvyamālā series and the Trivandrum series, the first containing the commentary *Alṁkāra-vimarśinī* and the second, the Vṛtti of Samudrabandha. There is also another commentary on it which has not yet been published, which is called *Alaṁkāra-sañjīvanī* by Vidyācakravarttī. It was probably written before Mallinātha's commentary, before the 14th century.

Ravivarma who was born in 1265 A.D. and he may have flourished towards the end of the 13th century or towards the beginning of the 14th century.

VĀGBHAṬA I

The *Vāgbhaṭālaṃkāra* of Vāgbhaṭa with a commentary by Siṃhadevagaṇi has been published in the Kāvyamālā series It is a small work containing 260 *kārikās*, divided into 5 chapters. The first chapter deals with the nature of Kāvya and holds that *pratibhā* is the source of Kāvya. *Pratibhā*, *vyutpatti* and *abhyāsa* are the three conditions which lead to the successful production of poetry. The second chapter is devoted to the description of languages in which Kāvya is written, such as *Saṃskṛta*, *Prākṛta*, *Apabhraṃśa* and *Bhūta-bhāṣa*. It divides Kāvya into metrical, non-metrical and mixed and deals with the eight *doṣas* of *pada*, *vākya* and *artha*. The 4th chapter deals with the *śabdālaṃkāras*, *citravakrokti*, *anuprāsa* and *yamaka* and 35 *arthālamkāras* and treats of two styles, *Vaidarbhī* and *Gauḍī*.

The author was a Jaina and his real name in Prākṛt is Bahata and he was probably the son of Soma. The examples are mostly the author's own. He probably wrote also a *Mahākāvya* called *Nemi-nirvāna*. He probably lived in the first half of the 12th century.

HEMACANDRA

His *Kāvyānuśāsana* is a small work of compilation with but little originality. It is written in the form of *sūtra* and *vṛtti*. The *sūtras* were probably called the *Kāvyānuśāsana* and the *vṛtti* was called *Alaṃkāra-cūḍāmaṇi*. There is a short commentary on the *Vṛtti* containing some examples. It is divided into eight chapters. The first deals with the nature of Kāvya, regarding what constitutes Kāvya, the various meanings of *śabda* and *artha*. The second deals with *rasa*, the third treats of *doṣa*, the fourth *guṇa*, the fifth figures of speech and so also the sixth. The 7th discusses the various kinds of heroes and heroines and the 8th classifies the Kāvya. He borrowed extensively from Rājaśekhara's *Kāvyamīmāṃsā*, *Kāvyaprakāśa*, *Dhvanyāloka* and *Locana*. In the commentary, however, he gives copious examples, but he exercises but little influence on his successors. He is primarily a grammarian. He was born in 1088 A.D. and died in 1172 A.D.

JAYADEVA

His *Candrāloka* contains 10 chapters of 350 verses. The first as usual is dedicated to the definition and condition of poethood and the classification of wards, the 2nd to *doṣa*, the 3rd to devices adopted by poets to heighten the charm of their words, the 4th to *guṇas*, the 5th to *alaṃkāras*, the 6th to *rasa*, the 7th to *vyañjanā*, the 8th to *guṇībhuta-vyaṅga*, the 9th to *lakṣaṇā* the 10th to *abhidhā*. The author was the son of Mahādeva and Sumitrā and wrote the celebrated Kāvya, *Prasanna-Rāghava*. He is different from the author of *Gītagovinda*, who was the son of Bhojadeva and Ramādevī and was an inhabitant of Kenduvilva in Bīrbhūm, Bengal. It is a much later work, probably not earlier than the 12th century A.D.

The text was published first in Madras, 1857, Calcutta, 1874, 1877, and 1906 by Jīvānanda; by Subrahmyaṇya at Vizagapatam in 1908; by Venkaṭācāryya Sāstrī, Palghat, 1912; by Nirṇayasāgara Press 1912-1917; with the commentary of *Candrāloka-niguḍhārtha-dīpikā*. The Madras edition containing the *Budha-rañjanī* commentary is a commentary on the *arthālaṃkāra* section and not on the whole of the text. It had also many other commentaries, such as, *Śāradāgama*, *Candrāloka-prakāśa* by Proddyota Bhaṭṭa, *Rākāgamasudhā* by Viśveśvara also called Gāgā Bhaṭṭa, *Ramā* by Vidyānātha Payaguṇḍa, a commentary by Vājacandra, *Śāradaśarvarī* by Virūpākṣa, and *Candrāloka-dīpikā* by an anonymous writer.

BHĀNUDATTA

His *Rasa-taraṅgiṇī* is a work in eight chapters, dealing merely with the various components of *rasa*, such as, *bhāva, sthāyibhāva, anubhāva, sāttvikabhāva, vyabhicāribhava* and various *rasas*, etc. The *Rasa-mañjarī* deals with the nature of the heros and heroines and the parts they play. He seems to have drawn much from *Daśa-rūpaka.* He was the son of Gaṇeśvara and belonged to the Videha country on the bank of the Ganges. He probably flourished towards the end of the 13th or the beginning of the 14th century. His *Gīta-gaurīśa* seems to have been modelled on Jayadeva's *Gītagobinda,* and Jayadeva is generally placed in the 12th century A.D. The commentary *Rasa-mañjarī-prakāśa*[1] was written in 1428. This also corroborates our conclusion about the date of Bhānudatta that he flourished sometime at the end of the 13th or the beginning of the 14th century.

VIDYĀDHARA

His work *Ekāvali* with the *Tarala* commentary by Mallinātha has been published by Trivedī in the Bombay Sanskrit Series. All the examples are Vidyādhara's own and contain panegyrics of King Narasiṃha of Utkala in whose court he lived, just as there are other works, *e.g., Pratāparudra-yaśobhūṣaṇa, Raghunātha-bhūpatīya.* This work is divided into eight chapters

[1] *Rasamañjarīprakāśa* was published in Madras 1872 and 1881, with *Vyaṅgārtha-kaumudī* of Anantapaṇḍita and *Rasamañjarīprakāśa* of Nāgojī Bhaṭṭa was published in the Benaras Sanskrit Series in 1904 and was also *Veṅkaṭācāryya Śāstrī,* Madras 1909. There were many commentaries as if apart from those mentioned above, such as, *Parimala* by Śeṣacintāmaṇi, 17th century, *Rasamañjarīvikāsa* by Gopāla Ācāryya, 15th century, *Rasikarañjanī* by Gopāla Bhaṭṭa, son of Harivaṁśa Bhaṭṭa, *Samañjasā* or *Vyaṅgyārtha-kaumudī* by Viśveśvara, son of Lakṣmīdhara, *Rasamañjaryāmoda* by Raṅgasvāmin, *Vyaṅgyārtha-dīpikā* by Anandaśarman, *Bhānubhāva-prakāśinī* by Mādhava, *Rasikarañjana* by Brajarāja Dīkṣita, and *Rasamañjarī-sthūlatātparyārtha* by an anonymous writer. The *Rasataraṅgiṇī* has also a number of commentaries, such as, *Naukā* by Gangārāma *Rasikarañjanī* by Veṇīdatta, *Setu* by Jīvarāja, *Rasodadhi* by Gaṇeśa, *Rasodadhi* by Mahādeva, *Sāhityaśudhā* by Nemisādhu, *Nūtanatari* by Bhagavadbhaṭṭa, a commentary by Divākara, another by Ayodhyāprasād.

or *unmeṣas*. The first deals with the conditions of being a poet, the nature of Kāvya and discusses the views of Mahimabhaṭṭa and others. The 2nd chapter deals with the threefold meanings of words, *abhidhā, lakṣaṇā,* and *vyañjanā* ; the third and fourth with *dhvani* and *guṇībhūta-vyaṅga* and the fifth with *guṇa* and *rīti*, the sixth with *doṣa*, the seventh with *śabdālaṃkāra* and the eighth with *arthālaṃkāra*. The work is based on the *Kāvya-prakāśa* and *Alaṃkārasarvasva*. Mr. Trivedī in his edition of the work brings out all the important data about his date and it appears that the author was patronised either by Keśava Narasiṃha (1282-1307) or by Pratāpa Narasiṃha (1307-1327). He therefore probably flourished in the 14th century.[1]

Vidyānātha

An excellent edition of Vidyānātha's *Pratāparudra-yaśo-bhuṣana* with a commentary called *Ratnāpaṇa* by Mallinātha's son Kumārasvāmī has been brought out by Trivedī in the Bombay Sanskrit Series. It consists of *kārikās, vṛttis,* and illustrations. The illustrations are all composed by the writer in honour of his patron. The patron is said to be a Kakatīya king of Telangana, Pratāparudradeva, also called Vīrarudra or Rudra whose capital was at Ekaśilā (Warangal). The work is divided into 9 chapters or *prakāśanas* and the following subjects are dealt with in order :—heros, nature of Kāvya, nature of *nāṭaka, rasa, doṣa, guṇa, śabdālaṃkāra, arthālaṃkāra, miśrālaṃkāra*. It deals with some new *alaṃkāras* not taken up by Mammaṭa, or described by him, such as *pariṇāma, ullekha, vicitra* and *vikalpa*. He flourished probably in the beginning of the 14th century. *Ratnāpaṇa* is an excellent commentary by Kumārasvāmī, son of Mallinātha.[2]

1 On discussions about his date see J.B.R.A.S., Vols. X. & XI ; Telang's article in Indian *Antiquary*, Vols. II & III ; Bühler's reports on Sanskrit Manuscripts 1874 ; *Rasārṇava-sudhākara*, p. 107 ; see also Dr. De's *Sanskrit Poetics* and Kane's Introduction to *Sāhitya darpaṇa*.

2 In addition to Trivedi's edition there were also two other editions of the wokr.

Vāgbhaṭa II

The *Kāvyānuśāsana* of Vāgbhaṭa has been published with the *Alaṃkāra-tilaka* commentary in the Kāvyamālā Series, written in the form of *sūtra, vṛtti* and examples. It is divided into 5 chapters. In the first he deals with the definition of Kāvya and the conditions of poets, the division of Kāvya as *gadya, padya* and *miśra* and the distinction between *mạhākāvya, ākhyāyikā, katha, campu* and *miśra-kāvya* including the 10 *rūpakas*. The 2nd chapter deals with the 16 *doṣas* of *pada*, 14 *doṣas* of *vākya* and 14 *doṣas* of *artha* and 10 *guṇas* according to Daṇḍin and Vāmana. But he holds that *guṇas* are really 3 in number, *mādhuryya, ojas* and *prasāda* and he admits 3 *rītis—gauḍī, vaidarbhī* and *pāñcālī*. In the 3rd chapter he describes 63 *arthālaṃkāras* and mentions among them some rare *alaṃkāras, anya, apara, pūrva, leśa, vihita, mata, ubhayanyāsa, bhāva* and *āśīḥ*. In the 4th chapter he deals with 6 *śabdālaṃkāras*, e.g., *citra, sleṣa, anuprāsa, vakrokti, yamaka,* and *punaruktavadābhāsa*. In the 5th he deals with the *rasas* and the varieties of heroes and heroines. He probably wrote a *mahākāvya* called *Ṛṣabha-deva-carita* and a work on metrics, *Chando'nuśāsana*. He was the son of Nemikumāra and probably lived in the 15th century A.D. He has but little originality in his work and has drawn his materials from *Kāvyamīmāṃsā* and *Kāvyaprakāśa*.

Viśvanātha

Viśvanātha's *Sāhitya-darpaṇa* is a very popular work on *alaṃkāra*. His great grand-father, Nārāyaṇa, was a very learned man and had written many works on Alaṃkāra, and his father Candraśekhara was a poet and he often quotes from his father's work. He mentions two works of his father, Puṣpamata and Bhāṣarṇava. In all probability he was an inhabitant of Orissa as he sometimes gives Oriya equivalents of Sanskrit words in his commentary on *Kāvyaprakāśa*. Both his father and he himself probably held high offices in the court of the king of Kaliṅga, and had the title *Sandhi-vaigrahika-mahāpātra.* He was probably a Vaiṣṇava in religion and was also a poet and he quotes his own verses both in Sanskrit and Prākṛt. He wrote a number of other works such as, *Rāghava-vilāsa, Kuvalayāśva-carita*—a Prākṛt kāvya, *Prabhāvatī* and *Candrakalā* (both *nāṭikās*), and also *Praśasti-ratnāvali* and a *karambhaka* in 16 languages. His *Sāhityadarpaṇa* was composed in 1384 A.D.[1] There are at least 4 commentaries on *Sāhityadarpaṇa,—Sāhityadarpaṇa-locana* by Anantadāsa, *Sāhityadarpaṇa-ṭippana* by Mathurānāth Śukla, *Sāhitya-darpaṇa-vivṛti* by Rāmacaraṇa Tarkavāgīśa and *Sahitya-darpaṇa-prabhā* by Gopīnātha.

Keśavamiśra

His *Alaṃkāra-śekhara,* written as *kārikā, vṛtti* and examples, has been published in the Kāvyamālā series. It is said in the *vṛtti* that the *kārikās* were written by one Śauddhodani. The author has drawn largly from *Kāvyādarśa, Kāvyamīmaṃsā, Dhvanyāloka, Kāvyaprakāśa,* and *Vāgbhaṭālaṃkāra.* It is divided into 8 chapters called *ratnas,* and deals with the conditions of kāvya, the *rītis,* the threefold meanings of words, the *doṣas,* the *guṇas* and the *alaṃkāras,* the nature of heroes and heroines, the conventions of poets, subjects to be described in a *kāvya,* tricks of words and the *rasas.* He also regards *rasa* as the soul of poetry. The work was written, as the writer says, at the instance of the King Māṇikyacandra, the son of Dharmacandra who flourished in the middle of the 16th century.

Appaya Dīkṣita

Appaya wrote 3 works on poetics, *Vṛtti-vārttika* in 2 chapters dealing with words and their meanings. *Kuvalayānanda,* is an elementary treatise of *alaṃkāra* in which he adds 24 more *alaṃkāras* to the 100 *alaṃkāras* already given in *Candrāloka.* His third work is *Citra-mīmāṃsā,* in which he deals with *dhvani,*

1 For a discussion on his date see P. V. Kane's Introduction to *Sāhityadarpaṇa.*

guṇībhutavyaṅga and *citrakāvya* and treats of a number of *alaṃkāras*. Jagannātha in his *Rasa-gaṅgādhara* tries to refute the doctrines of *Citramīmāṃsā* and calls his work *Citramīmāṃsā-khaṇḍana*, but curiously enough, he stops at *apahnuti*. Appaya Dīkṣita quotes from *Ekāvalī*, *Pratāparudra-yaśobhūṣaṇa* and *Alaṃkāra-sarvasva-sañjīvanī* and must therefore be later than the 14th century. Dr. Hultzsch in the *Epigraphica Indica*, Vol. 4, shows that the Veṅkaṭapati referred to in *Kuvalayānanda* was Veṅkaṭa I of Vijayanagara, one of whose grants is dated 1601 A.D. Appaya Dīkṣita therefore flourished in the first quarter of the 17th century.

JAGANNĀTHA

The *Rasa-gaṅgādhara* of Jagannātha together with its commentary *Marma-prakāśa* by Nāgeśabhaṭṭa has been published in the Kāvyamālā series. It is a standard work an poetics, of the same rank as *Dhvanyāloka* and *Kāvyaprakāśa*. The work consists of *kārikās*, *vṛttis* and examples which are all from the author's pen. He often boldly criticises celebrated writers of the past offering his own independent views. He holds that not *rasa* but *rāmaṇīyakatā* is the essence of good Kāvya.[1] The work suddenly breaks off in the second chapter while dealing with the *uttarālaṃkāra* and Nāgeśa's commentary also goes no further. It seems therefore probable that Jagannātha could not complete his work. His *vṛtti* is very erudite and contains references to his many views on the subject of the theory of *vyañjanā* or *dhvani* and the expression of *rasa*, which are not available in any other work of *alaṃkāra*. In addition to *Rasa-gaṅgādhara* and *Citra-mīmāṃsā-khaṇḍana* he wrote another work called *Bhāminī-vilāsa* published by L. R. Vaidya in the Kāvyamālā series. He wrote a criticism of Bhaṭṭoji Dīkṣita's *Manoramā* and called it *Manoramā-kuca-mardana*.

Jagannātha was a Tailaṅga Brāhmaṇa who studied under his own father Perubhaṭṭa, and Śeṣavīreśvara. The title

1 *rāmaṇīyakārtha-pratipādakas śabdaḥ kāvyam—Rasagaṅgādhara*.

Paṇḍitarāja was given to him by Shahjahan. He wrote a work called *Asafa-vilāsa*, probably mourning the death of the favourite Khan-Khanan who died in 1641 A.D. and praises Dara Siko in his *Jagadābharaṇa*. He probably lived in the middle of the 17th century.

Later Minor Writers

Quite a large number of Alaṃkāra works has been written in recent times and it may be worthwhile to mention some of their names :—Acyuta-Śarmā's *Sāhitya-sāra*, a work of 12 chapters, of the 19th century, Ajitasenācāryya's *Alaṃkāra-cintāmaṇi* and *Śṛṅgāra-mañjarī* (the writer was a Jaina), *Anuratna-maṇḍana* or Ratna-maṇḍana-gaṇi's *Jalpa-kalpa-latā*—probably of the 16th century, *Mugdha-medhākara* by the same author, Anantarāya's *Kavisamaya-kallola*, Ananta's *Sāhitya-kalpa-vallī*, Amṛtānanda Yogin's *Alaṃkāra-saṃgraha* (edited in Calcutta, 1887, with an English translation), Mallarāja's *Rasa-ratnā-dīpikā*, Indrajit's *Rasika-priyā*, Kacchapeśvara Dīkṣita's *Rāmacandra-yaśobhuṣaṇa*, Kāṇḍālayarya's *Alaṃkāra-sirobhuṣaṇa*, Kātyāyaṇa Subrahmaṇya Sūri's *Alaṃkāra-kaustubha* probably at the end of the 18th century, Kānticandra Mukhopādhyāya's *Kāvya-dīpikā* (Calcutta 1870 and 1876), Kāśīlakṣmaṇa Kavi's *Alaṃkāra-grantha*, Kṛṣṇa's *Sāhitya-taraṅgiṇī*, Kumbha's *Rasaratna-koṣa*, (15th century), Kṛṣṇabhaṭṭa's *Vṛtti-dīpikā*, Kṛṣṇa Dīkṣita's *Raghunātha-bhūpālīya*, Kṛṣṇa Śarman's *Mandāra-makaranda-campū*, (edited in the Kāvyamālā and the *Rasaprakāśa*). The writer was later than Appayya Dīkṣita. We have also Keśavabhaṭṭa's *Rasika-sañjīvanī*, Gaṅgānanda-maithila's *Karṇa-bhūṣaṇa* (probably in the 16th century). It is unnecessary, however, to enumerate these names of Alaṃkāra works of later writers which exceed one hundred in number. Besides these, there are more than fifty anonymous works on Alaṃkāra. Quite a large number of these names have been collected from the catalogue of Sanskrit Mss. in Dr. S. K. De's *Sanskrit Poetics*, Vol. I and also in P. V. Kane's Introduction to *Sāhityadarpaṇa*.

CHAPTER II

PRINCIPLES OF LITERARY TASTE AND CRITICISM

INTRODUCTORY

From the preceding sketch of the history of the old school of writers on Alaṃkāra and the works on Alaṃkāra it may appear that though our history of *alaṃkāra* begins with Bhāmaha or Bharata, the science of *alaṃkāra* must have begun in association with the grammatical ways of thinking, probably from the 2nd or the 3rd century B.C. I have pointed out elsewhere that *upamā* as a decorated form has been very well investigated by Yāska and Pāṇini. It seems natural therefore to think that the early efforts on the subject must have generally concentrated themselves on the discovery of these decorative forms of speech which go by the name of *alaṃkāra.* A close study of the Rudradaman inscription of Junāgaḍh in the 2nd century A.D. shows clearly that certain dignified ways of literary delivery were accepted as binding in high literary circles. It may naturally be regarded quite a feasible process of turning to the other topics of *alaṃkāra-śāstra* from an acute observation of the conditions under which a figure of speech becomes really an *alaṃkāra.* It was found that a literary composition must first of all be free from grammatical errors and must internally be logically coherent. Kauṭilya's *Arthaśāstra* gives us fairly elaborate canons for regulating the composition of different types of royal edicts. It also became evident to these early inquirers that different forms of compositions became effective in diverse ways and that these ways of composition were of a structural character which belonged to the composition as a whole and could not be located in any particular part of the composition. These were called the *rīti* or mode. No *Alaṃkāra* writer has obstruct the comprehension of sense, impossible descriptions, vulgar words and vulgar significance or the use of harsh words. When these are compared with the defects pointed out by Mammaṭa we find that with closer inspection many new defects have come out. Thus, according to Mammaṭa there are sixteen kinds of defects of words, e.g., use of harsh words, incorrect words, those not incorrect yet not current in usage, to use words in a wrong meaning, to use a word in an obscure sense ignoring the more patent meaning, to use words which are antagonistic to the emotions that are to be roused, to use words merely for the sake of keeping the metre, to use words in a meaning which it does not possess, obscenity, to use words in a doubtful meaning, to use words in such technical meanings in which they are used only in special works, to use vulgar words, to have recourse to ungraceful meanings, to create obscurities, to lay emphasis on the wrong place, to use words in such a manner that undesirable and unwholesome suggestions may be apparent, and so forth. To these Mammaṭa adds the defects not of words but of sentences : to use words contrary to the intended emotions, to make euphonic combinations in wrong places, to use more or less words than is necessary, to make an idea drop after rising to a height, after having finished an idea to take it up again, the absence of link between connected sentences not to give proper importance to an idea, to compose sentences in such a manner that one may be dependent on the other for its comprehension, to make compositions in such a manner that the meaning is not available without making insertions, wrong use of words, breaking of the expected order, to introduce all on a sudden an unexpected and contrary emotion. In addition to these, Mammaṭa has spoken of many defects of sense, such as, to describe such things which are not indispensable for the main purport of the speech ; to use words in such a manner that there may be difficulty in comprehending the sense ; to contradict oneself ; to use words in a wrong order ; to use sentences in a manner such that though their meaning is comprehended the purport remains obscure ; to speak unconventionally ; to fail to speak in a new manner.

If we consider the above-mentioned defects enumerated by Bhāmaha and Mammaṭa, we find that in a higher sense they may all be regarded as defects of style. In the modern European concept style signifies the manner in which a particular personality gives expression to himself. Whenever the question of personality comes there comes the question of the way of his enjoyment and the motive that is urged by such an enjoyment. Now, many of the defects enumerated are really defects of expression, *i.e.*, defects that delay the expression, obscure its clarity, or effects, the height of its vigour or bring in associations that operate to throw it out of gear. Mammaṭa regarded *śabda* and *artha* as being the body of literature. The body should not be such that it might give a false expression to the soul within. It is the soul within that out of the whole nature selects a particular part and enjoys it and returns to the world its enjoyment through the vehicle of thought and language so that similar enjoyments may be produced in others.

But in the earlier writings of Indian authors of Alaṃkāra the style was limited to the mere externals of *śabda* and *artha* though at times the true significance of *rasa*, of emotional enjoyment peeped in and through them. Mammaṭa had the advantage of the deep wisdom of Ānandavardhana and Abhinava and as such he had counted as defect whatever delayed the communication of the emotion or obscured it or arrested its heightening or laid it in the wrong channel, or to its partial apprehension. From Bhāmaha to Vāmana no one had given the right emphasis on aesthetic emotion and for that reason they could not see eye to eye to Mammaṭa's view that detraction from aesthetic enjoyment was what constituted defects. But Bhāmaha had so cleverly put the whole thing that it cannot be gainsaid that he regarded the sweetness of emotion as being the fundamental essential of literature. Against Mammaṭa it may be said that we notice some sort of hesitancy in such admission. Though in describing *doṣa* he defines them as those that hinder the expression of *rasa*, yet in defining kāvya he says—Kāvya is that which should not be marred by defects should have excellences, but may or may not have *alaṃkāras*. Now, such a definition would not necessarily mean that it is indispensable for poetry to be charged with emotion. Among later writers also Jagannātha did not admit this indispensable character of *rasa*. All the defects that have hitherto been pointed out lead to an obscurity of comprehension, undesirable suggestion or wheeling of the mind out of its track by impossible description which lead to the misapprehension of aesthetic enjoyment. Bhāmaha always insisted on the fact that the style of poetry should be easy of comprehension for if this is not so then even if the poems are charged with emotions they would fail to affect us. He had in many places contrasted literature and other sciences as honey and bitter pills. He had also told us that unless something is said in a striking manner it was no poetry. He was thus in a way hinting that aesthetic emotion and its unobstructed communication constituted the art of poetry. Daṇḍin has not said anything very definite about the relation between the defects and the excellences, yet he has admitted the relativity of some of the defects. He has also said that whatever is not available in the Vaidarbhī style should be regarded as defects. It would not be wrong to think that he had regarded the defects to be those which were opposed to the excellences. In the classification of *doṣas* there is hardly any agreement between the various writers on *alaṃkāra*. But it would be unfruitful for us to enter into that discussion. But from Bhāmaha to Mammaṭa most of the authors have signified the relative chapter of some of the *doṣas*. Thus, the use of harsh words may be a defect in amorous poetry but it should be an excellence in heroic poetry. Bhāmaha has said that it is by the manner of use that a defect may be an excellence or an excellence may be a defect.[1]

1 *sanniveśa-viśeṣāttu duruktam api śobhate*
nilaṁ palāśam ābaddham antarāle srajam iva
kiñcid āśraya-saundaryād dhatte śobhāmasādhvapi
kāntā-vilocana-nyastam malīmasam ivāñjanam.

Bhoja also counted a number of *doṣas* but there is no originality in it. Bhāmaha is unwilling to accept the rigidity of the classification of style as *Gauḍī, Vaidarbhī, Pāñcālī,* etc. and he dismisses also the list of ten *guṇas* accepted by Bharata. In their place he accepts only three, viz., sweetness, strength and simplicity. The excellences (*guṇas*) are integral to the structure of the style, whereas the figures of speech are comparatively external. This is the view that Udbhata has expressed in his commentary on Bhāmaha.[1]

Vāmana has described excellences as those that beautify speech and he defined *Alaṃkāra* as heightening the nature of speech. Mammaṭa has severely criticised this view of Vāmana. Vāmana has counted ten excellences depending on words and ten on its significance. He used the same terms in double senses to denote the excellence of words and the excellence of meaning. Thus, the word *ojas* means the thickness of word-structure but it also means gravity of meaning. *Prasāda* means on the one hand the loose structure of a sentence and on the other hand it means simplicity of meaning. *Śleṣa* means on the one hand smoothness of expression while on the other hand it also means the existence of various meanings of one word, and so on. Bharata, Daṇḍin and Bhāmaha practically followed the same principle in counting the excellences, but there is a difference of meaning in the terms used by them. Thus, what Daṇḍin called *'śleṣa'* is called *'ojas'* by Bhāmaha, and Vāmana's *'pṛthak-padatva'* and *'agrāmyakatā'* are equivalent to Daṇḍin's *mādhuryya*! There is no agreement between Vāmana's *'samādhi'* and Daṇḍin's *'samādhi;'* while *'ojas'*

[1] *yathā tadvad-asādhīyaḥ sudhiyaśca prayojayet*
tad grāhyaṁ surabhikusumaṁ grāmyametan nidheyam
dhatte sobhaṁ viracitamidam sthānamasyaitad asya
mālākāro racayati yathā sādhu vijñāya mālāṁ
yogyam kāvyeṣu avahita-dhiyā tadvad evābhidhānam.
—Bhāmaha *1. 54-55, 58-59.*

samavāyavṛttyā śauryyādayaḥ saṁyogavṛttyā tu hārādaya ityasmāt guṇālaṁkārāṇāṁ bhedaḥ, ojaḥprobhṛtīnāmanuprāsopamādināṁ cobhayeṣām api samavāyavṛttyā sthitiriti gaḍḍalikāpravāheṇaivaiṣāṁ bhedaḥ.

has been used by Bharata to mean 'solid structure' of long compounds with which Daṇḍin and Bhoja agree, while Hemcandra does not. According to Hemcandra *'ojas'* means 'to attribute greatness to the meaning.' The same may be said of Bhoja. His definitions sometimes agree with Vāmana and sometimes do not. We thus see that the technical names used to denote the various excellences by the different writers do not agree. Bhoja and others have mentioned new excellences which are absent in the treatment from Bharata to Vāmana. It also appears that not all our senses can be present in every case of literary structure. The existence of some may easily bar out others. Mammaṭa has emphasised the view that the excellences belong to the aesthetic emotion. For that reason the defects of aesthetic emotion will involve a difference of aesthetic qualities. Generally, the classification of the *guṇas* are of an arbitrary character. Thus Mammaṭa criticising Vāmana says that what Vāmana calls different *guṇas* are sometimes such that some of them are modifications of one *guṇa*. What Vāmana calls *śleṣa, samādhi, udāratā* and *prasāda* are included within *'ojas.'* It has been suggested that the *guṇas* are those excellences which influence the mind in a particularly favourable manner and makes its speech original. In many cases the so-called *guṇas* are but the absence of defects. Again, what has been counted as *guṇas* by some have been regarded by others as being only poetical skill.

Many of our modern writers have considered it advantageous to speak of the divergence of views of the different Alaṃkāra authors as being capable of being classified in the Western fashion, such as, the *Rīti* school, the *alaṃkāra* school or the *Dhvani* school. I am forced to submit a dissenting note, to this way of classification. From Bharata to Ānandavardhana everyone of the writers of Alaṃkāra understood the importance of *doṣa, guṇa, rīti, rasa,* and *alaṃkāra* as constituting the grounds of appraisal of the value of any kāvya. But of these writers if Vāmana regarded *rīti* or style to constitute the chief essence it cannot be regarded that he thereby formed a school by himself. We do not know of any other author who like Vāmana says, *ritirātmā kāvyasya*! Daṇḍin as well as most other writers have given much space to *rīti, doṣa, guṇa,* and *alaṃkāra.* The doctrine of *guṇas* was also an old doctrine and we find *mādhuryya, kānti,* and *udāratā* referred to there. Bharata enumerates 10 *guṇas* and they are more or less the same as those enumerated by Daṇḍin and Vāmana. But as *rasa* is more important for *Nāṭya-śāstra* Bhàrata laid greater stress on *rasa* than on *doṣa* or *guṇa,* whereas Daṇḍin gives greater preference to *doṣa, guṇa* and *alaṃkāra,* as almost the whole of his work is dedicated to *doṣa, guṇa* and *alaṃkāras.* Daṇḍin, however, expands the concept of *alaṃkāras* and includes the *guṇas* within them. We have already stated that the attention of the early writers was drawn primarily ro the literary embellishments found in figures of speech. But as thought advanced it was found that the literary embellishment would not really be embelishment unless certain other conditions be fulfilled, as for example, as Bhāmaha stated, that there must be a strikingness or archness (*vakrokti*) or originality and due exaggeration (*atiśayokti*) without which the *alaṃkāras* would not be *alaṃkāras* and Daṇḍin pointed out that the literary excellences or the *guṇas* also constitute *alaṃkāras* which form the essence of the *Kāvyamārga.* The word *mārga* means the way and this is very nearly the same as the *rīti* of Vāmana. The *guṇas* there refer to the way of speech or the style. The previous writer did not fully realise the value of the excellences or the *guṇas* as constituting the essence of good style. Daṇḍin however defines Kāvya as *iṣṭārtha-vyavacchinna-padāvalī.* The *padāvalī* should be *iṣṭārthavyavacchinna,* i.e., agreeable, plesent. Naturally the question would arise how should the words be arranged that they may produce the *iṣṭārtha.* The way of making the suitable arrangement of sound or sense should be such that they may be pleasureable. Even Kuntaka in later times laid emphasis on the particular *bandha* or arrangement of *śabda* and *artha* as constituting a good Kāvya and he said that such an arrangement can only be successful when it is manipulated by genius that knows how to make it striking. Daṇḍin had not definitely introduced the idea of the proper arrangement of sense or *artha* as Kuntaka did, he only spoke of *padāvalī* and did not introduce the concept of *artha* which, however, must have been latent in his mind. Kuntaka made it patent. What Kuntaka calls *bandha* is *vyavaccheda* or *mārga* in Daṇḍin. Bharata himself also spoke of the *kāvya-guṇas* but he does not speak of *rīti*. Daṇḍin as a matter of fact spread out his *guṇas* as indicating only two varieties of style, the *Vaidarbhī* and the *Gauḍī*. These names, however, are not Daṇḍin's own as we find them also in Bhāmaha. I have already pointed out that even at the time of Patañjali, different cultural centres in India had demonstrated their inclinations towards different styles of composition. Bāṇa in his *Harṣacarita* in a much later time confirms the view. Bhāmaha mentioned the *guṇas* independently of the style. But Daṇḍin included them within the style. Bharata also regarded the *guṇas* as belonging to the kāvya as a whole and not to the style, while the later writers like Mammaṭa and others regarded the *guṇas* as belonging to *rasa*. According to Daṇḍin it is the *Vaidarbhamārga* that carries within it the correct integration of the ten *guṇas* which may be regarded as the very life of the *Vaidarbhamārga* and are absent in the *Gauḍī*. The ten guṇas enumerated by Daṇḍin are neither logically distinct nor exhaustive.[1] Of the *guṇas* enumerated by Daṇḍin the *samādhi* is really *upamālaṃkāra* whereas the other *guṇas* refer to the sonorous effects of sound, compactness of words and clearness of meaning. Daṇḍin says that *alaṃkāras* are those qualities that produce the embellishment of kāvya (*kāvyaśobhākarān dharmān alaṃkārān pracakṣate*). In such a wide scope *guṇas*

1 The ten *guṇas* of Daṇḍin are:—*ṣleṣa* (compactness), *prasāda* (clearness), *samatā* (proper grouping of the word-sounds), *mādhuryya* (alliterative sweetness and absence of vulgarity), *sukumārata* (soft sounds), *arthavykti* (explicitness of sense, which is almost the same as *prasāda*), *udāratva* (expression of high spirit), *ojas* (force proceeding from the use of compounds), *kānti* (agreeableness, due to consonance of usage, convention and the like), *samādhi* (transference of characters, qualities and actions).

are also included within the concept of *alaṃkāra* and in chapter II, 3 he speaks of the *guṇas* constituting the *Vaidarbhī* style as *alaṃkāras* and distinguishes these from other *alaṃkāras* which may exist both in the *Gauḍī* and the *Vaidarbhī* style and these may be regarded as the general *alaṃkāras*.[1]

We thus find that Daṇḍin conceives of as kāvya that composition of words that produces pleasure. Here, of course, the idea of *rasa* is very dominant. As a matter of fact it is the very defining concept of kāvya, its very soul. For, if a particular composition did not produce pleasure it could not be kāvya at all. Bhāmaha also distinguishes kāvya from *śāstra* as honey and bitter *guḍucī*. But the production of pleasure being the common quality of all kāvya, a further criterion of superiority is added as depending on the presence or absence of further embellishment. If Daṇḍin could logically think it would have occurred to him, why do these embellishments add to the charm of poetry if poetry be that which produces pleasure? Is that not an introduction of new standard? If this is a new standard what constitutes the character of this standard? Or do these qualities add to the charm of poetry because they heighten or make it easy to enjoy the pleasure better! This would have naturally brought him to the position of Mammaṭa. He however, did not follow this line of thinking and regarded the *śobhā* of *kāvya* as being something different from the *'iṣṭārtha'* or desirability. But then a new difficulty occurred—the *guṇas* produce *śobhā*, so do the *alaṃkāras*. Therefore *guṇas* also must be *alaṃkāras*.[2]

1 *kaścin mārga-vibhāgārtham uktāḥ prāg apy alaṁkriyāḥ* |
sādhāraṇam alaṁkāra-jātam adya pradarśyate ||

—*Kāvyādarśa*.

i.e., in treating the *vaidarbhī* style we have shown some of the *alaṁkāras* (which are nothing but the *guṇas*), and now we are describing those *alaṁkāras* which are present in both *Gauḍī*- and *Vaidarbhī*.

2 Thus, Taruṇa Vācaspati in commenting on *Kāvyaprakāśa* II 3 says: *pūrvaṁ śleṣādayo daśa guṇā ityuktam, kathaṁ te'laṁkārā ucyante iti cet śobhākaratvaṁ hi alaṁkāra-lakṣaṇam, tallakṣaṇa-yogāt te'pyalaṁkārāḥ.........guṇā alaṁkāra eva ityācāryāḥ...... tataḥ śleṣādayaḥ guṇātmakālaṁkārāḥ pūrvam mārga-prabheda-pradarśanāya uktāḥ, idānīṁ tu mārga-dvaya sādhāraṇā alamkārā ucyante.*

In the treatment of the figures of speech that are common to *Vaidarbhī* and *Gauḍī* Daṇḍin takes up the *śabdālaṃkāras*, particularly *yamaka* and 35 *arthālaṃkāras*.[1]

As regards *doṣa* Daṇḍin generally regards the opposites of the *guṇas* as *doṣa*, but as three of the *guṇas* have no opposites, Daṇḍin counts the *doṣas* as seven. Daṇḍin does not discuss the question as to whether *doṣas* are positive or negative. He only holds that the *Vaidarbhī rīti* is free from the *doṣas* and that they are only to be found in the *Gauḍī rīti*. But Vāmana positively declares the *doṣas* as being the negations of *guṇas*. According to Vāmana *śabda* and *artha* form the body of kāvya, and *rīti*, the structural arrangement of words (*viśiṣṭa-pada-racanā*) is its soul. But if only a particular structure or regiment of words be the soul of good poetry what is this particular element ? Vāmana's answer is this that it is that structure that contains *guṇas*. He holds further that in *Vaidarbhī* we have all the ten kinds of *guṇas*, in the *Gauḍī* we have only *ojas* and *kānti* and in the *Pāñcālī* only *mādhuryya* and *saukumāryya*. But he does not discuss the question as to why a particular *guṇa* should be so called and should a particular structure containing particular *guṇas* be given preference to other structures. The *guṇas* are regarded by Vāmana as qualities of *śabda* and *artha*, but the commentator notes that the *guṇas* really belong to the *rīti*. Their existence is proved according to Vāmana by the testimony of men of taste. Vāmana's enumeration of *guṅas* or rather the names that he ascribed to the various *guṇas* is different from that of Daṇḍin. But in essence they may be regarded as a consequence of an expansion and systematization of Daṇḍin's ideas. It cannot also be said that the classifications and the definitions are all logically valid and they have been severely criticised by Mammaṭa. It may also be pointed out that some of the *guṇas* of Vāmana as well as Daṇḍin are really *alaṃkāras*. Following

1 Both Bhāmaha and Daṇḍin devote much time to *citrabandhas* called *prahelikā* Bāṇa and Māgha and Bhāravi as well had much preference for these. But Ānandavardhana entirely discredited them.

Bhāmaha the later writers of *alaṃkāra* have regarded *vakrokti* or *ukti-vaicitrya* the principal criterion for the admission of figures of speech.

It is because that none of these writers could discover the underlying principle of *guṇa* and *doṣa* that they tried to pick up in a haphazard manner some of the appealing qualities of a delightful poetic conversation. The difference in classification, enumeration and nomenclature among the various writers was therefore natural. But on the whole it was really Bharata's classification that has been developed upto its furthest limits by Vāmana. Vāmana, however, does not stop with the *guṇas* but he thinks that a kāvya is acceptable because it is *alaṃkāra* (*kāvyaṃ grāhyam alaṃkārāt*) and defines *alaṃkāra* as beauty (*saundaryyam alaṃkāram*). We find here a double scheme. *Rīti* is called the soul of kāvya, but a *kāvya* is acceptable only if there is *alaṃkāra* or *saundaryya*. The compromise has been arrived at by holding that while the *guṇas* are the permanent qualities constituting kāvya, and are hence called the *guṇas*, the *alaṃkāras* form additional charms. But why the *guṇas* constituting the *rīti* should be regarded as essential for kāvya ? The answer that we get is that they are indispensable qualities without which no beauty or charm of poetry can be produced (*guṇāḥ nityā tairvinā kāvyanāmānupapattiḥ*). The *alaṃkāras* produce only additional charms. The *guṇas* are said to be related to the *rīti* in the *samavāya* relation or the relation of inherence, whereas the *alaṃkāras* exist in the relation of *saṃyoga*. Mammaṭa has, however, pointed out that this view is not correct, for a *guṇa* like the *ojas* and an *alaṃkāra* like *anuprāsa* or *upmā*, should be regarded as being in *samavāya* relation. The upshot of the whole thing is that *alaṃkāras* cannot produce kāvya without the *guṇas* but the *guṇas* may produce kāvyas with out there being any *almkāra*. Vāmana does not pay much attention to the *alaṃkāras*. He counts only *anuprāsa* and *yamaka* and *śabdālaṃkāra* and regards all *arthālaṃkāras* as involving *upamā* or different modes of *upamā*.

It is desirable, however, that though here and there among the ancients there may have been people who are inclined to give a special emphasis to *rīti*, yet it would be wrong to speak of the writers of Alaṃkāras in the past as belonging to the *Rīti* school or the Alaṃkāra school. No such classification is current in the Indian tradition of Alaṃkāra and I do not know of a number of writers of a particular time as upholding the *rīti* theory so that they might be referred to as belonging to the *Rīti* school as we may very well find in the field of Indian Philosophy. When we find that from the time of Śaṅkara there is an unbroken chain of authors who held the monistic doctrine and supported it against the attack of the opponents, we can speak of these authors as belonging to the school of Śaṅkara. But if a writer here and a writer there have any special fondness for *rīti* we cannot call them as belonging to a particular school, any more than we can speak of Hegel as belonging to the Aristotelian school or Kant to the Platonic. The fact was that these early writers were groping in the dark for discovering a rational principle about the essential *sine qua non* constitution and the nature of kāvya and, they faltered in their attempts and ran into contradictions. Thus in Vāmana we may ask : what is *rīti* apart from the *guṇas* ? A *rīti* is a *viśiṣṭa-pada-racanā*, but this *viśiṣṭatā* of arrangement or *racanā* includes the *guṇas*. Vāmana therefore regards the *guṇas* as essential in poetry. If that is so there would be no *rīti* without them and it is said that they are in the *samavāya* relation with the *rīti*. That which is in a *samavāya* relation with any thing must be regarded as being such an indispensable character of the thing that the thing can hardly be conceived without that quality. We can hardly speak of any *rīti* without speaking of the *guṇas*. The *rīti*, therefore, which is supposed to be the soul of kāvya, would be only imaginable as an abstract and theoretical entity for upholding the *guṇas*. The *Ekāvali* points out that if the *guṇas* are the principal elements, they themselves cannot be regarded as adorning poetry, for they themselves should be the objects of adornment.

Prof. Kane says : "Vāmana is the foremost representative of the *rīti* school." But where are the others ? Mr. Kane further says that "The Alaṃkāra school looked upon the *alaṃkāras*, which are really of secondary importance, as very important. The *rīti* school marks a very real advance over the Alaṃkāra school, and though it did not reach the real essence of poetry it approached very near it. Instead of looking upon mere *alaṃkāras* as the essence of poetry it looked upon the *guṇas* as the essence. The *rīti* school was not yet quite aware of that to which the *guṇas* belonged. It is therefore that the *Dhvanikārikā* says about the *Rīti* school, "*asphuṭa-sphūritam*, etc."[1] But this seems hardly correct. Bhāmaha regarded *vakrokti* as the soul of all *alaṃkāras* and regarded honey-like sweetness to be the characteristic of *kāvya*.

Going back to Bhāmaha, Udbhaṭa and Rudraṭa we may say that here also to call them as belonging to the Alaṃkāra school is not quite correct. For, though Bhāmaha collects many *alaṃkāras* from the previous writers and regards them as embellishment as everyone does, he never regards *alaṃkāras* as the soul of kāvyas. As a matter of fact the problem as to what constitutes the essence of literature was not solved till the advent of Dhvanikāra. When Vāmana said, *rītir ātmā kāvyasya*' he probably simply meant that kāvya necessarily implies a *bandha* or arrangement of *śabdārtha*. Though he uses the word *ātman* yet by that word he really means *deha* (body) of kāvya, which is really *śabdārtha*.[2] But Bhāmaha was shrewd enough to perceive that it is not merely the *bandha* that constitutes a kāvya but the expression must be out of the commonplace. It must be *vakra*. Probably the word *vakra* has been suggested by the amorous glances of women. The glance made in a straightforward manner is simple vision but an arch-glance signifies the whole

1 *asphuṭa-sphuritaṁ kāvyam tattvam etad yathoditam* |
aśaknuvadbhirvyākartum rītayaḥ sampravartitāḥ ||
Dhvanikārikā III. 52

ātmā dehe dhṛtau jīve svabhāve paramātmani

situation of mental complex and emotion that fills us with a thrill. Similarly, an expression carries with it the heart of the poet when it is used in a special and unique manner and without that uniqueness mere communication of information is not a kāvya. For this reason he had dismissed the claims of *hetu, leśa,* etc., to the status of *alaṃkāra.*

Bhāmaha no doubt accepts two kinds of *alaṃkāras, śabda* and *artha,* but so does everybody. In his treatment of the object of kāvya he counts a number of external reasons, along with *prīti* or delight, which have been followed by other writers of *alaṃkāras* also.[1] Bhāmaha thus puts in *mokṣa* also as the object of a kāvya to bring in it a line with *darśanas.* Bharata had described the function of dramatic art as being of the nature of play or pleasure and uses the terms *krīḍanaka* and *vinodakaraṇa* (*Nāṭya-śāstra* I. 11 and I. 86).[2]

Bhāmaha regards kāvya as being the togetherness of *śabda* and *artha* implying thereby that both were equally important. He further conditioned it and said that it should be free from defects (*nirdoṣa*). He does not pay that attention to *rīti* that Daṇḍin and Vāmana gave. His emphasis was on *vakrokti.* This *vakrokti* was also the same as *atiśayokti.* He says that unless any composition can transcend the limits of its meaning it can neither be striking nor be poetic. He further says that unless this transcending character is found no *alaṃkāra* can claim any excellence. He therefore defines *atiśayokti* as *nimittato vaco yat tu lokātikrānta-gocaram* and this is paraphrased by Daṇḍin as—*vivaksā vā viśokaṣya lokasīmātivartinī.* Abhinava also in defining *vakratā* says *śabdasya hi vakratā, abhidheyasya ca vakratā lokottīrṇenaiva rūpeṇa avasthānaṁ.* The *vakratā*

1 These external reasons are :—

dharmārthakāmamokṣeṣu vaicakṣaṇyaṁ kalāsu ca |
karoti kīrttiṁ prītiṁ ca sādhukāvyaniṣevaṇam ||

2 But Abhinava says that the real essence of kāvya is *prīti* or joy without any further end and it is this which distinguishes kāvya from the commandatory scriptures and the r commendatory stories. Abhinava is probaby the first to distinguish between three kinds of *upadeśas, guru-sammita, suhṛt-sammita, kāntā-sammita.*

thus means according to Abhinava the same as the *atiśayokti* of Bhāmaha, namely, that words and their meaning should transcend their ordinary local limits. It cannot be denied that in laying his emphasis on *vakrakti* and *atiśayoktā* Bhāmaha had implicitly caught the secret of the charm of literature, which has been so explicitly brought out in the works of Ānandavardhana and Abhinava. From this point of view he had attained a state of literary perspective which underwent no improvement in the hands of his successors, until we come to Ānandavardhana. Kuntaka also admits the *vakratā* of Bhāmaha though he would call it a *bhaṅgi* or *vicchitti*, which constituted the special charm and strikingness of poetry as distinguished from common speech. Naturally enough he included the function of *rasa* within *alaṃkāra*. In II, 85 Bhāmaha says that *rasa* as well as *alaṃkāra* are produced from *vakrokti*. This meaning has been accepted by Abhinavagupta and it really means, though implicitly, that *rasa* is the result of *vyañjanā* and the *vyañjanā* is in reality the *vakrokti*. Bhāmaha, of course, never dealt with the subject of *vyañjanā* as a special topic but it is clear from his definition that implicitly at least he had caught the real purport of *vyañjanā* and its real function in poetry.

Bhāmaha in the treatment of his *alaṃkāras*, *paryyāyokta*, *vyājastuti*, *aprastutapraśaṃsā* and *samāsokti*, shows that in them all there is always an implied sense which is explained by Udbhaṭa as *vācyavācaka-vyaktibhyām śūnyenāvagamātmanā*. Thus there is an '*avagamyamāna artha*' or an implied meaning in these *alaṃkāras*. But Ānandavardhana criticises that mere *avagamyamāna* or implication is not enough to produce *dhvani*. The implication must be superior to the ordinary meaning, which should play only a subordinate role and this alone can produce *dhvani*. Udbhaṭa has also shown in detail that even in the case of the expressed poetic figures like *rūpaka*, etc., there may be an underlying current of implication. This has been admitted by the writer of the *Locana*. This brings out the fact that it is not true that Bhāmaha and Udbhaṭa denied *dhvani*, but they did not simply count *dhvani* as an independent and separate function but as included in the elements of the general structure of good poetry. Thus, again, Pratīhārenduraja, the commentator of Udbhaṭa, says that the *dhvani* which has been regarded by some writers as the soul of literature has not been specially treated by Udbhaṭa as it has been already dealt with in an implied manner in the treatment of *alaṃkāra*. Jagannātha also remarks that though Udbhaṭa and others never mentioned *dhvani* in an explicit manner, yet the fact of the implication playing a very important, nay, an indispensable, part in poetry was well-known to them. Ruyyaka also confirms this view. In Vāgabhaṭa and Hemacandra also we find the same view operating that Bhāmaha and Udbhaṭa had all perceived the essence of *dhvani* and its function in kāvya but had not treated them separately as the Dhvanikāra did. Kuntaka, however, develops and expands Bhāmaha's definition of *vakrokti* and founds on it his own doctrine of literary excellence. Udbhaṭa also, though he does not treat of *rasa* separately, does indeed treat of *rasa* in association with *alaṃkāras* and treats also of *bhāva* and *anubhāva*, which may be traced in Bhāmaha also. In both Bhāmaha and Udbhaṭa also there was but little distinction between the *guṇas* and *alaṃkāras*.[1] But Vāmana, as we have seen, distinguishes between *guṇas* and *alaṃkāras*. Again, while Bhāmaha simply mentioned the *rītis* but does not lay any importance to the rigidity of classification, Udbhaṭa does not even mention the *rītis* but only mentions the three *vṛttis* which are associated with *anuprāsa*, which correspond roughly to the three *guṇas* of Vāmana,[2] and so does Ānandavardhana. But it cannot be said that Udbhaṭa's *guṇas* tally wholly with the *rītis* of Vāmana or the three *guṇas* of Ānandavardhana. But while the *guṇas* are regarded by Udbhaṭa (according to Abhinavagupta) as belonging merely to the *saṅgaṭhana* or arrangement, such as, *a-samāsa*, *dīrgha-samāsa* or *madhyama-samāsa*, it does not seem that

1 *udbahṭādibhistu guṇālaṁkārāṇām prāyaśaḥ sāmyam eva sūcitam.*
Alaṁkārasarvasva, p. 7.

2 *rīter hi guṇeṣeva paryyavasitiḥ.*

Vāmana is specifically clear as to whether the *guṇas* are something over and above *saṅgaṭhana*. It is interesting here also to note that Pratīhārendurāja regards *rasa* as the soul of poetry and attributes the same view to Udbhaṭa whose work was commented upon by him.

Rudraṭa, again, does not attach much importance to the *rītis* or the *gṇas* but he descends straight away to the classification of *alaṃkāras, śabdālaṃkāras,* and *arthālaṃkāras* and their enumeration and definition. He no doubt speaks of *rasa* also but he does not give it the prominence it deserves.

I have so long combated the theory of many of my predecessors that the inquiry into the nature and genius of poetry could be sub-divided into a number of schools. But I contended from the very beginning that the study of *alaṃkāra* first attracted and in fact originated the inquiry into the science of poetics. I have also observed that a number of poetic figures were discovered in the time of Pāṇini in the grammar school, and a further investigation into which for specialised treatment passed into the hands of a school of writers who were regarded as writers on poetics. This early predilection towards the poetic figures had gained such traditional strength that even when as a result of further enquiry the essence of literature was considered by some to belong to the style, the absence of *doṣas,* and the possession of *guṇas* or to *dhvani* and *rasa,* elaborate treatment of the *alaṃkāras* never ceased. Indeed in the later writers we find more and more classification and ingenious distinction and dialectical skill were displayed in the treatment of *alaṃkaras.* These different writers, however, did not agree in their classification of the *alaṃkāras* or the subtle distinctions maintained by one or the other writer. This was largely due to the change of perspective due to a more recondite acquaintance with the principles of literature. A comparative study of this in itself may prove to be an interesting field by itself. Some of the writers had a much wider scope attached to a particular figure of speech than others. But it is needless for us to enter into the discussion of such elaborate details.

VAKROKTI

Bhāmaha in his work says that as the night is without the moon, as beauty is without the humility, so is dexterity of speech without poetic talents. Even a fool can be a scientist or learned in the Scriptures with the instructions of the teacher, but without genius it is not possible to be a poet. The literary body of a poet shines even greater at the fall of the physical one. Genius alone is not sufficient for the production of poetry but one must acquire a thorough acquaintance and experience with the words and their subtle meanings and must study also the literature of other poets. A poet should be careful to see that not one word used by him be defective or transferable. Poetry like a woman receives an enhancement of her beauty by adornments. But before all adornments the language must be faultless.

Kāvya or poetry consists of a co-operative conjunction of words and their meanings. Above all, such a conjuction must be significant and striking. By the word 'striking' or *vakra* Bhāmaha means that kind of expression where "more is meant than meets the ear." He therefore dismisses *svabhāvokti* or natural description from the status of *alaṃkāra* as it is simply informative of a particular scene. Real adornments belong to that special trait of expression by which it implies more than it says. It is this striking implication of expression on which depends the adornment of all *alaṃkāras*. Therefore there cannot be any *alaṃkāra* where there is no *vakrokti*. He thus says that such expressions as 'the sun has set', 'the moon has risen', 'the birds are flying', cannot constitute literature.[1]

All the faults that Bhāmaha had described as faults or *doṣas* because they obscure the significance of turn of expression. It is the peculiarity and uniqueness of the significance of an expression that constitutes the literary character of a composition.

[1] *saiṣā sarvaiva vakroktir anayārtho vibhāvyate !*
yatano' syāṁ kavinā kāryaḥ ko'laṁkāro' nayā vinā !!

....

gato' stam arko bhātīndur yānti vāsāya pakṣiṇaḥ ।
ityevamādi kim kāvyaṁ vārttāmenāṁ pracakṣate. ।।

This *vakrokti* of Bhāmaha has been differently understood by different later writers. Daṇḍin, Vāmana and Rudraṭa understood *vakrokti* as a *śabdālaṃkāra* depending upon the pun existing in the two meanings of a word, making it possible for the hearer to draw a different meaning from the expression that what was intended by the speaker.[1]

When Bhāmaha said that *vakrokti* is the same as the *atiśayokti* he probably meant that *vakrokti* leads to the implication of an extra sense of *atiśaya*. Ānandavardhana understood it rightly and agreed with Bhāmaha.[2] Abhinavagupta, however, does not agree with it. Daṇḍin takes *atiśayokti* in the sense of exaggeration and says that in all *alaṃkāras* we have an element of exaggeration. *Vakrokti*, therefore, which is the same as *atiśayokti*, is a name of *alaṃkāra* in general. *Alaṃkāra* is, therefore, twofold, *svabhāvokti* and *vakrokti*. Other *alaṃkāras* are subdivisions of *vakrokti*. Vāmana counts *vakrokti* as a separate *alaṃkāra*. Kuntaka, probably a contemporary of Abhinava, was the first to attach a special importance to *vakroti*. He says that though there are hundreds of works on the science of *alaṃkāra* there is no one among them which lays special importance to the transcendent delight and inexpressible joy that poetry produces. Compared with this joy all other pleasures are trifling. Though literature consists in the co-operative conjunction of words, yet until such a conjunction can produce a superfluity of transcendent joy, it cannot be called literature. The same idea may be expressed in two such different ways that one may have an appeal of beauty to us far excelling that of the other.[3]

1. *aho kenedṛśī buddhir dāruṇā tava nirmita* ।
triguṇā śrūyate buddhir na tu dārumayī kvacit ॥

Here there is a pun on the word *dāruṇā*, as cruel or made of wood.

2 *tatrātiśayoktirevam alaṁkāram adhitiṣṭhati kavi-pratibhā-vaśāt tasya cārutvātiśaya-yogo'nyasya tvalaṁkāramātrataiva iti sarvvālaṁkārānusāriṇā svīkaraṇa-yogyatvenābhedo. pacārāt saiva sarvvālaṁkāra-rūpā ityayamevārtho'vagantavyaḥ*—Ānandavardhana.

3 *māninī-jana-vilocana-pātān*
uṣṇa-vāṣpa-kaluṣān-abhigrhṇan.
manda-manda-muditaḥ prayayau khaṁ
bhī abhīta iva śīta-mayūkhaḥ ॥

Words commingle with words and sense with sense, and as if by mutual rivalry they are mutually rising into a climax, an ascension point where they again commingle together.[1] Here Kuntaka suggests that the function of art is in the production of a whole in which the sound and the sense co-operate together in purity and propriety to rise gradually in an ascending scale till they rise to a completion. Words and sense are two different elements and the harmony must be attained both in their individual sphere and their mutual sphere of co-operation. There should be nothing in the arrangement of words that would produce a shock to the progressive march of thought and *vice versa*. They should march towards a common end. The word *sāhitya* (literature) etymologically means unity of thought and language. Intuition and expression are here for the sake of analysis split up as two and the growth of intuition and expression must be of such an organic order that they may produce a whole without a hole.

The words should be so chosen that they may express exactly what the poet intends to express.[2]

kramādeka-dvi-tri-prabhṛti-paripāṭīḥ prakaṭayan
kalāḥ svairam svairaṁ nava-kamala-kandāṅkura-rucah ।
purandhrīṇāṁ preyo-viraha-dahanoddīpita-dṛśāṁ
kaṭākṣebhyo bibhyan nibhṛta iva candro'bhyudayate ॥

Of these two verses the idea is the same, but the second is far more beautiful than the first. This is due to the mode of expression. Words meet with words, sense with sense, until by their mutual combination they create a picture more beauteous than what the mere sense or the purport would have given.

1 *asāraṁ saṁsāram parimuṣitaratnaṁ tribhuvanaṁ*
nirālokaṁ lokaṁ maraṇaśaraṇaṁ bāndhavajanam ।
adarpaṁ kandarpaṁ jananayananirmāṇam aphalaṁ
jagajjīrṇāraṇyaṁ kathamasi vidhatuṁ vyavasitaḥ ॥

The verse is from *Mālatīmādhava* and idea after idea with the words co-operating with them rise into a greater and greater resonance of sound and sense until they attain a climax in the last line.

2 *kallola-vellita-dṛṣat-paruṣa-prahārai*
ratnānyamūni makarākara māvamaṁsthāḥ ।
kiṁ kaustubhena bhavato vihito na nāma
yācñā-prasārita-karaḥ purusottamo'pi ॥

In this verse of Bhallaṭa, p. 587, the ocean is asked not to treat harshly and disdain the jewels with its roaring billows, for even Lord Nārāyaṇa spreads out his hand to snatch the

What Kuntaka wants to say is that the things of the external world that take the forms of ideas and images in the mind of the poet are not exactly a mere copy or a mere symbol of these objects, but held within the emotion of the boiling soul of the poet, they assume new spiritual forms with new spiritual values. Thus, the external objects, to which the poet is supposed to refer, become spiritually metamorphosed, and they are as such largely different from the the objects themselves, and they in their turn react on the poet's mind in an ineffable manner such that, inspired by them, the poet, through an inward spiritual activity, of which he is not even explicitly aware, chooses words and phrases, meanings and ideas of such propriety that may assemble together for the creation of an undivided piece of art. The upshot of this is that the process by which external physical objects and our ideas relating to them become transformed into poetic intuition vibrating with emotion, is a transcendental affair. It is transcendental in the sense that in our ordinary affairs our thoughts are moved in the tune of self-interest, the fulfilment of a need or the removal of a sorrow. It has always an external end to fulfil. But in the case of poetic intuition, no such interest of fulfilment of needs plays any part. It is therefore unlike all our ordinary activities, cognitive or conative. It is therefore called transcendent (*alaukika-vyāpāra*). It is in consequence of the movement of the same process that suitable words, phrases, ideas and metres are churned out, as it were, unconsciously or subconsciosly from the ocean of our internal experience and set in order for the creation of an artistic whole. The poet's ordinary personality is treated as an instrument, as it were, by his poetic personality.

Kaustubha jewel from it. Now, the high value of the *Kaustubha* does not demonstrate the importance of other jewels which this illustration was intended to demonstrate. Therefore, the word *Kaustubha* is wrongly chosen and does not convey the sense which the poet wished to convey. If in the place of the third line we substitute '*ekena kim na vihito bhavatah* '*sa nāma*,' the idea would have been consistently expressed.

Poetry consists in the translation of a spiritual form in the form of words and meanings. Poetry consists of unique combination of a unique class of words and their meaning. It is that peculiar combination which shows itself as the aesthetic quality in a work of art that was designated as *vakratā* by Kuntaka. A natural description can only become poetic when somehow or other the poetic personality, intuition or perspective is infused into it. Kuntaka has dismissed the *svabhāvokti* of Daṇḍin in same manner as some Western art critics have dismissed portrait painting from the dignity of art. But both in *svabhāvokti* and portrait painting, if they are works of art, there may be infusion of personality, apprehension of perspective, choice, emphasis and attribution of grace, which will naturally make them supersede their originals in nature. If a particular piece of composition did not contain any exuberent excess, an overflowing of significance, sonorousness and joy far beyond that which is carried by the words in their simple meanings, the composition would be a dry piece of information but not poetry. It may be history and philosophy but no literature. As life is to the body, which being in the body exceeds it in an unspeakable manner and gives meaning to all its dreams, so does the poetic and aesthetic quality charge a piece of composition with an excellence and emotion, a life and a thrill, that is far beyond the words and their meanings. This is what we call the aesthetic quality, which arises out of that unique character of the constitution of proper words and their meanings which can transform them into literature. It is this quality which may be regarded as the spontaneous ebullition of life and this is what Kuntaka understands by *vakratā*.

Kuntaka in criticising Vāmana and Daṇḍin says that it is wrong to associate poetic styles with particular countries or to say that there are three kinds of style. Styles may be of infinite variety in accordance with the personality of the poet and it is impossible to enumerate them. It does not matter what name you might give to a particular style. It is not only unimportant but useless. What is important is whether it is beautiful or not. There are poets who are habituated to write in a soft and tender fashion, while there are others who write in a more forceful manner, and a poet may be great and distinguished in whatever form of style he may choose to write. As it is impossible to discover the mystery of the creation of the Lord so it is impossible to delve into the mystery of any particular kind of style.

He distinguishes between a subjective aesthetic quality and an objective aesthetic quality. A subjective aesthetic quality is an internal character belonging to the intuition itself. The objective quality is that which belongs to the expression. He calls the former *saubhāgya* and the latter *tāruṇya*. According to the difference in style of expression and the mode of intuition the nature and character of aesthetic qualities must also vary. The manner of style followed by poets like Kālidāsa and others has been designated by Kuntaka as *sukumāra*, *i.e.* delicate and tender.

Speaking of the *vicitra-rīti* or ornamented style, Kuntaka says that it is very difficult to write in this style, and unless the words and the sense flow in their own dynamic competing with each other for the production of a piece of art, without any effort on the part of the poet, it will be impossible to be successful to write in this style.[1] The writers of this style can make both the apparent and the implied meaning beautiful.[2] It is unnecessary for me to go into any further details and elaborate illustrations, indulged in by Kuntaka in his work. Kuntaka did not deny *rasa* as emotion but he regarded that only as a mode of *vakratā* which produces both *rasa* and beauty.[3]

1 *Yat kavi-prayatna-nirapekṣayaiva śabdārthaḥ svābhāvikaḥ ko'pi vakratāprakāraḥ parisphuran paridṛśyate.*

2 *he helā-jita-bodhi-sattva vacasāṁ kiṁ vistaraistoyadhe*
nāsti tvat-sadṛśaḥ paraḥ parahitādhāne gṛhīta-vrataḥ ।
tṛśyat-pāntha-janopakāra-ghaṭanā-vaimukhya-labdhāyaśo-
bhāra-prodvahane karoṣi kṛpayā sāhāyakaṁ yan-maroḥ ॥

3 *nirantara-rasodgāra-garbha-saundarya-nirbharāḥ* ।
giraḥ kavīnāṁ jīvanti na kathāmātram āśritāḥ ॥

Writers like Bhāmaha and Daṇḍin had said that when the *rasa* is subordinate to the ordinary meaning it is a *rasavat alaṃkāra*. But Kuntaka does not admit it. He says that whenever there is *rasa* that alone is predominant. Kuntaka had also admitted *dhvani* under another name but included that also within *vakratā*. Though later writers did not accord a high place to Kuntaka yet it appears clear that an all-round estimate of literature with emotion and beauty as its root, as conceived by Kuntaka, seems to beat even the authors of the *dhvani* school, who were more or less obsessed by the *dhvani* and the *rasa* perspectives.

The Theory of Rasa

We must start the theory of *rasa* or aesthetic emotion with Bharata's maxim, *vibhāvānubhāva-vyabhicāri-saṁyogād rasaniṣpattiḥ*. The meaning of this line has been a subject of much discussion to which we shall attend later. But after this, the later writers are not particularly eloquent about *rasa* until we come to Ānandavardhana. Bhāmaha was also acquainted with *rasa* as he speaks of *kāvya-rasa* with which as a first starting people are to be tempted to study the Scriptures.[1] Daṇḍin also had not only spoken of *rasavad-alaṃkāra* but had also spoken of the *mādhuryya rīti* as being *rasamayī*. But the word *rasa* has a general and a technical meaning. In the general sense *rasa* means taste, *rasamayī* means tasty, while in the technical sense it means the well-known dominant emotions, such as, the amorous, the ludicrous, the pathetic, the passionate, the heroic, the wonder-producing, the fearful and the repugnant (*śṛṅgārahāsya-karuṇa-raudra-vīra-bhayānaka-bībhatsādbhutaā iti*).[2]

In our current literary discussions there is much confusion between these two senses of *rasa*. In one sense it means merely

1 *svādu-kāvya-rasonmiśraṁ śāstram apyupayujyate |*
prathamālīḍha-madhurāḥ pibanti kaṭu-bheṣajam ||
—*Bhāmaha.*

2 *raso gandhe rasaḥ svāde tiktādau viṣa-rogayoḥ |*
śṛṅgārādau drave vīryye deha-dhātvambupārade ||

pleasant, in other sense it means that a particular dominant emotion constituting our personality has been affected and roused. A mere sonorousness of alliterative sound has been spoken of by Daṇḍin and Vāgbhaṭa, but it means nothing more than the pleasant jingles. But in the description of *mahākāvya* or epic, Daṇḍin says, that these should be inspired with *rasa* or *bhāva*. Abhinavagupta in his commentary on Bharata's maxim of *rasa* had said that Daṇḍin's view of *rasa* is very much like that of Bhaṭṭa Lollaṭa. But if that were so it cannot be denied that Daṇḍin had a fair acquaintance with the view that it is the dominant emotions that come to be expressed as *rasa*. But we find no further treatment of *rasa* in Daṇḍin. Vāmana has admitted *rasa* as an important quality of literature and calls it *kānti*. Udbhaṭa has also admitted *rasa* in the case of the *rasavad-alaṃkāra*. He says that a piece of kāvya can only be called living when it is inspired with *rasa*. Rudraṭa also accepted the view that there is an intimate relation between kāvya and *rasa*, but he could say nothing further about this intimate relation.

Before proceeding further it is necessary to explain a few of the technical terms that are continually associated with any discussion of *rasa* :—(1) *Vibhāva*, the objective condition of producing an emotion. *Vibhāva* may be of two kinds, (*i*) *ālambana* and *uddīpana*. *Ālambana-vibhāva* means a person or persons with reference to whom the emotion is manifested. *Uddīpana-vibhāva* means the circumstances that have excited the emotion. Thus a man may feel attracted to a woman if the circumstances are co-operating with it. Thus it is easier for a man to be attracted towards a woman of young age if they are thrown alone and there is a beautiful scenery before them, the moon peeping through the clouds, the fragrant breeze blowing, and the like. Any one of such circumstances may be regarded as *uddīpana-vibhāva*, whereas both the man and the woman are *ālambana-vibhāvas* to each other. (2) *Anubhāva* means bodily expression by which the emotion is expressed. Thus the arch glances of a lady, her inviting smile, may be regarded as *anubhāva*. (3) The *vyabhicārī* means a series of diverse emotions that feed the lamp of a dominant emotion. A woman in love anxiously waiting at the rendezvous to meet her lover may feel disappointed that he is not coming, may be anxious that something might have happened to him, may be jealous that he might have beed courted by another woman, may feel delight in remembering the coaxing words that he had whispered into her ears, and so on. Like pictures in a cinematograph emotions of diverse sorts may be passing in quick succession and may all at the same time be continuing the constitution of the same emotion.

The real discussion of *rasa* was started by Abhinavagupta in his commentary on Bharata's maxim on *rasa*.[1] The real point of discussion and diversity of opinion was on the two words *saṃyoga* (conjunction) and *rasa-niṣpatti* (expression of *rasa* or completion of *rasa*). Before proceeding further it is necessary to say a few words about the foundation of *rasa*. It is based upon a particular view of psychology which holds that our personality is constituted, both towards its motivation and intellection, of a few primary emotions which lie deep in the subconscious or unconscious strata of our being. These primary emotions are the sex, the ludicrous, the pathetic, the heroic, the passionate, the nauseating, the wonderous. Other aesthetic psychologists have in later times added to it the peaceful or intellectual, the devotional and the filial. These emotions are running through all natures in a permanent manner and may in that sense be called dominant emotions (*sthāyibhāva*). These dominant states that determine the particular internal temperaments are regarded as the dominant characteristics of those emotional states. Emotional states, such as, the amorous, the heroic and the others, show in their expressions the appearance of atomic formations, *i.e.*, each emotion in its manifestation shows a composition of diverse sentiments constantly shooting out and changing like the kinetic atoms and gases, like the

1 *vibhāvānubhāvavyabhicārisamyogād rasaniṣpattiḥ*

flamelets that continually come and go and thereby produce the appearance of the permanent, undivided whole of a flame ; there are continually passing little flames of diverse sentiments that give expression to the permanent emotion of love or hate, heroism or anger. It should, however, be noted that no emotion is called *rasa* unless it is aesthetically excited. When a young man falls in love with a young woman and his whole frame is shaken, we cannot speak of him as being the subject of *śṛṅgāra-rasa,* or when his son is dead and he is crying in tears, we cannot speak of him that he is the *karuṇa-rasa. Rasa* is an emotion excited by artistic circumstances or situations.

Now, the question that puzzled the old Alaṃkāra writers, was this : How can our dominant emotions be roused by aesthetic or artistic means ? Some writers like Bhaṭṭa Lollaṭa held that while the *vibhāva, anubhāva* and *vyabhicārī* are either ingeniously described or set forth vividly by mimic, they co-operate together and in their conjunction *rasa* is produced. As through hallucination we may perceive a snake and be afraid of it even if there be no snake, so though there is no real Rāma, no real Sītā, the mimic actors may by their acting produce a situation of reality in our minds and induce the amorous sentiments of Rāma in our minds. The internal datum which guarantees the production of such an illusory perspective is the fact that we have the amorous emotion running through subconscious stratum of our personality as our very constituent. Bhaṭṭa Lollaṭa says that when the *vibhāva* ideation of the situation and the person together with the atomic emotions that are the feeders of the sentiment of love, are made to coalesce with or penetrate into the inner vein of the dominant amorous, it is only then that a new superimposition of an illusory amorous emotion can be produced. In further explanations of the view of Lollaṭa, it appears that the actor tries to imitate the sentiment of the hero whose part he plays, but that the audience by the conjunction of the amorous situation and the projection of the person has in him the dominant stream of a particular emotion transformed into the aesthetic sentiment called *rasa*. Thus Mammaṭa, in speaking of Bhaṭṭa Lollaṭa, says that the dominant emotion of, say, the amorous, is roused or produced by the *vibhāvas* consisting of the woman on the one hand and the exciting circumstances, such as, the garden, the moon-light and others, and then this is made intelligible by the external gestures of the actors, and then this being heightened by the free flow of the associated emotions, one intuits the *rasa* mainly in the hero of the plot and also in the player who has tried to live up to him.[1] According to this view, a dominant emotion of the aesthetic type is produced by *vibhāvas* and they are made intelligible by *anubhāvas* and enriched by the associated, changing feelings (*vyabhicāri-bhāvas*). Though this emotion primarily excited in the dramatic personage (*e.g.*, Rāma or Sītā), yet by imitation or the assumption of the role of Rāma or Sītā it appears in the actor or by transference into the aesthetic audience who witness the play, and the emotion thus roused in the audience is called *rasa*.

But the above quotation from Mammaṭa (see footnote) does not tally with the actual statement now available in the *Abhinava-bhāratī*, the commentary by Abhinava on Bharata's *Nāṭya-śāstra*. It appears there as if *anubhāva* meant those feelings which are similar to *sthāyibhāva* in their nature as feelings, but were constantly changing. These are, no doubt, internal states but they are not co-existent with the dominant emotion. Yet contact of these loose and changeable feelings with the dominant emotions is possible only because the dominant emotion resides in the back of the mind as an instinctive character of it. The idea seems to be that the dominant emotion resides in the mind as a *vāsanā*. The concept of *vāsanā* in Indian thought is rather dsfficult and to some extent obscure also.

1 *vibhāvair lalanodyānādibhir ālambanoddīpana-karaṇaiḥ ratyādiko bhāvo gaṇitaḥ anubhāvaiḥ nāyakasya bhujākṣepa-prabhṛtibhiḥ kāryyaiḥ pratītiyogyaḥ kṛtaḥ vyabhicāribhir nirvvedābibhiḥ sahakārivhir upacito mukhyayā rāmādāv anukāryya tadrūpatānusandhānāt narttake'pi pratiyamāno rasāh iti Bhaṭṭalollaṭa-prabhṛtayaḥ.*

It means in the first instance the motivation within us, that spring of desire that adapts us to find our enjoyments in this or that particular way. It is supposed that in the animal world the behaviour of the animal, its impulse to action and its adaptation to find enjoyment in a particular mode of behaviour, is guided by its own particular *vāsanā*. *Vāsanā* thus means a complex integration of emotion and impulse. Man is born with a large number of such emotion-impulse complexes or *vāsanās*. Some of these lie dormant in him and may become active by external stimulus. It is peculiar in man that on the basis of these emotion-impulse complexes similar other complexes may spring into being through mere description, delineation or imitation. It is here that the artistic faculty finds its place. This second type of emotional complex is not directly connected with the *kleśas* or the affliction which are concerned with the moral career of a human being in his struggle with his environment. It, therefore, belongs to a new order of reality. The discussion among the scholars was about the nature, origin and character of these second-grade complexes. Bhaṭṭa Lollaṭa was of opinion that in addition to the dominant emotion-impulse complexes or *vāsanās* there were the changing feelings in and through which each dominant emotion expressed itself. He further held that feelings were also of the nature of *vāsanās* and that reason when aroused they could commingle with the dominant emotion and so enrich it as to make it shine through them.

On the point that in a dramatic performance the player imitates the dramatic personages and thereby produces feelings similar to them, Abhinava shows sharp opposition. He says that imitation produces laughter. Imitation is also done in a case where the thing itself cannot be completely done. Again, a dramatic emotion is supported by the situation and the person (*ālambana-* and *uddīpana-vibhāva*). Both these are of the nature of facts and entities and therefore cannot be imitated. It is not also possible to imitate a mental feeling. There is either a feeling there or not. If I have in my mind a feeling which is similar to a feeling of another, it is no longer an imitation ; for if I have the feeling, it is a real one, and if I have not got it, it does not exist. A mere imitation of external gestures is not an imitation of the internal thing. I do not also know in what particular manner Rāma expressed his sorrow at his separation from Sītā. We may at least imitate the gestures of an ordinary man of whom we have seen grieving. Abhinava says that the player in a drama does not go to the stage with the idea that he was going to imitate Rāma's gestures. But the whole situation, his dress, the music, the surroundings, the utterance of the poet's words as coming from Rāma, make him forget for the time his local personality, and while playing the part of Rāma, he spontaneously assumes Rāma's personality and the real world of his particular time and place slips away (*ucita-gītā-todya-carvaṇā-vismṛta-sāṃsārika-bhāvatayā*).

The upshot, then, is that according to Abhinava no imitation can produce the illusion which holds its sway both among the actors and the audience. On the other hand a conscious imitation would spoil the very illusion which is the business of the dramatic art to stir up. In our ordinary life the events that stir us up are present with us, and immediately affect our interest, excite and change our motives to the success or failure of our wishes leading to pleasure and pain. The criterion of truth in this field is a correspondence of the objective field in time, place and character with the subjective field of consciousness or it may also be that since the action of our operation of the external world is that all truth is rational and logically consistent, truth may as well mean consistency of the objective finding with the subjective expectation in time, place and character throughout the entire field of their application. Or truth may also mean that it may somehow or other affect our feelings, our beliefs and our wills. Most discussions about truth whether it be realistic, idealistic or pragmatic, are generally restricted to the field of occurrence through which our little selves have to run for their final fulfilment. In this field we ourselves are connected with the external world directly and intimately, and as such the manner in which we are affected by our intercourse with the external world seriously hurts or promotes our position in the external world and also in our minds. But if such be our nature that a presentation in a particular literary form of certain events, real or unreal, produces in us such a charm that the whole of the present environment slips off, as it were, like an enfolding garment, from our consciousness and we feel ourselves to be real participants of an imaginary situation, appearing no longer as imaginary, we can no longer judge the status of this appearance by our criteria of our living world and call it true, false or doubtful. Our judgments of truth and falsehood are merely in and through, and in terms of, the experiences of the living world. All our perspectives of truth and falsehood are from different points or sections of the living world with reference to which and relative to which our judgments of truth and falsehood are made. But with reference to the imaginary representations and experiences that introduce us to the field of poetry or drama, we can no longer set our limits to the real objective world. No co-ordinates from it can be drawn to find our location in the aesthetic world and consequently we can make no judgment of truth or reality about it. In witnessing a play as a result of the joint co-operation of all the factors including the music, we seem to indentify ourselves with the dramatic personages and feel ourselves to be one with them.

Abhinava's teacher in his work *Kāvya-kautuka* says that a dramatic play is not a physical occurrence. In witnessing a play we forget the actual perceptual experience of the individuals on the stage playing their different parts or their individuality as associated with their local names and habitations. The man who is playing the part of Rāma does not appear to us in his actual individual character and it does not also appear to us that he cannot be the Rāma about whom Vālmīki wrote. He stands somewhere midway between the pure actuality and the pure idealiy. This together with all the scenic associations and those of music produces an experience which vibrates with exhilaration ; and as a result thereof the whole presentation of actuality becomes veiled, as it were, in so far as it is an actual occurrence of presentative character. The past impressions, memories, associations, and the like, which were lying deeply buried in the mind, became connected with the present experience and thereby the present experience became affiliated and perceived in a new manner resulting in a dimension of new experience, revealing new types of pleasures and pains, unlike the pleasures and pains associated with our egoistic instincts and the success or failures of their strivings. This is technically called *rasāsvādana-camatkārā carvaṇā* which literally means—the expriencing of a transcendant exhilaration from the enjoyment of the roused emotions inherent in our own personality. A play or a drama is the objective content of such an experience. A drama or a play is not a physical occurrence. It is a pure spiritual enlightenment, a spiritual expression throbbing and pulsating with a new type of music, joyous and pensive. As a result of this experience a unity is effected between the individual's own experience and the expression of the art. This experience is, therefore, nothing else but the enlightenment of a universal. Or it may also rather be said that it is a new creation involving the personality of the individual and the objective dramatic contents as constituents—a new appearance, a revelation different from all other experiences and all external objects. If this analysis be true, dramatic experience and art can no longer be regarded as imitative.

Bhaṭṭatauta thought that on the one hand all the equipments of the stage together with the music release from our mind the hold of the impression that such and such a person has taken a particular part, and it also makes us indifferent to the suggestion of an impossibility that the player before us cannot be Rāma. Being cut off of its connection on two sides, namely, the positive connection of the play with the present actor as a known individual with the actuality of all his bearings, and on the other hand the impossibility of connecting the actor with the realised Rāma's character having lost its force, the suggestive influence can very naturally surcharge the mind with new exhilarations and feelings which can, without any relation to anything else, modify the state of the mind. In this state the previous experiences existing in the mind of the audience as impressions work up indepentently in association with the suggestion of the dramatic performance. The affiliation, apperception, and integration of these roused impressions and expectations produce new joys and new intuitions. The aesthetic content of a drama is all that is illuminated in such a process.

Mammaṭa repudiates Bhaṭṭa Lollaṭa's view that *rasa* is related to the *vibhāvas* in the relation of the produced and the producer, as effect and cause. He says that if the *vibhāvas* are to be regarded as cause they must be regarded as the cause of agency or the efficient cause—*nimitta-kāraṇa.* But in the case of *nimitta-kāraṇa,* we know that an action may remain intact even when the efficient agent is destroyed. There cannot be any *rasa* unless there is also the *vibhāva* and the *anubhāva.* The *vibhāvas,* etc., cannot also be regarded as a communicative agent, for a communicative agent pre-supposes the existence of the thing to be communicated, but the *rasa* does not exist before. It can be lived through only when it is suggested by the *vibhāvas* and the *rasa* has no other existence than being lived through and enjoyed. For, it should be remembered that the dominant emotions existing in the subconscious strata of the person are not themselves *rasas.* They acquired that designation only when they are aesthetically presentable and enjoyable. Bhaṭṭa Lollaṭa cannot also explain the method as to how the *rasa* produced in the player can infect the audience.

It is not the place here to enter into all the niceties of discussion into which the various exponents of the *rasa* theory entered, such as, Bhaṭṭa Lollaṭa, Śrī Śaṃkuka, Bhaṭṭatauta, Bhaṭṭa Nāyaka and Abhinava himself.[1]

Śrī Śaṃkuka introduced the similitude of painting to explain the enlightenment of aesthetic emotion. He said that just as of a painted horse it can be said that it is not a horse and that it is a horse, so of an aesthetic experience we can say that it is both real and unreal. Bhaṭṭa Nāyaka said that *rasa* is neither produced nor suggested, nor created by anything. He held that a proper aesthetic creation has the peculiar function of generating in us a new spiritual creation and we have in us a special function by which we can enjoy it. These two functions are called by him *bhāvakatva* and *bhojakatva*. The enlightenment of *rasa* is not the subject of ordinary psychology but of aesthetic psychology. For the presentation of the spiritual situation throbbing with exhilaration we are bound to admit two different functions, *bhāvakatva* and *bhojokatva,* without which the aesthetic experience cannot be explained. Abhinava, however, has combated the view with all the force that he can command. Abhinava is unwilling to admit these two extraordinary functions. Abhinava holds that in the case of a truly poetic composition, after having grasped the full significance of the words and their meanings, there is a mental intuition as a result of which the actual, temporal and spatial character of the situation is withdrawn from the mental field and the emotion suggested therein loses its individual character and also becomes dissociated from such conditions as might have led us to any motivation. The emotion is apprehended and intuited in a purely universal character and in consequence thereof the ordinary pathological symptoms of emotion lose their significance and through all the different emotions bereft of their pathological characters we have one enjoyment of joy. It is for this reason that in the experience of a tragedy we find as much enjoyment as in that of a comedy, for the experience of a grief would have

[1] For a more elaborate treatment of the subject, see the author's *Kāvya-vicāra.*

been unpalatable if it was associated with its pathological consequences. These pathological consequences are always due to a sense of self-struggle, self-motivation, loss, and the like. But in the intuition of the *rasa* we live through the experience of a pure sentiment bereft of all its local characters.

In the subconscious and unconscious regions there are always lying dormant various types of emotio-motive complexes. When through artistic creation a purely universal emotional fear, amour, etc. are projected in the mind they become affiliated to those types of emotio-motive complexes and this mutual affiliation or appreception or implicit recognition of identity immediately transforms the presented artistic universal into artistic joy or *rasa*. It is for this reason that in the rousing of artistic joy there is a kinship and identity among all art-enjoyers.

Here we find that the universalization of poetic art is of two kinds. First of all, the aesthetic composition by nature of its special suggestive force presents before our minds an aesthetic situation and an emotion that is devoid of all its local character. Secondly, the expression of this artistic enlightenment has a universal character in its manifestation in different minds. In the next stage this presented whole becomes commingled with various types of subconscious and unconscious feelings or emotio-motive complexes which are lying dormant in the minds of various people. It is easy to see that so far as these latter are concerned they are naturally different in different persons in accordance with the nature and diversity of experience. It is for this reason that the same artistic whole, though it be presented in the same manner in different minds, their artistic apperception of it would be different in accordance with the difference of diverse emotio-motive complexes. But neither in the universal whole presented to the mind nor in the motive complexes do we find any trace of any local character or colouration that are associated with the ego or the self in its practical commerce with the real objective world around it. It is therefore called transcendental, *i.e.*, *alaukika*, and its other name is *camatkāra*. The word *camatkāra* is in reality used in three different senses. It is sometimes used to denote the special aesthetic attitude of the mind produced by the commingling of the universal artistic situation and the stirred up emotio-motive complexes. It also means the aesthetic pleasure arising out of it ; and thirdly, the bodily manifestation of such an enjoyment. In addition to this, it is also used to denote that special mental function by which the whole thing is enjoyed.

It will again be out of place for us to enter into the various problems of *rasa* over which we have the accounts of the most recondite discussion.[1]

The view of *rasa* expressed by Abhinava had been accepted in later times as the almost unchallengeable gospel truth and as the last analysis of the aesthetic phenomenon as propagated through literature. Kṣemendra, however, in his *Aucitya-vicāra-carccā* tried to find the secret of poetry in propriety. But as many other Alaṃkāra writers have pointed out, the secret of the production of propriety is again nothing but the production of *rasa*. As *rasa* is soul of poetry, many prominent later writers, like Viśvanātha and others, have regarded *doṣa*, *guṇa* and *alaṃkāra* as belonging to the *rasa*. The *guṇa* and the *doṣa* belong permanently to the structure of the composition, whereas the *alaṃkāras* are additional charms. Jagannātha is disposed to take a more mataphysical view of the situation and thinks that the essence of *rasa* consists in pure consciousness as conditioned by the aesthetic situation and content. Jagannātha also gives us various definitions of *rasa*, mostly of a metaphysical character from the standpoint of different systems of philosophy.

DHVANI

We have indicated before that words have a two-fold function, primary (*abhidhā*) and indicatory (*lakṣaṇā*). In most cases

1 See the author's *Kāvya-vicāra*.

wherever there is an indicatory sense there is also a reflected and suggested sense. It is generally for giving scope to the reflected or suggested purport that a word is used in an indicatory sense instead of its primary sense. Thus instead of saying "The holy man lives on the side of the Ganges," one may say "The holy man lives on the very stream of the Ganges". The latter proposition being physically impossible, has the same purport as the first proposition. But yet the phraseology was so chosen in the second proposition that this meaning could be arrived at only by indirect indication. The reason for this was that the latter expression naturally suggests that the holy man lives so near the Ganges that he draws all its advantages. This suggested sense which arises separately, as it were, when the first two functions had ceased to operate, is called *dhvani*. The idea of *dhvani* has been drawn from the theory of *sphoṭa* of the grammarians. Bhartṛhari in his *Vākyapadīya* as well as later grammatical writers have elaborately maintained this view. It involves many obscure philosophical discussions which are out of place in the present context. But the general upshot of the theory is that the words and propositions in particular contexts and with reference to particular speakers and audience under particular circumstances and situations, may induce *rasa* or suggest important truths or ideas or *alaṃkāras*. Dhvanikāra says that from early times people had regarded *dhvani* or implicative suggestion as essence of poetry. But there have been some who held that there is no necessity of admitting *dhvani* and that the purpose of *dhvani* could be served by the extension of the primary sense as in the case of *lakṣaṇā*. There are others again who hold that apart from words, their meanings and *alaṃkāras*, there is nothing else that raises the beauty of literature, or that whatever heightens the beauty of literature must have to be regarded either as *guṇa* or *alaṃkāra*, that words and their meanings form the core of kāvya and that none of them could be regarded as *dhvani*. It is for refuting the views of such people that Dhvanikāra undertook his work.[1] It is thus evident that long before Dhvanikāra there had been thinkers of the *alaṃkāra* school some of whom not only admitted *dhvani* as a separate function of words and propositions but have been extremely enthusiastic over it, while there have been others who denied the existence of *dhvani* as a separate function.[2]

Udbhaṭa had said that the *abhidhā* function of words is two-fold, primary and subordinate. Vāmana had addmitted *lakṣaṇā* and called it *vakrokti*. Thus opinions differ not only about the existence of *dhvani* but also about its nature and function. But in spite of this difference of opinion people have always marked that there was some secret in the compositions of great poets which makes them charming, and Abhinava remarks that those who by constant association with literature can make their mind like a mirror, are the persons who can be called *sahṛdaya* or men of taste. It is they who can feel at once that *dhvani* is the essence of poetry.[3] Ānandavardhana further says that just as the loveliness of women is something over and above their limbs so in the words of great poets we find an exquisite charm which is over and above the words and their meanings, and this is *dhvani*. The *rasa*, of which so much has been spoken, is also communicated by the *dhvani*. But what is *dhvani* ? Let us take an example :

Holy father, go thou fearless thine way,
The dog that barked at thee lies dead quite near the bay
Mauled by the lion that on the banks of the Godā does rove
And loves to loiter in that shady grove.

1 *kāvyāsyatmā dhvanir iti budhair yaḥ samāmnāta-pūrvas*
tasyābhāvaṁ jagadur apare bhāktam āhustathānye
kecid vācaṁ sthitam aviṣaye tattvam ūcus tadīyaṁ
tena brūmaḥ sahṛdaya-manaḥprītaye tat-svarūpam.

2 Thus, Manoratha, the poet, who has been already referred to spoke of the newfangled admirers of *dhvani* in the following terms :—
yasmin nāsti vastu kiñcana manah-prahlādi sālaṁkṛtir
vyutpannair racitam ca naiva vacanair vakrokti śūnyaṁ ca yat
kāryaṁ tad dhvaninā samanvitamiti prītyā praśamsan jaḍo
no vidmo' bhidadhāti kiṁ sumatinā pṛṣṭaḥ svarūpam dhvaneḥ.

3 *yeṣāṁ kāvyānuśīlanābhyāsa-vaśāt viśadībhūte mano-mukure varṇanīyatanmoyībhavana-yogyatā te hṛdaya-saṁvāda-bhājaḥ sahṛdayāḥ.*

A lady had a place of assignment in a particular flowery grove, but a religious man used to disturb the solitude of the grove and despoiled it of its beautiful flowers. The lady in order to frighten the holy mam started a cock-and-bull story that a lion was seen in the grove and that it had killed a dog. But the lady addresses the holy man in quite a different manner. Her idea comes to this : A lion is loitering about in the grove and you may now walk about the place just as you please. Her words are, "go thou fearless thine way" The words, "go thou fearless thine way" is finished by signifying that the man may walk as he pleases. The primary meaning has not been barred by the context and therefore there cannot be any indicatory meaning (*lakṣaṇā*) by the extension of the primary. Yet we understand from the sentence very clearly that the holy man had been very politely warned. This significant suggestion comes only by the implication of *dhvani*, for this meaning is completely different from the primary meaning. Bhaṭṭa Nāyaka holds that it is a suggestion of fear by the introduction of lion that may be regarded as desisting the holy man from walking by that path. To this Abhinava's reply is that the warning becomes apparent only when the whole situation is taken into consideration and as such it is the suggestive sense of the whole context. And even if there has been any suggestion of fear that also would be possible only through implication. Abhinava gives another example :

Mother-in-law in deep slumber sleeping here,
While I lie quite on this side, dear,
Mark out cots in daylight clear,
Don't by chance come of me too near.

This is spoken by a spoilt lady who lived alone with her mother-in-law, who snored deeply in the night and the lady in showing the mutual positions of their sleeping places and in warning the guest not to come too near her bed is actually inviting him to come to her bed in the night, for the mother-in-law would be sleeping like a stick. Here the negative meaning suggests the positive meaning.

In the case of the manifestation of *rasa* also Abhinava said that it is the delineation of the exciting scenery and the circumstances as well as the various passing feelings and their expressions that jointly suggest to our minds by the process of *dhvani* an aesthetic situation which later on develops into *rasa.* By the suggestive process of *dhvani* one can indicate *rasa* through any particular suggestion, warning, admonition or the like, or an *alaṃkāra.* It is needless for me to enter into these scholastic discussions by the opponents of *dhvani* like Mahima Bhaṭṭa, who wanted to show that all cases of *dhvani* are but cases of inference, or Bhaṭṭa Nāyaka and others, who wanted to include it within *lakṣaṇā.* It may, however, be pointed out in this connection that just as in the *sphoṭa* theory it is supposed that the words and propositions as a whole conjointly signify a particular meaning, so it is held by the upholders of *dhvani,* like Ānandavardhana and Abhinava and others, that a whole situation, a context, the speakers, the words and their meanings, all may jointly co-operate to produce a suggestion. The consideration of the context and the situation is the most important condition of *dhvani.* Thus, in a story in the *Mahābhārata* when a baby was brought to the cremation ground, the jackal gives a speech that the attendants should sorrow over the death of the baby and wait till dusk, for by some good chance the baby may come to life. The vulture delivers a counter-speech that there is no use in further delay, weeping over the dead child, for no one who comes to the cremation ground ever revives. Both of them have cogent reasons on their side, but the real motive of their speech becomes obvious when we remember that if the baby is protected till nightfall, the vulture would have no share in the carcass, and the jackal would have to contend over the mastery of the carcass with the vulture, if the carcass is not protected till dark. So all their reasons emanate from their greedy look at the carcass.

They are like two European diplomats, and all the meaning and import of high-sounding moral speeches become apparent as soon as we can catch the suggestion of the real motive.

The upholders of the *dhvani* further urge that a piece of composition should not only contain implications or implied suggestion but it is when these suggestions are more beautiful and charming than the primary sense or when the suggestive meaning is the only meaning intended, then we can call a piece of composition a good piece of kāvya. When the suggestive sense is weaker than the ordinary sense or is less charming, the *dhvani* becomes weaker, and this type of kāvya is called *guṇībhūta-vyaṅgya.*

Ānandavardhana divides *dhvani* into two clases: (*i*) *avivakṣita-vācya, i.e.*, where the primary sense has to be absolutely ignored; (*ii*) the other type is *vivakṣitānyapara-vācya, i.e.*, where the primary sense remains in force but along with it a superior suggestive sense flashes out. The first class, namely, the *avivakṣita-vācya,* can again be divided into two classes: (*a*) *arthāntara-saṃkramita* and (*b*) *atyanta-tiraskṛta.* The *arthāntara-saṃkramita* is that where the implication modifies the primary sense, whereas *atyanta-tiraskṛta* is that where the implied sense entirely reverses the primary sense. Thus, in speaking to one's mortal enemy one says: "What immeasurable benefits have thou confered on me; what debts of magnanimity do I owe to thee. Behaving in the same manner, oh my friend, may you live a hundred years more". Here the implied suggestion is that for all the ill treatments he had received from the enemy he curses the latter. Here the implied sense completely reverses the primary sense. The *vivakṣitānyapara-vācya dhvani* is again of two kinds: (*a*) the *lakṣya,* and (*b*) the *alakṣya.* The *alakṣyakrama-dhvani* is that where the process of suggestion is so quick that it can not be apprehended. It is only in the case of the implication of the *rasa* that this *dhvani* occurs. The *lakṣyakrama-dhvani* is that where the process of the implied suggestion can be recognised.

The limits of my subject preclude me from entering into many interesting discussions on the nature of *dhvani* and the conflict of opinions, which forms a very interesting chapter on the study of the development of our aesthetic traditions. But on the whole it may be said that the *dhvani* theory came to stay in the field of Indian poetics, and no further notable progress has been made upon it through the centuries that have passed away.

SOME EARLIER WRITERS

A work called the *Pātālavijaya* or *Jāmbavatī-vijaya*, quotations from which are available in some of the anthological works, was probably written in the *kāvya* style as may be judged from the quotations found in these anthologies. If this work can really be attributed to Pāṇini, the grammarian, we have to admit that the *kāvya* style of writing was in vogue in the 4th or the 5th century B.C., when Pāṇini probably lived.[1] Patañjali quotes a number of passages written in the *kāvya* style which proves that the *kāvya* style of writing was promient in his days.[2] Again, in anthologies Patañjali has been quoted as the writer of some isolated verses.[3] The *Mahābhāṣya* also refers to a poem by Vararuci.[4] Piṅgala, who was probably a contemporary of

1 Winternitz thinks that the *Aṣṭādhyāyī* of Pāṇini was written in or about 350 B.C. He agrument is based on the fact that he mentions Yāska and Śaunaka.

Mr. K. C. Chatterjee has tried to prove that the poet Pāṇini is not the grammarian Pāṇini and the *Jāmbavatī-vijaya* and *Pātāla-vijaya* are one and the same work.

(See C.O.J., I. 1933.)

Pischel in Z.D.M.G. 39, 1885,95ff. has argued on behalf of the identity of the two and so also P. Peterson in J.B.R.A.S., 17, 1889, 57ff.; see also *Subhāṣita-ratnāvalī*, 54 ff. and J.R.A.S., 1891, 311ff.; Kane in *Indian Antiquary* 1, 1912, 125; H. R. Diwekar in *Les fleurs de Rhetorique dans l'Inde, Paris*, 1930, p. 32; and Dr. S. K. De in his *Treatment of Love in Sanskrit Literature*, Calcutta, 1929, p. 13, holds the same view; Thomas in his Introduction to *Kavīndra-vacana-samuccaya*, p. 61 ff., regards the question as undecided. Other writers such as F. Kielhorn in N G.W.G., 1885, 185 ff.; R. G. Bhandarkar in J.B.R.A.S. 16, 344; D.R. Bhandarkar in *Indian Antiquary* 41 1912, 125 n; and A. B. Keith in this *History of Sanskrit Literature* 203 f. have expressed themselves against the identity of the two. It is interesting to notice that Rājamukuṭa in his commentary on *Amarakoṣa* written in 1431, quotes the passage from *Jāmbavatī-vijaya*. The poet Pāṇini is also quoted by Ruyyaka. In *Sadukti-karṇāmṛta* a poet called Dākṣīputra (which is probably another name for Pāṇini) is praised.

2 Compare G. Bühler in his *Die indischen Inschriften und das Alter der indischen Kunstpoesie*, p. 72; F. Kielhorn, *Indian Antiquary*, 14, 326ff. and Dr. P. C. Chakravarty in I.H.Q.2. 1926, 464 ff.

3 Peterson, in J.R.A.S., 1891, 311 ff.

4 *Vārarucaṁ kāvyam—Mahābhāṣya*, 4, 3., 101.

The unknown poet Jāluka is also mentioned here.

O.P. 220—77

Patañjali presupposes in his Metrics the existence of love-lyrics written in the *kavya* style.

Again, the Hāthi-gumphā inscription of Khāravela written somewhere about the 1st or the 2nd century B.C. in a language allied to Pāli, contains rhythmic prose with alliterations and long compounds which reminds one of the *kāvya* style.[1]

The existence of the *kāvya* style in early times is proved by the existence of the *Bṛhat-kathā* of Guṇāḍhya which in its original form is not now available. In the Jaina *Aṅgas,* in didactic passages, in the life history of Mahāvira, in the Buddhist-Pāli canons and patticularly in the *Therīgāthās* we come across verses which are written in the *Kāvya* style.[2] A Nāsik inscription of about 154 A.D. illustrates various modes of prose and this inscription is written in Prākṛt.[3]

1 This inscription has been worked upon by various scholars such as Lüders, *Bruchstücke buddhistischer Dramen,* Berlin, 1911; *Epigraphica Indica,* X, Appendix pp. 160, Charpentier, W.Z.K.M., 29, 1915, 208ff; R. C. Mazumdar and K. G. Śaṅkara Iyer, *Indian Antiquary,* 47, 1918. 223ff; 48, 19, 214ff., Sten Konow in *Acta Or,* 1. 1933, pp. 12 ff; Smith, *Early Histoty,* pp. 219; B. M. Barua, I.H.Q., 4, 1928, pp. 511ff; Ramāprasād Chanda, I. H. Q., 5, 1929, 587ff.; and K. P. Jayaswal and R. D. Banerjee, *Epigraphica Indica,* 20, 1929-30, pp. 71ff.

Here in the latest researches the first half of the 2nd century B. C. is fixed as the date of the inscription. On the style of the old Brahmī Inscription, see B. M. Barua, I.H.Q., 4, 1928, pp. 525ff.

2 The theory of renaissance as propounded by Maxmuller in *India,—What Can It Teach Us, London,* 1882, has been completely refuted by G. Bühler, *Die indischen Inschriften und das Alter der indischen Kunstpoesie* (S.W.A., 1890); also by Haraprasāda Śāstri in J.A.S.B., 6, 1910, 305ff. K. G. Bhandarkar, *A Peep into the Early History of India,* J.B.R.A.S, 1900, pp. 407 ff., reprinted, Bombay, 1920, pp, 72 (b). There are some who do not believe in the theory of the complete interruption of Sanskrit literature, but think that during centuries of Buddhism from the 1st century B.C. to the 4th century A.D. the overflow of Prākṛt literature had slowed down the development of Sanskrit literature. F. Lacôte, of course, in his *Essai sur Guṇāḍhya et la Bṛhatkaṭhā,* Paris, 1908 and Jacobi in his *Ausgewählte Erzählungen in Mâhârâshṭri,* pp. 11 ff., hold that there is a special Prākṛt period in Indian literature. But there is no reason for accepting such a suggestion. Prākṛt poetry was limited to certain classes and probably to certain courts and to certain sects and there were also probably poets both in Prākṛt and Sanskrit, but there seems to be no period in Indian History in which people wrote only in Prākṛt and not in Sanskrit.

3 See Bühler, *Die indischen Inschriften und das Alter der indischen Kunstpoesie,* pp. 56ff.; also Smith's *Early History,* pp. 230, 231; also S. Lévi, *la Suite des Indies dans*

The Rudradāmana inscription at Girnar, written in the 2nd century A.D., appears to conform to Daṇḍin's *vaidarbhī* style.[1]

Aśvaghoṣa, who flourished about 100 A.D., in his works also confirms the same view. Aśvaghoṣa's *Buddha-carita* is well-known. In addition to this, he wrote also the *Sūtrālaṃkāra* and also the drama *Śāriputra-prakaraṇa*[2] and another *kāvya* dealing with the conversion of Nanda, the half-brother of Buddha, in 18 cantos, and this is called the *Saundarananda*.[3]

The other author of this period was Mātṛceṭa, wrongly regarded as Aśvaghoṣa by Tāranātha.[4]

les textes Sanskrites a propos d'une des inscriptions de Nāsik (*Cinquan—lumiere de l'eco'e Pratique des A. hautes etudes*, Paris, 1921). See also Dr. H. C. Raychaudhuri's *Political History of Ancient India*, Calcutta, 1923, pp. 261 ff.

1 This inscriptioh has been re-published by Kielhorn in *Epigraphica Indica* 8, 36 ff. and was dated by him as belonging to 151 or 152 A.D. and Bühler placed it between 160 and 170 A.D. It appears in the same rock of Girnar on which 18 edicts of Aśoka appear. See also Smith's *Early History*, pp. 222, 231 and Raychaudhuri's *Political History of Ancient India*, pp. 65 ff.

2 In 1911 Lüders discovered three pages from the Central Asian Collection of the drama of Aśvaghoṣa. See *Das Śāriputra-prakaraṇa, ein Drama des Aśvaghoṣa.* (SBA., 1911, pp. 388ff.)

The book was also called *Śāradvatī-putraprakaraṇa*. See also H. Luders, *Bruchstücke buddhistischer Dramen* (*Königlich Preussische Turfan—Expeditionen Kleinere Sanskrit texte*), Berlin, 1911 ; Also *Buddhistische Dramen aus vorklassischer Zeit* (*Internationale Wochenschrift* V, 1911, NR. 22) ; also *Die Vermutung* von Lüders. (SBA. 1911, S. 409.) The title-page of the drama *Śāriputra-prakaraṇa* gives the author's name as the son of Suvarṇākṣī. There is also another fragment of an allegorical drama containing *buddhi, dhṛti, kīrti*, etc., as personalities. It is possible that this drama was also written by Aśvaghoṣa.

3 See La vallée Poussin in B.S.O.S., 1918, 133ff. ; also Hultzsch, Z.D.M.G., 74, 1920, 293ff. and Gawronski. As Thomas says, there is another work attributed to Aśvaghoṣa called *Gaṇḍī-stotra*. See *Bulletin de l' Academie Imperiale*, 1911, pp. 1044. Another work of Aśvaghoṣa called *Vajra-sūcī* has been edited and translated by Weber in *Die Vajrasūcī des Acvagoṣa* (*Abhandlungen d. Königl. Akademie d. Wissenschaften zu Berlin*, 1859).

4 The following works are attributed to him :—

1. *Varṇanārha-varṇanā-stotra.*
2. *Śatapañcaśatka-stotra.*
3. *Samyag-buddha-lakṣaṇa-stotra.*
4. *Triratna-maṅgala-stotra.*
5. *Ekottarika-stotra.*
6. *Sugata-pañcatriratna-stotra.*
7. *Triratna-stotra.*
8. *Ārya-tārādevī-stotra.*
9. *Maticitra-gīti.*
10. *Catur-viparyaya-kathā.*
11. *Kaliyuga-parikathā.*

Āryaśūra also belongs to this time and had written *Jātakamālā*, *Pāramitā-samāsa*, *Prātimokṣa-sūtrapaddhati*, *Bodhi-sattva-jātaka-dharmagaṇḍī*, *Supathādeśa-parikathā* and *Subhāṣita-ratna-karaṇḍaka-kathā*.[1]

Closely connected with the *Jātakamālā* are the *Avadāna* literature, such as the *Avadāna-śataka*, the *Divyāvadāna*, and the *Mahāvastu* as well as the *Lalitavistara*, which are all written probably during the 1st 2nd century A.D. The *Avadāna* tales are generally of a didactic nature and so also are the *Jātaka* stories, but the *Bṛhatkathā* and the *Pañcatantra* relate stories from a different point of view. One of the versions of the entire *Pañcatantra* is styled the *Tantrākhyāyikā*.

Bhaṭṭikāvya and other Cognate Caritakāvyas

The oldest commentary, *Jayamaṅgalā*, has been edited by Govinda Śaṅkara Śāstrī Bāpaṭa in N.S.P., Bombay (1887) and the commentary of Mallinātha in B.S.S. (1898). Schütz translated the five Cantos XVIII to XXII in German in his *Fünf Gesānge des Bhaṭṭikāvya* in 1837. An experimental translation

Many other works of Aśvaghoṣa also exist in Tibetan, such as *Aṣṭavighna-kathā*, *Gaṇḍīstotra-gāthā*. *Daśā-kuśala-karma-patha-nirdeśa*, *Paramārtha-bodhi-citta-bhāvanā-kramavarṇa-saṁgraha*, *Maṇidīpamahākāruṇikadevapañca-stotra*, *Vajrayānamūlapattisaṁgraha*, *Śatapañcāśatka-nāmastrotra*, *Śoka-vinodana*, *Saṁvṛti-bodhi-citta-bhāvan-opadeśa-varṇa-saṁgraha*, *Sthūlā-patti*. The following works attributed to Aśvaghoṣa exist in Chinese :—*Fifty verses on the Rules for Serving a Teacher*; *Daśaduṣṭakarmamārga*; *Mahāyāna-bhūmiguhyavācamūla śāstra*; *Sūtrālaṅkāraśāstra*.

On Mātṛceta see Tāranātha's *Geschichte des Buddhismus* in *Indian. Aus dem Tibetieschen*, Petrograd. 1869.

See also F. W. Thomas—The *Works of* Āryasūra, Triratna-dāsa and Dharmika-suhūti in *Album Kern*, Leyden 1903, pp. 405 408.

Also Mātṛceṭa—and the *Muhārāja-kaṇīkālekhā* in *Indian Aniquary*, 32, 1903, pp. 45-60 Also see *Vārṇanārha-varṇanā* of Matṛceṭa, *Indian Antiquary*, 34, 1905, pp. 145-163. Also *Kavīndra-vacana-samuccaya*. (Introduction). Also Sylvain Lévi, *Notes sur les Indo-scythes* in J. A. 1896, pp. 447-449, pp. 455-456. Also L. de la Vallée Poussin, *Documents Sanscrities*.

1 Āryaśūra's work *Catuḥśataka* was translated into Chinese in 434 A.D.

in poetry has been given by Anderson in J. B. R. A. S., 3, 1850 (p. 20ff.). The first four cantos have been translated into English by V. G. Pradhana, Poona, 1897.

In Cantos X to XIII the most important figures of speech have been illustrated by Bhaṭṭi. This section shows striking similarity with Bhāmaha, Daṇḍin and Udbhaṭa though there are great differences in detail. In Cannot XIII the *bhāṣā-leśa* has been mentioned. It does not occur in the earliest *Alaṃkāra-śāstras* of which Ānandavardhana furnisheṣ one example. Cf. Trivedi's edition of *Bhaṭṭi*, Vol. II, Notes, p. 9 ; Kane, *Indian Antiquary*, 1912, p. 208 ; Kane, *Introduction to Sāhityadarpaṇa*, p. 14 ff. ; S. K. De's *poetics*, Vol. I, p. 50 ff. ; Nobels, *Studien Sum* 10, *Buch des Bhaṭṭikāvya* in *Le Muséon* 37, 1924, p. 281 ff. Ruyyaka also quotes *Bhaṭṭikāvya*. Kramadīśvara in his grammar *Saṃkṣiptasāra* quotes liberally from Bhaṭṭi. See Zachariae in *Bezz. Beitr.*, 5, 1880, p. 53 ff.

At the end of the 22nd Book, verse 33, the poet says that "this work is like a lamp for those whose eye is grammar, but is like a mirror in the hand of the blind or people without grammar. This poem must be understood with a commentary ; then it is a feast for the discerning ones. As I only like to deal with experts, fools will fare badly with this poem".[1]

Chronologically he may be regarded as being contemporary with .Bhartṛhari. Bhaṭṭi may be regarded as having lived in the court of Śrīdharasena in Valabhī.[2]

1 *vyākhyāgamyamyidaṁ kāvyam utsavaḥ sudhiyāmalam* । *hatā durmedhasaścāsmin vidvat-priyatayā mayā* ॥ Bhāmaha in criticising this view of Bhaṭṭi says *kāvyānyapi yadīmāni vyākhyāgamyānī śāstravat* । *utsavaḥ sudhiyāmeva hanta durmedhaso hatāḥ* ॥ That is, even if poetry has to be understood only through commentaries like the *śāstras*, then it is only the enjoyment of the intelligent and those who lack it are indeed cursed. This shows apart from other things that Bhaṭṭi was probably a contemporary of Bhāmaha or Bhaṭṭi may have been prior to Bhāmaha but not later. Bhaṭṭi has sometimes been associated with Bhartṛhari and sometimes he has been described as the son of the half-brother of Bhartṛhari. Some commentators regard him as the son of Śrīdhara Svāmin.

2 In the last verse of the *Bhaṭṭikāvya* we have the following line—*kāvyamidaṁ vihitaṁ mayā valabhyāṁ śrīdharasena-narendra-pālitāyām.*

Now there are four Dharasenas in Valabhī (modern Vala in Kathiāwad). The date of the first Dharasena is not known. The earliest grant of Dharasena II is 252 *samvat* of the Valabhī era, *i.e.*, about 571 A.D., and the latest grant of Dharasena IV is *samvat* 332 of the Valabhī era or 651 A.D. Dharasena I probably lived in 500 A.D. for Droṇasiṃha, the successor of Dharasena I, came to the throne in 502 A.D. Bhaṭṭi may therefore be placed between 500 and 600 A.D. He would thus be either a contemporary or predecessor of Bhāmaha as mentioned before. Some scholars identify him with Bhaṭṭibhaṭṭa, son of Bāppā who forms the object of a grant made by Dhruvasena III, son of Dharasena IV (653 A.D.). Dr. Hultzsch objects to this identification (see *Epigraphica, Indica.* Vol. I, p. 92). Mr. B. C. Mazumdar in J. R. A. S. (1904), pp. 395-97 identifies him with Vatsabhaṭṭi of the Mandasore Sun temple inscription (473 A.D.), because of the similarity between the verses of the inscription and the description of autumn by Bhaṭṭi. If this view is correct, Bhaṭṭi would be living under Dharasena I. Keith objects to this view, but both Keith and Mazumdar agree that Bhaṭṭi flourished before Bhāmaha and Daṇḍin and that he is not the Bhārtṛhari, the author of the *Vākyapadīya.*[1] The popularity of Bhaṭṭi may well be judged from the fact that Bhaṭṭikāvya has at least twelve commentators.[2]

The *Bhaṭṭikāvya* is not however the only *mahākāvya* which has been used for the purpose of illustrating grammar. We have to mention in this connection Bhaumaka or Bhaṭṭabhīma or Bhūma or Bhūmaka who wrote the *Rāvaṇārjunīya* in twenty-seven cantos.[3] The subject-matter is the fight of Arjuna

1 See Kane, Introduction to *Sāhityadarpaṇa*, pp. 15 and 16.

2 Commentary by Śaṅkarācārya; *Subodhinī* by Kumudānanda; commentary by Jayamaṅgala; *Bhaṭṭibodhinī* by Nārāyaṇa Vidyāvinoda; *Kalāpadīpikā* by Puṇḍarīkākṣa; *Mugdhabodhinī* by Bharatasena; commentary by Mallinātha; *Vyākyānanda* by Rāmacandra; *Subodhinī* by Rāmacandra Vācaspati; *Bhaṭṭicandrikā* by Vidyāvinoda; *Kalāpadīpikā* by Vidyāsāgara.

3 Edited in the *Kāvyamālā* series, 68, 1900. It is also cited under the name *Vyoṣa* or *Vyoṣakāvya*. See K. C. Chatterjee in I. H. Q., 1931, p. 628 and Zachariae, Z. I. I., 9.1932, p. 10 ff.

Kārttavīrya with Rāvaṇa after the legend told in the *Rāmāyaṇa*, VII. 31-33. The main purpose of the work is to illustrate the rules of Pāṇini's grammar.[1] Another work of the same kind primarily dedicated to grammatical lexicography and only secondarily a poem is the *Kavirahasya* by Halāyudhy.[2] It is a sort of lexicon of roots (*dhātupāṭha*) and at the same time a eulogy of Kṛṣṇarāja III of the Rāṣṭrakūṭa family who reigned in Deccan from 940-956 A.D. Hemacandra also wrote his historical epic *Kumārapālacarita* to illustrate his own grammar. Other grammatical poems are the *Vāsudevavijaya* by the poet Vāsudeva who probably lived in the court of Vikrama of Calicut in Kerala, and the supplement to it is a *dhātukāvya* by Nārāyaṇabhaṭṭa.

The story of Kṛṣṇa was utilised by Lolimbarāja in his epic poem *Harivilāsa*. He lived in the court of southern king Harihara, a contemporary of Bhoja.[3] *Harivilāsa* was written in five cantos.[4] Rāmacandra also wrote *Gopālalīlā* about the Kṛṣṇa legend in 1484 in Tailinga.[5] Kṣemendra's *Daśāvatāra-carita* in its 9th canto deals with the life of Buddha in which the Buddha and the Kṛṣṇa legends have been inter-mingled.[6] Kṣemendra's other two works *Bhāratamañjarī* and *Rāmāyaṇa-mañjarī* are well known.[7] The *Bhāratamañjarī* and the *Daśāvatāracarita* were probably written in 1037 and 1066.[8] About 200 years later

1 Kṣemendra quotes it in the *Suvṛtta-tilaka* as an example of the *Kāvya-śāstra*.

2 This has been edited in 2 recensions by L. Heller, Greifswald ; also see Bhandarkar's *Reports on Sanskrit Manuscripts*, 1883-1884. See also L. Heller, *Halāyudha's Kavirahasya*, Diss., Göttingen, 1894 ; Zachariae, *Die Indischen Wörterbücher*, p. 26.

3 See *Paṇḍit*, Vol II, p. 78 f. ; Weber, *Ind. Streifen* III, 210, 3. and Kṛṣṇamācārya, p. 120.

4 It has been published in *Paṇḍit* II, 79 ff. and the *Kāvyamālā*, Part XI, 1895, 94 133.

5 Published in *Paṇḍit*, Vol. VI.

6 Published in the Kāvyamālā series. 1891. See also Foucher, JA, 1892, and J. J. Meyer, *Altindische Schelmenbücher*, I, p. XXXIII ff. A part of Canto IX has been translated here.

7 Published in the Kāvyamālā series, 65, 1898 and 83, 1903.

8 See Lévi. JA. 1885, VI, 420.

Jaina Amaracandra, also called Amaracandra-sūri, Amarapaṇḍita and Amarajati wrote an abridgement of the *Mahābhārata* called the *Bālabhārata*.[1] The work was written under king Viśāladeva of Anhilvad, 1243-1261.

As there was a tendency of making abridgements from larger poetical works so there was also a tendency of some authors to make abridgements from prose works as well. Thus Abhinanda or Gauḍābhinanda wrote his *Kādambarī-kathāsāra* in the 9th century in which he abridged Bāṇa's romance *Kādambarī*.[2] He was the son of Bhaṭṭa Jayanta. One of his ancestors Śaktisvāmin was the minister of the Kashmiri king Muktāpīḍa (699-735). In one of the verses he refers to the dramatist Rājaśekhara who was his contemporary. He must be distinguished from the other Abhinanda, the son of Śatānanda whose time is not known. He had written an epic called the *Rāmacarita* in which he dealt with the story of Rāma.[3] The Indian poets, however, turned their attention to other directions also. It is, therefore, well worth noting here the name of Sandhyākara Nandī, the author of the *Rāmapālacarita*.[4] The verses have a double sense, one applying to the hero Rāma and the other to the king Rāmapāla, who lived towards the end of the 11th century. The story of the killing of Kīcaka is written in the *Yamaka-kāvya* called the *Kīcaka-vadha*, which has a commentary by Janārdanasena.[5]

1 Published in *Paṇḍit*, Vol. IV-VI and in *Kāvyamālā* 45, 1894. D. Galanos published a translation of it in Greek, 1847, Athens. See also Weber, ZDMG, 27, 1873, 710 ff.; *Ind. strifen* 3, 211 ff.

2 In this connection we may mention the name of *Padyakādambarī* of Kṣemendra. See Schönberg, *Kṣemendra's Kavikaṇṭhābharaṇa*.

3 Bühler, *Indian Antiquary* 2. 1873, 102 ff.; Thomas, p. 20. Aufrecht in ZDMG. 27, p. 4 quotes a verse where Abhinanda is associated with Kālidāsa as being equally celebrated.

4 Published by MM. Haraprasāda Śāstrī in J A.S.B. III, 1910, pp. 1-56. *Epigraphica Indica*, Vol. IX, p. 321 ff. See also H. C. Ray's *Dynastic History of Northern India*, I. 258, etc, Index, p. 641 ; Dr. Ray has used the materials of this book for historical construction ; *Cf.* also Ramāprasād Chanda, Modern Review, March, 1935, p. 349 ff.

5 Edited with an Introduction, notes and extracts from the commentary of Sarvānandanāga by Dr. S. K. De, 1929. The word is quoted in the manuals of poetics from the 11th

But two other writers tried to outshine the work of Sandhyākara Nandī by writing two works called the *Rāghavapāṇḍavīya* or the *Dvisandhānakāvya* and the *Rāghavanaiṣadhīya*. The first one was written by Dhanañjaya, a Digambara Jaina who probably wrote his work between 1123 and 1140.[1] This work, however, should not be confused with the *Rāghavapāṇḍavīya* by Kavirāja, which has at least six commentaries.[2] Dhanañjaya is a Carnatic man referred to by Vādirāja in the *Pārśvanāthacarita* (1025 A.D.), who lived probably in the 2nd half of the 10th Century.[3]

The other author of the *Rāghavapāṇḍavīya* called Kavirāja lived in the court of Kāmadeva II of the Kadamva family, who lived in the latter half of the 12th century. This poem is divided into 13 cantos.[4] But we hear of another *Rāghavapāṇḍavīya* written by Śrutakīrti. He is referred to in an inscription, dated the 1163 and it contains a verse which is quoted from the *Pampārāmāyaṇa*, 1105 A.D.[5] This *Rāghavapāṇḍavīya* was a work which, when read from left to right in the usual way, delineated the character of Rāma but when read from right to left it delineated the character of the Pāṇḍavas. We hear of another *Rāghavapāṇḍavīya*, which when read from right to left, delineated the story of Kṛṣṇa.[6] Kavirāja, the author of the *Rāghavapāṇḍavīya*, was a very famous man.

century onwards beginning with Bhoja (1050 A.D.) as well as in dictionaries and grammatical works. The verse I. 7. should be interpreted as an allusion to king Vigrahapāla. *Cf.* S. K. De's edition, p. XIII ff., 93 ff.; J. R. A. S. 1927, 109 f.; B. S. O. S., V. 3, 1929, 502 f., A. B. Keith in B. S. O. S., V. I. 1928, p. 31.

1 This work has been published in the Kāvyamālā series 49, and it consists of 18 cantos.

2 Commentaries by Cāritravardhana, Padmanandībhaṭṭāraka, Puṣpadanta, Lakṣmaṇapaṇḍita (*Sāracandrikā*), Visvanātha and Śaśadhara (*Prakāśa*).

3 *Cf.* A. Benkaṭasubbiah, in J.B.R.A.S., 1928, 135 ff.; See also K. B. Pāṭhak, J. B. R. A. S., 21, 1904, 1 ff.; Bhāndārkar, *Report on Sanskrit Mss.*, 1884-1887, p. 19 ff.; Zachariae *Die indischen Wörterbücher*, p. 27 ff.

4 It has been edited with the commentary of Śaśadhara in the Kāvyamālā series, 62.

5 See Narasiṁhachar, *Epigraphica Carnatica*, Vol. II, No. 64.

6 See Keith, *India Office Catalogue*, No. 7133.

Pāṭhak thinks that his real name was Mādhavabhaṭṭa.[1] Our Kavirāja says that no one can rival him in *vakrokti*.

The *Rāghhvanaiṣadhīya* was written by Haradatta Sūri.[2] We do not exactly know the date of the author. Every verse here has been interpreted on the one hand as describing Rāma's exploits and character and on the other, those of Nala.

There is, however, another *Rāghavapāṇḍavayādavīya* written by one Cidamvara, where every verse can be interpreted in three ways, as describing episodes of the *Mahābhārata*, the *Rāmāyaṇa* and the *Śrīmadbhāgavata*.[3]

Amaracandra, a pupil of Jinadatta Sūri, wrote, at the request of the minister Padma, a *mahā-kāvya* called the *Padmānanda*.[4] This work is of 19 cantos in which the life of the first Jina, Ṛṣabha, is treated in an ornate style. He has written another work called the *Caturviṃśati-jinendra-saṃkṣipta-caritāni*, in which he gives an account of the life of the Jinas. Hemacandra had written a *mahā-kāvya* in which the lives of the Jinas and Jina poets were described. There is also another work called the *Munisuvratakāvyaratna* edited in the Trivandrum series, 1931, in which the life of the 20th Jina is decribed by a poet of unknown age called Arhaddāsa. Amaracandra in drawing his short life of the 24 Jinas had to draw his materials from Hemacandra.

Ravideva, son of Nārāyaṇa, who wrote a commentary on the *Nalodaya*, wrongly attributed to Kalidāsa, wrote a small *kāvya* called the *Kāvyarākṣasa*, to which he added his own commentary.[5] We really know nothing of Ravideva's time.

1 See K. B. Pāṭhak, *J.B.R.A.S.*, 1905, 11 ff. But Benkaṭasubbiah does not agree with him. The name Kavirāja being used as a title, it is not possible to make out anything about the date of the author of the *Rāghavapāṇḍavīya* from the reference to the name Kavirāja in Vāmana's *Kāvyālaṁkārasūtravṛtti*, IV. 1. 10.: *kavirājamavijñāya kutaḥ kāvyakriyādaraḥ/kavirājañca vijñāya kutaḥ kāvyakriyādaraḥ.//*

2 It has been edited with the Poet's own commentary in the Kāvyamālā series, 1896.

3 See Aufrecht's *Catalogus Catalogorum*.

4 Critically edited by H. R. Kapadia, G. O. S, 58, 1932.

5 Peterson, *Three Reports*, p. 334 ff. ; *Report* IV, p. CV ; Bhandarkar, *Report*, 1883-84, p. 16 ; Aufrecht, *Catālogus Catalogorum* ; Pischel, Z.D.M.G. 1902, 626 ; 1904, 244.

The work has 4 commentaries, by Kavirāja (*Subodhinī*), Kṛṣṇacandra. Premadhara, and Vidyākara Miśra. Aufrecht says that the work is attributed to two other persons excluding Ravideva, *viz.*, Kālidāsa and Vararuci. In one commentary Vāsudeva, son of Ravideva, is mentioned as the author of the *Nalodaya.*[1]

Vāsudeva, son of Ravi, to whom the *Nalodaya* is attributed, wrote 3 other *kāvyas*, the *Tripuradahana*, the *Saurikathodaya* and the *Yudhiṣṭhiravijaya*[2]

We must now mention Kumāradāsa's *Jānakīharaṇa.*[3] Thomas thinks that Kumāradāsa is older than Rājaśekhara and probably lived in the 7th century. Aufrecht says that passages from the *Jānakīharaṇa* have been quoted by Rāyamukuṭa, who wrote a commentary on the *Amarakoṣa* in 1431. According to tradition, Kumāradāsa was a Simhalese king, who lived between 517 A.D. and 526 A.D. Kumāradāsa's style of writing resembles more that of Kālidāsa than that of Bhāravi and Māgha.

The *Kirātārjunīya* of Bhāravi is based upon a *Mahābhārata* story, in which considerable modification have been made. It has been quoted by Vāmana in his *Alaṃkārasutravṛtti*, by Kṣemendra in the *Suvṛttatilaka* and by Dhanapāla and Rājaśekhara, and is also quoted in some of the anthologies. Its popularity is evident from the fact that it has at least 20 commentaries.[4]

This book was published by A. Hoefer, *Sanskrit-Lesebuch*, Berlin, 1849. p. 86 ff.; K.P. Parab, Bombay, 1900; an Italian translation by Belloni-Filippi in G.S.A.I., 1906, 83 ff.; see also Weber, *Ind. Streifen*, II, 15.

1 Cf. Ramnatha Iyer, in *J.R.A.S.*, 1925, 263 ff.

2 Edited with Rajānakaratnakaṇṭha's commentary in the Kāvyamālā, 60, 1897. This commentary is called the *Pārthakathā*. See Zachariae, in Z.I.I., 4, 1926, 223 ff.

3 It was published in Bombay by G. R. Nandargikar. He wrote also a work, *Kumāradāsa and his place in Sanskṛit Literature* in 1908. Many writers had written about the poetry of Kumāradāsa, such as, J. d'Alwis, 1870; Zachariae, *Bezz. Beitr*, 5, 1880; G. G. A. 1887; Peterson, J. B. R. A. S., 17, 1889, 57 ff; E. Leumann, W. Z. K. M. 7, 1893, 226 ff.; F. W. Thomas, J. R. A. S. 1901 253 ff; A. B. Keith, J. R. A. S., 1901, 578 ff. The work has also been quoted in the *Śubhāṣitāvalī*, 24 f. and other works of anthology.

4 By Narahari, Ekanātha, Kāśīnatha, Gadasiṁha, Prakāśavarṣa, Jonarāja, Dāmodara Miśra (*Gaurava-dīpanī*), Dharmavijaya, Bhagīratha, Bharatasena,

Bhāravi indulges in many word-tricks. Sometimes there are verses with one alphabet and sometimes he writes verses which can be read vertically, from right to left and left to right. Bhāravi is particularly famous for his many pithy sayings and maxims which are often quoted as rules of conduct. He seems to have been very well read in Indian polity. As for the general estimate of his work, see Dr. De's treatment in the body of the book.

With Bhāravi our attention is drawn to Māgha's *Śiśupāla-vadha.*[1] Māgha also indulges like Bhāravi in many *alaṃkāras* and word-tricks.[2] Māgha based the scheme of his work on Bhāravi.[3] The story is based on the *Mahābhārata,* II, 41-45, and also, I. 287. According to Indian tradition Māgha is supposed to have the combination of depth of meaning, richness of imagery and sweetness of words. Māgha's *Śiśupālavadha,* though not a very excellent work in our judgment and poetical taste, attained a great popularity among the scholars of India as may well be judged by the fact that there are at least 16 or 17 commentaries on the *Śiśupalavadha.*[4]

Manohara Śarmā, Mallinātha, Mādhava, Rājakunda, Lokānanda, Bankimadāsa (*Vaiṣamyoddhāriṇī*), Vinayarāma (*Pradīpikā*). Harikaṇṭha and the commentary called the *Śabdārthadipikārasabodhinī*. An excellent edition of the commentary of Mallinātha has been published from the Nirṇayasāgara Press, Bombay. It was translated into German by Schütz, 1845. Translated into English by C. Cappeller in H.O.S., Vol. 15. The *kirātārjunīya* has also been quoted in the Kaśikā ; see Kielhorn, *Indian Antiquary*, 14, 327. The 4th canto has been translated by Haberlandt, in the *Wiener Landwirtschaftl Zeitung*, 1883.

1 Published with Mallinātha's commentary by the Nirṇayasāgara Press, Bombay. A German translation in prose of the first 11 cantos by Schütz appeared in 1843. A general introduction of it by C. Cappeller appeared in 1915, Stuttgart.

2 An example of word trick can be found in XIX, 3,

jajau jo ja ji jij jā ji
taṁ tato' ti ta tā ti tut ।
bhābho'bhibha bhi bhū bhā bhū
rā rā ri ra ri rī ra raḥ ॥

3 Jacobi, W.Z.K.M., 3, 1889, 121 ff ; 141 ff.

4 There are commentaries on the *Śiśupālabadha* by Ananta Devāyani Kavivallabha Cakravarti, Govinda, Candraśekhara (*Sandarbhacintāmaṇi*), Cāritravardhana, Dinakara,

Rājānaka Ratnākara in his *Haravijaya* appears to have been passionately influenced by Māgha's *Śiśupālavadha*. This work is written in 50 cantos and reveals an exhaustive study of Māgha's *Śiśupālabadha*. The poem is based upon a conquest of Andhakāsura by Śiva. But Rājānaka Ratnākara used all the opportunities of drawing materials from various subjects for drawing his pictures. Thus he brings his knowledge of *Nītiśāstra* into prominence in writting Cantos VIII-XVI, his knowledge of *Kāmaśāstra* in the 29th canto and devotes one canto to a hymn to the goddess Durgā (*Caṇḍīstotra*). The same writer is the author of another work called the *Vakrokti-pañcāsikā*.[1]

The other, who wrote an epic on the model of Māgha in 21 cantos, called the *Dharmaśarmābhyudaya*, a life of Dharmanāthatīrthaṅkara, was the Jaina Haricandra.[2] Haricandra lived later than Vākpati who wrote the *Gauḍavaha* and hence must have lived after the 8th century A.D.

The story of Nala has been utilised by many writers. Thus, we have many works on that subject, such as the *Nalacandra*, the *Nalacaritra* (a drama by Nīlakaṇṭha *Dikṣita*), the *Nalabhumipālarūpaka* (a drama), the *Nalayādavarāghavapāṇḍavīya* (a *kāvya*), the *Nalavarṇanakāvya* (by Lakśmīdhara), the *Nalānanda* (a drama by Jīvavibudha) and the *Nalodaya* to which reference has already been made.[3]

Devarāja, Bṛhaspati, Bhagadatta, Bhagīratha, Bharatasena, Bhavadatta (*Tattvakaumudī*) Mallinātha (*Sarvaṁkaṣā*); Maheśvara Pañcānana (*Māghatattvasamuccaya*), Lakṣmīnātha Śarmā, Vallabhadeva (*Sandehaviṣauṣadhi*), and Śrīraṅgadeva.

1 Rājānaka Ratnākara's *Haravijaya* has been published with the commentary of Alaka in the Kāvyamālā series, 22 1890; see also Schmidt, W. Z. K. M., 29, 259 ff. Jacobi says that Ratnākara himself says that he followed Baṇa. See also K. H. Dhruva, W. Z. K. M., 5, 1891, 25 ff. The *Vakroktipañcāśikā* with the commentary of Vallabhadeva has already appeared in the Kāvyamālā series. Bernheimer in Z. D. M. G , 63, 1909, 816 ff. gives a resume of the work. Ratnākara is also the author of another work, the *Dhvanigāthāpañjikā*. Both the works have been quoted by Ruyyaka.

2 Published in the Kāvyamālā series, No. 8, 1888 ; see also Jacobi, W.Z.K.M., 1889. 136 ff. There was another works of *kāvya* called the *Dharmaśarmābhyudaya* by Puṣpasena.

3 This work has no less than a dozen commentaries, by Ātreya Bhaṭṭa, Āditya Sūri, Keśavāditya, Gaṇeśa, Nṛsiṁha also called Nrsiṁhaśrama, Pratijñākara Miśra, Bharatasena,

But the most important work in which the Nala legends have been worked up into a massive *kāvya* is the *Naiṣadhacarita* by Śrīharṣa. It has been arbitrarily divided into two parts, the *Pūrva* and the *Uttara Naiṣdha* (I-XI and XII-XXII). The first half was edited by Premcand Tarkavāgīśa from the Sanskrit College, Calcutta, 1836. An edition of the second half with the commentary of Nārāyaṇa was published by E. Röer in the Bibliotheca Indica Series in 1855.[1]

It is based upon the story of Nala and Damayantī in the *Mahābhārata*. Śrīharṣa had a thorough knowledge of the *Alaṃkāraśāstra*, the *Kāmaśāstra*, the *Purāṇas*, the Metrics and Grammar and he tries to show all his learning in this work. Winternitz, in commenting on it, says: "What a difference between the delicate chastity with which the love between Nala and Damayantī is depicted in the *Mahābhārata* and the sultry erotics bordering on obscenity in Cantos XVIII-XX of the *Naiṣadhacarita*, which describe the love life of the newly wedded couple." And yet it cannot be denied that Śrīharṣa is a master of language and metrics, an artist in the invention of elaborate plays on words and that he has many good ideas in his description of Nature. Śrīharṣa also shows his philosophical learning and convinces us of his erudition in the Vedānta, Nyāya, Vaiśeṣika, Buddhistic systems and the Cārvāka. Śrīharṣa was the author, we know, of an abstruse dialectical

Mukunda Bhaṭṭa, Ravideva (*Jaṭāvabodhinī*), Rāmarśi, son of Vṛddhavyāsa, Hariratna (*Bālabodhinī*), the *Arthadīpikā*.

1 A complete edition with the commentary of Nārayaṇa was published in the Nirṇayasāgara Press, Bombay; W. Yates in his *Asiatic Researches*, Vol. 20, Part II, Calcutta, 1839, p. 318 ff. has given an excellent Introduction to this work. The whole work has been translated into English with critical notes from unpublished commentaries, appendices and vocabulary by Kṛṣṇakānta Handiqui, Lahore, 1934. It has no less than about two dozen commentaries, by Rājānaka Ānanda, Iśānadeva, Udayanācārya, Gopīnātha (*Harṣahṛdaya*), Caṇḍupaṇdita (written in the middle of the 15th century), Cāritravardhana Jinaraja, Narahari (*Naiṣadhīyaprakāśa*) Nārāyaṇa (*Naiṣadhaprakāśa*), Bhagīratha, Bharatasena, Bhavadatta, Mathurānātha Śukla, Mallinātha (*Jīvātu*), Mahādeva Vidyāvāgīśa, Rāmacandra Śeśa (*Bhāvadyotanikā*), Vaṁśīvadana Śarman, Vidyāraṇya Yogin, Viśveśvarācārya (*Padāvākyārthapañjkā*, quoted by Mallinātha in 1.5.118 and hence prior to him), and Śrīdatta, Śrīnātha (*Naiṣadhaprakāśa*) and Sadānanda.

work on the Vedānta called the *Khaṇḍanakhaṇḍakhādya*. The *Naīṣadhacarita* was a source of delight to the scholarly pundits. But yet there is a tradition to which Winternitz refers in his *History of Indian Literature*. The tradition is to the effect that Śrīharṣa showed his work to his maternal uncle Mammaṭa, the author of the *Kāvyaprakāśa*. Mammaṭa is said to have remarked after reading the book that had he read it before writing his *Kāvyaprakāśa*, he would have found in one place the examples of *doṣa* or faults of literary style and would have saved himself the trouble of hunting for it from book to book.[1]

Śrīharṣa was the son of Śrīhīrapaṇḍita and Śrīmāmalladevī, as is apparent from the concluding verse of each canto.[2] In the concluding verse of the *Khaṇḍanakhaṇḍakhādya*, Śrīharṣa says that he belonged to the court of Jayantacandra of Kānyakubja, as may be evident from his statement that he received two betel leaves from the king and had a seat assigned to him in the court. In that verse he also refers to his sweet *kāvya*, the *Naiṣadhacarita*.[3] From a land-grant it appears that Jayantacandra lived in 1165 A. D. This Jayantacandra was the grandson of Govindacandra, who is so renowned in the Hindi poems as Rājā Jayacānd whose daughter was carried off by the gallant Rai Pithorā of Ajmeer. He was known to the Mahammadan historians as the king of Benares, which was probably his capital. His territory extended from the borders

1 This tradition is referred to by Hall in his preface to the edition of the *Vāsavadattā*. He quotes it from a Bengali pomphlet entitled *Saṁskṛta Bhāṣā O Saṁskṛtasāhityaviṣayaka Prastāva*. But it has no historical validity. Anyhow, it represents one aspect of the opinion regarding Śriharśa.

2 *śrī harṣaṁ kavi-rāja-rājī-mukuṭālaṁkārahīraḥ sutam*
śrī-hīraḥ suṣuve jitendriya-cayaṁ māmalla-devī cayam ||
tac-cintā-maṇi-mantra-cintana-phale śṛṅgāra-bhaṅgyā mahā.
kāvye cāruṇi naiṣadhīyacarite sargo'yam ādirgataḥ ||

3 *tāmbūladvayamāsanaṁ ca labhate yaḥ kānyakubjeśvarāt*
yaḥ sākṣāt-kurute samādhiṣu para-brahma-pramodārṇavam ||
yat-kāvyaṁ modhu-varṣi dharṣita-parāstarkeṣu yasyoktayah
śrī-śrīharṣa-kave kṛtiḥ kṛti-mude tasyā'bhyudīyādiyam ||

of China to the province of Mālwa. He was defeated by Sāhābuddin about 1194 at Chandawar, in the Etawah district. His army was destroyed and he was also killed. Śrīharṣa thus lived in the end of the 12th century A.D. In addition to the *Khaṇḍanakhaṇḍakhādya,* he is said to have written two other *kāvyas* called the *Vijayapraśasti* and the *Gauḍorvīśakulapraśasti.* He quotes Vācaspati who lived in 976 A.D. He also quotes Udayana who lived in 984 A.D. So we may safely regard Śrīharṣa to belong to the 12th century A.D. Other works attributed to him are the *Arṇavavarṇana,* the *Śivaśaktisiddhi,* the *Sāhasāṅkacampū,* the *Īśvarābhisandhi,* and the *Sthairya-vicāraṇaprakaraṇa.* It seems from references in the *Naiṣadhacarita* that the *Kaṇḍanakhaṇḍakhādya* was written earlier than the *Naiṣadhacarita.*

Tradition runs that his father was defeated by a scholar in a debate. He felt so insulted that he died out of grief. At the time of his death he told his son Śrīharṣa that unless he took revenge on hehalf of his father by defeating his opponent in debate, his soul would not rest in peace. Śrīharṣa promised the same to his father and after long penances and adoration of Durgā he received a special charm (*cintāmaṇimantra*) and the gift of knowledge and wisdom. But after this he appeared so learned that nobody could understand his discussions and then he again adored Durgā to make his words intelligible. The goddess prescribed that he should take curd in the night and that thereby he would become more phlegmatic and duller and so be intelligible to others. That the story is partially true and that he offered penances to Durgā, is inferable from references in the *Naiṣadhacarita.*[1] The poet Kṛṣṇānanda not only wrote a commentary on the *Naiṣadhacarita,* but he also re-wrote the legend of Nala in an epic, the *Śahṛdayānanda* in 15 cantos probably in the 13th century.[2] In the 15th century

1 See Pandit Lakṣmaṇa Śāstrī Drāviḍa's Introduction to the *Khaṇḍanakhaṇḍakhādya*

2 Edited in the Kāvyamālā series, 32, 1892.

again, the poet Vāmanabhaṭṭabāṇa (or Abhinavabhaṭṭabāṇa) wrote the same legend in his *Nalābhyudaya.*[1] He was also the author of the *Śṛṅgārabhūṣaṇa,* the *Pārvatīpariṇaya* and the *Vemabhūpālacarita.* He imitated the prose style of Bhaṭṭabāṇa.[2] Vemabhūpāla, in whose court the poet Abhinavabāṇa lived, was himself also a learned man and had written the *Śṛṅgāradīpikā* and the *Saṅgītacintāmaṇi.* He was the ruler of the Triliṅga country. From a copper plate, dated the 1448 in the name of the son of Vema, it is possible to determine the time of his father Annavema or Vemabhūpāla as being the first half of the 15th century when the poet Abhinavabāṇa lived. The style of the *Nalābhyudaya* is quite simple.

We must now mention the name of the Kashmir poet Maṅkha and his book *Śrīkaṇṭhacarita.*[3] It deals with the story of the destruction of the demon Tripura by Śiva, but this is made only the occasion for the description of natural scenery in different seasons and the amusements of the court. In the 25th canto, of which we have a German translation, Maṅkha

1 A fragment of 8 cantos of this poem has been edited in the Trivandrum Sanskrit Series, No. 3, 1913, by Gaṇapati Śāstrī. He is also the author of the *Vemabhūpālacarita,* a prose novel after the style of *Harṣacarita.* Vema, the hero of this novel, was still living when Vamanabhaṭṭabāṇa wrote, probably in the first half of tne 15th century. Cf. Gaṇapati Śāstrī's Introduction and Suali in G.S.A.I., 26, 214.

2 Thus he says at the commencement of *Vemabhūpālacarita* :

bāṇakavīndradanye kāṇāḥ khalu sarasa-gadya-saraṇiṣu ।
iti jagati rūḍham-ayaśo vata sakulo vāmano'dhunā mārṣṭi ॥
kavirabhinava-bāṇaḥ kāvyamatyadbhutārtham
bhuvanamohita-bhūmir nāyako vemabhūpaḥ ।
tri-bhuvana-mahanīya-khyātimāneṣu yogaḥ
prakaṭayati na keṣāṁ paṇḍitānāṁ praharaṣm ॥

Again, at the end of the same work comes the passage :—

sarvo-tkarṣeṇa vartamānaḥ sākṣāl-lakṣmī-samuccāryamāṇa-jaya-śabdo viśva-viśvambharapāla-mauli-mālā-makaranda-surabhita-caraṇāravindo jayati viśvādhi-kavibhāve vemo-bhūpālaḥ.

See Introduction by Gaṇapati Śastrī.

3 This work with the commentary of Jonarāja (1417-1467 A.D.) was published in the Kāvyamālā series in 1887. The 25th Canto was translated into German by Elizabeth Kreyenborg (*Der XXV Gesang des Śrīkaṇṭha-caritam des Maṅkha, Ein beitrag zur altindischen literaturgeschichte. Diss, Münster* 1. W. 1929.

describes how after finishing his poem he read it out to a number of pundits in the house of his brother Alaṃkāra, the minister of Jayasiṃha and takes this opportunity of describing a *sabhā* of scholars. Maṅkha himself calls Ruyyaka the author of the *Alaṃkārasarvasva*, as his teacher.[1] It is curious, however, that Ruyyaka should quote in his *Alaṃkārasarvasva* verses from the *Śrīkaṇṭhacarita*. Kane thinks that though Ruyyaka had in the beginning written a commentary on the *Alaṃkārasarvasva*, this commentary was retouched by Maṅkha and he probably introduces his own verses into it. For this reason, while Kumārasvāmī, Jagannātha and Jayaratha attribute the commentary (*vṛtti*) to Ruyyaka himself, Samudrabandha, an author of the 13th century, attributes the commentary to Maṅkha. Maṅkha is sometimes called Maṅkhaka also and the *Rājataraṅgṇī* says that he was appointed minister for peace and war by king Jayasiṃha of Kashmir.[2] Now, Jayasiṃha of Kashmir ruled in 1128-1149 A.D, and according to Bühler, Maṅkha's *Śrīkaṇṭhacarita* was written between 1135 and 1145 A.D.

Rājānaka Jayadratha wrote a religious epic called the *Haracaritacintāmaṇi* in 32 cantos.[3] He probably lived in the first quarter of the 13th century. His elder brother Jayaratha wrote a commentary on the *Alaṃkārasarvasva*, called the *Vimarśinī*, which was quoted and criticised by Jagannātha. His great-grand-father's brother was a minister of king Ucchala (1101-1111 A.D.) and his father Śṛṅgāra was a minister of Rājarāja or Rājadeva (1203-1226). In the *Haracaritacintāmaṇi*, Jayadratha refers to the conquest of Pṛthvīrāja (*Pṛthvīrājavijaya*) which event took place in 1193. We may therefore safely put

1 See *Śrikaṇṭhacarita*, XXV, 26-30.

2 sāndhivigrahiko maṅkhakākhyo' laṅkarasodaraḥ ।
sa maṭhasyābhavatpraṣṭhaḥ śrīkaṇṭhasya pratiṣṭhayā ॥
(*Rājataraṅgiṇī*, VIII, 3354).
Vide also *Śrīkaṇṭhacarita* III, 66.

3 Published in Kāvyamālā, 61, 1197; see Bühler's *Report*, p. 61. Winternitz is mistaken in calling the author Jayaratha, which should be Jayadratha.

Jayadratha in the last quarter of the 12th century and the first quarter of the 13th century. Jayadratha was a pupil of Sughaṭadatta, Śiva and Śaṅkhadhara. In addition to the *Haracaritacintāmaṇi* he wrote the *Alaṃkāravimarśiṇī* and the *Alaṃkārodāharaṇa.* In the *Haracaritacintāmaṇi,* Jayadratha deals with the Śiva legends and doctrines of the Kashmir Śaivism.

The *Kathākautuka* was written by Śrīvara probably in the 15th century. It is an adaptation in 15 cantos of the Jami story "Yusuf U Zuleikha" in Persian. It glorifies Muhammad Shah who ascended the throne in 1481 A.D. and in whose reign Jami died. The story of Yusuf and Zuleikha is of Hebrew origin, which was the romantic theme of Jami. The amalgamation of this romantic Persian love lyric with the Indian Śaiva faith is indeed interesting. The 15th Canto of the work is dedicated entirely to the praise of Śiva.[1] Śrīvara was a pupil of Jonarāja and in addition to the *Kathākautuka* he also wrote the *Jinataraṅgiṇī.* The poet Bhānubhaṭṭa, also called Hari, wrote an epic called the *Haihayendracarita* dealing with the life of Kārtavīryārjuna according to the *Viṣṇupurāṇa,* on the model of Śrīharṣa's *Naiṣadhacarita.* He also wrote another historical poem called the *Śambhurājacarita,* Śambhurāja being the Marāṭha king Sambhājī, son of Śivājī. The work was complete in 1684 A.D.[2]

We now pass on to Nīlakaṇṭha Dīkṣita who wrote a poem on the descent of Gaṅgā to the world called the *Gaṅgāvataraṇa.*[3]

1 See R. Schmidt, *Das Kathākautukam des Śrīvara verglichen mit Dschāmīs Jusuf und Zuleikha,* Kiel, 1893. Text also in the Kāvyamālā series, 72, 1901. On the Persian poetry see P. Horn, *Geschichte der Persischen Litteratur,* 1901, p. 190 f. The epic *Delārāmakathāsāra* by the Kashmiri poet Rājānaka Bhaṭṭa Āhlādaka, published in the Kāvyamālā series, 77, 1902 (see Hertel, *Jinakirti's Geschichte von Pāla und Gopāla,* pp. 61 ff; 135 f.).

2 See Scherbatskoi *Uber das Haihayendracarita des Harikavi,* in Memories de l'Academie imp. des sciences de St. Petersburg,. VIII Series, t. IV, No. 9, 1900; and P. K. Gode in *Ann. Bh. Ins.* 16, 1935, p. 362 ff.

3 Edited in the Kāvyamālā series, No. 76, 1902.

The poet is the son of Nārāyaṇa Dīkṣita, a nephew of Appaya Dīkṣita. He also wrote another work called the *Śivalīlārṇava* in 21 cantos, in which he describes the 64 sports of *līlā* of Śiva according to the *Hālāsyamāhātmya* of the *Skandapurāṇa*.[1]

A woman poetess called Madhuravāṇī who was a court poetess of King Raghunātha of Tanjore, wrote the *Rāmāyaṇasāra* dealing with the principal tale of the *Rāmāyaṇa* in the 17th century.[2]

Two cantos of an epic *Rājapraśasti* by a poet Raṇacchoda of the end of the 18th century has come down to us in an inscription[3] Even as late as the end of the 18th and the beginning of the 19th century, Rūpanātha Upādhyāya wrote an epic called the *Rāmavijaya-mahākāvya*.[4]

SANSKRIT DRAMA

The *Nāṭṭyaśāstra* of Bharata, probably a work of the 2nd or the 3rd century A.D., preserves a tradition that *nātya* is the fifth Veda which men of all castes would enjoy and which was composed out of the elements of all four Vedas and that Viśvakarmā built a play-house and instructed Bharata into the practice of the art. The gods Śiva, Pārvatī and Viṣṇu, all contributed their portions essential to the effective practice of this creation. Originally practised in Heaven, it was brought to earth in an imperfect condition by Bharata. All through the epochs the holiness of the *Nāṭyaśāstra* and the Vedas has been preserved.

1 Edited by Gaṇapati Śāstrī, TSS No. 4, 1909; Cakrakavi was the author of another epic called the *Jānakīpariṇaya* edited in TSS No. 24, 1913. He was perhaps a contemporary of Nīlakaṇṭha Dīkṣita

2 See M. T. Narasimhienger, J.R A.S., 1908, p. 168.

3 See Kielhorn, *Epigraphica Indica*, Vol. V, Appendix no 321.

Published with Introduction by Pandit Nārāyāṇa Śāstrī Khiste, edited by Gaṇapatilāl Jhā, Benares, 1932. The Rāma epic *Raghuvīracarita*, edited in TSS No. 57, 1917, is by an unknown author in an unknown period. The *Bharatacita* dealing with the legend of Bharata, son of Duṣyanta, by a poet Kṛṣṇa. TSS No. 86, 1926, is also of an unknown period.

We cannot trace any drama in the Vedic literature. But there are many hints in the Vedas of the nature of dialogues.[1] Thus, the story of Yama and Yamī (*R.V.*, X. 10). the dialogue between Purūravā and Urvaśī (*R.V.*, X. 95), that between Nema Bhārgava and Indra (*R.V.*, VIII. 100), between Agastya, Lopāmudrā and their son (*R.V.*, I. 179), the debate between Indra, Indrānī and Vṛṣākapi, Saramā and the Paṇis (*R.V.*, X. 108), and many other instances like that, illustrate the existence of dialogues in the *Ṛgveda*. Maxmüller suggests in connection with his version of the *Ṛgveda*, I. 165 (SBE. XXXII, 182 f.) that the dialogue was repeated at sacrifices in honour of the Maruts or that two parties personating Indra and the Maruts enacting it. The suggestion was repeated by Lévi in his *Le Théâtre Indien*, Paris, 1890 (1. 307 ff.), who further urged that since the *sāma* hymns were sung, the art of music had developed in the Vedic age. We hear also of coquettish women in the *Ṛgveda* (I. 92.4), and the *Atharva-veda* (XII. 1.41) tells us that men used to sing and dance in Vedic times. It is thus possible that there were dramatic spectacular shows of a religious character in the Vedic age.

From this Prof. von Schroeder drew the elaborate theory that the drama developed in the Vedic atmosphere of dancing, singing, *soma*-drinking, out of the dialogues and monologues.[2]

Hertel lent support to the view that the dialogues were like the Mystery Plays and the hymns, when they were sung by various persons, and had in them the seeds of drama.[3] Hertel further seeks to discover a drama in the *Suparṇādhyāya*, a late chapter of the Vedic texts. A prototype of the old type of drama may be traced in the modern '*jātrās*' of Bengal.

It is indeed possible to discover dramatic elements in the *Ṛgveda*, but all the hymns of the *Ṛgveda* need not be ritualistic.

1 Keith, J.R.A.S., 1911, 981 ff.

2 *Mysterium und Mimus im Rigveda*, 1908 ; V. O. J., XXII, 223 ff. ; XXIII, 1 ff., 270 f.

3 V.O.J., XVIII. 59 ff., 137 ff. ; XXIII, 273 ff.; XXIV, 117 ff. Cf. Charpentier,

to try to find ritualistic explanations in all the hymns and to explain the origin of the drama in the rituals of the *Ṛgveda,* may certainly be regarded as a little over-straining the facts. In any case, sufficient arguments have not been brought forward in support of such a supposition.[1] Again, Hertel's suggestion that the dialogues of the *Ṛgveda* were always sung in accompaniment with dance, lacked confirmation in the vedic ritualistic texts. It is also practically certain that while in the *Sāma-veda* hymns were as a rule always sung, not all the *Ṛgveda* texts could be sung. Mr. Hertel has hardly proved his case that the *Suparṇādhyāya* represents a full-fledged drama. Windich, Oldenberg and Pischel think that Vedic hymns were originally associated with prose compositions which have not come down to us.[2] The suggestion is that these hymns and dialogues are dramatic. Pischel explained the combination of prose and verse in Sanskrit drama as a legacy from these hymns.[3] Our Vedic traditions do not support such a view. The tales of Śunaḥśepha in the *Aitareya Brāhmaṇa* and the tale of Purūravas and Urvaśī in the *Śatapatha Brāhmaṇa* are tales for explaining the ritual. It is therefore quite unsound to regard that Vedic texts at any time represented any form of the drama. No assumption of the dramatic nature of the hymns is at all necessary to explain the context. Prof. Geldner at one time supported Oldenberg's view but later on regarded the hymns as ballads.[4] The use of prose and verse in Indian dramas does not necessitate the theory that this should have a Vedic ancestry. Drama requires prose and verse for songs. It is moreover well-known that the Hindus are very fond of verses and that verse-forms are used even in books on law, astronomy, etc.

1 Keith, The *Sanskrit Drama,* p. 18 ; Detailed objections against such overstraining of the Vedic hymns have been made by Keith (Ibid, p. 18 et seq.)

2 Z.D.M.G., XXXVII, 54 ff. ; XXXIX, 52 ff. ; G.G.A., 1909, p. 66 ff.: G.N., 1911, p. 441 ff. ; *Zur Geschichte der altindischen Prosa* (1917), p. 53 ff. ; *Das Mahābhārata,* p. 21 ff.

3 Keith has contradicted the theory in J.R.A.S., 1911, p. 981 ff. ; 1912, p. 429 ff; *Ṛgveda Brāhmaṇas,* p. 68 ff.

4 *Die indische Balladendichtung,* 1913 ; G.M. Miller, *The Popular Ballad,* 1905.

It should be noted in this connection that the epithet drama can be given only in such cases where players act for giving pleasure. Even if there are imitative elements in some Vedic rituals, their intention being the production of magical effects, they cannot be as such regarded as dramas. In the Vedic ritual of the *mahāvrata* there are certain operations symbolising the victory of the Aryans over the non-Aryans. Again, in certain ceremonies sex unions or approaches resembling sex union are used as symbols of fertility. But from this it may be hazardous to think that pantomimes or mimic plays existed among the people from which they crept into the Vedic ritulas. We have nowhere the word *naṭa* or *nāṭaka* in the Vedic literature. The term *śailūṣa* is of course used, but there is no proof that that term denoted an actor. It might have denoted quite easily a musician or a singer, though in later literature the term is almost always used to denote a *naṭa*.[1]

We cannot, therefore, agree with Hillebrandt and Konow that the cases referred to above are instances of ritual-dramas and that they are borrowed from popular pantomimic plays.[2]

But the hymns of the *Sāmaveda* were sung and we have many instances of dancing as forming parts of the Vedic ceremonies. Thus at the *mahāvrata*, the maidens used to dance round the fire as a charm for causing rain and at the marriage ceremony matrons whose husbands were living, used to dance as a charm in order to make the marriage happy. Again, when a dead man was burnt, mourners moved round the vase containing the ashes and dancers were present who danced in accompaniment of music.[3] Judging from these materials it is possible to hold that the atmosphere which could produce drama was already being

1 Use of the term *śailūṣa* may be found in V.S., XXX. 4 ; T.B., III. 4-2,

2 *Über die Anfänge des indischen Dramas*, Munich, 1914, p. 22 ; *Das indische Dramā* Berlin, 1920, p. 42 ff.

3 Caland, *Die altindischen Todten und Bestattungsgebräuche*, p. 138 ff.

formed in the Vedic society. It is perfectly legitimate to surmise that these songs and dances were associated with the pantomimic gestures and postures. A little addition of prose and verse with a story behind it transforms it into a crude form of drama. Thus, it is reasonable to hold that though there were no actual dramas in the Vedic period, the surrounding and environment for the development of the drama was already being formed. Keith says, however, that unless the hymns of the *Rgveda* present us with real drama which is most implausible, we have not the slightest evidence that the essential synthesis of elements and the development of plot, which constituted the drama, were made in the Vedic age. On the contrary, there is every reason to believe that it was through the use of epic recitations that the latent possibilities of drama were evoked and the literary form created. Oldenberg[1] admits the importance of the epic on the development of drama but Keith holds that but for epic recitation dramas could not have evolved. Keith further points out that the vast majority of the stanzas were not sung but were only recited.

Admitting the importance of epic recitation, the present writer is of opinion that the prevalence of songs and dances had much to contribute to the development of the drama. According to Bharata it is the song, the music and the dance as well as the imitative acting of the actors that constitute the chief difference between dramas and *kāvyas*. The *Daśa-rūpaka* defines drama or *nāṭya* as imitation of a situation (*avasthānukṛti*).

Keith thinks that the drama developed out of the recitation of the epic poems, but he does not seem to adduce any plausible argument in his favour. The view as he states appears only as a conjecture. He points out that all those places where the works *naṭa* and *nartaka* are used in the *Mahābhārata* and the *Rāmāyaṇa*, are such that we could easily take it in the sense of

1 *Die Literatur des alten Indien*, p. 241.

a mimic or a dancer.[1] It is only in the *Harivaṃśa,* written somewhere about the 2nd century A.D., that we hear of a drama made out of the story elements of the *Rāmāyaṇa.* He then refers to some references to a much later period when the epics were recited, and he refers to a picture in Sāncī, which may be dated before the Christian era, in which we find a representation of a group of *kathakas,* who were reciting in accompaniment with music and dance. He further thinks that the term *bhārata* is an appellation of a comedian in the later texts, attesting the connection of the rhapsodes with the growth of the drama.[2] Keith derives the *bhāṭs* or the professional reciters from the word *bhārata.*[3] He derives the term *kuśīlava* from Kuśa and Lava of the *Rāmāyaṇa.* Later on, by a sort of witticism, *kuśīlava* came to refer to the bad morals of the actors.[4]

Pāṇini in IV. 3.110, 111 refers to the *Naṭasūtra* of Śilālin and Kṛṣāśva. The reference is made with regard to the derivation of the words *śailālin* and *kṛśāśvin.* The *sūtras* are : *pārāśaryya-śilālibhyām* and *karmanda-kṛśāśvādiniḥ.* The words *śilālin* and *kṛśāśva* get respectively the suffixes *ṇinī* and *ini* to denote the *naṭas* of the Śilālin and Kṛśāśva schools, the forms being *śailālino naṭāḥ kṛśāśvino naṭāḥ.* In other cases, the adjectives would be *śailālam* and *kārśāśvam.* It implies that there were two kinds of *Naṭa-sūtra* attributed to Śilālin and Kṛśāśva. The adherents were called *śailālins* and *kṛśāśvins.* The difficulty here is about the meaning of the word *naṭa-sūtra.* Does *naṭa* mean a mere 'dancer' or a 'dramatic player' ? Pāṇini's date is fairly fixed as being the 4th or the 5th century

1 Hopkins,—*The Great Epic of India,* p. 55 ff. ; *Nāṭaka* in Mbh. II. II. 36 is considered as very late ; J.R.A.S. 1903, p. 571 ; see *Mahābhārata,* XII. 140, 21 ; also XIII, 33.12 ; see *Harivaṁśa,* II. 88 ff ; see *Rāmāyaṇa* II.67.15 ; also II.69.3 ; also II. I, 27. where the word *vyāmiśraka* is used to denote plays in mixed languages according to the commentator ; see also Hillebrandt. ZDMG., LXXII : 229 n 1 ; see also Keith—*The Sanskrit Drama,* p. 29.

2 Macdonell and Keith, *Vedic Index,* Vol. II, 94 ff.

3 See Keith, *The Sanskrit Drama,* p. 30.

4 See Konow, *Das indische Drama,* Berlin p. 9 ; Lévi, *Le Théâtre Indien,* Paris., 1890 , p. 51, On the nature of the rhapsodes, see Jacobi, *Das Rāmāyaṇa,* p, 62 ff, ; GGA, 1889, p, 877 ff, ; Hopkins, *The Great Epic of India,* p, 364,

B.C., and if *naṭa* means a 'dramatic actor' then we could be sure of the existence of dramas in Pāṇini's times. Patañjali, the author of the *Mahābhāṣya*, who lived probably in 150 B.C., refers in his commentary, to a poetical line referring to the killing of Kaṃsa by Vāsudeva as an event of the past (*jaghāna kaṃsaṃ kila vāsudevaḥ*).

Again, in explaining Pānini's *sutra*, *hetumati ca*, III. 1. 26., Patañjali raises in the *Bhāṣya*, the question as to how to justify the causative suffix *ṇic* in such expressions as he makes Kaṃsa killed or makes Bali bound when Kaṃsa and Bali were respectively killed and bound long ago. He justifies the usage in the following manner:—He says the *śaubhikas* (*i.e.*, the teachers teaching the actors how to imitate the killing of Kaṃsa) demonstrate through the actor imitating Kaṃsa how they are to behave as Kaṃsa and be killed. So they do with reference to Bali and these are demonstrated before the public eyes. Then again, in pictures also scenes may be painted in which strokes are aimed and shown as cutting Kaṃsa. In the case of the *granthikas* also, though there is only a book in the hand and the audience before, he so describes the events that they appear to people almost in their objective external forms. Sometimes, however, there is a mixture of acting as well as recitations. The *granthikas* sometimes divided themselves into a few parties, one posing themselves as belonging to the side of Kaṃsa and the other as belonging to the party of Kṛṣṇa and they painted themselves red and black. It should be noted that since the objective occurrence of the fight between Kaṃsa and Kṛṣṇa was a matter of mental imposition, it was possible to describe the events in the present, past and future and it appears that Patañjali actually quotes phrases from some dramatic narration that existed in his time describing the killing of the king Kaṃsa as present, past and future (*gaccha hanyate kaṃsaḥ, gaccha ghānisyate kaṃsaḥ, kiṃ gatena hataḥ kaṃsaḥ*).[1]

[1] *Mahābhāṣya* by Patañjali, III. 1.26.

Lüders and Keith seem to have misunderstood the situation by misinterpreting the meaning of the word *śaubhika* and the function of the *granthikas*. The *śaubhikas* did not before the eyes of the spectators actually carry out—naturally in appearance only—the killing of Kaṃsa and the binding of Bali; nor are the *śaubhikas* persons who explained to the audience shadow-pictures. The *śaubhikas* are the teachers who trained the actors in the matter of actual acting, or demonstrating how Kaṃsa is killed by Kṛṣṇa or Bali is fettered. This demonstration is a visible demonstration by superintending over the acting of their disciples. The *śaubhikas* are the *prayojaka-kartā* or the causative nominative, because they direct their disciples as to how they should actually show the killing of Kaṃsa before the public eye. Kaiyaṭa gives the meaning of the word *śaubhika* as—*kaṃsānukāriṇāṃ naṭānāṃ vyākhyānopādhyāyāḥ* ; *kaṃsānukārī naṭaḥ sāmājikaiḥ kaṃsabuddhyā parigṛhītaḥ kaṃso bhāṣye vivakṣitaḥ*. This means that the *śaubhikas* are the teachers for explaining to the *naṭas* how to imitate Kaṃsa, and it is the *naṭa* that imitates Kaṃsa and is regarded by the audience as Kaṃsa and it is such a Kaṃsa that has been referred to in the *Bhāṣya*. The *naṭa* that plays the part of Vāsudeva is made to imitate the actor, the real, Vāsudeva, in killing Kaṃsa. Thus, Nāgeśa says in his *Uddyota*, *tādṛśenaiva vāsudevena*.

In our view, there were two schools of dancing and acting, one of Śilālin and the other of Kṛśāśva. There were dramatic schools in which there were teachers who taught pupils the art of acting and dancing. These teachers were called *śaubhikas*. Dancing itself in tableau forms sometimes attained the function of dramatic performance through speechless gestures. The gestures, the movements of the limbs, the postures, the various positions of fingers or of standing and sitting,—all came within the art of dancing as is well-evident from the *Nāṭya-śāstra* and the *Viṣnu-dharmottara Purāna*.

We must say that *nāṭya* is defined in the *Daśarūpaka* as *avasthānukṛti* or the imitation of situations, which need not necessarily be vocal. Even a non-vocal pantomimic performance will be called a *nāṭya*. A *nāṭya* is called a *rūpaka* because of the imposition of the characters of heroes upon the actor. Sometimes a dance with a mere song expressing a particular sentiment, forms the minimum requirements of a drama. Thus in the *Mālavikāgnimitra,* Mālavikā in the 2nd Act first sings a song and then expresses the sentiment of the song through dancing or acting (*tato yathārasamabhinayati*). The *Parivrājikā* explains the symbolic aspect of the dance.[1]

We next come to the meaning of the word *granthika*. The word *granthika* is used in the *Bhāṣya* on Pāṇini I. 4.29, and III.1.26. The meaning of the word *granthika* in the *Bhāṣya,* III.1.26, is given by Kaiyaṭa as being *kathaka*. As regards the word *śabda-grantha-gaḍḍa* in the phrase *granthikeṣu kathaṃ yatra śabda-grantha-gaḍḍamātram lakṣyate,* the reading is *gaḍḍa* and not *gaḍu* as taken by Keith. At least, that is the reading that had been accepted by Nāgeśa and *gaḍḍa* means 'crowd of men' (*manuṣya-saṅghātaḥ*), as interpreted by Nāgeśa. It appears from Nāgesa's interpretation that these *granthikas* explained the whole story from the beginning to the end ; *e.g.*, in the case of Kaṃsa, they described Kamsa's birth, his attainment of prosperity and destruction and thereby they made the impression of Kaṃsa so vivid that they were almost felt to be objectively present before the audience. It appeared to the audience through the impressive description of the *granthikas* that the whole episode appeared as if it were objectively enacted before them or as if the real Kaṃsa and Vāsudeva were present before them. The text of the *Bhāṣya* that follows, is rather a little obscure, but it appears that sometimes it was a mixed one (*vyāmiśrāśca dṛśyante*), *i.e.*, the entertaining description of the *granthika* was supplemented by the actual acting of the people

1 ***aṅgairantar-nihita-vacanaiḥ sūcitaḥ samyagarthaḥ***
pāda-nyāso layamupagatas-tanmayatvaṁ raseṣu/
śākhāyonirmṛdurabhinayas-tadvikalpā-nuvṛttau
bhāvo bhāvaṁ tudati viṣayād rāga-bandhaḥ sa eva//

coloured black and red to denote respectively the party of Kaṃsa and the party of Kṛṣṇa. The interpretation given by Keith is as follows :—"They also, while relating the fortunes of their subjects from their birth to their death, make them real to the minds of their audience, for they divide themselves into two parties, one set adhering to Kṛṣṇa, and one to Kamsa, and they adopt different colours, the adherents of Kaṃsa black, and those of Kṛṣṇa red." Keith's reading of the texts also differs from ours. Keith's reading is *ātaśca sato vyāmiśra hi dṛśyante.* In our reading of the text there is a full-stop after *ātaśca satah* and in the next passage we have *ca* instead of *hi.* That this reading is correct, is apparent from Nāgeśa's interpretation. After *vyāmiśrāśca,* Nāgeśa says *ca hetau, i.e.,* the *ca* here gives the reason. The reason is that two parties are formed, one for Kaṃsa and the other for Kṛṣṇa and that they make their parties impressive by dyeing them in different colours black and red. The meaning that has been given here, would be corroborated by a reference to the commentary of Helārāja on the *Vākyapadīya* III.7.5, which has been quoted in Kaiyaṭa's commentary.

The next question is with regard to the place where these performances were held and the further question as to whether they were purely pantomimic or whether there were actual dialogues in them. Keith says that this question cannot be decided. But here I should refer our readers to Patañjali's *Bhāṣya* on Pāṇini, 1.4.29. The *Bhāṣya* runs as follows :— *ākhyāto'payoge/ upayoga iti kimartham/ naṭasya śṛṇoti, granthikasya śṛṇoti/ upayoga iti ucyamāne'pi atra prāpnoti/ cṣo'pi hi upayogaḥ/ ātaśca upayogo yadārambhakā raṅgaṃ gacchanti naṭasya śroṣyāmaḥ granthikasya śroṣyāma iti/*

Now, the phrase *naṭasya śṛnoti* means that one listens to what the *naṭa* says. People go to the *raṅga* or stage with the definite purpose of listening to the vocal performance of the *naṭas* and *granthikas.* This settles the question that there was a stage when the *naṭas* and the *granthikas* played and that their performance included vocal speeches. Further evidence is derived from the fact that Patañjali in his *Bhāṣya,* III.1.26, quotes specimens of prose utterances of these actors : *gaccha hanyate kaṃsaḥ, gaccha ghāniṣyate kaṃsaḥ, kiṃ gatena hataḥ kaṃsaḥ.*

We have therefore now the decisive evidence that by the 2nd century B.C. there were actually the stage or the *raṅga* where the *naṭas* imitated the actions of the legendary heroes and that their performances included prose speeches at least. If this is accepted, we may also infer that the *Naṭa-sūtras* of Śilālin and Kṛśāśva mentioned by Pāṇini must have been written at a time when the performance of *naṭas* was very popular and since there were *Naṭa-sūtras,* there must have been *śaubhikas* for teaching the dramatic art. We therefore conclude that dramas were probably in existence in the 5th or 6th century B.C.

We regret we are quite unable to agree with Prof. Keith's view regarding the origin of the Indian drama from any analogy of the vegetation ritual in which the outworn spirit of vegetation represented in Kaṃsa is destroyed. There is not only the *Kaṃsa-vadha* drama referred to by Patañjali but also the *Bali-vandhana.* Its analogy with the *mahāvrata* ceremony seems to us as entirely out of place verging on absurdity. Neither Kaṃsa is a Śūdra nor Kṛṣṇa is a Vaiśya. His statement that because victory lies with the Vaiśya and defeat with the Śūdra we have no sorrow in Sanskrit drama, seems to us to be rather wild. We also fail to understand how the dramas *Kaṃsa-vadha, Uru-bhaṅga* and *Bāla-carita* support this theory. We also fail to understand how the religious origin of the drama can be adduced from the character of the *vidūṣaka.* His statement "It would be absurd to ignore in this regard the dialogue between the Brahmin and the hetaera in the Mahāvrata where the exchange of coarse abuse is intended as a fertility charm," is itself absurd for two reasons ; first of all, the supposition that the coarse abuse is intended as a fertility charm, is itself a wild conjecture ; secondly, the *vidūṣaka* in the Sanskrit drama does but seldom indulge in coarse abuse. The name *vidūṣaka* suggests nothing. The name *vidūṣaka* for the Fool in Sanskrit plays may simply imply that he always encouraged the king in his inappropriate love and adventures.

we need not go in details into Prof. Keith's treatment of the subject, for much of it seems to us quite out of place in proving his theory of the religious origin of the Sanskrit drama. Great legends of the past always had their appeal on the Indian mind, but some of our oldest dramas have no religious significance, *e.g.*, the *Cārudatta* and the *Svapnavāsavadattā* of Bhāsa, *Mṛcchakaṭikā* of Śūdraka, the *Vikramorvaśī*, the *Mālavikāgnimitra* and the *Abhijñānaśakuntalā* of Kālidāsa. We are prepared to admit that sometimes dramas were played on the occasion of religious festivities, but it cannot be proved that the dramas were played only or mostly at the time of religious festivities. On the other hand, the references to the *Mahābhāsya* quoted above do not reveal in the least the religious origin of the drama. But one fact remains that the Indians always regarded the drama to have a great educative value in which people of all classes would join.

Professors Konow and Hillebrandt support the theory of the secular origin of the drama.[1] They believe that though Vedic ceremonies may have their share, yet a popular mime existed. The existence of *naṭas* or *nartakas* is proved from the evidence of the *Mahābhāṣya* and the *Rāmāyaṇa*. Hillebrandt further thinks that a comedy is a natural expression of man's primitive life of pleasure. The simplicity of the Indian stage, the use of Sanaskrit and the dialects of the classical drama. claimed as an evidence of the popular origin of the drama, the popular nature of the *vidūṣaka*, the beginning of the drama with the *sūtradhāra* and the *naṭī*, his wife, are all regarded as evidence for the secular origin of the Indian drama. Prof. Konow thinks that we have even now the model of the old Indian drama in the *yātrās* and similar performances. Pischel goes

[1] I.D., p. 42 ff. ; A.I.D., p. 22 ff.

in for the puppet play.[1] But nothing can be proved from the existence of the puppet-shows that they represent the origin of the Indian drama. Lüder's view again that the *śaubhikas* explained the tale of what is explained in pictures, is clearly impossible.[2] Lüders endeavoured to prove that the function of the *śaubhikas* was to explain the shadow-plays, and he thought that these, united with the art of the old *naṭas*, explained the origin of the Indian drama. Konow suggests that the word *rūpa* in Aśoka's Edict No. 4 refers to some shadow-play. The word *nepathya* meaning dress was termed into the word *nepathya* meaning dressing-room and it was supposed that the shadow-plays were explained from behind the curtain. Keith thinks that the early existence of the shadow drama as held by Pischel, cannot be proved. There are indeed examples of *chāyā-nāṭya,* as in the case of the *Dūtāṅgada* by Subhaṭa in the 13th century and the *Dharmābhyudaya* of Meghaprabhācārya.[3] But it forms rather a very small part of the Indian drama.

In any case, the evidence adduced does not seem to be sufficient to prove the secular origin of the drama or its origin from puppet-plays or shadow-plays.

Our own position in the matter is that secular pantomimic dances associated with songs were, in all probablity, held mostly on religious occasions and with the growth of religious legends these were associated with plots drawn from those legends. We believe that since long before Pāṇini the two terms *kṛśāśvin* and *śailālin* denote two different schools of dancing and since also the art of dancing as we find in Bharata and later traditional works such as the *nātya-sūtra* in *Viṣṇu-dharmottara-purāṇa,* various forms of gestures, postures, positions intended to express sentiments and to communicate them to others, included within it all the functions of a dramatic actor. The infiltration of legendary

[1] See *Mahābhārata* III. 30. 23 ; V. 39.1. We have references to the puppet devices in the *Kathā-sarit-sāgara* and the *Bāla-rāmāyaṇa* of Rāja-śekhara.

[2] See Hillebrant, Z.D.M.G., LXXII, p. 230 f. ; Winternitz, Z D.M.G., LXXIV, 120 f,

[3] Z.D.M.G., LXXV., 69.

plots or symbolic plots must have taken place from very early times ; it would be impossible to distinguish therein the religious and the secular motive, both having interpenetrated into each other, into the production of the device of these performances at the time of religious festivities.

We know also that at the time of Patañjali the *naṭas* played on the stage with their wives called the *naṭa-bhāryā* or *naṭī* and that these *nāṭīs* took the parts of the wives or the objects of love of other *naṭas* playing the roles of different characters in different dramas and that they declared their love with relevant characters in proper speeches. The *naṭas* also wore different kinds of false hair and bread and dyed themselves as the occasion required, and they were generally persons amenablr to sentimental appeal. They also sang songs, danced and acted different parts, which they were called upon to play.[1]

We have further evidence that the science of drama existed, as distinguished from dancing and music, and that the teachers who taught these subjects to the courtesans and other persons, were paid out of the public revenue and we have the name *nātya* there along with *nṛtta*—a fact which definitely proves the existence of *nāṭya* as an art encouraged and recognised by the Government, There were also arrangements for higher teaching for the production of expert teachers of these subjects.[2]

Our interpretation of the passage of the *Mahābhāṣya* reading the *granthikas* in III. 1. 26., *viz.*, that two kinds of

---

[1] *agāsīt naṭah—Mahābhāṣya*, II. 4. 77.
rasiko naṭaḥ—Ibid. V. 2. 95.

vyañjanāni punar-naṭa-bhāryāvad bhavanti tad yathā naṭānāṁ striyo raṅga-gatā yo yaḥ pṛcchati kasya yūyaṁ kasya yūyam-iti taṁ taṁ tava tavetyāhuḥ evaṁ vyañjanāny-api yasya yasyā' caḥ kāryamucyate taṁ taṁ bhajante ।

—*Ibid.* VI. 1.2.

sarvakeśī naṭaḥ—Ibid. II. 1.66.

[2] *gīta-vādya--pāṭhya-nṛtta-nāṭyā-kṣara-citra-vīṇā-veṇu-mṛdaṅga paracittajñāna gandha-mālya-saṁyūhana-sampādana-saṁvāhana vaiśika-kalā-jñānāni-gaṇikā-dāsī-raṅgo-pajīviniśca grāhayato rāja-maṇḍalād-ājīvaṁ kuryāt* । *gaṇikā-putran raṅgo-pajīvinaśca mukhyān niṣpā-dayeyuḥ sarva-tālāvacaraṇaṁca* । *Arthaśāstra*, Chap. 48.

—Gaṇikādhyakṣa, Artha-śāstra, II. 27.

demonstrations, one depending solely on the descriptive power of the *granthikas* and the other where the descriptive performance of the *granthikas* was supplemented by actors differently dyed, as distinguished from the interpretation of other scholars like Keith and Lüders, could be found to be irreproachable on two grounds : firstly, when we consider the meaning of the word *vyāmiśra* and secondly, when we take the eleborate interpretation on it as given by Helā-rāja to explain Bhartṛhari's *Kārikā* in the *Vākyapadīya* interpreting the same point.[1]

Moreover, that *nāṭya* existed in the time of Pāṇini, is evident from the fact that he himself derived the word in his Rule IV. 3. 129, *chandogaukthikayājñikabahvṛcanaṭāññyaḥ, i.e.*, the *nāṭya* is formed by the suffix *ñya* to the word *naṭa*. The suffix *ñya* is used in the sense of *dharma*, i. e., character and

1 In the *Mahābhāṣya* II. 2. 111. we have the passage '*vyāmiśrāśca dṛśyante.*' The *ca* is interpreted by Kaiyaṭa as meaning *hetu* or cause (*ca hetam*). In the reading given by Keith (*vyāmiśrā hi dṛśyante*) we have *hi* instead of *ca*. But *hi* also means *hetu* (*hi hetāvavadhārane—Amarakośa*). The meaning of the word *vyāmiśra* will be evident on a reference to Patañjali's own use of the same word in another context, in the *Bhāṣya* to Pāṇini, III. 2. 41.

adya hyo'bhukṣmahīti ? । *adya ca hyaśca abhukṣmahīti vyāmiśre luñeva yathā syāt* । The *laṅ* is prescribed in *anadyatana*, but when *adyatana* and *anadyatana* both go together as in referring to my eating to-day and yesterday, that is when the eating of to-day and yesterday are combined, we have *vyāmiśra*. In such a case we have *luṅ* only.

As regards our interpretation that in one case the *granthikas* themselves created the objective illusion of the appearance of a fight between Kaṁsa and Kṛṣṇa occurring as if before the eyes of the audience, we quote the following passage from Helā-rāja's commentary, together with Bhartṛhari's kārikā which gives also a philosophical ground for it :—

śabdopahitarūpāṁśca buddherviṣayatāṁ gatān ।
pratyakṣamiva kaṁsādin sādhanatvena manyate ।।

tatra granthikāḥ kathakāyata iti vṛttirūpeṇaiva kaṁsavadhādyācakṣate । *tatra ca prakṛtirūpasyābhāvāt kathaṁ prayojyoprayojakatvamitī paryanuyogaḥ* । *tatra parihāra uktaḥ* । *te'pi hi teṣāmutpattiprabhṛtyāvināśād buddhirvyācakṣāṇāḥ santo buddhiviṣayān-prakāśayantīti cirakālātītatvāt kaṁsādīnāṁ bahirasattvāt buddhigocaratayā sato vidyamānāṁstān prakāśaynti śabdenāvabhāsayanti* । *buddhipratibhāsyeva hyākāraḥ śabdārtho na vastvarthaḥ* । *tathā ca kathakaḥ śrotari kaṁsādyākārapratyayajananāt buddhivāsudevena buddhikaṁsaṁ ghātayatīti prayojakatvasamāropāt prayogopapattiḥ* । *tathā hi kathako'tiśabdasāmarthyopakṣayāt rūpaviśeṣān śrotrabuddhigocaramāpatitān savyāpārarūpān kaṁsādīn karmādisādhanatayā bhāṣyakāro manyata iti buddhyovasthānibandhanaḥ sādhanavyavahāraḥ siddhaḥ* ।

—Helārājā's commentary on *Vākyapadiya*, III. 7.5.

habit and also the *āmnāya* or the traditional Scriptures belonging to them. Thus, *nāṭya* means, according to Pāṇini, the character and behaviour by virtue of which a *naṭa* is so called and also the dramatic science or scripture, the *Nāṭya-śāstra*. Roth and Böhtlingk give the meaning of the word *nāṭya* as *tanz* (dance), *mimik* (mimic) *darstellung auf der bühne* (performance upon the stage), *schauspielerkunst* (the science or art of stage performance).

Again, the *Kāma-sutra* of Vātsyayana is placed in the 2nd century B.C. by Schmidt.[1] This work (I. 3. 16) refers to *gītam, vādyam, nṛtyam* and *nāṭakākhyāyikā-darśanam*. Here music, dancing, songs and witnessing the performance of *nāṭaka* and *ākhyāyikā* referring probably to the performance of *naṭas* and *granthikas*, are mentioned as edifying and instructive. He further mentions that on specified days the *Kuśīlavas* came from different temples and gave performance at the temple of Sarasvatī. Those performances were called by him *prekṣaṇakas*. The festivities mentioned in I. 4. 42, are mostly spring festivities or seasonal festivities or religious festivities. We have also here the names and descriptions of *pīṭhamarda, viṭa* and *viduṣakas*. It is thus not true that the *viduṣakas* are Fools who attended the courts of kings only. They are mere comedians, who made their livelihood by their witticisms and also by friendly advice. They were generally also well-versed in some art or other and were trusty. The *pīṭhamardas* were generally well-versed in fine arts and came generally from distant places and often made their bread by being instructors to the courtesans. They were generally poverty-stricken fellows having no wife or children. The *viṭas* were those who had a family and had many good qualities and who had spent all their riches in luxury and made their living through the courtesans and those who visited them. We have thus the evidence here that the *vidūṣaka, pīṭhamarda* and *viṭa* were real characters in social life in

1 *Beiträge zur Indischen Erotik*, 3rd Edition, Berlin, 1922, p.9.

the 2nd century B.C. and were not merely dramatic invention.

There is an excellent literature in modern European languages on Sanskrit dramas, which is well worth reading. There is, first of all, H. H. Wilson's *Select Specimens of the Theatre of the Hindus*, London, 1827 (Wilson's *Works*, Vols. 11 and 12); out of this English translation the German translation was made called *Theater der Hindus*, 2 volumes, Weimar, 1828, 1831; Sylvain Lévi, *Le Théatre Indien*, Paris, 1890; J. L. Klein, *Geschichte des Dramas*, 3 volumes, Leipzig, 1866; M. Schuyler, *A Bibliography of the Sanskrit Drama*, New York, 1906 (C. U. I. S., 3); R. Pischel, G.G.A., 1883, p. 1217ff.; 1891, p. 353 ff.; A. Barth, *Revue Critique*, 1892, p. 185 ff.; G. A. Grierson, *Indian Antiquary*, 23. p. 190 ff.; A. Hillebrandt, *Alt-Indien*, p. 150 ff., and *Über die Anfänge des indischen Dramas* (S. Bay. A., 1914, 4. Abh.); E. J. Rapson, in E.R.E., IV, 883 ff.; Winternitz, *Österr. Monatschrift für den Orient*, 41, 1915, 173 ff.; H. Lüders, *Die Śaubhikas, ein Beitrag zur Geschichte des indischen Dramas*, S.B.A., 1916, 698 ff., and other works.

Vāmana thinks that of all forms of poetry or literary creations, the dramatic form is the best, for it is like a picture, and like a picture it manifests things in their complete concreteness (Vāmana's *Kāvyālaṅkāra* 1.3.31). R. Gottschall, in his *Poetik* II, p. 184 (Breslau, 1870) says that the drama is the flower of poetry as the union of epic and lyric elements is the spontaneous demonstration of life towards actual development. So Bharata also gives drama the most prominent place.

It is probable that poetry in earlier times written in a balladic form, such as the *śatakas* or the *praśastis*, could hardly be regarded as having any dramatic fulfilment. Under the circumstances, it is difficult to imagine how ballads could have been transformed into dramatic poetry.

Winternitz refers to a letter written to him by Grierson, his collaborator, on the subject of Buddhist *ākhyānas* (dated the

9th and the 19th December, 1912), in which he draws attention to what he has written about the *Rājasthānī Kheyāls*, written in the Marwar dialect. These attractive folk-stories were clothed in the form of dialogues in verse or prose composition mixed with dialogues in verse. These were either recited by a person loudly or played upon the stage involving the introduction of a stage-manager. It had probably neither any scenery nor any division into Acts. From the literary point of view, these could be called ballads in the form of dramas. E. Schlagintweit in his *India in Wort und Bild*, II, p. 12, pictures the development of the Indian drama. K. Rāmavarmarāja writes in J. R. A. S., 1910, p. 637, about the manner in which even to-day dramas are acted in Mālābār by the so-called Cakkyars, in demonstrating Purānic stories with moral teachings and also the *prabandhas* and *campūs*. From the picture of these Mālābār Brahmins, the Cakkyars, the successors of the Puranic *sūtas*, one realises how even to-day the difference between the dramatic performance and the epic recitations between the parts of the mimic actor and the reciting *naṭa*, is bridged over. We here understand the difference between the Sanskrit expressions, *bhārata* and *kuśīlava* and also the *sūtradhāra*.

There is also the theory that the drama evolved from the manner in which the Vedic texts were chanted. On this point, see A. Hillebrandt, *Die Sonnwendfeste in Altiindien*, p. 43; also *Vedische Mythologie*. In post-Vedic times, there were festivities in honour of Indra in the rainy season and festivities throughout the year in honour of the gods, Kṛṣṇa, Rāma and Śiva. On this point, see Haraprasāda Śāstrī, J.A.S.B., N.S. 5, 1909, 351 ff., where he tries to trace the origin of the Indian drama to the festivity of Indradhvaja. See also Hopkins, *Epic Mythology*, *Grundriss*, III, 1B, p. 125 ff. In the last mentioned work Hopkins gives us a description of the festivity of raising the banner of Indra, which probably took place in the end of the month of September. Bloch in Z.D.M.G., 62, 1908, p. 655 and L. V. Schroeder, in *Mysterium und Mimus im*

Rigveda, 17 ff., think that a great part of the origin of the Indian drama has to be attributed to the Śaiva cult. On the doctrine of the influence of the Kṛṣṇa cult on the origin of Indian drama, see Winternitz's article on the Kṛṣṇa Cult and its Contribution to Indian Drama, Z.D.M.G., 74, 1920, 118 ff. On the conjecture of A. B. Keith on the subject, see, A. B. Keith, Z.D.M.G., 64, 1910, 534 ff. and J.R.A.S., 1912, 411 ff.

The cult of Kṛṣṇa was often associated with some mimic dances. Winternitz gives a reference to the *Viṣṇu-purāṇa*, V. 13, where the *Rāsa* of Kṛṣṇa with the Gopinīs is described. He implies thereby that some kind of folk-dance and mimic must have been associated with the representation in the religious festivities associated with these. K. Th. Preuss, in *Archive für Anthropologie*, 1904, p. 158 ff., refers to Mexican spring festivities as associated with mimic dance in ceremonial dramas. The shadow plays of Jāvā have also a religious character (See W. W. Skeat, *Malay Magic*, London, 1900, 503 ff. and H. Bohatta, in *Mitteilungen der Anthropolog. Ges. in Wien*, 1905, 278 ff.). About China, see W. Grube, *Geschichte der Chinesischen Literatur*, p. 362 ff. and 396. About Japan, see K. Florenz, *Geschichte der Japanischen Litteratur*. About the subject in general, see W. Wundt, *Völkerpsychologie*, III and L. V. Schroeder.

The origin of the Indian drama from dancing is well-imaginable from the names, *nāṭaka, naṭa* and *nāṭya*. *Naṭa* means a 'dancer', *nāṭya* means 'mimic' or 'the art of spectacular show' and *nāṭaka* means 'mimical show'. The word *naṭa* is a Prākṛt form of the Sanskrit root *nṛt*—'to dance'. This view of Winternitz is somewhat modified if we refer to the meaning of *nāṭaka* as given in the *Nāṭya darpaṇa*. There it is said that *nāṭaka* is so called because it makes the heart of the audience dance, and Abhinavagupta says that *nāṭaka* is so called because it softens or bends down the mind. Though recitation of mere stories may also make the hearts of the people dance, yet it is not so much as a play that is divided into Acts and enacted in association with music and dress, etc. (see *Nāṭya-darpaṇa,* G.O.S. p. 28). The meaning of *nṛtta* given in the *Bhāva-prakāśana,* G.O.S., p. 46, includes gestures and postures also particularly when associated with songs and music, whereas *nartana* means merely the 'movements of the limbs.'[1] The *Viṣṇudharmottara-purāṇa* regards painting as only a part of dancing—a fuller treatment of what is only statically shown in painting.

The mimic dance and the play consequential to it is an ingredient of the religious cults. The religious associations is also evident from the *nāndī.* The *nāndī* is only a remnant of a longer religious ceremony which formed the *pūrva-raṅga,* associated with music, recitation and dance, in honour of a particular God. The *Nāṭya-darpaṇa* says that the *nāndī* refers to all that is to be performed in the *pūrva-raṅga,* some of which were of local nature or useless or not compulsory and hence they are not separately defined (*Nāṭya-darpaṇa,* G.O.S., p. 193). *Bharata's Nāṭya-śāstra,* V. 113, prescribes an *ijyā* or sacrificial ceremonial of an auspicious nature, to be performed.

Winternitz says that this religious motive explains the reason why in India the legends of gods and of the Buddha was so much utilised in the composition of the *kāvya* and the dramas. In popular religious feasts and holy places only those dramas were played which had a religious content.[2]

1 *naṭa-karmaiva nāṭyaṁ syāditi nāṭya-vidāṁ matam* ।
karaṇairaṅgahāraiśca nirvṛttaṁ nṛttamucyate ॥
vṛttibhiḥ sahitaṁ gītaṁ tathā vādyādibhiryutam ।
nartanaṁ gātra-vikṣepamātramityucyate budhaiḥ ॥

2 On this point see the description of Bhavāis in Guzerat in H. H. Dhruva, in O. C. IX, London, 1. 305-307 the *yātrās* in Bengal (Nishikanta Chatterjee, *Indische Essays.* Zürich, 1883). We have also similar priestly performances in the Punjab (see R. C. Temple, *Legends of the Punjab* vol. I, p. viii). In the *Daśaharā* festivals the Rāma legend is played in places like Ferozepure, etc. (R. C. Temple, *Indian Antiquary,* 10, 1881, 289). So also in the festivites associated with *Kālī-pūja, Durgā-pūjā, Vāsantī-pūjā* and the *Holi,* the legends of gods are demonstrated before the people in dramatic forms (see F. Rosen, *Die Indarsabhā des Amānat. Neuindisches Singspiel.,* Leipzig, 1892).

Winternitz thus holds that as in the present time so in ancient times the religious ceremonies and festivities were associated with dramatic displays as is well evidenced by the names, *naṭa*, *kuśīlava* and *śailūṣa*.

The Theory of the Greek Origin of the Indian Drama

Some European scholars had held that the Indian drama had developed under the Greek influence. A. Weber had for the first time given expression to the supposition that the dramas played in the court of the Greek princes in Bactria, the Punjab and Guzrat, had inspired the origin of dramas in India.[1] E. Windisch has also sought to prove the influence of Greek drama on Indian drama.[2] Jacobi, Pischel, Schroeder and Lévi have long ago shown the weakness of the argument in favour of the Greek influence. There is hardly any proof that at that time any Greek drama was enacted in India. Chronologically also the influence of Greek dramas in the development of Indian dramas would not appear probable. The question assumed a new form in 1903, through the book of Hermann Reich, *Der Mimus*. Reich was writing a history of mimic. He traced it not only in the old classical Greek dramas but also all over the world and tried to prove that this mimic wandering from Greece also came to India. Reich tried to show the similarity of Greek mimic which Indian *prakaraṇa* and repeated mostly the arguments of Windisch. The point arose about the drop-scene. Neither the Indians nor the Greeks had any drop-scene in the modern

[1] *Ind. litteratur Geschichte*, Berlin 1876 p 224 also *Die Griechen in Indien* S. B. A., 1890, 920 f.

[2] *Der griechische Einfluss im indischen Drama,* in O.C.V., Berlin, 1882; Th. Bloch, a pupil of Windisch believed in 1904 (Z. D. M. G. 58, 455 f.) that in some hole in Central India a Greek theatre could be discovered. But the archaeologists have with very good grounds spoken against the possibility of discovering any Greek theatre; see J. Burgess, *Indian Antiquary*, 34, 1905, 197 ff.; C. Glanneau, *Revue Archéologique*, 1904, 142 f.; V. Golonbew, *Ostasiat. Zeitschrift*, 3, 1914-15, 253 ff. Even so, one would be disappointed to find any reference to the difference that exists between Bharata's *Nāṭya-śāstra* and the *Poetics* of Aristotle. (See *Beiträge zur altindischen Rasalehre*, Leipzig, 1913.)

sense of the term. The stage is separated from the ante-room; the drop-scene separated the back-room from the stage and this separated the *nepathya*. The Indian *nepathya* corresponded to the post-scenium of the Graeco-Roman Theatre. The drop-scene in Sanskrit is called *yavanikā*.[1]

Another agreement between the Greek mimic and the Indian drama is to be found in the admixture of prose and verse and the introduction of the folk-dialect. The Indian *sūtradhāra* corresponded to the chief mimic in the Graeco-Roman type and we have also the wife of the *sūtradhāra* as in Greece. As the common people went to see the mimic so also in old Greece disreputable people went to these places and the women mimics were courtesans there as well as in India. The mimic stage of Greece corresponded with that of India in its simplicity. The scenic apparatus was very little and simple and much depended on the imagination of the spectator or whatever could be expressed through gestures. Consequently, there is also a disorderly change of scenes without retrogression upon the unity of time and place.[2] There is some similarity also between the wit of the mimic and the *vidūṣaka*. The only difference between the two is that while *vidūṣaka* is a Brahmin the wit in Greek plays is either a slave or a peasant. Reich believed that the Roman mimic influenced by the Greek, spread over and influenced the mimic plays over the whole of Europe in the middle ages. It passed off from Italy to the court of Queen Elizabeth and from there had influenced the writings of Shakespeare and so he thinks that the agreement between Shakespearean and Indian dramas can be explained.[3]

1 The word *yavanikā* may be regarded to mean as coming from *yavanas* or the Persians. Pischel thought that the word *yavanikā* is only the sanskritising of the Prākṛt word *yavanikā* (G. G. A., 1891, 354). We do not come across the word in Bhāsa.

2 Bharata indeed says that one act should not contain events of more than a day, but the poets do not observe this rule. Often a number of acts is devoted to describe the event of a day and between one act and another many years may pass. (See A. V. W. Jackson, *Time and Analysis of Sanskrit Plays*, J. A.O. S., 1897, 341ff.; 1900, 88 ff.)

3 On this point, see Schroeder, I. L. C., 602 f; *Reden und Aufsätze*, p. 105; H. H. Wilson's Works, Vol. XI, p, xii; Reich, *Der Minus*, 880 ff.; Klein, *Geschichte*

If Reich's theory is correct, then the Indian dramatic writers were either directly influenced by the Greek mimic or the Indian plays were somehow influenced by the introduction of the mimic influence. Both may be possible.

But on the other hand, it is possible that the Indians had invented the dramatic art before the Greeks and that Indian comedians had gone about quite independently of each other and had, thus, influenced the Greek mimic and this also explains the correspondence betwen Greek mimics and Sanskrit plays and also that between Shakespearean plays and the Sanskrit drama.

Against the possibility of any foreign influence we may say that it is remakable that in Indian drama as we find it the characters are peculiarly of Indian national type. When Indian astronomy and Indian sculpture let themselves to be influenced by Greek ideas the matter can be detected very easily. But in the development of the Indian drama we find essentially the the Indian spirit and Indian life. As it now stands. the development of Indian drama seems to be quite independent of Greek influence.

Again, Reich holds that his theory of transmission of the mimic from Greece to the whole of the world only indirectly affects the case of India. He has not given any direct evidence of the influence of Greek drama on the Indian, The chronological possibility does not seem to decide in favour of the influence of the Greek drama on the earlier Indian dramas.[1]

des Dramas III, 87 ; A. V. W. Jackson, *American Journal of Philology*, 1898, 241 ff. ; W. A. Clouston, *Asiatic Quarterly Review*, 1890, p. 206.

Another point of agreement between Indian and old English plays, as stated by Winternitz (*History of Indian Literature*, Vol III, p. 177) is that the curtain had different colours—black in the case of serious plays, variegated in the case of comic ones, white in the case of erotic and red in the case of violent display as battle and wars. In old English plays also the curtain had different colours.

1 See Pischel, S. B. A., 1906, p. 502 ; G. G. A., 1891, p. 354 and D. L. Z., 1905, p. 541 ; see also his paper, *Die Heimat des Puppenspiels* (Halle, 1900), in which Pischel tries to prove that the Indian drama arose from puppet-play and had developed from it and that it is in the puppet-play that we find the origin of the comic figure of the *vidūṣaka*. The

The whole of the Vedas do not seem to give any secure proof for the existence of spectacular shows and the idea of literary dramas, though there may have existed in the East singers, mimic dances and dialogues. Pāṇini refers to the *Naṭa-sūtras* which must have been a book of instruction for the dramatic art such as Bharata's *Nāṭya-sūtra,* and which might have dealt with religious mimic dances.[1] In Patañjali's *Mahābhāṣya* and in the epics *Mahābhārata* and *Rāmāyaṇa* and in the text of the old Buddhistic literature, we hear much of recitations, singers and dance's and leaders of plays. But we do not know of any literary drama of these types.[2]

It is only first in the *Hari-vaṃśa* and in the Buddhist Sanskrit text of the 1st century A.D. that we get evidence of actual literary dramas. These dramas seemed to be too good to be excluded and the Buddhists, therefore, imported them in their literature. We have a great enlightenment of the dramatic literature in the 1st century B.C. and the 1st century A.D. This was also the time of much Greek influence in India

introduction of the *sūtradhāra* and the *sthāpaka* also points to the same direction (see Sankar P. Pandit, in his edition of *Vikramorvaśiya*, B.S.S., 1879, Notes p. 4 and O. C. IX, London 1, 313f. But the puppet-play and its fool had his home in India and so also had the fool of Greek Mimus to be lead out of Indian puppet play to be conceived to be drawn away. It was right that the whole construction of Pischel had not the advantage of drawing sympathetic attention of specialists, It had to be simply ignored and so also the theory of shadow-play (Pischel, S. B. A. 1906, 482 ff. and Lüders, S. B. A., 1916, 698 ff.)

1 Pāṇini, 4, 3, 110 ; see also *Osterr. Monatsschrift. Orient*, 41. 1915, 180 f.

2 On Patañjali see Winternitz, Z.D.M.G., 1920, 118 ff. In the whole of the *Mahābhārata* there is one passage in II. 11.36—

nāṭakā vividhāḥ kāvyāḥ kathā-khyāyika-kārikaḥ ।
tatra tiṣṭhanti te puṇyāḥ ye cānye guru-pā'akāḥ ॥

The verse, however, does not occur in the South Indian recensions (Winternitz, J.R.A.S., 1903, 571 ff.) In the *Rāmāyaṇa* II, 69.4, we have the verses

vādayanti tadā śāntiṁ lāsayantyapi cāpare ।
nāṭakānyapare smāhur hāsyāni vividhāni ca ॥
sa tair mahātmā bharataḥ sakhibhiḥ priyabodhibhiḥ ।
goṣṭhīhāsyāni kurvadbhir na prāhṛṣyata rāghavaḥ ॥

But it is difficult to understand how the appellation of *nāṭaka* can suit the context, and it was at this time that the Graeco-Buddhistic sculpture flourished.[1]

Śakas and the Sanskrit Drama

Lévi held the view that Sanskrit rose to the position of a literary language more or less from the time that we find the use of Sanskrit in the inscriptions. The earliest Sanskrit inscription is that of Rudradāman in A.D. 150, or the Uṣabhadāta's inscription of 124 A.D. This implies that the Sanskrit Drama flourished at the time of the Kṣatrapas who had their capital in Ujjayinī where so many Sanskrit writers of repute had flourished. The discovery of the dramatic fragments of Aśvaghoṣa definitely repudiates the view. The arguments brought in favour do not seem to be sufficiently serious to deserve any criticism.[2]

Buddhistic Dramas[3]

The first evidence of the existence of literary dramas in India has to be found in the Buddhistic Sanskrit literature. In the *Avadāna-śataka* there is a reference to a dancing girl Kuvalayā, who had attained the highest stage of holiness because she had the opportunity of showing honour to one of the earlier Buddhas in the Buddhistic drama (*nāṭaka*). The *Lalita-vistara* notes that Buddha had in his young days received instructions on

1 In one Buddhistic collection of dramatic fragments (Lüders, *Bruchstücke buddhistischer Dramen*) Buddha is introduced as appearing in his holy light but his halo of light has a Greek tinge in it as Foucher has shown. It may also be noted that the story of king Udayana has in it a motive of a Trojan War, as has already appeared in Bhāsa's dramas. The resemblance of the *Bhāṇas* to the Greek mimologies has been pointed out by Lindeneau. The present editor is unable to subscribe to the view of Winternitz and other scholars that the Udayana story has a Greek motive in it. The improbability of it would appear in our treatment of Guṇāḍhya. We also cannot subscribe to the view that the Indian drama had its first beginnings between 1st centura, B.C. to 1st century A.D. Our reasons will appear in our treatment of Kālidāsa and Bhāsa.

2 See Keith's *Sanskrit Drama.*

3 See Lévi, 319 ff. ; Winternitz, W.Z.K.M., 27, 1913, 39 f.

nāṭya.[1] There is also the story of Māra and Upagupta, from which dramatic elements can be restituted and elements of it can be drawn from Aśvaghoṣa's *Sūtrālaṅkāra.*[2]

In 1911, H. Lüders found in a bundle of palm-leaves in Turfan three pages in Central Asian dialect which has been deciphered as being a fragment of a drama of Aśvaghoṣa called the *Sāriputra-prakaraṇa* or *Śāradvatī-putraprakaraṇa.*[3] The pages belong to the last Act of the piece and relates the story of Śāriputra and his friend Maudgalyāyana as related in the Buddhist canon of Mahāpadma in the *Vinaya-piṭaka.* The small remnant does not lead us very far regarding the worth and the general scheme of the drama but we can only understand that the dramatist Aśvaghoṣa was not inferior to the Aśvaghoṣa the writer of *Kāvya.* It seems that the scheme is that of the classical drama.

But the palm-leaf bundle contained two dramas together, which from paleographic evidence appeared to be manuscripts written in the Kuṣān times and both these probably were written by Aśvaghoṣa. But the title page in the other drama is missing. It seems to be an allegorical drama in which *buddhi, dhṛti, kīrti,* are playing their parts as personages. Both these seem to belong to the 1st century A.D. We have here the Introduction to the Act, the Vidūṣaka, the mixture of prose and verse and also of Sanskrit and Prākṛt and Lūders has shown that the Prākṛt here used is older than that of the classical dramas.

After this first discovery, another bundle has been found in which there are two dramas in Tukhārian dialect on the life of Buddha. It shows the influence on Indian drama of the Chinese theatre.[4] In classical Sanskrit there is no Buddhistic drama.

1 In *Avadāna,* 75 (VIII. 51); *Lalita-vistara,* XII. In *Jātaka-mālā,* 27.4 there is an allusion to *rasa* as was demonstrated in a drama by a good player.

2 W.Z.K.M., 27; 40. Winternitz thinks that Aśvaghoṣa is the first Indian poet who was the author also of a drama. This statement is highly doubtful as would appear from our treatment of Kālidāsa and Bhāsa.

3 See S.B.A., 1911, p. 388 ff.

4 Lévi, J.A., 1911, p. 10, Vol. 17, p. 139.

The drama *Nāgānanda* of Harṣadeva cannot be regarded as being Buddhistic in character. We have got a Tibetan translation of the drama called the *Lokānanda* of Candragomin, the poet and the grammarian.

I-Tsing says that Mahāsattva Candradāsa, a learned man in Eastern India had composed a poetic song about the prince Viśvāntara, hitherto known as Sudāna, and people all sing and dance to it through five centuries in India.[1] In Burma also even to-day the story of *Vessantara-jātaka* is played on the stage. In the Tibetan monasteries also Buddhist dramas find their place.

Lyric Poetry

We have already referred to the reputation of the *Megha-dūta*, the earliest and the best lyric that the Sanskrit literature possesses. Manuscripts and commentaries diverge as regards the number of verses (from 110-120) and as regards their order. The commentator Mallinātha, who belonged probably to the 14th century, already regards some verses as *prakṣipta* or interpolated and also refers to some different readings.[2] Earlier than Mallinātha we have the commentator Dakṣiṇāvarta-nātha, and still earlier, Vallabha-deva.[3] The earliest form of text is what

[1] See Takakusu's *I-Tsing*, p. 164 Lévi (B. E. F. E. O., 1903, 41 ff.). For the date of Candragomin, see Liebich, *Das Datum Candragomin's und Kālidāsa's*, Breslau, 1903, p. 9 ff.

[2] A verse by Mallinatha occurs in the Vijayanagara inscription of the year 1533-34 (Fleet, in *Indian Antiquary*, 5, p. 20 note). Mallinātha quotes the *Vasanta-rajya*, which was written about 1400 A.D. (See Hultzsch *Prākṛta-rūpāvatāra*, edited, 1909, p. IV. Note). Whether the poet Mallinātha as cited in Ballāla's *Bhoja-prabandha*, 16th century, Nirṇayasāgara Press edition, verse No. 222 is identical with the commentator Mallinātha, cannot be determined.

[3] See E. Hultzsch's edition of Māgha's *Śiśupāla-vadha*, German translation. Here he agrees with Pandit Durgā-prasād and K. P. Parab (Kāvya-mālā series, Part I, page 101, Note), that the latter lived at the beginning of the 10th century in Kashmir as he is identical with that Vallabha-deva whose grandson Kaiyata wrote a commentary on Ānanda-vardhana's *Devī-śataka* in the year 977. Pāṭhak in his edition, p. xvi ff., raised serious objections to this identification and has given good reasons for regarding Vailabhadeva as being precedent to the year 1100 A.D. See J. Nobel, *Foundations of Indian Poetry*, p. 15 N; and A.B. Keith in BSS V, 1 1928, p. 31f. and S. K. De in J.R.A.S., 1927, p. 472N. and B.S.O.S. v 3, 1929, p. 503.

is found in the *Pārśvā-bhyudaya* by Jinadāsa, who wrote his *Samasyā-pūraṇa* poem in the 9th century. The text of the *Megha-dūta* is embodied in the *Pārśvā-bhyudaya*. According to this text the poem has 120 verses, whereas the *Vidyullatā* commentary, edited by R. V. Krishnamachariar, Śrīraṅgam 1909, has only 110, Vallabha-deva 111, and Mallinātha 115 verses.[1]

We have also referred, in our section on Kālidāsa, to the number of imitations that was made regarding the *Megha-dūta*.

We now come to the *Caurī-surata-pañcāśikā* or the 50 Verses of clandestine amours, that is said to have been written by Bilhaṇa, who was a Kasmiri poet and lived in the court of a South Indian prince. The story goes that Bilhaṇa was secretly attached to the daughter of the king. Being discovered, he was sentenced to death and at the place of execution he composed these fifty verses full of voluptuous love experiences, each verse beginning with the phrase *adyāpi tām.*[2] It is said that the king was so much delighted to hear these verses referring to his daughter Vidyā that he pardoned Bilhaṇa and allowed him to marry his daughter.[3] It is curious that there is

1 See J. Hertel, in G. G. A. 1912, 403 ff., who suggests that Kālidāsa's number was 108; see also for criticism of the text Macdonell, J.R.A.S., 1913, 176 ff. and Hari Chand's *Kālidāsa*, p. 238 ff.

2 The verses are also called the *Caura-pañcāśikā* or *Cora-pañcāśat*. It was sometimes supposed that the name of the author was Cora, but according to Bühler (Report 48 f. and *Vikramāṅka-deva-carita*, p. 24), there is hardly any doubt that Bilhaṇa was the author of the poem. The text of the Middle Indian recension has been edited by Bohlen, Berolini, 1833, and Haeberlin, 217 ff. In the South Indian recension, which has been edited and translated by Ariel (J.A., 1848), as well as in the edition which appeared in the Kāvyamālā series, Part 13, 1903, pp. 145-69, the 50 stanzas form only an insertion in the short epic poem *Bilhaṇa-carita* in which the legend of Bilhaṇa's love for the princess is told, though differently in each of the two editions. The Kashmir recension of the *Pañcāśikā* has been discussed with textual criticism, edited and translated by W. Solf, Kiel, 1886; see also Jacobi in *Literaturblatt für orientalische Philologie*, III, 63 ff. and Winternitz in *Osterr Monatsschrift für den Orient*, 12, 1886, 155 ff.

3 This story, so far as the name of the princess is concerned, is found in the opening verse of the *Caura-pañcāśikā*:

adyāpi tāṁ kanaka-campaka-dāma-gaurīm
phullā-ravinda-vadanāṁ-tanu-loma-rājīm
supto-tthitāṁ-madana-vihval-ālasā-ṅgīm
vidyāṁ pramāda-guṇitām-iva cintayāmi

another *khaṇḍa-kāvya* called the *Vidyā-sundara* which is a dialogue between a young princess and her lover. The lover persuaded the princess to allow him to spend the night with her. The princess told him that, if detected, he would be beheaded, but she ultimately agreed to his undaunted overtures. In the morning he was discovered and the king's people took him to the place of execution. When he was asked by them to pray to God at the last moment of his life, the lover, called Caura, was supposed to say as follows ; but nothing follows. The following portion suits very well with the *Caura-pañcāśikā* as an Epilogue. The two seem to be the two parts of the same story. The style and the language are closely similar Both are equally erotic and sexually inspired.[1] The

These verses are capable of being interpreted also as an adoration to the goddess Kālī. The word *Vidyā* at the beginning of the 4th line means, on the one hand *mahāvidyā* or the goddess Kālī and also refers to the name of the princess whom Bilhaṇa loved. The legend forms a part of the poem in the edition by Ariel and in the Kāvyamālā and is also told by the commentator. The work has a number of commentaries, such as by Gaṇapati, Maheśvara Paṇḍita, Rāma Tarkavāgīśa, Rādhākṛṣṇa, etc. In Ariel's edition the princess is called Yāminī-pūrṇa-tilakā, daughter of the Pāñcāla king Madanā-bhirāma. In the Kāvyamālā edition, on the other hand, she is called Śaśi-kalā, Candra-kalā or Candra-lekhā, who is a daughter of king Vīra-siṁha of Mahilā-pattana. So we have in the Kāvyamālā series the name of the *Caura-pañcāśikā* as *Candra-lekhā-śakti-Bilhaṇa-kāvya*. In a manuscript from Guzerat, the beloved is a Caurā (*i.e.*, Cauḍā or Cāpatkaṭā) princess. The commentator Gaṇapati regards this as a *khaṇḍa-kāvya* and thinks that a Brahmin Caura had a love intrigue with a princess, *i. e.*, the proper theme of the poem was the love between a thief and a princess.

[1] The last verse of the *Vidyā-sundara* is as follows :—

rājā tānapi sevkān suvasanā-laṅkāra-bhūṣī-kṛtān
kṛtvā ghnantu vipakṣakaṁ kharataraṁ khaḍgaṁ samānīyate |
nītvā taṁ bhavanād vahir-vilasitaṁ rājā-tmajaṁ sāhasaṁ
dṛṣṭvā saṁsmara devatām iti tadāpyevaṁ sa cauro'vadat ||

The Bengali poet Bhārata-candra in the 18th century united the *Vidyā-sundara* and the *Caura-pañcāśikā* and formed one connected story and so also did Rāmaprasāda. Sundara is a prince of Kañcī who goes to Burdwan and becomes attached to the daughter of the king of Burdwan. He used to send love epistles to her through symbols in flower-garlands and used to meet the princess through a tunnel, which he made between his house and that of the princess. Ultimately he was discovered and taken to the place of execution, where he sang hymns of adoration to the goddess Kālī. In Haeberlin's edition Sundara is mentioned as the author of the *Caura-pañcāśikā*. In MM. Haraprasād's *Catalogue*, VII, No. 5114, Caura is mentioned as the poet of the *Vidyā-sundara*. But in the *Vidyā-sundara* text of the *Caura-pañcāśikā* is indeed all uncertain. Winternitz says that of the fifty verses only five have come down in all recensions.[1]

We come now to the *Ārya-saptaśatī* written by Govardhana in the 11th century. He is contemporary of Jayadeva. As he himself boasts in V. 52, he adapted for the first time the style of poetry as love lyrics in Sanskrit which was previously current in Prākṛt only. He evidently modelled his work on Hāla's *Gāthā-saptaśatī*. Each of the verses is a separate love-scene as in Hāla's book. Grierson points out that the Hindī poet Bihārīlāl composed his *Sat'saī* in the Hindī language after his model and Paramānanda wrote his *Śṛṅgāra-saptaśatikā* modelling it on Bihārīlāl's *Sat'saī*.[2] The *Ārya-saptaśatī* is inferior in poetic excellence to Hāla's work.

Side by side with the love lyrics we have the religious hymns in the form of *Śatakas* or centuries, such as the *Caṇḍī-śataka* of Bāṇa.[3] There are 102 verses in the *sragdharā* metre. It is the adoration of Caṇḍī as the *Mahiṣa-mardinī*.

Another poem dedicated to the Sun, like the *Mayūra-śataka*, is the *Sāmba-pañcāśika*, also called the *Paramāditya-stotra* and the *Brahmāditya-stava*, attributed to Śāmba, son of Kṛṣṇa.[4]

We nowhere find the name of Sundara. We find there the names Kumāra and Caura. The Kashmir recension has two introductory verses, the second of which looks like the poet's farewell to life. In the Calcutta Kāvya-saṁgraha edition also, in the 49th verse, the poet says that the only escape from the sorrow of his separation can be impending death.

1 See S.N. Tadpatrikar in *Ann. Bh. Inst.*, 9, 1927-28, p. 18 ff. The *Bilhaṇa-pañcāśat-pratyuttara* or *Bhūpajā-jalpitam*, recording the wailings of the princess Śaśi-kalā, is an imitation by a poet Bhūvara, which runs as a continuation of Bilhaṇa's *Caura-pañcāśikā*.

2 See J.R.A.S., 1894, p. 110.

3 Edited in the Kāvya-mālā, Part 4, 1 ff., with commentary; see Bühler, *Indian Antiquary*, 1, 1872, 111 ff; translated into English by Quackenbos, *The Sanskrit Poems of Mayūra* together with the text and translation of Bāṇa's *Caṇḍī-śataka*, pp. 243-357.

4 Edited with a commentary of Kṣema-rāja, in the Kāvyamālā series, 13, 1889, with another commentary by Śāmbaśiva Śāstrī, TSS, No. 104, 1930; In the *Varāha-purāṇa*. 177, 40 ff. (Bibliotheca Indica edition, *Cf.* TSS. 104, Preface, p. 2) it is related that, guided by Kṛṣṇa, Śāmba went to worship the Sun in Mathurā. There is also a *Sāmbopa-purāṇa* dedicated to the Sun-cult.

We come next to the *Śiva-mahimnaḥ-stotra* by Puṣpa-danta, a Gandharva. The story goes that Puṣpa-danta used to steal flowers from a king's garden for worshpping Śiva. The gardeners left scattered about some flowers with which Śiva had been worshipped. The Gandharva unwittingly treaded over those flowers and lost his power of flying and was caught by the gardeners. He composed the verses in order to escape punishment from the king. The *Mahimnaḥ-stotra* is popular among the Hindus. It has got over 20 commentaries. It is difficult to say anything about the author of the *Stotra.*[1]

Of the other hymns attributed to Śaṅkara we have the *Bhavānyaṣṭaka* and the *Ānanda-laharī.*[2]

There is another *Ānanda-laharī,* also called *Saundarya-laharī,* a work of 103 verses of *śikhariṇī,* the last one being in the *vasanta-tilaka* metre. It is really a *stotra* not in the praise of Śiva but of Śakti. It is said that Śiva can only function

1 Mr. J. C. Ghosh in C.O.J., 1, 1934 ff. suggests that the author was the Jain Puppha-yanta who was formerly a Śaiva Brahmin, in the 10th century, but nothing can be made out merely from the similarity of names. Among its celebrated commentators, we have the names of Śrīdhara-svāmī, Vopadeva and Madhusūdana Sarasvatī. It has been translated by Avalon. There is a suggestion that Śaṅkarācārya wrote a commentary on it. See MM. Haraprasāda's *Cat.* VII. Nos. 5, 8, 3.—5606. A collection of 8 such hymns with English translation is included in S. Venkaṭaramanan's *Select Works of Śrī Śaṅkarā-cārya,* Madras. A considerable number of hymns in minor works of Śaṅkarācārya has been published in the *Works of Śaṅkarācārya,* Vol, IV, edited by Hari-raghunātha Bhāgabat, Poona 1925 and the *Bṛhat-stotra-ratnākara*.

2 The former has been translated by A. Hoefer, *Sanskrit-Lesebuch,* Berlin, 1894 ; see also *Ind. Gedichte,* II, 157, ff. The latter has been edited and translated into French by A. Troyer in J. A., 1841. The text has also been published in Haeberlin, 246 ff. It has been translated into English by Avalon, with commentary, 2nd edition, Madras, 1924. Other hymns to Devī have been edited in KM., Part IX, 1893, 114 ff., 140 ff ; Part XI, 1895, 1 ff ; the *Ambā-ṣṭaka* or *Eight Stanzas to the Mother,* with commentary, in KM., Part II, 1886, 154 ff ; the *Pañca-stavī* (*Five Hymns to Durgā* by unknown authors) in KM., Part III, pp. 9-31 Hymns addressed to Śiva and attributed to Śaṅkara have been edited in Haeberlin, 496 ff., and in KM., Part VI, 1890, 1 ff ; a hymn to Viṣṇu in KM., Part II, 1886, 1 ff. There are other works also which pass by the name of *Ananda-laharī,* such as the *Ananda-laharī-kāvya* by Gopāla-kavi, the *Ananda laharī-kāvya* by Abhinava-nārāyan-endra Sarasvatī. This *Ānanda-laharī-stotra* in twenty *śikhariṇī* verses was published in the *Bṛhat-stotra-ratnākara.*

through the potency of Śakti.[1] It has no less than 25 commentaries. Some of the most celebrated commentators are Appaya Dīkṣita, Kavirāja, Jagannātha Pañcānana and Śrīkaṇṭha Bhaṭṭa.

Later authors often assumed that Śaṅkara was a follower of the Śakti cult. The confusion may have occurred from the fact that a Tāntrik author Śaṅkara existed in Bengal in the 15th century.[2]

There is another work called *Ṣaṭpadī* which is a hymn to Viṣṇu-nārāyaṇa which is attributed to Śaṅkarācārya.[3] This work consists of seven *āryā* stanzas and contains good poetry. A *Śataślokī-gītā* is attributed to Rāmānuja.

There is another work called the *Pañcaśatī* or Five-Hundred Verses which was written by Mūka, contemporary of Śaṅkara. But in the Kāvyamālā series, wherein it was printed in 1888, Mūka is said to be a modern poet. But Kṛṣṇamācārya says that tradition would place him as a contemporary of Śaṅkara. He is said to have been dumb originally and is said to have got his speech from the Deity. Ānanda-vardhana wrote *Devī-śataka.*[4] It is composed of 100 verses and is replete with all sorts of *alaṅkāras.* Utpaladeva, the teacher of Abhinava-gupta, wrote in the beginning of the 10th century a book of twenty hymns to Śiva.[5] In the 14th century, Jagaddhara composed thirty-eight hymns in honour of Śiva called the *Stuti-kusumāñjali.*[6] Utpaladeva is said to have been the son of Udayākara and disciple of Somānanda. He

1 A verse from the *Saundarya-laharī* is quoted in Vallabha-deva's *Subhāṣitā-valī* as being by Śaṅkara.

2 See Śivaprasāda Bhaṭṭācārya's article in I.H.Q., 1, 1925. p. 349, Notes; see also MM. Haraprasāda's *Cat.* VII, 5, 6, 7, 9. where he says that the author of the *Maṇikarṇikā-ṣṭaka* is Gauḍīya Śaṅkarācārya. But in the Bengali edition of the *Maṇikarṇikā-ṣṭaka,* published in the Kāvya-saṁgraha, it is said to have been cemposed by Gaṅgādharā-kavi.

3 See *Minor Works of Śaṅkarācārya,* p. 366, see also S.G. Kanhere, B.S.O.S., IV., 1926, 301 ff.

4 Edited in the Kāvyamālā series, 1803, with the commentary of Kayyaṭa, written in A.D. 978 (Hultzsch, *Kālidāsa's Megha-dūta,* p. ix).

5 Edited with the commentary of Kṣema-rāja in Chowkhamba Sanskrit series Benares 1902.

6 Edited with commentary in the Kāvyamālā series, 1891.

lived in 930 A.D. and wrote the *Ajaḍa-pramātṛ-siddhi*, the *Iśvara-pratyabhijñā-sūtra-vimarṣiṇī*, the *Parameśa-stotrā-valī* and the *Spanda-pradīpikā*. The *Stotrā-valī* contains twenty hymns to God Śiva.

The *Mukunda-mālā*[1] by Kulaśekhara is worthy of notice. There were several Kerala kings of the name Kulaśekhara between the 9th and 12th centuries. In this connection, we must mention the name of Līlā-śuka or the Kṛṣṇa-līlā-śuka also called Bilva-maṅgala, whose *Kṛṣṇa-karṇā-mṛta* is sung along with the songs of Jayadeva, the poet of the *Gīta-govinda*.[2] The *Kṛṣṇa-karṇā-mṛta* or *Kṛṣṇa-līlā-mṛta* has about 7 or 8 commentaries.[3] It is said that the *Kṛṣṇa-karṇā-mṛta* was brought by Śrī-Caitanya (1485-1533 A.D.) from the South. The text, however, varies in the Southern and in the Bengal recensions. In the Southern text it consists of three sections, the number of verses in each varying from 102 to 112, while the Bengal text gives only the first section containing 112 verses. Bilva-maṅgala's

1 Edited in Haeberlin, 515 ff., 22 verses ; the Kāvyamālā edition contains 34 verses ; Barnett in his *Cat*, 521, refers to an edition with free paraphrase in Canarese and English translation edited by M. B. Srinivasa-Iyengar, Bangalore. 1907. A verse from it is found quoted in an inscription of Pagan, 13th century ; see Hultzsch, *Epigraphia Indica*, 7, 197. *Mukunda-mālā* has been quoted in the *Sāhitya Darpaṇa*; see Śivaprasāda Bhaṭṭācārya, I.H.Q., 1935, 350 ; K. L. Pisharoti, I. H. Q., 7, 1931, 319 ff. Hultzsch holds that the reputation of the poem is due to the fact that the author is the first of the Vaiṣṇava Perumāls, who actively patronised the Vaiṣṇava faith to check Buddhism and Jainism in Kerala. Pisharoti thinks that he belonged to the middle of the 8th century, while K. G. S. Iyer, in I. H. Q., 7, 644 ff., 651, 724 ff. and 731, places him in the 11th or the 12th century ; see Gaṇapati in TSS, 11, p. 4, and A.S. Rāmnātha Iyer, in J.R.A.S., 1925, 272.

2 The Śrīvāṇīvilās Press publishes an edition of it with the commentary of Pāpayallaya Sūri, Srirangam, with 3 *āśvāsas* (chapters), consisting of 107, 110 and 112 verses respectively. The Rādhāramaṇa Press, Murshidabad, Bengal, published it in 1916, with the commentary of Kṛṣṇadās Kavirāja. Dr. De maintains (*Ann. Bh. Inst.*, 16, 1935, 173 ff.) it with some justice that the original text consisted only of the first *āśvāsa* and that the other two chapters had been interpolated later on. Kṛṣṇadāsa Kavirāja utilises another shorter commentary by Caitanyadāsa (see De, *l. c.*, 1786 and I. H. Q., 10, 1934, p. 315). An edition with Bengali metrical exposition etc., Calcutta 1913, is mentioned by Barnett, *Cat.*, 548.

3 Some of the commentaries are : *Karṇānanda-Prakāśinī*, *Sāraṅga-raṅgadā*, *Kṛṣṇa-vallabhā* by Gopāla, by Pāpayallaya Sūri, by Vṛndāvana Dāsa. by Kṛṣṇadāsa Kavirāja, by Śaṅkara. The work should be distinguished from the *Kṛṣṇa-karṇāmṛta-mahārṇava* by Madhvācārya.

other works are the *Kṛṣṇa-bāla-caritra*, the *Kṛṣṇāhnika-kaumudī*, the *Govinda-stotra*, the *Bāla-kṛṣṇa-krīḍā*, the *Bilvamaṅgala-stotra*. It is difficult to ascertain the date of Bilva-maṅgala. The poetess Gaṅgā-devī in the 14th century in her *Mādhurī-vijaya* (I, 12) praises the Kṛṣṇāmṛta-kavi immediately after Daṇḍin and Bhavabhūti (Wariyar, I.H.Q., 1931, 334 ff.). It has been suggested that Līlā-śuka, who is a commentator of one of Śaṅkara's works, refers to Padmācārya as his teacher. In that case he could be a contemporary of Padmapāda and must have lived in the 9th century A.D. It has been suggested by others that Līlā-śuka was the name of the writer who wrote the grammatical commentary *Puruṣakāra* at the end of the 12th or the 13th century.[1] It has also been suggested that the author of the *Kṛṣṇa-karṇāmṛta* also wrote the *stotras*, *Abhinava-kaustubha-mālā* and *Dakṣiṇā-mūrti-stava*.[2]

The Kashmiri poet Loṣṭaka of the 12th and the 13th century, wrote a *Dīnā-krandana-stotra* in 54 *vasanta-tilaka* verses.[3] Another Kashmiri poet Jagaddhara, son of Ratnadhara, published in the 14th century a *Stuti-kusumāñjali* consisting of 38 hymns in praise of Śiva.[4]

A *Śikṣāṣṭaka* of 8 verses is attributed to Śrī Caitanya and hymns to Caitanya himself were written by Sārvabhauma Bhaṭṭācārya, whom Caitanya had converted[5]

Rūpa Gosvāmī wrote the *Dūta-kāvyas* to which reference has already been made. Sixty hymns to Kṛṣṇa are included in his *Stava-mālā*[6] about 1550 A. D. Rūpa Gosvāmī, brother of

1 See S. Paramesvara Iyer, as quoted by Wariyar. *l.c.*, p. 334, and Gaṇapati Śāstrī in TSS., 1, Introduction, p. 2 ff.

2 Edited in TSS, 1907, The *Laghu-stuti*, a hymn to the goddess Bhāratī of uncertain date, has been published in TSS, 1917.

3 Kāvyamālā. Part VI, p. 21 ff.

4 Edited with the commentary of Rājānaka-ratnakaṇṭha in the Kāvyamālā texts, 1891.

5 See S. K. De's *Padyāvalī*, p. 213 ff. and I.C., 1, 1934, 21 ff.

6 Edited with the commentary of Jīvadeva in Kāvyamālā, 1903. Jīvadeva is probably Jīva Gosvāmī. A collection also contains the *Mukunda-muktāvalī* of an anonymous writer, published in the Kāvyamālā, Part II, 1886 157 ff. The *India Office Cat.*, 1469, refers to Rūpa as the author of the commentary.

Sanātana and Vallabha, son of Kumāra and grandson of Mukunda, was a prolific writer in Sanskrit. He wrote no less that 32 works among which there are many *stotras*.[1]

In the middle of the 16th century Madhusūdana Sarasvatī, the celebrated Vedantist, wrote the *Ānanda-mandākinī*, adoration hymn to Kṛṣṇa.[2] Madhusūdana Sarasvatī wrote also other hymns, dramas, kāvyas, commentaries and philosophical works. He was a pupil of Viśveśvara Sarasvatī and Srīdhara Sarasvatī and a teacher of Puruṣottama Sarasvatī. He is supposed to have been a native of Eastern Bengal.[3]

In the middle of the 16th century, Sūrya-deva wrote his *Rāmakṛṣṇa-kāvya* which can be read straight forwards and backwards, yielding two different meanings, one relating to Rāma and the other relating to Kṛṣṇa It consists of 38 verses.[4]

A Kerala writer Nārāyaṇa-bhaṭṭa completed towards the end of the 16th century the *Nārāyaṇīya*, a *stotra* in adoration of Nārāyaṇa, which is also a *kāvya* dealing with the subject-matter of the *Bhāgavata-purāṇa*.[5]

1 *Ujjvala-nīlamaṇi*, *Utkalikā-vallarī*, *Uddhava-dūta*, *Upadeśāmṛta*, *Kārpaṇya-puñjikā*, *Gaṅgā-ṣṭaka*, *Govinda-virudāvalī*, *Gaurāṅga-sura-kalpataru*, *Caitanyā-ṣṭaka*, *Chando-ṣṭādaśaka*, *Dāna-keli-kaumudi*, *Nāṭaka-candrikā*, *Padyā-valī*, *Paramārtha-sandarbha*, *Prīti-sandarbha*, *Premendu-sāgara*, *Bhakti-rasāmṛta-sindhu*, *Mathurā-mahimā*, *Mukunda-muktā-ratnāvalī-stotra-ṭīkā*, *Yamunā-ṣṭaka*, *Rasāmṛta*, *Lalita-mādhava-nāṭaka*, *Vidagdha-mādhava-nāṭaka* (1549), *Vilāpa-kusumāñjali*, *Vraja-vilāstava*, *Śikṣā-daśaka*, *Saṁkṣepā-mṛta*, *Sādhana-paddhati*, *Stava-mālā*, *Haṁsadūta-kāvya*, *Harināmā-mṛta-vyākaraṇa*, *Harekṛṣṇa-mahāmantrārtha-nirūpaṇa*.

2 Edited in the *Pandit*, N.S , 1, 498 ff. and Kāvyamālā, Part II, 1886, 138 ff.

3 The following books are attributed to him : *Advaita-siddhi*, *Advaita-ratna-rakṣaṇa*, *Ātma-bodha-ṭīkā*, *Ānanda-mandākini*, *Ṛgveda-jaṭādya-ṣṭa-vikṛti-vivaraṇa*, *Kṛṣṇa-kutūhala nāṭaka*, *Prasthāna-bheda*, *Bhakti-sāmānya-nirūpaṇa*, *Bhagavadgītā-gūḍhārtha-dīpikā*, *Bhagavad-bhakti-rasāyana*, *Bhāgavata-purāṇādyaślokatraya-vyākhyā*. *Bhāgavata-purāṇa prathama-śloka-vyākhyā*, *Mahimnaḥ stotra-ṭīkā*. *Rājñāṁ pratibodhaḥ*, *Veda-stuti-ṭīkā* *Vedānta-kalpa-latikā*, *Śāṇḍilya-sūtra-ṭīkā*, *Śāstra-siddhānta-leśa-ṭīkā*, *Saṁkṣepa-śārīraka-sāra-saṁgraha*, *Sarvavidyā siddhānta-varṇana*, *Siddhānta-tattva-vindu*, *Hari-līlāvyākhyā*.

4 Edited in Haeberlin, 463 ff, and Kāvyamālā, Part II, 1895, 147 ff.

5 Edited with the commentary of Gaṇapati Śāstrī in TSS, 1912. On his life and works see Pisharoti, in I.H.Q., 1933, 22ff. He is very famous in the Kerala country and there his *stotras* are daily read like the *Bhāgavata* by pious prrsons.

In the 17th century, Rāmabhadra Dīkṣita wrote various hymns in *kāvya* style in which he sang the glory of Rāma's arrows in the *Rāma-cāpa-stava*, the *Rāma-vāṇa-stava* and also a *Varṇamālā-stotra* which was a simple hymn in the alphabetical order.[1] In the same century Jagannātha Paṇḍita wrote his *Lakṣmī-laharī*,[2] *Gaṅgā-laharī* also called the *Pīyūṣa-laharī*[3] and he also wrote the *Sudhā-laharī*.[4]

Nīlakaṇṭha Dīkṣita, a teacher of Rāmabhadra, wrote a hymn called the *Ānanda-sāgara-stava*.[5]

Lakṣmaṇācārya wrote a hymn in 50 verses called the *Caṇḍī-kuca-pañcāśikā*, though it actually contains 83 verses.[6] Another semi-religious and semi-erotic poem was written by Śivadāsa called the *Bhikṣāṭana-kāvya*. It describes the feelings and actions of the female devotees of Śiva when they go about as religious mendicants.[7] The author is quoted in many of the anthologies.[8] Among the erotico-religious lyrics, the most famous is the *Gīta-govinda* by Jayadeva, the court-poet of Lakṣmaṇasena and son of Bhoja-deva of Kendubilva. The book has not only been famous in India for its melody but it

1 The Kāvyamālā, 1894, 1897, 1903. Rāmabhadra was a pupil of Nīlakaṇṭha and was also a dramatist. He is supposed to have written a commentary on the *Paribhāṣā-vṛtti* of Sīradeva.

2 Edited in Kāvyamālā 1896, 104 ff.

3 Jagannātha is said to have married a Mahammadan woman and was outcasted. At one time, sitting with his wife on the high bank of the Ganges, he was composing the verses of the *Gaṅgā-laharī*. With the composition of each verse the Ganges was rising up and with the composition of the 52nd and the last verse the Ganges rose higher and higher until at last is reached him and his wife and washed away their sins. They were drowned and were never seen again. The *Gaṅgā-laharī* is, however, famous all over India. See Vaidya's Introduction to his edition of the *Bhāminī-vilāsa*. Hymns to Gaṅgā are also ascribed to Vālmīki, Kālidāsa and Śaṅkara. The *Amṛta-laharī* is a hymn to the Jamunā,—Kāvyamālā, Part I, p 99 ff; the *Karuṇā-laharī*, edited in Kāvyamālā, Part II, p. 55 ff, sings of the misery of human existence.

4 Edited in the Kāvyamālā, Part I, 16 ff.

5 Kāvyamālā, Part XI, 1895, 76 ff.

6 Edited in the Kāvyamālā, Part IX, 1893, p. 80 ff.

7 Aufrecht in Z.D.M. G., 27, 12.

8 Eggeling *India Office Cal.*, p. 1448 ff.

has also attained great celebrity amongst the European writers.[1] There are many legends regarding Jayadeva. Some of these are recorded in the *Bhakta-māla*.[2] Jayadeva is said to have been an ascetic in young life and married, later on, Padmāvatī. The *Gīta-govinda* describes in melodious verses, which can be sung, the amours of Kṛṣṇa and Rādhā. Here and there benedictions are also inserted and in the concluding verse of each song the name of the poet is given. The *Gita-govinda* has no less than 30 commentaries.[3]

1 Editions: *Gīta-govinda, Jayadevae poetae Indici drama lyricum. Textum...... recognovit............interpretationem latinam adjecit*, C. Lassen, Bonnae ad Rh. 1836. The *Gīta-govinda* of Jayadeva with the commentaries *Rasika-priyā* of King Kumbua and *Rasa-mañjarī* of MM. Śaṅkara Miśra. Ed. by M. R. Telang and W. L. S. Paṇśikar, 3rd Ed. Bombay, 1910, NSP. An English translation by W. Jones already appeared in the year 1807 in the *Asiatic Researches*, 3, 184 ff. The last-named gave rise to the German rendering by F. H. v. Dalberg (Erfurt, 1802), F. Majer (in *Asiat. Magazin*, II, 294 ff.) and A. W. Riemenschneider (Halle, 1818). A German version by F. Rückert (first made after a Calcutta print in 1829, and then remodelled according to Lassen's edition) appeared in the *Zeitschrift für die Kunde des Morgenlandes*, 1, Göttingen 1837, p. 128 ff. (with grammatical notes, p. 286 ff.), also in *Rückert Nachlese*, I, 346 ff. in H. V. Glasenapp, *Indische Liebeslyrik*, pp. 114-175, also in *Inselbucheri*, No. 303. Translated into English by Edwin Arnold, London, 1875, into French, by H. Foucher, Paris, 1850, and by G. Courtillier (*avec une preface de S. Lévi*, Paris, 1904), into Dutch by B. Faddegon, Santpoort 1932. On the numerous commentaries on the *Gīta-govinda, Ind. Off. Cat.*, VII, p. 1454 ff., MM. Haraprasada *Cat.*, VII, Nos. 5159-5170. See Pischel, HL. p. 19 ff; Keith, HSL, 190 ff; S. K. De, *Treatment of Love in Sanskrit Literature*, p. 56 ff.

2 See Wilson's works 1, 65 ff. M. Garcin de Tassy, *Histoire de la Litteratur Hindone et Hindoustanie*, 2nd Edition Paris, 1870, II, 69 ff; Trumpp in S Bay A, 1879, 1, I, 6 ff; Macauliffe, *The Sikh Religion*, Oxford, 1909, V, 4 ff; M. Chakravarty in JASB, N. S. 2, 1906, 163 ff. Legend from the Sanskrit *Bhakta-māla* by Candradatta).

Rückert and Edwin Arnold arbitrarily omitted the religious accessories and thus gave a wrong perspective of the poems. The Indian editions and the French translation by Courtillier give the proper idea of the poem.

3 These commentaries are by: Kamalākara (*Ratnamālā*), Kumbhakarṇa-mahendra (*Rasika-priyā*), Udayanācārya (*Bhāva-vibhāvinī*), by Kṛṣṇa-datta, Kṛṣṇa-dāsa, Gopāla (*Artha-ratnāvali*), Nārāyaṇa-bhaṭṭa (*Pada-dyotinī*), Caitanya-dāsa, Nārāyaṇa-dāsa (*Sarvāṅga-sundarī*), Pītāmbara, Bhagavad-dāsa (*Rasa-kadamba-kallolinī*), Bhāvā-cārya, Mānāṅka, Rāma-tāraṇa (*Mādhurī*), Rāmadatta, Rūpadeva, (*Sānanda-govinda*), Lakṣmaṇa-bhaṭṭa, Lakṣmaṇa Sūri (*Śruti-rañjinī*), Banamālī Bhaṭṭa, Viṭṭhala-dikṣita (*Gīta-govinda-prathamāṣṭapadī-vivṛti*), Viśveśvara-bhaṭṭa *Śruti-rañjinī*), Śaṅkara-miśra (*Rasa-mañjari*), Śāli-nātha, Śeṣaratnākara (*Sāhitya-ratnākara*), Śrīkānta-miśra (*Pada-bhāvārtha-candrikā*), Śrīharṣa, Hṛdayābharaṇa (*Gīta-govinda-tilakottama*), *Bāla-bodhinī* and *Vacana-mālikā*.

The poem has been designated as a lyrical drama by Lassen and Schroeder and sometimes as a refined *yātrā*. But since the poet divided it into cantos he intended it to be treated as a *kāvya*. The *Gīta-govinda* is actually sung in many of the temples of Viṣṇu by the temple girls in accompaniment with dancing. Though the poem has an erotic form particularly to lay readers, to the devotees of Hari they do not excite any sex passion or idea but fill their minds with the splendour of the divine amour between Rādhā and Kṛṣṇa. It is not so much an expression of the longing of the human soul symbolised in Rādhā and God symbolised in Kṛṣṇa, but to a real Vaiṣṇava it appears as the delineation of the transcendental amours of Rādhā and Kṛṣṇa into which the devotee enters through religious sympathy and devotion. Goethe admired the poem even through the imperfect translation of Jones. Goethe had even expressed the intention to translate the poem himself.[1] Winternitz makes the following remark about the *Gīta-govinda* in the *History of Indian Literature,* Vol. III : "At the first glance it might seem as if, in the love lyric of the Indians in contrast to the love song of other nations, the sensual element outweighed all else. It is true that it is very prominent in Indian love songs, often all too prominent for the Western taste—beautiful women are crushed by the the weight of their breasts, their hips resembled elephants' trunks, lövers tear garments from the bodies of their beloved in their passion, and there is often mentioned biting and scratching, but these lovers, both men and women, also pine away with longing and die for love. It is also true that the Indian lyric being a branch of the ornate court poetry attaches too much importance to form for Western taste and that very frequently it is nothing more than a witty sport. And yet not infrequently we find true and deep sentiment and inward feeling in the erotic as well as in the religious lyric. Moreover, a deep feeling for Nature is genuine

1 *Goethes Werke,* **Jubiläumsausgabe,** Vol. 37, p. 210 ff. ; *Brief-wechsel zwischen Schiller und Goethe,* II, pp. 303, 309.

and unaffected in the Indian lyric as in Indian poetry in general." Thus, Goldstücker also said : "Deepest feeling for Nature has at all times been a characteristic trait of the Indian mind."[1]

The Indian *stotra* literature is indeed very large and it is impossible to give any complete idea of its extent and the hold that it had upon the religious life of the Hindus. Most religious persons of education would probably compose a *stotra* for himself and would recite other well-known *stotras* in the morning, after bath and while taking bath, and at the time of religious prayers in the morning, mid-day and evening. It forms a daily routine of the religiously-minded Hindus. The various Manuscript Libraries in India contain many manuscripts of *stotras*. The Tanjore Manuscript Library alone contains 204 *stotra* works and some thousands of them would be available in the various Manuscript Libraries of India.

Amaruśataka

The poet Amaru, the author of this collection, the exact number of verses of which is indeed uncertain, is also called Amarū and Amaruka. The collection has got a number of commentaries such as, *Amaru-darpaṇa, Rasika-sañjīvanī* by Arjunavarman, *Bhāva-cintāmaṇi* by Caturbhuja Miśra and also by Kokasambhava, Nandalāla, Ravicandra, Rāmarudra, Vemabhūpāla, Śaṅkarācārya, Hariharabhaṭṭa and by Jñānānanda Kalādharasena. The last commentator explains the poems in a double sense, *viz.*, from the side of love and of quietism. Arjunavarman's commentary has been published in the Kāvyamālā series, which was probably written between 1215 and 1218 A.D. The reputation of *Amaruśataka* is well evident from the traditional saying that each verse of Amaru is equal in value to 100 good works *ekam-evā-maroḥ ślokaḥ sat-prabandha-śatāya ca.*

[1] ***Allgemeine Betrachtungen über das indische Naturgefühl*** **in Alex. V. Humboldt, Kosmos, II. 115 ff.**

Though Ānandavardhana first refers to *Amaru-śataka* about 850 A.D. and Vāmana refers to Amaru's slokas, none of them mention his name, and as the work varies largely from recension to recension, it is very difficult to locate Amaru's date, as Dr. De has pointed out in the body of the text ; and there is no wonder that ślokas written by other persons had entered into the collection. We know nothing of his life. There is a traditional story that when Śaṅkara, the philosopher, was defeated in debate for his absence of knowledge in erotics, he entered the dead body of king Amaru and in that body he learnt everything about erotics and wrote the verses which pass by the name of *Amaru-śataka.*

Ravicandra, author of the Kāmadā commentary, thought that it had a double meaning, an erotic and a religious one.

It should be noted that wherever we find Śatakas like *Śṛṅgāra-śatakà, Amaru-śataka* and the like the number may be 100, less or more, the word "hundred" being used in the sense of 'many'.

Friedrich Rückert has translated 38 verses of Amaru. Schroeder has also translated some selected poems of Amaru in *Amaru-Mangoblūten,* p. 77 ff. and Hertel in *Indische Gedichte* and Hans Lindach under the pseudonym Hermann Weller, in *Im Lande der Nymphāen* has given a picture of amorous life from Amaru, 1908. The atmosphere created by Bohtlingk, in *Indischen Sprüchen,* seems also to smell of Amaru. Schroeder has given a beautiful description of Amaru's verses in *Reden und Aufsätze,* 1913, 158 ff.

Assuming that the verses referred to by Ānandavardhana are genuine verses of Amaru, we may suppose that Amaru had attained celebrity by the 8th century A.D.

BHARTṚHARI

If we can assume that the text of the *Śṛṅgāra-śātaka* as published in the Kāvya-saṃgraha series belongs to Bhartṛhari it would not be injudicious to think that the *Vairāgya-śataka* might in all probability also belong to Bhartṛhari. At least there need not be any objection on the score that the person writing on *Śṛṅgāra* could not be expected to write on *Vairāgya* as well. In the 99th verse of *Śṛṅgāra-śataka* of the Kāvya-saṃgraha series Bhartṛhari says : "When the ignorance produced by the movement of the darkness of sex-desire prevailed, the whole world was full of women for me. Now that with the effective collyrium of discrimination our eyes have attained their proper sight, I find the whole world full of Brahman." In verse 19 and 20 also he thinks that there are two alternatives for the male, either to be an ascetic in the Himalayas or to be given to the charms of women—a fact which shows that his mind sometimes oscillated between the two poles. In verse 44 again, the poet feels and refers to the cloyment of amorous indulgence. Again, in 46, the poet refers to the two alternatives, either enjoyment or taking to an ascetic's life (*yauvanaṃ vā vanaṃ vā*). He finds again, in 47, that women are extremely attractive and charming to him, yet they are the cause of all sorrow. In verses 73-92 he expressly manifests his disinclination towards women. In verses 94 *et seq.*, he abuses those women who are trying to attract him though he had already made up his mind to turn an ascetic. Moreover, verse 15 of the *Vairāgya-śataka* reminds one of verse 78 of the *Śṛṅgāra-śataka.* In verse 42 *et.seq.*, even in spite of his disinclination to worldly joys, amours with women are still considered by him as having a value worthy of this life.

It seems however doubtful whether the *Nīti-śataka* is actually the work of Bhartṛhari, the author of the *Śṛṅgāra* and the *Vairāgya-śataka*. The tone seems to be entirely different and the style is also different. There are a few verses also in the edition published in the Kāvya-saṃgraha series which may be traced to the *Pañca-tantra*. But the name Bhartṛhari is not associated with any of the *Śatakas* in the verses. It is only in conclusion of the verses that the name of Bhartṛhari occurs and not in the body of the book.

We know that the grammarian Bhartṛhari wrote a commentary on Patañjali's *Mahābhāṣya* and also a philosophy of grammar called the *Vākya-padīya*. The Chinese pilgrim I-Tsing refers to a learned Bhartṛhari who was a true supporter of Buddhism and was well-known throughout India and died forty years before I-Tsing came. I-Tsing wrote in 691, so this Bhartṛhari must have died in 651. I-Tsing does not say anything about the identity of the grammarian and writer of the *Vākya-padīya*. But he tells us a remarkable story about him ; he says that this Bhartṛhari seven times became an ascetic and seven times became a householder. I-Tsing also refers to a verse in which Bhartṛhari says that he is unable to cut asunder the bonds of the world. Max Müller has on this ground identified the grammarian and the poet. But certainly we cannot arrive at such a conclusion from the statement of I-Tsing. It is also surprising that though we have the name Bhartṛhari we should know nothing of the Bhartṛhari of whom reference has been made by I-Tsing. Bhartṛhari of the *Śatakas* is not a Buddhist but a Saiva in the Vedantist sense. It is possible to recognise Bhartṛhari as being first a poet then a saint of the Śaiva type but it requires a long stretch of imagination to regard him as having turned a Buddhist.[1]

I-Tsing says that Patañjali the grammarian had written a grammatical work called *Cūrṇi* in which he analysed the *sūtras* of Pāṇini and illustrated the *vṛtti* clearing up many difficulties. We know that the name of the *Mahābhāṣya* is *Cūrṇī* and it is by this name that Indurāja quotes the *Mahābhāṣya* in his commentary on *Udbhaṭālaṃkāra*. Then I-Tsing speaks of the *Bhartṛhari-śāstra* as the commentary on the *Cūrṇī*. He says that in this work Bhartṛhari deals with the principles of human life and the grammatical science and also relates the reasons of the rise and decline of many families. The author was intimately

K. B. Pathak in J.B.R.A.S., 1893, 341 ff., thinks that the grammarian Bhartṛhari was in all probability a Buddhist. In such a case of course the writer of the *Śatakas* will be different from the grammarian.

acquainted with the doctrine of sole knowledge (*Vidyāmātra*) and had skilfully discussed about the *hetu* and *udāharaṇa*. This scholar was famous throughout the five parts of India and his excellence was known everywhere. He believed deeply in the three jewels and diligently meditated on the two-fold nothingness (that of *ātman* and *dharma*). Having desired to embrace the excellent law, he became a homeless priest, but overcome by worldly desires he returned to the laity. He became seven times a priest and seven times returned to the laity. Unless one believes in the truth of cause and effect one cannot act strenuously. Bhatṛhari is said to have written a verse of selfreproach to the following effect : "Through the enticement of the world I return to the lady, being free from secular pleasures, again I wear the priestly cloak. How do these two impulses play with me as a child !" I-Tsing further says : "It is forty years since his death (A.D. 651-652)."

According to I-Tsing, Bhartṛhari is supposed to have written another work called the *Vākya-padīya*. It is supposed to be a book by Bhartṛhari on the inference supported by the authority of the sacred teaching and on inductive argument.

Now, if we are to believe in the testimony of I-Tsing, which is extremely definite with regard to Bhartṛhari the author of the *Vākya-padīya* and if we accept the story he relates about Bhartṛhari, it is not unlikely that the Bhartṛhari of the *Śṛṅgāra* and the *Vairāgya-Śatakas* who reveals in him to master passions, which are extremely opposite to each other, *viz*., passion for women and passion for being a recluse, is identical with the writer of the *Vākya-padīya*. Bhartṛhari's work on the *Mahābhāṣya* is now lost to us. We are therefore unable at the present moment to say anything about the truth or error of I-Tsing's remark about this work. But if we ignore the testimony of I-Tsing we should be most unwilling to believe that the Bhartṛhari of the *Śatakas* is identical with the Bhartṛhari of the *Vākya-padīya*. Not only the *Śatakas* do not seem to contain any similarity with *Vākya-padīya* so far as style, language or manner of speech are concerned, but there is not the slightest sign in the *śatakas* which may lead us to think that the writer was an expert in grammar. The monism of the *Vākya-padīya* does not seem to be in any way a Śaiva doctrine. Far less could we trace anything of Buddhism either in the writer of the *śatakas* or in the writer of the *Vākya-padīya.* They on the other hand seem to be quite antagonistic to Buddhism. If the testimony of I-Tsing is to be believed then we have to assume that Bhartṛhari lived in the middle of the 7th century and though I-Tsing does not say that Bhartṛhari was a poet, it would not be very far wrong to suppose that the Bhartṛhari of the *śatakas* is identical with the Bhartṛhari of the *Vākya-padīya.*

GNOMIC POETRY

Some moral stanzas are found in *ṚV.* and in fairly large numbers in the *Aitareya Brāhmaṇa,* the *Upaniṣads* and the *Mahābhārata. Dhammapada* and the Gītā are also full of such maxims. That rich store-house of stories, the *Pañcatantra,* may also be regarded as a great store-house of wise maxims. There are many collections of such wise sayings, particularly those which were useful for a successful career and individual well-being, such as, *Rāja-nīti-samuccaya, Cāṇakya-nīti, Cāṇakya-rājanīti, Vṛddha-Cāṇakya* and *Laghu-Cāṇakya.* See also, in this connection, O. Kressler, *Stimmen indischer Lebensklugheit,* 1907. There are Tibetan and Arabic versions of these also (SBA, 1895, p. 275 and Zachariae WZKM, xxviii, 182 ff ; for Galanos' source, see Bolling, JAOS, xli, 49 ff.). We do not exactly know the source of the collections that go by the name of Cāṇakya. As Keith says, its contents deal with general rules for the conduct of life for intercourse among men, general reflections on richness and poverty, on fate and human effort and on a variety of religious and ethical topics ; as also, as we find in the *Subhāṣitas* and animal stories of the *Hitopadeśa,* on the relation between master and his servants, the king and his ministers, different kinds of difficult situations, the character of women and the like. There are also many antithetic expressions.

We have also the *Nīti-śataka* of Bhartṛhari. Under Śaṅkara-varman (883-902) of Kashmir, we have the Bhallaṭa-kavi and his *Bhallaṭṭa-śataka*. We have also another work by Śilhaṇa, the Kashmirian poet, who was an admirer of Bhartṛhari and also borrows from the *Nāgānanda* of Harṣa. As the *Sadukti-karṇāmṛta* of 1205 quotes from him, he must have been anterior to it. Pischel thinks that Śilhaṇa is a mistake for Bilhaṇa. Śilhaṇa's book has been edited by K. Schönfeld, Leipzig, 1910 (also see Keith, JRAS, 1911, p. 257 ff.) We have discussed Bilhaṇa separately. Śambhu, who lived under Harṣa of Kashmir (1089-1101), wrote a work called *Anyokti-muktā-latā-śataka*, published in the Kāvyamālā series, in 108 verses. His *Rājendra-karṇapura*, in praise of Harṣa is cited by Vallabha-deva. We have the *Dṛṣṭānta-śataka* of Kusuma-deva, of unknown date, published in the Kāvya-saṃgraha series by Jīvānanda. The *Dṛṣṭānta-śataka* consists of 100 verses. In each verse we have the instruction in the first line and simile in the second line. The *Bhāva-śataka* of Nāgarāja and the *Upadeśa-śataka* of Gumāni, are worth referring to in this connection. The *Mugdhopadeśa* of Jalhaṇa, of the first half of the 12th century is another excellent work. Somapāla was the king of Kashmir at his time. It is a work on good conduct and contains 66 verses. We must also mention *Sudarśana-śataka* by Śrī-kuru-nārāyaṇa-kavi (published in the Kāvyamālā series), *Subhāṣitanīvi* by the celebrated Veṅkaṭ-ācārya of the 14th century, in 12 chapters (published in the Kāvyamālā series), *Anyopadeśa-śataka* by Madhusūdana-Kavi, son of Padmanābha, *Śānti-vilāsa*—By Nīlakaṇṭha-Dīkṣita son of Nārāyaṇa and grandson of the brother of Appaya-Dīkṣita (Kāvyamālā series), *Darpa-dalana*—by Kṣemendra—in 7 chapters, 619 verses.

The *Sabhā-rañjana-śataka* is another work of the same description, of 105 verses, by Nīlakaṇṭha Dīkṣita ; *Sevya-sevakopadeśa* by Kṣemendra ; so also *Cāru-caryā* of Kṣemendra, of 100 verses ; *Caturvarga-saṃgraha* by Kṣemendra, in 4 chapters, of 111 verses. *Kali-viḍambana* is an excellent work by Nīlakaṇṭha Dīkṣita, in which he describes the weakness and wickedness in various professions of life. It is extremely amusing that *Śṛṅgāra-vairāgya-taraṅgiṇī* by Somaprabhācārya, in 46 verses, can be interpreted both on the side of love and on the side of renunciation. We have the *Sahṛdaya-līlā* of Rājānaka Ruyyaka ; *Sudhā-laharī* by Jagannātha-paṇḍita ; *Kalā-vilāsa* of Kṣemendra is a work in 10 chapters, in which he deals with *dambha, lobha, kāma,* courtesans, the *kāyastha,* pride, songsters, goldsmith and various kinds of swindlers through stories and also in the 10th chapter instructs us about proper behaviour. We have again *Prāṇ-ābharana* by Jagannātha,, containing 53 verses and *Amṛta-laharī* also by the same author. Appaya Dīkṣita also wrote a *Vairāgya-śataka.*

Among the didactic works we must mention Śānti-deva's *Bodhi-caryāvatāra,* as also the *Śikṣā-samuccaya.* We have also the *Śata-ślokī* · attributed to Śaṅkara. It contains 101 *Sragdhārā* verses. Keith refers to the *Śṛṅgāra-jñāna-nirṇaya* (edited by J. M. Grandjean, AMG. X, 477 ff.) which gives a contest between the claims of love and of knowledge, the claims of love being espoused by Rambhā and those of philosophy by Śuka. We are reminded of a similar struggle between love and renunicia-tion in Bhartṛhari's *Vairāgya-śataka.*[1] We have a work on pornography called the *Kuṭṭanī-mata* by Dāmodara-gupta, minister of Jaya-pīḍa of Kashmir (778-813). Dāmodara-gupta is referred to by Kalhaṇa as a poet and Mammaṭa and Ruyyaka quote verses from him. The work has been published with a

[1] *Cf. Śṛṅgāra-śataka,* 19 :—

mātsaryam-utsārya vicārya Kāryam āryāḥ samaryādam-idaṁ vadantu ।
sevyā nitamvā kimu bhūdharāṇām uta smara smera-vilāsinīnāṁ ॥

O.P. 220—85

commentary called *Rasa-dīpikā* by the Guzerati Printing Press, 1924. It is also called *Śaṃbhalī-mata*. The poet vividly describes through the mouth of a procuress by name Vikarāla, the various cunning arts, wiles and devices, which are resorted to by courtesans to decoy and lead guileless, simple and weak-minded youngmen to ruin. He wrote the work, as he says in the last verse, to help people from being cheated by wicked women, rogues and procuresses. The story is: that a dancing girl Named Mālatī, who lived in Benares, being unable to attract lovers to herself seeks the advice of an old procuress called Vikarāla. Vikarāla succeeds in attracting the son of a king's high official, called Cintāmani. This she does by narrating the story of *Hāralatā* to Cintāmaṇi. She also advises Mālatī to behave like Mañjarī for ensnaring the youngmen and she relates the story of Mālatī.

Another work worthy of reference is the *Nīti-mañjarī* of Dyā Dviveda (1494) which illustrates about 200 verses of maxims by tales culled from Sāyaṇa's commentary on the *Ṛg-veda*.[1] The *Subhāṣita-ratna-sandoha* written about 994, and *Dharma-parīkṣā*, written about twenty years later, by Amitagati, brother of Kṣemendra, deal with the various aspects of Jaina ethics.[2]

Historical Kāvyas

Among the historical *kāvyas* we have the prose romance of Bāṇa (7th century), the Prakṛt kāvya *Gauḍa-vaha* by Vākpatirāja, the court-poet of King Yaśovarman of Kanauj (750 A.D.). Both the works are but fragmentary. They contain little historical material and are full of description of natural scenes, the seasons, etc. We have then the *Nava-sāhasāṅka-carita* by Padmagupta or Parimala, which deals in reality with a fairy-tale

See Keith, J.R.A.S, 1900, p. 127 ff. and 796 f.

2 Edited in Kāvyamālā series with translation by Schimdt and Hertel, Z.D.M.G, LIX and LXI; *Cf.*, also W.Z.K.M., XVII. 105 ff.; see also N. Mironov's *Die Dharmaparīkṣā des Amitagati*, 1903.

theme but mentions many historical names. It was written in glorification of his parton-king Sindhurāja Nava-sāhasāṅka. There was indeed some historical truth in the narrative of the fairy-tale and it was written about 1005 A.D. We have then the *Vikramāṅkadeva-carita* by Bilhaṇa. It deals with the historn of Someśvara I, Someśvara II, and specially Vikramāditya VI and the Cālukya princes reigning between 1076 and 1127. In the historical information given here as regards the war between the Cālukyas and the Colas we hear that the Colas were completely annihilated every time just as in the present war-news we hear that the Germans are completely annihilated and yet the city is occupied by them. The poet gets the better of the historian and he does not take any interest in giving us any information regarding the interval of time between two events. In the 18th and last chapter he gives his autobiography.[1] We have then the *Rāja-taraṅgiṇī* by Kalhaṇa of the 12th century. Kalhaṇa's great work was continued in the 15th and 16th centuries by chroniclers. Thus, Jona-rāja, who died in 1459, continued the history of Kashmiri princes down to the reign of Sultan Zainu-l-'abidin. His pupil Śrīvara wrote the *Jaina-rāja-taraṅgiṇī* dealing with the period between 1459 and 1486. The *Rājāvali-patākā* was begun by Prājya-bhaṭṭa and completed by his pupil Śuka a few years after the annexation of Kashmir by Akbar (1586).

Then again, Jalhaṇa in his poem *Somapāla-vilāsa* describes the life of king Somapāla of Rājapurī near Kashmir against whom war was made by the Kashmiri king Sussala. We have also the historical poem *Pṛthvīrāja-vijaya* by Jonarāja describing the victories of the Cauhān king Pṛthvīrāja of Ajmere and Delhi who fell in 1193. The work was probably written between 1178 and 1200 A.D.

[1] The work has been edited by Bühler in P.S.S., 1875. The *Rāja-taraṅgiṇī* is quite reliable for the description of events and things of Kalhaṇa's own time, but as for past history, it is almost mythical. It is also a valuable source for the history of culture. It is a mine of rich informations regarding the religious conditions, the sects, the Kashmiri popular beliefs, snake-cult, etc. The poetic charm of the book is also indeed very great.

The learned Jaina monk Hemacandra wrote his *Dvyāśraya-kāvya* in Sanskrit and Prākṛt with the twofold object of teaching grammar and relating the story of the Calukyas of Anhilvad. The Sanskrit part is in 20 cantos dealing with the Calukya rulers from Mūlarāja to Karṇa, the father of Jayasiṃha, the reign of Jayasiṃha and of the martial and pious deeds of Kumārapāla. It illustrates at the same time the rules of Sanskrit grammar by Hemacandra. The second part is a Prākṛt poem and deals in 8 cantos the life and deeds of Kumārapāla. The work could not have been written before 1163, for Kumārapāla was still living at the height of his fame when the poem was written.[1]

The *Kīrti-kaumudī* is the biography of Vastupāla, minister of the Vāghelā princes, Lavaṇa-prasāda and Vīra-dhavala, by Someśvara-deva who lived in Guzerat between 1179 and 1262. It deals with the history of the Vāghelā dynasty of Guzerat. It is a work of poetical value and contributes to the history of the Calukyas.[2] Someśvara-deva also wrote a romantic epic called the *Surathotsava* with a fairy-tale theme which has probably some historical background, and in the last canto the poet gives his family history.

The life of Vastupāla is also the subject-matter of a work called the *Vastupāla-caritā* by Jina-harṣa. The King Vastupāla was himself a poet who wrote a work called *Nara-nārāyaṇānanda* dealing with the story of the friendship of Arjuna and Kṛṣṇa and the abduction of Subhadrā by Arjuna (written between 1220 to 1230 A.D.).[3] The same minister Vastupāla was the hero of a later work called the *Sukṛta-saṅkīrtana* by Arisiṃha. It is important from the point of view of the history of Guzerat.[4] In

1 The Prākṛt *Dvyāśraya-kāvya* with the commentary of Pūrṇakalaśagaṇi, has been published in B.S.S., 1900, and the Sanskrit *Dvyāśraya-kāvya* in the same series in 1915 and again in 1921, with the commentary of Abhaya-tilaka-gaṇi.

2 Edited in B.S.S., 1883.

3 Edited, G.O.S., 1916.

4 Edited in the Śrījaina Ātmānanda Sabhā Series, 1916

this connection we have to mention Bālacandra Sūri's *Vasanta-vilasa-mahākāvya.*[1]

We have also the life and good deeds of a merchant Jagaḍū extolled in Sarvānanda's *Jagaḍū-carita* written in the 14th century.

In the 14th century the poetess Gaṅgādevi wrote an historical poem called the *Mathurā-vijaya* or *Vīrakamparāya-carita,* in which she describes the heroic deeds of her husband who led victorious expeditions against King Campa of Kāñcī and against the Mahomedan chief of Madura (Madhurā rājya).[2] The heroic deeds of Hammira, who distinguished himself in the war with the Moslems is described in the *Hammira-kavya* by the Jaina Nayacandra in the 15th century. Rudrakavi wrote a historical poem in 20 cantos called the *Rāṣṭrauḍha-vaṃśa-kāvya* dealing with the history of the Bāgulas of Mayūragiri from the founder of the dynasty Rāṣṭraudha down to Nārāyaṇa Sha in the 16th centnry.[3] About the middle of the 16th century, Mādhava, a son of Abhayacandra, a court official of the Vāghelarāja Vīrabhānu, wrote the *Vīra-bhānūdaya-Kāvya* in 12 cantos, which contained dates for the history of Rewa in the Moghul period. Nyāya-vācaspati Rudra, brother of Viśvanātha Tarkapañcānana and son of Vidyānivāsa wrote a panegyrical poem on king Bhāvasiṃha, called *Bhāva-vilāsa.*[4] Bhāvasiṃha was a contemporary of Akbar.

Again, Raghunātha in the 16th century wrote a work of 18 cantos called *Rasika-maraṇa* in which the life and work of the Vaiṣṇava teacher Durvāsas is related. The *Kṣitīśa-vaṃśāvali-carita* was written in the middle of the 18th century relating the

1 Edited in G.O.S., 1917.

2 Edited in Trivendrum, 1916. Another lady, Rāmabhadrāmbā wrote the *kāvya* called the *Raghunāthābhyudaya* edited by the University of Madras, 1934. The hero of the *kāvya* is Raghunātha-nāyaka who ruled in Tanjore in the first quarter of the 16th century.

3 Edited in G.O.S., 1917.

4 Edited in Kāvyamālā, Part II, 1886. This Rudra was the author of the *Bhramara-dūta.*

history of the ancestors of king Kṛṣṇa-candra of Navadvīpa in Bengal and their battles against the Moslems, and the destinies of the individual rulers as well as all kinds of court tales, anecdotes and even fairy tales. The work is written in a very simple prose.

There had been indeed many more historical *kāvyas* in Sanskrit and many also are the chronicles in Hindī, Rājasthānī, Bengali, Tāmil and Siṃhalese. But many of them have entirely disappeared because the general interest of the people for any particular prince or hero was only of a temporary character and could not be compared with the perennial interest and emotion that they could derive by harping on the legends of the *Rāmāyana*, the *Mahābhārata* and the *Puraṇas.* The motive of *dharma* as interlaced with pleasant emotion is not only the cause as to why so few of the historical poems had been written or preserved, but it also explains the manner in which these historical chronicles were written. The mere determination of the actual deeds of kings, martial or otherwise, or the relating of the nature of their political administration or the actual narration of their relations and the like, would have but little place in a work of *kāvya* and people in general would not be interested in such recitals. Even in dealing with the chronicles of history, the main attention of the poet was directed to two points, one, the creation of aesthetic emotion by lovely descriptions, scenes of love, natural scenes, and the beauty of nature, and two, the creation of ideals. The poet would thus even at the sacrifice of exactitude and sometimes by mythical accounts, try to portray a great deal. He would not mind so much about the inaccuracy of details, even if the story had dot sufficient evidence to be regarded as well-founded, provided the legend or the tradition was in consonance with the spirit of the character that a man possessed. A mere fact as fact was contingent and unimportant but what is important is a total effect, the transfiguration of the character as conceived in the poet's mind. The discussions on the nature of truth and falsity as found in the various parts of the *Mahābhārata* and elsewhere reveal to us the fact that mere verbal correctness and objective agreement of words was not really truth. Truth was that which was beneficial and good for humanity. Thus the *Mahābhārata* is very positive that there are occasions in which truth is false and false is truth.[1] The fundamental principle that determines the truth-value of truth is not the agreement of words with facts but with human good. Truth is not good for itself, but so far only as it leads to human good. With such an idea of truth the poet may well be expected to give a greater emphasis and to indulge in imagination for portraying a particular sentiment of his. This sentiment is again well-demonstrated in the exaggerations of facts through imagery in order to give poetic expression to a particular fact. The waist of a beautiful damsel may be slender but a poet like Śrīharṣa in order to emphasise the point of slenderness would describe the waist as *aṇu-madhyā* (*i.e.*, waist like an atom) or *sad-asat-saṃśaya-gocarodarī* (*i.e.*, the waist so slender that there is doubt whether it exists or not). The poet as well as other persons know it well that from the point of view of fact the description is false, but the Indian reader will not be shocked at such a description until he is told by his European masters that the description is ludicrous and false, for he knows that the technique of exaggeration is never intended to be taken in its literal character but only as intimating to us the poet's emphasis on slenderness. Bhāmaha, Abhinava-gupta and others, all proclaim that *atīśayokti* or exaggeration is the soul of all *alaṅkāras* or poetic adornments. This aesthetic doctrine follows directly from the view that expressions should be carriers more of the sentiments and impressions than agreement with actual facts. Mere agreement of words with facts has but little importance. What matters really, is the consequential effect on others.

1 ***bhavet satyaṁ na vaktavyaṁ vaktavyam-anṛtaṁ bhavet |***
yatrānṛtaṁ bhavet satyaṁ satyaṁ vāpyanṛtaṁ bhavet ||
***Mahābhārvta, Śāntiparva,* 109. 5.**

Thus, for example, Kalhaṇa in his *Rāja.taraṅgiṇī* describes the sense of justice that king Candrāpīḍa had (Book IV) as also the relation in which the meanest of subjects stood to the king. His description goes as follows : "Once when he wanted to build a temple, a leather-tanner—who belongs to the despised classes in Kashmir refused to give up his hut for the building site. When this was reported to the king he blamed the officials for not having first asked the tanner's permission. They should either not build, or else erect the temple elsewhere, he says :

'Who would sully a pious work by taking away the land from another ? If we, who are to see that justice is done, perform illegal actions, who would tread the right path ?'

As the tanner desires audience of the king, this is granted to him. The king asks him why he is hindering the pious work, as he could get a better hut or claim money as compensation for his present hut. The tanner replies to him :

'The body of man, who is born in the cycle of existences, is like a weak suit of armour, which is held together only, by the two nails "I" and "mine." The same feeling of "I" which lives in you, who are resplendent in ornaments of bracelets and necklaces, lives also in us poor people.

What this residence with the gleaming white palaces is to your Majesty, that is this hut, whose window is the neck of a pot, to me.

From my birth this hut has been, like a mother, the witness of my joys and sorrows and so I cannot bear to see it pulled down to-day.

The pain which men feel, whose home is taken forcibly away from them, can be described only by a God who has fallen out of his celestial chariot, or by a king who has lost his realm.

Nevertheless, I would give it up, if your Majesty were to come into my house and request me to do so, in accordance with propriety.'

Thereupon the king goes into the pariah's house, buys the hut from him, and is praised by him as a virtuous king."

This story brings out two important points, *viz.*, that the king's sense of justice was so universal as even to include a tanner. We know that in India, legal justice is also called *dharma.* It was a greater *dharma* for a king that he should not violate the right of the tanner than that he should erect a temple. Even the *dharma* to be acquired by the erection of a temple would be meaningless if it is based upon the violation of the rights of the meanest of man. On the other hand, the sense of right on the part of the tanner did not spring from any sense of political liberty or political rights of a citizen but from a supreme philosophy of the universal equality of all men as spirits. As pure spirit or self the tanner felt himself to be equal in rank and position with the king. He had therefore as much right to his property as the king had to his own property. It was not important for the poet to enquire as to the proofs of the authenticity of the story provided it represented the cultural conditions that prevailed among the people at the time and the bright sense of justice with which the king was credited. If the story has been able to impress upon us this fact, it has done its purpose. Its truth or falsehood as fact is not of much relevance. It is the inner essence of man and his relations to man in that aspect that was important to the poet and not actually the exactitude of the physical happenings.

The Prākṛt

The Prākṛt is the name given to a literary language which is in part artificial. It however at bottom represents a real language which has been conventionalised. It is distinguished on the one hand from Sanskrit and on the other from Apabhraṃśa. Daṇḍin speaks of works written in Sanskrit, Prākṛt and Apabhraṃśa. This is also the classification implied by Vararuci in his *Prākṛta-prakāśa* though he does not refer to Apabhraṃśa as being a form of Prākṛt. Nevertheless, the difference between Apabhraṃśa and

Prākṛt is very thin. The modern grammarians regard Apabhraṃśa as a form of Prākṛt as one may note in Hemachandra and in Mārkaṇḍeya-kavīndra. We sometimes find Apabhraṃśa coupled with Prākṛt as Śaurasena Apabhraṃśa, Mahārāṣṭra Apabhraṃśa and Māgadhī Apabhraṃśa side by side with Śaurasenī, Mahārāṣṭrī and Māgadhī Prākṛts. From the examples given by Hemacandra it appears that this Apabhraṃśa very nearly approached the spoken dialect. The Prākṛts were probably a compromise between the spoken dialect and the Sanskrit, or rather between the Apabhraṃśa and Sanskrit. For this reason, the grammarians sometimes speak of Prākṛt being the foundation of Sanskrit—a doctrine which is certainly false from the point of view of linguistics. But it has some justification when judged from the principle in which Prākṛt and Sanskrit were adapted to each other. Apabhraṃśa has often been regarded as a local dialect. This is the view of *Vāgbhaṭālaṅkāra* (*apabhraṃśas-tu yac-chud-dhaṃ tat-taddeśeṣu bhāṣitam*). It was in this *deśabhāṣā* that Guṇādhya wrote his work. But in writing in this Apabhraṃśa it became a literary language and came under the domination of grammar. It was probably in this way that Apabhraṃśa came to be regarded as a type of Prākṛt, having definite rules. Apabhraṃśa then came to be distinguished from *deśabhāṣā* or *grāmyabhāṣā*. It would not be right to hold that the Apabhraṃśa and the Prākṛt associated with particular local names such as Mahārāṣṭra, Sūrasena, Magadha, etc., were actually spoken by the people of those localities any more than the people of Gauḍa, Vidarbha or Pañcāla who wrote in those styles of Sanskrit which pass by the names of Gauḍī, Vaidarbhī or Pañcālī. We can only think that they were based on certain local dialects which were much modified and they came to be used in literature. It is on account of voluntary alterations that even the most ancient inscriptions have been written in a specially ordered court language which had no real currency but was conventionalised. These Prakṛts are comparable to Classical Sanskrit but not to the Sanskrit of the Brāhmaṇas.

The Paiśācī Prākṛt is one of the most ancient varieties of Prākṛt. In the existing leterary works the Paiśācī dialect is seldom used. The Prākṛt grammars indeed note many varieties of it but we do not find it actually employed in other works. The Tibetans however say that the doctrine of Sarvāstivādins hold that in ancient times the *sthaviras* of one of the four schools wrote their books in the Paiśācī dialect though the Sammitīyas did it in Apabhraṃśa, the Mahāsaṅghikas in Prākṛt and the Sarvāstivādins in Sanskrit. If we may believe the statement it proves that the Paiśācī existed as the written language. Tāranātha says that the name came from Vinītadeva. The name Paiśācī has been given to the language because it was an inferior and barbarous dialect. This tradition may at least mean that the Paiśācī was used by certain sects of Buddhism. But we cannot be positive about it.

Sénart suggests that Apabhraṃśa was sometimes called the Paiśācī. It is probable that Apabhraṃśa being similar to the Paiśācī, was identified with it and this may be the reason why Vararuci does not speak of Apabhraṃśa.

Celebrated Writers of the Past Little Known Now

There had been quite a number of writers in the past whose wroks are not now available, but who were very celebrated in their time. Thus, Vyāḍi was a great writer, who wrote a *Saṃgraha* on Pāṇini and probably other works. He is referred to by Rāja-śekhara (*Kāvya-mīmāṃsa*, p. 55). We have Saumilla and Kaviputra mentioned by Kālidāsa in the 1st century B.C. along with Bhāsa. Rūpa and Sūri are also mentioned by Rāja-śekhara. So we have also Meṇṭha, Bhartṛ-meṇṭha or Meṇṭha-rāja mentioned by Bāna and also by Rāja-śekhara. Medhāvī-rudra has been mentioned by Bhāmaha. We hear the name of the *Rāmābhyudaya* mentioned by Ānanda-vardhana, Dhanika and Viśvanātha, atributed to Yaśovarman, the patron of Bhava-bhūti and Vākpati. We hear also of Śivasvāmin who lived in the middle of the 9th century and was a contemporary of the poet

Ratnākara. He is said to have written many *nāṭakas, naṭikās* and *prakaraṇas,* but excepting a few verses on the anthologies we practically know nothing of him.

Again, Mātra-rāja, known to Ānanda-vardhana and Abhinava-gupta wrote his play *Tāpasa-vatsarāja-carita* mentioned in Hall's Catalogue (Pischel, ZDMG XXXIX 315, Hultzsch, NGGW, 1886, p. 224 ff.) and numerous quotations from it are available in the *Nāṭya-darpaṇa* and elsewhere. But Māyū-rāja's *Udātta-rāghava* is known only by name. He was probably a king of the Kalacuri dynasty (see Bhaṭṭanātha Svāmin, *Indian Antiquary,* XLI, 139 f ; Bhāndārkar's *Report,* 1897, p. 11, p, 18 ; also Peterson's *Report,* II, 59). He is cited in Dhanika's commentary on the *Daśa-rūpaka.* The *Pārvatī-pariṇaya* was at one time attributed to Bāṇa but now it is attributed to Vāmana Bhaṭṭa-bāṇa. The *Mallikā-māruta* was at one time thought to be a work of Daṇḍin but now it is known to be the work of Uddaṇḍin, of the 17th century. Bhaṭṭāra Haricandra, so much eulogised by Bāṇa, is now merely a name. Many of the works that have been mentioned and passages from which have been quoted by the *Nāṭya-darpaṇa* or the *Bhāva-prakāśikā* of the 12th century, are practically unknown now. Some of the these are, the *Anaṅga-vatī-nāṭikā,* the *Anaṅgasenā-harinandi-prakaraṇa* by Śukti-vāsakumāra, the *Abhinava-rāghava* by Kṣīra-svāmin, pupil of Bhaṭṭendu-rāja, the *Arjuna-carita,* a *mahā-kāvya* by Ānanda vardhana, the *Indu-lekhā,* both a *nāṭikā* and a *vīthī* ; the *Kṛtyā-rāvaṇa,* a *nāṭaka,* the *Kauśalikā,* a *nāṭikā* by Bhaṭṭa Bhavanuta-cūḍa, *Citrotpal-āvalambitaka-prakaraṇa by* Saṅkuka, *Chalita-rāma-nāṭaka, Jāmadagnya-jaya* (*vyāyoga*), *Taraṅga-datta* (*prakaraṇa*), *Devī-candragupta* (a *nāṭaka* by Viśākha-deva), *Payodhi-mathana, Pāṇḍav-ānanda, Pārtha-vijaya* (a *nāṭaka* by Trilocana), *Puṣpa-duṣitaka* (a *prakaraṇa*), *Pratimā-nirudha* (*a nāṭaka* by Vasunāga, son of Bhīma-deva), *Prayog-ābhyudaya, Bālikā-vañcitaka* (a *nāṭaka*), *Manoramā-vatsarāja* by Bhīmaṭa, *Mallikā-makaranda, Māyā-puṣpaka* (*nāṭaka*), *Yādav-ābhyudaya, Raghu-vilāsa.* Rāghav-*ābhyudaya* (*nāṭaka*), *Rādhā-vipralambha* by Bhejjala. *Rohiṇī-*

mṛgāṅka (*prakaraṇa*), *Vanamālā* (*nāṭikā*), *Vidhi-vilasita* (*nāṭaka*), *Vilakṣa-duryodhana*, *Sudhā-kalaṣa*, *Hayagrīva-vadha* (a *mahākāvya* by Bhartṛ-meṇṭha).

Again, Śārada-tanaya mentions a number of writers. These are : *Abdhi-mathana*, a poem in Apabhraṃśa quoted also in Vāgbhaṭa's *Alaṅkāra-tilaka*, *Amṛta-manthana* (a *samavakāra*), *Udātta-kuñjara* (an *uparūpaka*), *Kali-keli*, *Kusuma-ṣekhara* (an *īhāmṛga* ; it is also called *Kusuma-śekhara-vijaya* and is quoted in the *Sāhitya-darpaṇa*), *Keli-raivata* (a *hallīśa*, quoted also in the *Sāhitya-darpaṇa*), *Gaṅgā-taraṅgikā* (an *upaṛūpaka*), *Gauḍavijaya*, *Tārak-oddharaṇa* (a *ḍima*). *Tripura-dāha* a *kāvya* by Ravi-sūnu. There are also two other *kāvyas* of the name, *Tripura-daha* or *Tripura-dahana* by Nārāyaṇa-bhaṭṭa and Vāsudeva and there is also a *ḍima* of that name. We have also *Tripura-mardana* (an *uparūpaka*), *Devī-pariṇaya* (a drama in 9 Acts), *Devī-mahādeva* (an *uparūpaka*), *Nala-vikrama* (a drama of 8 Acts), *Nandi-māli* (a *bhāṇa*), *Nṛsiṃha-vijaya*, *Padmāvatī pariṇaya* (a *prakaraṇa*), *Māṇikya-vallikā* (an *uparūpaka*), *Mārica-vañcita*, *Menakā-nahuṣa* (a *troṭaka* in 9 Acts), *Vakulavīthī* (a *vīthī*), *Vṛtr-oddharaṇa* (a *ḍima*), *Sāgara-kaumudī* (a *prahasana*), *Sugrīva-kelana* (an *uparūpaka*), *Sairandhrikā* (a *prahasana*), *Stambhita-rambhaka* (a *toṭaka* of 7 Acts). Such and many others are the dramas that are lost to us.

It seems that the land of the dramatic literature of India beginning probably as early as the 5th or the 6th century B.C. to the 11th and the 12th century A.D., is almost a containent submerged within the briny ocean of forgetfulness. It is, therefore, quite injudicious for us to think that we can form a real estimate of the extent and worth of the Sanskrit dramatic literature from the few specimens that are yet left to us.

GUṆĀḌHYA

In Guṇāḍhya we have an author whose work the *Bṛhatkathā* was given a place parallel to the *Rāmāyaṇa* and the *Mahā-*

bhārata. Thus Govardhana says in the *Sapta-śatī* published in the Kāvyamālā series: "We salute the poets of the *Rāmāyaṇa*, the *Mahābhārata* and the *Bṛhatkathā*"; and he compares the eloquence of the three writers to the flow of three rivers. Guṇāḍhya is also referred to in the same work as Vyāsa who had returned to the world. Bāṇa also speaking of the people of Ujjayinī says that they are attached to the *Mahābhārata*, the *Rāmāyaṇa*, the *Purāṇas* and the *Bṛhatkathā*. The *Daśarūpa* refers to the *Bṛhatkathā* as a great mine of stories which are utilised by other dramatists. Dhanpāla in his Introduction to the *Tilakā-mañjarī* has rendered homage to Vālmīki and Vyāsa and the author of the *Setu-bandha* and immediately afterwards to the author of the *Bṛhatkathā* because other *kathās* in Sanskrit were derived from it. In Kashmir, Kṣemendra wrote 3 *mañjarī*, the *Bhārata-mañjarī*, *Rāmāyaṇa mañjarī* and *Bṛhatkathā-mañjarī*. The *Nepālamāhātmya* written on Nepal compares Guṇāḍhya with Vālmīki.

The existence of the *Bṛhatkathā* was doubted for a long time by European scholars such as Wilson and Lassen, but when Hall printed out his edition of the *Vāsava-dattā* of Subandhu (1859) and referred to the testimony of the *Kāvyādarśa*, it was practically proved that the work existed till the 7th century. In 1871 Būhler discovered the *Bṛhatkathā-mañjarī*. The impossibility of holding that Kṣemendra had abridged Somadeva's *Kathā-sarit-sagara* and other relevant facts strengthened the supposition that there must have been an original from which both had drawn. M.S. Lévi referred to a *śloka* in a Cambodian inscription in the last quarter of the 9th century where there is an irrefutable allusion to Guṇāḍhya and his work in Prākṛt. Barth referred to another *śloka*[1] in the same inscription which referred to Guṇāḍhya. Thus, the reality of Guṇāḍhya can no longer be denied. Further, a review of the external and internal

1 *pūradaḥ sthira-kalyāṇo guṇāḍhyaḥ prākṛta-priyaḥ* |
anītiryyo viśālākṣaḥ śūro nyakkṛtabhīmakaḥ ||

proofs of the existence of Guṇāḍhya can be referred to in Lacôte's *Essai sur Guṇāḍhya et la Bṛhatkathā.*

The Kashmirian and the Nepalese legends regarding Guṇāḍhya have been referred to by Dr. De in brief in the body of the text. Kṣemendra says that Guṇāḍhya was born in the Deccan on the river Godāvarī. Somadeva called the city Supratiṣṭhita instead of Pratiṣṭhāna. This Pratiṣṭhāna was the capital of the Andhra-Bhṛtyas who were the descendants of the Śātavāhana ings. In the *Mahābhārata* Pratiṣṭhāna is the place of pilgrimage near the confluence of the Ganges and the Jamuna. The *Bṛhatkathā* does not give any indication that Guṇāḍhya was a Southerner. On the other hand, there are reasons to believe that he lived in Ujjayinī or in Kauśāmbī. But there are many scholars who are disposed to identify Pratiṣṭhāna as a city on the Godāvarī.

The importance of Guṇāḍhya and the high esteem in which he was held and the reverence that was shown to him will appear from the remark of Jagaddhara, a commentator of the *Vāsavadattā,* when he says : *"Guṇāḍhyaḥ...............tena kila bhagavato Bhavānīpateḥ mukha-kamalāt upaśrutya Bṛhatkathā nibaddheti vārttā."*

We have no doubt that the *Kathā-sarit-sāgara* of Somadeva and the *Bṛhatkathā-mañjarī* of Kṣemendra had drawn upon the *Bṛhatkathā* itself or any other work based on the *Bṛhatkathā.* A critical analysis of the *Kathā-sarit-sāgara* of Somadeva shows that much of its defects is due to the defects of the Kashmirian *Bṛhatkathā* on which it was based. The model that Somadeva imitated was probably absolutely incoherent. If we had not another version than the *Kathā-sarit-sāgara* it would have been difficult to say whether Somadeva reproduced the plan of his original exactly or not. But at the same time it would not be impossible to judge that the Kashmirian *Bṛhatkathā* was not the *Bṛhatkathā* of Guṇāḍhya. Kṣemendra's *Bṛhatkathā-mañjarī* adapts the tale in a new form and as such it is not surprising that some of the stories are missing here. It does not prove that they did not exist in the Kashmirian *Bṛhatkathā* but the probability is that Kṣemendra had neglected them as he also supplemented the original with descriptions of his own.

The *Bṛhatkatha-manjarī* of Kṣemendra, however, seems to reproduce exactly the composition of the Kashmirian *Bṛhatkatha* with all its defects. When Kṣemendra tries to hide the incoherence of the model, he does it by artifices of form while Somadeva tries to correct the plan. It is evident that the Kashmirian *Bṛhatkathā* was not a work which had any logical unity in it but which is merely a collection denuded of any literary unity.

The Kashmirian *Bṛhatkathā* appears as a compilation and not as an original work. We do not know the name of its author. The Kashmirians, of course, believe that the author was Guṇāḍhya. It had probably suffered many editions and it is probable that the last compiler had made considerable improvements. The *Kathā-sarit-sāgara* says that it has followed the original loyally.[1]

The quotation given below would show that though he was loyal to the original, he had made considerable changes and tried to make a *kāvya* of it. Somadeva thus corrected the plan of the Kashmirian *Bṛhatkathā* and expressed the whole thing in a concise and easily comprehensible manner. Kṣemendra's taste is undoubtedly inferior to that of Somadeva. He is verbose and full of mannerisms and has a tendency particularly to dilate upon erotic pictures. Nevertheless, sometimes he seems to supplement Somadeva. He seems to conserve some of the details not found in Somadeva and it may be possible by laborious

[1] yathā mūlaṁ tathaivaitan na manāgapyatikramaḥ ।
grantha-vistara-saṁkṣepa-mātraṁ bhāṣā ca bhidyate ॥
aucityā-nvaya-rakṣā ca yathā-śakti vidhīyate ।
kathā-rasā-vighātena kāvyāṁśasya ca yojanā ॥
vaidagdhya-khyāti-lobhāya mama naivāyamudyamaḥ ।
kiṁtu nānā kathā-jāla-smṛti-saukarya-siddhaye ॥

Kathā-sarit-sāgara, I, 10-12.

In all probability the edition of *Bṛhat-kathā* used by Kṣemendra was entirely differnet from that used by Somadeva.

analysis of the two works to surmiṣe some of the impoatrnt details of the Kashmirian *Bṛhaṭkthā*. In brief, it has been suggested that Kṣemendra was more loyal with regard to the order and Somadeva with regard to the materials.[1]

It is, however, certain that we cannot regard the Kashmirian *Bṛhatkathā* as being the work of Guṇāḍhya. We cannot impute to Guṇāḍhya such incoherence as prevails in the Kashmirian *Bṛhatkathā*, nor the patternity of a good part of the material of *Bṛhatkathā*. Moreover, it does not seem also probable that Guṇāḍhya should have such an accurate knowledge of Kashmirian geography as is revealed in Somadeva's work. The Kashmirian *Bṛhatkathā*, therefore, is to be regarded as a local work.

[1] Sten Konow (I.A , XLIII, p. 6) holds with Lacôte that the source of the *Kathā-sarit-sāgara* and the *Bṛhatkathā-mañjarī* was based not on Guṇāḍhya but on a later work compiled in the 7th century A.D. Keith in his *History of Sanskrit Literature*, p. 275, and Winternitz in Vol. III of his *History of Indian Literature*, hold the same view. Bühler (I.A., Vol. I, p. 319) holds that Somadeva and Kṣemendra remodelled the Prākṛt original. Speyer in his *Studies about the Kathā-sarit-sāgara*, p. 27, agrees with Lacôte. Pandit Kṛṣṇam-ācārya in his Prefade to *Priytadarśikā* (V. V. Press. Srirangam) as well as Dr. A. Venkaṭa Subbiyah, in his articles on the *Pañcatantra* of Durgasiṁha (*Indian Culture*, Vol. I, Part II, p. 214) holds a different view. Now, the order of the *lambhakas* in the two does not agree. The general surmise has been that either Kṣemendra or Somadeva had changed the order of the original in Prākṛt. Mankowski (*Einleitung der auszug aus dem Pañcatantra*), Lacôte (*Essai*, p. 91 ff.) and Penzer in his *Ocean of Stories* and the *Terminal Essay*, Vol. IX, p. 115, hold that Somadeva has made the change of the order of the *lambhakas*, while Speyer thought that Kṣemendra had changed the order while Somadeva followed the original order faithfully. The basis of the view that Somadeva made the changes, is the verse beginning with *yathāmūlam*, etc., already quoted. S. Rangācār (IHQ, 1938) argues that the phrase *yathāmūlaṁ tathaivaitat* (as already quoted) refers to the fact that he was loyal to the order of the *lambhakas* of original. The only point in which Somadeva deviated from the original, is its division into *taraṅgas* as distinguished from its division into *gucchakas* and *lambhakas* of lhe original. But in the *Bṛhatkathā-mañjari* also the following verses occur :—

seyaṁ hara-mukhod-gīrṇā kathā-nugraha-kāriṇī ।
paiśāca-vāci patītā sañjātā vighnadāyinī ॥
ataḥ sukha-niṣevyā-sau kṛtā saṁskṛtayā girā ।
samāṁ bhuvamivā-nitā gaṅgā śvabhrā-valambinī ॥

Now, therefore, from their own statements it appears that they professed to be loyal to their own original. If this assumption is correct, we should be led to think that in their arrangement they followed the order of their own originals. But their own originals were different in their structures being two recensions of the original *Bṛhatkathā*.

It is difficult to determine the date of the Kashmirian *Bṛhatkathā*. But it is possible to some extent to determine the two limits. The work was regarded as very old in the time of Kṣemendra, and one may infer that it was written at least one or two centuries before Kṣemendra's time. On the one hand it could not have been very old. Somadeva in his *Praśasti* declared that the poem was written to please the grandmother of Harṣa and the mother of king Kalaśa. The *Kathā-sarit-sāgara* must therefore have been written between 1063 and 1082 A.D. These dates are also corroborated by the statement of the *Rāja-taraṅgiṇī*. Kṣemendra was a contemporary of Ananta, the father of Kalaśa and his *Bhārata-mañjarī* was written in 1037 A.D. His *Daśāvatāra carita* was written in 1066 in the second year of the reign of Kalaśa. But the exact date of the *Bṛhatkathā-mañjarī* cannot be ascertained. Assuming that it was written more or less at the same time as the *Bhārata-mañjarī*, we may say that it was written 25 to 30 years before the *Kathā-sarit-sāgara* of Somadeva.

We have the other work called the *Śloka-saṃgraha* of Buddha-svāmin or Budha-svāmin, which is a summary of the *Bṛhatkathā* and which has again a Nepalese and a Kashmirian version. The style is simple, the vocabulary is rich, and sometimes long compounds also occur. It is probable that the author lived in the 9th or the 10th century.

The *Śloka-saṃgraha* of Budha-svāmin seems to be pretty faithful to the Kashmirian *Bṛhatkathā*, though at times he also seems to introduce new details of adventure.

We must now turn to the *Bṛhatkathā*. By a comparison of the different adaptations of the *Bṛhatkathā* of Guṇāḍhya, Lacôte says that Buddhism had adopted some of the personages treated by Guṇāḍhya and has given them a high place in the gallery of kings contemporary to Buddha. We have no place here to discuss how far Guṇāḍhya was faithful to the legends which he found floating and about those which were availed of by the Buddhist writers and this cannot be done without any detailed and comparative examination of the stories, which our limitations of space would not permit us to do. Some of the stories are found in the Vedas and the Brāhmaṇas as well. The central personage seems to be Udayana rather than Nara-vāhana-datta as often maintained by many. The ideal of Nara-vāhana-datta was probably taken by Buddha himself. If we could transpose the history of Buddha in the world of adventures, we could very well imagine the formation of a Chakravartin king like Nara-vāhana-datta. The whole treatment of his character consisted in being a curious mixture of lyricism and realism so charcteristic of the manner of Guṇāḍhya. He chose for his heroes the Vidyādharas who were demi-gods and masters of the science of magic. The Vidyādharas who seemed to be the creation of popular imagination constituted the traits of old Gandharvas, Yogins and the Apsarasas. The *Ramāyaṇa* and the *Mahābhārata* knew the Vidyādharas. They are associated with the Gandharvas, Yakṣas, Siddhas, the Cāraṇas and the Kinnaras. But they are also, on the other hand, closely allied to the Daityas, Dānavas, Bhūtas, Piśācas and the Rākṣasas. We had before this suggested in the Introduction that the Hindu society, strangled on all sides by the rules of Smṛti, was largely dissociated from reality and looking forward to following the customs of a past and forgotten age, the poets had to choose their stories from divine and semi-divine circles. This is very clearly testified by the manner in which Guṇāḍhya chose his heroes from amongst the Vidyādharas. It is interesting to note that the choice was remakably good and the characters are dramatic and human. Udayana was a Hindu Don Juan who served as the model of many other dramatists. Hemacandra in his *Kāvyānuśāsana* regards Udayana as being of a light vein, tender, passionate, amorous, devoted to the arts and dancing and devoid of all kinds of barbarity. This type has been copied in the *Ratnāvalī* and the *Priyadarśikā*. The other type of character was that of Nara-vāhana-datta who showed in himself a living personality. He was not a popular character and he was made up of sterner qualities. He is sometimes passionate, violent and wilful. He has sometimes brusque explosions of unjust anger and sometimes uses cruel words of ingratitude and yet at other times is quite tender and amiable.

If Guṇāḍhya was not the first to compose the floating tales into a romance, there seems to be no doubt that he was indeed the first to construct a vast collection of floating literature or stories into the type of *kathā*. A work like that of Guṇāḍhya properly responds to the class of *kathā* referred to by Daṇḍin. It is probable that the *Bṛhatkathā* contained some verses but the fragments cited by Hemacandra are in prose and it is not improbable that the orginal work was written in prose and verse. Daṇḍin tells us that the *kathā* should be in prose and refers to the *Bṛhathathā* in illustrating his opinion. Under such circumstances it seems better to accept his testimony that the *Bṛhatkathā* was written in prose. Subandhu, Bāṇa and Trivikrama all refer to the *Bṛhatkathā*. Trivikrama regards Bāṇa as an imitator of Guṇāḍhya.[1] Dhanapāla says that the *Bṛhatkathā* is the source of other *kathās*. Somadeva in a list which is not chronological, names Guṇāḍya between Kaṇṭha and Vyāsa.

The story of Naravāhanadatta has been adoped by the Jaina story-book *Kathā-koṣa* and various other works where no strict borṛowing is traceable. There are indubitable reflections of its characterisations[2] Bosch shows that it contained the *Vetāla-pañca-viṃśati*. Subandhu finds in the *Bṛhatkathā* the history

1 śaśvadbāṇadvitīyena namad-ākāra-dhāriṇā ।
dhanuṣy-eva guṇāḍhyena niḥśeṣo rañjito janaḥ ॥

Nala-campū of Trivikrama-bhaṭṭa, I, Stanza 14.

2 See F. Lacōte's *Essai sur Guṇāḍhya et la Bṛhatkathā*, Paris, 1908 ; see J. Charpentier, JA, XVI. 1910, p. 600 ff. ; F.D K. Bosch, *The Legend of Jīmūta-vāhana in the Sanskrit Literature*, Leyden, 1914 ; see also *Mélanges Lévi*, p 253 ff. Hertel's *Tantrākhyāyikā*, I. 41 f ; also *Pañcatantra*.

Hertel thinks that in the *Tantrākhyāyikā* there is the recension No. 2 of the *Pañcatantra* and that Somadeva represents most exactly the ancient state of the *Pāñcatantra*. If this were the case, then the original of the *Pañcatantra* would be in the *Brhatkathā* of Guṇāḍhya. But this is doubtful.

of Vikramāditya.[1] Dhanañjaya quotes from the *Rāmāyaṇa*, the *Mahābhārata* and also from the *Bṛhatkathā*. In the heroine of the *Svapna-vāsavadattā* of Bhāsa we probably find a reflection of the heroine married to Sañjaya while Kālidāsa in the *Meghadūta* 1.30, refers to Avantī as the city of Udayana. Vallabha, the oldest commentator, finds here a reference to the *Bṛhatkathā*. A legend of Udayana appears in the *Aṭṭha-kathā* of Dhammapada and in the *Divyāvadāna*, and the same appears in the Chinese and Tibetan version of the *Vinaya* of the school of the Mūlasarvāstivādins. In the Cambodian inscription Guṇāḍhya is spoken of as a friend to the Prākṛt language.[2]

We have now to say a few words about the Paiśācī dialect of the *Bṛhatkathā*. A reference to the Paiśāci dialect is found in Hemacandra, IV, 303-324. Pischel has collected in his *De Grammatisis Pracritisis*, quotations given by Hemacandra of the Paiśācī Prākṛt. These quntations, when taken together, show that they were probably taken from the *Bṛhatkathā* of Guṇāḍhya as they tally with some passages in the *Kathā-sarit-sāgara*.[3]

Pischel believes that the Paiśācī dialect is related somehow to the dialect of Teufel or the dialect of the Daradas of the North-West[4]

It is believed that there was a recension which was probably written at the time of King Durvinīta of the Gaṅga dynasty in the 6th century A.D.[5] We have, of course, two other recensions of

1 *Vāsava-dattā* (Hall's edition), p. 110.

2 Lévi, J.A., 1885.

3 See F. Lacōte's *Essai*, etc., p. 202 *et seq*. Some of the passages as in Hemacandra, IV, 310, 316, etc., run as follows :—'*kiṁ pi kiṁ pi hitapake atthaṁ ciṁtayamānī*. Here, *hitapake* is *hṛdayake* and *ciṁtayamānī* is *cintayamānā*.

pudhumataṁsane savvassa yyeva sammānaṁ kīrate—Here *pudhumataṁsane* is *prathamadarśane*.

Again, *taṁ taṭṭhūna ciṁtitaṁ raññā kā eṣā huveyya*. Here *taṭṭhūna* is *dṛṣṭvā* and *huveyya* is *bhavet*.

4 See Pischel's *Grammatik der Prakrit-Sprachen* ; Grierson, *Indian Antiquary* 30, 1901, p. 556; Z.D.M.G., 66, 1912 : Anders Konow, Z.DM.G.; 64, 1910, 95 ff.; see also J. S. Speyer.

5 See R. Narasiṁhācāra,—*Indian Antiquary*, 42, 1932, 204 and J. R. A. S., 1913, 389 ff ; see also Fleet, *Indian Antiquary*, 30. 1901, 222; Kielhorn, *Epigraphica Indica*, VII, Appendix, p. 21 VIII, Appendix II, p. 4 note ; Krishnaswāmi Aiyengār in J.R.A.S., 1906,

the *Bṛhatkathā*—Kṣemendra's *Bṛhatkathā-mañjarī* and Somadeva's *Kathā-sarit-sāgara*, to which references have already been made, and a Nepalese recension by Buddha-svāmin or Budhasvāmin. The Nepalese version of Budha-svāmin bears the title of *Bṛhatkathā-śloka-saṃgraha.*[1] We are not certain about the date of Budha-svāmin. Lacôte places him in the 8th or the 9th century. While Budha-svāmin's book was written in verse and divided in *sargas* like the Epics, Guṇāḍhya's *Bṛhatkathā* was written in prose and in *lambhakas.*

Winternitz, in Vol. III of his *History of Indian Literature,* would like to place Guṇāḍhya in the 1st century A.D. But Keith, while holding that Guṇāḍhya cannot be later than 500 A.D., holds that to place him in the 1st century A.D. would be quite conjectural, though no other later date can be regarded as more assured. We in our turn are troubled with the question as to whether Bhāsa drew upon Guṇāḍhya's work, or whether he got the plot of the dramas of the *Svapna-vāsavadattā*, etc., from Guṇāḍhya's work or directly from the floating stories from which Guṇāḍhya himself got his materials. Since in our opinion Bhāsa flourished near about the 3rd century B.C., in the former supposition that Bhāsa had utilised Guṇāḍhya's book, Guṇāḍhya has to be placed earlier than Bhāsa. But if the latter supposition be true, then indeed we cannot argue anything from the existence of the story found both in Guṇāḍhya and in Bhāsa.

PANCA-TANTRA

We may assume that stories, didactic and otherwise, were current from very early times. It is difficult, of course, to

689 ff. and in *Ancient India*, London, 1911, p. 328 and 337, refers to the Tāmil work—*Udayana Kadai* or *Perungadai* as being a translation of the *Bṛhatkathā* made in the 2nd century A. D. Lacôte refers to the Tāmil and Persian versions of the *Bṛhatkathā* in his *Essai*, p. 197 ff.

1 See Haraprasāda Śāstrī, J.A.S.B., 62, 1893, 245 ff.; Lévi, in *Comptes Rendus de l'Académie des inscriptions et belles lettres*, 1899, p. 78, 84; Hertel *Südliches pañcatantra*; Speyer, *Studies about the Kathā-sārit-sāgara*, p. 56; Lacôte, J.A., 1906 and *Essai*, 146. This *Śloka-saṁgraha* consists of 28 *sargas* and has been translated by Lacôte, Paris, 1908,

discover tales of the type of the *Pañca-tantra* in the Vedas. But in *Rgveda* VII, 103 we have a passage in which Brahmins are compared to croaking frogs. There are indeed many stories associated with the life of the gods and we hear Dadhyañcas holding the head of a horse and divulging a secret after which his own head was returned to him. In *Ṛgveda* VIII and IX we hear of the king of the rats rejoiced at heart for having eaten up through his subject rats all the corns and oblations of Saubhari, son of Kaṇva, and there is an allusion there to Saubhari's being begotten in an animal's womb. In the Upaniṣads also we hear of the satire of the white dogs seeking a leader and the talk of two geese and the instruction of Satya-kāma first by a bull, then by a goose and an aquatic bird.[1] Here we have instances of instruction of man by animals. In the *Mahābhārata* also we find many fables scattered about throughout the work. We also know that the doctrine of rebirth had destroyed the ordinary barrier between men and animals. Such an atmosphere was suitable for the development of the animal fables. The *Jātaka* stories also abound with episodes of men and animals and we find many representations in which the animals are susceptible to the greatness of Buddha. In many of his past lives the Bodhisattva was born as various animals and in and through his dealing with other animals we have the character of men reflected among the animals. It was also a strong belief from very early times that the animals had intelligible speech and in Varāhamihira's work we have a *Virutādhyāya* in which an interpretation is given of the cries of various animals. The references in the *Mahā-bhāsya* to such expressions as *Kāka-tālīya* or *ajā-kṛpāṇīya* (II.1.3.) indicate that animal fables were current at that time. But the *Pañca-tantra* literature develops these stories in such a manner that they illustrate in a concrete way the precepts of *Nīti-śāstra* and *Artha-śāstra*. The *laukika nyāyas*, some of which have been collected in such

1 *Chāndogya* I, 12; IV. 1, 5, 7. Also see Keith's *History of Sanskrit Literature*, p. 242.

work as *Laukika-nyāya-saṃgraha* have also little stories to illustrate popular maxims which are freely used even in philosophical literature. While *Artha-śāstra* deals with scientific polity, the *Nīti-śāstra* deals with practical common-sense.

In the structure of the *Pañca-tantra* we have tales profusely interspersed with the instructive common-sense wisdom in easy verse. Thus the popular tales were turned into the fables of the *Pañca-tantra*. The *Pañca-tantra* is a definite Indian creation entirely different in structure from the AEsop's Fables.

In *Alaṃkāra* literature, *kathā* is distinguished from *ākhyāyikā* but the thinnes of this distiction is apparent from the fact that while the *Pañca-tantra* tales are often called *kathā* there is a version which calls it an *ākhyāyikā* and the work is called *Tantrākhyāyikā*.

The originals of the various works which have come down to us in the name of *Pañca-tantra,* are now lost. But we can get to the substance of it. The Pehlvi translation was made in 570 A.D. but its substance can be made out from an old Syriac and Arabic version of the same. Then we have the substance of the tale in the *Bṛhat-kathā* as preserved for us in the *Bṛhat-kathā-mañjarī* of Kṣemendra and the *Katha-sarit-sāgara* of Somadeva.

Pañca-tantra Texts

The *Pañca-tantra* texts are :—

(1) The *Tantrākhyāyikā,* in older and the later recension in Kashmirian and two Jain recensions from a similar work, but not the *Tantrākhyāyikā,* well known in the 'textus simplicior' edited by Bühler and Kielhorn and in Purṇabhadra's *Paṇca-tantra.*

(2) The text that was translated into Pehlvi.

This Pehlvi text is not really available to us but its Syriac and Arabic translations exist and these have flown into European languages and from these we can infer about the Pehlvi translation and their original.

(3) An extract from the *Pañcatantra* is dealt with in the Kashmirian *Bṛhat-kathā* and in two metrical compilations in Kṣemendra's *Bṛhat-kathā-mañjarī* and Somadeva's *Kathā-sarit-sāgara*. Kṣemendra had written the story of the *Pañcatantra* without any break and probably Somadeva also got it from the recension of the *Bṛhat-kathā* used by him. It is clear that the story in the *Bṛhat-kathā* was the source. In the *Kathā-sarit-sāgara* and the *Bṛhat-kathā-mañjarī* many parts seem to have been interpolated and the Nepalese version which is least charged with accretion, does not contain any *Pañcatantra*. Hertel thought that if the matter of the *Pañcatantra* formed any part, it might be in the 10th *sarga*, which he believes to be the 10th book of Somadeva, and in the colophon there calls it *kathāsaṃlapanam*. But the dimension of this *sarga*, although considerable, could not contain the whole of the *Pañcatantra*. As a matter of fact the 10th *sarga*, no more than the other contained various stories. It also has to be noted that the *Śloka-saṃgraha* does not contain any *Pañcatantra*. From this it would be right to argue that the *Pañcatantra* existed absolutely independent of the *Bṛhat-kathā*. In 1906 after the first edition of the *Pañcatantra*, Hertel received from Nepal a copy of a manuscript belonging to the Durbar at Katmundu, which he thought, must contain the *pañcatantra*. This was in reality the *Bṛhat-kathā-śloka-saṃgraha*. But the book of Śaktiyasas of the Kashmirian *Bṛhat-kathā* contains a really original version of the *Pañcatantra*. The result is that the *Pañcatantra* resembles that of Somadeva's oldest recensions. Kṣemendra had reduced the matter to a small section which may be regarded as dealing with the *Pañcatantra* materials. Somadeva, however, mixed up the fables of the *Pañcatantra* all through. Hertel thinks that it might be in the *Tantrākhyāyikā*, that Somadeva found represented most exactly the ancient state of the *Pañcatantra*. It cannot be doubted that the *Pañcatantra* was retouched variously by various compilers. It is hardly necessary to add that the Kashmirian *Bṛhat-kathā* must serve as a basis of any theory regarding the antiquity of the

available forms of stories of the *Pañcatantra*. This argument practically destroys Speyer's observations regarding the relative chronology of the *Pañcatantra* and the *Bṛhat-kathā*.

Winternitz says the story in the *Bṛhat-kathā* appears in a twisted form though the original may not seem to have been forgotten. We have the same kind of teaching with animal stories in the instruction given by Gomukha to Naravāhanadatta.[1] The same value is not attached to the stories. There is again a Southern edition of the *Pañcatantra*. As Hertel points out, it is based upon a North-Western edition of the 7th century. The importance of this text lies in the fact that it stands very near to the *Tantrākhyāyikā*.[2]

A Nepalese recension of the Southern *Pañcatantra* and the popular *Hitopadeśa* drawn from some earlier version stands very nearly to the text of the North-Western edition.[3]

The *Tantrākhyāyikā* is a work in the Sanskrit Kāvya style. The prose is the artistic one and as such consists of small compounds and verses containing *śleṣas* and double meanings and other *alaṃkāras*. The prose is widely different from the ornate language in the romance of Subandhu and Bāṇa and what is found in the *Jātaka-mālā*[4] Yet the editor is a man of taste and knows the Kāvya style very well. It may be held

1 See *Bṛhat-kathā-mañjarī* XVI, p. 255 ff ; *kathā-sarit-sāgara*, 60-64 ; Man kowski, *Der Auszug aus dem Pañcatantra in Kṣemendra's Bṛhat-kathā-mañjarī*, Einleitung, Text, Über-setzung und Anmerkungen, Leipzig, 1892 ; see also Speyer, *Studies about the Kathā-sarit-sāgara*, p. 36 f. ; also Hertel's *Das Pañcatantra*, p. 30 ff.

2 See M. Haberlandt in S. W. A., 107, 1884, pp. 397-476 ; a criticism of another recen-sion is given by Hertel, *Das südliche Pañcatantra*, XXIV, A.S.W., Leipzig, 1906 ; see also Hertel's *Das Pañcatantra*, p. 33 ff.

3 See Hertel's *Das südliche Pañcatantra* ; also Z.D.M.G., 1910, p. 58 ff. and *Das Pañcatantra*, p. 37 ff. Hertel has indeed been unable to prove that all these were drawn from one defective original.

4 Jacobi, G.G.A., 1905, p. 377 and Hertel's *Tantrākhyāyikā* (Translation, 1.22) which is the same as the *Jātaka-mālā*. But this belongs to another class ; it is a sort of *campū* with prose and verse written in Kāvya style. The *Tantrākhyāyikā* is not a *campū*, rather the verses have here a sort of twist and are also composed in a different manner.

that originally these tales were of folk-origin but the refinement with which it was later on worked up altogether changed its form.[1] The *Pañcatantra* contains five books. Of these the 4th and the 5th only are dovted to universal teachings of life. The first book deals with some lessons in Politics. Though the first book deals with politics, it also deals with lessons of good life. The whole work may be regaded as political text-book. There is a great integral relation as regards its instruction between. it, Kauṭilya's *Artha-śāstra* and the *Nīti-sāra.*[2]

When the history of the *Nīti-śāstrā* will be properly analysed, the atmosphere of the *Tantrākhyāyikā* and the oldest *Pañcatantra* will be discovered there. The *Tantrākhyāyikā* does not belong to the time of Cāṇakya in 300 B.C. as much as the *Pañcatantra* does not belong to king Khosru-Anoshirwan (531-579 A.D.) who had it translated in Pehlevi and later on in the year 570 it had a Syriac translation from the Pehlevi. These form more or less a universal teaching of polity. Though it deals with polity and teachings about successful life, yet as Dr. De points out in the body of the text, it is an extremely pleasant animal story book as well. Winternitz thinks that the work can be placed between 300-500 A.D. or at least undoubtedly it should be regarded as belonging to the early type of work belonging to the Kāvya style. The *Tantrākhyāyikā* must have been based on an older version of the *Pañcatantra.* The way of life taught in the *Tantrākhyāyikā* in undoubtedly Brahminic with a Viṣṇuite tinge. Its mythology is quite aware of the

1 In the Introductory portion of the *Tantrākhyāyikā* and so also in other versions of the *Pañcatantra,* Viṣṇuśarmā appears as the speaker. This is so also in the works of Pūrṇabhadra and Nārāyaṇa. Benfey (I. p. 29 ff.) has already shown that Viṣṇuśarmā is probably a changed form of Viṣṇugupta—the other name of Cāṇakya. Hertel in his *Tantrākhyāyikā* has discussed all these points. It seems unlikely that Viṣṇuśarmā was the real writer of the work or that it was written for the edification of children. See Winternitz, W.Z.K.M., 1911, p. 52 ff.; also Hertel's *Tantrākhyāyikā,* I. 23 and Z.D.M.G., 1906, p, 787 ff. and F.W. Thomas, J.R.A.S., 1910, p. 974 ff.

2 See A. Hillebrandt, *Über das Kauṭilīyaśāstra und Verwandtes.* Breslau, 1008, p. 9 ff.; Hertel's *Tantrākhyāyikā,* Ubersetzung I, p. 141 ff. und Ausgabe, p. 169 ff.

world of gods as taught in the Epic *Purāṇas*. The minister is a Brahmin and Brahminic supremacy is manifest. The ethical standpoint of the *Tantrākhyāyikā* is different from that of Buddhism.[1] Hertel translates the word *tantra* in the *Pañcatantra* or the *Tantrākhyāyikā* as *klugheitsfell* or a case of good sense. But I am afraid the word *tantra* has no such sense in Sanskrit. The meaning seems to be applicable here is *iti-kartavyatā* or way of procedure. Thus we have the *Trikāṇḍa-śeṣa* giving the meaning of the word as *iti-kartavyatā tantram upāyaśca dvi-sādhakaḥ*. It may also mean a body of conclusions, as in the *Amara-koṣa, tantraṃ pradhāne siddhānte.*

There is another edition of the *Pañcatantra* published under the name *Textus Simplicior* by Kielhorn and Bühler, B.S.S., I, III, V and translated by Fritze, Leipzig, 1884, which was best known as the genuine *Pañcatantra* Text, before the discovery of the *Tantrākhyāyikā*. It is new work based upon older grounds. The stories are given in clear and good language and in brighter ways than in the *Tantrākhyāyikā*. Of the 4th and 5th books only a few stories have been touched upon in the *Tantrākhyāyikā*. The text of the *Textus Simplicior* was probably based upon the North-west Indian texts upon which the Pehlevi translation and the South Indian texts are based. It was probably originally written in the North-West Indian language after which it was probably newly written.[2] The text was probably drawn up by an unknown Jaina between the 9th and the 11th century A.D. but it does not reveal any particular Jaina tendency.

[1] Regarding the Buddhistic frame of the *Pañcatantra*, the *Nīti* history and *Dharma* history, see Hertel, J.A., 1908, p. 399 ff. Regarding the Buddhistic origin of the *Pañcatantra* see the discussion by A. Barth (*Mélusine* IV, 1888-89, p. 558 ff.) and Bühler (*Verhandlungen der 42. Versammlung deutscher Philologen und Schulmänner in Wien*, 1893, p. 504). See also Ed. Huber (B.E.F.E.O. IV, pp. 707 and 755) and Hertel, W.Z.K.M. 20, 1906, p. 113 ff. Benefy, however, holds the view of the Buddhistic origin of the *Pañcatantra* and he tried to demonstrate it in various ways. It is true that much of the history of the *Pañcatantra* can be found in the *Jātaka* works. But this is probably due to the fact that many of the *Jātakas* originated from an older frame of the *Pañcatantra*. See Hertel, W.Z.K.M. 16, p. 269 ff.

[2] See Jacobi, G.G.A., 1905, p. 377 ff.

[3] See Hertel, B.S.G.W., 1902, p. 62 ff., also Jacobi, G.G.A., 1905, p. 380 ff.

There is a peculiar story here about a weaver impersonating as Viṣṇu based on the materials of the *Textus Simplicior* with the additions taken from the later recensions of the *Tantrākhyāyikā*. We have the *Pañcākhyānaka* or the *Pañcatantra* written by the Jaina monk Pūrṇabhadra in 1199. The *Tantrākhyāyikā* formed one of the earliest reductions of the *Pañcatantra* stories and this recension dates probably from about 200 B.C. A Kashmirian manuscript of it was got by Bühler written in the Sāradā character and Hertel had the good fortune to get a copy of this work in the Deccan College Library at Poona. In the many Indian recensions of this work the most important is that which has been commonly called by Western scholars the *Textus Ornatior* and its author is Pūrṇabhadra Sūri as we have just mentioned. An English translation of this work has been made by Mr. Paul Elmer More. Kosegarten's edition of the *Textus Simplicior* and his specimen were both uncritical and Hertel published a critical edition of it in the Harvard Oriental Series, 1908, though originally the venture was launched by Schmidt.

Pūrṇabhadra says in the colophon that by his time the *Pañcatantra* text had become extremely corrupted and the manuscripts were such that the letters were worn out, and correction was made with reference to every letter, word, sentence, episode and *śloka*.[1] It is probable, as judged from grammatical peculiarities, that Pūrṇabhadra had utilised some other Prākṛt work or works written in popular dialect.[2]

Another abridged text was made in the year 1659-1660 by the Jaina monk Meghavijaya which was called the *Pañcākhyānoddhāra*.[3] It contains some new stories. The chief source for Meghavijaya was a metrical Sanskrit work based upon *Pañcā-*

1 *pratyakṣaraṁ pratipadaṁ prativākyaṁ pratikathāṁ* ।
pratiślokaṁ śrīpūrṇabhadrasūrirviśodhayāmāsa śāstramidam ॥

See the excellent critical Introduction by Hertel in the Harvard Oriental Series Vols. XI-XII, 1908 and 1912.

2 **See Hertel, H.O.S., XII, p. 29 ff.**

3 **See Hertel, Z.D.M.G., 1903, p. 639 ff; and Z.V.V., 1906, p. 249 ff.**

khyāna-caupai, written in old Guzerati by one Jaina monk Vaccharāja in the year 1591-92.

Another text pretty far removed from Pūrṇabhadra's text appears as a Southern *Pañcatantra.* It contains many new stories probably derived from Tamil sources.[1]

There is another text published by Abbé J. A. Dubois, *Le Pantchatantra ou les cinq ruses.*

In Nepal we have another text called the *Tantrākhyāna.*[2] This edition has slight tinges of Jainism and Buddhism. The compilation was probably made at least in the 14th century. The date of the manuscript is not probably later than 1484.

The most important of all the new works based on the *Pañcatantra* is probably the Bengali work, *Hitopadeśa.* It seems to be wholly a new work. Its chief source seems to be the North-Western version of the *Pañcatantra* on which the Southern and the Nepalese versions are based. The author gives his name and that of his patron Dhavalacandra in the colophon.[3]

The *Pañcatantra* has played an important part in the whole world literature.

Benfey in the Introduction to his translation of the *Pañcatantra,* shows how the older books of literature of the three

1 On another Southern text of the *Pañcatantra*, see Z.D.M.G., 1906, p. 769 ff.

2 See C. Bendall, J.R.A.S., 1888, p. 465 ff., and also Hertel, Z.D.M.G., 1910, p. 58 ff.

3 We have critical forewords by Schlegel and Lassen (Bonn a. Rh., 1829-1832) and by P. Peterson, B.S.S., 1887 ; also Introduction given by Hertel over the text and the author of the *Hitopadeśa*, 1897, and *Pañcatantra*, p. 38 ff. See also Hertel's article over a MS. of the *Hitopadeśa*, Z.D.M.G., 1901, p. 487 ff. and Zachariae, *Z.D.M.G.*, 61, p. 342 ff.

An old Nepalese manuscript dated 1373 exists. Hultzsch has quoted from Māgha's *Śiśupāla-vadha* a verse in the *Hitopadeśa*. See Hertel's *Tantrākhyāyikā* (translated) I. p. 145 ff.

Winternitz points out that in the *Hitopadeśa*, *Bhaṭṭārakavāra* has been used for Sunday, but this reference to '*vāra*' of the week does not occur in Indian inscriptions before 500 A.D. and it became universal after 900 A.D. ; see Fleet, J.R.A.S., 1912, p. 1045 ff.

There are many translations of the *Hitopadeśa*, such as by Max Müller, 1844, Schoemberg, 1884, Fritze, 1888, Hertel, 1895. The West European translation is the English tramslation by Charles Wilkins, 1787, and the French translation by Langles. 1790.

Translations from the *Pañcatantra* exist in Hindi, Guzerati, Canarese, Tamil and Malayalam. Translations of the *Pañcatantra* exist also in Bengali, in the Brajabhāṣā, in Hindustani, Marathi and Newari.

continents have been invaded for many centuries by the stories of the *Pañcatantra.*

In the *Kathāmukha* of the *Tantrākhyāyikā* an adoration is paid to Manu, Vācaspati, Śukra and Parāśara, Vyāsa and Cāṇakya. Viṣṇuśarman here says that he has written the book by examining all works on polity.[1] It is possibible that the *Pañcatantra* had utilised the *Artha-śāstra* of Kauṭilya for the composition of the work. There is also an old *Nīti* work attributed to Cāṇakya, but the exact relation between Cāṇakya and the *Pañcatantra* cannot be determined. Nothing is known regarding any personal details or the time of the author and it has been held with some justice that the name Viṣṇuśarman is a pseudonym and that Viṣṇuśarman was probably Viṣṇugupta. But this can only be a possible conjecture.

Even before the *Pañcatantra* was rendered into Pehlevi in 570 A.D., it was a very well-known work. The translation was probably made from a North-Western recension into which many interpolations had crept in. Hertel tries to prove that the *Tantrākhyāyikā* is the earliest available recension of the *Pañcatantra.* Hertel holds that oldest Kashmir version of the *Tantrākhyāyikā* existed as early as 200 B.C. This Kashmir version through one or two transmissions was utilised by the pseudo-Guṇāḍhya in the Kashmirian *Bṛhat-kathā.* From these we have Kṣemendra's *Bṛhat-kathā-śloka-mañjarī* about 1040 and Somadeva's *Kathā-sarit-sāgara* about 1063 to 1082. From the Kashmirian version from another line there came the North-West Indian version from which the Pehlevi version was made in 570 A.D. and from this Syriac and Arabic versions were made which passed on to Asia, North Africa and Europe and after the 5th century from the same North-East Indian recension we have the Southern *Pañcatantra* and its Tamil version. From the

1 *manave vācaspataye śukrāya parāśarāya sasutāya* |
cāṇakyāya ca mahate namo'stu nṛpaśāstrakartṛbhyaḥ ||
sakalārthaśāstrasāraṁ jagati samālokya viṣṇuśarmā'pi |
tantraiḥ pañcabhīretaiścakāra sumanoharaṁ śāstram ||

North-East Indian version again sprang up the *Hitopadeśa* in Bengali by the 14th century and also the Nepalese version. There also sprang up another North-East Indian version after 850 A.D. which has been collected in the *Textus Simplicior*. Based upon the text of the *Textus Simplicior* (North-West Indian recension) and the Kashmir manuscript written in Sārada character before 1040 and probably from certain Prākṛt materials Pūrṇabhadra's compilation was made in Guzerat in 1199.

Holding the date of Cāṇakya from Kauṭilya's *Artha-śāstra* as being 300 B.C., the *Tantrākhyāyikā* must have been written between this limit and 570 A.D., when the work was translated into Pehlevi. From many considerations we regard the date of the original Kashmirian *Tantrākhyāyikā* to be 200 B.C.

The *Tantrākhyāyikā* is but the other name for *Pañcatantra*. It is supposed to be a summary account of the tales that have floated through tradition.[1] The Southern *Pañcatantra* I. 151 contains a verse which is identical with *Kumāra-sambhava* II. 55, from which we can infer that it was written after Kālidāsa. The date of the Nepalese recension is quite undecided. The *Hitopadeśa* of Nārāyaṇa has a manuscript which is dated 493 Nepalese era, *i.e.*, 1373 A.D. It quotes Kāmandaka and Māgha and it may be assumed that it was written sometime between 800-1373 A.D.

The popularity of the *Pañcatantra* is evident from the fact that excluding Hertel's works it has at least six German translations by Brockhaus, 1844, by Boltz, in 1868, Schoenberg, 1884, Fritze, 1888 ; and another in 1853. It has been translated into English by Charles Wilkins, Sir William Jones, Johnson Max Müller, Sir Edwin Arnold and by Hale-Wortham and by Manickchand

1 *granthavistarabhīrūṇāṁ bālānām alpacetasām* ।
bodhāya pañcatantrākhyam idaṁ saṁkṣipya kathyate ।
anyadiyo'pi likhitaḥ śloko yaḥ prakramāgataḥ ।
svalpatvāt granthavistaradoṣastena na jāyate ॥

Jain. Its French translation was made by Langlès, 1790, and Lancereaṇ, 1882. It was translated in Bengali by Lakṣmīnārāyana Nyāyalaṅkāra and also into Brajabhāṣā ; and also in Hindi, Hindustani, Marathi, Newari, Presian and Telugu.

Hertel had concluded that all the sources of the *Pañcatantra* and the *Tantrākhyāyikā* had been derived from a defective original which he designated by the letter T. But notwithstanding what has been said above, this has not been proved. He thought that the sources of the *Bṛhat-kathā-mañjarī, Kathā-sarit-sāgara* and *Tantrākhyāyikā* and *Pañcatantra* were derivable from two sources, the original of the *Tantrākhyāyikā* and the source of the other three groups and in part of the version B of the *Tantrākhyāyika* itself which he calls K. This also has not been proved and it seems in part implausible also because this would mean that the occurrence of any story in any two of the four versions should be a strong ground for assigning it to the original text. But according to Hertel's own view, such a significance would be plausible, only the story occurred in both the *Tantrākhyāyikā* and one of the K versions. Hertel further assumes apparently without much ground that there was another intermediate archetype, "N-W." which is the direct ancestor of the Pehlevi translation, the Southern *Pañcatantra* group and the Simplicitor of Bühler and Kielhorn. Further, it can also be argued with sufficient ground that the *Tantrākhyāyikā* recension was prior to others. Its omission of stories may not necessarily be the sign of its loyalty to the ultimate source. The recension containing fuller stories need not necessarily be the later one. The word *tantra* in the *Pañcatantra* probably means *śāstra* or *siddhānta*. Thus in the *Amara-koṣa* we have *tantra* in the sense of *siddhānta* and in the *Anekārtha-saṃgraha* the word *tantra* is used in the sense of *śāstra*. *Pañcatantra* thus means *Five Śāstras* or *Five Siddhāntas*. From the name it seems that the *Tantrākhyāyikā* represented the main story of the *Pañcatantra*. This explains why the *Tantrākhyāyikā* should contain less stories than the *Pañcatantra*.

BHASA

Bhasa was probably a Brahmin and a devotee of Viṣṇu. Our knowledge of Bhasa was first acquired merely from the reference to him along with the other poets Saumilla and Kaviputra as dramatists of great distinction by Kalidasa in the *Mālavikāgnimitra.*[1] But as yet we know nothing of Saumilla and Kaviputra. It is, however, difficult to say whether Kalidasa had used Bhasa as the model of the frame of his dramas as Winternitz suggests.[2] The poet Bāṇa in his introductory verse 16, of his *Harṣa-carita,* refers to Bhasa with high compliments.[3] Vakpati in his *Gauḍavaho* mentions Bhasa in verse 800.[4] In commentaries from the 9th to 12th century a drama *Svapna-nāṭaka* or *Svapna-vāsavadattā* is often quoted. But Rajaśekhara refers in a verse in a anthology called *Sūkti-muktāvali* to Bhasa's *Svapna-vāsavadattā* and Bhasa is generally referred to in most anothologies. This was all that was known about Bhasa till 1910 when Gaṇapati Śastrī discovered in South Travancore ten dramas of Bhasa in palm-leaf MSS. all in one bundle and this was regarded as a good ground for recognising in them the lost dramas of Bhasa. Later, however, two other dramas were found. There is an initial difference between the

1 *prathitayaśasāṁ bhāsa-saumilla-kaviputrādīnāṁ prabandhānatikramya vartamāna-kaveḥ kālidāsaya kriyāyāṁ kathaṁ bahumānaḥ.*

2 *Geschichte der indischen Litteratur,* p. 184.

3 *sūtradhārakṛtārambhair nāṭakairbahubhūmikaiḥ |*
sapatākairyaśo lebhe bhāso devakulairiva ||
—*Harṣa-carita,* Śl. 16.

4 *bhāsammi jalaṇamitte kantīdeve a jassa rahuāre |*
sobandhave a bandhammi hāriyande a āṇando || 800

5 For discussions on Bhāsa, see Pischel, G.G.A. 1883, p. 1232 ff; Gaṇapati Śāstrī's Introduction to his edition of *Svapnavāsavadattā* and *Pratimā-nāṭaka*; Jacobi, *Internat. Monatsschrift*. VII, 1913, p. 653 ff; A.A. Macdonell, J.R.A.S., 1913, p. 186 ff; V. A. Smith, *Indian Antiquary*, 1911, p. 87 ff; Suali in G.S.A.I., 25, 1912, p. 5 ff; Hertel, *Jina-kirtti's Geschichte von Pāla und Gopāla*, p. 152 ff; Max Lindenau, *Bhāsa-Studien, ein Beitrag zur Geschichte des altindischen Dramas* (Leipzig, 1918).

The verses of Bhāsa in the anthologies have been collected together and translated by Aufrech in *Ind. Stud.* 17, 168 ff; Z.D.M.G. 27, 65; 36, 370 ff; and Peterson, *Subhāṣita-muktāvali*, p. 80 ff; J.R.A.S., 1891, p. 331 ff. also pp. 105 and 159.

ordinary classical drama and the dramas of Bhāsa. In the ordinary classical dramas we find that after the *nāndī* the *sūtradhāra* steps in (*nāndyante sūtradhāraḥ*). But in the newly found dramas the *sūtradhāra* steps in after the *nāndī* and begins sometimes with an introductory adoration to Viṣṇu as in the *Avimāraka* and the *Dūta-ghaṭotkaca*; and at other times starts with introducing in the usual manner by suggestion the names of the important personages. In the ordinary classical dramas again we find a little praise of the drama and the name of the author, but it is not so in the newly found dramas. The plays are generally short and sometimes of one Act. The dramas generally begin with one adoration hymn and end also with one. But in the dramas of Bhāsa generally there is the same type of the *Bharata-vākya* called generally *sthapanā* in which a benediction is referred to the king, as in the *Svapna-nāṭaka*, the *Pratijñā-nāṭaka* and the *Pañcarātra-nāṭaka*. The king is often called Rājasiṃha.[1] We cannot ascertain that this Rājasiṃha is a Pallava king.

The *nāṭakas* of Bhāsa are as follows: *Svapna-nāṭaka*, *Pratijñā-nāṭaka*, *Pañcarātra*, *Cārudatta*, *Dūta-ghaṭotkaca*, *Avimāraka*, *Bālacarita*, *Madhyama-vyāyoga*, *Karṇa-bhāra*, *Ūru-bhaṅga*, *Abhiṣeka-nāṭaka*, *Pratimā-nāṭaka*. These were all in old Kerala characters.

That these dramas were written by one and the same person appears to be certain on account of the identity of style and the fact that some of the verses are repeated from drama to drama and the same ways of speech occur in several dramas.

1 *evam āryamiśrān vijñāpayāmi* |
aye, kiṁ nu khalu mayi vijñāpanavyagre śabda iva śrūyate |
aṅga ! *paśyāmi*.

This passage occurs in all the dramas excepting *Pratijñā*, *Cārudatta*, *Avimāraka* *Pratimā* and *Karṇa-bhāra*. Again, the passage

imāṁ sāgaraparyantāṁ himavad-vindhya-kuṇḍalām |
mahīmekātapatrāṅkām rājasiṁhaḥ praśāstu naḥ ||

occurs in *Svapna* and *Bāla-carita*. Again.

bhavantvarajas gāvaḥ paracakraṁ praśāmyatu |
imāmapi mahīṁ kṛtsnāṁ rājasiṁhaḥ praśāstu naḥ ||

The *Svapna-nāṭaka* has been referred to as *Svapna-vāsava-dattā* by Abhinavagupta and the name of Bhāsa has been referred to by Kālidāsa and Bāṇa. The *Svapna-nāṭaka* appears in another MS. as *Svapna-vāsavadattā*. It is from this scanty evidence that it has been suggested that Bhāsa was the author of these dramas. This raised a storm of discussion amongst scholars, both Indian and European. Since the publication of the new dramas by MM T. Gaṇapati Śāstrī, scholars like Jacobi (translation of the *Svapna-vāsavadattā*), Jolly (*Nachrichten*, 1916), Winternitz (*Festschrift Kuhn*, pp. 299-304), Konow (*Festschrift Kuhn*, pp. 106 *et seq.* and *Das Indischen drama*, p. 51 ; *Ind. Ant.*, 49, 1920, 233 ff.), M. Baston (translation of the *Svapna-vāsavadattā*), Suali (*Giornale della soc. As. Italiana*, XXV, p. 95), Pavolini (*Giornale della soc. As. Italiana*), Lesny, Dr. Lindenau (*Bhāsa Studien*), Dr. Morgenstierne, M. Lacôte, Dr. Printz,, Dr. Barnett, (B.S.O.S., I., 3, 1920, p. 35 ff) Dr. Thomas (J.R.A.S., 1922, 79 ff.), Pisharoti, Dr. Sukthankar (J.A.O.S., 40, 1920. 248 ff ; 41, 1921, 1 ff. ; J.B.R.A.S., 1925, p. 126) Rāmāvatāra Pāṇḍeya, Bhaṭṭanāthasvāmī (*Ind. Ant.*, 45, 1916, 189 ff.) Raṅgācārya, Ruddy, Kane and Stein, A. Banerjee-Sastri (J.R.A.S., 1921, p. 367) and many others have continued a controversy since the publication of the Bhāsa dramas by MM. Gaṇapati Śāstrī in 1912. If one has to give a full account of this controversy it may well-nigh fill a volume and yet the controversy cannot be regarded as having reached a conclusive stage. It cannot be expected of us to enter into any elaborate detail about this controversy, but it may be regarded desirable to state some of the salient features regarding the controversy.

occurs in *Pratijñā*, *Avimāraka* and *Abhiṣeka* and the 2nd line occurs also in *Pañcarātra*, Again, the passage.

limpatīva tamo'ṅgāni varṣatīvāñjanaṁ nobhaḥ |
asatpuruṣaseveva dṛṣṭir viphalatāṁ gatā ||

occurs in *Cārudatta* and *Bāla-carita*.

MM. Gaṇapati Śāstrī came across a bundle of palm-leaf MSS. of *nāṭakas* in the Manalikkara Maṭham near Padmanābhapuram, written in old Malayalam character. These MSS. proved to be 10 *rūpakas* and subsequently an eleventh *rūpaka* was found and later on he found from one Govinda Pisharodi two *nāṭakas* of a similar character named *Abhiṣeka-nāṭaka* and *Pratimā-nāṭaka*. Subsequently to this he found that the Palace Library of Travancore contained a MS. of each of these two books. So altogether these 13 *rūpakas* were discovered which were never seen or heard of before. In this connection it is well worth noting that there is the practice in the Malayalam country from very ancient times of having Sanskrit *nāṭakas* staged in the temples by the priests in which often kings participated.

In the ordinary *nāṭakas* generally a *nāndī* verse is given and then the stage-direction (*nāndyante sūtradhāraḥ*) but in the newly found dramas we have first the stage-direction (*nāndyante tataḥ praviśati sūtradhāraḥ*) and then we have a *maṅgala-śloka*. Again, instead of the word *prastāvanā* these *nāṭaks* use the *sthāpanā*. There is, again no mention of the name of the author and of the work in the *sthāpanā* as is usual to find in the *prastāvanā* of other dramas. In these dramas again there is at the end of the drama a sentence announcing the fact that such and such a drama (giving the name) is finished. In the dramas of Bhāsa we have always a prayer to the effect "May our greatest of kings or may our king rule the land."

Now, since the author's name is not given in any of the dramas, two questions naturally arise ; (1) who are the authors of the dramas, (2) are they all from the one hand, or they are written by different men ? Further questions arise as follows : Assuming, for reasons presently to be adduced, that Bhāsa is the author of one or two or all these dramas, was there one Bhāsa, or an earlier and a later Bhāsa ; and about some of these dramas a further question may be raised as to whether there was more than one drama of the same name written by different authors, or by two authors of the same name, an earlier and a later.

The earliest mention of Bhāsa is made by Kālidāsa in *Mālavikāgnimitra* along with Saumilla and Kaviputra. We know practically nothing of Saumilla and Kaviputra. MM. Gaṇapati Śāstrī has urged that these newly found dramas are the dramas of this pre-Kālidāsa Bhāsa. His view has been endorsed by most European scholars excepting Dr. Barnett. Dr. Ottoztein seems to be unable to pronounce any judgment while Dr. Barnett, Pisharoti and Rāmāvatāra Pāṇḍeya and some othe scholars hold that these dramas cannot be of any pre-Kālidāsa Bhāsa, but that they were probably written sometime in the 7th century A.D.

Regarding the supposition that all these dramas were written by the same author, MM. Gaṇapati Śāstrī points out that the verse *limpatīva* occurs both in *Cārudatta* and *Bāla-carita.* The sentence *kiṃ vakṣyatīti hṛdayaṃ pariśaṃkitaṃ me* occurs in the 6th Act of the *Svapna-nāṭaka* and the 4th Act of the *Abhiṣeka* and a few such other points of similarity can be detected in the plays.

On the point that Bhāsa was the author of the *Svapna-vāsavadattā,* he refers to the verse of Rājaśekhara in the *Kavi-vimarśa* quoted in the *Śūkti-muktāvali* and Bhāsa has been spoken of as being the author of the *Svapna-vāsavadatta.*[1] He also refers to Kālidāsa's allusion to Bhāsa as well as Bāṇa's.[2] From this MM. G. Śāstrī argues that the word *sūtradhārakṛtārambhaih* means a reference to the stage-direction found in these dramas and therefore here Bāṇa's reference proves that these dramas were written by Bhāsa ; and we have the *śloka* of Rājaśekhara that *Svapna-vāsavadattā* belonged to the group of Bhāsa dramas.

1 *bhāsanāṭakacakre'pi cchekaiḥ kṣipte parīkṣitum |*
svapnavāsavadattasya dāhako'bhūnna pāvakaḥ ||

2 *sūtradhārakṛtārambhair nāṭakairbahubhūmikaiḥ |*
sapatākairyaśo lebhe bhāso devakulairiva ||
—*Harṣa-carita, Śloka* 16.

Now, this argument does not appear to be conclusive. Pisharoti refers to the verses of the *Kavi-vimarśa* in the same context and shows that Rājaśekhara there attributes *Priyadarśikā* and *Ratnāvalī* to Bhāsa.[1] Rājaśekhara further in the same context says that Śrīharṣa made Bhāsa a *sabhā-kavi*. Doubts have also been raised by other scholars as to whether the *Kavi-vimarśa* is at all a work of Rājaśekhara or not. In any case, if this Bhāsa was the writer of the *Svapna-vāsavadattā* he flourished in Śrīharṣa's time and cannot be the pre-Kālidāsa Bhāsa. Again, all dramas are really begun by the *sūtradhāra*. In the ordinary dramas he is alrady on the stage, recites the *nāndīśloka* and then begins the drama. In the newly found dramas, it is suggested, that some one else or the *sūtradhāra* himself recites the *nāndī* without entering the stage and after the *nāndīśloka* has been recited probably from behind the stage the *sūtradhāra* enters and recites a verse in which he introduces the principal personages and in the course of that also offers a benediction. Under the circumstances, it is difficult to suppose that Bāṇa's reference *sūtradhārakṛtārambhaiḥ* refers the special feature of the introductory stage-direction of the dramas. Moreover Bāṇa seems to have introduced the word *sūtradhārakṛtārambhaiḥ* and *sapatākaiḥ* for maintaining his imagery through a double meaning. Had this not been so and had the verse any intention of offerring to the special features of Bhāsa's drama this would have applied to the terms *bahubhūmikaiḥ* and *saytākaiḥ* and such new features would have been discoverable in the newly published dramas.

It may be worthwhile to consider a few others references. Sarvānanda, who probably lived in the 13th or 14th century, wrote a commentary on the *Amara-koṣa* called *Amarakoṣa-ṭīkā-sarvasva*. In this work there is a reference to the *Svapna-vāsavadattā* and MM. Śāstrī holds that there is a reference to the

1 *ādau bhāsena racitā nāṭikā priyadarśikā |*
tasya ratnāvalī nūnam ratnamāleva rājate ||
See Pisharoti's articles on Bhāsa Problem, *India Historical Quarterly*, 1925, p. 103.

marriage of Udayana with Padmāvatī and Vāsavadattā here.[1] But owing to considrations discussed in the foot-note, it may well be doubted whether there is any reference here to the *Svapna-vāsavadattā* of MM. G. Śāstrī. Again, Abhinavagupta also mentions *Svapna-vāsavadattā* and *Daridra-carudatta*. Here also we have no reason to suppose that the *Daridra-carudatta* is the same as out *Cārudatta-nāṭaka* and all we can know from here is that there were these two *nāṭakas*, *Svapna-vāsavadattā* and *Daridra-cārudatta*, and we know really nothing of their authorship. Again, Vāmana in the 3rd *adhyay* of the 4th *adhikaraṇa* of his *Kāvyālaṅkāra-sūtravṛtti* quotes a passage without naming the book or the author and this passage is found in the printed text of *Svana-vāsavadattā* in the 4th Act. There are also two other quotations from Vāmana which may be traced in the 4th Act of the *Pratijñā-yaugandharāyaṇa* and the 1st Act of the *Cārudatta-nāṭaka*.[2] The verse *limpatīva tamo'ṅgāni* found

1 The passage in the *Amara-ṭīkā-sarvasva* is as follows :—

trividhaḥ śṛṅgāraḥ dharmārthakāmabhinnaḥ tatrādyo yathā nandayantyāṁ brāhmaṇabhojanaṁ dvitīyaḥ svadeśam ātmasāt kartum udayanasya padmāvatīpariṇayaḥ arthaśṛṅgārastṛtīyaḥ svapnavāsavadatte tasyaiva vāsavadattāpariṇayaḥ. The passage has been otherwise put by MM. G. Śāstrī in his Introduction to the *Svapna-vāsavadattā*: —*svadeśamātmasāt kartum udayanasya padmāvatipariṇayaḥ arthaśṛṅgāraḥ svapnavāsavadatte tṛtīyastasyaiva-vāsavadattāpariṇayaḥ Kāmaśṛṅgāraḥ*. It will be seen that by translating the word *svapna vāsavadatte* before *tṛtīya* the meaning has been absolutely changed. If the former is the right reading as I suppose it is, then the work *Svapna-vāsavadatta* referred to here, would describe *Vāsavadattā pariṇayaḥ* and not *Padmāvatī-pariṇayaḥ* as is found in the printed text of the *Svapna-vāsavadatta* publishrd by MM. G. Śastrī. Granting that MM, G. Śāstrī's reading is correct, we have only the evidence here of a *Svapna--vāsavadattā* in which two marriages are described of Padmāvatī and Vāsavadattā. But in the printed text only one marriage is described and even then, as a story is taken from an older source, it does not rule out that there may have been two *Svapna-vāsavadattās* and it does not prove that it is a work of Bhāsa.

See Pisharoti's article on Bhāsa Problem, *Indian Historical Quarterly*, 1925.

2 *śaracchaśāṅkagaureṇa vātāviddhena bhāmini |*
kāśapuṣpalavenedaṁ sāśrupātaṁ mukhaṁ mama ||

—Vāmana, IV. 3.

Cf. 4th Act of the *Svapna-vāsavadatta*.

yu bharttṛpiṇḍasya kṛte na yudhye t |

—Vāmana, V. 2,

Cf. 4th Act, *Pratijñā-yaugandharāyaṇa*.

in the *Kāvyādarśa* of Daṇḍin occurs also in the *Bālacarita* and the *Cārudatta*. But so far as these are concerned, these prove practically nothing regarding the authorship of the dramas or their being the works of the same hand. Again, in the 3rd *uddyota* of the *Dhvanyāloka-locana* a passage is quoted as belonging to the *Svapna-vāsavadatta*, but it does not occur in the printed text. This śloka is not only to be found in the *Svapna-vāsavadatta* but MM. G. Śastri himself admits that we cannot imagine any situation in the *Svapna-vāsavadatta* in which such a passage could have occurred. It is rather curious that an authority like Abhinavagupta should make any error of this type. Again, in the explanation of the 85th *kārikā* of the 6th chapter of the *Sāhitya-darpaṇa* a śloka is referred to as having been quoted from the *Bāla-carita* but this is not avaiable in the printed text nor can a proper situation be imagined for it, in it. But Bhāmaha gives a description of events in his chapter on *Nyāya-virodha* which tallies with similar descriptions in the *Pratijñā-nāṭaka* and a passage from it is found repeated in Prākṛt in the same *nāṭaka*. But Bhāmaha does not mention anything about the name of the *nāṭaka* or its author. Again, the same reference that is found in Sarvānanda's *Ṭīkā-sarvasva*, is found in the *Nāṭaka-lakṣaṇa-ratna-koṣa*. In the *Kaumudī-mahotsava* we find reference to Avimāraka the hero and Kuraṅgī the heroine but this is not probably a reference to the printed drama *Avimāraka*. A 14th century commentary on the *Śakuntalā* says that the *sūtradhāra* of the play *Cārudatta* uses Prākṛt and this is testified in the printed text of the *Cārudatt.a* The *Nātya-darpaṇa* again mentions a drama called the *Daridra-cārudatta* but the verse quoted in the *Nātya-darpaṇa* from the *Svapna-vāsavadatta* is not found in it though we may imagine a situation for it in *Svapna-vāsavadatta* IV. Again, in the *Nāṭaka-lakṣaṇa-ratna-koṣa* a verse is quoted from the *Cārudatta*, the contents of

Again, *yāsāṁ balirbhavati*, etc.

—Vāmana, V. I.

Cf. 1st Act of the *Cārudatta-nāṭaka*.

which is traceable to the *Mṛcchakaṭika* but not to the *Cārudatta-nāṭaka*. But we have nowhere in these passages any reference to Bhāsa. Again, Sāradātanaya has a quotation in his *Bhāva-prakāśana* from the *Svapna-vāsavadatta*. It is not available in the printed text but a situation corresponding to it can be imagined in the 5th Act of the *Svapna-vāsavadatta*. In an article MM. Gaṇapati Śāstrī refers to a passage from the *Śṛṅgāra-prakāśa* of Bhojadeva of the 11th century where in the plot of the 5th Act of the printed text of the *Svapna-vāsavadatta* is delineated, but unfortunately there is no mention here of Bhāsa as the author of the *Svapna-vāsavadatta*.[1] The *Nātya-darpaṇa*, however, mentions *Daridra-cārudatta* but not the author, but he refers to the *Svapna-vāsavadatta* as being a work of Bhāsa and gives a quatation from it, as we have already said.[2]

Now let us sum up the position. There is undoubted by an old pre-Kālidāsa Bhāsa. Bhāsa is known to Bāṇa-Bhaṭṭa, but whether this Bhāsa was the pre-Kālidāsa Bhāsa or if we believe the testimony of the *Kavi-vimarśa* of Rājaśekhara, a contemporary of himself, we do not know. Practically none of the verses quoted in different books as belonging to the *Svapna-vāsavadatta* or other texts, are found in the printed text. Of all the dramas only the *Svapna-vāsavadatta* has been mentioned as being the work of Bhāsa in the *Nātya-darpaṇa*, but the quotation does not tally with the text of the printed book. The quotation from the *Nāṭaka-lakṣaṇa-ratna-koṣa* also shows that there existed a version of the *Svapna-vāsavadatta* with at least a different *sthāpanā* and there were at least some scenes in it which were not found in the printed text. These and other evidences, when put together, lead us to conclude that we are prepared to agree that Bhāsa had written the *Svapna-vāsavadatta*. But that the present text

1 The *Śṛṅgāra-prakāśa* (11th century) describes the plot of the 5th Act as follows: *svapnavāsavadatte padmāvatīṁ asvasthāṁ draṣṭuṁ rājā samudragṛhakaṁ gataḥ | padmāvatīrahitaṁ ca tadavalokyā tasyā eva śayane suṣvāpa | vāsavadattāṁ ca svapnavad asvapne dadarśa | svapnāyamānaśca vāsavadattām ābabhāṣe | svapnaśabdena ceha svāpo vā svapnadārśanaṁ va svapnāyitaṁ vā vivakṣitam |*

2 *Nāṭyadarpaṇa*, pp. 53 *and* 84.

should be identically the same work is more than what we can say. It is strange that there should be no reference to the works of Bhāsa that are now attributed to him in the printed texts of the T. S. Series. It is also strange that the few quotations that have referred to the *Svapna-vāsavadatta* should not be available in the printed text and that other references to other texts, like the *Bāla-carita* or the *Daridracārudatta* should not be traceable to to the printed text. It may be that when other MSS. are available such quotations may be traceable. But I doubt it very much. In any case, until such MSS. are available we cannot say that the printed text of the *Svapna-vāsavadatta* is the *Svapna-vāsavadatta* of pre-Kālidasa Bhāsa.

Judging the evidences as a whole it seems to be probable that these works probably are texts adapted from the work of an old Bhāsa by castigation and insertion to suit the convenience of the theatrical audience at the temples in Travancore. It is for this reason that though the name of the drama is given in the end, the name of the author is not given, for the editor who pruned the text of Bhāsa could not pass it off as a work of Bhāsa before an audience which knew what Bhāsa's works were. Neither could he advertise his own name as an editor of Bhāsa, for the editing was made for the convenience of staging and not for the improvement of the text. It may in this connection be pointed out that the so-called *Svapna-vāsavadatta* of the T.S. Series is actually called the *Svapna-nāṭakam* and not the *Svapna-vāsavadatta.* The shortening was unnecessary if it was not intended to distinguish it from the *Svapna-vāsavadatta.* The fact that the *Uru-bhaṅga* is not a tragedy in one Act but a detached intermediate Act of some drama is also quite obvious. It seems to me, however, that probably all these dramas, to whosoever their authorship may be due, were edited either by the same editor or by the same circle of editors.

Much has been made by the different scholars regarding the difference between *nāndyante sūtradhāraḥ* and *nāndyante praviśati sūtradhāraḥ.* It should be observed in this connection that there may be three classes of *nāndī*—a *nāndī* may be *maṅgala-śloka*, written by the author of the drama, as is found both in the *Śakuntalā* and in the *Vikramorvaśī*. There is another class of *nāndī* which is an auspicious ceremony to be performed for the performance of the drama, which varied differently according to local custom and practice. As this did not form any part of the actual drama this was left out of consideration and was included within stage-directions. It is for this reason that this position is left off as *nāndyante, i.e.*, after the *nandī* has been finished. The writer of the drama does not bother himself as to what may be the nature of this *nāndī*. The third class of *nāndī* was an auspicious verse which was recited by a *sūtradhāra, pāripārśvika* or a *sthāpaka*. In a drama like the *Śakuntalā*, we have first the auspicious verse *yā sṛṣṭiḥ* etc. which is intended by the poet for the auspicious ending of the work. This is no part of the actual drama that is played. Then came the *nāndī*, about the nature of which the poet is silent. The *sūtradhāra* was present on the stage when the *nāndī* ceremony was performed. When the ceremony was over, he started his speech in order to introduce the drama. In the so-called Bhāsa plays the *sūtradhāra* is not supposed to be present when the *nāndī* ceremony was being done. I fancy that this may be due to the fact that some articles of the auspicious rights of the temple wherein the play was staged, was made and the *sūtradhāra* being of a lower caste was not present there. When this *nāndī* of auspicious rights was finished he entered the stage and recited his own *nāndī*. In most cases the sort of verse as prescribed for the *sūtradhāra's nāndī* tallies with the *sūtradhāra's nāndī* of the so-called Bhāsa play ; but it does not tally with the *nāndī* of Kālidāsa, for a *nāndī* should be either of 12 or 8 syllables ; which condition was not satisfied in a *sragdharā* or a *śārdūla-vikrīḍita* metre.

Regarding the date of Bhāsa, the argument of MM. Gaṇapati Śāstrī based on the priority of Bhāmaha to Kālidāsa and Bhāmaha's possible reference to the story contained in

Bhāsa's dramas, seems to be extremely improbable. His statement that Bhāmaha was prior to Guṇāḍhya is also wholly unbelievable. Our reasons for this contention may well be consulted in our treatment of Bhāmaha's date in the Chapter on *Alaṃkāra* and our note on Guṇāḍhya. But it cannot be gainsaid that Bhāsa was already a celebrated and old writer in the time of Kālidāsa, for Kālidāsa refers to him as *prathitayaśāḥ* (of well-spread celebrity) and contrasts himself as a new (*nava*) writer, while Bhāsa's work is regarded as old (*purāṇa*). We can, therefore, safely place him at least two to three centuries before Kālidāsa. There is no reference to Bhāsa in any pre-Kālidāsa documents. This pre-Kālidāsa Bhāsa may thus be believed to have lived in the 3rd century B. C. In the *Pratimā-nāṭaka* (5th Act) a reference is made to a *Mānavīya-Dharmaśāstra*, a *Bārhaspatya-Arthaśāstra*, a *Nyāyaśāstra* of Medhātithi and a *Prācetasa-Śrāddhakalpa*. But nothing can be made out of it. The *Yogaśāstra* and the *Arthaśāstra* have been referred to in the *Avimāraka* and the *Pratijña-yaugandharāyaṇa*. But nothing important can be made out of this, for the *Yogaśātra*, the *Artha-śāstra* and the *Mānavīya-Dharmaśastra* are certainly older than Bhāsa. We do not know of any *Nyāyaśastra* by Medhātithi. In language, the style of Bhāsa seems to stand between Kālidāsa and Aśvaghoṣa. The Prākṛt also is older than that used in the classical dramas. On this evidence, Winternitz would place Bhāsa in the 3rd century or the first half of the 4th century A.D.[1]

Most of the stories are drawn from *Mahābhārata*. Kṛṣṇa and Rāma legends also play their part in the *Bāla-carita* and the dramas *Pratimā-nāṭaka* and *Abhiṣeka-nāṭaka*. The story of the *Svapna-nāṭaka* and *Pratijñā-yaugandharāyaṇa* are drawn from Guṇāḍhya's *Bṛhat-kathā* and probably also that of *Avimāraka* and *Darīdra-cārudatta*.

1 See Lesny, Z.D.M.G., 1917, p. 203 ff., see also Lindenau, *Bhāsa Studien*, p. 14 ff., who believes Bhāsa to have lived after 200 A.D. Aśvaghoṣa and Bharata probably lived between 100 and 200 A.D.

The plays of Bhāsa have been differently classified by different people.[1] We may thus divide them as follows : (i) the Udayna plays—*Svapna* and *Pratijñā* ; (ii) Fiction or original plays—*Avimāraka* and *Cārudatta* ; (iii) the *Mahābhārata* plays—*Bālacarita, Duta-ghaṭotkaca, Dūta-vākya, Karṇabhāra, Pañca-rātra, Ūrubhaṅga, Madhyama-vyāyoga* ; (iv) the *Rāmāyaṇa* plays —*Pratimā* and *Abhiṣeka*—altogether 13 plays.

Some of the South Indian plays, e-g., the *Matta-vilāsa, Kalyāṇa-saugandhika, Tapatī-saṃvaraṇa,* etc. and the southern manuscripts of the *Śakuntalā* and the *Nāgānanda,* display some structural peculiarity.[2] But the plays of Bhāsa show some special structural peculiarity : (i) they begin with the same stage-direction.[3] (ii) The *sūtradhāra* recites only one *maṅgala-śloka* and in some of the dramas the dramatic persons are introduced in the *maṅgala-śloka.*[4] (iii) Excepting *Karṇabhāra* we have *sthāpanā* instead of *prastāvanā.* (iv) The name of the book is given in the conclusion but the author's name is absent. (v) Excepting some of they dramas, the all begin in the *sthāpanā* with the same kind of phraseology.[5] (vi) The epilogues are nearly identical.

The dramas of Bhāsa not only ignored the rules of the *Nātya-śāstra* in introducing death and violent action on the stage, but they also used the word *ārya-putra* as a term of address from a servant, whereas *ārya-putra* is generally the term of address from a wife to her husband. The dramatic devices

1 Winternitz, O.Z. IX, followed by Devadhara, Plays, etc. Lindenau, *Bhāsa Studien* p. 16 ; Jahagirdar, I.A. 1931, pp. 42-44 ; Svarupa, *Vision.* Introduction, p. 10.

2 See *Bhāsa—A Study, Pusalker,* 1940. They all begin with the lines : *aye kinnu khalu mayi vijñāpanavyagre śabda iva śrūyate.*

3 *nāndyante tataḥ praviśati sūtradhāraḥ.*

4 *Svapna, Pratijñā, Pañcarātra* and *Pratimā.*

5 *evam āryamiśrān vijñāpayāmi. aye, kinnu khalu mayi vijñāpanavyagre śabda iva śrūyate. aṅga paśyāmi.* The *Pratijñā, Cārudatta, Avimāraka* and *Pratimā* use a different form.

6 They use the verse :

imāṁ sāgaraparyantāṁ himavad-vindhya-kuṇḍalām |
mahīmekātapatrāṅkāṁ rājasiṁhaḥ praśāstu naḥ ||

Cārudatta and *Dūta-ghaṭotkaca* have no epilogues.

are also similar in most of the plays ; such as, the constant recourse to *ākāśabhāṣitam*, description of battles, duels, etc. The entrance of persons of high ranks preceded by the words *ussaraha, ussaraha*. The cammunication of the intervening events is by a chamberlain, who addresses the female door-keeper in somewhat the same phraseology. The door-keeper is often addressed with the same phraseology, such as *nivedyatām, nivedyatām*. The dramatic characters often know what is passing in others' minds.[1] We also often notice the same kind of ideas, such as, (*i*) the best weapon of a hero is his hand ; (*ii*) Nārada is described as inciting quarrels. (*iii*) Dhṛtarāṣṭra is described as having been made blind through the jealousy of the gods. (*iv*) Arjuna's exploits with the Kirāta is described in the same terms in *Dūta-vākya, Dūta-ghaṭotkaca* and *Uru-bhaṇga* (*v*) Inference of the existence of cities from the watering of trees. (*vi*) The idea that kings live in their sacrifice.

The dramatic device of *patākāsthāna* is used in *Pratiñā*, Act II, *Abhiṣeka*, V, *Avimāraka*; Act II, *Pañcarātra*, Act I, *Pratima*, Act I.

Again, similar forms of irony and dramatic situation *Prati*., V. 20 (p. 107) and *Abhiṣeka*, II. 18 (p. 27), in *Bāla*. (p. 61) and *Pañca*. (p. 87) are sometimes introduced. The same expressions are sometimes used in different dramas. The use of common imagery of a peculiar character, the introduction of similar dramatic scenes and even the use of similar unique exrressions and vocabulary and the recurrence of the same verses and long prose passages, grammatical solecisms and Prākṛt archaisms all go to prove that whatever may have been the original of these plays, they all were the products of the same hand.[2]

But howsoever Professor Pusalker and others may try to explain the absence of the verses quoted from Bhāsa by other writers in the printed T.S. texts by inventing situations where

1 See *Bhāsa*, Pusalker, p. 8.
2 See *Bhāsa* by Pusalker for details.

their verses might have occurred and by attributing everything to clerical error, the facts remain that these are not found in the T. S. texts, so even though we are willing to believe that the texts originally belonged to the author, it cannot be denied that they suffered much alteration and nothing is settled about the point that they were written by a pre-Kālidāsa Bhāsa.

Bāṇa refers to a Bhāsa and it is possible that this is a reference to a pre-Kālidāsa Bhāsa. Now *patākā* means *aṅka* and banner[1] and *bhūmikā* means composition and change of dress. Thus the verse may be translated thus :—Bhāsa attained fame by his introduction of dramas with the stage manager (carpenter) and with many actors and its division in many acts like the houses of gods which are commenced with the carpenter's line and have many floors and banners. It my opinion this suggests that Bhāsa was the first to start the classical drama as starting with a *Sūtradhāra* and a compound of many players in diverse dress and also of many acts. This would make Bhāsa a very old writer who according to Bāṇa gave the structure and from to the classical drama and therefore attained such great fame. But yet we have no evidence that this Bhāsa was the writer of the T.S.S. plays, as they now stand. But we are prepared to agree that though there may have been castigations, modifications and changes, on the whole they revel the composition of the old Bhāsa. Since we have placed Kālidāsa in the 1st century B.C. and since we find that there is no Aśokan influence of the prohibition of sacrifices and since we also find the great prevalence of image-worship at the time, and for sundry other reasons as

1 *sūtradhārakṛtārambhair nāṭakairbahubhūmikaiḥ |*
sapatākairyaśo lebhe bhāso devakulairiva ||
—Harṣa-carita.

patākā vaijayantyāṁ ca saubhāgye'ṅke dhvaje'pi ca
—Viśva

bhūmikāracanāyāṁ syād veśāntaraparigrahe
—Medinī

Kulaṁ janapade gṛhe
—Viśva

the style and the like, our conjecture is that he was probably a writer of the Mauryya times. It seems also probable that he lived at a time when the *Mahābhārata* tales had not been worked up in the present form. The characterisation of Duryyodhana and his consent in giving back to the Pāṇḍavas half the kingdom are such radical changes of the story of *Mahābhārata* that no writer could have introduced those tales without giving a rude shock to public feelings at a time when the *Mahābhārata* had been codified in the present form. His tendency to write different types of dramas also supports the view that he was writing at a time when these various forms of drama were gradually evolving out.

In the *Dūta-kāvya* a scene from the *Udyoga-parva* is depicted. Bhīṣma was being appointed as the general. When Kṛṣṇa comes with a message of conciliation and peace, Duryyodhana tries to insult him by looking at a picture portraying the scene of the pulling of Draupadī's hair and clothes and has a wordy conversation with him. After this he tries to arrest him but Kṛṣṇa shows his cosmic form and Duryyodhana flies away. Kṛṣṇa's weapons, *Sudarśana,* etc., appear but finding Kṛṣṇa pacified go away. Dhṛtarāṣṭra falls at his feet and mollifies him. The portrait scene and the appearance of Kṛṣṇa's weapons are new modifications on the story of the *Mahābhārata.* In the *Mahābhārata,* Dhṛtarāṣṭra is the Emperor but here Duryyodhana is the real Emperor as well as a mighty warrior, whereas in the *Mahābhārata* he is only a wicked man. It is either a *vyāyoga* or a *vīthi.*

KARṆA-BHĀRA

Karṇa was appointed general after Droṇa. He asked Śalya to drive the chariot where Arjuna was fighting. He is held back for a moment by the memory of his relationship with the Pāṇḍavas anh tells Śalya the story of how he received new weapons from Paraśurāma. In the meanwhile, Indra in the form of a Brahmin asked for his natural armour which he gives away to him in spite of the warning of Śalya. Indra sends Vimala, as Śakti, to Karṇa. Karṇa asks Śalya to drag the chariot to the battle-field.

In the Epic, the story of the giving away of the natural armour happens earlier, while the Pāṇḍavas were in the forest. The introduction of the episode in the midst of the war makes Karṇa appear nobler. Śalya is more sympathetic to Karṇa than in the Epic. It is a *vyāyoga* and also an instance ofu *tsṛṣṭikāṅka.*

DŪTA-GHATOṬKACA

In this play Ghaṭotkaca is represented as going to Dhṛtarāṣṭra on the death of Abhimanyu, to tell him that this foul deed will be avenged. Dhṛtarāṣṭra himself was quite angry with his sons and Jayadratha for the commision of the act and had assured them that nothing would save them from the arrows of the Pāṇḍavas. The embassy of Ghaṭotkaca is a new introduction, which does not occur in the Epic.

ŪRU-BHAṄGA

Whereas in the Epic the family of Duryyodhana is far away from the battle-field, in this drama after the club fight between Bhīma and Duryyodhana, when Duryyodhana was stuck in the thigh agains the rules of fight, the poet utilises the opportunity of demonstrating Duryyodhana's softer sentiments towards his father, wife and child. Duryyodhana also shows great partience and forbearance in trying to dissuade Balarāma and Aśvatthāmā from avenging his death by killing the Pāṇḍavas. He also confesses that he has done more ill to the Pāṇḍavas than they had done to him.

It is an *utsṛṣṭikāṅka.*

MADHYAMA-VYĀYOGA

It is a story which is wholly invented. It depicts the meeting of Bhīma and Ghaṭotkaca; the latter was out for securing a victim for his mother and the three sons of a Brahmin were all vying with one another for being made a victim. The middle one was chosen but as Ghaṭotkaca was calling for him as *madhyama, madhyama,* Bhīma appeared on the scene. Bhīma offers himself as a victim if Ghaṭotkaca was able to take him by force, in which he fails. Bhīma then accompanied Ghaṭotkaca to Hiḍimbā who recognised him.

Pañcarātra

In this play Duryyodhana performed a sacrifice with Droṇa as the priest and as the *dakṣiṇā* of the sacrifice Droṇa requests Duryyodhana to settle with the Pāṇḍavas by giving them half the Empire and Duryyodhana agreess if any news of the Pāṇḍavas would be got within five days. This being fulfilled, Duryyodhana agrees to part with half the kingdom in favour of the Pāṇḍavas. We have nowhere in the Epic the performance of the sacrifice, agreement with Droṇa and the final parting of half the kingdom to the Pāṇḍavas, which would have made the Kurukṣetra battle impossible. It is a *samavakāra.*

Abhiṣeka

The scene opens in Kiṣkindhyā and the agreement between Sugrīva and Rāma to help each other. Sugrīva challenges Bāli to fight but when he is worsted in the fight, Rāma kills him with an arrow. After the death of Bāli, Sugrīva is anointed king. There is much deviation here from the description in the *Rāmāyaṇa.*

Bāla-carita

It deals with the early life of Kṛṣṇa. There are some elements in it which does not tally with the description of Kṛṣṇa as we find elsewhere. Though the dancing of the Gopinīs is mentioned, we do not find any of the amorous scenes described in the *Bhāgavata* or the *Brahma-vaivartta.* The girl that is killed by Kaṃsa has been given birth to by Devakī. After Kṛṣṇa had killed Kaṃsa, the old king Ugrasena was released from prison. and was crowned.

Avimāraka

The story of the *Avimāraka* seems to have been taken either from the *Bṛhat-kathā* or from some floating stories of the time which were taken up by the *Bṛhat-kathā* ; yet the story, as it appears, is slightly different from that found in the *Kathā-sarit-sāgara*. It is a long story. It refers to the union of Kuraṅgī, daughter of a king, with Avimāraka, who was also a prince in disguise in clandestine ways. It is a full-fledged *nāṭaka*.

Pratima

The *Pratimā* which is a full-fledged *nāṭaka*, is based on the story of the *Rāmāyaṇa*, with many deviations, both as regards plot and as regards the depicting of characters.

Pratijñā-Yaugandharāyaṇa

It is a story from the *Bṛhat-kathā* with deviations. In this play king Pradyota, willing to give his daughter Vāsavadattā in marriage to Vatsarāja, took him by a ruse and carried him off to his country. There Vatsarāja fell in love with Vāsavadattā. By a cunning device of the minister Yaugandharāyaṇa, Vatsarāja succeeded in eloping with Vāsavadattā. It has been regarded by some as a *prakaraṇa* and by others as a *nāṭikā* and by others as an *īhāmṛga*.

Svapna-Vāsavadatta

Udayana Vatsarāja lost a part of his kingdom by the invasion of Āruṇi. The minister Yaugandharāyaṇa conceived of the plan of making Udayana marry the daughter of the king of

Madadha in order to make an ally of him for restoring the kingdom conquered by Āruṇi. Udayana's wife Vāsavadattā agrees with the plan fixed by Yaugandharāyaṇa and arives at Rājagṛha in an *āśramạ,* posing herself as a sister of Yaugandharāyaṇa. Padmāvatī, the daughter of the Magadha king, comes there and meets Vāsavadattā in disguise. Padmāvatī agrees to the request of Yaugandharāyaṇa to keep Vāsavadattā with her. A rumour is afloat that there is a great fire at Lavaṅka in which both Yaugandharāyaṇa and Vāsavadattā perished. Vāsavadattā describes to Padmāvatī the beauty of Udayana. A betrothal of Padmāvatī with Udhyana is arranged. The marriage of Udayana takes place. But the king Udayana, though he had heard of the death of Vāsavadattā in the Lavaṇaka fire and though he had married Padmāvatī, was still in very much grief for her. In one scene Udayana was asleep on bed and Vāsavadattā, mistaking him to be Padmāvatī sleeps beside him. But the king, in his dream calls out for Vāsavadattā and recognises Vāsavadattā. But she leaves hastily. Udayana then with the combined forces that belonged to him and the king of Magadha, regains his kingdom. His mother-in-law the Queen Aṅgāravatī, had sent him a picture of Udayana and Vāsavadattā. Padmāvatī recognises in the portrait Avantikā, who was in the disguise of Vāsavadattā with her. At this time a Brahmin, who was Yaugandharāyaṇa in disguise, is announced and Vāsavadattā is brought in and when her veil is removed, she is recognised and Padmāvatī pays her homage to Vāsavadattā.

CĀRRUDATTA

No precise information is available regarding the source of the story. It is very closely allied to the story of the *Mṛcchakaṭika.* It is a *prakaraṇa.*[1]

1 For material in the study of Bhāsa and a masterly treatment of the subject in detail reference may be made to *Bhāsa—A Study,* by A. D. Pusalker.

KĀLIDĀSA

Much has been written in the East and the West about the date of Kalidāsa.[1] There is a story that Kalidāsa was the son of a Brahmin, but early in life he was a cowherd boy. He, however, succeeded in marrying a princess and being shamed by her, he adored the goddess Kalī through whose grace he became a great scholar and poet. Hence his name was Kalidāsa.[2] Another Ceylones tradition makes him a contemporary of the poet Kumāradāsa of the 6th century A.D.[3] Hoernle says that Kalidāsa was like a hook to which many stories hanged, although they have no historical validity.[4]

All that we may learn from Kalidāsa's own works is that he was probably devoted to Śiva. He also adores Viṣṇu as the incarnation of Brahman and he praises Brahman as the original cause of the world. He seems to have been quite familiar to

1 See G. Huth, *Die Zeit des Kālidāsa*, Diss, Berlin, 1890 and B. Liebich, *Indogermanische Forschungen*, 1912-13, p. 198 ff.

2 See Tāranātha's *Geschichte des Buddhismus*, translated by A. Schiefner, p. 76 ff; R. Vāsudeva Tullu, *Indian Antiquary*, 1878, p. 115 ff; M. T. Narasimhiengar, *Indian Antiquary*, 1910, p. 236.

3 See T. W. Rhys Davids and C. Bendall, J,R.A.S., 1888, p. 148 ff., and p. 440; W. Geiger, *Literatur und Sprache der Singhalesan* (*Grunriss* I, 10), p. 3 ff. ; H.M. Vidyābhūṣaṇa, J.A.S.B., 1893, p. 212 ff; J, E. Seneviratne, *The Life of Kālidās*, Colombo, 1901. The life of Kālidāsa has been dramatised in Ceylon. The life of Kālidāsa is found in later works like the *Bhoja-prabandha* and is current in the oral tradition of the pundits, wherein he is said to have been at first a very foolish man who was cutting the branch of the tree on which he was sitting. A princess had made the wager that she would marry the scholar who would defeat her in discussion. Many scholars were defeated by her and some of them, wanting to take their revenge, put forth Kālidāsa as their teacher who was so wise that he remained silent. By a clever ruse they convinced the princess of the scholarship of the speechles man. The lady discovered her mistake in her bridal night. She kicked him out of her bed. He then adored Sarasvatī and became a great poet and went to see the princess. The princess asked him what he wanted. He replied—*asti kaşcid vāg-viśeṣah*. To immortalise his first speech with the princess he wrote three works beginning with *asti* (*Kumāra-sambhava*), *kaścit* (*Megh :-dūta*) and *vāk* (*Raghu-vaṁśa*).

4 Grierson and Hoernle, J.A R.S, 1906, p. 692 ff, and 699 ff; also see *Die Anekdoten über Kālidāsa in Ballala's Bhoja-prabandha* by Th. Pavie, J.A. 1854, pp. 385-431 ; S. M. Natesa Śastri, *Ind. Ant.*, 18, p, 40 ff. ; see also *Geschichten wie sie die Pandits von Ujjain noch heute erzählen* by Jackson, J.A.O.S., 1901, p. 331 ff.

the doctrine of Vedānta, Sāṃkhya and Yoga.[1] He seems to have travelled much over India and was well-acquainted with the geography of India and outside India. He shows his acquaintance with the geography of India in his *Megha-dūta* and it seems that he had carefully observed the actual progress of the monsoon in India. He was a well-known scholar and often loved to depict the old picture of living the *varṇāśrama-dharma*. He is not only acquainted with the science of poetry and dramaturgy but has sufficient knowledge of the pictorial art as well. He was well-versed in all the sciences including Astronomy and Grammar, as well as in Erotics and Polity.[2] He frequently in many places uses the *śabdālaṅkāra* called *yamaka* and refers to and uses many *alaṅkāras* in it.[3] He had also, as is evident from the *Vikramorvaśī*, sufficient knowledge of music, singing and dancing. From his special partiality to Ujjayinī it has been suggested that his home was probably in Ujjayinī. The title of the drama, *Vikramorvaśī* has an allusion, it has been suggested, to Vikramāditya, in whose court he might have lived.[4] Tradition says that he was one of the nine jewels of Vikramāditya's court,[5] the others being Vararuci, Dhanvantari, Kṣapaṇaka, Amarasiṃha, Śaṅku, Vetāla-bhaṭṭa, Ghaṭakarpara and Varāha-mihira. But this traditional account seems to

[1] See Harris, *An Investigation into some of Kālidāsa's Views*, Evansville, Indiana, 1884; M. T. Narasimhi Ivengar, *Kālidāsa's Religion and Philosophy*, *Indian Antiquary*, 1910, p. 236 ff.; also Kirsnamacharya, p. 73 ff.

[2] See Haraprasāda Śāstrī, J.B.O.R.S., 1916, p. 180. In his comparisons we find allusions to technical grammatical terms; Hillebrandt, *Kālidāsa*, p. 143; See also p. 20 ff.; N. G. Mazumdar's article in *Indian Antiquary*, 1918, p. 95; Tucci, R.S.O., 1923, p. 9 ff., p. 22 ff; A. H. Shah, *Kauṭilya and Kālidāsa*, in O.J.M.S., Vol. X No. 4 and Vol XI, 1-3.

[3] See Hillebrandt, *Kālidāsa*, p. 107 ff.

[4] See Bhāu Dāji in Nandargikar's Introduction to his edition of the *Raghu-vaṃśa*, p. 35 ff.

[5] Haraprasād Śāstrī, in J.B.O.R.S, I, 1915, p. 197 ff., thought that it could be proved that Kālidāsa's home was in Malva. Paṇḍit Lachmīdhar in his article, *The Birth-Place of Kālidāsa* (Delhi University publication No. I, 1926) says that his home was in Kashmir. It is also supposed by many that he was born in Vidarbha because he wrote in the Vaidarbhī style; N. G. Mazumder, *Indian Antiquary*, 1918, p. 264; F. G. Peterson, J.R.A.S., 1926, p. 725. Even Bengal has been claimed by some to have been the birth-place of the poet.

have little historical value.[1] Further, the astronomer Varāha-mihira lived probably in the first half of the 6th century. No king at his time had the title of Vikramāditya. The style of Kālidāsa as well as his astronomical views are other than those of Varāha-mihira.[2] So also Dhanvantari, the author of a medical glossary, is older than Amarasiṃha, and he has in his glossary utilised Kālidāsa.[3] Kṣapaṇaka was a lexicographer. He wrote a work called the *Anekārtha-koṣa,* which is quoted in the *Guṇa-ratna-mahodadhi.* Ghaṭakarpara wrote a *kāvya* called the *Ghaṭa-karpara-kāvya.* It has commentaries, such as, those by Vaidya-nātha, Vindhyeśvarīprasāda, Tāracandra, Govardhana, Kuśala-kavi and Abhinavagupta, the last-named one being called the *Ghaṭakarpara-kulaka-vṛtti.* Vararuci is known as a grammarian. About 22 books are ascribed to him of which 13 are works on grammar, one on lexicon, the Prākṛt Grammar, *Prākṛta-prakāśa,* one on medicine, one on *rāja-nīti* and two *kāvyas* called the *Rākṣasa-kāvya* and *Vararuci-vākya-kāvya* and other works. But it is doubtful whether all these were written by him. We know nothing of Śaṅku, but know one called Śaṅkuka, who wrote

1 It has been sometimes erroneously asserted that Kālidāsa had written an astrological text *Jyotirvidābharana* which was probably written in the 16th century A.D.; see A. Weber, Z.D.M.G., 1868. p. 708 ff.

A reference to the *nava-ratna* is found as early as 948 A.D. in an Inscription in Buddha-Gayā. The Inscription is however lost and it is only on the evidence of a doubtful copy of Wilmot and a translation of it by Charles Wilkins (*Asiatic Researches,* 1806, p. 284 ff.) that it is known. Winternitz says that Wilmot was a victim to erroneous belief. See also A. Holtzmann, *Über den griechischen Ursprung des indischen Tierkreises,* Karlsruhe, 1841, 18 ff., p. 27 ff. See also Zachariae, *Die indischen Wörterbücher,* p. 18 f; Fleet, *Indian Antiquary,* 1901, p. 3 f.

2 Jacobi, Z.D.M.G., 1876 p. 304 ff.

3 Zachariae, *Beiträge zur indischen Lexikographie,* Berlin, 1883, p. 37. Dhanvantari wrote a *Nighaṇṭa* called the *Dhanvantarinighaṇṭa.* Other works ascribed to him are: *Ouṣadha-prayoga, Kāla-jñāna, Cikitsā-tattva-vijñāna, Cikitsā-dīpikā Cikitsa-sāra. Bāla-cikitsā, Yoga-cintāmaṇi, Yoga-dīpikā, Vidyā-prakāśa-cikitsā.* Varāha-mihira in his *Pañca-siddhāntikā* takes 506 A. D. as the epoch year of his calculations. Many works of astronomy are attributed to him, such as, *Bṛhat-saṁhitā, Ārūḍha-jātaka, Kāla-cakra, Kriyākairava-candrikā, Jātaka-kalānidhi, Jātaka-sāra or Laghu-jātaka, Daivajña-vallabhā, Pañca-siddhān-tikā, Praśna-candrikā, Bṛhat-jātaka, Mayūra-citraka,, Muhūrta-grantha, Yoga-yātrā, Yogārṇava, Vaṭa-kalikā, Sārāvalī.*

Bhuvanābhyudaya and a work on *alaṃkāra* and also a commentary on Bharata's *Nāṭya-śāstra*. We know nothing of Vetālabhaṭṭa. Amarasiṃha was undoubtedly the celebrated writer of the lexicon called *Amara-koṣa* or *Nāmaliṅgānuśāsana*. It had no less than 37 commentaries, some of which have been published and the others are available in manuscripts. He is also reputed to be a grammarian and as such he has been mentioned in Bopadeva's *Kavikalpadruma*. It is difficult to say how many of the nine jewels lived in the court of Vikramāditya, but many scholars of the present day believe that at least Kālidāsa lived in the court of Vikramāditya of Ujjayinī, who is supposed to have started the Vikrama era to signalise his victory over the Śakas in the year 58 B. C.[1]

There has been a great controversy regarding the date of Kālidasa. Some have tried to prove that he belonged to the 1st or 2nd century B.C.[2] If it could be proved that Aśvaghoṣa in his *Saundarānanda* or the *Buddha-carita* borrowed from Kālidāsa, the contention could be proved[3] But on this point, no infallible judgment can be made, though there are evident similarities between the writings of the two authors.

Chandragupta II and Skandagupta assumed the title of Vikramāditya as evidenced by numismatic proofs. Chandragupta

1 See *Cambridge History of India*, Vol. I. p. 532 ff, 571, 581 (E.J. Rapson); Kielhorn, *Indian Antiquary*, 1890, p. 316, had for the first time demonstrated that the Vikrama era was identical with the Mālava era.

2 K. G. Śaṅkara, and K. M. Shembavnekar and Dhīrendranāth Mukerji in the latter's article on the Gupta era (*Daulatpur College Magazine*, 1934), tried to prove in an unconvincing manner that the Gupta era was identical with Vikrama era and thereby to prove that Kālidāsa lived in the 1st century B. C. A terracotta medallion found in Bhita near Allahabad is a scene of a hermitage and it belongs to the Suṅga period. It hae been suggested that the beautiful scene is that of the hermitage of the *Śakuntalā*. But Sir John Marshall says that it resembles the reliefs of Sanchi and probably represents a scene from the *Jātakas*. Sec. J. R. A. S., 1911, p. 138; *Cambridge History*, Vol. I. p. 643, Plate No. XXIX, 81; also Kṣetresh Bh. Chatterjee's artiele, *The Date of Kālidāsa*, where he tries to prove an earlier date of Kālidāsa.

3 Opinions are available on both sides. While Kṣetresh Ch. Chatterjee holds that Aśvaghoṣa was the borrower, MM. Haraprasāda Śāstrī, in J. B. O. R. S., 1916, p. 186, holds the opposite view.

II had his capital in Ujjayinī. Winternitz, following Bloch, thinks that the *Raghuvaṃśa* contains many allusions to Chandragupta II.[1]

The present writer does not think that there is any evidence that Kālidāsa lived in Ujjayinī for a long time or that the *Raghuvaṃśa* contains any allusion to Chandragupta II. The poet Kālidāsa, of course, is very reverential to Vālmīki, but he does not say of him as a mythical seer of antiquity as living in another *yuga*, as Winternitz says. Jacobi is supposed to have demonstrated that certain astrological data in Kālidāsa's epics reveal an acquaintance with Greek astrology and that the stage of Greek astrology as represented in the works of Indian astrologers correspond to that which is evidenced by Firmicus Meternus about the middle of the 4th century A.D.[2] Bühler has shown that the author of an inscription in the Sun temple at Mandasor, one called Vatsabhaṭṭi, had not only imitated the style of Kālidāsa but he actually borrowed some of Kālidāsa's poems as the model on his own verses.[3] If this is correct, Kālidāsa must have lived and attained fame before the year 473 A.D. But as the present writer is unable to weigh the astronomical evidence of Jacobi, he is unable to place the other limit of Kālidāsa's date to 350 A.D. But the argument for his date being 375 A.D. gains in strength if we can believe that he lived in the court of Vikramāditya and that this Vikramāditya was Chandragupta II. On this point we have no conclusive evidence. Our conclusion therefore is that Kālidāsa lived pretty long before the middle of the 6th century A.D. But how long it was we are unable to decide.

I now wish to adduce an altogether new point, which I hope, may throw some light on the date of Kālidāsa. The principle of inheritance in Kauṭilya's *Arthaśāstra* differs in a

1. T. Bloch, Z. D. M. G., 1908, p. 671 ff. In J. R. A. S., 1909, p. 740 ff, F. W. Thomas has tried to contradict this idea.

2. *Monatsberichte der Berliner Akademie der Wissenschaften* 1873, p. 554 ff. and Z.D.M.G., 1876, p. 302 ff.

3. *Die indischen Inschriften*, p. 18 ff. and 24. f; also Kielhorn, N. G. G. W., 1890, p. 251 ff.

very significant manner from those that are found in Yajñavalkya and others. In Kauṭilya's *Arthaśāstra*, in the chapter on *Dāya-vibhāga*, the sons share the father's property. In those cases in which any of the sons may be dead, his share would go to his direct descendants up to the 4th generation ; but when a man has no son, the property would go to the brothers, provided they are living together, as also the daughters. Under certain conditions the nephew also may share, but there is no provision for the property of a person going to distant relations, the inheritors being limited to sons, daughters, brothers and sons of brothers. In the case of those who have none of these the property should go to the king after providing for the maintenance of the wife and the funeral ceremony of the deceased excepting in the case of a Vedic Brahmin.[1] Now in the Manu or Yājñavalkya *smṛtis*, there is no such law and the property of a person may go to his wife and other relations. In the Yājñavalkya, in the absence of the son or sons the property would go first to the wife and then to daughters, if the wife is not living.[2] Nowhere in the Hindu legal literature

1 *adāyakaṁ rājā haret strī-vṛtti-preta-kāryavaryam, anyatra śrotriya-dravyāt, tat traividyebhyaḥ prayacchet*.—*Artha-śāstra*, III. 5.

2 *patnī-duhitaraściva pitarau bhrātarastathā* ।
tatsutā gotrajā bandhu-śiṣya-sabrahmacāriṇaḥ ॥
eṣāmabhāve pūrvasya dhanabhāguttarottaraḥ ।
svaryātasya hyaputrasya sarvavarṇeṣvayaṁ vidhiḥ ॥
—*Yājñavalkya*, II, 8. 135, 136.

Mitakṣarā in supporting this view quotes Vṛddhamanu
aputrā śayanaṁ bhartuḥ pālayanti vrate sthitā ।
patnyeva dadyāt tatpiṇḍaṁ kṛtsnamaṁśaṁ labheta ca ॥

Vṛddhaviṣṇu says—
aputradhanaṁ patnyabhigāmi.

Kātyāyana says—
patnī patyurdhanaharī.

Bṛhaspati also says—
asutasya pramītasya patnī tadbhāgahāriṇī.

Manu says—
anapatyasya putrasya mātā dāyamavāpnuyāt ।
mātaryapi ca vṛttāyāṁ piturmātā hareddhanam ॥—(IX, 217).

Manu further says—
pitā haredaputrasya rikthaṁ bhrātara eva vā ।

do we find that there is any provision for the property of a person to go to the king except in those extreme cases where not only no relatives are availablē but not even a disciple or a class-fellow of the person (*śiṣya* and *sabrahmacārin*) ia available.[1]

From a study of the older legal treatises it appears that it is quite against the spirit of Hindu law that property should be allowed to go to the king. It is only when no relations of any description, not even disciples and class-fellows, are available that property should go to the king. In Kauṭilya's *Arthaśastra* only do we find that in the absence of a *dāyāda,* property should go to the king but the number of *dāyādas* or inheritors is extremely limited, as we have shown above. This was probably due to the fact that the Mauryas were greedy and needed wealth and therefore changed the older Hindu laws in their own interest, so that by restricting the number of inheritors and by providing for transmission to the king in the absence of such limited inheritors, the state could acquire enormous wealth from rich merchants and others. That the Mauryas had the monopoly of making images for being sold, shows that they were often in want of money and took to such means as selling images for money which is quite undignified for a state.[2] It is quite consistent with such a behaviour of the Mauryas with regard to collection of money by any means whatsoever that they should revise the old Hindu law in their favour so that they could secure as much property of the people as possible by restricting the number of inheritors and by debarring the wife from inheriting the peoperty of the husband. Now in the 6th Act of the *Śakuntāla,* the minister sends a letter in which it is stated that a merchant named Dhanavṛddhi had died in an accident on the sea leaving

1 **Thus Manu (IX. 189) says :—**

itareṣāṁ tu varṇānāṁ sarvabhāve harennṛpaḥ

2 **See Pāṇini's rule *Jīvikārthe cāpaṇye* and the *Bhāṣya* on it—**

apaṇye ityucyate tatredaṁ na siddhati śivaḥ skandaḥ viśākhaḥ iti. kiṁ kāraṇam. mauryaih hiraṇyārthibhiḥ arccāḥ prakalpitāḥ, bhavettāsu na syāt yāstu etāḥ saṁprati pūjārthaḥ tāsu bhaviṣyati ||

no child and he had millions of gold and suggesting also that under the circumstances this gold should go to the state. The king, Duṣyanta, says that enquiry should be made if he had any among his wives who was pregnant. The *Pratihārī* replies that one of his wives is in a state of pregnancy and the king orders that the gold of the merchant should go to the child in the womb.[1] This would lead to the supposition that Kālidāsa who was in all probability referring to a law prevalent in his own days, lived at a time when the Maurya laws of inheritance were in force even with Hindu kings. This conclusioon seems so obvious that we think that we may rely on it and place Kālidāsa at a later period of the Suṅgas. He may have been either a contemporary of Agnimitra or came shortly after him.

We have now to see if there are any facts which can be adduced against such a conclusion. We find from the Gupta inscriptions that in the time of Chandragupta II or Skandagupta, Brahminic laws were in force. We know also that Puṣyamitra had performed an *Aśvamedha* sacrifice and probably thereby sought to establish his claim as an orthodox Hindu king and it is reasonable to imagine that he had made considerable or wholesale changes in the Maurya law and established the old Hindu laws. Consequenty, it is reasonable to imagine that Kālidāsa lives sometime after Puṣyamitra and Agnimitra, when the Brahminic renaissance had started and when the inheritance law of Yājñavalkya or the *Dharma-śāstras* had not yet been re-introduced by the repeal of the Maurya laws. Had he lived in later days, say in the time of Candragupta II, he would have found the state laws to be based entirely on old Hindu laws and

1 *Rājā—(vācayati) viditamastu devapādānāṁ dhanavṛddhiranāma vaṇik vāripathopajīvī nauvyasanena vipannaḥ. sa cānapatyaḥ. tasya cānekakoṭisaṅkhyaṁ vasu, tadidānīṁ rājasvatāmāpadyate. iti śrutvā devaḥ pramāṇamiti. (saviṣādam) kaṣṭaṁ khalvanapatyatā, Vetravati mahādhanatayā bahupatnīkenānena bhavitavyaṁ tadanviṣyatāṁ yadi kācidāpannasattvāsya bhāryā syāt.*

Pratihārī—dāṇiṁ jjeva sākeda urassa seṭṭhiṇo duhidā ṇivvutta-puṁsavaṇā tassa jā-ā suṇīadi.

Rājā—sa khalu grabhaḥ pitryamṛkthamarhati gatvaivamamātyaṁ brūhi ।

had no occasion to refer to a law prevalent during the Maurya time as codified in Kauṭilya's *Arthaśāstra*.

Now, we know by a reference to the 4th canto of the *Raghuvaṃśa* that Kālidāsa was aware of the Yavanas, the Huns and the Persians. Our contacts with the Persians and the Greeks are of a very early date and in the the 2nd century B.C. the Greeks had invaded the city of Sāketa. In the Bhitari inscriptions we have a passage.[1] Prof. Raychaudhuri in his *Political History of Ancient India* in commenting on this passage says that the enemies mentioned in this Bhitari inscription were outsiders, *e.g.*, the Puṣyamitras and the Huns. The Huns after the death of Atilla, their leader, gradually overcame the resistance of Persia when king Feroze was killed in 484 A.D. Swarms of these White Huns also assailed the Kuṣān kingdom of Kabul and thence poured into India. They at first came in a comparatively small body and were repelled by Skandagupta in 455 A.D. as is evident from the Bhitari inscription. About ten years after they came in a much greater force and overwhelmed the kingdom of Gāndhāra and Peshawar and penetrated into the heart of the Gangetic provinces and overthrew the Gupta Empire. The leader of this invasion was Toramāna, who established himself as a ruler of Malwa in Central India in A.D. 500. Thus if Kālidāsa had made reference after seeing the Huns in India, he must have written his *Raghuvaṃśa* sometime after 455 A.D. But in the inscription of Vatsabhaṭṭi he is already well-established as a great poet in 473 A.D. and this would be unaccountable and Kālidāsa's date in that case would not be the first half of the 4th century. We have, therefore, to assume that when Kālidāsa refers to the Huns in the 68th verse of the 4th Book of the *Raghuvaṃśa*, in the North beyond Kashmir on the banks of the Indus, he probably refers to some small settlements of Huns who

1 *pitari divamupete viplulāṁ vaṁśalakṣmim* |
bhujabalavijitārir yaḥ pratiṣṭhāpya bhūyaḥ ||
jitamiti paritoṣānmātaraṁ sāsrahetrām ||
hataripuriva kṛṣṇo devakīm abhyupetaḥ ||

had already migrated up to that region. They were undoubtedly the White Huns because Kālidāsa describes that their cheeks became ruddy through fear of Raghu's prowess. As regards our contact with China, we must first note that the author of the *Periplus* tells us of Thinæ a land of silk, situated where the sea-coast ends externally, whence we may gather that the Chryse of Pliny was conceived by him as an island lying not only to the east of the Ganges but also to the southward of the Chinese Empire. The great Western State of China, Ts'in, and the city called Thinæ (meant probably as the genitive of 'This') was its capital, situated not far above the confluence of the Wei river with the Hoang-ho river. The state of Ts'in gradually grew in power. The greatest of the Ts'in monarchs was Ts'in Chi Hwangti, who ruled from 221-209 B.C., and he was the p bn who began the Great Wall and who pushed the Chinese frontier across the Gobi desert making Hami under the Tien-shan Mountains his out-post and thus preparing the way for direct communication with Bactria. Regular caravan travel between China and Bactria is said to have begun in 188 B.C. We thus see that Chinese silk very well finds its place in India early in the 2nd century B.C. or even earlier. But there was another route also of the importation of silk from China by way of the Brahmaputra Valley, Assam and Eastern Bengal early in the Christian era. We have thus reasons to believe that if Kālidāsa lived in the 2nd century B.C. he would not be unacquainted with Chinese silk. A part of the Chinese trade was localised at the mouth of the Indus. Generally the Chinese silk was exchanged for frankincense which was much valued in China. Through India the silk yarn passed on to Arabia and Syria and thence found its way to the Roman market. A part of the trade also passed through Persia, and Aristotle gives an excellent account of silk and how it was produced.[1]

There are some scholars who believe that Kālidāsa lived towards the close of the 5th century and was a contemporary of

1 See Schoff—*Periplus of the Erythroean Sea*, pp. 261-270.

Kumāragupta and Skandagupta.[1] In such a case Kālidāsa would have lived from about 390 to 460 A.D. There are others again who believe that Kālidāsa lived in the 6th century A.D.[2] But except for the slight difficulty regarding the possibility of Kālidāsa's knowledge of the Hun settlement in the North, I am convinced that there is no other difficulty in holding that Kālidāsa lived in the 2nd century B. C. and was probably a contemporary of Patañjal, the writer of the *Mahābhāṣya.* If Kālidāsa had a real knowledge of the Huns he would not have located them on the banks of the Indus.[3] After conquering the Huns, Raghu passed on to Kāmboja which was the north-eastern part of Afghanistan. In the Girnar and Dhauli inscriptions of Asoka, Kāmboja is mentioned as Kāmbocha.[4] If Raghu met the Huns on the banks of the Indus and then passed on to Kāmboja and if that part of the Indus be such as to produce

[1] M. Chakravarti, J.R.A.S., 1903, p. 183 ff., 1904, p. 158 ff., B. C. Mazumdar, J.R.A.S., 1909, p. 731 ff.; B. Liebich, *Indogerman. Forschungen*, 31, p, 200, relies mainly on the description of Raghu's conquering expedition in the 4th canto of the *Raguvaṁśa*; Bühler, in his *Die indischen Inschriften*, p. 82, had warned us against making such sweeping conclusions; see also k. B. Pāṭhak *Indian Antiquary*, 1912, p. 265 ff.; A. Gawroński in the work *The Digvijaya of Raghu and some connected problems* (*Roznik Oryentalistyczny, Polnisches Archiv für Orientalistik*, Krakau, 1914-1915) sought also to prove on the same grounds that Kālidāsa came to the court in the reign of Kumāragupta and became the famous court poet under Skandagupta. Sten Konow in *Festschrift Wackernael*, 1923, p. 4, regards the *Kumāra-sambhava* as being written in celebration of the birth of the Gupta Emperor Kumāragupta or of his successor Skandagupta. See also E. Windisch, *Geschichte der Sanskriphilologie* Grundriss I, IB), p. 175, Note 2.

[2] A.F.R. Hoernle, *Indian Antiquary*, 1912, p. 156, says that Yaśodharman who defeated or helped to defeat the Huns in the legendary Vikramāditya, though Yaśodharman is not known to have ever borne the title to Vikramāditya. Such a view is held by D. R. Bhāndārkar, (*Ann. Bh. Inst.*, 8, 1926-27, p. 200 ff. and *Asutosh Memorial Volume*, p. 72 ff; MM. Haraprasāda Śāstrī (J. B. O. R. S., 2. 1916, p. 31 ff., p. 391 ff.) as also B. C. Mazumder, *Ibid.* p. 388 ff.) believed that Kālidāsa be'onged to the second half of the period between 404 and 533 A. D,

[3] The verse runs as follows:

vinītādhvaśramāstasya sindhutīraviceṣṭanaiḥ |
dudhuvurvājinaḥ skandhān lagnakuṅkumakeśarān ||
tatra hūṇāvarodhānāṁ bhartṛṣu vyaktavikramam |
kapolapāṭalādeśi babhūva raghuceṣṭitam |

—*Raghuvaṁśa*, IV, 67-8.

[4] See N. L. De's *The Geographical Dictionary of Ancient and Medieval India.*

he must have passed through the Gāndhāra country on the border of Kashmir, gone westwards and then southwards to Kamboja'. At the time of return he is said to have mounted up on the Himalayas and then come down. It is not described that he crossed the Himalayas for reaching the land of the Huns. Now, we know that Kashmir is the only country that produces saffron. It seems, therefore, that some parts of the Kāśhmīra-Gāndhāra country was regarded by him as being the home of the Huns. Now, this would be impossible, for the Huns lived in the Oxus Valley and when they invaded India they over-ran the whole country and in such a case there would be no meaning in supp sing the Gāndhāra-Kāśmīra country on the banks of the Indus to be the home of the Huns. It may, therefore, be reasonably supposed that Kālidāsa had no direct knowledge of the Huns. He only knew probably by hearsay that the Huns lived in the north and located them on the banks of the Indus quite erroneously. It is not impossible for a cultured man living in the 2nd century B.C. to have heard the name of the White Huns who lived somewhere in the north. The reference to the Huns therefore does not imply that he lived at the time of the Hun invasion or that he had any definite knowledge of the Huns excepting that they were White and that they lived somewhere in the north.[1]

Just as there is a great controversy regarding the date of Kālidāsa so there is not yet a complete unanimity regarding Kālidāsa who had already established his fame on the most firm basis by the first half of the 7th century. He is mentioned by the great poet Bāṇa and also in an inscription of the year 634, as a famous poet.[2]

1 The Huns are freely mentioned in the *Rāmāyaṇa* and the *Mahābhārata* and it cannot be argued that all such passages were interpolated after the 5th century A. D. The Huns may have had small settlements in the Northern mountains yet unerthed by historical researches and they may have floated into India as mercenaries seeking employment.

2 Refer to the inscription of the Megati temple, Aihole ; see Fleet, *Indian Antiquary*, 1879, p. 237 ff. and Kielhorn *Epigraphica Indica*, 6. p. 1-12 ; also *Indian Antiquary* 20, 1891, p. 190. It seems also evident from the researches of the above scholar that the authors of the *Praśaśti* inscriptions of the 6th century and even of the inscriptions of Cambodia of the beginning of the 7th centnry were familiar with Kālidāsa's *Raghu-vaṁśa*.

Aufrecht has enumerated the names of the works that pass under the name of Kālidāsa. The verses of Kālidāsa quoted in the anthologies[1] have been collected by Aufrecht and Thomas.[2] Some later poets also called themselues Nava-kālidāsa or Abhinava-kālidāsa.[3] It is said that there were three Kālidāsas : one under Vikramāditya, one under Bhoja and one under the Emperor Akbar.[4] In the anthology *Harihārāvali* an Ākbarīya Kālidāsa is quoted.

But it seems certain that Kālidāsa was the author of a drama called the *Abhijñāna-Śakuntala,* a drama called the *Vikramorvaśī* and a drama called the *Mālavikāgnimitra,* an epic poem called the *Raghuvaṃśa,* a semi-epic poem called the *Kumara-sambhava,* a lyric poem called the *Megha-dūta* and another lyrical piece called the *Ṛtu-saṃhāra.*[5]

Kālidāsa has been regarded as one of the greatest poets of India not only on the testimony of Indian authors but also that of European authors.[6] Kālidāsa wrote two epics, *Kumāra-sambhava* and *Raghu-vaṃśa,* of which probably *Kumāra-sambhava* is earlier.

1 See *Indian Antiquary*, 1872, 340 ff. and C. C., I, 99.

2 Z.D.M.G., 1885, 306 ff. : *Kavīndra-vacana-samuccaya*, 30 ff.

3 Aufrecht, C.C., I, 24, 280.

4 Weber, Z.D.M.G., 22, 713 ; 27, 175 f. and 182 ; Peterson, *Subhāṣita*, 18 ff.

5 Other works attibuted to him are *Śṛṅgāra-śataka*, *Śṛṅgāra-tilaka*, *Nalodaya*, a poem of 4 cantos, and *Dvātriṁśatputtalikā*. A number of other works are attributed to Kālidāsa in Aufrecht's *Catalogus Catalogorum* ; *Ambāstava*, *Kālīstotra*, *Kāvyanāṭakālaṅkāra*, *Caṇḍikādaṇḍakastotra*, *Durghaṭa-kāvya*, *Navaratna-mālā*, *puṣpabāṇa-vilāsa*, *Rākṣasa-kāvya*, *Rāma-setu*, *Laghu-stava*, *Vidvadvinodakāvya*, *Vṛndāvana-kāvya*, *Śṛṅgāra-sāra*, *Śyāmalā-daṇḍaka*, *Śruta-bodha*. I have already spoken of three Kālidāsas. But there are at least 7 or 8 Kālidāsas. In addition to Ākbarīya Kālidāsa, we have Kālidāsa the writer of *Gaṅgāstava and Maṅgalāṣṭaka* ; Kālidāsa the writer of *Jyotirvidābharaṇa* : Kālidāsa the writer of lexicon *Ratna koṣa* ; Kālidāsa-Gaṇaka the writer of *Śatru-parājaya-svara-śāstra-sāra* ; Kālidāsa, the author of *Śuddhi-candrikā* ; Kālidāsa, son of Balabhadra, author of *Kuṇḍa-pravandha* ; Kālidāsa, son of Rāmagovinda of the 18th century, the author of *Tripurasundarī-stuti-kāvya*. There is also a Kālidāsa Nandin who was a poet and a Kālidāsa Miśra grandfather of Muralīdhara. Most of these MSS. are available.

6 Thus see *Harihāravali* *Śārṅga-dhara-paddhati* (the testimony of Kṛṣṇabhaṭṭa). *Kālidāsa et l'art Poetique*, Paris, 1917, p. 119 ff. ; also *A Literary Estimate of Kālidāsa* by A. Hillebrandt *Kālidāsa*, Breslau, 1921. Keith, *History of Sanskrit Literature*.

The *Kumara sambhava*[1] deals with the story that the gods being terrorised by Tārakāsura first approached Brahmā and then being advised that only a son of Śiva could defeat him, tried through the help of Indra to fascinate Śiva with the grace and beauty of Pārvatī but failed. Pārvatī, however, resorted to *tapas* and thereby attracted Śiva and they were then married. This forms the story of the first eight cantos over which the most celebrated commentator, Mallinātha, has written a commentary. The other nine cantos deal with the birth of Kumāra, his leadership of the gods' army and the final destruction of Tārakāsura. It has been often doubted with justice whether the later nine cantos were written by Kālidāsa or not. No definite opinion can be pronounced on the matter. A commentary on these later nine

1 The first 7 cantos of *Kumārasambhava* were edited and translated into Latin by A. F. Stenzler, London, 1838. The first 8 cantos with Mallinātha's commentary, edited with English and Bengali translation by Śrish Ch. Chakravartī, Dacca, 1901. Cantos 1-5, with English translation by M. R. Kale and S. R. Dharaṇīdhara, Bombay, 1907; with commentary of Mallinātha on *sargas* I-VIII and of Sītārāma on VIII-XVII, ed. by V.L.S Bansikar N.S.P., 4th ed, 1908; *sargas* I-VIII with two commentaries by Gaṇapati Śāstrī in T.S.S. Nos. 27, 32, 36, 1913-14. With commentaries ed. by Kanakalatā Thakkura, Benares, 1923 (Haridas Sanskrit series, No. 14). Cantos I-V with a Sanskrit commentary (*Bālabodhinī*) by S. D. Gajendragadkar, Introd., translation, etc. by R. D. Karmakar, Bombay, 1923. English translation of the first seven cantos by R. T. H. Griffith (*The Birth of the War-God, a Poem by Kālidāsa*, 2nd Ed., London 1879.) German translation of cantos I-VIII in prose by Walter, München-Leipzig, 1913. Cantos III-V translated into German by Hannah Neckel in *Beitrage zur Sprachund Volkerkunde, Festschrift Hillebrandt*. Halle, 1913. A French translation by H. Franche (*Kālidāsa, Oeuvres complètes*, 1860). Cantos VIII-XVII were first published in Pandit, Vol I, 1866. In the same journal (I, 656, 128 ff., 141 f.; III, 88) the question of the authenticity of these cantos was discussed by Indian scholars; on this see Weber in Z.D.M.G., 27, 174 ff., and *Indisch Streifen*, 3, 217 ff., 241 ff. The story of the *Kumārasambhava* was acted in 18 tableaux by Indian women and children according to the translation by Griffith at the Court Theatre in London in March, 1912 (As. Quart Rev., N. S., 1, 1913, p. 327)-

Many commentaries were written on the *Kumārasambhava*, such as *Padārtha-dīpikā Anvaya-lāpikā* by Kṛṣṇapati Śarman; also commentaries by Kṛṣṇamitrācārya, Gopālananda (*Sārāvalī*), by Govindarāma (*Dhīrañjanikā*), by Caritravardhana (*Śiśuhitaiṣiṇī*), by Jinabhadra Sūri (*Bālabodhinī*), by Narahari. Nārayaṇa, Prabhākara, Bṛhaspati Bharatasena (*Sābodhā*), Bhīṣmamiśra Maithila, Munī-Matīratna (*Avacūri*). Mallinātha (*Sañjivanī*), Raghupati (*Vyākhyāsudhā*), Vatsa, Ānandadevayāni Vallabha, Vallabhadeva, Vindhyeśvarīprasāda (*Kathambhūtikā*), Vyāsavatsa (*Śiśuhitaiṣiṇī*) and Haricaraṇa Dāsa (*Devasenā*).

Most of these MSS. are available.

cantos by Sītārāma Kavīśvara has been printed by the Nirṇayasāgara Press in 1893. The first canto deals with the description of the Himalayas which fails to impress upon us the sublimity of the great mountain as well as the childhood of Pārvatī. The second canto deals with the philosophical hymn of adoration to Brahmā on Sāmkhya lines. The third canto deals with the advent of untimely spring in the hermitage of Śiva, the effort of Madana to captivate Śiva, his destruction by the anger of Śiva and the final disappearance of Śiva from the scene of disturbance. The fourth canto deals with the sorrowing of Kama's wife Rati, which does not rouse our sympathy so much for the sufferer as it rouses the amorous sentiments due to the amorous reminiscences of the wife as expressed in weeping The fifth canto shows the determination of Pārvatī to attain holy and immortal grace through *tapas* whereby she attracts Śiva who comes to her as a *brahmacārī* and we have an excellent dialogue between Śiva and Pārvatī as also the description of Pārvatī's *tapas*. The 6th, 7th and 8th refer to the arrangement and final execution of the marriage. The 5th canto as well as portions of the 3rd canto are of real poetic value.[1]

1 The authenticity of the 8th canto has been objected to on the ground that the description of the amorous pleasure of Pārvatī and Śiva is as unsuitable as the description of such pleasurs on the part of one's parents. But Ānandavardhana in his *Dhvanyāloka*, III, 6, p. 137, holds that it depends upon the talent of the poet and he himself refers to the canto VIII of the *Kumārasambhava*. Mammaṭa in his *Kāvyaprakāśa*, VII criticises the description of the love-scenes of Śiva and Pārvatī. Vāmana cites examples from this canto in two passages of his Poetics (4.3.33). The passage, referred to by Vāmana, is *Kumārasambhava*, 8.63. Thus in Vāmana's time the 8th canto was in existence. Mallinātha however wrote a commentary only on cantos I-VIII. The earlier commentator Aruṇagirinātha (Gaṇapati Śāstrī. T.S.S., 37, Preface) also commented on the first 8 *sargas*. There is a great similarity between the *Śivarahasya* of the *Śaṅkarasaṁhitā* of the *Skandapurāṇa* and *Kumārasambhava*. This can be explained on the assumption that the author of the *Śivarahasya* had utilised the first 8 cantos of the *Kumarasambhava* and the latter part of it may have been the original of the spurious cantos of the *Kumārasambhava*—see Weber, in Z. D. M. G., 27, 179, 190 ff. and Pandit, Vol. III, 19 ff, 85. In the 14th century the Jaina Jayaśekhara wrote another epic called the *Kumārasambhava*, (Peterson III, Rep., Extra, 251 ff.) Udbhaṭa also composed a *Kumārasambhava*, verses from which are quoted in his *Alaṁkara-Saṁgraha*. Thus we had three *Kumārasambhavas*.

Mainly on the ground that Mallinatha's commentary is not available for cantos IX-XVII, it has been held by many that these cantos did not belong to Kalidasa. But the style and the manner of expression in these cantos do not seem to reveal an alien hand. All that was objectionable was the 8th canto but since that canto was in existence in the time of Vamana, there is no internal evidence that these cantos did not belong to Kalidasa. There is practically no external evidence that they did not belong to Kalidasa. On the other hand the existence of the contents of all these cantos in the *Śiva-rahasya* may be regarded as a proof that these cantos of Kalidasa were known to the author of the *Śiva-rahasya*. There seems to be no point in the argument that only the first 8 cantos were utilised by the author of the *Śiva-rahasya* and that the other portion of the *Śiva-rahasya* was the original from which these cantos of the *Kumara-sambhava* have been spuriously put forth by some unknown author. A reference to the contents of the *Śiva-rahasya* shows that the story given there does not agree so closely either in the first or in the second part, as could convince us that the author of the *Śiva-rahasya* had based his plot of the first part on Kalidasa's first 8 cantos of the *Kumara-sambhava*, or that the so-called spurious part of the *Kumara-sambhava* was based on the other part of the story in the *Śiva-rahasya* though there are occasional similarities of description. There are some very essential divergences. This compels us to think that both Kalidasa and the author of the *Śiva-rahasya* had based their story on some other version of it which was available to both Kalidasa and the author of the *Śiva-rahasya*. The argument, therefore, that this spurious part of the *Kumara-sambhava* was based on the *Śiva-rahasya*, falls to the ground.

The other epic written by Kalidasa is *Raghu-vaṃśa* or the story on Raghu's line, in which the poet takes up the life and deeds of some of Rama's ancestors and descendants.

1 Text with Latin translation, edited by A.F. Stenzler, London, 183?. Among the Indian editions, that by Shanker P. Pandit in BSS, 1869-1874, with Mallinātha's commen

It is indeed difficult to ascertain what may have been the original source from which the materials regarding the king of the line of Raghu were drawn upon. It was certainly not the *Rāmāyaṇa*, for the *Rāmāyaṇa* deals mainly with the story of Rāma and partly with that of Daśaratha. As for the story of Dilīpa, Raghu, Aja and others, we are unable to locate the exact sources. It seems to us that Kalidāsa had some purpose before his mind which stimulated him to paint in glorious colours the character, the exploits and the adventures of the old kings of the glorious days of the supremacy of the Hindu kings. Though the *Raghu-vaṃśa* paints before us in golden colours the character of Dilīpa, Raghu and his descendants and as such may be regarded as a world devoid of unity, yet we can never feel it. It never strikes us that as Kālidāsa passes from one to another, there is any real break in the treatment of new personalities. There is one pattern of life through most of these personalities. As we pass from one king to another, we feel as if the same character is being displayed from aspect to aspect, from one side to another. It appears that most of these characters could be combined and rolled up as if they delineated the same hero in different circumstances and perspectives.

Thus, in the first two cantos we have the description of king Dilīpa anxious for his progeny for fear of suspension of libations and offerings of food to the ancestors. He goes to the hermitage of the priest Vaśiṣṭha and is told of his transgression

tary, and that by G. R. Nandargikar (3rd Ed., Bombay, 1897) with Mallinātha's commentary, numerous explanatory notes and a complete English translation in prose, are to be recommended. English translation by P. de Lacy Johnstone, London, 1902. Book I of the *Raghu-vaṁśa* translated in verse by J. Murray Mitchell in J.B.R.A,S., No. VI. Oct, 1843, p, 308 ff. Extracts translated by Ralph T. H. Griffith, from the Sanskrit, Allahabad, 1912. There is a beautiful, though a very free and abridged, translation in German verse by Ad. Fr, Graf von Schack, *Orient und Occident, III*; Stuttgart, 1890. There is a poetical German translation of the first 31 verses by E. Leumann in *Festschrift Windisch*, p. 43 ff. and a complete German prose translation by O. Walter, München-Leipzig, 1914, and is advised expiation by tending the divine cow of his hermitage. The cow tests the king by creating a phantom lion ready to kill the cow. By her magic she arrests the king's hands. The king cannot strike the lion but offers his body to the lion in lieu of the life of the cow. The cow is pleased and the king has the benediction that a child will be born to him. Here two traits of the pattern king of the golden age are shown: (1) A king should marry for the sake of the progeny who can offer food and water to the ancestors. (2) A Kṣattriya should offer his own life in protecting one who seeks his protection. The scene changes. His wife Sulakṣaṇā becomes pregnant in the 3rd canto and Raghu is born and the king is relieved from his debt to his ancestors. Raghu grows and is made the crown-prince. Dilīpa performs the *Aśvamedha* sacrifice and Raghu is appointed in charge of the horse and fights with Indra and though he is defeated, he secures the boon from Indra that his father should have the merit of the *Aśvamedha* sacrifice. Dilīpa takes *vānaprastha* and in the 4th canto king Raghu starts his conquering career (*digvijaya*). In the 5th canto Kautsa, a disciple of Varatantu, approaches Raghu, when he had just finished the sacrifice in which he had given away his all, for the payment of his fees to the teacher and Raghu draws the money for him from Kuvera. Raghu has a son called Aja. The son grows, is educated and is sent to the *svayaṃvara* of Indumatī, sister of Bhoja. In the 6th canto we have the description of the *svayṃvara* of Indumatī, in which Aja succeeds in being chosen by Indumatī among a large number of kings. In the 7th canto he marries Indumatī and is attacked by her unsuccessful suitors and comes out victorious. In the 8th canto Aja becomes king but by the accident of a heavenly garland falling upon Indumatī, she dies and we have the pathetic grief of Aja for her. In the 9th, Aja's son Daśaratha becomes king and we have the hunting scene of Daśaratha. In the 10th, we have the sons born to Daśaratha and from the 11th begins the career of Rāma. Kālidāsa had the good sense not to attempt rivalling the great master Vālmīki and he passed off the general episodes of Rāma's story described in the *Rāmāyaṇa* in a brief manner. He tried to show his skill in new descriptions of events and episodes which Vākmīki had not emphasised. He banishes Sītā though he knew that she was sinless and in the character of Sītā we have the character of an ideal Hindu wife who is prepared to bear any suffering that is imposed on her by her husband with sweetness and good grace. Execution of Śambuka is described with approbation and in the 15th canto we have the tragedy of Lakṣmana's renouncing his life in the Sarayū and Rāma also proceeds northwards and ultimately becomes merged in his own divine form. In the 16th canto Kuśa, Rāma's son, ascends the throne and he rebuilds the city of Ayodhyā which was deserted by the citizens of Ayodhyā when Rāma departed for Heaven. There is also here charming descriptions of amorous love scenes and Kuśa is married to Kumudvatī, daughter of the Nāga king. In the 17th canto Kuśa begets a son called Atithi. Kuśa dies fighting the demons as an ally to Indra and Kumudvatī also dies with him. Ministers make Atithi the king and we have the description of the ascension ceremony. We have here the description of the manner in which a dutiful king conducted his affairs. Atithi also performs an *Aśvamedha* ceremony. He had married the daughter of the king of the Niṣāda and after him his son Nala becomes the king. He had a son called Puṇḍarīka and thus we have a series of other kings until we come to Agnivarṇa. He was a debauchee and spent his time with women and ultimately died having no son and suffering from diseases. At his death the ministers and the people made the chief queen the Regent and with this description in the 19th canto the work closes.

If we review the characters of the different kings that have been emphasised we find that in each of them various royal traits have been described. The race of the king degenerated by marrying princesses of Non-Aryan tribes like the Niṣādas and the Nāgas and we have the tragic end of the race with the king Agnivarṇa who spends his time in debauchery.

Kālidāsa (Raghuvaṃśa)

It has been remarked that in drawing Agnivarṇa's character, Kālidāsa was displaying and illustrating his knowledge of the *Kāmā-śastra,* but it does not seem to us to be correct ; for, in the first place, mere delineation of sensuality is not an illustration from the *Kāma-śāstra,* and in the second place, Kālidāsa is never known to us to demonstrate any pedantry. J. J. Meyer in the Introduction to his edition of *Daśa-kumāra-carita* appreciates the joyous and purely amorous life of Agnivarṇa, though his end is so tragic. R. Schmidt in his work on the *Love and Marriage in Ancient and Modern India,* Berlin, 1904 also refers to it.

Winternitz in the third volume of his *History of Indian Litrature* assures us that in Dhāra there existed copies of *Raghu-vaṃśa* containing 26 cantos, and S. P. Pandit in 1874, in the Preface to his edition of *Raghu-vaṃśa,* says that a person in Ujjayinī had a manuscript of *Raghu-vaṃśa* up to the 25th canto But the commentators do not know anything more than the 19th canto.

Kālidāsa's *Abhijñāna-śakuntalā* is the most famous of all Sanskrit dramas. It is one of the first works of Sanskrit literature that was known early in Europe. Sir William Jones translated it in 1789, thirty-two years after the Battle of Plassey and in 1791 it was translated by George Forster into German. Herder and Geothe were struck with wonder on reading this drama in translation. Geothe expressed his appreciation of Śakuntalā in a poem in 1791 and many years later he wrote to Chezy, the French publisher of Sanskrit texts of Śakuntalā in 1830 in the most appreciative manner.

There is a story both in the *Mahābhārata* and in the *Padma-purāṇa* which corresponds in general with the story of the Śakuntalā of Kālidāsa but the kernel of the story has been worked by Kālidāsa in an entirely different and masterly manner. Kālidāsa's story, however, is more akin to the *Padma-purāna* than to the *Mahābhārata.*[1] There is a native saying that Śakuntalā is the best product of Kālidāsa and therein also the 4th Act is the best.[2] The work *Abhijñāna-śakuntalam* had many commentaries in the past.[3] The simple story of the drama is that king Duṣyanta had on his hunting tour visited the hermitage of Kaṇva, where he met Śakuntalā and her two friends Priyaṃvadā and Anasūyā. He fell in love with Śakuntalā when Kaṇva was away and after spending some time with her, returned to the city promising to send for her shortly. In the meanwhile, while Śakuntalā was plunged in a state of grief through the separation, she failed to hear the call of the angry sage Durvāsā asking hospitality and was crused by him, On account of the curse Duṣyanta forgot all about Śakuntalā. Kaṇva on his return found his adopted child Śakuntalā (daughter of Viśvāmitra and the heavenly nymph Menakā) in a state of pregnancy and sent her to Duṣyanta's court. The latter failed to recognise her and sent her away. She was taken by her mother up in Heaven. Śakuntalā had dropped the ring that the king had given her in water. This ring was later found and the king at once remembered the whole thing and was smitten with grief. Duṣyanta later on had to go to Heaven in order to help Indra in his fight with the demons. There he met Śakuntalā and his son and they were again united.

1 Winternitz had written in 1897 that Kālidāsa had followed the version of *Padma-purāṇa* as available in the Southern recension of the *Śakuntalopākhyāna* ; *Indian Antiquary*, 1898, p. 136. But Beharilal Sircar in his Bengali book *Śakuntalā-rahasya* had already expressed the view in 1896. But the point in question is as to whether Kālidāsa borrowed from the *Padmapurāṇa* or the writer of the *Padmapurāṇa* borrowed from Kālidāsa. It is also an unfortunate matter that we have no reliable edition of the *Padmā-purāṇa* from which we may make a proper judgment. A careful comparison has been made between the *Mahābhārata* episode and the story of Śakuntalā by Berthold Müller in his article *Kālidāsa's Śakuntalā and Its Source* in 1874.

2 *kālidāsasya sarvasvam abhijñānaśakuntalam |*
tatrāpi ca caturtho'ṅko yatra yāti śakuntalā ||

—Quoted by G. R. Nandargikar in the Introduction in his *Raghuvaṁśa*.

3 Commentary by Abhirāma Bhaṭṭa, Kāṭayavema (*Kumāragirirājīya*) Kṛṣṇanātha Pañcānana, Candraśekhara, Damaruvallabha, Nārāyaṇa Bhaṭṭa (*Prākṛta-vivṛti*), Rāghava Bhaṭṭa (*Artha-dyotanikā*), Rāmabhadra, Śaṅkara (*Rasa-candrikā*) and by Śrīnivāsa Bhaṭṭa.

The character of Śakuntalā was very sweet so far as in her tenderness and sympathy she had made herself one as it were with the trees and animals of the hermitage but she was more spirited than Sītā and gave Duṣyanta some hot words when she was repulsed. Duṣyanta was a type of the old Hindu kings who indulged in *Gāndharva* marriage and whose behaviour was quite in consonance with Vedic customs. It has been suggested that the *Gāndharva* marriage was at this time going out of practice and that Kālidāsa's opinion was that such passionate marriages proved often disastrous. We do not find any *Gāndharva* marriage among the kings of the Raghu line.

The *Vikramorvaśī* is a drama of 5 Acts, while *Śakuntalā* is one of 7 Acts. The story is as follows :—

When Urvaśī, a heavenly nymph, was returning from Kuvera, she was attacked by the demon Keśī. The king Pururavā on hearing her cries saved her from the demon and they became mutually attracted towards each other. Urvasī then approached the king and left a note of love to him. But she had to hurry away for a dramatic performance in Heaven. Urvaśī again returned to the king. The king then went to the Kailāsa mountain for enjoyment. There finding Pururavā attached to a Vidyādhara girl called Udakavatī, Urvaśī became jealous and in straying about entered into a prohibited garden where she was changed into a creeper and the love-sick king went about from place to place searching her. The maddened king began to sing songs and dance. Urvaśī, however, came to life with the touch of a jewel. They again returned to the kingdom. In the meanwhile the jewel was carried away by a bird. The jewel, however, fell down from the sky with an arrow attached to it containing the name of Āyu, the son of Pururavā and Urvaśī. At that time an ascetic woman came with a boy, who was the son of Urvaśī and Pururavā. At this time Urvaśi entered. Urvaśī then told him that she had a curse that when she sees the face of her son, she should return to Heaven and for that reason she had sent away the son for training without looking at his face and now she has to return. The king then arranged for anointing his son. Nārada came at this time and told him that Indra had allowed Urvaśī to stay with him all his life.

The story of the *Vikramorvaśī* is based upon the brief story given in the *Matsya-purāṇa,* Chapter 24.

The title *Vikramorvaśī* means *vikrameṇa hṛtā urvaśī i.e.,* Urvaśī who was taken from the hands of a demon by bravery. In the commentary of Kāṭayavema the title is explained as the drama of Vikrama and Urvaśī.[1]

The *Mālavikāgnimitra* is a drama in 5 Acts, relating the love story between king Agnimitra and Mālavikā. It is probable that *Mālavikāgnimitra* was the first drama written by Kalidāsa. The second probably was *Vikramorvaśī,* and the third *Abhijñāna-śakuntalam.*[2] The hero Agnimitra was the son of Puṣyamitra, a king of the Suṅga dynasty, who lived in 185 A.D.

The *Megha-dūta* of Kalidāsa wherein a *Yakṣa,* separated from his wife, is supposed to address the cloud to bear his

1 In many of the MSS. the drama has been described as *nāṭaka,* in other as *troṭaka.* A critical edition of the *Vikramorvaśī* by R. Lenz (Berlin, 1813) and a German translation were published by Bollensen in 1846 and Śankara P. Paṇḍit also published an edition in 1789 in Bombay. The Southern recension was published by R. Pischel (*Monatsberichte der akademie der Wissenschaften zu Berlin,* 1875).

Śaṅkara P. Paṇḍit in the Introduction to his edition and so also T. H. Bloch in his work on Vararuci and Hemacandra, 1893, expressed a doubt regarding the authenticity of the *Prākṛt ślokas* in *apabhraṁśa* in the 5th Act. H. Jacobi also in his *Bhavisattakhā* of Dhanapāla says that the liberty in *apabhraṁśa* found here is probably due to pantomimic conditions of dancing. Pischel in his *Materialien zur kenntanis des apabhraṁśa,* Berlin, 1920, and Konow (G. G. A. 1890, 475 ff.) hold the verses to be genuine.

K. G. A. Hoefer, Berlin, 1837, B. Hirgel, 1838, Lobedanz, 1861 and Fritze had translated *Vikramorvaśī* into German. Wilson, of course, had translated it in his *Hindu Theatre* but the work had also been translated in French, Swedish, Italian, Spanish and Czech. A. Hillebrandt and Muir also wrote on the subject of *Vikramorvaśī.*

2 It was published by Śaṅkara P. Paṇḍit, in *B.S.A Series* in 1869. O. F. Tulberg published in Bonn, 1840, an uncritical edition of the work. A critical introduction to it was written by C. Cappeller, *Observationes ad Kālidāsae Mālavikāgnimitram,* Diss., Regimonti, 1858 ; F. Haag, *Zur text Kritik und Erklarund von Kālidāsa Mālavikāgnimitra,* Frauenfeld, 1872 ; see also Bokensen, Z.D.M.G., 1859, 480 ff. ; A. Weber, Z.D.M.G., 1860, 261 ff,

message to his wife, is the best known lyric in Sanskrit literature. It is divided into two parts. In the first part the Yakṣa is supposed to describe the route that his messenger should take from Rāmagiri to Alakā and we have here a description of natural scenes of the various countries through which the cloud passed. The second part, called the *Uttara-megha*, deals with the description of Alakā and the message.[1] Kālidāsa's *Megha-dūta* has been not only widely appreciated in India through centuries but also by many Western scholars and poets. Thus, Goethe speaking of *Megha-dūta* said; "The first acquaintance with this work made an epoch in our life".

The *Megha-dūta* had many commentaries.[2] The *Megha-dūta* had many imitations. One of these is *Pavana-dūta*, written by the poet Dhoyī, in which a Gandharva maiden sends the wind as her messenger to king Lakṣmaṇasena.[3] Rūpa-goswāmī in the 16th century wrote his *Haṃsa-dūta*, where

1 It was published by Gildemeister in Bonn, and the critical Introduction and Glossary by A. F. Stenzler, Breslau, 1874. The commentary of Mallinātha with the text was published by N. B. Godabole and K. K. Paraba, Bombay, 1886. The best edition is that of E. Hu tzeh with the old commentary of Vallabhadeva, 1911. It was translated into English verse by H. H. Wilson in 1813 together with parallel passages from classical and English poetry. We have another edition with prose translation by C. Schutz, Bielepeld 1859. Maxmuller published a metrical translation (Königsberg, 1847). E. Muir gave another rendering of it in his *Classical Poetry of India*, III, 90 ff., another by L. Fritze (Chemnitz, 1879) in which he had utilised the manuscript prose translation by Stenzler. A French translation was made by A. Guerinot, Paris, 1902. An anonymous English translation appeared in Paṇḍit, Vol. II. English prose translation was made by Jacob, Pathak and Nandargikar.

2 Some of these commentaries are:—*Avacūri*, *Kathambūtī*, *Meghalatā*, *Mālatī* by Kalyāṇamalla, *Manoramā* by Kavicandra, *Rasadīpikā* by Jagaddhara, *Tattva-dīpikā* by Bhagīratha Miśra, *Sañjīvanī* by Mallinātha, *Muktāvalī* by Rāmanātha, *Śiṣya-hitaiṣiṇī* by Lakṣminivāsa, *Durbodha-pada-bhañjikā* by Viśvanātha, *Megha-dūtārtha-muktāvalī* by Viśvanātha Miśra, *Tātparya-dīpikā* by Sanātana Śarmā, *Meghadūtā vacūri* by Sumativijaya; also commentaries by Haridāsa, Śaśvata, Vallabha, Vācaspatigovinda, Rāma Upādhyāya, Mahimasiṁhagaṇi, Bharatasena, Divākara, Janendra, Janārdana, Cintāmaṇi, Kṣemasiṁhagaṇi, Kṛṣṇadāsa, Uddyotakara and others.

There was another Jaina *Megha-dūta* written by Merutunga of the 14th century who wrote *Prabandha-cintāmaṇi* in 1306 and a medical work called *Kaṅkālā-dhyāya-vārttika*.

3 It was published by N. Chakravarty in J.A.S.B., 1905; see Pischel also and Aufrecht, Z.D.M.G., 1900, 616 ff, There is also another *Pavana-dūta* by Vādicandra Sūri.

the swan is made the messenger of Radha to Kṛṣṇa. *Padāṅka-dūta* by Kṛṣṇabhaṭṭa Sarvabhauma (1723 A.D.), a blind imitation of *Megha-dūta* called the *Śuka-saṅdeśa* by Lakṣmīdasa and two works bearing the title of *Uddhava-dūta* by one unknown author and by the poet Mādhava of the 17th century.[1] The poet Viṣṇudāsa wrote the *Mano-dūta*. Another work of the same name was written by Vrajanātha in 1758. *Megha-dūta* was again translated into Singhalese and imitations also took place there. It was also translated into Tibetan about the 13th century and it exists in the Tangyur collection. This version was translated into German by Beckh in 1906.[2]

Ṛtu-saṃhāra is a work which describes the six seasons in beautiful poems.[3] The work *Śṛṅgāra-tilaka* is also ascribed to Kālidāsa.[4]

The work called *Ghaṭa-karpara* is a small work written in 22 verses, in which a young woman sends in the rainy season her greetings to her husband through the cloud.[5]

1 *Śuka-sandeśa* has been published by Mahārāja Rāmavarman of Travancore (J.R.A.S. 1884, p. 401 ff.). The work is well-known in the Malabar (J.R.A S,, 1910, p. 638).

2 See also the article by Buth and Beck in SBA., 1895, 268 f. and 281 ff. (*Ein Beitrāg zur Textkritik von Kālidāsas Meghadūta*, Berlin, 1?0).

3 The genuineness of the *Ṛtu-saṁhāra* has been doubted in many quarters. See J. Nobel (Z.D.M.G., 1912, 275 ff., 1919, 194 f,. J.R.A.S., 1913, 401 ff.) wherein he attempts to prove that the *Ṛtu saṁhāra* is a genuine work of Kālidāsa. He is supported in it by A. B. Keith. (J.R.A.S., 1912, 1066 ff); It is universally believed that it is a genuine work of Kālidāsa. Yet in the Mandasor inscription of 472 A.D. verses from *Ṛtu-saṁhāra* are also found imitated. It is curious however that verses from the *Ṛtu-saṁhāra* should not be found quoted either in the works of authority of Sanskrit verses or in works of the poetics. See Harichand's *Kālidāsa*, p. 240 ff. Viśveśvara, however, in his *Ṣaḍ-ṛtu varṇana* written in the 18th century imitated verses from the *Ṛtu-saṁhāra*.

4 The *Megha-dūta* and the *Śṛṅgāra-tilaka* were edited by Gildemeister, Bonn, 1811. There is also a work called *Śṛṅgāra-śataka*, which is attributed to Kālidāsa. It is, however, a sort of compilation. Another work called *Śyāmalā-daṇḍaka*, in prose, is also attributed to Kālidāsa, It consists of hymns to the goddess Durgā, interspered with prose and has been translated into Tibetan as the *Sarasvatīstotra* and *Maṅgalāṣṭaka* (see F. W. Thomas, J.R.A.S., 1903, p. 785 ff. The *Maṅgalāṣṭaka* exists also in Sanskrit MS.).

5 Published with translation by G M. Dursch, Berlin, 1828; Haeberlin, 120 ff; French translation by Chézy (J.A., 1823, II, p. 39 ff); German translation by Hoefer (*Indische Gedichte*, Vol. II. p. 129 ff., and Bohlen, *Das alte Indien*, Kōnigsberg, 830, 380 ff; see also Eggeling's *India Office Catalogue*, VII, p, 1427 f.

I have already pointed out that there is really no justification in thinking that Kalidasa belonged to the court of Vikramaditya. But, be that as it may, it appears that Prof. Shemvanekar's article as published in the *Journal of the University of Bombay*, I, pp. 232-246, seems definitely to prove that the son of Mahendraditya assumed the title of Vikramaditya in the 1st century B.C. This would fit in with the Vikramaditya tradition of Kalidasa as well. Aśvaghoṣa is generally placed in the 1st century A.D. Cowell had argued that Kalidasa is indebted to Aśvaghoṣa. Since then scholars have been dubious as to the exact relation between Aśvaghoṣa and Kalidasa. It seems to us, however, that the arguments put forward by Prof. Chatterjee (*Allahabad University Studies*, No. 2, pp. 80-114) and Prof. Roy (*Śakuntalā*, Introduction, pp. 19-28) definitely prove Kalidasa to be the model and fountain of inspiration of Aśvaghoṣa. We have already shown that the Huns were known to the Indians from pretty early times, and on this subject one may also consult J. U. B., I, p. 245 ; *Allahabad University Studies*, pp. 126-33 ; J. I. H., Madras, No. 15. pp. 93-102. The researches of other scholars, such as Daśaratha Śarman on *Kaumudī-mahotsava*, I. H. Q., X, 1763-66 ; XI, pp. 147-48 ; *Proceedings and Transactions of the All-India Oriental Conferences*, Vol. VIII ; Summaries, pp. 25-26 ; *Annals of Bhandarkar's Oriental Research Institute*, Poona, XVI, pp. 155-57 ; and Introduction to *Padma-cūḍāmaṇi*. All these point to the same direction that Kalidasa probably lived in the 1st century B.C. On this subject, particularly as regards religious, political and social environment and astronomical knowledge of the period, one may consult further, Roy's *Śakuntalā*, Introduction, pp. 1-19 and 28-30, Vaidya's *Lokaśikṣaṇā*, VII, pp. 9-17. K. Roy, *Evolution of Gītā*, pp. 201-22, Dhruva, *Thakkar Lectures*, pp. 207-13. Apte, Kane and Paranjpe also incline more

We have a Ghaṭa-karpara as one of the nine jewels in the court of Vikramāditya. It is impossible to say whether this was actually written by the Ghaṭakarpara or whether it could be attributed to Kālidāsa.

or less to the same view. Further, Prof. Shemvanekar has adduced sufficient evidence to prove (*loc. cit.*) that the Guptas were Vaiṣṇavas and that Chandragupta II was not the first Vikramāditya. For all these reasons I should be inclined to think that Kālidāsa lived in the 1st century B.C. It may also be incidentally mentioned that, judging from internal evidence, one may point out that Kālidāsa had no knowledge of the Sāṃkhya as schemed out by Iśvarakṛṣṇa in his *Kārikās*, which were probably written in the 3rd century A.D. It may also be mentioned with force that he had no knowledge of the Sāṃkhya that is said to have been preached by Arāḍa as reported in Aśvaghosa's *Buddha-carita*, or the Sāṃkhya of the *Caraka-saṃhitā*. The knowledge of Sāṃkhya displayed by Kālidāsa in Canto II of the *Kumāra-sambhava* and in Canto X of the *Raghu-vaṃśa* is a positively monistic doctrine as found in the *Upaniṣads*, or rather the Sāṃkhya philosophy in the *Gītā* (see my History of Indian Philosophy, Vol. II, p. 461 *et seg.*).

SUBANDHU

Among the older prose romances (*gadya kāvya*), the *Daśa-kumāra-carita*, *Harṣa-carita*, *Kādambarī*, *Vāsavadattā*, *Tilaka-mañjarī*, *Gadya-cintāmaṇi* and *Vīra-nārāyaṇa-carita* are available, whereas the prose work of Bhattāra-Hāricandra, *Taraṅgavatī* and *Trailokya-sundarī*, though referred to by Bāṇa, are not easily accessible.

For a fuller discussion of Subandhu's date see Introduction to *Vāsavadattā* published from Śrīraṅgam, 1906.[1] The *Vāsava-dattā* of Subandhu belongs to the Kathā literature. Patañjali mentions *Vāsavadattā* as an *ākhyāyikā* in IV. 2.60 (and not in IV. 3.87 as Winternitz says). We do not know if Bāṇa's reference to *Vāsavadattā* is to this older *Vāsavadattā*, but Cartellieri (W Z K M, 1, 1887, 115 ff.), Thomas (W Z K M,

1 Published in 1859, Bibliotheca Indica series, Calcuta, with the commentary of Śivarāma Tripathi; English Translation by L. H. Gray from a text in Telugu character. New York, C U I S, Vol. VIII, 1913. See also Weber, *Indische Streifen* I, p. 369 ff.

12, 1898, 21 ff.) and Man'kowski (W Z K M, 15, 1901, 246 f.) hold that the reference to *Vāsavadattā* in Bāṇa is to Subandhu's *Vāsavadattā*.[1]

BANA

Many works are attributed to Bāṇa, such as *Kādambarī*, *Caṇḍī-śataka*, *Pārvatī-pariṇaya-rūpaka*, *Mukuṭa-tāḍitaka-nāṭaka* quoted by Caṇḍapāla in his commentary on *Damayantī-kāvya*, *Sarvacarita-nāṭaka*, *Harṣa-carita*. Kṣemendra quotes verses of Bāṇa in his *Aucitya-vicāra-carcā* and we have verses from Bāṇa in *Sūkti-muktāvalī* and *Subhāṣitāvalī*.[2]

The historical elements in Bāṇa's *Harṣa-carita* cannot very well be utilised. Thus, Keith says : "Historically we may say that the work is of minimal value, though in our paucity of actual records it is something even to have this. But chronology is weak and confused, it is extremely difficult to make out the identity of the king of Mālava[3] and even the Gauḍa king is only indirectly indicated as Śaśāṅka, whose name is given by Hiuen Tsang.[4] Bāṇa has not attempted to make intelligible the course of events which rendered it possible for the Gauḍa king to come into hostile contact with Rājyavardhana in or near Mālava and it is difficult not to suppose that he desired, writing at a considerable distance of time, to leave what was long past in a vague position. What he does supply to history is the vivid pictures of the army, of the life of the court, of the different sects and their relations to the Buddhists and the avoca-

1 The *Vāsavadattā* has a number of commentaries :—*Tattvadīpanī* by Jagaddhara, commenntary by Narasiṁhasena, by Nārāyaṇa, *Cūrṇikā* by Prabhākara, *Tattvakaumudī* by Rāmadeva, *Vyākhyāyikā* by Vikramarddhi, *Kāñcana-darpaṇa* by Śivarāma and also commentaries by Śṛṅgāragupta and Sarvacandra.

2 His Harṣa-carita was published with the commentary of Śaṅkara by A. A. Führer, Bombay, 1909, BSS ; translated into English by E. B. Cowell and F. W. Thomas, London, 1897 ; see also Bhāu Dāji in J. B. R. A. S., X, 1871, 38 ff. ; also, Führer, O. C. VI, Leiden, III, 2, 199 ff. ; R. W. Frazer, *Literary History of India*, p. 255 ff.

3 See Smith, EHI, p. 350. ff ; R. Mookerjee, *Harṣa*, p. 50 ff.

4 For a defence of him, see Majumdar, *Early History of Bengal*, p. 16 ff.

tions of a Brahmin and his friends."[1] Even the time of the birth of his hero king Harṣa is not also probably correct.[2]

His other important work is *Kādambarī*.[3] It has a number of commentaries.[4]

ŚŪDRAKA

We have only one work of Śūdraka called the *Mṛcchakaṭika*. The work has attracted much notice in the West.[5]

The discovery of the *Cārudatta* by Bhāsa, which was probably the original of his *Mṛcchakaṭika*, fixes the upper limit of Śūdraka, the author of the *Mṛcchakaṭika*, but we cannot decide whether he was prior to Kālidāsa or not. Vāmana recognises him in III. 2. 4 ; Daṇḍin cites the verse *limpatīva*, etc., which is found in the *Mṛcchakaṭika* but it is now known to be a citation on the part of the author of the *Mṛcchakaṭika* from Bhāsa.

1 Keith's *History of Sanskrit Literature*, pp. 318-19.

2 See Winternitz, *Geschichte*, Vol. III ; Fleet, *Indian Antiquary*, 1901, 12f ; see also Bühler's *Vikramāṅkadevacarita*, Introduction, p. 4 ff. ; *Epigraphica Indica*, 1, 67 ff. 4 208 ff., and Rapson, J. R. A. S. 1898, 448 ff.

3 Edited by Peterson, Bombay, 1883, BSS ; Translated with occasional omissions by C. M. Ridding, London, 1896 ; see also Weber, *Indische Streifen*, 1, 352 ff and Lacôte in *Mélanges Lévi*, 259 ff.

4 These commentaries are by Bālakṛṣṇa, by Mahādeva, *Viṣamapadavṛtti* by Vaidyanātha Pāyaguṇḍe, by Śivarāma, by Siddhacandragaṇi and Sukhakāra.

5 A critical edition of the *Mṛcchakaṭika* was published from Bonn in 1847 by A. F. Stenzler. It was published also with two commentaries by N. B. Godbole, *B.S.S.*, 1896, and by P. H. M. Sanna Śāstrī and K. P. Parab, in *N.S.P.* 3rd Edition Bombay, 1909, with a commentary. German Translation by O. Böhtlingk, St. Petersburg, 1877, L. Fritze, 1879 and H. C. Kellner, 1894 ; English Translation by H. H. Wilson (*Select Specimens*, Vol. I.) and by A. W. Ryder, in *H.O.S.*, Vol. IX. See also continuation in *J.A.O.S.*, 1906, 418 ff. : French Translation by P. Regnaud, Paris, 1876 ; there are translations, in Dutch, Swedish, Danish, Italian and Russian. See also an Introduction by Cappeller in *Festgruss an Böhtlingk*, p. 20 ff. and A. Gawronski in *Kuhns Zeitschrift für vergl. Sprach*, 44, 1911, 224 ff. The drama has been played often on the European stage. In France, it was translated by Méry and Gérard de Nerval, in 1850, and in a new work by V. Barrucand ; Emil Pohl translated in German in 1892, Stuttgart, and called in *Vasantasenā*, for the German stage. A free German translation was also made under the title *Vasantasenā* by Haberlandt, Leipzig, 1893. A new adaptation for the stage was made by Lion Feuchtwanger, München, 1916. The editor had the opportunity of witnessing a performance of the drama under the name of *Vasantasenā* in 1929 on the chief stage of Vienna.

The play represents Śūdraka, a king, as the author ; king Śūdraka is described as a king in Kalhaṇa's *Rāja-taraṅgiṇī*, III. 643. The *Skanda-purāṇa* makes him the first king of the Andhrabhṛtyas and the *Vetāla-pañcaviṃśati* refers to him and gives his capital as Vardhamāna or Śobhāvatī. In the *Kādambarī* he is located in Vidiśā. The *Harṣa-carita* also refers to the artifice by which he relieved himself of his enemy Candraketu, king of Cakora, and the *Daśa-kumāra-carita* of Daṇḍin refers to his adventures in different lives. The fact that Rāmila and Somila wrote a *Kathā* on him, indicates that he was a legendary character of that time.[1] Rājaśekhara mentions Śūdraka along with Śatavāhana.[2] From all these divergent references Keith considers him to be merely a legendary person. Prof. Konow, however, regards him as a historical person and recognises in him the Ābhīra prince Śivadatta whose son Iśvarasena is regarded by Fleet to have overthrown the last king of the Andhra dynasty and to have founded the Cedī era (248-49).[3] This inference is drawn by Konow on the ground that in the *Mṛcchakaṭika*, Pālaka, the king of Ujjayinī, is defeated by Āryyaka, son of a herdsman Gopāla, and the Ābhīras are essentially herdsmen. But Keith thinks that these names, Pālaka and Gopāla, are merely of a legendary character and that it is wrong that they should be taken as proper names along with Āryyaka. But Bhāsa in the *Pratijñā-yaugandharāyaṇa* speaks of

1 Rājaśekhara tells us that Rāmila and Somila composed a work called *Śūdraka-kathā* and he also refers to Saumilla along with Bhāsa. Kālidāsa himself in his *Mālavikāgnimitra* speaks of Kavi-putra and Saumilla. The *Śarṅgadhara-paddhati* quotes a verse from Rāmila and Somila, (see Keith, *Sanskrit Drama*, pp. 127-128).

2 Vāsudeva-śātavāhana-śūdraka-sāhasāṅkādīn sakalān sabhāpatīn dāna-mānābhyām a ukuryyāt/

—Rājaśekhara's Kāvya-mīmāṁsā, p. 55.

Keith says that he is later the hero of a *parikathā*, *Śudraka-vadha* (Rāyamukuṭa, *Z.D.M.G.*, XXVIII, p. 117) and of a drama called *Vibhrānta-śūdraka* (*Sarasvatī-kaṇṭhābharaṇa*, p. 378) ; Keith's, *Sanskrit Drama*, p. 129 n.

3 *K.F.*, p. 107 ff ; also Bhandarkar's *Ancient Hist. of India*, p. 64 f. ; C.H.I., I. 311 ; laso Keith's *Sanskrit Drama*, p. 129.

Gopala and Palaka as being sons of Pradyota of Ujjayini, and it is probable that the *Bṛhatkathā* contained the story of Gopala as surrendering the kingdom on Pradyota's death to Palaka and Palaka had to make room for Āryyaka, his brother's son.[1] But Keith brushes it aside and regards Śūdraka as being merely a legendary person. We are ourselves unable to believe either Prof. Konow or Prof. Keith. The universal tradition of the existence of a poet called Śūdraka cannot be regarded as purely mythical or legendary. All that we can say is that he probably flourished after Bhasa. The reference to Śakāra and Viṭa as in a comparatively respectable position, in which the *gaṇikā* Vasanta-sena is also placed, clearly refers to an atmosphere of social existence depicted in the *Kāma-sūtra,* which was probably written in the 2nd century B.C. Our conjecture is that Śūdraka probably lived between the 1st century B.C. and the 1st century A.D. It is peculiar that when Cārudatta is asked in the court scene why he, a respectable person, should associate with a *gaṇikā,* he fearlessly replied that it was a fault of youth and not of character.

The *Mṛcchakaṭika* has a number of commentaries by Gaṇapati, Prthvīdhara, Rāmamaya Śarmā and Lallā Dīkṣita.

Harṣa the Dramatist

Three dramas, *Nāgānanda, Ratnāvalī* and *Priyadarśikā,* are attributed to Śrīharṣa, the patron of Bāṇabhaṭṭa, of the 7th century. Nāgojī Bhaṭṭa in his commentary to the *Kāvyapradīpa* said that an author called Dhāvaka wrote the *Ratnāvalī* under the name of king Harṣa in return for money received from him. But this late version of the story cannot be relied upon. In most manuscripts the name Bāṇa is mentioned, which probably means that Bāṇa received money from the king Harṣa not in lieu of allowing king Harṣa to enjoy the reputation of authorship of a new work written by Bāṇa, but for his own poetical talents. Nāgeśa's version of the story is also found in Mammaṭa, but as

1 *Ibid,* p. 130.

has been pointed out, this is a wrong reading of Dhāvaka for Bāṇa (see Bühler, *Indische Studien*, 14, 407).

Over the three dramas, see F. Cimmino in *O.C.*, XIII, Hamburg, 1902, p. 31 ff.; and Jackson in *J.A.O.S.*, 1900, 88 f.

The *Ratnāvalī* was published by C. Cappeller in O. Böhtlingk's *Sanskrit Chrestomathie*, III, 1909, p. 326 ff.; also N. B. Godbole and K. P. Parab, 2nd Edition, *N.S.P.*, Bombay, 1890 and with the commentary of Nārāyaṇa Śarmā by Kṛṣṇa Rao Joglekar, Bombay, 1913, *N.S.P.*; German translation by L. Fritz, 1878; English Translation by Wilson. The *Ratnāvalī* has another commentary by Bhīmasena. The *Priyadarsikā* was published by V. D. Gadre, Bombay, 1884, *N.S.P.*, French Translation by G. Strehly, Paris, 1880.

The drama *Priyadarśikā* has been modelled on the *Mālavikāgnimitra*, but the story was utilised by Bhāsa and also by Mātrarāja or Anaṅgaharṣa in his drama called the *Tāpasa-vatsarāja-carita*. The *Nātya-darpaṇa* quotes profusely from this work. See also E. Hultzsch in *N. G. G. W.*, 1886, 224 ff. Abhinavagupta also cites from it. The work must have, therefore, been written before the 9th century. Probably Mātrarāja utilised the story of the *Bṛhatkathā* of Guṇāḍhya. See also C. Lacôte, *J. A.*, 1919, 508 f.

The *Nāgānanda* has been published by G. B. Brahme and D. M. Paranjape, Poona, 1893 and by Ganapati Śāstrī, in the *Trivendum Series*, with the commentary of Śivarāma. Translated into English by Palmer Boyd, London, 1872 and into French by Bergaigne, Paris, 1879 and into Italian by Cimmino, 1903.

The story of the *Nāgānanda* is drawn from the *Kathāsaritsāgara* and Kṣemendra's *Bṛhatkathā-manjarī*. The story is unknown in the older *avadāna* literature. I-Tsing, however, refers to king Silāditya's story of Bodhisattva Jīmūtavāhana and that this story was shown on the stage of his time. The *Nāgānanda* has a commentary by Ātmārāma.

Viśākhadatta

Viśākhadatta is the author of the celebrated work *Mudrārākṣasa*. It was published by K. T. Telang, BSS. Bombay, 1884, with the commentary of Dhuṇḍhi-rāja and also by Hillebrandt, Breslau, 1912. See also Hillebrandt, ZDMG., 1885, p. 107 ff. ; also in NGGW, 1905, 129 ff. and *Über das Kauṭilīya-śāstra und Verwandtes,* Breslau, 1908. Translated into German by L. Fritze ; in English by H. H. Wilson ; in French by V. Henry, Paris, 1888 ; in Italian by A. Marazzi, Milan, 1874.

In many manuscripts, however the name given is not Viśākhadatta but Viśākhadeva.

There is a discussion as to whether Viśākhadatta lived in the time of Candragupta II. On this subject, see Jayaswal, *Indian Antiquary,* 1913, p. 265 ff., wherein he gives the date as 410 A.D. See also Konow, *Indian Antiquary,* 1914, p. 64 ff. ; V. A. Smith, *Early History of India,* 120 n ; Hillebrandt, *Über das Kautilīya-śāstra,* 25 ff. ; ZDMG, 1915, 363. Hillebrandt places Viśākhadatta in the 4th century A.D. and so does also Tawney (JRAS, 1908 p. 910). In some manuscripts, in the *bharatā-vākya,* Avantī-varmā is mentioned instead of Candragupta. See the discussion of Jacobi, WZKM, 1888, 212 ff., Dhruva, WZKM, 1891, 25 ff. ; Telang his own Introduction to his Editions ; Keith, J.R.A.S., 1909, 148 ff. ; Rapson, ERE, IV, p 886. We know thus with certainty that he cannot be later than the 10th century A.D. as he is cited in the commentary of the *Daśarūpaka.*

Murāri

Murāri is later than Bhavabhūti, as he cites from the *Uttaracarita,* as the verses 31 and 32 of the 6th Act of the *Uttaracarita* are cited in the 6th and 7th Slokas of the 1st Ac of the *Anargharāghava.* Ratnākara (9th century A.D.) in his

Haravijaya refers to Murārī.[1] Konow does not believe that Ratnākara referred to Murārī but he believes that Maṅkha's *Śrīkaṇṭha-carita* (A.D. 1135) refers to Murārī. Konow thinks that Murārī was earlier than Rājaśekhara.[2] The *Daśa-rūpaka* also refers to the *Anargha-rāghava* (III.21) in his II. 1. Keith further thinks that Jayadeva imitated the *Prasanna-rāghava* (*cf.* Jayadeva, II.34 with the *Prasanna-rāghava*, VII.83). But no definiteness can be arrived at regarding Murārī.

CATURBHĀṆĪ

vararucirīśvardattaḥ śyāmilakaḥ śūdrakaśca catvāraḥ ।
ete bhāṇān vabhaṇuḥ kā śaktiḥ kālidāsasya ॥

The above verse—which says that *bhāṇa* could only be written by Vararuci, Iṣvaradatta, Śyāmilaka and Śūdraka, and that Kālidāsa was incapable of writing any *bhāṇa*—occurs at the end of the *Padma-prabhṛtaka*.

It is difficult to say which Vararuci is here referred to. In the *Mahābhāṣya* we hear of a Vararuci (*vārarucāḥ ślokāḥ*) According to the *Kathāsaritsāgara*, Vararuci was a co-pupil with Paṇini. Vyāḍi is said to have introduced him to his preceptor Upavarṣa. According to the *Avantīsundraīkathāsāra*, Vararuci said to have lived somewhere on the bank of the Godavarī. He wrote on grammar, astrology and *dharma-śāstra* and two *Kāvyas* called *Kaṇṭhābharaṇa* and *Cārumatī*. A verse from the *Cārumatī* is quoted in the *Subhāṣitāvalī* and Bhoja-deva also in his *Śṛṅgāra-prakāsa* quotes a verse.

After Vararuci we have Śūdraka, the author of the *Mṛccha-kaṭika* and the *Vatsarāja-carita*. It is said that Śūdraka was a Brahmin attached to the court of Svātī, an Andhara-bhṛtya king of Ujjayinī. When still young, he quarrelled with the king and

1 Bhaṭṭa-nātha Svāmin, in *Indian Antiquary*, XLI. 141, and Lévi in his *Indian Theatre*, Vol. I, p. 277, contradicts it.
2 *Indian Drama* p. 83.

his friends. His intimate friend Vandhudatta saved him from difficulties and he had also later in life given him a good turn, when a Bhikṣu called Saṅghilaka was prevented from his murderous attempt on him by Śūdraka. The adventure of Śūdraka as have been described in the *Avantīsundarī-kathā* by Daṇḍin, have much resemblance with the heroes and the plot of the *bhāṇa* ascribed to Śūdraka, The adventures of Śūdraka are also found in the *Śūdraka-kathā* of Rāmila and Somila, the *Vikrānta-śūdraka* and the *Śūdraka-carita* by Pañcaśikha.

In this *bhāṇa* we have Devadattā as the heroine, her sister Vipulā and the friend Śaśa. These characters are referred to by Bāṇa in his *Kādambarī*. *Kāmadatta*, a work referred to in this *bhāṇa*, was probably a *prakaraṇa* written by Śūdraka himself.

Īśvara-dattā, author of the other *bhāṇa*, leaves nothing behind him by which we can infer his date. He is mentioned by Bhojadeva in his *Śṛṅgāra-prakāśa* and also by Hema-candra. We also find a verse in the *Subhāṣitāvalī* under the name of Īśvara-sena and it is not improbable that Īśvara-datta and Iśvara-sena are the same persons.

Śyāmilaka was probably a native of Kashmir. He has been referred to by Kṣemendra in his *Aucitya-vicāra* and Abhinavagupta quotes from the *Pāda-tāḍitaka*. It is not improbable that he may have lived between 800 A.D. and 900 A.D.

The above four poets, Śūdraka, Īśvara-datta, Vararuci and Śyāmilaka, wrote respectively the four *bhāṇas*, viz., *Padma-prabhṛtaka*, *Dhūrtta-viṭa-saṃvāda*, *Ubhayābhisārika* and *Pāda-tāḍitaka*. All the four *bhāṇas* consist of poems and prose.

BHAṬṬA-NĀRĀYAṆA

His work, *Beṇī-saṃhāra* is quoted by Vāmana, Ānanda-vardhana, Ruyyaka, Nami, Kṣemendra, the *Kāvya-prakāśa* and the *Daśa-Rūpaka*. It was published by J.Grill, Leipzig, 1871, and with the commentary of Jagaddhara, by K. P. Parab and K. R. Modgavkar, Bombay, 1898, 2nd Edition, 1905, NSP.

A free translation of it has been made by S. M. Tagore Calcutta, 1880.

BHAVABHŪTI

Bhavabhūti's three dramas, the *Mahavīra-carita,* the *Uttara carita* and the *Mālatī-mādhava,* are famous in Sanskrit literature The first two are based on the legend of Rāma. The *Mahāvīra-carita* was published by F. H. Trithen, London, 1848, with the commentary of Vīra-rāghava, by T. R. Ratnam Aiyar S. Raṅga-cariar and K. P. Parab, 2nd Edition, Bombay, 1901, NSP. See also the English Translation by Wilson ; also English Translation by Pickford, 1871.

The *Uttara-carita* has been published with the commentary of Vīra-rāghava by T. R. Ratnam Aiyar and V. L. Sh. Panasīkar, 4th Edition, Bombay 1911, NSP. English Translation by Wilson, Vol. I, p. 275 ff. and C. H. Tawney, 2nd Edition ; Calcutta, 1874. French Translation by F. Neve, Brussels and Paris, 1880 ; Senart, JA, 1881, XVII, 562 ff. A scene of the 4th Act has been translated by Oldenberg, LAI, p. 278 ff. The *Mālatī-mādhava* was published by R. G. Bhandarkar with the commentary of Jagaddhara, BSS, Bombay 1876, 2nd Edition, 1905 ; and also with the commentary of Tripurāri and Jagaddhara by M. R. Telang and W. Sh. Panasikar, Bombay, 1905, NSP ; also English Translation by M. R. Kale, 1913 ; German Translation by Fritze, 1844 ; French Translation by G. Strehly with a preface by Bergaigne.

Klein in his *History of Dramas,* Vol. III, p. 51, describes Bhavabhūti as the Indian Shakespeare.

KUMARADĀSA

For General information regarding his poems, see J. d'Alwis, 1870 ; Zachariae, *Beiträge zur Kunde der indogermanischen Sprachen,* 5, 1880, p. 52 and GGA, 1887, p. 95 ; Peterson. JBRAS., 17, 1889, 57 ff. and *Subhāṣita-muktāvalī,* 24 ff. ;

E. Leumann, WZKM, 7, 1893, 226 ff; F. W. Thomas, JRAS, 1901, 253 ff.; A. B. Keith, *Ibid*, 578 ff. *Jānakīharaṇa*, edition of Ceylon, 1891; Cantos I-X, Bombay, 1907; Canto XVI, BSOS, IV, 285 ff.

Rāja-sekhara mentions him as an example of genius, though blind, in the sentence *yā śabda-grāmam ratha-sārtham alaṅkāra-tantra-yukti-mārgam anyadapi tathāvidham adhihṛdayaṃ pratibhāsayati sā pratibhā* । *apratibhasya padārtha-sārthaḥ parokṣa iva* । *pṛtibhāvataḥ punarapaśyato'pi pratyakṣa iva* । *yato medhāvi-rudrakumāradāsādayo jātyandhāḥ kavayaḥ śrūyante* ॥ This proves that he must have flourished long before Rāja-sekhara. Keith thinks that he knew the *Kāśikā Vṛtti* (A.D. 650) and that Vāmana (about A.D. 800) also refers to Kumāradāsa, when he censures the use of *khalu* as the first word. Keith further thinks that he was earlier than Māgha. See also O. Walter, *Übereín-stimmungen in Gedanken Vergleichen und Wendungen bei indischen Kunstdichtern*, Leipzig, 1905, 0. 18 ff.

Nīlkaṇṭha Dīkṣita

He was not only the author of *Śiva-līlārṇava* but also of *Kali-viḍambana*, *Sabhā-rañjana-śataka*, *Anyopadeśa-śataka*, *Śānti-vilāsa*, *Vairāgya-śataka* and *Ānanda-sāgara-stava*. His major works are, besides *Śiva-līlārṇāva*, *Gaṅgāvataraṇa*, *Nala-carita-nāṭaka*, *Kaiyyaṭa-vyākhyāna* and *Śiva-tattva-rahasya*. He lived in the middle of the 16th century near Conjeevaram and was a grandson of the brother of Appaya Dīkṣita. Contemporaneous to Appaya Dīkṣita there was a number of well-reputed poets, such as (1) Ratna-kheṭa who wrote *Śiti-kaṇṭha-vijaya-kāvya* and *Bhāvanā-puruṣottama-nāṭaka*, (2) Bhaṭṭojī Dīkṣīta, (3) Govinda Dīkṣita. Ānanda-rāya Makhin's father Nṛsiṃha-rāya wrote *Tripura-vijaya-campū* and the nephew of Bhagavanta-rāya was the author of *Mukunda-vilāsa-kāvya* and *Rāghavābhyudaya-nāṭaka*. Ānanda-rāya Makhin wrote at least two dramas, *Vidyā-pariṇaya* and *Jīvānanda*, in the 18th century. Govinda Dīkṣita, father of Venkaṭesvara Makhin, who was the teacher of Nīlakaṇṭha Makhin, not only wrote a commentary on Kumārila's philosophy but also a drama called *Raghunātha-vilāsa*. He also wrote a work called *Harivaṃsa-sāra-carita*, a *mahā-kāvya* of 23 cantos, on which Appaya Dīkṣita wrote a commentary. Veṅkaṭeśvara Makhin's teacher and elder brother Yajña-nārāyaṇa Dīkṣita wrote at least 3 works, *Raghunātha-bhupa-vijaya*, *Raghunātha-vilāsa-nāṭaka* and *Sāhitya-ratnākara*. The great scholars who were contemporaneous with Yajña-nārāyaṇa Dīkṣita, were Kṛṣṇayajvan, Somanātha, Kumāra-tātācāryya, author of the *Pārijātanāṭaka*, Rāja-cūdāmaṇi Dīkṣita and Bhāskara Dīkṣita. Cokkanātha Makhin also was a contemporary of Nīlakaṇṭha Dīkṣita. The great poet Veṅkaṭeśvara also lived at this time who wrote a *mahā-kāvya* called *Rāma-candrodaya*. Nīlakaṇṭha Makhin's younger brother Atirātra-yajvan wrote *Kuśa-kumudvatī-nāṭaka*. Śrī-cakra-kavi of this time wrote *Citra-ratnākara*, *Rukminī-parinaya*, *Jānakī-pariṇaya*, *Gauri-pariṇaya* and *Draupadī-pariṇaya*. Nīlakaṇṭha's son Gīrvāṇendra wrote a *bhāṇa* called *Śṛṅgāra-koṣa*.

Mahendravikrama-varman

Mahendravikrama-varman, the son of the Pallava king Siṃhaviṣṇuvarman was a contemporary of Harṣa and was himself a king. His work *Matta-vilāsa* has been published in the Trivendrum Series. The scene of the drama is Kāñcī, where he ruled in the 7th century A.D. It is a *prahasana* and it comes from the South and shows the same technique as regards the *prastāvanā* and *sthāpanā* as we find in Bhāsa. The *Matta-vilāsa* is probably the earliest of the *prahasanas* that have come to us. The story is amusing and probably suggests a reflection on the character of the degenerate Buddhists and the Kāpālikas.

Veṅkaṭanātha

Veṅkaṭanātha was primarily a writer on Rāmānuja's system of philosophy. The details of his philosophy and his works may be found in Vol. III of the *History of Indian Philosophy* by the present editor. But Veṅkaṭanātha was not only a philosopher but a writer of good poetry as well, as may be seen from many of the poems of the *Yādavābhyudaya*, a work on the life of Kṛṣṇa. He does not appear to be in any way a laborious writer but his diction is rather simple and charming and in many places he indulges in now forms of imagery. Thus for instance in Canto II of the *Yādavābhyudaya* there is the following verse :—

diśastadānīmavanīdharāṇāṃ
sagairikaiḥ pāradapaṅkalepaiḥ ।
cakāśire candramaso mayūkhaiḥ
pañcāyudhasyeva śaraiḥ pradīptaiḥ ॥

Udayasundarī-kathā

(11th Century)

Soḍḍhala, a native of Guzerat, wrote a *Campū* called *Udayasundarī-kathā.* He belonged to the Kāyastha caste. He lost his father when a mere boy and was brought up by his maternal uncle Gaṅgādhara. He went to Sthānaka, the capital of Kaṅkaṇa. There he flourished in the court of three royal brothers Cehiṭṭa-rāja, Nāgārjuna and Mummani-rāja. He was a contemporay of Vatsa-rāja. The *Udayasundarī-kathā* was written between 1026 A.D. and 1050 A.D. The author compares himself to Bāṇa and Vālmīki and is quite proud of his achievement. The *Udayasundarī-kathā* is based upon an original story. King Vatsa-rāja, at whose suggestion the work was written, was a king of the Lāṭa country (Southern Guzerat including Khandesh).

Udayavarma-carita

(11th Century)

The *Udayavarmā-cartia* is a small work in verse describing the glory of king Udayavarmā who was a Kerala king and lived in the latter half of the 11th century. The author of the work is one called Mādhavācāryya. This Mādhavācāryya could not be the same as Vidyāraṇya or the author of the *Sarva-darśana-saṃgraha* who lived in the 14th century. But there was a Mādhava Paṇḍita who is reputed to have written a commentary on the *Sāmaveda,* who was attached to king Udayavarmā. His father Nārāyaṇa was a contemporary of Skanda-svāmī, who along with Nārāyaṇa and Udgītha wrote a commentary on the *Ṛgveda.* The work has been published in the T.S. series by K. Śāmbaśiva Śāstrī. There are also other conjectures about Udayavarman's date but I prefer to accept the conclusion of the learned editor.

KUMĀRAPĀLA-PRATIBODHA

(12th Century)

The author Somaprabhācārya is a well-known Jaina scholar who lived towards the end of the 12th century and wrote his work in 1195 A.D., only 11 years after King Kumārapāla had died. He was thus a contemporary of King Kumārapāla and his preceptor Hemachandra. He composed the work dwelling in the residence of the poet Siddhapāla, son of the poet-king Śrī Śrīpāla, was one of the best poets of Guzerat. Śrīpāla's son Siddhapāla was also a poet and a friend of King Kumārapāla. Somaprabhācārya was the author also of *Sumatinātha-carita, Sūktimuktāvalī* and *Śatārtha-kāvya.* The author's aim, as usual with such other poets, was not writing a history, but to write a *kāvya* with special emphasis upon religion. We find here a picture of Hemachandra and his relation with Kumārapāla who was converted into Jainism. Information about Kumārapāla is also available from the three works of Jayasiṃha Sūri—*Prabhāvaka-carita, Prabandha-cintāmanī, Kumārapāla-carita,* and Cāritrasundara's *Kumārpāla-carita* and Jinamaṇḍana's *Kumārapāla-prabandha.*

We know that Kumārapāla held his court at Anhilwara and he zealously preached the sanctity of animal life and had censors like Aśoka's for the preaching of *dharma* to the people. The *Kumārapāla-pratibodha* is a sort of *campū* written in Prākṛt prose and verse and is full of the principles of Jaina religion and contains many stories.

RŪPAKA-ṢAṬKA

(12th Century)

We have a collecton of six dramas by Vatsa-rāja, the minister of Paramardi-deva, whose reign extended from 1163 to 1203 A.D. and the reign of his son Trailokya-deva extended till the end of the first halt of the 13th centnry. Vatsa-rāja lived between the second half of the 12th century and the first half of the 13th century. Paramardi-deva was the immediate successor of Madana-varmā who was defeated by Siddha-rāja, king of Guzerat. Both Madana-varmā and Paramardi-deva lived a luxurious life according to the description of the *Prabandha-cintāmami*. Paramardi was so much given to cruel pastimes that he killed a cook every day at the time when he served him and people called him Kopakālānala. Paramardi was defeated by Pṛthvī-rāja as recorded in a short inscription at Madanapura in 1183 A.D. He was also later on defeated by Kutubuddin Ibak in 1203 A.D. His son Trailokya-varmā, however, recovered the capital of Kāliñjara. Paramardi was also a poet as we know by his composition of a long *praśasti* to Śiva. But actually the composition was done by Vatsa-rāja and an allusion to it is found in the *Karpūra-carita*. This *Rupaka-ṣaṭka* was edited by Mr. C. D. Dalal, Baroda 1918. It contains a *vyāyoga* on the same subject as Bhāravi's *Kirāṭārjunīya*, and an *īhāmṛga* called *Rukmiṇī-haraṇa*, a *ḍima* called *Tripura-dāha*; a *samavakāra* called *Samudra-mathana* and a *bhāṇa* called *Karpura-carita* describing the revelry, gambling and love of a gambler with a courtesan and *Hāsya-cūḍāmaṇi*, a frace in one Act in which an *ācārya* of the Bhāgavata school is ridiculed.

A verse from Vatsa-rāja is found quoted in Jalhaṇa's *Sūkti-muktāvalī*. The style is excellent and the plot well-executed.

Partha-Parākrama

Mr. Dalal in his Introduction to *Pārtha-parākrama* states that the entire Sanskrit Dramatic Literature of India consists of about 600 works. He gives us a list of contributions from Guzerat as given below, which is not out of interest :—

Bilhaṇa's *Karṇa-sundarī* (already printed) ; Rāmacandra's *Raghu-vilāsa, Nala-vilāsa, Yadu-vilāsa, Kaumudi-mitrānanda* (printed), *Nirbhayabhīma-vyāyoga, Satyahariśchandra, Vanamālikā-nāṭikā, Mallikā-makaranda*. Then we have Devacandra's *Candralekhāvikrīḍana-nāṭikā* and *Māna-mudrā-bhañjana* ; Yaśaścandra's *Mudrita-kumuda-candra* (printed) and *Rājīmatī-prabodha* ; Rāmacandra's *Prabuddha-rauhiṇeya*, Subhaṭa's *Dūtāṅgada* (printed), Prahlādana's *Pārtha-parākrama*. Someśvara's *Ullāgha-rāghava*, Narendra-prabha's *Kākutstha-keli*, Bālacandra's *Karuṇā-vajrāyudha* (printed), Vijayapāla's *Draupadi-svayaṃvara*, Yaśaḥpāla's *Moha-parājaya*, Megha-prabha's *Dharmābhyudayacchāyā-nāṭaka*, Vyāsa-mokṣaditya's *Bhīma-parākrama*, Gaṅgādhara's *Gaṅgadāsapratāpa-vilāsa*, Ravidāsa's *Mithyājñānakhaṇḍana*.

We have also taken a more or less detailed note of a number of other Gurjara works in other sections of these Editorial Notes.

There were other dramas of this type, such as *Dhanañjaya-vijaya* of Kañcanācarya, *Nirbhaya-bhīma* of Rāmacandra, *Kirātārjunīya* of Vatsa-rāja, *Narakāsura-vijaya* of Dharma-paṇḍita, *Pracaṇḍabhairava* of Sadāśiva, *Saugandhikā-haraṇa* of Viśvanātha and *Vinatānandana* of Govinda.

Our author was the son of Yaśodhavala. He was not only a poet but also a great warrior. He is described by Someśvara as having attained his celebrity as a Lord of Victory. He is also presented as being a great philanthropist in *Surathotsava* of

Someśvara. He founded a city called Prahlādanapura, the modern Pālanpur, in Guzerat.

NARANĀRĀYAṆĀNANDA

(13th Century)

The poem *Naranārāyaṇānanda* is a *kāvya* in 16 cantos describing the friendship of Arjuna and Kṛṣṇa and the abduction of Subhadrā by Arjuna. Vastupāla the author, also called Vasantapāla, who wrote the work in 1277 Saṃvat, was the minister of king Vīradhavala of Dholka, and was celebrated for his tolerance and cosmopolitanism. He even built a mosque for the Mahomedans. His glories are not only sung in the *Prabandha-cintāmaṇī*, and the *Caturviṃśati-prabandha* but also in the *Kīrti-kaumudī* of Someśvara and the *Sukṛta-sāṅkīrtana* by Nṛsiṃha and also in the *mahā-kāvya Vasanta-vilāsa* by Bāla-candra and in Jinaharṣa's *Vastupāla-carita*. He was a minister, warrior, philanthropist, a builder of public places and temples, a patron of poets and himself a poet. He had established three great libraries. He encouraged the writting of great works and *Kathā-ratna-sāgara* of Bāla-candra Sūri and *Alaṅkāra-mahodadhi* of Narendra-prabha were composed at his patronage. He was very liberal in his gifts to the poets and patronised such writers as Someśvara, Harihara, Arisiṃha, Dāmodara, Nānaka, Jaya-deva, Madana, Vikala, Kṛṣṇa-siṃha and Śaṅkara-svāmī. He was himself a great poet and his verses have been quoted in works of anthology, such as *Sūkti-muktāvalī* and *Śārṅgadhara-paddhati*. The work *Naranārāyaṇānanda* is excellent in style and poetic fancy.

SRĪNIVĀSA-VILĀSA-CAMPŪ

(*c.* 14th Century)

Śrīnivāśa-vilāsa-campū is a *campū* in which Bāṇa's alliteration and *śleṣa* or punning have been imitated with a vengence. It is, however, a pleasant love-story of a Southern king Śrīnivāsa.

It was written by Veṅkṭādhvarin or Venkaṭeśa. It is written in two parts, a *pūrva-bhāga* with 5 *ucchvāsas* and the *Uttara-bhāga* with 5 *ucchvāsas*. The poet seems to have been a disciple of Vedānta-deśika of the 14th century and Śrīnivāsa, a Southern Chief, was his patron.

NALĀBHYUDAYA

(15th Century)

It is a work by Vāmana Bhaṭṭabāṇa, who is the author of *Śṛṅgāra-bhūṣaṇa, Pārvatī-pariṇaya* and *Vemabhūpāla-carita.* He was also called Abhinava Bhaṭṭabāṇa. At the commencement of his work *Vemabhūpāla-carita,* the poet says that it has long been said that none but Bāṇa could write charming prose—Vāmana now will wipe away that bad name (*bāna-kavīndrādanye kāṇāh khalu sarasa-gadya-saraṇiṣu iti jagati rūḍhamayaśo vatsakulo vāmano' dhunā mārṣṭi*).

Vemabhūpala was the ruler of the Triliṅga country during the middle of the 15th century and he was himself well-versed in all arts and wrote a commentary on *Amaru-śataka,* called *Śṛṅgāra-dīpikā,* and *Saṅgīta-cintāmaṇi.*

The *Nalābhyudaya* is a *mahā-kāvya* in 8 cantos and the style is lucid and clear. As a matter of fact, the style seems to be approaching Kalidāsa in sweetness. The work has been published in the Trivendrum Sanskrit Series by MM. T. Gaṇapati Śāstrī.

KATHĀ-KAUTUKA

(15th Century)

The *Kathā-kautuka* is based on the story of Yusuf-Zuleikhā of the Persian poet Jāmī, written by the Kashmir poet Śrīvara, who lived in the 15th century. This is one of the few successful adaptations of Persian tales into Sanskrit poetry. The work is written in easy Sanskrit poetry and divided into 15 chapters called *kautukas.* The author seems to have been well-versed in

Persian and Arabic as he calls himself *yavana-śāstra-pārangama*. But he does not follow the text of Yusuf-Zuleikhā in any faithful manner.

RĀṢṬRAUḌHA-VAṂŚA-MAHĀKĀVYA

(16th Century)

The *Rāṣṭrauḍha-vaṃśa* is a *mahā-kāvya* in 20 cantos. It is a historical poem containing the history of the Bāgulas of Mayūragiri, from the orginator of the dynasty, Rāṣṭrauḍha, king of Kanauj, to the reign of Nārāyaṇa Shāh, ruler of Mayūragiri and patron of the author (1596 A.D.). Rudra-kavi wrote another work called *Jāhāṅgīr-shāh-carita* in prose, at the order of Pratāp Shāh, son of Nārāyaṇa Shāh. Mayūragiri is in the Nāsik district. The work is historically more faithful than other works of this nature.

KAMALINĪ-KALAHAṂSA

(16th Century)

Kamalinī-kalahaṃsa was written by Rāja-cūḍāmani, son of Srīnivāsa Dīkṣita and Kāmākṣī Devī, towards the end of the 16th century. Rāja-cūḍāmaṇi wrote a number of works of a philosophical type. But he also wrote *Śṛṅgāra-sarvasva* (a *bhaṇa*), a supplementary work on *Bhoja-campū*, the *Bhārata-campū Śaṅkarābhyudaya, Ratnakheṭa-vijaya, Mañju-bhāṣinī, Kaṃsa-vadha, Rukmiṇī-Pariṇaya, Ānandarāghava-nāṭaka* and many other works.

ACYUTARĀYĀBHYUDAYA

(By Śrī Rānjanātha)

(16th Century)

Acyuta-rāya was the son of Narasiṃha who succeeded his brother Kṛṣṇa-rāya to the throne in the year 1527–30 and ruled from 1530 to 1542, as the Emperor of Vijayanagara. In the poem *Acyutarāyābhyudaya* the poet describes the geneologieal history of King Acyuta-rāya. There was once a king named Timma among the Tuluva dynasty of kings in Vijayanagara, who had a wife called Devakī and their son Īśvara had a wife called Bukkāmmā. Their eldest son Narasiṃha became the Emperor and captured the Fort of Mānavadurga, but when the Nizam of the place submitted himself to him and begged his pardon he returned the fort to him and then took Seringapatam. He then overcame the Marawas and took hold of Mādura and conquered Konetirāja and made Vijayanagara his capital. His three sons became king one after another and Acyuta-rāya was the youngest. His queen was Varadāmbal. Being informed that the Cola king had fled from his kingdom and sought refuge with the king of Chera, who had usurped the Pāṇḍya kingdom, Acyuta-rāya marched to Kālahastī and Viṣṇukāñcī and finally went to Srīraṅgam. After this he sent one of his generals to punisn the Chera king. A regular fight took place later on between the king of Travancore and Acyuta-rāya ; Acyuta-rāya became victorious. The Chera king took refuse with Prince Salaga-rāja who gave the Pāṇḍya chief his former dominions. He then went to the Malaya mountain in the sea. This story is narrated in the first six cantos of this *Kāvya*.

The work *Acyutarāyābhyudaya* was published in the Śrīvāṇī-vilāsa Press, Srīraṅgam, in 1907 and bears with it a commentary by Srīkṛṣṇa Sūri.

ĀNANDAKANDA-CAMPŪ

(17th Century)

This work is attributed to Mitra-miśra. He is the reputed author of the *Vīramitrodaya*, a work an Dharma-sāstra. He also wrote a commentary on Yājñavalkya Smṛti and also a mathematical work, both of which were called *Vīramitrodaya*. But it appears that Mitra-miśra used to get many books written by other schlars, to all of which the name *Vīramitrodaya* is given. Thus in the commentary on Yājñavalkya Smṛti it is said that the commentary was written by Sri Sadānanda under the orders of Mitra-miśra. So also was the mathematical work written by Rāma-daivajña and called *Vīramitrodaya*. So Dharmayya Dīkṣita wrote a commentary on *Advaitavidyā-tilaka* under the suggestion of Mitra-miśra.

Mitra-miśra's patron, Raja Vīrasiṃha-deva of Orchha, reigned from 1605 to 1627, and as Mr. Gopinath Kaviraja says, was probably identical with Birsing Deo who is said to have killed Abul Fazl. The *Ānandakanda-campū* treats of the birth of the Divi ✻ Joy as Śrīkṛṣṇa. The Editor, Pandit Nanda Kisore Sarman, says that the work was composed in 1632 A.D. It is divided into 8 *ullāsas* or chapters.

NĀRAYAṆĪYA

This work by Nārāyana Bhaṭṭa with the commentary Bhaktapriyā, by Deśamaṅgala Vāryya, has been published by K. Sāmbaśiva Sāstrī in the Trivendrum Sanskrit Series. Its essence has been culled from the *Bhāgavata-purāṇa* by Nārāyaṇa Bhaṭṭapāda. It is one of the finest examples of the *stotra* literature and consists of 100 *daśakas* or decades. It is not only a *stotra* but also an excellent *kāvya* on account of its poetic merit. It is regarded in the Kerala country as reverentially as the *Śrīmad-bhagabad-gītā*. The author was born in the Mepputtur Illam in the village of Perumanam on the river Nila in North Malabar. His fame as a poet grew very high and excellence of his works was recognised by all and he was entertained at the court of king Deva-nārāyana. He wrote the following works :—(1) *Nārāyaṇīya*, (2) *Māna-meyodaya*, (3) *Aṣṭamī-campūkāvya*, (4) *Prakriyā-sarvasva*, (5) *Dhātu-kāvya*, (6) *Kailāsa-śaila-varṇana*, (7) *Kaunteyāṣṭaka* (8) *Ahalyā-śāpa-mokṣa*, (9) *Śūrpaṇakhā-pralapā*, (10) *Rāma-kathā*, (11)*Dūta-vākya-prabandha*, (12) *Nalayani-carita*, (13) *Nṛga-*

mokṣa-prabandha, (14) *Rājasūya-prabandha,* (15) *Subhadrā-haraṇa-prabandha,* (16) *Svāhā-sudhākara,* (17) *Saṅgīta-ketu-śṛṅgāra-līlā-carita.*

BHARATA-CARITA

Bharata-carita, a *mahā-kāvya* of 12 cantos, was written in different metres on the life of Bharata, son of Duṣyanta, by Kṛṣṇakavi. It has been published in the Trivendrum Sanskrit Series by MM. T. Ganapti Sastri. Nothing can be made out regarding the identity or nativity of Kṛṣṇakavi, the author of this poem.

CANDRAPRABHĀ-CARITA

This work has been published in the Kāvyamālā Series, 1902, Bombay, by MM. Pandit Durga Prasad and Mr. K. P. Parab. It was written by Vīranandī, a pupil of Abhayanandī, who again was a pupil of Guṇa-nandī. The poem consists of 18 cantos and contains many charming scenes and descriptions. The style is lucid and clear.

KĀVYA-RATNA

The author of this work is Arhaddāsa and it has been published in the Trivendrum Sanskrit Series by K. Sāmvaśiva Śāstrī It deals with the life of Muni Suvrata, a Jaina Tīrthaṅkara and it is also called *Muni-suvrata-kāvya.* Muni Suvrata is said to have been a teacher of Mallinātha. It is difficult to say whether this Mallinātha is identical with the commentator Mallinātha.

BĀLA-MĀRTAṆḌA-VIJAYA

This is a drama in 5 Acts by Devarāja-kavi, published in the Trivendrum Sanskrit Series edited by K. Sāmbaśiva Śāstrī. According to tradition, the poet Deva-rāja belonged to a Brahmin family that migrated from Pattamadai in the Tinnevelly district and settled at Asrama, a village near Suchindram in South Travancore. He was patronised by Prince Rāma-varmā, a nephew of his Highness Mārtaṇḍa-varmā and became the chief of the pandits attached to the palace. His father Śeśādri was a Vedic scholar. King Mārtaṇḍa-varmā ruled from 1729 to 1758. The drama deals with the conquests of King Mārtaṇḍa-varmā and the dedication of his Empire to the deity Śrīpadmanābha, reserving to himself the position of Viceroy and servant of the deity and governing the country in his name.

The dramatist tries to follow the style of Kālidāsa and in this work one can sometimes trace expressions similar to those of Kālidāsa. Sometimes he follows also the style of Viśākhadatta's *Mudrā-rākṣasa*. Mārtaṇḍa-varmā has figured largely in Malayalam literature also.

INDEX

A

A. A. Führer, 168*, 22*, 755
A. A. Macdonell, 708*, See Macdonell
A. A. Maria Sharpe, 225*
A. Banerji Sastri, lxxiv, 494* See Banerji-Sastri
A. Barth, 646, 702. See Barth
Abbé J. A. Dubois, 704
Abdallah ibn'l Muquffa, 89*
Abdhimathana, 687
A. Benkatasubbiah, 619*
A. Bergainge. See Bergaigne
Abhandl, d. Berliner Akad. 71*
Abhayacandra, 679
Abhayadeva Sūri, 395
Abhayanandī, 775
Abh für kunde d°., 96*
Abhaya-tilaka-gaṇi, 678*
Abhidharma, 10, 70
Abhidharmakoṣa, xix, cxiv
Abhidhā, 534* 545, 554, 560, 562
Abhidhā-vṛtti-mātṛkā, 189*, 530*
Abhijñāna-Śakuntala xxx, xxxv, 53*, 58, 60, 133, 134-36, 140-46, 162*, 270*, 641, 747
Abhimanyu, 112, 113, 724
Abhinaya, 539
Abhinaya-darpaṇa, 524*
Abhinanda, author of *Kādambarī-kathā-sāra*, (q. v), 324, 618
Abhinanda, author of *Rāmacarita* (q. v.), cxxviii, 201, 324
Abhinanda, Gauḍa, 324
Abhinava Bāṇa. See Bāṇa, Vāmana Bhaṭṭa,
Abhinava-bhāratī, 523, 524*, 535*, 548, 596
Abhinavagupta, xli, xlii, xliv, xlvi, lxxvi, lxxvii, lxxxv, lxxxvi, cxv, 54*, 66, 105*, 171, 249, 271*, 299*, 300, 301, 302*, 323*, 324, 369*, 401*, 427*, 523, 524, 525*, 527, 535, 539*, 540-45, 548, 550, 551. 552, 556, 557, 582*, 583, 584, 587, 593, 594, 596-99, 602, 604, 606 607, 608, 648, 661, 681, 686, 715, 730, 759, 762. See *Locana*
Abhinava-kaustubha-mālā, 386*, 663
Abhinava-nārāyaṇendra Sarasvatī, 668
Abhinava-rāghava, 302*, 464, 686
Abhirāma, 140*
Abhisārikā. lxiv, 271*
Abhisārikā- vañcitaka, 271*, 302
Abhiṣeka-nāṭaka, 101, 109*, 114, 302* , 709, 710, 711, 720, 721
A. B. Keith, 1*, 2*, 556*, 612*, 621*, 648, 691, 752, 757, 758, 764. See Keith
ABORI, 107*, 415*, 464*, 477*
Aboriginal, lxxxvii, cxxiii
Absolutism, xxvii
Abul Fazl, 774
Academies, lvii
Acala, 8*
Acaleśvara (deity), 466*
Accā Dikṣita, 334*
Accents, vi, cxxiii
Accoda lake, 235
Acintyaram Sarman, 324*
A. Conrady, 510*
Action, dramatic, 116, 117, 135, 141, 257, 258, 259, 262, 264, 267, 271, 273, 275, 282, 284, 286, 287, 288, 301, 303, 494, 501, 505
Acyuta-lilodaya, 338*
Acyutarāya (of Vijayanagara), 361, 371*, 418, 438
Acyutarāyābhyudaya, 361*, 773
Acyuta-Śarmā, 566
Adbhuta-darpaṇa, 464
Ad. Fr. Graf Von Schack, 744*
A. D. Pusalker, 102*
Advaitaratna-rakṣaṇa 664
Advaitasiddhi. 664
Advaita Vedānta, 463
Advaitavidyātilaka, 774
Advaitins, 438, 772, 773
Adyr Library, 333*
Aesop's Fables, 698
A. Esteller. 506*, See Esteller
Aesthetic, xxi, xxxv, xl, xlii, xliii, xliv, xlvi, xlvii, xlix, lii, lxxvii, 25, 29, 309, 571, 572, 575, 592, 602; 603, 604, 608, 601, 666, 670, 681
Afghanistan, 738
A. F R. Hoernle, 738*, See Hoernle.
A. F. Stenzler, 126*, 129*' 132*, 239*, 741, 743, 751, 756, See Stenzler.
Agashe, 208*, 209*, 210*, 211*, 215*, 503* See G. J. Agashe
Agastya, 464, 631,
A. Gawroński, 69*, 124*, 738*, 756*, See Gawroński
Aghoraghaṇṭa, 283
Agni-purāṇa, xiii, 66, 426*, 427*, 539, 553
Agnimitra, c, cviii, 137, 139, 151, 735, 750
Agni-varṇa, lxxxi, 131, 132*, 746, 747
A. Guerinot, 751*
Aguru, lvi
Ahalyā-śāpa-mokṣa, 774
A. Hamilton, 90*
A. H. Franche, 422*

A. Hillebrandt, 44*, 46*, 262*, 646*, 647. See Hillebrandt.
A. Hoefer, 121*, 621*
A. Holtzmann, 730*
A. H. Shah, 729*
A. I. D., 641*
Aihole inscription, xix, 15, 124*, 178
Aitareya Brāhmaṇa. 632, 673
Aja (king), xxx, 130, 131, 150*. 745
Ajaḍa-pramātṛ-siddhi, 662
Ajantā, cxi
Ajaya (river), 390
Ajayapāla, 404, 463*
Ajātaśatru, cvii
Ajiravatī (river), 226
Ajita-senācārya, 506
Ajitāpīḍa, 121*, 302, 349
Ajmere, 360, 469, 625, 677
Akālajalada, 454
Akbar, 315 359*. 402*, 468*, 677, 679, 740
Akbariya Kālidāsa, 740
A. K. Pisharoti, 102*
Alaka, 320, 623*
Alakadatta, 354
Alakāpūrī, cxxvi, 133, 751
Alaṁkāra (a scholar called Laṅkaka), 322
Alaṁkāra or *Alaṁkāras* xi, xvi, xvii, xviii, xix, xxix, li, 514-20, 526, 530, 532*, 534-38 545, 548-50, 553, 557, 563, 564, 566-69, 573-75, 578, 579, 581, 582, 584-87. 592, 593, 595, 605, 606, 608, 615, 622, 661, 681, 685, 700, 719, 729, 731
Alaṁkāra-cintāmaṇi, 566
Alaṁkāra-cūḍāmaṇi, 559
Alāṁkāra-grantha, 566
Alamkāra-kaustubha, 566
Alaṁkāra-mahodadhi, 770
Alaṁkāra, minister of Jayasiṁha, 628
Alaṁkārānusāriṇī, 558
Alaṁkārodāharaṇa, 629
Alaṁkāra-saṁgraha (of Udbhata), 533, 742*
Alaṁkāra-saṁgraha (of Amṛtānanda-yogin), 566
Alaṁkāra-sañjīvanī, 548*
Alaṁkāra-sarvasva. 322. 323* 360*, 531*, 545, 552 556, 557*, 558, 562, 584* 628
Alaṁkāra-sarvasva-sañjīvanī, 565
Alaṁkāra-sāra-saṁgraha-laghu-vṛtti, 545
Alaṁkāra-śāstra, lxxv, 517, 520-523, 615,
Alaṁkāra school, 502, 517, 519, 538, 571, 580, 581, 604, 628, 638
Alaṁkāra-śekhara, 564
Alaṁkāra-śirobhūṣaṇa, 566
Alaṁkāra-sūtras, 557
Alaṁkāra-sūtrarvṛtti, 621
Alaṁkāra-tilaka, 563. 687
Alaṁkāra vimarśinī, 558*, 629
Album Kern, 614*
A. L. Chézy, 140*. See Chézy
A l'étude de la Musique Hindue, 522*
Alexander, ciii
Alex V. Humbold, 668
Alfred de Musset, liv
Allaṭa or Alāṭa, 555
Allahabad, 18, 102*, 497*, 535*, 731*, 744*
Allahabad University Studies, 124*, 753
Allegorical, 332, 374, 479, 481, 485, 487*, 613
Allgemeine Betrachtungen über das° 668
Alliteration, 15, 33, 169, 187, 202*, 236, 382, 395, 612
Almora, 370, 371, 403
Alt. Indien, 64
Altindische Schelmeubücher, 617*
Alwar, ciii
Amaracandra Sūri, Jaina Amaracandra. Amarajati, or Amarapaṇḍita, 331, 344, 429, 618
Amaracandra (author of *Padmānanda*), 620
Amara-koṣa, 7, 413, 539*, 611*, 621, 707
Amarakoṣa-ṭīkāsarvasva, 713, 714, 721
Amaraśakti (king), 88
Amarasiṁha or Amara, lvii, 5*, 28*, 204*, 729, 730
Amaru, Amaruka or Amarū, 2, 36, 155, 156-162, 164-166, 239, 306, 364, 366, 415, 668
Amaru-darpaṇa, 668
Amaru-Mangoblüten 660
Amaru-śataka. 155-62, 555*, 668, 669, 771
A. Marazzi, 760
Ambara-karaṇḍaka (a sport), 491*
Ambā (mother of Cakrakavi), 331
Ambālikā, story of, 216
Ambāṣṭaka, 660
Ambāstava, 740
Amer, Journ. of Philology, 29*, 211*
American Orient. Soc., 88*, 421*
A.M.G., 675
Amir Shikar (Hammīra), 478
Amitagati, 404
Ammal Ācārya, See Varadācārya
Amorous, lxxxiii, lxxxiv, lxxxv, lxxxix, 28, 38, 137, 193, 250, 384, 491, 572, 581, 592, 594, 595, 596, 666, 670, 693, 742, 746. 747
Amṛtabhānu, 319
Amṛtalaharī of Jagannātha, 383, 675
Amṛtamanthana, 687
Amṛtananda, 73*
Amṛtānanda Yogin, 566
Amṛtodaya, 486
Amsterdam, 94, 510*
Amusement, xxi, lxxix, 20, 21, 351, 363, 627,
Anacdote or Anecdotal, 83, 427, 428
Anaṅgaharsa Mātrarāja, 300, 759
Anaṅgasenā (courtesan), 497
Anaṅgasenā-harinandi, 475, 686
Anaṅgavatī, 471, 686
Anaṅgavāṇa, lix
Anaṅgāpīda, 356
Ananta (author of the *Sāhityakalpa-valli*), 556
Anantabhaṭṭa, 437
Ananta, commentator, 370*
Anantadāsa, 564
Anantadeva, 468
Anantadevāyani, 622*
Ananta, King, 96, 404, 409, 553, 554, 692
Anantanārāyaṇa, 341
Anantanārāyaṇa (god), 477*

Ananta paṇḍita, 561*
Anatācārya, lxxviii
Anāntāmmā, 438
Ananvaya, 526, 534, 536
Anargha rāghava, 449-53, 462, 760, 761
Anateomical, lxviii
Ancint India, 92*, 696*
Anders Konow, 695*
Anderson, 615
Andhaka (demon), 319, 623
Andhra, c, ci, cvii, 212, 757
Andhrabhṛtyas, ci, 241, 757, 761
Anekārtha-saṁgraha, 707
Anesaki. See M. Anesaki
Aṅgada, 186, 502, 464
Aṅhilvad, 343, 351, 428, 471, 472* (Aṅahilla-pāṭaka), 603, 618
Anhilwāra, cxii, 768
Animal fable 691
Annals of Orient. Research, 132*
Annales de Musee Guimet, 81*, 83*
Annals of the Bhandarkar Oriental Research Institute, 629*, 753
Annamalainagar, 381*
Annamalai University Sanskrit Series, 381*
Annavema, 627
Annayārya, 439
Anquetil Duperron, v
Anthologia, Sanskritica, 497*
Anthology, Anthological or Anthologist, xcix, 4, 8, 9, 10*, 16, 17*, 40, 104, 119, 120, 121*, 122, 157, 158*, 160, 162, 165, 166, 167, 168, 170, 173, 177, 186, 197, 209*, 242, 256*, 270, 280*, 299*, 300*, 306, 320, 324, 364, 366, 377, 389, 394, 401, 411-17, 435, 454, 461, 477, 611, 621, 665, 686, 708, 770
Antichüs the Great, ciii
Antigone, lxviii
Antiquary, 659, 748
Anubhāva, 539, 561, 584, 593, 595, 596, 601
Aṇugadāra, 201*,
Anumāna, 246, 552
A. N. Upadhye, 343*
Anuprāsa, 526, 528*, 530, 534, 536, 537, 559, 563, 579, 584
Anuratnamaṇḍana, 566
Anuśāsana-parvan (Mahābhārata), 195
Anuṣṭubh (metre), 2*, 14*
Anvaya, 537
Anvaya-lāpika, 741*
Anyopadeśa-śataka of Madhusūdana, 403, 674 ; of Nīlakantha Dīkṣita 403, 764 ; and of Viśveśvara, 403
Anyokti-muktāvalī, 403
Apabhraṁśa, viii, 139*, 194, 203, 314, 390*, 394, 395, 427, 430*, 508, 510, 526, 537, 559
Apahāravarman, 221, 281*
Apahnuti, 526, 530, 536, 553
Appayya Dīkṣita, 332*, 334, 400, 439*, 564, 565, 566, 630, 661, 674, 675, 764, 765
Aprastutapraśaṁsā, 520, 526, 530, 534, 536, 583
Apsarases, 75*, 179, 190, 334, 693
Apte, 455*, 753, See V. S. Apte
Arab, Arabia or Arabic, xxi, cxvi, 89, 673, 698, 705, 737, 772
Arabina Sea, cviii
Archaism, 10, 15, 105, 343*, 721
Archipelago (Malayan), cxi
Architectural, xc, xci, cxi
Archive für Anthropologie, 648
Ardhamāgadhī, ix
Ardhanārīśvara-stotra, 382
Arhaddāsa, 620, 775
Arhats 82
Ariel, 368*, 567*, 568*, See J. Ariel.
Arikeśarin, 400, 435
Arisiṁha, 331*, 363, 678, 770
Aristophanes, iv
Aristotle, 53*, 650, 737
Arjuna, 167, 178, 190, 275, 332, 616, 678, 721, 723, 770
Arjunacarita, 686
Arjunavarmadeva, 158*, 170*, 472, 555*, 668
Arkasvāmin, 321
Army, 626, 741, 755
Arṇava-varṇana, 626
Arṇava vivaraṇa, 326*
A. R. Ramanatha Ayar, 121*
Artha lxxv, lxxxi, lxxxv, lxxxvi, 415, 549, 559, 563, 764
Artha dīpikā, 624*
Arthakrama, 522
Arthapati (in the *Kādambarī*), 225
Arthhapāla, (story of), 212, 232
Artha-śāstra, xiii, lviii, lx, xcvii, cxxiv, 15, 85, 86*, 105, 522, 567, 643, 698, 701, 705, 706, 719, 732, 733, 734, 736
Artha-śleṣa, 521
Arthaśṛṅgāra, 714
Arthālaṁkāra, 539, 552, 556, 557, 559, 560, 562, 566, 579, 585
Arthāntaranyāsa, 526, 530, 534, 536
Arthopamā, 518, 519, 553
Art of war and weapons, 26
Aruṇagiri, 126*, 129*
Aruṇagirinātha, 742
Arya Aryan, or Aryans, v, xxi, lxv, lxvii, lxxi, lxxii, lxxxvii, cxxiv, 613,* 633
Asafā vilāsa, 566
Asaṅga, cvi
Asia, Central, cxi, 22, 43, 72, 77, 79*, 244, 705
Asiatic Quarterly Review, 523,* 741*
Asiatic Researches, 624*, 660*
Asiatic Society of Bengal, 354*, 413*
Asmakavaṁsa, 527
Aśoka, viii, cix, cx, cxxiv, 73, 82, 290, 355, 356, 613, 768
Aśokadatta, 280*
Aśokan edicts, 290, 642
Aśokan inscription, cx, cxx, cxxiv
Aśokāvadāna, cvi, 81*, 82
A. S Ramanatha Ayyar, 338*
Assam 737
Aśṭakālika-Līlā. 333
Aṣṭavighnakathā, 614*
Aṣṭādhyāyī, 336, 611*, See Pāṇini
Astrology, Astronomy or Astronomical, 26* 492. 553, 632, 652, 730, 732, 753

Asura Bāna, 463
Asura or Asuras, lxxi, cxxiii, 50. See Demon
Asutosh Memorial Volume, 738*
Aśvaghoṣa, ix, xvi, xviii, lxxxviii, c, civ, cvi, 4, 6, 9*, 10*, 13, 15, 18, 19*, 35, 43, 51, 69-79, 80, 101, 118, 123*, 124, 128*, 156, 164, 167, 200, 316, 345, 364, 378,* 479, 520, 613, 655.
Aśvalallta (metre), 12, 184*
Aśvamedha, 735, 746
Aśvatthāman, 273, 275, 724
Aśvavarman (king), cxi
A. T. D., 641*
Atilla, 736
Atirātra yajvan, 765
Atiśayokti, li, 518, 526, 530, 534, 536, 538, 582, 583, 587
Atharvaveda, xiii, lxxv, 20, 631
Atithi (king), 746
Atri, xxv
A. Troyer, 660*
Aṭṭhakathā, 695
Aucitya-vicāra-carcā, 19*, 120, 166*, 186*, 299*. 531*, 542, 548, 604, 755, 762
Aucitya-vicāra-cintamani, 535*
Aufrecht, 7*, 8* 9, 158*, 162*, 166*, 170*, 320*, 413*, 414*, 506*, 553, 554, 618*, 620*, 621*, 665 , 708*, 740, 751
Aupacchandasika (metre), 14*, 120*, 150, 181*
Aupajaṅgham, xxv
Aupakāyana, 521
Ausgabe, 701*
Ausgwählte Erzählungen in Māhārashtrī, 612*
Auśīnari (queen), 139
Auszug aus dem Pañcatantra, 89*
Avacūri, 741*
Avadāna literature, 71, 81-83, 321, 405, 613, 759
Avadānas, cvi, 655
Avadānaśataka, cxv, 614, 654
Avalon, 380*, 660*
Avaloka, 243*
Avalokiteśvara, 373, 412
Avantikā (*rīti*), 553
Avantikā (in *Svapnavāsava-dattā*), 727
Avantisundarī, 211*, 454
Avantisundarī-kathā, 211* 762
Avantisundarī-kathāsara, 211*, 761
Avantivarman, Maukhari, 263 ; King of Kashmir, cxvi, 263, 319, 320, 356, 536, 544, 760
Avantī, 110, 695
Avasthānukṛti, 56, 631, 637
Avatāra, 321*, 324
Avatāra, poet, 335*, 382
Avecune preface de's levi, 666*
Avimāraka, 101, 109*, 115-16, 141*, 244*, 709, 710, 715, 719, 720, 721, 726
Avitathā (metre), 187*
A. V. Kathvate, 361*
A. Von Staél-Holstein, 71*
A. V. W. Jackson, 110*, 161*, 255*, 256*, 652 See Jackson.
A. Weber, 48*, 52*, 140*, 427*, 498*, 650*, 750*. See Weber.
A. W. Ryder, 207, 239
Ayodhya, lxiii, cviii, cxvii, 69, 131, 186, 292, 342*, 359, 452, 504, 746
Ayodhyāprasād, 561*
Ābhīra, cvii, 240*, 249*, 757
Ācārya, 768.
Ācikhyasāu-upamā, 532*
Āḍhyarāja, cxv, 16. 17
Ādigrantha, 390*
Ādi-kavi, 460
Ādinātha, temple of-363*
Ādiparvan (*Mahābhārata*), 140
Ādi-Purāna, 374*
Ādiśura, cxv, 272
Āditya Sūri, 623*
Āgamodaya Samiti Series 344*
Āhavamalla, 351
Ākhaṇḍalaka, lix
Ākhyāna, Vedic, 3, 43*, 44, 85, 87, 200*, 435
Ākhyāyikā, xviii, 11, 84, 88*, 200-05, 211*, 864*, 431*, 433, 526, 530, 532*, 539, 563
Ākhyāyikā and Kathā in Classical Sanskrit, 202*
Ākṣepa, 526, 530, 534, 536, 545, 553
Ālambana, 593, 597
Āmnāya 645
Ānandadevayāni Vallabha, 741
Ānandakanda-campū, 774
Ānadda-kośa, 494
Ānanda-laharī, 380, 660
Ānanda-latikā, 504
Ānanda-mandākinī, 382, 664
Ānandaram Barua. 277*, 535
Ānanda-rāghava-nāṭaka, 772
Ānandarāya Makhin, 486, 764
Ānandaśarman, 561*
Ānanda-sāgara-stava, 383, 403*, 665
Ānandavardhana, 8*, 25, 27*, 29*, 120*, 147, 158, 160, 166*, 168*, 179*, 188, 221, 226*, 271, 276, 299, 301, 335*, 382, 391*, 401, 426* 455, 519, 524, 538, 540-44, 546, 568, 571, 574, 578, 583, 584, 587, 592, 606, 608, 609, 615, 556, 661, 669, 685, 686, 742*, 762
Ānanda-vṛndāvana-campū, 396*, 440
Ānandayaiñeśvara. 555
Āndhra-rāmāyaṇa. 417
Āpaddharma, xvii
Āpadeva. 468
Āpastamha, xxv, 522
Ārabhaṭī (Vṛtti) 63, 539
Āruṇi, 726,727
Ārūḍhjātaka, 730*
Ārvars, cxviii
Āryabhaṭa, cx
Āryadeva, 81*
Āryaka, 757, 758
Ārya Śūra, xviii, cvi, 8*, 15, 80, 614
Āryā (metre), 12, 77*, 196*, 199, 204, 243*, 285*, 337, 338*, 339, 370, 371, 400, 402, 404, 406, 661
Āryā-saptaśati of Govardhana, 370-71, 659 ; of Viśveśvara, 371

Āryā-tārā-sragdhārā-stotra, 378
Āsapha-vilāsa, 364*
Āśādhara, Jaina commentator, 539
Āścarya-cūḍāmaṇi, 102*, 302
Āśiḥ, 526, 530, 563
Āśram, (village), 776
Āśrama, xxxii, 727
Ātmabodha-ṭīkā, 664*
Ātmaram Sasti Vetal, 189*
Ātma-ṣaṭka, 380
Ātmārāma, 759
Ātreya Bhaṭṭa, 623
Ātreya Gotry, 438
Āvantī, ix
Āyu, 749

B

B. A. Hirszbant, 407*
Bactria, 650, 737
Badarīnātha, 340*
Baḍu Caṇḍīdāsa, 391*
Bahuśrutikā, 19, 69
Baital Pacīsī, 422*
Baka-demon, 465
Balabhadra, 740
Balabhadra (in *Daśakumāra-carita*), 281*
Baladeva, 190, 344
Baladeva Bidyābhūṣaṇa, 556
Balarāma, 724
Bali, 11, 636, 725
Bali-vandhana, 640
Ballad, Ballad-play, 43*, 631, 647
Ballāla, 429
Banamālī Bhaṭṭa, 666*
Bandha, 575, 576, 581
Bandhumatī, 477*
Banerjee-Sastri, lxxiv, See A. Banerjee-Sastri
Bangalore, 300* 417*
Bankimadāsa, 622*
Banner festival, 50
Bansikar, 741
Bappabhaṭṭi, 379
Bari, 73*
Barnett, 105*, 106*, 254*, 550*, 662*, 710. See L D. Barnett
Baroda, 8*, 66*, 120*, 169*, 171*, 201*, 271*, 299*, 324*, 332*, 344* 360*, 362*, 363*, 414*, 431, 463*, 465*, 466*, -473*, 478*, 484*, 489*, 490*, 768
Barth, 688
Battle, xiii, xiv, lxxxvii, xc, xcvii, 191, 320 345, 461, 652, 680, 720, 724, 725, 747
Bauddha-saṁgatyalaṁkāra, 217
Baudhāyana, xiii, xxv
Fāgula, 360, 679, 772
Bāla-bhārata, 331, 344, 457, 547, 618
Bāla-bodhinī, 6?4*, 666*
Bālacandra, author of *Karuṇā-vajrāyudha*, 769, 770
Bālacandra, Ācarya, 470
Bāla-carita, 60, 101, 109*, 114, 115, 530*, 640, 709, 710, 712, 715, 717, 719, 720
Bāla-cikitsā, 730*
Bāla-cittānurañjanī, 556
Bāla-gopāla-stuti, 386*
Bāla kāṇḍa (*Rāmāyaṇa*), 331
Bālakṛṣṇa, 756*
Bālakṛṣṇa (Jagannātha's father), 469
Bālamanoramā Press, 102*, 277*, 302*, 437*, 465
Bāla-mārtaṇḍa-vijaya, 479, 775
Bāla-rāmāyaṇa, lxxxv, 55 , 280*, 450*, 454, 455-57, 460, 506*, 552, 642*
Bāla-sarasvatī, 472
Bāla-vālmiki, 40
Bālāditya, cxiii
Balikā-vañcitaka, 686
Bāṇabhaṭṭa or Bāṇa, xix, xxi, lii, lviii, lx, ci, cxiii, cxiv, cxix, 5*, 16-18, 92, 93, 101, 104, 107, 120*, 155, 158*, 166-168, 169*, 170-172, 178, 191*, 200, 201, 203, 204, 205, 209, 210, 213, 215-19, 222-39, 241, 250*, 253-55, 256*, 258 , 261, 271, 278-80, 298, 299, 306, 324, 335, 340, 346, 349, 350*, 352, 353, 357, 359, 378, 384 , 405, 419, 429-33, 435, 436, 464*, 553, 576, 578 , 618, 623, 659, 676, 685, 686, 688, 694, 700, 708, 710, 712, 713, 716, 722, 739, 754, 755, 758, 759, 766, 770, 771
Bāṇa, Vāmana Bhaṭṭa, 299, 331, 433, 489, 627, 771
Bāṇeśvara Vidyālaṁkāra, 439*
Bāppa, 516
Bārhaspatya Arthaśāstra, 729
Bārhut Stūpa, 85*
B. C. Majumdar, 183*, 218, 616
Beast-fable, 4, 155, 204, 205
Beatrice, 38
Beau, lvi
Beef-eating, xxiv
B. E. F. E. O , 702
Beharilal Sircar, 748
Beiträge, zur ütteren Geschichte des Alaṁkāraśāstra, 520*, 529*
Beiträge zur altin dischen, 53
Beiträge zur Indischen Erotik, 645*
Beiträge zur indischen Lexikographie, 730*
Beiträge zur kunde der indoger°, 763
Beiträge zur sprach und volkerkunde 741*
Beiträge znr Textkritik von Kālidāsa's Meghadūta, 133*
Belloni Filippi, 192*, 621*,. See F. Belloni Fillippi
Belvalkar, 108*, 242 , 278*, 279*, 280*, 288*, 529*
Benares, civ, cxvii, 196*, 197, 198, 326*, 331*, 344*, 371*, 374*, 435*, 439*, 455*, 462*, 465*, 473*, 476*, 486*, 490*, 535*, 625, 530, 676, 741*, See Vārāṇasī
Benares Sanskrit Series, 561*
Bendall, 189*. See C. Bendall
Benfey, 86*, 701*, 702*, 704*
Bengal, xxv, xxxix, lxiii, cxvi, 272, 326*, 333, 339, 359, 371, 372*, 373*, 374*, 377, 378, 387, 389-91, 392*, 397, 398, 413, 414, 415, 424, 439*, 440, 450*, 468, 470, 485, 499, 560, 631, 662, 729
Bengali, lxii, xcii, cxxiii, op, 368*, 382, 394, 533, 625, 704, 706, 707, 741*, 748
Bengal Vaiṣṇava, 333, 440

Benīsaṁhāra, cxv, 762. See *Venīsaṁhāra*
Ben John on, 147
Benkaṭasubbiah, 620*
Beokh, 752
Berar, 278, 436*
Bergaigne, 371*, 759, 763
Berhampur, 397*, 468*
Berlin, 44*, 45*, 52*, 77*, 86*, 87*, 89*, 90*, 120*, 121*, 124*, 127*, 133*, 136*, 138*, 161*, 209*, 218*, 300*, 367*, 469*, 520*, 612*, 613*, 621*, 633*, 645*, 650*, 728*, 730*, 747*, 752*
Bern Heimer, 533*
Berthold Müller, 748
Besch, 694
Besnagar, cii
Beyrouth, 89*
Bezz Beitr, 615, 621
B. Faddegon, 666
B. G. Yogi, 439
Bhadanta, 69, 165
Bhagadatta, 623
Bhagadajjukīya, 255 , 488, 494-95
Bhagavadbhakti-rasāyana, 664*
Bhagavadbhaṭṭa, 561*
Bhagavaddāsa, 666
Bhagavadgītā, xvii, xlix, 535*, 673, 754
Bhagavantarāya, 764
Bhagīratha, 334
Bhagīratha (commentator), 533*, 621 -24*
Bhagīratha Miśra, 751
Bhaimarthī, xviii, 11, 200
Bhairavānanda, 458
Bhaktamāl (Hindi), *Bhakta-mālā*, 389*
Bhaktāmara-stotra, 172, 379
Bhakti, ciii, 70, 72, 375, 376, 379, 384, 385, 389, 397, 415, 468, 482, 483, 511*
Bhakti-dūta, 374*
Bhaktipriyā, (commentary), 774
Bhakti-rasāmṛta-sindhu, 664
Bhakti-śataka, 378
Bhattaṭa-kavi, 588*, 674
Bhallaṭa-śataka, 401, 674
Bhandarkar, 7*, 278*, 279 , 553*, 617*, 619*, 629*, 686, 757*
Bhandarkar Comm. Vol., 240*, 520*, 531*
Bhandarkar Oriental Institute, 360*
Bhaṅgī 583
Bharadvāja, xxv, xcvi, 484 (Gotra)
Bharata, xli, lxxvi, lxxviii, 14*, 15, 43, 50, 51*, 52, 53*, 54*, 63*, 66, 103, 120*, 198, 250, 253*, 271*, 300*, 301*, 493, 506*, 513, 518, 521-24, 526, 527, 530*, 531*, 550, 555, 556, 569, 574-76, 579, 592-94, 596, 630, 634, 642, 646, 653
Bharata, Bhāṭa, 51*
Bharata-carita, 630*, 775
Bharata, (Daśaratha's son), 113
Bharata, Duṣyanta's son, 630*, 775
Bharata-mallika, 183*, 325*
Bharatasena, 616* 621*, 623*, 624*, 741*, 751*
Bharaṭaka-dvātriṁśikā, 426
Bharata-vākya, 104, 106, 262, 524*, 709
Bhartṛhari, 8*, 10*, 16, 35, 155, 156, 159, 161-65, 166, 183, 194, 293, 263*, 306, 364, 366, 367*, 400, 401*, 402, 428, 479*, 516, 605, 615, 616, 644, 669-75
Bhartṛhari-nirvede, 161*, 479
Bhartṛhari Śāstra, 671
Bhatṛhari, story, of 428
Bhartṛmeṇṭha or Meṇṭha, 5*, 120, 321, 460, 685
Bhaṭṭa-bhavantacūḍā, 686
Bhaṭṭa Bhīma, Bhauma or Bhaumaka, cxv, 336, 616
Bhaṭṭagopāla (Bhavabhūti's grandfather), 278*
Bhaṭṭa-jayanta, 618
Bhaṭṭa Kumāra, same as Kumaradāsa (q. v.), 185
Bhaṭṭa Lollaṭa, 593, 595-97, 600, 602
Bhaṭṭa Narayana, cxv, 156, 211*, 239, 270, 271-77, 441, 444, 453, 762. See *Veṇī-Saṁhāra.*
Bhattanātha Svāmin, 102*, 450*, 686, 710, 761*
Bhaṭṭanāyaka, 523, 524, 550, 602, 607, 608
Bhaṭṭatauta, 523, 544, 548, 600, 602
Bhaṭṭāra, Haricandra, lvii, cxv, 8*, 16-17, 201, 219, 344, 686, 754
Bhaṭṭenduräja, 302*, 464, 535*, 544, 686
Bhaṭṭi, cx, cxvi, cxiv, cxx, 156, 161*, 175, 177, 183-86, 239, 305, 315, 316, 322, 334, 336, 528, 529, 615, 616
Bhaṭṭibodhinī, 616*
Bhaṭṭibhaṭṭa, 616
Bhaṭṭicandrikā, 616*
Bhaṭṭidālaka, 78*
Bhaṭṭikāvya or *Rāvaṇavadha*, 27*, 161*, 183-85, 336, 337, 614-16
Bhaṭṭodbhaṭa, 555
Bhaṭṭojī Dīkṣita, 341*, 514, 565, 764
Bhaumī-pariṇaya, 465*
Bhavabhūti, xxi, li, cxiv, cxvi, cxix, cxxviii, cxxix, 5*, 8*, 9*, 37, 39, 60, 104, 153-56, 170, 219*, 235, 239, 244*, 245, 257*, 270, 276*, 277-98, 299, 300, 303, 415, 429, 441, 443, 444, 447, 449-51, 453, 455*, 456, 459, 460, 464, 473, 474, 477*, 553, 663, 685, 760, 763
Bhavadatta, 334*, 345*, 397*, 403*, 404*, 430*, 468*, 623*, 624*
Bhavadeva Chatterji, 340*
Bhavanicharan Sarman, 481*
Bhavatanucūḍā Bhaṭṭa, 471, 686
Bhavānyaṣṭaka, 660
Bhaveśa (Kṛṣṇadatta's father), 392*
Bhavisatta-kaha, 240*, 524*, 750*
Bhavanagar, 343*, 362*, 363*, 374*, 471*, 475*, 476*, 503*
Bhayahara Stotra, 172
Bhayānaka, 592
Bhāgavata, 341, 373*, 385, 3 1, 437, 440, 480, 664, 725, 774
Bhāgavata-campū of Cidambara, of Rājānatha and of Rāmabhadra, 437
Bhāgavatapurāṇādya-ślokatraya-vyākhyā 664*

Bhāgavata (school), lxii, cii, 474, 492*, 768
Bhāgurāyaṇa, 269, 459, 461
Bhāmaha, xv, li, 17, 26*, 110, 133*, 174*, 183*, 202, 203, 209*, 513, 516, 517, 519, 520, 525-29, 530*, 531-34, 537, 538, 539*, 544, 548, 555, 556, 567-69, 571-73, 575-77, 579, 581-84, 586, 587, 592, 615, 616, 681, 685, 715, 718, 719
Bhāmaha-vivaraṇa, 527
Bhāminī-vilāsa, 371, 400, 565, 665*
Bhāṇa, lxxxii, lxxxvi, lxxxvii, 23, 62, 66, 156, 197, 213, 239, 242*, 244*. 248-55, 299, 465*, 474, 487-93, 496, 654*, 761, 762, 765, 768, 772
Bhāṇikā, 468
Bhānubhaṭṭa, 629
Bhānubhāva-prākāśinī, 561*
Bhānucandra, 218, 229*
Bhānudatta, 396*, 561
Bhānumatī, 479*
Bhānumatī (queen of Duryodhana), 273
Bhārata, (*Epic*), 11. See *Mahābhārata*
Bhārata-campū, 437, 772
Bhārata-candra, 658*
Bhārata-mañjarī, 554, 617, 688, 692, 772
Bharatī (*vṛtti*), 63, 539
Bhāravi, xix, lvii, cx, 8*, 9*, 15, 23, 120*, 156, 167, 173-75, 177-82, 187-94, 209*, 223, 239, 305, 321, 325, 469. 473, 477*, 578, 621, 622, 768
Bhāsa, ix, xxix, lx, lxiii, lxxxi, lxxxviii, cii, cxiii, cxvii, cxix, cxxv, 16, 101-17, (dramas ascribed to), 118, 156, 218*, 219, 240, 241, 242*, 254*, 255*, 272, 301*, 496*, 504, 529*, 530*, 641, 651*, 654*, 655*, 685, 695, 696, 708-10, 712, 713, 717-22, 756, 757-59, 765
Bhāsa and Authorship of the Trivandrum Plays, 102*
Bhāsa—*a Study*, 102
Bhāsa-studien, 103*, 719*, 720*
Bhāsa's Prakrit, 105*
Bhāsa's Works, 102*
Bhāṣā (Bhuta-), 7, 94, 559
Bhāsārṇava, 563
Bhāskara, 464, 556
Bhāskaradatta, Mahārāja, 262
Bhāskara Dīkśita, 765
Bhāskaragupta, 20
Bhāṣya of Medhātithi on Manu, 105
Bhāṣya on Nyāyasūtra, cxiv
Bhāṣya of Patañjali, cxxi, 638-40. See *Mahābhāṣya*
Bhāṭs, 635
Bhāu Dāji, 729*, 755
Bhāva, 524*, 538, 553, 561, 563
Bhāvacintamani 668
Bhāvadevī, 416, 764
Bhāvakatva, 602
Bhāvanā purusottama, 486*
Bhāva prakāśa, 299, 494
Bhāva prakāśana, lxv, lxxxv*, 649
Bhāva prakāśikā, 686
Bhāvasama, 528*
Bhāva-sandhi, 557
Bhāva-śataka, 335*, 402, 674
Bhāvasiṁha, 403, 679
Bhāvasvāmin, 486*
Bhāva-vilāsa, 402, 679
Bhāvācārya, 666*
Bhāvartha-cintāmaṇi, 556
Bhāvika, 526, 528*, 530, 534
Bhāvodaya, 557
Bhejjala, 686
Bhikṣāṭana, 333, 370, 655
Bhikṣu, 69, 422*, 762
Bhikṣusūtra, 523
B. Hirgel, 750*
Bhita, 731*
Bhīma, 271*, 301*, 302
Bhīma (Pāṇḍava), 113, 178, 191, 273-75, 299, 337, 467, 724, 725
Bhīmadeva, 301, 472* 686
Bhīmagupta (king), 538
Bhīmaparākrama, 769
Bhīmasena, 336*, 556, 759
Bhīmaṭa, 301*, 686
Bhīṣma, 167, 189, 193, 723
Bhīṣmamiśra, 741
Bhoja or Bhojarāja, cxvii, 16*, 119*, 168*, 170*, 189*, 196, 201, 210*, 211*, 241*, 271*, 299, 301*, 302*, 324, 332*, 350, 417*, 424, 428, 429, 430*, 435*, 437, 438*, 506, 533, 551, 552, 553, 556, 573, 574, 617, 619*, 740, 745
Bhojacampu, 772
Bhojadeva (jayadeva's father), 389, 560, 665, 761, 762
Bhojakatva, 602
Bhoja-prabandha, 5*, 19, 189*, 429, 506, 553*, 728
Bholānātha, 373*
Bhramara-dūta, 374*
Bhramara-vilasita (metre), 12
Bhṛgu, xxv
Bhujaṅgaprayāta (metre), 121*, 380
Bhujaṅgaśekhara (in *Mukundānanda*), 490
Bhuluya (in Noakhali), 499
Bhuvanakośa, 455
Bhuvanābhyudaya, 121*, 321*, 523, 731
Bhūdeva Śukla, 486
Bhūmmī, 212
Bhūpojā-jālpitam, 650*
Bhūśaṇa Bhaṭṭa, 229, 231, 232
Bhūsaṇā, 207*
Bhūta bhāṣā. See Bhāṣā
B. H. Wortham, 161*
Bibhatsādbhuta, 592
Bibhīṣaṇa, 502
Bibl. Buddh. 71*, 81*
Bibliography of the Sanskrit Drama, 239*, 646
Bibliotheca Indica Series or Bib. Ind., 74*, 83*, 96*, 217*, 325*, 340*, 342*, 360*, 378*, 412*, 428*, 485*, 539*, 556*, 624, 754
Bibliothek Orientalischer°, 422*
Bihārīlal, 659
Bilhaṇa, 350-53, 354, 357, 359, 360, 368, 369, 471, 553*, 657, 658, 769
Bilhaṇa-carita, 657*
Bilhaṇa-kāvya, 368

Bilhaṇa-pañcāśat-pratyuttara, 659*
Bilvamaṅgala, 387, 619. See Līlāśuka
Bilvamaṅgala-stotra, 386*
Biography or Biographical ixxxviii, 42, 83, 93, 238, 333*
Biology or Biological, xxii, lxvii, cxix, 291,
Birbhum, 390, 560
Birsing Deo, 774
Birth of the War-God, a poem by Kālidāsa, 741*
B. Jülg, 422*
Black Yajurveda, 278
B. Liebich, 124*, 728*, 738*
Bloch, Th, 50*, 732
Bloomfield, 29*, 211*, 344*,. See M. Bloomfield
B. M. Barua, 612*
Bodhāyana, 225*, 494
Bodhāyana, Vṛttikāra, 495
Bodhicaryāvatāra, 81*, 675
Bodhisattva, 80, 81, 84, 259, 591*, 697
Bodhisattva-jātaka-dharmagaṇḍī, 614
Bodhisattva Jīmūtavāhana, 759*
Bodhisattvāvadāna-mālā, 81
Bodleian Catalogue, 506*
Bohlen, 162*, 369*, 657*, 752*. See P. Von Bohlen
Bohtliṅgk, 10*, 54*, 256*, 645, 669. See O. Bohtlingk.
Bois-le-roi, 277
Bokensen, 750*
Bollensen, F, 136*, 750*
Bolling, 673
Boltz, 706
Bombay, 17*, 89*, 95*, 96*, 119*, 121*, 122*, 126*, 128*, 129*, 132*, 136*, 138*, 139*, 140*, 158*, 161*, 168*, 169*, 178*, 183*, 189*, 196*, 197*, 200*, 201*, 207*, 221*, 226*, 229*, 239*, 241*, 256*, 271*, 277*, 298*, 299*, 316*, 319*, 320*, 323*, 324*, 325*, 331*,-37*, 340*,-45*, 353*, 354*, 362*, 368*,-71*, 374*, 379*, 380*, 383*, 388*, 391*, 396*, 403*, 404*, 405*, 428*, 429*, 430*, 435*,-39*, 449*, 457*, 462*, 464*, 467*,-69*, 472*, 478*, 479*, 481*, 485*, 486*, 490*, 496*, 502*, 506*, 533*, 550*, 612*, 621*, 622*, 624*, 744*, 755*, 756*, 759, 760, 762-64, 775
Bombay Skt. Ser., 89*, 90*, 129*, 136*, 138*, 161*, 183*, 226*, 229*, 239*, 262*, 277*, 279*, 349*, 350*, 361*, 362*, 413*, 414*, 526, 561, 562
Bombay University Journal, 390*
Bonn, 102*, 127*, 132*, 140*, 158*, 277*, 388*, 497*, 756*
Bopadeva, 731
Borneo, cxi
Bower manuscripts, viii
Brahmacārī, xxxii, 742
Brahmadatta, 521
Brahmaputra vallcy, 737
Brahmasutra, xxvii
Brahmavaivarta Purāṇa, 391, 725
Brahmā, 521, 741, 742
Brahmāditya stava, 659
Brajabhāsā, 704, 707
Brajarāja Dīksita, 561*
B. R. Arte, 457*
Brāhmaṇa (literature), vi, xvii, 3, 20, 87, 112, 195, 693
Bresalau, 52*, 122*, 124*, 132*, 140*, 262*, 656*, 740, 760
Bṛhadratha Mauryya, c
Bṛhaduddyota, 556
Bṛhaspati, xxv, xcvi, 623*, 733*, 741*
Bṛhat-jātakā, 730*
Bṛhatkatha, cii cvi, 15, 16, 83, 84, 89, 92-100, 110, 155, 200, 205, 215, 218, 230, 231, 244*, 250*, 258*, 265, 280, 404, 421, 527, 612, 614, 687-92, 694-96, 698, 699, 700, 719, 726, 758, 759
Bṛhatkathā-mañjarī, 89*, 95*, 230*, 258*, 265*, 325*, 421, 554, 688, 689, 690, 692, 696, 698, 699, 700, 705, 707, 759
Bṛhatkathā-ślokā-saṁgraha, 96, 696
Bṛhat-saṁhita, 730*
Bṛhatstotra-ratnākara, 380*, 660*
Bṛhat-subhadraka, 494
Brief Wechsel zwischen° 667*
Brindāban, 440*. See Vṛndāvana
British, xcii, 315
Broach, 478
Brockhaus, 706
Bruchstücke buddhistischer Dramen, 77*, 612, 613*
Bruchstücke der Kalpnāmaṇḍitikā des Kumāralāta, 72*
Bruchstücke indischer Scauspiele° 469*
Brussels, 763
Bruxelles, 277*
B. S. A., 750*
BSGW 89*, 421*, 424, 427*
BSOS, 11*, 48*, 66*, 102, 105*, 185*, 202*, 241*, 254*, 413*, 467*, 613*, 656, 710*, 764
BSS, 614, 678, 743*
Bstan-hayur, 71, 173*
Buddha, xvii, cv, cvi, 19, 70, 73-75, 77, 81-83, 162, 167, 173, 252, 258, 321, 322, 325*, 345, 379, 384, 412, 527, 613, 617, 649, 692, 693 697
Buddhagayā, cviii, 730*
Buddhaghosa, 345
Buddhism, xix, lxvi, civ, cv, cx, cxi, cxii, 70, 71, 78, 85 290, 321, 355, 482, 4 5, 662*, 671, 673, 685, 701
Buddhist, vii, xviii, xcvi, c, civ, cv, cvi, (Stotras), cviii, cx, cxi, cxiii, cxvi, cxvii, 6, 15, 19, 50, 52*, 69, 72, 74, 75, 77, 79, 83, 119, 161, 165, 166, 172, 195, 214, 227, 252, 254, 258, 260*, 281, 321, 326, 345, (Kāvya), 346, 377, 378-79 (Stotras), 401, 405, 409, 412, 470, 497, 518, 526-28, 532*, 533, 612, 647 (Ākhyānas), 655, 671, 755, 765
Buddhi, 613, 65?
Buddhi-vinoda-kāvya, 122*
Buddha rañjani, 560
Buddhasvāmin, 96, 98-100, 421, 692, 696
Bühler, 5*, 9*, 17*, 89, 92*, 96*, 320*, 322*, 323*, 349*, 360*, 389, 536*, 539*, 553*, 558*, 562*, 613*, 618*, 628*, 657*, 659*,

677*, 691*, 698*, 702*, 703*, 732*, 738*, 756*, 759*, See G. Bühler
Bukka, 418
Bukkāmma, 773
Bulletin de l' Academie Imperiale, 613
Bulletin de l' E'cole°, 217*
Bunyan, 481, 484
Burdwan, 439*, 658*
Burgess, 363
Burglary, 211*, 213
Burnell, 396*, 486*
Burzoé, 88*
Buth, 752*

C

Cahuan, or Cahumāna or Cauhāna, 360, 363, 454, 469, 677
Caitanya, cxviii, 333, 372*, 391, 397, 398, 440, 468, 511*
Caitanya-candrāmṛta, 397
Caitanya-candrodaya, 78, 485
Caitanya-dāsa, 386*, 388*, 391*, 662*
Caitanyāṣṭaka, 664*
Cakkyar, 103, 647
Cakora, 757
Cakorākṣa, lix
Cakra-kavi, 331, 630
Cakrapāṇi Dīkṣita, 210
Cakravartins (Jaina), 344
Cakravākikā, lix
Cakrāyudha, cxvii
Cakṣurapidhāna (sport), 491*
Caland, 510. See Caland
Calcutta, cvii, cxxiii, 13*, 17*, 52*, 73*, 74* 83*, 96*, 102*, 120*, 121*, 122*, 126*, 132*, 136*, 140*, 158*, 159*, 161*, 171*, 173*, 183*, 185*, 194*, 210*, 217*, 230*, 240*, 246*, 248*, 249*, 256*, 271*, 277*, 298*, 300*, 325*, 339*, 340*, 343*, 354*, 359*, 367*, 368*, 372*, 373*, 375*, 378*, 388*, 389* 391*, 394*, 412*, 416*, 424*, 428*, 429*, 439*, 440*, 449*, 455*, 469*, 470*, 481*, 485*, 489*, 498*, 504*, 506*, 529*, 533*, 539*, 550*, 552, 560, 566, 611*' 613*, 624*, 662*, 666*, 754*, 763
Calcutta Kāvya Saṁgraha edition, 659*
Calcutta Oriental Journal or C.O.J., 11*, 415*, 611*, 660*
Calcutta Oriental Series, 262*
Calcutta Sanskrit College, 529
Calcutta University, x, 457*
Calicut, 298
Caliphs, xciv
Callet, 429*
Calukya Somadeva 341
Camatkāra, xliv. 600
Camatkāra-candrikā, 398
Cambodia, 93*, 739
Cambodian inscription, 93*, 688, 695
Cambridge, 47*, 52*, 82*, 89*, 140*, 209*, 239*, 424*, 457*
Cambridge History of India, 731
Campa, king, 679
Campaka, 354
Campaka-śreṣṭhi-kathānaka, 427
Campā, 211, 450 (in Gauda)
Camphor Land, 98
Campū, xcix, 306, 307, 326*, 331*, 333*, 341, 343*, 362, 371, 376, 417, 419, 420, 430, 431, 433-40, 508, 563, 647, 700, 766, 768, 770
Canarese, 340*, 662*
Cañcālakṣī (metre), 13
Caṇḍabhārgava, 141*
Caṇḍaka, lix
Caṇḍakauśika, 469-70
Candanadāsa, 265, 267
Caṇḍapāla, 299, 435*
Candapala (king), 458, 755
Caṇḍasena, lviii
Caṇḍasena (King's general), 477
Caṇḍāla, cix, 115, 171
Caṇḍāla Divākara, 171
Caṇḍella, 481
Caṇḍī or Caṇḍikā, 167, 170, 171, 172*, 233, 320, 384
Caṇḍīkuca-pañcāśikā, 384, 665
Caṇḍi-śataka, cxiii, 168*, 169*, 170-71, 238, 384*, 659, 755
Candra, cxiii
Candradatta, 389*
Candradāsa, cxiii
Candradeva, cxvi
Candra-dūta of Jambū, 373* ; of Kṛṣṇcandra Tarkālaṁkāra, 374*
Candragomin, lvii, cvi, cvii, cix, cx, cxiii, 80*, 81*,, 119, 656
Candragupta (Maurya), cvii, cviii, 196, 262, 266, 268, 271 ; (Gupta) I and II, 18, 125, 262, 263, 272, 477*, 731, 754, 760
Candragupta (merchant's son), 407
Candraka or Candaka, cxiii, 119
Candrakala (nātikā), 564
Candraketu, 289, 757
Candralekhā (queen), 351, 352, 368*
Candralekhā-śakti-Bilhaṇa-kāvya, 658*
Candralekhā-vikrīḍana-nāṭikā, 769
Candramauli Dīkṣita, 210
Candramita, 321
Candraprabhā-carita, 775
Candraśekhara, 506*, 563, 622*
Candrāditya (Kaiyaṭa's father), 538
Candrāditya, 477*, 532*
Candrāloka, 462, 560, 565
Candrāloka-dīpikā, 560
Candrāloka-nigūḍhārtha-dīpikā, 560
Candrāloka-prakāśa, 560
Candrāpīḍa in *Kādambarī*, 230, 234, 299*
Candrāpiḍa, king, 682
Candrāvatī, 466
Candrikā (Commentary), 533*, 540
Candrikā (metre), 181*
Cape Comorin. cvi
Caraka, xciv
Caraka-saṁhitā, xviii, 754
Caravan travel, 737
Caritā-kāvyas, lxxxviii, xcix, 614
Cariyā-piṭaka, 80
Carlyle, lxviii
Carnatik, 618

Carpaṭa-pañjarikā, 380
Cartellieri, 220*, 754
Cartesian Co-ordinates, xc
C. A. Rylands, 207*
Catalogus Catalogorum, 620*
Catalogue, (Eggeling's) 502* ; (Haraprasāda's) 658*, 660*-62*
Catalogue of India Office Manuscripts, 473*
Catalogue of Manuscripts in Central Provinces, 480*
Catalogue of Manuscripts in the British Museum, 504*
Catalogue of Sanskrit Manuscripts in the Tanjore Palace Library, 170*
Catuḥ-śataka, 81*
Catuḥ-śataka-stotra, 79
Caturaṅga-vihāra (sport), 491*
Caturbhāṇī, 209, 242*, 343-55, 487, 489, 492, 493, 761
Caturbhuja 396, 668* (Miśra)
Caturhārāvali-citrastava, 335*
Caturvarga-cintāmaṇi, 425
Caturvarga-saṁgraha, 406
Caturviṁśati-jinastuti or *Caturviṁśikā* of Śobhana, 338, 379 ; of various poets, 379
Caturviṁśati-jinānanda-stuti of Meruvijaya-gaṇi, 344*
Caturviṁśati-jinendra-saṁksipta-caritāni, 620
Caturviṁśati-prabandha, 770
Caturtviparyaya-kathā, 613*
Cauḍa, or Cāpotkaṭa family, 363, 368*
Cauhan King Hammira, 478*
Caulukya Kumārapāla, 467, 484
Caurapallī, 368*
Caura-pañcāśikā, 367, 553*, 567*, 658*, 659*
Caurī-ṣurata-pañcāśikā, 657
Cālukya or Caulukya, 341, 351, 362, 363, 428, 435, 467, 471, 484, 502, 677, 678
Cālukya Arikeśarin III, 435
Cālukya Karuṇadeva, 471
Cāṇakya, 162, 194, 195, 264*, 265*, 266-69, 288, 673, 701, 705
Cāṇakyakathā, 262*
Cāṇakyanīti, *Cāṇakyanīti-darpaṇa*, *Cāṇakya-nīti-śāstra*, *Cāṇakyanīti-śataka*, *Cāṇakya-śataka*, *Cāṇakya-śloka*, 196. See Laghu-cāṇakya and Vṛddha-cāṇakya
Cāṇḍupaṇḍita, 325*, 326*, 624*
Cūṇḍātī. ix
Cāritrasundara, 345, 362*, 374*, 767
Cāritravardhana, 126*, 132*, 325*, 619*, 622*, 624*
Cārucaryā, 406, 675
Cārudatta. 101, 107*, 108, 109, 240-42, 244*, 245, 248, 252, 712
Cārumatī, 11*, 200, 761
Cārubāsinī (metre), 13
Cārvāka, 272, 326, 482, 624
Cārvāka (demon), 273
C. Bendall, 704*
C. Cappeller or Cappeller, 73*, 136*, 140*, 178*, 189*, 256*, 457*, 497-99*, 535*, 622*, 756*, 759*
C. D. Dalal or Dalal, 332*, 360*, 363*, 431*, 466*, 478*, 489*, 493, 768, 769
Cedi, 189, 450, 470*, 481, 757
Cehiṭṭarāja 766
Central Asia or Central Asian, cvi, 613, 655
Central India, cxii, cxiii, 94*
Cetodūta, 374*
C. E. Vaughan, 141*
Ceylon or Ceylonese, cviii, cxi, cxv, 132*, 169*, 185, 186*, 378, 728
C. Formichi, 73*
Chandas, 7
Chandawar, 626
Chandīdāsa, 556
Chandonuśāsana, 563
Chandoratnāvali, 331*
Chandovicitti. 530*
Chandrakumar Bhattacharya, 506*
Charles Wilkins, 706
Charpentier, 240*, 245*, 263*, 612, 631*, See J. Charpentier
Charudev Sastri, 138*
Chatterji (Kshetresh), 753
Chavillākara, 355
Chāndogya Upaniṣad. 518, 522, 697
Chāyā nāṭaka, 48, 501, 503, 504, 507, 642. See Shadow-play
Chekānuprāsa. 534, 557
Chemnitz, 751*
Chenab (river), cviii
Chera, 773
Chézy, 752*
Chikago, 71*, 89*, 207*
China or Chinese, xxiii, civ, cv, cvi, cxii, cxv, cxvi, cxviii 13, 69*, 70-73, 79-82, 255, 539, 626, 648, 655, 737
Chinda, *chinda-praśasti*, 326*
Chintaharan Chakravarti, 134*, 372*, 373*
Chintāmaṇi (son of an official) 197
Chittagong, cxxiii
Chittarāja (of Koṅkaṇa), 432
Chosroes Anūshīrwān, 88*
Chowkhamba Skt. Ser., 132*, 371*, 381*, 435*, 661*
Chowringhee, xxxix
Christ, xlii, lxxxviii, ci, 387
Christian, xviii, xxv, xlix, xxxiii, liv, lxiii, lxxxvi i, ciii, cv, cxi, 4, 5, 6, 78, 92, 387, 520, 522, 523, 524*, 635, 737
Chryse, 737
C. H. Tawney, 96*, 136*, 161*, 277*, 427* 428*, 763. See Tawney,
Cidambara, 341, 437, 620
Cikitsā-dīpikā, 730*
Cikitsā-sāra. 730*
Cikitsā-tattva-vijñāna. 730*
Cimmino, 759. See F. Cimmino
Cintamaṇi Bhaṭṭa, 425, 751*
Cintāmaṇi in *Kuṭṭanimata*, 676
Cintāmaṇi (in *Vāsavadattā*), 220
Cintāmaṇi-mantra, 626
Cippaṭa Jayāpīḍa, 319
Citra, 521, 557, 563
Citrabandha, 179*, 191 318, 320, 322, 335 382, 530, 537, 554, 565, 578*
Citrabandha-rāmāyaṇa, 335*
Chitrabhānu (Bāṇa's father) 225
Citrabhārata, 465
Citra-compū, 439*

Citra-kāvya, 335*, See Citrabandha.
Citral, 95
Citralekhā (metre) 13, 14*
Citra mīmāṁsā, 564, 565
Citra-mīmaṁsā-khaṇḍana, 565
Citra-ratnākara, 765
Citra yajña 505
Citrāṅgada, 521
C. J. Ogden, 107*, 256
C. Kunhan Raja, 102*, 132*, 301*
C. Lacôte or Lacôte 756*, 759. See Lacôte
C. Lassen, 277,, 497*, 666*
Classical Poetry of India, 751*
Classical Sanskrit Literature, x, 375*
C. M. Ridding, 229*, 756*
Cock-fight, 21, 212, 214, 419
Coins, cvii, cx
Cokkanātha Makhin, 765
Cola, 351, 352, 470*, 633, 677, 773
Colebrooke, v
Coleridge, 111*
Collected Works 388*-89*
Collins, 207*. See Mark Collins.
Colombo, 133*, 169*, 185*
Colonel Jacob, 132*, 526, 533, 537*. See Jacob
Columbia University, 550*
Columbia University Indo-Iranian Series, 168*
Columbia University Press, 217*, 256*
Comedy, 39, 54, 65, 155, 138, 197, 199, 244 (Greek), 245 (of Errors), 248, 253, 257, 259, 260, 261, 273, 294, 446, 456* (of Errors), 462-74, 492, 493, 602, 641
Comic, lxxxvii, 39, 62, 65, 197, 198, 250, 252, 260, 281, 473, 492, 652*
Compounds, xxi, 15, 34, 149, 169, 182, 184, 202* 206, 216, 221, 23[illegible], 23[illegible], 275, 284, 285*, 445, 568, 574, 612, 6[illegible], 700
Comptes Rendus de l'Académic inscriptions, 696*
Conjeeveram (Kāñci), 254, 438, 487*, 764
Connecticut, 421*
Cora or Caura, 368*, 369, 567, 568
Corpus Inscriptionum Indicarum 17
Court, xiii, xx, xxxix, lv, lviii, lxi, ciii, cix, cx, 5, 53, 121*, 168, 171, 186, 228, 255*, 320, 334, 341, 342*, 350, 353, 364*, 470, 498, 502, 558*, 561, 563, 612, 615, 617, 625, 627, 645, 657, 667, 679, 680, 64, 731*, 738, 747, 753, 754, 767, 768, 774
Court-epic, 41
Courtesan, xxxi, xxxviii, lvi, lvii, lxi, lxxi, lxxxiii, lxxxvi, 21, 78, 98, 138, 197, 198, 211, 214, 240, 244*, 251, 252, 302, 404, 410, 491, 492, 494, 495, 497, 498, 643, 645, 768
Court-language, ci
Court life, lx, lxi, 136, 257, 279, 443, 458, 461, 462
Court-poet, 370, 676
Court-theatre, 741
Cowell. See E. B. Cowell
C. R. Devadhar, 101*, 102*, 242*
C. R. Lanman, 457*
C. R. Narsiṁha Sarmā, 159*, 165*
Cromwell, lxvii
Criminal law, cix
C. Sankararaja Sastri, 302*
C. Sankararama Sastri, 207*, 277*, 437*, 465*
C. Schutz, 751*
C. S. Gulleri, 360*
C U. I S, 754
Cukhala, 544
Cult, ciii (Śiva and Vāsudeva), 166, 169 (of the Sun), 222, 377, 482 (Soma), 648 (Kṛṣṇa and Śaiva), 661 (Śakti), 677* (Snake)
Cūḍāmaṇi, 302
Cūrṇikā, 755
Cū ṇī, 671
C W. Gurner, 69*, 661*
C. Wilkins, 90*
Cyavāna, xxv
Czech, 750*

D

Dacca, 33*, 386*, 468*, 741
Dacca University Orient., 337*, 373*, 415*, 498*
Dacca University Studes, 29*, 386*
Dadhīca, 225
Dadhyañcas, 697
Daivajña Sūrya, 342, 437
Daivajña-vallabhā, 730*
Daivāsuram, 11*
Dakṣa, 505
Dakṣiṇabhāratī Series, 476*
Dakṣiṇāmūrti-stava, 386*, 663
Dakṣiṇāpatha, 303, 321
Dakṣiṇāvartanātha, 132, 656
Dalal. See C. D. Dalal
Damaruvallabha (commentator), 74[illegible]*
Damaruvallabha Sarman, 489*
Damayanīt, 326-29, 435, 624
Damayantī-kathā or *Nalacampū*, 435
Damayantī-kāvya, 755
Dambha, 675
Dance or Dancing, xviii, lvi, lviii, lix, lxxi, lxxiv, lxxvi, lxxvii, lxxxiii, lxxxiv, 20, 44, 45, 50, 56, 62, 67, 213, 390*, 491, 524*, 631, 632, 634, 635, 637, 642-45, 648, 649, 653, 654, 656, 676, 693, 725, 729, 749 750*
Dancing Girl, lix, lxxiii, 198, 390*, 491, 500, 654
Daṇḍaka (forest), 151, 153, 293
Daṇḍaka (metre), 285*
Daṇḍanīti, xcvii, 527
Daṇḍin, xx, xxviii, cxiv, 17, 21*, 28*, 33*, 92, 94, 120*, 155, 174, 178*, 179*, 191, 197, 200, 202, 203 205-17, 222, 223, 237, 241, 289, 321, 340*, 419, 429, 433, 434, 475, 476*, 477* 521, 527-31, 537, 538, 545, 548, 553, 569, 572-78, 582, 587, 590, 592, 593, 613, 615, 616, 663, 683, 686, 694, 756, 757, 762
Danish, 756
Dantivarman, 263
Danton, 213
Danturā (in *Laṭak-melaka*), 437
Daradas, 695
Dardic dialect, 94, 95

Darduka, 433
Daridr -cārudatta, 714, 719
Darpa-dalana, 407
Daśaduṣṭa-karmamārga, 614*
Daśaharā, 649
Daśa-kumāracarita, cxiv, 92*, 206-17, 219*, 231, 232*, 281*, 476, 530, 531, 747, 754, 757
Daśakuśala-karmapatha-nirdeśa, 614*
Das alte Indien, 752*
Das altindische Schattenspiel, 47*
Daśapura, 18
Daśaratha, xxx, 60, 114, 132, 186, 451, 456, 477, 744, 745, 753
Daśaratha Sarma, 477*
Daśarūpaka, 51, 66, 243*, 244*, 256*, 264*, 265*, 272, 274*, 299*, 300, 301*, 302, 369*, 449, 455*, 493, 506*, 634, 637, 686, 688, 760-62
Daśa-ślokī Stotra, 380
Daśāvatāra-carita, 321*, 324, 617, 692
Das Daśarūpa ist viel°, 550*
Das Datum des Candrogomin's und Kālidāsa's 124*, 656*
Dasgupta, 533*
Das ind. Drama, 45*, 633*, 635*, 674, 710
Das Kathākautukam des Śrivara verglichen°, 629*
Das Leben des Buddha von Aśvaghoṣa, 73*
Das Mahābhārata, 632*
Das Pañcatantra, 88*, 90*
Das Rāmāyaṇa, 120*, 635*
Das Śariputra Prakaraṇa ein Drama des Aśvaghoṣa, 76*, 613*
Date of Kālidāsa, The, 731*
Dattaka, 477*
Dattakalasi, 252
Dattaka-sarvāśraya, 189
Dattila, 525*
Daulatpur College Magazine, 731*
Dāhala, 350
Dākṣiṇātyā, ix
Dāmaka-prahasana, 495
Dāmalipta, 212
Dāmodara, 770
Dāmodara (father of Līlāśuka), 387
Dāmodara (father of Sārṅgadhara), 414
Dāmodaragupta, 197-99, 251, 255, 404-6, 410 675
Dāmodara Miśra, 506, 621*
Dāna-keli-kaumudī, 468, 664*
Dāna-stuti, 3
Dāra Shikoh, v, 364*, 566
Dāyabibhāga, 733
Dāyāda, 734
D. B. Diskalkar, 17*
D. C. Bhattacharyya, 189*
D. C. Sarcar, 12*
De xvii, xx, xlvi, 524, 527, 538, 562, 622. 662*, 669, 689. See S. K. De
Deccan, 88, 210, 530, 617, 689
Deccan College Libray, 703
Defects, 517, 568-72, 574, 582. See *Doṣas*
De Grammatisis Pracritisis, 695
De Kālidāsae Cakuntali recensionibus, 140*
Delarama-kathasara, 629*
Delārāmā-kathāsāra, 629*
De Legende van Zīmūtavāhana, 258*
Delhi, cxvii, 360, 402, 627
Demetrios, ciii
Democracy, liv
Demon, 11*, 65, 115, 139, 168, 170, 171, 212, 273, 320, 357, 473, 746, 748-50
Denarius. See Dināra
Der Auszug aus dem Pañcatantra°, 89*, 700*
Der Budhismus, 69*
Der griechische Einfluss im indischen Drama, 52*, 650*
Der Mimus, 650, 651*
Der Textus Ornatior der Śukasaptati, 425*
Der XXV Gesang des Srīkaṇṭhacaritam, 627*
Deśabhāṣā, 684
Deśaladevi, 469
Deśamaṅgala Vāryya, 774
Des Cat. Trivandrum Palace, 400*
Descriptive Cat. Madros Govt. Orient. Library, 400*, 414*, 439*
Descriptive Cat. of MSS. in ihe Jaina Bhandar, 201*
Desdemona,, xlviii
Deśopadeśa, 408-9
Devabhūti, c
Devacandra 769
Devadattā (hetaera), 250, 762
Devadāsī, lxxv
Devadhara, 720*
Devagiri, 342*
Devakinandan Press, 440*
Devakī, 726
Devakī (Timma's wife), 773
Devakumāraka, 416
Devapattana, 503
Devapāla 324*, 378
Devaprabha Sūri, 332, 345
Devarāja, 479, 623*
Devarāja-kavi, 775
Devasenā, 250
Deva-senā (Commentary), 741*
Devasūri, 476
Devavijaya-gaṇi, 338
De Vidūṣaka in het indischtoonel, 46*
Devī-candragupta, 271* 302, 686
Devī-caritrodaya, 338*
Devī-mahādeva, 687
Devī-pariṇaya, lxxxv, 687
Devī-śataka, 27*, 335*, 382*, 656*, 661
Devotional Poetry, 375
D. Galanos, 618*
Dhammapada, 673, 675
Dhanadadeva, 370
Dhanadeva, 476, 484
Dhanañjaya, lxxvi, 250, 550, 551, 619
Dhanañj ya-nāma-mālā, 340*
Dhananjaya, Śrutakīrti Traividya, 340
Dhanañjaya-vijaya, 467, 769 (of Kāñcanācārya)
Dhanapāla (Digambara), author of *Bhabisatta-kaha*, 430*
Dhanapala (Śevetambara), author of *Tilakamañjarī*, 201, 229, 430, 431, 621, 688, 694
Dhaneśvara 497
Dhanika, 265*, 369*, 550, 686

Dharaṇī, cvi
Dharasena, I, II, III and IV, 616
Dharma, xxv, lxxii, lxxiii, lxxiv, lxxv. lxxvi, lxxviii, lxxix, lx, 290, 415, 644, 672, 680, 687. 696, 702*, 729, 768
Dharmadāsa Sūri, 335*
Dharmakathā, 201*
Dharmakīrti, cxiv, 71, 165, 217, 218, 528, 532
Dharmanābha, 189
Dharmanātha, Saint, 17*
Dharmanātha, (story of), 344
Dharmanāthatīrthaṅkara, 623
Dharmapaṇḍita, 769
Dharmaparīkṣā, 676
Dharmavācaspati, 533*
Dhakkī, ix
Dharmapāla, cxvi, 324*
Dharmarāma Sthavira, 185*
Dharma-saṁhitā. xxv, xxvi, xxvii, li, lxxiii, xciiI, xcvii
Dharma-śāstra, 86, 290, 553, 735, 761, 773
Dharma-sūtra, xxv
Dharma-vijaya, 486, 621*
Dharmayya Dīkṣita, 774
Dharmābhyudaya, 503, 642
Dharmābhyudaya-chāya-nāṭaka, 769
Dharma-śarmābhyudaya, 17*, 344, 437, 623
Dharmika-suhūti, 614*
Dhauli (inscription), 738*
Dhavala candra, 90, 704
Dhāra, 747
Dhāravarṣa. 466
Dhārā, 158*, 168*, 332*, 340*, 349, 350, 428-31, 472
Dhāriṇī (queen), 137, 139
Dhātu-kāvya, 336, 617
Dhātu-pāṭha, 336
Dhāvaka, 255*, 758, 759
Dhirendranath Mukherjee, 731*
Dhīraśānta, lxxxiii
Dhīrāñjanikā, 741*
Dhīreśvara, 497
Dhīṣaṇa, 521
Dholka, 332, 770
Dhoyi, 373*, 374*, 390
Dhṛtarāṣṭra, 273, 275, 721, 723, 724
Dhṛti, 613. 655
Dhruva, 753, 760. See H. H. Dhruva
Dhruvādevī, 271*
Dhuṇḍhirāja, 262*, 760
Dhūrta-carita, 494
Dhūrta-nartaka, 500
Dhūrta-samāgama, 488*, 497
Dūrta-viṭa-saṁvāda, 248-50, 768
Dhūrtila, 525*
Dhvajamaha, 50
Dhvani, 517, 524*, 535, 539, 543, 545, 546, 551, 564, 565, 583-85, 592, 604, 605-10
Dhvanikāra, 516, 536, 556, 568, 569, 581, 584, 605, 606
Dhvani-kārikā, 581*
Dhvanigāthā-pañjikā, 623*
Dhvanvantari, 5*, 729, 780
Dhvanvantari-nighaṇṭa, 730*
Dhvanyāloka, cxiv, cxv, 29*, 158*, 168*, 188*, 221*, 226, 271*, 299*, 391*, 539-42, 545, 565, 742
Dhvanyāloka-locana, 715
Dialect, viii, ix, 93, 94, 95, 105*, 444
Dialogue, 44-7, 57, 243, 505, 509, 510, 631, 632, 639, 640, 647, 651, 653, 658
Dialogue hymns, 43, 45, 85
Dice, lix, 250, 404
Didactic, xc, xcix, cvi, 2, 51, 194, 364, 367, 372, 398, 399, 406, 407, 410, 411, 425, 427, 479, 483, 517, 614, 675, 696
Diddā, 356
Die altindischen Todten°, 633*
Die alteste Rezension des Mahānāṭaka, 506*
*Die Anekdoten über Kālidāsa**, 728*
Die Anfänge, 46*
Die Dharmaparīkṣā des Amitagati, 676*
Die Griechen in Indien, 52*
Die Heimgt des Puppenspiels, 47*, 652*
Die Hofdtchier desa Lakṣmaṇasena, 340*
'Die in bücher eingeteilte Erzählungssammlung', 88*
Die indarsabhā desamanat°, 649*
Die indische Balladendichtung, 632*
Die indischen Inschriften und das Alter der°, 5*, 17*, 611*, 612*, 732*, 738*
Die indischen Wortebücher, 617*, 619*, 730
Die Lehre des Udbhaṭa°, 543*
Die Litteratur des alten Indien, x, 20*, 25*, 141*, 520*, 634*
Die Poetic und Aesthetic der Inder°, 520*
Die Recensionen der Śakuntalā, 52*, 140*
Die Rezensionen der Cakuntalā, 140*
Die Saubhikas ein beitrāg zur°, 47*, 646
Die Sonnwendfeste in Attundien, 647
Die Svrophen d Mādhavānalakathā, 424*
Die Vajraśūci des Acvaghoṣa, 613*
Die Vermutung von Lüders, 613*
Die Zeit des Kālidāsa, 124*, 728*
Digambara, Jaina, ix, 340. 379*, 404, 422, 429, 430, 432, 435, 437, 476, 497, 619
Digambara Jaina Granthabhandar, 379*
Digambara Jaṭāsura, 497
Digambara Kumudacandra, 476
Digvijaya of Raghu, The, 124*
Dima, lxxxii, lxxxiv, lxxxvii, 65, 474, 687, 717, 724, 768
Dinakara, 622*
Dināra, 82. See Denarius.
Dinnāga, xix, cxiv, 124*, 464*
Diplomat, 609
Divākara, 751*
Divyāvadāna, 52*, 82, 614, 695
Dīlipa, xxix, xxx, lx, 130, 744
Dīnā-krandana-stotra, 663
Dipaka, 530, 534, 536, 556, 569
Dīpakarṇi, cii
Dīpikā commentary, 506*
Dīrgha-samāsa, 584
D. L. Z., 652*
D. M. Paranjape, 759
Doctrine, ix, 72-74, 81, 321, 393, 62 685, 693 (of rebirth), 754
Documents Sanscritics, 614*
Doḍhaka (metre), 12

Dogma, liii, 25
Dombikā, 302
Don A. de Silva Devarakkita Baṭuvantuḍave 169*
Don Juan, 693
Doṣa, 517, 532, 536, 539, 559-62, 564, 571-75, 578, 579, 585, 586, 604, 625. See Defects
Dosādhikārikā, 521
Drama, xxxvi, xxxviii, xlvi, xlvii, xlix, lxiv, lxxiv, lxxv. lxxix, lxxxi, lxxxii, lxxxvi, lxxxix, xcviii, xcix, cxxi, 2, 4, 11, 16, 22, 36, 37, 38, 40, 41, 62-68 (origin and characteristics), 76-78 (of Aśva-ghoṣa), 101-11 (ascribed to Bhāsa), 118, 123, 125, 126, 131-48 (of Kālidāśa), 150, 151, 160, 202, 213, 229, 239-48 (of Śūdraka), 248-53, (Caturbhāṇī), 254-55 (of Mahendra-vikrama), 255-62 (of Harṣa), 262-71 (of Bhaṭṭa Nārāyaṇa), 277-98 (of Bhava-bhūti), 298-300 (of Yaśovarman and others), 346, 362, 376, 441-511 (Later Decadent), 554, 569, 598, 599, 600 (related to *rasa*), 613 (of Aśvaghoṣa), 623 (of Nil-akaṇṭha Dīkṣita), 630-35, 638, 641-43 (origin), 646-48 (European literature on it), 654-56 (Buddhistic dramas).
Dramas and Dramatic Dances of Non-European Races, 47*
Dramaturgy, xviii, lxxvi, 15, 26*, 52, 62, 103, 169, 523
Draupadī, 273-75, 331* 337, 372, 457, 467, 504
Draupadī-pariṇaya, 765
Draupadī-svayaṁbarā, 467, 769
Dravidian or Draviḍa, viii, xxii, ciii, 94*, 95, 138*, 233, 450
D. R. Bhandark r, 435*, 524*, 611*, 738*
D. R. Bhandarkar Volume, 52*
D. R. Iyengar, 487*
D. R. Mankad, 51*, 56*, 65*, 66*, 122*, 477*. See Mankad.
Droṇa, 273, 723, 725
Droṇasiṁha, 616
Dṛṣṭānta, 534
Dṛṣṭānta-kalikā-śataka, 402
Dṛṣṭānta-śataka, 674
Drum plays, 107
Drutavilmbita (metre), 12, 120*, 121*, 159*, 196*, 285*, 329
Dualism, xxvii
Dugald Stewart, v
Duḥśāsana, 273
Durācāra, 497
Durboda-pada-bhañjikā, 751*
Durgadasa Cakravartin, 505
Durgaprasad, 96*, 189*, 197*, 319*, 322*, 324*, 331*, 344, 353, 359*, 370*, 382*, 405*, 413*, 435*, 437*, 471*, 479*, 486*, 496*, 502*, 556*, 775
Durgā, 213, 338*, 391*, 499, 623, 626, 752
Durgāpūjā, 497, 649*
Durgāsiṁha, 691*
Durgā-stava, 381
Durghaṭa-kavya, 335*, 470*
Duritārṇava, 499
Durlabhavardhana, 356
Durvāsā, xxxvi, 144, 381, 464, 679, 748
Durvinīta, 92*, 695
Duryodhana, 113, 273, 372, 504, 723-25
Duṣkaracitra-prakāśikā, 553*
Duṣyanta, lx, xlii, lxiii, lxxxii, 57, 292, 463, 620, 735, 748, 749, 775
Dutch 225*, 666*, 756*
Dūta-ghaṭotkaca, 709, 720, 721
Dūta-kāvyas, 372, 75, 663
Dūta-vākya, 101, 109*, 112
Dūtāṅgada, 465*, 471 , 501-4, 507
Dvaita forest, 178
Dvādaśa-pañjarikā Stotra, 194, 380 See *Mohamudgara*
Dvārakā, 396
Dvātriṁśat-puttalikā, 740*
Dvi-saṁdhāna kāvya, 340, 619
Dvyāśraya-kāvya, 678. See *Kumārapāla-carita.*
Dya Dviveda, 676
Dynastic History of Northern India, 618*

E

Early History of Bengal, 755*
Early History of India, 760
Early History of Vaiṣṇava Faith°, 391* 398*
Eastern and Indian Studies in honour of F. W. Thomas, 371*
Eastern Bengal, 664, 737
Eastern India, 656
E. B. Cowell, cv, 69*, 73*, 82*, 138, 226*, See Cowell
Edgerton, 5*, 86*-89*, 421*, 424*. See F. Edgerton
Edict, 522, 613
Edwin Arnold, 368*, 666*
Een onb ekend Indish tooneel stuk, 510*
Eggeling, 210*, 338*, 396*, 493*, 473*, 502, 504, 665*, 752*
E. H. Barlingame, 29*
E. H. Johnston. See Johnston
E. Hultzsch. See Hultzsch
Ein Beiträg zur Geschichte des indschen Dramas, 646
Ein Beiträg zur Textkritik von Kālidāsa's Meghadūta, 133*, 752*
Einfluss, 242*
E J. Bril, 355*
E. J. Rapson, 54*, 646, 731*
Ekanātha (commentator), 621*
Ekāvalī, 549, 561, 565, 580
Ekottarika stotra, 613*
Elegy, 132
Elephant-lore, 110, 240
E. Leuman, 201*, 621*, 744*, 764
Elizabeth, 651
Elizabethan, 46, 55, 141*, 223
Elizabeth Kreyenborg, 627
E. Lovarini, 427*
Ember Krisnamacharya, 360*, 414*, 431*
Emil Pohl, 756*
Emotion, xliii, xcii, 22, 568-70, 572, 581, 589, 590, 594-97, 601
Emperor of India Press, 380*

Empirical, 64, 174
E. Muir, 751*
Encyclop of Religion and Ethics, 361*
England, xci, 50
Epic, lxxv, lxxxviii, lxxxix, xcix, 1-4, 10*, 11, 12, 20, 35, 41, 45, 50, 51, 52*, 53, 58, 72, 85, 91, 100, 101, 112-16, 140, 156, 166, 173*, 177, 178, 186, 190, 195, 196, 272, 273, 275, 290, 295, 327, 328, 331, 340, 358, 381, 384, 386, 398, 402, 404, 437, 462, 505, 507, 618, 623, 626, 629, 630, 634, 646, 696, 702, 724, 725, 732, 740, 742*, 743
Epic Mythology, 647
Epigram, 329
Epigrammatic, 91, 407
Epigraphica Carnatica, 619*
Epigraphical, 6, 195
Epi. Ind. or *Epigraphica Indica* or E, I., 14*, 15*, 189*, 381*, 435*, 466*, 547*, 550, 612*, 613*, 616, 618*, 630, 662*, 595*, 739*, 756*
Epilogue, 658, 720.
Episode, xxx, xxxvi, xxxviii, xlvii, lix, l. lii, lxxxiii, lxxxvii, 11, 99, 111, 156, 178, 238, 244, 287, 299, 331, 337, 390, 415, 437, 477, 485, 496, 638, 697, 703, 724, 746, 748*
E. R. E., 54*, 646
Erfurt, 666*
Ernest Leroux, 196*
E. Röer, 325*, 624
Erotic, lxii, c, 9, 13, 15, 21, 22, 38, 40. 62-65, 67, 115, 156, 157, 159, 187, 190, 197, 198 204, 206, 253, 265, 310, 328, 333, 345, 364-67, 370-72, 384 386, 396, 399, 404, 490-94, 652*, 658, 665, 667, 669, 690, 729
Erotic Poetry, lxiv, 22, 23, 156-66, 181, 193, 206, 213, 220, 234-35, 364-75
E. Schalgintweit, 647
Espionage, 418
Essai sur Gunādhya et la Bṛhatkathā, 92* 97*, 99*, 612*, 689, 691*, 694*, 696*
Etawah, 626
E. Teza, 196*
Ethical, 673, 702
Eugéne Monseur, 196*
Eukratides, ciii
Eupheus, 223
Euphonic ccmbination, 569, 570
Euripides, 141*
Europe, v, lxx, cxxv, 89, 214, 651, 747
European, v, lxx, lxxi, 24, 315, 517, 609, 646, 650, 651, 666, 681, 688, 698, 704*, 710, 712, 740, 756*
Evansville, 729*
E. V. Vira Raghavacharya, 341*, 487*
E. Windisch, 650, 738*
Excellence, 568, 569, 573, 574, 590, See *Guṇa*
Expiation, xlviii, 745

F

Fable, 28, 38, 42, 83-100, 195, 204, 205, 272, 427, 437, 697-99
See Popular Fable
Faery Queene, 234
Fa Hien, cix
Fairy Tale, lxxiv, 100, 112, 205, 350, 427, 676-78, 680
Farce, 246, 254, 255*, 260, 474. 492*, 768
Farcical plays, 254, 487-500
Fateh Shah, 486
F. Belloni Filippi, 121*
F. Benary, 121*
F. Bollensen, 136*. See Bollensen
F. Cimmino, 523*, 759
F. D. K. Bosch, 258*, 694*
Feast, 649
F. Edgerton. See Edgerton
Feer, 82*
Felix Neve, 277*, 763
Ferenze, 192*
Fermicus Maternus, 732
Feroze, King, 736
Ferozepur, 649*
Fertility rite, 45
Festgabe Harmann Jacobi, 102*
Festgruss an Böhltingk, 756*
Festschrift Ernst Windisch, 28*, 744*
Festscrift Hillebrandt, 741*
Festscrift M. Winternitz, 391*
Festscrift Wackernagel, 738*
F. G. Peterson, 729*
F. Haag, 136*, 750*
F. Hall, 92*, 171*, 201*, 217*-19*, 522*, 550*, 625*, 686, 695*
F. H. Trithen, 763
F. H. v. Dalberg, 666*
Fiction, 37, 214, 227, 228, 239, 254*, 346, 720
Fifty Verses on the Rules for serving a teacher, 614*
Figure of speech, 567-69, 573, 575, 578, 579, 585, 615
Fine art, 645
Fire-ordeal, 292, 302, 303, 463
F. Kielhorn, 454*, 469*, 611. See Kielhorn
F. Lacôte, 92*, 96*, 107*, 612*, 694*, 695*, See Lacôte
Flanders xci
Fleet, 5. 17, 92, 656*, 695*, 704*, 730*, 739*, 756*, 757
F. Majer, 666*
Folk-dance, 648
Folk-dialect, 651
Folk-literature, 4, 156, 157
Folk-lore, 49
Folk-tale, 3, 4, 11*, 42, 53, 84, 115, 138, 155, 201, 205, 206, 214, 217, 232, 235, 282, 291, 419, 422
Fool, The, in Elizabethan drama, 46, 55
Foucher, 617*, 654*
Foundations of Indian Poetry, 656*
Fourth Reports, 345*, 404*
France, lxix
Frauenfela, 136*, 138*, 750
Frazer, x
French, 81, 136, 207, 239, 240, 371, 389, 481, 660*, 666*, 704*, 70-*, 741*, 747*, 756* 763
Friedrich Rückert or F. Rückert, 666*

Fritze. See L. Fritze
F. Rosen, 649*
Funeral ceremony, 733
Fünf Gesänge des Bhaṭṭikāvya, 614
Führer, 755*
F. Weller, 73*
F. W. Thomas, 5*, 8*, 17*, 26*, 71*, 78* 79, 80*, 95*. 104*, 124*, 218*, 226*, 248*, 412*, 764. See Thomas

G

Gadasiṁha, 621*
Gadya, 529, 530, 539, 563, 564
Gadya-cintāmaṇi, 432, 754
Gadya-kāvya, 754
Gaekwad's Orient Series or GOS, 8*, 54*, 66*, 78*, 120*, 171*, 185*, 201*, 271*, 299*, 324*, 332*, 344*, 360*, 362*, 363*. 414*, 431*, 463*, 465*, 466*, 473*, 478*, 484*, 489*, 490*, 523, 546, 620*, 649, 678*, 679
G. A. Jacob, 520*, 533*
Gajagati (metre), 12
Gajapati Kusuma-Kanduka (sport), 491*
Gajapati Narsimhadeva, 511*
Gajapati Pratāparudra, 485
Galanos, 673*. See D. Galanos.
Gambling, 26*, 211, 213, 246, 474, 485, 491, 768
Gaṇa-kārikā, 218*
Gaṇapati, 367*
Gaṇapati (commentator) 658*, 662*, 758
Gaṇapatilāl Jhā, 630
Gaṇapati Śāstri, 529*, 552, 627, 630, 658*, 663, 664*, 708, 712, 718, 741*, 742*, See T. Ganapati Sastri
Gandharva, lxiii, lxxxiv, 179, 190, 234, 439, 502, 660, 693, 749, 751
Gandharva-veda 524*
Gaṇḍī, 71
Gaṇḍīstotra-gāthū, 71, 167, 378*, 113*, 614*
Gaṇeśa (commentator), 561*, 623*
Gaṇeśa (deity), 391*
Gaṇeśvara, 561
Gaṅgā, 382*, 391*, 629, 691*
Gaṅgādāsa Pratāpadeva, 479*
Gaṅgādāsa-pratāpa-vilāsa, 479, 769
Gaṅgādevī, 361, 418, 663, 679
Gaṅgādhara, 479, 661* (kavi), 766, 769
Gaṅgādvāra, 88,
Gaṅgā-laharī, 383, 665
Gaṅgāmbikā, 437
Gangānanda Maithila, 566
Gangānāth Jhā, Sir, 535*
Gangārāma, 561*
Gaṅgāṣṭaka, 664*
Gaṅgāstava, 740
Gaṅgā-taranginī, 687
Gaṅgāvataraṇa, 334, 629, 764
Ganges, lxxii, ci, 164, 334, 561, 664, 665*, 689, 737
Gaṇikādhyakṣa, 643*
Garbha-sandhī, lxxxii
Gardabhilas cvii
Garuḍa, 115, 259
Gauḍa, 88, 169*, 171, 227, 228, 324, 326*, 352, 409, 450, 472, 684, 755
Gauda Abhinanda, 324, 618, See Abhinanda
Gauḍavaha, 219, 278*, 279, 314, 350*, 623, 676, 708
Gauḍa-vijaya, 687
Gauḍi Rīti, 218*, 526, 530, 532*, 535, 537, 568, 684
Gauḍorvīśa-praśasti, 326*, 626
Gaurava-dīpanī, 621*
Gaurāṅga-līlāmṛta, 398
Gaurāṅgasurakalpataru, 664*
Gaurishankar, 320*, 321*
Gaurī, 258, 259, 331*
Gaurī-pariṇaya, 765
Gaurī, woman-poet, 416
Gautama, xiii xxv
Gautamī, ci, 145
Gawronski, 613*. See A. Gawronski
Gāṅā Bhaṭṭa, 560
Gāndharva (marriage), xxxiv, xxxvi, xxxvii, 749
Gāndhāra, 94, ciii, cv, 736, 739
Gāṅga dynasty, 695
Gārgya, xxv
Gārgya Gotra, 341
Gārgya (Grammarian), 518
Gāthā, vii, 82
Gāthā-saptaśatī, See Sattasaī
G. B. Brahme, 256*
G. Bühler, 209 , 326*, 349*, 350*, 361*, 611*, 612*. See Bühler
G. C. O. Haas, 265*, 550*
G. Courtillier, 389*
G. de Blonay, 378*
G. Deveze, 481*
Geographical Data of the Raghuvaṁśa and the Daśakumāracarita, The, 208*
Geography, 208, 209, 218*, 263*, 455, 729
George, Forster, 747
George Grierson, viii, See. G. Grierson
Gerard de Nerval, 756
German, cxxvi, 73*, 89*, 119*, 120*, 122*, 138*, 178*, 189*, 197*, 239*, 262*, 401*, 407*, 469*, 481*, 558*, 614, 622, 627, 656, 666*. 677, 706, 741*. 744* 747, 750*, 752*, 756*, 759, 760, 763
Geschichte, 756
Geschichte der Chinesischen Litteratur, 648
Geschichte der Indischen Litteratur x, 543*, 708*
Geschichte der Japanischen Litteratur, 648
Geschichte der Sanskrit Philologie und Indischen Altertumskunde. x, 738*
Geschichte des Buddhismus in Indian aus dem, 614*, 728*
Geschichte des dramas, 646, 651*, 652*
Geschicten wie sie die Pandits von Ujjain°, 728*
Geva-rūpaka, 67*
G. G. A., 621*, 632, 635, 646, 651*, 652*, 657*, 700*, 702*, 708*, 750*, 763
G. Grierson or Grierson, 94*, 95*, 371*, 389*, 422*, 510*, 646, 659, 695*, 728*

Ghanaśyāma, 277*
Ghaṇṭā-Māgha, 193
G. Harihara Sastri, 178*, 209*
Ghaṭakarpara, 5*, 120, 156, 157, 335, 337, 338, 364, 730, 752*, 753*
Ghaṭakarpara-kāvya, 730
Ghatotkaca, 724, 725
Ghaṭikāśata Sudarśanācārya, 487*
Ghost, lxxxiv, lxxxvii, 141*, 280* 282
G. Huth, 124*, 533*, 728*. See Huth
G. I. L., 86*, 99*, 102*, 140*, 201*, 240*
Gildemeister, 751*, 752*
Giornale de la Societa Asiatic Italiana, 523*
Girnar, ci, cxii, cxxi
Gīrvāṇendra, 765
Gīta-digambara, 396*
Gīta-gaṅgādhara, 396*
Gīta-gaurīpati, 396*
Gīta-gaurīśa, 562
Gīta-giriśa, 396*
Gīta-gopāla, 396*
Gīta-govinda, 157, 314, 371, 376, 388-96, 509, 510, 560, 561, 662, 665-67
*Gītagovinda, Jayadeva poetae Indico**, 666*
Gītagovinda-prathamāsṭapadī-vivṛti, 666*
Gītagoviuda-tilakottama, 666*
Gīta-rāghava, 396*
Gītā. See *Bhagavadgītā*
Gītāvalī, 396*, 397
G. J. Agashe, 207*. See Agashe
G. K. Nariman, 256
G. K. Srigondekar, 465*
Glanneau, 650*
G. M. Dursch, 120*, 232*, 752*
G. M. Miller, 632*
G. N. 632*
Gnomic poetry, 3, 11, 38, 42, 87, 91, 121, 155, 194-96, 402, 673
Gobi, desert, 737
Gods, xxiii, 11*, 20, 65, 82, 98, 111, 128, 166-69, 171, 178, 193, 214, 230, 327, 328, 352, 438, 473, 515, 534*, 630, 649, 658, 667, 697
Godāvari, ci, 93, 473*, 606, 689, 761
Goethe, 143, 147, 667, 747, 751
Goethe's Works, 667*
Gokula, poet, 333
Gokulanātha, 486
Goldsmith, lix, 675
Goldstücker, 668
Gommi, tale of, 212
Gomukha, 100, 700
Gomūtrika (type of *Kāvya*), 530
Gonanda, 355, 356
Gondephares, ciii
Gopal Narayan Co, 331*, 396*
Gopāla Ācārya, 561*
Gopāla Bhaṭṭa, 386*, 561*
Gopālacampū, 396*, 440
Gopāla (Commentator), 662, 666*
Gopāla kathā, 332*
Gopāla-Kavi, 660*
Gopāla keli-candrikā, 444, 467, 509-10
Gopāla, King, 481
Gopālalīlā, 617
Gopālananda, 741*
Gopendra, commentator, 535*
Gopinath Kaviraj, 774
Gopi, 338, 372*, 373*, 384, 391, 490, 510
Gopīnātha Cakravartin, 498-99
Gopīnātha (commentator), 564, 624*
Gopīnātha, Mahārājādhirāja, 210
Gorakṣanātha, 479
Gotra, 225, 278, 341, 402, 438, 449, 462, 464, 469*, 486, 733*
Göttinginsche gelehrte Anzeigen, 133*, 444*, 470*, 520*, 524*
Göttingen, 336*, 340*, 371*, 380*, 520*, 522*, 550*, 666*
Gottimger nachrichten, 189*
Govardhana, 659, 668, 730
Govardhana Ācarya, 370-71, 390
Govinda, the writer, lix, 622*
Govinda, author of Vinatānandana, 769
Govindacandra of Kanauja, 496
Govindabhaṭṭa, 467*
Govindabirudāvalī, 397, 664*
Govindadev Sastri, 455*, 462*
Govinda, Dīkṣita, 764
Govindalīlāmṛta, 333, 396
Govinda Pisharodi, 711
Govinda Sankar Bapat, 183*
Govindastotra, 663
Govinda Thakkura, 556
Govindāṣṭaka, 380*
Govt. Oriental Library, 374*
Govt. Orient MSS Library, 186*, 476*
G. P. Quackenbos, 121*, 168*, 169*, 170*, See Quackenbos
Grace Abounding, 481
Graeco-Buddhistic, 654
Graeco-Roman, ciii, cv, 651
Grahavarman, 227, 263
Grahāditya, lix
Grammar or Grammarian, vi, cix, cxxi, cxxii, cxxiii, cxxiv, 7-9, 10, 11*, 12, 26*, 93, 95, 107*, 119, 161, 170, 180, 183, 187, 192, 221, 242*, 278, 310, 336, 337*, 350, 361*, 362, 387, 513, 515, 517-19, 521, 530*, 539, 545, 554, 560*, 585, 604, 611, 615-17, 656, 678, 684, 685, 729, 730
Grammatik der Prakrit-Sprachen, 243*, 444*, 695*
Gray Thomas, 298
Gray. See L. H. Gray
Grāmya, 534, 684 (-bhāṣā)
Granthamālā, 340*, 371*, 468*, 469*, 496*
Granthapradarśanī series, 535*
Granthika, 11, 49, 636-38, 644, 645
Great Epic of India, The, 635*
Greece or Greek, xxii, iv, lxviii, cii, ciii, 5, 41, 43, 47, 49, 52, 53-6, 62, 86*, 94*, 227, 202, 242, 618, 650-53, 654*, 732, 736
Greek in Bactria and India, 52*
Greifswald, 336*
Gṛhyasūtra, xxv
Grill. See J. Grill
G. R. Nandargikar, 132*, 621*, 744*, 748*. See Nandargikar
Groningen, 46*
Grundriss, 336*, 647, 728
G. S. A. I., 121*, 141*, 427*, 621*, 627, 708*

G. Strehly, 277*, 763
Gujarat of Guzerat, cvii, cxxiv, 331, 332, 345, 361-63 ; 432, 476, 478, 479, 484, 492, 510, 650, 658*, 706, 766-70
Gujarati New Press, 380*
Gujarati painting, 390*
Gujrati Printing Press, 126*, 426.*
Gumani, 402, 674
Guṇa, 518, 526, 532*, 536, 546, 552, 554 574-79, 581, 584, 585, 604, 505. See Excellence
Guṇabhadrācārya, 344, 433, 436
Guṇacandra, 105*, 120*, 121*, 271*, 463
Guṇadoṣa-bodha, 554
Guṇamati, cxii
Guṇaratnamahodadhi, 730
Guṇasāgara, 368*
Guṇaupādānika, 521
Guṇāḍhya, lii, lxiv, lxxix, lxxxxvii, lxxxviii, xc, cii, cvi, cxv, 4, 15, 84, 89, 92-100, 155, 205, 218, 265, 280, 404, 421. 612, 654*, 684 686, 687, 689-96, 705, 719, 759
Guṇā nanda, 775
Guṇībhūta vyañga, 538, 554, 609
Guṇībhūta-vyañjanā, xvii
Gupta (dynasty), cx, cxi, cxii, cxvii, 5*, 17, 118, 124, 225, 249, 263, 271*, 731*, 735, 736, 738, 754
Gurjara, cxii, 492, 769
Gurkha, cxvi
Guruveyoor, 382

H

Haberlandt, 622*, 756*
Haeberliu, 120*, 121*, 161*, 169*, 194*, 196*, 335*, 338*, 342*, 367*, 372*, 373*, 380*, 381*, 388*, 401*, 568*, 657*, 660*, 662*, 664*, 752*
Haihaya, 504
Haihayendra-carita, 629
Halāyuddha, 336, 617
Halāyudha's Kavirahasya, 339*, 617
Hale Wartham, 256*, 706
Haliodorus, Greek ambassador, cii
Hall. See F. Hall
Halle, 47*, 83*, 424*, 652*, 666*, 741*
Hammira-kāvya, 679
Hammīra (or Mewar), 363, 478*, 679, (Amīr Shikār), 478
Hammīra-mada mardana, 362*, 363*, 478
Hammīra-mahākāvya, 363*, 478
Haṁsa-dūta of Rūpa Gosvāmin. 372*, 373* 664*, 751 ; of Veṅkatadeśika, 373*, 374*
Haṁsaruta (metre), 12
Haṁsa-saṁdeśa, 332*, 373*, 375*
Haṁs.avijaya-gaṇi, 403*
Handiqui, 327*, See K. K. Handiqui
Hannah Neckel, 741*
Hannes Skold, Dr. cxxiv, 424
Hannover 122*
Hansh Lindach, 669
Hanūmat, 303, 451
Hanūmat as author 505, 506
Hanūmat (Bhīma's half brother), 46, 71
Hara, 396
Haracarita-cintāmaṇī, 323, 628, 629
Haradatta, author of *Padamañjarī*, 528
Haradatta Sarman, 413*
Haradatta Sūri 341, 620
Haragovinda Das, 465*
Hara-keli, 469
Haramikā, lix
Haraprasad Sastri, 50*, 74*, 96*, 339*, 374*, 378*, 391*, 470*, 612*, 618*, 647*, 660*, 661*, 696*, 729*, 738*
Harasiṁha or Harisiṁha, 497
Haravijjaya, 167, 319-20, 382*, 450, 623, 761
Hara-vilāsa, 455, 547
Har Bilas Sarda, 360*
Harekṛṣṇa-mahāmanṭrārthanirūpaṇa, 664*
Harekrishna Mukherjee, 388*
Hari, also called Bhānubhatta, 415, 629
Hari (deity), 667
Haribhadra, 344
Haribhadra Sūri, 363, 470
Hari Bhāskara, 415
Haricandra (Jaina), 17*, 437, 623
Haricandra, Bhaṭṭāra. See Bhaṭṭāra Haricandra
Haricaraṇa Dāsa, 741*
Harichand Hirachand, 372*
Harichānd Sastri, 122*, 126*, 133*, 140*
Harichand, 520*, 528, 529*, 558*, 657*, 752*
Haridas Das, 398*
Haridas Sankrit Series, 741*
Haridas Sastri, 185*
Haridāsa, 480*
Haridāsa (commentator), 751*
Haridūta, 504
Harigovinda, 390
Harihara, 372*, 404*, 429
Harihara (author of *Bhartṛhari-nirveda*), 161*, 479
Hariharabhaṭṭa, 668
Hariharadeva of Mithilā, 510*
Harihara Sastri, 418*
Harihara-subhāṣita, 372*, 404*, 429
Harihārāvalī, 740
Harikaṇṭha, 622*
Hari Kavi, 415
Harikṛṣṇa Vyāsa, 553*
Harināmāmrta-Vyākarana, 664*
Harinātha, 533*
Harinīpluta (metre), 12, 77*, 159*, 196*, 285* 329*
Hariraghunātha Bhāgavata, 660*
Hariratna, 624*
Hariśaṁkara, 396*
Hariścandra, 469, 470
Hariścandra-nṛtya, 510*
Harisena, cvii, cx, xix, 18
Harivaṁśa, ci, 51, 52*, 101*, 440, 466, 635 653
Harivaṁsa Bhaṭṭa, 561*
Harivaṁśa-sāra-carita, 765
Harivijaya, 761
Hari-vilāsa, 332, 617
Harlot, 407
Harman Weller, 669
Harries, 729*

Harṣa, cxiii, cxv, 173*, 354, 356, 358, 363, 402, 656, 674, 756, 765
Harṣacarita, cii. cxiii, lx. 16, 84, 92*, 93, 168*, 169, 173*, 201, 204, 218, 225-29, 271*, 272, 341, 349, 350, 433, 456. 459, 471, 576, 627. 708, 712*, 722*, 754, 757
Harsacarita-vārttika, 558
Harsahṛdaya, 624*
Harṣavardhana of Kanauj, 16, 17*, 18, 55*, 105, 110, 111 138, 156, 162, 168, 169, 171-73, 189*, 198, 209, 226, 227, 237, 239, 249, 254-62, 270, 301*
Harṣa-vikramāditya, 525
Harvard O.S. or H.O.S. or 80*, 89*, 140*, 178*, 239*, 277*, 424*, 457*, 622*, 703, 756*
Hastāmalaka, 380
Hastimalla, 467*
Hastings, 94*
Hastipaka, 120*
Hataera, 46, 491, 640
Haṭha-yoga, 479
Hayagrīva-vadha, 120, 687
Hāla or Hāla Sātavāhana, ix, c, cii, 4, 5*, 15, 16, 93, 94, 155-57, 159, 201, 241, 371, 391*, 428, 659
Hāla Saptaśatī, cii
Hālāsya-māhātmya, 334, 630
Hāralatā, 676
Hāravarṣa Yuvarāja, 324*
Hārīta, xxv
Hāsya-cuḍāmaṇi, lxxxvii, 474, 492*, 494, 768
Hāsyārṇava, 498
Hāthi-gumpha, 612
H. Bohatta, 648
H. Brokhaus, 96*, 481*
H. C. Kellner, 756*
H. C. Raychaudhury, Dr. 613*, 618*
Hebrew, 629
Hecuba, 141*
Hegel 580
Heinrich Blatt, 89*, 90*
Heinrich Uhle, 421*
Helārāja 355, 639, 644
Heldengedicht, 129
Heledorus, cii
Hellenic, vi
Hemacandra, viii, 29*, 67*, 95*, 197, 241*, 249, 265*, 336, 343-45, 361, 429, 455, 462*, 464*, 465, 469, 484, 485, 525*, 27, 542, 574, 584, 617, 620, 678, 684, 693-95, 750*, 762, 767
Hemavijaya-gaṇi, 427
Hemādri, 425
Herder, 747
Herman Beckh, 133*
Hermann Reich, 650
Hermann Weller, 669
Hermitage, xxxvi, xxxix, lxxx, 40, 128, 143, 144, 232, 451, 731*, 742, 744, 745, 749
Hertel, 87*, 88, 89*, 90, 263*, 421*, 424*, 426*, 631, 632, 669, 676*, 694*, 696*, 699*, 700, 701*, 702, 703, 704*, 705, 707, 708*, See J. Hertel.
Hertford, 138*
Hetu, 526, 530, 538, 582, 672
H. Fauche, 207*, 741*
H. Foucher, 666*. See Foucher
H. D. Dhruva, 523*, 649*. See Dhruva.
H. H. Wilson, 132*, 207*, 646, 651*, 756*, 760
Hiḍimba, 725
Hillebrandt, 48*, 122*, 124*, 132*, 149*, 262*, 270*, 444*, 633, 635, 641, 642*, 701*, 729*, 760. See A. Hillebrandt.
Himālaya, 38, 133, 153, 179, 190, 234, 332, 445, 670, 739, 742
Hindi, 371, 389, 467*, 621, 659, 680, 704*, 707
Hindu, vii, xxiii, xlix, lx, lxi, lxiii, lxxxix, xc, xciii, cv, cx, cxi, cxvi, cxvii, cxviii, 166, 364, 377-79, 400, 437, 631, 660, 668, 693, 733-35, 744, 749, 750*
Hindu Law of Partition Inheritance and Adoption, 240*
Hindusthānī, 704*, 707
Hindu Theatre, 486*
Hirananda Sastri, 102*, 107*
Hiralal Hansaraj, 343*, 345*, 362*, 424*, 427*
Hiraṇyabāhu (river Śona), 225
Hiraṇyakeśin Dharmasūtras, xxv
Historical Writings, xi, lxxx, 38, 42, 228, 306, 345-64, 474-79, 676-680, 755
Historie de la Litterature, 666*
History of Dramas, 763
History of Indian Literature or H. I. L., 14*, 69*, 71*, 74*, 79*, 82*, 124*, 172*, 331*, 345*, 378*, 379*, 652*, 667, 691*, 696
History of Indian Literature, by Weber, x
History of Indian Philosophy, 754, 766
History of Sanskrit Literature, or H. S. L. x, 2*, 26*. 77*, 86*. 94*, 201*, 209*, 611* 666*, 691*. 697, 740*
Hitopadeśa, 90, 502*, 673, 700, 704, 706
Hitopadeśa nach Nepalischen Handschrift 90*
Hiuen-Tsang, cviii, 755
Hīnayāna, vii
H. Jacobi, 2*, 120*, 172*, 189, 343*, 379* 530*, 750*. See Jacobi
H. Kreyenborg, 122*
H. L. 666*
H. Lüders, 47*, 72, 76*, 77*, 501*, 613*, 646 655. See Lüders
H. M. Vidyābhūṣaṇa, 728*
Hoangho. 737
Hoefer, 752*
Hoernle, 218*, 539*, 728
H. Ojha, 360*
H. Oldenberg, 20*, 44*, 87*, 132*, 141*, 165*
Holf dichter des Lakṣmanasena, 371*, 388*
Holi Festival, 49, 649*
Holland, xci
Holtzmann, 730
Homer, 127, 173*
Hopkinṣ, 635*, 647
Horse-sacrifice, cii, 46, 241. See *Aśvamedha*
H. R. Bhagavat, 380*

Hṛdaya-darpaṇa, 524, 656
Hṛdaya-dūta, 372*, 374*
Hṛdayaṅgama (commentary), 521, 533*
Hṛdayābharana, 666*
H. R. Diwakar, 611*
Hrishikesh Series, 391*
H. R. Kapadia, 620*
H. Sarma, 8*
Huber, 72*, 702*
Hugli, 440
Hultzsch, 132*, 133*, 183*, 189*, 300*, 381*, 444*, 450*, 467*, 470*, 475*, 476*, 481*, 503*, 565, 613 , 616, 656*, 661*, 662*, 686, 704*, 751*, 759
Humburg, 759
Humour, 197, 198, 211, 215, 223, 233, 244, 253, 270, 295
Hun or Hūṇa, xxii, cxii, cxiii, cxv, cxviii, 227, 263*, 356, 736, 738, 739, 753
Huṣka, 356
Huth, 125*, See G. Huth
H. V. Glasṣenapp, 666*
Hymmology, 167, 377

I

IA or *Indian Antiquary*, 5*, 9*, 12*, 71*, 79*, 92*, 102*, 161 , 242*, 262*, 263*, 286*, 340 , 363*, 450*, 465*, 470*, 481*, 520*, 524*, 529*, 530*, 533*, 547*, 550*, 562 , 611, 612*, 615, 618*, 622*, 646*, 650*, 656*, 686*, 691*, 695*, 708*, 710, 729*,-31*, 738*,-40*, 748*, 756*, 760, 761*,
Iceland, 86*
I.D.641*, 761*, (*Indian Drama*)
Inealistic or Idealism, lxxx, cxxxvii, 57, 292*, 598
I. H. Q. 12*, 54*, 56*, 102*, 122*, 124*, 134*, 167*, 178*, 209*, 211*, 219*, 243*, 263*, 372*, 373*, 402*, 437*, 548*, 477*, 501*, 507*, 508*, 611*, 612*, 615*, 661*, 691*, 713*, 714*, 753
I, Ir. Series, 550*
I. L. C. 651*
Imagery, 152, 176, 192, 233, 369, 393, 492, 519, 721, 766
Image-worship, 722
Im Lande der Nymphäen, 669
Incarnation, 93, 325, 437. See Avatāra.
Ind. Culture, 11*, 12*, 326*, 341*, 438*, 470*, 691*
Ind. Erzahler, 207*
India, v, vii, xxvii, xxxv, xl, lxi, lxvii, lxx, lxxi, lxxiv, lxxviii, lxxix, lxii, xcii, xciii, c, ciii-vii, cx, cxi, cxviii, cxix, cxxv, cxxviii, 4-6, 9, 21, 24, 25, 33, 40, 41, 43-45, 47-50, 52-55, 57, 59, 80, 86*, 90*, 94, 122-25, 129, 133, 139*, 141, 191, 193, 194, 205, 211, 216, 228, 235, 252, 257*, 266, 277, 281, 290, 302, 332, 333, 343*, 347, 351*, 360*, 369, 374*, 377, 387, 389, 403, 410, 415, 437, 438, 489, 507, 510, 520, 529*, 547, 649, 650, 653, 654, 665, 671, 672, 729, 736, 737, 739, 740, 751, 769
Indian in wort und Bild°, 647
Indian Literature, modern, reaction on Sanskrit, 314-15, 538-9, 511
Indian Review, 417*
Indian Song or Songs, The, 389*
Indian studies in honour of Lanman, 209*
Indian Theatre, 761*
India Office Cat., 124*, 126*, 210*, 335*, 338*, 373*, 396*, 421*, 424*, 429*, 438*, 479*, 619 , 665*, 666*, 752*
India office Library, 525*
India office Ms. 210*, 502*, 504
India—what it ca teach us, 171*, 539*, 612*
Indiens Litteratur und kultur, x
Indische Alterthumskunde, 5*
Indische Drama, 77*, 106*, 240*, 262*, 272*
Indische Essays, 649*
Indische Gedichte 660*, 669, 752*
Indische Leibeslyrik, 666*
Indischen Sprüchen, 669
Ind Litteratur geschichte 650*
Indo-Aryan, 94*, 95
Indo-European, 44
Indo-Germanic, v
Indogerm Forschungen, 124*, 728*, 738*
Indo-Parthian, ci, ciii
Indra, 43, 49, 50, 130, 138, 140, 178, 190, 334, 571, 631, 647, 723, 724, 744, 745, 748, 750
Indradhvaja, 647
Indra-dhvaja-pūja, 49
Indra III, 435, 570*
Indrjajit, 566
Indramatī, 745
Indraprastha, 190
Indrapura, 469
Indravajrā (metre), 12, 196*, 243
Indrāṇī, 43, 631
Indrāyudha, cxvi
Ind. Streifen, 127*, 209*, 218*, 235*, 331*, 617*, 618*, 621*, 741*, 754*, 756*
Ind. Stredien, 52*, 166*, 172*, 192*, 210*, 424*, 708*, 759
Indudūta, 373*
Indulekhā, 471, 686
Indumatī (princess), 130
Indumatī (Mādhava Bhaṭṭa's mother), 467
Indumatī (Princess), 130
Indurāja, 671
Indus, lxxi, cxvi, cxvii, 736-39
Ind Worterbucher, 336*, 361*
Inselbucheri, 666*
Inscription, vii, viii, ix, xi, xvi, xviii, xxi, ci, cii, cxi, cxxiv, 4, 6, 14, 15, 17, 18, 79, 93*, 118, 123, 173*, 178, 179*, 183, 189, 207, 254, 343*, 346, 352, 355, 390, 400, 435, 469, 481, 553*, 612, 616, 619, 630, 654, 662, 684, 688, 704*, 732, 735, 736, 738, 739, 768
Ionian, 54
Iran, v, lxxii
Iranian, 169
Iranic, vi
Irāvatī queen, 137*
Irony, 145, 721
Islam, cxvi
Italian, 621, 656, 750*, 756*, 759, 760

Italic, vi
Italy, 651
Itihāsa, xiv, xvii, xcix, vlix, lxxix, 1, 41, 43*, 173*
I. Tsing, cxi, 656, 671-73, 759, 760
Ihāmṛga, lxxxvii, 65, 473, 687, 726, 768
Iśāna, lviii
Iśānadeva, 249*, 623*
Iśānadeva (Līlāśuka's preceptor), 387
Iśvara, 773
Iśvaradatta, 156, 213, 249, 761, 762
Iśvarakṛṣṇa, cxiv
Iśvara-pratyabhijñāsūtra-vimarśinī, 662
Iśvara-śataka, 335*, 382
Iśvarasena, 249*, 757, 762
Iśvarābhisandhi, 626

J

J. A., 69*, 70*, 72*, 79*, 81*, 93*, 95*, 102*, 107*, 194*, 367*, 378*, 421*, 429*, 550*, 655*, 657*, 660*, 674*-96*, 702*, 728, 752*, 759, 763
Jacobi, 13, 120*, 127 , 190*, 192*, 240*, 263*, 319*, 322*, 424*, 524*, 529*, 533*, 536, 537*, 543, 548, 550*, 551, 558*, 612*, 622*, 623, 635, 650, 657*, 700*, 702*, 708*, 730*, 732, 760, See H. Jacobi
Jackson, 18*, 55*, 173*, 256*, 651*, 728*, 759*. See A. V. W. Jackson
Jagaddhara, 217, 271*, 277*, 553*, 661, 663, 689, 751*, 755*, 762, 763
Jagaddhara Zadoo, 355*
Jagadābharaṇa, 364*, 566
Jagadīśvara, 498
Jagaḍū, 679
Jagaḍu-carita, 679
Jaganmohan Tarkālaṁkāra, 469*
Jagannātha, 469
Jagannātha Pañcānana, 661
Jagannātha Paṇḍita, 665, 675
Jagannatha, Tailaṅga, 364, 371, 372, 383, 400, 527, 555, 565, 572, 584, 604, 628, 675
Jagannatha (temple of) 450*
Jagannātha-vallabha, 396, 468, 511*
Jagatī (metre), 2*, 12
Jaghana-capala (metre), 417
Jaghana-capalā, womanpoet, 417
Jāhāgirdār, 720*
Jahlaṇa or Jalhaṇa, 7, 8*, 16, 185, 300, 360, 410, 414, 417*, 473*, 542, 677, 769
Jaina, vii, ix, xcvii, cv, 7*, 17*, 50, 72, 89, 122*, 166, 168 172, 189*, 195, 201, 211, 214, 325, 326, 331, 338, 340, 342-45 (Mahākāvyas), 361-63 (Poems with Historical Theme), 364 373-75, (Dūta-kāvyas), 377, 379 (Stotras), 400, 404, 424, 426-29, 430*, 431-33 (Prose kāvyas), 462*, 472, 539, 559 (Writers), 612 (*Aṅgas*), 676 (Ethics), 678, 679 (Authors), 694 (Story-book), 698 (Recension), 703, 742*, 751, 767 (Writers), 768 (Religion), 775 (Tirthaṅkara)
Jaina Ātmānanda Granthamalā, 374*, 471*, 475, 476*, 503*
Jaina Ātmānanda Sabhā, 362*, 363*, 467*
Jaina Bhāskarodaya Press, 362*, 424*, 427*
Jaina Dharmapraśāraka Sabhā, 343*
Jaina Haricandra 17*
Jaina Jayaśekhara 742*
Jaina *Meghadūta*, 751*
Jaina-Nayacandra, 679
Jaina Padmānanda, 400
Jaina Puppharyanta, 660*
Jaina Rāja-Śekhara, 7, 325-26
Jaina-rāja-taraṅginī, 677
Jaina Tīrthaṅkara, 775
Jaina Yaśovijaya Granthamālā, 476*
Jainism, 172, 361, 482, 484, 485, 662*, 704, 767
Jaipur, 403
Jaitrasiṁha, 363
Jaladharamālā (metre), 181*
Jalāpa (Nāgarāja's father), 402
Jaloddhatagati (metre), 181*
Jalpa-kalpa-latā, 566
Jambhaladatta, 421, 423
Jambū, 373*
Jami, 629
Jammu cat, 229*
Jamnagar, 343*, 362*, 424*
Jamunā, cvii, 665*, 689
Janaka, 788
Janārdana (commentator of *Meghadūta*), 751
Janārdana Gosvāmin, 370
Janārdana-sena, 337
Janendra, 751*
Jaṅgamas, 492*
Jantuketu (in *Laṭaka-melaka*), 497
JAOS, 29*, 46*, 55*, 86*, 89* 107*, 140 , 161*, 165 , 168*, 242*. 45 260*, 277*, 344*, 404*, 421*, 455*. 7* 479*, 481*, 502*, 651*, 673, 710, 728* 756*, 759
Japal, cvi
Japan, 648
Japanese, cvi
J. Ariel, 367*, See Ariel
Jarjara-pūjā, 49, 50
ARS, 728*
Jasahara-cariu, 436
JASB, 69*, 80*, 263*, 373*, 381*, 389*, 390*, 413*, 524*, 612*, 618*, 647, 666*, 696*, 728*, 751*
Jaṭasiṁhanandī, 343
Jaṭāvabodhinī, 624*
Java, cxi 48, 86*, 648
Javanese, 48
Javanikā or Jamanikā, 54*
Jaya, 439
Jayacandra of Kanauj, lviii, 326, 428
Jayadeva author of *Candrāloka*, 560
Jayadeva, author of *Gīta-govinda* (q. v.), 314, 325*, 371, 373*, 388-90, 468, 509, 510* 561, 659, 662, 666, 761
Jayadeva, author of *Prasannarāghava*, 369 389*, 462-63
Jayadeva Pakṣadhara, 462
Jayadratha, 724

Jayadratha (author), 323, 628, 629
Jayamaṅgala, 183*, 528*, 616*
Jayanta, xix
Jayanta Bhaṭṭa (Abhinanda's father), 324, 555
Jayanta Bhaṭṭa, author of *Nyāyamañjari*, 381*
Jayantabhaṭṭa (commentator of *Kāvya-prakāśa*), 555
Jayantacandra, 625
Jayanta-maṅgalam, 494*
Jayantapurī, 340
Jayanta Siṁha, 478
Jayanta-vijaya, 345
Jayantī-kṣetra, 340*
Jayaratha, 323*, 360, 557, 558, 628, 629*
Jayarāma, 555, 556
Jayaśaṁkara, 278
Jaysena, lix
Jayasiṁha of Gujarat, 345, 476
Jayasiṁha of Kashmir, 19, 323, 351, 354, 553*, 628, 678
Jayasiṁha Sūri, (author of *Hammīra-mada-mardana*, 362*, 478
Jayasiṁha Sūri, author of *Kumāra-pāla-caritā*, 362*, 363*, 767
Jayasiṁhābhyudaya, 359*
Jayaswal, 263*, 402*, 477*, 760. See K. P. Jayaswal
Jayatilaka Sūri, 335*
Jayatīrtha, cxviii
Jayā, 171
Jayānaka, 360*
Jayāpīḍa, Cippata of Kashmir, cxvi, 197, 319, 536
Jābāli, 230, 231
Jāhāngīra-sāha-carita, 360*, 772
Jāluka, 611*
Jāmadagnya-jaya or *Jāmadagnya-vijaya*, 464, 686
Jāmbavatī, 8
Jāmbavatī-jaya or *Jāmbavatī-vijaya*, xviii, 7, 611
Jāmī, Persian poet, 771
Jānakī-haraṇa, cxv, 127*, 185-88. 621, 764
Jānakī-pariṇaya, 331, 456*, 464, 630, 765
Jāṅgulika, 168*
Jāṅgulī, 475
Jātaka, xviii, 4. 72, 80, 81, 83, 5, 87, 133*, 141*, 258, 369*, 434, 697. 702*, 731*
Jātaka-kalānidhi, 730*
Jātaka-mālā, cvii, 80-1. 614, 655*, 700
Jātaka-sāra, 730*
Jātukarṇa, xxv
Jātukarṇī, 278
Jātrā, 631, See Yātrā
J.B.A.R.S., 671*, 676*, 710
J. B. Chaudhuri, 373*, 375*, 416*, 417*
J. B. Modaka, 435*, 437*
J. B. O. R. S, 72, 470*, 477*, 494*, 510*, 731*, 738*
J. B. R. A. S., 60*, 102*, 105*, 108*, 121*, 161*, 166*, 189*, 218*, 278*, 320*, 326*, 340*, 531*, 542*, 562*, 611*, 612*, 615*, 619*-21*, 744*, 755*, 763.
J. B. T. S., 378*
J. Burgess, 650*
J. C. Ghosh, 470*, 660*
J. Charpentier, 107*, 240*, 263*, 684*, See Charpentier
J. d' Alwis, 621*
Jena, 497*, 498*, 535*
J. E. Seneviratne, 728
J. F. Fleet, 454*
Jester, 257, 260*. See Vidūṣaka
Jewellery. 173
J. Gildemeister. 132*, 158*
J. Grill, 271*, 272*, 762. See Grill
J. Grosset, 522*
J. Haeberlin. See Haeberlin
Jhalkikar, lxiv.
J. Hertel, 44*, 86*, 89*, 90*, 133*. 207*, 404*, 426*, 427*, 657**. See Hertel
J. Huizinga, 46*
Jina, 172, 214, 344, 379
Jinabhadra Sūri, 741*
Jinadatta Sūri, 331
Jinadāsa, 657
Jinaharṣa, 770
Jinakīrti, 427
Jinakirtis Geschichte von Pala and Gopāla, 427*, 629*
Jinamaṇḍana, 362*, 767
Jina Pārśvanātha, 172*
Jinaprabha Sūri, 172*, 379, 476
Jinaraja 325*, 624*,
Jina Ṛṣabha, 172
Jinasena, 132*, 374*
Jinataraṅginī, 629
Jinavijaya, 428*. See Muni Jinavijaya
Jinānanda, 676
Jinendrabuddhi, 189*, 528
Jintaguptal, cxii
Jivananda or Jivananda Vidyasgar, 120*, 121*. 161*, 169*, 194*, 196*, 217*, 298*, 325*, 338*, 342*, 368*, 369*, 373*, 380*, 381*, 424*, 429*, 469*, 489*, 506*, 560
Jīmūta, lix
Jīmūtavāhana, story of, lxxxiv, 19, 60, 258-60, 759
Jīva Gosvāmin, 396*, 397, 440, 663*
Jīvaṁdhara, 344, 433, 437
Jīvaṁdhara-campū, 344, 437
Jīvaṁdhara-carita, 344
Jīvarāja, 561
Jīvānanda, 486, 764
J. J. Meyer, 157*, 207*, 617, 747
J. Jolly or Jolly, 240*, 496*, 710
J. L. Kein, 646
J. M. Grandjean, 675
J. M. Kennedy, 161*
J. Murray Michell, 744*
Jnānanidhi, 278
Jnānaśrī, 474
Jnānānanda Kalādhara, 158*, 668
Jnanendra Bhiksu, 514
J. Nobel, 122*, 173*, 202*, 520*, 529*, 656*, 752*. See Nobel
J. N. Tarkaratna, 183*
Jodhpur, 373*
John Pickford, 277*

Johnson, 706
Johnston, 9*, 13*, 14*, 69*, 70*-74*, 76*-78*, 122*. See E. H. Johnston
Jonarāja, 322*, 354*, 359, 360, 415, 621*, 627, 629
Jones, 393, 667
JORM, 470*
Jaurnal of Indian History 122*
Journal of Orient. Research or JOR, 102*, 119*, 271*, 300*, 302, 332*, 414*, 415*
Journal of the Annamalai Univ., 137*
Journal of the University of Bombay, 390*, 752*
Journal of Veṅkaṭeśvara Oriental Institute, 487*
JPASB, 50*
JRAS, 8*, 17*, 29*, 47*-9*, 71*, 79*, 81*, 88*, 89*, 92*, 95*, 102*, 104*, 105*, 107*, 108*, 122*, 124*, 133*, 169*, 173*, 183*, 185*, 186*, 189*, 200*, 201*, 218*, 240*, 243*, 245*, 248*, 254*, 263*, 278*, 300*, 322*, 338*, 360*, 371*, 378*, 401*, 413*, 417* 464*, 490*, 504, 520*, 525*, 526, 531*, 533, 537*, 539*, 540*, 550*, 552, 616*, 619*, 621*, 630*-32*, 635*, 647, 648, 656*, 657*, 659*, 662*, 674, 695*, 701*, 704*, 708*, 710, 728, 729*, 731*, 732*, 738*, 752*, 755*, 759, 760, 764
Jṛmbhaka weapon), 53*
J. S. Hosing, 189*
J. S. Speyer, 80*, 92*, 695*. See Speyer
J. Thakakusu, 256*. See Takakusu
J. Taylor, 481*
J. biläumsaugabe, 667*
Julius Caesar, 33*
Junāgaḍ, cxii, 567
Juṣka, 356
Jyeṣṭhakalaśa, 350
Jyotirīśvara Kaviśekhara, 497
Jyotirvidābharaṇa, 5*, 730*, 740*

K

Kabul, civ, 736
Kacchapeśvara Dīkṣita, 566
Kadamba family, 619
Kadphises I and II, civ
Kafirstan, 94
Kahlaṇa or Kalhaṇa, 119, 120*, 121*, 197, 198, 241, 279, 299, 320. 321*, 322*, 349, 343-59, 360*, 382. 523, 536, 675, 677, 682
Kaikeyī, 113, 114, 287, 456
Kailāsa, 322, 450, 452
Kailāsa-śailavarṇana, 774
Kaiśikī (*vṛtti*) 539
Kaiyaṭa, 538, 637-39, 644*, 656*
Kaiyyaṭa-vyākhyāna, 764
Kalakaṇṭha, 298
Kalasa, king, cxvi, 96*, 553*, 692
Kalatrapatrikā, 791
Kalāpadīpikā, 616*
Kalā-vilāsa, 407-8, 675
Kali, 327, 410, 658*
Kalikāla-Vālmīki, 339
Kali-keli, 494, 687
Kalilag wa Damnag, Kalīlā-wa Dimna, 89*
Kaliṅga, cxxi, 212, 473, 563
Kaliṅga-senā (courtesan), 98
Kaliṅga-rāya, 400*, 414
Kalivarjyas, xxiv
Kali-viḍambana, 403*, 410, 675, 764
Kalyuga-parikathā, 613*
Kalmuch, 422*
Kalpanā-n-aṇḍitikā or *Kalpanālaṁkṛtikā*, 72
Kalpataru Press, 380
Kalyāṇa 341, 351
Kalyāṇa, an author, 396*
Kalyāṇamalla, 751*
Kalyāṇa-mandira, 172*, 379
Kalyāṇa-saugandhika, 467, 720
Kalyāṇavarman, 477
Kamalākara, author of *Ratnamālā* (commentary), 666*
Kamalākara Bhatta, 555, 556, 666*
Kamalākara bhikṣu, 218*
Kamalā-vilāsa 551*
Kamalinī-kalahaṁsa 472, 772
Kampanāya or Vīra-Kampana, 418
Kaṁsa, 11, 49, 60, 115, 332, 336, 636-39, 640*, 644*
Kaṁsa-vadha, xviii, 437*, 468, 640, 772
Kaṇabhakṣa, 527
Kanaka-jānakī, 565*
Kanakalata Thakura, 741*
Kanakaprabhā ((metre), 13
Kanauj, cxv-cxvii, 16, 326, 361, 496, 676, 772
Kandarpa-keli, 494
Kandarpaketu, Prince, 219-21
Kanduka-krīdā, 491*
Kandukavatī, Princess of Dāmaliptā 212, 216
Kane, 189*, 525*, 527, 530, 532, 533*, 536, 538, 540*, 542, 543*, 550*, 552*, 556, 562*, 581, 611*, 615, 616*, 628, 710, 753, See P. V Kane
K. A. Nilkantha Sastri, 470*
Kaniṣka civ, cvi, cx. 13, 14*, 18, 70, 73, 80, 81*. 356
Kankaṇa 766
Kaṅkā, 218*
Kaṅkālādhyāya-vārttika, 751*
Kaṅkālī, 405
Kant, 580
Kaṇṭhābharaṇa, 761
Kanticandra Mukophadhyay, 566
Kaṇva, xxv, c, 40, 144, 145, 697, 747
Kapālakuṇḍalā, 283
Kapi-dūta, 373, 374*
Kapilarudra, 525*
Kapilavastu, 75
Kapiñjala family, 331
Kapiśā, cxvi
Kapphiṇa, King, 321
Kapphiṇābhyudoya, cxv, 320
Karatāla, 351
Karañja, 436*
Karanja Jaina Series, 436*
Karālakeśā, lix
Karkoṭa dynasty 356
Karkya, 325*
Karlsruhe, 730*
Karman, 60, 81
Karṇa, 112-13, 327, 275, 678, 722

Larṇa-bhāra, 101, 109*, 112, 709, 720
Karṇabhūṣaṇa, 566
Karṇa, Cedi king, 350
Karṇadeva Trailokyamalla, 359, 471
Karṇaparva (*Mahābhārata*), xiii
Karṇa-sundarī, 350, 471-72, 769
Karnatak Press, 439*
Karṇānanda Prakāśinī, 662*
Karṇāṭa, 343, 470*, 497,
Karṇīputra Mūladeva, 250, 407
Karpaṭi Gotra, 402
Karpaṭika, 120*
Karpūra-caritu, lxxxvii, 474, 489, 492*, 768
Karpūra-mañjarī, 454, 457-58, 547
Karpūratilaka, King of Kaliṅga, 473
Karuna (*rasa*), 555, 592, 595
Karuṇā-laharī, 383, 665*
Karuṇā-vajrāyudha, 363, 769
Kashgar, civ, cxvi
Kashi Skt. Ser., 189*
Kashmir or Kashmirian civ, cv, cxiii, cxv, cxvi, 19, 72, 88, 89, 90, 93, 95, 96, 98, 99, 119, 120, 121*, 173*, 197, 199, 230, 249*, 255*, 263, 279, 280, 302, 316, 319-24, 326*, 336, 349, 350, 354-59, 369, 377, 378, 381, 382, 401-11, 415, 421, 422, 423, 471, 525*, 535, 544, 553*, 554, 618, 627-29, 656*, 659*, 674-75, 677, 682, 688-92 698-99, 700*, 705, 706, 729*, 736, 762. 771
Kashmir Report, 91*, 320*, 322*, 389*, 554*
Kashmir Series of Texts and Studies, 408*
Kathaka, 508*, 635, 638
Kathambhūti, commentary, 751*
Khatā, xvii, lxxv, xcix, 84, 94, 200-5, 211*, 222, 419, 431, 433-34. 532*, 539, 563, 635, 638, 653*, 688, 694, 698-99, 754, 757
Kathā and Ākhyāyikā in Classical Sanskrit, The, 84*
Kathā-kautuka, 316*, 629, 711
Kathā-kośa, 427, 694
Katkā-mukha, 705
Kathānaka, 426
Kathā-ratna-sāgara, 770
Kathā-ratnākara, 427
Kathā-sarit-sāgara, lxiv. 29*, 89*, 92*, 96, 138*, 230*, 231. 258*, 421*, 642*, 688-90, 691*, 692. 695-96, 698-99, 700*, 705, 707, 722, 759, 761
Kathā-trayī, 341
Kathiawad, cviii, 3 2, 503, 616
Katmundu, 699
Kaumudī-mahotsava, 257*
Kaumudī-mahotsava, 476, 715, 758
Kumudi-mitrananda, 450*, 475, 769
Kauṇḍinya Gotra, 462
Kauntaleśvara dautya, 119*
Kaunteyāṣṭaka, 774
Kaurava, 178, 273, 274
Kauśalikā, 171, 686
Kauśāmbi, cix, 689
Kauśikāyana Gotra, 469*
Kausikī (Vṛtti), 63, 66*
Kauṭilya xiii, xcvi, xcvii, 15, 522, 567, 701, 706, 732-33, 735-36
Kauṭilya and Kālidāsa, 729*
Kautsa, 745
Kautuka-ratnākara, 499
Kautuka-sarvasva, 498-99
Kavicandra, 751*
Kavi-kaṇṭhābharana, 10*, 29*, 324*, 365*, 554*, 618*
Kavikarṇapūra, Paramānanda Sena, 78, 396*
Kavimalla, 331
Kaviputra, 16, 101, 685, 712, 757*
Kavi-rahasya, 336, 521, 617
Kavirāja, 18 (title), 33, 454, 459, 460, (title)
Kavirāja, author of *Rāghavapāṇḍavīya*, 340, 619-21
Kavirāja, commentator, 661
Kavirājamārga, 531*
Kavi-samaya, 26*, 28
Kavi samaya-kallola, 566
Kavitarkika, son of Vāṇīnātha, 499
Kavitārkika-siṁha Vedāntācārya, 439, See Vedāntācārya
Kavivallabha Cakravartī, 622*
Kavi vimarśa, 713
Kavīndra-kaṇṭhābharaṇa, 335*
Kavīndra-vacana-samuccaya, 5*, 8, 16*, 19*, 71*, 119*, 158*, 173*, 186*, 300*, 412, 455*, 681*, 740*
Kayyaṭa, 48*, 382*
Kādambarī, 230, 232, 234, 299*
Kādambarī, cxiii, 84, 170*, 201, 204, 218, 225, 227, 229-35, 238, 405, 430*, 431, 436, 474, 618, 754-55, 757, 762
Kādambarī-kathā sāra, 324, 618
Kādambas, 340
Kāka-dūta, 375*
Kākaṭīya, 467, 479*, 562
Kākutstha-keli, 769
Kālacakra, 730*
Kālacuri, 301, 450, 454, 504, 686
Kālajñāna, 730
Kālañjara, 301*, 473, 489
Kālapriyanātha, 279
Kālidāsa, vii, ix, xvii, xix, xx, xxi, xxix-xxixi, xxxv-xxxviii, li, lvii, lx, lxiii, lxxx, xcvii, xcxiii, c. cii, cv, cviii, cx, cxvii, cxix, cxxv-cxxvii, cxxxix, 2, 5*, 8*, 9*, 16, 18, 23, 25*, 35, 38-40 51, 55, 60, 69, 74, 78, 101, 104, 105, 110, 118-54 (predecessors, date and works), 185-60, 159, 167, 170, 173, 175, 176-79, 180-181, 185, 187, 188, 191, 194, 200, 201, 210*, 219, 235, 239, 241, 245, 257, 260*, 261, 263, 264, 270, 277, 279*, 280, 283, 285*, 289, 294, 295, 297, 305, 306, 316, 317, 321, 322, 325, 331, 337, 345, 372, 374*, 375, 381, 429, 444, 464, 477*, 522, 525*, 529*, 538, 553 591, 618*, 620, 621, 641, 654, 655, 657-58, 665*. 685, 695, 706, 708, 710, 712, 716-18, 722, 729-32, 735, 737-41, 743-44, 747-48, 750-54, 757*, 761, 771
Kālidāsa and Padmapurāṇa, 140*
Kālidāsa, author of *Gaṅgāstava*, 740*
Kālidāsa, author of *Jyotirvidābharaṇa*, 740*
Kālidāsa, author of *Kuṇḍa-prabandha*, 740*

Kālidāsa, author of *Ratnakoṣa*, 740*
Kālidāsa, author of *Śuddhi-candrikā*, 740*
Kālidāsa, author of *Tripurasundarīstutikāvya*, 740*
Kālidāsa et l' Art poetique de l' Inde, 126*, 520*, 528, 548*, 550*, 558, 657*, 740*
Kālidāsa-Gaṇaka, 740*
Kālidāsa (Hillebrandt's) 124*, 149*, 740*
Kālidāsa Miśra, 740*
Kālidāsa Nandin, 740*
Kālidāsa Maghadūta, 661*
Kālidāsa's Religion and Philosophy, 729*
Kālidāsa's Śakuntalā and Its Source, 748*
Kāliñjara, 768
Kālīprasāda, 374*
Kālī, 368*, 473, 658*, 728
Kālīpūjā, 649*
Kālī-stotra, 740*
Kāma, lxxv, lxxx, lxxxi, lxxxv, lxxxvi, lxxxix, 128, 151, 675, 742
Kāmadatta, 762
Kāmadā commentary, 669
Kāmadeva, 340
Kāmadeva II, 619
Kāmadeva, Kādamba, 340
Kāmadeva Trailokyamalla, 350-51
Kāmadhenu, 527, 529*, 535*
Kāmamañjarī (courtesan), 21, 211, 281*
Kāmandaka, 706
Kāmandakī, 281, 282, 284
Kāmandakīya Nīti-śāstra, 91
Kāmarāja Dīkṣita, 370
Kāmarūpa, cvii, 352, 364, 473
Kāma-śāstra, xxxi, lxxv, xcix, 23, 281*, 290, 291, 328, 385, 487, 623, 624, 747, See Vātsyāyana
Kāma-sṛṅgāra, 714*
Kāma-sūtra, xxxiii, lxii, lxiv, 21, 405, 645, 758
Kāmavilāpa Jātaka, 133*
Kāmbocha, 738
Kāmboja, 738-39
Kāmeśvara, 469
Kāmyaka forest, 178
Kāñcanamālā, 257
Kāñcanapallī, 485
Kāñcanācārya, 467, 769
Kāñcī, cxiii, 254, 332, 384, 450, 487*, 489, 491, 568*, 658*, 679, 765
Kāṇḍālayarya, 566
Kāntotpīḍā (metre), 13
Kānti, 575, 576*, 593
Kānyakubja, 227, 255, 272, 279, 299, 325, 350, 470, 625
Kāpālika, 281, 282, 476, 497, 765
Kārikā of Bhartṛhari, 644
Kārikās (of Dhvanikāra), 540-44
Kārpaṇya-pañjikā, 664*
Kārttikeya, xxxii, xxxvii
Kārtyavīryārjuna, 336, 616-17, 629
Kārtyāyanī, 115
Kāśikā, cxiii, cxiv, 178*, 186*, 189*, 336*, 536, 622, 764
Kāśīlakṣmaṇa Kavi, 566
Kāsīnātha, 621*
Kāśīpati Kavirāja, 490
Kāśyapa, xxv
Kāśyapa, a writer of *alaṁkara*, 520, 521
Kāśyapa Gotra, 278
Kātantra or Kātantrika, cii, 93, 252
Kāṭya, xxv,
Kātyavema, 136, 138*, 748*, 750
Kātyāyana, vi, vii, 10*, 11, 93, 200, 514, 519, 535 (Gotra), 733*
Katyāyana Subrahmaṇya, 566
Kātyāynikā, lix
Kāvya, Characteristics vii, viii, xi, xv, xvi, xvii, xviii, vxi, xxvii, xxviii, xxx, xxxii, xxxv, xxxviii, xl, xli, xlvi, xlix, li, lii, lxii, lxiv*, lxxv, lxxviii, lxxix, lxxx, xcix*, cvi, cxx ; Origin and Sources 1-18 ; Environment and characteristics 18-42, 3, 74, 75, 76, 78, 79, 80, 84, 99, 117, 118, 119, 122*, 127*, Sataka and Stotra-kāvya 156-173 ; Mahākāvya 173-94, 316-45 ; Prose 200-39, 429-33 ; 306, 307 ; Historical 345-64 ; Erotic 364-75 ; Devotional, 375-98 ; Didactic and Satiric 194-99, 398-411 ; Anthologies and Women Poets 411-18 ; Campū 433-40 ; Definition, constituents and classification of *Kāvya* as in Alaṁkāra Śāstra 518, 526, 535-37 540*, 544, 559, 562, 563, 572, 574-82, 584, 586, 592*, 593, 609 ; Some earlier Kāvyas 611-13 ; Bhaṭṭikavya and other cognate Caritakāvyas 617*, 621, 623, 625-26 ; Drama and Kāvya 634, 649, 653 ; Khaṇḍa Kāvya or Lyric poetry 658, 664, 665, 667, Historical Kāvya 679*, 680, 687, 690 ; Pañcatantra 700, 701 ; Miscellaneous 730, 761, 767, 700, 773-74
Kāvya-darpaṇa, 556
Kāvyadhvani, 540*
Kāvya-dīpikā, 566
Kāvya-kalāpa, 368*, 372*, 373*
Kāvya-kalpalatā, 28, 331
Kāvyakaraṇa, xviii
Kāvya-karaṇa-grantha, 522
Kāvya-kautuka, 544-45, 548, 599
Kāvyaliṅga (*alaṁkāra*), 534
Kāvyamālā (Series), 170*, 172*, 197*, 256, 271* 332*, 333*. 335*, 336, 338*, 342*, 363*, 364*, 368*-73*, 379*, 384*, 397*, 400*-03*, 406*, 407*, 410*, 487*, 523*, 535*, 536, 557, 558*, 559, 563-66, 616*-21*, 623*. 626*, 629*, 656*-59*, 661*, 662*, 663*, 665*, 668, 674, 688, 751, 775
Kāvya-mīmāṁsā, 7*, 19*, 28*, 29*, 78*, 185, 271*, 381*, 454-55, 525*, 542*, 546-47, 560, 563-64, 685
Kāvya-nāṭakālaṁkāra, 740*
Kāvya-nirṇaya, 550
Kāvya-pradīpa, 758
Kāvya-prakāśa, xvii*, liii, 255*, 439*, 525*, 548, 552, 554, 560, 563-65, 577*, 625, 742*, 762
Kāvyaprakāśa-darpaṇa, 556
Kāvya-prakāśa-dīpikā, 556
Kāvyaprakāśa-nidarśanā, 556
Kāvyaprakāśa-saṁketa, 525*, 548, 555, 558,
Kāvyaprakāsa-saṁketa, of Māṇikyacandra, 558

Kāvyaprakāśa-tilaka, 556
Kāvyaprakāśa-viveka, 556
Kāvyasaṁgraha (Series), 161*, 194*, 338*, 342*, 367*, 368*, 372*, 373*, 659*, 661*, 669*, 674
Kāvyavicāra, 520*, 524, 533*, 602*, 604*
Kāvyādarśa, cxiv, 28*, 94, 203, 207-09, 222, 236, 433, 477*, 521, 525*, 529, 530*, 531, 532*, 533, 553, 564, 577*, 688, 715
Kāvyādarśa (Commentary on *Kāvyaprakāśa*), 556
Kāvyālaṁkāra, (Bhāmaha's) 526, 527, 533; (Rudrat's), 7, 337*, 525*, 536; (Vāmana's) 158*, 188*, 219*, 226*, 242*, 271*, 280*, 646
Kāvyālaṁkāra-sarvasva, 558
Kāvyalaṁkāra-sūtra, 535
Kāvyālaṁkāra-sūtravṛtti, 620*, 714
Kāvyāloka, Same as *Dhvanyāloka*, See *Dhvanyāloka*.
Kāvyānuśāsana, 29*, 67*, 249, 464*, 548, 559, 693 (of Hemacandra): 563 (of Vāgbhaṭa)
Kāvyetihāsa-saṁgraha (Series), 437*, 468*
Kāyastha, 331, 408, 409, 431, 468, 675, 766
K. B. Pathak, 132*, 619*, 620*, 671. See Pathak.
K. Burkhard, 140*
K. C. Chatterjee, 611*, 616*
K. C. Mehendale or Mehendale, 240, 243*,
Kedarnath, 384*, 403*, 435*, 438*, 439*, 485*
Keith, x, xi, cxxiv-cxxvi, 10*, 11*, 26*, 43*, 47*, 50*. 52*, 53*, 77*, 86*, 92*, 94*, 100, 102*, 105*, 123*-25*, 183*, 185*, 192*, 201*, 209*, 218*, 240*, 242*-43, 278*, 299, 301*, 401, 413*, 497*, 508, 509, 616, 619, 631*, 632*, 634-35, 637-42, 644, 654, 666*, 673-75, 676*, 696-97, 740*, 755-58, 760, 761, See A. B. Keith.
Kekaya, 94, 95*
Keliraivata, 687
Kendubilva or Kendulī, 389, 390, 560, 665.
Kerala, 103, 107, 121*, 336, 337, 343*, 369*, 371, 381, 382, 465, 467, 468, 490, 494, 617, 662*, 766, 774
Keralikā, lix.
Keśava, 360
Keśava Bhaṭṭa, 437, 566
Keśavamiśra, 533*, 538, 564
Keśava Narasiṁha, 562
Keśavaditya, 623*
K. F., 757*
K. Florenz, 648
K. G. A. Hoefer, 750*
K. Glaser, 299*
K. G. Sankar, 124*, 731*
K. G. S. Iyer, 612*, 662*
Khaṇḍana-khaṇḍa-khādya, 326, 625, 626
Khaṇḍana-khaṇḍa-khādya, Introduction to the, 626*
Khāndesh, 766
Khāravela, 612
K. H. Dhruva, 262*, 263*, 623*
Khosru-Anoshirwan, 701
Kiel, 140*, 158*, 316*, 424*, 657*
Kielhorn, 5, 11*, 12*, 89*, 178*, 189*, 466*, 480*, 481*, 528*, 611*, 613*, 622*, 630*, 695, 698, 702, 707, 731*, 732*, See F. Kielhorn
Kilpauk, 400*
Kinnara, 993
Kirātārjunīya, of Bhāravi, 178-82, 187, 191, 621-22, 768-69; of Vatsaraja, 473
Kiṣkindhyā, 725
Kiṣorikā (poetess), 477*
Kīcaka, 337, 618
Kīcaka-vadha, 337, 339, 618
Kīrti-kaumudi, 362, 678, 770
Kīrti-lata, 391*
Kīrtimati, 477
Kirtisena, Yādava King, 477
Kīrtivarman, 481
K. K. Handiqui, 325*, 624*, See Handiqui
Klasse, 522*
Kilen, (J. L.) 646, 651*, 763
Klienere Sanskrit-Texte, 72*, 77*
K. L. Pisharoti, 662*
K. L. V. Sastri, 325*
K. Markandeya Sarma, 400*
K. M. Banerji, 381*
K. M. Shembavnekar, 731*
K. Narayanacharya, 487*
K. N. Sane, 435*, 437*
Kohalācarya, 525*
Kokasambhava, 158*, 668
Kolāmbapura, 466
Kolāhalapura, 492
Koṇamukha, 350
Koṇḍaviḍu, 299, 433
Kongl Preuss Turfan Expeditionen, 72*, 77*
Königsberg, 481*, 751*, 752
Koṅkaṇa, 432
Konow, 263*, 277*, 633, 641-42, 710, 750*, 757-58, 760-61. See Sten Konow (q. v.).
Kopakālānala, 768
Koppala, 343*
Korea, cvi
Kosegarten, 705*
Koṭiliṅgapura, 490
Koṭi-vīraha, 371
K. P. Jayaswal, 262*, 477*, 612*. See Jayaswal.
K. P. Parab, 119*, 121*, 126*, 131*, 136*, 140*, 169*, 178*, 226*, 229*, 239*, 256*, 271*, 277*, 316*, 319*, 322*, 323*,-25* 331*, 332*, 334*, 336*, 337*, 340*, 341*, 345*, 370*, 371*, 397*, 403*, 405*, 430*, 437*, 439*, 449*, 457*, 462*, 464*, 467*, 468*, 471*, 479*, 486*, 489*, 490*, 496*, 621*, 656*, 751*, 759, 762, 763
K. P. Trivedi, or Trivedi, 183*, 528*, 529*, 530, 567-62, 675
Krakau, 124*
Kramadīśvara, 615
K. Rāmavarmarāja, 647
Kressier. See Oscar Kressler
Krishnaji Ganapat Press, 437*
Krishna Sastri Gurjara Press, 469*
Krishnath Nyayapanchanan, 256*
Kriyā-kairava-candrikā, 730*

K. R. Modgarkar, 762
K. Roy, 753
K. R. Pisharoti, 102*, 137*, 381*
Kṛśāṇu (Gandharva), 439
Kṛśāśva, 52*, 523, 635, 637, 630
Kṛṣṇa, 8, 40, 49, 50, 101, 112, 115, 167, 189, 190, 193, 273, 275, 332, 333, 338, 341, 342. 372*, 373*, 374, 382, 383, 384, 385, 386, 387, 390, 391, 392, 393, 396, 397, 415, 426, 437, 440, 466, 467, 468, 474. 485, 487, 490, 510. 511, 617, 619, 630, 636, 639, 640, 644*, 647. 648, 659, 663, 664, 666, 667, 678, 719, 725, 752. 766, 770, 772
Kṛṣṇa, author of *Bharata-carita*, 630*, 775
Kṛṣṇa, author of *Sāhitya-taraṅgiṇī*, 566
Kṛṣṇa-bāla-carita, 663
Kṛṣṇā-bhakti candrikā, 468
Kṛṣṇa-bhaṭṭa, 566, 740*, 752
Kṛṣṇa-bhāvanāmṛta, 333*, 398
Kṛṣṇa-candra, 621, 680
Kṛṣṇacandra Tarkālaṁkāra, 374*
Kṛṣṇadatta, 480*, 666*
Kṛṣṇadatta, commentator, 392*
Kṛṣṇadāsa, commentator of *Meghadūta*, 751*
Kṛṣṇadasa Kavirāja, 333, 386*, 398, 662*, 755*
Kṛṣṇa Dīkṣita 566
Kṛṣṇa-karṇāmṛta, 386-88, 662
Kṛṣṇa-karṇāmṛta-mahārṇava, 662*, 663*
Kṛṣṇakānta Tarkavāgīśa, 533*
Kṛṣṇa, king of Dāhala, 350
Kṛṣṇa-kutūhala-nāṭaka, 664*
Kṛṣṇalīlā, 338
Kṛṣṇalīlāmṛta, same as *Kṛṣṇa-karṇāmṛta*
Kṛṣṇa-līlāśuka. See Līlāśuka
Kṛṣṇalīlā-taraṅgiṇī, 396
Kṛśṇamācārya, 617*, 661, 691*, 729*
Kṛṣṇamiśra, 77, 448, 480-84, 487
Kṛṣṇamitrācārya, 741*
Kṛṣṇanātha-pañcānana, 748*
Kṛṣṇanātha Sārvabhauma Bhaṭṭācārya, 505
Kṛṣṇapati Śarman, 741*
Kṛṣṇa, poet, 369, 43
Kṛṣṇarāja III, 336, 616, 617
Kṛṣṇa Rao Joglekar, 759
Kṛṣṇa, Rāṣṭrakūṭa king, 435
Kṛṣṇa Śarman, same as Kṛṣṇa, poet, 566
Kṛṣṇa Sārvabhauma, 373*
Kṛṣṇasiṁha, 770
Kṛṣṇa-stotra, 386*
Kṛṣṇasvāmī Aiyenger, 695*
Kṛṣṇavallabhā, 662*
Kṛṣṇayajvan, 765
Kṛṣṇa, Yādava king, 414
Kṛṣṇa-yātrā, 393, 510
Kṛṣṇāhnika-kaumudī, 333*, 397, 398*, 663
Kṛṣṇānanda, 331, 626
Kṛṣṇānandinī, *Tippanī*, 556
Kṛṣṇilaka, Śreṣṭhiputra, 252
Kṛtyārāvaṇa, 301, 686
Kṣaharāṭa, ci
K. Sambasiva Sastri, 479*, 774-75
Kṣapaṇaka (lexicographer), 5*, 729, 730
Kṣatra-cūḍāmaṇi, 344, 438*
Kṣatrapa, 6, 94, 106*, 654
K. Schönfeld, 401*, 674
Kṣemaṁkara Muni, 424
Kṣemarāja, 381*, 382, 659*, 661*
Kṣemasiṁha, 751*
Kṣemendra, cvi 9, 19*, 29*, 89, 90, 96, 98, 99, 119*, 120, 166*, 186*, 199, 230*, 249, 265*, 280, 299*, 320, 321*, 324, 325, 336, 355, 401*, 404-10, 421, 422*, 423, 461, 465, 471, 531*, 535*, 542, 548, 552, 554, 604 617, 618*, 621, 674-76, 688-92, 696*, 698, 699, 705, 755, 759, 762
Kṣemīśvara, 448, 465*, 469-70
Kshetresh Chattopadhyaya, 124*, 731
Kṣitīśa-vaṁśāvalī-carita, 679
Kṣīrasvāmin, 302
K. S. Ramaswami Sastri, 324*
K. Srinivasacharya, 487*
K. St. J. M. de Vreese, 355*
K. Th. Preuss, 648
K. T. Telang, 161*, 262*, 299*, 326*
Kubera, 225, 467, 521
Kuberadatta, 251
Kucamāra, 521
Kucha, cxv
Kuhns Zeitschrift für vergla Sprach, 756*
Kukkuṭakroḍa, 298
Kulaśekhara of Kerala, lxxviii, 121*, 337, 338*, 381, 465, 467*, 662
Kulapatyaṅka, 300
Kumāra, 127, 659*, 664, 741
Kumārabhaṭṭa, same as Kumāradāsa (q. v.) 185
Kumāradatta, iix
Kumāradāsa, cxv, 19*, 127*, 156, 175, 177, 185-88, 239, 305, 621, 728, 764
Kumāradāsa and his place in Skt. Lit., 185* 621*
Kumāradevī, Licchavi Princess, cvii
Kumāradhātusena, 185
Kumāragiri-rājīya, 748*
Kumāragupta, cx, 738
Kumārajīva, 69*, 72
Kumāralāta xviii, 15, 72, 73*, 79, 82
Kumāramaṇi, 186*
Kumārapāla of Anhilvād, 343, 361-62, 428, 463*, 467, 484, 485, 503, 678, 767-68,
Kumārapāla-carita, of Hemacandra 336, 361-62, 617, 767 ; of Jayasiṁha Sūri 362* ; of Cāritrasundara 362*, 767
Kumārapāla-prabandha, 767
Kumārapāla-pratibodha, 362*, 768
Kumāra-sambhava, xxi, xxxvii, lxxx, cv, cxiv, 23, 105*, 123*, 125*, 126-28, 150, 167, 187, 299, 383, 533, 706, 728*, 738*, 740-43, 754
Kumāra (Someśvara's father), 332
Kumāra-svāmī, 557, 563, 628
Kumāra-tātācārya, 765
Kumārila, xxv, xxxv, 278*, 765
Kumbha, 388*, 190*, 666*
Kumbha, author of *Rasaratna-kośa*, 566
Kumbhakarna mahendra, 666*
Kumbkakonam, 487*
Kumbha-Nikumbha, 324
Kumudānanda, 616*
Kumudikā, story of, 244*,
Kumudvatī, 746

Kundadantī (metre), 13
Kundamālā 53*, 464
Kundaprabandha, 740*
Kuṇḍina (in Mahārāṣṭra) 450
Kunnamkulam, 338*
Kuntaka, 120*, 249, 300, 301, 302, 369*, 401* 542, 548-50, 775-76, 583, 584, 587-92
Kuntala, 119*, 298, 368
Kuppusvami Sastri, 301*, 302*,
Kuraṅgī, (story of), 477*, 715
Kuravirāma, 551
Kuru, 112, 113, 466
Kurukṣetra, 725
Kürzefre Textf rm 140*
Kuśa, 51, 635, 746
Kuśa Dynasty, 80
Kuśa-kumudvatī-nāṭaka, 765
Kuśalakavi, 730
Kuṣāṇa, ci, 5, 43, 80, 655, 736
Kuśīlava, 51, 635, 645, 647, 650
Kusumadeva, 203
Kusumalatāvellita, (metre) 14*,
Kusumapura, 218, 251
Kusuma-sékhara, 687
Kusuma-śekhara-vijaya, 687
Kuṭilā (metre), 181*
Kuṭṭanī-mata, xxxiii, 197, 198, 199, 251, 256, 407, 525, 675
Kutubuddin Ibak, 768
Kuvalayavati, 373*
Kuvalayā (dancing girl), 654
Kuvalayananda, 557, 564, 565
Kuvalyāśva-carita, 564
Kuvalayāśva (legend of), 471
Kuvera, 749
Kūrma, 325*
K. Viraraghava Tatacarya, 487*
K. V. Krishnamachariar or Krishnamachariar, 132*, 222*

L

Lachmīdhar, 729*
Lacote, 89*, 92*, 94*, 95*, 96*, 97*, (F. Lacote) 99*, 110*, 201*, 689, 691, 692, 696, 756*. See C. Lacote.
Laghu-cāṇakya, 196, 673. See Cāṇakya
Laghu-dīpikā, 207*
Laghu-jātaka, 743*
Laghūs tava, 740*,
Laghuddyota, 556
Laharīs, five, (*Amṛta-*, *Sudhā-*, *Gaṅgā-*, *Ka uṇā-*, and *Lakṣmī*)- of Jagannātha, 383, 665
Lahore, 8 , 138*, 320*, 325*, 355, 417*, 467*, 496*, 498*
Lakṣmaṇa, 154, 292, 300*, 451*, 456*, 465
Lakṣmaṇa Ācārya, 384, 665
Lakṣmaṇabhaṭṭa, 437, 666*
Lakṣmaṇabhaṭṭa Aṇkolakara, 415
Lakṣmaṇaguru, 545
Lakṣmaṇamāṇikya, 499
Lakṣmaṇa Paṇḍita, 619*
Lakṣmaṇa Śāstrī Drāviḍa, 626*
Lakṣmaṇasena of Bengal, 371, 373*, 390, 413 428, 429, 751
Lakṣmaṇa Sūri, 340*, 666*
Lakṣmī, 383*, 473
Lakṣmīdāsa, 752
Lakṣmīdhara, 316, 414, 561*, 623
Lakṣmīlaharī, 383, 665
Lakṣmī (mother of Jagannātha Tailaṅga), 371, 469
Lakṣmī (mother of Someśvara), 332
Lakṣmī (mother of Śrīnivāsa Atirātrayājin), 486*,. See Śrīnivāsa Atīrātrayājin.
Lakṣmīnātha Bhaṭṭa, 553
Lakṣhmīnātha Śarmā, 623*
Lakṣmīnārāvana Nyāyālaṁkāra, 707
Lakṣmīnivāsa, 751*
Lakṣmī, woman poet, 416*
Lalita-mādhava, 468
Lalita-ratnamālā, 471
Lalitaśūradeva, lxxx
Lalita-vista a, 52*, 83, 345, 522, 614, 654, 655
Lalitāditya of Kashmir, 279
Lallā Dīkṣita, 239*, 758
La Metrica degli. Indi, 192
Lancereau, 707
Langles, 704*, 707
Laṅkā, 131, 183, 286, 463, 464, 502, 504
Laṇkāvatāra, cvi
Lanman, 298*
La Rhetotique Sanskrite 520*, 522*
L' Art poetıque de l' Inde, 122*
Lassen, 5,. 388*, 393, 497*, 666*, 667, 688, 704*. See C. Lassen.
La suite des Indies dans les, 612 -13*
Laṭaka—melaka, 494, 496-97
Latin, v, xi, xii, 12*, 122*, 126*, 129*, 138* 161*, 741*, 743,
Laukika-nyāya-saṁgraha, 698
Lava, 289, 635
Lavaṇasiṁha, 363
Lavaṇaprasāda, 428, 678
Law, xxiv, 26*, 72, 242*, 632, 734, 735
Lāsya, 50, 66*.
Lāṭa, 432, 766
Lāṭānuprāsa, 557
Lāṭī (rīti), 537
L. B. Gandhi, 201*
L. Cheikho, 89*
L. D. Barnett, 102*, 185*, 254*, 467*, See Barnett
L. de la Vallee Poussin, 72*, 79*, 613*, 614*
Lear, King, xlviii, 447
Leiden, 79 , 258*, 355 , 614*
Legal literature, lxi, lxiii, lxxiii, xciii, xciv.
Legend or Legendary, xxxiv, xxxv, xli, lxxxiv, lxxxv, xc, ciii, 3, 4*, 5, 22, 26*, 28, 44, 49, 50, 55, 60, 65, 69, 72, 73, 74, 75, 80, 82, 83, 84, 85, 93, 94, 97, 98, 101, 107*, 110, 111, 115, 116, 119, 124, 128, 129, 130, 138, 140, 148, 150, 151, 161, 168, 169, 172, 185 189, 206, 210*, 219, 226*, 240, 241, 244, 256, 257, 258, 272, 289, 290, 324, 342, 343, 344, 356, 357, 368, 376, 378, 387, 389, 402, 406, 438, 439, 442, 624, 626, 627, 629, 630*, 640-42, 649*, 658*, 666, 680, 689, 692, 695, 719, 738*

Legend of Jīmūtavāhana, The, 674*,
Legends of the Punjab, 649*
Leipzig, 44*, 45*, 77*, 89*, 90*, 96*, 103*, 122*, 138*, 140*, 189*, 196*, 197*, 207*, 209*, 256*, 262*, 271*, 277*, 298*, 391*, 401*, 404*, 421*, 422*, 424*, 426*, 427*, 469*, 472*, 480*, 498*, 506, 510, 533 , 646, 649*, 650*, 674*, 700*, 708*, 756*, 762.
Leipzig Catalogue, 162*,
Le Museon, 615
Leo Von Mankowski, 89*
Le Pancatantra ou les cinq ruses, 704
Leśa (*alaṁkāra*) 526, 563
Les fleurs de Rhetorique dans l' Inde, 611*
Less Litteratures de l' Inde, x, 136*
Lesny, 719*. See V. Lesny
Le Theatre Indien, 631, 646
Letto-Slavic, vi
Leumann, 186*. See E. Leumann
Leuven, 225*
Lévi, 48*, 51*, 52*, 53*, 79*, 217*, 406*, 421*, 497*, 501*, 504*, 522, 551, 617*, 631, 635*, 650*, 654*, 655*, 695*, 696*, 761. See Lévy
Lexicography, lexicon, or lexicographer, 26*, 107*, 170, 187, 192, 204, 310, 323*, 340*, 337*, 430*, 539, 545, 617, 730, 740*
L. Feer, 81*, 82*
L. Fritze, 138*, 262*, 277*, 469* 702-3, 704*, 706, 750*, 751*, 756*, 760, 763. See Fritze
L. Heller or Heller, 336*, 617*
L. H. Gray, 141*, 161*, 165*, 201*, 211*, 217*, 218*, 219*, 220*, 223*, 230*, 232*, 242*, 243*, 257*, 457*, 479*, 502. See Gray
Licchavi, cvii, 477
Liebich, 656*
Lindeneau, Dr., 654*, 710, 719*, 720*. See Maxa Lindeneau
Lingānuśāsana, ascribed to Vararuci, 11*
Lingua franca, ix
Linguistic Survey, 94*
Lit. d. alten Indien 87*, 165*
Literary History of India, x
Literaturblatt für orientalische Philologie, 657*
Literature of the Śvetāmbaras of Gujarat, 426*
Līlā-madhukara, 490*
Līlāśuka or Bilvamaṅgala, 386-88, 389, 391, 392, 396-7, 662-3
Līlāvati, 20, 342*
Lobedanz, 750*
Locana (on *Dhvanyāloka*), cxv, 301*, 369*, 527, 540, 541*, 542, 543*, 544, 545, 548, 560, 583
Locana-vyākhyāna-kaumudī, 546
Logic or logician, xxvi, 26, 165, 278, 326, 462, 554
Lohara, dynasty, 356
Lokanātha, 331
Lokānanda-nāṭaka, cxiii, 81*, 119, 622*, 656
Lokeśvara-śataka , 378, 384*
Lokokti-muktāvalī, 403
Lolimbarāja, 332, 617
Lollaṭa, 523
London, 4*, 119*, 126*, 129*, 140*, 161*, 207*, 226*, 229*, 256*, 277*, 368*, 380*, 389*, 649*, 653*, 696*, 741*, 744*, 759
Lopāmudrā, 631
L. Oster, 429*
Louvain, 173*
Love and Marriage in modern and ancieut India, 747
Love-drama, love-poetry or love-story, 136, 156-57, 161, 201*, 244, 280, 302, 319, 364, 365, 367, 391
L R. Vaidya, 272*, 372*, 565
L. Sarup, 101*, 467*
Lüders, 11*, 48, 76*, 77*, 504, 612*, 613*, 637, 642, 644*, 653*, 654*,. See H. Lüders
Luptopamā, 518
L. Von Schroeder, x, 44* 647, 648
Lyly and his *Eupheus*, 223
Lyric or lyrical, xxxviii, lxxv, xcix, 2*, 3, 4, 12, 13, 33, 38, 52, 57, 58, 132, 134, 135, 139, 147 (Drama), 150, 157 (on Love), 159, 181, 184*, 192, 194, 297, 302, 314, 332, 366, (on Love), 387, 390, 393, (Drama) 441, 442, 445, 510, 612 629 (on Love), 646, 656, 659, 665, 667 (on Love), 751

M

Macaultiffe, 666*
Macbeth, 141*
Macdonell, x, 635*, 657*
Madana, xxi, 742
Madanadeva, king, 370
Madana, king, 93
Madanakīrti, Digambara, 429
Madanamañjarī 280*, 497
Madanamañjukā, 97, 98, 100, 244*
Madanapāla of Bengal, 339
Madana, poet, 338, 770 ; of Gauḍa 472
Madanapura, 768
Madana-senikā (courtesan), 251
Madanavarman, king, 429, 768*
Madanābhirāma, king, 368* 658*
Madan Mohan Tarkalamkar, 210*
Madayantikā, 281, 282, 284
Madālasā-campū, 435*
Madhukara, lix
Madhumati (commentary), 556
Madhuravāṇī, poetess, 630
Madhurā-vijaya, 361, 418, 663
Madhusudan Das, 440*
Madhusūdana, commentator, 169*
Madhusūdana Kaul, 408*
Madhusūdana, redactor, 506
Madhusūdana Sarasvatī, 382, 660*, 664
Madhusūdana Kavi, 674
Madhyama, 101, 709, 720, 722
Madiravatī, 280*
Madras 185*, 186*, 207*, 211*, 246*, 271*, 277*, 298*, 300*, 301*, 302*, 320*, 332*, 333*, 338*, 345*, 380*, 396*, 414*, 415*, 417*, 429*, 432*, 437*, 476*, 494*, 529*, 560, 561*, 660*, 753
Madras Government Oriental Manuscript Library, 377*

Madura, 334, 361, 383, 400, 418, 679, 773
Magadha, cxii, 568, 684, 727
Magic, 26*, 28*, 46, 85, 100, 115*, 138, 141*, 179, 205, 212, 213, 214, 220, 234, 260*, 280*, 298, 303, 346, 419, 422, 463, 472, 491, 745
Mahābhārata, vii, xiv, xvii, xxiii, xxix, xxxiii, xxxvii, xlix, lii, lxii, lxxviii, lxxix, lxxxvii*, xcvi*, xcviii, cxxix, 1, 2, 4, 47, 60*, 101, 108, 112, 128*, 133*, 140, 141*, 170, 173*, 177, 178, 189, 195, 200*, 272, 299, 326, 327, 331, 332, 337, 341, 356, 457, 465, 568, 608, 618, 620-22, 624. 634, 635*, 642*, 653, 673, 680, 681, 687-89, 673, 695, 697, 719, 720, 722, 739*, 747, 748
Māhabhārata-mañjari, 325*
Mahābhāsya, viii, cxxi, 5*, 10, 48, 51, 350, 512, 516, 519, 530*, 532*, 568, 611, 635, 641, 643, 644, 653, 671, 672, 697, 738, 761
Mahādeva (author), 464, 465
Mahādeva, author of *Rasodadhi*, 561*, 629
Mahādeva, commentator of *Kādambarī*, 756*
Mahādeva, father of the author of Candrāloka, 560
Mahādeva, Jayadeva's father, 389*, 462
Mahādeva Vidyāvagīśa, 624*
Mahākavi, 69, 278, 454
Mahākāla, 279
Mahākāvya, lxxviii, 7, 73, 129, 156, 167 ; from Bhāravi to Māgha 173-94, 305 ; Later 316-45 ; 364, 366, 430, 539, 559, 563, 593, 616, 620, 686, 765, 770, 772. See Kāvya
Mahākṣatrapa, 14
Mahāmātra, 251
Mahānaṭaka, 444, 449*, 465*, 501, 502*, 503, 504, 505-10
Mahāpadma, 655
Mahāpātra, 331
Mahārāja-kaṇikā-lekhā, 80, 614*
Mahārāṣtra or Maratha, 415, 439*, 450, 547, 629, 684
Mahārāṣṭrī or Maratri, ix, x cxx, 243*, 261*, 270*, 424, 684, 705, 707
Mahāsattva Candradāsa, 656
Mahāsāghika, 69, 685
Mahāsena Pradyota, 111
Mahāśvetā, 230. 231, 233, 235
Mahā-ummaga Jātaka, 369*
Mahāvagga, 75, 77
Mahāvastu, 83, 614
Mahāvādin, 69
Mahāvibhāṣa, cv
Mahāvidyā, 648*
Mahāvīra, ix, 612
Mahāvīra-carita, 277, 278*, 280*, 289*, 285-88, 297*, 449, 452, 502, 763
Mahāvrata ceremony, 45, 46, 533*, 635*, 640
Mahāyāna, civ, cvi, cxi, cxii, cxvi, 70*, 71, 72, 79, 82, 377, 379
Mahāyāna-bhūmiguhyavācamūla-śāstra, 614*
Mahāyāna-sraddhotpāda-śāstra, 71
Mahāyāna-sūrālaṅkāra, cv
Mahāyāntrika, 498
Mahendrapāla, cxvii, 454, 455, 547*
Mahendravikrama, cxiii, 239, 254, 494, 765
Mahendita, 753
Maheśvara, 535*, 555
Maheśvara Nāyālaṁkāra, 556
Maheśvara Pañcānana, 623*
Maheśvarapaṇḍita, 658
Mahilāpattana, 368*, 658*, 660*, 661*
Mahilārophya, 88
Mahima Bhaṭṭa, 524, 530*, 542, 550-52, 555, 608
Mahima-siṁhagaṇi, 751*
Mahimnaḥ-stotraṭikā, 664*
Mahiṣamardinī, 659
Mahīpāla, 345
Mahīpāla Bhuvanaikamalla of Kānyaāubja or Mahodaya, 454, 455, 470
Mahīpāla-carita, 345
Mahīpāla II of Bengal, 339, 470
Mahīpāla, King, 547*
Mahodaya, 454. See Mahīpāla Bhuvanikamalla
Maithila or Maithili, 121*, 393, 426, 486, 497, 511
Maithilī-kalyāṇa, 497*
Maitreya, 246
Majumdar, 755*
Makaranda, 220, 281-85
Malabar, ciii, cxi, 338*, 476, 647, 752*, 774
Maladhārin Devaprabha Sūri, 332
Malaya bill, 373*, 773
Malayaketu, 263*, 266-68
Malay Archipelago, cvi
Malayavati, 259
Malayavāhana, King, 432
Malayālam, 104, 105, 108, 185*, 371, 704*, 776
Malayālam Journal, 102*
Malay Magic, 648
Mallarāja, 566
Mallācārya, 331
Malleśvaram, 417*
Mallikā, daughter of Vidyādhara King 298
Mallikā-makaranda, 475, 686, 769
Mallikā-māruta, 289, 474, 686
Mallinātha, 122, 126, 129*, 132*, 178*, 183*, 189, 325*, 558*, 561, 562, 614, 622*, 623*, 624*, 656, 657, 741, 742*, 743, 751*, 775
Malva, 729*
Mammaṭa, xx, zl, liii, lxiv, 169*, 179* 197, 255*, 325*, 401*, 439*, 516, 531*, 534*, 538, 552, 555-57, 562, 570-79, 596, 600, 625, 675, 742*, 758
Manalikkara Maṭham, 711
Maṇḍaleśvara Bhaṭṭa, 467
Mandara, Mount, 319
Mandasor, 18, 123, 183, 616, 732*, 752*
Mandākinī, female magician, 298
Mandākrāntā (metre), 9*, 12, 121*, 132, 150, 151, 159*, 184*, 196*, 285*, 329, 372, 382
Mandaraka, lix
Mandāra-makaranda-campū, 431, 566
Mandārika, 231
Mandodarī, 303, 502
M. Anesaki, 70*, 71*
Maṅgala, 525*

Mańgla-śloka, 711, 720
Mańgalāṣṭaka, 740*, 752*
Mangalodaya Press, 129*
Manickchand Jain, 706-7
Maṇidīpa-mahākāruṇika-devapañca-stotra, 614*
Maṇiguptaka, 491*
Manikacandra Digambara Granthamālā, 467*
Maṇikarṇikā, Princess, 212
Maṇikarṇilkāṣṭak , 661*
Maṇirāma, 122*
Maṇitāra, Town, 226
Mañijarī (dancing girl), 198, 676
Mañjarī (metre), 12
Mañju-bhāṣiṇī, 772*
Mañjubhaṣinī (metre), 13, 285
Mankad, 67*. See D. R. Mankad
Mańkha or Mańkhaka, 19, 120*, 322-23, 350*, 360, 382*, 449, 557, 558, 627, 628, 761
Mańkha-koṣa, 323*
Mańkowski, 218*, 691*, 700*, 755
Manmatha, Mańkhaka's grandfather, 322
Manmatha-mohana, 469*
Manodūta, of Vrajanātha 327, 374*, 752; of Viṣṇudāsa 372*, 374*, 752
Monohara Śarmā, 622
Monomohan Chakravarti, 389*, 413*
Manoramā, 301*
Manoramā, 565 (of Bhaṭṭojī Dīkṣita): 751* (of Kavicandra)
Monoramā-kuca-mardana, 565
Monoramā-vatsarāja, 301*, 686
Manorathagupta, 544
Mohoratha, poet, 540*, 543, 544, 686*
Mantharā, 287, 303, 451, 465
Mantra, xxiv
Mantragupta, 212, 213
Manu. xiii, xxv, xxvi, xxix, xxxvi, cx, 72, 105, 705, 719, 733, 734
Marawa, 773
Marīci, ascetic 211
Mark Collins, 248*, 209*
Marly, liv
Marmaprakāśa, 565
Marriage, xiii, lxxii, 22, 97, 168, 187, 252, 259, 280*, 281, 283, 285, 286, 290, 291, 292, 302, 327, 331, 332, 333, 341, 351, 454, 458, 471, 497, 633
Marwar, 647
Marx, xciv
M. A. Stein, 353*
Mata (*alamkara*), 538, 653
Matańga, 525*
Match-maker, 272, 281*
Materialien zur kenntnis des apabhraṁśa, 750*
Meteriaux pour servir ā l'historic de la déesse Buddhique Tārā 378*
Mathuraprasad Misra, 196*
Mathurā, cii. 49, 81*, 93, 350, 373*, 659*
Mathurādāsā. Kāyastha, 468
Mathurā-mahimā, 664*
Mathurānātha Śukla, 564, 624*
Mathurā-vijaya, 679
Maticitragīti, 613*
Matsya-purāṇa, 138*, 750
Mattamayūrā (metre), 181*
Matta-vilāsa cxiii, 104*, 254-55, 487, 494, 765
Maudgalāyana (Kumāradāsa's father), 185
Maudgalya. xxv, 449
Maudgalyāyana, 77*, 655
Maukhari, 227, 263
Maurya, lviii, lxi, lxxiv, lxxvii, xciv, xcv, c, cxvii, 262, 265*, 266, 268, 722, 734, 735
Max Lindenau, 53*, 103*, 708*
Max Müller, xxvii, 4-6, 171*, 539*, 612*, 630, 671, 704*, 706, 751*
Maypole ceremony, 50
Mayūkha, xxvi
Mayūra, 121*, 155, 1 8*, 166, 167, 168, 169*, 170, 171, 172, 239, 378, 538
Mayūra-citraka, 730*
Mayūragiri, 361, 679, 772
Mayūraka lix, 168*
Mayūrāṣṭaka, 168, 659
Mādhava, 336
Mādhava, author of *Bhānubhāva-prakāśinī*, 561*
Mādhava, author of *Uddhava-dūta*, 752
Mādhava, author of *Vīra-bhānudaya*, 379
Mādhava Bhaṭṭa, probable name of Kavirāja, 340, 620
Mādhava Bhaṭṭa, 467
Mādhava Bhaṭṭa, Viśvanātha Bhaṭṭa's father, 473*
Mādhava-campū, 439*
Mādhava, commentator, 622*
Mādhava Ācārya, commentator of *Parāśara Smṛti*, xcviii, 662*, 762
Mādhava in *Mālatīmādhava* 281-83, 285, 288
Mādhava Paṇḍita, 767
Mādhava, Śakalyamalla's father, 331
Mādhava Śarman, 373*
Mādhavānala-kathā, 424*
Mādhurī, 666*
Mādhurya, xv, 522, 526, 528, 563, 572, 573, 575, 576*, 578, 592
Mādhyamika, 71
Māgadhī (*bhāṣa*), 537, 553, 568
Māgadhī (Prakrit), ix, 270*, 276*, 684
Māgha, xvi, cxiv, 23, 155, 156, 173, 174, 175, 177, 179, 188-94, 223, 239, 305, 306, 315, 316, 319, 321, 325, 334, 344, 429, 528, 538, 553, 578*, 661-23, 656*, 704*, 706, 764
Māghatattva-samuccaya, 623*
Māhārāṣṭrī (Prakrit), 13, 243*, 261*, 270*. See Mahārāṣṭrī
Māhiṣmatī, 450
Mālatī, commentary, 751*
Mālatī, courtesan, 197, 676
Mālatī in *Mālatī-mādhava*, 281-83, 285
Mālatī-mādhava, 53*, 219*, 244*, 277, 278, 280-85, 287, 297*, 298, 452, 474-75, 553*, 588*, 763
Mālatī (metre), 12
Mālava or Malwa, cviii, cxii, 227, 539, 626 736, 755
Mālavarudra, 525*, 531*
Mālavikā, xxxi, 137, 638

Mālavikāgnimitra, xxxi, xxxvi, c, 16, 53*, 136-38, 143, 257, 260*, 288, 638, 641, 708, 712, 740, 750, 759
Mālā (metre), 12
Malinī (metre), 14*, 77*, 159*, 173, 196*, 285*, 373
Mālayabhāra (metre), 285*
Mālyavat, 286-88, 449, 451, 456
Mānameyodaya, 774
Māna-mudrā-bhañjana, 769
Mānatuṅga, 172, 379
Mānavadurga, 773
Mānavikrama, 298*
Mānavīya Dharmaśāstra. See *Manu*
Mānāṅka, 338, 666*
Māṇīkkavachahara ciii
Māṇikyacandra, 525*, 547-49, 558, 564
Māṇikya Sūri, 343
Māṇikya-vallikā, 687
Māra, 19, 20, 73, 74, 345, 655
Mārijjanā, 533*
Mārīca xxxvi
Mārīca-vañcita, 687
Mārkaṇḍeya, Kavīndra, 684
Markaṇḍeya (Prakrit Grammar), 95*
Mārtaṇḍavarman, king, 479*, 779
Mārula, woman poet, 417*
Māruta, Kuntala prince, 298
Mātaṅga-Divākara, 171
Mātrarāja 686
Mātṛceṭa, xvii, cv, 15, 79-80, 613, 614*
Mātṛcitra, 80
Mātṛgupta, 5*, 119, 120, 523*, 525*
Mātṛsena, lviii
Māyā-puṣpaka, 301, 686
Māyurāja, 298, 300, 686
M. Bloomfield, 28*, 212*, 250*, 254 See Bloomfield
M. B. Emeneau, 404*, 421*
M. B. Srinivasa Iyengar, 662*
M. Chakravarty, 666*, 738*
M. Dillor, 299*
Medhātithi, xcvii, xcviii, 105, 719
Medhāvin, cxiv, 520, 525, 527, 532*
Medhāvirudra, 525*, 685
Medinī, 721*
Megasthenes, xcv
Meghadūta, xxxvii, cii, cxxvi, 40, 120, 123, 124*, 125*, 131, 132-34, 150, 151, 156, 157, 364, 372, 374*, 396, 528, 553*, 656, 657, 695, 728*, 729, 750, 752
Meghadūta-samasyā-lekha, 374*
Megha-dutārtha-muktavali, 751*
Meghadūtāvacuri, 751*
Megha-latā, 751*
Meghaprabhācārya, 503, 642, 769
Meghavarṇa, cviii
Meghavijaya, 375*, 703
Mekhalā, 459
Mélanges Lévi, 92, 694*, 756*
Melodrama or melodramatic, 55, 111, 115, 116, 139, 141, 259*, 260, 282, 284, 301, 393, 395, 510
Memoires de I' Academie imp, des Sciences de St. Petersburg, 629*
Menakā, xxxi, 748
Menakā-nahuṣa, 687
Meṇṭha or Bhartṛmeṇṭha, lvii, cxvi, 120, 685,
Meṇṭharāja, 685
Mepputtura, Illam, 774
Merchant of Venice, 33*
Meru, Mount, 452,
Merutuṅga, 189*, 428, 340*, 751*
Meruvijaya-gaṇi, 344*,
Metaphor, 2, 34, 35, 39, 123, 151, 169*, 191, 195, 233, 329
Metre, cxxv, cxxxi, 2, 9, 11, 12, 13, 14, 17, 20, 26*, 42, 52, 71, 75, 77, 83, 94, 95, 107*, 120, 121, 125*, 131, 132, 134, 150, 151, 158*, 159, 165*, 167, 168, 169, 170, 171, 172, 173, 174, 180, 181, 184*, 187, 190, 192, 194, 195, 196, 201, 202, 203, 204, 211*, 219*, 225, 226, 243, 255*, 261*, 270, 276, 385*, 308, 317, 320, 323, 327, 329, 333, 387, 359, 363, 366, 368, 378, 380, 390, 394, 397, 510, 524*, 659, 660
Metres of Bhartṛhari, The, 165*
Mesopotamia, civ
Mewar, 363
Mexican, 648
Meyer, 209*,
M. Garcin de Tassy, 666
M. Ghosh or Manomohan Ghosh, 12 , 444*, 454*, 457*
M. Haberlandt, 700*. See Haberlandt
Mihirakula, cxii, cxiii, 356
Milan, 760
Mildred C. Tawney, 47*, See Tawney
Milindapañho, 254*
Milton 173, 298*
Minader, c, cii, ciii
Minor Poems of Nīlakaṇṭha Dīkṣita, 403*
Minor Works of Śaṅkarācārya, 661*,
Miracle, 81, 114, 172, 229, 321, 346, 357
Mirzapore, 196*,
Miśra (alaṁkara), 652
Miśra (Kāvya), 539, 563
Mitākśara, xxxiv, xxvi, 553, 733*
Mithilā, 186, 389, 392 , 396*, 403, 426*, 451, 462, 479*, 497. See Maithila
Mithradates, cii
Mithyājñāna-khaṇḍana, 769
Mitragupt, 212
Mitramiśra, 773, 774
Mitra (R. L.), 374*, See Rajendralal Mitra
Mitrananda, 475
Mitteilungen d r Anthropology. Ges in Wien, 648
Mīmaṁsā, xxiii, 276, 516
Mīṇākṣī, 313
M Krishnamacharier, 375*
Mleccha, cxxii, 2,622, 263*, 266, 478
M. L. Ettinghausen, 173*
MM. Sastri, 522, 523*, 524*. See Haraprasad Sastri.
M. N. Dutta, 539*
Modern Review, 373*, 618*
Modern Vernaculara Lit. of Hindustan, 389*, 422*
Moḍha family, 484
Moha-mudgara, 194, 380
Mohana-dāsa, 506*

Moha-parājaya, 362*, 484, 769
Monastery, cviii, 228, 656
Monatsberichte der akademie der Wissenschaften zu Berlin 732*, 750*
Monatsber. d. kgl. preuss Akad zu Berlin, 138*,
Monier Williams, 138*, 140
Monk, cvii, cix, 75, 78, 81*, 211, 214, 254, 321, 343, 345, 404, 497
Monody, 132, 157
Monologue Play, 10*, 66, 156, 248, 250, 631
Moral or morality, xlviii, 1, lxxv, lxxxix, lxxx, xci, xcvii, 214, 609. See Didactic
Morgenstierne, 107-8*, 109
Morikā, woman poet, 417*
Mount Abu, 374*, 466*
Mṛcchakaṭika, xxxiii, xlvii, lxiv, lxxxiii, lxxxvi, 53*, 58, 60, 78, 100, 107, 108, 109*, 209*, 211*, 213, 239-48, 252-53, 264, 269, 270*, 291, 443, 479, 530*, 641, 716, 727, 756-58, 761
Mṛdaṅga, 643
Mṛdaṅga-vāsulaka, 252
Mṛgarāja-lakṣman, title of Bhaṭṭa Nārāyaṇa, 272
Mṛgavatī-caritra, 345
Mṛgāṅkadatta, 98
Mṛgāṅka-lekhā, 473
Mṛgāṅkāvatī, 459
M. R. Kale, 207*, 741*, 763
M. R. Kavi, 211*, 248*, 464*, 476*
M. R. Majumdar, 390*
M. R. Telang, 138*, 277*, 298*, 371*, 388*, 666*, 763. See Telang
M. Schuyler 40*, 46, 239*, 277*, 646. See Schuyler
M. S. Levi, 688. See Levi and S. Levi
M. T. Narasimha Aiyanger, 403*, 531*, 537*, 552*, 630, 728
Mudrā-rākṣasa, xlvii, cxv, 53*, 58, 110, 162* 243*, 262, 264-71, 443, 474, 476, 760, 776
Mudrita-kumudacandra, 476, 769
Mugdha-bodhinī, 660
Mugdha-medhākara, 566
Mugdhopadeśa, 410, 674
Muhammadan or Muslim or Moslem, lxxii, xcii, cxvi, cxvii, cxviii, 315, 447, 478, 625, 665*, 679, 680
Mu'ammad Shah II, 479*, 629
Muhūrta-grantha 730*
Mutkā-carita, 440
Muktāphala-ketu, story of, 98
Muktāpīḍa, cxvii, 618
Muktāvatī of Narasiṁha Sūri, 533*
Muktāvalī of Rāmanātha, 751*
Muktigarbha, 521
Mukulabhaṭṭa, 188*, 535, 536, 540*, 541*
Mukunda Bhaṭṭa, 624*
Mukunda-mālā, 381 662
Mukunda muktāvalī 397, 663*, 664
Mukunda-vilāsa-kāvya, 764
Mukundānanda, 490, 492*
Mukuṭa-tāḍitaka, cxiii, 299, 755
Mulachandra Tulsidas Televala, 396
Mullā Jāmī Nur-ud-din, 316*
Mummuṇirāja, of Konkaṇa, 432
München, 425, 427*, 744*, 756*
Muṇḍaka (Upaniṣad), xvii
Muni Caturvijaya, 471*, 484*
Munich, 240*, 633
Muni Jinavijaya, 467*
Muni Puṇyavijaya, 475*, 476*, 503*
Munisuvrata, 478
Munisuvrata-kāvya, 775
Munisuvrata-kāvyaratna, 620
Muñja of Dhara, 340*, 428, 430, 550, 553*. See Vākpatirāja Muñja
Muralidhara, 740*
Murāri, 448-53, 455, 457, 459, 462, 463, 760, 761
Murshidabad, 397*, 468*, 662*
Music, lvi, lviii, lxxvii, xci, xciv, cviii, cxxviii, 20-22, 44, 56, 58*, 62, 67, 76, 110, 246, 598, 599, 600, 631, 634, 635, 643, 645, 649, 729. See Song.
Mūka-kavi, 384, 661
Mūkārbhaka Śaṁkara, 384
Mūladeva, Karṇīputra, 250, 407
Mūla-kārikā, 541
Mūlarāja, 678
Mūlasarvāstivādins, 695
Mysore, cxxiv, 159, 374*, 380*
Mysterium und Mimus in Rgveda, 44*, 631*, 647, 648
Mystery Play, 44, 46, 631
Myth or mythical xxxv, xxxviii, cxxviii, 128, 150, 170, 179, 180, 235, 241, 324, 357, 406, 547, 680, 732, 758
Mythology, v, lii, lxii, cv, 128, 166, 701

N

Nachrichten d Göttingischen Gesselschaft, 300* 710
Nachrichten von der Kgl. Gesellschaft der Wissenschaften, 520*, 522*
Nagna-śramaṇa, 252
Nahapāna, ci
Naiṣadha-carita, cxvii, 30, 325-30, 624, 625, 626, 629,
Naiṣadha-prakāśa, 624*
Naiṣadhānanda, 465*
Naiṣadhīya-prakāśa, 624*
Nakṣatra, xiv
Nala 326-29, 331, 337, 341, 435, 620, 623, 624, 626, 746
Nala-bhūmipāla-rūpaka, 623
Nala-campū, 299, 435, 694*
Nala-carita, 465*, 623, 764
Nala-rāmāyaṇa, 547
Nala-varṇana-kāvya, 623
Nalavikrama, lxxxv, 687
Nala-vilāsa, 462*, 465, 469, 769
Nalayani-carita, 774
Nala-yādava-rāghava-pāṇḍavīya, 623
Nalābhyudaya, 331, 627, 771
Nalānanda, 623
Nallā Dīkṣita, 490
Nalodaya, 121, 337, 338*, 620-23, 740*
Nami sādhu, 11*, 525*, 531*, 532*, 536*, 538
Nanda, 74, 75, 156, 264*, 265*, 266, 568
Nanda, Buddha's half-brother, 613
Nandalāla, 668

Nandana, 281
Nandana (metre), 184*
Nandargikar, 5*, 123*, (G. R.), 124*, 185*, 729*, 751*
Nandayantī, 302
Nandighoṣa-vijaya, 511*
Nandikeṣvaıa, 521, 524*
Nandimāli, 687
Nandisvāmī, 521
Nañjarāja-yaśobhūṣaṇa, 490*
Narahari, commentator, 325*, 621*, 624 741*
Narahari, poet, 370
Narahari SarasvatItIrtha, 556
Narakāsura-vijaya, 769
Naranārayaṇānanda, 332, 678, 770
Narasiṁhadeva, Gajapati, 511*
Narasiṁha, king of Utpaıa, 561
Narasiṁha-manīṣā 556
Narasiṁha, of Vijayanagara, 497*
Narasiṁha, Sena, 755*
Narasiṁha Sūri, 533*
Narasiṁha Thakkura, 556
Naravāhanadatta, 97-100, 693, 694, 700
Naradataka (metre), 285*
Narendraprabha, 759, 770
Narendravardhana, 300
Nariman, 18*
Narkūṭaka (metre), 184*
Narma-mālā, 408-410,
Nasik, 15, 612, 772
Naṭa, 51*, 52*, 633-35, 637, 639-44, 647, 648, 650
Naṭa-sūtra, 52*, 523, 636, 640
Native Opinion Press, 380*
Naukā, 561*,
Nausari, 435
Navadvipa or Nadia, xxiv, 373*, 485
Nava Kālidāsa, 740
Navamālikā, Princess of Śrāvasti, 212
Navaratna-mālā, 740*
Navasāhasāṅka, 553*
Nava-sāhasāṅka-carita, 168, 349-50, 676
Navasāhasāṅka-carita-campū, 326*
Nawāb Asaf Khān, 364*
Nayacandra Sūri, 363
Nābhādāsa, 389*
Nāgabhaṭa, cxvii,
Nāgadevi, 350
Nāgaraka, 20-22, 24 62, 246
Nāgarāja, 335* 403, 674
Nāgasena, 254*
Nāgānanda, lxxxiv, cxiii, 19, 53*, 60, 173, 189*, 255, 256, 258-60, 656, 674, 720, 759.
Nāgārjuna, cvi, cxviii, 80*, 81*,
Nāgārijuna, king, 432, 766
Nāgeśabhata, 565, 637-39, 758
Nāgojībhaṭṭa, 556, 561*,
Nāmaliṅgānuśāzana, 731
·Nānaka 770
Nāṇḍillagopa, 481*
Nāndī, 50, 104*, 109*, 649, 709, 711, 718
Nāndī Bharata, 524*
Nāndīśloka, 713
Nānyadeva, 277*
Nārada, 116, 190, 721, 750
Nārāśaṁsa hymns, 3
Nārāyaṇa, author of *Hitopadeśa*, 90,. 701*, 706
Nārāyanṇa, author of *Vṛtta-ratnākara*, 527
Nārāyaṇabhatta, 382, 617, 687, 748*, 774
Nārāyaṇa, commentator, 126*, 129*, 277*, 325*, 624, 741*, 755*
Nārāyaṇa, commentator of *Rgveda*, 767
Nārāyaṇa (deity), 664
Nārāyaṇa Dīkṣita, 630, 674
Nārāyaṇa, father of the poet Krśna, 369
Nārāyana, poet, lviii, 336, 368*. 371
Nārāyaṇa, Ravideva's father, 620
Nārāyaṇa Sāha, 361, 679, 772
Nārāyaṇatīrtha, 396
Nārāyaṇa Vidyāvinoda, 616*
Nārāyaṇa, Visvanatha's great grand-father, 563
Nārāyaṇīya (Stotra), 371,, 382 , 664
Nāṭaka, lxxvii, lxxxii, lxxxiii, lxxxv lxxxviii, 64, 65, 67, 139*, 258, 299, 301, 302, 457, 462, 505, 506* (Mahā-), 507*, 562, 633, 635*, 645, 648, 653*, 655, 686, 709, 711, 714, 715. See Drama.
Nāṭaka-candrikā, 664*
Nāṭaka-lakṣaṇa-ratna-kośa, 299*, 300*, 715, 716
Nāṭaka-mīmāṁsā, 558
Nāṭa-vāṭa-prahasana, 496
Nāṭikā, 67, 256, 457, 462, 471-72, 473, 484, 686. 726. See Drama.
Nāṭya-darpaṇa, lxxvii, 66* 105*, 120*, 121*, 244*, 271*, 299*, 300*, 301, 302, 450*, 463, 468, 471, 475, 648, 649, 686, 715, 716, 759
Nāṭya pradīpa, 525*
Nāṭya Śāstra, ix, x lxxv-lxxviii, xcix, cxiv, 51*, 52, 53* 56, 250, 521, 518, 522-25, 530*, 532,* 539*, 550, 575, 582, 596, 630, 642, 645, 650*, 731
Nāṭyasūtra, xli, 512, 548, 652, 650
Naṭya-veda-vivṛti, 525*
N. B. Godabole. 140*, 178*, 207*, 272, 759
N. B. Parvanikar, 126*
N. B. Utgikar, 279*
N. Chrkravarty, 751*
Nema Bhārgava, 631
Nemāditya, 435*
Nemi-dūta. 374*
Nemi-kumāra, 563
Neminātha, 345, 374
Nemi-nirvāṇā, 345, 559
Nemisādhu 561*
Nepal Ms., 389*
Nepal or Nepalese, cviii, cxvi, 73*, 90, 93, 95, 96-98, 412, 421, 510*, 688, 689, 692, 696, 699, 700, 706
Nepāla-māhātmya, 93, 688
Nebudda, c
Newāri, 321, 704*, 707
New Attic (Greek) Comedy, 53, 242
New Haven. 88, 421
New Ind. Antiquary, 324*, 326*
New York, 239*, 240*, 256*, 646, 754*
N. G. Banerji, 339*
N. G. G. W., 262*, 469*, 686, 732*, 760

N. G. Mazumdar, 729
N. G. W. G., 611
N. I. A., 371*
Nibandhas, xxvi, cxviii
Nidarśanā (*alaṁkāra*), 526, 530, 536*
Nidāna-kathā, 67*
Nighaṇṭu, 518, 730*
Nila (river) in North Malabar, 774
Nilkantha Janardan Kirtane, 363*
Nimbavatī, 281*
Nindopamā, 532*
Nipātas, vii
Nirbhaya-bhīma, 465, 769
Nirbhaya Narendra, 547*
Nirmalāta, 189
Nirṇaya-sindhu xxvi
Nirukta, cxxiv, 518
Nirvāṇa-ṣaṭka, 380
Nishikanta Chatterjee, 649*
Nītyasyarup Brahmacari, 325*, 440*
Niyoga, lxiii
Nizam, 773
Nilakaṇṭha, author of *Mayūkha*, xx, xxvi
Nīlkaṇṭha (Bhaṭṭa Gopāla's father), 278
Nīlkaṇṭha (Commentator of *Mahābhārata*) 47*
Nīlakṇṭha Dīkṣita, 334, 383, 403, 510, 438, 457*, 464*, 465, 467, 623, 629, 630*, 665, 674, 675
Nīlkaṇṭha Makhin, 765
Nīlkaṇṭha-vijaya-campū, 334*, 437-38, 464*
Nīlamata-purāṇa, 355
Nīti, 195, lxxv, xcix, 704*, 705
Nīti-dviṣaṣṭikā, 400
Nīti kalpataru, 404
Nīti mañjarī, 676
Nīti-pradīpa, 121
Nīti-ratna, 11*
Nīti-sataka, (of Bhartṛhari) 161, 162, 163, 164, 194, 263*, 401*, 670, 674; of Dhanadadeva and others, 370
Nī i-sāra, 121
Nīti śāstra, 86, 623, 697, 698, 701
Nītivarman, 337
Nītivākyāmṛta, xcvii
N. K. Bhattacharya, 326*
N. L. Dey, 738*
N. Mironow, 676*
N. M. Penzer, 96*. See Penzer (q.v.)
Nobels, 615
North Africa, 705
Notes sur les Indo-scythes, 614*
Notices, 374*
Notices, of R. L. Mitra, 480*
Nṛgamokṣa prabandha, 775
Nṛpāvalī, 355
Nṛsiṁha, 325*
Nṛsiṁha Bhaṭṭa, 551
Nṛsiṁha-campū, of Daivajña Sūrya 437; of Keśavabhaṭṭa 437; of Saṁkarsaṇa 437
Nṛsiṁha of Bhāradvāja Gotra, 486
Nṛsiṁha, poet, 490*
Nṛsiṁha-rāya, 764
Nṛsiṁha Śarmā 623*
Nṛsiṁha, Śeṣa Kṛṣṇa, 468
Nṛsiṁha-vijaya, 687
Nṛtya-prakāra, 67*
N. S., 664*
N. S. P. or Nirnay Sagar Press, 89*, 95* 96*, 119*, 121*, 122*, 126*, 132*, 138*, 140*, 158*, 161*, 168*, 178*, 183*, 188*, 189*, 197*, 207*, 221*, 226*, 229*, 239*, 241*, 249*, 256*, 271*, 277*, 298*, 299*, 316*, 319*, 323*, 324*, 325*, 331*, 332*, 334*, 336*, 337*, 340*, 341*, 342*, 345*, 360*, 363, 368*, 369*, 370*, 371*, 374*, 379*, 380*, 383*, 384*, 391*, 401*, 403*, 404*, 405*, 415*, 429*, 430*, 435*, 437*, 438*, 449*, 457*, 462*, 464*, 467*, 468*, 469*, 471*, 479, 481*, 485*, 486, 489*, 496*, 502*, 533, 560, 614, 622*, 624, 656*, 666*, 742, 759, 762, 763
N. S. Panse, 462*
Nun, Buddhist, lix, 281. See Parivrājikā
Nūtānatarī, 561*
Nyāya, 406, 515, 624, 69[illegible] (*Laukika*), 698 (*Laukika*)
Nyāyabindu 532*
Nyāya śāstra 719
Nyāyasūtra cxiv
Nyāyavācaspati Rudra, 679
Nyāya-virodha, 715

O

Oak, Mr., 529*
O. Böhtlingk, 533, 756*, 759. See Böhtlingk
Observations ad Kālidāsae Mālavikāgnimitram, 136, 750*
O.C., 649*, 653*, 755*, 759
Ocean of Story, 88*, 95*, 96*, 422*, 691*
O. C V., 650*
Odeyadeva Vādībhasiṁha, 344, 432
Oḍiyā, 321*
Oedipus, 447
Oesterly, 422*
O. F. Tullberg, 750*
Ogden, 18*, 173*, 256* (C. J. Ogden).
Ojas, xv, 275, 526, 563, 573, 574, 576, 578, 579
O. J. M. S., 279*
O. Kressler, 673. See Oscar Kressler
Oldenberg, x, 25, 200*, 524*, 632, 634, 763, See H. Oldenberg
Oṁkaṇṭha, 8*
One-act Play, 112, 464, 466, 467, 473, 474, 487, 500, 504
One-character Play, 112
Orientalia, 470*. See *Sir Asutosh Jubilee Comm. Vol.*
Orient und Occident, 744*
Origin and Development of Bengal Language, 394*
Origin of the Vidūṣaka, The, 46*
Grissa, 389, 468, 485, 511*, 563
Oriyā, 563
Ornatior Text, 89, 90, 420, 422. See Textus Ornatior
Oscar Kressler, 196*. 673
Ostasiat Zeitschrist., 650*
Osterr. Monatsschrift für den Orient, 646, 653*, 657*

Ottoztein, Dr., 712
Ouṣadha-prayoga, 730*
Outlines of the History of Alaṁkāra Literature, 520*
O. Walter, 744*, 764. See Walter
Oxford, 11*, 73, 666*
Oxford University Press, 74*, 80*, 101*, 277*.
Oxus Valley, 739

P

Pada, 559
Pada-bhāvārtha-candrika, 666*
Pada-candrikā, 207*
Pada-dīpikā, 207*
Padadoṣa, 552
Pada-dyotinī, 666*
Pada-mañjari, 528
Padavākyārtha-pañjikā, 624*
Padāṅka-dūta, 373*, 752
Padārtha-dīpikā, 741*
Padārthasārtham, 764
Padāvalī, 575, 576, 630
Padma, 620
Padmacandra, 476
Padmagupta, 168*, 349-50, 353, 357, 676
Padma-mihira, 355
Padma, minister, 344
Padmanandibhaṭṭāraka, 619*
Padmanābha, 403*
Padmanābhapuram, 711
Padmapāda, 663
Padma-prābhṛtaka, 248, 249, 250, 761
Padmapura 278
Padmapurāṇa, 138*. 140, 747, 748*
Padmasambhava (sage), cxvi
Padmānanda, 331*, 344, 400, 620
Padmānanda, Jaina, 400
Padmāvatī, (Jayadeva's wife), 389, 390*, 666
Padmāvatī (mother of the poet Soḍḍhala) 431
Padmāratī-pariṇaya, 687
Padmāvatī (Udayana's love-lady), 98, 300, 714
Padmāvatī, woman-poet, 416
Padya, 529, 539, 563
Padya-cūḍām ıṇi, 345
Padya-kadambari, 324*
Padya-racana, 415, 416
Padya-venī, 415
Padyāmṛta-taraṅginī, 415
Padyāvalī, 8*, 324*, 397, 415, 663*, 664*
Pagan, 662*
Pahlavi, 87, 88
Pahlave, version of the *Pañcatantra*, 87, 88
Painting, xci, cxi, 57, 469
Paiśāca, 691*, 693
Paiśācī (Prakrit), ix cvi, 93, 94, 95, 537, 685, 695
Paiṭhīnasi, xxv
Pajjhaṭikā (metre), 194
Palace Library of Travancore, 711
Paleographic, 655
Palghat, 325*
Paliyam Manuscript Library, 494*
Pallava, cxiii, 254, 709, 765
Palmer Boyd, 256*, 759
Pampā-rāmāyana, 619
Pañcabāna-vijaya 490
Pañcarātra, 101, 109, 112, 113, 272, 709, 710*, 720, 721
Pañcarātra-nāṭaka, 709
Pañcarātrins, xcix
Pāñcaśatī, 384, 661
Pañca-sāyaka, 498
Pañca-siddhāntikā, 730*
Pañcaśikha, 241*, 762
Pañca-stavī, 660*
Pañcatantra, 15, 83, 84, 85, 86-92, 95, 98, 155, 200, 204, 207, 224, 231, 263*, 400, 419, 420, 425. 614, 670, 673, 691*, 694*, 696, 699, 700, 701-07
Pañcatantra Reconstructed, The, 88*
Pañcavaṭī, 289, 293, 450
Pañcākhyāna, 89, 704
Pañcākhyānaka, 703
Pañcākhyānoddhāra, 703
Pañcanana, 743*,
Paṇḍit, 126 , 324*, 331*, 382*, 440*, 455*, 457*, 462*, 487*, 617*, 618*, 664*, 741*, 742*, 751*
Paṇḍita-pīḍa-viśārada, 499
Panegyrics, xiv, xcix, cx, 3, 14, 18, 79, 167, 170, 190. 193, 238, 326*, 346, 362, 363, 3 7, 383
Paṇis, 631
Panjab Univ. Orient. Publication Series, 73*, 320*
Pannalal Choudhuri, 379*
Pantomime or Pantomimic, 67, 634, 638, 639 642
P. Anujan Achan, 494*
Papal, xciv
Parab, 95*, 168*, 299*. See K. P. Parab
Paramardideva, 473, 768
Paramāditya-stotra, 659
Paramānanda Cakravarttī, 556
Paramānanda-dāsa-sena Kavikarṇapūra, 333 398, 440, 485
Paramāra (dynasty), 349, 428, 431, 472
Paramāra Sindhurāja, 349
Paramārtha, cxii
Paramārtha-bodhi-citta-bhāvānukrama-varṇa-saṁgraha, 614*
Paramārtha-sandarbha, 664*
Paramātma-prakāśa, 139*
Parameśa-stotrāvalī, 662
Parameśvara Iyer, 663*
Parameśvarācārya, 546
Paranjape, 753
Paraśurama, 287, 288, 325, 451, 456, 723
Paratriṁśikā-vivaraṇa, 544
Paravanikar, 126*
Parākramabāhu, King, 378
Parāśara, xcviii, 521, 705
Parikarālamkāra, 555
Parikathā, 757*
Parimala, same as Padmagupta (q.v,)
Pariṇāma (*alaṁkāra*), 557, 562
Paris, 83*, 92*. 126*, 262*, 371*, 378*, 389*, 429*, 481*, 522*, 611*-13*, 631 635*, 646, 666*, 694*, 696, 751*, 756*, 759

Pariśiṣṭa-parvan, 265*, 343
Parivrājikā, xxxi, 252, 282, 301, 638
Parivṛtti (*alaṁkāra*). 526, 530, 534, 536
Parnadatta, cxii
Parody, xxxii
Paronomasia, 33, 34, 221, 222, 223, 236, 334, See Śleṣa and Pun
Parthian, ci, 5
Paruṣavṛtti, 534
Paryyāyokta (*alaṁkāra*), 526, 534, 545, 583
Paspaśāhnika, cxxi, 568*. See *Mahābhāṣya*
Patanjali, vi, vii, viii, xviii, xix, xx, lviii, cii, cviii, cxxi, cxxii, cxxiii, cxxiv, 5*, 6*, 10, 11, 13, 19, 48, 49. 52, 54, 186*, 200, 513, 516, 521, 522, 568, 576, 611, 612, 635, 640, 643, 644*, 653, 671, 738, 754. See *Mahābhāṣya*
Pātakā, 109*, 721, 722
Pathak, 132*, 133*, 161*, 189*, 340*, 528*, 531*, 620, 656*, 751*, See K. B. Pathak
Pathak Commemoration Volume, 454*, 506*
Pathological, 602, 603
Pathos, 39, 114, 131, 135, 146, 151, 261, 292, 296, 452, 461, 470
Patna, lxi. lxxiv
Patralekhā, 230, 233
Pattamadai, 775
Paulastya, 93
Paul Elmer More, 703
Pavana-dūta, of Dhoyi, 373*, 374*, 751 ; of Vādicandra Suri, 373*
Pavolini, 523* See P. E. Pavolini
Payodhi-manthana, 686
Pāda-tāḍitaka, 248, 249, 251, 253, 762
Pādukā-sahasra, 332*, 384*
Pāiya-lacchī-nāma-mālā, 430*
Pāla-gopāla-kathānaka, 427
Pālaka, 97, 244*, 245*, 758
Pālanpur, 770
Pālas of Bengal, 470*
Pāli, cx, 80, 321, 345, 434, 612
Pāli-jātakas, xviii, 80. See Jātaka
Pāñcastavī, 660
Pāñcāla, 568, 658*, 684
Pāñcālī (*rīti*), 535, 537, 553, 563, 565, 568, 573, 578, 684
Pāṇḍava, 113, 178, 337, 340, 457, 619, 723-25
Pāṇḍavā-carita, 332
Pāṇḍavābhyudaya, 504
Pāṇḍavānanda, 301, 686
Pāṇḍu, 337
Pāṇḍya kingdom, 773
Pāṇḍya Rājasiṁha I, 106*
Pāṇḍya-Ter-Mā an-Rājasiṁha, 106*
Pāṇini, vi, xvi, xviii, lvii, c, cviii, cxxi, 4, 6, 7. 8, 9, 10, 52*, 93, 178*, 252. 336, 513, 514, 516, 518-20, 523, 527, 567, 585. 611, 617, 634, 636. 638-40, 642, 644, 645, 653, 671, 685, 734*
Pāṇini, Poet, 611, 653*
Pāṇinian, cxxii, cxxiii
Pāntha-dūta, 373*
Pāpabuddhi dharmabuddhi-kathānaka, 427
Pāpayallaya Sūri, 386*, 662*
Pāpācāra, 500
Pāramitās (perfections of a Bodhisattva), 80
Pāramitā-samāsa, 614
Pārijāta-haraṇa, 340*, 510-11
Pārijāta-haraṇa-campū, 437
Pārijāta-mañjarī, 472
Pārśva, 70
Pārśvanātha, 374
Pārśvanātha-carita, 343*, 619
Pārśvābhyudaya, 132*, 374*, 656, 657
Pārtha-kathā, 621*
Pārtha, King, cxvi
Partha-parākrama, 466, 769
Pārthapura, 342
Pārtha-vijaya, 686
Pārvati, xxxi, xxxvii, lxxx, 341, 396, 630, 741, 742
Pārvatī-pariṇaya, cxiii, 298, 469, 627, 686, 755, 771
Pārvatī-rukmiṇīya, 341
Pāśupata, 254
Pāśupata, son of Kubera, 225
Pāṭaliputra, lviii, cvi, cvii, cviii, cix, 220, 263* 477
Pātāla-vijaya, 7, 611
Pāyaguṇḍi, 756
P. Bohlen, 161*, 367. See Bohlen
P. d' Alheim, 277*
P. de Lacy Johnstone, 744*
P. D. Gune, 107*
P. E. Foucaux 83*, 138*
Pehlevi, 698, 701, 702, 705
Penance, xxxii, lxxx, 626
Penzer, 29*, 95*, 422*, 691*. See N. M. Penzer
P. E. Pavolini, 141*, 710. See Pavolini
Perikles, 22
Periplus of the Erythroean Sea, 737
Persia, 736, 737
Persian, v, lxxii, cii, 89*, 316*, 629, 696*, 707, 771, 772
Perubhaṭṭa, 565
Perumanam, 774
Perumāls, Vaiṣnava, 662*
Peshawar. ciii, civ, 736
Pessimism, lxxxi, 10, 36
P. Goldschmidt, 119*
Phallic rites, 50
Phidias, lxviii
Philolog—Histor., 522*
Philology, v
Philosophical or Philosophy, v, xxii, xxiii, xxvi, xxvii, xlvii, xlviii, lxvi, lxxii, lxxv, lxxxii, xc, xci, xciv, cxvii, cxviii, cxx 26*, 42, 71, 81*, 157*, 161, 164, 167, 195, 328, 332, 347, 357, 375, 377, 380, 382, 385, 483, 494, 516, 544-45, 580, 590, 604, 605, 625, 671, 675, 683, 698, 742, 765
Phonetical, cxxiv
P. Horn, 629
Phraseology, 32, 35, 181, 184, 192, 412, 605, 720, 721
Phuṅkaṭamiśra, 497
Pickford, 763
Pilgrim's Progress, 481
Piṇāka-nandin, 339
Piṅgala, lvii, cviii, 12, 611
Piśācas, 693

Pischel, viii, 9*, 17*, 47*, 52*, 95*, 121*, 138*, 140*, 243*, 298*, 340*, 371*, 389*, 393, 394, 413*, 444*, 470, 503*, 524*, 537, 558, 620*, 632, 642, 650, 652*, 653*, 666*, 674, 686, 695, 708*, 750*, 751*. See R. Pischel
Pisharoti, 381*, 662*, 664*, 710, 712, 713, 714*. See K. R. Pisharoti
Pīḍita(alaṃkāra), 538
Pītāmbara, 486, 666*
Pīṭhamarda, 645
Piyūṣa-laharī, 665
Piyūṣavarṣa, 462
P. K. Gode, 122*, 149*, 415*,
Plassey, 747
Plato, lv, 486*, 629*
Platonic, 165*
Pliny, 737
Pluralism, xxvii, lxx
Pluta (accent), cxxii
Plutarch, xxxiv
P. L. Vaidya, 361*, 436*
Poems of Mayūra, 121*
Poetics, xvi, 15, 22, 29, 37, 52, 62, 63, 160, 309, 323, 366, 521, 529, 536, 585, 610, 618, 667, 742*. See *Alaṃkāra*
Poetics (referring to *Sanskrit Poetics*), 615
Poetics of Aristotle, 650*
Poetik, 646
Poetry, xvi, xv, xvi, xx, xxviii, xli, lxii, lxvi, cxxv, cxxix, 4, 11, 12, 13, 22, 23, 24, 25, 39, 58, 121, 134, 149, 151-53, 156, 157, 160, 165, 167, 176, 177, 182, 184, 185, 188, 192 194, 232, 235, 246, 250, 260, 292, 306, 314, 315, 318, 348, 359, 364-67, 369, 375, 376, 385, 394, 398, 399, 404, 418, 419, 453, 460, 461, 481, 542, 546, 548, 549, 550, 551, 554, 568, 572, 577, 578-81, 583-86, 590, 599, 604, 606, 621*, 629*, 656, 729, 751*
Political, liv, lxxv, xcii, ciii, cxvii, cxix, 24*, 74, 91, 111, 174, 245, 264, 265, 266, 332, 339, 354, 363, 447, 477, 478, 680, 683
Political History of Ancient India, 736
Politics or Polity, xcvi, cxvi, cxvi, 26*, 265, 357, 622, 698, 701, 705, 729
Poona, 101*, 123*, 132*, 140*, 149*, 185*, 240*, 242*, 256*, 262*, 272*, 279*, 360*, 361*, 380*, 408*, 435*, 473*, 462, 468, 529*, 660*, 703
Popular Ballad, The, 632*
Pornography, 675
P. Peterson or Peterson 8*, 9*, 10*, 90, 119*-21*, 162* 166*, 172*, 207*, 218, 229*, 230*, 235*, 278*, 320*, 345*, 611*, 620, 621, 686, 704, 708*
P. P. S. Śāstrī, 335*, 341*, 361*, 417*, 437*, 740*, 742, 756*, 768
Prabandha-cintāmaṇi, 19, 189*, 428, 751*, 767, 770
Prabandha-kośa, 7*, 326, 428
Prabhakara Sastri Veturi, 494*
Prabhā (commentary), 556
Prabhākara, 396*, 741*, 755
Prabhākara-vardhana, 227, 233
Prabhāvaka-carita, 767
Prabhāvati, 466, 564
Prabhudevī, 417
Prabodha-candrodaya, lxxxviii, 77, 480-84, 486*, 487*
Prabodhānanda, 369*, 397
Prabuddha-rauhiṇeya, 476, 769
Pracaṇḍabhairava, 769
Pracaṇḍa-pāṇḍava, same as *Bāla-bhārata* (q. v.), 547
Pracaṇḍa-sepha, 499
Pracetāyana, 521
Pradīpaka 622*
Pradyota, 110, 726, 758
Pradyumna, 466
Pradyumnābhyudaya, 466
Pragmatic, cxviii, cxxvii, 598
Praharaṇakalikā (metre), 184*
Praharṣiṇī (metre), 12, 14*, 181*, 190
Prahasana, lxxxii, lxxxiii, lxxxvi, lxxxvii, 62, 66, 244*, 254, 255, 411, 474, 487, 488, 493-500, 687, 765
Prahelikā, 530, 578*,
Prahlāda, 437
Prahlādanadeva, Yuvarāja, 466, 769, 770
Prajāpati, xxv
Prajāpati-nandin, 339
Prajñākara-miśra, 121*
Prakaraṇa, lxxxii, lxxxiii, lxxxv-lxxxvii, 65, 67, 76, 121*, 244*, 298, 301, 302, 474, 475, 476, 650, 686, 726, 727
Prakaraṇikā, 67*
Prakāśavarṣa, 621*
Prakāśendra, 404
Prakrit, vii, viii, ix, x, xi, xvii, xviii, lix, ci, cii, cxx, cxxi, cxxiv, 3, 4, 5, 11*, 15, 17*, 41, 46, 49, 67, 77, 87*, 92, 94, 95, 96, 105, 107, 119, 139, 155, 156, 157, 161* 172*, 201, 219, 242*, 243, 253, 255*, 261*, 262*, 270, 276, 279, 283*, 285*, 314, 322, 350*, 361, 362, 425, 427, 428, 430*, 444-45, 458, 461, 489, 503, 537, 612, 683, 684, 688, 691*, 695, 703, 719, 721, 730, 750*
Prakritism, 15, 82
Prakriyā-sarvasva, 774
Pramadā (metre), 13
Pramāṇas, 553
Pramāṇavidyā, xcix
Pramitākṣarā (metre), 12, 13, 181*
Prarocanā, 505
Praśaṃsopamā, 157* 167, 532*
Praśanna-rāghaa, 146, 369, 389*, 426-63, 464 502, 761
Praśasti, viii, lxxx, lxxxviii, xcix, cvi, 6, 14, 17, 18, 345, 520, 646, 692, 739, 768
Praśasti-ratnāvalī, 564
Prasāda, xv, 149, 526, 563, 573, 574, 576
Prasenajit, 321
Prastāvanā, 104, 590, 604, 605, 624, 664, 675, 683, 698, 711, 742, 754, 765, 772
Praśna-candrikā, 730*
Prasthāna-bheda, 664*
Pratāpa Narasiṃha, 562
Pratāparudra-deva, 562
Pratāparudra, Gajapati, 485
Pratāparudra-kalyāṇa, 478
Pratāparudra, Kākatīya 467, 470*, 531*
Pratāparudra of Warangal, 467, 479*

Pratāparudra-yaśobhūṣaṇa, 479*, 526, 529*, 561, 562, 565
Pratāpa Sāha, 360, 772
Pratijñā-cāṇakya, 271*, 301*, 301-2
Pratihārendurāja, 527, 530*, 533, 535, 536, 538, 541*, 542, 543*, 545, 584, 585
Pratijñākara, Misra, 623*
Pratijñā-nāṭaka, 709, 710*, 517, 720, 721
Pratijñā-yaugandharāyaṇa, 101, 108, 109, 110, 115, 116-17, 265, 301*, 302*, 714, 719, 757
Pratiloma (marriage), xiii
Pratimā-nāṭaka, 60, 101, 109*, 113, 114, 708*, 709, 719, 720, 726
Pratimāniruddha, 301, 686
Pratimokṣa-sūtrapaddhati, 614
Pratimukha-sandhi, lxxxii
Pratiṣṭhāna, ci, 93, 94, 95
Prativastūpamā, 526, 536
Pratyobhijñā school, 544, 545
Pravarapura, 350
Pravarasena, cxv, 16, 119
Pravartaka, 263*, 264*
Prayāga, 88, 301, 350, 450
Prayāgābhyudaya, 686
Prayoga-pārijāta, xxvi
Prācetasa-śrāddhakalpa, 719
Prācyā (Prākṛta), ix
Prājyabhaṭṭa, 354, 359, 677
Prākṛta-prakāśa 11*, 683, 730
Prākṛta-rūpāvatāra, 656*
Prākṛta-vṛtti, 748*
Prāṇānārāyana, 364
Prāṇābharaṇa, 364, 675
Prātimokṣa-sūtra-paddhati, 614
Prātiśākhyas viii
Pre-caitanya Vaiṣṇavism in Bengal in *Festschrift M. Winternitz*, 391*
P. Regnaud, 520*. See Regnaud
Prekṣāṇakas, 464, 645
Premacandra Tarkavāgīśa, 325*, 340*, 449, 624*
Premadhara, 621
Premendusāgara, 664*
Pretakārya, 733*
Preyas (*alaṃkāra*), 526, 534, 536, 557
Printz, Dr., 107*, 710. See W. Printz
Privy Council, xiii
Priyadarśikā, 301*
Priyadarśikā, lxxxvi, cxiii, 18* 55*, 110*, 173*, 255, 256-58, 260, 261, 383, 691*, 693, 713, 758, 759
Priyaṃvadā, 748
Priyaṅgu, 11
Prītikūṭa, 225
Prītisandarbha, 664*
Problem of the Mahānāṭaka, 501
Proceedings and Transactions of the All India Oriental Conference, 753
Proceedings of the Fifth Orient. Conf., 127*
Proceedings of the First Orient. Conf., 107*, 149*
Proceedings of the Second Orient, Conf., 126* 338
Proceedings of the Tenth All India Orient. Conference, 338*, 497*
Proddyota Bhaṭṭa, 560
Prose, lxv, cxvi, cxix, 6, 14, 17, 18, 34, 37, 38, 42, 44, 45, 49, 55, 57, 80, 82, 83, 87, 94, 118, 155, 171, 200-39, 429-32 (Prose Kāvya); 261, 276, 296, 303, 418-20 (Later Prose Literature); 420-29 (Prose Tale); 433-34 (Prose in Campū); 569, 612, 618*, 622, 627, 632, 634, 640, 647, 655, 676 (Romance); 678, 680, 694, 700, 721, 751, 752, 754, 768, 771
Prosody, 12, 188, 310, 331*, 439*
Pṛthakpadatva 573
Pṛthu, 262
Pṛthvīdhara, 758
Pṛthvī (metre), 196*
Pṛthvīrāja, 360, 628, 677, 768
Pṛthvīrāja-vijaya, 360, 628, 677
Przyluski, 81*
Psychological or Psychology, 22, 32, 139, 244, 294, 365, 376, 385, 388, 594, 602
Pulakeśin II, 178
Pulastya 521
Pulinda or Pulindha, 229*, 431
Pun, xxi, 33, 148, 169*, 171, 172, 182, 191, 206, 210, 222, 236, 328, 334, 335, 337, 339, 341, 360, 370, 382, 431, 435, 587, See Paronomasia and Śleṣa
Punarukta-vadābhāsa, 534, 556, 563
Puṇḍarīka, 230, 746
Puṇḍarīkākṣa, 616*
Puṇḍravardhana, 339
Punishment, xcvi, 660
Punjab, ciii, civ, cviii, cxvii, 649, 650, 656
Puṇyaketu, 484
Puṇyavaśas, 70
Puppet-play, 47, 642, 652*, 653*
Puragupta, cxii
Purañjana-carita, 480*
Purañjana-nāṭaka, 480*
Purāṇa or Purāṇic, vii, xiii, xxvi, xxxiv, xxxv, xli, xlii, lxxiii, lxxix, lxxxviii, xcix, cvii, 83, 93, 101, 115, 128, 132*, 137*, 138*, 140*, 166, 169, 170, 195, 322, 325, 331, 332, 342, 346, 377*, 378, 381, 384, 385, 402, 437, 462, 466, 469, 508*, 539, 624, 647, 680, 687
Puri, 331, 450*, 485, 511*
Purohita, xcv
Purusakāra, grammatical commentary, 663
Puruṣa-parīkṣā, 426
Puruṣottama Sarasvatī, 664
Puruvana, 336
Purūravā, 85, 138, 139, 151, 283, 385, 463, 464, 631, 632
Pusalker, 721, 727*. See A. D. Pusalker
Puṣkara, 88
Puṣpabāṇa-vilāsa, 740*
Puṣpabhūti, 227
Puṣpadanta, 381, 436, 619*, 660
Puṣpa-dūṣitaka (or °*bhūṣitaka*), 301, 302, 686
Puṣpamata, 563
Puspasena, 432, 623*
Puṣpitāgrā (metre), 14*, 120*, 150, 181*, 196*
Puṣyamitra, lx, ci, cii, cxii, cxvii, 568, 735, 736

Pūrṇabhadra, 89, 425, 698, 701, 703, 704, 706
Pūrṇacandra De, 380*
Purṇakalasagaṇi, 678*
Pūrṇa-Sarasvatī, 132*
Pūrṇavarman, cxi
Pūrva (*alaṁkāra*), 563
P. V. Kane, 173*, 229*, 520-525*, 529*, 531, 564, 566. See Kane
P. Von Bohlen, 367*. See Bohlen
P. V. Ramanujasvami, 258*
P. W. Jacob, 207*

Q

Quakenbos, 168*, 170*, 172*, 659*. See G, P. Quakenbos.
Quarterly Jour. of Andhra Research Soc., 476*
Queen Diddā, cxvi. See Diddā

R

Rabi, 556
Rabindranath, xx, xxxvi, xxxvii, xxxix, xcii, 134
Race, xxii, lxviii, lxx, lxxi, lxxix, xc
Racine, liv
Raghu, xxx, lxi, 130, 132, 150*, 185*, 737, 748, 743-45, 749
Raghukāra (=Kālidāsa), 8*, 129*,
Raghunandana xxiv, cxviii
Raghunātha-bhūpatīya, 561
Raghunātha-bhūpa-vijaya 765
Raghunātha-bhūpālīya, 566
Raghunātha-dāsa, 397, 440
Raghunātha, father of Veṅkaṭādhvarin, 438
Raghunātha, King of Tanjore, 630
Raghunātha Nāyaka, 333, 361, 417, 472
Raghunātha Rāya of Nadia, 373
Raghunātha-vilāsa, 765
Raghunāthābhyudaya, 361, 417, 679*
Raghupati, 741*
Raghuvaṁśa, xxx, xxxvii, lxxxi, cv, 5*, 8* 30, 74*, 122*, 123*, 125*, 126, 129, 132, 150, 151, 167, 185*, 187, 263*, 289, 452, 729*, 732, 736, 738*, 739, 740, 743, 744, 747-48
Raghu-vilāsa, 464, 686, 769
Raghuvīracarita, 630*
Rai Pithora, 625
Rajendralala Mitra. See R. L. Mitra,
Rajkot, 17*
Rajputana, 403
Rakrila-gomin, xv, 526, 527
Ramabatar Sarma, 102*, 413
Ramachandra Dinanath, 428*
Ramalal Kanjilal, 355*
Ramaprasad Chanda, 612*, 618*. See R. P. Chanda
Ramā, 560
Ramādevī, 560
Rambhā, 675
Ramcharan Chakravarti, 439
Raṇacchoḍa, 630
R. Anantakrishna Sastri, 332*
Raṇāditya, 356
Raṅga, 639, 640
Raṅganātha, 138*, 298*
Raṅga-pīṭha and Raṅga-śīrṣa, 54
Raṅgasvāmin, 561*
Raṅgācārya, 490
Raṅgācārya, Śāstrī, Reddī, 529*, 531*, 710
R. A. Niel, 82*
Rantivarman, 263
Rapson, 756*, 760, See E. J. Rapson
Rasa or Rasika, viii, xxx, lxiv, 22, 24, 25, 37, 56, 64, 385, 517, 524*, 537, 546-48, 550, 552, 554, 559, 561, 562, 564, 565, 569, 572, 574-77, 583-85, 591-95, 601-5, 608, 609, 655*
Rasabehari, Saṁkhyatirtha, 440*
Rasa-candrikā, 748*
Rasadhvani, 545
Rasadīpikā, 676
Rasa-gaṅgādhara, 527, 565
Rasakadamba-kallolinī, 666*
Rasakārikā, 556
Rasa-mañjarī, 561, 666*
Rasa-mañjarī-prakāśa, 561,
Rasamañjarī-sthūlatātparyārtha, 561*
Rasamañjarī-vīkāśa, 561*
Rasamañjaryāmoda, 561*
Rasaniṣpatti, 594
Rasa-prakāśa, 439*, 566
Rasaratna-dīpikā, 566
Rasaratnakoṣa, 566
Rasa-sadana, 490
Rasa-śāstra, 392
Rasa-taraṅgiṇī, 539, 553*, 561
Rasavat (*alaṁkāra*), 526, 530, 534, 546, 557, 592-93
Rasa-vilāsa, 486*
Rasābhāsa, xxxv, lxiv, lxv, 546
Rasādhikā ikā, 521
Rasārṇava-sudhākara, 474, 494, 525*, 562*
Rasika-maraṇa, 679
Rasika-priyā, 566
Rasikapriyā, commentary *of Gīta-govinda*, 666*
Rasika-rañjana, of Ramacandra, 342, 370 ; of Śrīnāsācārya, 490
Raskia-rañjani of Gopāla Bhaṭṭa and Veṇī-datta, 561*
Rasika-sañjīvani 568
Rasodadhi, 561*
Rasodgara, 597*
Rathakāra, xiii, xiv
Ratha-yātrā, festival, 511*
Rathoddhatā (metre), 120*, 150*, 196*, 329*,
Rathore dynasty cxvii
Rati xxi, 131, 150*, 742
Rati-kollolinī, 487
Rati-manmatha, 469
Ratnadarpaṇa, 553
Ratnadhara, 663
Ratnakheṭa Dīkṣita, 465*, 764
Ratnakheṭa-vijaya, 772
Ratnakoṣa, 740*
Ratnam Aiyar. See T. R. Ratnam A yar
Ratnamaṇḍanagaṇi, 566
Ratnamālā, 666*

Ratnapāṇi, 557
Ratnāharaṇa, 527
Ratnākara, 9*, 167, 263*, 319-20, 321, 335*, 382, 450*, 455, 538, 686, 760, 761
Ratnāpaṇa, 557, 562,
Ratnāvalī lxxxi, lxxxvi, cxiii, 53*, 162, 173, 198, 255, 256-58, 260-62, 272, 274*, 383, 443, 458, 472, 693, 713, 758, 759
Ratnāvalī, 281*
Ratneśvara, 553
Raudra (*rasa*), 592
Ravicandra, 157*, 158*, 668, 669
Ravideva or Ravi, 121*, 337, 620 624*
Ravideva, Vāsudeva's father, 621
Ravinartaka, 262*
Ravi-sūnu, 687
Ravivarman of Kerala, 466, 559
Rāḍha, 368*, 752
Rādhā, 40, 333, 374, 383, 390, 391, 392, 396, 415, 426*, 440, 485, 666, 667
Rādhākṛṣṇa, commentator, 658*
Rādhāraman Press, 397*, 468*, 662*
Rādhā-vipralambha, 686
Rāgas, 390
Rāghava, 340
Rāghavabhaṭṭa, commentator of *Śakuntalā*, 140*, 525*, 531*, 478*
Rāghava-naiṣadhīya, 341, 619, 620
Rāghava-pāṇḍava-yādavīya, 341, 620
Rāghava-pāṇḍavīya of Dhanañjaya, 340, 619 ; of Kavirāja, 340, 619 ;
Rāghava-vilāsa, 564
Rāghavābhyudaya, 461, 686
Rāghavendra, 381*
Rāhula Bhaṭṭa, 525*
Rājacūḍāmaṇi Dīkṣita, 333, 437*, 472, 765, 772
Rājadeva of Kashmir, 323*, 628
Rājadharma, xcvii
Rājagṛha, 727
Rājakuṇḍa, 622*
Rājamaṇḍala, 643*
Rājamati, 374*
Rāja-mārtaṇḍa, 553
Rājamitra, 527
Rājamṛgāṅka, 553
Rājamukuṭa, 611*
Rājanātha, 361*, 437
Rājanīti samnccaya, 673
Rājapraśasti, 630
Rājapurī (Kashmir), 360, 677
Rājaśekhara, His Life and Writings, 454*
Rājaśekhara, quoted by Jahlaṇa, 7, 9*, 10*, 16, 168*, 171, 208*, 300, 417*
Rājaśekhara Sūri, Jaina, 326, 428, 429
Rājaśekhara the dramatist, 7*, 19, 26, 28*, 29*, 78*, 94*, 120*, 138, 185, 271*, 280, 300 301*, 314, 381*, 401*, 417*, 444, 448, 450, 453-61, 462, 463, 470, 471, 521, 525*, 530*, 538, 542, 544, 546, 547*, 553, 560, 642*, 713, 716, 757, 761, 764
Rājasthānī, 680
Rājasthānī-kheyāls, 624*
Rājasūya, c
Rājasūya-prabandha 775
Rāja-taraṅgiṇī, 119, 279*, 353-59, 525*, 535*, 544, 628, 677, 682, 692, 757
Rājavāhana, 211
Rājā Jayacand, cxvii, 625
Rājānaka Ānanda, 555, 556, 624*
Rājānaka Bhaṭṭa Āhlādaka 629*
Rājānaka Jayadratha, 628
Rājānaka Ratnakaṇṭha, 556, 621*, 663*
Rājānaka Ratnākara, 337*, 623, See Ratnākara
Rājānaka Ruyyaka, 765
Rājānaka-tilaka, 558
Rājāvalī, 554
Rājāvalī-patākā, 359, 677
Rājā Vīrasiṁhadeva, 774
Rājendra Cola, 470*
Rājendra-karṇapūra, 363, 674
Rājīmatī-prabodha, 769
Rājnām pratibodha, 664*
Rājyadevī, 226
Rājyapāla, cxvii
Rājyaśrī, 227, 263
Rājyavardhana, 227, 755
Rākāgama-suddhā, 560
Rākṣasa, lxxi, lxxxiv, 465, 693
Rākṣasa-kavya, 121, 122*, 720
Rākṣasa or Rākṣasa Paṇḍita, 122, 266-69, 286
Rāma, xlix, lxxix, cxxvii, 40, 114, 130, 131, 154 183, 186, 187, 286, 288, 289, 292, 393, 300, 303, 325, 338, 339, 341, 342, 348, 350, 360, 374, 396, 451, 456, 463-65, 502, 504, 506, 595, 598, 599, 600, 611, 618, 619, 630*, 647, 649*, 664, 665, 763,
Rāma, a pramatist, 469*
Rāma-bāṇa-stava, 383*, 665
Rāmabhadra, 769
Rāmabhadra, commentator, 748*
Rāmabhadra Dīkṣita, 383, 456, 465, 489, 665,
Rāmabhadry, Jaina, 476
Rāmabhadrāmbā, 361, 417, 679*
Rāmabhaṭṭa, 396*
Rāmacandra, author of *Gopālalīlā*, 617
Rāmacandra, author of *Nāṭya-darpaṇa*, 105*, 120*, 121*, 271*, 450, 462, 463-64, 465, 468, 469, 471, 473*, 475
Rāmacandra Budhendra, 161*, 277*, 437*
Rāmacandra Cirañjīva Bhaṭṭācārya, 439
Rāmacandra, commentator, 616*
Rāmacandra Kavibhāratī, 378
Rāmacandra, King, xxx
Rāmacandra, poet, 342, 370
Rāmacandra Śesa, 624*
Rāmacandra Tailanga, 332*
Rāmacandra Vācaspati, 616*
Rāmacandra-yaśobhūṣaṇa, 566
Rāmacandrodaya, 338, 765
Rāmacaraṇa Tarkavāgīśa, 564
Rāma-carita of Abhinauda, 201, 324, 618 ; of Saṁdhvākara Nandin, 339, 359
Rāma cāpa-stava, 383* 665
Rāmadatta, 666
Rāmadāsa, 119*
Rāmadāsa Dīkṣita, 481*
Rāmadeva, commentator, 755*
Rāmadeva Vyāsa, 504
Rāmagiri, 133, 751
Rāmagovinda, 740*
Rāmakathā, 774

Rāma, Kaviśvara, lxxx
Rāmakṛṣṇa, 468, 510
Rāmakṛṣṇakāvya, 664
Rāma-kṛṣṇa-viloma-kāvya 342
Rāmamaya Śarmā, 758
Rāmanatha, 751
Rāma of Devagiri, 342 ; of Kerala, 121*
Rāmapāla carita, 618
Rāmapāla, king, 339, 359, 618
Rāmaprasāda, 658*
Rāmarṣi, 624*
Rāmarudra, 158*, 668
Rāmasetu, 740*
Rāma Tarkavāgīśa, 658*
Rāmatāranā. 666*
Rāma Upādhyāya, 751*
Rāmavarman, Mahārāja of Travancore, 752*
Rāmavarman Vañci, 468
Rāmavarmā, Prince, 776
Rāmavijaya-mahākāvya, 630
Rāma-yamakārṇava, 338
Rāmābhyudaya, lxxxv, 299, 504 (of Rāmadeva Vyāsa), 685 (of Yaśovarman)
Rāmādevi, 389
Rāmānandanātha, 158*
Rāmānada Rāya, 396, 468, 511*
Rāmānuja, cxviii, 487, 495, 661, 768
Rāmāṣṭaprāsa, 383*
Rāmāvatāra Pāṇḍeya, 710, 712
Rāmāyaṇa, vii, xiv, xvii, xxix, xxx, xxxiii, xlix, li, lii, lxii, lxxxviii, xcviii, cxxvii, cxxix, 1, 2, 51, 60, 69, 101, 113, 114, 128*, 131, 133, 150*, 173*, 177, 183, 277, 289, 300, 303, 324, 331, 339, 341, 450, 455, 465* 487, 505, 507, 568, 617, 620, 634, 635, 641, 653, 680, 687, 688, 693, 695, 720, 725, 726, 739, 744, 746
Rāmāyaṇa-campū, 437, 438*
Rāmāyaṇa-kathā-sāra, 417
Rāmāyaṇa-manjarī, 325*, 617, 688
Rāmāyaṇasāra, 630
Rāmeśvara, 497
Rāmila, 16, 201, 241, 757
Rāmilaka, 16*
Rāsa-līlā, 391, 397, 648
Rāsāmṛta. 664
Rāṣṭrakuta, 336, 435, 470*, 617
Rāṣṭraudha king, 361, 679, 772
Rāṣṭrandha-vaṁś, 360, 679, 772
Rāvaṇa, lxxix, cxxvii, cxxviii, 64, 131, 186, 286, 303, 336, 381, 451, 452, 456, 457, 461, 463, 464, 502, 617
Rāvaṇā-vadha or *Bhaṭṭi-kāvya* (q. v.), 183-85, 186
Rāvaṇa-vadha or *Setubandha* (prakrit), 119
Rāvaṇārjunīya, cxv, 376, 616
Rāyapura, 504
Rāyamukuṭa, 7, 8*, 9, 10*, 241*, 621*, 757*
R C Majumdar, 339*, 612*
R. C. Temple, 649*
R .D. Banerji, 470*, 612*
K D. Karmakar, 126*, 741*
Realism or Realistic, lxvi, xci, cxxvii, cxxviii, 24, 61, 153, 215, 230, 292. 404, 406, 419, 456, 484, 598, 693
Recitation 636, 649, 652, 653
Record of Buddhist Religion, A, 256*
Reddi, 299, 433
Reden und Aufsätze, 651*, 669
Regimonti, 136
Regnaud. 524*. See P. Regnaud.
Reich, 650, 651, 652. See Hermann Reich
Religion or religious, vii, xxii, xxix, lvi, lxv, lxvi, lxxi, lxxii, lxxiv, lxxix, lxxxiii, lxxxvii, lxxxviii, xc. xciii, cxix, 6, 26* 45*, 48, 50, 70, 76, 166, 167*, 208, 228, 265, 291, 354, 370, 374, 376-80, 382*, 386, 388, 389, 392, 393, 395, 396, 400, 428, 436, 440, 468, 496, 510, 564, 628, 631, 640, 641, 643, 645, 648, 649, 650, 652, 653, 659, 666*, 667, 668, 669, 673, 677*, 767
Renaissance of Sanskrit, xvii, 5, 612*, 735
Report, (of Bühler) 628 ; (of R. G. Bhandarkar) 7*, 121*, 336*, 340*, 402*, 414*, 686; (of Peterson) 686 ; (of Śesāgiriśastri) 396*;
Report of Sanskrit and Tamil Mss., 320*
Revā, 505
Rev. De la Linguistique et de Philologie- 481
Revue Arceélogiaque, 650*
Rewa, 679
R. G. Basak, 243 , 839*
R. G. Bhandarkar 10*, 121*, 189*, 336* 346*, 396*, 402*, 414*, 611*, 612*, 763
R. Gottschall, 646
Ṛgveda, vi, lxxiii, 43, 44, 45, 85, 138, 240, 518, 631, 632, 634, 673, 697, 767
Ṛgveda-jaṭādyaṣṭa-vikṛti-vivaraṇa, 664*
Rhetoric or rhetorician, xxviii, cxix, 26*, 27, 29, 31, 32, 76, 104, 105, 111, 116, 122, 127*, 147, 148, 153, 160, 169, 170, 172, 173, 174, 177, 180, 183, 188, 191, 192, 193, 196. 202, 204, 207, 208, 209*, 213, 221, 223, 224, 233, 236, 270, 272, 275, 277, 278, 305, 312, 319, 322, 327, 328, 330, 334, 376, 377, 379, 397, 462. See *Alaṁkāra* and Poetics.
Rhyme, 334*
Rhythm, 207
Richard Schmidt. See R. Schmidt
Ridgeway, 47
Ritual, lxviii, lxx, lxxi, cvi, 49, 633
Ritual drama, 44, 45, 46, 633
Rīti, 218*, 536, 539, 546, 554, 564, 567, 574-76, 578, 579, 580, 582, 584
Rītinirṇaya, 521
Rītischool, 574, 580, 581
R. Lenz, 138*, 750*
R. L. Mitra or Rajendralala Mitra, 83*, 127* 480*, 485*, 501*, 529*. See Mitra
R. L. Turner, 105*
R, Narasiṁha, 529*
R. Narasiṁhācāra, 695*
Rohasena, 242*
Rohiṇī-mṛgāṅka, 475, 686-87
Roma Chaudhuri, 416*
Romaharṣaṇa, xiii
Ramance or Romantic, xxxi, xxxii, xxxvi, 11*, 21*, 22, 37, 38, 41, 42, 58, 71, 84, 94, 100, 106, 110, 130, 131, 135, 138, 146,

147, 155, 200, 201*, 202, 205, 206, 208, 209, 210, 213, 214, 215, 216, 217, 218, 219, 228, 232, 234, 235, 236, 237, 241, 247, 253, 256, 260, 261, 265, 277, 284, 315, 324, 327, 330, 346, 352, 357, 419, 432, 471, 678, 694, 700
Romāvalī-śataka, 370
Romeo and Juliet, 282
Rome or Roman, xcv, civ, 50, 59, 82, 158*, 299*, 469*, 737
Roth, 645
Roy, Prof., 753
Roychaudhuri, 736
Rozinik Oryentalistyczny°, 738
R. P. Chanda, 326*
R. Pischel, 47*, 520*, 524*, 646, 750*. See Pischel
R. P. Oliver, 239*
R. Ramamurthi, 271*, 302*
Ṛsabha, 620
Ṛṣabha-deva-carita, 563
Ṛṣabha-pañcāśikā, 430*
R. Śarma, 8*
R. Schmidt, 298*, 299*, 316*, 319*, 404*, 407*, 425*, 469*, 747. See Schmidt
R. Simon, 158*
R. S. O., 729*
R. T. H. Griffith, 741*, 744*
Ṛtu-saṃhāra, cxxvii, 40, 122-23, 740, 752
Ṛucaka, 558
Rucipati Upādhyāya, 449*
Rucirā (metre), 13, 14*
Rückert, cxxvi, 666*. See F. or Friedrich Rückert.
Rückert-Nachlese, 666*
Ruddy, 710
Rudrabhaṭṭa, 157*
Rudradāmana, xvi, xviii, ci, cii, 14, 18, 531*, 567, 613, 654.
Rudramadeva, 158*
Rudra Nyāyavācaspati, 374*, 402*, 403
Rudra, poet, 360, 431 679, 772
Rudra, scholar, lvii
Rudrasena, cix
Rudrasiṃha, I, 106*
Rudraṭa, xxviii, cxv, 7, 26*, 174, 179*, 204, 337*, 525*, 531*, 537, 538, 553, 555, 556, 581, 585, 587, 593
Rukmiṇī, 331*, 333, 341
Rukmiṇī-haraṇa, 468, 473, 768
Rukmiṇī-kalyāṇa, 333
Rukmiṇi of the Modha family, 484
Rukmiṇi-pariṇaya, 468, 765, 772
Russian, 756*
Ruthnorton, 29*
Ruyyaka, 322, 323, 360*, 527, 557, 558, 584, 611*, 615, 628, 675.
Rūpa, lvii, 685
Rūpadeva, 666*
Rūpa Gosvāmin, 372, 373*, 392, 396*, 397, 414, 415, 440, 468, 663, 751
Rūpaka, lxxvi, 51*, 64, 67, 711
Rūpaka (*alaṃkāra*), 518, 520, 526, 530, 534, 563, 569, 583.
Rūupaka-nirūpaṇīya, 521
Rūpaka-ṣaṭka, 473-74, 489
Rūpanātha Upādhyāya, 630
Rūpiṇikā in *Bṛhatkrathā*, 244*
Rūpopamā, 518
R. V. Krishnamachariar, 217*, 298*, 433*
R. W. Frazer, 755*. See Frazer

S

Śabda, 547, 559, 571, 575, 578, 581, 582, 591* 764
Śabdaśleṣa, 521, 534*
Śabdālaṃkāra, 531*, 537, 539, 552-54, 556 557, 559, 578, 579, 585, 587, 729
Śabdārtha-vṛtti, 342*
Śabdopamā, 553
Śabhā-rañjana, 403, 675
Sachinandan Goswami, 333*
Sacred Books of the Buddhists, 80*
Sacrifice or Sacrificial lix, lx, lxi, lxviii, lxx, lxxv, cxxii, cxxiii, 568, 631, 721, 722, 725, 745.
Sadācāra, xxxvi
Sadānanda, 621
Sadāśiva, 769
Sadukti-karṇāmṛta, 8, 10*, 16*, 17*, 122* 256*, 324*, 389*, 390, 401, 413, 611*, 674
Sahabuddin Ghori, 539
Sahadeva, 536
Sahajiyā, 391*, 392*
Sahasrākṣa, 521
Sohokti (*alaṃkāra*), 534, 536
Sahṛdaya, 24, 540*, 541*, 542, 543*, 606
Sahṛdayalīlā, 551, 675
Sahṛdayānanda, 338, 626
Sailālin, 635
Sailendranath Mitra, 368*
Sailūṣa, 633, 650
Sairaṃdhrikā, 494, 687
Śaiva or Śaivism, xcix, ciii, cx, cxi, 93, 161, 252*, 254, 319, 321, 323*, 324, 333, 354, 377, 381, 382, 409, 426, 439, 492*, 503, 629, 671, 673
Śaka or Scythian, cii, ciii, cvii, cviii, cxviii, 4*, 5, 6, 54, 271*, 654, 731
Śaka Satrap, ci, cix, cx
Śakaṭadāsa, 269
Śakāra, 54, 57, 242*, 246, 248, 257, 758
Sakhāvardhana, 527
Śakti, lxxi, 534, 536, 660, 668, 724
Śaktibhādra, 102*, 301*, 302
Śaktism, 172
Śaktisvāmin, 618
Śaktivega, 98
Śakuni, 113
Sakuntalā, xxxi, xxxviii, lvii, lxiii, lxxx, lxxxii, lxxxv, 128, 140, 143, 145, 247
Śakuntalā, lxxxii, 525*, 531*, 731*, 747, 748, 749, 753. See *Abhijñana-śakuntalam*.
Śakuntala-rahasya, 748*
Śakuntalopākhyāna, 748*
Salagarāja, Prince, 773
Śalya, 723, 724, 773
Sama, 505
Samañjasā (or *Vyaṅgyārtha-kaumudi*), 561*
Samantabhadra, 379
Samarabhaṭa, 198

Samarapuṇgava Dīkṣita, 438
Samasyā-pūraṇa, a type of Kāvya, 338, 374
Samasyā-pūraṇa poem of Jinadāsa, 657
Samavakāra, lxxxii, lxxxiv, lxxxvii, 65, 473, 474, 475, 768
Samavāya, 579, 580
Samaya-mātṛkā, 405
Samaya-vidyā, xcix
Samādhi, 573, 574
Samāhita (*alaṃkāra*), 526, 530, 534, 536, 557
Samāsokti (*alaṃkāra*), 526, 530, 534, 536, 545, 553, 583
Samasiva Sastri, 375*, 414*, 659*
Sambat era, 125*, 531*, 553*
Sambhājī, 415, 629
Śaṃbhali-mata, 676
Śambhu, 363, 402
Śambhurāja-carita, 415*, 629
Sambhurāja, Same as Sambhaji
Śambuka, xxx, 746
Saṃdhilaka, 252
Saṃdhyākara Nandin, 339, 359, 618, 619
Saṃghadāsikā, 252
Saṃgīta-cintāmaṇi, 627, 771
Saṃgīta-gaṅgādhara, 490*
Saṃgīta-mādhava, 396*
Saṃgita-nātaka, 468, 511*
Saṃgraha of Vyāḍi on Pāṇini, 685
Saṃgrāmapāla, 360
Saṃkalpa-sūryodaya, 332. 486*, 487
Saṃkara (*alaṃkāra*), 534
Śaṃkara, commentator, 226*, 755*
Śaṃkara, dramatist, 490
Śaṃkara or Śaṃkarācārya, xix, xxvii, cxviii, 194, 377, 380, 384, 558*, 562*, 566, 580, 616*, 660, 661, 663, 665*, 668, 669, 675, 748
Śaṃkara Miśra, 388*, 390*, 666*
Saṃkaravarman, 401, 674
Śaṃketa, 515, 555
Śaṃkirṇa, 530
Saṃkṣepa śārīrakasāra-saṃgraha, 664*
Saṃkṣepāmṛta, 664*
Saṃkṣiptasāra, 615
Sammitīyas, 685
Saṃskṛta Bhāṣā O Saṃskṛta Sāhitya-Viṣayaka Prastāva, 625*
Saṃsṛṣṭi (*alaṃkāra*), 536
Samudrabandha, commentator, 557, 558, 628
Samudradatta, 302
Samudragupta, xix, cvii, cviii, cix, cxiii, cxiv, 18, 263, 268*
Samudra-manthana, lxxxiv, 473, 479*, 768*,
Samudrānanda, 545
Saṃvāda-sūkta, 43*
Saṃvāda-Ākhyāna, 3, 43*
Saṃvṛti-bodhi-citta-bhāvanopadeśa-varṇa-samgraha, 614*
Samyag buddha-lakṣaṇa-stotra, 613*
Samyaktva-kaumudī, 427
Sanātana, 664
Sanātana-gopāla-kāvya, 416
Sanātana Śarmā, 751*
Sanchi, 731*. See Sāñcī
Sandeha (*alaṃkāra*), 536
Sandhi-vaigrahika-mahāpātra, 564
Saṅghilaka, 762
Saṅgita-ketu-śṛṅgāra-līlā-carita, 775
Sañjīvanī, 751*
Śaṅkara Miśra, MM, 666*
Śaṅkara saṃhitā, 742*
Śaṅkarābhyudaya, 772
Śaṅkarācārya, Gauḍīya, 661*
Sankar, P. Pandit, 653*
Śaṅkha, xxv
Śaṅkhadhara, 496, 629
Śaṅku, 5
Śaṅkuka or Amātya Śaṅkuka, 121*, 302, 321*, 349, 523, 535*, 552, 686, 729, 730
Sanskrit College, 624
Sanskrit Chrestomathie, 256*, 759
Sanskrit Drama, The, or S. D. 11*, 43, 48*, 49*, 50*, 52*, 125*, 632*, 635*, 654*, 757*
Sanskrit Lesibuch, 621*, 660*
Sanskrit Poetesses, 416*, 417*
Sanskrit Poems of Mayūra, The, 168*, 659*, See *Poems* of *Mayūra*
Sanskrit Poetics, 7*, 11*, 26*, 29*, 119*, 121*, 183*, 309*, 322*, 323*, 331*, 333*-35*, 361*, 370*-72*, 381*, 396*, 403*, 404*, 439*, 454*, 455*, 462*, 479*, 519*, 520*, 523*, 524*, 527*, 529*, 531*, 533*, 549*, 551*, 552*, 553*, 558*, 562*, 566
Sanskrit Sāhitya Pariṣat, 372*, 504*
Santpoort, 666*
Santrakṣita, cxvi
Saptaśatī, c, 688
Sarabhā (metre), 14*
Sarabhoj of Tanjore, 486
Saramā, 43, 631
Sarasvatī, lvi, 327, 645
Sarasvatī-Bhavana Studies, 326*
Sarasvatī-kanṭhamaṇi, 533*, 757*
Sarasvatī-kanṭhabharaṇa, 17*, 211*, 241*, 435*, 551-53
Sarasvatī-kanṭhābharaṇa-mārjjanā, 553*
Sarasvatī-kanṭhābharaṇa-ṭīkā, 553*
Sarasvatītīrtha, 555
Sarasvatī-stotra, 752*
Sarasvatīvilāsa Series, 343*, 344*
Śarva, a name of Buddha, 527
Sarvacarita nāṭaka- cxiii, 755
Sarvadarśana-saṃgraha, 767
Sarvajnamitra, 378
Sarvavarman, ci, cii, 93
Sarvavidyā-siddhānta-varṇana, 664*
Sarvānanda-nāga, 337*, 618*
Sarvānanda, Vandyaghaṭīya, 413
Sarvāṅga-sundarī, 666*
Śarvārthasiddhī, 74, 264*, 266
Sarvāstivāda, cv
Sarvāstivādin, 70, 73
Śaśa, 250
Śaśadhara, 340*, 619*
Sasandeha (*alaṃkāra*), 526, 534
Śaśāṅka, 755
Śaśikalā, 659*
Śāśilekhā, 392*
Śaśiprabhā, 349
Śaśivadanā (metre), 13
Sassanian, ci, cvii

Śatakas, of Amaru, lxxxix, 155-62 ; of Bāṇa 158*, 166, 170-71, 172, 378 ; of Bhartṛhari 16, 35, 155, 156, 161-65, 194, 367*, 401*; of Mayūra, 155, 156*, 166, 170, 171, 172, 378 ; in general lxiv, lxxix, xcix, 157, 160, 161, 162, 166, 364, 367-72, 399, 400, 646, 659, 669, 671, 672, 673
Śatapañcāśatka-nāmastotra, 614*
Śatapañcāśatka-stotra, 79, 613*
Śatapatha Brahmaṇa, 138*, 518, 632
Śataśloka-gītā, 661
Śataślokī, 675
Śatārthakāvya, 767
Satire or Satiric poem and play, 85, 137*, 194, 197-99, 214, 215, 246, 250, 252, 253, 254, 255, 306, 404-11, 419, 438, 484, 492, 493, 496
Ṣaṭpadī, 661
Śatru-parājaya-svara-śāstra-sāra, 740*
Saṭṭaka, 67, 458*
Sattasaī, Saptaśatī of Hāla, 15, 155, 156, 157, 391, 659
Ṣaṭtriṃśanmata, xxv
Sattva, xlix
Satya-hariścandra, 469, 769
Satyam, 681*
Satyatapaḥ-kathodaya, 338*
Śaubhika, 11, 48, 636, 637, 640, 642
Śauddhodanī, 564
Saugandhikāharaṇa, 467, 769
Saumilla or Somila, 16, 101, 201, 241, 685, 757
Śaunaka, xxv, 43*, 611*
Saundarānanda, c, 6*, 70*, 73, 74-76, 361, 613, 731
Saundarya-laharī, 660, 661*
Śaurasenī (Prakrit), cxx, 49, 243*, 261*, 270*, 276*, 537
Saurāṣṭra, 251
Śaurīndra M. Tagore, 271*
Śauri-kathodaya, 338*, 621
Sautrāntika, 72, 73
Śavara, xix, xx
Sādhana-paddhati, 664*
Sāgaradatta, 302
Sāgara-kaumudī, 494, 689
Sāgarikā, lxxxi, lxxxii, 257
Sāhasāṅka, 17*, 757*
Sāhasāṅka-campū, 626
Sāhajī of Tanjore, 486
Sāhābuddin, 626. See Sahabuddin Ghori
Sāhitya-darpaṇa, 517, 521*, 523*, 524*, 525*, 542, 550*, 552*, 557*, 562*, 563, 564, 566, 615, 662*, 687
Sāhityadarpaṇa-locana, 564
Sāhityadarpaṇa-prabhā, 564
Sāhityadarpaṇa-ṭippanī, 564
Sāhityadarpaṇa-vivṛti, 564
Sāhitya-kalpāvalī, 566
Sāhitya-kaumudī, 555, 556
Sāhitya-mīmāṃsā, 558
Sāhitya-ratnākara, 765
Sāhitya-sarvasva, 535*
Sāhitya sāra, 566
Sāhityasudhā, 561*
Sāhitya-taraṅgiṇī, 566
Śākalyamalla, 331
Śākambharī, 469, 476
Śākya-bhikṣu, 252
Śālāturīya, 527
Śālibhadra-carita, 344
Śālinātha, 666
Śālinī (metre), 12, 77*, 196*
Śālivāhana, ci, 17*, 201*
Śālivāhana-kathā, 424*
Sāmarāja Dikṣita, 370, 486, 500
Sāmanta Vilāsraradatta, 262
Sāmaveda 45, 240, 632, 767
Sāmānya, 518
Sāmba, legend of, 169
Sāmba-pañcāśikā, 382, 659
Sāmbopa-purāṇa, 659*
Sām, Iranian story of, 169
Sāṃkhya, xix, lxvi, 72, 278, 729, 742, 754
Sāṃkhya-kārikā, cxiv
Sāmya (alaṃkāra), 538
Sānanda-govinda, 666*
Sāñcī, cvi, 635. See Sanchi
Sāndilya, 525*
Sāṇḍilya-sūtra-ṭīkā, 664*
Śāntanava, 519
Śāntideva, 81*, 675
Śānti-parvan (*Mahābhārata*), xvii*, 195
Śānti-śataka, 401
Śānti-vilāsa, 403, 674
Śārabodhinī, 556
Śāradā-candrika, 292
Śāradāgama, 560
Śāradā (script), 196, 396
Śāradātanaya, lxv, lxxxv*, 299, 302*, 494, 506*, 687
Śāradā-tilaka (Bhāṇa), 490, 491, 492*
Śāradvata, xxxix, lx, 225
Śāradvatī-putra-prakaraṇa, same as *Śāriputra-prakaraṇa*, 655
Sāraṅga-raṅgadā, 662*
Sāra-samuccaya, 354*
Sārasvatabhadra, 252
Sārāvalī, 730*
Sārāvalī, commentary, 741*
Śārdūlavikrīḍita (metre), 9, 12, 14*, 77*, 121*, 158*, 159*, 168, 170*, 184*, 196*, 243*, 261*, 270*, 276*, 285*, 326*, 373, 382, 383, 400*, 403*, 410, 456, 461, 462*
Śāriputra, 655
Śāriputra-prakaraṇa, lxxxviii, 73, 76-79, 655
Śārṅgadeva, 390*
Śārṅgadhara, 16, 414, 532*
Śārṅgadhara-paddhati, 8*, 333*, 414, 417*, 496*, 535*, 740*
Śārṅgarava, xxxix, lx, 145
Śārṅgarava, author, 551
Sārvabhauma Bhaṭṭācārya, 663
Sārvabhauma-nāgara, 252
Śāstrasiddhānta-leśa-ṭīkā, 664*
Śāsvata, commentator of *Meghadūta*, 751*
Sātakarṇi, cii
Sātavāhana, ci, cii, See Hāla Sātavāhana

Śātātapa, xxv
Sāttvati (Vṛtti), 63, 539
Sāyaṇa, lxxiii
S.B.A., 646, 652*, 655*
S. B. A. W., 47*, 52*
S. Bay A., 666*
Scherbatskoi, 629*
Schmidt, 89*, 623*, 645
Schönberg, 618*
Schroeder, 393, 650, 651, 667
Schulthess, 89*
Schyler, 277*
S. C. Law, 262*
Sculpture, 625, 654
S. C. Vidyabhushan, 80*, 378*,-79*
Scythians, xxii, See Śaka
S. D. Gajendragadkar, 741*
Sea voyage, xxiv
Śekhara, xx
Selections from Inscriptions, 17*
Select Specimens, 262*, 277*, 646
Select Works of Śaṃkarācārya, 380*, 660*
Semetic, lxvii
Senart, 685, See E. Senart
Senas (of Bengal), 390
Seneca, 141*
Seriṅgapatam, 773
Serge d' Oldenberg, 81*
Śeṣa, 521
Śeṣa Cintāmaṇi, 468
Sesagiri Sastri, 320*, 396*
Śeṣa Kṛṣṇa, 437, 461
Śeṣaratnākara, 667*
Śesavireśvara, 565
Śeṣādri Iyer, 371*
Setubandha, cxv, See *Rāvaṇa-vadha*
Sevya-sevakopadeśa, 406, 675
Sexology, lxxv
S. G. Kanhere, 661*
S. Goldschmidt, 119*
Shadow-play, 47, 48, 49, 501, 503, 504, 505, 637, 642, 653*. See Chāyā-nāṭaka
Shahabuddin Ghori, 360. See Sahabuddin Ghori
Shah Jahan, 315, 364*, 372, 566
Shah, Muhammad, 629
Shahpur I, cvii
Shakespeare, xxxiv, xxxv, xlviii, 33, 141*, 147, 148, 154, 244, 248, 444, 651
Shemvanekar, Prof. 753, 754
Shepherd's Calender, 123
Siddāpur Edicts, cxxi
Siddhacandra, 229*
Siddhacandragaṇi, 756*
Siddha, poet, 189*, 259
Siddharāja, 768
Siddhasena Divakāra, lix, 172*, 379
Siddhānta-tattvavindu, 664*
Siddhārthaka, 269
Siddhi Narasiṃha, 510*
Siddhipriya Stotra, 338
Siddhopamā, 518
Seiglin, 79*
Sikh, 390
Śikhaṇḍaka, lix
Śikhariṇī (metre), 9, 14*, 77*, 159*, 196*, 270*, 276*, 285*, 329, 372, 380, 383, 660
Śikṣā, 513
Śikṣā-daśaka, 664*
Śikṣāpada, 254*
Śikṣā-samuccaya, 695
Śikṣāṣaṭka, 663
Śilahāra (dynasty), 351
Śilābhaṭṭārikā, woman poet, 416, 417*
Śīlā ditya, 255, 428, 759
Śīlā-dūta, 374*
Śilālin, 52*, 523, 635, 640
Śihlaṇa, 401, 402, 674
Sikh Religion, The, 666*
Siṃhabhūpāla, 525*
Siṃpalese, 621 See Sinhalese
Siṃhavarman, 254
Siṃhaviṣṇuvarman, 765
Siṃhāsana-dvātriṃśikā, 11*, 424
Simile, 2, 14, 15, 24*, 34, 35, 39, 151, 169*, 171, 193, 196, 221, 223, 236, 270, 329, 519
Simon, 158*. See R. Simon
Simplicitor Text, 89, 80. See Textus Siṃhlicior
Sin, lxxxix, 665*
Sindhu, 404
Sindhurāja (Paramāra), 349
Śinhalese, 133*, 185, 186, 752. See Siṃpalese
Siṅghabhūpāla, 331, 490*. See Siṃhabhūpāla
Singing, lvi, lxxxiii, xviii. See Song
Siri Pālitta, 201*, 431
Siri Pulumāyi, 15
Śiśu-hitaiṣiṇī of Caritra-vardhana and Vyāsavatsa, 741*
Śiśupāla, King of Cedis, 189
Śiśupāla-vadha, 167, 188*, 189-94, 263*, 622, 623, 656*
Śiṣya-hitaiṣiṇī, 751*
Śiṣya-lekha, 80*, 81*
Sitavenga, 54*
Śitikaṇṭha-vijayakāvya, 764
Sitzungsberichte d Berliner Akad, 76*, 349*,
Śiva, xxxi, xxxii, lxxi, lxxx, xc, ciii, cv, cvii, cxiii, 50, 93, 128, 162, 167, 171, 179, 241, 258*, 278, 319-21, 333, 338*, 341, 352, 391, 393, 623, 627, 629, 630, 647, 648, 660-63, 665, 728, 741, 742
Śivadatta, 95*, 119*, 189*, 240*, 249*, 299*, 316*, 323*, 325*, 331*, 332*, 336*, 337*, 430*, 345*, 757
Śivadāsa, 421, 423, 424, 665
Śivalīlārṇava, 334, 630, 764
Śiva-mahimnaḥ-stotra, 381, 660
Śivanārāyaṇa-dāsa, 511*
Śivaprasad Bhattacharjee, 127*, 219, 508*, 661*
Śivapuri, 248*
Śiva-rahasya, 742*, 743
Śivarāma, 256*, 465*, 756*, 759*
Śivarāma Tripāṭhin, 217*
Śivarāmānanda tīrtha, 396
Śiva-sakti-siddhi, 326*, 626
Śivasiṃha of Mithilā, 426*
Śivasvāmin, cxv, 120*, 320-22, 685

Śivājī, 629
Śivāparādha-ksamāpaṇa-stotra, 380
Śivodaya, 338*
Sītā, xlix, lxxviii, cxxviii, 40, 114, 131, 185*, 187, 247, 286-89, 292-3, 300, 303, 324, 331, 374, 396, 429, 451, 456-57, 463-65, 504, 595, 598, 647, 731, 735, 736, 738, 746, 749
Sītā, poetess, 429
Sītārāma, Kavīśvara, 126*, 127*, 741*
Skandagupta, cxii, 179, 233
Skanda-purāṇa, 334, 630, 757
S. K. Belvalker, 107*, 277*
S. K. Chatterjee, 394*, 497*
S. K. De, xi, xii, 7*, 8*, 26*, 29*, 48*, 84* 119*,-21*, 159*, 165*, 178*, 183*, 185* 202*, 208*, 209*, 217*, 241*, 246*, 248* 271, 286*, 299*, 300*, 309*, 322*, 323* 324*, 326*, 331*, 335*, 337*, 361*, 363* 370*, 371* 381*, 391*, 396*, 398*, 403*, 404*, 413*, 415*, 435*, 430*, 454*, 455* 462*, 464*, 505*, 507*, 519*, 520*, 523*, 524*, 529*, 531*, 533*, 548*, 549*, 551*, 552*, 553*, 558*, 562*, 566*, 611, 615*, 618, 619, 656*, 663*, 666*, See De
S. K. Ramananda Sastri, 248*
S. Kuppusvami, 298*
S. Lefmann, 83*
Śleṣa, 33*, 218*, 221, 334, 335, 337, 339, 340*, 341, 342, 359, 526, 530, 534*, 536, 563, 574, 756*. See Paronomasia and Pun.
Śleṣa-kāvya, 335, 337-42
S. Levi, 1, 44*, 70*, 79*, 92*, 93*, 95*, 101*, 612*, 614*, 666*, See Levi
Śloka (metre), xxi, lxiv, 2, 9, 12, 79, 93, 94 96, 120, 121*, 131, 150, 167, 184*, 195, 196, 243*, 270*, 275*, 285*, 316*, 323, 324, 327, 329*, 336*, 344, 359, 402, 403, 404, 405, 406, 423, 424
Śloka-saṃgraha, 692
Śloka-vārttika, 12
Smārta Pañcopāsaka, 391*
Smith, cix*, 612, 613, 755* See V.A. Smith
S. M. Paranjpe, 256*
Smṛti, xxii, xxiii, xxiv, xxvi, xxviii, xxix, xxxi, xxxii, xxxiv, xxxvi, xxxix, xl, xlvii, lxii, xciii, xcv, xcix, cxviii, 290, 391, 693. See *Dharmaśāstra*
Snake-charm, Snake-doctor, 168, 212, 475, 491. See Jāṅgulika
S. N. Tadpatrikar, 659*
Śobhana, 338, 379
Soḍḍhala, 324*, 431-32, 455*, 766
Śoka vinodana, 614*
Solecism, 8*, 107, 209, 343*, 721
Solomon, 387
Soma, lix, 278, 559, 631
Somadatta, Prince, 78, 210*
Somadeva, 89, 90, 96, 98, 99, 230*, 231, 241, 244*, 280, 421, 422*, 423, 455, 688-92, 694, 696
Somdeva, Cālukya, 341
Somadeva, dramatist, 469, 479*
Somadeva Sūri, 343*, 432*, 435-36
Somagiri, 387
Somanātha, 765
Somapāla, 360, 677
Somapāla-vilāsa, 360, 410*, 677
Somaprabha, 432*
Somaprabhācārya, Jaina, 342, 362*, 370, 675, 767
Somānanda, 381, 661
Someśvara, 332, 350*, 362, 466*
Someśvara, commentator, 547-49, 555, 556
Someśvaradeva, 678
Someśvara II, 351, 677
Someśvara of Kalyāṇa, 341, 769, 770
Somila. See Saumilla
Song, lviii, lix, 20, 44, 45, 47, 51, 62, 67, 139*, 387, 510, 749, See Music
Sophocles, lxviii
Spandapradīpikā, 662
South or Southern India, civ, 400*, 403*, 437, 438, 467, 489, 653*, 720
Southern Guzerat, 766
Southern Pañcatantra, 89
South Travancore, 776
Sovani, Prof., 520*, 540*, 543*
Spenser, 230, 234, 484
Speyer, 82*, 99*, 265*. See J. S. Speyer
Sphoṭa, theory, 520, 527, 605, 608
Sports, lvi, 20, 491
S. P. Pandit or Pandit 125*, 129*, 132*, 136*, 138*, 278*, 279*, 361*
Spring festival, 645
Śraddhotpādasūtra, cv
Sragdharā, (metre), 9, 13, 71, 77*, 159*, 165*, 168, 169, 170, 184*, 196*, 261*, 270*, 276*, 285*, 329, 378, 380, 403*, 456, 461, 659
Śramaṇa, 422*
S. Rangacariar, 763
Śrauti, 519
Śravya, xlvi
Śrāvastī, 201*, 212, 321
S. R. Dharaṇīdhara, 741*
Srigopal Basu Mallik Lectures on Vedanta Philosophy, 380*
Śrībhūtirāja, 535*
Śrīcaitanya, 662, 663, See Caitanya
Śrīdatta, 340*, 624*
Śrīdāma carita, 486, 500
Śrīdevī, 340
Śrīdhara, author of *Kāvyaprakāśa-viveka*, 556
Śrīdharadāsa, 390, 401, 413
Śrīdhara Press, 418*
Śrīdhara Sarasvatī, 664
Śrīdharasena, 528, 615
Śrīdharasvāmin, 615*, 660*
Śrīgadita, 467
Śrīharṣa, lviii, cxvi, 325-30, 351, 429, 553, 625, 626, 627, 629, 666, 681, 758
Śrīhirapaṇḍita, 325, 625
Śrīkaṇṭha Bhaṭṭa, 661
Śrīkaṇṭha-carita, 19, 322-23, 350*, 382*, 449, 557, 558, 627, 628, 761
Śrīkaṇṭha-stava, 558
Śrīkaṇṭha, title of Bhavabhūti, 278, 298
Śrīkānta-miśra, 666*
Śrīkṛṣṇa, 774. See Kṛṣṇa.

Śrīkṛṣṇa-kīrtana, 391*
Śrīkṛṣṇa Sūri, 773
Śrīmad-bhagavad-gītā, 774, See *Gītā*
Śrīmadbhāgavata, 385, 620. See *Bhāgavata*
Śrīmāmalladevī, 625
Śrīnagara, cv
Śrīnātha, 624*
Śrīnivāsa Atirātrayāyin, 486*
Śrīnivāsa Dīkṣita, 772
Śrīnivāsa, king, 770, 771
Śrīnivāsa-vilāsa-campū, 439*, 748*, 770
Śrīnivāsācārya, 490
Śrīpadmanābha, 776
Śrīpādalipta. See Siri Pālitta
Śrīpulamāyi Vaśisthaputra, ci
Śrīraṅgam, 140, 217*, 219*, 298*, 332*, 334*, 380*, 403*, 433*, 487*, 535*, 657, 662*, 754, 773
Srirampore College Library, 413*, 424*
Śrī Rājanātha, 772
Śrī-sadānanda, 774
Śrīsaṃkuka, 602
Śrīsh Ch. Chakravarti, 741*
Śrīśrīpāla, 767
Śrīvara, 119, 120*, 316*, 354*, 359, 415, 629, 677, 771
Śrīvāṇīvilāsa Press, 217*, 256*, 298*, 331*, 332*, 334*, 361*, 380*, 403*, 433*, 487*, 773
Śrīvāṇīvilāsa Series, 535*, 662*
Śrīvijaya-praśasti, 326*
Śṛṅgāra, 357, 553, 555*, 592, 595, 672
Śṛṅgāra-bhūṣaṇa, 299, 489, 491*, 627, 771
Śṛṅgāra, brother of Maṅkhaka, 322
Śṛṅgāra-dīpikā, 627, 771
Śṛṅgāra-jñāna-nirṇaya, 675
Śṛṅgāragupta, 755*
Śṛṅgārā-kalikā-triśatī, 370
Śṛṅgāra-kośa, 765
Śṛṅgara-mañjarī, 490*, 566
Śṛṅgāra, minister of Rājadeva, 628
Śṛṅgāra-prakāśa, 16*, 201, 241*, 271*, 299, 301*, 553, 761, 762
Śṛṅgāra-rasa-maṇḍana, 392*, 396
Śṛṅgāra-saptaśatika, 659
Śṛṅgāra-sarvasva, 490, 491*, 772
Śṛṅgāra-śataka, of Bhartṛhari, 161, 162-63, 163-65; of Dhanadadeva, Janārdana, and Narahari, 370, 669, 670, 740, 752*
Śṛṅgāra-śekhara, 220
Śṛṅgārasāra, 740*
Śṛṅgāra-tilaka, of Ramabhadra, 465*, 489; of Rudra Bhaṭṭa, 157*, 298*, 537, 558*, 740*
Śṛṅgara-vairāgya-taraṅgini, 342, 370*, 675
Śṛṅgāra-vāṭika (or *vāpikā*), 473*
Śṛṅgārāmṛta-laharī, 487*
Śrutabodha, 740*
Śrutakīrti Traividya, 340, 619
Śrutasāgara Suri, 435*
Śrutānupālini, 521
Śruti, xcix
Śrutirañjanī, 666*
S. Srikantha Sastri, 263*
Stage, 107, 116, 135, 3*, 254*, 278, 647, 722. See Theatre
Statuary art, xc
Stambhita-rambhaka, 687
Stavamālā, 397, 663, 664*
Stavāvalī, 397
Sten Konow, 1, 43, 77, 94*, 106*, 136*, 140*, 239*, 240*, 242*, 262*, 272*, 277*, 298*, 301*, 504, 612*. See Konow
Stenzler, 132*. See A. F. Stenzler
Sthairya-vicāra-prakaraṇa, 326*, 626
Sthavira school, cviii, 685
Sthavirāvalī, 343
Sthānaka, 766
Sthāṇvīśvara, 226, 255
Sthāpaka or Sthāpana, 47, 104, 653*, 709, 711, 716, 718. See Sūtradhāra
Sthāyibhāva, 539, 561
Sthiramati, cxii
Sthūlāpatti, 614*
Sticu, 594, 596, 710
Stimmen indischer Lebensklugheit, 196*
Stotra, lxxv, xcix, cvi, 79, 150*, 166-73, 194, 306, 314, 332*, 333*, 338, 375-98, 430* 664, 668*, 774
Stotra Saṃgraha, Jaina, 379*
Stotrāvalī, 381
Strassburg, 243*
Strīparva (*Mahābhārata*), xvii
Studien Sum 10, *Buch des Bhaṭṭikāvya*, 615
Studies about the Kathāsarit sāgara, 691*, 700*
Studies about the Sanskrit Buddhist Lit., 69*
Studies on Sanskrit Lit., 159*
Stuti-kusumāñjali, 661, 663
Stuttgart, 20*, 189*, 520*, 524*
Stuti-saṃgraha, 379*
Stūpa, cv
Style, 224, 228-29, 232, 236, 239, 261, 269, 270, 287, 394, 402, 418, 420, 423, 426, 427, 517, 522, 530, 531*, 535, 537, 547, 571, 672, 684, 692, 709, 719, 723, 744, 769, 770. See *Rīti*
Suali, 627*
Subandhu, cxiv 5*, 8*, 16, 33, 92, 120, 155 191, 200, 201, 203, 205, 213, 216, 217-25, 227, 232, 236, 253, 330, 335, 340, 429, 435, 439*, 520, 688, 694, 755
Subarṇanābha, 521
Subhadrā, 332, 403*, 770
Subhadrā-dhanañjaya, 465
Subhadrā-haraṇa, 467
Subhadrā-haraṇa-prabandha, 775
Subhadrā-pariṇaya, 504
Subhaṭa, 502. See *Dūtāṅgada*
Subhāṣita-hārāvalī, 415
Subhāṣita-nīvi, 403, 674
Subhāṣita-ratna-karaṇḍaka-kathā, 614
Subhāṣita-ratna-sandoha, 401, 676
Subhāṣita-ratnāvali, 611*
Subhāṣitas, 673
Subhāṣita-triśatī (Bhartṛhari), 161*
Subhāṣitāvalī, of Śrīvara, 415; of Vallabhadeva, cxiii, 8*, 10*, 16, 119, 120*, 121*, 122*, 171, 173*, 320*, 333*, 389*, 400*, 402, 413, 414, 415, 535*, 538, 621*, 661*, 755, 761
Subodhā, 741*

Subodhinī, 616*, 621
Sucivāṇa, lix.
Sudarśana, 723
Sudarśana-śataka, 674
Sudāna, same as Viśvāntara, 656*
Śuddhicandrikā, 740*
Sudhālaharī, 383, 665, 675
Sudhākalasa, 687
Sudhāsāgara, 556
Sudṛṣṭi, lix
Sugata-pañcatriratna-stotra, 613*
Sughaṭadatta, 629
Sugrīva, cxxvii
Sugrīvakelana, 687
Suhma country, 212
Suhṛllekha, 80*, 81*
Suja-uddaulah, 439
Śuka, 359*, 677
Śukanāsa, 232, 234
Śukasandeśa, 752
Śuka-saptati, 420, 425-26
Sukhākara, 756*
Śukra, xcviii
Sukṛta-kīrti-kallolinī, 363
Sukṛta-saṃkīrtana, 363, 678
Sukthankar, 60*, 102*, 105*, 106*, 107*, 108*, 242*
Sulakṣaṇā, 745
Sumaṅgala-stotra, 368*
Sumanottarā, xviii, 11, 200
Sumanta, xxv
Sumati, lix
Sumatinātha-carita, 767
Sumati-vijaya, 751*
Sumatra, cxi, 389*, 426, 475
Sumila, lix
Sumitrā, 560
Śunaḥsepa, 85, 112, 632
Sunandā, 251, 252
Sundara, 368, 369, 658*, 659*
Sundaraka, Kaurava messenger, 273
Sundaranātha (Śiva), 334, 383
Sundaramiśra, 525*
Sundara-pāṇḍya, 400
Sundararāja, 468
Sundarī (metre), 14*, 75, 120*, 156. See Viyoginī
Sundarī-śataka, 370
Suṅga, c, ciii, 750
Sun-worship 172
Suparṇādhyāya, 631, 632
Supathādeśa-parikathā, 614
Supernatural, lxix, lxxxvii
Suprabhadeva, 189
Suprabha (or *Suprabhāta*) *stotra*, 173
Surapāla, 218*
Surata-mañjarī, 97
Suratha, 332
Surathotsava, 332, 350*, 362, 466*, 678, 769
Surānanda, 459
Susaṅgata, lxxxii
Susarman, Kāṇva king, c
Sussala of Kashmir, 354, 358
Suvadanā (metre), 14*, 77*
Suvarṇākṣī, 613*
Suvrata, 355
Suvṛtta-tilaka, 9, 120*, 249*, 336*, 617*, 621
Suyodhana, 179
Suzanne Karpales, 378*
Suzuki, 71*. See T. Suzuki
Sūdraka, xxix, xxxviii, lvii, lxiv, cx, cxix, cxxv, 22, 57, 108, 109*, 156, 213, 239-48, 249, 264, 270, 295, 302, 756, 757-58, 761-62
Śūdraka-carita, 762
Śūdraka-kathā, of Pañcaśikha,, 241*; of Somila, 16, 201, 241, 757*, 762
Śūdraka-vadha, 241*, 757*
Sūkti-muktāvalī of Jahlaṇa, 7, 8*, 10*, 120*, 168*, 171, 185, 300, 322*, 324*, 333*, 389*, 414, 417*, 455*, 473*, 755, 767, 769, 770
Sūkti-ratna-hāra, 400*, 414
Sūktivāsa-kumāra, 686
Śūra, Ārya, 80-81
Śūrasena, 568
Sūri, poet, 685
Śūrpaṇakhā, 287, 303
Śūrpaṇakhā-pralāpa, 774
Śūryadeva, 664
Sūryamati, Princess of Jalandhara, 96
Sūryaprabhā, 98
Sūrya-prakāśa, 352
Sūrya-śataka, 168-70
Sūtra, xxvii, cv, 535, 563
Sūtradhāra, 47, 103, 104*, 510, 641, 647, 651, 653*. See Sthāpaka
Sūtrālaṃkāra, cv, cvi, 72, 613, 655
Sūtrālaṃkāra-śāstra, 614*
Svabhāvokti (*alaṃkāra*), 526, 530, 534, 538, 586-87, 590
Svapna-daśānana, 301*
Svapna-nāṭaka or *Svapna-vāsavadattā*, 101, 105, 108, 109, 111, 116, 117, 136, 260*, 300, 529*, 531, 641, 695, 696, 719
Svarasthāna, 530
Svayambara, xc, 130, 286, 327, 351, 353, 451, 457, 504
Svayamutprekṣita-līlā, 397
Svāgatā (metre), 181*, 190*, 329*, 462*
Svāhā-sudhākara, 371, 775
Svāti, Andhra-bhṛtya king, 761
S. Venkataraman, 660*
Śvetāmbara Jaina, 361, 425, 430, 476, 537
Śvetāśvatara, xvii
S. W. A., 299*
Swang, 510
Sweet Valley, 94
Śyāmala, 552
Śyāmala-daṇḍaka, 752*
Śyāmalika, 156, 213, 249, 761, 762
Sylvain Levi, 240*, 646. See S. Levi and Levi.
Symbolism, 233
Syriac version of *Pañcatantra*, 89

T

T. A. Gopinath Rao, 343*, 418
Tagore, xxvii. See Rabindranath
Tagore Law Lectures, 240*
Tailaka, 553*
Tailaṅga, 371, 372*, 383, 565, 617, 627

Tailapa, king, 351
Taine, liv
Taittirīya Śākhā (Yajurveda), 278
Takakusu, 71*, 656*. See J. Takakusu, 256*
Tale, 38, 42, 53, 72, 80, 81, 82, 83-100, 110, 112, 116, 155, 172, 195, 198, 200, 205, 206, 211, 212, 214, 215, 216, 220, 227, 230, 231, 234, 235, 261, 344, 420-29.
Tales from Sanskrit Dramatists, 246*
Tamil, lxxviii, 92* 680, 698*, 704, 705
Tanasukhram Manasukhram Tripathi, 197*
Tangyur, 752
Tanjore, 333, 334, 343*, 344*, 361, 417, 464, 465*, 472, 486, 533*, 557 630, 668, 679*
Tanjore Catalogue, 335*, 338*, 341*, 396*, 417*, 437*
Tantra, viii, lxxv, 88, 166, 377*, 379, 458, 702, 707
Tantrākhyāna, 704
Tantrākhyāyikā, xiv, 15, 84, 88, 89, 90, 162*, 200, 263*, 614, 694*, 698-707
Tantrāloka, 12
Tantrāloka-viveka, 558
Tantrik, cxv, 377, 379, 459, 661
Tanvī (metre), 13
Tapas or *Tapasyā*, xxxvi, xxxvii, 741, 742
Tapatī, 466
Tapatī-saṃvaraṇa, 465, 720
Tarala, poet, 454
Taralā commentary, 561
Taraṅgadatta, 302, 686
Taraṅgalolā, 201*
Taraṅgavatī, 201, 431, 754
Taruṇa Vācaspati, 531*, 532*, 533*, 577*
Tatsama (Prākṛta), cxxiv
Tattva-bodhinī, 514
Tattva-dipanī, 755*
Tattvadīpikā, 751*
Tattva-guṇādarśa, 439
Tattva-kaumudī, 623*, 755*
Tattvoktikoṣa, 552
T. Aufrecht, 12*,
Tauṇḍikoki Viṣṇunāga, 251
Tawney, 29*, 230*, 430*, 760. See C. H. Tawney
Taxila, 72
Tālas, 390
Tāmralipti, cvii
Tāmraparṇī, 450
Taṇḍava, 50, 319
Tāṇḍavikā, lix
Tāpasa-vatsarāja carita, 300, 686, 759
Tārakoddharaṇa, lxxxiv, 687
Tārā, Buddhist deity, 378
Tārācandra, 730
Tārānātha, 613, 614*, 685, 728*
Tārāpīḍa, 234
Tārā-śaśāṅka, 369
Tāra, wife of Vidyānareśa, 373*
Tāṭakā, 451, 456
Tātparya-dīpikā, 751*
T. B. Panabokke, 133*
Technical Sciences, xi
Telang, 161*, 539*, 565, 760. See K. T. Telang and M. R. Telang
Telegu, 341*, 707, 754*
Telengana, 562
Terminal Essays, 691*
Terracotta, lxi, 731*
Teufel, 695
Teutonic, vi
Textus Ornatior, 425*, 703. See Ornatior Text
Textus Simplicior, 425*, 702, 703, 706, See Simplicior Text
T. Ganapati Sastri, 101, 102*, 109*, 126*, 178*, 254*, 256*, 331*, 334*, 382*, 386*, 465*, 466*, 548*, 550*
Thakkar Lectures, 753
Thaneswar, 16
Thānā, modern name of Sthānaka, 432
Th. Bloch, 54*, 650*, 750*
Theater der Hindus, 646
Theatre, 54, 56, 67, 651, 741*. See Drama and Stage.
Theâtre indien, 11*, 92*, 101*
Theft, 190, 250, 254, 485; (art of) 211
Theism, xxvii
Theocracy, xciv
Théodore Paviein, 429*
Theological or Theology, cv, 166, 385, 392, 440 483, 485, 486
Therīgāthās, 612
Thinae, 737
T. H. Kuppusvami Sastry, 472*
Thomas, 8*, 108*, 158*, 166*, 170*, 173*, 186*, 249, 454*, 611*, 613*, 618*, 621, 710, 754. See F. W. Thomas
Thomas Gray, 298*
Ph. Pavie, 728*
Three Reports, 121*, 402*, 465*, 620*
Thyestes, 141*
Th. Zachariae, 349*, 361*. See Zachariae
Tiberius, Roman Emperor, civ
Tibet or Tibetan, cvi, cxvi, 13, 71, 73, 79, 80, 119, 132*, 166*, 422*, 533*, 614*, 656, 673, 685, 752
Tien-shan Mountains, 737
Tilaka, 555
Tilaka-mañjarī, 201, 229*, 430-31, 688
Time and Analysis of Sanskrit Plays, 651*
Timma, 773
Tinnevelly, 468*, 775
Tirumala Nāyaka, 334
Tirumalāmbā, 361*, 417, 438
Tithis, xiv
Tīkā-sarvasva, 715
T. Narasimghyengar, 529*
Todar Mall, 277*, 278*, 280*, 286*, 468*
Tomematsu, 72*
Toramāṇa, 356, 736
Toṭaka, 687
Toṭaka (metre), 12
Tragedy, 141*
Tragedy or tragic, xxi, xxxii, xxxvi, xlix, 36, 39, 49, 59-61, 104, 112, 113, 128, 138, 139, 140, 142, 154, 244, 246, 248, 259, 260, 267, 283, 294, 446-47, 602, 717, 746, 747
Trailokyadeva, 768
Trailokya-sundarī-kathā, 431, 754
Trailokyavarmā, 768
Trajan, Roman Emperor, civ
Travancore, 468, 479, 708, 717, 773, 776

T. R. Cintamani, 119*, 361*, 437*
Treasury, xcv
Treatment of Love in Sanskrit Literature, 159*, 246*, 611*, 666*
Tribhuvanacandra, 533*
Tribhuvanapāla, commentator, 169*
Tribhuvanpāla, king, 502
Trichur, 129*, 248*
Tridaṇḍa-mālā, 72*
Trigarta, 113
Trikāṇḍa-śeṣa, 525*, 702
Triliṅga country, 771
Trilocana, 686
Trimaladeva, 473
Tripiṭaka, cv
Tripura, 322, 323, 474, 627
Tripura-dahana, 121*, 338*, 621, 687
Tripura-dāha, lxxxiv, 474, 687, 768
Tripura-mardana, 687
Tripura-sundarī-stutikāvya, 740*
Tripuravijaya-campū, 764
Tripurāri, 277*, 763
Tripurī, 455
Triratnadāsa, 614*
Triratna-stotra, 613*
Triśaraṇataṭabhīma, 533*
Triṣaṣṭi-śalākā-puruṣa-carita, 343
Triṣṭubh-Jagatī (metre), 2*, 12, 150
Trithen, 277*
Trivandrum, 16, 60*, 101, 104, 105, 106, 107, 109*, 112, 178*, 418*, 477*, 479*, 545, 620, 627, 679*
Trivandrum Sanskrit Series or TSS., 254*, 256*, 331*, 334*, 375*, 382*, 386*, 413* 465*, 466*, 479*, 548*, 550*, 551, 552, 558*, 620*, 627*, 630*, 659*, 662*, 663*, 717, 721, 722, 759, 765, 767, 771, 774, 775
Trivarga, lxxv, lxxxvi, lxxxiv, cxvii
Trivedi, 526, 528, 530*, 531*, 561, 562, 615, See K. P. Trivedi
Trivikramabhaṭṭa, 435, 694
Trivikaramasena, Same as Vikramasena (q.v.)
Trojan War, 654*
Troṭaka, 67, 139*, 687, 750*
T. R. Ratnam Aiyar, 277*, 286*, 298*, 763
Trübner, 161*, 368*, 389*
Trumpp, 666*
Ts'in Chi Hwangti, 737
T. S. Kuppusvami Sastri, 344*, 432*, 437*, 465*
T. Suzuki, 70*, 71*
Tucci, 729*
Tukhārian, 655
Tulasī-dūta, 373*
Tulasī plant 373
Tuluva dynasty, 773
Tulyayogitā (alaṃkāra), 530, 534, 536
Tuñjina of Kashmir, 119
Turfan, cxv, 655
Turks, cxv, cxvi cxviii
Turkistan, cvi
Turuṣka, 356
Tvaritagati (metre), 12
Types of Sanskrit Drama, 51*, 60*, 64*
Types of Tragic Drama, 141*

U

Über Bāṇa's Pārvatīpariṇayanāṭaka, 299*, 730*
Über Begriff und Wesen Der poetischen Figuren in der indischen Poetik, 520*, 701*, 760
Über das Kauṭilīyaśāstra und Verwandtes, 701*, 760
Über das Leben des Jaina-Mönches Hemacandra, 361*
Über das Navasāhasāṅkacarita, 349*
Über das Verhaltnis zwischen Cārudatta und Mṛcchakaṭika, 107*
Über das Zeitalter, 96*
Über den grichischen Ursprung des indischen Tierkreises, 730*
Über die Anfänge des indischen Dramas, 44*, 633*, 646
Über die Jaina Recensionen des Pañcatantra, 89*
Über die Vajraśūci, 71*
Über einen südlichen textus amplior des Pañcatantra, 89
Übereinstimmungen in Gedanken Vergleichen und Wendungen bei indischen Kunstdichten, 764
Über Kṣemendra's Darpadalana, 407*
Über-setzung und Anmerkungen, 700*, 701*
Ubhayanyāsa (alaṃkāra), 563
Ubhayābhisārikā, 11*, 248, 249, 251, 762
Uccala of Kashmir, 354, 356, 358
Ucchala, king, 628
Udakavatī, 749
Udayana, lxxxi, lxxxii, 97, 100, 110, 111, 201*, 271*, 300, 345, 471, 477*, 693, 695, 714, 720, 727
Udayana Kadai or *Perungadai*, 696*
Udayana-kathā, cii
Udayana Vatsarāja, 726
Udayanācārya, 624*, 666*
Udayaprabha Sūri, 363
Udayasundarī-kathā, 324*, 431-432, 455*, 766
Udayavarmā, 766, 767
Udayākara (father of Utpaladeva), 661
Udāra-rāghava, 331
Udāratā or *Udārtva (guṇa)*, 574, 575, 576*
Udātta, 534, 538
Udātta-kuñjara, 687
Udātta-rāghava, 300, 686
Udbhaṭa, xxviii, cxiv, 519, 523, 527, 528, 531, 534, 537, 569, 573, 581, 583, 584, 585, 593, 606, 615
Udbhaṭālaṃkāra, 671
Uddaṇḍin or Uddaṇḍanātha, 298, 474, 686
Uddhava, 190, 373
Uddhava-dūta, 373*, 664*, 752
Uddhava-saṃdeśa, 373*
Uddīpana, vibhāva, 593, 597
Udgatā (metre), 14*, 181*
Udambara, surname of Bhavabhūti, 278
Udyoga-parvan (*Mahābhārata*), 112, 195, 723
Uddyota, 637, 715
Uddyotakara, 217, 218, 751*

Udgītha, 767
Ugrasena, 726
Ujjayinī, lvii, cviii, cix, 4*, 93, 94, 95*, 125, 230, 232, 233, 234, 245*, 250, 251, 279, 373*, 450, 654, 688, 689, 731, 732, 757, 758, 761
Ujjvaladatta, 127*, 455
Ujjvalanīlamaṇi, 664*
Ullāgha-rāghava, 769
Ullekha (*alaṃkāra*), 562
Umā, 128
Umādevī, 486
Umāpatidhara, 390
Umāpati Upādhyāya, 510
Umbekācārya, 278*
Uṇādi, viii
Uṇādi-sūtra, 127*
Une Té trade on drame, hymne roman et poéme, 207*
United Provinces, lxxviii
University of Dacca, xii
University of Madras, 679*
University of Nālandā, cxii
University Press, 101*
Univ. Studies, 124*
Unmatta-kumāra-carita, 427
Unmatta-rāghava, 464
Unmattāvanti, King, cxvi
Unmāda-vāsavadattā, 301*, 302*
U. N. Upadhye, 139
Upadeśa-śataka, 674
Upadeśāmṛta, 664*
Upagupta, 655
Upahāravarman, 212
Upajāti (metre), 9, 14*, 77*,120*, 121*, 184*, 243*, 247, 285*, 329*
Upmanyu, 521
Upamā, xvi, 149*, 518-20, 525-27, 531*, 532* 534, 536, 538, 569, 576, 579. See Simile
Upamārtha, 519
Upamā-rūpaka, 534
Upamita, 518
Upaniṣad, v, vi, xvii, xviii, xxvii, lxviii, lxxv, 20, 85, 278, 482, 673, 697, 754
Uparūpaka, 51*, 64, 66, 67, 687
Upasthitapracupita (metre), 14*
Upavarṣa, lvii, cviii, 761
Upendravajrā (metre), 12
Upper Valley of the Indus, cxvii
U. S. A. 239*
Uṣabhadāta's inscription, 654
Uśanas, xxv
Utathya, 521
Utkala, 561. See Orissa
Utkalikavāllarī, 664*
Utpaladeva, 381, 661
Utpala, King, 356
Utprekṣā, 520, 525, 526, 530, 534, 536
Utprekṣāvallabha, 333, 370
Utprekṣāvayava, 534, 536
Utsṛṣṭāṅka, lxxxii, 65, 66, 724
Uttaramegha in *Meghadūta*, 751
Uttara-purāṇa, 344, 433, 436, 437
Uttara-rāma-carita, xlix, cxiv, 53*, 55*, 60, 277, 278*, 280*, 284, 285*, 287, 288-95, 297*, 449*, 452, 464, 760*, 763
Uttarālaṃkāra, 565
Urjasvī, 526, 534
Urubhaṅga, 60, 101, 109*, 112, 640, 717, 720, 721, 724
Urvasī, lxxx, 43, 60, 85, 139, 631, 632, 749, 750
Uṣas, lxxiii, 3

V

Vacana-mālikā, 666*
Vaidarbha Mārga, 208, 572
Vaidarbhī (*rīti*) 526, 553, 563, 572, 573. 576-78, 613, 729*
Vaidarbhī-vāsudeva, 468
Vaidya Bhānu Paṇḍita, 414*
Vaidyanātha (commentator), 730, 756*
Vaidyanātha-praśasti, 416*
Vaikhānasa, xxv
Vaikhānasa-smārta-sūtra, xiii
Vaimalya-vidhāyinī, 533*
Vainodaka, 521
Vairāgya-śataka, of Bhartṛhari, 161, 162, 163, 164, 194, 670, 672, 675; of Dhanadadeva, Janārdana and others, 370, 764 (of Nīlakaṇṭha Dīkṣita)
Vaiśampāyana, 230
Vaiṣamyoddhāriṇī, 622*
Vaiśeṣika, xix, 72, 624
Vaiśika Upacāra or Vaiśikī Kalā, 198, 643*
Vaiṣṇava or Vaiṣṇavism, vii, xxiii, lxii, lxxi, cix, cxi, cxvii, 252*, 333, 372*, 374, 375, 377, 381, 385, 389, 391, 392, 413, 414, 415, 439, 440, 489, 492*, 564, 662*, 667, 679, 754
Vaiṣṇava Faith and Movement in Bengal, 485*. See *Early History of Vaiṣṇava Faith and Movement in Bengal.*
Vainṣava Perumāl, 662*
Vaiśvadevī (metre), 196*, 243*
Vaitālīya (metre), 14*, 150, 181*, 196*, 329*
Vajradatta, 378, 384*
Vajrasūcī, cv, 71, 613*
Vajrayānamūlapatti-saṃgraha, 614*
Vakraghona, lix
Vakrokti, li, 33*, 518, 526, 536, 537, 549, 563, 575, 579, 581-84, 586. 587, 606, 620
Vakrokti-jīvita, 120*, 369*, 548, 552, 556, See Kuntaka
Vakrokti-pañcāśikā, 335*, 382*, 623
Vaktra (metre), 12, 159*, 201, 202, 203
Vakulavīthi, lxxxiv, 687
Valabhī, 183, 528, 615, 616
Vallabha, brother of Rūpa Gosvāmī, 664
Vallabha, commentator, 695, 751*
Vallabhadeva, 8*, 132*, 189, 382*, 402, 413, 414, 415, 421, 623*, 656, 657, 661*, 674. See *Subhāṣitāvalī*
Vallabhācārya or Vallabhācārī sect, 392, 396
Vaman Islampurkar, 349*
Vaṃśamaṇi, 396*
Vaṃśapatrapatita (metre), 181*
Vaṃśasthavila (metre), 9, 12, 14*, 77*, 121*, 159*, 196*, 329*
Vaṃśīvadana, 325*, 624*
Vanamālā, 771, 789

Vanamālikā-nāṭikā, 769
Vana-parvan (*Mahābhārata*), 178, 467*
Vanavāsi, known as Jayantī-kṣetra, 340*
Vandhudatta, 762
Varadarāja, 468
Varadācārya, 487, 489, 490
Varadāmbal, 773
Varadāmbikā-pariṇaya, 361*, 417, 438
Vararuci, xviii, lviii, cviii, 5*, 10, 93, 95*, 156, 195, 200, 248, 368,* 369, 424, 520, 527, 611, 621, 683, 685, 729, 730, 750*, 761, 762
Vararuci-vākya-kāvya, 730
Varatantu, 745
Varāha (incarnation), 325*
Varāhamihira, 5*, 697, 729, 730
Varāha-purāṇa, 659*
Varāṅga-carita, 342-43
Vardhamāna, 241, 757
Vardhamāna (Burdwan), 439*
Varendra Research Society, 339
Varmala or Varmalāta (king), 189
Varṇamālā-stotra, 383, 665
Varṇanārha-varṇana, 79*, 614*
Varṇāśrama, xxii, xxxi, l, xcvi, 729
Varṣa, lvii
Varuṇa, 475
Vasantaka, 257
Vasantapāla, 770
Vasantarājya, 656*
Vasantasenā, lxiv, 60, 100, 246, 247, 758, 770
Vasantasenā (drama translated from *Mṛcchakaṭika*), 756*
Vasantatilaka (Bhāṇa), 486
Vasantatilaka (metre), 9*, 12, 13, 14*, 77*, 120*, 121*, 159*, 172*, 196*, 243*, 270*, 276*, 285*, 320*, 329*, 368, 369, 372, 383*, 461, 462*, 660, 663
Vasanta-vilāsa, 363, 679, 770
Vasantotsava, 257*
Vaśiṣṭha, xxv, lx, 130, 289, 744
Vaśiṣṭha (Dharmasūtra), xiii
V. A. Smith, 481*
Vastupāla, 332, 362-64, 428, 478, 678, 770
Vastupāla-carita, 678, 770
Vasubandhu, xix, cvi, cviii, cxiv, 73*
Vasudeva, 190
Vasudeva, Minister, c
Vasunāga, 301, 686
Vaṭakalikā, 730*
Vaṭeśvaradatta, Sāmanta, 262
Vatsa, ancestor of Vātsāyana-gotra, 225
Vatsabhaṭṭi, cx, 18, 123, 183, 615, 616, 732, 736
Vatsa, commentator, 741*
Vatsarāja-carita, 761
Vatsarāja in *Pratijñā-yaugandharāyaṇa*, 726
Vatsarāja of Kālañjara, lxxxiv, 473, 489, 492*, 494, 768, 769
Vatsarāja of Lāṭa, 432, 443
Vatseśa, Story of, 527
Vaṭudāsa, 413
Vavilla Press, 494*
Vavilla Ramanujacharya, 489*
Vācaspati, 626
Vācaspati-govinda, 751
Vādhūla-gotra, 438
Vādicandra Sūri, 373*, 751*
Vādijaṅghāla, 533*
Vadirāja Sūri, 343, 436, 619
Vādya, 643*, 645
Vāgbhaṭa, author of *Alaṃkaratilaka*, 687
Vāgbhaṭa, author of *Kāvyānuśāsana*, 563, 584
Vāgbhaṭa, author of *Nemi-nirvāṇa*, 345, 593
Vāgbhaṭa, author of *Vāgbhaṭālaṃkāra*, 559
Vāgbhaṭālaṃkāra, 559, 564, 684
Vāghelarāja Vīrabhānu, 679
Vāghelā, 362, 678
Vāhlika, cvii
Vājacandra, 560
Vājapeya (Sacrifice), 278
Vākāṭaka (dynasty), 119*
Vākovākya, xlix
Vākpati or Vākpatirāja, cxvi, 201, 219, 279, 280, 285*, 299, 350, 623, 644, 676, 685
Vakpatirāja Muñja, 349*, 430. See Muñja
Vākya-padiya, 161, 516, 520, 605, 616, 639, 671-73
Vālin, 287, 288, 300*, 451, 452
Vālmīki, xvi, xvii, xxx, lxxxviii, cxxvii, cxxviii, 120*, 130, 131, 289, 303, 381, 599, 665*, 688, 732, 745, 766. See *Rāmāyaṇa*
Vāmana, xxviii, cxiv, cvx, 8*, 26*, 158, 174, 186*, 188, 203, 219, 226*, 242, 271, 280, 519, 527, 528, 631*, 535-38, 563, 569, 571, 573, 574, 575-82, 584, 585, 587, 590, 593, 606, 620*, 621, 646, 669, 714, 742*, 743, 756, 762, 764. See *Kāvyālaṃkāra-sūtra*.
Vāmanabhaṭṭa Bāṇa, cxiii, 627, 686, 771, See Bāṇa Vāmanabhaṭṭa
Vānaprastha, 745
Vaṅmaṇḍana-guṇa-dūta, 375*
Vāraruca Kāvya, 10, 611*
Vārāṇasī, 88, 350, 450. See Benares
Vārtā-śāstra, lxxv, xcvi
Vārttā (alaṃkāra), 526
Vārttika or Vārttika-kāra, 10*, 11*, 12, 200, 519
Vāsanā,, 596, 597
Vāsantikā, 473*
Vāsantī, 289, 293
Vāsantī-pūjā, 641*, 649*
Vāsavadattā, 111, 112, 219, 265, 300, 301
Vāsavadattā, xviii, lxiii, cxiv, 11, 16, 92*, 171*, 200, 217-25, 227, 625*, 688, 689, 695*, 714, 726, 727, 754, 755
Vāsiṣka (king), cvi
Vāsiṣṭhiputra, Śrīpulumāyi, ci
Vāsudeva Cayani, 496
Vāsudeva, commentator, 457*
Vāsudeva, Dhanañjaya's father, 340
Vāsudeva I (King), cvii, cx
Vasudeva (King), lvii, 757*
Vāsudeva (Kṛṣṇa), ciii, 114
Vāsudeva, poet, 121*, 336, 337, 338*, 617, 621, 637, 638, 687
Vāsudeva-vijaya, 336, 617
Vātsya, 525*
Vātsyāyana, xix, cxiv, 15, 21, 22, 198, 405, 491, 645. See *Kāma-sūtra*
Vātyāyana-gotra, 225
Vāyupurāṇa, xiv

Vāyu-vikāra, lviii
V. Barrucand, 756*
V. D. Gadre, 256*, 759
Veda or Vedic, v, vi, vii, viii, xvi, xvii, xxiii, xxiv, xxvi, xxxi, xxxv, lx, lxv, lxx, lxxi, lxxii, lxxiii, lxxiv, lxxviii, lxxix, xc, xcvi, cxxi, cxxii, cxxviii, 2*, 3, 4, 7, 12, 26*, 44, 45, 46, 85, 87, 156, 166, 200*, 278, 415, 438, 630, 631, 633-35, 641, 647, 653, 697, 733, 749, 776
Veda-kavi, 486
Veda-sāra-śiva-stuti, 380
Vedastuṭikā, 664*
Veda-vedāntā-mandira, 417*
Vedāṅga, lxxv
Vedānta, lxvi, 161, 326, 376, 379, 380, 483, 625, 729
Vedāntadeśika, 439, 771
Vedāntakalpa-Latikā, 664
Vedānta-sūtra, cxiv, 487*
Vedānta-vilāsa, 487
Vedāntācārya-vijaya, 439
Vedāranya, 338*
Vedic Index, 635*
Vedische Mythologie, 647
Vegavatī (metre), 12
Vegetation ritual, 640
Vema or Vemabhūpāla, 157*, 158*, 299, 433, 627, 668, 771
Vemabhūpāla-carita, 361*, 433, 627, 771
Veṇīdatta, 415, 561
Veṇī-saṃhāra, 271, 272-77, 443
Veṅkaṭa, cxviii
Vaṅkaṭadeśika or Veṅkaṭanātha, 332, 373*, 384*, 487, 765, 766
Veṅkaṭa I of Vijayanagara, 341, 565
Veṅkatarāja, 437
Veṅkaṭācārya, 674
Veṅkaṭācārya Śāstrī, 560, 561*
Veṅkaṭādhvarin, 341, 438, 439*, 771
Veṅkaṭeśa, 338, 771
Veṅkaṭeśa, father of Samarapuṅgava Dīkṣita, 438
Veṅkaṭeśvara, 335*
Veṅkaṭeśvara Makhin, 765
Veṅkaṭeśvara Press, 439*, 506*
Versailles, liv
Veṇu, 643*
Versailles, liv
Verhandl. des V oriental isten Congress, 127*, 192*, 702*
Verhandlungen der 42, *Versammlung deutsche Philologen*°, 702*
Vessantara, cxiii
Vessantara-Jātaka, 656
Vetālabhaṭṭa, 5*, 121, 195, 729, 731
Vetāla-pañcaviṃśati, 98,212,231,421-23,694,757
V. Golonbew, 650*
V. G. Pradhana, 615
V. Henry, x, 136*, 262*
Vibhāṣā commentary on Abbidharma, 70
Vibhāṣā scholar Pārśva, 70
Vibhāva, 593, 595, 596, 601
Vibhāvanā, 526, 534, 592
Vibhrānta-śūdraka, 757*
Vicchitti, 583
Vicitra (*alaṃkāra*), 562
Vicitrā (*rīti*), 591
Victor Hugo, liv
Victorian, 213
Vidagdha and Vidvat, 26, 27*
Vidagdha-mādhava, 468, 664*
Vidagdha-mukha-maṇḍana, 335*
Vidarbha, 210*, 213, 278, 568, 729*
Viddha-śālabhañjikā, 454, 457, 459, 472
Videha, 561
Vidhi-vilasita, 687
Vidiśā, cviii, 241, 757
Vidūṣaka, 46, 54, 55, 77, 78, 115, 137, 244*, 260, 458, 459, 461, 488, 495, 496, 498, 640, 641, 645, 651, 652, 655
Vivad-vinoda-kāvya, 122*, 740*
Vidvan-moda-taraṅgiṇī, 439
Vidyā, daughter of the king of Kashmir, 657, 658
Vidyācakravarttī, 558*
Vidyādhara, 97, 98, 249, 749
Vidyādhara, author of *Ekāvalī*, 561
Vidyādhara, commentator, 325*, 326
Vidyādhara Jātaka, 258
Vidyādharamalla, 459
Vidyādhara of Karpaṭi Gotra, 402
Vidyākaśa Miśra, 621
Vidyāmādhava, 341
Vidyāmātra, 672
Vidyā-nareśa, 373*
Vidyānātha, 479, 562
Vidyānātha Payaguṇḍa, 560
Vidyānivāsa, 679
Vidyā-pariṇaya, 486, 764
Vidyāpati, 391, 392, 426
Vidyāpati (title), 320, 351
Vidyā-prakāśa-cikitsā, 730*
Vidyāraṇya, 464*, 767
Vidyāraṇya Yogin, 624*
Vidyāsāgara, commentator of *Bhaṭṭikāvya*, 616*
Vidyā-sundara, 368*, 658
Vidyātaraṅgiṇī Press, 341*
Vidyāvatī, woman poet, 416*
Vidyullatā, 657
Vidyāvinoda, commentator of *Bhaṭṭikāvya*, 616*
Vidyunmālā (metre), 12, 13, 243*
Vienna, 756
Vigrahapāla, 619*
Vihārilāl, 371
Vihita (*alaṃkāra*), 563
Vijaya, 439
Vijaya-bhaṭṭārikā, 477*, 532
Vijayacandra, 326
Vijayanagara, 341, 361, 418, 438, 497*, 565, 773
Vijayapāla, 467, 769
Vijayaprabha Sūri, 375*
Vijayapraśasti, 626
Vijayaśrī, same as *Pārijāta-mañjarī* (q. v.)
Vijayā, 171
Vijayānanda, 533*
Vijayāṅkā, 417*
Viijā or Vijjakā, woman poet, 416, 477
Vijñapti-mātra-siddhi, 72*
Vijñapti-patra, 374*, 375
Vijñāna-vāda, 71

Vijñāneśvara, xxv, xcvii
Vikala, 770
Vikalpa (*alaṃkāra*), 562
Vikarālā, 197, 676
Vikaṭanitambā, woman poet, 416, 417
Vikrama, lx
Vikrama-carita, 5*, 424
Vikrama Era, (Fergusson's theory), 4*, 5
Vikrama of Calicut, 617
Vikrama, poet, 374*
Vikramarddhi, 755*
Vikramasena, 422
Vikramaśila, 324*
Vikramāditya, cvii, cix, 4*, 5, 10*, 17*, 18, 98, 125, 161*, 218*, 422, 424, 428, 677, 695, 729-32, 738*, 740, 753, 754
Vikramāditya VI Tribhuvanamalla, 351, 352
Vikramāṅkadeva-carita, 350-53, 651, 657*, 677
Vikramodaya, 424*
Vikramorvaśīya, xxxi, xxxvii, lxxxv, 53*, 136*, 138-40, 143, 301, 457, 522, 641, 652*, 653*, 729, 740, 749, 750
Vikrānta-kaurava, 467*
Vikrānta-śūdraka, 241*, 762
Vilakṣa-duryodhana, 687
Vilāpa-kusumāñjali, 664*
Vilgammūla Mahāṭhera, 169*
Vimalā, 724
Vimarśa, lxxxi, lxxxii, lxxxiv, 274
Vimarśinī, 628
Vinatā-nandana, 769
Vinaya, 695
Vinaya-piṭaka, 655
Vinayarāma, 622*
Vinayavijaya-gaṇi, 373*
Vināyaka, 211*
Vindhya, ix, lxxii, civ, cvii, 93, 94, 95, 220, 232
Vindhyavāsinī, 477-78
Vindhyeśvarīprasāda, 730, 741*
Vipulā, 762
Virādhagupta, 269
Virāṭa, 337, 466
Virāṭa-parvan (*Mahābhārata*), 113, 381
Virodha (*alaṃkāra*), 526
Virodhābhāṣa, 221
Virutādhyāya, 697
Virūpākṣa, 560
Viśaladeva of Gujarat, 331, 332, 362, 618
Viśaladeva Vigraharāja of Śākambharī, 469
Viṣama-pada-vṛtti, 756*
Viśākhadatta, cxv, 156, 239, 262-71, 295, 302*, 760, 776
Viśākhadeva, 686, 760
Viśeṣokti (*alaṃkāra*), 526, 530
Vision, 720*
Viṣṇu, xxv, lxxi, cxi, 49, 112, 114, 115, 187, 384, 391*, 483, 630, 667, 703, 708, 709, 728
Viṣṇudāsa, 372*, 752
Viṣṇu, Dhanañjaya's father, 550
Viṣṇudharmottara Purāṇa 637, 642, 649
Viṣṇu Dh. s., xiii
Viṣṇudviṣas, 344
Viṣṇugupta, 701*, 705
Viṣṇukāñcī, 773
Viṣṇunāga, 251
Viṣṇu-nārāyaṇa, 661
Visnuprasad Bhandari, 381*
Viṣṇu-purāṇa, xiii, 138*, 522, 524*, 629, 648
Viṣṇuśarman, 88, 701*, 705
Viśruta, story of, 210, 213
Viśvabandhu, 498
Viśvaguṇādarśa Campū, 341, 438-39
Viśvakarmā, 630
Viśva(koṣa), 722*
Viśvalaka, 251
Viśvanātha, author of *Mṛgāṅkalekhā*, 473
Viśvanātha, author of *Saugandhikāharaṇa*, 467, 769
Viśvanātha, author of *Sāhitya-darpaṇa* 28*, 66*, 179*, 334*, 470*, 493*, 506*, 516, 653, 604, 685
Viśvanātha-bhaṭṭa, 473*
Viśvanātha Chakravartin, 33*, 398, 440*
Viśvanātha (commentator), 619, 751*
Viśvanātha Tarkapañcānana, 679
Viśvāmitra, xxxi, 144, 451, 456*, 465, 470, 748
Viśvānatara, 656
Viśvāvarta, Maṅkhaka's father, 322
Viśvāvasu, Gandharva, 439
Viśveśvara, 335*, 752*
Viśveśvara, bhaṭṭa, 666*
Viśveśvara, author of *Rākāgama-sūtra*, 560
Viśveśvara, author of *Romāvalī-śataka*, 370, 371, 403
Viśveśvara, author of *Vyaṅgārtha-kaumudī*, 561*
Viśveśvara Sarasvatī, 664
Viśveśvarācārya, 624*
Viṭa, 54, 57, 66, 250, 251, 252, 253*, 260, 409, 474, 488, 490, 493, 645, 758
Vithala Sastri, 126*
Viṭṭhala-dīkṣita, 666*
Viṭṭhaleśvara, 392*, 396
Viyoginī (metre), 14*, 150*, See Sundarī
Vivakṣitānya-para-vācya-dhvani, 609, *Vivṛti*, 533*
Vizagapatam, 560
Vīṇā, lv, 301*, 643
Vīṇa-vāsavadattā, 301*
Vīrabhānūdaya-kāvya, 679
Vīracandra, 440*
Vīra carita, cxiv, 424*
Vīradeva, lix
Vīradhavala, 332, 362, 428, 478, 678, 770
Vīra era, 465*, 476*
Vīra-kamsaparāya-carita, 361, 418, 679
Vīramitrodaya, 773, 774
Vīranandī, 775
Vīranāga or Dhīranāga, 464
Vīranārāyaṇa, 433
Vīranārāyana-carita, 754
Vīra (*rasa*), 592
Vīrarāghava, 277*, 763
Vīrarudra. See Pratāparudra
Vīrasena, 18
Vīrasiṃha, 468, 568*, 658*
Vīrasiṃha-deva, Rājā, 777
Vīravarman, lix

Vīreśvara, 375*
Vīthī, lxxxii, lxxxiii, 65, 686, 723
V. J. Antani, 263*
V. Lesny, 105*
V. L. Panshikar, 89*, 207*, 229*, 325*, 429*, 438*, 439*, 465*, 481*, 485*, 763
V. L. S. Bansikar, 741*
V. O. J., 631*
Volkerpsychologie, 648
Von. Schroeder, 631. See L. V. Shroedor or Shroeder
Vopadeva, 660*
V. Raghavan, 414*
Vrajanātha, 372, 752
Vraja-vilāsa-stava, 664*
V. Ramasvami Sastrulu, 490*
Vṛddha-cāṇakya, 196, 673
Vṛddha-viṣṇu, 733*
Vṛddhavyāsa, 624*
Vṛndāvana, 338*, 372*, 390, 397, 440
Vṛndāvana Dāsa, 662*
Vṛndāvana-kāvya, 740*
Vṛndāvana-yamaka, 338
Vṛṣabhānujā, 468
Vṛṣākapi (Hymn), 43, 631
Vṛtroddharaṇa, lxxxiv, 387
Vṛttaratnākara, 527
Vṛtta-ratnāvalī, 439*
Vṛttidīpikā, 566
Vṛttikāra Bodhāyana 495
Vṛttis (dramatic), 63, 493*
Vṛttivārttika, 564
V. S. 633*
V. S. Apte, 454*
V. S. Sastri, 418*
V. S. Sukthankar, 102*, 107*
V. Venkatarama Sastri, 496*
V. V. Mirashi, 454
V. V. Press, 691*
Vyabhicārī (*bhāva*), 561, 592, 593, 595, 596
Vyaktiviveka, 530*, 551, 556, 558
Vyaktiviveka-vicāra, 558
Vyaṅgārtha-dīpikā, 561*
Vyaṅgārtha-kaumudī, of both Anantapaṇḍita and Viśveśvara, 561*
Vyañjanā xvii, 519, 546, 554, 562, 565, 583
Vyasanākara, 497
Vyatireka (*alaṃkāra*), 530, 536
Vyādhisindhu, 498
Vyāḍi, lviii, cviii, 10*, 93, 685, 761
Vyājastuti, 526, 534, 536, 583
Vyājokti, 530, 536
Vyākaraṇa, xvii, 516, 525. See Grammar
Vyākaraṇa Mahābhāṣya, 568. See *Mahābhāṣya*
Vyākhyānanda, 616*
Vyākhyāyikā, commentary of *Vāsavadattā*, 755*
Vyāmiśraka, 635*, 644
Vyāsa, 162, 178, 190, 381, 688, 694, 705. See *Mahābhārata*
Vyāsadāsa, title, 404
Vyāsa-mokṣāditya, 769
Vyāsatīrtha, cxviii
Vyāsavatsa, 741*
Vyāyoga, lxxxii, lxxxiii, 65*, 462, 464-67, 473, 686, 723, 724, 768
Vyoṣakāvya, 616*

W

W. A. Clouston, 652*
Walter, 741*, See O. Walter
War, lxxii, xc, cvii, 190, 652*
Warangal, 467, 479*
Wariyar, 663
Warrior, 114, 723, 769
W. Caland, 510*. See Caland
W. C. Woolner, 101*, 464*
Weapon, 112, 115, 178, 179, 723
Weber, x, 5*, 11*, 48*, 52*, 71*, 127*, 136*, 140*, 196*, 235, 300*, 331*, 372*, 424, 427*, 613*, 617*, 618*, 621*, 740*, 741*, 742*, 750*, 754*, 756. See A Weber
W. E. Clarke, 102*
Weimar, 646
Wei (river), 737
Western India, 252, 506
Westminster, 353*
W. Geiger, 728*
W. Grube, 648
W. Heymann, 522*
White Huns, cxv, 736, 737, 739
Wien, 140*, 361*
Wiener Landwirtschaft. Zeitung, 622*
Wiener Zeitschrift Für die Kunde des Morgenlandes, 537*
Wilson, 210*, 213*, 277*, 486*, 498*, 500*, 505, 646*, 666, 688, 750*, 763. See H. Wilson
Windisch, x 52*, 54*, 242*, 632, 659. See E. Windisch
Winternitz, x, xi, xiii, xv, xvi, 49*, 52*, 69*, 70*, 71*, 74*, 79*, 82*, 86*, 99*, 102*, 115*, 124*, 172*, 200*, 201*, 240*, 331*, 345*, 353*, 378*, 379*, 402*, 501*, 510*, 567*, 611*, 624, 625, 628*, 642*, 646, 648, 649, 650, 652*, 653, 654*, 655*, 657*, 659, 667, 691*, 696, 701, 704*, 708, 710, 719, 720, 730*, 732, 747, 748*, 754
W. Jones (William Jones), v, 122*, 140* 666*, 706, 747
W. L. Panshikar, 126*, 388*, 403*, 666
W. Macneille Dixon, 141*
W. Norman Brown, 29*
Woerterbücher, 361*
Woman poets, 361, 416-18, 429, 438, 477
Woolner Comm. Volume, 102*
Wordsworth, 206
Word-tricks, 622
Works, 646, 651*, 666*
Works of Āryaśūra, 614*
Works of Śaṅkarācārya, 66*
W. Printz, 105*. See Printz
W. Sh. Panasikar, 763
W. Solf, 368*, 657*
W. Wassiljew, 69*
W. W. Skeat, 648
W. W. Tarn, 52*
W. Wundt, 648

W. Yates, 121*, 664*
W. Z. K. M., 44*, 52*, 141*, 189*, 191*, 211*, 218*, 220*, 230*, 232*, 257*, 263*, 407*, 612, 621*, 622*, 623*, 653*, 654*, 655*, 673, 701*, 702*, 754, 760

X

Xaxartes cxvi

Y

Yadugiri Yatirāja, 300*
Yadunandana, 496
Yaduvilāsa, 769
Yajña-nārayana Dīkṣita, 765
Yajñarāma Dīkṣita, 465
Yajñaśrī, cl
Yajñeśvara, 169*
Yajurveda, Black, 278
Yakṣa, lxxx, cxxvi, 133, 693, 750, 751
Yama, xxv, 43, 495, 631
Yamaka, 120, 334, 337, 338, 373, 379, 521, 526, 530, 531*, 534, 563, 569, 578, 579 618, 729
Yamaka Kāvya, 121, 335, 337, 338
Yamaka-kāvya, 618
Yama-yamī (hymn), 43
Yamī, 45, 631
Yamunā, 40, 114, 383*
Yamunāṣṭaka, 664*
Yarkānd, civ
Yaśaḥpāla, 362*, 484, 769
Yaśaścandra, 476, 769
Yaśatilaka-cmapū, 343*, 432*, 435*36
Yaśodhara, 436
Yaśodhara-caritu, of Māṇikyacandra Sūri, 343; of Vadiraja, Sūri, 343, 436
Yaśodharman, cxiii, 738*
Yaśodhavala, 769
Yaśovanta Siṃha, 439*
Yaśovarman, cxvi, 279, 298, 299-300, 676, 685
Yaśovijaya Jaina Granthamālā, 344*, 374*, 379*, 465*. See Jaina Yaśovijaya Granthamālā
Yaśovijaya Jaina Saṃskṛta Pāṭhaśālā, 379*
Yathāsaṃkhya, 525
Yatirāja-vijaya, same as *Vedāntavilāsa* (q. v.)
Yaugandharāyaṇa, 111, 300, 459, 461, 726, 727
Yavakrita, 11
Yavana, cvii, 54, 736
Yavana-śāstra-pāraṅgama, 772
Yavanikā, 54
Yayāti, 11
Yādava, 477
Yādava-rāghavīya, 341, 438
Yādavābhyudaya of Rāmacandra, 468, 686 of Veṅkaṭadeśika, 332, 766
Yājñavalkya, xxv, xxvi, xxxiii, xxxiv, cx 381, 463, 522, 733, 735
Yājñavalkya-smṛti, xiii, xxvi, 773, 774
Yāminī-pūrṇa-tilaka, 368*, 658*
Yāska, xvi, xxv, cxxiv, 43*, 518, 567, 611
Yātrā, 34, 393, 395, 505, 508, 509, 501, 641, 667
Yātrā-prabandha, 438
Yāyāvara, 453
Yi-tsing, 71, 79, 80, 161, 256
Yoga, lxxi, 70*, 278, 485, 495, 729
Yoga-cintāmaṇi, 730*
Yoga-dīpikā, 730*
Yoga-yātrā, 730*
Yogācāra, 70*
Yogārṇāva, 730*
Yogiraj, Panditacharya, 374*
Yuan Chwang, 72, 255, 258*
Yudhiṣṭhira, 179, 189, 190, 192, 275, 348, 355
Yudhiṣṭhira-vijaya, 121*, 337, 338*, 621
Yueh-chis, ciii, civ
Yugmāygma-darśana (sport), 491*
Yusuf, 317*, 629
Yusuf U Zuleikha, 629, 771, 772
Yuvarāja I Keyūravarṣa, 454

Z

Zachariae, 336*, 361*, 615, 616*, 617*, 619* 621*, 673, 704*, 763. See Th. Zachariae
Zain-u' l-Ābidin of Kashmir, 316*, 359*, 677
Zamorin Mānavikrama, 298
Z. D. M. G., 5*, 7*, 8*, 9*, 10*, 11*, 13*, 43*, 44*, 48*, 49*, 50*, 54*, 87*, 89*, 94*, 105*, 115*, 121*, 122*, 127*, 136*, 158*, 166*, 183*, 235*, 241*, 262*, 263*, 320*, 329*, 331*, 407*, 414*, 422*, 427*, 444*, 450*, 467*, 469*, 475*, 500*, 501*, 503*, 520*, 529*, 533*, 537*, 611*, 618*, 620*, 623*, 632*, 635*, 642*, 647*, 648, 650*, 653*, 676*, 686, 695*, 700*, 701*, 703, 704*, 730*, 740*, 741*, 742*, 750*, 751*, 757*
Zeitschrift f. Ind. und Iran, 102*
Zeitschrift für die kunde des Morgenlandes, 666*
Z. M. D. G., 665*
Zuleikha, 629
Zur Geschichte der altindischen Prosa, 87*, 632*
Zur kritik des Mudrā-rākṣasa, 262*
Zur Textkritik und Erklärung von Kālidasa's Malavikagnimitra, 136*, 750*
Z. V. V., 703*